D0466525

continued on back inside cover

businesses in order to help the business firms they manage to succeed in the e-commerce era.

It would be foolish to ignore the lessons learned in the early period of e-commerce. Like so many technology revolutions in the past—automobiles, electricity, telephones, television, and biotechnology—there was an explosion of entrepreneurial efforts, followed by consolidation. By 2005, the survivors of the early period were moving to establish profitable businesses while maintaining rapid growth in revenues. In 2012, e-commerce is entering a new period of explosive entrenpreneurial activity focusing on social networks, and the mobile digital platform created by smartphones and tablet computers. These technologies and social behaviors are bringing about extraordinary changes to our personal lives, markets, industries, individual businesses, and society as a whole. In 2012, the stock values of Apple, Google, and Amazon hit new highs, along with many start-ups. E-commerce is generating thousands of new jobs for young managers in all fields from marketing to management, entrepreneurial studies, and information systems. Today, e-commerce has moved into the mainstream life of established businesses that have the market brands and financial muscle required for the long-term deployment of e-commerce technologies and methods. If you are working in an established business, chances are the firm's e-commerce capabilities and Web presence are important factors for its success. If you want to start a new business, chances are very good that the knowledge you learn in this book will be very helpful.

BUSINESS. TECHNOLOGY. SOCIETY.

We believe that in order for business and technology students to really understand e-commerce, they must understand the relationships among e-commerce business concerns, Internet technology, and the social and legal context of e-commerce. These three themes permeate all aspects of e-commerce, and therefore, in each chapter, we present material that explores the business, technological, and social aspects of that chapter's main topic.

Given the continued growth and diffusion of e-commerce, all students—regardless of their major discipline—must also understand the basic economic and business forces driving e-commerce. E-commerce has created new electronic markets where prices are more transparent, markets are global, and trading is highly efficient, though not perfect. E-commerce has a direct impact on a firm's relationship with suppliers, customers, competitors, and partners, as well as how firms market products, advertise, and use brands. Whether you are interested in marketing and sales, design, production, finance, information systems, or logistics, you will need to know how e-commerce technologies can be used to reduce supply chain costs, increase production efficiency, and tighten the relationship with customers. This text is written to help you understand the fundamental business issues in e-commerce.

We spend a considerable amount of effort analyzing the business models and strategies of "pure-play" online companies and established businesses now employing "bricks-and-clicks" business models. We explore why many early e-commerce firms fail and the strategic, financial, marketing, and organizational challenges they face.

- Governments around the world increase surveillance of Internet users and Web sites in response to national security threats; Google continues to tussle with China and other countries over censorship and security issues.

- Venture capital investing in e-commerce explodes for social, mobile, and local software applications in the first half of 2012, and then recedes as social and game firms lose market value.

WELCOME TO THE NEW E-COMMERCE

Since it began in 1995, electronic commerce has grown in the United States from a standing start to a $362 billion retail, travel, and media business and a $4.1 trillion business-to-business juggernaut, bringing about enormous change in business firms, markets, and consumer behavior. Economies and business firms around the globe are being similarly affected. During this relatively short time, e-commerce has itself been transformed from its origin as a mechanism for online retail sales into something much broader. Today, e-commerce has become the platform for media and new, unique services and capabilities that aren't found in the physical world. There is no physical world counterpart to Facebook, Twittter, Google search, or a host of other recent online innovations from Groupon and iTunes to Tumblr. Welcome to the new e-commerce!

Although e-commerce today has been impacted by the worldwide economic recession, in the next five years, e-commerce in all of its forms is still projected to continue growing at high single-digit rates, becoming the fastest growing form of commerce. Just as automobiles, airplanes, and electronics defined the twentieth century, so will e-commerce of all kinds define business and society in the twenty-first century. The rapid movement toward an e-commerce economy and society is being led by both established business firms such as Walmart, Ford, IBM, JCPenney, and General Electric, and newer entrepreneurial firms such as Google, Amazon, Apple, Facebook, Yahoo, Twitter, YouTube, and Photobucket. Students of business and information technology need a thorough grounding in electronic commerce in order to be effective and successful managers in the next decade. This book is written for tomorrow's managers.

While newer firms such as Facebook, Tumblr, YouTube, Twitter, Pinterest, Flickr, and Blinkx have grown explosively in the last two years and grab our attention, the traditional forms of retail e-commerce and services also remain vital and have proven to be more resilient than traditional retail channels in facing the economic recession that has occurred during the past year. The experience of these firms from 1995 to the present is also a focus of this book. The defining characteristic of these firms is that they are profitable, sustainable, efficient, and innovative, with powerful brand names. Many of these now-experienced retail and service firms, such as eBay, Amazon, E*Trade, Priceline, and Expedia, are survivors of the first era of e-commerce, from 1995 to spring 2000. These surviving firms have evolved their business models, integrated their online and offline operations, and changed their revenue models to become profitable. Students must understand how to build these kinds of e-commerce

- E-books take off and expand the market for text, supported by the iPad, Kindle, Nook, and iPhone.
- Streaming of popular TV shows and movies (Netflix, Amazon, and Hulu.com) becomes a reality, as Internet distributors and Hollywood and TV producers strike deals for Web distribution that also protects intellectual property.
- "Free" and "freemium" business models compete to support digital content.
- New mobile payment platforms emerge to challenge PayPal.
- B2B e-commerce exceeds pre-recession levels as firms become more comfortable with digital supply chains.

Technology

- Smartphones, tablets, and e-book readers, along with associated software applications, and coupled with 3G/4G cellular network expansion, fuel rapid growth of the mobile platform.
- Investment in cloud computing increases, providing the computing infrastructure for a massive increase in online digital information and e-commerce.
- Cloud-based streaming services for music and video replace sales of downloads and physical product.
- Nearly a million software apps fuel growth in app sales, marketing, and advertising; transforming software production and distribution.
- Touch interface operating systems emerge: Windows 8 introduced with a touch screen interface, mimicking Apple's iOS and Google Android smartphones.
- The cost of developing sophisticated Web sites continues to drop due to declining software and hardware prices and open source software tools.
- Internet and cellular network capacity is challenged by the rapid expansion in digital traffic generated by mobile devices; bandwidth caps begin to appear in 2012.
- Internet telecommunications carriers support differential pricing to maintain a stable Internet; opposed by Net neutrality groups pushing non-discriminatory pricing.

Society

- The mobile, "always on" culture in business and family life continues to grow.
- Congress considers legislation to regulate the use of personal information for behavioral tracking and targeting consumers online.
- States heat up the pursuit of taxes on Internet sales by Amazon and others.
- Intellectual property issues remain a source of conflict with significant movement toward resolution in some areas, such as Google's deals with Hollywood and the publishing industry, and Apple's and Amazon's deals with e-book and magazine publishers.
- P2P piracy traffic declines as paid streaming music and video gains ground, although digital piracy of online content remains a significant threat to Hollywood and the music industry.

PREFACE

WHAT'S NEW IN THE NINTH EDITION

Currency

The 9th edition features all new or updated opening, closing, and "Insight on" cases. The text, as well as all of the data, figures, and tables in the book, have been updated through October 2012 with the latest marketing and business intelligence available from eMarketer, Pew Internet & American Life Project, Forrester Research, comScore, Gartner Research, and other industry sources.

New Themes and Content

The 9th edition spotlights the following themes and content:

Headlines

- Social, Mobile, Local: New content about social networks, the mobile platform, and local e-commerce appears throughout the book.
  - » Social networks such as Facebook, Twitter, and LinkedIn continue their rapid growth, laying the groundwork for a "social e-commerce platform" and continued expansion of social marketing opportunities.
  - » The mobile Internet platform composed of smartphones and tablet computers takes off and becomes a major factor in search, marketing, payment, retailing and services, and online content. Mobile device use poses new security and privacy issues as well.
  - » Location-based services lead to explosive growth in local advertising and marketing.
- Online privacy continues to deteriorate, driven by a culture of self-revelation and powerful technologies for collecting personal information online without the knowledge or consent of users.
- Internet security risks increase; cyberwarfare becomes a new way of conducting warfare among nation-states and a national security issue.

Business

- E-commerce revenues surge after the recession.
- Internet advertising growth resumes, at a faster rate than traditional advertising.
- Social marketing/advertising grows faster than search or display advertising.

E-commerce

business. technology. society.

NINTH EDITION

Kenneth C. Laudon
New York University

Carol Guercio Traver
Azimuth Interactive, Inc.

PEARSON

Boston Columbus Indianapolis New York San Francisco Upper Saddle River
Amsterdam Cape Town Dubai London Madrid Milan Munich Paris Montreal Toronto
Delhi Mexico City São Paulo Sydney Hong Kong Seoul Singapore Taipei Tokyo

Editor In Chief: Stephanie Wall
Executive Editor: Bob Horan
Editorial Project Manager: Kelly Loftus
Director of Marketing: Maggie Moylan
Senior Marketing Manager: Anne Fahlgren
Senior Managing Editor: Judy Leale
Senior Production Project Manager: Karalyn Holland
Operations Specialist: Maura Zaldivar
Creative Director: Blair Brown
Art Director: Steve Frim
Cover Designer: DePinho Design
Cover Image: Shutterstock VLADGRIN
Media Editor: Denise Vaughn
Media Project Manager: Lisa Rinaldi
Full Service Project Management: Azimuth Interactive, Inc.
Composition: Azimuth Interactive, Inc.
Printer/Binder: Edwards Brothers Malloy
Cover Printer: Lehigh-Phoenix Color/Hagarstown
Text Font: ITC Veljovic Std. Book, 9.5pt

Credits and acknowledgements borrowed from other sources and reproduced, with permission, in this textbook appear on page C-1.

Library of Congress Cataloging-in-Publication Information Is Available

10 9 8 7 6 5 4 3 2

ISBN 10: 0-13-273035-9
ISBN 13: 978-0-13-273035-8

Deniz Aksen, Koç University (Istanbul)

Carrie Andersen, Madison Area Technical College

Dr. Shirley A. Becker, Northern Arizona University

Prasad Bingi, Indiana-Purdue University, Fort Wayne

Christine Barnes, Lakeland Community College

Cliff Butler, North Seattle Community College

Joanna Broder, University of Arizona

James Buchan, College of the Ozarks

Ashley Bush, Florida State University

Mark Choman, Luzerne City Community College

Andrew Ciganek, Jacksonville State University

Daniel Connolly, University of Denver

Tom Critzer, Miami University

Dursan Delen, Oklahoma State University

Abhijit Deshmukh, University of Massachusetts

Brian L. Dos Santos, University of Louisville

Robert Drevs, University of Notre Dame

Akram El-Tannir, Hariri Canadian University, Lebanon

Kimberly Furumo, University of Hawaii at Hilo

John H. Gerdes, University of California, Riverside

Philip Gordon, University of California at Berkeley

Allan Greenberg, Brooklyn College

Bin Gu, University of Texas at Austin

Peter Haried, University of Wisconsin-La Crosse

Sherri Harms, University of Nebraska at Kearney

Sharon Heckel, St. Charles Community College

David Hite, Virginia Intermont College

Gus Jabbour, George Mason University

Ellen Kraft, Georgian Court University

Gilliean Lee, Lander University

Zoonky Lee, University of Nebraska, Lincoln

Andre Lemaylleux, Boston University, Brussels

Haim Levkowitz, University of Massachusetts, Lowell

Yair Levy, Nova Southeastern University

Richard Lucic, Duke University

John Mendonca, Purdue University

Dr. Abdulrahman Mirza, DePaul University

Kent Palmer, MacMurray College

Karen Palumbo, University of St. Francis

Wayne Pauli, Dakota State University

Jamie Pinchot, Thiel College

Kai Pommerenke, University of California at Santa Cruz

Barry Quinn, University of Ulster, Northern Ireland

Michelle Ramim, Nova Southeastern University

Jay Rhee, San Jose State University

Jorge Romero, Towson University

John Sagi, Anne Arundel Community College

Patricia Sendall, Merrimack College

Dr. Carlos Serrao, ISCTE/DCTI, Portugal

Neerja Sethi, Nanyang Business School, Singapore

Amber Settle, DePaul CTI

Vivek Shah, Texas State University-San Marcos

SUPPORT PACKAGE

The following supplementary materials are available to qualified instructors through the Online Instructor Resource Center. Contact your Prentice Hall sales representative for information about how to access them.

- **Instructor's Manual with solutions** This comprehensive manual pulls together a wide variety of teaching tools so that instructors can use the text easily and effectively. Each chapter contains an overview of key topics, a recap of the key learning objectives, additional topics for class discussion and debate, lecture tips, discussion of the chapter-ending case, and answers to the Case Study Questions, Review Questions, and Student Projects.

- **Test Bank** For quick test preparation, the author-created Test Bank contains multiple-choice, true/false, and short-essay questions that focus both on content and the development of critical/creative thinking about the issues evoked by the chapter. The Test Bank is available in Microsoft Word and TestGen format. The TestGen is also available in WebCT and BlackBoard-ready format. TestGen allows instructors to view, edit, and add questions.

- **PowerPoint lecture presentation slides** These slides illustrate key points, tables, and figures from the text in lecture-note format. The slides can be easily converted to transparencies or viewed electronically in the classroom. The slides also include additional questions for the opening cases and the "Insight on" vignettes throughout the book. These questions are very useful for in-class discussions, or quizzes.

- **Learning Tracks** These additional essays, created by the authors, provide instructors and students with more in-depth content on selected topics in e-commerce.

- **Video Cases** The authors have created a collection of video case studies that integrate short videos, supporting case study material, and case study questions. Video cases can be used in class to promote discussion or as written assignments.

ACKNOWLEDGMENTS

Pearson Education sought the advice of many excellent reviewers, all of whom strongly influenced the organization and substance of this book. The following individuals provided extremely useful evaluations of this and previous editions of the text:

Chapter-Closing Case Studies Each chapter concludes with a robust case study based on a real-world organization. These cases help students synthesize chapter concepts and apply this knowledge to concrete problems and scenarios such as evaluating Pandora's freemium business model, ExchangeHunterJumper's efforts to build a brand, and the fairness of the Google Books settlement.

Chapter-Ending Pedagogy Each chapter contains extensive end-of-chapter materials designed to reinforce the learning objectives of the chapter.

Key Concepts Keyed to the learning objectives, Key Concepts present the key points of the chapter to aid student study.

Review Questions Thought-provoking questions prompt students to demonstrate their comprehension and apply chapter concepts to management problem solving.

Projects At the end of each chapter are a number of projects that encourage students to apply chapter concepts and to use higher level evaluation skills. Many make use of the Internet and require students to present their findings in an oral or electronic presentation or written report. For instance, students are asked to evaluate publicly available information about a company's financials at the SEC Web site, assess payment system options for companies across international boundaries, or search for the top 10 cookies on their own computer and the sites they are from.

Web Resources Web resources that can extend students' knowledge of each chapter with projects, exercises, and additional content are available at www.azimuth-interactive.com/ecommerce9e. The Web site contains the following content provided by the authors:

- Additional projects, exercises, and tutorials
- Information on how to build a business plan and revenue models
- Essays on careers in e-commerce

"Insight on" Cases Each chapter contains three real-world cases illustrating the themes of technology, business, and society. These cases take an in-depth look at relevant topics to help describe and analyze the full breadth of the field of e-commerce. The cases probe such issues as the ability of governments to regulate Internet content, how to design Web sites for accessibility, the challenges faced by luxury marketers in online marketing, and smartphone security.

Margin Glossary Throughout the text, key terms and their definitions appear in the text margin where they are first introduced.

Real-Company Examples Drawn from actual e-commerce ventures, well over 100 pertinent examples are used throughout the text to illustrate concepts.

PEDAGOGY AND CHAPTER OUTLINE

The book's pedagogy emphasizes student cognitive awareness and the ability to analyze, synthesize, and evaluate e-commerce businesses. While there is a strong data and conceptual foundation to the book, we seek to engage student interest with lively writing about e-commerce businesses and the transformation of business models at traditional firms.

Each chapter contains a number of elements designed to make learning easy as well as interesting.

Learning Objectives A list of learning objectives that highlights the key concepts in the chapter guides student study.

Chapter-Opening Cases Each chapter opens with a story about a leading e-commerce company that relates the key objectives of the chapter to a real-life e-commerce business venture.

Pinterest:

A Picture Is Worth A Thousand Words

Like all of the most successful e-commerce companies, Pinterest taps into a simple truth. In Pinterest's case, the simple truth is that people love to collect things, and show off their collections to others. And like other Internet firms that have goals of global scope, such as Google, Facebook, and Amazon, Pinterest also has a global mission: to connect everyone in the world through the things they find interesting. How? Founded in 2009 by Ben Silbermann, Evan Sharp, and Paul Sciarra and launched in March 2010, Pinterest allows you to create virtual scrapbooks of images, video, and other content that you "pin" to a virtual bulletin board or pin board on the Web site. For instance, on a recent August day, the home page of the site was populated with a truly eclectic collection of images: luscious chocolate chip cookies, crochet high-heeled shoes, an intricate and colorful Japanese painting of a tiger, an R2D2 trash can, and a close-up of various nail designs, among others. Categories range from Animals to Videos, with Food & Drink, DIY & Crafts, and Women's Fashion among the most popular. Find something that you particularly like? In addition to "liking" and perhaps commenting on it, you can re-pin it to your own board, or follow a link back to the original source. Find someone whose taste you admire or who shares your passions? You can follow one or more of that pinner's boards to keep track of everything she or he pins.

According to comScore, Pinterest is one of the fastest growing Web sites it has ever tracked, growing an astounding 4,377% from May 2011 to May 2012. Reportedly the fastest Web site in history to reach 10 million visitors a month, Pinterest currently has around 20 million monthly visitors, an estimated 70% to 80% of them women. According to some tracking services, it is now the third largest social network in the United States, behind Facebook and Twitter. It is also one of the "stickiest" sites on the Web—according to comScore, users spend an average of 80 minutes per session on Pinterest, and almost 60% of users with accounts visit once or more a week. Jeff Jordan, a partner at Andreessen Horowitz, a venture capital firm and investor in Pinterest, says he has seen

© Blaize Pascall / Alamy

3

types of online payment systems (credit cards, stored value payment systems such as PayPal, digital wallets such as Google Wallet and others), and the development of mobile payment systems.

Part 3, "Business Concepts and Social Issues," focuses directly on the business concepts and social-legal issues that surround the development of e-commerce. Chapter 6 focuses on e-commerce consumer behavior, the Internet audience, and introduces the student to the basics of online marketing and branding, including online marketing technologies and marketing strategies. The use of social networks and social marketing campaigns to create and sustain brands is also discussed. Chapter 7 is devoted to online marketing communications, such as display advertising, social network marketing, mobile marketing, e-mail marketing, and search-engine marketing. Chapter 8 provides a thorough introduction to the social and legal environment of e-commerce. Here, you will find a description of the ethical and legal dimensions of e-commerce, including a thorough discussion of the latest developments in personal information privacy, intellectual property, Internet governance, jurisdiction, and public health and welfare issues such as pornography, gambling, and health information.

Part 4, "E-commerce in Action," focuses on real-world e-commerce experiences in retail and services, online media, auctions, portals, and social networks, and business-to-business e-commerce. These chapters take a sector approach rather than a conceptual approach as used in the earlier chapters. E-commerce is different in each of these sectors. Chapter 9 takes a close look at the experience of firms in the retail marketplace for both goods and services. Chapter 9 also includes an "E-commerce in Action" case that provides a detailed analysis of the business strategies and financial operating results of Amazon, which can be used as a model to analyze other e-commerce firms. Additional "E-commerce in Action" cases will be available online at the authors' Web site for the text, www.azimuth-interactive.com/ecommerce9e. Chapter 10 explores the world of online content and digital media, and examines the enormous changes in online publishing and entertainment industries that have occurred over the last two years, including streaming movies, e-books, and online newspapers. Chapter 11 explores the online world of social networks, auctions, and portals. Chapter 12 explores the world of B2B e-commerce, describing both electronic Net marketplaces and the less-heralded, but very large arena of private industrial networks and the movement toward collaborative commerce.

Special Attention to the Social and Legal Aspects of E-commerce We have paid special attention throughout the book to the social and legal context of e-commerce. Chapter 8 is devoted to a thorough exploration of four ethical dimensions of e-commerce: information privacy, intellectual property, governance, and protecting public welfare on the Internet. We have included an analysis of the latest Federal Trade Commission and other regulatory and nonprofit research reports, and their likely impact on the e-commerce environment.

A major theme through out this chapter, and the remainder of the book, is the impact of social, mobile, and local commerce on how consumers use the Internet.

Writing That's Fun to Read Unlike some textbooks, we've been told by many students that this book is actually fun to read and easy to understand. This is not a book written by committee—you won't find a dozen different people listed as authors, co-authors, and contributors on the title page. We have a consistent voice and perspective that carries through the entire text and we believe the book is the better for it.

OVERVIEW OF THE BOOK

The book is organized into four parts.

Part 1, "Introduction to E-commerce," provides an introduction to the major themes of the book. Chapter 1 defines e-commerce, distinguishes between e-commerce and e-business, and defines the different types of e-commerce. Chapter 2 introduces and defines the concepts of business model and revenue model, describes the major e-commerce business and revenue models for both B2C and B2B firms, and introduces the basic business concepts required throughout the text for understanding e-commerce firms including industry structure, value chains, and firm strategy.

Part 2, "Technology Infrastructure for E-commerce," focuses on the technology infrastructure that forms the foundation for all e-commerce. Chapter 3 traces the historical development of the Internet I and thoroughly describes how today's Internet works. A major focus of this chapter is mobile technology, Web 2.0 applications, and the near-term future Internet that is now under development and will shape the future of e-commerce. Chapter 4 builds on the Internet chapter by focusing on the steps managers need to follow in order to build a commercial Web site. This e-commerce infrastructure chapter covers the systems analysis and design process that should be followed in building an e-commerce Web presence; the major decisions regarding outsourcing site development and/or hosting; and how to choose software, hardware, and other tools that can improve Web site performance. Chapter 5 focuses on Internet security and payments, building on the e-commerce infrastructure discussion of the previous chapter by describing the ways security can be provided over the Internet. This chapter defines digital information security, describes the major threats to security, and then discusses both the technology and policy solutions available to business managers seeking to secure their firm's sites. This chapter concludes with a section on Internet payment systems. We identify the stakeholders in payment systems, the dimensions to consider in creating payment systems, and the various

In-depth Coverage of Marketing and Advertising The text includes two chapters on marketing and advertising. Marketing concepts, including social, mobile, and local marketing, market segmentation, personalization, clickstream analysis, bundling of digital goods, long-tail marketing, and dynamic pricing, are used throughout the text.

In-depth Coverage of B2B E-commerce We devote an entire chapter to an examination of B2B e-commerce. In writing this chapter, we developed a unique and easily understood classification schema to help students understand this complex arena of e-commerce. This chapter covers four types of Net marketplaces (e-distributors, e-procurement companies, exchanges, and industry consortia) as well as the development of private industrial networks and collaborative commerce.

Current and Future Technology Coverage Internet and related information technologies continue to change rapidly. The most important changes for e-commerce include dramatic price reductions in e-commerce infrastructure (making it much less expensive to develop sophisticated Web sites), the explosive growth in the mobile platform such as iPhones, iPads, tablet computers, and expansion in the development of social technologies, which are the foundation of online social networks. What was once a shortage of telecommunications capacity has now turned into a surplus, PC prices have continued to fall, smartphone and tablet sales have soared, Internet high-speed broadband connections are now typical and are continuing to show double-digit growth, and wireless technologies such as Wi-Fi and cellular broadband are transforming how, when, and where people access the Internet. While we thoroughly discuss the current Internet environment, we devote considerable attention to describing Web 2.0 and emerging technologies and applications such as the advanced network infrastructure, fiber optics, wireless Web and 4G technologies, Wi-Fi, IP multicasting, and future guaranteed service levels.

Up-to-Date Coverage of the Research Literature This text is well grounded in the e-commerce research literature. We have sought to include, where appropriate, references and analysis of the latest e-commerce research findings, as well as many classic articles, in all of our chapters. We have drawn especially on the disciplines of economics, marketing, and information systems and technologies, as well as law journals and broader social science research journals including sociology and psychology.

We do not use references to Wikipedia in this text, for a variety of reasons. Most colleges do not consider Wikipedia a legitimate or acceptable source for academic research and instruct their students not to cite it. Material found on Wikipedia may be out of date, lack coverage, lack critical perspective, and cannot necessarily be trusted. Our references are to respected academic journals; industry sources such as eMarketer, comScore, Hitwise, Nielsen, and Gartner; newspapers such as the *New York Times* and *Wall Street Journal*; and industry publications such as *Computerworld* and *InformationWeek*, among others. Figures and tables sourced to "authors' estimates" reflect analysis of data from the U.S. Department of Commerce, estimates from various research firms, historical trends, revenues of major online retailers, consumer online buying trends, and economic conditions.

FEATURES AND COVERAGE

Strong Conceptual Foundation The book emphasizes the three major driving forces behind e-commerce: business development and strategy, technological innovations, and social controversies and impacts. Each of these driving forces is represented in every chapter, and together they provide a strong and coherent conceptual framework for understanding e-commerce. We analyze e-commerce, digital markets, and e-business firms just as we would ordinary businesses and markets using concepts from economics, marketing, finance, sociology, philosophy, and information systems. We strive to maintain a critical perspective on e-commerce and avoid industry hyperbole.

Some of the important concepts from economics and marketing that we use to explore e-commerce are transaction cost, network externalities, information asymmetry, social networks, perfect digital markets, segmentation, price dispersion, targeting, and positioning. Important concepts from the study of information systems and technologies play an important role in the book, including Internet standards and protocols, client/server computing, multi-tier server systems, cloud computing, mobile digital platform and wireless technologies, and public key encryption, among many others. From the literature on ethics and society, we use important concepts such as intellectual property, privacy, information rights and rights management, governance, public health, and welfare.

From the literature on business, we use concepts such as business process design, return on investment, strategic advantage, industry competitive environment, oligopoly, and monopoly. We also provide a basic understanding of finance and accounting issues, and extend this through an "E-commerce in Action" case that critically examines the financial statements of Amazon. One of the witticisms that emerged from the early years of e-commerce and that still seems apt is the notion that e-commerce changes everything except the rules of business. Businesses still need to make a profit in order to survive in the long term.

Currency Important new developments happen almost every day in e-commerce and the Internet. We try to capture as many of these important new developments in each annual edition. You will not find a more current book for a course offered during the 2013 academic year. Many other texts are already six months to a year out of date before they even reach the printer. This text, in contrast, reflects extensive research through October 2012, just weeks before the book hits the press.

Real-World Business Firm Focus and Cases From Akamai Technologies to Google, Microsoft, Apple, and Amazon, to Facebook, Twitter, and Tumblr, to Netflix, Pandora, and Elemica, this book contains hundreds of real-company examples and over 60 more extensive cases that place coverage in the context of actual dot.com businesses. You'll find these examples in each chapter, as well as in special features such as chapter-opening, chapter-closing, and "Insight on" cases. The book takes a realistic look at the world of e-commerce, describing what's working and what isn't, rather than presenting a rose-colored or purely "academic" viewpoint.

We also discuss how e-commerce firms learned from the mistakes of early firms, and how established firms are using e-commerce to succeed. Above all, we attempt to bring a strong sense of business realism and sensitivity to the often exaggerated descriptions of e-commerce. As founders of a dot.com company and participants in the e-commerce revolution, we have learned that the "e" in e-commerce does not stand for "easy."

The Web and e-commerce have caused a major revolution in marketing and advertising in the United States. We spend two chapters discussing how marketing and advertising dollars are moving away from traditional media, and towards online media and their huge audiences, creating significant growth in search engine marketing, targeted display advertising, online rich media/video ads, and social marketing techniques.

E-commerce is driven by Internet technology. Internet technology, and information technology in general, is perhaps the star of the show. Without the Internet, e-commerce would be virtually nonexistent. Accordingly, we provide three chapters specifically on the Internet and e-commerce technology, and in every chapter we provide continuing coverage by illustrating how the topic of the chapter is being shaped by new information technologies. For instance, Internet technology drives developments in security and payment systems, marketing strategies and advertising, financial applications, media distribution, business-to-business trade, and retail e-commerce. We discuss the rapid growth of the mobile digital platform, the emergence of cloud computing, new open source software tools and applications that enable Web 2.0, and new types of Internet-based information systems that support electronic business-to-business markets.

E-commerce is not only about business and technology, however. The third part of the equation for understanding e-commerce is society. E-commerce and Internet technologies have important social consequences that business leaders can ignore only at their peril. E-commerce has challenged our concepts of privacy, intellectual property, and even our ideas about national sovereignty and governance. Google, Facebook, Apple, Amazon, and assorted advertising networks maintain profiles on millions of shoppers and consumers worldwide. The proliferation of illegally copied music and videos on the Internet, and the growth of social networking sites often based on displaying copyrighted materials without permission, are challenging the intellectual property rights of record labels, Hollywood studios, and artists. And many countries—including the United States—are demanding to control the content of Web sites displayed within their borders for political and social reasons. Tax authorities in the United States and Europe are demanding that e-commerce sites pay sales taxes just like ordinary brick and mortar stores on mainstreet. As a result of these challenges to existing institutions, e-commerce and the Internet are the subject of increasing investigation, litigation, and legislation. Business leaders need to understand these societal developments, and they cannot afford to assume any longer that the Internet is borderless, beyond social control and regulation, or a place where market efficiency is the only consideration. In addition to an entire chapter devoted to the social and legal implications of e-commerce, each chapter contains material highlighting the social implications of e-commerce.

Seung Jae Shin, Mississippi State University

Sumit Sircar, University of Texas at Arlington

Hongjun Song, University of Memphis

Pamela Specht, University of Nebraska at Omaha

Esther Swilley, Kansas State University

Tony Townsend, Iowa State University

Bill Troy, University of New Hampshire

Susan VandeVen, Southern Polytechnic State University

Hiep Van Dong, Madison Area Technical College

Mary Vitrano, Palm Beach Community College

Andrea Wachter, Point Park University

Catherine Wallace, Massey University, New Zealand

Biao Wang, Boston University

Haibo Wang, Texas A&M International University

Harry Washington, Lincoln University

Rolf Wigand, University of Arkansas at Little Rock

Erin Wilkinson, Johnson & Wales University

Alice Wilson, Cedar Crest College

Dezhi Wu, Southern Utah University

Gene Yelle, SUNY Institute of Technology

David Zolzer, Northwestern State University

We would like to thank eMarketer, Inc. and David Iankelevich for their permission to include data and figures from their research reports in our text. eMarketer is one of the leading independent sources for statistics, trend data, and original analysis covering many topics related to the Internet, e-business, and emerging technologies. eMarketer aggregates e-business data from multiple sources worldwide.

In addition, we would like to thank all those at Prentice Hall who have worked so hard to make sure this book is the very best it can be. We want to thank Bob Horan, Executive Editor of the Prentice Hall MIS list, and Karalyn Holland, Senior Production Project Manager, for their support; Judy Leale for overseeing production of this project; and DePinho Design for the outstanding cover design. Very special thanks to Robin Pickering, Megan Miller, and Will Anderson at Azimuth Interactive, Inc., for all their hard work on the production of, and supplements for, this book.

A special thanks also to Susan Hartman, Executive Editor for the first and second editions and to Frank Ruggirello, Publisher at Addison-Wesley when we began this project, and now Vice President and Editorial Director at Benjamin-Cummings.

Finally, last but not least, we would like to thank our family and friends, without whose support this book would not have been possible.

Kenneth C. Laudon
Carol Guercio Traver

Brief Contents

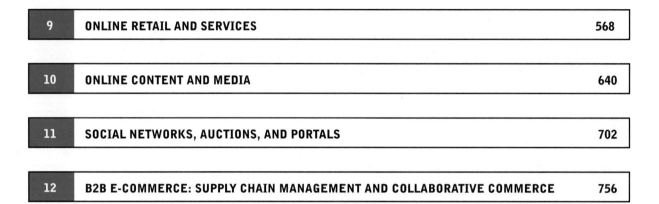

Contents

PART 2 Technology Infrastructure for E-commerce

5	E-COMMERCE SECURITY AND PAYMENT SYSTEMS	256

PART 3 Business Concepts and Social Issues

| 6 | E-COMMERCE MARKETING CONCEPTS: SOCIAL, MOBILE, LOCAL | 334 |

PART 4 E-commerce in Action

10	**ONLINE CONTENT AND MEDIA**	**640**

11 SOCIAL NETWORKS, AUCTIONS, AND PORTALS   702

Introduction to E-commerce

CHAPTER 1

The Revolution Is Just Beginning

LEARNING OBJECTIVES

After reading this chapter, you will be able to:

- Define e-commerce and describe how it differs from e-business.
- Identify and describe the unique features of e-commerce technology and discuss their business significance.
- Recognize and describe Web 2.0 applications.
- Describe the major types of e-commerce.
- Discuss the origins and growth of e-commerce.
- Understand the evolution of e-commerce from its early years to today.
- Identify the factors that will define the future of e-commerce.
- Describe the major themes underlying the study of e-commerce.
- Identify the major academic disciplines contributing to e-commerce.

Pinterest:

A Picture Is Worth A Thousand Words

Like all of the most successful e-commerce companies, Pinterest taps into a simple truth. In Pinterest's case, the simple truth is that people love to collect things, and show off their collections to others. And like other Internet firms that have goals of global scope, such as Google, Facebook, and Amazon, Pinterest also has a global mission: to connect everyone in the world through the things they find interesting. How? Founded in 2009 by Ben Silbermann, Evan Sharp, and Paul Sciarra and launched in March 2010, Pinterest allows you to create virtual scrapbooks of images, video, and other content that you "pin" to a virtual

© Blaize Pascall / Alamy

bulletin board or pin board on the Web site. For instance, on a recent August day, the home page of the site was populated with a truly eclectic collection of images: luscious chocolate chip cookies, crochet high-heeled shoes, an intricate and colorful Japanese painting of a tiger, an R2D2 trash can, and a close-up of various nail designs, among others. Categories range from Animals to Videos, with Food & Drink, DIY & Crafts, and Women's Fashion among the most popular. Find something that you particularly like? In addition to "liking" and perhaps commenting on it, you can re-pin it to your own board, or follow a link back to the original source. Find someone whose taste you admire or who shares your passions? You can follow one or more of that pinner's boards to keep track of everything she or he pins.

According to comScore, Pinterest is one of the fastest growing Web sites it has ever tracked, growing an astounding 4,377% from May 2011 to May 2012. Reportedly the fastest Web site in history to reach 10 million visitors a month, Pinterest currently has around 20 million monthly visitors, an estimated 70% to 80% of them women. According to some tracking services, it is now the third largest social network in the United States, behind Facebook and Twitter. It is also one of the "stickiest" sites on the Web—according to comScore, users spend an average of 80 minutes per session on Pinterest, and almost 60% of users with accounts visit once or more a week. Jeff Jordan, a partner at Andreessen Horowitz, a venture capital firm and investor in Pinterest, says he has seen only one other site with similar numbers—Facebook. But unlike Facebook, Pinterest currently doesn't accept paid advertisements, nor does it have a clear business model for producing revenue. Despite this, it is poised to become a major factor in the social e-commerce wave sweeping through the e-commerce landscape.

Whole Foods, the natural foods supermarket chain, was one of the first companies to develop a presence on Pinterest, and now has more than 55,000 followers. It doesn't use Pinterest to advertise its own products in an overt way. Instead, it uses Pinterest as a way to communicate Whole Foods' core values, such as caring about the community and the environment, promoting healthy eating, and selling high-quality organic and natural food, through carefully curating and presenting images relevant to those values. Pinterest is also having an impact on the magazine world. For instance, Time Inc.'s *Real Simple,* also an early adopter, is one of the most-followed brands on Pinterest, with more than 150,000 followers. Pinterest has become a leading source of traffic to the Real Simple Web site, providing twice as many referrals as Facebook and Twitter combined. Its success has not gone unnoticed. Other publishers, such as Hearst, Martha Stewart, and Condé Nast are now using Pinterest for their own magazines, and experiencing similar results. Fashion icons such as Oscar de la Renta and Badgley Mischka have used Pinterest to "live pin" their fashion shows and preview their collections.

For consumers, Pinterest can function both as a source of inspiration and aspiration. It has proven to be very popular for creating shopping wish lists and a great way to get ideas. Retailers, in particular, have taken notice and for good reason: several recent reports have shown that Pinterest helps drive shoppers to make purchases. For example, a study of 25,000 online stores using the Shopify e-commerce platform found there was as much traffic originating from Pinterest as from Twitter, and that Pinterest users spend an average of $80 each time they make an online purchase, twice the amount of Facebook users. Bizrate Insights found that almost a third of online shoppers surveyed have made a purchase based on what they'd seen on Pinterest and other image-sharing sites; an even higher percentage (37%) have seen items they want to buy but have not yet purchased. Wayfair, a furniture and home goods retailer, boosted conversions more than 100% and average order size by almost half in four weeks after a scavenger hunt it hosted on Pinterest. As a result, savvy retailers are starting to work Pinterest into their marketing mix. A recent Responsys study found that almost 25% of large retailers are highlighting Pinterest in their marketing e-mail, and it will likely soon overtake YouTube as the third most promoted social media site in retailers' e-mails behind Facebook and Twitter. eBay and Amazon are also getting into the act, and have added Pinterest buttons that allow users to share product images and page links directly from eBay and Amazon.

Pinterest's Web site was created using Django, an open source Web 2.0 framework that uses the Python programming language, which enables rapid development and reusability of components, coupled with elegant design. The Pinterest Web site reportedly went through 30 to 40 different iterations before settling on the final design. As with Facebook and Twitter, many third-party developers have also joined the party, with additional apps, browser extensions, and other third-party content that leverage off of the Pinterest platform. For instance, Zoomingo offers both a Web site and a mobile shopping app that allows you to find and get sale alerts for items you and others have pinned. Pinterest is also aggressive about leveraging ties to other social networks such as Facebook and Twitter—when you register, you can do so via Facebook, Twitter, or e-mail. Once you've registered, you can easily add Pinterest to your Facebook Timeline or link to your Twitter account.

On the mobile front, Pinterest introduced its own iPhone app in March 2011 and has frequently updated it since then, and an iPad app is also available for purchase. However, rather than develop additional stand-alone apps for Android, BlackBerry, or Windows smartphones, Pinterest chose a different route: to create a mobile version of the Web site using HTML5. Unlike an app, Pinterest Mobile runs inside the smartphone's browser rather than as a stand-alone program, and is able to serve multiple platforms.

Despite all the recent good news for Pinterest, there are some significant issues lurking just behind the scenes that may cloud its future; chief among them is copyright infringement. The basis of Pinterest's business model involves users potentially violating others' copyrights by posting images without permission and/or attribution. Although Pinterest's Terms of Service puts the onus on its users to avoid doing so, the site knowingly facilitates such actions by, for example, providing a "Pin it" tool embedded in the user's browser toolbar. Much of the content on the site reportedly violates its Terms of Service. Pinterest has provided an opt-out code to enable other sites to bar its content from being shared on Pinterest, but some question why they should have to take action when Pinterest is creating the problem. Further, the code does not necessarily resolve the issue since it does not prevent someone from downloading an image and then uploading it to Pinterest. Another thing Pinterest has done to try to ameliorate the problem is to automatically add citations (attribution) to content coming from certain specified sources, such as Flickr, YouTube, Vimeo, Etsy, Kickstarter, and SlideShare, among others. It also complies with the Digital Millenium Copyright Act, which requires sites to remove images that violate copyright, but this too requires the copyright holder to be proactive and take action to demand the images be removed. Some have suggested that Pinterest follow YouTube's lead and implement a filter system, coupled with a revenue sharing platform. Although no major copyright cases have been filed against it so far, how Pinterest resolves this issue may have a major impact on its ultimate success.

Pinterest is also not immune to the spam and scams that plague many e-commerce initiatives. The security company McAfee has discovered several money-making scams aimed at Pinterest users. For example, one scam pushes you to pin a scammer's site to your Pinterest profiles. If you do so, clicking on the link gets redirected and the scammer gets a referral fee if you ultimately buy something. Other scammers promise free products for repinning images and filling out a survey, and then redirect you to a phishing site that collects personal details. Fake apps on Google Play claim to be official Pinterest apps for Android, and display ads and gather personal data, unbeknownst to the user. Security analysts believe Pinterest will have to adapt its systems to deal with scammers and warn users to be wary of requests to pin content before viewing it and to be suspicious of "free" offers, surveys, and links with questionable titles. Pinterest has acknowledged the problem and has promised to improve its technology.

SOURCES: "Meet Django," Djangoproject.com, accessed August 13, 2012; "Going Mobile with Pinterest," Pinterestinvite.org, accessed August 13, 2012; "Pinterest Gives Copyright Credit to Etsy, Kickstarter, SoundCloud," by Sarah Kessler, Mashable.com, July 19, 2012; "Whole Foods: The King of Pinterest?," by Vicky Garza, *Austin Business Journal,* July 13, 2012; "Wayfair Finds Profits in a Pinterest Scavenger Hunt," by Amy Dusto, InternetRetailer.com, July 12, 2012; "Pinterest on Wish List of Rakuten, Japan's Amazon," by Evelyn M. Rusli, *New York Times,* July 12, 2012; "A Mobile Shopping App Takes an Interest in Pinterest," by Katie Deatsch, InternetRetailer.com, July 11, 2012; "Pinterest Tops Tumblr in National Popularity?," by Stephanie Mlot, *PC Magazine,* June 28, 2012; "BadgleyMischka Previews Resort Collection via Pinterest," by Jessica C. Andrews, *New York Times,* June 8, 2012; "Pinterest Whets Consumer Desire with Images that Turn Window Shoppers into Online Buyers," by Matt Butter, *Forbes,* June 6, 2012; "Gemvara Raises $25 Million," by Stefany Moore, InternetRetailer.com, June 5, 2012; "Pinterest Raises $100 Million with $1.5 Billion Valuation," by Pui-Wing Tam, *Wall Street Journal,* May 17, 2012; "Japanese E-commerce Company Rakuten Invests in Pinterest," by Zak Stambor, InternetRetailer.com, May 17, 2012; "Now on Pinterest: Scams," by Riva Richmond, *New York Times,* May 16, 2012; "Real Simple is First Print Mag to Reach 100K Pinterest Followers," *Advertising Age,* May 11, 2012; "Pinterest Plagued by More Scams, Fake Android Apps," by Fahmida Y. Rashid, PCMag.com, April 30, 2012; "Nearly 1/3 Online Shoppers Have Made Purchases from What They've Seen on Pinterest," by Zak Stambor, InternetRetailer.com, April 25, 2012; "E-commerce Giants Amazon and eBay Add Pinterest Buttons," by Kate Kaye, ClickZ.com, April 11, 2012; "Many Magazines Racing to Capitalize on Pinterest, *Advertising Age,* April 2, 2012; Interest in Pinterest Skyrockets," by Zak Stambor, InternetRetailer.com, March 23, 2012; "Is Pinterest the Next Napster," by Therese Poletti, *Wall*

Street Journal, March 14, 2012; "A Site That Aims to Unleash the Scrapbook Maker in All of Us," by Jenna Wortham, *New York Times*, March 11, 2012; "What Marketers Can Learn from Whole Foods' Organic Approach to Pinterest," by Lauren Drell, Mashable.com, February 23, 2012; "Pinterest Releases Optional Code to Prevent Unwanted Image Sharing," by Andrew Webster, Theverge.com, February 20, 2012; "A Scrapbook on the Web Catches Fire," by David Pogue, *New York Times*, February 15, 2012.

Another issue facing Pinterest is competition. Will Pinterest be like MySpace, destined to be eclipsed by a later entrant? Although some similar firms preceded Pinterest into the "visual collection" space, such as Polyvore and StyleCaster, Pinterest can be considered a first mover and as such has some significant advantages. However, other competitors are quickly springing up, such as Juxtapost (which allows private boards), Manteresting (aimed at the male demographic), and most recently, The Fancy. The Fancy has a revenue model based on linking its users to transactions, taking a 10% cut of purchases in the process, and has backing from co-founders of both Twitter and Facebook. In August 2012, Apple was reportedly in talks to purchase The Fancy, and if the acquisition is completed, The Fancy could become a formidable rival to Pinterest.

In 1994, e-commerce as we now know it did not exist. In 2012, less than 20 years later, around 150 million American consumers are expected to spend about $362 billion, and businesses more than $4.1 trillion, purchasing goods and services online or via a mobile device. A similar story has occurred throughout the world. And in this short period of time, e-commerce has been reinvented not just once, but twice.

The early years of e-commerce, during the late 1990s, were a period of business vision, inspiration, and experimentation. It soon became apparent, however, that establishing a successful business model based on those visions would not be easy. There followed a period of retrenchment and reevaluation, which led to the stock market crash of 2000–2001, with the value of e-commerce, telecommunications, and other technology stocks plummeting by more than 90% in the space of a year. After the bubble burst, many people were quick to write off e-commerce, predicting that its growth would stagnate, and the Internet audience would plateau. But they were wrong. The surviving firms refined and honed their business models, ultimately leading to models that actually produced profits. Between 2002–2008, retail e-commerce grew at more than 25% per year.

Today, we are in the middle of yet another transition: a new and vibrant social, mobile, and local model of e-commerce growing alongside the more traditional e-commerce retail sales model exemplified by Amazon. Social network sites such as Facebook, Twitter, YouTube, and Pinterest, which enable users to distribute their own content (such as videos, music, photos, personal information, blogs, and software applications), have rocketed to prominence. Spurred by the explosive growth in smartphones such as iPhones and Androids, tablet computers, and netbooks, a new e-commerce platform is emerging called "social e-commerce" because it is so closely intertwined with social networks, mobile computing, and heretofore private social relationships. Never before in the history of media have such large audiences been aggregated and made so accessible. Businesses are grappling with how best to approach this audience from an advertising and marketing perspective. Companies such as Groupon are seeking to combine these large audiences, social networks, and localization into new local marketing models. Governments, private groups, and industry players are trying to understand how to protect privacy on this new e-commerce platform. Social networks and user-generated content sites are also examples of technology that is highly disruptive of traditional media firms. The movement of eyeballs towards these sites means fewer viewers of cable and broadcast television and Hollywood movies, and fewer readers of printed newspapers and magazines, and so those industries are also facing a transition. It's probably safe to predict that this will not be the last transition for e-commerce, either.

1.1 E-COMMERCE: THE REVOLUTION IS JUST BEGINNING

In fact, the e-commerce revolution is just beginning. For example, in 2012:

- Online consumer retail sales in the United States are expected to grow by more than 15% compared to traditional retail growth of only about 3.4%. Around 150 million Internet users make at least one purchase during the year, and an additional 35 million use the Web to gather information about potential product purchases (eMarketer, Inc., 2012a; National Retail Foundation, 2012). Globally, growth rates are even higher: in Europe, business-to-consumer (B2C) e-commerce grew more than 18% to an estimated $260 billion, compared to flat traditional retail sales (Internet Retailer, 2012a). And in emerging markets such as China, India, and Brazil, growth rates are even higher, ranging from an astronomical 140% for China, 40% for India, to 22% in Brazil (eMarketer, Inc., 2012x).

- Mobile e-commerce in the United States has exploded, almost doubling from $6.7 billion in 2011 to an estimated $11.6 billion in 2012 (eMarketer Inc., 2012b).

- An "app economy" has developed in parallel with Internet e-commerce. E-commerce conducted through millions of apps is expected to produce an estimated $13 billion in revenue worldwide in 2012 (Yankee Group, 2012).

- Social e-commerce, although still in its infancy, has tripled in the United States, from $1 billion in 2011 to an estimated $3 billion in 2012, and the rest of the world is expected to spend about double that amount ($6 billion) (eMarketer, Inc., 2012c).

- Local e-commerce, the third dimension of the social, mobile, local e-commerce wave, also is growing in the United States, from $1.6 billion in 2011 to an estimated $2.9 billion in 2012 (eMarketer, Inc, 2011a).

- The number of individuals of all ages online in the United States is expected to increase to about 239 million, up from 232 million in 2011. (The total population of the United States is about 314 million.) Of these, about 193 million are adults (over 18) (eMarketer, Inc., 2012d, 2012e; U.S. Census Bureau, 2012a). Worldwide, around 2.3 billion are online, about 33% of the world's population.

- Of the total 119 million households in the United States, the number online is estimated to increase to about 89 million (or about 75% of all households) (eMarketer, Inc., 2011b).

- On an average day, around 82% of adult U.S. Internet users go online. About 59% send e-mail, 59% use a search engine, 48% use a social network. Around 45% get news, 28% watch an online video or look for information about a product or service they are thinking of buying, 24% do online banking, and 17% look for information on Wikipedia. (Pew Internet & American Life Project, 2012).

- B2B e-commerce—the use of the Internet for business-to-business commerce—will total about $4.1 trillion, comprising about 36% of all business-to-business trade in the United States (U.S. Census Bureau, 2012b; authors' estimates).

- The Internet technology base gained greater depth and power, as around 82.2 million households (about 69% of all U.S. households) have broadband cable, DSL, or wireless/satellite access to the Internet and 122 million people access the Internet via mobile devices (eMarketer, Inc., 2012f). Worldwide, around 594 million households have broadband access and 1.4 billion are mobile Internet users (eMarketer, 2012b).

These developments signal many of the themes in the new edition of this book (see **Table 1.1**). Social networks are becoming a new e-commerce platform that will rival traditional e-commerce platforms by providing search, advertising, and payment services to vendors and customers. Who needs Google when you can have a swarm of friends recommend music, clothes, cars, and videos, or see ads on a social site where you spend most of your time online? The mobile platform based on smartphones like the iPhone, tablet computers like the iPad, and netbooks has also finally arrived with a bang, making true mobile e-commerce a reality.

More and more people and businesses are using the Internet to conduct commerce; smaller, local firms are learning how to take advantage of the Internet as Web services and Web site tools become very inexpensive. New e-commerce brands emerge while traditional retail brands such as Sears, JCPenney, and Walmart further extend their multi-channel, bricks-and-clicks strategies and retain their dominant retail positions by strengthening their Internet operations. At the societal level, other trends are apparent. The Internet has created a platform for millions of people to create and share content, establish new social bonds, and strengthen existing ones through social networks, blogging, and video-posting sites. These same social networks have created significant privacy issues. The major digital copyright owners have increased their pursuit of online file-swapping services with mixed success, while reaching broad agreements with the big technology players like Apple, Amazon, and Google to protect intellectual property rights. States have successfully moved toward taxation of Internet sales, while Internet gaming sites have been severely curtailed through criminal prosecutions in the United States. Sovereign nations have expanded their surveillance of, and control over, Internet communications and content as a part of their anti-terrorist activities and their traditional interest in snooping on citizens. Privacy seems to have lost some of its meaning in an age when millions create public online personal profiles.

THE FIRST 30 SECONDS

It is important to realize that the rapid growth and change that has occurred in the first 17 years of e-commerce represents just the beginning—what could be called the first 30 seconds of the e-commerce revolution. The same technologies that drove the first decade and a half of e-commerce (described in Chapter 3) continue to evolve at exponential rates. This underlying ferment in the technological groundwork of the Internet and Web presents entrepreneurs with new opportunities to both create new businesses and new business models in traditional industries, and also to destroy old businesses. Business change becomes disruptive, rapid, and even destructive, while offering entrepreneurs new opportunities and resources for investment.

Improvements in underlying information technologies and continuing entrepreneurial innovation in business and marketing promise as much change in the next decade as was seen in the last decade. The twenty-first century will be the age of a digitally enabled social and commercial life, the outlines of which we can barely perceive at this time. Analysts estimate that by 2016, consumers will be spending about $542 billion and businesses about $5.7 trillion in online transactions. In 2020, industry

TABLE 1.1	MAJOR TRENDS IN E-COMMERCE 2012–2013

BUSINESS

- A new "social e-commerce" platform continues to emerge based on social networks and supported by advertising.
- A new app-based online economy grows alongside traditional Internet e-commerce.
- Retail e-commerce in the United States continues double-digit growth (over 15%), building on its 2010 and 2011 resurgence, after slow growth in 2008 and 2009 due to the recession.
- Facebook continues to grow, with more than 1 billion active users worldwide.
- Twitter continues to grow, with more than 140 million active users worldwide.
- Mobile retail e-commerce explodes to more than $11 billion in the United States.
- Localization of e-commerce expands with group marketing and localized tracking of mobile consumers.
- Consumer packaged goods begin to find their online market.
- Search engine marketing continues to challenge traditional marketing and advertising media as more consumers switch their eyes to the Web.
- Social and mobile advertising platforms show strong growth and begin to challenge search engine marketing.
- Online population growth in the United States slows, but the amount of the average purchase expands.
- The online demographics of shoppers continue to broaden with the fastest growth among tweens, teens, and older adults.
- Online businesses continue to strengthen profitability by refining their business models and leveraging the capabilities of the Internet.
- The breadth of e-commerce offerings grows, especially in entertainment, retail apparel, luxury goods, appliances, and home furnishings.
- Small businesses and entrepreneurs continue to flood into the e-commerce marketplace, often riding on the infrastructures created by industry giants such as Apple, Facebook, Amazon, Google, and eBay.
- Brand extension through the Internet continues to grow as large firms such as Sears, JCPenney, L.L.Bean, and Walmart pursue integrated, multi-channel bricks-and-clicks strategies.
- B2B supply chain transactions and collaborative commerce in the United States continue to strengthen and grow beyond the $4.1 trillion mark.

TECHNOLOGY

- A mobile computing and communications platform based on iPhones, BlackBerrys, and other smartphones, netbook computers, and the iPad (the "new client") becomes a reality and begins to rival the PC platform.
- More than 1 million apps in Apple's and Google's app stores create a new platform for online transactions, marketing, and advertising.
- The Internet broadband foundation becomes stronger in households and businesses. Bandwidth prices fall as telecommunications companies expand their capacities with new technologies.
- Computing and networking component prices continue to fall dramatically.

TABLE 1.1	MAJOR TRENDS IN E-COMMERCE 2012–2013

- As firms track the trillions of online interactions that occur each day on the Web, a flood of data, typically referred to as "Big Data," is being produced.
- In order to make sense out of Big Data, firms turn to sophisticated software called business analytics (or Web analytics) that can identify purchase patterns as well as consumer interests and intentions in milliseconds.
- Cloud computing completes the transformation of the mobile platform by storing consumer content and software on Internet servers and making it available to any consumer-connected device from the desktop to a smartphone.
- Real-time advertising becomes a reality as firms gain in computing power and database speeds.
- The global population using the Internet continues to expand by about 8.5%, with around 32% now online.

SOCIETY

- Consumer- and user-generated content, and syndication in the form of social networks, tweets, blogs, and wikis, continue to grow and provide an entirely new self-publishing forum that engages millions of consumers.
- The amount of data the average American consumes each day (currently around 34 gigabytes) continues to increase.
- Social networks encourage self-revelation, while threatening privacy.
- Traditional media such as television, newspapers, books, and magazines continue to lose subscribers, and adopt online, interactive models and mobile apps that offer new advertising and revenue platforms.
- E-books finally gain wide acceptance and today account for about half of all book sales.
- Conflicts over copyright management and control continue, but there is substantial agreement among Internet distributors and copyright owners that they need one another.
- Explosive growth continues in online and mobile viewing of video and television programs.
- Participation by adults in social networks on the Internet increases; Facebook becomes ever more popular in all demographic categories.
- Taxation of Internet sales becomes more widespread and accepted by large online merchants.
- Surveillance of Internet communications by both repressive regimes and Western democracies grows.
- Concerns over commercial and governmental privacy invasion increase as firms provide government agencies with access to private personal information.
- Internet security continues to decline as major sites are hacked and lose control over customer information.
- Spam remains a significant problem despite legislation and promised technology fixes.
- Invasion of personal privacy on the Web expands as marketers extend their capabilities to track users.
- Google becomes the target of anti-competitive and antitrust claims because of its search engine dominance.

analysts are calling for e-commerce to be about 17% of all retail sales (Deatsch, 2010). It appears likely that e-commerce will eventually impact nearly all commerce, and that most commerce will be e-commerce by the year 2050.

Is there a terminal point towards which e-commerce is hurtling? Can e-commerce continue to grow indefinitely? It's possible that at some point, e-commerce growth may slow simply as a result of overload: people may just not have the time to watch yet another online video, open another e-mail, or read another blog, tweet, or Facebook update. However, currently, there is no foreseeable limit to the continued rapid development of Internet and e-commerce technology, or limits on the inventiveness of entrepreneurs to develop new uses for the technology. Therefore, for now at least, it is likely that the disruptive process will continue.

Business fortunes are made—and lost—in periods of extraordinary change such as this. The next five years hold out extraordinary opportunities—as well as risks—for new and traditional businesses to exploit digital technology for market advantage. For society as a whole, the next few decades offer the possibility of extraordinary gains in social wealth as the digital revolution works its way through larger and larger segments of the world's economy, offering the possibility of high rates of productivity and income growth in an inflation-free environment.

As a business or technology student, this book will help you perceive and understand the opportunities and risks that lie ahead. By the time you finish, you will be able to identify the technological, business, and social forces that have shaped the growth of e-commerce and extend that understanding into the years ahead.

WHAT IS E-COMMERCE?

e-commerce

the use of the Internet, the Web, and apps to transact business. More formally, digitally enabled commercial transactions between and among organizations and individuals

Our focus in this book is **e-commerce**—the use of the Internet, the World Wide Web (Web) and mobile apps to transact business. Although the terms Internet and Web are often used interchangeably, they are actually two very different things. The Internet is a worldwide network of computer networks, and the Web is one of the Internet's most popular services, providing access to billions of Web pages. An app (short-hand for application) is a software application. The term is typically used when referring to mobile applications, although it is also sometimes used to refer to desktop computer applications as well. (We describe the Internet, Web, and apps more fully later in this chapter and in Chapter 3 and Chapter 4.) More formally, we focus on digitally enabled commercial transactions between and among organizations and individuals. Each of these components of our working definition of e-commerce is important. *Digitally enabled transactions* include all transactions mediated by digital technology. For the most part, this means transactions that occur over the Internet, the Web and/or via mobile apps. *Commercial transactions* involve the exchange of value (e.g., money) across organizational or individual boundaries in return for products and services. Exchange of value is important for understanding the limits of e-commerce. Without an exchange of value, no commerce occurs.

The professional literature sometimes refers to e-commerce as "digital commerce" in part to reflect the fact that in 2012, apps account for a small but growing amount of e-commerce revenues. For our purposes, we consider "e-commerce" and "digital commerce" to be synonymous.

THE DIFFERENCE BETWEEN E-COMMERCE AND E-BUSINESS

There is a debate among consultants and academics about the meaning and limitations of both e-commerce and e-business. Some argue that e-commerce encompasses the entire world of electronically based organizational activities that support a firm's market exchanges—including a firm's entire information system's infrastructure (Rayport and Jaworski, 2003). Others argue, on the other hand, that e-business encompasses the entire world of internal and external electronically based activities, including e-commerce (Kalakota and Robinson, 2003).

We think it is important to make a working distinction between e-commerce and e-business because we believe they refer to different phenomena. E-commerce is not "anything digital" that a firm does. For purposes of this text, we will use the term **e-business** to refer primarily to the digital enabling of transactions and processes *within* a firm, involving information systems under the control of the firm. For the most part, in our view, e-business does not include commercial transactions involving an exchange of value across organizational boundaries. For example, a company's online inventory control mechanisms are a component of e-business, but such internal processes do not directly generate revenue for the firm from outside businesses or consumers, as e-commerce, by definition, does. It is true, however, that a firm's e-business infrastructure provides support for online e-commerce exchanges; the same infrastructure and skill sets are involved in both e-business and e-commerce. E-commerce and e-business systems blur together at the business firm boundary, at the point where internal business systems link up with suppliers or customers (see **Figure 1.1**). E-business applications turn into e-commerce precisely when an exchange of value occurs (see Mesenbourg, U.S. Department of Commerce, 2001, for a similar view). We will examine this intersection further in Chapter 12.

e-business
the digital enabling of transactions and processes within a firm, involving information systems under the control of the firm

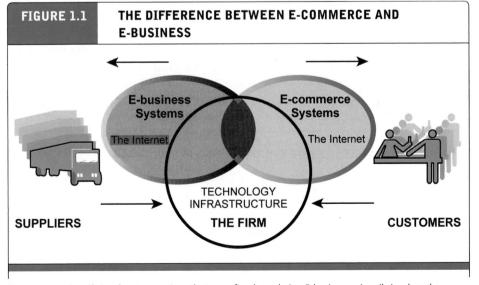

FIGURE 1.1 THE DIFFERENCE BETWEEN E-COMMERCE AND E-BUSINESS

E-commerce primarily involves transactions that cross firm boundaries. E-business primarily involves the application of digital technologies to business processes within the firm.

WHY STUDY E-COMMERCE?

Why are there college courses and textbooks on e-commerce when there are no courses or textbooks on "TV Commerce," "Radio Commerce," "Railroad Commerce," or "Highway Commerce," even though these technologies had profound impacts on commerce in the twentieth century and account for far more commerce than e-commerce?

The reason for the interest specifically in e-commerce is that e-commerce technology (discussed in detail in Chapters 3 and 4) is different and more powerful than any of the other technologies we have seen in the past century. E-commerce technologies—and the digital markets that result—are bringing about some fundamental, unprecedented shifts in commerce. While these other technologies transformed economic life in the twentieth century, the evolving Internet and other information technologies are shaping the twenty-first century.

Prior to the development of e-commerce, the marketing and sale of goods was a mass-marketing and sales force–driven process. Marketers viewed consumers as passive targets of advertising campaigns and branding "blitzes" intended to influence their long-term product perceptions and immediate purchasing behavior. Companies sold their products via well-insulated channels. Consumers were trapped by geographical and social boundaries, unable to search widely for the best price and quality. Information about prices, costs, and fees could be hidden from the consumer, creating profitable "information asymmetries" for the selling firm. **Information asymmetry** refers to any disparity in relevant market information among parties in a transaction. It was so expensive to change national or regional prices in traditional retailing (what are called *menu costs*) that "one national price" was the norm, and dynamic pricing to the marketplace let alone to individuals in the marketplace—changing prices in real time—was unheard of. In this environment, manufacturers prospered by relying on huge production runs of products that could not be customized or personalized. One of the shifts that e-commerce is bringing about is a reduction in information asymmetry among market participants (consumers and merchants). Preventing consumers from learning about costs, price discrimination strategies, and profits from sales becomes more difficult with e-commerce, and the entire marketplace potentially becomes highly price competitive. At the same time, online merchants gain considerable market power over consumers by using consumer personal information in ways inconceivable 10 years ago to maximize their revenues.

information asymmetry
any disparity in relevant market information among parties in a transaction

EIGHT UNIQUE FEATURES OF E-COMMERCE TECHNOLOGY

Table 1.2 lists eight unique features of e-commerce technology that both challenge traditional business thinking and explain why we have so much interest in e-commerce. These unique dimensions of e-commerce technologies suggest many new possibilities for marketing and selling—a powerful set of interactive, personalized, and rich messages are available for delivery to segmented, targeted audiences. E-commerce technologies make it possible for merchants to know much more about consumers and to be able to use this information more effectively than was ever true in the past.

TABLE 1.2	EIGHT UNIQUE FEATURES OF E-COMMERCE TECHNOLOGY
E-COMMERCE TECHNOLOGY DIMENSION	**BUSINESS SIGNIFICANCE**
Ubiquity—Internet/Web technology is available everywhere: at work, at home, and elsewhere via mobile devices, anytime.	The marketplace is extended beyond traditional boundaries and is removed from a temporal and geographic location. "Marketspace" is created; shopping can take place anywhere. Customer convenience is enhanced, and shopping costs are reduced.
Global reach—The technology reaches across national boundaries, around the earth.	Commerce is enabled across cultural and national boundaries seamlessly and without modification. "Marketspace" includes potentially billions of consumers and millions of businesses worldwide.
Universal standards—There is one set of technology standards, namely Internet standards.	There is a common, inexpensive, global technology foundation for businesses to use.
Richness—Video, audio, and text messages are possible.	Video, audio, and text marketing messages are integrated into a single marketing message and consuming experience.
Interactivity—The technology works through interaction with the user.	Consumers are engaged in a dialog that dynamically adjusts the experience to the individual, and makes the consumer a co-participant in the process of delivering goods to the market.
Information density—The technology reduces information costs and raises quality.	Information processing, storage, and communication costs drop dramatically, while currency, accuracy, and timeliness improve greatly. Information becomes plentiful, cheap, and accurate.
Personalization/Customization—The technology allows personalized messages to be delivered to individuals as well as groups.	Personalization of marketing messages and customization of products and services are based on individual characteristics.
Social technology—User content generation and social networks.	New Internet social and business models enable user content creation and distribution, and support social networks.

Potentially, online merchants can use this new information to develop new information asymmetries, enhance their ability to brand products, charge premium prices for high-quality service, and segment the market into an endless number of subgroups, each receiving a different price. To complicate matters further, these same technologies make it possible for merchants to know more about other merchants than was ever true in the past. This presents the possibility that merchants might collude on prices rather than compete and drive overall average prices up. This strategy works especially well when there are just a few suppliers (Varian, 2000a). We examine these different visions of e-commerce further in Section 1.2 and throughout the book.

Each of the dimensions of e-commerce technology and their business significance listed in Table 1.2 deserves a brief exploration, as well as a comparison to both traditional commerce and other forms of technology-enabled commerce.

Ubiquity

marketplace

physical space you visit in order to transact

ubiquity

available just about everywhere, at all times

marketspace

marketplace extended beyond traditional boundaries and removed from a temporal and geographic location

In traditional commerce, a **marketplace** is a physical place you visit in order to transact. For example, television and radio typically motivate the consumer to go some place to make a purchase. E-commerce, in contrast, is characterized by its **ubiquity**: it is available just about everywhere, at all times. It liberates the market from being restricted to a physical space and makes it possible to shop from your desktop, at home, at work, or even from your car, using mobile e-commerce. The result is called a **marketspace**—a marketplace extended beyond traditional boundaries and removed from a temporal and geographic location. From a consumer point of view, ubiquity reduces *transaction costs*—the costs of participating in a market. To transact, it is no longer necessary that you spend time and money traveling to a market. At a broader level, the ubiquity of e-commerce lowers the cognitive energy required to transact in a marketspace. *Cognitive energy* refers to the mental effort required to complete a task. Humans generally seek to reduce cognitive energy outlays. When given a choice, humans will choose the path requiring the least effort—the most convenient path (Shapiro and Varian, 1999; Tversky and Kahneman, 1981).

Global Reach

reach

the total number of users or customers an e-commerce business can obtain

E-commerce technology permits commercial transactions to cross cultural, regional, and national boundaries far more conveniently and cost-effectively than is true in traditional commerce. As a result, the potential market size for e-commerce merchants is roughly equal to the size of the world's online population (more than 2.2 billion) (Internet Worldstats, 2012). More realistically, the Internet makes it much easier for start-up online merchants within a single country to achieve a national audience than was ever possible in the past. The total number of users or customers an e-commerce business can obtain is a measure of its **reach** (Evans and Wurster, 1997).

In contrast, most traditional commerce is local or regional—it involves local merchants or national merchants with local outlets. Television and radio stations, and newspapers, for instance, are primarily local and regional institutions with limited but powerful national networks that can attract a national audience. In contrast to e-commerce technology, these older commerce technologies do not easily cross national boundaries to a global audience.

Universal Standards

universal standards

standards that are shared by all nations around the world

One strikingly unusual feature of e-commerce technologies is that the technical standards of the Internet, and therefore the technical standards for conducting e-commerce, are **universal standards**—they are shared by all nations around the world. In contrast, most traditional commerce technologies differ from one nation to the next. For instance, television and radio standards differ around the world, as does cell phone technology. The universal technical standards of the Internet and e-commerce greatly lower *market entry costs*—the cost merchants must pay just to bring their goods to market. At the same time, for consumers, universal standards reduce *search costs*—the effort required to find suitable products. And by creating a single, one-world marketspace, where prices and product descriptions can be inexpensively displayed for all to see, *price discovery* becomes simpler, faster, and more accurate (Banerjee, et al., 2005; Bakos, 1997; Kambil, 1997). Users of the Internet, both businesses and individuals, also experience *network externalities*—benefits that arise because everyone uses the same technology. With e-commerce technologies, it is possible for the first time in history to easily find many of the suppliers, prices, and delivery terms of a specific product anywhere in the world, and to view them in a coherent, comparative environment. Although this is not necessarily realistic today for all or even many products, it is a potential that will be exploited in the future.

Richness

Information **richness** refers to the complexity and content of a message (Evans and Wurster, 1999). Traditional markets, national sales forces, and small retail stores have great richness: they are able to provide personal, face-to-face service using aural and visual cues when making a sale. The richness of traditional markets makes them a powerful selling or commercial environment. Prior to the development of the Web, there was a trade-off between richness and reach: the larger the audience reached, the less rich the message. The Internet has the potential for offering considerably more information richness than traditional media such as printing presses, radio, and television because it is interactive and can adjust the message to individual users. Chatting with an online sales person, for instance, comes very close to the customer experience in a small retail shop. The richness of the Web allows retail and service merchants to market and sell "complex" goods and services that heretofore required a face-to-face presentation by a sales force. Complex goods have multiple attributes, are typically expensive, and cannot be compared easily (Fink, et al., 2004).

richness
the complexity and content of a message

Interactivity

Unlike any of the commercial technologies of the twentieth century, with the possible exception of the telephone, e-commerce technologies allow for interactivity, meaning they enable two-way communication between merchant and consumer and among consumers. Traditional television, for instance, cannot ask viewers questions or enter into conversations with them, or request that customer information be entered into a form. In contrast, all of these activities are possible on an e-commerce Web site and are now commonplace with smartphones, social networks, and Twitter. **Interactivity** allows an online merchant to engage a consumer in ways similar to a face-to-face experience.

interactivity
technology that allows for two-way communication between merchant and consumer

Information Density

The Internet and the Web vastly increase **information density**—the total amount and quality of information available to all market participants, consumers, and

information density
the total amount and quality of information available to all market participants

merchants alike. E-commerce technologies reduce information collection, storage, processing, and communication costs. At the same time, these technologies greatly increase the currency, accuracy, and timeliness of information—making information more useful and important than ever. As a result, information becomes more plentiful, less expensive, and of higher quality.

A number of business consequences result from the growth in information density. In e-commerce markets, prices and costs become more transparent. *Price transparency* refers to the ease with which consumers can find out the variety of prices in a market; *cost transparency* refers to the ability of consumers to discover the actual costs merchants pay for products (Sinha, 2000). But there are advantages for merchants as well. Online merchants can discover much more about consumers; this allows merchants to segment the market into groups willing to pay different prices and permits them to engage in *price discrimination*—selling the same goods, or nearly the same goods, to different targeted groups at different prices. For instance, an online merchant can discover a consumer's avid interest in expensive exotic vacations, and then pitch expensive exotic vacation plans to that consumer at a premium price, knowing this person is willing to pay extra for such a vacation. At the same time, the online merchant can pitch the same vacation plan at a lower price to more price-sensitive consumers. Merchants also have enhanced abilities to differentiate their products in terms of cost, brand, and quality.

Personalization/Customization

personalization
the targeting of marketing messages to specific individuals by adjusting the message to a person's name, interests, and past purchases

customization
changing the delivered product or service based on a user's preferences or prior behavior

E-commerce technologies permit **personalization**: merchants can target their marketing messages to specific individuals by adjusting the message to a person's name, interests, and past purchases. Today this is achieved in a few milliseconds and followed by an advertisement based on the consumers profile. The technology also permits **customization**—changing the delivered product or service based on a user's preferences or prior behavior. Given the interactive nature of e-commerce technology, much information about the consumer can be gathered in the marketplace at the moment of purchase. With the increase in information density, a great deal of information about the consumer's past purchases and behavior can be stored and used by online merchants. The result is a level of personalization and customization unthinkable with existing commerce technologies. For instance, you may be able to shape what you see on television by selecting a channel, but you cannot change the contents of the channel you have chosen. In contrast, the online version of the *Wall Street Journal* allows you to select the type of news stories you want to see first, and gives you the opportunity to be alerted when certain events happen. Personalization and customization allow firms to precisely identify market segments and adjust their messages accordingly.

Social Technology: User Content Generation and Social Networking

In a way quite different from all previous technologies, the Internet and e-commerce technologies have evolved to be much more social by allowing users to create and share content in the form of Web and Facebook pages, text, videos, music, and photos with a worldwide community. Using these forms of communication, users are able to create new social networks and strengthen existing ones. All previous mass media in modern history, including the printing press, use a broadcast model (one-to-many) where content is created in a central location by experts (professional writers, editors, directors, actors, and producers) and audiences are concentrated in huge aggregates to consume a standardized product. The telephone would appear to be an exception but it is not a "mass communication" technology. Instead the telephone is a one-to-one technology. The Internet and e-commerce technologies have the potential to invert this standard media model by giving users the power to create and distribute content on a large scale, and permit users to program their own content consumption. The Internet provides a unique, many-to-many model of mass communication.

WEB 2.0: PLAY MY VERSION

Many of the unique features of e-commerce and the Internet come together in a set of applications and social media technologies referred to as Web 2.0. The Internet started out as a simple network to support e-mail and file transfers among remote computers. Communication among experts was the purpose. The Web started out as a way to use the Internet to display simple pages and allow the user to navigate among the pages by linking them together electronically. You can think of this as Web 1.0—the first Web. By 2007 something else was happening. The Internet and the Web had evolved to the point where users could create, edit, and distribute content to others; share with one another their preferences, bookmarks, and online personas; participate in virtual lives; and build online communities. This "new" Web was called by many **Web 2.0,** and while it draws heavily on the "old" Web 1.0, it is nevertheless a clear evolution from the past.

> **Web 2.0**
> a set of applications and technologies that allows users to create, edit, and distribute content; share preferences, bookmarks, and online personas; participate in virtual lives; and build online communities

Let's take a quick look at some examples of Web 2.0 applications and sites:

- Twitter is a social network/micro-blogging service that encourages users to enter 140-character messages ("tweets") in answer to the question "What are you doing?" Twitter has more than 140 million active users worldwide, sending around 340 million tweets per day and more than 10 billion tweets a month. Twitter has begun to monetize its subscribers by developing an ad platform and providing marketing services to firms that want to stay in instant contact with their customers.

- YouTube, owned by Google after a $1.65 billion purchase, is the world's largest online consumer-generated video-posting site. In 2012, YouTube is morphing into a premium video content distributor and video producer, offering feature length movies, television series, and its own original content. In April 2012, YouTube had around 158 million unique viewers in the United States, and more than 800 million a month worldwide. According to Google, 72 hours of video are posted to the site every minute! YouTube reportedly streams more than 4 billion videos per day, including more than 600 million a day on mobile devices. However, although YouTube's revenues reportedly doubled in 2010 to nearly $1 billion and increased yet again to $1.6 billion in 2011, it is not known whether it has ever shown a profit. (YouTube, 2012; comScore, 2012a; Lawler, 2011; Yahoo Finance, 2011).

- The Apple iPhone (with more than 244 million sold worldwide through June 2012) supports mobile versions of Web 2.0 applications such as WordPress for the iPhone (which enables users to write posts, post photos, and manage comments to their blog via an iPhone or iPod touch), Mint (a personal financial manager), Borange (an iPhone app for sharing social availability), Tag It Like It's Hot (a social bookmarking application), and more than 650,000 other apps for business and personal use. Apple's iPad, introduced in 2010, builds on the iPhone foundation for a truly mobile e-commerce capability. As of June 2012, about 84 million iPads had been sold since its introduction.

- Instagram is a mobile photo-sharing application available for Androids and iPhones that allows users to easily apply a variety of different photo filters and borders, and then post the photos to social networks such as Facebook, Twitter, Foursquare, Tumblr and Flickr. Launched in November 2010, Instagram quickly attracted more than 50 million users and in April 2012 was purchased by Facebook for $1 billion (Buck, 2012).

- Wikipedia allows contributors around the world to share their knowledge and in the process has become the most successful online encyclopedia, far surpassing "professional" encyclopedias such as Encarta and Britannica. Wikipedia is one of the largest collaboratively edited reference projects in the world, with more than 3.9 million articles available in English and more than 21 million in total, in 285 languages. Wikipedia relies on volunteers, makes no money, and accepts no advertising. Wikipedia is consistently ranked as one of the top 10 most visited sites on the Web (Wikipedia.org, 2012; Wikimedia Foundation, 2011; comScore, 2012b).

- StumbleUpon helps users discover and rate online content targeted to their personal interests using collaborative filtering and social networks. In 2012, StumbleUpon had around 8–9 million monthly unique visitors (Compete.com, 2012a). Digg, Reddit, Delicious, Kaboodle, Mixx, Newsvine, Diigo, and Tip'd offer similar social bookmarking or tagging systems. Twitter is a major competitor of these sites.

- Tumblr is a combination of blog platform and social network. It allows users to easily post text, photos, links, music, videos and more. As of June 2012, Tumblr hosts almost 60 million blogs, containing almost 25 billion posts. On a typical day, users make over 65 million posts (Tumblr.com, 2012). Tumblr has more than doubled in size since September 2011. Wordpress is another company that provides software that allows you to easily create and publish a blog or Web site on the Web. WordPress is an open source product built by a community of volunteers and available for use free of charge. According to WordPress, more than 350 million people read blogs on WordPress.com, and users produce about 5.5 million new posts and 10 million new comments during a typical week. (WordPress.com, 2012).

What do all these Web 2.0 applications and sites have in common? First, they rely on user- and consumer-generated content. These are all "applications" created by people, especially people in the 18–34 year-old demographic, and in the 7–17 age group as well. "Regular" people (not just experts or professionals) are creating, sharing, modifying, and broadcasting content to huge audiences. Second, easy search capability is a key to their success. Third, they are inherently highly interactive, creating new opportunities for people to socially connect to others. They are "social" sites because they support interactions among users. Fourth, they rely on broadband connectivity to the Web. Fifth, many of them are currently only marginally profitable, and their business models are unproven despite considerable investment. Nevertheless, the potential monetary rewards for social sites with huge audiences is quite large. Sixth, they attract extremely large audiences when compared to traditional Web 1.0 applications, exceeding in many cases the audience size of national broadcast and cable television programs. These audience relationships are intensive and long-lasting interactions with millions of people. In short, they attract eyeballs in very large numbers. Hence, they present marketers with extraordinary opportunities for targeted marketing and advertising. They also present consumers with the opportunity to rate and review products, and entrepreneurs with ideas for future business ventures. Last, these sites act as application development platforms where users can contribute and use software applications for free. Briefly, it's a whole new world from what has gone before.

TYPES OF E-COMMERCE

There are several different types of e-commerce and many different ways to characterize them. **Table 1.3** lists the major types of e-commerce discussed in this book.[1] For the most part, we distinguish different types of e-commerce by the nature of the

TABLE 1.3	MAJOR TYPES OF E-COMMERCE
TYPE OF E-COMMERCE	EXAMPLE
B2C—business-to-consumer	Amazon is a general merchandiser that sells consumer products to retail consumers.
B2B—business-to-business	Go2Paper.com is an independent third-party marketplace that serves the paper industry.
C2C—consumer-to-consumer	On a large number of Web auction sites such as eBay, and listing sites such as Craigslist, consumers can auction or sell goods directly to other consumers.
Social e-commerce	Facebook is both the leading social network and social e-commerce site.
M-commerce—mobile e-commerce	Mobile devices such as tablet computers and smartphones can be used to conduct commercial transactions.
Local e-commerce	Groupon offers subscribers daily deals from local businesses in the form of "Groupons," discount coupons that take effect once enough subscribers have agreed to purchase.

[1] For the purposes of this text, we subsume business-to-government (B2G) e-commerce within B2B e-commerce, viewing the government as simply a form of business when it acts as a procurer of goods and/or services.

market relationship—who is selling to whom. Social, mobile, and local e-commerce can be looked at as subsets of these types of e-commerce.

Business-to-Consumer (B2C) E-commerce

business-to-consumer (B2C) e-commerce
online businesses selling to individual consumers

The most commonly discussed type of e-commerce is **business-to-consumer (B2C) e-commerce**, in which online businesses attempt to reach individual consumers. B2C commerce includes purchases of retail goods, travel services, and online content. Even though B2C is comparatively small (about $342 billion in 2012 in the United States), it has grown exponentially since 1995, and is the type of e-commerce that most consumers are likely to encounter. Within the B2C category, there are many different types of business models. Chapter 2 has a detailed discussion of seven different B2C business models: portals, online retailers, content providers, transaction brokers, market creators, service providers, and community providers.

Business-to-Business (B2B) E-commerce

business-to-business (B2B) e-commerce
online businesses selling to other businesses

Business-to-business (B2B) e-commerce, in which businesses focus on selling to other businesses, is the largest form of e-commerce, with about $4.1 trillion in transactions in the United States in 2012. There was an estimated $11.5 trillion in business-to-business exchanges of all kinds, online and offline, suggesting that B2B e-commerce has significant growth potential. The ultimate size of B2B e-commerce is potentially huge. There are two primary business models used within the B2B arena: Net marketplaces, which include e-distributors, e-procurement companies, exchanges and industry consortia, and private industrial networks, which include single firm networks and industry-wide networks.

Consumer-to-Consumer (C2C) E-commerce

consumer-to-consumer (C2C) e-commerce
consumers selling to other consumers

Consumer-to-consumer (C2C) e-commerce provides a way for consumers to sell to each other, with the help of an online market maker such as eBay or Etsy, or the classifieds site Craigslist. Given that in 2012, eBay is expected to generate around $65 billion in gross merchandise volume around the world, it is probably safe to estimate that the size of the global C2C market in 2012 is more than $80 billion (eBay, 2012). In C2C e-commerce, the consumer prepares the product for market, places the product for auction or sale, and relies on the market maker to provide catalog, search engine, and transaction-clearing capabilities so that products can be easily displayed, discovered, and paid for.

Social E-commerce

Social e-commerce
e-commerce enabled by social networks and online social relationships

Social e-commerce is e-commerce that is enabled by social networks and online social relationships. It is sometimes also referred to as Facebook commerce, but in actuality is a much larger phenomenon that extends beyond just Facebook. The growth of social e-commerce is being driven by a number of factors, including the increasing popularity of social sign-on (signing onto Web sites using your Facebook or other social network ID), network notification (the sharing of approval or disapproval of products, services, and content via Facebook's Like button or Twitter tweets), online collaborative shopping tools, and social search (recommendations from online trusted friends). Social e-commerce is still in its infancy, but, as noted previously, has tripled in the United States, from $1 billion in 2011 to an estimated $3 billion in 2012, with the rest of the world expected to spend about double that amount ($6 billion) (eMarketer, Inc., 2012c).

Mobile E-commerce (M-commerce)

Mobile e-commerce, or m-commerce, refers to the use of mobile devices to enable transactions on the Web. Described more fully in Chapter 3, m-commerce involves the use of cellular and wireless networks to connect laptops, netbooks, smartphones such the iPhone, Android, and BlackBerry, and tablet computers such as the iPad to the Web. Once connected, mobile consumers can conduct transactions, including stock trades, in-store price comparisons, banking, travel reservations, and more. Mobile retail purchases are expected to reach approximately $11.6 billion in 2012 (almost double that of 2011) and to grow rapidly in the United States over the next five years (eMarketer, 2012b).

mobile e-commerce (m-commerce)
use of mobile devices to enable transactions on the Web

Local E-commerce

Local e-commerce, as its name suggests, is a form of e-commerce that is focused on engaging the consumer based on his or her current geographic location. Local merchants use a variety of online marketing techniques to drive consumers to their stores. Local e-commerce is the third prong of the social, mobile, local e-commerce wave, and is expected to grow in the United States from $1.6 billion in 2011 to an estimated $2.9 billion in 2012 (eMarketer, Inc, 2011a).

Local e-commerce
e-commerce that is focused on engaging the consumer based on his or her current geographic location

GROWTH OF THE INTERNET AND THE WEB

The technology juggernauts behind e-commerce are the Internet and the Web. Without both of these technologies, e-commerce as we know it would be impossible. We describe the Internet and the Web in some detail in Chapter 3. The **Internet** is a worldwide network of computer networks built on common standards. Created in the late 1960s to connect a small number of mainframe computers and their users, the Internet has since grown into the world's largest network. It is impossible to say with certainty exactly how many computers and other wireless access devices such as smartphones are connected to the Internet worldwide at any one time, but the number is clearly more than 1 billion. The Internet links businesses, educational institutions, government agencies, and individuals together, and provides users with services such as e-mail, document transfer, shopping, research, instant messaging, music, videos, and news.

Internet
worldwide network of computer networks built on common standards

One way to measure the growth of the Internet is by looking at the number of Internet hosts with domain names. (An *Internet host* is defined by the Internet Systems Consortium as any IP address that returns a domain name in the in-addr.arpa domain, which is a special part of the DNS namespace that resolves IP addresses into domain names.) In January 2012, there were over 888 million Internet hosts in over 245 countries, up from just 70 million in 2000 (Internet Systems Consortium, 2012).

The Internet has shown extraordinary growth patterns when compared to other electronic technologies of the past. It took radio 38 years to achieve a 30% share of U.S. households. It took television 17 years to achieve a 30% share. It took only 10 years for the Internet/Web to achieve a 53% share of U.S. households once a graphical user interface was invented for the Web in 1993.

World Wide Web (the Web)

the most popular service that runs on the Internet; provides easy access to Web pages

The **World Wide Web (the Web)** is the most popular service that runs on the Internet infrastructure. The Web is the "killer app" that made the Internet commercially interesting and extraordinarily popular. The Web was developed in the early 1990s and hence is of much more recent vintage than the Internet. We describe the Web in some detail in Chapter 3. The Web provides access to billions of Web pages indexed by Google and other search engines. These pages are created in a language called *HTML (HyperText Markup Language)*. HTML pages can contain text, graphics, animations, and other objects. You can find an exceptionally wide range of information on Web pages, ranging from the entire collection of public records from the Securities and Exchange Commission, to the card catalog of your local library, to millions of music tracks and videos. The Internet prior to the Web was primarily used for text communications, file transfers, and remote computing. The Web introduced far more powerful and commercially interesting, colorful multimedia capabilities of direct relevance to commerce. In essence, the Web added color, voice, and video to the Internet, creating a communications infrastructure and information storage system that rivals television, radio, magazines, and even libraries.

There is no precise measurement of the number of Web pages in existence, in part because today's search engines index only a portion of the known universe of Web pages, and also because the size of the Web universe is unknown. Google reported that its system had, as of July 2008, identified 1 trillion unique URLs, although many of those pages did not necessarily contain unique content. By 2012, it is likely that Google indexes at least 120 billion Web pages, if not more. In addition to this "surface" or "visible" Web, there is also the so-called "deep Web" that is reportedly 1,000 to 5,000 times greater than the surface Web. The deep Web contains databases and other content that is not routinely indexed by search engines such as Google. Although the total size of the Web is not known, what is indisputable is that Web content has grown exponentially since 1993.

Read *Insight on Technology: Spider Webs, Bow Ties, Scale-Free Networks, and the Deep Web* for the latest view of researchers on the structure of the Web.

ORIGINS AND GROWTH OF E-COMMERCE

It is difficult to pinpoint just when e-commerce began. There were several precursors to e-commerce. In the late 1970s, a pharmaceutical firm named Baxter Healthcare initiated a primitive form of B2B e-commerce by using a telephone-based modem that permitted hospitals to reorder supplies from Baxter. This system was later expanded during the 1980s into a PC-based remote order entry system and was widely copied throughout the United States long before the Internet became a commercial environment. The 1980s saw the development of Electronic Data Interchange (EDI) standards that permitted firms to exchange commercial documents and conduct digital commercial transactions across private networks.

INSIGHT ON TECHNOLOGY

SPIDER WEBS, BOW TIES, SCALE-FREE NETWORKS, AND THE DEEP WEB

The World Wide Web conjures up images of a giant spider web where everything is connected to everything else in a random pattern, and you can go from one edge of the Web to another by just following the right links. Theoretically, that's what makes the Web different from a typical index system: you can follow hyperlinks from one page to another. In 1968, sociologist Stanley Milgram put forth the "small-world" theory for social networks by positing that every human was separated from any other human by only six degrees of separation. In the "small world" theory of the Web, every Web page was thought to be separated from any other Web page by an average of about 19 clicks. The theory was supported by early research on a small sampling of Web sites. But subsequent research conducted jointly by Andrei Broder and scientists at IBM, Compaq, and AltaVista found something entirely different. These scientists used a Web crawler to identify 200 million Web pages and follow 1.5 billion links on those pages.

The researchers discovered that the Web was not like a spider web at all, but rather like a bow tie. The bow-tie Web had a "strongly connected component" (SCC) composed, at that time, of about 56 million Web pages. On the right side of the bow tie was a set of 44 million OUT pages that you could get to from the center, but could not return to the center from. OUT pages tended to be corporate intranet and other Web site pages that are designed to trap you at the site when you land. On the left side of the bow tie was a set of 44 million IN pages from which you could get to the center, but that you could not travel to from the center. These were recently created pages that had not yet been linked to by many center pages. In addition, 43 million pages were classified as "tendrils," pages that did not link to the center and could not be linked to from the center. Finally, there were 16 million pages totally disconnected from everything. Subsequent research has replicated these findings. Although the numbers of Web pages and links have obviously exponentially increased, the basic structure of the Web discovered by Broder persists.

Further evidence for the non-random and structured nature of the Web is provided in research performed by Albert-Laszlo Barabasi at the University of Notre Dame. Barabasi's team found that far from being a random, exponentially exploding network of billions of Web pages, activity on the Web was actually highly concentrated in "very-connected super nodes" that provided the connectivity to less well-connected nodes. Barabasi dubbed this type of network a "scale-free" network. As its turns out, scale-free networks are highly vulnerable to destruction: destroy their super nodes, and transmission of messages breaks down rapidly. On the upside, if you are a marketer trying to "spread the message" about your products, place your products on one of the super nodes and watch the news spread.

More recently, researchers at the University of Michigan found the Web had significantly changed shape in the period 2005–2010. Rapid growth and consolidation of backbone telecommunications providers, a consolidation of applications (video is expected to account for 90% of Web traffic by 2014), and expansion of cloud computing and huge data centers, has created a Web where a significant part of Internet traffic does not flow through the backbone networks

(continued)

of giant Internet companies like AT&T or Level 3. Rather, so-called "hyper-giant" companies such as Google, Yahoo, Comcast, Amazon, and IBM are hooking their networks together in "peering arrangements." A significant part of Web traffic now occurs at the edges in what some call "fat tubes."

Thus, the picture of the Web that emerges from this research is quite different from earlier reports. The notion that most pairs of Web pages are separated by a handful of links, almost always under 20, and that the number of connections would grow exponentially with the size of the Web, is not supported. In fact, there is a 75% chance that there is no path from one randomly chosen page to another. The early notion that Internet traffic moves freely across a network of routers, choosing whatever path happens to work and be available, is replaced by the notion that today's Internet traffic moves along a small number of very big highways, say, from Amazon to IBM cloud computing centers, or Google's YouTube and Akamai's edge network. The Internet developed haphazardly in the past, and today's Internet is dominated by a few very large telecommunications carrier firms. The big nodes of the past have become the hyper-giants of the present. The rich have become richer.

The problem becomes more severe as the Internet goes global. Google's English language crawler does not crawl Chinese Web sites, and you will rarely see a Chinese language answer to a Google English query. The crawlable Web is only some unknown part of the much larger "deep Web." Content in the deep Web is not easily accessible to Web crawlers that most search engine companies use. Instead, these pages are either proprietary (not available to crawlers and non-subscribers), such as the pages of the *Wall Street Journal*, airline schedule and price information, and medical research findings, or are stuck in databases that themselves are not linked to other pages. The existence of the deep Web means that search engines are often unable to answer common questions like "What's the cheapest fare to Europe from New York this week?"

Given this understanding of the structure of the Web, the implications for entrepreneurs and marketers are clear. Because e-commerce revenues inherently depend on customers being able to find a Web site using search engines, Web site managers need to take steps to ensure their Web pages are part of the connected central core, or "super nodes," of the Web. One way to do this is to make sure the site has as many links as possible to and from other relevant sites, especially to other sites within the SCC. If your site is part of the deep Web, get out, and make it more accessible to crawlers. If you want to be global, develop foreign language versions of your main site. If you want to optimize your search engine rankings, put a lot of links on your pages to pages on other sites (become a hub). Last, get as many other sites to link to your pages as you possibly can (become an authority). It's called search engine optimization, and the more you know about the structure of the Web, the more effective your Web sites will be.

SOURCES: "Tubes: A Journey to the Center of the Internet," by Andrew Blum, Ecco Press, 2012; "The Deep Web: Deep Web FAQs," Brightplanet.com, accessed August 25, 2011; "Scientists Strive to Map the Shaper-Shifting Net," by John Markoff, *New York Times*, March 1, 2010; Networks, Crowds, and Markets: Reasoning About a Highly Connected World, by David Easley and Jon Kleinberg, Cambridge University Press, 2010; "Atlas Internet Observatory Report," by C. Labovitz , S. Lekel-Johnson, D. McPherson (Arbor Networks), J Oberheide (University of Michigan), and M. Karir (Merit Network, Inc.), Arbornetworks.com, 2010; "III-COR Discovering and Organizing Hidden-Web Sources," by Juliana Freire, University of Utah. Grant application. National Science Foundation, IIS Division of Information & Intelligent Systems, IIS -0713637. April 2009; "Exploring a 'Deep Web' That Google Can't Grasp," by Alex Wright, *New York Times*, February 23, 2009; "Invisible or Deep Web: What it is, Why it exists, How to find it, and Its inherent ambiguity," www.lib.berkeley.edu, accessed August 2008; "Accessing the Deep Web," by Bin He, Mitesh Patel, Zhen Zhang, and Kevin Chen-Chuan Chang; *Communications of the ACM (CACM)* 50 (2): 94–101, May 2007; "The Bowtie Theory Explains Link Popularity," by John Heard, Searchengineposition.com, June 1, 2000; "Graph structure in the Web," by Andrei Broder et al. In Proc. 9th International World Wide Web Conference, pages 309–320, 2000.

In the B2C arena, the first truly large-scale digitally enabled transaction system was deployed in France in 1981. The Minitel was a French videotext system that combined a telephone with an 8-inch screen. By the mid-1980s, more than 3 million Minitels were deployed, and more than 13,000 different services were available, including ticket agencies, travel services, retail products, and online banking. The Minitel service continued in existence until December 31, 2006, when it was finally discontinued by its owner, France Telecom.

However, none of these precursor systems had the functionality of the Internet. Generally, when we think of e-commerce today, it is inextricably linked to the Internet. For our purposes, we will say e-commerce begins in 1995, following the appearance of the first banner advertisements placed by AT&T, Volvo, Sprint, and others on Hotwired.com in late October 1994, and the first sales of banner ad space by Netscape and Infoseek in early 1995. Since then, e-commerce has been the fastest growing form of commerce in the United States. **Figure 1.2** and **Figure 1.3** chart the development of B2C e-commerce and B2B e-commerce, respectively, with projections for the next

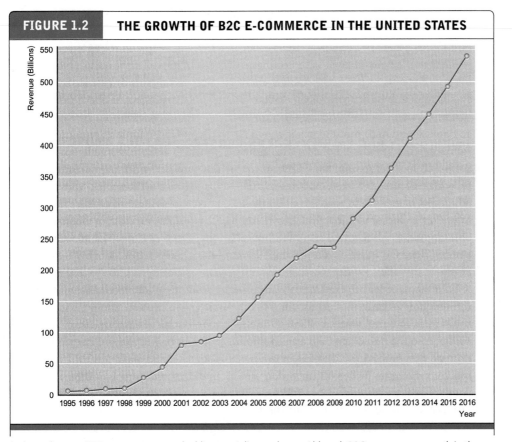

| FIGURE 1.2 | THE GROWTH OF B2C E-COMMERCE IN THE UNITED STATES |

In the early years, B2C e-commerce was doubling or tripling each year. Although B2C e-commerce growth in the United States slowed in 2008–2009 due to the economic recession, it resumed growing at about 13% in 2010 and has continued to grow at double-digit rates in 2011 and 2012.

SOURCES: Based on data from eMarketer, Inc., 2012; authors' estimates.

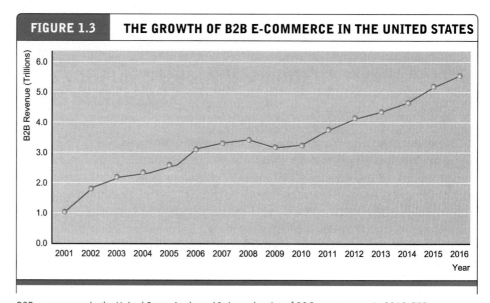

FIGURE 1.3 **THE GROWTH OF B2B E-COMMERCE IN THE UNITED STATES**

B2B e-commerce in the United States is about 10 times the size of B2C e-commerce. In 2016, B2B e-commerce is projected to be about $5.6 trillion. (Note: Does not include EDI transactions.)
SOURCES: Based on data from U.S. Census Bureau, 2012b; authors' estimates.

several years. Both graphs show a strong projected growth rate, but the dollar amounts of B2B e-commerce dwarf those of B2C.

TECHNOLOGY AND E-COMMERCE IN PERSPECTIVE

Although in many respects, e-commerce is new and different, it is also important to keep e-commerce in perspective. First, the Internet and the Web are just two of a long list of technologies that have greatly changed commerce in the United States and around the world. Each of these other technologies spawned business models and strategies designed to leverage the technology into commercial advantage and profit. They were also accompanied by explosive early growth, which was characterized by the emergence of thousands of entrepreneurial start-up companies, followed by painful retrenchment, and then a long-term successful exploitation of the technology by larger established firms. In the case of automobiles, for instance, in 1915, there were more than 250 automobile manufacturers in the United States. By 1940, there were five. In the case of radio, in 1925, there were more than 2,000 radio stations across the United States, with most broadcasting to local neighborhoods and run by amateurs. By 1990, there were fewer than 500 independent stations. There is every reason to believe e-commerce will follow the same pattern—with notable differences discussed throughout the text.

Second, although e-commerce has grown explosively, there is no guarantee it will continue to grow forever at these rates and much reason to believe e-commerce growth will cap as it confronts its own fundamental limitations. For instance, B2C retail e-commerce is still a small part (around 6%) of the overall $3.7 trillion retail market in the United States. Under current projections, in 2016, B2C retail e-commerce (estimated to be around $362 billion) will still be less than Walmart's fiscal 2012 revenue ($444 billion). Walmart is the world's largest and most successful retailer. On the other hand, with only around 6% of all retail sales revenue now being generated online, there is tremendous upside potential. At current double-digit rates, e-commerce is expected to be around 17% of all retail commerce by 2020.

POTENTIAL LIMITATIONS ON THE GROWTH OF B2C E-COMMERCE

The data suggests that, over the next five years, B2C e-commerce in the United States will grow by about 10% annually, slower than in earlier years, but much faster than traditional retail sales (about 4%). Nevertheless, there are several reasons to believe that e-commerce revenues from goods and services together will not expand forever at these rates. As online sales become a larger percentage of all sales, online sales growth will likely eventually decline to that growth level. This point still appears to be a long way off. Online content sales, everything from music, to video, medical information, games, and entertainment, have an even longer period to grow before they hit any ceiling effects.

There are other limitations on B2C e-commerce that have the potential to cap its growth rate and ultimate size. **Table 1.4** describes some of these limiting factors.

Some limitations may be minimized in the next decade. For instance, the price of an entry-level computer such as a tablet computer or netbook has fallen to around $250, although this still represents a substantial amount of money to many. Other

TABLE 1.4	LIMITATIONS ON THE GROWTH OF B2C E-COMMERCE
LIMITING FACTOR	COMMENT
Expensive technology	Using the Internet requires an investment of at least $200 to $300 for a computer and a connect charge ranging from about $10 to $50 a month depending on the speed of service.
Sophisticated skill set	The skills required to make effective use of the Internet and e-commerce capabilities are far more sophisticated than, say, for television or newspapers.
Persistent cultural attraction of physical markets and traditional shopping experiences	For many, shopping is a cultural and social event where people meet directly with merchants and other consumers. This social experience has not yet been fully duplicated in digital form (although social shopping is a major new development).
Persistent global inequality limiting access to telephones and personal computers	Much of the world's population does not have telephone service, PCs, or cell phones.
Saturation and ceiling effects	Growth in the Internet population slows as it approaches the size of the total population.

Internet-client devices such as smartphones are within this price range now. This, coupled with enhancements in capabilities such as integration with television, access to entertainment film libraries on a pay-per-view basis, and other software enhancements, will likely raise U.S. Internet household penetration rates to the level of cable television penetration (about 80%) by 2015. The PC operating system will also likely evolve from the current Windows platform to far simpler interfaces.

The most significant technology that can reduce barriers to Internet access is the wireless mobile platform (described in more detail in Chapter 3). Today, consumers can access the Internet via a variety of different mobile devices, such as mobile computers (laptops, netbooks, and tablets such as the iPad) and smartphones. In 2012, around 122 million people (over 50% of Internet users in the United States) use a mobile device to access the Internet, and this number is expected to grow to 199 million (75% of all Internet users in the United States) by 2016 (eMarketer, Inc., 2012g). **Figure 1.4** illustrates the rapid growth projected for mobile Internet access during the period 2009–2016.

On balance, the current technological limits on e-commerce growth, while real, are likely to recede in importance over the next decade. The social and cultural limitations of e-commerce are less likely to change as quickly, but the Web is fast developing virtual

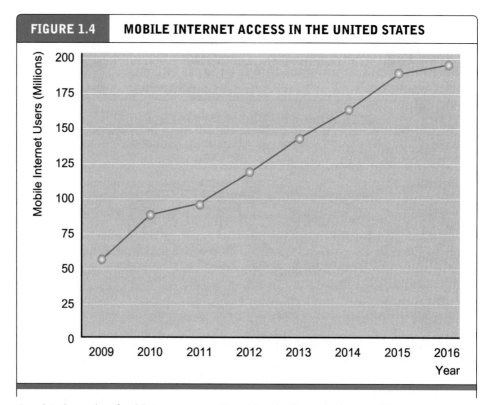

FIGURE 1.4   MOBILE INTERNET ACCESS IN THE UNITED STATES

Growth in the number of mobile Internet users will provide a significant stimulus to mobile e-commerce.
SOURCE: Based on data from eMarketer, Inc., 2012g.

social shopping experiences and virtual realities that millions find as entertaining as shopping or seeing their friends face to face.

1.2 E-COMMERCE: A BRIEF HISTORY

Although e-commerce is not very old, it already has a tumultuous history. The history of e-commerce can be usefully divided into three periods: 1995–2000, the period of invention; 2001–2006, the period of consolidation; and 2007–present, a period of reinvention with social, mobile, and local expansion. The following examines each of these periods briefly, while **Figure 1.5** places them in context along a timeline.

E-COMMERCE 1995–2000: INVENTION

The early years of e-commerce were a period of explosive growth and extraordinary innovation, beginning in 1995 with the first widespread use of the Web to advertise products. During this Invention period, e-commerce meant selling retail goods, usually quite simple goods, on the Internet. There simply was not enough bandwidth for more complex products. Marketing was limited to unsophisticated static display ads and not very powerful search engines. The Web policy of most large firms, if they had one at all, was to have a basic static Web site depicting their brands. This period of explosive growth was capped in March 2000 when stock market valuations for dot-com companies reached their peak and thereafter began to collapse.

The early years of e-commerce were also one of the most euphoric of times in American commercial history. It was also a time when key e-commerce concepts were developed and explored. Thousands of dot-com companies were formed, backed by

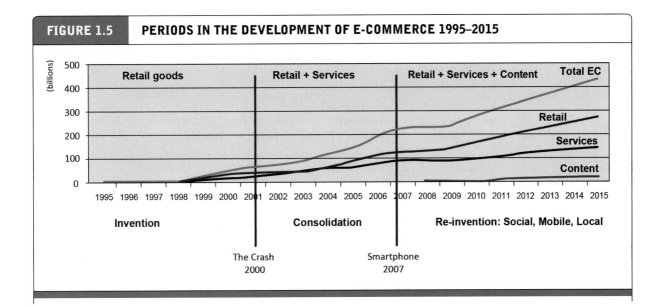

FIGURE 1.5   PERIODS IN THE DEVELOPMENT OF E-COMMERCE 1995–2015

more than $125 billion in financial capital—one of the largest outpourings of venture capital in United States history. While venture investment has trended markedly lower since 2000, it is still significantly larger than pre-1996 levels, and investing in dot-com and Internet businesses began to increase once again in 2010 after dramatically decreasing in the latter half of 2008 and early 2009 due to the recession. In 2011, venture capital investment in Internet-related companies increased significantly, by almost 70% more than the amount invested in 2010, to $6.9 bilion -- the highest amount invested in over a decade (PricewaterhouseCoopers, National Venture Capital Association MoneyTree Report, Data: Thomson Reuters, 2012).

For computer scientists and information technologists, the early success of e-commerce was a powerful vindication of a set of information technologies that had developed over a period of 40 years—extending from the development of the early Internet, to the PC, to local area networks. The vision was of a universal communications and computing environment that everyone on Earth could access with cheap, inexpensive computers—a worldwide universe of knowledge stored on HTML pages created by hundreds of millions of individuals and thousands of libraries, governments, and scientific institutes. Technologists celebrated the fact that the Internet was not controlled by anyone or any nation, but was free to all. They believed the Internet—and the e-commerce that rose on this infrastructure—should remain a self-governed, self-regulated environment.

For economists, the early years of e-commerce raised the realistic prospect of a nearly perfect competitive market: where price, cost, and quality information are equally distributed, a nearly infinite set of suppliers compete against one another, and customers have access to all relevant market information worldwide. The Internet would spawn digital markets where information would be nearly perfect—something that is rarely true in other real-world markets. Merchants in turn would have equal direct access to hundreds of millions of customers. In this near-perfect information marketspace, transaction costs would plummet because search costs—the cost of searching for prices, product descriptions, payment settlement, and order fulfillment—would all fall drastically (Bakos, 1997). New shopping bot programs would automatically search the entire Web for the best prices and delivery times. For merchants, the cost of searching for customers would also fall, reducing the need for wasteful advertising. At the same time, advertisements could be personalized to the needs of every customer. Prices and even costs would be increasingly transparent to the consumer, who could now know exactly and instantly the worldwide best price, quality, and availability of most products. Information asymmetry would be greatly reduced. Given the instant nature of Internet communications, the availability of powerful sales information systems, and the low cost involved in changing prices on a Web site (low menu costs), producers could dynamically price their products to reflect actual demand, ending the idea of one national price, or one suggested manufacturer's list price. In turn, market middlemen—the distributors, wholesalers, and other factors in the marketplace who are intermediaries between producers and consumers, each demanding a payment and raising costs while adding little value—would disappear (**disintermediation**). Manufacturers and content originators would develop direct market relationships with their customers. The

disintermediation

displacement of market middlemen who traditionally are intermediaries between producers and consumers by a new direct relationship between producers and consumers resulting intense competition, the decline of intermediaries, and the lower transaction costs would eliminate product brands, and along with it, the possibility of *monopoly profits* based on brands, geography, or special access to factors of production. Prices for products and services would fall to the point where prices covered costs of production plus a fair, "market rate" of return on capital, plus additional small payments for entrepreneurial effort (that would not last long). Unfair competitive advantages (which occur when one competitor has an advantage others cannot purchase) would be eliminated, as would extraordinary returns on invested capital. This vision was called **friction-free commerce** (Smith et al., 2000).

For real-world entrepreneurs, their financial backers, and marketing professionals, the idea of friction-free commerce was far from their own visions. For these players, e-commerce represented an extraordinary opportunity to earn far above normal returns on investment. The e-commerce marketspace represented access to millions of consumers worldwide who used the Internet and a set of marketing communications technologies (e-mail and Web pages) that was universal, inexpensive, and powerful. These new technologies would permit marketers to practice what they always had done—segmenting the market into groups with different needs and price sensitivity, targeting the segments with branding and promotional messages, and positioning the product and pricing for each group—but with even more precision. In this new marketspace, extraordinary profits would go to **first movers**—those firms who were first to market in a particular area and who moved quickly to gather market share. In a "winner take all" market, first movers could establish a large customer base quickly, build brand name recognition early, create an entirely new distribution channel, and then inhibit competitors (new entrants) by building in *switching costs* for their customers through proprietary interface designs and features available only at one site. The idea for entrepreneurs was to create near monopolies online based on size, convenience, selection, and brand. Online businesses using the new technology could create informative, community-like features unavailable to traditional merchants. These "communities of consumption" also would add value and be difficult for traditional merchants to imitate. The thinking was that once customers became accustomed to using a company's unique Web interface and feature set, they could not easily be switched to competitors. In the best case, the entrepreneurial firm would invent proprietary technologies and techniques that almost everyone adopted, creating a network effect. A **network effect** occurs where all participants receive value from the fact that everyone else uses the same tool or product (for example, a common operating system, telephone system, or software application such as a proprietary instant messaging standard or an operating system such as Windows), all of which increase in value as more people adopt them.[2] Successful first movers would become the new intermediaries of e-commerce, displacing traditional retail merchants and suppliers of content, and becoming profitable by charging fees of one sort or another for the value customers perceived in their services and products.

friction-free commerce
a vision of commerce in which information is equally distributed, transaction costs are low, prices can be dynamically adjusted to reflect actual demand, intermediaries decline, and unfair competitive advantages are eliminated

first mover
a firm that is first to market in a particular area and that moves quickly to gather market share

network effect
occurs where users receive value from the fact that everyone else uses the same tool or product

---

[2] The network effect is quantified by Metcalfe's Law, which argues that the value of a network grows by the square of the number of participants.

To initiate this process, entrepreneurs argued that prices would have to be very low to attract customers and fend off potential competitors. E-commerce was, after all, a totally new way of shopping that would have to offer some immediate cost benefits to consumers. However, because doing business on the Web was supposedly so much more efficient when compared to traditional "bricks-and-mortar" businesses (even when compared to the direct mail catalog business) and because the costs of customer acquisition and retention would supposedly be so much lower, profits would inevitably materialize out of these efficiencies. Given these dynamics, market share, the number of visitors to a site ("eyeballs"), and gross revenue became far more important in the earlier stages of an online firm than earnings or profits. Entrepreneurs and their financial backers in the early years of e-commerce expected that extraordinary profitability would come, but only after several years of losses.

Thus, the early years of e-commerce were driven largely by visions of profiting from new technology, with the emphasis on quickly achieving very high market visibility. The source of financing was venture capital funds. The ideology of the period emphasized the ungoverned "Wild West" character of the Web and the feeling that governments and courts could not possibly limit or regulate the Internet; there was a general belief that traditional corporations were too slow and bureaucratic, too stuck in the old ways of doing business, to "get it"—to be competitive in e-commerce. Young entrepreneurs were therefore the driving force behind e-commerce, backed by huge amounts of money invested by venture capitalists. The emphasis was on *deconstructing* (destroying) traditional distribution channels and disintermediating existing channels, using new pure online companies who aimed to achieve impregnable first-mover advantages. Overall, this period of e-commerce was characterized by experimentation, capitalization, and hypercompetition (Varian, 2000b).

The crash in stock market values for Internet-related companies throughout 2000 is a convenient marker for ending the early period in the development of e-commerce. Looking back at the early years of e-commerce, it is apparent that e-commerce has been, for the most part, a stunning technological success as the Internet and the Web ramped up from a few thousand to billions of e-commerce transactions per year, and this year will generate an estimated $333 billion in total B2C revenues and around $4.1 trillion in B2B revenues, with around 150 million online buyers in the United States. With enhancements and strengthening, described in later chapters, it is clear that e-commerce's digital infrastructure is solid enough to sustain significant growth in e-commerce during the next decade. The Internet scales well. The "e" in e-commerce has been an overwhelming success.

From a business perspective, though, the early years of e-commerce were a mixed success, and offered many surprises. Only about 10% of dot-coms formed since 1995 have survived as independent companies in 2012. Only a very tiny percentage of these survivors are profitable. Yet online B2C sales of goods and services are still growing. Consumers have learned to use the Web as a powerful source of information about products they actually purchase through other channels, such as at a traditional bricks-and-mortar store. This is especially true of expensive consumer durables such as appliances, automobiles, and electronics. This "Internet-influenced" commerce is very difficult to estimate, but is believed to have been somewhere around $1.2 trillion in 2012 (Forrester Research, 2011). Altogether then, B2C retail e-commerce (both actual purchases and purchases influenced by Web shopping but actually buying in a store) are expected to amount to over $1.4 trillion in 2012, or over 40% of total retail sales in the United States. The "commerce" in e-commerce is basically very sound, at least in the sense of attracting a growing number of customers and generating revenues.

E-COMMERCE 2001–2006: CONSOLIDATION

In the second period of e-commerce, from 2000 to 2006, a sobering period of reassessment of e-commerce occurred, with many critics doubting its long-term prospects. Emphasis shifted to a more "business-driven" approach rather than being technology driven; large traditional firms learned how to use the Web to strengthen their market positions; brand extension and strengthening became more important than creating new brands; financing shrunk as capital markets shunned start-up firms; and traditional bank financing based on profitability returned.

During this period of consolidation, e-commerce changed to include not just retail products but also more complex services such as travel and financial services. This period was enabled by widespread adoption of broadband networks in American homes and businesses, coupled with the growing power and lower prices of personal computers that were the primary means of accessing the Internet, usually from work or home. Marketing on the Internet increasingly meant using search engine advertising targeted to user queries, rich media and video ads, and behavioral targeting of marketing messages based on ad networks and auction markets. The Web policy of both large and small firms expanded to include a broader "Web presence" that included not just Web sites, but also e-mail, display, and search engine campaigns; multiple Web sites for each product; and the building of some limited community feedback facilities. E-commerce in this period was growing again by more than 10% a year.

E-COMMERCE 2007—PRESENT: REINVENTION

Beginning in 2007 with the introduction of the iPhone, to the present day, e-commerce has been transformed yet again by the rapid growth of online social networks, widespread adoption of consumer mobile devices such as smartphones and tablet computers, and the expansion of e-commerce to include local goods and services. The defining characteristics of this period are often characterized as the "social, mobile, local" online world. In this period, entertainment content begins to develop as a major source of e-commerce revenues and mobile devices become entertainment centers, as well as an on-the-go shopping devices for retail goods and services. Marketing is transformed by the increasing use of social networks, word-of-mouth, viral marketing, and much more powerful data repositories and analytic tools for truly personal marketing. Firms' online policies expand in the attempt to build a digital presence that surrounds the online consumer with coordinated marketing messages based on their social network memberships, use of search engines and Web browsers, and even their personal e-mail messages, social networks, the mobile platform, and local commerce. This period is as much a sociological phenomenon as it is a technological or business phenomenon. Few of the new mobile, social, and local firms in this period have been able to monetize their huge audiences into profitable operations yet, but many eventually will. The *Insight on Business* case, *Is the Party Already Over?*, examines the rise of yet another Internet investment bubble, this time centered around social media, and the fall-out resulting from the problems surrounding Facebook's initial public offering.

Table 1.5 summarizes e-commerce in each of these three periods.

ASSESSING E-COMMERCE: SUCCESSES, SURPRISES, AND FAILURES

Although e-commerce has grown at an extremely rapid pace in customers and revenues, it is clear that many of the visions, predictions, and assertions about e-commerce developed in the early years have not have been fulfilled. For instance, economists' visions of "friction-free" commerce have not been entirely realized. Prices are sometimes lower on the Web, but the low prices are sometimes a function of entrepreneurs selling products below their costs. Consumers are less price sensitive than expected;

TABLE 1.5	EVOLUTION OF E-COMMERCE	
1995–2000 INVENTION	**2001–2006 CONSOLIDATION**	**2007–PRESENT RE-INVENTION**
Technology driven	Business driven	Mobile technology enables social, local, and mobile commerce
Revenue growth emphasis	Earnings and profits emphasis	Audience and social network connections emphasis
Venture capital financing	Traditional financing	Smaller VC investments; early small-firm buyouts by large online players
Ungoverned	Stronger regulation and governance	Extensive government surveillance
Entrepreneurial	Large traditional firms	Entrepreneurial social and local firms
Disintermediation	Strengthening intermediaries	Proliferation of small online intermediaries renting business processes of larger firms
Perfect markets	Imperfect markets, brands, and network effects	Continuation of online market imperfections; commodity competition in select markets
Pure online strategies	Mixed "bricks-and-clicks" strategies	Return of pure online strategies in new markets; extension of bricks-and-clicks in traditional retail markets
First-mover advantages	Strategic-follower strength; complementary assets	First-mover advantages return in new markets as traditional Web players catch up
Low-complexity retail products	High-complexity retail products and services	Retail, services, and content

INSIGHT ON BUSINESS

IS THE PARTY ALREADY OVER?

In 2011 and early 2012, with the successful initial public offerings (IPOs) of LinkedIn, Zynga, Groupon, and Pandora Media, rampant interest in the forthcoming Facebook IPO, and increased venture capital investment in other social media companies such as Twitter, many felt the times were reminiscent of the dot-com bubble of 1998–2000, when venture capitalists poured an estimated $120 billion into around 12,500 dot-com start-up ventures and more than 1,500 companies went public, raising almost $115 billion. And, in an eerie similarity, just as the dot-com bubble burst to a crash in mid-2000, so too has the new "social media" bubble shown signs of serious leakage in mid-2012.

The problems first began to surface with the eagerly anticipated Facebook IPO in May 2012. Facebook went public with a valuation of over $100 billion, the biggest IPO valuation ever, and a share price of $38, making it unlikely that its shares would experience the traditional first day "pop" in price that was the hallmark of Internet IPOs back in the heyday of the dot-com bubble. Investors both large and small were inevitably disappointed as the shares declined rather than rose from its initial price. As spring turned into summer there was more bad news. With the release of Facebook's first public quarterly earnings report in July, which showed slowing growth in the total number of users and a net loss of $157 million, as well as continued uncertainty over how Facebook would be able to monetize its user base, the shares continued to lose value. By August, its share price had declined by more than 40% to the $20 range, cutting Facebook's valuation almost by half, to around $65 billion. At the same time, other Internet-related public companies, such as Zynga and Groupon, which had also gone public

with much fanfare, were experiencing similar troubles. Zynga's share price experienced a precipitous drop, by more than 75% from its high, as investors became concerned that a company built on virtual goods like online games might not have staying power. Questions about Groupon's business model and accounting methods, as well as slower growth and revenue that was below expectations, reduced its gleam for investors as well as its share price.

So, is the bloom totally off the social media rose? Is the party really already over? The answer is not by a long shot. The "old guard"—Amazon, Google, and Apple—are all doing just fine. Some of the "new guard," such as LinkedIn, are holding relatively steady. And the news for start-ups remains rosy. Starting an Internet-related company has, in some ways, never been easier or more potentially profitable. The technology required to begin a business has become very inexpensive and much more accessible, and, if necessary, many aspects of the process can be outsourced. It's the idea that is paramount. If it takes off and goes viral, the company can be worth millions before you even realize it. Pinterest, examined in the opening case, is a case in point. Other recent success stories include Yammer, a social network for businesses that was started in 2008 and acquired by Microsoft in June 2012 for $1.2 billion, and Instagram, started in 2009 and acquired by Facebook for $1 billion in April 2012. As a result, many believe that this is still a phenomenal time to be an entrepreneur. Venture capital firms remain undaunted and have raised billions for new funds that are ready to invest. These venture capital firms believe that the world of 2012 is much different from the earlier dot-com era, and that the barriers to creating a global start-up have never been lower. As a result, despite the turmoil in the stock markets, many

(continued)

young companies are still raising seed capital based on high valuations. Silicon Valley remains at the epicenter, but other areas, such as New York City, with its proximity to media, advertising and fashion industries, are also seeing increased activity. For instance, almost 500 start-ups in New York have received venture capital funding between 2007 and 2011, with the number of deals rising by 32% during that time.

Sectors that remain particularly hot include, not surprisingly, anything related to the mobile platform, and security. In the first quarter of 2012, the number of venture capital investments in the mobile sector reached an all-time high, with many of the deals related to mobile photo or video technology, which some have dubbed the Instagram Effect. Mobile payments are another strong area, with Square, which enables cell phones to accept credit card payments, attracting the majority of attention. Launched in October 2010, Square already is valued at more than $1 billion and has

recently announced an alliance with Starbucks that is likely to make it even more valuable.

On the security front, in 2011, venture capital firms invested almost $1 billion in security companies, nearly double their investments in 2010. Start-ups attracting significant investments include Bit9, a leader in advanced threat protection that has tripled its client base in two years; Lookout, which blocks malware and spyware on mobile devices; Zenprise, which brings business-level security to consumer phones; Appthority, which tracks suspicious behavior by mobile apps; and Solera Networks, which tracks intrusions in real time. Interest in security start-ups has also been heightened by some big-ticket acquisitions, including Apple's purchase of AuthenTec for $356 million and EMC Corporation's acquisition of NetWitness for a reported $400 million.

So while the party may have slowed for the moment on Wall Street, in the rest of the Internet world, it is by no means over!

SOURCES: "In Silicon Valley, Finding the Next Big Thing in the Ordinary," by Steven M. Davidoff, *New York Times*, August 14, 2012; "Groupon Posts Mixed Results, and Stock Falls," by Quentin Hardy, *New York Times*, August 13, 2012; "A Steep Climb Back for Facebook's Stock," by Somini Sengupta, *New York Times*, August 12, 2012; "Security Start-Ups Catch Fancy of Investors," by Nicole Perlroth and Evelyn M. Rusli, *New York Times*, August 5, 2012; "In Sliding Internet Stocks, Some Hear Echo of 2000," by David Streitfeld and Evelyn M. Rusli, *New York Times*, July 27, 2012; "Facebook Delivers an Earnings Letdown," by Somini Sengupta, *New York Times*, July 26, 2012; "The News Isn't Good for Zynga, Maker of Farmville," by David Streitfeld and Jenna Wortham, *New York Times*, July 25, 2012; "Venture Capital Investments Pick Up, with Strong Emphasis on Mobile," by Eliza Kern, Gigaom.com, July 16, 2012; "A Reality Series Finds Silicon Valley Cringing," by David Streitfeld, *New York Times*, July 9, 2012; "For Tech Start-Ups, New York Has Increasing Allure," by Joshua Brustein, *New York Times*, May 27, 2012.

surprisingly, the Web sites with the highest revenue often have the highest prices. There remains considerable persistent and even increasing price dispersion on the Web: online competition has lowered prices, but price dispersion remains pervasive in many markets despite lower search costs (Levin, 2011; Ghose and Yao, 2010). By some estimates, the standard deviation in Web prices is about 10% of the average price for the same product on the Web. Shop around! The concept of one world, one market, one price has not occurred in reality as entrepreneurs discover new ways to differentiate their products and services. While for the most part Internet prices save consumers about 20% on average when compared to in-store prices, sometimes prices on the Web are higher than for similar products purchased offline, especially if shipping costs are considered. For instance, prices on books and CDs vary by as much as 50%, and prices for airline tickets as much as 20% (Alessandria, 2009; Aguiar and Hurst, 2008; Baye, 2004; Baye, et al., 2004; Brynjolfsson and Smith, 2000; Bailey, 1998a, b). Merchants have adjusted to the competitive Internet environment by engaging in "hit-and-run pricing" or changing prices every day or hour (using "flash pricing" or "flash sales") so competitors never know what they are charging (neither do customers); by making their prices hard to discover and sowing confusion among consumers by "baiting and switching" customers from low-margin products to high-margin products with supposedly "higher quality." Finally, brands remain very important in e-commerce—consumers trust some firms more than others to deliver a high-quality product on time (Rosso and Jansen, 2010).

The "perfect competition" model of extreme market efficiency has not come to pass. Merchants and marketers are continually introducing information asymmetries. Search costs have fallen overall, but the overall transaction cost of actually completing a purchase in e-commerce remains high because users have a bewildering number of new questions to consider: Will the merchant actually deliver? What is the time frame of delivery? Does the merchant really stock this item? How do I fill out this form? Many potential e-commerce purchases are terminated in the shopping cart stage because of these consumer uncertainties. For some product areas, it is easier to call a trusted catalog merchant on the telephone than to order on a Web site. Finally, intermediaries have not disappeared as predicted. Most manufacturers, for instance, have not adopted the Dell model of online sales (direct sales by the manufacturer to the consumer), and Dell itself has moved towards a mixed model heavily reliant on in-store sales where customers can "kick the tires" by trying the keyboard and viewing the screen. Apple stores are the most successful stores in the world, with sales of about $5,600 per square foot, about 20 times the average for retail stores. People still like to shop in a physical store.

If anything, e-commerce has created many opportunities for middlemen to aggregate content, products, and services into portals and search engines and thereby introduce themselves as the "new" intermediaries. Yahoo, MSN, and Amazon, along with third-party travel sites such as Travelocity, Orbitz and Expedia, are all examples of this kind of intermediary. As illustrated in **Figure 1.6**, e-commerce has not driven

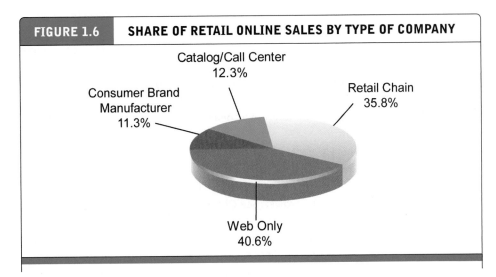

FIGURE 1.6 **SHARE OF RETAIL ONLINE SALES BY TYPE OF COMPANY**

Catalog/Call Center 12.3%

Consumer Brand Manufacturer 11.3%

Retail Chain 35.8%

Web Only 40.6%

Web-only firms account for the largest share of online retail sales, followed closely by online sales by traditional retail chain stores.

SOURCE: Based on data from Internet Retailer, 2012b.

existing retail chains and catalog merchants out of business, although it has created opportunities for entrepreneurial Web-only firms to succeed.

The visions of many entrepreneurs and venture capitalists for e-commerce have not materialized exactly as predicted either. First-mover advantage appears to have succeeded only for a very small group of sites. Historically, first movers have been long-term losers, with the early-to-market innovators usually being displaced by established "fast-follower" firms with the right complement of financial, marketing, legal, and production assets needed to develop mature markets, and this has proved true for e-commerce as well. Many e-commerce first movers, such as eToys, FogDog (sporting goods), WebVan (groceries), and Eve.com (beauty products) are out of business. Customer acquisition and retention costs during the early years of e-commerce were extraordinarily high, with some firms, such as E*Trade and other financial service firms, paying up to $400 to acquire a new customer. The overall costs of doing business on the Web—including the costs of technology, site design and maintenance, and warehouses for fulfillment— are often no lower than the costs faced by the most efficient bricks-and-mortar stores. A large warehouse costs tens of millions of dollars regardless of a firm's Web presence. The knowledge of how to run the warehouse is priceless, and not easily moved. The start-up costs can be staggering. Attempting to achieve or enhance profitability by raising prices has often led to large customer defections (as can be seen from Netflix's recent experience). From the e-commerce merchant's perspective, the "e" in e-commerce does not stand for "easy."

PREDICTIONS FOR THE FUTURE: MORE SURPRISES

Given that e-commerce has changed greatly in the last several years, its future cannot be predicted except to say "Watch for more surprises." There are five main factors that will help define the future of e-commerce. First, there is little doubt that the technology of e-commerce—the Internet, the Web, and the growing number of wireless devices that make up the mobile platform, including smartphones such as the iPhone, Android, and BlackBerry, and tablet computers such as the iPad—will continue to propagate through all commercial activity. The overall revenues from e-commerce (goods and services) in the United States rose in 2011 by around 14% and are expected to continue to rise, most likely at an annualized rate of about 10% per year through 2016. The number of products and services sold on the Web and the size of the average purchase order will both continue to grow at near double-digit rates. The number of online shoppers in the United States will also continue to grow, although at a much more modest rate of about 1% per year. There has also been a significant broadening of the online product mix compared to the early years when books, computer software, and hardware dominated e-commerce (see **Table 1.6**). This trend will continue as trust in e-commerce transactions grows. (See Chapter 9 for changes in retail products and services.)

Second, e-commerce prices will rise to cover the real costs of doing business on the Web, to price-in the benefits provided to customers shopping online, and to pay investors a reasonable rate of return on their capital. Third, e-commerce *margins*

TABLE 1.6	ONLINE RETAIL SALES BY CATEGORY, 2011
CATEGORY	ANNUAL SALES (IN BILLIONS)
	2011
Mass merchant/Department store	$74.2
Computers/Electronics	$28.9
Office supplies	$19.9
Apparel/Accessories	$22.2
Books/Music/Video	$6.2
Housewares/Home furnishings	$4.6
Health/Beauty	$4.1
Hardware/Home improvement	$4.4
Specialty/non apparel	$4.0
Food/Drug	$4.2
Flower/Gifts	$1.3
Sporting goods	$2.6
Toys/Hobbies	$2.3
Jewelry	$1.2
Automotive parts/Accessories	$0.75

SOURCES: Based on data from Internet Retailer, 2012b; authors' estimates.

(the difference between the revenues from sales and the cost of goods) and profits will rise to levels more typical of all retailers. Fourth, the cast of players will change radically. Traditional well-endowed, experienced Fortune 500 companies will play a growing and dominant role in e-commerce, while new start-up ventures will quickly gain large online audiences for new products and services not dominated by the large players. There will also be a continuation of audience consolidation on the Internet in general, with the top 100 sites garnering over 80% of all online sales (Internet Retailer, 2012b). **Table 1.7** lists the top 25 online retailers, as ranked by

TABLE 1.7	TOP 25 ONLINE RETAILERS RANKED BY ONLINE SALES
ONLINE RETAILER	ONLINE SALES (2011) (IN BILLIONS)
Amazon	$48.1
Staples	$10.6
Apple	$6.7
Walmart	$4.9
Dell	$4.6
Office Depot	$4.1
Liberty Interactive	$3.8
Sears	$3.6
Netflix	$3.2
CDW	$3.0
Best Buy	$3.0
OfficeMax	$2.9
Newegg	$2.7
Macy's	$2.2
W.W. Grainger	$2.2
Sony	$2.0
Costco	$1.9
L.L.Bean	$1.7
Victoria's Secret Direct	$1.6
JCPenney	$1.6
HP Home and Home Office	$1.6
Gap	$1.6
Target	$1.5
Williams Sonoma Inc.	$1.4
Systemax	$1.4

SOURCES: Based on data from Internet Retailer, 2012b; company reports on Form 10-K filed with the Securities and Exchange Commission.

2011 online sales. The table shows an unmistakable trend toward the appearance of some very well-known, traditional brands from strong traditional retail chains, with Staples, Walmart, Office Depot, Sears, Best Buy, OfficeMax, and Macy's all in the top 15.

Fifth, the number of successful pure online companies will remain smaller than integrated online/offline stores that combine traditional sales channels such as physical stores and printed catalogs with online efforts. For instance, traditional catalog sales firms such as L.L.Bean have transformed themselves into integrated online and direct mail firms with more than half of their sales coming from the online channel. Procter & Gamble will continue to develop informative Web sites such as Tide.com; and the major automotive companies will continue to improve the content and value of their Web sites even if they do not enter into direct sales relationships with consumers, but instead use the Web to assist sales through dealers (thereby strengthening traditional intermediaries and channels).

The future of e-commerce will include the growth of regulatory activity both in the United States and worldwide. Governments around the world are challenging the early vision of computer scientists and information technologists that the Internet should be a self-regulating and self-governing phenomenon. The Internet and e-commerce have been so successful and powerful, so all-pervasive, that they directly involve the social, cultural, and political life of entire nations and cultures. Throughout history, whenever technologies have risen to this level of social importance, power, and visibility, they become the target of efforts to regulate and control the technology to ensure that positive social benefits result from their use and to guarantee the public's health and welfare. Radio, television, automobiles, electricity, and railroads are all the subject of regulation and legislation. Likewise, with e-commerce. In the U.S. Congress, there have already been a number of bills passed (as well as hundreds proposed) to control various facets of the Internet and e-commerce, from consumer privacy to pornography, gambling, and encryption. We can expect these efforts at regulation in the United States and around the world to increase as e-commerce extends its reach and importance.

A relatively new factor that will influence the growth of e-commerce is the cost of energy, in particular gasoline and diesel. As fuel costs rise, traveling to shop at physical locations can be very expensive. Buying online can save customers time and energy costs. There is growing evidence that shoppers are changing their shopping habits and locales because of fuel costs, and pushing the sales of online retailers to higher levels.

In summary, the future of e-commerce will be a fascinating mixture of traditional retail, service, and media firms extending their brands to online markets; early-period e-commerce firms such as Amazon and eBay strengthening their financial results and dominant positions; and a bevy of entirely new entrepreneurial firms with the potential to rocket into prominence by developing huge new audiences in months. Firms that fit this pattern include Facebook, Twitter, Pinterest, and Tumblr.

1.3   UNDERSTANDING E-COMMERCE: ORGANIZING THEMES

Understanding e-commerce in its totality is a difficult task for students and instructors because there are so many facets to the phenomenon. No single academic discipline is prepared to encompass all of e-commerce. After teaching the e-commerce course for several years and writing this book, we have come to realize just how difficult it is to "understand" e-commerce. We have found it useful to think about e-commerce as involving three broad interrelated themes: technology, business, and society. We do not mean to imply any ordering of importance here because this book and our thinking freely range over these themes as appropriate to the problem we are trying to understand and describe. Nevertheless, as in previous technologically driven commercial revolutions, there is an historic progression. Technologies develop first, and then those developments are exploited commercially. Once commercial exploitation of the technology becomes widespread, a host of social, cultural, and political issues arise.

TECHNOLOGY: INFRASTRUCTURE

The development and mastery of digital computing and communications technology is at the heart of the newly emerging global digital economy we call e-commerce. To understand the likely future of e-commerce, you need a basic understanding of the information technologies upon which it is built. E-commerce is above all else a technologically driven phenomenon that relies on a host of information technologies as well as fundamental concepts from computer science developed over a 50-year period. At the core of e-commerce are the Internet and the World Wide Web, which we describe in detail in Chapter 3. Underlying these technologies are a host of complementary technologies: cloud computing, personal computers, smartphones, tablet computers, local area networks, relational and non-relational databases, client/server computing, data mining, and fiber-optic switches, to name just a few. These technologies lie at the heart of sophisticated business computing applications such as enterprise-wide computing systems, supply chain management systems, manufacturing resource planning systems, and customer relationship management systems. E-commerce relies on all these basic technologies—not just the Internet. The Internet, while representing a sharp break from prior corporate computing and communications technologies, is nevertheless just the latest development in the evolution of corporate computing and part of the continuing chain of computer-based innovations in business. **Figure 1.7** illustrates the major stages in the development of corporate computing and indicates how the Internet and the Web fit into this development trajectory.

To truly understand e-commerce, you will need to know something about packet-switched communications, protocols such as TCP/IP, client/server and cloud

FIGURE 1.7	THE INTERNET AND THE EVOLUTION OF CORPORATE COMPUTING

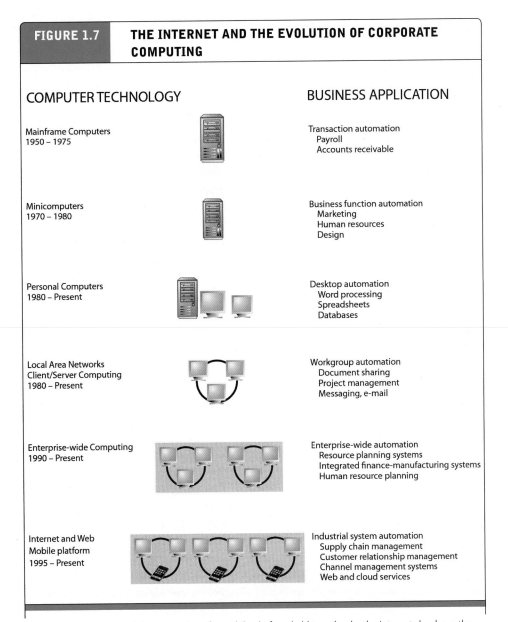

COMPUTER TECHNOLOGY | BUSINESS APPLICATION

Mainframe Computers
1950 – 1975

Transaction automation
    Payroll
    Accounts receivable

Minicomputers
1970 – 1980

Business function automation
    Marketing
    Human resources
    Design

Personal Computers
1980 – Present

Desktop automation
    Word processing
    Spreadsheets
    Databases

Local Area Networks
Client/Server Computing
1980 – Present

Workgroup automation
    Document sharing
    Project management
    Messaging, e-mail

Enterprise-wide Computing
1990 – Present

Enterprise-wide automation
    Resource planning systems
    Integrated finance-manufacturing systems
    Human resource planning

Internet and Web
Mobile platform
1995 – Present

Industrial system automation
    Supply chain management
    Customer relationship management
    Channel management systems
    Web and cloud services

The Internet and Web, and the emergence of a mobile platform held together by the Internet cloud, are the latest in a chain of evolving technologies and related business applications, each of which builds on its predecessors.

computing, mobile digital platforms, Web servers, HTML5, CSS, and software programming tools such as Flash and JavaScript on the client side, and Java, PHP, Ruby on Rails, and ColdFusion on the server side. All of these topics are described fully in Part 2 of the book (Chapters 3–5).

BUSINESS: BASIC CONCEPTS

While technology provides the infrastructure, it is the business applications—the potential for extraordinary returns on investment—that create the interest and excitement in e-commerce. New technologies present businesses and entrepreneurs with new ways of organizing production and transacting business. New technologies change the strategies and plans of existing firms: old strategies are made obsolete and new ones need to be invented. New technologies are the birthing grounds where thousands of new companies spring up with new products and services. New technologies are the graveyard of many traditional businesses, such as record stores. To truly understand e-commerce, you will need to be familiar with some key business concepts, such as the nature of digital markets, digital goods, business models, firm and industry value chains, value webs, industry structure, digital disruption, and consumer behavior in digital markets, as well as basic concepts of financial analysis. We'll examine these concepts further in Chapter 2 , Chapters 6 and 7, and also Chapters 9 through 12.

SOCIETY: TAMING THE JUGGERNAUT

With more than 193 million adult Americans now using the Internet, many for e-commerce purposes, and more than 2.2 billion users worldwide, the impact of the Internet and e-commerce on society is significant and global. Increasingly, e-commerce is subject to the laws of nations and global entities. You will need to understand the pressures that global e-commerce places on contemporary society in order to conduct a successful e-commerce business or understand the e-commerce phenomenon. The primary societal issues we discuss in this book are individual privacy, intellectual property, and public welfare policy.

Since the Internet and the Web are exceptionally adept at tracking the identity and behavior of individuals online, e-commerce raises difficulties for preserving privacy—the ability of individuals to place limits on the type and amount of information collected about them, and to control the uses of their personal information. Read the *Insight on Society* case, *Facebook and the Age of Privacy,* to get a view of some of the ways e-commerce sites use personal information.

Because the cost of distributing digital copies of copyrighted intellectual property—tangible works of the mind such as music, books, and videos—is nearly zero on the Internet, e-commerce poses special challenges to the various methods societies have used in the past to protect intellectual property rights.

The global nature of e-commerce also poses public policy issues of equity, equal access, content regulation, and taxation. For instance, in the United States, public telephone utilities are required under public utility and public accommodation laws to make basic service available at affordable rates so everyone can have telephone service. Should these laws be extended to the Internet and the Web? If goods are purchased by a New York State resident from a Web site in California, shipped from a center in Illinois, and delivered to New York, what state has the right to collect a sales tax? Should some heavy Internet users who consume extraordinary amounts

INSIGHT ON SOCIETY

FACEBOOK AND THE AGE OF PRIVACY

In a January 2010 interview, Mark Zuckerberg, the founder of Facebook, proclaimed that the "age of privacy" had to come to an end. According to Zuckerberg, social norms had changed and people were no longer worried about sharing their personal information with friends, friends of friends, or even the entire Web. This view is in accordance with Facebook's broader goal, which is, according to Zuckerberg, to make the world a more open and connected place. Many Facebook features are premised on this position. Supporters of Zuckerberg's viewpoint believe the 21st century is an age of "information exhibitionism," a new era of openness and transparency.

However, not everyone is a true believer. For instance, the end to the age of privacy came as blockbuster news to historians and legal scholars who noted that some of the basic concepts of privacy, such as limiting the power of institutions to intrude on the personal papers and activities of ordinary citizens, originated in the Constitution of the Roman Republic around 542 B.C. Nearly every important founding political document in Western societies provides limitations on the power of government to snoop on private citizens. Privacy—limitations on what personal information government and private institutions can collect and use—is a founding principle of democracies. The age of privacy has a very long history. A decade's worth of privacy surveys in the United States show that well over 80% of the American public fear the Internet is a threat to their privacy.

With more than 1 billion users worldwide, and about 190 million in North America,

Facebook's privacy policies are going to shape privacy standards on the Internet for years to come. The economic stakes in the privacy debate are quite large, involving billions in advertising and transaction dollars. Social network sites such as Facebook use a privacy-destruction business model that encourages and sometimes requires users to give up their claim to control their personal information and hence their privacy. The model is based on building a database of hundreds of millions of users who post personal information, preferences, and behaviors, and who are encouraged, or deceived, into relinquishing control over their information, which is then sold to advertisers and outside third parties. Privacy destruction is the primary way social network sites can make a profit. It's called, politely, "monetization of the user base."

Facebook's current privacy policies are quite a flip-flop from its original privacy policy in 2004, which promised users near complete control over who could see their personal profile. The default option then was that only immediate friends who you invited were given access. Other users in your network could not get much information about you at all. People outside that network could find nothing about you. This was the privacy environment that millions of Facebook users originally signed up for. However, every year since 2004, Facebook has attempted to extend—most often abruptly and without prior notice—its control over user information and content. Along the way, though, Facebook has learned that people actually do care about the use, control, and ownership of their personal information. For instance, in 2007, Facebook

(continued)

introduced the Beacon program, which was designed to broadcast users' activities on participating Web sites to their friends. A Facebook-based group created by MoveOn.org to resist the program soon had thousands of members. Class action suits followed. Facebook initially tried to mollify members by making the program "opt in" but this policy change was discovered to be a sham as personal information continued to flow from Facebook to various Web sites. Facebook finally terminated the Beacon program in 2009, and paid $9.5 million to settle the class action suits.

In 2009, undeterred by the Beacon fiasco, Facebook unilaterally decided that it would publish users' basic personal information on the public Internet, and announced that whatever content users had contributed belonged to Facebook, and that its ownership of that information never terminated. However, as with the Beacon program, Facebook's efforts to take permanent control of user information resulted in users joining online resistance groups and it was ultimately forced to withdraw this policy as well. The widespread user unrest prompted Facebook to propose a new Facebook Principles and Statement of Rights and Responsibilities, which was approved by 75% of the members who voted in an online survey. The new policy explicitly stated that users "own and control their information." Facebook also improved account deletion features, limited sublicenses of information about users, and reduced data exchanges with outside developers. These moves quieted the uproar for a time. Unfortunately, the resulting privacy policy was so complicated that users typically defaulted to "share" rather than work through over 170 information categories that users could choose to make public or private to various groups, the public, and

the Internet. Subsequently, Facebook announced further revisions designed to allow users to more easily specify who will see material they post: just friends, everyone on the Internet (now called "public"), or a customized group. Instead of having to click through pages of privacy options in Settings, the privacy options now appear right next to the material being posted.

In 2009, Facebook also introduced the Like button, and in 2010 extended it to third-party Web sites to alert Facebook users to their friends' browsing and purchases. In 2011, it began publicizing users' "likes" of various advertisers in Sponsored Stories (i.e., advertisements) that included the users' names and profile pictures without their explicit consent, without paying them, and without giving them a way to opt out. This resulted in yet another class action lawsuit, which Facebook settled for $20 million in June 2012. As part of the settlement, Facebook agreed to make it clear to users that information like their names and profile pictures might be used in Sponsored Stories, and also give users and parents of minor children greater control over how that personal information is used.

In 2011, Facebook enrolled all Facebook subscribers into its facial recognition program without asking anyone. When a user uploads photos, the software recognizes the faces, tags them, and creates a record of that person/photo. Later, users can retrieve all photos containing an image of a specific friend. Any existing friend can be tagged, and the software suggests the names of friends to tag when you upload the photos. This too raised the privacy alarm, forcing Facebook to make it easier for users to opt out. But concerns remain. A German data-protection agency is taking legal action against Facebook and seeking to fine it as a

(continued)

result. In May 2012, Facebook purchased Face.com, which provides the technology that powers its facial recognition program. Some have expressed concern about the possible expansion of this type of technology by Facebook. In July 2012, the U.S. Senate subcommittee on Privacy, Technology, and the Law called Facebook before it to discuss the technology and its future plans.

In May 2012, Facebook went public, creating more pressure on it to increase revenues and profits to justify its stock market value. Shortly thereafter, Facebook announced that it was launching a new mobile advertising product that will push ads to the mobile news feeds of users based on the apps they use through the Facebook Connect feature, without explicit permission from the user to do so. Facebook reportedly may also decide to track what people do on their apps. It also announced Facebook Exchange, a new program that will allow advertisers to serve ads to Facebook users based on their browsing activity while not on Facebook. Privacy advocates have raised the alarm yet again and more lawsuits have been filed by users who claim that Facebook has invaded their privacy by tracking their Internet use even after they have logged off from Facebook. Although Facebook is not yet combining this data with its own database of user personal information, there are concerns that it may do so in the future. And that database is truly huge. For instance, Max Schrems, an Austrian law student, was able to use the European Union's stronger privacy protections to force Facebook to release a copy of the data that Facebook had compiled on him over a three-year period. He received 1,222 pages covering 57 categories of personal data, such as date and time of log-ins, geographic location, deleted Wall posts and messages, e-mail addresses, and more. And even this was not a full copy—Facebook reportedly retains 84 different categories of data about every user. In response to increased European Union scrutiny of its data collection practices, Facebook recently agreed to provide users with more information about the data it stores, and will begin rolling out the new policy in Europe and Canada, and then later in the United States.

It appears that Zuckerberg's proclamation that the age of privacy is over was premature. Instead, Facebook's posture on privacy may turn out to be an enduring headache and perhaps ultimately its Achilles heel. As Facebook itself notes in its S-1 filing with the Securities and Exchange Commission, if it adopts "policies or procedures related to areas such as sharing or user data that are perceived negatively by our users or the general public," its revenue, financial results, and business may be significantly harmed. And this, more than anything else, may be the savior for privacy at Facebook.

SOURCES: "Facebook to Face Senate Hearing on Facial Recognition," by Katy Bachman, AdWeek.con, July 16, 2012; "Facebook to Target Ads Based on App Usage," by Shayndi Raice, *Wall Street Journal*, July 6, 2012; "Facebook's Facial-Recognition Acquisition Raises Privacy Concerns," by Samantha Murphy, Mashable.com, June 25, 2012; "Facebook Exchange Ads Raise Privacy Concerns," by Mikal E. Belicove, CNBC.com, June 21, 2012; "Facebook About to Launch Facebook Exchange, Real-Time Ad Bidding," by Jessica Guynn, *Los Angeles Times*, June 13, 2012; "Facebook Suit Over Subscriber Tracking Seeks $15 Billion," by Kit Chellel and Jeremy Hodges, Bloomberg.com, May 19, 2012; Facebook Inc. Form S-1/A filed with the Securities and Exchange Commission, May 16, 2012; "Facebook and Your Privacy," by Consumer Reports Staff, ConsumerReports.org, May 3, 2012; "Facebook Offers More Disclosure to Users," by Kevin J. O'Brien, *New York Times*, April 12, 2012; "German State to Sue Facebook over Facial Recognition Feature," by Emil Protalinski, ZDnet.com, November 10, 2011; "Facebook Aims to Simplify Privacy Settings," by Somini Sengupta, *New York Times*, August 23, 2011; "Facebook Again in Spotlight on Privacy," by Geoffrey Fowler, *Wall Street Journal*, June 8, 2011; "Facebook Redesigns Privacy Controls," by Ben Worthen, *Wall Street Journal*, May 27, 2010; "How Facebook Pulled a Privacy Bait and Switch," by Dan Tynan, *PC World*, May 2010; *The Constitution of the Roman Republic*, Andrew Lintott, Oxford University Press, 1999.

of bandwidth be charged extra for service, or should the Internet be neutral with respect to usage? What rights do nation-states and their citizens have with respect to the Internet, the Web, and e-commerce? We address issues such as these in Chapter 8, and also throughout the text.

ACADEMIC DISCIPLINES CONCERNED WITH E-COMMERCE

The phenomenon of e-commerce is so broad that a multidisciplinary perspective is required. There are two primary approaches to e-commerce: technical and behavioral.

Technical Approaches

Computer scientists are interested in e-commerce as an exemplary application of Internet technology. They are concerned with the development of computer hardware, software, and telecommunications systems, as well as standards, encryption, and database design and operation. Management scientists are primarily interested in building mathematical models of business processes and optimizing these processes. They are interested in e-commerce as an opportunity to study how business firms can exploit the Internet to achieve more efficient business operations.

Behavioral Approaches

In the behavioral area, information systems researchers are primarily interested in e-commerce because of its implications for firm and industry value chains, industry structure, and corporate strategy. The information systems discipline spans the technical and behavioral approaches. For instance, technical groups within the information systems specialty also focus on data mining, search engine design, and artificial intelligence. Economists have focused on consumer behavior at Web sites, pricing of digital goods, and on the unique features of digital electronic markets. The marketing profession is interested in marketing, brand development and extension, consumer behavior on Web sites, and the ability of Internet technologies to segment and target consumer groups, and differentiate products. Economists share an interest with marketing scholars who have focused on e-commerce consumer response to marketing and advertising campaigns, and the ability of firms to brand, segment markets, target audiences, and position products to achieve above-normal returns on investment.

Management scholars have focused on entrepreneurial behavior and the challenges faced by young firms who are required to develop organizational structures in short time spans. Finance and accounting scholars have focused on e-commerce firm valuation and accounting practices. Sociologists—and to a lesser extent, psychologists—have focused on general population studies of Internet usage, the role of social inequality in skewing Internet benefits, and the use of the Web as a social network and group communications tool. Legal scholars are interested in issues such as preserving intellectual property, privacy, and content regulation.

No one perspective dominates research about e-commerce. The challenge is to learn enough about a variety of academic disciplines so that you can grasp the significance of e-commerce in its entirety.

CASE STUDY

The Pirate Bay:
The World's Most Resilient Copyright Infringer?

The Pirate Bay (TPB), a Swedish Web site (thepiratebay.se), is one of the world's most popular pirated music and content sites, offering free access to millions of copyrighted songs and thousands of copyrighted Hollywood movies. It bills itself as the world's largest BitTorrent tracker. In July 2012, The Pirate Bay reported that it had almost 6 million registered users. It is regularly in the top 100 Web sites in the world in terms of global traffic, with about 20% of the visitors coming from the United States. In Sweden, Norway, and the Netherlands, it often ranks as one of the top 20 sites. It even has a Facebook page and Twitter feed. This despite the fact that TPB has been subjected to repeated legal efforts to shut it down. In fact, the authorities pursuing TPB must feel as if they are engaged in a never-ending game of Whack-a-mole, as each time they "whack" TPB, it somehow manages to reappear. But the battle is far from over. The Internet is becoming a tough place for music and video pirates to make a living in part because of enforcement actions, but more importantly because of new mobile and wireless technologies that enable high-quality content to be streamed for just a small fee.

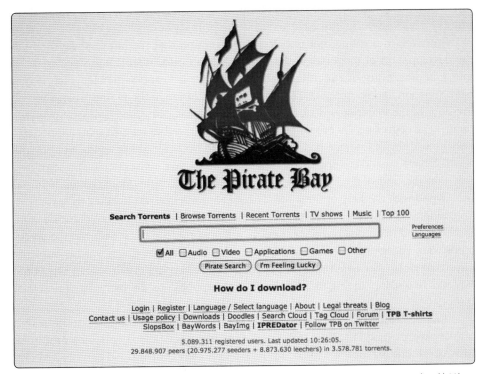

© Tommy (Louth) / Alamy

First some background. The Pirate Bay is part of a European social and political movement that opposes copyrighted content and demands that music, videos, TV shows, and other digital content be free and unrestricted. In a unique twist on prior efforts to provide "free" music, The Pirate Bay does not operate a database of copyrighted content. Neither does it operate a network of computers owned by "members" who store the content, nor create, own, or distribute software (like BitTorrent and most other so-called P2P networks) that permit such networks to exist in the first place. Instead, The Pirate Bay simply provides a search engine that responds to user queries for music tracks, or specific movie titles, and generates a list of search results that include P2P networks around the world where the titles can be found. By clicking on a selected link, users gain access to the copyrighted content, but only after downloading software and other files from that P2P network.

Voila! In The Pirate Bay's view, as the old saying goes, "no body, no crime." What could be illegal? The Pirate Bay claims it is merely a search engine providing pointers to existing P2P networks that it does not itself control. It says that it cannot control what content users ultimately find on those P2P networks, and that it is no different from any other search engine, such as Google or Bing, which are not held responsible for the content found on sites listed in search results. From a broader standpoint, The Pirate Bay's founders also claim that copyright laws in general unjustly interfere with the free flow of information on the Internet, and that in any event, they were not violating Swedish copyright law, which they felt should be the only law that applied. And they further claimed they did not encourage, incite, or enable illegal downloading. Nevertheless, the defendants have never denied that theirs was a commercial enterprise. Despite all the talk calling for the free, unfettered spread of culture, The Pirate Bay was a money-making operation from the beginning, designed to produce profits for its founders, with advertising as the primary source of revenue.

However, in a ruling that puts to rest the notion that the law is always behind the development of technology, the First Swedish Court in Stockholm declared the four founders guilty of violating Swedish copyright law, and sentenced each to one year in prison and payment of $3.5 million in restitution to the plaintiffs, all Swedish divisions of the major record label firms (Warner Music, Sony, and EMI Group among them). The court said "By providing a website with ... well-developed search functions, easy uploading and storage possibilities, and with a tracker linked to the website, the accused have incited the crimes that the file sharers have committed." The court also said that the four defendants had been aware of the fact that copyrighted material was shared with the help of their site. The prison sentence was justified by "extensive accessibility of others' copyrights and the fact that the operation was conducted commercially and in an organized fashion." In other words, the court believed the defendants were engaged in a commercial enterprise, the basis of which was encouraging visitors to violate the copyrights of owners. In fact, the primary purpose of The Pirate Bay was to violate copyrights in order to make money for the owners (commercial intent).

"Enable," "induce," and "encourage" copyright infringement and "intent to sell" are key words in this ruling and The Pirate Bay case. These concepts grounded in Western law are not "disabled" by new technology, but instead can be, and are, extensible to new technologies, and used to shape technology to society's needs and wishes. Indeed, there's a consensus developing among prosecutors and courts worldwide that infringement is not justified simply because it's technically possible to do it on the Internet.

Meanwhile, the U.S. government pressured the Swedish government to strengthen its copyright laws to discourage rampant downloading. In Sweden, downloading music and videos from illegal sites was very popular, engaged in by 43% of the Swedish Internet population. To strengthen its laws, Sweden adopted the European Union convention on copyrights, which allows content owners to receive from Internet providers the names and addresses of people suspected of sharing pirated files. In France, participating in these pirate sites will result in banishment from the Internet for up to three years. As a result, Internet traffic in Sweden declined by 40%, and has stayed there.

The Pirate Bay is appealing the court judgment, has paid no fine, and its owners have, as yet, never spent a night in jail although one of its founders, Peter Sunde, is expected to begin serving an 8-month sentence sometime during the summer of 2012. The Pirate Bay Web site continues to operate in Sweden much as before. Well, almost. In 2011, the firm moved its servers into caves in Sweden, and dispersed multiple copies of its program to other countries just in case Swedish police try to confiscate its servers again.

And since then, like the fight against the original Caribbean pirates of the seventeenth century, global forces continue to marshal against The Pirate Bay. Not the British Navy this time, but a loose coalition of a number of European countries and the United States. The firm has been hounded by lawsuits, police raids, and confiscation of servers in France, Finland, Italy, Germany, Denmark, Ireland, the U.K., and Greece. These countries have in some cases refused to allow Internet service providers in their countries to host The Pirate Bay, or link to The Pirate Bay, no matter where in the world its servers are located although The Pirate Bay has in some cases been able to circumvent this by frequently changing its IP address. The Pirate Bay has caused England, France, Malaysia, Finland, and most recently the United States, to consider strong intellectual property protection laws that will prevent domestic search engines and ISPs from linking to infringing sites, or resolving their domain names although thus far proposed legislation in the United States (known as the Protect IP Act) has been stalled due to opposition from civil liberties groups and search engine firms such as Google. Meanwhile, the world's largest advertising agency, GroupM, keelhauled The Pirate Bay and 2,000 other sites worldwide in 2011 by putting the sites on its blacklist of copyright infringing sites where it will not buy advertising space. Pirating intellectual property is, above all, about the money, as any good pirate knows.

The Pirate Bay case is just the latest in a saga of court cases involving the record industry, which wants to preserve its dominance of copyrighted music, and Internet users who want free music. In 2005, after several years of heated court battles, the case of *Metro-Goldwyn-Mayer Studios v. Grokster, et al.* finally reached the U.S. Supreme Court. In June 2005, the Court handed down its unanimous decision: Internet file-sharing services such as Grokster, StreamCast, BitTorrent, and Kazaa could be held

SOURCES: alexa.com/siteinfo/ thepiratebay.se, July 10, 2012; "Pirate Bay Founder Submits Emotional Plea for Pardon," by Ernesto, TorrentFreak, July 7, 2012; "The Pirate Bay Evades ISP Blockade with IPv6, Can Do It 18 Quintillion More Times," by Sebastian Anthony, Extremetech. com, June 8, 2012; "World's Biggest Ad Agency Keelhauls 2,000 Pirate Sites," by Natalie Apostolu, *The Register*, June 14, 2011; "Internet Piracy and How to Stop It," *New York Times*, June 8, 2011; "The "Pirate Bay: Five Years After the Raid," by Ernesto, Torrentfreak.com, May 31, 2011; "Why Google Would Defend Pirate Bay?," by Parmy Olson, *Forbes*, May 19, 2011; "The Protect IP Act: COICA Redux," by Abigail Phillips, Electronic Frontier Foundation, May 12, 2011; "Preventing Real Online Threats to Economic Creativity and Theft of Intellectual Property (Protect IP Act) of 2011," United States Senate, 112th Congress, 1st Session, 2011; "Pirate Bay Keeps Sinking: Another Law Suit Coming," by Stan Schroeder, mashable.com , June 22, 2010; "Idea Man of LimeWire at a Crossroads," by Joseph Plambeck, *New York Times*, May 23, 2010; "Pirate Bay Sunk by Hollywood Injunction For Now," by Charles Arthur, *The Guardian*, May 17 2010; "British Put Teeth in Anti-Piracy Proposal," by Eric Pfanner, *New York Times,* March 14, 2010.

liable for copyright infringement because they intentionally sought to induce, enable, and encourage users to share music that was owned by record companies. Indeed, it was their business model: steal the music, gather a huge audience, and monetize the audience by advertising or through subscription fees. Since the court ruling, Kazaa, Morpheus, Grokster, BearShare, iMesh, and many others have either gone out of business or settled with the record firms and converted themselves into legal file-sharing sites by entering into relationships with music industry firms. In May 2010, Mark Gorton, founder of the largest U.S. pirate site, LimeWire, lost a copyright infringement case. In May 2011, admitting his guilt ("I was wrong"), and having facilitated the mass piracy of billions of songs over a 10-year period, Gorton and his file-sharing company agreed to compensate the four largest record labels by paying them $105 million.

These legal victories, and stronger government enforcement of copyright laws, have not proven to be the magic bullet that miraculously solves all the problems facing the music industry. The music industry has had to drastically change its business model and decisively move towards digital distribution platforms. They have made striking progress, and, for the first time, in 2011 sales of music in a purely digital format accounted for more revenue than sales of music in a physical format. To do so, the music industry employed a number of different business models and online delivery platforms, including Apple's iTunes pay-per-download model, subscription models, streaming models and now music in the cloud. We will discuss each of these models in more detail in Chapter 10.

In each of these new media delivery platforms, the copyright owners—record companies, artists, and Hollywood studios—have struck licensing deals with the technology platform owners and distributors (Apple, Amazon, and Google). These new platforms offer a win-win solution. Consumers are benefitted by having near instant access to high-quality music tracks and videos without the hassle of P2P software downloads. Content owners get a growing revenue stream and protection for their copyrighted content. And the pirates? The Pirate Bay and other pirate sites may not be able to compete with new and better ways to listen to music and view videos. Like the real pirates of the Caribbean, technology and consumer preference for ease of use may leave them behind.

Case Study Questions

1. Do you think The Pirate Bay can continue to survive in a global Internet world? Why or why not?

2. Why is legislation like The Protect IP Act opposed by Google and civil liberties groups?

3. Why does cloud computing threaten pirate sites?

KEY CONCEPTS

■ Define e-commerce and describe how it differs from e-business.

- E-commerce involves digitally enabled commercial transactions between and among organizations and individuals. Digitally enabled transactions include all those mediated by digital technology, meaning, for the most part, transactions that occur over the Internet, the Web and/or via mobile apps. Commercial transactions involve the exchange of value (e.g., money) across organizational or individual boundaries in return for products or services.
- E-business refers primarily to the digital enabling of transactions and processes within a firm, involving information systems under the control of the firm. For the most part, e-business does not involve commercial transactions across organizational boundaries where value is exchanged.

■ Identify and describe the unique features of e-commerce technology and discuss their business significance.

There are eight features of e-commerce technology that are unique to this medium:

- *Ubiquity*—available just about everywhere, at all times, making it possible to shop from your desktop, at home, at work, or even from your car.
- *Global reach*—permits commercial transactions to cross cultural and national boundaries far more conveniently and cost-effectively than is true in traditional commerce.
- *Universal standards*—shared by all nations around the world. In contrast, most traditional commerce technologies differ from one nation to the next.
- *Richness*—refers to the complexity and content of a message. It enables an online merchant to deliver marketing messages with text, video, and audio to an audience of millions, in a way not possible with traditional commerce technologies such as radio, television, or magazines.
- *Interactivity*—allows for two-way communication between merchant and consumer and enables the merchant to engage a consumer in ways similar to a face-to-face experience, but on a much more massive, global scale.
- *Information density*—is the total amount and quality of information available to all market participants. The Internet reduces information collection, storage, processing, and communication costs while increasing the currency, accuracy, and timeliness of information.
- *Personalization* and *customization*—merchants can target their marketing messages to specific individuals by adjusting the message to a person's name, interests, and past purchases. Because of the increase in information density, a great deal of information about the consumer's past purchases and behavior can be stored and used by online merchants. The result is a level of personalization and customization unthinkable with previously existing commerce technologies.
- *Social technology*—provides a many-to-many model of mass communications. Millions of users are able to generate content consumed by millions of other

users. The result is the formation of social networks on a wide scale and the aggregation of large audiences on social network platforms.

- ■ **Describe and identify Web 2.0 applications.**

- • A set of applications has emerged on the Internet, loosely referred to as Web 2.0. These applications attract huge audiences and represent significant new opportunities for e-commerce revenues. Web 2.0 applications such as social networks, photo- and video-sharing sites, and blog platforms support very high levels of interactivity compared to other traditional media.

- ■ **Describe the major types of e-commerce.**

There are five major types of e-commerce:
- • B2C involves businesses selling to consumers and is the type of e-commerce that most consumers are likely to encounter. In 2012, consumers in the United States will spend about $362 billion in B2C transactions.
- • B2B e-commerce involves businesses selling to other businesses and is the largest form of e-commerce, with an estimated $4.1 trillion in transactions in the United States in 2012.
- • C2C is a means for consumers to sell to each other. In C2C e-commerce, the consumer prepares the product for market, places the product for auction or sale, and relies on the market maker to provide catalog, search engine, and transaction clearing capabilities so that products can be easily displayed, discovered, and paid for.
- • Social e-commerce is e-commerce that is enabled by social networks and online social relationships.
- • M-commerce involves the use of wireless digital devices to enable transactions on the Web.
- • Local e-commerce is a form of e-commerce that is focused on engaging the consumer based on his or her current geographic location.

- ■ **Understand the evolution of e-commerce from its early years to today.**

E-commerce has gone through three stages: innovation, consolidation, and reinvention. The early years of e-commerce were a period of explosive growth, beginning in 1995 with the first widespread use of the Web to advertise products and ending in 2000 with the collapse in stock market valuations for dot-com ventures.
- • The early years of e-commerce were a technological success, with the digital infrastructure created during the period solid enough to sustain significant growth in e-commerce during the next decade, and a mixed business success, with significant revenue growth and customer usage, but low profit margins.
- • E-commerce during its early years did not fulfill economists' visions of perfect friction-free commerce, or fulfill the visions of entrepreneurs and venture capitalists for first-mover advantages, low customer acquisition and retention costs, and low costs of doing business.

- E-commerce entered a period of consolidation beginning in 2001 and extending into 2006.
- E-commerce entered a period of reinvention in 2007 with the emergence of the mobile digital platform, social networks and Web 2.0 applications that attracted huge audiences in a very short time span.

■ **Identify the factors that will define the future of e-commerce.**

Factors that will define the future of e-commerce include the following:
- E-commerce technology (Internet, Web, and the mobile platform) will continue to propagate through all commercial activity, with overall revenues from e-commerce, the number of products and services sold and the amount of Web traffic all rising.
- E-commerce prices will rise to cover the real costs of doing business.
- E-commerce margins and profits will rise to levels more typical of all retailers.
- Traditional well-endowed and experienced Fortune 500 companies will play a growing and more dominant role.
- Entrepreneurs will continue to play an important role in pioneering new social applications that will rival search engines as advertising and e-commerce platforms.
- The number of successful pure online companies will continue to decline, and many successful e-commerce firms will adopt an integrated, multi-channel bricks-and-clicks strategy.
- Regulation of e-commerce and the Web by government will grow both in the United States and worldwide.

■ **Describe the major themes underlying the study of e-commerce.**

E-commerce involves three broad interrelated themes:
- *Technology*—To understand e-commerce, you need a basic understanding of the information technologies upon which it is built, including the Internet and the Web, and a host of complementary technologies— cloud computing, personal computers, smartphones, tablet computers, local area networks, client/server computing, packet-switched communications, protocols such as TCP/IP, Web servers, HTML, and relational and non-relational databases, among others.
- *Business*—While technology provides the infrastructure, it is the business applications—the potential for extraordinary returns on investment—that create the interest and excitement in e-commerce. New technologies present businesses and entrepreneurs with new ways of organizing production and transacting business. Therefore, you also need to understand some key business concepts such as electronic markets, information goods, business models, firm and industry value chains, industry structure, and consumer behavior in digital markets.
- *Society*—Understanding the pressures that global e-commerce places on contemporary society is critical to being successful in the e-commerce marketplace. The primary societal issues are intellectual property, individual privacy, and public policy.

■ **Identify the major academic disciplines contributing to e-commerce.**

There are two primary approaches to e-commerce: technical and behavioral. Each of these approaches is represented by several academic disciplines. On the technical side:

- Computer scientists are interested in e-commerce as an application of Internet technology.
- Management scientists are primarily interested in building mathematical models of business processes and optimizing them to learn how businesses can exploit the Internet to improve their business operations.
- Information systems professionals are interested in e-commerce because of its implications for firm and industry value chains, industry structure, and corporate strategy.
- Economists have focused on consumer behavior at Web sites, and on the features of digital electronic markets.

On the behavioral side:

- Sociologists have focused on studies of Internet usage, the role of social inequality in skewing Internet benefits, and the use of the Web as a personal and group communications tool.
- Finance and accounting scholars have focused on e-commerce firm valuation and accounting practices.
- Management scholars have focused on entrepreneurial behavior and the challenges faced by young firms that are required to develop organizational structures in short time spans.
- Marketing scholars have focused on consumer response to online marketing and advertising campaigns, and the ability of firms to brand, segment markets, target audiences, and position products to achieve higher returns on investment.

QUESTIONS

1. What is e-commerce? How does it differ from e-business? Where does it intersect with e-business?
2. What is information asymmetry?
3. What are some of the unique features of e-commerce technology?
4. What is a marketspace?
5. What are three benefits of universal standards?
6. Compare online and traditional transactions in terms of richness.
7. Name three of the business consequences that can result from growth in information density.
8. What is Web 2.0? Give examples of Web 2.0 sites and explain why you included them in your list.
9. Give examples of B2C, B2B, C2C, and social, mobile, and local e-commerce besides those listed in the chapter materials.
10. How are the Internet and the Web similar to or different from other technologies that have changed commerce in the past?
11. Describe the three different stages in the evolution of e-commerce.
12. What are the major limitations on the growth of e-commerce? Which is potentially the toughest to overcome?
13. What are three of the factors that will contribute to greater Internet penetration in U.S. households?

14. Define disintermediation and explain the benefits to Internet users of such a phenomenon. How does disintermediation impact friction-free commerce?

15. What are some of the major advantages and disadvantages of being a first mover?

16. Discuss the ways in which the early years of e-commerce can be considered both a success and a failure.

17. What are five of the major differences between the early years of e-commerce and today's e-commerce?

18. What factors will help define the future of e-commerce over the next five years?

19. Why is a multidisciplinary approach necessary if one hopes to understand e-commerce?

PROJECTS

1. Define "social e-commerce" and describe why it is a new form of advertising, search, and commerce.

2. Search the Web for an example of each of the major types of e-commerce described in Section 1.1. Create an electronic slide presentation or written report describing each Web site (take a screenshot of each, if possible), and explain why it fits into one of the category of e-commerce to which you have assigned it.

3. Choose an e-commerce Web site and assess it in terms of the eight unique features of e-commerce technology described in Table 1.2. Which of the features does the site implement well, and which features poorly, in your opinion? Prepare a short memo to the president of the company you have chosen detailing your findings and any suggestions for improvement you may have.

4. Given the development and history of e-commerce in the years from 1995–2012, what do you predict we will see during the next five years of e-commerce? Describe some of the technological, business, and societal shifts that may occur as the Internet continues to grow and expand. Prepare a brief electronic slide presentation or written report to explain your vision of what e-commerce will look like in 2016.

5. Follow up on events at Facebook and other social network sites since September 2012 (when the opening case was prepared). Has Facebook continued to challenge Google as an advertising and search platform? Has it launched any new e-commerce initiatives? Prepare a short report on your findings.

CHAPTER 2

E-commerce Business Models and Concepts

LEARNING OBJECTIVES

After reading this chapter, you will be able to:

- Identify the key components of e-commerce business models.
- Describe the major B2C business models.
- Describe the major B2B business models.
- Understand key business concepts and strategies applicable to e-commerce.

Tweet Tweet:

What's Your Business Model?

Twitter, the social network site based on 140-character text messages, is the latest in a series of unpredicted developments on the Internet. You can think of these as "Black Swan" events that have had, for the most part, very positive consequences. In fact, most of the wildly successful Internet applications and e-commerce businesses were not predicted by experts and technology gurus who we expect to tell us about the future.

Who could have predicted, for instance, that in 2012, in the United States, 191 million people would use search

© Kennedy Photography / Alamy

engines to conduct 17 to 18 billion online searches each month, 184 million would spend an average of 22.25 hours a month watching videos online, and 72 million would read blogs? Who knew that America's population was so starved for communication? No one, least of all the Internet technorati.

In 2012, social network sites continue this long tradition of surprising everyone. Twitter continues to be the buzz social network phenomenon of the year. Like all social network sites, such as Facebook, Pinterest, YouTube, Flickr, and others, Twitter provides a platform for users ("Tweeple," "twitterers," or "tweeters") to express themselves, by creating content and sharing it with others called "followers" who sign up to receive someone's "tweets." And like most social network sites, Twitter faces the problem of how to make a profit. In 2011, Twitter produced $140 million in revenue but zero profits despite over $1 billion in funding since its inception. Management is still trying to understand how best to exploit the buzz and user base it has unexpectedly created.

Twitter began in 2006 as a Web-based version of popular text messaging services provided by cell phone carriers. There are around 6 billion cell phones worldwide, and SMS text messaging is the most popular service after voice. The idea originated in March 2006 within a podcasting company called Odeo as executives searched for a new product or service to grow revenues. Jack Dorsey, originator of the idea, along with other executives, bought out other venture investors in Odeo, and eventually split Twitter off from Odeo to become a stand-alone, private company called Twitter.com.

The basic idea was to marry short text messaging on cell phones with the Web and its ability to create social groups. You start by establishing a Twitter account online. By typing a short message called a "tweet" online or to a code on your cell phone (40404), you can tell your followers what you are doing, your location, or whatever else you might want to say. You are limited to 140 characters, but there is no installation required and no charge. Kaboom: a social network messaging service to keep your buddies informed. Smash success.

Coming up with solid numbers for Twitter is not easy. By 2012, Twitter had an estimated 500 million registered users worldwide, although it is not clear how many continue to actively use the service after signing up. According to Twitter itself, it had 140 million "active" users worldwide as of March 2012. But according to eMarketer, there are actually far fewer active U.S. adult users (those who use Twitter at least once a month): eMarketer estimates their number to be around 30 million. Industry observers believe Twitter is the second largest social network worldwide, behind Facebook.

What started out in 2006 with 5,000 tweets has turned into a deluge of 340 million daily tweets worldwide. There were more than 150 million tweets about the 2012 Olympics, and more than 80,000 tweets per minute about Usain Bolt's 200-meter victory. Some celebrities, such as Lady Gaga, have millions of followers (in Lady Gaga's case, 28 million as of mid-2012). On the other hand, experts believe that the vast majority of tweets are generated by a small percentage of users. Twitter also has an estimated 60% churn rate: only 40% of users remain more than one month. Obviously, many users lose interest in learning about their friends' breakfast menu, and many feel "too connected" to their "friends," who in fact may only be distant acquaintances, if that.

The answers to these questions about unique users, numbers of tweets, and churn rate are critical to understanding the business value of Twitter as a firm. To date, Twitter has not generated a profit. But since its founding, it is reported to have raised more than $1 billion in venture capital funding, with the last round in December 2011, valuing the company at $8.4 billion.

So how can Twitter make money from its users and their tweets? What's its business model and how might it evolve over time? To start, consider the company's assets and customer value proposition. The main asset is user attention and audience size (eyeballs per day). The value proposition is "get it now" or real-time news on just about anything from the mundane to the monumental. An equally important asset is the database of tweets that contains the comments, observations, and opinions of the audience, and the search engine that mines those tweets for patterns. These are real-time and spontaneous observations.

Yet another asset has emerged: Twitter is a powerful alternative media platform for the distribution of news, videos, and pictures. Once again, no one predicted that Twitter would be among the first to report on terrorist attacks in Mumbai, the Iranian rebellion in June 2009, the political violence in Bangkok and Kenya in May 2010, and the uprisings in Egypt, Tunisia, and other areas in the Mideast and Africa in 2011.

How can these assets be monetized? Advertising, what else! In April 2010, Twitter announced its first foray into the big-time ad marketplace with Promoted Tweets. Promoted Tweets are Twitter's version of Google's text ads. In response to a user's query to Twitter's search function for tablet computers, for example, a Best Buy tweet about tablets will be displayed. Twitter claims Promoted Tweets are not really ads because they look like all other tweets, and are part of the tweet stream of messages. Twitter has since expanded the display of Promoted Tweets to other sites in the Twitter ecosystem, such as HootSuite. In April 2011, Twitter announced that it would offer geo-targeted Promoted Tweets. Many companies are now using the service, ranging from Best Buy, to Ford, to Starbucks, to Virgin America. According to Twitter, Promoted Tweets are producing greater engagement with viewers than traditional Web advertisements.

A second Twitter monetization effort announced in June 2010 is called Promoted Trends. "Trends" is a section of the Twitter home page that lets users know what's hot, what a lot of people are talking about. A company can place a Promoted Trends banner at the top of the Trends section and when users click on the banner, they are taken to the follower page for that movie or product. Promoted Trends are reportedly Twitter's most consistent source of revenue, costing advertisers between $100,000 to $120,000 a day. Currently, Twitter only sells one of these per day, but plans are afoot to create localized versions of the page, which would enable Twitter to increase its revenue stream.

In October 2010, Twitter launched Promoted Accounts, which are suggestions to follow various advertiser accounts based on the list of accounts that the user already follows. Like Promoted Tweets, Promoted Accounts can be geo-targeted at both the country level and the Nielsen DMA (Designated Marketing Area, roughly equivalent to a city and its suburb) level. Twitter added Enhanced Profile Pages for brands in February 2012. For a reported $15,000 to $25,000, companies get their own banner to display images, and the ability to pin a tweet to the top of the company's Twitter stream. In March 2012, Twitter began testing Promoted Tweets and Promoted Accounts on iOS and Android devices, and by June 2012 was reporting that it was generating the majority of its revenues from ads on mobile devices rather than on its Web site.

Another monetizing service is temporal real-time search. If there's one thing Twitter has uniquely among all the social network sites, it's real-time information. In 2010, Twitter entered into agreements with Google, Microsoft, and Yahoo to permit these search engines to index tweets and make them available to the entire Internet. This service gives free real-time content to the search engines as opposed to archival content. It is unclear who's doing whom a service here, and the financial arrangements are not public. Microsoft extended the deal for two years in September 2011, but Google let its deal with Twitter expire.

Other large players are experimenting. Dell created a Twitter outlet account, @DellOutlet, and is using it to sell open-box and discontinued computers. Dell also maintains several customer service accounts. Twitter could charge such accounts a commission on sales because Twitter is acting like an e-commerce sales platform similar to Amazon. Other firms have used their Twitter follower fan base to market discount air tickets (JetBlue) and greeting cards (Someecards).

Freemium is another possibility. Twitter could ask users to pay a subscription fee for premium services such as videos and music downloads. However, it may be too late for this idea because users have come to expect the service to be free. Twitter could charge service providers such as doctors, dentists, lawyers, and hair salons for providing their

SOURCES: "Twitter Embraces Changing Identity" by Nick Bilton, *New York Times*, July 30, 2012; "Analyst: Twitter Passed 500M Users in June 2012, 140M of Them in US; Jakarta 'Biggest Tweeting' City," by Ingrid Lunden, Tech-crunch.com, July 30, 2012; "Apple Officials Said to Consider Stake in Twitter," by Evelyn M. Rusli and Nick Bilton, July 27, 2012; "Twitter's Mobile Ads Begin to Click," by Shira Ovide, *Wall Street Journal*, June 28, 2012; "Micro-soft's Bing Extends Twitter Search Deal," by David Roe, Cmswire.com, September 2011; "Twitter Stats," Business.twitter.com/basics/what-is-twitter, August 22, 2012; "40 Fast Facts on Twitter," by Jennifer Lawinski, August 8, 2011; "Twitter Raises Big Bucks to Buy Back Shares," Denverpost.com, July 23, 2011; "How Twitter Makes Money," by Harry Gold, ClickZ.com, April 26, 2011, "Twitter to Launch Geo-targeted Promoted Tweets and Data for Marketers," by Sarah Shearnman, Brandrepublic.com, April 7, 2011; "Twitter Users: A Vocal Minority," by Paul Verna, eMarketer, March 2011; "Twitter as Tech Bubble Barometer," by Spencer E. Ante, Amir Efrati, and Anupreeta Das, *Wall Street Journal*, February 10, 2011; "Promoted Promotions," Blog.twitter.com October 4, 2010; "The Blogo-sphere: Colliding with Social and Mainstream Media" by Paul Verna, eMarketer, September 21, 2010; "Will Twitter's Ad Strategy Work," by Erica Naone, *Technology Review*, April 15, 2010; "Twitter Rolls Out Ads," by Jessica Vascel-laro and Emily Steel, *Wall Street Journal*, April 14, 2010.

customers with unexpected appointment availabilities. But Twitter's most likely steady revenue source might be its database of hundreds of millions of real-time tweets. Major firms such as Starbucks, Amazon, Intuit (QuickBooks and Mint.com), and Dell have used Twitter to understand how their customers are reacting to products, services, and Web sites, and then make corrections or changes in those services and products. Twitter is a fabulous listening post on the Internet frontier.

The possibilities are endless, and just about any of the above scenarios offer some solution to the company's problem, which is a lack of profits. The company is coy about announcing its business model, what one pundit described as hiding behind a "Silicon Valley Mona Lisa smile." These Wall Street pundits are thought to be party poopers in the Valley. For instance, notwithstanding Twitter's lack of profits, in July 2012, Apple was said to be interested in making a strategic investment in Twitter at a valuation in the absolutely astounding $10 billion range.

The story of Twitter illustrates the difficulties of turning a good business idea with a huge audience into a successful business model that produces revenues and even profits.

In the early days of e-commerce, thousands of firms discovered they could spend other people's invested capital much faster than they could get customers to pay for their products or services. In most instances of failure, the business model of the firm was faulty from the beginning. In contrast, successful e-commerce firms have business models that are able to leverage the unique qualities of the Web, provide customers real value, develop highly effective and efficient operations, avoid legal and social entanglements that can harm the firm, and produce profitable business results. In addition, successful business models must scale. The business must be able to achieve efficiencies as it grows in volume. But what is a business model, and how can you tell if a firm's business model is going to produce a profit?

In this chapter, we focus on business models and basic business concepts that you must be familiar with in order to understand e-commerce.

2.1   E-COMMERCE BUSINESS MODELS

INTRODUCTION

A **business model** is a set of planned activities (sometimes referred to as *business processes*) designed to result in a profit in a marketplace. A business model is not always the same as a business strategy although in some cases they are very close insofar as the business model explicitly takes into account the competitive environment (Magretta, 2002). The business model is at the center of the business plan. A **business plan** is a document that describes a firm's business model. A business plan always takes into account the competitive environment. An **e-commerce business model** aims to use and leverage the unique qualities of the Internet and the World Wide Web (Timmers, 1998).

EIGHT KEY ELEMENTS OF A BUSINESS MODEL

If you hope to develop a successful business model in any arena, not just e-commerce, you must make sure that the model effectively addresses the eight elements listed in **Table 2.1**. These elements are: value proposition, revenue model, market opportunity, competitive environment, competitive advantage, market strategy, organizational development, and management team (Ghosh, 1998). Many writers focus on a firm's value proposition and revenue model. While these may be the most important and most easily identifiable aspects of a company's business model, the other elements are equally important when evaluating business models and plans, or when attempting to understand why a particular company has succeeded or failed (Kim and Mauborgne, 2000). In the following sections, we describe each of the key business model elements more fully.

business model
a set of planned activities designed to result in a profit in a marketplace

business plan
a document that describes a firm's business model

e-commerce business model
a business model that aims to use and leverage the unique qualities of the Internet and the World Wide Web

TABLE 2.1	KEY ELEMENTS OF A BUSINESS MODEL
COMPONENTS	KEY QUESTIONS
Value proposition	Why should the customer buy from you?
Revenue model	How will you earn money?
Market opportunity	What marketspace do you intend to serve, and what is its size?
Competitive environment	Who else occupies your intended marketspace?
Competitive advantage	What special advantages does your firm bring to the marketspace?
Market strategy	How do you plan to promote your products or services to attract your target audience?
Organizational development	What types of organizational structures within the firm are necessary to carry out the business plan?
Management team	What kinds of experiences and background are important for the company's leaders to have?

Value Proposition

value proposition
defines how a company's product or service fulfills the needs of customers

A company's value proposition is at the very heart of its business model. A **value proposition** defines how a company's product or service fulfills the needs of customers (Kambil, Ginsberg, and Bloch, 1998). To develop and/or analyze a firm's value proposition, you need to understand why customers will choose to do business with the firm instead of another company and what the firm provides that other firms do not and cannot. From the consumer point of view, successful e-commerce value propositions include: personalization and customization of product offerings, reduction of product search costs, reduction of price discovery costs, and facilitation of transactions by managing product delivery (Kambil, 1997; Bakos, 1998).

For instance, before Amazon existed, most customers personally traveled to book retailers to place an order. In some cases, the desired book might not be available and the customer would have to wait several days or weeks, and then return to the bookstore to pick it up. Amazon makes it possible for book lovers to shop for virtually any book in print from the comfort of their home or office, 24 hours a day, and to know immediately whether a book is in stock. Amazon's Kindle takes this one step further by making e-books instantly available with no shipping wait. Amazon's primary value propositions are unparalleled selection and convenience.

Revenue Model

revenue model
describes how the firm will earn revenue, produce profits, and produce a superior return on invested capital

A firm's **revenue model** describes how the firm will earn revenue, generate profits, and produce a superior return on invested capital. We use the terms *revenue model* and *financial model* interchangeably. The function of business organizations is both to generate profits and to produce returns on invested capital that exceed alternative investments. Profits alone are not sufficient to make a company "successful" (Porter,

1985). In order to be considered successful, a firm must produce returns greater than alternative investments. Firms that fail this test go out of existence.

Retailers, for example, sell a product, such as a personal computer, to a customer who pays for the computer using cash or a credit card. This produces revenue. The merchant typically charges more for the computer than it pays out in operating expenses, producing a profit. But in order to go into business, the computer merchant had to invest capital—either by borrowing or by dipping into personal savings. The profits from the business constitute the return on invested capital, and these returns must be greater than the merchant could obtain elsewhere, say, by investing in real estate or just putting the money into a savings account.

Although there are many different e-commerce revenue models that have been developed, most companies rely on one, or some combination, of the following major revenue models: the advertising model, the subscription model, the transaction fee model, the sales model, and the affiliate model.

In the **advertising revenue model**, a Web site that offers its users content, services, and/or products also provides a forum for advertisements and receives fees from advertisers. Those Web sites that are able to attract the greatest viewership or that have a highly specialized, differentiated viewership and are able to retain user attention ("stickiness") are able to charge higher advertising rates. Yahoo, for instance, derives a significant amount of revenue from display and video advertising.

In the **subscription revenue model**, a Web site that offers its users content or services charges a subscription fee for access to some or all of its offerings. For instance, the online version of *Consumer Reports* provides access to premium content, such as detailed ratings, reviews, and recommendations, only to subscribers, who have a choice of paying a $6.95 monthly subscription fee or a $30.00 annual fee. Experience with the subscription revenue model indicates that to successfully overcome the disinclination of users to pay for content on the Web, the content offered must be perceived as a high-value-added, premium offering that is not readily available elsewhere nor easily replicated. Companies successfully offering content or services online on a subscription basis include Match.com and eHarmony (dating services), Ancestry.com (see **Figure 2.1**) and Genealogy.com (genealogy research), Microsoft's Xboxlive.com (video games), Rhapsody.com (music), and Hulu.com.

In the **transaction fee revenue model**, a company receives a fee for enabling or executing a transaction. For example, eBay provides an online auction marketplace and receives a small transaction fee from a seller if the seller is successful in selling the item. E*Trade, an online stockbroker, receives transaction fees each time it executes a stock transaction on behalf of a customer.

In the **sales revenue model**, companies derive revenue by selling goods, information, or services to customers. Companies such as Amazon (which sells books, music, and other products), LLBean.com, and Gap.com, all have sales revenue models.

In the **affiliate revenue model**, sites that steer business to an "affiliate" receive a referral fee or percentage of the revenue from any resulting sales. For example, MyPoints makes money by connecting companies with potential customers by offering special deals to its members. When they take advantage of an offer and

advertising revenue model
a company provides a forum for advertisements and receives fees from advertisers

subscription revenue model
a company offers its users content or services and charges a subscription fee for access to some or all of its offerings

transaction fee revenue model
a company receives a fee for enabling or executing a transaction

sales revenue model
a company derives revenue by selling goods, information, or services

affiliate revenue model
a company steers business to an affiliate and receives a referral fee or percentage of the revenue from any resulting sales

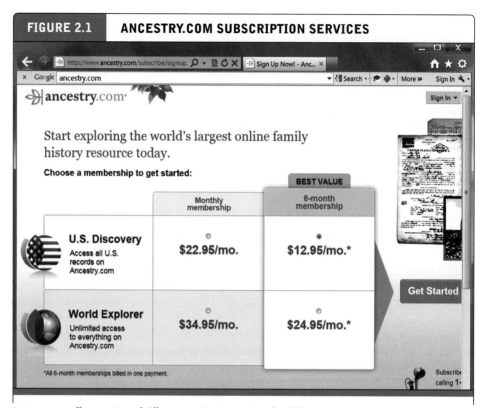

| FIGURE 2.1 | ANCESTRY.COM SUBSCRIPTION SERVICES |

Ancestry.com offers a variety of different membership options for different subscription fees.
SOURCE: Ancestry.com, 2012.

make a purchase, members earn "points" they can redeem for freebies, and MyPoints receives a fee. Community feedback sites such as Epinions receive much of their revenue from steering potential customers to Web sites where they make a purchase.

Table 2.2 on page 71 summarizes these major revenue models. The *Insight on Society* case, *Foursquare Checks Out a Revenue Model,* examines some of the issues associated with Foursquare's business and revenue model.

Market Opportunity

The term **market opportunity** refers to the company's intended **marketspace** (i.e., an area of actual or potential commercial value) and the overall potential financial opportunities available to the firm in that marketspace. The market opportunity is usually divided into smaller market niches. The realistic market opportunity is defined by the revenue potential in each of the market niches where you hope to compete.

For instance, let's assume you are analyzing a software training company that creates software-learning systems for sale to corporations over the Internet. The overall size of the software training market for all market segments is approximately $70 billion. The overall market can be broken down, however, into two major market segments:

market opportunity
refers to the company's intended marketspace and the overall potential financial opportunities available to the firm in that marketspace

marketspace
the area of actual or potential commercial value in which a company intends to operate

INSIGHT ON SOCIETY

FOURSQUARE CHECKS OUT A REVENUE MODEL

First the Internet made it possible for you to find products and friends. Now the Internet finds you to sell you products and check in with your friends. Foursquare is one of a host of companies that combine a social network business model with location-based technology. Foursquare's niche: a mobile social application that allows users to check in to a restaurant or other location, and automatically lets friends on Facebook and other programs learn where you are. If you're in a new town, the app transmits your location and sends you information about popular spots close by, with reviews from other Foursquare users. After starting up Foursquare on a smartphone, you'll see a list of local bars and restaurants based on your cell phone's GPS position. Select a location, ``check in,'' and a message is sent to your friends. Foursquare has a widely accepted loyalty program. Each check-in awards users points and badges. Visitors to places compete to become ``Mayors'' of the venue based on how many times they have checked in over a month's time. Mayors receive special offers.

Foursquare was founded by Dennis Crowley and Naveen Selvadurai. They began building the first version of the application in Fall 2008, originally working in the kitchen of Crowley's East Village New York apartment. They debuted the application at the South by Southwest Interactive Festival in March 2009, and soon attracted venture capital. As of April 2012, Foursquare had over 20 million members worldwide, split fairly evenly between the United States and the rest of the world, who have checked in over 2.5 billion times.

Foursquare shares many similarities with other social networks like Facebook and Twitter, which began operating without a revenue model in place. Like those companies, Foursquare has been able to command high valuations from venture capital investors ($600 million during its last round of funding in June 2011), despite its lack of significant revenue or profit. How is this possible? The answer lies in the coupling of its social network business model with smartphone-based technology that can identify where you are located within a few yards. There's potentially a great deal of money to be made from knowing where you are. Location-based data has extraordinary commercial value because advertisers can then send you advertisements, coupons, and flash bargains, based on where you are located. The market for location-based services in 2012 is expected to be more than $3 billion, and will rise to $10.3 billion by 2015.

Just as Facebook and Twitter have now begun to monetize their user bases, so too has Foursquare. It has now begun to migrate to an advertising-based, social retail sales model. Foursquare 2.0, released in late 2010, directs users to new locations rather than just sharing locations with friends. The New York Times, Wall Street Journal, Zagat, and others have added an ``Add to my Foursquare'' button, which automatically adds the location to the user's To-Do list. In June 2011, Foursquare partnered with American Express to offer discounts to cardholders when they check in on their cell phone to certain shops and restaurants. In tests of the program, American Express found that those in the test program spent 20% more on average than did those without access to the program. In July 2012, Foursquare announced the next steps in the monetization of its business model: Local Updates and Promoted Updates. Local Updates allow retailers to deliver geo-targeted offers and messages to customers, while Promoted Updates, similar to Twitter's Promoted Tweets, are geo-targeted paid advertisements.

(continued)

As the popularity of location-based services like Foursquare has grown, so too have concerns about privacy. The revelations by the *Wall Street Journal* in Spring 2011 that Apple and Google were surreptitiously and continuously collecting personal, private location data from iPhone and Android phones spurred privacy groups and Congress to launch investigations. In June 2011, the Federal Communications Commission, in cooperation with the Federal Trade Commission, sponsored a forum to discuss the social impact of location-based services, both positive and negative. Industry representatives from Facebook, Google, and Foursquare argued that existing apps as well as corporate policies were adequate to protect personal privacy because they rely on user permissions to share location (opt-in services). The industry argued as well that consumers get real benefits from sharing location data, otherwise they would not voluntarily give this data. Privacy advocates pointed out that 22 of the top 30 paid apps have no privacy policy, that most of the popular apps transmit location data to their developers after which the information is not well controlled, and that these services are creating a situation where government, marketers, creditors, and telecommunications firms will end up knowing nearly everything about citizens, including their whereabouts.

As a case in point, in April 2012, Foursquare was hit by a privacy landmine when an app called Girls Around Me surfaced that used Foursquare's application programming interface to show photos of women currently checked in around a particular neighborhood by pulling public photos of the women from their Facebook profiles linked to their Foursquare accounts. Foursquare quickly shut down the app and shortly thereafter made changes to its application programming interface to eliminate the ability of users to see strangers checked into a venue without being checked into the same place themselves. Illustrating the continuing issues Foursquare faces on the privacy front, the new version of its mobile app, introduced June 2012, allows users to see all of their friends' check-ins from the prior two weeks. As the ACLU noted, historical location data can reveal far more about a person than individual location records. Many users may not truly understand how much of their location history is available to their friends. Nor is there an easy way for users to control the visibility of their location history—users are limited to either deleting specific check-ins individually or being off the grid completely.

The Electronic Frontier Foundation, a privacy watchdog, has expressed increasing concern about location-based services. It noted numerous instances of governments seeking access to user location data from services such as Twitter and others in 2011 and 2012. In June 2012, it released its 2012 Privacy scorecard, based on the following criteria: public commitment to tell users when their data is sought by government, their transparency about when and how they provide data to government, and their willingness to fight for users' privacy rights in the courts and Congress. Foursquare received zero stars.

SOURCES: "Three Reasons Why Foursquare's New Advertising Model Might Work," by Anne Marie Kelly, *Forbes*, August 22, 2012; "Foursquare Will Test Paid Ads," by Stuart Elliott, *New York Times*, July 25, 2012; "Foursquare's New App Needs New Privacy Controls," by Chris Conley, Aclunc.org, July 2, 2012; "EFF's New Privacy Scorecard: Twitter Wins, Foursquare Loses," by Violet Blue, Zdnet.com, June 2, 2012; "When the Government Comes Knocking, Who Has Your Back?," Electronic Frontier Foundation, June 2012; "Wrap Up on Privacy and Location Based Services," by Prof. Peter Swire, Ohio State University, FCC Forum: Helping Consumers Harness the Potential of Location Based Services, June 28, 2011; "Technology and Privacy," by Prof. Matt Blaze, University of Pennsylvania, FCC Forum: Helping Consumers Harness the Potential of Location Based Services, June 28, 2011; "Companies Try to Allay Fears at FCC-FTC Hearing," by Brad Reed, *Network World*, June 28, 2011; "A Start-Up Matures, Working With AmEx," by Jenna Wortham, *New York Times*, June 22, 2011; "Apple, Google Collect User Data," by Julia Angwin and Jennifer Valentino-Devries, *Wall Street Journal*, April 22, 2011; "Telling Friends Where You Are (or Not)," by Jenna Wortham, *New York Times*, March 14, 2010.

TABLE 2.2	FIVE PRIMARY REVENUE MODELS	
REVENUE MODEL	EXAMPLES	REVENUE SOURCE
Advertising	Yahoo	Fees from advertisers in exchange for advertisements
Subscription	WSJ.com Consumerreports.org	Fees from subscribers in exchange for access to content or services
Transaction Fee	eBay E*Trade	Fees (commissions) for enabling or executing a transaction
Sales	Amazon L.L.Bean Gap iTunes	Sales of goods, information, or services
Affiliate	MyPoints	Fees for business referrals

instructor-led training products, which comprise about 70% of the market ($49 billion in revenue), and computer-based training, which accounts for 30% ($21 billion). There are further market niches within each of those major market segments, such as the Fortune 500 computer-based training market and the small business computer-based training market. Because the firm is a start-up firm, it cannot compete effectively in the large business, computer-based training market (about $15 billion). Large brand-name training firms dominate this niche. The start-up firm's real market opportunity is to sell to the thousands of small business firms that spend about $6 billion on computer-based software training and who desperately need a cost-effective training solution. This is the size of the firm's realistic market opportunity (see **Figure 2.2**).

FIGURE 2.2	MARKETSPACE AND MARKET OPPORTUNITY IN THE SOFTWARE TRAINING MARKET

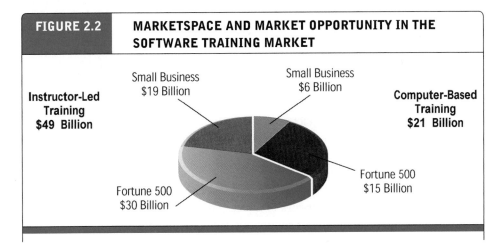

Marketspaces are composed of many market segments. Your realistic market opportunity will typically focus on one or a few market segments.

Competitive Environment

A firm's **competitive environment** refers to the other companies selling similar products and operating in the same marketspace. It also refers to the presence of substitute products and potential new entrants to the market, as well as the power of customers and suppliers over your business. We discuss the firm's environment later in the chapter. The competitive environment for a company is influenced by several factors: how many competitors are active, how large their operations are, what the market share of each competitor is, how profitable these firms are, and how they price their products.

Firms typically have both direct and indirect competitors. Direct competitors are those companies that sell products and services that are very similar and into the same market segment. For example, Priceline and Travelocity, both of whom sell discount airline tickets online, are direct competitors because both companies sell identical products—cheap tickets. Indirect competitors are companies that may be in different industries but still compete indirectly because their products can substitute for one another. For instance, automobile manufacturers and airline companies operate in different industries, but they still compete indirectly because they offer consumers alternative means of transportation. CNN.com, a news outlet, is an indirect competitor of ESPN.com, not because they sell identical products, but because they both compete for consumers' time online.

The existence of a large number of competitors in any one segment may be a sign that the market is saturated and that it may be difficult to become profitable. On the other hand, a lack of competitors could either signal an untapped market niche ripe for the picking, or a market that has already been tried without success because there is no money to be made. Analysis of the competitive environment can help you decide which it is.

Competitive Advantage

Firms achieve a **competitive advantage** when they can produce a superior product and/or bring the product to market at a lower price than most, or all, of their competitors (Porter, 1985). Firms also compete on scope. Some firms can develop global markets, while other firms can only develop a national or regional market. Firms that can provide superior products at the lowest cost on a global basis are truly advantaged.

Firms achieve competitive advantages because they have somehow been able to obtain differential access to the factors of production that are denied to their competitors—at least in the short term (Barney, 1991). Perhaps the firm has been able to obtain very favorable terms from suppliers, shippers, or sources of labor. Or perhaps the firm has more experienced, knowledgeable, and loyal employees than any competitors. Maybe the firm has a patent on a product that others cannot imitate, or access to investment capital through a network of former business colleagues or a brand name and popular image that other firms cannot duplicate. An **asymmetry** exists whenever one participant in a market has more resources—financial backing, knowledge, information, and/or power—than other participants. Asymmetries lead to some firms having an edge over others, permitting them to come to market with better products, faster than competitors, and sometimes at lower cost.

For instance, when Apple announced iTunes, a service offering legal, download-able individual song tracks for 99 cents a track that would be playable on any PC or digital device with iTunes software, the company had better-than-average odds of success simply because of Apple's prior success with innovative hardware designs, and the large stable of music firms that Apple had meticulously lined up to support its online music catalog. Few competitors could match the combination of cheap, legal songs and powerful hardware to play them on.

One rather unique competitive advantage derives from being a first mover. A **first-mover advantage** is a competitive market advantage for a firm that results from being the first into a marketplace with a serviceable product or service. If first movers develop a loyal following or a unique interface that is difficult to imitate, they can sustain their first-mover advantage for long periods (Arthur, 1996). Amazon provides a good example. However, in the history of technology-driven business innovation, most first movers often lack the **complementary resources** needed to sustain their advantages, and often follower firms reap the largest rewards (Rigdon, 2000; Teece, 1986). Indeed, many of the success stories we discuss in this book are those of companies that were slow followers—businesses that gained knowledge from failure of pioneering firms and entered into the market late.

Some competitive advantages are called "unfair." An **unfair competitive advantage** occurs when one firm develops an advantage based on a factor that other firms cannot purchase (Barney, 1991). For instance, a brand name cannot be pur-chased and is in that sense an "unfair" advantage. As we will discuss in Chapter 6, brands are built upon loyalty, trust, reliability, and quality. Once obtained, they are difficult to copy or imitate, and they permit firms to charge premium prices for their products.

In **perfect markets**, there are no competitive advantages or asymmetries because all firms have access to all the factors of production (including information and knowledge) equally. However, real markets are imperfect, and asymmetries leading to competitive advantages do exist, at least in the short term. Most competi-tive advantages are short term, although some—such as the competitive advantage enjoyed by Coca-Cola because of the Coke brand name—can be sustained for very long periods. But not forever: Coke is increasingly being challenged by fruit, health, and unique flavor drinks. In fact, many respected brands fail every year.

Companies are said to **leverage** their competitive assets when they use their competitive advantages to achieve more advantage in surrounding markets. For instance, Amazon's move into the online grocery business leverages the company's huge customer database and years of e-commerce experience.

Market Strategy

No matter how tremendous a firm's qualities, its marketing strategy and execution are often just as important. The best business concept, or idea, will fail if it is not properly marketed to potential customers.

first-mover advantage
a competitive market advantage for a firm that results from being the first into a marketplace with a serviceable product or service

complementary resources
resources and assets not directly involved in the production of the product but required for success, such as marketing, management, financial assets, and reputation

unfair competitive advantage
occurs when one firm develops an advantage based on a factor that other firms cannot purchase

perfect market
a market in which there are no competitive advantages or asymmetries because all firms have equal access to all the factors of production

leverage
when a company uses its competitive advantages to achieve more advantage in surrounding markets

market strategy

the plan you put together that details exactly how you intend to enter a new market and attract new customers

Everything you do to promote your company's products and services to potential customers is known as marketing. **Market strategy** is the plan you put together that details exactly how you intend to enter a new market and attract new customers.

For instance, Twitter, YouTube, and Pinterest have a social network marketing strategy that encourages users to post their content on the sites for free, build personal profile pages, contact their friends, and build a community. In these cases, the customer is the marketing staff!

Organizational Development

Although many entrepreneurial ventures are started by one visionary individual, it is rare that one person alone can grow an idea into a multi-million dollar company. In most cases, fast-growth companies—especially e-commerce businesses—need employees and a set of business procedures. In short, all firms—new ones in particular—need an organization to efficiently implement their business plans and strategies. Many e-commerce firms and many traditional firms that attempt an e-commerce strategy have failed because they lacked the organizational structures and supportive cultural values required to support new forms of commerce (Kanter, 2001).

organizational development

plan describes how the company will organize the work that needs to be accomplished

Companies that hope to grow and thrive need to have a plan for **organizational development** that describes how the company will organize the work that needs to be accomplished. Typically, work is divided into functional departments, such as production, shipping, marketing, customer support, and finance. Jobs within these functional areas are defined, and then recruitment begins for specific job titles and responsibilities. Typically, in the beginning, generalists who can perform multiple tasks are hired. As the company grows, recruiting becomes more specialized. For instance, at the outset, a business may have one marketing manager. But after two or three years of steady growth, that one marketing position may be broken down into seven separate jobs done by seven individuals.

For instance, eBay founder Pierre Omidyar started an online auction site, according to some sources, to help his girlfriend trade PEZ dispensers with other collectors, but within a few months the volume of business had far exceeded what he alone could handle. So he began hiring people with more business experience to help out. Soon the company had many employees, departments, and managers who were responsible for overseeing the various aspects of the organization.

Management Team

management team

employees of the company responsible for making the business model work

Arguably, the single most important element of a business model is the **management team** responsible for making the model work. A strong management team gives a model instant credibility to outside investors, immediate market-specific knowledge, and experience in implementing business plans. A strong management team may not be able to salvage a weak business model, but the team should be able to change the model and redefine the business as it becomes necessary.

Eventually, most companies get to the point of having several senior executives or managers. How skilled managers are, however, can be a source of competitive advantage or disadvantage. The challenge is to find people who have both the experience and the ability to apply that experience to new situations.

To be able to identify good managers for a business start-up, first consider the kinds of experiences that would be helpful to a manager joining your company. What kind of technical background is desirable? What kind of supervisory experience is necessary? How many years in a particular function should be required? What job functions should be fulfilled first: marketing, production, finance, or operations? Especially in situations where financing will be needed to get a company off the ground, do prospective senior managers have experience and contacts for raising financing from outside investors?

Read *Insight on Business: Is Groupon's Business Model Sustainable?* for a look at some of the issues involved in developing a successful business model.

CATEGORIZING E-COMMERCE BUSINESS MODELS: SOME DIFFICULTIES

There are many e-commerce business models, and more are being invented every day. The number of such models is limited only by the human imagination, and our list of different business models is certainly not exhaustive. However, despite the abundance of potential models, it is possible to identify the major generic types (and subtle variations) of business models that have been developed for the e-commerce arena and describe their key features. It is important to realize, however, that there is no one correct way to categorize these business models.

Our approach is to categorize business models according to the different major e-commerce sectors—B2C and B2B—in which they are utilized. You will note, however, that fundamentally similar business models may appear in more than one sector. For example, the business models of online retailers (often called e-tailers) and e-distributors are quite similar. However, they are distinguished by the market focus of the sector in which they are used. In the case of e-tailers in the B2C sector, the business model focuses on sales to the individual consumer, while in the case of the e-distributor, the business model focuses on sales to another business. Many companies use a variety of different business models as they attempt to extend into as many areas of e-commerce as possible. We look at B2C business models in Section 2.2 and B2B business models in Section 2.3.

A business's technology platform is sometimes confused with its business model. For instance, "mobile e-commerce" refers to the use of mobile devices and cellular and wide area networks to support a variety of business models. Pundits sometimes confuse matters by referring to mobile e-commerce as a distinct business model, which it is not. All of the basic business models we discuss below can be implemented on both the traditional Internet/Web and mobile platform. Likewise, although they are sometimes referred to as such, social e-commerce and local e-commerce are not business models in and of themselves, but rather sub-sectors of B2C and B2B e-commerce in which different business models can operate.

Finally, you will also note that some companies use multiple business models. For instance, Amazon has multiple business models: it is an e-retailer, content provider, market creator, e-commerce infrastructure provider, and more. eBay is a market

INSIGHT ON BUSINESS

IS GROUPON'S BUSINESS MODEL SUSTAINABLE?

Groupon is a business that offers subscribers daily deals from local merchants. The catch: a group of people (usually at least 25) have to purchase the discounted coupon (a "Groupon"). If you really want to go to that Italian restaurant in your area with a 50% discount coupon, you will need to message your friends to pay for the coupon as well. As soon as the minimum number of coupons is sold, the offer is open to everyone.

Here's how it works. Most Groupon deals give the customer 50% off the retail price of a product or service offered by a local merchant. For example, a $50 hair styling is offered at $25. The Groupon offer is e-mailed to thousands of potential customers within driving distance of the retailer. If enough people sign up and buy the Groupon, the deal is on, and the customer receives a Groupon by e-mail. Groupon takes a 50% cut of the revenue ($12.50), leaving the merchant with $12.50. In other words, the merchant takes a haircut of 75%! Instead of generating $50 in revenue for hair styling, the merchant receives only $12.50.

Who wins here? The customer gets a hair styling for half price. Groupon gets a hefty percentage of the Groupon's face value. The merchant receives many (sometimes too many) customers. While merchants may lose money on these single offers, they are hoping to generate repeat purchases, loyal customers, and a larger customer base. Moreover, the deals are short term, often good for only a day. The hope: lose money on a single day, make money on all the other days when regular prices are in effect. It's a customer acquisition cost.

Groupon combines two of the major trends in e-commerce: localization and social networks. Started in November 2008 by Andrew Mason, Groupon rocketed to prominence in less than three years, going public in June 2011. By that time, it operated in 43 countries, had 83 million subscribers, and had sold more than 70 million Groupons. It went public at a price of $20 per share, which gave the company a whopping $13 billion valuation.

But even then, there were questions. At the time, Groupon financials showed a loss of $456 million on revenues of $713 million for 2010, and $146 million on revenues of $645 million for the first quarter of 2011. Its biggest expense was customer acquisition. It spent $263 million in marketing for 2010 and almost equal to that amount ($208 million) in the first quarter of 2011 alone. Analysts and investors wondered if the Groupon business model would work. The critics pointed out that Groupon's revenue per customer was falling, the conversion rate of customers into subscribers was slowing down, the tens of millions of e-mails Groupon used to inform users of deals were poorly targeted, there were fewer Groupons being sold per customer, and the revenue per Groupon was falling. Groupon was spending so much on marketing that they were having a difficult time turning a profit despite healthy revenues.

The company responded by arguing that all these trends were typical of the early years of Amazon, Netflix, and even Google. While a company focuses on growing its customer base, revenues per customer and profits will decline. Senior management said the huge customer acquisition costs would continue for a few years, as would losses, until it reached sufficient size. The

(continued)

solution, according to the company, was scale: get big really quick, develop scale, and develop the brand so that competitors would never be able to find an audience.

But questions continue to abound. It is still not clear whether Groupon's business model is sustainable. Much of the skepticism regarding Groupon's prospects for future growth stems from small businesses expressing dissatisfaction with their results. "Deal fatigue" has begun to set in among both businesses and consumers alike. Though businesses were initially excited about the prospects of attracting new customers, many companies have found that the deals only attracted customers who were willing to spend the bare minimum for services, and who would not return if they could not get similar deals in the future. Many of Groupon's partner businesses that did experience an increase in their customer base still ended up losing money. For instance, a study of 150 Groupon merchants found that one-third of the deals were unprofitable for the merchants, and 42% of the merchants said they would not run a Groupon promotion again. In other cases, customers are discovering that some businesses have begun to discriminate against customers that use Groupons, and that oftentimes, Groupons can expire before they can be used, and the customer will lose they money they spent on them.

A year after Groupon went public, the jury remains out. In the last six months of 2011, nearly 800 daily deal sites went out of business. At the same time, some heavy hitters have joined the fray: Google Offers and Amazon Local. During that time, Groupon's stock price has steadily dropped from its initial price, and it currently sits at approximately $5 per share, just 25% of its initial value. On the plus side, its revenue for the first six months of 2012 compared to the same time period in 2011 almost doubled to over $1 billion, and it showed its first profit ever, even if it was only a comparatively meager $27 million.

In April, Groupon hired Kal Raman, formerly an Amazon retail executive, to take over primary responsibility for operations from Groupon's co-founder and CEO, Andrew Mason. Raman has begun to overhaul Groupon's sales and payment systems and will be introducing new technology to make its sales force more efficient. Groupon has also embarked on an acquisition spree during the first part of 2012, purchasing companies such as Uptake, Hyperpublic, Adku, and FeeFighters, which it believes will help its position in the small and medium-sized business market.

Nevertheless, many of Groupon's initial investors are still skeptical about whether the company can continue to push towards further profits. In 2012, two of its biggest venture backers, Battery Ventures and Andreessen Horowitz, sold 15.99 million and 5.1 million shares of Groupon stock, respectively. However, other prominent Groupon backers, like Morgan Stanley and T. Rowe Price, have increased their holdings this year. Groupon's earliest and largest backer, New Enterprise Associates, has held onto its full stake of shares since the company went public. Which of these companies is making the right choice?

SOURCES: "Groupon's New Operations Czar Grasps Shaky Helm," by Alistair Barr, Reuters, August 22, 2012; "Groupon Investors Give Up," by Shayndi Raice and Shira Ovide, *Wall Street Journal*, August 20, 2012; "Groupon Venture Backers Battery, Andreessen Horowitz Sell Stakes," by Lisa Rapaport and Douglas MacMillan, Businessweek.com, August 20, 2012; "Ready to Ditch the Deal," by Stephanie Clifford and Claire Cain Miller, *New York Times*, August 17, 2012; Groupon Quarterly Report on Form-Q, filed with the Securities and Exchange Commission, August 14, 2012; "Groupon Reports Mixed 2Q - Analyst Blog," by Zacks Equity Research, August 14, 2012; "Groupon Posts Mixed Results, and Stock Falls," by Quentin Hardy, *New York Times*, August 13, 2012; "Google Offers a Two-Pronged Attack on Groupon's Business Model," by Chunka Mui, *Forbes*, June 29, 2011; "How Does Groupon Work? Is Its Business Model Sustainable?" by Don Dodge, Dondodge.wordpad.com, June 11, 2011; "Is Groupon's Business Model Sustainable?" by Michael de la Merced, *New York Times*, June 8, 2011; "Groupon Plans I.P.O. With $30 Billion Valuation," by Evelyn Rusli and Michael de la Marcede, *New York Times*, June 2, 2011; "How Effective are Groupon Promotions for Businesses," by Utpal M. Dholakia; Rice University, March 12, 2011; "Google Beware: Groupon Is No YouTube," by Utpal Dholakia, Harvard Business Review Blog, December 3, 2010.

creator in the B2C and C2C e-commerce sectors, using both the traditional Internet/ Web and mobile platforms, as well as an e-commerce infrastructure provider. Firms often seek out multiple business models as a way to leverage their brands, infrastructure investments, and assets developed with one business model into new business models.

2.2 MAJOR BUSINESS-TO-CONSUMER (B2C) BUSINESS MODELS

Business-to-consumer (B2C) e-commerce, in which online businesses seek to reach individual consumers, is the most well-known and familiar type of e-commerce. **Table 2.3** illustrates the major business models utilized in the B2C arena.

E-TAILER

e-tailer
online retail store

Online retail stores, often called **e-tailers**, come in all sizes, from giant Amazon to tiny local stores that have Web sites. E-tailers are similar to the typical bricks- and-mortar storefront, except that customers only have to connect to the Internet to check their inventory and place an order. Some e-tailers, which are referred to as "bricks-and-clicks," are subsidiaries or divisions of existing physical stores and carry the same products. REI, JCPenney, Barnes & Noble, Walmart, and Staples are examples of companies with complementary online stores. Others, however, operate only in the virtual world, without any ties to physical locations. Amazon, Blue Nile, and Drugstore.com are examples of this type of e-tailer. Several other variations of e-tailers—such as online versions of direct mail catalogs, online malls, and manufacturer-direct online sales—also exist.

Given that the overall retail market in the United States in 2012 is estimated to be around $3.7 trillion, the market opportunity for e-tailers is very large (Bureau of Economic Analysis, 2012). Every Internet user is a potential customer. Customers who feel time-starved are even better prospects, since they want shopping solutions that will eliminate the need to drive to the mall or store (Bellman, Lohse, and Johnson, 1999). The e-tail revenue model is product-based, with customers paying for the purchase of a particular item.

barriers to entry
the total cost of entering a new marketplace

This sector, however, is extremely competitive. Since **barriers to entry** (the total cost of entering a new marketplace) into the Web e-tail market are low, tens of thousands of small e-tail shops have sprung up on the Web. Becoming profitable and surviving is very difficult, however, for e-tailers with no prior brand name or experience. The e-tailer's challenge is differentiating its business from existing stores and Web sites.

Companies that try to reach every online consumer are likely to deplete their resources quickly. Those that develop a niche strategy, clearly identifying their target market and its needs, are best prepared to make a profit. Keeping expenses low, selection broad, and inventory controlled are keys to success in e-tailing, with inventory being the most difficult to gauge. Online retail is covered in more depth in Chapter 9.

TABLE 2.3	B2C BUSINESS MODELS			
BUSINESS MODEL	VARIATIONS	EXAMPLES	DESCRIPTION	REVENUE MODEL
E-tailer	Virtual Merchant	Amazon iTunes Bluefly	Online version of retail store, where customers can shop at any hour of the day or night without leaving their home or office	Sales of goods
	Bricks-and-Clicks	Walmart.com Sears.com	Online distribution channel for a company that also has physical stores	Same
	Catalog Merchant	LLBean.com LillianVernon.com	Online version of direct mail catalog	Same
	Manufacturer-Direct	Dell.com Mattel.com SonyStyle.com	Manufacturer uses online channel to sell direct to customer	Same
Community Provider		Facebook LinkedIn Twitter Pinterest	Sites where individuals with particular interests, hobbies, common experiences, or social networks can come together and "meet" online	Advertising, subscription, affiliate referral fees
Content Provider		WSJ.com CBSSports.com CNN.com ESPN.com Rhapsody.com	Information and entertainment providers such as newspapers, sports sites, and other online sources that offer customers up-to-date news and special interest how-to guidance and tips and/or information sales	Advertising, subscription fees, affiliate referral fees
Portal	Horizontal/ General	Yahoo AOL MSN Facebook	Offers an integrated package of content, content-search, and social network services: news, e-mail, chat, music downloads, video streaming, calendars, etc. Seeks to be a user's home base	Advertising, subscription fees, transaction fees
	Vertical/ Specialized (Vortal)	Sailnet	Offers services and products to specialized marketplace	Same
	Search	Google Bing Ask.com	Focuses primarily on offering search services	Advertising, affiliate referral
Transaction Broker		E*Trade Expedia Monster Travelocity Hotels.com Orbitz	Processors of online sales transactions, such as stockbrokers and travel agents, that increase customers' productivity by helping them get things done faster and more cheaply	Transaction fees
Market Creator		eBay Etsy Amazon Priceline	Web-based businesses that use Internet technology to create markets that bring buyers and sellers together	Transaction fees
Service Provider		VisaNow.com Carbonite RocketLawyer	Companies that make money by selling users a service, rather than a product	Sales of services

COMMUNITY PROVIDER

community provider

sites that create a digital online environment where people with similar interests can transact (buy and sell goods); share interests, photos, and videos; communicate with like-minded people; and receive interest-related information

Although community providers are not a new entity, the Internet has made such sites for like-minded individuals to meet and converse much easier, without the limitations of geography and time to hinder participation. **Community providers** are sites that create an online environment where people with similar interests can transact (buy and sell goods); share interests, photos, videos; communicate with like-minded people; receive interest-related information; and even play out fantasies by adopting online personalities called avatars. The social network sites Facebook, LinkedIn, Twitter, and Pinterest, and hundreds of other smaller, niche sites all offer users community-building tools and services.

The basic value proposition of community providers is to create a fast, convenient, one-stop site where users can focus on their most important concerns and interests, share the experience with friends, and learn more about their own interests. Community providers typically rely on a hybrid revenue model that includes subscription fees, sales revenues, transaction fees, affiliate fees, and advertising fees from other firms that are attracted by a tightly focused audience.

Community sites such as iVillage make money through affiliate relationships with retailers and from advertising. For instance, a parent might visit RightStart.com for tips on diapering a baby and be presented with a link to Huggies.com; if the parent clicks the link and then makes a purchase from Huggies.com, RightStart gets a commission. Likewise, banner ads also generate revenue. Some of the oldest communities on the Web are The Well (Well.com), which provides a forum for technology and Internet-related discussions, and The Motley Fool (Fool.com), which provides financial advice, news, and opinions. The Well offers various membership plans ranging from $10 to $15 a month. Motley Fool supports itself through ads and selling products that start out "free" but turn into annual subscriptions.

Consumers' interest in communities is mushrooming. Community is, arguably, the fastest growing online activity. While many community sites have had a difficult time becoming profitable, many have succeeded over time, with advertising as their main source of revenue. Both the very large social network sites such as Facebook, Twitter, and LinkedIn as well as niche sites with smaller dedicated audiences are ideal marketing and advertising territories. Traditional online communities such as The Well, iVillage, and WebMD (which provides medical information to members) find that breadth and depth of knowledge at a site is an important factor. Community members frequently request knowledge, guidance, and advice. Lack of experienced personnel can severely hamper the growth of a community, which needs facilitators and managers to keep discussions on course and relevant. For the newer community social network sites, the most important ingredients of success appear to be ease and flexibility of use, and a strong customer value proposition. For instance, Facebook has leapfrogged over its rival MySpace by encouraging users to build their own revenue-producing applications that run on their profiles, and even take in advertising and affiliate revenues.

Online communities benefit significantly from offline word-of-mouth, viral marketing. Online communities tend to reflect offline relationships. When your friends say they have a profile on Facebook, and ask you to visit, you are encouraged to build your own online profile.

CONTENT PROVIDER

Although there are many different ways the Internet can be useful, "information content," which can be defined broadly to include all forms of intellectual property, is one of the largest types of Internet usage. **Intellectual property** refers to all forms of human expression that can be put into a tangible medium such as text, CDs, or on the Web (Fisher, 1999). **Content providers** distribute information content, such as digital video, music, photos, text, and artwork, over the Web. It is estimated that, U.S. consumers will spend more than $19 billion for online content such as movies, music, videos, television shows, e-books, and newspapers during 2012.

Content providers make money by charging a subscription fee. For instance, in the case of Rhapsody.com, a monthly subscription fee provides users with access to thousands of music tracks. Other content providers, such as WSJ.com (the *Wall Street Journal* online newspaper), *Harvard Business Review*, and many others, charge customers for content downloads in addition to or in place of a subscription fee. Micropayment systems technology provides content providers with a cost-effective method for processing high volumes of very small monetary transactions (anywhere from $.25 to $5.00 per transaction). Micropayment systems have greatly enhanced the revenue model prospects of content providers who wish to charge by the download.

Of course, not all online content providers charge for their information: just look at CBSSports.com, CIO.com, CNN.com, and the online versions of many newspapers and magazines. Users can access news and information at these sites without paying a cent. These popular sites make money in other ways, such as through advertising and partner promotions on the site. Increasingly, however, "free content" is limited to headlines and text, whereas premium content—in-depth articles or video delivery—is sold for a fee.

Generally, the key to becoming a successful content provider is owning the content. Traditional owners of copyrighted content—publishers of books and newspapers, broadcasters of radio and television content, music publishers, and movie studios—have powerful advantages over newcomers to the Web who simply offer distribution channels and must pay for content, often at oligopolistic prices.

Some content providers, however, do not own content, but syndicate (aggregate) and then distribute content produced by others. *Syndication* is a major variation of the standard content provider model. Another variation here is Web aggregators, who collect information from a wide variety of sources and then add value to that information through post-aggregation services. For instance, Shopping.com collects information on the prices of thousands of goods online, analyzes the information, and presents users with tables showing the range of prices and Web locations. Shopping.com adds value to content it aggregates, and resells this value to advertisers who advertise on its site.

Any e-commerce start-up that intends to make money by providing content is likely to face difficulties unless it has a unique information source that others cannot access. For the most part, this business category is dominated by traditional content providers. The *Insight on Technology* case, *Battle of the Titans: Music in the Cloud*, discusses how changes in Internet technology are driving the development of new business models in the online content market by Internet titans Apple, Google, and Amazon.

Online content is discussed in further depth in Chapter 10.

intellectual property
refers to all forms of human expression that can be put into a tangible medium such as text, CDs or on the Web

content provider
distributes information content, such as digital news, music, photos, video, and artwork, over the Web

INSIGHT ON TECHNOLOGY

BATTLE OF THE TITANS: MUSIC IN THE CLOUD

Business models are closely related to the technologies available to produce and distribute products and services. Nowhere is this more apparent than in the recorded music business, whose foundations since the early 20th century have been based on the technology on hand, from sheet music, to records, tape cassettes, CDs, to music videos for television sets. Always there was a physical product and a device on which to play the product. The Internet has enabled two new business models: the online store download-and-own model used by Amazon or Apple's iTunes where you purchase songs and store them on your computer or devices, and the subscription service model used by Rhapsody, Pandora, and many others where for a monthly fee you can listen to an online library of songs streamed to your devices. In this business model you don't own the music, and if you miss a payment, it's gone.

Both the download-and-own and subscription service models have significant shortcomings that detract from the customer experience. If you download music to a PC, you need cables and software to get the music to your smartphone, and you will be limited as to how many devices you can use. You may download using different devices and then face a problem coordinating them. Subscription services have confusing pricing schemes, typically cost $15 a month or more, and require you to have Internet access. Many services don't allow you to store songs locally on a device for off-the-Net play, while others allow local storage of music that will not be playable if you miss the monthly payment. Many of the inconveniences of these existing business models were created by record companies who feared, legitimately, that their music would be ripped off and their revenue decimated. Both happened.

Changes in technology are introducing yet a third recorded music business model: cloud streaming. Here, you own the music and you can store it on a single online cloud drive and play it from any device you choose—one music collection, no coordination issues, and local storage for offline playback. The technology behind this new business model is cloud computing, a model of computing where your software and files are stored on servers located on the Internet rather than on your local devices like PCs and local servers in your office or corporate headquarters. In 2012, cloud computing is the fastest growing corporate computing platform, with spending on cloud services estimated to top $100 billion. While cloud computing started out as a new and less-expensive method of information processing for large corporations, it is spreading to consumer services such as music, file storage, productivity software, and calendars. What makes cloud computing possible is mammoth data centers stocked with hundreds of thousands of computer processors, and cheap broadband networks that can move your files and software instructions rapidly back and forth from your local devices to cloud servers. For instance, Apple, Google, and Facebook have built some of the world's largest cloud data centers in South Carolina, where land and electricity are very inexpensive. Amazon, a leader in corporate cloud computing, has equally impressive cloud data centers located in rural Virginia and Washington State.

In 2012, Apple, Amazon, and Google, three of the largest Internet players, with annual revenues of $108 billion, $48 billion, and $38 billion, respectively, introduced their cloud-based music models. The resulting competition is a battle royale amongst Internet titans to preserve existing advantages for each firm, and to dominate the future of music distribution.

(continued)

Amazon was the first to announce its cloud music service, in March 2011. Using a "music locker" business model, Amazon's Cloud Player allows you to upload MP3 and ACC music files, store the music on Cloud Player, and play the music on any number of supported digital devices, such as your PC, Mac, Kindle Fire, Android Phone, iPhone, or iPod Touch. If you are a paid subscriber of Amazon's Cloud Drive storage service, you can access Cloud Player at no additional cost. If not, you can subscribe for $24.99 a year, which entitles you to import up to 250,000 songs. Presto: your music is no longer tied to a single digital device or platform. Amazon also sells music; it is the second largest music retailer in the world, with 20 million songs for sale.

Amazon's announcement was followed by Google's announcement in May 2011 of its own music locker service, called Google Music Beta, and now known as Google Play. This is another music locker service based on cloud computing. You download a Google music uploader app called Music Manager and it searches your hard drive or smartphone for music files, and automatically uploads them to the Google cloud. You get free storage for 20,000 songs, and you can play the songs from Android smartphones and tablets as well as PCs, but not iPhones or Windows phones yet. The Google Play store has millions of songs available for purchase.

Both Amazon and Google planned on beating Apple's cloud offering to market. In June 2011, Apple finally joined the party, announcing its own cloud service player and storage system, iCloud. Apple is the largest retailer of music in the world with more than 400 million credit card accounts (customers) and an inventory of more than 28 million songs. Apple's iCloud service allows you to store all your digital files, including music files, on Apple's cloud drive, and then play your music on any Apple device or PC connected to the Internet. Apple's approach is a "matching service" where you do not need to upload any of your music files. In a unique agreement with the four largest music firms, Apple's iCloud software identifies the music titles stored on your device and places high-quality copies into your iCloud drive automatically. This apparently applies to files you have illegally downloaded as well. iTunes Match is available on a subscription basis for the same price as Amazon's Cloud Player, $24.99 a year. Without it, you are limited only to the music you have purchased through iTunes. You can also upload digital documents, from photos and calendars to spreadsheets and papers, to the iCloud. Apple provides 5 gigabytes of storage for free, with additional amounts available for purchase. Apple's iCloud drive service is coordinated with its iOS 5 operating system for smartphones and i-devices. The new operating system does not require a PC or Mac base station, and you can manage all your digital content online using just an iPhone.

It's still too early to tell which of these giants will prevail in the music distribution business, but all will continue to be the dominant players. While there are mostly similarities among the various cloud services (they all will play on any device you choose), some differences may have business significance. For instance, Google and Amazon require users to upload their music, which can take many hours or even days, and some of your music tracks might be very low quality. Apple's service matches your local collection and places high-quality versions of the music online automatically. It's unclear if this is a permanent advantage because both Google and Amazon could negotiate similar terms from the music companies. Both Amazon and Apple appear to be advantaged because they can sell music as well as store it and play it back, whereas Google does not yet have a music store, although it does plan to develop one. Google and Apple can sell users expensive smartphones to play cloud music, whereas Amazon has no proprietary music player.

Setting aside fleeting advantages and minor differences among cloud services, where's the

(continued)

money in cloud music? Downloaded music is about a $4 billion market in 2012, out of a total online content market of $19 billion. While $4 billion is a large number, it's not huge. But music is just the first online content to go onto cloud servers. It will soon be followed by movies, television shows, books, and magazines, and revenues in these online markets are growing at double digits. In addition, the presence of all this content will drive consumers to buy hand-held mobile devices, where revenues and profits are much higher. None of the titans plan to miss out on this opportunity for cloud-based business models and mobile digital devices. There's also money for the content producers. The streaming music cloud services promise to provide a rich and stable stream of revenue for the content producers and artists. Instead of fighting each other, for once it appears the content owners and the Internet content distributors have reached a consensus on a mutually profitable business model for content.

SOURCES: "Web Services to Drive Future Growth for Amazon," by Trefis Team, Forbes.com, August 21, 2012; "Top Cloud Services for Storing and Streaming Music," by Paul Lilly, *PCWorld*, July 29, 2012; "Apple's Stash of Credit Card Numbers is Its Secret Weapon," by Nick Bilton, *New York Times*, June 11, 2012; "The Cloud That Ate Your Music," by Jon Pareles, *New York Times*, June 22, 2011; "Amazon's and Google's Cloud Services Compared," by Paul Boutin, *New York Times*, June 6, 2011; "Apple, Google, Facebook Turn N.C. Into Data Center," *Computerworld*, June 3, 2011; "For a Song, Online Giants Offer Music in a Cloud," by Walter Mossberg, *Wall Street Journal*, May 19, 2011; "Apple's Cloud Music Service Might Crush the Competition," by Mikko Torikka, VentureBeat.com, May 19, 2011; "Amazon Beats Apple and Google to Cloud Music," by Dean Takahashi, VentureBeat.com, March 28, 2011.

PORTAL

portal

offers users powerful Web search tools as well as an integrated package of content and services all in one place

Portals such as Yahoo, MSN, and AOL offer users powerful Web search tools as well as an integrated package of content and services, such as news, e-mail, instant messaging, calendars, shopping, music downloads, video streaming, and more, all in one place. Initially, portals sought to be viewed as "gateways" to the Internet. Today, however, the portal business model is to be a destination site. They are marketed as places where consumers will want to start their Web searching and hopefully stay a long time to read news, find entertainment, and meet other people (think of destination resorts). Portals do not sell anything directly—or so it seems—and in that sense they can present themselves as unbiased. The market opportunity is very large: in 2012, around 240 million people in the United States accessed the Internet at work or home. Portals generate revenue primarily by charging advertisers for ad placement, collecting referral fees for steering customers to other sites, and charging for premium services.

Although there are numerous portal/search engine sites, the top five sites (Google, Yahoo, MSN/Bing, AOL, and Ask.com) gather more than 95% of the search engine traffic because of their superior brand recognition (comScore, 2012). Many of the top sites were among the first to appear on the Web and therefore had first-mover advantages. Being first confers advantage because customers come to trust a reliable provider and experience switching costs if they change to late arrivals in the market. By garnering a large chunk of the marketplace, first movers—just like a single telephone network—can offer customers access to commonly shared ideas, standards, and experiences (something called *network externalities* that we describe in later chapters).

The traditional portals have company: Facebook and other social network sites are now the initial start or home page (portal) for millions of Internet users in the United States.

Yahoo, AOL, MSN, and others like them are considered to be horizontal portals because they define their marketspace to include all users of the Internet. Vertical portals (sometimes called vortals) attempt to provide similar services as horizontal portals, but are focused around a particular subject matter or market segment. For instance, Sailnet specializes in the consumer sailboat market that contains about 8 million Americans who own or rent sailboats. Although the total number of vortal users may be much lower than the number of portal users, if the market segment is attractive enough, advertisers are willing to pay a premium in order to reach a targeted audience. Also, visitors to specialized niche vortals spend more money than the average Yahoo visitor. Google and Ask.com can also be considered portals of a sort, but focus primarily on offering search and advertising services. They generate revenues primarily from search engine advertising sales and also from affiliate referral fees.

TRANSACTION BROKER

Sites that process transactions for consumers normally handled in person, by phone, or by mail are **transaction brokers**. The largest industries using this model are financial services, travel services, and job placement services. The online transaction broker's primary value propositions are savings of money and time. In addition, most transaction brokers provide timely information and opinions. Sites such as Monster.com offer job searchers a national marketplace for their talents and employers a national resource for that talent. Both employers and job seekers are attracted by the convenience and currency of information. Online stock brokers charge commissions that are considerably less than traditional brokers, with many offering substantial deals, such as cash and a certain number of free trades, to lure new customers.

transaction broker
site that processes transactions for consumers that are normally handled in person, by phone, or by mail

Given rising consumer interest in financial planning and the stock market, the market opportunity for online transaction brokers appears to be large. However, while millions of customers have shifted to online brokers, many have been wary about switching from their traditional broker who provides personal advice and a brand name. Fears of privacy invasion and the loss of control over personal financial information also contribute to market resistance. Consequently, the challenge for online brokers is to overcome consumer fears by emphasizing the security and privacy measures in place, and, like physical banks and brokerage firms, providing a broad range of financial services and not just stock trading. This industry is covered in greater depth in Chapter 9.

Transaction brokers make money each time a transaction occurs. Each stock trade, for example, nets the company a fee, based either on a flat rate or a sliding scale related to the size of the transaction. Attracting new customers and encouraging them to trade frequently are the keys to generating more revenue for these companies. Job sites generate listing fees from employers up front, rather than charging a fee when a position is filled.

Competition among brokers has become more fierce in the past few years, due to new entrants offering ever more appealing offers to consumers to sign on. Those who prospered initially were the first movers such as E*Trade, Ameritrade, Datek, and Schwab. During the early days of e-commerce, many of these firms engaged in expensive marketing campaigns and were willing to pay up to $400 to acquire a single customer. However, online brokerages are now in direct competition with traditional brokerage firms that have joined the online marketspace. Significant consolidation is occurring in this industry. The number of job sites has also multiplied, but the largest sites (those with the largest number of job listings) are pulling ahead of smaller niche companies. In both industries, only a few very large firms are likely to survive in the long term.

MARKET CREATOR

market creator
builds a digital environment where buyers and sellers can meet, display products, search for products, and establish a price for products

Market creators build a digital environment in which buyers and sellers can meet, display products, search for products, and establish prices. Prior to the Internet and the Web, market creators relied on physical places to establish a market. Beginning with the medieval marketplace and extending to today's New York Stock Exchange, a market has meant a physical space for transacting business. There were few private digital network marketplaces prior to the Web. The Web changed this by making it possible to separate markets from physical space. A prime example is Priceline, which allows consumers to set the price they are willing to pay for various travel accommodations and other products (sometimes referred to as a reverse auction) and eBay, the online auction site utilized by both businesses and consumers.

For example, eBay's auction business model is to create a digital electronic environment for buyers and sellers to meet, agree on a price, and transact. This is different from transaction brokers who actually carry out the transaction for their customers, acting as agents in larger markets. At eBay, the buyers and sellers are their own agents. Each sale on eBay nets the company a commission based on the percentage of the item's sales price, in addition to a listing fee. eBay is one of the few Web sites that has been profitable virtually from the beginning. Why? One answer is that eBay has no inventory or production costs. It is simply a middleman.

The market opportunity for market creators is potentially vast, but only if the firm has the financial resources and marketing plan to attract sufficient sellers and buyers to the marketplace. As of June 30, 2012, eBay had more than 113 million active registered users, and this makes for an efficient market (eBay, 2012). There are many sellers and buyers for each type of product, sometimes for the same product, for example, laptop computer models. New firms wishing to create a market require an aggressive branding and awareness program to attract a sufficient critical mass of customers. Some very large Web-based firms such as Amazon have leveraged their large customer base and started auctions. Many other digital auctions have sprung up in smaller, more specialized vertical market segments such as jewelry and automobiles.

In addition to marketing and branding, a company's management team and organization can make a difference in creating new markets, especially if some managers have had experience in similar businesses. Speed is often the key in such situations. The ability to become operational quickly can make the difference between success and failure.

SERVICE PROVIDER

service provider
offers services online

While e-tailers sell products online, **service providers** offer services online. There's been an explosion in online services that is often unrecognized. Web 2.0 applications such as photo sharing, video sharing, and user-generated content (in blogs and social network sites) are all services provided to customers. Google has led the way in developing online applications such as Google Maps, Google Docs, and Gmail. ThinkFree and Adobe Buzzword are online alternatives to Microsoft Word provided as services rather than boxed software (a product). More personal services such as online medical bill management, financial and pension planning, and travel recommender sites are showing strong growth.

Service providers use a variety of revenue models. Some charge a fee, or monthly subscriptions, while others generate revenue from other sources, such as through advertising and by collecting personal information that is useful in direct marketing. Some services are free but are not complete. For instance, Google Apps' basic edition is free, but a business edition with advanced tools costs $5/user/month or $50/user/year. Much like retailers who trade products for cash, service providers trade knowledge, expertise, and capabilities, for revenue.

Obviously, some services cannot be provided online. For example, dentistry, medical services, plumbing, and car repair cannot be completed via the Internet. However, online arrangements can be made for these services. Online service providers may offer computer services, such as information storage (as does Carbonite), provide legal services (RocketLawyer), or offer advice and services to high-net-worth individuals, such as at HarrisMyCFO.com. Grocery shopping sites such as FreshDirect and Peapod are also providing services.[1] To complicate matters a bit, most financial transaction brokers (described previously) provide services such as college tuition and pension planning. Travel brokers also provide vacation-planning services, not just transactions with airlines and hotels. Indeed, mixing services with your products is a powerful business strategy pursued by many hard-goods companies (for example, warranties are services).

The basic value proposition of service providers is that they offer consumers valuable, convenient, time-saving, and low-cost alternatives to traditional service providers or—in the case of search engines and most Web 2.0 applications—they provide services that are truly unique to the Web. Where else can you search 50 billion Web pages, or share photos with as many people instantly? Research has found, for instance, that a major factor in predicting online buying behavior is *time starvation*. Time-starved people tend to be busy professionals who work long hours and simply do not have the time to pick up packages, buy groceries, send photos, or visit with financial planners (Bellman, Lohse, and Johnson, 1999). The market opportunity for service providers is as large as the variety of services that can be provided and potentially is much larger than the market opportunity for physical goods. We live in a service-based economy and society; witness the growth of fast-food restaurants, package delivery services, and wireless cellular phone services. Consumers' increasing demand for convenience products and services bodes well for current and future online service providers.

Marketing of service providers must allay consumer fears about hiring a vendor online, as well as build confidence and familiarity among current and potential customers. Building confidence and trust is critical for service providers just as it is for retail product merchants.

---

[1] FreshDirect and other e-commerce businesses can also be classified as online retailers insofar as they warehouse commonly purchased items and make a profit based on the spread between their buy and sell prices.

2.3 MAJOR BUSINESS-TO-BUSINESS (B2B) BUSINESS MODELS

In Chapter 1, we noted that business-to-business (B2B) e-commerce, in which businesses sell to other businesses, is more than 10 times the size of B2C e-commerce, even though most of the public attention has focused on B2C. For instance, it is estimated that revenues for all types of B2B e-commerce in the United States will total around $4.12 trillion in 2012, compared to about $362 billion for all types of B2C e-commerce. Clearly, most of the dollar revenues in e-commerce involve B2B e-commerce. Much of this activity is unseen and unknown to the average consumer.

B2B e-commerce relies overwhelmingly on a technology called electronic data interchange (EDI) (U.S. Census Bureau, 2012). EDI is useful for one-to-one relationships between a single supplier and a single purchaser, and originally was designed for proprietary networks, although it is migrating rapidly to the Internet. Many firms have supplemented their EDI systems, however, with more powerful Web technologies that can enable many-to-one and many-to-many market relationships where there are many suppliers selling to a single or small group of very large purchasers, or, in the case of independent exchanges, where there are many sellers and many buyers simultaneously in the marketplace. EDI is not designed for these types of relationships. **Table 2.4** lists the major business models utilized in the B2B arena.

E-DISTRIBUTOR

e-distributor

a company that supplies products and services directly to individual businesses

Companies that supply products and services directly to individual businesses are **e-distributors**. W.W. Grainger, for example, is the largest distributor of maintenance, repair, and operations (MRO) supplies. MRO supplies are thought of as indirect inputs to the production process—as opposed to direct inputs. In the past, Grainger relied on catalog sales and physical distribution centers in metropolitan areas. Its catalog of equipment went online in 1995 at Grainger.com, giving businesses access to more than 1 million items. Company purchasing agents can search by type of product, such as motors, HVAC, or fluids, or by specific brand name.

E-distributors are owned by one company seeking to serve many customers. However, as with exchanges (described on the next page), critical mass is a factor. With e-distributors, the more products and services a company makes available on its site, the more attractive that site is to potential customers. One-stop shopping is always preferable to having to visit numerous sites to locate a particular part or product.

E-PROCUREMENT

e-procurement firm

creates and sells access to digital electronic markets

Just as e-distributors provide products to other companies, **e-procurement firms** create and sell access to digital electronic markets. Firms such as Ariba, for instance, have created software that helps large firms organize their procurement process by creating mini-digital markets for a single firm. Ariba creates custom-integrated online catalogs (where supplier firms can list their offerings) for purchasing firms. On the sell side, Ariba helps vendors sell to large purchasers by providing software to handle

BUSINESS MODEL	EXAMPLES	DESCRIPTION	REVENUE MODEL
TABLE 2.4	**B2B BUSINESS MODELS**		
(1) NET MARKETPLACE			
E-distributor	Grainger.com Partstore.com	Single-firm online version of retail and wholesale store; supply maintenance, repair, operation goods; indirect inputs	Sales of goods
E-procurement	Ariba PerfectCommerce	Single firm creating digital markets where sellers and buyers transact for indirect inputs	Fees for market-making services; supply chain management, and fulfillment services
Exchange	OceanConnect	Independently owned vertical digital marketplace for direct inputs	Fees and commissions on transactions
Industry Consortium	Exostar Elemica	Industry-owned vertical digital market open to select suppliers	Fees and commissions on transactions
(2) PRIVATE INDUSTRIAL NETWORK			
	Walmart Procter & Gamble	Company-owned network that coordinates supply chains with a limited set of partners	Cost absorbed by network owner and recovered through production and distribution efficiencies

catalog creation, shipping, insurance, and finance. Both the buy and sell side software is referred to generically as "value chain management" software.

B2B service providers make money through transaction fees, fees based on the number of workstations using the service, or annual licensing fees. They offer purchasing firms a sophisticated set of sourcing and supply chain management tools that permit firms to reduce supply chain costs. In the software world, firms such as Ariba are sometimes also called **application service providers (ASPs)**; they are able to offer firms much lower costs of software by achieving scale economies. **Scale economies** are efficiencies that result from increasing the size of a business, for instance, when large, fixed-cost production systems (such as factories or software systems) can be operated at full capacity with no idle time. In the case of software, the marginal cost of a digital copy of a software program is nearly zero, and finding additional buyers for an expensive software program is exceptionally profitable. This is much more efficient than having every firm build its own supply chain management system, and it permits firms such as Ariba to specialize and offer their software to firms at a cost far less than the cost of developing it.

EXCHANGES

Exchanges have garnered most of the B2B attention and early funding because of their potential market size even though today they are a small part of the overall B2B picture. An exchange is an independent digital electronic marketplace where hundreds of suppliers meet a smaller number of very large commercial purchasers (Kaplan and

B2B service provider
sells business services to other firms

application service provider (ASP)
a company that sells access to Internet-based software applications to other companies

scale economies
efficiencies that arise from increasing the size of a business

exchange
an independent digital electronic marketplace where suppliers and commercial purchasers can conduct transactions

Sawhney, 2000). Exchanges are owned by independent, usually entrepreneurial start-up firms whose business is making a market, and they generate revenue by charging a commission or fee based on the size of the transactions conducted among trading parties. They usually serve a single vertical industry such as steel, polymers, or aluminum, and focus on the exchange of direct inputs to production and short-term contracts or spot purchasing. For buyers, B2B exchanges make it possible to gather information, check out suppliers, collect prices, and keep up to date on the latest happenings all in one place. Sellers, on the other hand, benefit from expanded access to buyers. The greater the number of sellers and buyers, the lower the sales cost and the higher the chances of making a sale. The ease, speed, and volume of transactions are summarily referred to as *market liquidity*.

In theory, exchanges make it significantly less expensive and time-consuming to identify potential suppliers, customers, and partners, and to do business with each other. As a result, they can lower transaction costs—the cost of making a sale or purchase. Exchanges can also lower product costs and inventory-carrying costs—the cost of keeping a product on hand in a warehouse. In reality, as will be discussed in Chapter 12, B2B exchanges have had a difficult time convincing thousands of suppliers to move into singular digital markets where they face powerful price competition, and an equally difficult time convincing businesses to change their purchasing behavior away from trusted long-term trading partners. As a result, the number of exchanges has fallen to less than 200, down from more than 1,500 in 2002, although the surviving firms have experienced some success

INDUSTRY CONSORTIA

Industry consortia are industry-owned *vertical marketplaces* that serve specific industries, such as the automobile, aerospace, chemical, floral, or logging industries. In contrast, *horizontal marketplaces* sell specific products and services to a wide range of companies. Vertical marketplaces supply a smaller number of companies with products and services of specific interest to their industry, while horizontal marketplaces supply companies in different industries with a particular type of product and service, such as marketing-related, financial, or computing services. For example, Exostar is an online trading exchange for the aerospace and defense industry, founded by BAE Systems, Boeing, Lockheed Martin, Raytheon, and Rolls-Royce in 2000. Exostar connects with more than 300 procurement systems and has registered more than 70,000 trading partners in 95 countries around the world.

Industry consortia have tended to be more successful than independent exchanges in part because they are sponsored by powerful, deep-pocketed industry players, and also because they strengthen traditional purchasing behavior rather than seek to transform it.

PRIVATE INDUSTRIAL NETWORKS

Private industrial networks constitute about 75% of all B2B expenditures by large firms and far exceed the expenditures for all forms of Net marketplaces. A **private industrial network** (sometimes referred to as a private trading exchange or PTX) is a digital network (often but not always Internet-based) designed to coordinate the flow of communications among firms engaged in business together. The network is owned by a single large purchasing firm. Participation is by invitation only to trusted long-term suppliers of direct inputs. These networks typically evolve out of a firm's own enterprise resource planning (ERP) system, and are an effort to include key suppliers in the firm's own business decision making. For instance, Walmart operates one of the largest private industrial networks in the world for its suppliers, who on a daily basis use Walmart's network to monitor the sales of their goods, the status of shipments, and the actual inventory level of their goods.

We discuss the nuances of B2B commerce in more detail in Chapter 12.

2.4 E-COMMERCE ENABLERS: THE GOLD RUSH MODEL

Of the nearly 500,000 miners who descended on California in the Gold Rush of 1849, less than 1% ever achieved significant wealth. However, the banking firms, shipping companies, hardware companies, real estate speculators, and clothing companies such as Levi Strauss built long-lasting fortunes. Likewise in e-commerce. No discussion of e-commerce business models would be complete without mention of a group of companies whose business model is focused on providing the infrastructure necessary for e-commerce companies to exist, grow, and prosper. These are the e-commerce enablers: the Internet infrastructure companies. They provide the hardware, operating system software, networks and communications technology, applications software, Web designs, consulting services, and other tools that make e-commerce over the Web possible (see **Table 2.5** on page 92). While these firms may not be conducting e-commerce per se (although in many instances, e-commerce in its traditional sense is in fact one of their sales channels), as a group they have perhaps profited the most from the development of e-commerce. We will discuss many of these players in the following chapters.

2.5 HOW THE INTERNET AND THE WEB CHANGE BUSINESS: STRATEGY, STRUCTURE, AND PROCESS

Now that you have a clear grasp of the variety of business models used by e-commerce firms, you also need to understand how the Internet and the Web have changed the business environment in the last decade, including industry structures, business strategies, and industry and firm operations (business processes and value chains). We will return to these concepts throughout the book as we explore the e-commerce phenomenon. In general, the Internet is an open standards system available to all players, and this fact inherently makes it easy for new competitors to enter the marketplace and offer substitute products or channels of delivery. The Internet tends to intensify competition. Because information becomes available to everyone, the Internet inherently shifts power to buyers who can quickly discover the lowest-cost provider on the Web. On the other hand, the Internet presents many new opportunities for creating value,

TABLE 2.5	E-COMMERCE ENABLERS
INFRASTRUCTURE	PLAYERS
Infrastructure	Players
Hardware: Web Servers	IBM, HP, Dell, Oracle
Software: Server Software	Microsoft, RedHat Linux, Apple
Cloud Providers	Amazon Web Services, Rackspace, Google, IBM,
Hosting Services	Rackspace, Webintellects, 1&1 Internet, HostGator, Hostway
Domain Name Registration	Go Daddy, Network Solutions, Dotster
Content Delivery Networks	Akamai, Limelight
Site Design	GSI Commerce, Fry, Oracle
E-commerce Platform Providers	GSI Commerce, Magento, IBM, ATG, Demandware
Mobile Commerce Hardware Platform	Apple, Samsung, Google
Mobile Commerce Software Platform	Apple, Google, Adobe, Usablenet, Unbound Commerce, Branding Brand
Streaming, Rich Media, Online Video	Adobe, Apple, Easy 2 Technologies, Channel Advisor
Security and Encryption	VeriSign, Checkpoint, GeoTrust, Entrust, EMC, Thawte, McAfee
Payment Systems	PayPal, Authorize.net, Chase Paymentech, Cybersource
Web Performance Management	Compuware Gomez, AlertSite, Keynote Systems
Comparison Engine Feeds/Marketplace Management	Channel Advisor, Mercent, Channel Intelligence
Customer Relationship Management	Oracle, SAP, GSI Commerce, Salesforce.com, NetSuite
Order Management	RedPrairie, GSI Commerce, Stone Edge
Fulfillment	RedPrairie, GSI Commerce, CommerceHub
Social Marketing	Buddy Media, HootSuite, Context Optional
Search Engine Marketing	iProspect, Channel Advisor, Rimm-Kaufman
E-mail Marketing	Constant Contact, Experian CheetahMail, Bronto Software, MailChimp
Affiliate Marketing	Commission Junction, Google Affiliate Network, LinkShare
Customer Reviews and Forums	Bazaarvoice, PowerReviews, BizRate
Live Chat/Click-to-Call	LivePerson, BoldChat, Oracle
Web Analytics	Google Analytics, Adobe Omniture, IBM Coremetrics

for branding products and charging premium prices, and for enlarging an already powerful offline physical business such as Walmart or Sears.

Recall Table 1.2 in Chapter 1 that describes the truly unique features of e-commerce technology. **Table 2.6** suggests some of the implications of each unique feature for the overall business environment—industry structure, business strategies, and operations.

TABLE 2.6	EIGHT UNIQUE FEATURES OF E-COMMERCE TECHNOLOGY
FEATURE	**SELECTED IMPACTS ON BUSINESS ENVIRONMENT**
Ubiquity	Alters industry structure by creating new marketing channels and expanding size of overall market. Creates new efficiencies in industry operations and lowers costs of firms' sales operations. Enables new differentiation strategies.
Global reach	Changes industry structure by lowering barriers to entry, but greatly expands market at same time. Lowers cost of industry and firm operations through production and sales efficiencies. Enables competition on a global scale.
Universal standards	Changes industry structure by lowering barriers to entry and intensifying competition within an industry. Lowers costs of industry and firm operations by lowering computing and communications costs. Enables broad scope strategies.
Richness	Alters industry structure by reducing strength of powerful distribution channels. Changes industry and firm operations costs by reducing reliance on sales forces. Enhances post-sales support strategies.
Interactivity	Alters industry structure by reducing threat of substitutes through enhanced customization. Reduces industry and firm costs by reducing reliance on sales forces. Enables Web-based differentiation strategies.
Personalization/ Customization	Alters industry structure by reducing threats of substitutes, raising barriers to entry. Reduces value chain costs in industry and firms by lessening reliance on sales forces. Enables personalized marketing strategies.
Information density	Changes industry structure by weakening powerful sales channels, shifting bargaining power to consumers. Reduces industry and firm operations costs by lowering costs of obtaining, processing, and distributing information about suppliers and consumers.
Social technologies	Changes industry structure by shifting programming and editorial decisions to consumers. Creates substitute entertainment products. Energizes a large group of new suppliers.

INDUSTRY STRUCTURE

E-commerce changes industry structure, in some industries more than others. **Industry structure** refers to the nature of the players in an industry and their relative bargaining power. An industry's structure is characterized by five forces: *rivalry among existing competitors*, the *threat of substitute products, barriers to entry into the industry*, the *bargaining power of suppliers*, and the *bargaining power of buyers* (Porter, 1985). When you describe an industry's structure, you are describing the general business environment in an industry and the overall profitability of doing business in that

industry structure
refers to the nature of the players in an industry and their relative bargaining power

environment. E-commerce has the potential to change the relative strength of these competitive forces (see **Figure 2.3**).

When you consider a business model and its potential long-term profitability, you should always perform an industry structural analysis. An **industry structural analysis** is an effort to understand and describe the nature of competition in an industry, the nature of substitute products, the barriers to entry, and the relative strength of consumers and suppliers.

E-commerce can affect the structure and dynamics of industries in very different ways. Consider the recorded music industry, an industry that has experienced significant change because of the Internet and e-commerce. Historically, the major record label firms owned the exclusive rights to the recorded music of various artists. With the entrance into the marketplace of substitute providers such as Napster and Kazaa, millions of consumers began to use the Internet to bypass traditional music labels and their distributors entirely. In the travel industry, entirely new middlemen such as Travelocity have entered the market to compete with traditional travel agents. After Travelocity, Expedia, CheapTickets, and other travel services demonstrated the power

industry structural analysis

an effort to understand and describe the nature of competition in an industry, the nature of substitute products, the barriers to entry, and the relative strength of consumers and suppliers

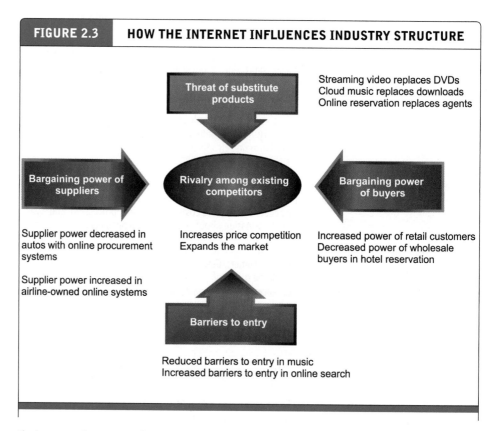

FIGURE 2.3 | **HOW THE INTERNET INFLUENCES INDUSTRY STRUCTURE**

Threat of substitute products
Streaming video replaces DVDs
Cloud music replaces downloads
Online reservation replaces agents

Bargaining power of suppliers

Rivalry among existing competitors

Bargaining power of buyers

Supplier power decreased in autos with online procurement systems

Supplier power increased in airline-owned online systems

Increases price competition
Expands the market

Increased power of retail customers
Decreased power of wholesale buyers in hotel reservation

Barriers to entry

Reduced barriers to entry in music
Increased barriers to entry in online search

The Internet and e-commerce have many impacts on industry structure and competitive conditions. From the perspective of a single firm, these changes can have negative or positive implications depending on the situation. In some cases, an entire industry can be disrupted, while at the same time, a new industry is born. Individual firms can either prosper or be devastated.

of e-commerce marketing for airline tickets, the actual owners of the airline seats—the major airlines—banded together to form their own Internet outlet for tickets, Orbitz, for direct sales to consumers (although ultimately selling the company to a private investor group). Clearly, e-commerce and the Internet create *new industry dynamics* that can best be described as the give and take of the marketplace, the changing fortunes of competitors.

Yet in other industries, the Internet and e-commerce have strengthened existing players. In the chemical and automobile industries, e-commerce is being used effectively by manufacturers to strengthen their traditional distributors. In these industries, e-commerce technology has not fundamentally altered the competitive forces—bargaining power of suppliers, barriers to entry, bargaining power of buyers, threat of substitutes, or rivalry among competitors—within the industry. Hence, each industry is different and you need to examine each one carefully to understand the impacts of e-commerce on competition and strategy.

New forms of distribution created by new market entrants can completely change the competitive forces in an industry. For instance, when consumers gladly substitute free access to Wikipedia for a $699 set of World Book encyclopedias, or a $40 DVD, then the competitive forces in the encyclopedia industry are radically changed. Even if the substitute is an inferior product, consumers are able to satisfy their anxieties about their children's education at a much lower cost (Gerace, 1999). As we describe in Chapter 10, the content industries of newspapers, books, movies, games, and television have been transformed by the emergence of new distribution platforms.

Inter-firm rivalry (competition) is one area of the business environment where e-commerce technologies have had an impact on most industries. In general, the Internet has increased price competition in nearly all markets. It has been relatively easy for existing firms to adopt e-commerce technology and attempt to use it to achieve competitive advantage vis-à-vis rivals. For instance, the Internet inherently changes the scope of competition from local and regional to national and global. Because consumers have access to global price information, the Internet produces pressures on firms to compete by lowering prices (and lowering profits). On the other hand, the Internet has made it possible for some firms to differentiate their product or services from others. Amazon has patented one-click purchasing, for instance, while eBay has created a unique, easy-to-use interface and a differentiating brand name. REI, Inc.—a specialty mountain climbing–oriented sporting goods company—has been able to use its Web site to maintain its strong niche focus on outdoor gear. Therefore, although the Internet has increased emphasis on price competition, it has also enabled businesses to create new strategies for differentiation and branding so that they can retain higher prices.

It is impossible to determine if e-commerce technologies have had an overall positive or negative impact on firm profitability in general. Each industry is unique, so it is necessary to perform a separate analysis for each one. Clearly, e-commerce has shaken the foundations of some industries, in particular, information product industries (such as the music, newspaper, book, and software industries) as well as other information-intense industries such as financial services. In these industries, the power of consumers has grown relative to providers, prices have fallen, and overall profitability has been challenged. In other industries, especially manufacturing, the Internet has not greatly changed relationships with buyers, but has changed relationships with suppliers. Increasingly, manufacturing firms in entire industries have banded together to aggregate purchases, create industry digital exchanges or marketplaces, and outsource industrial processes in order to obtain better prices from suppliers. Throughout this book, we will document these changes in industry structure and market dynamics introduced by e-commerce and the Internet.

INDUSTRY VALUE CHAINS

value chain

the set of activities performed in an industry or in a firm that transforms raw inputs into final products and services

While an industry structural analysis helps us understand the impact of e-commerce technology on the overall business environment in an industry, a more detailed industry value chain analysis can help identify more precisely just how e-commerce may change business operations at the industry level. One of the basic tools for understanding the impact of information technology on industry and firm operations is the value chain. The concept is quite simple. A **value chain** is the set of activities performed in an industry or in a firm that transforms raw inputs into final products and services. Each of these activities adds economic value to the final product; hence, the term *value chain* as an interconnected set of value-adding activities. **Figure 2.4** illustrates the six generic players in an industry value chain: suppliers, manufacturers, transporters, distributors, retailers, and customers.

By reducing the cost of information, the Internet offers each of the key players in an industry value chain new opportunities to maximize their positions by lowering costs and/or raising prices. For instance, manufacturers can reduce the costs they pay for goods by developing Web-based B2B exchanges with their suppliers.

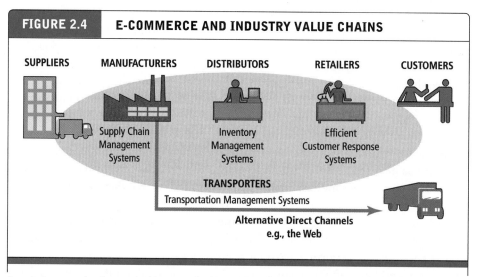

FIGURE 2.4 **E-COMMERCE AND INDUSTRY VALUE CHAINS**

SUPPLIERS   MANUFACTURERS   DISTRIBUTORS   RETAILERS   CUSTOMERS

Supply Chain Management Systems

Inventory Management Systems

Efficient Customer Response Systems

TRANSPORTERS
Transportation Management Systems

Alternative Direct Channels e.g., the Web

Every industry can be characterized by a set of value-adding activities performed by a variety of actors. E-commerce potentially affects the capabilities of each player as well as the overall operational efficiency of the industry.

Manufacturers can develop direct relationships with their customers through their own Web sites, bypassing the costs of distributors and retailers. Distributors can develop highly efficient inventory management systems to reduce their costs, and retailers can develop highly efficient customer relationship management systems to strengthen their service to customers. Customers in turn can use the Web to search for the best quality, fastest delivery, and lowest prices, thereby lowering their transaction costs and reducing prices they pay for final goods. Finally, the operational efficiency of the entire industry can increase, lowering prices and adding value to consumers, and helping the industry to compete with alternative industries.

FIRM VALUE CHAINS

The concept of value chain can be used to analyze a single firm's operational efficiency as well. The question here is: How does e-commerce technology potentially affect the value chains of firms within an industry? A **firm value chain** is the set of activities a firm engages in to create final products from raw inputs. Each step in the process of production adds value to the final product. In addition, firms develop support activities that coordinate the production process and contribute to overall operational efficiency. **Figure 2.5** illustrates the key steps and support activities in a firm's value chain.

firm value chain
the set of activities a firm engages in to create final products from raw inputs

The Internet offers firms many opportunities to increase their operational efficiency and differentiate their products. For instance, firms can use the Internet's communications efficiency to outsource some primary and secondary activities to specialized, more efficient providers without such outsourcing being visible to the consumer. In addition, firms can use the Internet to more precisely coordinate the steps in

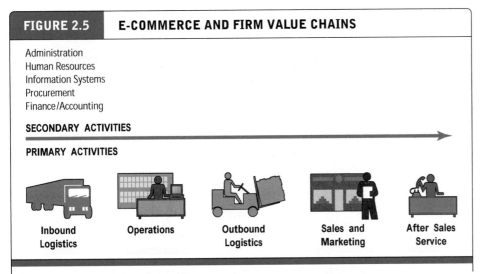

FIGURE 2.5   E-COMMERCE AND FIRM VALUE CHAINS

Administration
Human Resources
Information Systems
Procurement
Finance/Accounting

SECONDARY ACTIVITIES

PRIMARY ACTIVITIES

| Inbound Logistics | Operations | Outbound Logistics | Sales and Marketing | After Sales Service |

Every firm can be characterized by a set of value-adding primary and secondary activities performed by a variety of actors in the firm. A simple firm value chain performs five primary value-adding steps: inbound logistics, operations, outbound logistics, sales and marketing, and after sales service.

the value chains and reduce their costs. Finally, firms can use the Internet to provide users with more differentiated and high-value products. For instance, Amazon uses the Internet to provide consumers with a much larger inventory of books to choose from, at a lower cost, than traditional book stores. It also provides many services—such as instantly available professional and consumer reviews, and information on buying patterns of other consumers—that traditional bookstores cannot.

FIRM VALUE WEBS

value web

networked business ecosystem that coordinates the value chains of several firms

While firms produce value through their value chains, they also rely on the value chains of their partners—their suppliers, distributors, and delivery firms. The Internet creates new opportunities for firms to cooperate and create a value web. A **value web** is a networked business ecosystem that uses Internet technology to coordinate the value chains of business partners within an industry, or at the first level, to coordinate the value chains of a group of firms. **Figure 2.6** illustrates a value web.

A value web coordinates a firm's suppliers with its own production needs using an Internet-based supply chain management system. We discuss these B2B systems in Chapter 12. Firms also use the Internet to develop close relationships with their

| FIGURE 2.6 | **INTERNET-ENABLED VALUE WEB** |

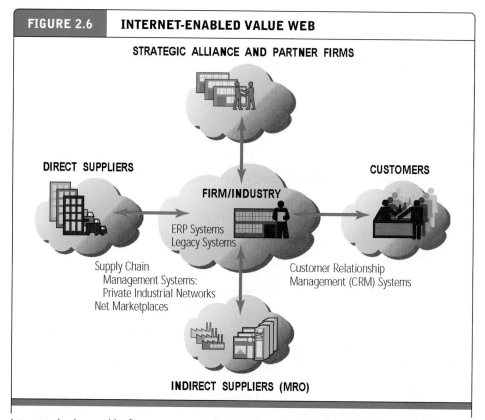

Internet technology enables firms to create an enhanced value web in cooperation with their strategic alliance and partner firms, customers, and direct and indirect suppliers.

logistics partners. For instance, Amazon relies on UPS tracking systems to provide its customers with online package tracking, and it relies on the U.S. Postal Service systems to insert packages directly into the mail stream. Amazon has partnership relations with hundreds of firms to generate customers and to manage relationships with customers. (Online customer relationship management systems are discussed in Chapter 6.) In fact, when you examine Amazon closely, you realize that the value it delivers to customers is in large part the result of coordination with other firms and not simply the result of activities internal to Amazon. The value of Amazon is, in large part, the value delivered by its value web partners. This is difficult for other firms to imitate in the short run.

BUSINESS STRATEGY

A **business strategy** is a set of plans for achieving superior long-term returns on the capital invested in a business firm. A business strategy is therefore a plan for making profits in a competitive environment over the long term. **Profit** is simply the difference between the price a firm is able to charge for its products and the cost of producing and distributing goods. Profit represents economic value. Economic value is created anytime customers are willing to pay more for a product than it costs to produce. Why would anyone pay more for a product than it costs to produce? There are multiple answers. The product may be unique (there are no other suppliers), it may be the least costly product of its type available, consumers may be able to purchase the product anywhere in the world, or it may satisfy some unique needs that other products do not. Each of these sources of economic value defines a firm's strategy for positioning its products in the marketplace. There are four generic strategies for achieving a profitable business: differentiation, cost, scope, and focus. We describe each of these below. The specific strategies that a firm follows will depend on the product, the industry, and the marketplace where competition is encountered.

Although the Internet is a unique marketplace, the same principles of strategy and business apply. As we will see throughout the book, successful e-commerce strategies involve using the Internet to leverage and strengthen existing business (rather than destroy your business), and to use the Internet to provide products and services your competitors cannot copy (in the short term anyway). That means developing unique products, proprietary content, distinguishing processes (such as Amazon's one-click shopping), and personalized or customized services and products (Porter, 2001). Let's examine these ideas more closely.

Differentiation refers to all the ways producers can make their products unique and distinguish them from those of competitors. The opposite of differentiation is **commoditization**—a situation where there are no differences among products or services, and the only basis of choosing a product is price. As economists tell us, when price alone becomes the basis of competition and there are many suppliers and many customers, eventually the price of the good falls to the cost to produce it (marginal revenues from the nth unit equal marginal costs). And then profits are zero! This is

business strategy
a set of plans for achieving superior long-term returns on the capital invested in a business firm

profit
the difference between the price a firm is able to charge for its products and the cost of producing and distributing goods

differentiation
refers to all the ways producers can make their products unique and different to distinguish them from those of competitors

commoditization
a situation where there are no differences among products or services, and the only basis of choosing products is price

an unacceptable situation for any business person. The solution is to differentiate your product and to create a monopoly-like situation where you are the only supplier.

There are many ways businesses differentiate their products. A business may start with a core generic product, but then create expectations among users about the "experience" of consuming the product—"Nothing refreshes like a Coke!" or "Nothing equals the experience of driving a BMW." Businesses may also augment products by adding features to make them different from those of competitors. And businesses can differentiate their products further by enhancing the products' abilities to solve related consumer problems. For instance, tax programs such as TurboTax can import data from spreadsheet programs, as well as be used to electronically file tax returns. These capabilities are enhancements to the product that solve a customer's problems. The purpose of marketing is to create these differentiation features and to make the consumer aware of the unique qualities of products, creating in the process a "brand" that stands for these features. We discuss marketing and branding in Chapters 6 and 7.

In their totality, the differentiation features of a product constitute the customer value proposition we described in earlier sections of this chapter. The Internet and the Web offer some unique ways to differentiate products. The ability of the Web to personalize the shopping experience and to customize the product or service to the particular demands of each consumer are perhaps the most significant ways in which the Web can be used to differentiate products. E-commerce businesses can also differentiate products by leveraging the ubiquitous nature of the Web (by making it possible to purchase the product from home, work, or on the road); the global reach of the Web (by making it possible to purchase the product anywhere in the world); richness and interactivity (by creating Web-based experiences for people who use the product, such as unique interactive content, videos, stories about users, and reviews by users); and information density (by storing and processing information for consumers of the product, such as warranty information on all products purchased through a site or income tax information online).

Adopting a *strategy of cost competition* means a business has discovered some unique set of business processes or resources that other firms cannot obtain in the marketplace. Business processes are the atomic units of the value chain. For instance, the set of value-creating activities called Inbound Logistics in Figure 2.5 is in reality composed of many different collections of activities performed by people on the loading docks and in the warehouses. These different collections of activities are called *business processes*—the set of steps or procedures required to perform the various elements of the value chain.

When a firm discovers a new, more efficient set of business processes, it can obtain a cost advantage over competitors. Then it can attract customers by charging a lower price, while still making a handsome profit. Eventually, its competitors go out of business as the market decisively tilts toward the lowest-cost provider. Or, when a business discovers a unique resource, or lower-cost supplier, it can also compete effectively on cost. For instance, switching production to low-wage-cost areas of the world is one way to lower costs.

Competing on cost can be a short-lived affair and very tricky. Competitors can also discover the same or different efficiencies in production. And competitors can also move production to low-cost areas of the world. Also, competitors may decide to lose money for a period as they compete on cost.

The Internet offers some new ways to compete on cost, at least in the short term. Firms can leverage the Internet's ubiquity by lowering the costs of order entry (the customer fills out all the forms, so there is no order entry department); leverage global reach and universal standards by having a single order entry system world-wide; and leverage richness, interactivity, and personalization by creating customer profiles online and treating each individual consumer differently—without the use of an expensive sales force that performed these functions in the past. Finally, firms can leverage the information intensity of the Web by providing consumers with detailed information on products, without maintaining either expensive catalogs or a sales force.

While the Internet offers powerful capabilities for intensifying cost competition, which makes cost competition appear to be a viable strategy, the danger is that competitors have access to the same technology. The *factor markets*—where producers buy supplies—are open to all. Assuming they have the skills and organizational will to use the technology, competitors can buy many of the same cost-reducing techniques in the marketplace. Even a skilled labor force can be purchased, ultimately. However, self-knowledge, proprietary tacit knowledge (knowledge that is not published or codified), and a loyal, skilled workforce are in the short term difficult to purchase in factor markets. Therefore, cost competition remains a viable strategy.

Two other generic business strategies are scope and focus. A *scope strategy* is a strategy to compete in all markets around the globe, rather than merely in local, regional, or national markets. The Internet's global reach, universal standards, and ubiquity can certainly be leveraged to assist businesses in becoming global competitors. Yahoo, for instance, along with all of the other top 20 e-commerce sites, has readily attained a global presence using the Internet. A *focus strategy* is a strategy to compete within a narrow market segment or product segment. This is a specialization strategy with the goal of becoming the premier provider in a narrow market. For instance, L.L.Bean uses the Web to continue its historic focus on outdoor sports apparel; and W.W. Grainger—the Web's most frequently visited B2B site—focuses on a narrow market segment called MRO: maintenance, repair, and operations of commercial buildings. The Internet offers some obvious capabilities that enable a focus strategy. Firms can leverage the Web's rich interactive features to create highly focused messages to different market segments; the information intensity of the Web makes it possible to focus e-mail and other marketing campaigns on small market segments; personalization—and related customization—means the same product can be customized and personalized to fulfill the very focused needs of specific market segments and consumers.

Industry structure, industry and firm value chains, value webs, and business strategy are central business concepts used throughout this book to analyze the viability of and prospects for e-commerce sites. In particular, the signature case studies found at the end of each chapter are followed with questions that may ask you to identify the competitive forces in the case, or analyze how the case illustrates changes in industry structure, industry and firm value chains, and business strategy.

2.6	**CASE STUDY**

Pandora

and the Freemium Business Model

P andora is the Internet's most successful subscription radio service. As of April 30, 2012, it had approximately 150 million registered users in the United States, and continues to add more than 1 million new subscribers a week—that's one new subscriber about every second! Pandora now accounts for more than 70% of all Internet radio listening hours. Radio? In the Internet age of iTunes, Rhapsody, and listen-to-what-you-want-anywhere-anytime? Why would anyone want an online radio station to choose the music they will be able to hear? That's so old school.

Not exactly. At Pandora, users select a genre of music based on a favorite musician, and a computer algorithm puts together a personal radio station that plays not only the music of the selected artist but also closely related music by different artists. How does the computer know about closely related music and music genres? Can a computer understand music? Not really. Instead a team of professional musicians listens to new songs each day and classifies the music according to more than 400 musical criteria including male or female vocal, electric vs. acoustical guitar, distortion of instruments,

© NetPhotos / Alamy

presence of background vocals, strings, and various other instruments. These criteria are used in a computer algorithm to classify new songs into five genres: Pop/Rock, Hip-Hop/Electronica, Jazz, World Music, and Classical. Within each of these genres are hundreds of sub-genres. Like Taylor Swift? Create a radio station on Pandora with Taylor Swift as the artist and you can listen all day not only to some Taylor Swift tracks but also to musically related artists such as Carrie Underwood, Rascal Flatts, Anna Nalick, and others.

The algorithm used to identify genres of songs is a result of the Music Genome Project conceived by Will Glaser and Tim Westergren in 1999. Westergren, a jazz musician, and Glaser believed it was possible to identify genres of music, and sub-genres, using their expertise (and that of other musicians) to identify similarities among artists and songs. They identified more than 400 factors to help classify songs, and leave it up to the computer program to select appropriate matches based on a user's input of a selected artist. To some extent they are mimicking disc jockeys and radio program managers who had no trouble creating jazz radio, classical radio, and pop/electronica stations, and within these general categories, sub-groups of musicians who shared musical characteristics.

In 2005, Glaser and Westergren launched Pandora.com, a music service based on the Music Genome Project. Their biggest challenge was how to make a business out of a totally new kind of online radio station when competing online stations were making music available for free, many without advertising, and online subscription services were streaming music for a monthly fee and finding some advertising support as well. Online music illegally downloaded from P2P networks for free was also a significant factor, as was iTunes, which by 2005 was a roaring success, charging 99 cents a song with no ad support, and 20 million users at that time. The idea of a "personal" radio station playing your kind of music was very new.

Facing stiff odds, Pandora's first business model was to give away 10 hours of free access to Pandora, and then ask subscribers to pay $36 a month for a year after they used up their free 10 hours. Result: 100,000 people listened to their 10 hours for free and then refused to use their credit cards to pay for the annual service. People loved Pandora but were unwilling to pay for it, or so it seemed in the early years.

Facing financial collapse, in November 2005 Pandora introduced an ad-supported option. Subscribers could listen to a maximum of 40 hours of music in a calendar month for free. After the 40 hours were used up, subscribers had three choices: (a) pay 99 cents for the rest of the month, (b) sign up for a premium service offering unlimited usage, or (c) do nothing. If they chose (c), the music would stop, but users could sign up again the next month. The ad-supported business model was a risky move because Pandora had no ad server or accounting system, but it attracted so many users that in a few weeks they had a sufficient number of advertisers (including Apple) to pay for their infrastructure. In 2006, Pandora added a "Buy" button to each song being played and struck deals with Amazon, iTunes, and other online retail sites. Pandora now gets an affiliate fee for directing listeners to Amazon where users can buy the music. In 2008, Pandora added an iPhone app to allow users to sign up from their smartphones and listen all day if they wanted. This added 35,000 new users a day. By 2009, this "free" ad-supported model had attracted 20 million users. All of Pandora's plans come with restrictions required by the music companies that own the music, including the inability to hear a song on demand, no replay, and a skip limit of six skips per hour per station. Also, the music cannot be used commercially or outside the United States. After struggling for years showing nothing but losses, threatened by the music labels who wanted to raise their Internet radio rates, Pandora finally had some breathing room.

Still not giving up on its premium service, in late 2009, the company launched Pandora One, a premium service that offered no advertising, higher quality streaming music, a desktop app, and fewer usage limits. The service cost $36 a year. By July 2010, Pandora had 600,000 subscribers to its premium service, about 1% of its then 60 million users. At the end of 2009, Pandora reported $55 million in annual revenue, mostly from ads. The remainder of its revenue came from subscriptions and payments from iTunes and Amazon when people bought music. In 2010, Pandora achieved even greater success. Revenue more than doubled, to $137 million, with about $120 million coming from advertising and $18 million from subscriptions. Pandora's "new" business model has proven so successful that it filed for an initial public offering in early 2011, and went public in June 2011. For 2012, revenues again doubled, to $274 million, with about 87% ($239 million) coming from advertising and the remainder from subscriptions and other sources. However, it has not yet shown a profit, and does face competition from services such as Spotify, which also is using the freemium strategy.

Pandora is an example of the "freemium" business revenue model. The model is based on giving away some services for free to 99% of the customers, and relying on the other 1% of the customers to pay for premium versions of the same service. As Chris Anderson, author of *Free: The Future of a Radical Price,* has pointed out, since the marginal cost of digital products is typically close to zero, providing free product does not cost much, and potentially enables you to reach many more people and if the market is very large, even getting just 1% of that market to purchase could be very lucrative. There are many other examples of successful freemium model companies. For many traditional print media like newspapers and magazines, the freemium model may be their path to survival. But it won't work for every online business.

While it clearly has worked for Pandora, there is ongoing debate among e-commerce CEOs and venture capitalists about the effectiveness of the freemium model. The crux of the issue is that while freemium can be an efficient way to gather a large group of potential customers, companies have found that it's a challenge to convert eyeballs into those willing to pay. Absent subscriber revenue, firms need to rely on advertising revenues.

MailChimp's story is both a success and a cautionary tale. The company lets anyone send e-mail newsletters to customers, manage subscriber lists, and track the performance of an e-mail marketing campaign. Despite the powerful tools it gives marketers, and its open applications programming interface, after 10 years in business, the company had only 85,000 paid subscribers.

In 2009, CEO Ben Chestnut decided that it was time to implement new strategies to attract additional customers. MailChimp began giving away its basic tools and charging subscription fees for special features. The concept was that as those customers' e-mail lists grew, they would continue using MailChimp and be willing to pay for enhanced services. These services included more than just the ability to send e-mails to a greater number of people. Clients would pay to use sophisticated analytics to help them target their e-marketing campaigns more efficiently and effectively.

In just over a year, MailChimp went from 85,000 to 450,000 users. E-mail volume went from 200 million a month to around 700 million. Most importantly, the number of paying customers increased more than 150%, while profit increased more than 650%! Sounds great, but there was also a price to pay. The company also saw a significant increase in abuse of its system, and a related increase in legal costs. Much of the abuse was "fuzzy spam," where spammers were able to successfully disguise their efforts so software such as SpamAssassin couldn't find and block their messages.

Instead of abandoning the freemium model, MailChimp developed Project Omnivore, an optimization algorithm that could find bad e-mails. Between September 2009 and September 2010, the company sent around 70,000 warnings, suspended almost 9,000 accounts, and shut down about 1,900 users. Fortunately for MailChimp, the algorithm can add additional value for customers because it can find positive trends and estimate the odds that users will open a given e-mail in an e-marketing campaign.

For MailChimp, freemium has been worth the price. It currently supports more than 2 million subscribers worldwide, sending 3.2 billion e-mails per month. However, Ning, a company that enables users to create their own social networks, tried freemium and came to a different conclusion. They abandoned it in July 2010.

Marc Andreessen, co-author of Mosaic, the first Web browser, and founder of Netscape, launched Ning in 2004. With his assistance, the company has raised $119 million in funding. Despite being the market's leading social network infrastructure platform, Ning was having a common problem—converting eyeballs into paying customers. While 13% of customers were paying for some premium services, the revenue was not enough. The more free users Ning acquired, the more it cost the company.

In May 2010, Ning announced the impending end of the freemium model. The company shed staff, going from 167 to 98, and began using 100% of its resources to capture premium users. Since shifting to a three-tier paid subscription model, Ning has experienced explosive growth, increasing the number of paying customers from 17,000 to more than 100,000 and growing revenue by more than 500%. By September 2011, Ning had more than 100 million registered user social profiles and its social networks reached more than 60 million monthly unique users. In December 2011, Ning was acquired by Glam Media, a leading social media company, for $200 million.

So when does it make sense to include freemium in a business plan? It makes sense when the product is easy to use and has a very large potential audience, preferably in the millions. A solid customer value proposition is critical. It's helpful if a large user network increases the perceived value of the product (i.e., a dating service). Freemium may work when a company has good long-term customer retention rates and the product produces more value over time. An extremely important part of the equation is that the variable costs of providing the product or service to additional customers for free must be low.

For example, Evernote, a personal note-taking service, added freemium to its business model and has since grown its user base to 34 million. The company has over 1.4 million paying users. Typically, 2% to 5% of freemium users convert from the

SOURCES: "When Freemium Fails," by Sarah E. Needleman and Angus Loten, *Wall Street Journal*, August 22, 2012; "Evernote Opens Up about Tripling Its Revenue," by Patrick Hoge, Bizjournals.com, July 27, 2012; "MailChimp Announces Integration with Customer Analytics Platform," press release, July 26, 2012; "Pandora Faces Rivals for Ears and Ads," by Ben Sisario, *New York Times*, June 20, 2012; "Evernote by the Numbers: 34M Users, 1.4M Paying, and the Relative Merits of Different Platforms," by Ingrid Lunden, Techcrunch.com, June 19, 2012; Pandora Media Inc. Annual Report on Form 10-K, March 2012; "An Interview with Phil Libin (Evernote)," Doeswhat.com, February 25, 2012; "Glam Media Completes Ning Acquisition," press release, December 5, 2011; "Gling? Glam Buys Ning for $200 Million, Mostly in Stock," by Kara Swisher, Allthingsd.com, September 20, 2011; "Pandora IPO Prices at $16; Valuation $2.6 Billion," by Eric Savitz, Blogs.forbes.com, June 14, 2011; "Social-Networking Site Ning: Charging Users Works for Us," by Jennifer Valentino-DeVries, *Wall Street Journal*, April 13, 2011; "Explainer: What Is the Freemium Business Model," by Pascal-Emmanuel Gobry, *San Francisco Chronicle*, April 8, 2011; "Shattering Myths About 'Freemium' Services: Mobility is Key," by Martin Scott, WirelessWeek, April 7, 2011; "Evernote Statistics—89% User Acquisition via Word of Mouth," Plugged.in, April 5, 2011; Pandora Media Inc, Amendment No. 2 to Form S-1, filed with Securities and Exchange Commission, April 4, 2011; "Going Freemium: One Year Later," by Ben Chestnut, Blog.mailchimp.com, September 27, 2010; "Update on Omnivore, New 3 Strikes Rule," by Ben Chestnut, Blog.mailchimp.com, August 27, 2010; "How To Avoid The Traps and Make a 'Freemium' Business Model Pay," Anna Johnson, Kikabink.com, June 14th, 2010; "6 Ways for Online Business Directories to Convert More Freemium to Premium," BusinessWeek.com, April 14, 2010; "Case Studies in Freemium: Pandora, Dropbox, Evernote, Automattic and MailChimp," by Liz Gannes, Gigacom.com, Mar. 26, 2010; *Free: The Future of a Radical Price*, by Chris Anderson, Hyperion, 2009.

free product to the paid version. Evernote currently has a conversion rate of around 4–5%, within the range of what is expected. But Evernote has also discovered that the longer a subscriber remains an active user, the more likely he or she is to convert to a premium subscription. For instance, 12% of those who continue to use Evernote for at least two years become premium subscribers. Evernote currently is taking in about $30 million in revenues and recently raised funding of $100 million that valued the company at $1 billion, clear proof that the freemium model can add tremendous value.

Companies also face challenges in terms of what products and/or services to offer for free versus what to charge for (this may change over time), the cost of supporting free customers, and how to price premium services. Further, it is difficult to predict attrition rates, which are highly variable at companies using freemium. So, while freemium can be a great way to get early users and to provide a company with a built-in pool for upgrades, it's tough to determine how many users will be willing to pay and willing to stay.

A freemium strategy makes sense for companies such as Pandora, where there is a very low marginal cost, approaching zero, to support free users. It also makes sense for a company where the value to its potential customers depends on a large network, like Facebook. Freemium also works when a business can be supported by the percentage of customers who are willing to pay, like Evernote and Pandora, especially when there are other revenues like affiliate and advertising fees that can make up for shortfalls in subscriber revenues. Freemium has also become the standard model for most apps, with over 75% of the top 100 apps in Apple's app store using a freemium strategy.

Case Study Questions

1. Compare Pandora's original business model with its current business model. What's the difference between "free" and "freemium" revenue models?

2. What is the customer value proposition that Pandora offers?

3. Why did MailChimp ultimately succeed with a freemium model but Ning did not?

4. What's the most important consideration when considering a freemium revenue model?

2.7 REVIEW

KEY CONCEPTS

■ **Identify the key components of e-commerce business models.**

A successful business model effectively addresses eight key elements:

- *Value proposition*—how a company's product or service fulfills the needs of customers. Typical e-commerce value propositions include personalization, customization, convenience, and reduction of product search and price delivery costs.
- *Revenue model*—how the company plans to make money from its operations. Major e-commerce revenue models include the advertising model, subscription model, transaction fee model, sales model, and affiliate model.
- *Market opportunity*—the revenue potential within a company's intended marketspace.
- *Competitive environment*—the direct and indirect competitors doing business in the same marketspace, including how many there are and how profitable they are.
- *Competitive advantage*—the factors that differentiate the business from its competition, enabling it to provide a superior product at a lower cost.
- *Market strategy*—the plan a company develops that outlines how it will enter a market and attract customers.
- *Organizational development*—the process of defining all the functions within a business and the skills necessary to perform each job, as well as the process of recruiting and hiring strong employees.
- *Management team*—the group of individuals retained to guide the company's growth and expansion.

■ **Describe the major B2C business models.**

There are a number of different business models being used in the B2C e-commerce arena. The major models include the following:

- *Portal*—offers powerful search tools plus an integrated package of content and services; typically utilizes a combined subscription/advertising revenue/transaction fee model; may be general or specialized (vortal).
- *E-tailer*—online version of traditional retailer; includes virtual merchants (online retail store only), bricks-and-clicks e-tailers (online distribution channel for a company that also has physical stores), catalog merchants (online version of direct mail catalog), and manufacturers selling directly over the Web.
- *Content provider*—information and entertainment companies that provide digital content over the Web; typically utilizes an advertising, subscription, or affiliate referral fee revenue model.
- *Transaction broker*—processes online sales transactions; typically utilizes a transaction fee revenue model.
- *Market creator*—uses Internet technology to create markets that bring buyers and sellers together; typically utilizes a transaction fee revenue model.
- *Service provider*—offers services online.

- *Community provider*—provides an online community of like-minded individuals for networking and information sharing; revenue is generated by advertising, referral fees, and subscriptions.

■ **Describe the major B2B business models.**

The major business models used to date in the B2B arena include:
- *E-distributor*—supplies products directly to individual businesses.
- *E-procurement*—single firms create digital markets for thousands of sellers and buyers.
- *Exchange*—independently owned digital marketplace for direct inputs, usually for a vertical industry group.
- *Industry consortium*—industry-owned vertical digital market.
- *Private industrial network*—industry-owned private industrial network that coordinates supply chains with a limited set of partners.

■ **Understand key business concepts and strategies applicable to e-commerce.**

The Internet and the Web have had a major impact on the business environment in the last decade, and have affected:
- *Industry structure*—the nature of players in an industry and their relative bargaining power by changing the basis of competition among rivals, the barriers to entry, the threat of new substitute products, the strength of suppliers, and the bargaining power of buyers.
- *Industry value chains*—the set of activities performed in an industry by suppliers, manufacturers, transporters, distributors, and retailers that transforms raw inputs into final products and services by reducing the cost of information and other transaction costs.
- *Firm value chains*—the set of activities performed within an individual firm to create final products from raw inputs by increasing operational efficiency.
- *Business strategy*—a set of plans for achieving superior long-term returns on the capital invested in a firm by offering unique ways to differentiate products, obtain cost advantages, compete globally, or compete in a narrow market or product segment.

QUESTIONS

1. What is a business model? How does it differ from a business plan?
2. What are the eight key components of an effective business model?
3. What are Amazon's primary customer value propositions?
4. Describe the five primary revenue models used by e-commerce firms.
5. Why is targeting a market niche generally smarter for a community provider than targeting a large market segment?
6. Besides music, what other forms of information could be shared through peer-to-peer sites? Are there legitimate commercial uses for P2P commerce?
7. Would you say that Amazon and eBay are direct or indirect competitors? (You may have to visit the Web sites to answer.)

8. What are some of the specific ways that a company can obtain a competitive advantage?
9. Besides advertising and product sampling, what are some other market strategies a company might pursue?
10. What elements of Groupon's business model may be faulty?
11. Why is it difficult to categorize e-commerce business models?
12. Besides the examples given in the chapter, what are some other examples of vertical and horizontal portals in existence today?
13. What are the major differences between virtual storefronts, such as Drugstore.com, and bricks-and-clicks operations, such as Walmart.com? What are the advantages and disadvantages of each?
14. Besides news and articles, what other forms of information or content do content providers offer?
15. What is a reverse auction? What company is an example of this type of business?
16. What are the key success factors for exchanges? How are they different from portals?
17. What is an application service provider?
18. What are some business models seen in the C2C and P2P e-commerce areas?
19. How have the unique features of e-commerce technology changed industry structure in the travel business?
20. Who are the major players in an industry value chain and how are they impacted by e-commerce technology?
21. What are four generic business strategies for achieving a profitable business?
22. What is the difference between a market opportunity and a marketspace?

PROJECTS

1. Select an e-commerce company. Visit its Web site and describe its business model based on the information you find there. Identify its customer value proposition, its revenue model, the marketspace it operates in, who its main competitors are, any comparative advantages you believe the company possesses, and what its market strategy appears to be. Also try to locate information about the company's management team and organizational structure. (Check for a page labeled "the Company," "About Us," or something similar.)

2. Examine the experience of shopping on the Web versus shopping in a traditional environment. Imagine that you have decided to purchase a digital camera (or any other item of your choosing). First, shop for the camera in a traditional manner. Describe how you would do so (for example, how you would gather the necessary information you would need to choose a particular item, what stores you would visit, how long it would take, prices, etc.). Next, shop for the item on the Web. Compare and contrast your experiences. What were the advantages and disadvantages of each? Which did you prefer and why?

3. Visit eBay and look at the many types of auctions available. If you were considering establishing a rival specialized online auction business, what are the top three market opportunities you would pursue, based on the goods and auction community in evidence at eBay? Prepare a report or electronic slide presentation to support your analysis and approach.

4. During the early days of e-commerce, first-mover advantage was touted as one way to success. On the other hand, some suggest that being a market follower can yield rewards as well. Which approach has proven to be more successful— first mover or follower? Choose two e-commerce companies that prove your point, and prepare a brief presentation to explain your analysis and position.

5. Prepare a research report (3 to 5 pages) on the current and potential future impacts of e-commerce technology, including mobile devices, on the book publishing industry.

6. Select a B2C e-commerce retail industry segment such as pet products, online gaming, gift baskets, and analyze its value chain and industry value chain. Prepare a short presentation that identifies the major industry participants in that business and illustrates the move from raw materials to finished product.

7. The ringtone industry is a profitable segment of the music industry. Research the ringtone industry in terms of industry structure, value chains, and competitive environment. Is there room in this industry for another competitor, and if so, what kind of business model and market strategy would it folllow?

Technology Infrastructure for E-commerce

CHAPTER 3

E-commerce Infrastructure: The Internet, Web, and Mobile Platform

After reading this chapter, you will be able to:

- Discuss the origins of the Internet.
- Identify the key technology concepts behind the Internet.
- Describe the role of Internet protocols and utility programs.
- Discuss the impact of the mobile platform and cloud computing.
- Explain the current structure of the Internet.
- Understand the limitations of today's Internet.
- Describe the potential capabilities of the Internet of the future.
- Understand how the Web works.
- Describe how Internet and Web features and services support e-commerce.
- Understand the impact of m-commerce applications.

Google Glass:

Augment My Reality

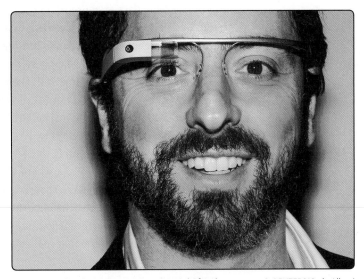

© REUTERS/Carlo Allegri

Walk down the street in any major metropolitan area and count the number of people pecking away at their iPhones or Androids. Roam your campus—how many of your friends are texting, tweeting, or watching a YouTube video on their smartphone? Ride the train and observe how many fellow travelers are reading an online newspaper on their phone or tablet computer. Today, the primary means of accessing the Internet, both in the United States and worldwide, is through smart-phones such as the Apple iPhone, Android, or BlackBerry and tablet computers such as the iPad. Traditional desktop and laptop PCs will, of course, remain important e-commerce and Internet tools, but the action has shifted to the mobile platform. Rather than being just another channel to the Internet, mobile devices are becoming THE channel. This means the primary platform for e-commerce products and services will also change to the mobile platform. The number of mobile Internet users is expected to grow to more than 75% of all Internet users in the United States, about 200 million people, by 2016.

The mobile platform provides the foundation for a number of unique new services. One of the most exciting examples is augmented reality. Augmented reality refers to content (text, video, and sound) that is superimposed over live images in order to enrich the user's experience. The technology brings together location and context, helping the user understand his or her environment better. Only recently have mobile devices and their associated networks improved to the point where augmented reality tools are feasible, but a growing number of businesses are investing in augmented reality services for their mobile clients, and a recent study by Semico Research predicted that by the end of 2016, revenue produced by the augmented reality industry will total more than $600 billion. There is a wealth of possibilities for augmented reality, and many companies are already exploring them. Many of those companies are smaller software companies, but you've probably heard of at least one of them: Google.

In 2012, Google began releasing information about its prototype augmented reality glasses, and co-founder Sergey Brin was seen wearing a trial version in public. The small, wrap-around glasses have a clear display mounted above the eye, and they stream information directly to the lenses. The wearer can use voice commands to access features of the glasses, which also have a camera that can snap pictures or record video. Most importantly, the glasses have an augmented reality display, which will allow users to overlay graphics and other images on top of their vision that adjust based on the line of sight of the wearer.

Promotional videos released by Google suggest the device will perform a wide array of functions for the user, including calling up maps, accessing reviews on the fly, displaying schedule reminders at appropriate times, and integrating fully with other Google services, like Google+. Google's involvement in augmented reality is a major step in the maturation of the technology, and Apple has filed for patents that suggest it is planning its own augmented reality foray, which may be the final push needed to put augmented reality squarely into the mainstream. Still, skeptics worry that the technology is more flash than substance, and that it might not deliver on the optimistic earnings projections cited today. Other critics worry that the technology will be too distracting. Google engineers counter that augmented reality displays will help users to connect more seamlessly with the real world, rather than obscuring it.

It's not hard to figure out where the e-commerce might reside in these tools. How would you like your business to show up on the Google glasses of users visiting or searching for points of interest in your neighborhood? Yellow Pages is testing the use of augmented reality to overlay advertisements, paid for by businesses, to street views where its app is used. Another variation is a real estate app tested by RightMove that allows users to point their phone up and down a street and find out what is for sale or for rent, and how much it costs. It also provides contact information for each of the properties.

How much would you pay to have an online travel guide with you all the time for that next trip abroad? Yelp, TripAdvisor, and Lonely Planet are just a few of the travel companies that have introduced some aspects of augmented reality to their apps. Wikitude is an online augmented reality mobile platform that uses the same kind of wiki tools that power Wikipedia, the online encyclopedia. The application is available for the iPhone, Android, and Symbian mobile operating systems. The Wikitude browser displays information about whatever the user's phone camera is pointed at. Using the smartphone's GPS, accelerometer, and compass, the browser knows where it is located, and what direction it is pointing. The browser then accesses the Wikitude database to provide text information on the object being looked at by the user, including identifying the object or scene, history, and related points of interest. You can think of Wikitude as a very sophisticated travel guide, which is precisely its most common use. In addition, merchants can advertise their local offerings and discount coupons based on where the user is located. Wikitude is therefore an advertising platform as well as a travel guide. Other companies, like Layar, offer competing services.

Many companies are using augmented reality as part of their mobile applications to allow users to see how a prospective purchase would look before buying. For example, Blinds.com's Window Shopper app allows consumers to take a photo of a window in their house using their mobile phone, and then overlay different styles of blinds on the photo to see how the end result would look before they finalize their purchase. Because the top reason that people provide for not buying blinds online is not being able to see what they would look like, augmented reality is helping Blinds.com drive more online sales than ever before.

In the same vein, Lumber Liquidators added a feature to its Floor Finder mobile app called the Visualizer. Just as with Blinds.com, customers take a picture of the floor of any room in their house, and the app can overlay flooring of the customer's choice on top of that area. Yet another current use of augmented reality is to allow users to simulate "trying on" the product. For instance, eBay's Fashion iPhone app lets users virtually try on sunglasses using the phone's front-facing camera to take a picture of themselves and then virtually "fit" the sunglasses to their face. Watchmaker Neuvo offers a similar app that lets users virtually try on watches, while a Converse app lets you do the same with Converse shoes. Software from Zugara allows you try on clothing from online shops.

Gaming is another area where augmented reality is expected to make a big splash. Qualcomm, a leading digital wireless telecommunication development firm, has released an augmented reality game software development kit for both Android and iOS devices, and many games with this feature are expected to be released in 2012. Many believe that augmented reality will ultimately become essential to consumers' mobile experiences, just as mobile devices themselves have become essential. The challenge is to get past the tendency to view augmented reality as a science fiction come to life and instead look at it as a tool that businesses and consumers can use to connect and communicate.

SOURCES: "How Augmented Reality Will Change the Way We Live," by Mez Breeze, thenextweb.com, August 25, 2012; "Augmented Reality is a New Reality for a Forward Thinking Retailer," by Allison Enright, Internetretailer.com, August 24, 2012; "Augmented Reality is Finally Getting Real," by Rachel Metz, *Technology Review*, August 2, 2012; "Is the Floor Beneath Your Feet Real?" by Bill Siwicki, Internetretailer.com, July 31, 2012; "You Will Want Google Goggles," by Farhad Manjoo, *Technology Review*, July 2012; "Google Begins Testing Its Augmented-Reality Glasses," by Nick Bilton, *New York Times*, April 4, 2012; "Apple Patent Hints at Augmented Reality Camera App," by Josh Lowensohn, News.cnet.com; August 18, 2011; "Augmented Reality Kills the QR Code Star," by Kit Eaton, Fastcompany.com, August 4, 2011; "Qualcomm's Awesome Augmented Reality SDK Now Available for iOS," Techcrunch.com, July 27, 2011; "Real Life or Just Fantasy," by Nick Clayton, *Wall Street Journal*, June 29, 2011; "Augmented Reality Comes Closer to Reality," by John Markoff, *New York Times*, April 7, 2011; "Augmented Reality's Industry Prospects May Get Very Real, Very Fast," by Danny King, Dailyfinance.com, March 11, 2011; "Even Better Than the Real Thing," by Paul Skelton, *Wall Street Journal*, February 15, 2011; "Wikitude Goes Wimbledon 2010," press release, Wikitude.com, June 20, 2010.

T his chapter examines the Internet, Web, and mobile platform of today and tomorrow, how it evolved, how it works, and how its present and future infrastructure enables new business opportunities.

The opening case illustrates how important it is for business people to understand how the Internet and related technologies work, and to be aware of what's new. This is true for small businesses in particular, with new local advertising possibilities enabled by smartphones and tablet computers. It could change your business drastically, and open up new opportunities as well. Operating a successful e-commerce business and implementing key e-commerce business strategies such as personalization, customization, market segmentation, and price discrimination requires that business people understand Internet technology and keep track of Web and mobile platform developments.

The Internet and its underlying technology is not a static phenomenon in history, but instead continues to change over time. The Internet happened, but it is also happening. Computers have merged with cell phone services; broadband access in the home and broadband wireless access to the Internet via smartphones, tablet computers, and laptops is expanding rapidly; self-publishing on the Web via blogging, social networking, and podcasting now engages millions of Internet users; and software technologies such as Web services, cloud computing, and smartphone apps are revolutionizing the way businesses are using the Internet. Looking forward a few years, the business strategies of the future will require a firm understanding of these technologies to deliver products and services to consumers. **Table 3.1** summarizes some of the most important developments in e-commerce infrastructure for 2012–2013.

3.1 THE INTERNET: TECHNOLOGY BACKGROUND

What is the Internet? Where did it come from, and how did it support the growth of the Web? What are the Internet's most important operating principles? How much do you really need to know about the technology of the Internet?

Let's take the last question first. The answer is: it depends on your career interests. If you are on a marketing career path, or general managerial business path, then you need to know the basics about Internet technology, which you'll learn in this and the following chapter. If you are on a technical career path and hope to become a Web designer, or pursue a technical career in Web infrastructure for businesses, you'll need to start with these basics and then build from there. You'll also need to know about the business side of e-commerce, which you will learn about throughout this book.

Internet
an interconnected network of thousands of networks and millions of computers linking businesses, educational institutions, government agencies, and individuals

As noted in Chapter 1, the **Internet** is an interconnected network of thousands of networks and millions of computers (sometimes called *host computers* or just *hosts*) linking businesses, educational institutions, government agencies, and individuals. The Internet provides approximately 2.3 billion people around the world (including about 239 million people in the United States) with services such as e-mail, apps,

TABLE 3.1	TRENDS IN E-COMMERCE INFRASTRUCTURE 2012–2013

BUSINESS

- Explosion of Internet content services and mobile access devices strains the business models of Internet backbone providers (the large telecommunication carriers).
- Internet backbone carriers initiate differential pricing models so that users pay for bandwidth usage.
- Mobile devices become the primary access point to social network services and a rapidly expanding social marketing and advertising platform, and create a foundation for location-based Web services and business models.
- The growth in cloud computing and bandwidth capacity enables new business models for distributing music, movies, and television.
- Search becomes more social and local, enabling social and local commerce business models.

TECHNOLOGY

- "Big data" produced by the Internet creates new business opportunities for firms with the analytic capability to understand it.
- Mobile devices such as smartphones and tablet computers are well on their way to becoming the dominant mode of access to the Internet. The new client is mobile.
- The explosion of mobile apps threatens the dominance of the Web as the main source of online software applications and leads some to claim "the Web is dead."
- HTML5 grows in popularity among publishers and developers and makes possible Web applications that are just as visually rich and lively as so-called native mobile apps.
- Cloud computing reshapes computing and storage, and becomes an important force in the delivery of software applications and online content.
- The Internet runs out of IPv4 addresses; transition to IPv6 begins.
- The shipment of tablet computers exceeds the shipment of PCs.
- The decreased cost of storage and advances in database software leads to explosion in online data collection known as "big data."

SOCIETY

- ICANN, which manages the Internet's domain name system, okays vast expansion of top-level domain names.
- Governance of the Internet becomes more involved with conflicts between nations.
- Government control over, and surveillance of, the Internet is expanded in most advanced nations, and in many nations the Internet is nearly completely controlled by government agencies.
- The growing Web-based infrastructure for tracking online and mobile consumer behavior conflicts with individual claims to privacy and control over personal information.

newsgroups, shopping, research, instant messaging, music, videos, and news (Internetworldstats.com, 2012). No single organization controls the Internet or how it functions, nor is it owned by anybody, yet it has provided the infrastructure for a transformation in commerce, scientific research, and culture. The word Internet is derived from the word *internetwork*, or the connecting together of two or more

The Web

one of the Internet's most popular services, providing access to more than 100 billion Web pages

computer networks. The **Web** is one of the Internet's most popular services, providing access to billions, perhaps trillions, of Web pages, which are documents created in a programming language called HTML that can contain text, graphics, audio, video, and other objects, as well as "hyperlinks" that permit users to jump easily from one page to another. Web pages are navigated using browser software.

THE EVOLUTION OF THE INTERNET: 1961—THE PRESENT

Today's Internet has evolved over the last 60 or so years. In this sense, the Internet is not "new;" it did not happen yesterday. Although journalists talk glibly about "Internet" time—suggesting a fast-paced, nearly instant, worldwide global change mechanism—in fact, it has taken about 60 years of hard work to arrive at today's Internet.

The history of the Internet can be segmented into three phases (see **Figure 3.1**). In the first phase, the *Innovation Phase,* from 1961 to 1974, the fundamental building blocks of the Internet were conceptualized and then realized in actual hardware and software. The basic building blocks are: packet-switching hardware, a communications protocol called TCP/IP, and client/server computing (all described more fully later in this section). The original purpose of the Internet, when it was conceived in the 1960s, was to link large mainframe computers on different college campuses. This kind of one-to-one communication between campuses was previously only possible through the telephone system or postal mail.

In the second phase, the *Institutionalization Phase,* from 1975 to 1995, large institutions such as the Department of Defense (DoD) and the National Science Foundation (NSF) provided funding and legitimization for the fledging invention called the Internet. Once the concepts behind the Internet had been proven in several government-supported demonstration projects, the DoD contributed $1 million to further develop

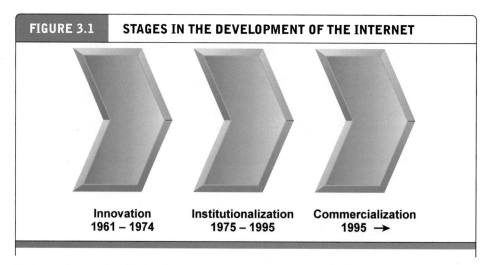

| **FIGURE 3.1** | **STAGES IN THE DEVELOPMENT OF THE INTERNET** |

Innovation
1961 – 1974

Institutionalization
1975 – 1995

Commercialization
1995 →

The Internet has developed in three stages over a 50-year period from 1961 to the present. In the Innovation stage, basic ideas and technologies were developed; in the Institutionalization stage, these ideas were brought to life; in the Commercialization stage, once the ideas and technologies had been proven, private companies brought the Internet to millions of people worldwide.

them into a robust military communications system that could withstand nuclear war. This effort created what was then called ARPANET (Advanced Research Projects Agency Network). In 1986, the NSF assumed responsibility for the development of a civilian Internet (then called NSFNET) and began a 10-year-long $200 million expansion program.

In the third phase, the *Commercialization Phase*, from 1995 to the present, government agencies encouraged private corporations to take over and expand both the Internet backbone and local service to ordinary citizens—families and individuals across America and the world who were not students on campuses. By 2000, the Internet's use had expanded well beyond military installations and research universities. See **Table 3.2** for a closer look at the development of the Internet from 1961 on.

TABLE 3.2	DEVELOPMENT OF THE INTERNET TIMELINE	
YEAR	EVENT	SIGNIFICANCE
INNOVATION PHASE 1961–1974		
1961	Leonard Kleinrock (MIT) publishes a paper on "packet switching" networks.	The concept of packet switching is born.
1972	E-mail is invented by Ray Tomlinson of BBN. Larry Roberts writes the first e-mail utility program permitting listing, forwarding, and responding to e-mails.	The first "killer app" of the Internet is born.
1973	Bob Metcalfe (XeroxParc Labs) invents Ethernet and local area networks.	**Client/server computing is invented.** Ethernet permitted the development of local area networks and client/server computing in which thousands of fully functional desktop computers could be connected into a short-distance (<1,000 meters) network to share files, run applications, and send messages. Although the Apple and IBM personal computers had not yet been invented, at XeroxParc Labs, the first powerful desktop computers connected into a local network were created in the late 1960s.
1974	"Open architecture" networking and TCP/IP concepts are presented in a paper by Vint Cerf (Stanford) and Bob Kahn (BBN).	**TCP/IP invented.** The conceptual foundation for a single common communications protocol that could potentially connect any of thousands of disparate local area networks and computers, and a common addressing scheme for all computers connected to the network, are born.
		These developments made possible "peer-to-peer," "open" networking. Prior to this, computers could only communicate if they shared a common proprietary network architecture, e.g., IBM's System Network Architecture. With TCP/IP, computers and networks could work together regardless of their local operating systems or network protocols.

(continued)

TABLE 3.2	DEVELOPMENT OF THE INTERNET TIMELINE (CONTINUED)

INSTITUTIONAL PHASE 1975–1995

1980	TCP/IP is officially adopted as the DoD standard communications protocol.	The single largest computing organization in the world adopts TCP/IP and packet-switched network technology.
1980	Personal computers are invented.	Altair, Apple, and IBM personal desktop computers are invented. These computers become the foundation for today's Internet, affording millions of people access to the Internet and the Web.

YEAR	EVENT	SIGNIFICANCE
1984	Apple Computer releases the HyperCard program as part of its graphical user interface operating system called Macintosh.	The concept of "hyperlinked" documents and records that permit the user to jump from one page or record to another is commercially introduced.
1984	Domain Name System (DNS) introduced.	DNS provides a user-friendly system for translating IP addresses into words that people can easily understand.
1989	Tim Berners-Lee of the physics lab CERN in Switzerland proposes a worldwide network of hyperlinked documents based on a common markup language called HTML—HyperText Markup Language.	**The concept of an Internet-supported service called the World Wide Web based on HTML pages is born**. The Web would be constructed from "pages" created in a common markup language, with "hyperlinks" that permitted easy access among the pages. The idea does not catch on rapidly and most Internet users rely on cumbersome FTP and Gopher protocols to find documents.
1990	NSF plans and assumes responsibility for a civilian Internet backbone and creates NSFNET.[1] ARPANET is decommissioned.	The concept of a "civilian" Internet open to all is realized through non-military funding by NSF.
1993	The first graphical Web browser called Mosaic is invented by Marc Andreessen and others at the National Center for Supercomputing at the University of Illinois.	Mosaic makes it very easy for ordinary users to connect to HTML documents anywhere on the Web. The browser-enabled Web takes off.
1994	Andreessen and Jim Clark form Netscape Corporation.	The first commercial Web browser—Netscape—becomes available.
1994	The first banner advertisements appear on Hotwired.com in October 1994.	**The beginning of e-commerce**.

COMMERCIALIZATION PHASE 1995–PRESENT

1995	NSF privatizes the backbone, and commercial carriers take over backbone operation.	**The fully commercial civilian Internet is born**. Major long-haul networks such as AT&T, Sprint, GTE, UUNet, and MCI take over operation of the backbone. Network Solutions (a private firm) is given a monopoly to assign Internet addresses.
1995	Jeff Bezos founds Amazon; Pierre Omidyar forms AuctionWeb (eBay).	E-commerce begins in earnest with pure online retail stores and auctions.
1998	The U.S. federal government encourages the founding of the Internet Corporation for Assigned Names and Numbers (ICANN).	Governance over domain names and addresses passes to a private nonprofit international organization.

[1] "Backbone" refers to the U.S. domestic trunk lines that carry the heavy traffic across the nation, from one metropolitan area to another. Universities are given responsibility for developing their own campus networks that must be connected to the national backbone.

(continued)

TABLE 3.2	DEVELOPMENT OF THE INTERNET TIMELINE (CONTINUED)	
1999	The first full-service Internet-only bank, First Internet Bank of Indiana, opens for business.	Business on the Web extends into traditional services.
2003	The Internet2 Abilene high-speed network is upgraded to 10 Gbps.	A major milestone toward the development of ultra-high-speed transcontinental networks several times faster than the existing backbone is achieved.
YEAR	EVENT	SIGNIFICANCE
2005	NSF proposes the Global Environment for Network Innovations (GENI) initiative to develop new core functionality for the Internet.	Recognition that future Internet security and functionality needs may require the thorough rethinking of existing Internet technology.
2006	The U.S. Senate Committee on Commerce, Science, and Transportation holds hearings on "Network Neutrality."	The debate grows over differential pricing based on utilization that pits backbone utility owners against online content and service providers and device makers.
2007	BBN Technologies is selected by the NSF to plan and design the next-generation Internet (GENI).	Work begins on the new Internet, which can provide differential service levels, guaranteed service levels, and differential pricing.
2008	The Internet Society (ISOC) identifies Trust and Identity as a primary design element for every layer of the Internet, and launches an initiative to address these issues.	The leading Internet policy group recognizes the current Internet is threatened by breaches of security and trust that are built into the existing network.
2008	National LambdaRail develops the first 40 Gbps network and the first transcontinental Ethernet network.	Using Cisco optical routers, this leading consortium of universities and businesses provides a nationwide platform for experimentation in very high-speed Internet platforms.
2008	Internet "cloud computing" becomes a billion-dollar industry.	Internet capacity is sufficient to support on-demand computing resources (processing and storage), as well as software applications, for large corporations and individuals.
2009	Internet-enabled smartphones become a major new Web access platform.	Smartphones extend the reach and range of the Internet to more closely realize the promise of the Internet anywhere, anytime, anyplace.
2009	Broadband stimulus package and Broadband Data Improvement Act enacted.	President Obama signs stimulus package containing $7.2 billion for the expansion of broadband access in the United States.
2011	ICANN expands domain name system.	ICANN agrees to permit the expansion of generic top-level domain names from about 300 to potentially thousands using any word in any language.
2012	World IPv6 Launch day.	Major ISPs, home networking equipment manufacturers, and Web companies begin to permanently enable IPv6 for their products and services as of June 6, 2012.

SOURCES: Based on Leiner, et al., 2000; Zakon, 2005; Gross, 2005; Geni.net, 2007; nlr.net, 2010; ISOC.org, 2010; arstechnica.com, 2010; ICANN, 2011a; Internet Society, 2012.

THE INTERNET: KEY TECHNOLOGY CONCEPTS

In 1995, the Federal Networking Council (FNC) took the step of passing a resolution formally defining the term *Internet* (see **Figure 3.2**).

Based on that definition, the Internet means a network that uses the IP addressing scheme, supports the Transmission Control Protocol (TCP), and makes services available to users much like a telephone system makes voice and data services available to the public.

Behind this formal definition are three extremely important concepts that are the basis for understanding the Internet: packet switching, the TCP/IP communications protocol, and client/server computing. Although the Internet has evolved and changed dramatically in the last 30 years, these three concepts are at the core of the way the Internet functions today and are the foundation for Internet II.

Packet Switching

Packet switching is a method of slicing digital messages into discrete units called **packets**, sending the packets along different communication paths as they become available, and then reassembling the packets once they arrive at their destination (see **Figure 3.3**). Prior to the development of packet switching, early computer networks used leased, dedicated telephone circuits to communicate with terminals and other computers. In circuit-switched networks such as the telephone system, a complete point-to-point circuit is put together, and then communication can proceed. However, these "dedicated" circuit-switching techniques were expensive and wasted available communications capacity—the circuit would be maintained regardless of whether any

packet switching

a method of slicing digital messages into packets, sending the packets along different communication paths as they become available, and then reassembling the packets once they arrive at their destination

packet

the discrete units into which digital messages are sliced for transmission over the Internet

FIGURE 3.2	RESOLUTION OF THE FEDERAL NETWORKING COUNCIL

"The Federal Networking Council (FNC) agrees that the following language reflects our definition of the term 'Internet.'

'Internet' refers to the global information system that—

(i) is logically linked together by a globally unique address space based on the Internet Protocol (IP) or its subsequent extensions/follow-ons;

(ii) is able to support communications using the Transmission Control Protocol/Internet Protocol (TCP/IP) suite or its subsequent extensions/follow-ons, and/or other IP-compatible protocols; and

(iii) provides, uses or makes accessible, either publicly or privately, high level services layered on the communications and related infrastructure described herein."

Last modified on October 30, 1995.

SOURCE: Federal Networking Council, 1995.

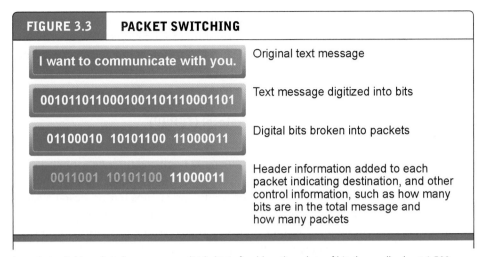

FIGURE 3.3	PACKET SWITCHING

I want to communicate with you. — Original text message

0010110110001001101110001101 — Text message digitized into bits

01100010 10101100 11000011 — Digital bits broken into packets

0011001 10101100 11000011 — Header information added to each packet indicating destination, and other control information, such as how many bits are in the total message and how many packets

In packet switching, digital messages are divided into fixed-length packets of bits (generally about 1,500 bytes). Header information indicates both the origin and the ultimate destination address of the packet, the size of the message, and the number of packets the receiving node should expect. Because the receipt of each packet is acknowledged by the receiving computer, for a considerable amount of time, the network is not passing information, only acknowledgments, producing a delay called latency.

data was being sent. For nearly 70% of the time, a dedicated voice circuit is not being fully used because of pauses between words and delays in assembling the circuit segments, both of which increase the length of time required to find and connect circuits. A better technology was needed.

The first book on packet switching was written by Leonard Kleinrock in 1964 (Kleinrock, 1964), and the technique was further developed by others in the defense research labs of both the United States and England. With packet switching, the communications capacity of a network can be increased by a factor of 100 or more. (The communications capacity of a digital network is measured in terms of bits per second.[2]) Imagine if the gas mileage of your car went from 15 miles per gallon to 1,500 miles per gallon—all without changing too much of the car!

In packet-switched networks, messages are first broken down into packets. Appended to each packet are digital codes that indicate a source address (the origination point) and a destination address, as well as sequencing information and error-control information for the packet. Rather than being sent directly to the destination address, in a packet network, the packets travel from computer to computer until they reach their destination. These computers are called routers. A **router** is a special-purpose computer that interconnects the different computer networks that make up the Internet and routes packets along to their ultimate destination as they travel. To ensure that packets take the best available path toward their destination, routers use a computer program called a **routing algorithm**.

router
special-purpose computer that interconnects the computer networks that make up the Internet and routes packets to their ultimate destination as they travel the Internet

routing algorithm
computer program that ensures that packets take the best available path toward their destination

[2] A bit is a binary digit, 0 or 1. A string of eight bits constitutes a byte. A home telephone dial-up modem connects to the Internet usually at 56 Kbps (56,000 bits per second). Mbps refers to millions of bits per second, whereas Gbps refers to billions of bits per second.

protocol

a set of rules and standards for data transfer

Transmission Control Protocol/Internet Protocol (TCP/IP)

the core communications protocol for the Internet

TCP

protocol that establishes the connections among sending and receiving Web computers and handles the assembly of packets at the point of transmission, and their reassembly at the receiving end

IP

protocol that provides the Internet's addressing scheme and is responsible for the actual delivery of the packets

Network Interface Layer

responsible for placing packets on and receiving them from the network medium

Internet Layer

responsible for addressing, packaging, and routing messages on the Internet

Transport Layer

responsible for providing communication with the application by acknowledging and sequencing the packets to and from the application

Application Layer

provides a wide variety of applications with the ability to access the services of the lower layers

Packet switching does not require a dedicated circuit, but can make use of any spare capacity that is available on any of several hundred circuits. Packet switching makes nearly full use of almost all available communication lines and capacity. Moreover, if some lines are disabled or too busy, the packets can be sent on any available line that eventually leads to the destination point.

Transmission Control Protocol/Internet Protocol (TCP/IP)

While packet switching was an enormous advance in communications capacity, there was no universally agreed-upon method for breaking up digital messages into packets, routing them to the proper address, and then reassembling them into a coherent message. This was like having a system for producing stamps but no postal system (a series of post offices and a set of addresses). The answer was to develop a **protocol** (a set of rules and standards for data transfer) to govern the formatting, ordering, compressing, and error-checking of messages, as well as specify the speed of transmission and means by which devices on the network will indicate they have stopped sending and/or receiving messages.

Transmission Control Protocol/Internet Protocol (TCP/IP), which has become the core communications protocol for the Internet (Cerf and Kahn, 1974). **TCP** establishes the connections among sending and receiving Web computers, and makes sure that packets sent by one computer are received in the same sequence by the other, without any packets missing. **IP** provides the Internet's addressing scheme and is responsible for the actual delivery of the packets.

TCP/IP is divided into four separate layers, with each layer handling a different aspect of the communication problem (see **Figure 3.4**). The **Network Interface Layer** is responsible for placing packets on and receiving them from the network medium, which could be a LAN (Ethernet) or Token Ring network, or other network technology. TCP/IP is independent from any local network technology and can adapt to changes at the local level. The **Internet Layer** is responsible for addressing, packaging, and routing messages on the Internet. The **Transport Layer** is responsible for providing communication with the application by acknowledging and sequencing the packets to and from the application. The **Application Layer** provides a wide variety of applications with the ability to access the services of the lower layers. Some of the best-known applications are HyperText Transfer Protocol (HTTP), File Transfer Protocol (FTP), and Simple Mail Transfer Protocol (SMTP), all of which we will discuss later in this chapter.

IP Addresses

The IP addressing scheme answers the question "How can billions of computers attached to the Internet communicate with one another?" The answer is that every computer connected to the Internet must be assigned an address—otherwise it cannot send or receive TCP packets. For instance, when you sign onto the Internet using a dial-up, DSL, or cable modem, your computer is assigned a temporary address by your Internet Service Provider. Most corporate and university computers attached to a local area network have a permanent IP address.

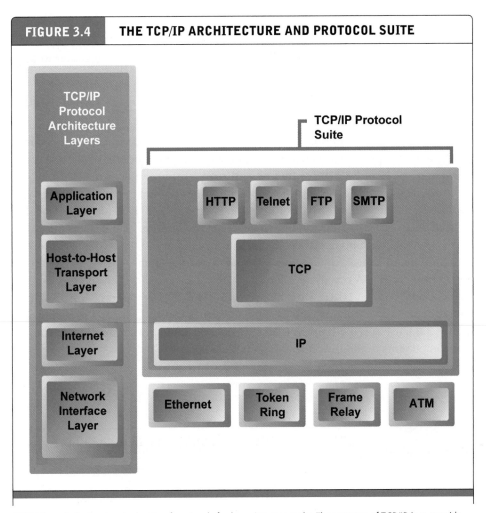

FIGURE 3.4   **THE TCP/IP ARCHITECTURE AND PROTOCOL SUITE**

TCP/IP is an industry-standard suite of protocols for large internetworks. The purpose of TCP/IP is to provide high-speed communication network links.

There are two versions of IP currently in use: IPv4 and IPv6. An **IPv4 Internet address** is a 32-bit number that appears as a series of four separate numbers marked off by periods, such as 64.49.254.91. Each of the four numbers can range from 0–255. This "dotted quad" addressing scheme supports up to about 4 billion addresses (2 to the 32nd power). In a typical Class C network, the first three sets of numbers identify the network (in the preceding example, 64.49.254 is the local area network identification) and the last number (91) identifies a specific computer.

Because many large corporate and government domains have been given millions of IP addresses each (to accommodate their current and future work forces), and with all the new networks and new Internet-enabled devices requiring unique IP addresses being attached to the Internet, by 2011, there were only an estimated 76 million IPv4 addresses left, declining at the rate of 1 million per week. IPv6 was created to address

IPv4 Internet address
Internet address expressed as a 32-bit number that appears as a series of four separate numbers marked off by periods, such as 64.49.254.91

IPv6 Internet address

Internet address expressed as an 128-bit number

this problem. An **IPv6 Internet address** is 128 bits, so it can support up to 2^{128} (3.4×10^{38}) addresses, many more than IPv4.

Figure 3.5 illustrates how TCP/IP and packet switching work together to send data over the Internet.

Domain Names, DNS, and URLs

domain name

IP address expressed in natural language

Domain Name System (DNS)

system for expressing numeric IP addresses in natural language

Uniform Resource Locator (URL)

the address used by a Web browser to identify the location of content on the Web

Most people cannot remember 32-bit numbers. An IP address can be represented by a natural language convention called a **domain name**. The **Domain Name System (DNS)** allows expressions such as Cnet.com to stand for a numeric IP address (cnet. com's numeric IP is 216.239.113.101).[3] A **Uniform Resource Locator (URL)**, which is the address used by a Web browser to identify the location of content on the Web, also uses a domain name as part of the URL. A typical URL contains the protocol to be used when accessing the address, followed by its location. For instance, the URL http://www.azimuth-interactive.com/flash_test refers to the IP address 208.148.84.1 with the domain name "azimuth-interactive.com" and the protocol being used to access the address, HTTP. A resource called "flash_test" is located on the server directory path /flash_test. A URL can have from two to four parts; for example, name1.name2.name3.org. We discuss domain names and URLs further in Section 3.4. **Figure 3.6** illustrates the Domain Name System and **Table 3.3** summarizes the important components of the Internet addressing scheme.

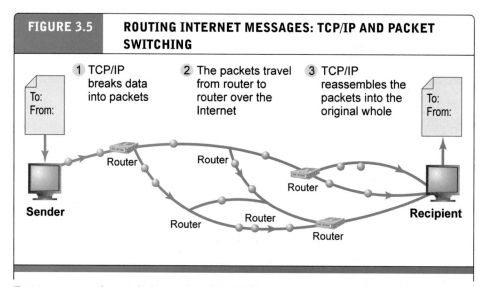

| FIGURE 3.5 | ROUTING INTERNET MESSAGES: TCP/IP AND PACKET SWITCHING |

The Internet uses packet-switched networks and the TCP/IP communications protocol to send, route, and assemble messages. Messages are broken into packets, and packets from the same message can travel along different routes.

---

[3] You can check the IP address of any domain name on the Internet. In Windows 7 or Vista, use Start/cmd to open the DOS prompt. Type ping < Domain Name >. You will receive the IP address in return.

FIGURE 3.6	THE HIERARCHICAL DOMAIN NAME SYSTEM

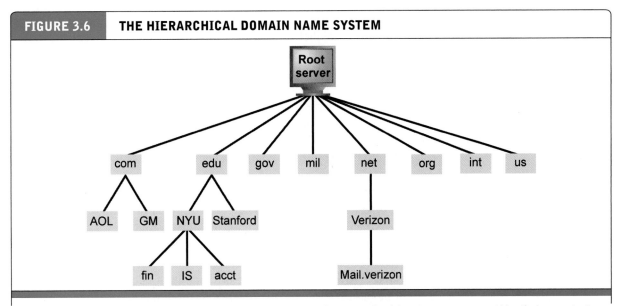

The Domain Name System is a hierarchical namespace with a root server at the top. Top-level domains appear next and identify the organization type (such as .com, .gov, .org, etc.) or geographic location (such as .uk [Great Britain] or .ca [Canada]). Second-level servers for each top-level domain assign and register second-level domain names for organizations and individuals such as IBM.com, Microsoft.com, and Stanford.edu. Finally, third-level domains identify a particular computer or group of computers within an organization, e.g., www.finance.nyu.edu.

Client/Server Computing

While packet switching exploded the available communications capacity and TCP/IP provided the communications rules and regulations, it took a revolution in computing to bring about today's Internet and the Web. That revolution is called client/server computing and without it, the Web—in all its richness—would not exist. **Client/server computing** is a model of computing in which powerful personal computers and other Internet devices called **clients** are connected in a network to one or more server computers. These clients are sufficiently powerful to accomplish complex tasks such

client/server computing
a model of computing in which powerful personal computers are connected in a network together with one or more servers

client
a powerful personal computer that is part of a network

TABLE 3.3	PIECES OF THE INTERNET PUZZLE: NAMES AND ADDRESSES
IP addresses	Every device connected to the Internet must have a unique address number called an Internet Protocol (IP) address.
Domain names	The Domain Name System allows expressions such as Pearsoned.com (Pearson Education's Web site) to stand for numeric IP locations.
DNS servers	DNS servers are databases that keep track of IP addresses and domain names on the Internet.
Root servers	Root servers are central directories that list all domain names currently in use for specific domains; for example, the .com root server. DNS servers consult root servers to look up unfamiliar domain names when routing traffic.

server

networked computer dedicated to common functions that the client computers on the network need

as displaying rich graphics, storing large files, and processing graphics and sound files, all on a local desktop or handheld device. **Servers** are networked computers dedicated to common functions that the client computers on the network need, such as file storage, software applications, utility programs that provide Web connections, and printers (see **Figure 3.7**). The Internet is a giant example of client/server computing in which millions of Web servers located around the world can be easily accessed by millions of client computers, also located throughout the world.

To appreciate what client/server computing makes possible, you must understand what preceded it. In the mainframe computing environment of the 1960s and 1970s, computing power was very expensive and limited. For instance, the largest commercial mainframes of the late 1960s had 128k of RAM and 10-megabyte disk drives, and occupied hundreds of square feet. There was insufficient computing capacity to support graphics or color in text documents, let alone sound files, video, or hyperlinked documents.

With the development of personal computers and local area networks during the late 1970s and early 1980s, client/server computing became possible. Client/server computing has many advantages over centralized mainframe computing. For instance, it is easy to expand capacity by adding servers and clients. Also, client/server networks are less vulnerable than centralized computing architectures. If one server goes down, backup or mirror servers can pick up the slack; if a client computer is inoperable, the rest of the network continues operating. Moreover, processing load is balanced over many powerful smaller computers rather than being concentrated in a single huge computer that performs processing for everyone. Both software and hardware in client/server environments can be built more simply and economically.

Today there are more than 1.6 billion personal computers in existence worldwide. Personal computing capabilities have also moved to smartphones and tablet computers (all much "thinner clients" with a bit less computing horsepower, and limited memory,

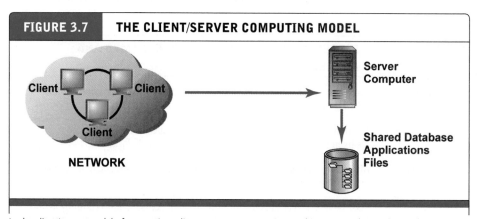

FIGURE 3.7 | **THE CLIENT/SERVER COMPUTING MODEL**

In the client/server model of computing, client computers are connected in a network together with one or more servers.

but which rely on Internet servers to accomplish their tasks). In the process, more computer processing will be performed by central servers.

THE NEW CLIENT: THE MOBILE PLATFORM

There's a new client in town. In a few years, the primary means of accessing the Internet both in the United States and worldwide will be through highly portable smartphones and laptop computers, and not traditional desktop or laptop PCs. This means that the primary platform for e-commerce products and services will also change to a mobile platform.

The change in hardware has reached a tipping point. The form factor of PCs has changed from desktops to laptops and tablet computers such as the iPad (and more than 100 other competitors). Tablets are lighter, do not require a complex operating system, and rely on the Internet cloud to provide processing and storage. And, while there are an estimated 1.6 billion PCs in the world, the number of cell phones long ago exceeded the population of PCs. In 2011, there are an estimated 4 billion worldwide mobile phone users, with 243 million in the United States, around 880 million in China, and 470 million in India (eMarketer, Inc., 2012a). The population of mobile phone users is more than twice that of PC owners. About 25%, or 950 million, of the world's mobile phone users are smartphone users. In the United States, about 122 million people access the Internet using mobile devices, mostly smartphones and tablets. Briefly, the Internet world is turning into a lighter, mobile platform. The tablet is not replacing PCs so much as supplementing PCs for use in mobile situations.

Smartphones are a disruptive technology that radically alters the personal computing and e-commerce landscape. Smartphones involve a major shift in computer processors and software that is disrupting the 40-year dual monopolies established by Intel and Microsoft, whose chips, operating systems, and software applications have dominated the PC market since 1982. Few cell phones use Intel chips, which power 90% of the world's PCs; only a small percentage of smartphones use Microsoft's operating system (Windows Mobile) and that's mostly in Asia. Instead, smartphone manufacturers either purchase operating systems such as Symbian, the world leader, or build their own, such as Apple's iPhone iOS and BlackBerry's OS, typically based on Linux and Java platforms. Around 90% of the 1.5 billion cell phones shipped in 2011 use some version of Advanced RISC Machine (ARM) chips, licensed by ARM Inc. and manufactured by many firms. For instance, Apple's 4G iPhone uses an Apple A4 ARM-based chip that runs at 1 gigahertz (GHz) and includes a built-in graphics processor. The A4 is manufactured by Samsung. The A4 uses only .45 milliwatts of power (compared to a typical laptop dual-core mobile Intel processor that uses 25 watts—about 500 times more power consumption). Smartphones do not need fans. Cell phones do not use power-hungry hard drives but instead use flash memory chips with storage up to 32 megabytes that also require much less power.

The mobile platform has profound implications for e-commerce because it influences how, where, and when consumers shop and buy.

FIGURE 3.8	THE CLOUD COMPUTING MODEL

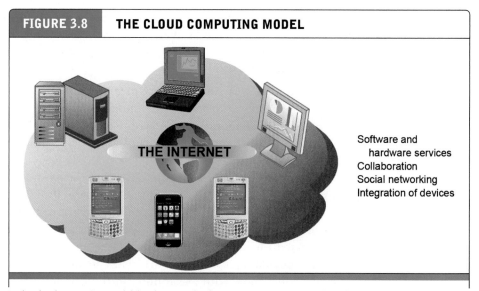

In the cloud computing model, hardware and software services are provided on the Internet by vendors operating very large server farms and data centers.

THE INTERNET "CLOUD COMPUTING" MODEL: SOFTWARE AND HARDWARE AS A SERVICE

The growing bandwidth power of the Internet has pushed the client/server model one step further, towards what is called the "cloud computing model" (**Figure 3.8**). **Cloud computing** refers to a model of computing in which firms and individuals obtain computing power and software applications over the Internet, rather than purchasing the hardware and software and installing it on their own computers. Currently, cloud computing is the fastest growing form of computing, with an estimated market size in 2012 of $100 billion.

Hardware firms such as IBM, HP, and Dell have built very large, scalable cloud computing centers that provide computing power, data storage, and high-speed Internet connections to firms that rely on the Internet for business software applications. Amazon, the Internet's largest retailer, is also one of the largest providers of cloud infrastructure and software services.

Software firms such as Google, Microsoft, SAP, Oracle, and Salesforce.com sell software applications that are Internet-based. Instead of software as a product, in the cloud computing model, software is a service provided over the Internet (referred to as SaaS—software as a service). For instance, Google claims there are around 40 million active users and 4 million businesses that use Google Apps, its suite of office software applications such as word processing, spreadsheets, and calendars, that users access over the Internet. More than 100,000 firms and organizations use Salesforce.com's customer relationship management software.

Microsoft, which in the past has depended on selling boxed software to firms and individuals, is adapting to this new marketplace with its own "software plus service" (buy the boxed version and get "free" online services), Windows Live, and Online Technology initiatives.

cloud computing

model of computing in which firms and individuals obtain computing power and software over the Internet

Cloud computing has many significant implications for e-commerce. For e-commerce firms, cloud computing radically reduces the cost of building and operating Web sites because the necessary hardware infrastructure and software can be licensed as a service from Internet providers at a fraction of the cost of purchasing these services as products. This means firms can adopt "pay-as-you-go" and "pay-as-you-grow" strategies when building out their Web sites. For instance, according to Amazon, hundreds of thousands of customers use Amazon's Web Services arm, which provides storage services, computing services, database services, messaging services, and payment services. For individuals, cloud computing means you no longer need a powerful laptop or desktop computer to engage in e-commerce or other activities. Instead, you can use much less-expensive netbooks or smartphones that cost a few hundred dollars. For corporations, cloud computing means that a significant part of hardware and software costs (infrastructure costs) can be reduced because firms can obtain these services online for a fraction of the cost of owning, and they do not have to hire an IT staff to support the infrastructure. These benefits come with some risks: firms become totally dependent on their cloud service providers.

OTHER INTERNET PROTOCOLS AND UTILITY PROGRAMS

There are many other Internet protocols and utility programs that provide services to users in the form of Internet applications that run on Internet clients and servers. These Internet services are based on universally accepted protocols—or standards—that are available to everyone who uses the Internet. They are not owned by any organization, but they are services that have been developed over many years and made available to all Internet users.

Internet Protocols: HTTP, E-mail Protocols, FTP, Telnet, and SSL/TLS

HyperText Transfer Protocol (HTTP) is the Internet protocol used to transfer Web pages (described in the following section). HTTP was developed by the World Wide Web Consortium (W3C) and the Internet Engineering Task Force (IETF). HTTP runs in the Application Layer of the TCP/IP model shown in Figure 3.4 on page 125. An HTTP session begins when a client's browser requests a resource, such as a Web page, from a remote Internet server. When the server responds by sending the page requested, the HTTP session for that object ends. Because Web pages may have many objects on them—graphics, sound or video files, frames, and so forth—each object must be requested by a separate HTTP message. For more information about HTTP, you can consult RFC 2616, which details the standards for HTTP/1.1, the version of HTTP most commonly used today (Internet Society, 1999). (An RFC is a document published by the Internet Society [ISOC] or one of the other organizations involved in Internet governance that sets forth the standards for various Internet-related technologies. You will learn more about the organizations involved in setting standards for the Internet later in the chapter.)

E-mail is one of the oldest, most important, and frequently used Internet services. Like HTTP, the various Internet protocols used to handle e-mail all run in the Application Layer of TCP/IP. **Simple Mail Transfer Protocol (SMTP)** is the Internet protocol used to send e-mail to a server. SMTP is a relatively simple, text-based protocol that was developed in the early 1980s. SMTP handles only the sending of e-mail. To retrieve

HyperText Transfer Protocol (HTTP)
the Internet protocol used for transferring Web pages

Simple Mail Transfer Protocol (SMTP)
the Internet protocol used to send mail to a server

Post Office Protocol 3 (POP3)

a protocol used by the client to retrieve mail from an Internet server

Internet Message Access Protocol (IMAP)

a more current e-mail protocol that allows users to search, organize, and filter their mail prior to downloading it from the server

File Transfer Protocol (FTP)

one of the original Internet services. Part of the TCP/IP protocol that permits users to transfer files from the server to their client computer, and vice versa

Telnet

a terminal emulation program that runs in TCP/IP

Secure Sockets Layer (SSL) /Transport Layer Security (TLS)

protocols that secure communications between the client and the server

Ping

a program that allows you to check the connection between your client and the server

e-mail from a server, the client computer uses either **Post Office Protocol 3 (POP3)** or **Internet Message Access Protocol (IMAP)**. You can set POP3 to retrieve e-mail messages from the server and then delete the messages on the server, or retain them on the server. IMAP is a more current e-mail protocol supported by all browsers and most servers and ISPs. IMAP allows users to search, organize, and filter their mail prior to downloading it from the server.

File Transfer Protocol (FTP) is one of the original Internet services. FTP runs in TCP/IP's Application Layer and permits users to transfer files from a server to their client computer, and vice versa. The files can be documents, programs, or large database files. FTP is the fastest and most convenient way to transfer files larger than 1 megabyte, which some e-mail servers will not accept. More information about FTP is available in RFC 959 (Internet Society, 1985).

Telnet is a network protocol that also runs in TCP/IP's Application Layer and is used to allow remote login on another computer. The term Telnet also refers to the Telnet program, which provides the client part of the protocol and enables the client to emulate a mainframe computer terminal. (The industry-standard terminals defined in the days of mainframe computing are VT-52, VT-100, and IBM 3250.) You can then attach yourself to a computer on the Internet that supports Telnet and run programs or download files from that computer. Telnet was the first "remote work" program that permitted users to work on a computer from a remote location.

Secure Sockets Layer (SSL)/Transport Layer Security (TLS) are protocols that operate between the Transport and Application Layers of TCP/IP and secure communications between the client and the server. SSL/TLS helps secure e-commerce communications and payments through a variety of techniques, such as message encryption and digital signatures, that we will discuss further in Chapter 5.

Utility Programs: Ping and Tracert

Packet InterNet Groper (Ping) allows you to check the connection between a client computer and a TCP/IP network (see **Figure 3.9**). Ping will also tell you the time it takes for the server to respond, giving you some idea about the speed of the server and the Internet at that moment. You can run Ping from the DOS prompt on a personal

| FIGURE 3.9 | THE RESULT OF A PING |

A ping is used to verify an address and test the speed of the round trip from a client computer to a host and back.

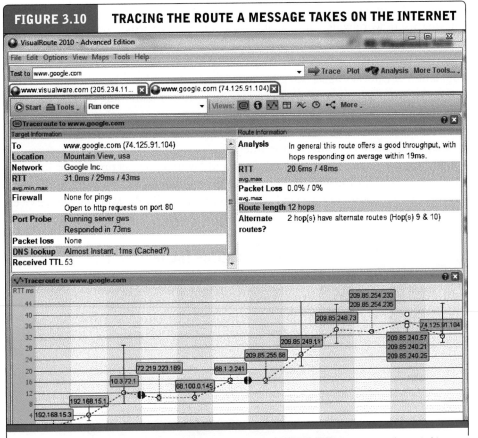

FIGURE 3.10 **TRACING THE ROUTE A MESSAGE TAKES ON THE INTERNET**

VisualRoute and other tracing programs provide some insight into how the Internet uses packet switching. This particular message traveled from a computer in Ashburn, Virginia, to San Antonio, Texas.
SOURCE: Visualware, Inc., 2011.

computer with a Windows operating system by typing: ping < domain name >. We will discuss Ping further in Chapter 5, because one way to slow down or even crash a domain server is to send it millions of ping requests.

Tracert is one of several route-tracing utilities that allow you to follow the path of a message you send from your client to a remote computer on the Internet. **Figure 3.10** shows the result of a message sent to a remote host using a visual route-tracing program called VisualRoute (available from Visualware).

Tracert
one of several route-tracing utilities that allow you to follow the path of a message you send from your client to a remote computer on the Internet

3.2 THE INTERNET TODAY

In 2012, there are an estimated 2.3 billion Internet users worldwide, up from 100 million users at year-end 1997. While this is a huge number, it represents only about 30% of the world's population (Internetworldstats.com, 2012). Although Internet user growth has slowed in the United States to about 1% annually, in Asia, Internet growth is about 10% annually, and by 2015, it is expected that there will be about 2.9 billion Internet users worldwide. One would think the Internet would be overloaded with such incredible growth; however, this has not been true for several reasons. First, client/server computing is highly extensible. By simply adding servers and clients, the population of Internet users can grow indefinitely. Second, the Internet architecture is built in layers so that each layer can change without disturbing developments in other layers. For instance, the technology used to move messages through the Internet can go through radical changes to make service faster without being disruptive to your desktop applications running on the Internet.

Figure 3.11 illustrates the "hourglass" and layered architecture of the Internet. The Internet can be viewed conceptually as having four layers: Network Technology Substrates, Transport Services and Representation Standards, Middleware Services,

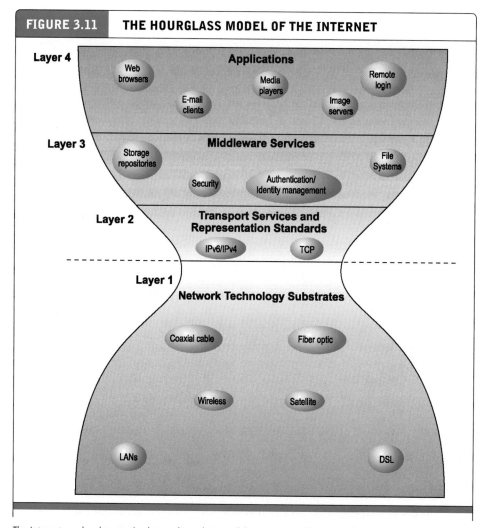

FIGURE 3.11 THE HOURGLASS MODEL OF THE INTERNET

The Internet can be characterized as an hourglass modular structure with a lower layer containing the bit-carrying infrastructure (including cables and switches) and an upper layer containing user applications such as e-mail and the Web. In the narrow waist are transportation protocols such as TCP/IP.

and Applications.[4] The **Network Technology Substrate layer** is composed of telecommunications networks and protocols. The **Transport Services and Representation Standards layer** houses the TCP/IP protocol. The **Applications layer** contains client applications such as the World Wide Web, e-mail, and audio or video playback. The **Middleware Services layer** is the glue that ties the applications to the communications networks and includes such services as security, authentication, addresses, and storage repositories. Users work with applications (such as e-mail) and rarely become aware of middleware that operates in the background. Because all layers use TCP/IP and other common standards linking all four layers, it is possible for there to be significant changes in the Network layer without forcing changes in the Applications Layer.

THE INTERNET BACKBONE

Figure 3.12 illustrates some of the main physical elements of today's Internet. Originally, the Internet had a single backbone, but today's Internet has several backbones that are physically connected with each other and that transfer information from one private network to another. These private networks are referred to as

Network Technology Substrate layer
layer of Internet technology that is composed of telecommunications networks and protocols

Transport Services and Representation Standards layer
layer of Internet architecture that houses the TCP/IP protocol

Applications layer
layer of Internet architecture that contains client applications

Middleware Services layer
the "glue" that ties the applications to the communications networks and includes such services as security, authentication, addresses, and storage repositories

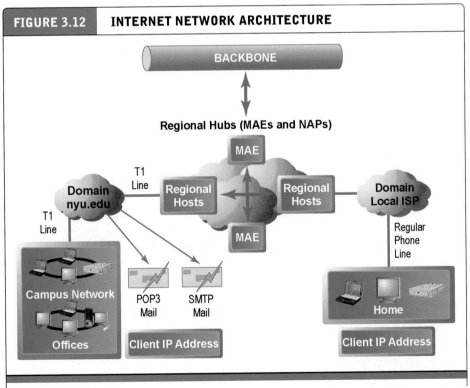

| FIGURE 3.12 | **INTERNET NETWORK ARCHITECTURE** |

Today's Internet has a multi-tiered open network architecture featuring multiple national backbones, regional hubs, campus area networks, and local client computers.

---

4 Recall that the TCP/IP communications protocol also has layers, not to be confused with the Internet architecture layers.

Network Service Provider (NSP)

owns and controls one of the major networks comprising the Internet's backbone

backbone

high-bandwidth fiber-optic cable that transports data across the Internet

bandwidth

measures how much data can be transferred over a communications medium within a fixed period of time; is usually expressed in bits per second (bps), kilobits per second (Kbps), megabits per second (Mbps),or gigabits per second (Gbps)

redundancy

multiple duplicate devices and paths in a network

Internet Exchange Point (IXP)

hub where the backbone intersects with local and regional networks and where backbone owners connect with one another

campus area network (CAN)

generally, a local area network operating within a single organization that leases access to the Web directly from regional and national carriers

Network Service Providers (NSPs), which own and control the major backbone networks (see **Table 3.4**). For the sake of clarity we will refer to these networks of backbones as a single "backbone." The **backbone** has been likened to a giant pipeline that transports data around the world in milliseconds. In the United States, the backbone is composed entirely of fiber-optic cable with bandwidths ranging from 155 Mbps to 2.5 Gbps. **Bandwidth** measures how much data can be transferred over a communications medium within a fixed period of time and is usually expressed in bits per second (bps), kilobits (thousands of bits) per second (Kbps), megabits (millions of bits) per second (Mbps), or gigabits (billions of bits) per second (Gbps).

Connections to other continents are made via a combination of undersea fiber-optic cable and satellite links. The backbones in foreign countries typically are operated by a mixture of private and public owners. The backbone has built-in redundancy so that if one part breaks down, data can be rerouted to another part of the backbone. **Redundancy** refers to multiple duplicate devices and paths in a network.

INTERNET EXCHANGE POINTS

In the United States, there are a number of hubs where the backbone intersects with regional and local networks, and where the backbone owners connect with one another (see **Figure 3.13**). These hubs were originally called Network Access Points (NAPs) or Metropolitan Area Exchanges (MAEs), but now are more commonly referred to as **Internet Exchange Points (IXPs)**. IXPs use high-speed switching computers to connect the backbone to regional and local networks, and exchange messages with one another. The regional and local networks are owned by local Bell operating companies (RBOCs—pronounced "ree-bocks") and private telecommunications firms; they generally are fiber-optic networks operating at more than 100 Mbps. The regional networks lease access to ISPs, private companies, and government institutions.

CAMPUS AREA NETWORKS

Campus area networks (CANs) are generally local area networks operating within a single organization—such as New York University or Microsoft Corporation. In fact, most large organizations have hundreds of such local area networks. These organizations are sufficiently large that they lease access to the Web directly from regional and national carriers. These local area networks generally are running Ethernet (a

TABLE 3.4	MAJOR U.S. INTERNET BACKBONE OWNERS
AT&T	Verio
AOL Transit Data Network (ATDN)	CenturyLink
Cable & Wireless	Sprint
Level 3 Communications	Verizon

FIGURE 3.13 — SOME MAJOR U.S. INTERNET EXCHANGE POINTS (IXPs)

Region	Name	Location	Operator
EAST	MAE East	Virginia and Miami	MCI
	New York International Internet Exchange (NYIIX)	New York	Telehouse
	Peering and Internet Exchange (PAIX)	New York, Philadelphia and Northern Virginia	Switch and Data
	NAP of the Americas	Miami	Terremark
CENTRAL	MAE Chicago	Chicago	MCI
	Chicago NAP	Chicago	SBC
	MAE Central	Dallas and Atlanta	MCI
	Peering and Internet Exchange (PAIX)	Atlanta	Switch and Data
WEST	MAE West	San Jose and Los Angeles	MCI
	Peering and Internet Exchange (PAIX)	Palo Alto, San Jose and Seattle	Switch and Data
	Los Angeles International Internet Exchange (LAIIX)	Los Angeles	Telehouse

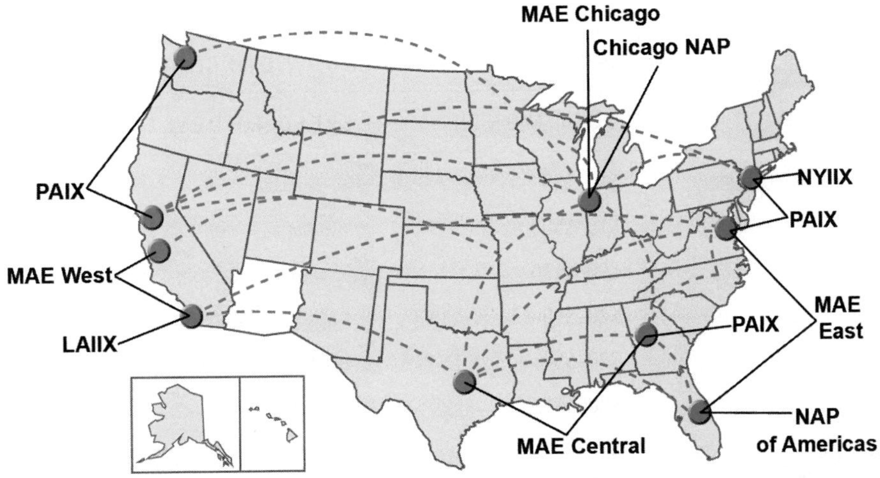

local area network protocol) and have network operating systems such as Windows Server or Linux that permit desktop clients to connect to the Internet through a local Internet server attached to their campus networks. Connection speeds in campus area networks are in the range of 10–100 Mbps to the desktop.

INTERNET SERVICE PROVIDERS

The firms that provide the lowest level of service in the multi-tiered Internet architecture by leasing Internet access to home owners, small businesses, and some large institutions are called **Internet Service Providers (ISPs)**. ISPs are retail providers. They deal with "the last mile of service" to the curb—homes and business offices. ISPs typically connect to IXPs with high-speed telephone or cable lines (45 Mbps and higher).

There are a number of major ISPs, such as AT&T, Comcast (Optimum Online), Cablevision, Cox, Time Warner Cable, Verizon, Sprint, and CenturyLink (formerly Qwest), as well as thousands of local ISPs in the United States, ranging from local telephone companies offering dial-up and DSL telephone access to cable companies offering cable modem service, to small "mom-and-pop" Internet shops that service a small town, city, or even county with mostly dial-up phone access. If you have home or small business Internet access, an ISP likely provides the service to you. Satellite firms also offer Internet access, especially in remote areas where broadband service is not available.

Table 3.5 summarizes the variety of services, speeds, and costs of ISP Internet connections. There are two types of ISP service: narrowband and broadband. **Narrowband** service is the traditional telephone modem connection now operating at 56.6 Kbps (although the actual throughput hovers around 30 Kbps due to line noise that causes extensive resending of packets). This used to be the most common form of connection worldwide but is quickly being replaced by broadband connections in the United States, Europe, and Asia. Broadband service is based on DSL, cable modem, telephone (T1 and T3 lines), and satellite technologies. **Broadband**, in the context of

Internet Service Provider (ISP)

firm that provides the lowest level of service in the multi-tiered Internet architecture by leasing Internet access to home owners, small businesses, and some large institutions

narrowband

the traditional telephone modem connection, now operating at 56.6 Kbps

broadband

refers to any communication technology that permits clients to play streaming audio and video files at acceptable speeds—generally anything above 100 Kbps

TABLE 3.5	ISP SERVICE LEVELS AND BANDWIDTH CHOICES	
SERVICE	COST/MONTH	SPEED TO DESKTOP (KBPS)
Telephone modem	$10–$25	30–56 Kbps
DSL	$15–$50	768 Kbps–7 Mbps
FiOS	$90–$130	15 Mbps–50 Mbps
Cable modem	$20–$50	1 Mbps–20 Mbps
Satellite	$20–$50	768 Kbps–5 Mbps
T1	$300–$1,200	1.54 Mbps
T3	$2,500–$10,000	45 Mbps

Internet service, refers to any communication technology that permits clients to play streaming audio and video files at acceptable speeds—generally anything above 100 Kbps. In the United States, broadband users surpassed dial-up users in 2004, and in 2012, there are an estimated 82 million broadband households (about 70% of all households) (eMarketer, Inc., 2012b).

The actual throughput of data will depend on a variety of factors including noise in the line and the number of subscribers requesting service. Service-level speeds quoted are typically only for downloads of Internet content; upload speeds tend to be much slower. T1 lines are publicly regulated utility lines that offer a guaranteed level of service, but the actual throughput of the other forms of Internet service is not guaranteed.

Digital Subscriber Line (DSL) service is a telephone technology that provides high-speed access to the Internet through ordinary telephone lines found in a home or business. Service levels range from about 768 Kbps up to 7 Mbps. DSL service requires that customers live within two miles (about 4,000 meters) of a neighborhood telephone switching center.

Cable modem refers to a cable television technology that piggybacks digital access to the Internet using the same analog or digital video cable providing television signals to a home. Cable Internet is a major broadband alternative to DSL service, generally providing faster speeds and a "triple play" subscription: telephone, television, and Internet for a single monthly payment. Cable modem services range from 1 Mbps up to 15 Mbps. Comcast, Time Warner Road Runner, Cox and Cablevision are the largest cable Internet providers.

T1 and T3 are international telephone standards for digital communication. **T1** lines offer guaranteed delivery at 1.54 Mbps, while T3 lines offer delivery at a whopping 45 Mbps. T1 lines cost about $300–$1,200 per month, and **T3** lines between $2,500 and $10,000 per month. These are leased, dedicated, guaranteed lines suitable for corporations, government agencies, and businesses such as ISPs requiring high-speed guaranteed service levels.

Satellite companies provide high-speed broadband Internet access, primarily to homes and offices located in rural areas where DSL or cable access is not available. Access speeds and monthly costs are comparable to DSL and cable, but typically require a higher initial payment for installation of a small (18-inch) satellite dish. Satellite providers typically have policies that limit the total megabytes of data that a single account can download within a set period, usually 24 hours. The major satellite providers are HughesNet, WildBlue, and StarBand.

Nearly all large business firms and government agencies have broadband connections to the Internet. Demand for broadband service has grown so rapidly because it greatly speeds up the process of downloading Web pages and increasingly, large video and audio files located on Web pages (see **Table 3.6**). As the quality of Internet service offerings expands to include Hollywood movies, music, games, and other rich media-streaming content, the demand for broadband access will continue to swell. In order to compete with cable companies, telephone companies provide an advanced form of DSL called FiOS (fiber-optic service) that provides up to 50 Mbps speeds for households, which is much faster than cable systems.

Digital Subscriber Line (DSL)
delivers high-speed access through ordinary telephone lines found in homes or businesses

cable modem
piggybacks digital access to the Internet on top of the analog video cable providing television signals to a home

T1
an international telephone standard for digital communication that offers guaranteed delivery at 1.54 Mbps

T3
an international telephone standard for digital communication that offers guaranteed delivery at 45 Mbps

TABLE 3.6	TIME TO DOWNLOAD A 10-MEGABYTE FILE BY TYPE OF INTERNET SERVICE	
TYPE OF INTERNET SERVICE	**TIME TO DOWNLOAD**	
NARROWBAND SERVICES		
Telephone modem	25 minutes	
BROADBAND SERVICES		
DSL @ 1 Mbps	1.33 minutes	
Cable modem @ 10 Mbps	8 seconds	
T1	52 seconds	
T3	2 seconds	

INTRANETS AND EXTRANETS

The very same Internet technologies that make it possible to operate a worldwide public network can also be used by private and government organizations as internal networks. An **intranet** is a TCP/IP network located within a single organization for purposes of communications and information processing. Internet technologies are generally far less expensive than proprietary networks, and there is a global source of new applications that can run on intranets. In fact, all the applications available on the public Internet can be used in private intranets. The largest provider of local area network software is Microsoft, followed by open source Linux, both of which use TCP/IP networking protocols.

Extranets are formed when firms permit outsiders to access their internal TCP/IP networks. For instance, General Motors permits parts suppliers to gain access to GM's intranet that contains GM's production schedules. In this way, parts suppliers know exactly when GM needs parts, and where and when to deliver them. Extranets will receive some attention as a technology that supports certain types of B2B exchanges (described in Chapter 12).

WHO GOVERNS THE INTERNET?

Aficionados and journalists often claim that the Internet is governed by no one, and indeed cannot be governed, and that it is inherently above and beyond the law. What these people forget is that the Internet runs over private and public telecommunications facilities that are themselves governed by laws, and subject to the same pressures as all telecommunications carriers. In fact, the Internet is tied into a complex web of governing bodies, national governments, and international professional societies. There is no one single governing organization that controls activity on the Internet. Instead, there are several organizations that influence the system and monitor its operations. Among the governing bodies of the Internet are:

intranet

a TCP/IP network located within a single organization for purposes of communications and information processing

extranet

formed when firms permit outsiders to access their internal TCP/IP networks

- The *Internet Architecture Board (IAB)*, which helps define the overall structure of the Internet.
- The *Internet Corporation for Assigned Names and Numbers (ICANN)*, which assigns IP addresses and manages the top-level Domain Name System. ICANN was created in 1998 by the U.S. Department of Commerce.
- The *Internet Engineering Steering Group (IESG)*, which oversees the setting of standards with respect to the Internet.
- The *Internet Engineering Task Force (IETF)*, a private-sector group that forecasts the next step in the growth of the Internet, keeping watch over its evolution and operation.
- The *Internet Society (ISOC)*, which is a consortium of corporations, government agencies, and nonprofit organizations that monitors Internet policies and practices.
- The *World Wide Web Consortium (W3C)*, a largely academic group that sets HTML and other programming standards for the Web.
- The *International Telecommunication Union (ITU)*, which helps set technical standards.

While none of these organizations has actual control over the Internet and how it functions, they can and do influence government agencies, major network owners, ISPs, corporations, and software developers with the goal of keeping the Internet operating as efficiently as possible. ICANN comes closest to being a manager of the Internet and reflects the powerful role that the U.S. Department of Commerce has played historically in Internet governance.

In addition to these professional bodies, the Internet must also conform to the laws of the sovereign nation-states in which it operates, as well as the technical infrastructures that exist within each nation-state. Although in the early years of the Internet there was very little legislative or executive interference, this situation is changing as the Internet plays a growing role in the distribution of information and knowledge, including content that some find objectionable.

The U.S. Department of Commerce originally created ICANN with the intent that it take temporary control of the Domain Name System and the 13 root servers that are at the heart of the Internet addressing scheme. Beginning in 2000, ICANN and the Department of Commerce suggested they would turn over control of the DNS to some unspecified international body. However, this is no longer the case. The United States changed its policy in June 2005, when the Department of Commerce announced it would retain oversight over the root servers. There were several reasons for this move, including the use of the Internet for basic communications services by terrorist groups, and the uncertainty that might be caused should an international body take over. In 2008, the Department of Commerce reaffirmed this stance, stating that it "has no plans to transition management of the authoritative root zone file to ICANN" (U.S. Department of Commerce, 2008). At the same time, growing Internet powers China and Russia are lobbying for more functions of the Internet to be brought under the control of the United Nations, raising fears that governance of the Internet could become even more politicized (Pfanner, 2012).

Read *Insight on Society: Government Regulation and Surveillance of the Internet* for a further look at the issue of censorship of Internet content and substance.

3.3	**THE FUTURE INTERNET INFRASTRUCTURE**

The Internet is changing as new technologies appear and new applications are developed. The next era of the Internet is being built today by private corporations, universities, and government agencies. To appreciate the potential benefits of the Internet of the future, you must first understand the limitations of the Internet's current infrastructure.

LIMITATIONS OF THE CURRENT INTERNET

Much of the Internet's current infrastructure is several decades old (equivalent to a century in Internet time). It suffers from a number of limitations, including:

- *Bandwidth limitations.* There is insufficient capacity throughout the backbone, the metropolitan switching centers, and most importantly, the "last mile" to the house and small businesses. The result is slow peak-hour service (congestion) and a limited ability to handle high volumes of video and voice traffic.

- *Quality of service limitations.* Today's information packets take a circuitous route to get to their final destinations. This creates the phenomenon of **latency**—delays in messages caused by the uneven flow of information packets through the network. In the case of e-mail, latency is not noticeable. However, with streaming video and synchronous communication, such as a telephone call, latency is noticeable to the user and perceived as "jerkiness" in movies or delays in voice communication. Today's Internet uses "best-effort" quality of service (QOS), which makes no guarantees about when or whether data will be delivered, and provides each packet with the same level of service, no matter who the user is or what type of data is contained in the packet. A higher level of service quality is required if the Internet is to keep expanding into new services, such as video on demand and telephony.

- *Network architecture limitations.* Today, a thousand requests for a single music track from a central server will result in a thousand efforts by the server to download the music to each requesting client. This slows down network performance as the same music track is sent out a thousand times to clients that might be located in the same metropolitan area. This is very different from television, where the program is broadcast once to millions of homes.

- *Language development limitations.* HTML, the language of Web pages, is fine for text and simple graphics, but poor at defining and communicating "rich documents," such as databases, business documents, or graphics. The tags used to define an HTML page are fixed and generic.

- *Wired Internet.* The Internet is largely based on cables—fiber-optic and coaxial copper cables. Copper cables use a centuries-old technology, and fiber-optic cable is expensive to place underground. The wired nature of the Internet restricts mobility

latency

delays in messages caused by the uneven flow of information packets through the network

INSIGHT ON SOCIETY

GOVERNMENT REGULATION AND SURVEILLANCE OF THE INTERNET

On December 17, 2010, a Tunisian street vendor named Mohamed Bouazizi set himself on fire to protest police confiscation of his wares and long-term harassment and humiliation. Within hours, news of the incident spread throughout Tunisia and the rest of world through Internet services such as Twitter and Facebook, and cell phone networks. Within days, tens of thousands of Tunisians took to the streets in what they called the "Jasmine Revolution." By January, President Ben Ali resigned and fled the country after 23 years in power. In the following weeks and months, the news of the Tunisian uprising spread throughout the Arab world, leading hundreds of thousands of protestors to take on their respective dictatorships in Egypt, Syria, Libya, Bahrain, and Yemen, along with smaller protests in other Arab countries. Called the "Arab Spring," the Internet and cell phone–based message services like Twitter played a critical role in helping young protestors discover one another, organize, and act together.

Events like the Jasmine Revolution and the Arab Spring, along with many earlier incidents, encourage us all to think of the Internet and the Web as an extraordinary technology unleashing torrents of human creativity, innovation, expression, and sometimes, popular rebellion. On a scale much larger than the invention of movable type by Gutenberg in fifteenth century Germany, the Internet allows hundreds of millions of people to e-mail, Facebook, Twitter, and Google (all verbs that are new to our age, the Internet age). How ironic then that the same Internet has spawned an explosion in government control and surveillance of individuals on the Internet! Totalitarian dictators of the twentieth century

would have given their eyeteeth for such a marvelous technology that can track what millions of people do, say, think, and search for in billions of e-mails, searches, blogs, and Facebook posts.

Many people assume that because the Internet is so widely dispersed, it must be difficult to control or monitor. Legions of music and video pirates believe they are anonymous on the Internet and cannot possibly be held accountable for what they do. Unfortunately, with contemporary surveillance technologies, these beliefs are either false or misleading. In reality, just about all governments assert some kind of control and surveillance over Internet content and messages. There's a tug of war going on between sophisticated users of the Internet and state-sponsored censors and security police around the world.

Internet traffic in all countries runs through large fiber-optic trunk lines. In China, there are three such lines, and China requires the companies that own these lines to configure their routers for both internal and external service requests. When a request originates in China for a Web page in Chicago, Chinese routers examine the request to see if the site is on a blacklist, and then examine words in the requested Web page to see if they contain blacklisted terms. Blacklisted terms include "falun" (a suppressed religious group in China) and "Tiananmen Square massacre" (or any symbols that might lead to such results such as "198964" which signifies June 4, 1989, the date of the massacre), among many others. The system is often referred to as "The Great Firewall of China" and is implemented with the assistance of Cisco Systems (the U.S. firm that is the largest manufacturer of routers in the world). Other U.S. Internet firms

(continued)

are also involved in China's censorship and surveillance efforts, including Yahoo, Microsoft, and Juniper Networks, among many others.

When U.S. search engines (Microsoft, Google, and Yahoo) moved into China in 2002, the firms agreed to censor the search results of Chinese citizens according to criteria dictated by China's Internet agency in return for access to the China market. For instance, in 2002, the Chinese government summarily shut off access from inside China to Google's offshore servers in Hong Kong, which did not exercise self-censorship. Even before this action, Google's results were often slowed by the Great Firewall. After this incident, Google decided in 2006 to locate its servers on Chinese soil (Google.cn), where they became directly subject to China's censorship regime, which bans from the Internet anything that damages the honor or interests of the state, disturbs the public order, or infringes upon national customs and habits.

Flash forward to January 2010: Google announced it was leaving China after a massive cyber assault was launched from Taiwan but that was allegedly instigated by the Chinese government in an effort to steal user information (such as what Chinese citizens were searching for). Thirty-four other U.S. companies were targeted, all high-tech Internet-related concerns. Google claimed it could no longer abide by China's growing demands for censorship and surveillance although the attack was also a direct threat to Google's business algorithms and proprietary technology. In other words, this attack was aimed at Google's jugular. Google began automatically redirecting all Chinese mainland traffic to its uncensored Hong Kong servers. The Chinese government objected. Google, in a minor compromise, stopped the automatic redirect and instead put a button on the screen that users could click to search the Hong Kong site, otherwise they would default to the censored Chinese site. The Chinese government objected again and threatened to withdraw Google's license to operate in China. In March 2011, Google accused the Chinese government of disrupting Gmail service inside China and making it appear like a technical problem with Google. And as the Arab Spring spread throughout the Middle East and Africa, China strengthened its efforts to censor the Internet. The word "freedom" is now censored on Chinese search engines, along with "Jasmine" and "Arab Spring."

China is hardly the only government that exercises powerful controls over its citizens' use of the Internet. In June 2009, the video of Neda Agha-Soltan, who had been shot by a squad of Iranian riot police and was bleeding to death on the streets of Tehran, quickly raced around the world via the Internet and cell phone networks despite the efforts of the Iranian government, which had completely shut down text messaging in the country; blocked access to selected sites such as YouTube, MySpace, and Facebook; and slowed all Internet traffic in Iran by 90% so it could sift through e-mail messages. In the protests that followed the disputed Iranian election of June 2009, Twitter became the primary organizing tool of the protestors, and an important source of information for the rest of the world, along with YouTube and other social sites to which protestors were able to connect, despite the best efforts of Iranian government censors.

Iran's Internet surveillance of its citizens is considered by security experts to be one of the world's most sophisticated mechanisms for controlling and censoring the Internet, allowing it to examine the content of individual online communications on a massive scale, far more sophisticated than even China's Internet surveillance activities. The Iranian system

(continued)

goes far beyond preventing access to specific sites such as BBC World News, Google, and Facebook. Because the techniques for getting around government site access censorship are widely known (generally find a proxy server in another country that will allow you access to a forbidden site), governments need to do much more to control access and to figure out what their citizens are really thinking. One technique is deep packet inspection of every e-mail, text, or Twitter tweet. Deep packet inspection allows governments to read messages, alter their contents for disinformation purposes, and identify senders and recipients. It is accomplished by installing computers in the line between users and ISPs, opening up every digitized packet, inspecting for keywords and images, reconstructing the message, and sending it on. This is done for all Internet traffic including Skype, Facebook, e-mail, tweets, and messages sent to proxy servers. These operations can slow down Internet service, but this delay can be avoided by installing additional servers. Iran's Internet Monitoring Center is located in the government telecommunications monopoly, a central choke point for all Internet traffic in the country. Iran has some of the world's finest deep packet monitoring equipment supplied by a joint venture called Nokia Siemens Networks. There are, of course, reasons why Iran's government did not simply shut down the Internet entirely. Some traffic is required for business purposes, and keeping the Internet functioning allows the state to identify its enemies and critics.

Not to be outdone, both Europe and the United States have at various times taken steps to control access to Internet sites, censor Web content, and engage in extensive surveillance of communications, although not to the extent of Iran, China, and many other nations. For instance, Britain has a list of blocked sites, as does Germany and France. A proposed

Communications Data Bill in Great Britain would allow bulk, warrantless, surveillance of all Internet traffic by government agencies in the United Kingdom. A similar law has also been proposed in Australia, although it remains tabled pending the next election there. The Australian Communications and Media Authority has developed a list of several hundred Web sites that have been refused registration in Australia, mostly violent video game and online pornography sites. The United States and European countries generally ban the sale, distribution, and/or possession of online child pornography. Both France and Germany bar online Nazi memorabilia. Even in South Korea, one of the world's most wired countries, reports have surfaced that the government is monitoring its citizens' Internet usage and cracking down on freedoms.

In response to terrorism threats and other crimes, European governments and the U.S. government have also initiated deep packet inspection of e-mail and text communications. This surveillance is not limited to cross-border international data flows and includes large-scale domestic surveillance and analysis of "ordinary" e-mail, tweets, and other messages. For instance, the FBI has recently created a secret Internet surveillance unit, the Domestic Communications Assistance Center, in a collaborative effort with the U.S. Marshals Service and the Drug Enforcement Agency. The DCAC's mission is to assist in the development of new surveillance technologies that will allow authorities to increase the interception of Internet, wireless, and VoIP communications. Although it may seem preposterous that any U.S. government agency could read an estimated 150 billion daily e-mails, this task is, in reality, only slightly more complicated than Google's handling of 10 to 12 billion search queries per month. Governments and private technology companies are partnering

(continued)

to use software to analyze millions of e-mails, tweets, and other messages in an effort to preemptively fight terror and stop other crimes. Governments and telecommunications companies are also increasingly working together to monitor Internet users. While the Internet has unleashed an explosion of expression, and even enabled several rebellions and revolutions around the world, at the same time it has become a testing and proving ground for new government surveillance capabilities for both democratic and totalitarian regimes.

SOURCES: "Sir Tim Berners-Lee Accuses Government of 'Draconian' Internet Snooping," by Lucy Kinder, *The Telegraph*, September 6, 2012; "Korea Policing the Net. Twist? It's South Korea," by Choe Sang-Hun, *New York Times*, August 12, 2012; "How Governments and Telecom Companies Work Together on Surveillance Laws," by Ryan Gallagher, Slate.com, August 14, 2012; "Internet Surveillance Put Off Until After the Election," by Philip Dorling, *The Sydney Morning Herald*, August 10, 2012; "FBI Quietly Forms Secret Net-Surveillance Unit," by Declan McCullagh, News.Cnet.com, May 22, 2012; "Catching Scent of Revolution, China Moves to Snip Jasmine," by Andrew Jacobs and Jonathon Ansfield, *New York Times*, May 10, 2011; "Google Accuses Chines of Blocking Gmail Service," by David Barboza and Claire Cain Miller, *New York Times*, March 20, 2011; "Bullets Stall Youthful Push for Arab Spring," by Michael Slackman, *New York Times*, March 17, 2011; "OpenNet Initiative Releases 2010 Year in Review," Berkman Center for Internet and Society, Harvard University, March 22, 2011; "Google Co-founder Sergey Brin Urges US to Act Over China Web Censorship," by Bobbie Johnson, TheGuardian.co.uk, May 10, 2010; "Journalists' E-mails Hacked in China," by Andrew Jacobs, *New York Times,* March 31, 2010; "Enemies of the Internet. Countries Under Surveillance," Reporters Without Borders, www.rsf.org, March 12, 2010; "Google Hack Smells More and More Like Chinese Government Job," by Katherine Noyes, Technewsworld.com, February 22, 2010; "Google Warns of China Exit Over Hacking," by Jessica Vascellaro, *Wall Street Journal*, January 13, 2010; "Foreign Intelligence Surveillance Act (FISA)," *New York Times*, July 23, 2009.

of users although it is changing rapidly as Wi-Fi hotspots proliferate, and cellular phone technology advances. However, cellular systems are often overloaded due to the growth in the number of smartphones.

Now imagine an Internet at least 1,000 times as powerful as today's Internet, one that is not subjected to the limitations of bandwidth, protocols, architecture, physical connections, and language detailed previously. Welcome to the world of the future Internet, and the next generation of e-commerce services and products!

THE INTERNET2® PROJECT

Internet2®
advanced networking consortium of more than 350 member institutions working in partnership to facilitate the development, deployment, and use of revolutionary Internet technologies

Internet2® is an advanced networking consortium of more than 350 member institutions including universities, corporations, government research agencies, and not-for-profit networking organizations, all working in partnership to facilitate the development, deployment, and use of revolutionary Internet technologies.[5] The broader Internet2 community includes more than 66,000 institutions across the United States and international networking partners in more than 50 countries. Internet2's work is a continuation of the kind of cooperation among government, private, and educational organizations that created the original Internet.

The advanced networks created and in use by Internet2 members provide an environment in which new technologies can be tested and enhanced. For instance, Internet2 provides a next-generation, nationwide 100 gigabit-per-second network that not only makes available a reliable production services platform for current high-performance needs but also creates a powerful experimental platform for the development of new network capabilities. The fourth generation of this network, built through

[5] The Internet2® project is just one aspect of the larger second-generation Internet we call Internet II.

a federal stimulus grant from the National Telecommunications and Information Administration's Broadband Technology Opportunities Program, began to be deployed in 2011 (see **Figure 3.14**). The hybrid optical and packet network provides 8.8 terabits of capacity with the ability to seamlessly scale as requirements grow, includes over 15,000 miles of owned fiber optic cable, and will reach into underserved areas of the country, supporting connectivity for approximately 200,000 U.S. community anchor institutions (schools, local libraries, and museums), and enabling them to provide citizens across the country with telemedicine, distance learning, and other advanced applications not possible with consumer-grade Internet services. The infrastructure will support a wide range of IP and optical services already available today and also stimulate a new generation of innovative services. The goal is to create an intelligent global ecosystem that will enable researchers, scientists, and others to "turn on" high-capacity network connections whenever and wherever they are needed. Other initiatives involve science and engineering (advanced network applications in support of distributed lab environments, remote access to rare scientific instruments, and distributed large scale computation and data access), health sciences and health networks (telemedicine, medical and biological research, and health education and awareness), and arts and humanities (collaborative live performances, master classes, remote auditions, and interactive performing arts education and media events).

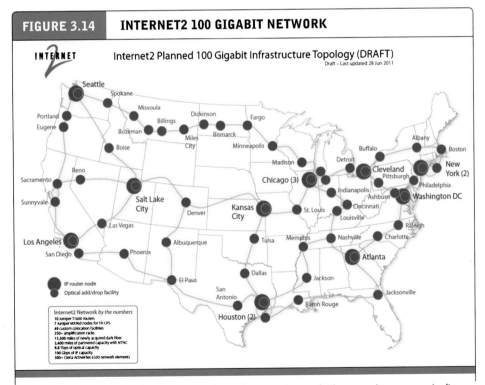

| FIGURE 3.14 | **INTERNET2 100 GIGABIT NETWORK** |

Internet2 is in the process of deploying a 100 gigabit-per-second network. The network represents the first national implementation of 100 gigabit Ethernet capabilities across the entire network.

SOURCE: Internet2.edu, 2011.

THE FIRST MILE AND THE LAST MILE

The Internet2 project is just the tip of the iceberg when it comes to future enhancements to the Internet. In 2007, the NSF began work on the Global Environment for Network Innovations (GENI) initiative. GENI is a unique virtual laboratory for exploring future internets at scale. GENI aims to promote innovations in network science, security technologies, services, and applications. GENI is a partnership of leading academic centers and private corporations such as Cisco, IBM, and HP, among many others. To date, awards have been made to 83 academic/industry teams for various projects to build, integrate, and operate early prototypes of the GENI virtual laboratory (Geni.net, 2012). In June 2012, the NSF announced that it would be building on the GENI project as part of US Ignite, a White House initiative aimed at realizing the potential of fast, open, next-generation networks. GENI will underly US Ignite and provide a virtual laboratory for experiments that the NSF hopes will transform cybersecurity, network performance, and cloud computing research (National Research Foundation, 2012).

The most significant privately initiated (but often government-influenced) changes are coming in two areas: fiber-optic trunk line bandwidth and wireless Internet services. Fiber optics is concerned with the first mile or backbone Internet services that carry bulk traffic long distances. Wireless Internet is concerned with the last mile—from the larger Internet to the user's smartphone, tablet computer, or laptop.

Fiber Optics and the Bandwidth Explosion in the First Mile

fiber-optic cable

consists of up to hundreds of strands of glass or plastic that use light to transmit data

Fiber-optic cable consists of up to hundreds of strands of glass that use light to transmit data. It often replaces existing coaxial and twisted pair cabling because it can transmit much more data at faster speeds, with less interference and better data security. Fiber-optic cable is also thinner and lighter, taking up less space during installation. The hope is to use fiber optics to expand network bandwidth capacity in order to prepare for the expected increases in Web traffic once Internet II services are widely adopted.

During the early years of e-commerce, there was an enormous increase in long-haul backbone capacity. By 2001, more than $90 billion of fiber-optic cable had been installed throughout the United States. Then, demand declined, due in part to the continued technical improvement in switching equipment, which allows firms to achieve exponentially higher throughput from the existing fiber-optic cables by improvements in processors and techniques. As a result, the cost of using fiber optic cable has fallen significantly. Currently, thousands of miles of fiber-optic cable in the United States are still "dark" or "unlit." The Federal Communications Commission has encouraged the utilization of this dark fiber by allowing schools and libraries to use federal technology funds to obtain access to these unused lines, as part of the Obama administration's drive to implement a national broadband plan.

In addition, the existing installed base of fiber optic cable represents a vast digital highway that is currently being exploited by YouTube (Google), Facebook, and other high-bandwidth applications. Telecommunications companies are recapitalizing and building new business models based on market prices for digital traffic. The net result is that society ultimately benefited from extraordinarily low-cost, long-haul, very high-bandwidth communication facilities that are already paid for.

Demand for fiber-optic cable has begun to strengthen as consumers demand integrated telephone, broadband access, and video from a single source. In 2011, around 19 million miles of optical fiber were installed in the United States, the most since 2000. In some cases it is location, rather than a need for capacity, that is driving new demand (Troianovski, 2012). Interactive online television, online movies, inexpensive Voice over Internet Protocol (VoIP) telephone, and Internet access all from the same company that provides a single cable into the home is the vision driving Verizon, other local Bells, and cable firms. In 2004, Verizon began building its FiOS fiber-optic Internet service, network infrastructure, and since then, it has spent $23 billion expanding the service. In 2012, there are about 5 million Verizon FiOS broadband customers. FiOS provides download speeds of up to 50 Mbps and upload speeds of up to 10 Mbps. **Table 3.7** illustrates several optical bandwidth standards and compares them to traditional T lines.

Figure 3.15 gives a comparative look at bandwidth demand for various applications.

The Last Mile: Mobile Internet Access

Fiber-optic networks carry the long-haul bulk traffic of the Internet—and in the future will play an important role in bringing BigBand to the household and small business. The goal of the Internet2 and GENI projects is to bring gigabit and ultimately terabit bandwidth to the household over the next 20 years. But along with fiber optics, arguably the most significant development for the Internet and Web in the last five years has been the emergence of mobile Internet access.

Wireless Internet is concerned with the last mile of Internet access to the user's home, office, car, smartphone, or tablet computer, anywhere they are located. Up until 2000, the last-mile access to the Internet—with the exception of a small satellite Internet connect population—was bound up in land lines of some sort: copper coaxial TV cables or telephone lines or, in some cases, fiber-optic lines to the office. Today, in comparison, high-speed cell phone networks and Wi-Fi network hotspots provide a major alternative.

TABLE 3.7	HIGH-SPEED OPTICAL BANDWIDTH STANDARDS
STANDARD	**SPEED**
T1	1.544 Mbps
T3	43.232 Mbps
OC-3	155 Mbps
OC-12	622 Mbps
OC-48	2.5 Gbps
OC-192	9.6 Gbps

Note: "OC" stands for Optical Carrier and is used to specify the speed of fiber-optic networks conforming to the SONET standard. SONET (Synchronous Optical Networks) includes a set of signal rate multiples for transmitting digital signals on optical fiber. The base rate (OC-1) is 51.84 Mbps.

FIGURE 3.15	BANDWIDTH DEMAND OF VARIOUS WEB APPLICATIONS

Narrowband	**Broadband**	**BigBand**	
Peripheral sharing	Video conferencing	TV, HDTV	
	Multimedia distance learning	Interactive TV	
		Hollywood on the Web	
Telemetry	File transfer	Extensive cloud services	
Radio e-mail	VoIP	Medical images	
	CD transfer rates	Remote labs	
Wireless alarms, pagers, text, e-mail	Simulations	Multi-person video conferencing	
	High-definition graphics		
	Cloud services possible		

1 Kbps	1 Mbps	1 Gbps	1 Tbps

Protocol: Modem vbis90 56.6Kbps Ethernet 10Mbps FDDI/SONET 100Mbps ATM

Media: Cellular/WAP   Twisted Pair   DSL   Coax Cable   Fiber Cable   OC-68

The really exciting e-commerce applications such as high definition television (HDTV) and interactive TV and movies require higher levels of bandwidth to the home than are typically currently available in the United States.

In 2012, more tablet and laptop computers with wireless networking functionality built in are expected to be sold in the United States than desktop computers. And more smartphones will be sold than PCs of any kind in 2012. Smartphones are the fastest growing mobile devices with respect to Internet access. Clearly, a large part of the future Internet will be mobile, access-anywhere broadband service for the delivery of video, music, and Web search. According to eMarketer, there are already 122 million mobile Internet users in the United States in 2012, and more than 1.4 billion worldwide (eMarketer, Inc., 2012c).

Telephone-based versus Computer Network-based Wireless Internet Access There are two different basic types of wireless Internet connectivity: telephone-based and computer network-based systems.

Telephone-based wireless Internet access connects the user to a global telephone system (land, satellite, and microwave) that has a long history of dealing with thousands of users simultaneously and already has in place a large-scale transaction billing system and related infrastructure. Cellular telephones and the telephone industry are currently the largest providers of wireless access to the Internet today. In 2011, there were more than 1.5 billion mobile phones sold worldwide, with a similar amount expected to be sold in 2012. The percentage of smartphones sold (about 44%) is continuing to climb (International Data Corporation, 2012).

In the United States, there are two basic types of cellular networks—those based on Global System for Mobile Communications (GSM) standards (used worldwide and in the United States by AT&T and T-Mobile) and those based on Code Division Multiple

Access (CDMA, used primarily in the United States by Verizon and Sprint). In 2012, 4G networks using a technology known as Long-Term Evolution (LTE) (adopted by both AT&T and Verizon) can deliver downloads at up to 100 Mbps, with the potential to provide up to 50 Mbps upload speeds. **Table 3.8** summarizes the various telephone technologies used for wireless Internet access.

Smartphones, such as an iPhone, Android, or BlackBerry, combine the functionality of a cell phone with that of a laptop computer with Wi-Fi capability. This makes it possible to combine in one device music, video, Web access, and telephone service.

Once a connection is established with a user's smartphone, there are a number of different ways to deliver Web pages. The iPhone and Android phones have such high resolution and large screens that Web pages are delivered as ordinary HTML pages and the user can scroll around the page to navigate. Ordinary cell phones with less capable screens either use Wireless Application Protocol (WAP) or i-mode, a proprietary standard owned by the Japanese company NTT DoCoMo.

Wireless local area network (WLAN)-based Internet access derives from a completely different background from telephone-based wireless Internet access. Popularly known as **Wi-Fi**, WLANs are based on computer local area networks where the task is to connect client computers (generally stationary) to server computers within local areas of, say, a few hundred meters. WLANs function by sending radio signals that are broadcast over the airwaves using certain radio frequency ranges (2.4 GHz to 5.875 GHz, depending on the type of standard involved). The major technologies here are

Wi-Fi
Wireless standard for Ethernet networks with greater speed and range than Bluetooth

TABLE 3.8	WIRELESS INTERNET ACCESS TELEPHONE TECHNOLOGIES		
TECHNOLOGY	SPEED	DESCRIPTION	PLAYERS
3G (THIRD GENERATION)			
CDMA2000 EV-DO HSPA (W-CDMA)	144 Kbps–2 Mbps	High-speed, mobile, always on for e-mail, browsing, instant messaging. Implementing technologies include versions of CDMA2000 EV-DO (used by CDMA providers) and HSPDA (used by GSM providers). Nearly as fast as Wi-Fi.	Verizon, Sprint, AT&T, T-Mobile, Vodafone
3.5G (3G+)			
CDMA2000 EV-DO, Rev.B	Up to 14.4 Mbps	Enhanced version of CDMA 2000 EV-DO.	Verizon, Sprint
HSPA+	Up to 11 Mbps	Enhanced version of HSPA.	AT&T, T-Mobile
4G (FOURTH GENERATION)			
Long-Term Evolution (LTE)	Up to 100 Mbps	True broadband on cell phone.	AT&T, Verizon, Sprint, T-Mobile (in 2013)

the various versions of the Wi-Fi standard and Bluetooth. Other WLAN technologies include WiMax, Ultra-Wideband (UWB), and ZigBee (see **Table 3.9**).

In a Wi-Fi network, a *wireless access point* (also known as a "hot spot") connects to the Internet directly via a broadband connection (cable, DSL telephone, or T1 line) and then transmits a radio signal to a transmitter/receiver installed in a laptop computer or PDA, either as a PC card or built-in at manufacture (such as Intel's Centrino processor, which provides built-in support for Wi-Fi in portable devices). **Figure 3.16** illustrates how a Wi-Fi network works.

Wi-Fi offers high-bandwidth capacity from 11 Mbps to 70 Mbps—far greater than any 3G or 4G service currently in existence—but has a limited range of 300 meters, with the exception of WiMax discussed below. Wi-Fi is also exceptionally inexpensive. The cost of creating a corporate Wi-Fi network in a single 14-story building with an access point for each floor is less than $100 an access point. It would cost well over $500,000 to wire the same building with Ethernet cable. Admittedly, the Ethernet cable would be operating at a theoretical 100 Mbps—10 times as fast as Wi-Fi. However, in some cases, this capacity is not needed and Wi-Fi is an acceptable alternative.

TABLE 3.9	WIRELESS INTERNET ACCESS NETWORK TECHNOLOGIES		
TECHNOLOGY	RANGE/ SPEED	DESCRIPTION	PLAYERS
Wi-Fi (IEEE 802.11 a/b/g/n)	300 feet/ 11–70 Mbps	Evolving high-speed, fixed broadband wireless local area network for commercial and residential use	Linksys, Cisco, and other Wi-Fi router manufacturers; entrepreneurial network developers
WiMax (IEEE 802.16)	30 miles/ 50–70 Mbps	High-speed, medium-range, broadband wireless metropolitan area network	Clearwire, Sprint, Fujitsu, Intel, Alcatel, Proxim
Bluetooth (wireless personal area network)	1–30 meters/ 1–3 Mbps	Modest-speed, low-power, short-range connection of digital devices	Sony Ericsson, Nokia, Apple, HP, and other device makers
Ultra-Wideband (UWB) (wireless personal area network)	30 feet/ 5–10 Mbps	Low-power, short-range, high-bandwidth network technology useful as cabling replacement in home and office networks	Intel, Freescale
ZigBee (wireless personal area network)	30 feet/ 250 Kbps	Short-range, very low-power, wireless network technology useful for remotely controlling industrial, medical, and home automation devices	ZigBee Alliance, Texas Instruments Norway AS, Freescale, Mitsubishi, Motorola, Digi, San Juan Software

| **FIGURE 3.16** | **WI-FI NETWORKS** |

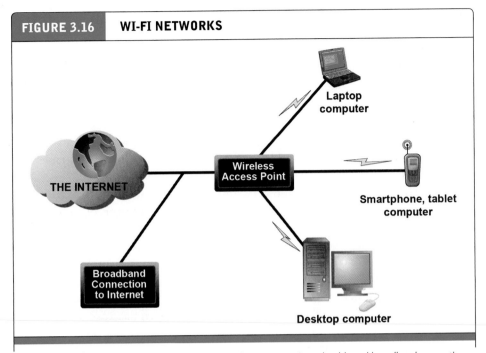

In a Wi-Fi network, wireless access points connect to the Internet using a land-based broadband connection. Clients, which could be laptops, desktops, or tablet computers, connect to the access point using radio signals.

While initially a grass roots, "hippies and hackers" public access technology, billions of dollars have subsequently been poured into private ventures seeking to create for-profit Wi-Fi networks. The most prominent network has been created by Boingo Wireless with more than 500,000 hot spots around the globe. AT&T Wi-Fi Services (formerly Wayport) created another large network that provides Wi-Fi service at hotels, airports, McDonald's, and IHOP restaurants, and Hertz airport rental offices, with around 30,000 hot spots in the United States. T-Mobile and Sprint have also established nationwide Wi-Fi services at 2,000 Starbucks coffee shops and thousands of other public locations. Apple, in turn, has made Wi-Fi automatically available to iPhone and iPad devices as an alternative to the more expensive and much slower 3G and 4G cellular systems.

Will WLAN compete directly against far more expensive telephone 4G services? The answer is "eventually, but not right now." Wi-Fi was originally a local area network technology of limited range, for stationary client computers, but with high capacity suitable for most Web surfing and some corporate uses with modest bandwidth demands. Cellular phone systems are wide area networks of nearly unlimited range, for mobile client computers and handhelds, and with modest but rapidly increasing capacity suitable for e-mail, photos, and Web browsing (on very small screens). However, the rock-bottom price of Wi-Fi coupled with ambitious plans for a 30-mile-range WiMax (802.16) service suggests that Wi-Fi could drain significant business from far more capital-intensive cellular systems.

Bluetooth

technology standard for short-range wireless communication under 30 feet

A second WLAN technology for connecting to the Internet, and for connecting Internet devices to one another, is called Bluetooth. **Bluetooth** is a personal connectivity technology that enables links between mobile computers, mobile phones, PDAs, and connectivity to the Internet (Bluetooth.com, 2012). Bluetooth is the universal cable cutter, promising to get rid of the tangled mess of wires, cradles, and special attachments that plague the current world of personal computing. With Bluetooth, users can wear a cell phone wireless earbud, share files in a hallway or conference room, synchronize their smartphone with their laptop without a cable, send a document to a printer, and even pay a restaurant bill from the table to a Bluetooth-equipped cash register. Bluetooth is also an unregulated media operating in the 2.4 GHz spectrum but with a very limited range of 30 feet or less. It uses a frequency hopping signal with up to 1,600 hops per second over 79 frequencies, giving it good protection from interference and interception. Bluetooth-equipped devices—which could be cell phones or laptops—constantly scan their environments looking for connections to compatible devices. Today, almost all cell phones and mobile devices are Bluetooth-enabled.

Table 3.10 summarizes some of the e-commerce services that are supported by wireless Internet access. Some of these services are *push services*—the transmission of data at a predetermined time, or under determined conditions. This could include unsolicited information such as news delivery or stock market values. Other services are *pull services*—transmission of data resulting from user requests. Geographical information services—advertising for local pizza shops, restaurants, and museums—are a major growth area for cell phone services in part due to the Wireless Communications and Public Safety Act of 1999, which required all cell phone carriers in the United States to feature E911 technology. E911 (Enhanced 911) service allows a person's cell phone to be located at a physical address when that person calls the 911 emergency number used throughout the United States. This requires all cell phones to be equipped with GPS receivers, which provide a fairly precise latitude and longitude location. In fact, all cell phone carriers can identify the GPS location of a cell phone regardless of what number is called. This enhanced geographic locating capability can easily be used to send locally based advertising to cell phone users either over the Web or using the cellular network itself.

THE FUTURE INTERNET

The increased bandwidth and expanded wireless network connectivity of the Internet of the future will result in benefits beyond faster access and richer communications. First-mile enhancements created by fiber-optic networks will enhance reliability and quality of Internet transmissions and create new business models and opportunities. Some of the major benefits of these technological advancements include latency solutions, guaranteed service levels, lower error rates, and declining costs. Widespread wireless access to the Internet will also essentially double or even triple the size of the online shopping marketspace because consumers will be able to shop and make purchases just about anywhere. This is equivalent to doubling the physical floor space of all shopping malls in America. We describe some of these benefits in more detail in the following sections.

TABLE 3.10	WIRELESS INTERNET E-COMMERCE SERVICES
SERVICE	DESCRIPTION
Horizontal Market Services	**Services that apply across industries and firms**
Personalized information	Stock values, news, and quotes based on user profiles and needs
Location-based local content	Local maps, hotel finders, movie locations and times, and restaurant locations and reviews
Media services	Videos, movies, photos, news, and music
Banking services	Balance checking, money transfer, bill payment, and overdraft alerts
Financial services	Trading, stock alerts, and interest rates based on user account information
Vertical Market Services	**Services that apply within a firm or industry**
Sales support	Stock and production information, remote orders, calendars, and planning information
Reservation systems	Airline, train, hotel, and event reservations coordinated with inventory
Dispatching	Communication of job details, parts information, and repair routines
Fleet management	Control of fleet delivery or service staff; monitoring locations and work schedules
Parcel delivery	Tracking of packages, queries, and performance monitoring
Home automation	Coordinating alarm and other digital services and devices in a home
Industrial automation	Coordinating machine controllers in a factory

Latency Solutions

One of the challenges of packet switching, where data is divided into chunks and then sent separately to meet again at the destination, is that the Internet does not differentiate between high-priority packets, such as video clips, and those of lower priority, such as self-contained e-mail messages. Because the packets cannot yet be simultaneously reassembled, the result can be distorted audio and video streams.

Differentiated quality of service (**diffserv**) is a technology that assigns levels of priority to packets based on the type of data being transmitted. Video conference packets, for example, which need to reach their destination almost instantaneously, receive much higher priority than e-mail messages. In the end, the quality of video and audio will skyrocket without undue stress on the network. Differential service is very controversial because it means some users may get more bandwidth than others, and potentially they may have to pay a higher price for more bandwidth.

differentiated quality of service (diffserv)
a new technology that assigns levels of priority to packets based on the type of data being transmitted

Guaranteed Service Levels and Lower Error Rates

In today's Internet, there is no service-level guarantee and no way to purchase the right to move data through the Internet at a fixed pace. Today's Internet promises only "best effort." The Internet is democratic—it speeds or slows everyone's traffic alike. In the future, it will be possible to purchase the right to move data through the network at a guaranteed speed in return for higher fees.

Declining Costs

As the Internet pipeline is upgraded, the availability of broadband service will expand beyond major metropolitan areas, significantly reducing the cost of access. More users means lower cost, as products and technology catch on in the mass market. Higher volume usage enables providers to lower the cost of both access devices, or clients, and the service required to use such products. Both broadband and wireless service fees are expected to decline as geographic service areas increase, in part due to competition for that business.

The Internet of Things

Internet of Things (IoT)

Use of the Internet to connect a wide variety of devices, machines, and sensors

No discussion of the future Internet would be complete without mentioning the **Internet of Things (IoT)**, also sometimes referred to as the Industrial Internet. Internet technology is spreading beyond the desktop, laptop, and tablet computer, and beyond the smartphone, to consumer electronics, electrical appliances, cars, medical devices, utility systems, machines of all types, even clothing – just about anything that can be equipped with sensors that collect data and connect to the Internet, enabling the data to be analyzed with data analytics software. The Internet of Things builds on a foundation of existing technologies, such as RFID, and is being enabled by the availability of low cost sensors, the drop in price of data storage, the development of "Big Data" analytics software that can work with trillions of pieces of data, as well implementation of IPV6, which will allow Internet addresses to be assigned to all of these new devices. Funding and research for the Internet of Things is being spear-headed by the European Union and China (where it is known as the Sensing Planet), and in the United States by companies such as IBM's Smarter Planet initiative. Although challenges remain before the Internet of Things is fully realized, it is coming closer and closer to fruition.

3.4 THE WEB

Without the Web, there would be no e-commerce. The invention of the Web brought an extraordinary expansion of digital services to millions of amateur computer users, including color text and pages, formatted text, pictures, animations, video, and sound. In short, the Web makes nearly all the rich elements of human expression needed to establish a commercial marketplace available to nontechnical computer users worldwide.

While the Internet was born in the 1960s, the Web was not invented until 1989–1991 by Dr. Tim Berners-Lee of the European Particle Physics Laboratory, better known as CERN (Berners-Lee et al., 1994). Several earlier authors—such as Vannevar Bush (in 1945) and Ted Nelson (in the 1960s)—had suggested the possibility of organizing knowledge as a set of interconnected pages that users could freely browse (Bush, 1945; Ziff Davis Publishing, 1998). Berners-Lee and his associates at CERN built on these ideas and developed the initial versions of HTML, HTTP, a Web server, and a browser, the four essential components of the Web.

First, Berners-Lee wrote a computer program that allowed formatted pages within his own computer to be linked using keywords (hyperlinks). Clicking on a keyword in a document would immediately move him to another document. Berners-Lee created the pages using a modified version of a powerful text markup language called Standard Generalized Markup Language (SGML).

Berners-Lee called this language HyperText Markup Language, or HTML. He then came up with the idea of storing his HTML pages on the Internet. Remote client computers could access these pages by using HTTP (introduced earlier in Section 3.1 and described more fully in the next section). But these early Web pages still appeared as black and white text pages with hyperlinks expressed inside brackets. The early Web was based on text only; the original Web browser only provided a line interface.

Information being shared on the Web remained text-based until 1993, when Marc Andreessen and others at the National Center for Supercomputing Applications (NCSA) at the University of Illinois created a Web browser with a graphical user interface (GUI) called **Mosaic** that made it possible to view documents on the Web graphically—using colored backgrounds, images, and even primitive animations. Mosaic was a software program that could run on any graphically based interface such as Macintosh, Windows, or Unix. The Mosaic browser software read the HTML text on a Web page and displayed it as a graphical interface document within a GUI operating system such as Windows or Macintosh. Liberated from simple black and white text pages, HTML pages could now be viewed by anyone in the world who could operate a mouse and use a Macintosh or PC.

Mosaic
Web browser with a graphical user interface (GUI) that made it possible to view documents on the Web graphically

Aside from making the content of Web pages colorful and available to the world's population, the graphical Web browser created the possibility of **universal computing**, the sharing of files, information, graphics, sound, video, and other objects across all computer platforms in the world, regardless of operating system. A browser could be made for each of the major operating systems, and the Web pages created for one system, say, Windows, would also be displayed exactly the same, or nearly the same, on computers running the Macintosh or Unix operating systems. As long as each operating system had a Mosaic browser, the same Web pages could be used on all the different types of computers and operating systems. This meant that no matter what kind of computer you used, anywhere in the world, you would see the same Web pages. The browser and the Web have introduced us to a whole new world of computing and information management that was unthinkable prior to 1993.

universal computing
the sharing of files, information, graphics, sound, video, and other objects across all computer platforms in the world, regardless of operating system

Netscape Navigator

the first commercial Web browser

Internet Explorer

Microsoft's Web browser

In 1994, Andreessen and Jim Clark founded Netscape, which created the first commercial browser, **Netscape Navigator**. Although Mosaic had been distributed free of charge, Netscape initially charged for its software. In August 1995, Microsoft Corporation released its own free version of a browser, called **Internet Explorer**. In the ensuing years, Netscape fell from a 100% market share to less than .5% in 2009. The fate of Netscape illustrates an important e-commerce business lesson. Innovators usually are not long-term winners, whereas smart followers often have the assets needed for long-term survival. Much of the Netscape browser code survives today in the Firefox browser produced by Mozilla, a non-profit heavily funded by Google.

HYPERTEXT

hypertext

a way of formatting pages with embedded links that connect documents to one another, and that also link pages to other objects such as sound, video, or animation files

Web pages can be accessed through the Internet because the Web browser software on your PC can request Web pages stored on an Internet host server using the HTTP protocol. **Hypertext** is a way of formatting pages with embedded links that connect documents to one another and that also link pages to other objects such as sound, video, or animation files. When you click on a graphic and a video clip plays, you have clicked on a hyperlink. For example, when you type a Web address in your browser such as http://www.sec.gov, your browser sends an HTTP request to the sec.gov server requesting the home page of sec.gov.

HTTP is the first set of letters at the start of every Web address, followed by the domain name. The domain name specifies the organization's server computer that is housing the document. Most companies have a domain name that is the same as or closely related to their official corporate name. The directory path and document name are two more pieces of information within the Web address that help the browser track down the requested page. Together, the address is called a Uniform Resource Locator, or URL. When typed into a browser, a URL tells it exactly where to look for the information. For example, in the following URL:

http://www.megacorp.com/content/features/082602.html

http = the protocol used to display Web pages

www.megacorp.com = domain name

content/features = the directory path that identifies where on the domain Web server the page is stored

082602.html = the document name and its format (an HTML page)

The most common domain extensions (known as general top-level domains, or gTLDs) currently available and officially sanctioned by ICANN are shown in **Table 3.11**. Countries also have domain names, such as .uk, .au, and .fr (United Kingdom, Australia, and France, respectively). These are sometimes referred to as country-code top-level domains, or ccTLDs. In 2008, ICANN approved a significant expansion of gTLDs, with potential new domains representing cities (such as .berlin), regions (.africa), ethnicity (.eus), industry/activities (such as .health), and even brands (such

TABLE 3.11	TOP-LEVEL DOMAINS		
GENERAL TOP-LEVEL DOMAIN (GTLD)	YEAR(S) INTRODUCED	PURPOSE	SPONSOR/ OPERATOR
.com	1980s	Unrestricted (but intended for commercial registrants)	VeriSign
.edu	1980s	U.S. educational institutions	Educause
.gov	1980s	U.S. government	U.S. General Services Administration
.mil	1980s	U.S. military	U.S. Department of Defense Network Information Center
.net	1980s	Unrestricted (but originally intended for network providers, etc.)	VeriSign
.org	1980s	Unrestricted (but intended for organizations that do not fit elsewhere)	Public Interest Registry (was operated by VeriSign until December 31, 2002)
.int	1998	Organizations established by international treaties between governments	Internet Assigned Numbers Authority (IANA)
.aero	2001	Air-transport industry	Societé Internationale de Telecommunications Aeronautiques SC (SITA)
.biz	2001	Businesses	NeuLevel
.coop	2001	Cooperatives	DotCooperation LLC
.info	2001	Unrestricted use	Afilias LLC
.museum	2001	Museums	Museum Domain Name Association (MuseDoma)
.name	2001	For registration by individuals	Global Name Registry Ltd.
.pro	2002	Accountants, lawyers, physicians, and other professionals	RegistryPro Ltd
.jobs	2005	Job search	Employ Media LLC
.travel	2005	Travel search	Tralliance Corporation
.mobi	2005	Web sites specifically designed for mobile phones	mTLD Top Level Domain, Ltd.
.cat	2005	Individuals, organizations, and companies that promote the Catalan language and culture	Fundació puntCAT
.asia	2006	Regional domain for companies, organizations, and individuals based in Asia	DotAsia Organization
.tel	2006	Telephone numbers and other contact information	ICM Registry
.xxx	2010	New top-level domain for pornographic content	None yet approved

SOURCE: Based on data from ICANN, 2011b.

as .deloitte). In 2009, ICANN began the process of implementing these guidelines. In 2011, ICANN removed nearly all restrictions on domain names, thereby greatly expanding the number of different domain names available. As of September 2012, more than 2000 applications for new gTLDs had been filed and ICANN has announced that it will begin evaluating them as a batch beginning in December 2012, in a process that might take up to a year to complete.

MARKUP LANGUAGES

Although the most common Web page formatting language is HTML, the concept behind document formatting actually had its roots in the 1960s with the development of Generalized Markup Language (GML).

HyperText Markup Language (HTML)

HyperText Markup Language (HTML)

GML that is relatively easy to use in Web page design. HTML provides Web page designers with a fixed set of markup "tags" that are used to format a Web page

HyperText Markup Language (HTML) is a GML that is relatively easy to use. HTML provides Web page designers with a fixed set of markup "tags" that are used to format a Web page (see **Figure 3.17**). When these tags are inserted into a Web page, they are read by the browser and interpreted into a page display. You can see the source HTML code for any Web page by simply clicking on the "Page Source" command found in all browsers. In Figure 3.17, the HTML code in the first screen produces the display in the second screen.

| FIGURE 3.17 | **EXAMPLE HTML CODE (A) AND WEB PAGE (B)** |

(a)   (b)

HTML is a text markup language used to create Web pages. It has a fixed set of "tags" that are used to tell the browser software how to present the content on screen. The HTML shown in Figure 3.17 (a) creates the Web page seen in Figure 3.17 (b).

HTML defines the structure and style of a document, including the headings, graphic positioning, tables, and text formatting. Since its introduction, the major browsers have continuously added features to HTML to enable programmers to further refine their page layouts. Unfortunately, some browser enhancements may work only in one company's browser. Whenever you build an e-commerce site, you should take care that the pages can be viewed by the major browsers, even outdated versions of browsers. HTML Web pages can be created with any text editor, such as Notepad or WordPad, using Microsoft Word (simply save the Word document as a Web page), or any one of several Web page development tools such as Microsoft Expression Web or Adobe Dreamweaver.[6]

The most recent version of HTML is HTML5. HTML5 introduces features like video playback and drag-and-drop that in the past were provided by plug-ins like Adobe Flash. HTML5 applications have many of the rich interactive features found in smartphone apps. The *Insight on Technology* case, *Is HTML5 Ready for Prime Time?* examines some of the issues associated with use of HTML5.

eXtensible Markup Language (XML)

eXtensible Markup Language (XML) takes Web document formatting a giant leap forward. XML is a markup language specification developed by the W3C that is similar to HTML, but has a very different purpose. Whereas the purpose of HTML is to control the "look and feel" and display of data on the Web page, XML is designed to describe data and information. For example, consider the sample XML document in **Figure 3.18**. The first line in the sample document is the XML declaration, which is always included; it defines the XML version of the document. In this case, the document conforms to the 1.0 specification of XML. The next line defines the first element of the document (the root element): < note >. The next four lines define four child elements of the root (to, from, heading, and body). The last line defines the end of the root element. Notice that XML says nothing about how to display the data, or how the

eXtensible Markup Language (XML)
a markup language specification developed by the World Wide Web Consortium (W3C) that is designed to describe data and information

FIGURE 3.18	A SIMPLE XML DOCUMENT

```
<?xml version="1.0"?>
<note>
<to>George</to>
<from>Carol</from>
<heading>Just a Reminder</heading>
<body>Don't forget to order the groceries from FreshDirect!</body>
</note>
```

The tags in this simple XML document, such as <note>, <to>, and <from> are used to describe data and information, rather than the look and feel of the document.

---

[6] A detailed discussion of how to use HTML is beyond the scope of this text.

INSIGHT ON TECHNOLOGY

IS HTML5 READY FOR PRIME TIME?

Can HTML5 save businesses billions of dollars in development costs and bring about the demise of the native app? Possibly! The newest standard for how Web pages should be rendered by a browser has been welcomed by developers far in advance of its scheduled 2014 ratification by the World Wide Web Consortium (W3C). One key development that has jazzed developers and spurred corporate battles alike is the video element. Advocated by Apple founder Steve Jobs as the preferred method for displaying video on the Web, the video element replaces plug-ins such as Flash, QuickTime, and RealPlayer, a dramatic breakthrough in Web page design. Apple refused to allow Adobe Flash software to be used on iOS mobile devices, and ultimately has prevailed: Adobe has abandoned development of mobile Flash and agreed to use HTML5 to develop future tools.

In the interim, HTML5 has become a catch-all term that encompasses not only the video element but also the use of the newest versions of Cascading Style Sheets (CSS3) and JavaScript, and another new tool, HTML5 Canvas. The canvas element essentially provides an application programming interface (API) to draw rectangular block-level objects. Also intended to replace plug-ins, it is used with a set of JavaScript functions to render simple animations, which reduces page load time. Multi-platform Web developers began using HTML5 because these new elements provided device independence, but soon discovered that they could do even more. The built-in functionality of mobile devices, including GPS and swiping, can be accessed, enabling m-commerce sites to build Web-based mobile apps that can replicate the native app experience. Web-based mobile apps (HTML5 apps) work just like Web pages. When a user navigates to the page containing the mobile app, the page content, including graphics, images, and video, are loaded into the browser from the Web server, rather than residing in the mobile device hardware like a native app. This concept was embraced by mobile developers who naturally dream of being able to reach all platforms with a single product.

For businesses, the cost savings are obvious. A single HTML5 app requires far less labor hours to build than multiple native apps for the iOS, Android, Windows Phone, and other platforms. Furthermore, Apple charges a 30% commission on apps purchased through their stores as well as on app subscriptions they broker. Businesses that build their own Web-based apps can spend less on product development and avoid these distribution costs. The bad news for Apple is that if HTML5 apps proliferate and native apps correspondingly decline, some analysts are predicting sharply decreasing profit margins and market share for its iOS platforms. Further good news for other businesses is that embedded video and HTML5 apps can more easily be linked to and shared on social networks, encouraging viral distribution. Some HTML5 apps can even be designed so that they can be run on mobile devices when they are offline. Differences in how apps run across different platforms and workarounds are eliminated.

One company quick to capitalize on the Web-based mobile app trend was Usablenet, a software platform provider. Usablenet released an HTML5 mobile platform in April 2011. The Usablenet Mobile 2.0 system provides m-commerce proprietors with a set of tools for building HTML5 sites that are optimized for touch-based browsers and can exploit mobile device functionality. Photo galleries can be swiped through, individual photos can be double-tapped to zoom in, scrolling promotions and expanding and collapsing menus

(continued)

can be incorporated, and consumers can search for nearby store locations based on their current whereabouts. Amtrak, Delta, Expedia, FedEx, Hilton, Marks & Spencer, Sprint, JCPenney, and Victoria's Secret are among the Fortune 1000 companies who have already discovered the advantages of an HTML5 m-commerce site built with Usablenet Mobile 2.0.

An April 2012 Usablenet study examined the experiences of 50 retail and travel companies who had built HTML5 m-commerce sites using its system and found that 28% enjoyed increased site traffic as well as an 11% increase in the number of page views per visit. ShopNBC, one of the top 100 m-commerce proprietors according to Internet Retailer, upgraded its m-commerce site and found that mobile customers not only spent more time on their site but also began streaming their broadcast channel in greater numbers. ShopNBC had used the HTML5 video element one year previously to stream their live television feed to smartphone and tablet users without the need for a plug-in. It was this experience that prompted them to undergo a complete HTML5 redesign. What's more, ShopNBC and other study participants' users were 15% less likely to enter the site and immediately leave, a statistic referred to as the bounce rate. While ShopNBC still maintains numerous apps for multiple platforms, it might discontinue them to conserve resources. The prospect of focusing the company's IT resources on maintaining and managing one mobile site as opposed to multiple mobile apps is undoubtedly enticing.

Another company that is delighted with its HTML5 revamp is ideeli.com, a members-only discount fashion flash-sales site that offers sales from as many as 40 designers at a time, beginning at noon each day and lasting for 40 hours. Because its iPad traffic had increased 70% over the previous year, ideeli needed an upgrade to optimize for small screen size and speed load time. The results were impressive. iPad visitors increased by 70% and now comprise between 10% and 20% of its customers. What's more, this translated to a 25% increase in average order value. Ideeli achieved increased page-load times because HTML5 can cache data in the mobile browser. After a user has visited the site, part of ideeli's database is stored there, decreasing the number of times the browser must ping the database. This boosts site responsiveness, particularly between 12:00 and 12:15 PM when flash sales are just taking off and ideeli records 15% of its daily traffic. HTML5 has also enabled ideeli to maintain just one Web site for all users, both desktop and mobile. This is yet another huge cost-savings benefit for some retailers, who can go back to creating just one Web site by incorporating contact points for HTML5 apps.

The biggest challenge of HTML5 apps is to meet and then attempt to surpass the user experience and performance level of native apps. Although HTML5 sites load faster than first-generation mobile commerce sites, native apps generally still trump HTML5 apps on speed because a great deal of the interface already resides on the mobile device. Only newly requested data must be loaded. The mobile device platform also provides a standard user interface that native app developers can exploit to provide ease of execution for the user. Wooga, a German social games developer that supplies games to Facebook, cancelled its plans for an HTML5 site in June 2012 because it could not replicate the speed of its native apps. It also found that it was difficult to get users to create a link on their home screens so that they could easily access its HTML5 apps. Furthermore, mobile device users could not play their HTML5 games while offline as they could with native apps. Facebook was disappointed in this development because it was hoping to ditch its commission fees and gain more control over its platform. Later, however, Facebook concurred with Wooga's conclusions regarding speed and replaced its iPhone app, which had mainly served as a portal to its HTML5 mobile site, with an iOS native app.

(continued)

According to Sir Tim Berners-Lee, founder and chief of the W3C and an ardent opponent of native apps because they remove functionality from the Web, HTML5 security and access control issues are currently being addressed. For instance, HTML5 does not support digital rights management (DRM). In the past, media companies developed their own copy protection standards based on geographical region and/or whether payment had been proffered. These were enforced through their own media players. Since HTML5 does not require plug-ins to play video (or audio), and further, since HTML5 is an official W3C standard charged with remaining vendor neutral, this presents a challenge to the HTML5 working group.

Although HTML5 is being widely adopted on e-commerce and m-commerce sites, all of the major browser companies are diligently adapting to exploit its capabilities, and some businesses have been able to develop useful HTML5 apps, so far the outlook is not great for the demise of native apps, as Berners-Lee so hopes to see. Instead, native apps are incorporating HTML5 code into a kind of hybrid or mixed mode app. A March 2012 survey from Appcelerator and research firm IDC found that 79% of developers planned to work on a mixed-mode mobile app that combines elements of HTML5 with the performance-oriented abilities of their native apps. Only 6% planned to create HTML5 apps. While the lure of reaching all platforms with a single product is potent, if developers cannot produce a product that equals the performance of native apps, they will stick with the side their bread is buttered on and continue to develop native apps for the top sellers.

SOURCES: "Why HTML5 Is in Trouble on the Mobile Front," by David Meyer, ZDNet, September 5, 2012; "A Technology Switch Bears Mobile Commerce Fruit," by Kevin Woodward, Internet Retailer, August 30, 2012; "HTML5: Don't Believe the Hype Cycle," by Dan Rowinski, ReadWriteWeb.com, August 21st, 2012; "Is HTML5 the End of Native Mobile Apps?," by Hernán Gonzalez, ClickZ.com, August 17, 2012; "ShopNBC.com Targets More App-like Features in its Mobile Site Update," by Kevin Woodward, Internet Retailer, July 2, 2012; "What Do You Get by Adding HTML5 to Your Mobile Site?," by Bill Siwicki, Internet Retailer, April 12, 2012; "HTML5 Mobile Sites Give Apps a Run for their Money," by Bill Siwicki, Internet Retailer, February 3, 2012; "HTML5 Is Popular, Still Unfinished," by Don Clark, Wall Street Journal, November 11, 2011; "Adobe's Flash Surrender Proves Steve Jobs And Apple Were Right All Along With HTML5," by Nigam Arora, Forbes, November, 9, 2011; "Financial Researcher: HTML5 Adoption Might Hurt Apple's Profit," by Loek Essers, Macworld, Sep 12, 2011.

text should look on the screen. HTML is used for information display in combination with XML, which is used for data description.

Figure 3.19 shows how XML can be used to define a database of company names in a company directory. Tags such as < Company >, < Name >, and < Specialty > can be defined for a single firm, or an entire industry. On an elementary level, XML is extraordinarily easy to learn and is very similar to HTML except that you can make up your own tags. At a deeper level, XML has a rich syntax and an enormous set of software tools, which make XML ideal for storing and communicating many types of data on the Web.

XML is "extensible," which means the tags used to describe and display data are defined by the user, whereas in HTML the tags are limited and predefined. XML can also transform information into new formats, such as by importing information from a database and displaying it as a table. With XML, information can be analyzed and displayed selectively, making it a more powerful alternative to HTML. This means

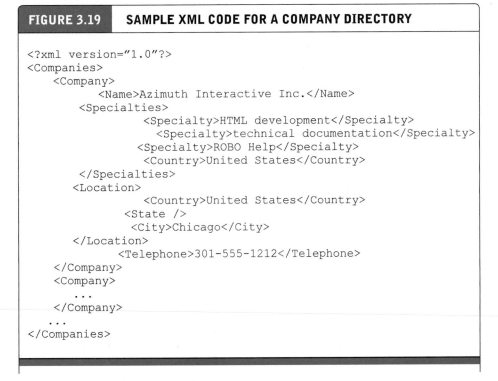

FIGURE 3.19 **SAMPLE XML CODE FOR A COMPANY DIRECTORY**

```
<?xml version="1.0"?>
<Companies>
    <Company>
            <Name>Azimuth Interactive Inc.</Name>
        <Specialties>
                    <Specialty>HTML development</Specialty>
                    <Specialty>technical documentation</Specialty>
                <Specialty>ROBO Help</Specialty>
                <Country>United States</Country>
        </Specialties>
        <Location>
                    <Country>United States</Country>
                <State />
                <City>Chicago</City>
        </Location>
                <Telephone>301-555-1212</Telephone>
    </Company>
    <Company>
        . . .
    </Company>
    . . .
</Companies>
```

This XML document uses tags to define a database of company names.

that business firms, or entire industries, can describe all of their invoices, accounts payable, payroll records, and financial information using a Web-compatible markup language. Once described, these business documents can be stored on intranet Web servers and shared throughout the corporation.

WEB SERVERS AND CLIENTS

We have already described client/server computing and the revolution in computing architecture brought about by client/server computing. You already know that a server is a computer attached to a network that stores files, controls peripheral devices, interfaces with the outside world—including the Internet—and does some processing for other computers on the network.

But what is a Web server? **Web server software** refers to the software that enables a computer to deliver Web pages written in HTML to client computers on a network that request this service by sending an HTTP request. The two leading brands of Web server software are Apache, which is free Web server shareware that accounts for about 64% of the market, and Microsoft's Internet Information Services (IIS), which accounts for about 14% of the market (Netcraft, 2012).

Aside from responding to requests for Web pages, all Web servers provide some additional basic capabilities such as the following:

Web server software
software that enables a computer to deliver Web pages written in HTML to client computers on a network that request this service by sending an HTTP request

- *Security services*—These consist mainly of authentication services that verify that the person trying to access the site is authorized to do so. For Web sites that process payment transactions, the Web server also supports SSL and TLS, the protocols for transmitting and receiving information securely over the Internet. When private information such as names, phone numbers, addresses, and credit card data needs to be provided to a Web site, the Web server uses SSL to ensure that the data passing back and forth from the browser to the server is not compromised.

- *FTP*—This protocol allows users to transfer files to and from the server. Some sites limit file uploads to the Web server, while others restrict downloads, depending on the user's identity.

- *Search engine*—Just as search engine sites enable users to search the entire Web for particular documents, search engine modules within the basic Web server software package enable indexing of the site's Web pages and content and permit easy keyword searching of the site's content. When conducting a search, a search engine makes use of an index, which is a list of all the documents on the server. The search term is compared to the index to identify likely matches.

- *Data capture*—Web servers are also helpful at monitoring site traffic, capturing information on who has visited a site, how long the user stayed there, the date and time of each visit, and which specific pages on the server were accessed. This information is compiled and saved in a log file, which can then be analyzed. By analyzing a log file, a site manager can find out the total number of visitors, average length of each visit, and the most popular destinations, or Web pages.

The term *Web server* is also used to refer to the physical computer that runs Web server software. Leading manufacturers of Web server computers include IBM, Dell, and Hewlett-Packard. Although any personal computer can run Web server software, it is best to use a computer that has been optimized for this purpose. To be a Web server, a computer must have the Web server software installed and be connected to the Internet. Every public Web server computer has an IP address. For example, if you type http://www.pearsonhighered.com/laudon in your browser, the browser software sends a request for HTTP service to the Web server whose domain name is pearsonhighered.com. The server then locates the page named "laudon" on its hard drive, sends the page back to your browser, and displays it on your screen. Of course, firms also can use Web servers for strictly internal local area networking in intranets.

Aside from the generic Web server software packages, there are actually many types of specialized servers on the Web, from **database servers** that access specific information within a database, to **ad servers** that deliver targeted banner ads, to **mail servers** that provide e-mail messages, and **video servers** that provide video clips. At a small e-commerce site, all of these software packages might be running on a single computer, with a single processor. At a large corporate site, there may be hundreds or thousands of discrete server computers, many with multiple processors, running specialized Web server functions. We discuss the architecture of e-commerce sites in greater detail in Chapter 4.

A **Web client**, on the other hand, is any computing device attached to the Internet that is capable of making HTTP requests and displaying HTML pages. The most

database server
server designed to access specific information with a database

ad server
server designed to deliver targeted banner ads

mail server
server that provides e-mail messages

video server
server that serves video clips

Web client
any computing device attached to the Internet that is capable of making HTTP requests and displaying HTML pages, most commonly a Windows PC or Macintosh

common client is a Windows or Macintosh computer, with various flavors of Unix/Linux computers a distant third. However, the fastest growing category of Web clients are not computers at all, but smartphones, tablets, and netbooks outfitted with wireless Web access software. In general, Web clients can be any device—including a printer, refrigerator, stove, home lighting system, or automobile instrument panel—capable of sending and receiving information from Web servers.

WEB BROWSERS

A Web browser is a software program whose primary purpose is to display Web pages. Browsers also have added features, such as e-mail and newsgroups (an online discussion group or forum). The leading Web browser is Microsoft Internet Explorer, with about 49% of the market as of August 2012. Mozilla Firefox is currently the second most popular Web browser, with about 18% of the U.S. Web browser market (Marketshare.hitslink.com, 2012). First released in 2004, Firefox is a free, open source Web browser for the Windows, Linux, and Macintosh operating systems, based on Mozilla open source code (which originally provided the code for Netscape). It is small and fast and offers many features such as pop-up blocking and tabbed browsing. The third most popular browser, with about a 17% market share, is Google's Chrome, a small, yet technologically advanced open source browser. Apple's Safari browser is fourth, with about 11% of the market.

3.5 THE INTERNET AND THE WEB: FEATURES AND SERVICES

The Internet and the Web have spawned a number of powerful software applications upon which the foundations of e-commerce are built. You can think of these all as Web services, and it is interesting as you read along to compare these services to other traditional media such as television or print media. If you do, you will quickly realize the richness of the Internet environment.

E-MAIL

Since its earliest days, **electronic mail**, or **e-mail**, has been the most-used application of the Internet. Worldwide, there are an estimated 3.3 billion e-mail accounts, sending an estimated 145 billion e-mails a day. About 75% of these e-mail accounts (2.5 billion) are consumer accounts and about 25% (850 million) are corporate e-mail accounts (Radicati Group, 2012). Estimates vary on the amount of spam, ranging from 40% to 90%. E-mail marketing and spam are examined in more depth in Chapter 7.

E-mail uses a series of protocols to enable messages containing text, images, sound, and video clips to be transferred from one Internet user to another. Because of its flexibility and speed, it is now the most popular form of business communication—more popular than the phone, fax, or snail mail (the U.S. Postal Service). In addition to text typed within the message, e-mail also allows **attachments**, which are files inserted within the e-mail message. The files can be documents, images, sounds, or video clips.

electronic mail (e-mail)
the most-used application of the Internet. Uses a series of protocols to enable messages containing text, images, sound, and video clips to be transferred from one Internet user to another

attachment
a file inserted within an e-mail message

INSTANT MESSAGING

Instant messaging (IM) allows you to send messages in real time, one line at a time, unlike e-mail. E-mail messages have a time lag of several seconds to minutes between when messages are sent and received. IM displays lines of text entered on a computer almost instantaneously. Recipients can then respond immediately to the sender the same way, making the communication more like a live conversation than is possible through e-mail. To use IM, users create a buddy list they want to communicate with, and then enter short text messages that their buddies will receive instantly (if they are online at the time). And although text remains the primary communication mechanism in IM, users can insert audio clips or photos into their instant messages, and even participate in video conferencing. Instant messaging over the Internet competes with wireless phone Short Message Service (SMS) texting, which is far more expensive than IM.

The major IM systems are Microsoft's Windows Live Messenger, Skype, Yahoo Messenger, Google Talk and AIM (AOL Instant Messenger). Facebook also offers instant messaging services via Facebook Chat. IM systems were initially developed as proprietary systems, with competing firms offering versions that did not work with one another. In 2011, there still is no built-in interoperability among the major IM systems. The number of worldwide IM accounts is around 2.7 billion (Radicati Group, 2012).

SEARCH ENGINES

No one knows for sure how many Web pages there really are. The surface Web is that part of the Web that search engines visit and record information about. For instance, Google currently searches billions of Web pages and stores information about those pages in its massive computer network located throughout the United States. But there is also a "deep Web" that could contain more than a trillion additional Web pages, many of them proprietary (such as the pages of the online version of the *Wall Street Journal*, which cannot be visited without an access code) or behind corporate firewalls.

But obviously with so many Web pages, finding Web-specific pages that can help you or your business, nearly instantly, is an important problem. The question is: how can you find the one or two Web pages you really want and need out of the billions of indexed Web pages?

Search engines solve the problem of finding useful information on the Web nearly instantly and are one of the "killer apps" of the Internet era. Almost 60% of all adult American Internet users use a search engine on any given day, generating about 17 billion queries a month (Pew Internet & American Life Project, 2012; comScore, 2012a). There are hundreds of different search engines, but the vast majority of the search results are supplied by the top five providers (see **Figure 3.20**).

Web search engines started out in the early 1990s shortly after Netscape released the first commercial Web browser. Early browsers were relatively simple software programs that roamed the nascent Web, visiting pages and gathering information about the content of each Web page. These early programs were called variously crawlers,

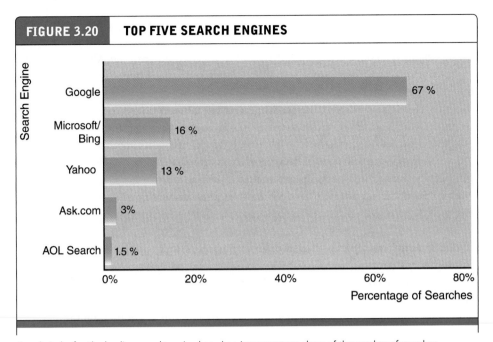

FIGURE 3.20	TOP FIVE SEARCH ENGINES

Google is, by far, the leading search engine based on its percentage share of the number of searches.
SOURCE: Based on data from comScore, 2012a.

spiders, and wanderers; the first full-text crawler that indexed the contents of an entire Web page was called WebCrawler, released in 1994. AltaVista (1995), one of the first widely used search engines, was the first to allow "natural language" queries such as "history of Web search engines" rather than "history + Web + search engine."

The Google search engine is continuously crawling the Web, indexing the content of each page, calculating its popularity, and caching the pages so that it can respond quickly to your request to see a page. The entire process of scanning a page takes about one-half of a second.

The first search engines employed simple keyword indexes of all the Web pages visited. They would count the number of times a word appeared on the Web page, and store this information in an index. These search engines could be easily fooled by Web designers who simply repeated words on their home pages. The real innovations in search engine development occurred through a program funded by the Department of Defense called the Digital Library Initiative, designed to help the Pentagon find research papers in large databases. Stanford, Berkeley, and three other universities became hotbeds of Web search innovations in the mid-1990s. At Stanford in 1994, two computer science students, David Filo and Jerry Yang, created a hand-selected list of their favorite Web pages and called it "Yet Another Hierarchical Officious Oracle," or Yahoo!. Yahoo initially was not a real search engine, but rather an edited selection of Web sites organized by categories the editors found useful. Yahoo later developed "true" search engine capabilities.

In 1998, Larry Page and Sergey Brin, two Stanford computer science students, released their first version of Google. This search engine was different: not only did it index each Web page's words, but Page had discovered that the AltaVista search engine not only collected keywords from sites but also calculated what other sites linked to each page. By looking at the URLs on each Web page, they could calculate an index of popularity. AltaVista did nothing with this information. Page took this idea and made it a central factor in ranking a Web page's appropriateness to a search query. He patented the idea of a Web page ranking system (PageRank System), which essentially measures the popularity of the Web page. Brin contributed a unique Web crawler program that indexed not just keywords on a Web page, but combinations of words (such as authors and their article titles). These two ideas became the foundation for the Google search engine (Brandt, 2004). **Figure 3.21** illustrates how Google works.

Search engine Web sites have became so popular and easy to use that they also serve as major portals for the Internet (see Chapter 11). The search marketplace has become very competitive despite the dominance of Google. Both Microsoft and Yahoo have invested more than $1 billion each to match Google's search engine. In 2009, Yahoo finally threw in the towel and agreed to adopt Microsoft's Bing search engine instead, in return for 88% of the advertising revenues generated by search on Yahoo's sites.

Initially, few understood how to make money from search engines. That changed in 2000 when Goto.com (later Overture) allowed advertisers to bid for placement on their search engine results, and Google followed suit in 2003 with its AdWords

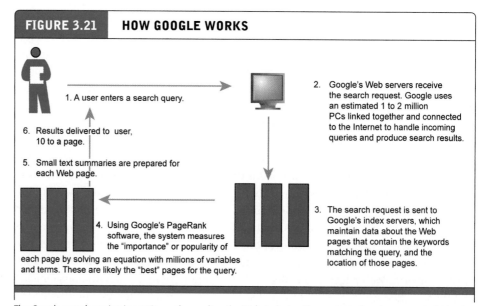

FIGURE 3.21 HOW GOOGLE WORKS

1. A user enters a search query.

6. Results delivered to user, 10 to a page.

5. Small text summaries are prepared for each Web page.

4. Using Google's PageRank software, the system measures the "importance" or popularity of each page by solving an equation with millions of variables and terms. These are likely the "best" pages for the query.

2. Google's Web servers receive the search request. Google uses an estimated 1 to 2 million PCs linked together and connected to the Internet to handle incoming queries and produce search results.

3. The search request is sent to Google's index servers, which maintain data about the Web pages that contain the keywords matching the query, and the location of those pages.

The Google search engine is continuously crawling the Web, indexing the content of each page, calculating its popularity, and caching the pages so that it can respond quickly to your request to see a page. The entire process takes about one-half of a second.

program, which allowed advertisers to bid for placement of short text ads on Google search results. The spectacular increase in Internet advertising revenues (which have been growing at around 20%–25% annually over the last few years), has helped search engines transform themselves into major shopping tools and created an entire new industry called "search engine marketing." Search engine marketing has been the fastest growing form of advertising in the United States, reaching about $19.5 billion in 2012. When users enter a search term at Google, Bing, Yahoo, or any of the other Web sites serviced by these search engines, they receive two types of listings: sponsored links, for which advertisers have paid to be listed (usually at the top of the search results page), and unsponsored "organic" search results. In addition, advertisers can purchase small text ads on the right side of the search results page. Although the major search engines are used for locating general information of interest to users, search engines have also become a crucial tool within e-commerce sites. Customers can more easily search for the product information they want with the help of an internal search program; the difference is that within Web sites, the search engine is limited to finding matches from that one site. In addition, search engines have extended their services to include news, maps, satellite images, computer images, e-mail, group calendars, group meeting tools, and indexes of scholarly papers. In 2012, Google and Bing have added social search terms to their search results. Whatever these search engines can glean from your e-mails and social network posts they can use in response to your searches to make the results more "personal" and social. Outside of e-mail, search engines are the most common online daily activity and produce the largest online audiences.

ONLINE FORUMS AND CHAT

An **online forum** (also referred to as a message board, bulletin board, discussion board, discussion group, or simply a board or forum) is a Web application that enables Internet users to communicate with each other, although not in real time. A forum provides a container for various discussions (or "threads") started (or "posted") by members of the forum, and depending on the permissions granted to forum members by the forum's administrator, enables a person to start a thread and reply to other people's threads. Most forum software allows more than one forum to be created. The forum administrator typically can edit, delete, move, or otherwise modify any thread on the forum. Unlike an electronic mailing list (such as a listserv), which automatically sends new messages to a subscriber, an online forum typically requires that the member visit the forum to check for new posts. Some forums offer an "e-mail notification" feature that notifies users that a new post of interest to them has been made.

online forum
a Web application that allows Internet users to communicate with each other, although not in real time

Online chat differs from an online forum in that, like IM, chat enables users to communicate via computer in real time, that is, simultaneously. However, unlike IM, which works only between two people, chat can occur among several users. Typically, users log in to a "chat room" where they can text message others. Some chat rooms offer virtual chat, which enable users to incorporate 2-D and 3-D graphics along with avatars (an icon or representation of the user) into their chat, or offer the ability to communicate via audio and/or video. Chat systems include Internet Relay

online chat
enables users to communicate via computer in real time, that is, simultaneously. Unlike IM, chat can occur among several users

Chat (IRC), Jabber, Yahoo, and MSN chat, and a number of proprietary systems based on the Microsoft Windows or Java platform. E-commerce firms typically use online forums and online chat to help develop community and as customer service tools. We will discuss the use of online forums as a community-building tool further in Chapter 11.

STREAMING MEDIA

streaming media

enables music, video, and other large files to be sent to users in chunks so that when received and played, the file comes through uninterrupted

Streaming media enables live Web video, music, video, and other large-bandwidth files to be sent to users in a variety of ways that enable the user to play back the files. In some situations, such as live Web video, the files are broken into chunks and served by specialized video servers to users in chunks. Client software puts the chunks together and plays the video. In other situations, such as YouTube, a single large file is downloaded from a standard Web server to users who can begin playing the video before the entire file is downloaded. Streamed files must be viewed "live"; they cannot be stored on client hard drives without special software. Streamed files are "played" by a software program such as Windows Media Player, Apple Quick-Time, Flash, and RealMedia Player. There are a number of tools used to create streaming files, but one of the most common is Adobe's Flash program. The Flash player has the advantage of being built into most client browsers; no plug-in is required to play Flash files.

Sites such as YouTube, Metacafe, and Facebook have popularized user-generated video streaming. Web advertisers increasingly use video to attract viewers. Streaming audio and video segments used in Web ads and news stories are perhaps the most frequently used streaming services. As the capacity of the Internet grows, streaming media will play an even larger role in e-commerce.

COOKIES

cookie

a tool used by Web sites to store information about a user. When a visitor enters a Web site, the site sends a small text file (the cookie) to the user's computer so that information from the site can be loaded more quickly on future visits. The cookie can contain any information desired by the site designers

A **cookie** is a tool used by a Web site to store information about a user. When a visitor enters a Web site, the site sends a small text file (the cookie) to the user's computer so that information from the site can be loaded more quickly on future visits. The cookie can contain any information desired by the Web site designers, including customer number, pages visited, products examined, and other detailed information about the behavior of the consumer at the site. Cookies are useful to consumers because the Web site will recognize returning patrons and not ask them to register again. Cookies are also used by advertisers to ensure visitors do not receive the same advertisements repeatedly. Cookies can also help personalize a Web site by allowing the site to recognize returning customers and make special offers to them based on their past behavior at the site. Cookies allow Web marketers to customize products and segment markets—the ability to change the product or the price based on prior consumer information (described more fully in later chapters). As we will discuss throughout the book, cookies also can pose a threat to consumer privacy, and at times they are bothersome. Many people clear their cookies at the end of every day. Some disable them entirely using tools built into most browsers.

WEB 2.0 FEATURES AND SERVICES

Today's broadband Internet infrastructure has greatly expanded the services available to users. These new capabilities have formed the basis for new business models. Digital content and digital communications are the two areas where innovation is most rapid. Web 2.0 applications and services are "social" in nature because they support communication among individuals within groups or social networks.

Online Social Networks

If there is a "killer app" on the Internet in 2012 and going forward, it is social networks. Online social networks are described throughout this book in many chapters because they have developed very large worldwide audiences and form the basis for new advertising platforms and for social e-commerce (see chapters 6, 7, and 11). Online social networks are services that support communication within networks of friends, colleagues, and entire professions. The largest social networks are Facebook (1 billion worldwide), LinkedIn (175 million worldwide), Twitter (more than 140 million active users worldwide), and Pinterest (more than 100 million). These networks rely on user-generated content (messages, photos, and videos) and emphasize sharing of content. All of these features require significant broadband Internet connectivity and equally large cloud computing facilities to store content.

Blogs

A **blog** (originally called a **weblog**) is a personal Web page that typically contains a series of chronological entries (newest to oldest) by its author, and links to related Web pages. The blog may include a blogroll (a collection of links to other blogs) and track-backs (a list of entries in other blogs that refer to a post on the first blog). Most blogs allow readers to post comments on the blog entries as well. The act of creating a blog is often referred to as "blogging." Blogs are either hosted by a third-party site such as Blogger.com (owned by Google), LiveJournal, TypePad, Xanga, WordPress, and Tumblr, or prospective bloggers can download software such as Movable Type to create a blog that is hosted by the user's ISP. Blog pages are usually variations on templates provided by the blogging service or software and hence require no knowledge of HTML. Therefore, millions of people without HTML skills of any kind can post their own Web pages, and share content with friends and relatives. The totality of blog-related Web sites is often referred to as the "blogosphere."

Blogs have become hugely popular. While estimates on the number of blogs vary, BlogPulse, a blog research firm, estimates that there are more than 180 million blogs as of the end of 2011 (Nielsen, 2012a). According to eMarketer, there are an estimated 25 million active U.S. bloggers, and 72 million U.S. blog readers (eMarketer, Inc., 2012d, 2012e). No one knows how many of these blogs are kept up to date or are just yesterday's news. And no one knows how many of these blogs have a readership greater than one (the blog author). In fact, there are so many blogs you need a blog search engine just to find them (such as Google's or Technorati's search engine), or you can just go to a list of the most popular 100 blogs and dig in. We discuss blogs further in

blog
personal Web page that is created by an individual or corporation to communicate with readers

Chapters 6 and 7 as a marketing and advertising mechanism, and in Chapter 10 as a part of the significant growth in user-generated content.

Really Simple Syndication (RSS)

Really Simple Syndication (RSS)
program that allows users to have digital content, including text, articles, blogs, and podcast audio files, automatically sent to their computers over the Internet

The rise of blogs is correlated with a distribution mechanism for news and information from Web sites that regularly update their content. **Really Simple Syndication (RSS)** is an XML format that allows users to have digital content, including text, articles, blogs, and podcast audio files, automatically sent to their computers over the Internet. An RSS aggregator software application that you install on your computer gathers material from the Web sites and blogs that you tell it to scan and brings new information from those sites to you. Sometimes this is referred to as "syndicated" content because it is distributed by news organizations and other syndicators (or distributors). Users download an RSS aggregator and then "subscribe" to the RSS "feeds." When you go to your RSS aggregator's page, it will display the most recent updates for each channel to which you have subscribed. RSS has rocketed from a "techie" pastime to a broad-based movement.

Podcasting

podcast
an audio presentation—such as a radio show, audio from a movie, or simply a personal audio presentation—stored as an audio file and posted to the Web

A **podcast** is an audio presentation—such as a radio show, audio from a movie, or simply a personal audio presentation—stored as an audio file and posted to the Web. Listeners download the files from the Web and play them on their players or computers. While commonly associated with Apple's iPod portable music player, you can listen to MP3 podcast files with any MP3 player. Podcasting has transitioned from an amateur independent producer media in the "pirate radio" tradition to a professional news and talk content distribution channel.

Wikis

wiki
Web application that allows a user to easily add and edit content on a Web page

A **wiki** is a Web application that allows a user to easily add and edit content on a Web page. (The term wiki derives from the "wiki wiki" (quick or fast) shuttle buses at Honolulu Airport.) Wiki software enables documents to be written collectively and collaboratively. Most wiki systems are open source, server-side systems that store content in a relational database. The software typically provides a template that defines layout and elements common to all pages, displays user-editable source code (usually plain text), and then renders the content into an HTML-based page for display in a Web browser. Some wiki software allows only basic text formatting, whereas others allow the use of tables, images, or even interactive elements, such as polls and games. Since wikis by their very nature are very open in allowing anyone to make changes to a page, most wikis provide a means to verify the validity of changes via a "Recent Changes" page, which enables members of the wiki community to monitor and review the work of other users, correct mistakes, and hopefully deter "vandalism."

The most well-known wiki is Wikipedia, an online encyclopedia that contains more than 4 million English-language articles on a variety of topics, appears in 285 languages, and has 365 million readers worldwide. It is more popular than iTunes. The

Wikimedia Foundation, which operates Wikipedia, also operates a variety of related projects, including Wikibooks, a collection of collaboratively written free textbooks and manuals; Wikinews, a free content news source; and Wiktionary, a collaborative project to produce a free multilingual dictionary in every language, with definitions, etymologies, pronunciations, quotations, and synonyms.

Music and Video Services

With the low-bandwidth connections of the early Internet, audio and video files were difficult to download and share, but with the huge growth in broadband connections, these files are not only commonplace but today constitute the majority of Web traffic. Spurred on by the worldwide sales of more than 410 million iOS devices (iPhones, iPads, and iPod Touches) through June 30, 2012, as well as millions of other smartphones and MP3 players, the Internet has become a virtual digital river of music files. Today, the iTunes Store has a catalog with more than 28 million tracks, 85,000 television episodes, and 45,000 movies, including more than 3,000 in high definition (Arar, 2012).

Online video viewing has also exploded in popularity. In July 2012, around 184 million Americans watched 37 billion videos for an average of 22.5 hours per viewer (comScore, 2012b). By far, the most common type of Internet video is provided by YouTube, with more than 4 billion videos streamed and viewed each a day (120 billion a month), most of them short clips taken from television shows, or user-generated content. The largest sources of legal, paid television content are the iTunes Store, where you can purchase specific episodes or entire seasons of TV shows, and Hulu, which is owned by major television producers NBCUniversal, News Corp., The Walt Disney Company, and Providence Equity Partners.

Internet advertising makes extensive use of streaming video ads: in July 2012, Americans watched 9.6 billion video ads, almost double the amount in the previous year! Companies that want to demonstrate use of their products have found video clips to be extremely effective. And audio reports and discussions have also become commonplace, either as marketing materials or customer reports.

Future digital video networks will be able to deliver better-than-broadcast-quality video over the Internet to computers and other devices in homes and on the road. High-quality interactive video and audio makes sales presentations and demonstrations more effective and lifelike and enable companies to develop new forms of customer support. The Internet is well on its way to becoming a major distribution channel for movies, television shows, and sporting events (see Chapter 10).

Internet Telephony

If the telephone system were to be built from scratch today, it would be an Internet-based, packet-switched network using TCP/IP because it would be less expensive and more efficient than the alternative existing system, which involves a mix of circuit-switched legs with a digital backbone. Likewise, if cable television systems were built from scratch today, they most likely would use Internet technologies for the same reasons.

IP telephony

a general term for the technologies that use VoIP and the Internet's packet-switched network to transmit voice and other forms of audio communication over the Internet

Voice over Internet Protocol (VoIP)

protocol that allows for transmission of voice and other forms of audio communication over the Internet

Already, nearly all pre-paid phone cards use the Internet for the long distance portion of calls. About 30% of the international calls from or to the United States use the Internet. Internet telephony is not entirely new. **IP telephony** is a general term for the technologies that use **Voice over Internet Protocol (VoIP)** and the Internet's packet-switched network to transmit voice, fax, and other forms of audio communication over the Internet. VoIP avoids the long distance charges imposed by traditional phone companies.

There were about 175 million residential VoIP subscribers worldwide in 2012, and this number is expanding rapidly as cable systems provide telephone service as part of their "triple play": voice, Internet, and TV as a single package (Burger, 2012).

VoIP is a disruptive technology. In the past, voice and fax were the exclusive provenance of the regulated telephone networks. With the convergence of the Internet and telephony, however, this dominance is already starting to change, with local and long distance telephone providers and cable companies becoming ISPs, and ISPs getting into the phone market (see **Table 3.12**). Independent service providers such as VoIP pioneers Vonage and Skype accounted for more than 60% of VoIP service in the United States in 2004, but this percentage dropped significantly by 2011 as traditional players such as Comcast, Time Warner, Verizon, AT&T, Cox, and other telephone and cable companies moved aggressively into the market.

Video Conferencing and Telepresence

Although video conferencing has been available for years, few have used it due to the cost of video equipment and telephone line rental fees. However, in recent years, Internet-based video conferencing has begun to overtake traditional telephone-based

TABLE 3.12	KEY IP TELEPHONY PLAYERS
SPECIALTY	**COMPANY**
Independent Facilities-based Service Providers	Vonage
	Time Warner Digital
	Comcast Digital Voice
	Cablevision/Optimum Voice
	Cox Digital Phone
	Verizon
	AT&T
	SBC
Client-based Service Providers	Skype
	Net2Phone
	MSN
	Yahoo Messenger
	Google Talk

systems. Internet video conferencing is accessible to anyone with a broadband Internet connection and a Web camera (webcam). The most widely used Web conferencing suite of tools is WebEx (now owned by Cisco). VoIP companies such as Skype and ooVoo also provide more limited Web conferencing capabilities, commonly referred to as video chatting.

Telepresence takes video conferencing up several notches. Rather than single persons "meeting" by using webcams, telepresence creates an environment in a room using multiple cameras and screens, which surround the users. The experience is uncanny and strange at first because as you look at the people in the screens, they are looking directly at you. Broadcast quality and higher screen resolutions help create the effect. Users have the sensation of "being in the presence of their colleagues" in a way that is not true for traditional webcam meetings. Providers of telepresence software and hardware include Cisco, HP, and Teliris.

Online Software and Web Services: Web Apps, Widgets, and Gadgets

We are all used to installing software on our PCs. But as the Web and e-commerce move towards a service model, applications increasingly will be running off Web servers. Instead of buying a "product" in a box, you will be paying for a Web service instead. There are many kinds of Web services now available, many free, all the way from full-function applications, such as Microsoft Office 365, to much smaller chunks of code called "widgets" and "gadgets."

Widgets pull content and functionality from one place on the Web to a place where you want it, such as on your Web page, blog, or Facebook page. You can see Web widget services most clearly in photo sites such as Picnik.com, which offers a free photo-editing application that is powerful and simple to use. Facebook's Like button is a widget that is used by more than 50 million people a day in the United States. Walmart, eBay, and Amazon, along with many other retailers, are creating shopping widgets that users can drag to their blogs or profile pages on various social networks so visitors can shop at a full-function online store without having to leave the page. Yahoo, Google, MSN, and Apple all have collections of hundreds of widgets available on their Web sites.

Gadgets are closely related to widgets. They are small chunks of code that usually supply a single limited function such as a clock, calendar, or diary. You can see a collection of gadgets at http://www.google.com/ig/directory?synd=open.

Intelligent Personal Assistants

The idea of having a conversation with a computer, having it understand you, and be able to carry out tasks according to your direction, has long been a part of science fiction, from the 1968 Hollywood movie *2001: A Space Odyssey*, to an old Apple promotional video depicting a professor using his personal digital assistant to organize his life, gather data, and place orders at restaurants. That was all fantasy. But Apple's Siri, billed as an intelligent personal assistant and knowledge navigator and released in October 2011 for the iPhone 4S, has many of the capabilities of the computer assistants found in fiction. Siri has a natural language, conversational interface, situational awareness, and is capable of carrying out many tasks based on verbal commands by delegating requests to a variety of different Web services. For instance, you can ask Siri to find a restaurant nearby that serves Italian food. Siri may show you an ad for a local restaurant in the process. Once you have identified a restaurant you would like to eat at, you can ask Siri to make a reservation using OpenTable. You can also ask Siri to place an appointment on your calendar, search Google (or Bing) for airline flights, and figure out what's the fastest route between your current location and a destination using public transit. The answers are not always completely accurate, but critics have been impressed with its uncanny abilities. Siri is currently available on the iPhone 4S, the iPhone 5, the third generation iPad, and the fifth generation iPod Touch.

In July, 2012, Google released its version of an intelligent assistant for Android-based smartphones, which it calls Google Now. Google Now is part of the Google Search application. While Google Now has many of the capabilities of Apple's Siri, it attempts to go further by predicting what users may need based on situational awareness, including physical location, time of day, previous location history, calendar, and expressed interests based on previous activity, as described in its patent application (United States Patent Office, 2012). For instance, if you often search for a particular musician or style of music, Google Now might provide recommendations for similar music. If it knows that you go to a health club every other day, Google Now will remind you not to schedule events during these periods. If it knows that you typically read articles about health issues, the system might monitor Google News for similar articles and make recommendations.

3.6 MOBILE APPS: THE NEXT BIG THING IS HERE

The use of mobile Internet access devices such as smartphones, iPads and other tablet computers, and laptops in e-commerce has truly exploded in 2012. From nearly zero mobile commerce prior to 2007, today, mobile commerce revenue in the United States from mobile retail purchases ($11.3 billion), mobile advertising ($2.6 billion), location-based services ($1 billion), games ($1 billion), e-book sales ($2.1 billion), and app sales ($6.7 billion) is approaching $25 billion. Worldwide, mobile payment transactions will reach an estimated $250 billion in 2012 (Juniper Research, 2012). More than 70% of U.S. mobile phone owners are expected to use their mobile devices to research and browse products and services in 2012, and the percentage is steadily increasing. More than 35% are expected to make at least one purchase via mobile phone in 2012, more than double the number in 2010 (eMarketer, Inc., 2012f). While mobile commerce is more widespread among younger consumers, there is evidence that even those over 55 are beginning to use this channel more frequently.

Tablets are being added into the mix. More than 50% of tablet owners have reported using their tablets at least once a week to shop, particularly on nights and weekends, and often from the comfort of couch or bed. More than 40% have made a purchase using their tablet (eMarketer, 2012g). As a result, companies are rapidly increasing their investment in mobile commerce technologies. For instance, a Forrester

Research survey found that more than 50% of U.S. online retailers planned to make mobile commerce a high-priority technology investment in 2011, significantly higher than the 18.6% who so indicated in 2010 (Oracle, 2011). An Internet Retailer survey found that almost 90% of merchants surveyed believed mobile commerce is important to their future online business, and that around 70% are planning to increase the size of the mobile commerce budgets. As with many other aspects of e-commerce, Amazon is a leader, with more than $2 billion in mobile sales worldwide in 2011. More than $4 billion in mobile sales worldwide were transacted using eBay (Internet Retailer, 2012).

Mobile capabilities include making sure Web sites are compatible with mobile browsers, are optimized for use on various devices (discussed further in Chapter 4), and provide downloadable mobile apps. Although both are important, right now, mobile apps appear to be attracting most of the attention. According to Nielsen, the average consumer spends about an hour a day interacting with the Web and apps on their smartphone, with more than two-thirds of that time spent on mobile apps. In the travel area, the disparity is even more glaring: users spent 95% of their time accessing travel information from mobile apps, compared to only 5% from the mobile Web (Nielsen, 2011, 2012b). *Insight on Technology: Apps For Everything: The App Ecosystem* gives you some further background on mobile apps.

PLATFORMS FOR MOBILE APPLICATION DEVELOPMENT

Unlike mobile Web sites, which can be accessed by any Web-enabled mobile device, apps are platform-specific. Applications for the iPhone, iPad, and other iOS devices are written in the Objective-C programming language using the iOS SDK (software developer kit). Applications for Android operating system–based phones are typically written using Java, although portions of the code may be in the C or C++ programming language. BlackBerry apps are also written in Java. Applications for Windows mobile devices are written in C or C++.

APP MARKETPLACES

Once written, applications are distributed through various marketplaces. Android apps for Android-based phones are distributed through Google Play, which is controlled by Google. iPhone applications are distributed through Apple's App Store. BlackBerry applications can be found in RIM's App World, while Microsoft operates the Windows Phone Marketplace for Windows mobile devices. Apps can also be purchased from third-party vendors such as Amazon's Appstore. It is important to distinguish "native" mobile apps, which run directly on a mobile device and rely on the device's internal operating system, from Web apps referred to in Section 3.6, which install into your browser, although these can operate in a mobile environment as well.

INSIGHT ON BUSINESS

APPS FOR EVERYTHING: THE APP ECOSYSTEM

When Steve Jobs introduced the iPhone in January 2007, no one—including himself—envisioned that the device would launch a revolution in consumer and business software, or become a major e-commerce platform, let alone a game platform, advertising platform, and general media platform for television shows, movies, videos, and e-books. In short, it's become the personal computer all over again, just in a much smaller form factor.

The iPhone's original primary functions, beyond being a cell phone, were to be a camera, text messaging device, and Web browser. What Apple initially lacked for the iPhone were software applications that would take full advantage of its computing capabilities. The solution was software developed by outside developers—tens of thousands of outside developers—who were attracted to the mission by potential profits and fame from the sale or free distribution of their software applications on a platform approved by the leading innovator in handheld computing and cellular devices. More than two-thirds of apps are free. Every month, Apple receives more than 20,000 new apps from independent developers who may be teenagers in a garage, major video game developers, or major publishers, as well as Fortune 500 consumer products firms using apps for marketing and promotion.

In July 2008, Apple introduced the App Store, which provides a platform for the distribution and sale of apps by Apple as well as by independent developers. Following in the footsteps of the iTunes music store, Apple hoped that the software apps—most free—would drive sales of the iPhone device. It was not expecting the App Store itself to become a major source of revenue. Fast forward to 2012: there are now an estimated 725,000 approved apps available for download from the App Store. Other smartphone developers also followed suit: there are also thousands of apps available for Android

phones, BlackBerrys, and Windows phones. As of June 2012, Apple reported more than 30 billion apps had been downloaded and over 46 million apps are downloaded each day. Apple does not report its app revenues separately, but it does report the amount of money it pays out to app developers, which allows analysts to guess at how much money Apple makes on app sales. Analysts believe apps will generate more than $2 billion for Apple in 2012. Although this is just a fraction of Apple's gross revenues, Apple's primary goal in offering apps is not to make money from them, but instead to drive sales of devices—the iPhones, iPads, and iPods that need software to become useful. It's the reverse of printer companies who make cheap printers in order to sell expensive ink. At the same time, apps tie the customer to a hardware platform: as you add more and more apps to your phone, the cost of switching to, say, an Android, rises with each new app installed.

The app phenomenon, equally virulent on Android and BlackBerry operating system platforms, has spawned a new digital ecosystem: tens of thousands of developers, a wildly popular hardware platform, and millions of consumers looking for a computer in their pocket that can replace their now clunky desktop-laptop Microsoft Windows computers, do a pretty good job as a digital media center while on the road, and, by the way, serve as a cell phone.

The range of applications among the 725,000 or so apps on the Apple platform is staggering and defies brief description. Categories include Business, Travel, Sports & Fitness, Social Networking, News, Lifestyle, Games, Entertainment, Education, Family & Kids, Music, and Apps by Apple. You can use the Genius feature to recommend new apps based on ones you already have. There are so many apps that searching for a particular app can be a problem unless you know the name of the app or the developer. Google is probably the

(continued)

best search engine for apps. Enter a search term like "Kraft app" and you'll find that Kraft has an app called iFood Assistant that provides recipes using Kraft products. The most popular app categories are games, education, entertainment, books, and lifestyle.

The implications of the app ecosystem for e-commerce are significant. The smartphone in your pocket not only becomes a general-purpose computer, but also an always present shopping tool for consumers, as well as an entirely new marketing and advertising platform for vendors. Early e-commerce applications using desktops and laptops were celebrated by pundits as allowing people to shop in their pajamas. Smartphones extend this range from pajamas to office desktops to trains, planes, and cars, all fully clothed. You can shop anywhere, shop everywhere, and shop all the time, in between talking, texting, watching video, and listening to music.

Almost all of the top 100 brands have a presence in at least one of the major app stores, and more than 85% have an app in the Apple App Store. Here are a few examples of how some different firms are using apps to advance and support their brands:

- Benjamin Moore's Color Capture: Enables users to match colors and paints
- Colgate-Palmolive's Max White Photo Recharger: Enables users to whiten their teeth in photos
- Tiffany's Engagement Ring Finder: Lets users view diamonds by size, shape, setting, metal, and design
- Charmin's SitOrSquat: Restroom Finder: Provides users with locations of nearest public bathrooms, including cleanliness reviews, availability of changing tables, and handicapped access.

There are, of course, dangers in any ecosystem dominated by a single company. The Apple iOS platform is closed and proprietary, a walled garden, a limiting sandbox. The apps you buy there can play nowhere else. Many apps are incredibly single-purposed and limited in applicability. While this cannot be said of general-purpose readers, it is true of proprietary e-readers like the New York Times and Wall Street Journal e-readers. Do we need two? Do we need an e-reader for every publication? The apps don't come with any warranty. Because Apple controls who can play in the sandbox, there is the possibility, even the likelihood, that Apple acts as a censor of content, or worse, a monopolist that prevents certain applications from entering the marketplace, or more likely, an arbitrary, inscrutable bureaucratic machine that decides which apps will play and which will not. For instance, in 2010, Apple removed more than 5,000 applications because of sexually themed content. Such programs often appear on the store's list of most-downloaded apps. Clearly Apple is concerned the App Store might become an adult digital theme park that would turn off parents and families who are the target audience for iPhone and iPad sales. Nevertheless, critics note that a Sports Illustrated swimsuit app and a Playboy app survived the purge. But apps from some smaller companies did not and lost substantial business as a result. In 2012, for the first time, Apple was forced to remove malware from its App Store. A Russian app entitled "Find and Call" purported to simplify users' contacts lists, but instead stole those contacts and uploaded the address book to a remote server, spamming those addresses. Clearly, the app ecosystem is not immune to many of the same issues that apply to the Internet and e-commerce at large.

SOURCES: "App Store Metrics," 148Apps.biz, accessed September 10, 2012; "First Instance of iOS App Store Malware Detected, Removed," by Christina Bonnington, Wired.com, July 5, 2012; "iOS Devs Earned $2.5B from Apps Year over Year," by Jolie O'Dell, VentureBeat.com, June 11, 2012; "The Apps Strategies of the Top 100 Brands," by Haydn Shaughnessy, Forbes.com, October 27, 2011; "iSuppli: Apple's App Store Will Dominate the Market Through 2014," by Leslie Horn, PCMag.com, May 4. 2011; "Apple More Than Doubles 2010 Apps Revenue, but Its Market Share Slips," by Danny King, Dailyfinance. com, February 15, 2011; "The State of Mobile Apps," by The Nielsen Company, June 1, 2010; "Mobile Apps and Consumer Product Brands," by Tobi Elkin, eMarketer, March 2010; "Apple Bans Some Apps for Sex-Tinged Content," by Jenna Wortham, *New York Times*, February 22, 2010; "Apple App Store Has Lost $450 Million To Piracy," by Garrett McIntyre and Phil MacDonald, 247Wallstreet.com, January 13, 2010; "Inside the App Economy," by Douglas MacMillan, *BusinessWeek*, October 22, 2009.

Akamai Technologies:
Attempting to Keep Supply Ahead of Demand

I n 2012, the amount of Internet traffic generated by YouTube alone is greater than the amount of traffic on the entire Internet in 2000. In the last year, Netflix's subscriber base jumped by 16 million to more than 27 million subscribers, most of whom are now streaming movies over the Internet and, in June 2012, those subscribers logged approximately one billion hours of content-viewing. Because of video streaming and the explosion in mobile devices demanding high-bandwidth applications, Internet traffic has increased 800% since 2007 and is predicted to triple by the end of 2016. Internet video is now 51% of Internet traffic and will reach 55% by 2016, according to networking giant Cisco Systems. Mobile platform traffic from

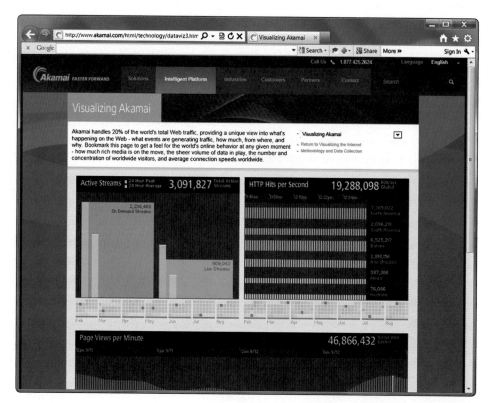

smartphones and Wi-Fi devices is growing at 60% and will soon push cellular networks and the Internet to their capacities. Cisco estimates that annual global Internet traffic will be around 1.3 zettabytes in 2016: that's 1,300 exabytes, or, in other words, 13 with 19 zeroes behind it!

Experts call services like YouTube, Netflix, and high definition streaming video "net bombs" because they threaten the effective operation of the Internet. At some point, demand will exceed capacity, and either there will be "brownouts" where everyone's connection speed slows down or "capping" of bandwidth hogs (those 10% of Internet users who consume 60% of the Internet's capacity because of extensive video downloading).

Analysts differ on how fast Internet capacity is growing. Large telecommunication companies (AT&T, Verizon, Comcast, and Level3) argue that demand will overwhelm capacity by 2015, while other experts argue that Internet bandwidth can double every year for a very long time and easily keep up with demand. Perhaps they're both right: Internet capacity can expand to keep up with demand if sufficient capital is invested in backbone and local networks. That's a big "if." As a result, and in order to raise capital, nearly all the large ISPs such as Comcast, Charter, Cox, and AT&T have bandwidth caps in place where heavy users of video are charged more for their Internet service. More charges based on usage are in the pipeline.

Is Internet bandwidth capacity doubling every year? The proof is in the pudding. How much faster has your home or office bandwidth connection become in the last year? Chances are, your Internet connection speed has not changed in several years, and you may be seeing the effects online. For instance, in 2012, millions of viewers streamed the summer Olympics, including 1.5 million users watching the women's gymnastics team final live. Throughout the first week of events, online viewers reported an avalanche of dropped connections, choppy frame rates, and other technical problems. Even on a regular Friday or Saturday night, the average Internet home viewer will experience stuttering video and sound. This is hardly the stuff of a bright future for mass audience video over the Web.

In today's broadband environment, the threshold of patience is probably much lower than even a few seconds. Increased video and audio customer expectations are bad news for anyone seeking to use the Web for delivery of high-quality multimedia content such as CD-quality music and high definition video. If you are SiriusXM Radio and you want to stream online music to several million users a day, you will definitely need some help. If you are Apple iTunes and want to provide music or and video downloads to your 400 million online customers, you will also need some help. Akamai is one of the Web's major helpers, and each of the preceding companies, along with an overwhelming majority of the Web's top companies, use Akamai's services to speed the delivery of content. Akamai serves more than 3,000 hours of content every minute.

Slow-loading Web pages and Web content—from music to video—sometimes result from poor design, but more often than not, the problem stems from the underlying infrastructure of the Internet. As you have learned in this chapter, the Internet was originally developed to carry text-based e-mail messages among a relatively small group of researchers, not bandwidth-hogging graphics, sound, and video files to tens of millions of people all at once. The Internet is a collection of networks that has to pass information from one network to another. Sometimes the handoff is not smooth. Every 1,500-byte packet of information sent over the Internet must be verified by the receiving server and an acknowledgment sent to the sender. This slows down not only the distribution of content such as music, but also slows down interactive requests, such as purchases, that require the client computer to interact with an online shopping cart. Moreover, each packet may go through many different servers on its way to its final destination, multiplying by several orders of magnitude the number of acknowledgments required to move a packet from New York to San Francisco. The Internet today spends much of its time and capacity verifying packets, contributing to a problem called "latency" or delay. For this reason, a single e-mail with a 1 megabyte attached PDF file can create more than 50 megabytes of Internet traffic and data storage on servers, client hard drives, and network back up drives.

Akamai (which means intelligent, clever, or "cool" in Hawaiian) Technologies was founded by Tom Leighton, an MIT professor of applied mathematics, and Daniel Lewin, an MIT grad student, with the idea of expediting Internet traffic to overcome these limitations. When Timothy Berners-Lee, founder of the World Wide Web, realized that congestion on the Internet was becoming an enormous problem, he issued a challenge to Leighton's research group to invent a better way to deliver Internet content. The result was a set of breakthrough algorithms that became the basis for Akamai. Lewin received his master's degree in electrical engineering and computer science in 1998. His master's thesis was the theoretical starting point for the company. It described storing copies of Web content such as pictures or video clips at many different locations around the Internet so that one could always retrieve a nearby copy, making Web pages load faster.

Officially launched in August 1998, Akamai's current products are based on the Akamai Intelligent Platform, a cloud platform made up of over 105,000 servers within over 1,000 networks in 78 countries around the world, and all within a single network hop of 90% of all Internet users. Akamai software on these servers allows the platform to identify and block security threats and provide comprehensive knowledge of network conditions, as well as instant device-level detection and optimization. Specific products include Aqua Web Solutions for site performance, mobile performance, and data collection and online marketing; Terra Enterprise Solutions that enable businesses to leverage Akamai's cloud platform; Kona Security Solutions and Sola Media Solutions that focus on the delivery of interactive HD quality video on multiple devices; and Aura Network Solutions. Akamai's site performance products allow customers to move their Web content closer to end users so a user in New York City, for instance, will be served L.L.Bean pages from the New York Metro area Akamai servers, while users of the L.L.Bean site in San Francisco will be served pages from Akamai servers in San Francisco. Akamai has a wide range of large corporate and government clients: 1 out of every 3 global Fortune 500 companies, the top 30 media and entertainment companies, 92 of the top 100 online U.S. retailers, all branches of the U.S. military, all the top Internet portals, all the major U.S. sports leagues, and so on. In 2012, Akamai delivers between 15% and 30% of all Web traffic, and over 2 trillion daily Internet interactions.

Other competitors in the content delivery network (CDN) industry include Blue Coat, Limelight, Savvis, and Mirror Image Internet.

Accomplishing this seemingly simple task requires that Akamai monitor the entire Internet, locating potential sluggish areas and devising faster routes for information to travel. Frequently used portions of a client's Web site, or large video or audio files that would be difficult to send to users quickly, are stored on Akamai's servers. When a user requests a song or a video file, his or her request is redirected to an Akamai server nearby and the content served from this local server. Akamai's servers are placed in Tier 1 backbone supplier networks, large ISPs, universities, and other networks. Akamai's software determines which server is optimum for the user and then transmits the "Akamaized" content locally. Web sites that are "Akamaized" can be delivered anywhere from 4 to 10 times as fast as non-Akamaized content. Akamai has developed a number of other business services based on its Internet savvy, including targeted advertising based on user location and zip code, content security, business intelligence, disaster recovery, on-demand bandwidth and computing capacity during spikes in Internet traffic, storage, global traffic management, and streaming services. Akamai also offers a product called Advertising Decision Solutions, which provides companies with intelligence generated by the Internet's most accurate and comprehensive knowledge base of Internet network activity. Akamai's massive server deployment and relationships with networks throughout the world enable optimal collection of geography and bandwidth-sensing information. As a result, Akamai provides a highly accurate knowledge base with worldwide coverage. Customers integrate a simple program into their Web server or application server. This program communicates with the Akamai database to retrieve the very latest information. The Akamai network of servers is constantly mapping the Internet, and at the same time, each company's software is in continual communication with the Akamai network. The result: data is always current. Advertisers can deliver ads based on country, region, city, market area, area code, county, zip code, connection type, and speed. You can see several interesting visualizations of the Internet that log basic real-time Web activity by visiting the Akamai Web site.

The shift towards cloud computing and the mobile platform as well as the growing popularity of streaming video have provided Akamai with new growth opportunities. As more businesses and business models are moving to the Web, Akamai has seen its client base continue to grow beyond the most powerful Internet retailers and online content providers. In 2012, Akamai launched its Aqua Mobile Accelerator service, which automatically senses the quality of a wireless Internet connection and optimizes it continuously. It also detects the type of device submitting a request for data, whether a PC-based browser, smartphone, or tablet, and optimizes content delivery for that platform. Akamai customers report that Aqua Mobile Accelerator has equalized the performance of mobile Web sites and traditional desktop-accessible Web sites. Akamai has also continued to develop the Akamai Intelligent Platform as an alternative to traditional content delivery methods.

Akamai is also acutely aware of the increase in cybercrime as more traffic migrates to the Internet. Growth in Internet traffic is good news for Akamai, but the company

SOURCES: "Facts & Figures," Akamai.com, accessed September 10, 2012; "The State of the Internet, 1st Quarter 2012 Report," by Akamai Technologies, Inc., August 9, 2012; "Akamai Shares Jump on Cloud-Computing Profit Boost," by Sarah Frier, Bloomberg.com, July 26, 2012; "Olympics Website Leans on Open Source, Akamai for Winning Results," by Bernard Golden, CIO.com, June 26, 2012; "You Think the Internet is Big Now? Akamai Needs to Grow 100-Fold," by Mathew Ingram, GigaOM.com, June 20, 2012; Cisco Visual Networking Index, 2011-2016," by Cisco Systems, Inc., May 30, 2012; "Akamai Eyes Acceleration Boost for Mobile Content," by Stephen Lawson, *Computerworld*, March 20, 2012; "Akamai Now Running 105,000 Servers," by Rich Miller, datacenterknowledge.com, March 8, 2012; "To Cash In on Wave of Web Attacks, Akamai Launches Standalone Security Business," by Andy Greenberg, Forbes.com, February 21, 2012; "Internet Data Caps Cometh," by Holman Jenkins, *Wall Street Journal*, May 11, 2011; "Wider Streets for Internet Traffic," by Anne Eisenberg, *New York Times*, October 9, 2010; "Google TV, Apple TV, and Roku's Biggest Enemy: A Lack of Internet Bandwidth," by Steven Vaughan-Nichols, zdnet.com, October 8, 2010; "Obama Pledges to Increase Internet Capacity," by Stephanie Kirchgaessner and Kenneth Li, FT.com, June 29, 2010.

must also now deal with politically motivated cyberattacks, organized crime online, and state-sponsored cyberwarfare. In 2012, Akamai unveiled its Kona Site Defender tool, which offers a variety of security measures for Akamai clients. The tool protects against Distributed Denial of Service (DDoS) attacks and includes a firewall for Web applications. Analysts also expect Akamai to acquire Web security companies to bolster that aspect of their business, with a focus on companies offering the ability to block viruses, prevent data loss, and control bandwidth through the Internet rather than with traditional software or hardware. With so many businesses now dependent on the uninterrupted flow of content over the Internet, Akamai is in a very strong position to sell security services to its customers. However, as impressive as Akamai's operation has become, it may not be nearly enough to cope with the next 5 to 10 years of Internet growth.

Case Study Questions

1. Why does Akamai need to geographically disperse its servers to deliver its customers' Web content?

2. If you wanted to deliver software content over the Internet, would you sign up for Akamai's service? What alternatives exist?

3. What advantages does an advertiser derive from using Akamai's service? What kinds of products might benefit from this kind of service?

4. Why don't major business firms distribute their videos using P2P networks like BitTorrent?

5. Do you think Internet users should be charged based on the amount of bandwidth they consume, or on a tiered plan where users would pay in rough proportion to their usage?

3.8 REVIEW

KEY CONCEPTS

■ Discuss the origins of the Internet.

The Internet has evolved from a collection of mainframe computers located on a few U.S. college campuses to an interconnected network of thousands of networks and millions of computers worldwide. The history of the Internet can be divided into three phases:

- During the *Innovation Phase* (1961–1974), the Internet's purpose was to link researchers nationwide via computer.
- During the *Institutionalization Phase* (1975–1995), the Department of Defense and National Science Foundation provided funding to expand the fundamental building blocks of the Internet into a complex military communications system and then into a civilian system.

- During the *Commercialization Phase* (1995 to the present), government agencies encouraged corporations to assume responsibility for further expansion of the network, and private business began to exploit the Internet for commercial purposes.

■ **Identify the key technology concepts behind the Internet.**

The Internet's three key technology components are:
- *Packet switching*, which slices digital messages into packets, routes the packets along different communication paths as they become available, and then reassembles the packets once they arrive at their destination.
- *TCP/IP*, which is the core communications protocol for the Internet. TCP establishes the connections among sending and receiving Web computers and makes sure that packets sent by one computer are received in the sequence by the other, without any packets missing. IP provides the addressing scheme and is responsible for the actual delivery of the packets.
- *Client/server technology*, which makes it possible for large amounts of information to be stored on Web servers and shared with individual users on their client computers (which may be desktop PCs, laptops, netbooks, tablets, or smartphones).

■ **Discuss the impact of the mobile platform and cloud computing**
- The mobile platform is becoming the primary means for accessing the Internet.
- The number of cellphone subscribers worldwide far exceeds the number of PC owners.
- The form factor of PCs has changed from desktops to laptops and tablet computers such as the iPad.
- Smartphones are a disruptive technology that radically alters the personal computing and e-commerce landscape.
- Cloud computing refers to a model of computing in which firms and individuals obtain computing power and software applications over the Internet, rather than purchasing the hardware and software and installing it on their own computers. Cloud computing is the fastest growing form of computing.

■ **Describe the role of Internet protocols and utility programs.**

Internet protocols and utility programs make the following Internet services possible:
- *HTTP* delivers requested Web pages, allowing users to view them.
- *SMTP* and *POP* enable e-mail to be routed to a mail server and then picked up by the recipient's server, while *IMAP* enables e-mail to be sorted before being downloaded by the recipient.
- *SSL* and *TLS* ensure that information transmissions are encrypted.
- *FTP* is used to transfer files from servers to clients and vice versa.
- *Telnet* is a utility program that enables work to be done remotely.
- *Ping* is a utility program that allows users to verify a connection between client and server.
- *Tracert* lets you track the route a message takes from a client to a remote computer.

■ Explain the structure of the Internet today.

The main structural elements of the Internet are:
- The *backbone*, which is composed primarily of high-bandwidth fiber-optic cable operated by a variety of providers.
- *IXPs*, which are hubs that use high-speed switching computers to connect the backbone with regional and local networks.
- *CANs*, which are local area networks operating within a single organization that connect directly to regional networks.
- *ISPs*, which deal with the "last mile" of service to homes and offices. ISPs offer a variety of types of service, ranging from dial-up service to broadband DSL, cable modem, T1 and T3 lines, and satellite link service.
- *Governing bodies*, such as IAB, ICANN, IESG, IETF, ISOC, W3C, and ITU. Although they do not control the Internet, they have influence over it and monitor its operations.

■ Understand the limitations of today's Internet.

To envision what the Internet of tomorrow—Internet II—will look like, we must first look at the limitations of today's Internet:
- *Bandwidth limitations.* Today's Internet is slow and incapable of effectively sharing and displaying large files, such as video and voice files.
- *Quality of service limitations.* Data packets don't all arrive in the correct order, at the same moment, causing latency; latency creates jerkiness in video files and voice messages.
- *Network architecture limitations.* Servers can't keep up with demand. Future improvements to Internet infrastructure will improve the way servers process requests for information, thus improving overall speed.
- *Language development limitations.* The nature of HTML restricts the quality of "rich" information that can be shared online. Future languages will enable improved display and viewing of video and graphics.
- *Limitations arising from the "wired" nature of the Internet.* The Internet is based primarily on physical cables, which restricts the mobility of users.

■ Describe the potential capabilities of the Internet of the future.

Internet2 is a consortium working together to develop and test new technologies for potential use on the Internet. In addition to the Internet2 project, other groups are working to expand Internet bandwidth via improvements to fiber optics. Wireless LAN and 4G technologies are providing users of smartphones and tablet computers with increased access to the Internet and its various services. The increased bandwidth and expanded connections will result in a number of benefits, including latency solutions; guaranteed service levels; lower error rates; and declining costs. The Internet of Things will be a big part of the Internet of the future, with more and more sensor-equipped devices machines and devices connected to the Internet.

■ Understand how the Web works.

The Web was developed during 1989–1991 by Dr. Tim Berners-Lee, who created a computer program that allowed formatted pages stored on the Internet to be linked using keywords (hyperlinks). In 1993, Marc Andreessen created the first graphical Web browser, which made it possible to view documents on the Web graphically and created the possibility of universal computing. The key concepts you need to be familiar with in order to understand how the Web works are the following:

- *Hypertext*, which is a way of formatting pages with embedded links that connect documents to one another and that also link pages to other objects.
- *HTTP*, which is the protocol used to transmit Web pages over the Internet.
- *URLs*, which are the addresses at which Web pages can be found.
- *HTML*, which is the programming language used to create most Web pages and which provides designers with a fixed set of tags that are used to format a Web page.
- *XML*, which is a newer markup language that allows designers to describe data and information.
- *Web server software*, which is software that enables a computer to deliver Web pages written in HTML to client computers that request this service by sending an HTTP request. Web server software also provides security services, FTP, search engine, and data capture services. The term Web server also is used to refer to the physical computer that runs the Web server software.
- *Web clients*, which are computing devices attached to the Internet that are capable of making HTTP requests and displaying HTML pages.
- *Web browsers*, which display Web pages and also have added features such as e-mail and newsgroups.

■ **Describe how Internet and Web features and services support e-commerce.**

Together, the Internet and the Web make e-commerce possible by allowing computer users to access product and service information and to complete purchases online. Some of the specific features that support e-commerce include:

- *E-mail*, which uses a series of protocols to enable messages containing text, images, sound, and video clips to be transferred from one Internet user to another. E-mail is used in e-commerce as a marketing and customer support tool.
- *Instant messaging*, which allows messages to be sent between two users almost instantly, allowing parties to engage in a two-way conversation. In e-commerce, companies are using instant messaging as a customer support tool.
- *Search engines*, which identify Web pages that match a query submitted by a user. Search engines assist users in locating Web pages related to items they may want to buy.
- *Online forums* (message boards), which enable users to communicate with each other, although not in real time, and online chat, which allows users to communicate in real time (simultaneously), are being used in e-commerce as community-building tools.
- *Streaming media*, which enables music, video, and other large files to be sent to users in chunks so that when received and played, the file comes through uninterrupted. Like standard digital files, streaming media may be sold as digital content and used as a marketing tool.
- *Cookies*, which are small text files that allow a Web site to store information about a user, are used by e-commerce as a marketing tool. Cookies allow Web sites to personalize the site to the user and also permit customization and market segmentation.

Web 2.0 features and services include:

- *Social networks*, which are online services that support communication within networks of friends, colleagues, and even entire professions.
- *Blogs*, which are personal Web pages that typically contain a series of chronological entries (newest to oldest) by the author and links to related Web pages.
- *RSS*, which is an XML format that allows users to have digital content, including text, articles, blogs, and podcast audio files, automatically sent to their computers over the Internet.
- *Podcasts*, which are audio presentations—such as a radio show, audio from a movie, or simply personal audio presentations—stored as audio files and posted to the Web.
- *Wikis*, which are Web applications that allow a user to easily add and edit content on a Web page.
- *Music and video services*, such as iTunes and digital video on demand.
- *Internet telephony*, which uses VoIP to transmit audio communication over the Internet.
- *Online software and services*, such as Web apps, widgets, and gadgets.

■ **Understand the impact of m-commerce applications.**

- M-commerce applications are part of the larger $25 billion m-commerce market. They facilitate many aspects of this larger market, and sales of mobile apps currently account for about $6.7 billion in annual revenue.
- The average consumer spends about an hour a day interacting with the Web and apps on their smartphone, with more than two-thirds of that time spent on mobile apps.
- There are a variety of different platforms for mobile application development including Objective-C (for iOS devices), Java (BlackBerrys and Android smartphones), and C and C++ (Windows mobile devices and some BlackBerry coding).
- Mobile apps for the iPhone are distributed through Apple's App Store, for BlackBerrys through RIM's App World, for Android devices through Google Play, and for Windows mobile devices through Microsoft's Windows Phone Marketplace. There are also third-party vendors such as Amazon's Appstore.

QUESTIONS

1. What are the three basic building blocks of the Internet?
2. What is latency, and how does it interfere with Internet functioning?
3. Explain how packet switching works.
4. How is the TCP/IP protocol related to information transfer on the Internet?
5. What technological innovation made client/server computing possible?
6. What is cloud computing, and how has it impacted the Internet?
7. Why are smartphones a disruptive technology?
8. What types of companies form the Internet backbone today?
9. What function do the IXPs serve?
10. What is the goal of the Internet2 project?
11. Compare and contrast intranets, extranets, and the Internet as a whole.
12. What are some of the major limitations of today's Internet?

13. What are some of the challenges of policing the Internet? Who has the final say when it comes to content?
14. Compare and contrast the capabilities of Wi-Fi and 3G/4G wireless networks.
15. What are the basic capabilities of a Web server?
16. What are the major technological advancements that are anticipated to accompany the Internet of the future? Discuss the importance of each.
17. Why was the development of the browser so significant for the growth of the Web?
18. What advances and features does HTML5 offer?
19. Name and describe five services currently available through the Web.
20. Why are mobile apps the next big thing?

PROJECTS

1. Review the opening case on augmented reality. What developments have occurred since the date this case was written in September 2012?

2. Locate where cookies are stored on your computer. (They are probably in a folder entitled "Cookies" within your browser program.) List the top 10 cookies you find and write a brief report describing the kinds of sites that placed the cookies. What purpose do you think the cookies serve? Also, what do you believe are the major advantages and disadvantages of cookies? In your opinion, do the advantages outweigh the disadvantages, or vice versa?

3. Call or visit the Web sites of a cable provider, DSL provider, and satellite provider to obtain information on their Internet services. Prepare a brief report summarizing the features, benefits, and costs of each. Which is the fastest? What, if any, are the downsides of selecting any of the three for Internet service (such as additional equipment purchases)?

4. Select two countries (excluding the United States) and prepare a short report describing their basic Internet infrastructure. Are they public or commercial? How and where do they connect to backbones within the United States?

5. Investigate the Internet of Things. Select one example and describe what it is and how it works.

CHAPTER 4

Building an E-commerce Presence: Web Sites, Mobile Sites, and Apps

After reading this chapter, you will be able to:

- Explain the process that should be followed in building an e-commerce Web site.
- Describe the major issues surrounding the decision to outsource site development and/ or hosting.
- Identify and understand the major considerations involved in choosing Web server and e-commerce merchant server software.
- Understand the issues involved in choosing the most appropriate hardware for an e-commerce site.
- Identify additional tools that can improve Web site performance.
- Understand the important considerations involved in developing a mobile Web site and building mobile applications.

Tommy Hilfiger

Replatforms

Tommy Hilfiger is one of the world's best known premium lifestyle brands in the United States for the 18–35 age demographic. Founded in 1985 by Tommy Hilfiger, a young designer in New York City, the brand expanded its line of casual clothing for men, women, and children through specialty retailers, department stores, and more than 1,000 apparel stores and outlets throughout the world. In 2010, the company was purchased by Phillips-Van Heusen, owner of the Calvin Klein brand, for $3 billion. The resulting company is the world's largest clothing

© incamerastock / Alamy

company, with $5.9 billion in revenues in 2011, with Tommy Hilfiger generating $3.1 billion of those revenues.

A significant part of the company's growth since 2007 has occurred through its online stores. The company had developed a Web store in 2000 as a simple catalog of products available at retailers and then expanded into online sales by 2004. By 2006, it was clear that effective online retailing required more than just a storefront with a catalog, and more than a database responding to customer requests for products. The existing Web site did not fit the contemporary needs and expectations of customers or company merchandisers. For instance, it was difficult to change prices, move products around the online catalog depending on demand, measure results, build promotions, or personalize the offerings based on customer histories and online behavior. There was no recommender system that could suggest clothing to online customers based on their prior behavior. Instead, products were promoted based on what marketing managers wanted or needed to sell regardless of what the customer wanted. If you're buying a pair of jeans, chances are good, based on prior customer behavior, that you will want to consider a new belt or shoes.

Hilfiger did not want to hire an entire new IT staff to rebuild its Web site, and it did not want to make the investment in hardware and telecommunications that would be required for a new Web site. Instead it turned to Art Technology Group (ATG), a firm specializing in e-commerce software and hardware solutions. The ATG e-commerce platform software provided Hilfiger managers with a state-of-the-art e-commerce platform with automated recommendations that can deliver a personalized experience to each customer, and easy marketing and promotional campaign support to Hilfiger managers through a cutting-edge Business Control Center. Best of all, the ATG platform solution was an on-demand, online software platform. Hilfiger did not have to buy any hardware or software infrastructure, or hire IT staff, to build the new Web site. One way to "right-size" a Web site's infrastructure is to shift the risks and costs of infrastructure to external, specialized firms that can operate the infrastructure for you. From a "look and feel" standpoint, the Web site distinctly captured the Tommy Hilfiger "vibe," also an important consideration. Advancing the brand experience through the Web site was a major driver in its redesign. The result was a smashing success: online sales for Hilfiger increased 30% in the first year of operation.

But success comes with costs: in 2011, Tommy Hilfiger decided to replatform its global IT infrastructure because of the growth in its complex business, and because of the demands of customers using its Web sites and partner sites like eBay who needed far more support as sales expanded. Hilfiger had swiftly transformed from a bricks-and-mortar retailer into a more complex retail operation with substantial online sales, and now had to deal with online service issues, returns, payments, shipping, and customer support issues on a global basis. The challenge was implementing a new platform that would allow all regions to grow, while meeting the needs of different markets. The company turned to SAP to create a new global enterprise infrastructure and help build out its mobile Web applications both for retail customers but also for its global suppliers and retailers.

In 2012, Hilfiger continues to build on its e-commerce success. Its Facebook page has more than 4.4 million Likes, and almost 70,000 people talking about the company's clothing on Facebook. Hilfiger has also broadened its social visual site presence through an extensive photo blog on Tumblr and a smaller presence on Pinterest. It has a Twitter feed, and an iPhone app that allows customers to try on digital versions of select pieces in virtual fitting rooms. For the iPad, Hilfiger has created the iPad Fit Guide, which uses video imaging to capture a 360-degree view of the clothing. Customers can compare the fit of different products, view alternative styling suggestions, and read about the specifics of the cut and rise of each pant.

For start-ups and small businesses, there are of course many less-costly alternatives to using a sophisticated tool like ATG's or SAP's sophisticated e-commerce platforms. For instance, one solution is to build a Web site using pre-built templates offered by Yahoo! Merchant Solutions, Amazon, eBay, Network Solutions, or hundreds of other online sites. Fees range from a few hundred dollars to several thousand. These firms host your Web site and they worry about capacity and scale issues as your firm grows. For instance, Yahoo Merchant Solutions offers three different packages: Starter, Standard, and Professional. As the business grows, you can move up to a more comprehensive package. Amazon will even handle the fulfillment of orders for you and probably do a much better job than you or your limited staff can do.

The cost of building Web sites has fallen drastically, not just because of the fall in hardware costs, but also because the cost of software needed to build and operate Web sites has fallen, sometimes to zero. There are thousands of open source software tools available to develop Web sites and associated databases that will cost you nothing. Many of these tools can be used by amateurs, some are as simple to use as blog software tools, while others require a technical background and training. Analysts believe that a Web site costing more than $1 million in 2000 could be built for less than $50,000 in 2012. For instance, you can obtain the Linux operating system to run your Web site for next to nothing, along with osCommerce, an open source shopping cart order system. In the past, building your own custom shopping cart could easily cost $250,000 and up to several million dollars. However, building the Web business yourself will cost you dearly in time, and delay your entrance to the market. How much is your time worth? Remember, the "e" in e-commerce does not stand for easy.

SOURCES: "How Do You Know When It's Time to Replatform," by Jared Blank, slide presentation, June 14, 2012; PVH Corporation, "SEC Form 10-K for the Fiscal Year 2011," Securities and Exchange Commission, filed on March 28, 2012; "Tommy Hilfiger Bolsters in-store Summer Traffic via iPad App," by Rimma Kats, Mobilemarketer.com, June 30, 2011; "Virtual Fitting Room...In Reality," by Justin Disandro, Socialtechpop.com, May 5, 2011; "Interview: Jared Blank, VP E-commerce for Tommy Hilfiger," Patperdue.com, March 23, 2011; "ShopTommy.com Dresses For Online Success—On Demand," Case Study, ATG.com, June 2010; "Finding the Right Fit for Multi-Channel Commerce: American Eagle Outfitters," Case Study, ATG.com, June 2010; "Technology for the Solo Entrepreneur," by William Bulkeley, *Wall Street Journal*, May 17, 2010; "Calvin Klein Owner Buys Tommy Hilfiger," BBCnews.co.uk, March 15, 2010.

I n Chapter 3, you learned about e-commerce's technological foundation: the Internet, Web, and the mobile platform. In this chapter, you will examine the important factors that a manager needs to consider when building an e-commerce presence. The focus will be on the managerial and business decisions you must make before you begin, and that you will continually need to make. Although building a sophisticated e-commerce presence isn't easy, today's tools are much less expensive and far more powerful than they were during the early days of e-commerce. You do not have to be Amazon or eBay to create a successful Web e-commerce presence. In this chapter, we focus on both small and medium-sized businesses as well as much larger corporate entities that serve thousands of customers a day, or even an hour. As you will see, although the scale may be very different, the principles and considerations are basically the same.

4.1 IMAGINE YOUR E-COMMERCE PRESENCE

Before you begin to build a Web site or app of your own, there are some important questions you will need to think about and answer. The answers to these questions will drive the development and implementation of your online presence.

WHAT'S THE IDEA? (THE VISIONING PROCESS)

Before you can plan and actually build a Web presence, you need to have a vision of what you hope to accomplish and how you hope to accomplish it. The vision includes not just a statement of mission, but also identification of the target audience, characterization of the market space, a strategic analysis, an Internet marketing matrix, and a development timeline. It starts with a dream of what's possible, and concludes with a timeline and preliminary budget for development of the Web presence.

If you examine any successful Web site, you can usually tell from the home page what the vision that inspires the site is. If the company is a public company, you can often find a succinct statement of its vision or mission in the reports it files with the Securities and Exchange Commission. For Amazon, it's to become the largest marketplace on earth. For Facebook, it's to make the world more open and connected. For Google, it's to organize the world's information and make it universally accessible and useful. The Web presence you want to build may not have such all encompassing ambitions, but a succinct statement of mission, purpose, and direction is the key factor in driving the development of your project. For instance, the Tommy.com Web site reflects the brand image of Tommy Hilfiger Inc., whose primary mission is (as noted in its annual report) to combine fresh American style with unique details to give time-honored classics an updated look for customers who desire high quality, designer apparel at competitive prices under a number of different labels. Most Web sites and presences are much more focused. For instance, Texture Media, which operates NaturallyCurly.com, described in the Insight on Business case later in this chapter, describes itself as a social media company empowering, embracing and connecting the world of curls, kinks and waves. The NaturallyCurly Web site is clearly aimed at creating a community of women surrounding the topics of hair, fashion, and health. The mission of Theknot.com is to be the Internet's comprehensive, one-stop wedding planning solution.

WHERE'S THE MONEY: BUSINESS AND REVENUE MODEL

Once you have defined a mission statement, a vision, you need to start thinking about where the money will be coming from. You will need to develop a preliminary idea of your business and revenue models. You don't need detailed revenue and cost projections at this point. Instead, you need a general idea of how your business will generate revenues. The basic choices have been described in Chapter 2. Basic business models are portal, e-tailer, content provider, transaction broker, market creator, service provider, and community provider (social network).

The basic revenue model alternatives are advertising, subscriptions, transaction fees, sales, and affiliate revenue. There's no reason to adopt a single business or revenue model, and in fact, many firms have multiple models. For instance, the New York Times digital business model is to both sell subscriptions and sell ad space. In addition, they sell unique photographs and gifts. At Theknot.com, a vertical portal for the wedding industry, you will find ads, affiliate relationships, and sponsorships from major creators of wedding products and services, including a directory to local wedding planners, all of which produce revenue for Theknot.com. Petsupplies.com and Petsmart.com, the most popular pet Web sites in the United States, have more focused sales revenue models, and present themselves almost entirely as etailers of pet supplies.

WHO AND WHERE IS THE TARGET AUDIENCE

Without a clear understanding of your target audience, you will not have a successful Web presence. There are two questions here: who is your target audience and where are they on the Web? Your target audience can be described in a number of ways: demographics, behavior patterns (lifestyle), current consumption patterns (online vs. offline purchasing), digital usage patterns, content creation preferences (blogs, social networks, sites like Pinterest), and buyer personas (profiles of your typical customer). Understanding the demographics of your target audience is usually the first step. Demographic information includes age, income, gender, and location. In some cases, this may be obvious and in others, much less so. For instance, Harley-Davidson sells motorcycles to a very broad demographic range of varying ages, incomes, and locations, from 34-year-olds to 65-year-olds. Although most of the purchasers are middle-aged men, with middle incomes, many of the men ride with women, and the Harley-Davidson Web site has a collection of women's clothing and several Web pages devoted to women riders. While the majority of men who purchase Harley-Davidsons have modest incomes, a significant group of purchasers are professionals with above-average incomes. Hence, the age and income demographic target is quite broad. What ties Harley-Davidson riders together is not their shared demographics, but their love of the motorcycles and the brand, and the lifestyle associated with touring the highways of America on a powerful motorcycle that sounds like a potato popper. In contrast, a site like Theknot.com is aimed at women in the 18–34-year-old range who are in varying stages of getting married, with lifestyles that include shopping online, using smartphones and tablets, downloading apps, and using Facebook. This audience is technologically hip. These women read and contribute to blogs, comment on forums, and use Pinterest to find ideas for fashion. A "typical" visitor to Theknot.com would be a 28-year-old woman who has an engagement ring, is just starting the wedding planning process, has an income of $45,000, lives in the Northeast, and is interested in a beach wedding. There are of course other "typical" profiles. For each profile for your Web site you will need to develop a detailed description.

WHAT IS THE BALLPARK? CHARACTERIZE THE MARKETPLACE

The chances of your success will depend greatly on the characteristics of the market you are about to enter, and not just on your entrepreneurial brilliance. Enter into a declining market filled with strong competitors, and you will multiply your chances of failure. Enter into a market that is emerging, growing and has few competitors, and you stand a better chance. Enter a market where there are no players, and you will either be rewarded handsomely with a profitable monopoly on a successful product no one else thought of (Apple) or you will be quickly forgotten because there isn't a market for your product at this point in time (the Franklin e-book reader circa 1999).

Features of the marketplace to focus on include the demographics of the market and how a Web presence fits into the market. In addition, you will want to know about the structure of the market: competitors and substitute products.

What are the features of the marketplace you are about to enter? Is the market growing, or receding in size? If it's growing, among which age and income groups? Is the marketplace shifting from offline to online delivery? If so, is the market moving towards traditional Web sites, mobile, and/or tablets? Is there a special role for a mobile presence in this market? What percentage of your target audience uses a Web site, smartphone, or tablet? What about social networks? What's the buzz on products like yours? Are your potential customers talking about the products and services you want to offer on Facebook, Twitter, or blogs? How many blogs focus on products like yours? How many Twitter posts mention similar offerings? How many Facebook Likes (signs of customer engagement) are attached to products you want to offer?

The structure of the market is described in terms of your direct competitors, suppliers, and substitute products. You will want to make a list of the top five or ten competitors and try to describe their market share, and distinguishing characteristics. Some of your competitors may offer traditional versions of your products, while others will offer new renditions or versions of products that have new features. You need to find out everything you can about your competitors. What's the market buzz on your competitors? How many unique monthly visitors (UMVs) do they have? How many Facebook Likes, Twitter followers, and/or Pinterest followers? How are your competitors using social sites and mobile devices as a part of their online presence. Is there something special you could do with social networks that your competitors do not? Do a search on customer reviews of their products. You can find online services (some of them free) that will measure the number of online conversations about your competitors, and the total share of Internet voice each of your competitors receives. Do your competitors have a special relationship with their suppliers that you may not have access to? Exclusive marketing arrangements would be one example of a special supplier relationship. Finally, are there substitutes for your products and services? For instance, your site may offer advice to the community of pet owners, but local pet stores or local groups may be a more trusted source of advice on pets.

WHERE'S THE CONTENT COMING FROM?

Web sites are like books: they're composed of a lot pages that have content ranging from text, to graphics, photos, and videos. This content is what search engines catalog as they crawl through all the new and changed Web pages on the Internet. The content is why your customers visit your site and either purchase things or look at ads which generate revenue for you. Therefore, the content is the single most important foundation for your revenue and ultimate success.

There's generally two kinds of content: static and dynamic. Static content is text and images that do not frequently change, such as product descriptions, photos, or text that you create to share with your visitors. Dynamic content is content that changes regularly, say, daily or hourly. Dynamic content can be created by you, or increasingly, by bloggers and fans of your Web site and products. User generated content has a number of advantages: it's free, it engages your customer fan base, and search engines are more likely to catalog your site if the content is changing. Other sources of content, especially photos, are external Web sites that aggregate content such as Pinterest, discussed in the opening case in Chapter 1.

KNOW YOURSELF: CONDUCT A SWOT ANALYSIS

A **SWOT analysis** is a simple but powerful method for strategizing about your business and understanding where you should focus your efforts. In a SWOT analysis you describe your strengths, weaknesses, threats, and opportunities. In the example SWOT analysis in **Figure 4.1**, you will see a profile of a typical start-up venture that includes a unique approach to an existing market, a promise of addressing unmet needs in this market, and the use of newer technologies (social and mobile platforms) that older

SWOT analysis
describes a firm's strengths, weaknesses, opportunities, and threats

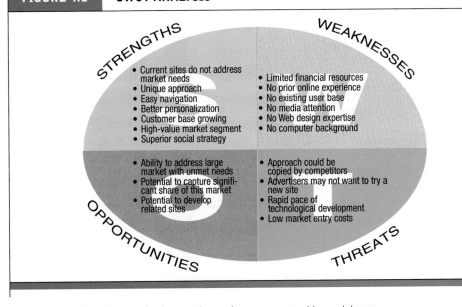

| FIGURE 4.1 | SWOT ANALYSIS |

A SWOT analysis describes your firm's strengths, weaknesses, opportunities, and threats.

competitors may have overlooked. There are many opportunities to address an large market with unmet needs, as well as the potential to use the initial Web site as a home base and spin-off related or nearby sites, leveraging the investment in design and technology. But there are also weaknesses and threats. Lack of financial and human resources are typically the biggest weakness of start-up sites. Threats include competitors that could develop the same capabilities as you, and low market entry costs which might encourage many more start-ups to enter the marketplace.

Once you have conducted a SWOT analysis, you can consider ways to overcome your weaknesses and build on your strengths. For instance, you could consider hiring or partnering to obtain technical and managerial expertise, and looking for financing opportunities (including friends and relatives).

DEVELOP AN E-COMMERCE PRESENCE MAP

E-commerce has moved from being a PC-centric activity on the Web to a mobile and tablet-based activity as well. While 80% or more of e-commerce today is conducted using PCs, increasingly smartphones and tablets will be used for purchasing. Currently, smartphones and tablets are used by a majority of Internet users in the United States to shop for goods and services, explore purchase options, look up prices, and access social sites. Your potential customers use these various devices at different times during the day, and involve themselves in different conversations depending what they are doing—touching base with friends, tweeting, or reading a blog. Each of these are "touch points" where you can meet the customer, and you have to think about how you develop a presence in these different virtual places. **Figure 4.2** provides a roadmap to the platforms and related activities you will need to think about when developing your e-commerce presence.

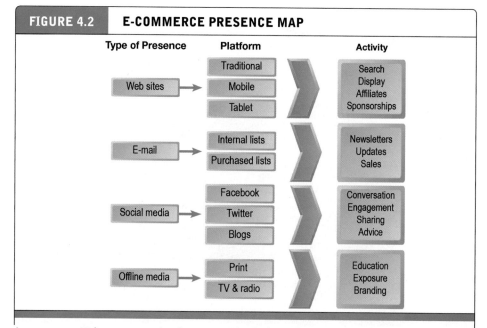

FIGURE 4.2   **E-COMMERCE PRESENCE MAP**

An e-commerce Web presence requires firms to consider the four different kinds of Web presence, and the platforms and activities associated with type of presence.

Figure 4.2 illustrates four different kinds of an e-commerce presence: Web sites, e-mail, social media, and offline media. For each of these types there are different platforms that you will need to address. For instance, in the case of Web site presence, there are three different platforms: traditional desktop, tablets, and smartphones, each with different capabilities. And for each type of e-commerce presence there are related activities you will need to consider. For instance, in the case of Web sites, you will want to engage in search engine marketing, display ads, affiliate programs, and sponsorships. Offline media, the fourth type of e-commerce presence, is included here because many firms use multiplatform or integrated marketing where print ads refer customers to Web sites. The marketing activities in Figure 4.2 are described in much greater detail in Chapters 6 and 7.

DEVELOP A TIMELINE: MILESTONES

Where would you like to be a year from now? It's a good idea for you to have a rough idea of the time frame for developing your e-commerce presence when you begin. You should break your project down into a small number of phases that could be completed within a specified time. Six phases are usually enough detail at this point. **Table 4.1** illustrates a one-year timeline for the development of a start-up Web site devoted to teenage fashions.

HOW MUCH WILL THIS COST?

It's too early in the process to develop a detailed budget for your e-commerce presence, but it is a good time to develop a preliminary idea of the costs involved. How much you spend on a Web site depends on what you want it to do. Simple Web sites can be built and hosted with a first-year cost of $5,000 or less if all the work is done in-house by yourself and others willing to work without pay. A more reasonable budget for a small Web start-up would be $25,000 to $50,000. Here the firm owner would develop all the content at no cost, and a Web designer and programmer would be hired to implement

TABLE 4.1	E-COMMERCE PRESENCE TIMELINE	
PHASE	ACTIVITY	MILESTONE
Phase 1: Planning	Envision Web presence; determine personnel	Web mission statement
Phase 2: Web site development	Acquire content; develop a site design; arrange for hosting the site	Web site plan
Phase 3: Web Implementation	Develop keywords and metatags; focus on search engine optimization; identify potential sponsors	A functional Web site
Phase 4: Social media plan	Identify appropriate social platforms and content for your products and services	A social media plan
Phase 5: Social media implementation	Develop Facebook, Twitter, and Pinterest presence	Functioning social media presence
Phase 6: Mobile plan	Develop a mobile plan; consider options for porting your Web site to smartphones	A mobile media plan

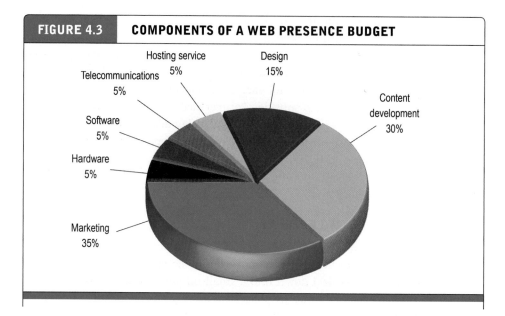

FIGURE 4.3 **COMPONENTS OF A WEB PRESENCE BUDGET**

While hardware and software costs have fallen dramatically, Web sites face significant design, content development, and marketing costs.

the initial Web site. As discussed later, the Web site would be hosted on a cloud-based server. The Web sites of large firms that offer high levels of interactivity and linkage to corporate systems can cost several hundred thousand to millions of dollars a year to create and operate.

While how much you spend to build a Web site depends on how much you can afford, and, of course, the size of the opportunity, **Figure 4.3** provides some idea of the relative size of various Web site costs. In general, the cost of hardware, software, and telecommunications for building and operating a Web site has fallen dramatically (by over 50%) in the last decade, making it possible for very small entrepreneurs to build fairly sophisticated sites. At the same time, while technology has lowered the costs of system development, the costs of marketing, content development, and design have risen to make up more than half of typical Web site budgets. The longer term costs would also have to include site and system maintenance which are not included here.

4.2 BUILDING AN E-COMMERCE PRESENCE: A SYSTEMATIC APPROACH

Once you have developed a vision of the Web presence you want to build, it's time to start thinking about how to build and implement the Web presence. Building a successful e-commerce presence requires a keen understanding of business, technology, and social issues, as well as a systematic approach. E-commerce is just too important to be left totally to technologists and programmers.

The two most important management challenges are (1) developing a clear understanding of your business objectives and (2) knowing how to choose the right technology to achieve those objectives. The first challenge requires you to build a plan for developing your firm's presence. The second challenge requires you to understand some of the basic elements of e-commerce infrastructure. Let the business drive the technology.

Even if you decide to outsource the development effort and operation to a service provider, you will still need to have a development plan and some understanding of the basic e-commerce infrastructure issues such as cost, capability, and constraints. Without a plan and a knowledge base, you will not be able to make sound management decisions about e-commerce within your firm (Laudon and Laudon, 2012).

PIECES OF THE SITE-BUILDING PUZZLE

Let's assume you are a manager for a medium-sized industrial parts firm in the United States. You have been given a budget of $100,000 to develop an e-commerce presence for the firm. The purpose will be to sell and service the firm's customers, who are mostly small machine and metal fabricating shops, and to engage your customers through a blog and user forum. Where do you start? In the following sections, we will examine developing an e-commerce Web site, and then, at the end of the chapter, discuss some of the considerations involved in developing a mobile site and building mobile applications.

First, you must be aware of the main areas where you will need to make decisions (see **Figure 4.4**). On the organizational and human resources fronts, you will have to bring together a team of individuals who possess the skill sets needed to build and manage a successful e-commerce Web site. This team will make the key decisions about business objectives and strategy, technology, site design, and social and information policies. The entire development effort must be closely managed if you hope to avoid the disasters that have occurred at some firms.

You will also need to make decisions about hardware, software, and telecommunications infrastructure. The demands of your customers should drive your choices of technology. Your customers will want technology that enables them to find what they want easily, view the product, purchase the product, and then receive the product from your warehouses quickly. You will also have to carefully consider design. Once you have identified the key decision areas, you will need to think about a plan for the project.

FIGURE 4.4	PIECES OF THE E-COMMERCE SITE-BUILDING PUZZLE

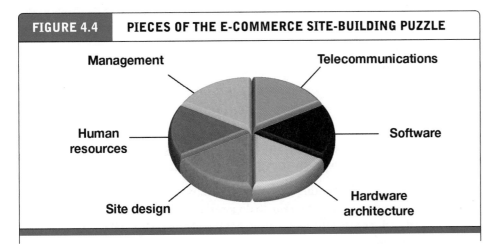

Building an e-commerce Web site requires that you systematically consider the many factors that go into the process.

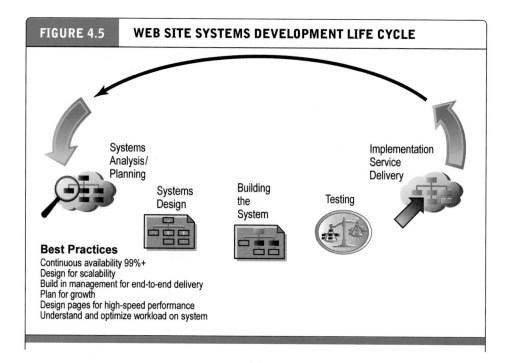

FIGURE 4.5   WEB SITE SYSTEMS DEVELOPMENT LIFE CYCLE

PLANNING: THE SYSTEMS DEVELOPMENT LIFE CYCLE

Your second step in building an e-commerce Web site will be creating a plan document. In order to tackle a complex problem such as building an e-commerce site, you will have to proceed systematically through a series of steps. One methodology is the systems development life cycle. The **systems development life cycle (SDLC)** is a methodology for understanding the business objectives of any system and designing an appropriate solution. Adopting a life cycle methodology does not guarantee success, but it is far better than having no plan at all. The SDLC method also helps in creating documents that communicate objectives, important milestones, and the uses of resources to management. **Figure 4.5** illustrates the five major steps involved in the systems development life cycle for an e-commerce site:

- Systems analysis/planning
- Systems design
- Building the system
- Testing
- Implementation

systems development life cycle (SDLC)

a methodology for understanding the business objectives of any system and designing an appropriate solution

SYSTEMS ANALYSIS/PLANNING: IDENTIFY BUSINESS OBJECTIVES, SYSTEM FUNCTIONALITY, AND INFORMATION REQUIREMENTS

In the systems analysis/planning step of the SDLC, you try to answer the question, "What do we want this e-commerce site to do for our business?" The key point is to let the business decisions drive the technology, not the reverse. This will ensure that your technology platform is aligned with your business. We will assume here that you have identified a business strategy and chosen a business model to achieve your strategic objectives (see Chapter 2). But how do you translate your strategies, business models, and ideas into a working e-commerce Web site?

One way to start is to identify the specific business objectives for your site, and then develop a list of system functionalities and information requirements. **Business objectives** are simply capabilities you want your site to have.

System functionalities are types of information systems capabilities you will need to achieve your business objectives. The **information requirements** for a system are the information elements that the system must produce in order to achieve the business objectives. You will need to provide these lists to system developers and programmers so they know what you as the manager expect them to do.

Table 4.2 describes some basic business objectives, system functionalities, and information requirements for a typical e-commerce site. As shown in the table, there are nine basic business objectives that an e-commerce site must deliver. These objectives must be translated into a description of system functionalities and ultimately into a set of precise information requirements. The specific information requirements for a system typically are defined in much greater detail than Table 4.2 indicates. To a large extent, the business objectives of an e-commerce site are not that different from those of an ordinary retail store. The real difference lies in the system functionalities

business objectives
capabilities you want your site to have

system functionalities
types of information systems capabilities you will need to achieve your business objectives

information requirements
the information elements that the system must produce in order to achieve the business objectives

TABLE 4.2	SYSTEM ANALYSIS: BUSINESS OBJECTIVES, SYSTEM FUNCTIONALITY, AND INFORMATION REQUIREMENTS FOR A TYPICAL E-COMMERCE SITE	
BUSINESS OBJECTIVE	**SYSTEM FUNCTIONALITY**	**INFORMATION REQUIREMENTS**
Display goods	Digital catalog	Dynamic text and graphics catalog
Provide product information (content)	Product database	Product description, stocking numbers, inventory levels
Personalize/customize product	Customer on-site tracking	Site log for every customer visit; data mining capability to identify common customer paths and appropriate responses
Engage customers in conversations	On site blog	Software with blogging and community response functionality
Execute a transaction	Shopping cart/payment system	Secure credit card clearing; multiple payment options
Accumulate customer information	Customer database	Name, address, phone, and e-mail for all customers; online customer registration
Provide after-sale customer support	Sales database	Customer ID, product, date, payment, shipment date
Coordinate marketing/advertising	Ad server, e-mail server, e-mail, campaign manager, ad banner manager	Site behavior log of prospects and customers linked to e-mail and banner ad campaigns
Understand marketing effectiveness	Site tracking and reporting system	Number of unique visitors, pages visited, products purchased, identified by marketing campaign
Provide production and supplier links	Inventory management system	Product and inventory levels, supplier ID and contact, order quantity data by product

and information requirements. In an e-commerce site, the business objectives must be provided entirely in digital form without buildings or salespeople, 24 hours a day, 7 days a week.

SYSTEM DESIGN: HARDWARE AND SOFTWARE PLATFORMS

system design specification
description of the main components in a system and their relationship to one another

logical design
describes the flow of information at your e-commerce site, the processing functions that must be performed, the databases that will be used, the security and emergency backup procedures that will be instituted, and the controls that will be used in the system

physical design
translates the logical design into physical components

Once you have identified the business objectives and system functionalities, and have developed a list of precise information requirements, you can begin to consider just how all this functionality will be delivered. You must come up with a **system design specification**—a description of the main components in the system and their relationship to one another. The system design itself can be broken down into two components: a logical design and a physical design. A **logical design** includes a data flow diagram that describes the flow of information at your e-commerce site, the processing functions that must be performed, and the databases that will be used. The logical design also includes a description of the security and emergency backup procedures that will be instituted, and the controls that will be used in the system.

A **physical design** translates the logical design into physical components. For instance, the physical design details the specific model of server to be purchased, the software to be used, the size of the telecommunications link that will be required, the way the system will be backed up and protected from outsiders, and so on.

Figure 4.6(a) presents a data flow diagram for a simple high-level logical design for a very basic Web site that delivers catalog pages in HTML in response to HTTP requests from the client's browser, while **Figure 4.6(b)** shows the corresponding physical design. Each of the main processes can be broken down into lower-level designs that are much more precise in identifying exactly how the information flows and what equipment is involved.

BUILDING THE SYSTEM: IN-HOUSE VERSUS OUTSOURCING

outsourcing
hiring an outside vendor to provide the services you cannot perform with in-house personnel

Now that you have a clear idea of both the logical and physical design for your site, you can begin considering how to actually build the site. You have many choices and much depends on the amount of money you are willing to spend. Choices range from outsourcing everything (including the actual systems analysis and design) to building everything yourself (in-house). **Outsourcing** means that you will hire an outside vendor to provide the services involved in building the site rather than using in-house personnel. You also have a second decision to make: will you host (operate) the site on your firm's own servers or will you outsource the hosting to a Web host provider? These decisions are independent of each other, but they are usually considered at the same time. There are some vendors who will design, build, and host your site, while others will either build or host (but not both). **Figure 4.7** on page 208 illustrates the alternatives.

Build Your Own versus Outsourcing

Let's take the building decision first. If you elect to build your own site, there are a range of options. Unless you are fairly skilled, you should use a pre-built template to create the Web site. For example, Yahoo Merchant Solutions, Amazon Stores, and eBay

FIGURE 4.6   A LOGICAL AND PHYSICAL DESIGN FOR A SIMPLE WEB SITE

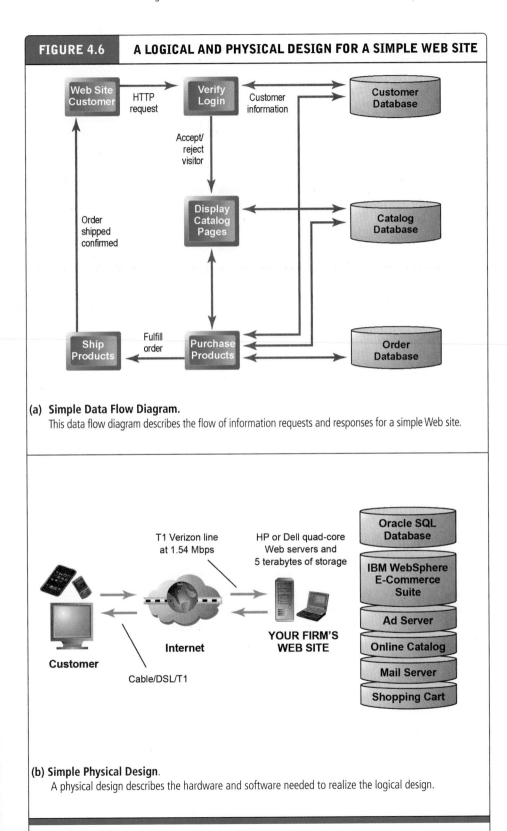

(a) **Simple Data Flow Diagram.**
This data flow diagram describes the flow of information requests and responses for a simple Web site.

(b) **Simple Physical Design.**
A physical design describes the hardware and software needed to realize the logical design.

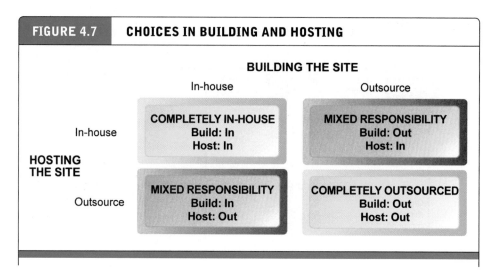

FIGURE 4.7 **CHOICES IN BUILDING AND HOSTING**

You have a number of alternatives to consider when building and hosting an e-commerce site.

WordPress

open source content management and blog Web site design tool

content management system (CMS)

organizes, stores, and processes Web site content

all provide templates that merely require you to input text, graphics, and other data, as well as the infrastructure to run the Web site once it has been created.

If your Web site is not a sales-oriented site requiring a shopping cart, one of the least expensive and most widely used site building tools is WordPress. **WordPress** is a blogging tool with a sophisticated content management system. A **content management system (CMS)** is a database software program specifically designed to manage structured and unstructured data and objects in a Web site environment. A CMS provides Web managers and designers with a centralized control structure to manage Web site content. WordPress also has thousands of user-built plug-ins and widgets that you can use to extend the functionality of a Web site. Web sites built in WordPress are treated by search engines like any other Web site: their content is indexed and made available to the entire Web community. Revenue-generating ads, affiliates, and sponsors are the main sources of revenue for WordPress sites. While these are the least costly sources of a Web presence, you will be limited to the "look and feel" and functionality provided by the template and infrastructure provided by these vendors.

If you have some experience with computers, you might decide to build the site yourself "from scratch." There are a broad variety of tools, ranging from those that help you build everything truly "from scratch," such as Adobe Dreamweaver and Microsoft Expression, to top-of-the-line prepackaged site-building tools that can create sophisticated sites customized to your needs. **Figure 4.8** illustrates the spectrum of tools available. We will look more closely at the variety of e-commerce software available in Section 4.3.

The decision to build a Web site on your own has a number of risks. Given the complexity of features such as shopping carts, credit card authentication and processing, inventory management, and order processing, the costs involved are high, as are the risks of doing a poor job. You will be reinventing what other specialized firms have already built, and your staff may face a long, difficult learning curve, delaying your entry to market. Your efforts could fail. On the positive side, you may be better

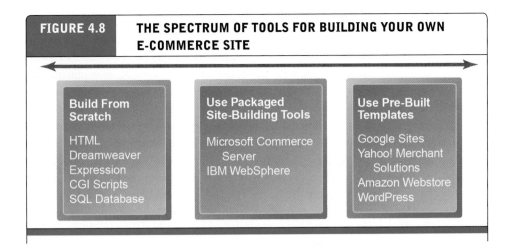

FIGURE 4.8   **THE SPECTRUM OF TOOLS FOR BUILDING YOUR OWN E-COMMERCE SITE**

Build From Scratch

HTML
Dreamweaver
Expression
CGI Scripts
SQL Database

Use Packaged Site-Building Tools

Microsoft Commerce Server
IBM WebSphere

Use Pre-Built Templates

Google Sites
Yahoo! Merchant Solutions
Amazon Webstore
WordPress

able to build a site that does exactly what you want, and, more importantly, develop the in-house knowledge to allow you to change the site rapidly if necessary due to a changing business environment.

If you choose more expensive site-building packages, you will be purchasing state-of-the art software that is well tested. You could get to market sooner. However, to make a sound decision, you will have to evaluate many different packages and this can take a long time. You may have to modify the packages to fit your business needs and perhaps hire additional outside vendors to do the modifications. Costs rise rapidly as modifications mount. A $4,000 package can easily become a $40,000 to $60,000 development project (see **Figure 4.9**). If you choose the template route, you will be limited to the functionality already built into the templates, and you will not be able to add to the functionality or change it.

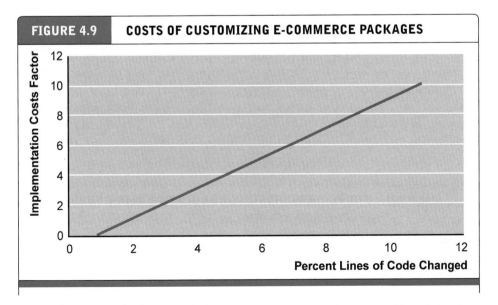

FIGURE 4.9   **COSTS OF CUSTOMIZING E-COMMERCE PACKAGES**

While sophisticated site development packages appear to reduce costs and increase speed to market, as the modifications required to fit the package to your business needs rise, costs rise rapidly.

In the past, bricks-and-mortar retailers in need of an e-commerce site typically designed the site themselves (because they already had the skilled staff in place and had extensive investments in information technology capital such as databases and telecommunications). However, as Web applications have become more sophisticated, larger retailers today rely heavily on vendors to provide sophisticated Web site capabilities, while also maintaining a substantial internal staff. Small start-ups may build their own sites from scratch using in-house technical personnel in an effort to keep costs low. Medium-size start-ups will often purchase a Web site design and programming expertise from vendors. Very small mom-and-pop firms seeking simple storefronts will use templates or blogging tools like WordPress. For e-commerce sites, the cost of building has dropped dramatically in the last five years, resulting in lower capital requirements for all players (see *Insight on Business: Curly Hair and Appillionaires.*)

Host Your Own versus Outsourcing

Now let's look at the hosting decision. Most businesses choose to outsource hosting and pay a company to host their Web site, which means that the hosting company is responsible for ensuring the site is "live," or accessible, 24 hours a day. By agreeing to a monthly fee, the business need not concern itself with many of the technical aspects of setting up a Web server and maintaining it, telecommunications links, nor with staffing needs.

co-location

when a firm purchases or leases a Web server (and has total control over its operation) but locates the server in a vendor's physical facility. The vendor maintains the facility, communications lines, and the machinery

You can also choose to *co-locate*. With a **co-location** agreement, your firm purchases or leases a Web server (and has total control over its operation) but locates the server in a vendor's physical facility. The vendor maintains the facility, communications lines, and the machinery. Co-location has expanded with the spread of virtualization where one server has multiple processors (4 to 16) and can operate multiple Web sites at once with multiple operating systems. In this case, you do not buy the server but rent its capabilities on a monthly basis, usually at one-quarter of the cost of owning the server itself. See **Table 4.3** for a list of some of the major hosting/co-location providers. There is an extraordinary range of prices for co-location, ranging from $4.95 a month, to several hundred thousands of dollars per month depending on the size of the Web site, bandwidth, storage, and support requirements.

While co-location involves renting physical space for your hardware, you can think of using a cloud service provider as renting virtual space in your provider's infrastructure. Cloud services are rapidly replacing co-location because they are less expensive, and arguably more reliable. Unlike with co-location, your firm does not own the hardware. Cloud service providers offer a standardized infrastructure, virtualization technology, and usually employ a pay-as-you-go billing system.

TABLE 4.3	KEY PLAYERS: HOSTING/CO-LOCATION/CLOUD SERVICES
Amazon EC2	IBM Global Services
Bluehost	Rackspace
CenturyLink	ServerBeach
GoDaddy	Verio
GSI Commerce	Verizon/Terremark

INSIGHT ON BUSINESS

CURLY HAIR AND APPILLIONAIRES

With so many big companies with national brand names dominating the e-commerce scene, and with the top 100 retail firms collecting more than 90% of the revenues, you may wonder if there's a chance for the little guy anymore, the amateurs. The answer is yes: there are still billions left in potential online retail sales, with additional money to be made from advertising revenues. In fact, there's an e-commerce frenzy going on in 2012 that nearly rivals the dot-com era with one exception: the start-ups have much leaner development models made possible in part by much cheaper technology, and social network sites that can bring inexpensive marketing and sales (no national television marketing budget needed). If you can create or identify a community of people with shared interests and issues, you'll have a built-in audience.

NaturallyCurly.com is a good example of a low-entry-cost, niche-oriented site that actually created an online community where none existed before. Two reporters, Gretchen Heber and Michelle Breyer, started the site with $500 in 1998. Both had naturally curly hair and often had long discussions about the difficulty of dealing with it on muggy days. Or they'd talk about how good it looked on other days. Based on a hunch that other people also needed help coping with curly hair issues, they launched NaturallyCurly.com. They spent $200 on the domain name, and bought some curly hair products to review on the site. The site was built with a simple Web server and the help of a 14-year-old Web page designer. The idea was to act as a content site with community feedback. They added a bulletin board for users to send in their comments.

(continued)

There were no competitors at first, and even without advertising on Google, they started showing up in Google searches for "curly hair" near or at the top of the search results list. In 2000, after a year of operation, they got an e-mail from Procter & Gamble, the world's largest personal care products company, asking if they would accept advertising for $2,000 a month for two years. From there, the site grew by adding additional advertising from leading hair care products companies and now generates revenue in excess of $1 million from advertising and sales of products on curlmart.com, its online boutique for curly hair products. In May 2007, the firm received an investment of $600,000 from a venture capital firm that was used to hire a marketing person and support staff, improve its Web technology, and expand its shipping and handling operations. In September 2010, Naturally-Curly unveiled a new Web site, one that offers a more personalized experience for its users. The revamp included hair-type–specific content, an upgraded geo-targeted Salon and Stylist finder, and an upgraded "Frizz Forecast."

The firm has moved aggressively into social marketing by establishing a Facebook page and a Twitter account. Curlmart.com, its e-commerce site, now showcases 60 different brands and 550 community-vetted products. In 2011, Naturally-Curly moved into mobile apps after deciding not to create a mobile Web site which simply replicated its Web sites. Curls on-the-Go is a free app that personalizes advice to its users based on their hair characteristics and preferred styles. The app is designed to sell products, provide reviews from visitors to its Web sites, and to help users find local salons. Other apps include CurlTalk and CurlyNikki.

By 2012, the Naturally Curly Network of hair style sites morphed into TextureMedia Inc. which sells ad space for its network of six related, branded Web sites: CurlMart, TextureTrends, Curl-niki, curlStylist, Curls on-the-Go (mobile app), and the mother ship Naturallycurly.com. The combined sites generate more than 2 million unique visitors a month, and the firm is profitable.

Other start-up firms are finding that cloud computing and social marketing greatly reduce the costs of building a Web site and starting a company. Christian Gheorghe started Tidemark Systems on a shoestring, but not by buying his own computers or building the IT infrastructure of a typical company. Tidemark Systems produces a Web-based business analytic software package that client companies use to track and analyze everything from sales to employee benefits. Rather than purchase office productivity software, he uses Google Docs and open source alternatives for databases. For a phone system, he uses Skype for free, and his e-mail is handled by Gmail. Instead of buying his own servers, he rents computing time from Amazon's cloud service for roughly twelve cents an hour. If Tidemark purchased its own servers it would have to purchase enough computing power to handle peak demands, but most of the time, the computers would be sitting idle. If Gheorghe was lucky, 15% of the computing power would be used. With cloud services, he's paying for the computer power he is actually using. Storing 100 gigabytes of data in the cloud costs Tidemark $10 a month.

Like cloud computer and social networks, the app economy has changed the economics of software production and e-commerce and has led to a small group of Appillionaires—a very small group of apps creators who make it big. One of the best known appillionaires is Chris Stevens, author of the Alice for the iPad app, an interactive rendering of the classic Sir John Tenniel illustrated edition of Lewis Carroll's *Alice in Wonderland*. Within a few months of its release, Alice for iPad was reviewed on Oprah Winfrey's television show and rose to the top ranks of apps in the iTunes store. What kind of infrastructure did Chris Stevens need to build this interactive book (and a series of related apps in the interactive book format)? An iMac and an iPhone, along with three months of 15-hour days. Stevens has been a reporter, graphic designer, and a writer for CNET. Along with a friend, who like Stevens had been recently fired from their jobs, he co-founded Atomic Antelope Inc., an interactive app

(continued)

book publisher. His friend provided the programming. In March 2012, Atomic Antelope's second hit app, Alice for the iPad II: Alice in New York, won a Kirkus Star Award, the second for the company.

It isn't just hardware that's getting so inexpensive, but other services as well that are vital for the success of small start-ups. Market intelligence, public relations, and even design services can be found online for a fraction of the cost of traditional service firms. Anne Kallus founded an online wedding-dress store, FairyGownMother.com, and used her Facebook presence to gain insights into shoppers' tastes by testing a variety of sales pitches. Cost: $300. While not a statistically valid sampling of customers (which would have cost thousands from a market research firm), the online

survey helped her identify key themes that worked with her potential customers. Need a logo or Web site design? 99Designs.com bills itself as the fastest growing design marketplace in the world. It crowdsources design projects to participating designers and artists. Typical projects have six to ten designers submitting several designs each for a $300 job. Successful bidders on recent projects have come from Italy, Indonesia, Slovakia, and New Zealand.

The moral of the story: its never been cheaper to start an e-commerce company. In fact, the recession may be an entrepreneur's best friend. In a poor economy, failures are not so noticeable, which creates a better environment for risk-taking, which encourages innovation.

SOURCES: "Behind the Curls: TextureMedia Becomes a Big Hairy Deal," by Sandra Zaragoza, *Austin Business Journal*, August 12, 2012; Community and the Value of a Kinky Idea," by Laura Lorber, Entrepreneur.com, August 2012; "TextureMedia Launches New Offer Platform," Press Release, TextureMedia Inc., April 2012; "Chris Stevens on Alice for the iPad, Book Apps, and Toronto," *Toronto Review*, January 9, 2012; "Striking It Rich In The App Store: For Developers, It's More Casino Than Gold Mine," by Chris Stevens, *FastCompany*, November 2, 2011; "Retail Online Integration," by Melissa Campanelli, Retailonlineintegration.com, October 2011; *Appillionaires: Secrets from Developers Who Struck It Rich on the App Store*, by Chris Stevens, Wiley, September 2011; "World's Leading Social Media Company for Curly-, Kinky- and Wavy-Haired Women Relaunches as TextureMedia, Inc." Press Release, TextureMedia Inc., September 27, 2011; "The NaturallyCurly Network Launches Curls on the Go," Naturallycurly.com, July 7, 2011; "The NaturallyCurly Network Captures $1.2 Million in Additional Angel Investment," Naturallycurly.com, June 22, 2011; "NaturallyCurly.com Unveils New Look," NaturallyCurly.com, September 27, 2010; "NaturallyCurly Expands Network and Content Coverage with Acquisition of CurlyNikki.com," NaturallyCurly.com, September 16, 2010; "Web Start Up Frenzy 2.0," by Sharon Machlis, Computerworld.com, April 29, 2010; "Splitting Hairs," by Virginia Heffernan, *New York Times*, April 4, 2010; "Launching an E-commerce Site With Social Networking," Marketingsherpa.com, March 3, 2010; "Software and Technology Services NaturallyCurly.com, Inc.," Business-Week.com, July 28, 2009; "The New Internet Startup Boom: Get Rich Slow," by Josh Quittner, Time.com, April 9, 2009.

Hosting, co-location, and cloud services have become a commodity and a utility: costs are driven by very large providers (such as IBM) who can achieve large economies of scale by establishing huge "server farms" located strategically around the country and the globe. This means the cost of pure hosting has fallen as fast as the fall in server prices, dropping about 50% every year! Telecommunications costs have also fallen. As a result, most hosting services seek to differentiate themselves from the commodity hosting business by offering extensive site design, marketing, optimization, and other services. Small, local ISPs also can be used as hosts, but service reliability is an issue. Will the small ISP be able to provide uninterrupted service, 24x7x365? Will they have service staff available when you need it?

There are several disadvantages to outsourcing hosting. If you choose a vendor, make sure the vendor has the capability to grow with you. You need to know what kinds of security provisions are in place for backup copies of your site, internal monitoring of activity, and security track record. Is there a public record of a security breach at the vendor? Most Fortune 500 firms have their own private cloud data centers so they can control the Web environment. On the other hand, there are risks to hosting your own site if you are a small business. Your costs will be higher than if you had used a large outsourcing firm because you don't have the market power to obtain low-cost hardware and telecommunications. You will have to purchase hardware and software, have a physical facility, lease communications lines, hire a staff, and build security and backup capabilities yourself.

TESTING THE SYSTEM

Once the system has been built and programmed, you will have to engage in a testing process. Depending on the size of the system, this could be fairly difficult and lengthy. Testing is required whether the system is outsourced or built in-house. A complex e-commerce site can have thousands of pathways through the site, each of which must be documented and then tested. **Unit testing** involves testing the site's program modules one at a time. **System testing** involves testing the site as a whole, in the same way a typical user would when using the site. Because there is no truly "typical" user, system testing requires that every conceivable path be tested. Final **acceptance testing** requires that the firm's key personnel and managers in marketing, production, sales, and general management actually use the system as installed on a test Internet or intranet server. This acceptance test verifies that the business objectives of the system as originally conceived are in fact working. It is important to note that testing is generally under-budgeted. As much as 50% of the software effort can be consumed by testing and rebuilding (usually depending on the quality of the initial design).

IMPLEMENTATION AND MAINTENANCE

Most people unfamiliar with systems erroneously think that once an information system is installed, the process is over. In fact, while the beginning of the process is over, the operational life of a system is just beginning. Systems break down for a variety of reasons—most of them unpredictable. Therefore, they need continual checking, testing, and repair. Systems maintenance is vital, but sometimes not budgeted for. In general, the annual system maintenance cost will roughly parallel the development cost. A $40,000 e-commerce site will likely require a $40,000 annual expenditure to maintain. Very large e-commerce sites experience some economies of scale, so that, for example, a $1 million site will likely require a maintenance budget of $500,000 to $700,000.

Why does it cost so much to maintain an e-commerce site? Unlike payroll systems, for example, e-commerce sites are always in a process of change, improvement, and correction. Studies of traditional systems maintenance have found 20% of the time is devoted to debugging code and responding to emergency situations (for example, a new server was installed by your ISP, and all your hypertext links were lost and CGI scripts disabled—the site is down!) (Lientz and Swanson, 1980; Banker and Kemerer, 1989). Another 20% of the time is concerned with changes in reports, data files, and links to backend databases. The remaining 60% of maintenance time is devoted to general administration (making product and price changes in the catalog) and making changes and enhancements to the system. E-commerce sites are never finished: they are always in the process of being built and rebuilt. They are dynamic—much more so than payroll systems.

The long-term success of an e-commerce site will depend on a dedicated team of employees (the Web team) whose sole job is to monitor and adapt the site to changing market conditions. The Web team must be multi-skilled; it will typically include programmers, designers, and business managers drawn from marketing, production, and sales support. One of the first tasks of the Web team is to listen to customers' feedback on the site and respond to that feedback as necessary. A second task is to develop a systematic monitoring and testing plan to be followed weekly to ensure all the links are operating, prices are correct, and pages are updated. A large business may have thousands of Web pages, many of them linked, that require systematic monitoring. Other important tasks of the Web team include **benchmarking** (a process in which the site is compared with those of competitors in terms of response speed, quality of layout, and design) and keeping the site current on pricing and promotions. The Web is a competitive environment where you can very rapidly frustrate and lose customers with a dysfunctional site.

benchmarking

a process in which the site is compared with those of competitors in terms of response speed, quality of layout, and design

FACTORS IN OPTIMIZING WEB SITE PERFORMANCE

The purpose of a Web site is to deliver content to customers and to complete transactions. The faster and more reliably these two objectives are met, the more effective the Web site is from a commerce perspective. If you are a manager or marketing executive, you will want the Web site operating in a way that fulfills customers' expectations. You'll have to make sure the Web site is optimized to achieve this business objective. The optimization of Web site performance is more complicated than it seems and involves at least three factors: page content, page generation, and page delivery (see **Figure 4.10**). In this chapter, we describe the software and hardware choices you will need to make in building an e-commerce site; these are also important factors in Web site optimization.

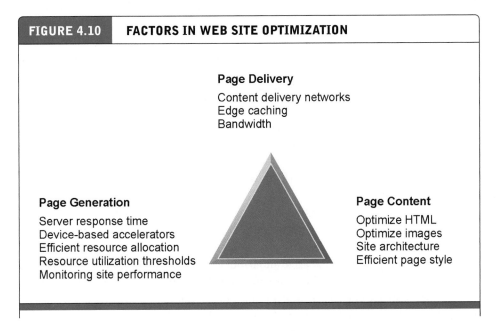

| FIGURE 4.10 | FACTORS IN WEB SITE OPTIMIZATION |

Page Delivery
Content delivery networks
Edge caching
Bandwidth

Page Generation
Server response time
Device-based accelerators
Efficient resource allocation
Resource utilization thresholds
Monitoring site performance

Page Content
Optimize HTML
Optimize images
Site architecture
Efficient page style

Web site optimization requires that you consider three factors: page content, page generation, and page delivery.

Using efficient styles and techniques for *page design* and *content* can reduce response times by two to five seconds. Simple steps include reducing unnecessary HTML comments and white space, using more efficient graphics, and avoiding unnecessary links to other pages in the site. *Page generation* speed can be enhanced by segregating computer servers to perform dedicated functions (such as static page generation, application logic, media servers, and database servers), and using various devices from vendors to speed up these servers. Using a single server or multiple servers to perform multiple tasks reduces throughput by more than 50%. *Page delivery* can be speeded up by using edge-caching services such as Akamai, or specialized content delivery networks such as RealNetworks, or by increasing local bandwidth. We will discuss some of these factors throughout the chapter, but a full discussion of Web site optimization is beyond the scope of this text.

4.3 CHOOSING SOFTWARE AND HARDWARE

Much of what you are able to do at an e-commerce site is a function of the software and hardware. Along with telecommunications, hardware and software constitute the infrastructure of a Web presence. As a business manager in charge of building the site, you will need to know some basic information about both. The more sophisticated the hardware and software, and the more ways you can sell goods and services, the more effective your business will be. This section describes the software and hardware needed to operate a contemporary e-commerce site.

SIMPLE VERSUS MULTI-TIERED WEB SITE ARCHITECTURE

system architecture
the arrangement of software, machinery, and tasks in an information system needed to achieve a specific functionality

Prior to the development of e-commerce, Web sites simply delivered Web pages to users who were making requests through their browsers for HTML pages with content of various sorts. Web site software was appropriately quite simple—it consisted of a server computer running basic Web server software. We might call this arrangement a single-tier system architecture. **System architecture** refers to the arrangement of software, machinery, and tasks in an information system needed to achieve a specific functionality (much like a home's architecture refers to the arrangement of building materials to achieve a particular functionality). The SteamShowers4Less and NaturallyCurly sites both started this way—there were no monetary transactions. Tens of thousands of dot-com sites still perform this way. Orders can always be called in by telephone and not taken online.

However, the development of e-commerce required a great deal more interactive functionality, such as the ability to respond to user input (name and address forms), take customer orders for goods and services, clear credit card transactions on the fly, consult price and product databases, and even adjust advertising on the screen based on user characteristics. This kind of extended functionality required the development of Web application servers and a multi-tiered system architecture to handle the processing loads. *Web application servers*, described more fully later in this section, are specialized software programs that perform a wide variety of transaction processing required by e-commerce.

In addition to having specialized application servers, e-commerce sites must be able to pull information from and add information to pre-existing corporate databases. These older databases that predate the e-commerce era are called *backend* or *legacy* databases. Corporations have made massive investments in these systems to store their information on customers, products, employees, and vendors. These backend systems constitute an additional layer in a multi-tiered site.

Figure 4.11 illustrates a simple two-tier and more complex multi-tier e-commerce system architecture. In **two-tier architecture**, a Web server responds to requests for Web pages and a database server provides backend data storage. In a **multi-tier architecture**, in contrast, the Web server is linked to a middle-tier layer that typically includes a series of application servers that perform specific tasks, as well as to a

two-tier architecture
e-commerce system architecture in which a Web server responds to requests for Web pages and a database server provides backend data storage

multi-tier architecture
e-commerce system architecture in which the Web server is linked to a middle-tier layer that typically includes a series of application servers that perform specific tasks as well as to a backend layer of existing corporate systems

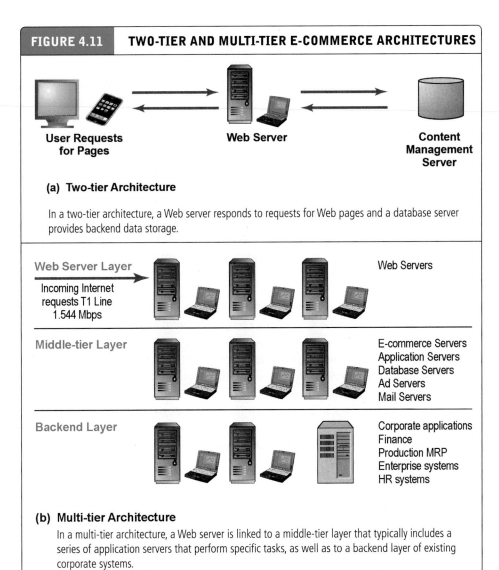

| FIGURE 4.11 | TWO-TIER AND MULTI-TIER E-COMMERCE ARCHITECTURES |

User Requests for Pages   **Web Server**   **Content Management Server**

(a) Two-tier Architecture

In a two-tier architecture, a Web server responds to requests for Web pages and a database server provides backend data storage.

Web Server Layer — Web Servers
Incoming Internet requests T1 Line 1.544 Mbps

Middle-tier Layer — E-commerce Servers / Application Servers / Database Servers / Ad Servers / Mail Servers

Backend Layer — Corporate applications / Finance / Production MRP / Enterprise systems / HR systems

(b) Multi-tier Architecture

In a multi-tier architecture, a Web server is linked to a middle-tier layer that typically includes a series of application servers that perform specific tasks, as well as to a backend layer of existing corporate systems.

backend layer of existing corporate systems containing product, customer, and pricing information. A multi-tiered site typically employs several physical computers, each running some of the software applications and sharing the workload across many physical computers.

The remainder of this section describes basic Web server software functionality and the various types of Web application servers.

WEB SERVER SOFTWARE

All e-commerce sites require basic Web server software to answer requests from customers for HTML and XML pages.

When you choose Web server software, you will also be choosing an operating system for your site's computers. Looking at all servers on the Web, the leading Web server software, with about 66% of the market, is Apache, which works with Linux and Unix operating systems. Unix is the original programming language of the Internet and Web, and Linux is a derivative of Unix designed for the personal computer. Apache was developed by a worldwide community of Internet innovators. Apache is free and can be downloaded from many sites on the Web; it also comes installed on most IBM Web servers. Literally thousands of programmers have worked on Apache over the years; thus, it is extremely stable. There are thousands of utility software programs written for Apache that can provide all the functionality required for a contemporary e-commerce site. In order to use Apache, you will need staff that is knowledgeable in Unix or Linux.

Microsoft Internet Information Services (IIS) is the second major Web server software available, with about 16% of the market. IIS is based on the Windows operating system and is compatible with a wide selection of Microsoft utility and support programs. These numbers are different among the Fortune 1000 firms, and different again if you include blogs, which are served up by Microsoft and Google at their own proprietary sites.

There are also at least 100 other smaller providers of Web server software, most of them based on the Unix or Sun Solaris operating systems. Note that the choice of Web server has little effect on users of your system. The pages they see will look the same regardless of the development environment. There are many advantages to the Microsoft suite of development tools—they are integrated, powerful, and easy to use. The Unix operating system, on the other hand, is exceptionally reliable and stable, and there is a worldwide open software community that develops and tests Unix-based Web server software.

Table 4.4 shows the basic functionality provided by all Web servers.

Site Management Tools

In Chapter 3, we described most of the basic functionality of the Web servers listed in Table 4.4. Another functionality not described previously is site management tools. **Site management tools** are essential if you want to keep your site working, and if you want to understand how well it is working. Site management tools verify that links on pages are still valid and also identify orphan files, or files on the site that are not linked to any pages. By surveying the links on a Web site, a site management tool can

site management tools
verify that links on pages are still valid and also identify orphan files

TABLE 4.4	BASIC FUNCTIONALITY PROVIDED BY WEB SERVERS
FUNCTIONALITY	DESCRIPTION
Processing of HTTP requests	Receive and respond to client requests for HTML pages
Security services (Secure Sockets Layer)	Verify username and password; process certificates and private/public key information required for credit card processing and other secure information
File Transfer Protocol	Permits transfer of very large files from server to server
Search engine	Indexing of site content; keyword search capability
Data capture	Log file of all visits, time, duration, and referral source
E-mail	Ability to send, receive, and store e-mail messages
Site management tools	Calculate and display key site statistics, such as unique visitors, page requests, and origin of requests; check links on pages

quickly report on potential problems and errors that users may encounter. Your customers will not be impressed if they encounter a "404 Error: Page Does Not Exist" message on your Web site. Links to URLs that have moved or been deleted are called dead links; these can cause error messages for users trying to access that link. Regularly checking that all links on a site are operational helps prevent irritation and frustration in users who may decide to take their business elsewhere to a better functioning site.

Even more importantly, site management tools can help you understand consumer behavior on your Web site. Site management software and services, such as those provided by Webtrends, can be purchased in order to more effectively monitor customer purchases and marketing campaign effectiveness, as well as keep track of standard hit counts and page visit information. **Figure 4.12** on page 220 shows a screenshot that illustrates WebTrends Analytics 10.

Dynamic Page Generation Tools

One of the most important innovations in Web site operation has been the development of dynamic page generation tools. Prior to the development of e-commerce, Web sites primarily delivered unchanging static content in the form of HTML pages. While this capability might be sufficient to display pictures of products, consider all the elements of a typical e-commerce site today by reviewing Table 4.2 (on page 205), or visit what you believe is an excellent e-commerce site. The content of successful e-commerce sites is always changing, often day by day. There are new products and promotions, changing prices, news events, and stories of successful users. E-commerce sites must intensively interact with users who not only request pages but also request product, price, availability, and inventory information. One of the most dynamic sites is eBay—the auction site. There, the content is changing minute by minute. E-commerce sites are just like real markets—they are dynamic. News sites, where stories change constantly, are also dynamic.

The dynamic and complex nature of e-commerce sites requires a number of specialized software applications in addition to static HTML pages. Perhaps one of the

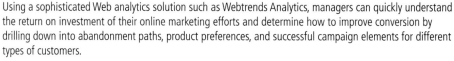

Using a sophisticated Web analytics solution such as Webtrends Analytics, managers can quickly understand the return on investment of their online marketing efforts and determine how to improve conversion by drilling down into abandonment paths, product preferences, and successful campaign elements for different types of customers.

SOURCE: Webtrends, Inc., 2011.

dynamic page generation

the contents of a Web page are stored as objects in a database, rather than being hard-coded in HTML. When the user requests a Web page, the contents for that page are then fetched from the database

most important is dynamic page generation software. With **dynamic page generation**, the contents of a Web page are stored as objects in a database, rather than being hard-coded in HTML. When the user requests a Web page, the contents for that page are then fetched from the database. The objects are retrieved from the database using Common Gateway Interface (CGI), Active Server Pages (ASP), Java Server Pages (JSP), or other server-side programs. CGI, ASP, and JSP are described in the last section of this chapter. This technique is much more efficient than working directly in HTML code. It is much easier to change the contents of a database than it is to change the coding of an HTML page. A standard data access method called *Open Database Connectivity (ODBC)* makes it possible to access any data from any application regardless of what database is used. ODBC is supported by most of the large database suppliers such as Oracle, Sybase, and IBM. ODBC makes it possible for HTML pages to be linked to backend corporate databases regardless of who manufactured the database. Web sites must be able to pull information from, and add information to, these databases. For example, when a customer clicks on a picture of a pair of boots, the site can access the product catalog database stored in a DB2 database, and access the inventory database stored in an Oracle database to confirm that the boots are still in stock and to report the current price.

Dynamic page generation gives e-commerce several significant capabilities that generate cost and profitability advantages over traditional commerce. Dynamic page generation lowers *menu costs* (the costs incurred by merchants for changing product descriptions and prices). Dynamic page generation also permits easy online *market segmentation*—the ability to sell the same product to different markets. For instance, you might want variations on the same banner ad depending on how many times the customer has seen the ad. In the first exposure to a car ad, you might want to emphasize brand identification and unique features. On the second viewing you might want to emphasize superlatives like "most family friendly" to encourage comparison to other brands. The same capability makes possible nearly cost-free *price discrimination*—the ability to sell the same product to different customers at different prices. For instance, you might want to sell the same product to corporations and government agencies but use different marketing themes. Based on a cookie you place on client computers, or in response to a question on your site that asks visitors if they are from a government agency or a corporation, you would be able to use different marketing and promotional materials for corporate clients and government clients. You might want to reward loyal customers with lower prices, say on DVDs or musical tracks, and charge full price to first-time buyers. Dynamic page generation allows you to approach different customers with different messages and prices.

Dynamic page generation also enables the use of a content management system. As previously described, a CMS is used to create and manage Web content. A CMS separates the design and presentation of content (such as HTML documents, images, video, audio) from the content creation process. The content is maintained in a database and dynamically linked to the Web site. A CMS usually includes templates that can be automatically applied to new and existing content, WYSIWYG editing tools that make it easy to edit and describe (tag) content, and collaboration, workflow, and document management tools. Typically, an experienced programmer is needed to install the system, but thereafter, content can be created and managed by non-technical staff. There are a wide range of commercial CMSs available, from top-end enterprise systems offered by Autonomy, EMC/Documentum, OpenText, IBM, and Oracle, to mid-market systems by Ixiasoft, PaperThin, and Ektron, as well as hosted software as a service (SaaS) versions by Clickability, CrownPeak Technology, and OmniUpdate. There are also several open source content management systems available, such as WordPress, Joomla, Drupal, OpenCms, and others.

APPLICATION SERVERS

Web application servers are software programs that provide the specific business functionality required of a Web site. The basic idea of application servers is to isolate

Web application server
software programs that provide specific business functionality required of a Web site

the business applications from the details of displaying Web pages to users on the front end and the details of connecting to databases on the back end. Application servers are a kind of middleware software that provides the glue connecting traditional corporate systems to the customer as well as all the functionality needed to conduct e-commerce. In the early years, a number of software firms developed specific separate programs for each function, but increasingly, these specific programs are being replaced by integrated software tools that combine all the needed functionality for an e-commerce site into a single development environment, a packaged software approach.

Table 4.5 illustrates the wide variety of application servers available in the marketplace. The table focuses on "sell-side" servers that are designed to enable selling products on the Web. So-called "buy-side" and "link" servers focus on the needs of businesses

TABLE 4.5	APPLICATION SERVERS AND THEIR FUNCTION
APPLICATION SERVER	FUNCTIONALITY
Catalog display	Provides a database for product descriptions and prices
Transaction processing (shopping cart)	Accepts orders and clears payments
List server	Creates and serves mailing lists and manages e-mail marketing campaigns
Proxy server	Monitors and controls access to main Web server; implements firewall protection
Mail server	Manages Internet e-mail
Audio/video server	Stores and delivers streaming media content
Chat server	Creates an environment for online real-time text and audio interactions with customers
News server	Provides connectivity and displays Internet news feeds
Fax server	Provides fax reception and sending using a Web server
Groupware server	Creates workgroup environments for online collaboration
Database server	Stores customer, product, and price information
Ad server	Maintains Web-enabled database of advertising banners that permits customized and personalized display of advertisements based on consumer behavior and characteristics
Auction server	Provides a transaction environment for conducting online auctions
B2B server	Implements buy, sell, and link marketplaces for commercial transactions

to connect with partners in their supply chains or find suppliers for specific parts and assemblies. These buy-side and link servers are described more fully in Chapter 12. There are several thousand software vendors that provide application server software. For Linux and Unix environments, many of these capabilities are available free on the Internet from various sites. Most businesses—faced with this bewildering array of choices—choose to use integrated software tools called merchant server software.

E-COMMERCE MERCHANT SERVER SOFTWARE FUNCTIONALITY

E-commerce merchant server software provides the basic functionality needed for online sales, including an online catalog, order taking via an online shopping cart, and online credit card processing.

Online Catalog

A company that wants to sell products on the Web must have a list, or **online catalog**, of its products, available on its Web site. Merchant server software typically includes a database capability that will allow for construction of a customized online catalog. The complexity and sophistication of the catalog will vary depending on the size of the company and its product lines. Small companies, or companies with small product lines, may post a simple list with text descriptions and perhaps color photos. A larger site might decide to add sound, animations, or videos (useful for product demonstrations) to the catalog, or interactivity, such as customer service representatives available via instant messaging to answer questions. Today, larger firms make extensive use of streaming video.

Shopping Cart

Online **shopping carts** are much like their real-world equivalent; both allow shoppers to set aside desired purchases in preparation for checkout. The difference is that the online variety is part of a merchant server software program residing on the Web server, and allows consumers to select merchandise, review what they have selected, edit their selections as necessary, and then actually make the purchase by clicking a button. The merchant server software automatically stores shopping cart data.

Credit Card Processing

A site's shopping cart typically works in conjunction with credit card processing software, which verifies the shopper's credit card and then puts through the debit to the card and the credit to the company's account at checkout. Integrated e-commerce software suites typically supply the software for this function. Otherwise, you will have to make arrangements with a variety of credit card processing banks and intermediaries.

MERCHANT SERVER SOFTWARE PACKAGES (E-COMMERCE SUITES)

Rather than build your site from a collection of disparate software applications, it is easier, faster, and generally more cost-effective to purchase a **merchant server software package** (also called an **e-commerce server suite**). Merchant server

---

e-commerce merchant server software
software that provides the basic functionality needed for online sales, including an online catalog, order taking via an online shopping cart, and online credit card processing

online catalog
list of products available on a Web site

shopping cart
allows shoppers to set aside desired purchases in preparation for checkout, review what they have selected, edit their selections as necessary, and then actually make the purchase by clicking a button

merchant server software package (e-commerce server suite)
offers an integrated environment that provides most or all of the functionality and capabilities needed to develop a sophisticated, customer-centric site

software/e-commerce suites offer an integrated environment that promises to provide most or all of the functionality and capabilities you will need to develop a sophisticated, customer-centric site. An important element of merchant sofware packages is a built-in shopping cart that can display merchandise, manage orders, and clear credit card transactions. E-commerce suites come in three general ranges of price and functionality.

Basic packages for elementary e-commerce business applications are provided by Bizland, HyperMart, and Yahoo Merchant Solutions. Webs.com also offers free Web building tools and hosting services. OSCommerce is a free, open source e-commerce suite used by many small start-up sites. PayPal can be used as a payment system on simple Web sites, and widgets can add interesting capabilities.

Midrange suites include IBM WebSphere Commerce Express Edition and Ascentium Commerce Server (formerly Microsoft Commerce Server). High-end enterprise solutions for large global firms are provided by IBM WebSphere's Commerce Professional and Enterprise Editions, ATG, GSI Commerce, Demandware, Magento, and others. There are several hundred software firms that provide e-commerce suites, which raises the costs of making sensible decisions on this matter. Many firms simply choose vendors with the best overall reputation. Quite often this turns out to be an expensive but ultimately workable solution.

Choosing an E-commerce Suite

With all of these vendors, how do you choose the right one? Evaluating these tools and making a choice is one of the most important and uncertain decisions you will make in building an e-commerce site. The real costs are hidden—they involve training your staff to use the tools and integrating the tools into your business processes and organizational culture. The following are some of the key factors to consider:

- Functionality
- Support for different business models
- Business process modeling tools
- Visual site management tools and reporting
- Performance and scalability
- Connectivity to existing business systems
- Compliance with standards
- Global and multicultural capability
- Local sales tax and shipping rules

For instance, although e-commerce suites promise to do everything, your business may require special functionality—such as streaming audio and video. You will need a list of business functionality requirements. Your business may involve several different business models—such as a retail side and a business-to-business side; you may run auctions for stock excess as well as fixed-price selling. Be sure the package can support all of your business models. You may wish to change your business processes, such as order taking and order fulfillment. Does the suite contain tools for modeling business process and work flows? Understanding how your site works will require visual reporting tools that make its operation transparent to many different people in your business. A poorly designed software package will drop off significantly in performance as visitors and transactions expand into the thousands per hour, or minute. Check for performance and scalability by stress-testing a pilot edition or obtaining data from the vendor about performance under load. You will have to connect the e-commerce suite to your traditional business systems. How will this connection to existing systems be made, and is your staff skilled in making the connection? Because of the changing technical environment—in particular, changes in mobile commerce platforms—it is important to document exactly what standards the suite supports now, and what the migration path will be toward the future. Finally, your e-commerce site may have to work both globally and locally. You may need a foreign language edition using foreign currency denominations. And you will have to collect sales taxes across many local, regional, and national tax systems. Does the e-commerce suite support this level of globalization and localization?

BUILDING YOUR OWN E-COMMERCE SITE: WEB SERVICES AND OPEN SOURCE OPTIONS

While existing firms often have the financial capital to invest in commercial merchant server software suites, many small firms and start-up firms do not. They have to build their own Web sites, at least initially. There are really two options here, the key factor being how much programming experience and time you have. One option is to utilize the e-commerce merchant services provided by hosting sites such as Yahoo Merchant Solutions. For a $50 setup fee, and a starter plan of $39.95, the service will walk you through setting up your Web site and provide Web hosting, a shopping cart, technical help by phone, and payment processing. Bigstep.com takes users step by step through the process of building an online store. Entrabase.com and Tripod provide easy-to-use site-building tools and e-commerce templates for e-commerce sites. An e-commerce template is a pre-designed Web site that allows users to customize the look and feel of the site to fit their business needs and provides a standard set of functionality. Most templates today contain ready-to-go site designs with built-in e-commerce suite functionality like shopping carts, payment clearance, and site management tools.

One of the most popular low-cost tools for creating a Web site without having to have any programming skills is Homestead.com. Building a Web site at Homestead involves three steps: choosing a design from over 2,000 templates, customizing the design with logos and content, and publishing it on the Web on Homestead servers with your own unique IP address, and e-mail. Once you build the Web site, Homestead provides a comprehensive set of services such as PayPal and credit card payment clearing, online catalog, shopping cart, real-time transaction processing, and custom shipping tables. Marketing support is available in the form of search engine optimization for your site, and advertising on Google, Amazon, and MSN. There is a 30-day free trial, and basic service for $4.99 a month, with charges for additional services.

If you have considerable, or at least some, programming background, you can consider open source merchant server software. **Open source software** is software devel-

open source software
software that is developed by a community of programmers and designers, and is free to use and modify

TABLE 4.6	OPEN SOURCE SOFTWARE OPTIONS
MERCHANT SERVER FUNCTIONALITY	**OPEN SOURCE SOFTWARE**
Web server	Apache (the leading Web server for small and medium businesses)
Shopping cart, online catalog	Many providers: Zen-Cart.com, AgoraCart.com, X-Cart.com, osCommerce.com
Credit card processing	Many providers: Echo Internet Gateway; ASPDotNetStorefront. Credit card acceptance is typically provided in shopping cart software but you may need a merchant account from a bank as well.
Database	MySQL (the leading open source SQL database for businesses)
Programming/scripting language	PHP (a scripting language embedded in HTML documents but executed by the server providing server-side execution with the simplicity of HTML editing). Perl is an alternative language. JavaScript programs are client-side programs that provide user interface components. Ruby on Rails (RoR, Rails) is another popular open source Web application framework.
Analytics	Analytics keep track of your site's customer activities and the success of your Web advertising campaign. You can also use Google Analytics if you advertise on Google, which provides good tracking tools; most hosting services will provide these services as well. Other open source analytic tools include Piwik, CrawlTrack, and Open Web Analytics.

oped by a community of programmers and designers, and is free to use and modify. **Table 4.6** provides a description of some open source options.

The advantage of using open source Web building tools is that you get exactly what you want, a truly customized unique Web site. The disadvantage is that it will take several months for a single programmer to develop the site and get all the tools to work together seamlessly. How many months do you want to wait before you get to market with your ideas?

One alternative to building a Web site first is to create a blog first, and develop your business ideas and a following of potential customers on your blog. Once you have tested your ideas with a blog, and attract a Web audience, you can then move on to developing a simple Web site.

THE HARDWARE PLATFORM

hardware platform

refers to all the underlying computing equipment that the system uses to achieve its e-commerce functionality

As the manager in charge of building an e-commerce site, you will be held accountable for its performance. Whether you host your own site or outsource the hosting and operation of your site, you will need to understand certain aspects of the computing hardware platform. The **hardware platform** refers to all the underlying computing equipment that the system uses to achieve its e-commerce functionality. Your objective is to have enough platform capacity to meet peak demand (avoiding an overload condition), but not so much platform that you are wasting money. Failing to meet peak demand can mean your site is slow, or actually crashes. Remember, the Web site may be your only or principal source of cash flow. How much computing and telecommunications capacity is enough to meet peak demand? How many hits per day can your site sustain?

To answer these questions, you will need to understand the various factors that affect the speed, capacity, and scalability of an e-commerce site.

RIGHT-SIZING YOUR HARDWARE PLATFORM: THE DEMAND SIDE

The most important factor affecting the speed of your site is the demand that customers put on the site. **Table 4.7** lists the most important factors to consider when estimating the demand on a site.

Demand on a Web site is fairly complex and depends primarily on the type of site you are operating. The number of simultaneous users in peak periods, the nature of customer requests, the type of content, the required security, the number of items

TABLE 4.7	FACTORS IN RIGHT-SIZING AN E-COMMERCE PLATFORM				
SITE TYPE	PUBLISH/ SUBSCRIBE	SHOPPING	CUSTOMER SELF-SERVICE	TRADING	WEB SERVICES/ B2B
Examples	WSJ.com	Amazon	Travelocity	E*Trade	Ariba e-procurement exchanges
Content	Dynamic Multiple authors High volume Not user-specific	Catalog Dynamic items User profiles with data mining	Data in legacy applications Multiple data sources	Time sensitive High volatility Multiple suppliers and consumers Complex transactions	Data in legacy applications Multiple data sources Complex transactions
Security	Low	Privacy Non-repudiation Integrity Authentication Regulations	Privacy Non-repudiation Integrity Authentication Regulations	Privacy Non-repudiation Integrity Authentication Regulations	Privacy Non-repudiation Integrity Authentication Regulations
Percent secure pages	Low	Medium	Medium	High	Medium
Cross session information	No	High	High	High	High
Searches	Dynamic Low volume	Dynamic High volume	Non-dynamic Low volume	Non-dynamic Low volume	Non-dynamic Moderate volume
Unique items (SKUs)	High	Medium to high	Medium	High	Medium to high
Transaction volume	Moderate	Moderate to high	Moderate	High to extremely high	Moderate
Legacy integration complexity	Low	Medium	High	High	High
Page views (hits)	High to very high	Moderate to high	Moderate to low	Moderate to high	Moderate

in inventory, the number of page requests, and the speed of legacy applications that may be needed to supply data to the Web pages are all important factors in overall demand on a Web site system.

Certainly, one important factor to consider is the number of simultaneous users who will likely visit your site. In general, the load created by an individual customer on a server is typically quite limited and short-lived. A Web session initiated by the typical user is **stateless**, meaning that the server does not have to maintain an ongoing, dedicated interaction with the client. A Web session typically begins with a page request, then a server replies, and the session is ended. The sessions may last from tenths of a second to a minute per user. Nevertheless, system performance does degrade as more and more simultaneous users request service. Fortunately, degradation (measured as "transactions per second" and "latency" or delay in response) is fairly graceful over a wide range, up until a peak load is reached and service quality becomes unacceptable (see **Figure 4.13**).

Serving up static Web pages is **I/O intensive**, which means it requires input/output (I/O) operations rather than heavy-duty processing power. As a result, Web site performance is constrained primarily by the server's I/O limitations and the telecommunications connection, rather than speed of the processor.

Other factors to consider when estimating the demand on a Web site is the user profile and the nature of the content. If users request searches, registration forms, and order taking via shopping carts, then demands on processors will increase markedly.

RIGHT-SIZING YOUR HARDWARE PLATFORM: THE SUPPLY SIDE

Once you estimate the likely demand on your site, you will need to consider how to scale up your site to meet demand. We have already discussed one solution that requires very little thought: outsource the hosting of your Web site to a cloud-based service. See Chapter 3 for a discussion of cloud-based computing services. However, if you decide to host your own Web site, scalability is an important consideration. **Scalability** refers to the ability of a site to increase in size as demand warrants. There are three steps you can take to meet the demands for service at your site: scale hardware vertically, scale hardware horizontally, and/or improve the processing architecture of the site (see **Table 4.8** on page 230). **Vertical scaling** refers to increasing the processing power of individual components. **Horizontal scaling** refers to employing multiple computers to share the workload and increase the "footprint" of the installation (IBM, 2002).

You can scale your site vertically by upgrading the servers from a single processor to multiple processors. You can keep adding processors to a computer depending on the operating system and upgrade to faster chip speeds as well.

There are two drawbacks to vertical scaling. First, it can become expensive to purchase additional processors with every growth cycle, and second, your entire site becomes dependent on a small number of very powerful computers. If you have two such computers and one goes down, half of your site, or perhaps your entire site, may become unavailable.

Horizontal scaling involves adding multiple single-processor servers to your site and balancing the load among the servers. You can then partition the load so some servers handle only requests for HTML or ASP pages, while others are dedicated to

stateless

refers to the fact that the server does not have to maintain an ongoing, dedicated interaction with the client

I/O intensive

requires input/output operations rather than heavy-duty processing power

scalability

the ability of a site to increase in size as demand warrants

vertical scaling

increasing the processing power of individual components

horizontal scaling

employing multiple computers to share the workload

FIGURE 4.13	**DEGRADATION IN PERFORMANCE AS NUMBER OF USERS INCREASES**

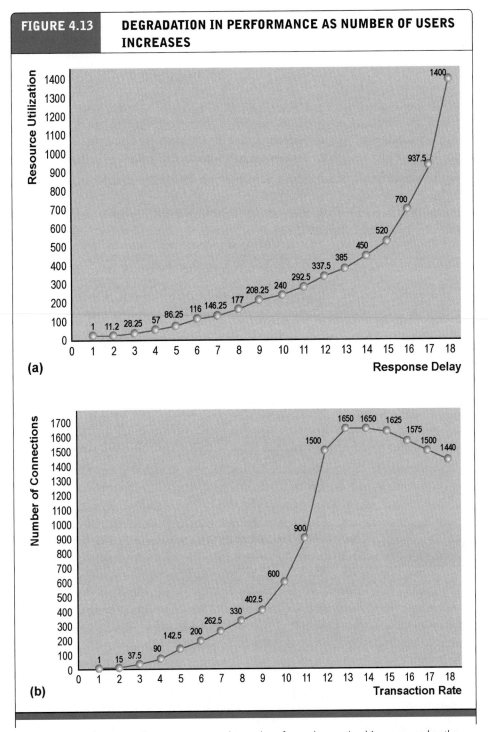

(a)

(b)

Degradation in Web server performance occurs as the number of users (connections) increases, and as the system's resources (processors, disk drives) become more utilized. In (a), user-experienced delay rises gracefully until an inflection point is reached, and then delay rises exponentially to an unacceptable level. In (b), the transaction rate rises gracefully until the number of users rapidly escalates the transaction rate, and at a certain inflection point, the transaction rate starts declining as the system slows down or crashes.

TABLE 4.8	VERTICAL AND HORIZONTAL SCALING TECHNIQUES
TECHNIQUE	**APPLICATION**
Use a faster computer	Deploy edge servers, presentation servers, data servers, etc.
Create a cluster of computers	Use computers in parallel to balance loads.
Use appliance servers	Use special-purpose computers optimized for their task.
Segment workload	Segment incoming work to specialized computers.
Batch requests	Combine related requests for data into groups, process as group.
Manage connections	Reduce connections between processes and computers to a minimum.
Aggregate user data	Aggregate user data from legacy applications in single data pools.
Cache	Store frequently used data in cache rather than on the disk.

handling database applications. You will need special load-balancing software (provided by a variety of vendors such as Cisco, Microsoft, and IBM) to direct incoming requests to various servers.

There are many advantages to horizontal scaling. It is inexpensive and often can be accomplished using older PCs that otherwise would be disposed of. Horizontal scaling also introduces redundancy—if one computer fails, chances are that another computer can pick up the load dynamically. However, when your site grows from a single computer to perhaps 10 to 20 computers, the size of the physical facility required (the "footprint") increases and there is added management complexity.

A third alternative—improving the processing architecture—is a combination of vertical and horizontal scaling, combined with artful design decisions. **Table 4.9** lists some of the more common steps you can take to greatly improve performance of your

TABLE 4.9	IMPROVING THE PROCESSING ARCHITECTURE OF YOUR SITE
ARCHITECTURE IMPROVEMENT	**DESCRIPTION**
Separate static content from dynamic content	Use specialized servers for each type of workload.
Cache static content	Increase RAM to the gigabyte range and store static content in RAM.
Cache database lookup tables	Use cache tables used to look up database records.
Consolidate business logic on dedicated servers	Put shopping cart, credit card processing, and other CPU-intensive activity on dedicated servers.
Optimize ASP code	Examine your code to ensure it is operating efficiently.
Optimize the database schema	Examine your database search times and take steps to reduce access times.

site. Most of these steps involve splitting the workload into I/O-intensive activities (such as serving Web pages) and CPU-intensive activities (such as taking orders). Once you have this work separated, you can fine-tune the servers for each type of load. One of the least expensive fine-tuning steps is to simply add RAM to a few servers and store all your HTML pages in RAM. This reduces load on your hard drives and increases speed dramatically. RAM is thousands of times faster than hard disks, and RAM is inexpensive. The next most important step is to move your CPU-intensive activities, such as order taking, onto a high-end, multiple processor server that is dedicated to handling orders and accessing the necessary databases. Taking these steps can permit you to reduce the number of servers required to service 10,000 concurrent users from 100 down to 20, according to one estimate.

4.4 OTHER E-COMMERCE SITE TOOLS

Now that you understand the key factors affecting the speed, capacity, and scalability of your Web site, we can consider some other important requirements. You will need a coherent Web site design that makes business sense—not necessarily a site to wow visitors or excite them, but to sell them something. You will also need to know how to build active content and interactivity into your site—not just display static HTML pages. You must be able to track customers who come, leave, and return to your site in order to be able to greet return visitors ("Hi Sarah, welcome back!"). You will also want to track customers throughout your site so you can personalize and customize their experience. You will definitely want the ability for customers to generate content and feedback on your site to increase their engagement with your brand. Finally, you will need to establish a set of information policies for your site—privacy, accessibility, and access to information policies.

In order to achieve these business capabilities, you will need to be aware of some design guidelines and additional software tools that can cost-effectively achieve the required business functionality.

WEB SITE DESIGN: BASIC BUSINESS CONSIDERATIONS

This is not a text about how to design Web sites. (In Chapter 7, we discuss Web site design issues from a marketing perspective.) Nevertheless, from a business manager's perspective, there are certain design objectives you must communicate to your Web site designers to let them know how you will evaluate their work. At a minimum, your customers will need to find what they need at your site, make a purchase, and leave. A Web site that annoys customers runs the risk of losing the customer forever. For instance, a survey by Hostway found that about 75% of respondents said they were extremely or somewhat unlikely to visit an offending site again and to unsubscribe from the offending company's promotional messages when they encounter one of their "pet peeves," and around 71% said they might refuse to purchase from the Web site and would view the company in a negative way. About 55% said they would complain about the Web site to friends and associates, and 45% said they might even

TABLE 4.10	E-COMMERCE WEB SITE FEATURES THAT ANNOY CUSTOMERS
• Requiring user to view ad or Flash introduction before going to Web site content • Pop-up and pop-under ads and windows • Too many clicks to get to the content • Links that don't work • Confusing navigation; no search function • Requirement to register and log in before viewing content or ordering • Slow loading pages • Content that is out of date	• Inability to use browser's Back button • No contact information available (Web form only) • Unnecessary splash/flash screens, animation, etc. • Music or other audio that plays automatically • Unprofessional design elements • Text not easily legible due to size, color, format • Typographical errors • No or unclear returns policy

refuse to make purchases in the company's offline stores (Hostway, 2007). See **Table 4.10** for a list of the most common consumer complaints about Web sites.

Some critics believe poor design is more common than good design. It appears easier to describe what irritates people about Web sites than to describe how to design a good Web site. The worst e-commerce sites make it difficult to find information about their products and make it complicated to purchase goods; they have missing pages and broken links, a confusing navigation structure, and annoying graphics or sounds that you cannot turn off. **Table 4.11** restates these negative experiences as positive goals for Web site design.

TOOLS FOR WEB SITE OPTIMIZATION

A Web site is only as valuable from a business perspective as the number of people who visit. Web site optimization (as we use it here) means how to attract lots of people to your site. One solution is through search engines such as Google, Bing, Ask.com, and several hundred others. The first stop for most customers looking for a product or service is to start with a search engine, and follow the listings on the page, usually starting with the top three to five listings, then glancing to the sponsored ads to the right. The higher you are on the search engine pages, the more traffic you will receive. Page 1 is much better than Page 2. So how do you get to Page 1 in the natural (unpaid) search listings? While every search engine is different, and none of them publish their algorithms for ranking pages, there are some basic ideas that work well:

- **Metatags, titles, page contents:** Search engines "crawl" your site and identify keywords as well as title pages and then index them for use in search arguments. Pepper your pages with keywords that accurately describe what you say you do in your metatag site "description" and "keywords" sections of your source code. Experiment: use different keywords to see which work. "Vintage cars" may attract more visitors than "antique cars" or "restored cars."

TABLE 4.11	THE EIGHT MOST IMPORTANT FACTORS IN SUCCESSFUL E-COMMERCE SITE DESIGN	
FACTOR	**DESCRIPTION**	
Functionality	Pages that work, load quickly, and point the customer toward your product offerings	
Informational	Links that customers can easily find to discover more about you and your products	
Ease of use	Simple fool-proof navigation	
Redundant navigation	Alternative navigation to the same content	
Ease of purchase	One or two clicks to purchase	
Multi-browser functionality	Site works with the most popular browsers	
Simple graphics	Avoids distracting, obnoxious graphics and sounds that the user cannot control	
Legible text	Avoids backgrounds that distort text or make it illegible	

- **Identify market niches:** Instead of marketing "jewelry," be more specific, such as "Victorian jewelry," or "1950s jewelry" to attract small, specific groups who are intensely interested in period jewelry and closer to purchasing.

- **Offer expertise:** White papers, industry analyses, FAQ pages, guides, and histories are excellent ways to build confidence on the part of users and to encourage them to see your Web site as the place to go for help and guidance.

- **Get linked up:** Encourage other sites to link to your site; build a blog that attracts people and who will share your URL with others and post links in the process. List your site with Yahoo Directory for $300 a year. Build a Facebook page for your company, and think about using Twitter to develop a following or fan base for your products.

- **Buy ads:** Complement your natural search optimization efforts with paid search engine keywords and ads. Choose your keywords and purchase direct exposure on Web pages. You can set your budget and put a ceiling on it to prevent large losses. See what works, and observe the number of visits to your site produced by each keyword string.

- **Local e-commerce:** Developing a national market can take a long time. If your Web site is particularly attractive to local people, or involves products sold locally, use keywords that connote your location so people can find you nearby. Town, city, and region names in your keywords can be helpful, such as "Vermont cheese" or "San Francisco blues music."

TOOLS FOR INTERACTIVITY AND ACTIVE CONTENT

As a manager responsible for building a Web site, you will want to ensure that users can interact with your Web site quickly and easily. As we describe in later chapters, the more interactive a Web site is, the more effective it will be in generating sales and encouraging return visitors.

Although functionality and ease of use are the supreme objectives in site design, you will also want to interact with users and present them with a lively, "active" experience. You will want to personalize the experience for customers by addressing their individual needs, and customize the content of your offerings based on their behavior or expressed desires. For example, you may want to offer customers free mortgage calculations or free pension advice, based on their interaction with programs available at your site. In order to achieve these business objectives, you will need to consider carefully the tools necessary to build these capabilities. Simple interactions such as a customer submitting a name, along with more complex interactions involving credit cards, user preferences, and user responses to prompts, all require special programs. The following sections provide a brief description of some commonly used software tools for achieving high levels of site interactivity.

Bling for Your Blog: Web 2.0 Design Elements

widget

a small, pre-built chunk of code that executes automatically in your HTML Web page; capable of performing a wide variety of tasks

One easy way to pump up the energy on your Web site is to include some appropriate widgets (sometimes called gadgets, plug-ins, or snippets). **Widgets** are small chunks of code that execute automatically in your HTML Web page. They are pre-built and many are free. Social networks and blogs use widgets to present users with content drawn from around the Web (news headlines from specific news sources, announcements, press releases, and other routine content), calendars, clocks, weather, live TV, games, and other functionality. You can copy the code to an HTML Web page. A good place to start is Google Gadgets and Yahoo Widgets.

Mashups are a little more complicated and involve pulling functionality and data from one program and including it another. The most common mashup involves using Google Maps data and software and combining it with other data. For instance, if you have a local real estate Web site, you can download Google Maps and satellite image applications to your site so visitors can get a sense of the neighborhood. There are thousands of Google Map mashups, from maps of Myanmar political protests, to maps of the Fortune 500 companies, all with associated news stories and other content. Other mashups involve sports, photos, video, shopping, and news.

The point of these Web 2.0 applications is to enhance user interest and engagement with your Web site and brand.

Common Gateway Interface (CGI)

Common Gateway Interface (CGI)

a set of standards for communication between a browser and a program running on a server that allows for interaction between the user and the server

Common Gateway Interface (CGI) is a set of standards for communication between a browser and a program running on a server that allows for interaction between the user and the server. CGI permits an executable program to access all the information within incoming requests from clients. The program can then generate all the output required to make up the return page (the HTML, script code, text, etc.), and send it back to the client via the Web server. For instance, if a user clicks the My Shopping Cart button, the server receives this request and executes a CGI program. The CGI program retrieves the contents of the shopping cart from the database and returns it to the server. The server sends an HTML page that displays the contents of the shopping cart on the user's screen. Notice all the computing takes place on the server side (this is why CGI programs and others like it are referred to as "server-side" programs).

CGI programs can be written in nearly any programming language as long as they conform to CGI standards. Currently, Perl is the most popular language for CGI scripting. Generally, CGI programs are used with Unix servers. CGI's primary disadvantage is that it is not highly scalable because a new process must be created for each request, thereby limiting the number of concurrent requests that can be handled. CGI scripts are best used for small to medium-sized applications that do not involve a high volume of user traffic. There are also Web server extensions available, such as FastCGI, that improve CGI's scalability (Doyle and Lopes, 2005).

Active Server Pages (ASP)

Active Server Pages (ASP) is Microsoft's version of server-side programming for Windows. Invented by Microsoft in late 1996, ASP has grown rapidly to become the major technique for server-side Web programming in the Windows environment. ASP enables developers to easily create and open records from a database and execute programs within an HTML page, as well as handle all the various forms of interactivity found on e-commerce sites. Like CGI, ASP permits an interaction to take place between the browser and the server. ASP uses the same standards as CGI for communication with the browser. ASP programs are restricted to use on Windows 2003/2000/NT Web servers running Microsoft's IIS Web server software.

Active Server Pages (ASP)
a proprietary software development tool that enables programmers using Microsoft's IIS package to build dynamic pages

Java, Java Server Pages (JSP), and JavaScript

Java is a programming language that allows programmers to create interactivity and active content on the client computer, thereby saving considerable load on the server. Java was invented by Sun Microsystems in 1990 as a platform-independent programming language for consumer electronics. The idea was to create a language whose programs (so-called Write Once Run Anywhere [WORA] programs) could operate on any computer regardless of operating system. This would be possible if every operating system at the time (Macintosh, Windows, Unix, DOS, and mainframe MVS systems) had a Java Virtual Machine (VM) installed that would interpret the Java programs for that environment.

Java
a programming language that allows programmers to create interactivity and active content on the client computer, thereby saving considerable load on the server

By 1995, it had become clear, however, that Java was more applicable to the Web than to consumer electronics. Java programs (known as Java applets) could be downloaded to the client over the Web and executed entirely on the client's computer. Applet tags could be included in an HTML page. To enable this, each browser would have to include a Java VM. Today, the leading browsers do include a VM to run Java programs. When the browser accesses a page with an applet, a request is sent to the server to download and execute the program and allocate page space to display the results of the program. Java can be used to display interesting graphics, create interactive environments (such as a mortgage calculator), and directly access the Web server.

Java Server Pages (JSP), like CGI and ASP, is a Web page coding standard that allows developers to use a combination of HTML, JSP scripts, and Java to dynamically generate Web pages in response to user requests. JSP uses Java "servlets," small Java programs that are specified in the Web page and run on the Web server to modify the

Java Server Pages (JSP)
like CGI and ASP, a Web page coding standard that allows developers to dynamically generate Web pages in response to user requests

JavaScript

a programming language invented by Netscape that is used to control the objects on an HTML page and handle interactions with the browser

Web page before it is sent to the user who requested it. JSP is supported by most of the popular application servers on the market today.

JavaScript is a programming language invented by Netscape that is used to control the objects on an HTML page and handle interactions with the browser. It is most commonly used to handle verification and validation of user input, as well as to implement business logic. For instance, JavaScript can be used on customer registration forms to confirm that a valid phone number, zip code, or even e-mail address has been given. Before a user finishes completing a form, the e-mail address given can be tested for validity. JavaScript appears to be much more acceptable to corporations and other environments in large part because it is more stable and also it is restricted to the operation of requested HTML pages.

ActiveX and VBScript

ActiveX

a programming language created by Microsoft to compete with Java

VBScript

a programming language invented by Microsoft to compete with JavaScript

Microsoft—not to be outdone by Sun Microsystems and Netscape—invented the **ActiveX** programming language to compete with Java and **VBScript** to compete with JavaScript. When a browser receives an HTML page with an ActiveX control (comparable to a Java applet), the browser simply executes the program. Unlike Java, however, ActiveX has full access to all the client's resources—printers, networks, and hard drives. VBScript performs in the same way as JavaScript. Of course, ActiveX and VBScript work only if you are using Internet Explorer. Otherwise, that part of the screen is blank.

ColdFusion

ColdFusion

an integrated server-side environment for developing interactive Web applications

ColdFusion is an integrated server-side environment for developing interactive Web applications. Originally developed by Macromedia and now offered by Adobe, ColdFusion combines an intuitive tag-based scripting language and a tag-based server scripting language (CFML) that lowers the cost of creating interactive features. ColdFusion offers a powerful set of visual design, programming, debugging, and deployment tools.

PERSONALIZATION TOOLS

You will definitely want to know how to treat each customer on an individual basis and emulate a traditional face-to-face marketplace. *Personalization* (the ability to treat people based on their personal qualities and prior history with your site) and *customization* (the ability to change the product to better fit the needs of the customer) are two key elements of e-commerce that potentially can make it nearly as powerful as a traditional marketplace, and perhaps even more powerful than direct mail or shopping at an anonymous suburban shopping mall. Speaking directly to the customer on a one-to-one basis, and even adjusting the product to the customer is quite difficult in the usual type of mass marketing, one-size-fits-all commercial transaction that characterizes much of contemporary commerce.

There are a number of methods for achieving personalization and customization. For instance, you could personalize Web content if you knew the personal background of the visitor. You could also analyze the pattern of clicks and sites visited for every customer who enters your site. We discuss these methods in later chapters on marketing. The primary method for achieving personalization and customization is through the placement of cookie files on the user's client computer. As we discussed in Chapter 3, a cookie is a small text file placed on the user's client computer that can contain any kind of information about the customer, such as customer ID, campaign ID, or purchases at the site. And then, when the user returns to the site, or indeed goes further into your site, the customer's prior history can be accessed from a database. Information gathered on prior visits can then be used to personalize the visit and customize the product.

For instance, when a user returns to a site, you can read the cookie to find a customer ID, look the ID up in a database of names, and greet the customer ("Hello Mary! Glad to have you return!"). You could also have stored a record of prior purchases, and then recommend a related product ("How about the wrench tool box now that you have purchased the wrenches?"). And you could think about customizing the product ("You've shown an interest in the elementary training programs for Word. We have a special 'How to Study' program for beginners in Office software. Would you like to see a sample copy online?").

We further describe the use of cookies and their effectiveness in achieving a one-to-one relationship with the customer in Chapter 8.

THE INFORMATION POLICY SET

In developing an e-commerce site, you will also need to focus on the set of information policies that will govern the site. You will need to develop a **privacy policy**—a set of public statements declaring to your customers how you treat their personal information that you gather on the site. You also will need to establish **accessibility rules**—a set of design objectives that ensure disabled users can effectively access your site. There are more than 50 million Americans who are disabled and require special access routes to buildings as well as computer systems (see *Insight on Society: Designing for Accessibility*). E-commerce information policies are described in greater depth in Chapter 8.

privacy policy
a set of public statements declaring to your customers how you treat their personal information that you gather on the site

accessibility rules
a set of design objectives that ensure disabled users can effectively access your site

4.5 DEVELOPING A MOBILE WEB SITE AND BUILDING MOBILE APPLICATIONS

Today, building a Web site is just one part of developing an e-commerce presence. Given that 122 million U.S. Internet users (about 50% of all Internet users) access the Web at least part of the time from mobile devices, firms today need to develop mobile Web sites, mobile Web apps, as well as native apps, in order to interact with customers, suppliers, and employees. Deciding which of these extended Web presence tools to use is a first step.

There are three kinds of mobile e-commerce software offerings to consider, each with unique advantages and costs. A **mobile Web site** is a version of a regular Web site that is scaled down in content and navigation so that users can find what they want and move quickly to a decision or purchase. You can see the difference between a regular Web site and a mobile site by visiting the Amazon Web site from your desktop computer and then a smartphone or tablet computer. Amazon's mobile site

mobile Web site
version of a regular desktop Web site that is scaled down in content and navigation

INSIGHT ON SOCIETY

DESIGNING FOR ACCESSIBILITY

Ever see a popular YouTube video with captions that can be read by the hearing impaired? Ever roll your mouse over an Amazon product page with your Internet Explorer accessibility features turned on and hear an audio description of the products and prices so sight-impaired people can understand the page? Chances are the answer in both cases is "No." Why not? There are approximately 38 million Americans with hearing loss and 25 million with significant vision loss. The prevalence of disabilities in the population will only increase as the population ages.

These and other disabilities often can be addressed with intelligent software and hardware design. But, for the most part, this has not yet occurred. As a result, the Internet and mobile devices are unfriendly places for many disabled in America. For instance, according to a Pew Research Center report, only 54% of American adults with disabilities use the Internet, compared to 81% of those who are not. And even when the disabled do get online, the problems don't end there.

To begin to remedy these issues, the Federal Communications Commission published a white paper in April 2010 calling for stronger accessibility legislation for broadband service devices, from smartphones to social network sites. In October 2010, the 21st Century Communications and Video Accessibility Act was signed into law. Title I of the act addresses making products and services (including smartphones) using broadband fully accessible to people with disabilities. Title II of the act requires programs shown on television and the Internet to include closed captioning. The FCC is currently in the process of issuing regulations and pilot programs to implement the act, and the act is expected to take full effect over the next three years. September 30, 2012, was the deadline for online video services to implement closed captioning as part of the act.

Disability advocates are also using lawsuits to move the ball forward. In January 2010, Arizona State University (ASU) reached an agreement with blind plaintiffs represented by the National Federation of the Blind and the American Council of the Blind. In July 2009, both had sued ASU to stop ASU's planned use of Kindle e-book reading devices in a pilot program that would be inaccessible to blind students. Although the Kindle has audio capabilities, and some books would be available in audio form, the menu structure of the Kindle cannot be driven by verbal commands, and most books would not have audio editions. Working with the support of Amazon, ASU planned to roll out the Kindle reader campus-wide sometime in 2010 as an experiment and demonstration. For students, Kindle textbooks are available at roughly half the price of a standard book. Five other universities (Princeton, Case Western Reserve, Reed College, Pace University, and University of Virginia) involved in the Amazon trial rollout agreed along with ASU to shelve the Kindle reader experiment until these devices can be used fully by blind students. Amazon is working on changes to the Kindle that make it more friendly for disabled persons, but the National Federation of the Blind criticized newer versions of the Kindle in 2012, saying that Amazon had not done enough to make their devices accessible.

The lawsuit and settlement raised concerns at the Department of Education and the Justice Department. In June 2010, the Department of Education sent a letter to university presidents and deans requiring colleges that use e-book devices in the classroom to ensure these devices are fully functional for blind students. Otherwise, the universities would be in violation of federal

(continued)

law. Similar requirements apply to all K-12 educational institutions in the United States.

In 1998, Congress amended the Rehabilitation Act to require U.S. agencies, government contractors, and others receiving federal money to make electronic and information technology services accessible to people with disabilities. Known as Section 508, this legislation requires Web sites of federally funded organizations to be accessible to users who are blind, deaf, blind and deaf, or unable to use a mouse. However, the legislation applies only to U.S. agencies, government contractors, and others receiving federal money, and not to the broader e-commerce environment of private business firms.

In one of the first lawsuits seeking to enforce Section 508 for Internet services, Access Now Inc., an advocacy group for the disabled, sued Southwest Airlines in 2001 on behalf of more than 50 million disabled Americans for operating a Web site that was inaccessible to the disabled, on the grounds that this violated the 1990 Americans with Disabilities Act (ADA). In November 2002, a Federal District Court in Florida, in one of the first court decisions on the applicability of the ADA to Web sites, ruled that ADA applies only to physical spaces, not virtual spaces. However, the judge noted in a footnote that she was surprised that a customer-oriented firm like Southwest Airlines did not "employ all available technologies to expand accessibility to its Web site for visually impaired customers who would be an added source of revenue."

Since this early decision, however, both the interpretation of the law and public sentiment have resulted in many well-known Web sites attempting to conform to the spirit of Section 508, sometimes voluntarily and sometimes under threat from advocacy groups. For instance, RadioShack, Amazon, Ramada, and Priceline have entered into agreements with the American Council for the Blind and the American Foundation for the Blind. Meanwhile, the National Federation of the Blind (NFB) brought a class-action

suit against Target for failing to make its site accessible for the blind. They claimed that blind people could not use Target's shopping cart because it required use of a mouse, used inaccessible image maps and graphics, and lacked compliant alt-text, an invisible code embedded beneath graphics that allows screen reading software to vocalize a description of the image. Target claimed the ADA did not apply to Web sites.

In September 2006, a federal district court ruled that ADA did indeed apply to Web sites. The court held "the 'ordinary meaning' of the ADA's prohibition against discrimination in the enjoyment of goods, services, facilities, or privileges is that whatever goods or services the place provides, it cannot discriminate on the basis of disability in providing enjoyment of those goods and services." The court thus rejected Target's argument that only its physical store locations were covered by the civil rights laws, ruling instead that all services provided by Target, including its Web site, must be accessible to persons with disabilities. In October 2007, the court granted class-action status to the lawsuit.

In August 2008, Target and the NFB settled the suit. Target made no admission or concession that its Web site violated the ADA, but agreed to bring it into compliance with certain online assistive technology guidelines by February 28, 2009, and to have the NFB certify that it is compliant with those guidelines. In addition, Target agreed to pay damages of $6 million. Many accessibility advocates expressed disappointment that the resolution of the case via a settlement failed to provide any clear legal precedent. Nevertheless, a prudent e-commerce firm with a customer orientation will use available technologies to expand accessibility to its Web site for impaired customers both to expand its customer base and avoid costly and embarrassing litigation.

In 2012, a district court in Massachusetts ruled that Web sites can be considered "public accommodation," and as such fall under the jurisdiction of the ADA (*National Association of the*

(continued)

Deaf, et al., v. Netflix Inc.). For example, Netflix's "Watch Instantly" feature does not provide equal access, which it must do as a "place of exhibition or entertainment." Netflix and other companies have appealed the ruling, which it views as too drastic a deviation from precedent.

So how does a blind person access the Web, and how should designers build in accessibility for the blind? Most blind persons use the same computers as everyone else. But a blind person's computer uses screen-reader software that translates text information on the screen into synthesized speech or Braille. Internet Explorer is the Web browser most typically used, although other browsers are also available, such as Lynx (a text-only browser written originally to run under Unix), which generate their own speech.

A blind person navigates a Web page by checking the hypertext links on the page, usually by jumping from link to link with the Tab key; the screen-reader software automatically reads the highlighted text as the focus moves from link to link. If the highlighted text is something like "How to Contact Us," a blind user will likely be able to make sense out of the link. If, however, the highlighted text is "Click Here," or "Here," it will be difficult, if not impossible, for a blind user to interpret the meaning of the link without using a different navigation strategy. With the more recent screen-reader software/browser combinations, it is possible for a blind Web surfer to explore the page one line at a time, thus alleviating this problem. However, being forced to examine every detail of a Web page just to learn the meaning of a hypertext link is a time-consuming process that, ideally, should be avoided. The important point to keep in mind is that the screen-reader software is looking for ASCII text, which it can convert to speech or Braille.

Once the desired hypertext link has been located, the blind person presses the Enter key (clicks on the link) to go where the link points. If there is a form to fill out on the page, the blind person will usually tab to the appropriate input field and type the information in the usual way. Other controls such as checkboxes, combo boxes, radio buttons, and the like can all be used if the screen-reader software can detect them. There are several simple strategies Web designers can use to improve accessibility. Embedding text descriptions behind images is one example that allows screen readers to announce those descriptions. So instead of saying "Image," when a screen reader passes over an image, the visually impaired user can hear "Photo of a cruise ship sitting in a harbor." Allowing users to set the color and font schemes can also make a difference for the visually impaired. Adding screen magnification tools and sound labels where hyperlinks appear are two additional ways to increase accessibility.

These are examples of "equivalent alternatives" to visual content that disability advocates suggest should be required, both for visual and auditory content, to ensure individuals with disabilities have equal access to information that appears on-screen. Guidelines for creating accessible Web pages include ensuring that text and graphics are understandable when viewed without color, using features that enable activation of page elements via a variety of input devices (such as keyboard, head wand, or Braille reader), and providing clear navigation mechanisms (such as navigation bars or a site map) to aid users.

The World Wide Web Consortium (W3C) issued Web Content Accessibility Guidelines (WCAG) 2.0 in June 2010 (final draft form) that provide all organizations with strategies in Web design for accommodating people with many different kinds of disabilities. Some of the problems encountered by disabled users include so-called "captchas" or distorted text that people are supposed to read and then reenter into a text box to gain access to a site, check-out buttons that are images rather than text and cannot be read by text-reading software, and YouTube videos without captions.

(continued)

Ensuring accessibility of mobile devices has its own set of issues, in many instances ones that are even more challenging than those associated with the Web. There is only a limited selection of mobile devices with built-in accessibility features. The small size of the device, screen, and keypad presents its own problems. Third-party applications, such as text-to-speech/screen readers and screen magnifiers, are starting to become available, but much work still needs to be done. For instance, many mobile devices come equipped with voice control capabilities and audio alerts, which could be helpful to those with vision or motor difficulties, but in most cases, these are still limited to simple tasks, and do not provide access to the full functionality of the device. In addition, the deaf community cannot rely on audio content or alerts, so developers need to provide text or other alternatives for auditory information. Those with impaired motor functionality also face great challenges in dealing with input to mobile devices. To deal with these challenges, the WC3 recommends that mobile content developers follow Section 508, WCAG 2.0, and its guidelines on mobile Web best practices.

Many companies are experimenting with mobile apps for visually impaired smartphone users. Blind shoppers can scan for product information using DirectionsForMe.org's mobile app. Customers at supermarkets will be able to determine the brand name and other details about a product on their own. Verizon also announced that it was releasing a series of Android apps for the visually impaired, which use voice recognition to perform a variety of tasks on their phones. These include the ability to set alarms, browse the Web, compose and send e-mails, and more.

SOURCES: "National Federation of the Blind Comments on New Kindles," marketwatch.com, September 6, 2012; "A New Mobile View," by Amy Dusto, Internetretailer.com, September 5, 2012; "FCC: Online Video Caption Requirements Go Forward," by Chris Tribbey, Homemediamagazine.com, August 29, 2012; "FCC tells Web TV Providers to Start Using Online Captions Next Month," by Jim Barthold, Fierceonlinevideo.com, August 22, 2012; "Verizon Wireless Introduces Mobile Accessibility App for Customers Who Are Visually Impaired," dailymarkets.com, August 17, 2012; National Association of the Deaf, et al. ("NAD"), versus Netflix Inc. 2012; United States District Court of Massachusetts, June 19, 2012; "Can A Web Site be a Public Accommodation Under the ADA?" Timothy Springer, webaccessibility.com, June 5, 2012; "Mobile Web Accessibility," by Tim Shelton, Accessibletech.com, July 2011; "For the Disabled, Just Getting Online is a Struggle," by Wilson Rotham, Technolog.msnbc.msn.com, January 21, 2011; "Americans Living with Disability and their Technology Profile," by Susannah Fox, Pewinternet.org, January 21, 2011; "Federal Government Requiring Colleges to Include Blind-Friendly Electronic Book Readers," by Dorie Turner, Associated Press, June 29, 2010; "W3C Web Accessibility Initiative [Final Draft]," WC3.org, June 2010; "A Giant Leap and a Big Deal: Delivering on the Promise of Equal Access to Broadband for People with Disabilities," Federal Communications Commission, April 23, 2010; "21st Century Communications and Video Accessibility Act of 2009," Hearings, 111th Congress, House of Representatives, H.R. 3101, April 2010; "A Giant Leap & a Big Deal," by Elizabeth Lyle, Federal Communications Commission, Working Paper Series No. 2, April 2010; "Blindness Organizations and Arizona State University Resolve Litigation Over Kindle," National Federation of the Blind, Press Release, January 11, 2010; "Web Accessibility: Making Your Site Accessible to the Blind," by Curtis Chong, National Federation of the Blind, accessed August 14, 2009.

is a cleaner, more interactive site suitable for finger navigation, and efficient consumer decision making. Like traditional Web sites, mobile Web sites run on a firm's servers, and are built using standard Web tools such as server side HTML, Linux, PHP and SQL. Like all Web sites, the user must be connected to the Web and performance will depend on bandwidth. Generally, mobile Web sites operate more slowly than traditional Web sites viewed on a desktop computer connected to a broadband office network. Most large firms today have mobile Web sites.

A new trend in the development of mobile Web sites is the use of **responsive Web design** tools and design techniques, which make it possible to design a Web site that automatically adjust its layout and display according to the user's screen resolution, whether a desktop, tablet, or smartphone. Responsive design tools include HTML5 and CSS3 and its three key design principles involve using flexible grid-based layouts, flexible images and media, and media queries.

responsive Web design
Tools and design principles that automatically adjust the layout of a Web site depending on user screen resolution

mobile Web app

application built to run on the mobile Web browser built into a smartphone or tablet computer

A **mobile Web app** is an application built to run on the mobile Web browser built into a smartphone or tablet computer. In the case of Apple, the native browser is Safari. Generally they are built to mimic the qualities of native apps using HTML5 and Java. Mobile Web apps are specifically designed for the mobile platform in terms of screen size, finger navigation, and graphical simplicity. Mobile Web apps can support complex interactions used in games and rich media, perform real-time, on-the-fly calculations, and can be geo-sensitive using the smartphone's built-in global positioning system (GPS) function. Mobile Web apps typically operate faster than mobile Web sites but not as fast as native apps.

native app

application designed specifically to operate using the mobile device's hardware and operating system

A **native app** is an application designed specifically to operate using the mobile device's hardware and operating system. These stand-alone programs can connect to the Internet to download and upload data, and can operate on this data even when not connected to the Internet. Download a book to an app reader, disconnect from the Internet, and read your book. Because the various types of smartphones have different hardware and operating systems, apps are not "one size fits all" and therefore need to be developed for different mobile platforms. An Apple app that runs on an iPhone cannot operate on Android phones. As you learned in Chapter 3, native apps are built using different programming languages depending on the device for which they are intended, which is then compiled into binary code, and which executes extremely fast on mobile devices, much faster than HTML or Java-based mobile Web apps. For this reason, native apps are ideal for games, complex interactions, on-the-fly calculations, graphic manipulations, and rich media advertising.

PLANNING AND BUILDING A MOBILE WEB PRESENCE

What is the "right" mobile Web presence for your firm? The answer depends on identifying the business objectives, and from these, deriving the information requirements of your mobile presence. The same kind of systems analysis and design (SAD) reasoning described earlier in the chapter is needed for planning and building a mobile presence, although there are important differences.

The first step is to identify the business objectives you are trying to achieve. **Table 4.12** illustrates the thought process for the analysis stage of building a mobile presence. Why are you developing a mobile presence? Is it to drive sales by creating an easily browsed catalog where users can shop and purchase? Strengthen your brand by creating an engaging, interactive experience? Enable customers to interact with your customer community? How are your competitors using their mobile presence? Once you have a clear sense of business objectives, you will be able to describe the kind of system functionality that is needed and specify the information requirements for your mobile presence.

After you have identified the business objectives, system functionality, and information requirements, you can think about how to design and build the system. Now is the time to consider which to develop: a mobile Web site, a mobile Web app, or a native app. From our previous discussion, if your objective is branding or building community, then a native app is recommended because you can display rich interactive media and highly interactive, efficient games. If your objective is to drive sales, advertise, or gather feedback on specific products, all of which require an online

TABLE 4.12	SYSTEMS ANALYSIS FOR BUILDING A MOBILE PRESENCE	
BUSINESS OBJECTIVE	SYSTEM FUNCTIONALITY	INFORMATION REQUIREMENTS
Drive sales	Digital catalog; product database	Product descriptions, photos, SKUs, inventory
Branding	Showing how customers use your products	Videos and rich media; product and customer demonstrations
Building customer community	Interactive experiences, games with multiple players	Games, contests, forums, social sign-up to Facebook
Advertising and promotion	Coupons and flash sales for slow-selling items	Product descriptions, coupon management, and inventory management
Gathering customer feedback	Ability to retrieve and store user inputs including text, photos, and video	Customer sign-in and identification; customer database

database of products, then a mobile Web site or mobile Web app is recommended because high-speed interactions are not needed, and these objectives are really just an extension of your main desktop Web site.

MOBILE WEB PRESENCE: DESIGN CONSIDERATIONS

Designing a mobile presence is somewhat different from traditional desktop Web site design because of different hardware, software, and consumer expectations. **Table 4.13** describes some of the major differences.

Designers need to take mobile platform constraints into account when designing for the mobile platform. File sizes should be kept smaller and the number of files sent to the user reduced. Focus on a few, powerful graphics, and minimize the number of images sent to the user. Simplify choice boxes and lists so the user can easily scroll and touch-select the options.

TABLE 4.13	UNIQUE FEATURES THAT MUST BE TAKEN INTO ACCOUNT WHEN DESIGNING A MOBILE WEB PRESENCE
FEATURE	IMPLICATIONS FOR MOBILE PLATFORM
Hardware	Mobile hardware is smaller, and there are more resource constraints in data storage and processing power.
Connectivity	The mobile platform is constrained by slower connection speeds than desktop Web sites.
Displays	Mobile displays are much smaller and require simplification. Some screens are not good in sunlight.
Interface	Touch-screen technology introduces new interaction routines different from the traditional mouse and keyboard. The mobile platform is not a good data entry tool but can be a good navigational tool.

MOBILE WEB PRESENCE: PERFORMANCE AND COST CONSIDERATIONS

If you don't have an existing Web site, the most efficient process is to build a site in the first instance using responsive Web design, as previously described. If you already have a Web site that don't want to totally redevelop, the least expensive path is to resize it to create a smartphone-friendly mobile site. Doing so typically will not require a complete redesign effort. You will need to reduce the graphics and text, simplify the navigation, and focus on improving the customer experience so you do not confuse people. Because your customers might still use a relatively slow 3G cell connection, you will need to lighten up the amount of data you send. Also, given the difficulty of customer data entry on a mobile device, you cannot expect customers to happily enter long strings of numbers or text characters. For marketing clarity, make sure the brand images used on the mobile Web site match those on the traditional Web site. Small companies can develop a mobile Web site for under $10,000 using the same consultants and servers as their existing Web site.

Building a mobile Web app that uses the mobile device's browser requires more effort and cost than developing a mobile Web site, suffers from the same limitations as any browser-based application, but does offer some advantages such as better graphics, more interactivity, and faster local calculations as, for instance, in mobile geo-location applications like Foursquare that require local calculations of position and then communication with the site's Web server.

The most expensive path to a mobile presence is to build a native app. Native apps can require more extensive programming expertise. In addition, virtually none of the elements used in your existing Web site can be re-used, and you will need to redesign the entire logic of the interface and carefully think out the customer experience. For instance, there is a fairly stable HTML traditional Web site interface with buttons, graphics, videos, and ads that has developed over the last decade. This is not true for apps. There is no set of standards or expectations even on the part of users—every app looks different from every other app. This means the user confronts large variations in app design, so your interface must be quite simple and obvious. Many of the bells and whistles found on the large desktop Web site screen cannot be used in mobile apps. You'll need even greater simplification and focus. These weaknesses are also native apps' greatest strength: you have the opportunity to create a really stunning, unique customer experience where users can interact with your brand. If you want an intense branding experience with your customers, where interaction between your brand and customers is effortless and efficient, then native apps are the best choice.

The *Insight on Technology* case, *Building a Mobile Presence,* takes a further look at some of the considerations involved for three very different companies-- Decker Outdoors Corporation, USAA, and Ryland Homes.

INSIGHT ON TECHNOLOGY

BUILDING A MOBILE PRESENCE

In 2012, almost every company with a Web presence is thinking about or developing mobile applications and mobile Web sites. Increasingly, their customers are going mobile. By 2013, more people will use their mobile phones than PCs to go online, and there will be one mobile device for every person on earth by 2015. The number of Web searches performed on mobile devices has more than quadrupled since 2010. Customers expect, and even demand, to be able to use a mobile device of their choice to obtain information or perform a transaction anywhere and at any time. So, if a company wants to stay connected to its customers, it needs some sort of mobile presence.

Developing mobile apps or a mobile Web site has some special challenges. The user experience on a mobile device is fundamentally different from that on a PC. There are special features on mobile devices such as location-based services that give firms the potential to interact with customers in meaningful new ways. Firms need to be able to take advantage of those features while delivering an experience that is appropriate to a small screen. There are multiple mobile platforms to work with—iPhone, Android, BlackBerry, and Windows, and a firm may need a different version of an application to run on each of these. You can't just port a Web site or desktop application to a smartphone or tablet. It's a different systems development process.

It's important to understand how, why, and where customers use mobile devices and how these mobile experiences change business interactions and behavior. For example, do customers who use an app conduct a greater number of transactions (like purchasing) on apps when compared to a mobile browser? When compared to a tablet computer, do customers spend more or less time researching products and shopping from a smartphone? If tablets are primarily used for browsing, not purchasing, then how should tablet sites be designed?

Deckers Outdoor Corporation, the parent company of brands such as UGG Australia, Teva, and Simple Shoes, spent considerable time studying its customers' mobile behavior. It looked at how customers use their mobile devices while shopping and researching brands to find out how consumers would connect with its brand through the mobile channel. When people use mobile devices, how do they research products? What information do they want about a brand? Are they looking for information about product features, product reviews, or retail store locations?

Decker's customer analysis showed that when consumers use mobile devices inside a Deckers store, what is most important is a seamless interaction. Customers want to be able to look at a product on their phones and see the same information inside the store, plus some additional information, such as consumer reviews.

A mobile strategy involves much more than selecting mobile devices, operating systems, and applications. It also involves changes to business processes—changing the way people work and the way a firm interacts with its customers. Mobile technology can streamline processes, make them more portable, and enhance them with capabilities such as touch interfaces, location and mapping features, alerts, texting, cameras, and video functionality. The technology can also create less efficient processes or fail to deliver benefits if the mobile application is not properly designed.

USAA, the giant financial services company serving members of the U.S. military and their families, is acutely aware of the need to ensure that mobile technology is aligned with its customer-facing business processes and leads to

(continued)

genuine improvements. The company is using mobile technology to refine its business processes and provide simpler and more powerful ways for customers to interact with the company.

USAA launched its Web site in 2000 and went mobile 10 years later, with about 90% of its interactions with customers taking place on these two self-service channels. In 2011, USAA handled 183 million customer contacts through the mobile channel alone, and expects the mobile channel will be its primary point of contact with customers in the next two years. USAA has 100 dedicated mobile developers writing apps for devices using the iPhone, iPad, and Android operating systems, along with apps for the BlackBerry and Windows Phone. USAA developed a smartphone accident report and claims app that enables customers to snap a photo and submit a claim directly from the site of an accident using their phones. The app is also able to send geographic information system (GIS) data to a towing service and display nearby car rental locations. Another mobile app supports photo deposits: a customer can capture an image of a check with a smartphone and automatically submit it to the bank. The money is instantly deposited in the customer's account. This system eliminates the labor and expense of processing paper checks, and the time required to mail the check and wait three days for the deposit to clear. In 2011, USAA Federal Savings Bank processed $6.4 billion in deposits through this mobile app.

The mobile app also displays loan and credit card balances, shopping services, homeowners and auto insurance policy information, Home Circle and Auto Circle buying services, retirement products and information, ATM and taxi locators, and a community feature that lets users see what others are posting about USAA on Twitter, Facebook, and YouTube.

A real estate company may want to display a completely different site to mobile users who are looking for house information after driving by a "For Sale" sign. The realtor may want to optimize the mobile interface to include specific listing and contact information to capture the lead immediately and keep the load time fast. If the mobile site is simply a more user-friendly version of the desktop site, the conversions may not be as high.

Ryland Homes, one of the top U.S. new home builders, has a conventional Web site, but it wanted to be able to engage customers using mobile technology as well. The company revamped its mobile Web site in March 2011 to increase sales leads by helping potential customers with mobile phones find its locations, look at its products, register with the company, and call directly. Ryland's development team made the site easier to read and capable of fitting on a smartphone or tablet screen without requiring users to pinch and zoom. It used jQuery Mobile software and responsive Web design to create variations of the site that were appropriate for different smartphone or tablet models employed by users. The jQuery Mobile framework allows developers to design a single Web site or application that will work on all popular smartphone, tablet, and desktop platforms, eliminating the need to write unique apps for each mobile device or operating system. Ryland focused on features such as location-based driving directions to nearby communities, clickable phone numbers, and brief online registrations to increase the chances of making a sale. The site shows nearby communities in order of distance, based on the location of the mobile device.

SOURCES: "Mobility Transforms the Customer Relationship," by Samuel Greengard, *Baseline*, February 2012; "How Deckers Used a Mobile Application to Build Customer Traffic," by William Atkinson, *CIO Insight*, November 9, 2011; "Going Mobile: A Portable Approach to Process Improvement," Business Agility Insights, June 2012, and Google Inc., Ryland Homes Opens Doors to Local Sales with Mobile Site for Home-Buyers, 2011.

Orbitz Charts
Its Mobile Trajectory

When it comes to mobile apps and gauging their impact on consumers and business, there's no better industry to look at than the online travel industry and its airline and hotel reservation systems. And there's no better company in this industry in developing mobile apps than Orbitz Worldwide Inc., the leading online travel site. Orbitz connects consumers to plane tickets from 400 airlines, hotel rooms from 80,000 hotels worldwide, as well rental cars, cruises, and vacation packages. On a busy day, consumers will make an estimated 2 million searches for airline reservations and more than 1 million hotel reservations. In June 2012, Orbitz released its latest Apple iOS app which has all the power, and is much faster, than its desktop reservation system. The new app allows users to arrange for flight, lodging, and car rental reservations in a continuous stream with minimal data entry from the user. Orbitz claims it is the fastest mobile travel app in the industry. For travelers on the go, the new app provides nearly real-time travel planning anywhere and anytime—no desktop needed.

As early as 1999, fledgling Internet travel companies such as Priceline, Expedia, Travelocity, and Galileo were already transforming the travel industry. Recognizing the threat, and the opportunity, five major airlines—United, Delta, Continental, Northwest, and American—banded together to form a new venture that would become Orbitz. By the time the site launched in 2001, six other airlines had invested and anti-trust objections from consumer groups and competitors had been rejected by the U. S. Department of Transportation. Even at that early date, the Orbitz management team was forward-thinking, including the capability for consumers to access flight updates and cancellations via pagers and mobile phones. By the time the Department of Justice had completely cleared Orbitz for takeoff and it had completed its IPO in November 2003, Orbitz had recruited more than 100 independent hotels in addition to its initial TravelWeb syndicate, which included the big players such as Marriott, Hilton, and Hyatt.

By 2006, Orbitz had technologically surpassed its U.S. competitors when it was the first Internet travel company to offer a WML-only (Wireless Markup Language) mobile Web site. (Expedia had a mobile site for its UK customers.) Users could check flight statuses for 27 airlines, some of which did not yet have a mobile site, and search for hotels in the 19 largest destination markets in the United States and in Cancun, Mexico. They also had access to a personal page dedicated to itineraries for Orbitz-booked trips and links to autodial Orbitz customer service. Additional services added in 2007 included enabling mobile users to view average wait times to get through security and available Wi-Fi services for a particular airport. A data feedback system was instituted to compute check-in delays and taxi line wait-times based on customer inputted experiences. The year 2008 saw the addition of an iPhone/iPod–specific app with the same capabilities for itinerary, flight status, WiFi availability, and wait-time checking as well as the ability to view weather and traffic conditions, reports from other travelers, and information about where to park and ground transportation. Customers could also now use technology specifically designed for touch-based Safari browsers to book a hotel room during inclement weather.

By 2010, market research had pushed Orbitz to increase its investment in mobile technology. A redesigned mobile Web site was launched in July, and a smartphone app for Google Inc.'s Android operating system was unveiled in November along with an updated iPhone app. Users of any Web-enabled device could now access a tool set comparable to the standard e-commerce site to purchase flights, book car rentals, and secure hotel accommodations, including same-day reservations. The native apps and redesigned mobile site, developed in-house with input from an unnamed outside vendor, also offered the standard e-commerce site service called Price Assurance, which guarantees consumers an automatic refund if another Orbitz customer books the same service for less.

In July 2011, Orbitz added a hotel-booking app for iPad users, "Hotels by Orbitz." When launched, the GPS-enabled app displays a map of the user's current location. Pins dot the map to indicate hotel locations, which can be touched to display the establishment name, address, phone number, and cost, providing instant price comparison. Hotels can also be selected from a scrolling list to the left of the map. Expanding a tile supplies additional details including pictures, reviews, and lists of room features and establishment amenities. Users can also toggle to a data table view, enabling comparisons based on multiple features and amenities in addition to price. If the user's current location is not the desired target, a search by city, address, zip code, or landmark can be conducted instead. Lodging choices can be filtered and sorted according to various criteria including price, user-rated review score, distance from destination, and a star-based rating. Orbitz tackled lodging first because market research indicated that iPad users were most interested in securing accommodations. The full complement of hotels available on the e-commerce site is offered at the same rate on the m-commerce site, including all special offers. At this point, this included thousands of locations worldwide. Chris Brown, Orbitz's vice president of product strategy, explained that native touch-based apps appeal to a set of consumers who prefer this style of interaction, not yet available on the Web, and in particular to those searching for same-day accommodations. While only 12 to 14% of traditional e-commerce Web site shoppers want to reserve a room for the day on which they are searching, smartphone and other Web-enabled device users book for that night between 60 and 65% of the time. Barney Harford, CEO of Orbitz Worldwide, touted the ability to book a hotel room "in just three taps."

Only three months earlier, Orbitz had been first-to-market with an m-commerce site designed specifically for business users. Orbitz knew that since most business travelers were already carrying a smartphone or other Web-enabled mobile device, and mobile Internet access was overtaking conventional desktop access, there was no time to waste. Since corporate travel managers must adhere to company-specific, business logic rules that include preferred vendors, cost prerequisites, mandatory services, and compulsory documentation, the platform must be able to store and abide by these dictates. Because each company has its own business logic rules, the mobile commerce platform would have to be customized for each firm. Orbitz decided that the optimal solution was to construct a mobile Web site that could be accessed from any Web-enabled device rather than build native apps for multiple different devices. The goals were to exclude no one, provide a uniform and yet native app-like experience for each type of device, and deliver full travel policy compliance for business clients. The Orbitz for Business mobile Web site delivers the same set of tools enjoyed by the consumer market, applies saved policy controls to new reservations, and delivers both global and company-specific messages on both the home page and in search results to assist business travelers in adhering to company guidelines. Business-specific tools include the ability to enter and modify the trip purpose, search results that give precedence to preferred vendors, and access company-specific reference data. Orbitz is sure that converting business customers from passive viewers of travel updates and weather conditions to active mobile purchasers of all facets of a professional trip is dependent only upon the short juncture it will take for them to become at ease with the technology and familiar with the integration possible between Orbitz for Business and their corporate travel policy. New customer acquisition can be triggered, at least initially, by offering last-minute promotions and deals to a customer base that is often searching for same-day reservations.

Despite all of these changes, upgrades, and additions to their mobile platforms in what would normally be considered a narrow business time frame, the rapidly expanding and changing mobile environment called for further investments. When the m-commerce site was redesigned to support transactions, Orbitz had pursued a minimalist approach. According to Brown, the m-commerce site, as well as the initial rollouts of the Android and iPhone apps, were valuable learning experiences for the company that enabled them to assemble skilled teams. This prepared them to create second-generation applications that could meet evolving consumer expectations. Three main improvements were made to the second-generation m-commerce site. First, it was optimized to accommodate the small screen size of any Web-enabled mobile device. Second, it was updated to accommodate swiping gestures, and third, it was revamped to expedite touch screen transactions.

Swiping, once the exclusive province of apps, can now be accomplished using the newest version of Hypertext Markup Language, HTML5. What's more, HTML5 enables m-commerce sites to incorporate capabilities identical to mobile apps simply by tapping into the built-in functionality of mobile devices, including GPS. Orbitz employed HTML5 to enable customers to swipe through pictures of hotels. Mobile transaction speed was given a boost through the implementation of a new proprietary global online travel agency platform. The platform speeds up page loading by essentially creating mobile Web pages on the fly from the standard e-commerce Web page and eliminating redirects. The standard Web page is passed through a page-rendering framework tool that instantly produces an HTML5 version that can exploit inherent smartphone capabilities. Faster browsing is not the only advantage, however. Brown stressed the reduced labor hours required in contrast to having to create mobile-optimized counterparts for each standard Web page.

Consumers could also now book vacation packages, view the savings accrued from the simultaneous booking of a flight and hotel room, and create an online profile linked to their credit card to speed the check-out process. GPS capabilities enabled

SOURCES: "Orbitz, Inc. History," FundingUniverse.com, accessed September 2, 2012; "How to Embark upon an M-commerce Redesign," by Kevin Woodward, *Internet Retailer*, August 10, 2012; "Top 10 Mobile Commerce Apps of Q2," by Rimma Kats, *Mobile Commerce Daily*, July 6, 2012; "Orbitz Revamps iPhone App with Focus on Streamlined Booking, Deals," by Lauren Johnson, *Mobile Commerce Daily*, June 22, 2012; "Orbitz Rolls Out Major Update to App for iPhone and iPod Touch," Orbitz, June 21, 2012; "Orbitz Releases New Travel App," by Emily Brennan, *New York Times*, June 21, 2012; "Orbitz Launches New iPhone App, Bets on Mobile Growth," by Erica Ogg, Gigaom.com, June 21, 2012; "Orbitz: Mobile Searches May Yield Better Hotel Deals," by Barbara De Lollis, *USA Today*, May, 10, 2012; Orbitz Worldwide Inc., Form 10-K for the fiscal year ended December 31, 2011, Securities and Exchange Commission, filed March 31, 2012; "Orbitz Launches Revamped Mobile Site, Daily Deals to Capitalize on Last-Minute Travel," by Lauren Johnson, *Mobile Commerce Daily*, December 13, 2011; "Orbitz Travels the M-commerce Site Redesign Route," by Bill Siwicki, *Internet Retailer*, December 13, 2011; "Orbitz Unveils Powerful New Mobile Website and Introduces New 'Mobile Steals' Program Offering Discounted Mobile-only Rates on Hotels," Orbitz, December 12, 2011; "Orbitz Creates Intuitive Search-and-Book Experience via iPad App," by Rimma Kats, *Mobile Commerce Daily*, July 7, 2011; "Get a Room," by Kevin Woodward, *Internet Retailer*, July 7, 2011; "Orbitz Launches New 'Orbitz Hotels' App for iPad®," Orbitz, July 6, 2011; "Orbitz for Business Debuts Mobile Booking Site Targeting Corporate Travelers," by Dan Butcher, *Mobile Commerce Daily*, April 15, 2011; "Two Travel Providers Make Mobile moves," by Katie Deatsch, *Internet Retailer*, November 16, 2010; "Orbitz Launches Native iPhone® and Android™ Applications That Allow Consumers to Shop and Book

consumers to locate nearby hotels and conduct price, distance, and rating comparisons. Likewise, improved search and sorting and filtering capabilities enabled consumers to compare flights and car rentals based on various criteria, including traveler type, and to access customer reviews. Looking to capitalize on the market research findings that highlighted the burgeoning role of Web-enabled mobile devices in securing same-day accommodations, Orbitz also instituted mobile-exclusive same-day deals. These specials, called Mobile Steals, are available both on the m-commerce site and through the Hotels by Orbitz app, which was also released for the Android and iPhone. Last-minute perishable goods are available in more than 50 markets worldwide, benefitting both lodging proprietors and consumers. Proprietors are able to fill rooms that might otherwise remain vacant, and consumers enjoy savings of up to 50% off the standard rate.

Even so, with mobile transaction customers doubling in one year's time, Orbitz decided that an overhaul of its native iPhone app was also in order. When re-launched in June 2012, the iOS app included an improved filtering tool that enabled users to search and compare offerings by cost, distance from destination, and star ratings. Like Hotels by Orbitz, an improved GPS-enabled mapping function displayed nearby hotels and Mobile Steals, providing instant price comparisons. Securing flight, lodging, and car rental reservations was simplified, eliminating browser screens and data entry repetition, and allowing users to perform all three operations in a continuous in-app stream unassociated with a mobile Web site. This was the heart of the redesign: to eliminate the mobile Web site and consolidate the entire search and reservation process within the native app so that users would no longer experience disruptive and time-consuming redirects either to Orbitz's mobile site or to an airline, hotel, or car rental agency site to complete the booking. The goal was to trump its competitors on speed and ease of use.

Brown believed that although mobile transactions in 2012 still represented less than 10% of Orbitz's total bookings, the investment would be rewarded by the broad opportunity presented by the rapidly escalating m-commerce market. New customer acquisition was expected as users discovered the increased transaction speed provided by the app. Increased speed is particularly attractive to consumers looking to book same-day reservations, which also comprise about 50% of Orbitz's mobile car rental purchases.

In order to verify that its goals for the app had been achieved, Orbitz commissioned a speed comparison study with Atmosphere Research Group and C + R Research. The travel apps, m-commerce sites, and e-commerce sites of its major competitors, including Kayak, Expedia, Priceline, and Travelocity, were pitted against the Orbitz iPhone app. The study found that Orbitz iPhone app users were able to book a round-trip flight to Hilton Head, South Carolina, a hotel reservation, and a car rental in slightly more than seven minutes, twice as fast as its iPhone app competitors. Only 60% of study participants using a competitor's product (aggregated) were able to complete the task as quickly. The Orbitz iPhone app transaction speed also surpassed comparable iPad and Android apps as well as desktop e-commerce site experiences. Study participants overwhelming awarded positive marks to the completely in-house–built Orbitz iPhone app in comparison to its competitors, 92% and 30%, respectively.

To speed the identification and fulfillment of future needs, customers' search history, personal information, frequent flyer program data, and travel preferences are saved within the app, enabling one-tap access to recent searches and automatic search suggestions. Itineraries can be accessed even while offline, and flight status and gate change data can be accessed with a single tap. Trips can also be easily added to the Apple Calendar app, formerly called iCal, used by many iPhone and iPod touch users.

Orbitz's future plans include optimizing consumers' ability to fulfill future travel needs by incorporating a synchronization mechanism between their mobile devices and their desktops. Integrating purchases from separate platforms will enable Orbitz to present better recommendations and target market more effectively. As market conditions dictate, an app for tablets that use the Android operating system will be developed, and plans are already underway to update the iPad app so that it is a full-service rather than just hotel-booking tool.

Flight, Hotel and Car Rental Options," Orbitz, Nov 15, 2010; "Orbitz for iPhone Review," by Joe Seifi, AppSafari.com, November 13th, 2008; "Orbitz Goes Mobile," by Russell Buckley, MobHappy.com, September 6, 2007;"Orbitz Mobile," by Dennis Bournique, WAPReview.com, August 15, 2006.

Case Study Questions

1. When compared to traditional desktop customers, why are mobile phone users much more likely to book a room or airline reservation for the same day?

2. In the mobile design project of 2011, why did Orbitz management decide to construct a mobile web site for corporate users rather than a native app?

3. What is "business logic" and why was it important for corporate travelers to have online reservation systems that included business logic?

4. Why did Orbitz reverse policy in 2012 and build native apps for each mobile platform (iOS and Android) instead of a single mobile Web site?

4.7 REVIEW

KEY CONCEPTS

■ **Explain the process that should be followed in building an e-commerce Web site.**

Factors you must consider when building an e-commerce site include:
- Hardware architecture
- Software
- Telecommunications capacity
- Site design
- Human resources
- Organizational capabilities

The systems development life cycle (a methodology for understanding the business objectives of a system and designing an appropriate solution) for building an e-commerce Web site involves five major steps:

- Identify the specific business objectives for the site, and then develop a list of system functionalities and information requirements.
- Develop a system design specification (both logical design and physical design).
- Build the site, either by in-house personnel or by outsourcing all or part of the responsibility to outside contractors.
- Test the system (unit testing, system testing, and acceptance testing).
- Implement and maintain the site.

The nine basic business and system functionalities an e-commerce site should contain include:

- *Digital catalog*—allows a site to display goods using text and graphics.
- *Product database*—provides product information, such as a description, stocking number, and inventory level.
- *Customer on-site tracking*—enables a site to create a site log for each customer visit, aiding in personalizing the shopping experience and identifying common customer paths and destinations.
- *Shopping cart/payment system*—provides an ordering system, secure credit card clearing, and other payment options.
- *Customer database*—includes customer information such as the name, address, phone number, and e-mail address.
- *Sales database*—contains information regarding the customer ID, product purchased, date, payment, and shipment to be able to provide after-sale customer support.
- *Ad server*—tracks the site behavior of prospects and customers that come through e-mail or banner ad campaigns.
- *Site tracking and reporting system*—monitors the number of unique visitors, pages visited, and products purchased.
- *Inventory management system*—provides a link to production and suppliers in order to facilitate order replenishment.

■ **Describe the major issues surrounding the decision to outsource site development and/or hosting.**

Advantages of building a site in-house include:
- The ability to change and adapt the site quickly as the market demands
- The ability to build a site that does exactly what the company needs

Disadvantages of building a site in-house include:
- The costs may be higher.
- The risks of failure may be greater, given the complexity of issues such as security, privacy, and inventory management.
- The process may be more time-consuming than if you had hired an outside specialist firm to manage the effort.
- Staff may experience a longer learning curve that delays your entry into the market.

Using design templates cuts development time, but pre-set templates can also limit functionality.

A similar decision is also necessary regarding outsourcing the hosting of the site versus keeping it in-house. Relying on an outside vendor to ensure that the site is live 24 hours a day places the burden of reliability on someone else, in return for a monthly hosting fee. The downside is that if the site requires fast upgrades due to heavy traffic, the chosen hosting company may or may not be capable of keeping up. Reliability versus scalability is the issue in this instance.

■ Identify and understand the major considerations involved in choosing Web server and e-commerce merchant server software.

Early Web sites used single-tier system architecture and consisted of a single-server computer that delivered static Web pages to users making requests through their browsers. The extended functionality of today's Web sites require the development of a multi-tiered systems architecture, which utilizes a variety of specialized Web servers, as well as links to pre-existing backend or legacy corporate databases.

All e-commerce sites require basic Web server software to answer requests from customers for HTML and XML pages. When choosing Web server software, companies are also choosing what operating system the site will run on. Apache, which runs on the Unix system, is the market leader.

Web servers provide a host of services, including:
* Processing user HTML requests
* Security services
* File transfer
* Search engine
* Data capture
* E-mail
* Site management tools

Dynamic server software allows sites to deliver dynamic content, rather than static, unchanging information. Web application server programs enable a wide range of e-commerce functionality, including creating a customer database, creating an e-mail promotional program, and accepting and processing orders, as well as many other services.

E-commerce merchant server software is another important software package that provides catalog displays, information storage and customer tracking, order taking (shopping cart), and credit card purchase processing. E-commerce suites can save time and money, but customization can significantly drive up costs. Factors to consider when choosing an e-commerce suite include its functionality, support for different business models, visual site management tools and reporting systems, performance and scalability, connectivity to existing business systems, compliance with standards, and global and multicultural capability.

■ Understand the issues involved in choosing the most appropriate hardware for an e-commerce site.

Speed, capacity, and scalability are three of the most important considerations when selecting an operating system, and therefore the hardware that it runs on.

To evaluate how fast the site needs to be, companies need to assess the number of simultaneous users the site expects to see, the nature of their requests, the type of information requested, and the bandwidth available to the site. The answers to these questions will provide guidance regarding the processors necessary to meet customer demand. In some cases, adding additional processing power can add capacity, thereby improving system speed.

Scalability is also an important issue. Increasing processing supply by scaling up to meet demand can be done through:

- *Vertical scaling*—improving the processing power of the hardware, but maintaining the same number of servers
- *Horizontal scaling*—adding more of the same processing hardware
- *Improving processing architecture*—identifying operations with similar workloads and using dedicated, tuned servers for each type of load

■ **Identify additional tools that can improve Web site performance.**

In addition to providing a speedy Web site, companies must also strive to have a well-designed site that encourages visitors to buy. Building in interactivity improves site effectiveness, as does personalization techniques that provide the ability to track customers while they are visiting the site. Commonly used software tools for achieving high levels of Web site interactivity and customer personalization include:

- *Common Gateway Interface (CGI) scripts*—a set of standards for communication between a browser and a program on a server that allows for interaction between the user and the server
- *Active Server Pages (ASP)*—a Microsoft tool that also permits interaction between the browser and the server
- *Java applets*—programs written in the Java programming language that also provide interactivity
- *JavaScript*—used to validate user input, such as an e-mail address
- *ActiveX and VBScript*—Microsoft's version of Java and JavaScript, respectively
- *Cookies*—text files stored on the user's hard drive that provide information regarding the user and his or her past experience at a Web site

■ **Understand the important considerations involved in building a mobile Web site and developing mobile applications.**

- When developing a mobile presence, it is important to understand the difference between a mobile Web site, mobile Web apps, and native apps.
- The first step is to identify business objectives, since they help determine which type of mobile presence is best.
- Design should take into account mobile platform constraints.
- Developing a mobile Web site is likely to be the least expensive option; mobile Web apps require more effort and cost; native apps are likely to be the most expensive to develop.

QUESTIONS

1. Name the six main pieces of the e-commerce site-building puzzle.
2. Define the systems development life cycle and discuss the various steps involved in creating an e-commerce site.
3. Discuss the differences between a simple logical and simple physical Web site design.
4. Why is system testing important? Name the three types of testing and their relation to each other.
5. Compare the costs for system development and system maintenance. Which is more expensive, and why?
6. Why is a Web site so costly to maintain? Discuss the main factors that impact cost.

7. What are the main differences between single-tier and multi-tier site architecture?
8. Name five basic functionalities a Web server should provide.
9. What are the three main factors to consider when choosing the best hardware platform for your Web site?
10. Why is Web server bandwidth an important issue for e-commerce sites?
11. Compare and contrast the various scaling methods. Explain why scalability is a key business issue for Web sites.
12. What are the eight most important factors impacting Web site design, and how do they affect a site's operation?
13. What are Java and JavaScript? What role do they play in Web site design?
14. Name and describe three methods used to treat customers individually. Why are they significant to e-commerce?
15. What are some of the policies e-commerce businesses must develop before launching a site, and why must they be developed?

PROJECTS

1. Go to Webs.com or NetworkSolutions.com. Both sites allow you to create a simple e-tailer Web site for a free trial period. Create a Web site. The site should feature at least four pages, including a home page, product page, shopping cart, and contact page. Extra credit will be given for additional complexity and creativity. Come to class prepared to present your e-tailer concept and Web site.

2. Visit several e-commerce sites, not including those mentioned in this chapter, and evaluate the effectiveness of the sites according to the eight basic criteria/functionalities listed in Table 4.11. Choose one site you feel does an excellent job on all the aspects of an effective site and create an electronic presentation, including screen shots, to support your choice.

3. Imagine that you are the head of information technology for a fast-growth e-commerce start-up. You are in charge of development of the company's Web site. Consider your options for building the site in-house with existing staff, or outsourcing the entire operation. Decide which strategy you believe is in your company's best interest and create a brief presentation outlining your position. Why choose that approach? And what are the estimated associated costs, compared with the alternative? (You'll need to make some educated guesses here—don't worry about being exact.)

4. Choose two e-commerce suite software packages and prepare an evaluation chart that rates the packages on the key factors discussed in the section "Choosing an E-commerce Suite." Which package would you choose if you were developing a Web site of the type described in this chapter, and why?

5. Choose one of the open source Web content management systems such as WordPress, Joomla, or Drupal or another of your own choosing and prepare an evaluation chart similar to that required by Project 4. Which system would you choose and why?

CHAPTER 5

E-commerce Security and Payment Systems

LEARNING OBJECTIVES

After reading this chapter, you will be able to:

- Understand the scope of e-commerce crime and security problems.
- Describe the key dimensions of e-commerce security.
- Understand the tension between security and other values.
- Identify the key security threats in the e-commerce environment.
- Describe how technology helps protect the security of messages sent over the Internet.
- Identify the tools used to establish secure Internet communications channels and protect networks, servers, and clients.
- Appreciate the importance of policies, procedures, and laws in creating security.
- Describe the features of traditional payment systems.
- Identify the major e-commerce payment systems in use today.
- Describe the features and functionality of electronic billing presentment and payment systems.

Cyberwar:

MAD 2.0

Over the past several years, Google and China have been fighting an undeclared war. In March 2011, Google blamed the Chinese government for manipulating and disrupting Gmail and Google Talk. The attack was apparently related to efforts by the Chinese government to control a global outbreak of democratic fever and public demonstrations inspired by the Tunisian and Egyptian street revolutions in the spring of 2011. In June 2012, Google advised many of its Gmail users in China, the United States, and Japan that its new warning system had detected a possible "state-sponsored" cyberattack against their account. The company would not release details of how it knew such attacks were occurring, nor who the sponsoring state was, but that this was yet another censorship/privacy battle in the China vs. Google war seemed certain.

© Rafal Olechowski / Fotolia

Previously, in January 2010, Google considered shutting down its Chinese operations because of sophisticated cyberattacks on its computer systems worldwide, which were aimed at the Gmail user accounts of Chinese activists. A simple phishing instant message (IM) was sent to a Google employee in China who clicked on a link—hardly a sophisticated attack. The unsuspecting employee downloaded software that took over his computer and ultimately gained access to the computers of Google software developers in California responsible for the password system. Some of Google's proprietary source code was stolen. When Google revealed the theft, it was a stark departure from how U.S. companies generally handle cyberburglaries. Of the 34 other companies struck, only Adobe and Intel also went public. While most companies prefer to handle these matters internally, far more—according to congressional testimony, 94%—are not even aware that their networks have been compromised. As serious as Google considered these issues, a November 2011 report by 14 U.S. intelligence agencies revealed that the theft of intellectual property was far more pervasive than even Google imagined.

The report detailed a concerted government-based cyberwarfare strategy that comprises a significant plank in China's economic policy. At least 17 cyberespionage rings based in China have been identified. Their modus operandi is to insert spyware through phishing e-mails. Evidence that this is a well-financed, centralized effort includes a division of labor among several groups, with some concentrating on network penetration and others on data extraction, a sophisticated support infrastructure, and suspected command-and-control (C&C) servers operated by China's People's Liberation Army. The seven economic objectives in China's 12th Five-Year Plan (2011–2015) parallel the corporate and research targets. For example, in the biotechnology sector, drug manufacturers Wyeth and Abbott Laboratories and medical device maker Boston Scientific were hit. The computing center for the Food and Drug Administration, where sensitive information including chemical formulas and drug trial documents are stored, was also infiltrated. In the manufacturing sector, the networks of Cypress Semiconductor Corp, Aerospace Corp, and Environmental Systems Research Institute were compromised, possibly yielding China data regarding the manufacture of telecommunication chips, semiconductors, mapping software, and documents pertaining to national security space programs. Small strategic targets such as iBahn, the company that provides Internet access to business travelers at the Marriott and other large hotel chains, have exposed access points into numerous corporate networks as well as access to millions of confidential, and possibly encrypted, e-mail messages.

According to 2012 congressional testimony, over the past 12 years, China has penetrated the networks of at least 760 ISPs, corporations, research universities, and government agencies. Cyberespionage is a far quicker and cheaper path to economic dominance than independent research and development. Representative Mike Rogers estimated that China had garnered $500 billion worth of U.S. corporate assets. The magnitude of this wealth transfer is difficult to quantify because there are so many unknown variables. How quickly can source code, blueprints, chemical formulas, and other data be translated into products that can outcompete?

In another 2012 incident, China is suspected of infiltrating the e-mail system used by the U.S.-China Economic and Security Review Commission. The hackers showed great initial interest in communications from National Foreign Trade Council (NFTC) head William Reinsch, the former chairman of the commission. Cybersecurity experts speculate that Reinsch's NFTC account was targeted because it offered a less secure back door into the U.S.-China commission. Like the iBahn incursion, this type of "blended attack" is structured so that the objective is reached by first penetrating a weaker network with whom or through whom the target regularly communicates.

In response to these revelations, the Obama administration publicly called out the Chinese government, which has staunchly denied all allegations, naming it the top cyberthreat to U.S. firms. Rogers and Representative Dutch Ruppersberger introduced the Cyber Intelligence Sharing and Protection Act (CISPA), which passed the House of Representatives in April 2012. CISPA would allow ISPs and other Internet companies to collect, analyze, and share with the National Security Agency (NSA) and other agencies activities perceived as possible threats. Likewise, it establishes conditions and procedures through which agencies would be permitted to share evidence, including classified information, with companies. Respected digital rights advocacy groups such as the Electronic Frontier Foundation oppose it because the language is so ambiguous as to not rule out ISPs, e-mail providers, and other Internet companies collecting virtually unlimited dossiers on their users. What's more, it contains no provisions for judicial oversight and cancels out privacy protections in several current laws by inserting a cybersecurity exception. The corresponding Senate bill, the Cybersecurity Act of 2012, has not passed.

Few viable deterrents are available. A U.N. Security Council resolution aimed at curtailing cyberespionage would not be able to pass because the five permanent members, of which China is one, have veto power. Sanctions carry the risk of initiating a trade war. With CISPA stalled in Congress, and deeming it ineffectual in any event, Richard Clarke, former special adviser on cybersecurity to U.S. President George W. Bush, penned an April 2012 New York Times editorial calling on President Obama to pass an executive order. Without authorization, no government agency can step in to stop corporate attacks. Internal documents indicate that the administration is crafting an order to establish a Department of Homeland Security program, leaving current privacy protections intact. Privacy advocates favor this route because there would be no cybersecurity exception granting immunity to corporations.

While China has been busy employing cyberespionage to climb its way to the unrivaled apex of the economic heap, other nations are engaged in a different form of cyberwarfare. U.S. cyberspies concentrate on national security. Foreign governments, military, and terrorist groups are targeted for defense purposes. The Stuxnet worm is a high-visibility example of this. First discovered in June 2010, Stuxnet was designed to disable the computers that control the centrifuges in Iran's uranium enrichment process. A secret joint United States-Israel operation code-named Olympic Games is believed to have created Stuxnet. In another strike against Iran in April 2012, malware wiped computers in the Iranian Oil Ministry and the National Iranian Oil Company clean. Initial reports identified the malware as a Trojan dubbed Flame. Flame was suspected of pursuing multiple Iranian objectives including key oil export hubs. Iran's National Computer Emergency Response Team released a tool to detect and destroy Flame in early May.

In August 2012, security firm Kaspersky Labs announced that it believed there were actually two different malware agents launched in separate attacks: Flame, an espionage agent, and Wiper, a data deletion agent. Flame was found to be closely related to both Stuxnet and the Duqu worm. Believed to be created by Stuxnet's developers, Duqu, discovered in September 2011, is designed to collect passwords, take desktop screenshots to monitor user's actions, and pilfer various kinds of documents. Also in August 2012, Kaspersky announced the detection of another cyber-surveillance tool. Given the moniker Gauss, it was likely used to "follow the money" in Middle Eastern banking transactions. With an online banking module, and laden with encrypted malicious code, the Trojan is designed to collect the banking credentials of patrons of multiple Lebanon-based banks, Citibank, and PayPal. So far, Kaspersky has been unable to decrypt the malware payload, because soon after its discovery, Gauss became inactive when its C&C servers shut down. Gauss is built on the same platform as Flame and is closely related to, and probably built in the same laboratory as, Stuxnet. Added together, the evidence suggests a possible effort by the U.S. government to root out terrorist group funding networks.

Although cyberattacks are reported as discrete incidents, they are in fact ongoing activities punctuated by major events. In the United States, the public Web, air-traffic control systems, healthcare, and telecommunications services have all been attacked.

SOURCES: "Malware Aimed at Iran Hit Five Sites, Report Says," by John Markoff, *New York Times*, February 11, 2011; "Israeli Test on Worm Called Crucial in Iran Nuclear Delay," by William Broad, *New York Times*, January 15, 2011; "Stuxnet Malware is 'Weapon' Out to Destroy...Iran's Bushehr Nuclear Plant?", by Mark Clayton, *Christian Science Monitor*, September 21, 2010; "Steps Taken to End Impasse Over Cybersecurity Talks," by John Markoff, *New York Times*, July 16, 2010; "Obama and Cyber Defense," by L. Gordon Crovitz, *Wall Street Journal*, June 29, 2009; Cyberattack on Google Said to Hit Password System," by John Markoff, *New York Times*, April 10, 2010; *Cyber War: The Next Threat to National Security and What to Do About It*, by Richard A. Clarke and Robert K. Knake, Ecco/HarperCollins Publishers, March 2010; "Mutually Assured Destruction 2.0," *New York Times*, January 26, 2010; "Cyberwar: In Digital Combat, U.S. Finds No Easy Deterrent," by John Markoff, David Sanger, and Thom Shanker, *New York Times*, January 26, 2010; "Google, Citing Attack, Threatens to Exit China," by Andrew Jacobs, *New York Times*, January 12, 2010.

Both China and Russia have been caught trying to infiltrate the U.S. electric-power grid, leaving behind software code to be used to disrupt the system. In July 2010, after 10 years of debate, 15 nations including the United States and Russia agreed on a set of recommendations that it was hoped would lead to an international treaty banning computer warfare. It never materialized. Kaspersky Labs founder, Eugene Kaspersky, continued to advocate for its passage at CeBIT Australia in May 2012. Because, as Kaspersky points out, cyberweapons are both cheap and potent, more than 100 nations have cyberwarfare capabilities and programs. Digital security companies can only discover a fraction of the existing malware. And because telecommunication security necessarily requires inspecting content, democratic nations' attempts to pass cybersecurity legislation will meet opposition from privacy groups. An international treaty seems our best hope of avoiding MAD 2.0, the modern version of the Cold War era "mutually assured destruction," in which cyber-offensive actions are engaged in to destroy aggressors' Internet and other critical infrastructure.

Powerful states can launch cyberattacks but cannot easily defend against them. Offense has the advantage. First strike is an attractive option. Perhaps because this is so, the United States and China have conducted two cyberwar game events, with a third in the works. Designed as a preventative measure against a conventional arms confrontation should either side feel threatened in cyberspace, they gave the United States the opportunity to confront China about its cyberespionage, apparently to little effect. According to Jim Lewis, director of the Centre for Strategic and International Studies think tank, which coordinated the games in conjunction with a Chinese think tank, China believes the United States is in decline, putting it in the one-up position. Organizing the games through think tanks rather than government channels enables government and intelligence agency officials to meet in an atmosphere that allows for candid discussion as opposed to more formal talks. Dubbed "Track 1.5" diplomacy, events such as these allow the Chinese to express that they too have been afflicted by cyberespionage and believe they have been unfairly scapegoated. Participants of the first event were tasked with developing a response to a cyberattack from a malware agent such as Stuxnet. In the second, they were specifically asked to outline their response if they knew that the attack had been perpetrated by the other party. This purportedly went poorly. Lewis' impression is that the present balance of power in China favors factions that support conflict over those that support cooperation.

With the United States refocusing its military attention on China as a dual cyber-weapon/conventional military threat, any attempt to reduce the distrust and ignorance that fuel arms races are welcome. Even if a complete ban on cyberweapons is unrealistic, measures such as prohibiting infrastructure and financial system attacks might be achievable. Better yet, persuading nations to agree that they will not perpetrate a first strike would go a long way in preventing MAD 2.0.

A s *Cyberwar: Mutually Assured Destruction* illustrates, the Internet and Web are increasingly vulnerable to large-scale attacks and potentially large-scale failure. Increasingly, these attacks are led by organized gangs of criminals operating globally—an unintended consequence of globalization. Even more worrisome is the growing number of large-scale attacks that are funded, organized, and led by various nations against the Internet resources of other nations. Currently there are few if any steps that individuals or businesses can take to prevent these kinds of attacks. However, there are several steps you can take to protect your business Web sites and your personal information from routine security attacks. Reading this chapter, you should start thinking about how your business could survive in the event of a large-scale "outage" of the Internet.

In this chapter, we will examine e-commerce security and payment issues. First, we will identify the major security risks and their costs, and describe the variety of solutions currently available. Then, we will look at the major payment methods and consider how to achieve a secure payment environment. **Table 5.1** highlights some of the major trends in online security in 2012–2013.

TABLE 5.1	WHAT'S NEW IN E-COMMERCE SECURITY 2012–2013

- Mobile malware presents a tangible threat as smartphones and other mobile devices become more common targets of cybercriminals.
- Certificate authorities and the digital encryption regime that provides a basis for trust within the Internet infrastructure tighten standards in an attempt to prevent further attacks after several high-profile hacks in 2011.
- The amount of spam decreases as a result of the demise of Rustock, the largest spam-sending botnet in the world, in 2011.
- Hackers and cybercriminals continue to focus their efforts on social network sites to exploit potential victims.
- Politically motivated, targeted attacks by hacktivist groups such as Anonymous and LulzSec and others continue, as well as advanced persistent threats.
- Nations continue to engage in cyberwarfare and cyberespionage; Duqu, created from the same code base as Stuxnet, is discovered, raising concerns that it may be used for similar future attacks.
- Large-scale data breaches continue to expose data about individuals to hackers and other cybercriminals.
- Malicious attacks targeting Mac computers increase.

5.1 THE E-COMMERCE SECURITY ENVIRONMENT

For most law-abiding citizens, the Internet holds the promise of a huge and convenient global marketplace, providing access to people, goods, services, and businesses worldwide, all at a bargain price. For criminals, the Internet has created entirely new—and lucrative—ways to steal from the more than 1 billion Internet consumers worldwide. From products and services to cash to information, it's all there for the taking on the Internet.

It's also less risky to steal online. Rather than rob a bank in person, the Internet makes it possible to rob people remotely and almost anonymously. Rather than steal a CD at a local record store, you can download the same music for free and almost without risk from the Internet. The potential for anonymity on the Internet cloaks many criminals in legitimate-looking identities, allowing them to place fraudulent orders with online merchants, steal information by intercepting e-mail, or simply shut down e-commerce sites by using software viruses and swarm attacks. The Internet was never designed to be a global marketplace with a billion users, and lacks many basic security features found in older networks such as the telephone system or broadcast television networks. Who ever heard of the telephone system being hacked and "brought down" by programmers in Eastern Europe? By comparison, the Internet is an open, vulnerable-design network. The actions of cybercriminals are costly for both businesses and consumers, who are then subjected to higher prices and additional security measures. However, the overall security environment is strengthening as business managers and government officials make significant investments in security equipment and business procedures.

THE SCOPE OF THE PROBLEM

Cybercrime is becoming a more significant problem for both organizations and consumers. Bot networks, DDoS attacks, Trojans, phishing, data theft, identity theft, credit card fraud, and spyware are just some of the threats that are making daily headlines. Social networks such as Facebook, Twitter, and LinkedIn have also had security breaches. For example, in June 2012, LinkedIn revealed that Russian hackers had obtained almost 6.5 million user passwords and posted them online. In July 2012, Twitter was hit by a widespread spam attack involving malicious tweets that included a user's Twitter name, which ultimately redirected the user to a Russian Web site containing the Blackhole exploit kit. But despite the increasing attention being paid to cybercrime, it is difficult to accurately estimate the actual amount of such crime, in part because many companies are hesitant to report it due to the fear of losing the trust of its customers, and because even if crime is reported, it may be difficult to quantify the actual dollar amount of the loss.

One source of information is the Internet Crime Complaint Center ("IC3"), a partnership between the National White Collar Crime Center and the Federal Bureau of Investigation. The IC3 data is useful for gauging the types of e-commerce crimes most likely to be reported by consumers. In 2011, the IC3 processed almost 315,000 Internet crime complaints, the second-highest number in its 11-year history. Over half the complainants reported a financial loss, with the total reported amount almost $500 million. The average amount of loss for those who reported a financial loss was more than $4,100. The most common complaints were for scams involving the FBI, identity theft, and advance fee fraud (National White Collar Crime Center and the Federal Bureau of Investigation, 2012).

The Computer Security Institute's annual *Computer Crime and Security Survey* is another source of information. In 2011, the survey was based on the responses of 351 security practitioners in U.S. corporations, government agencies, financial institutions, medical institutions, and universities. The survey reported that 46% of responding organizations experienced a computer security incident within the past year. The most common type of attack experienced was a malware infection (67%), followed by phishing fraud (39%), laptop and mobile hardware theft (34%), attacks by botnets (29%), and insider abuse (25%). Not all of these necessarily involve e-commerce, although many do. Few companies were willing to share their estimated security loss numbers. But in the previous year's survey, of those that did report, the total loss reported was $41.5 million, with an average annual loss of $288,000. The most expensive security incidents were financial fraud, which averaged $500,000, followed by dealing with bot computers within the organization's network ($345,000) (Computer Security Institute, 2011, 2010). These figures represent only direct losses and not the costs of the security systems or personnel. Security experts believe underreporting of losses is growing in the last few years because of public attention.

Reports issued by security product providers, such as Symantec, are another source of data. Symantec issues a semi-annual *Internet Security Threat Report*, based on 64.6 million sensors monitoring Internet activity in more than 200 countries. In 2011, Symantec identified more than 405 million variants of malware versus 286 million in 2010. The sheer volume of Web-based attacks was up by more than 80% in 2011. Advances in technology have greatly reduced the entry costs and skills required to enter the cybercrime business. According to Symantec, low cost and readily available Web attack kits, which enable hackers to create malware without having to write software from scratch, are responsible for more than 60% of all malicious activity. In addition, there has been a surge in polymorphic malware, which enables attackers to generate a unique version of the malware for each victim, making it much more difficult for pattern-matching software used by security firms to detect. Other findings indicate that targeted attacks are increasing; social networks are helping criminals identify individual targets; and mobile platforms and applications are increasingly vulnerable. According to Symantec, 2011 marked the first year that mobile malware presented a tangible and significant threat, with a 93% increase in the number of vulnerabilities identified compared to 2010 (Symantec, 2012a). However, Symantec does not attempt to quantify actual crimes and/or losses related to these threats.

Online credit card fraud and phishing attacks are perhaps the most high-profile form of e-commerce crimes. Although the average amount of credit card fraud loss experienced by any one individual is typically relatively small, the overall amount is substantial. The research firm CyberSource estimates online credit card fraud in the United States amounted to about $3.4 billion in 2011. Online fraud peaked in 2008 at $4 billion, suggesting that merchants are managing their credit card payment risks much better than earlier (CyberSource, 2012). The overall rate of online credit card fraud is estimated to be about .6% of all online card transactions. As a percentage of all e-commerce revenues, credit card fraud is declining as merchants and credit companies expand security systems to prevent the most common types of low-level fraud. But the nature of credit card fraud has changed greatly from the theft of a single credit card number and efforts to purchase goods at a few sites, to the simultaneous theft of millions of credit card numbers and their distributions to thousands of criminals operating as gangs of thieves. The emergence of "identify theft," described in detail later in this chapter, as a major online/offline type of fraud, may well increase markedly the incidence and amount of credit card fraud, since identity theft often includes the use of stolen credit card information and the creation of phony credit card accounts. According to the Identity Fraud Report by Javelin Strategy & Research, identity fraud increased by 13% in 2011, with the total number of victims increasing to 11.6 million adults. However, the total dollar amount stolen as a result of identity fraud has not increased, holding steady at about $18 billion (Javelin Research & Strategy, 2012).

The Underground Economy Marketplace: The Value of Stolen Information

Criminals who steal information on the Internet do not always use this information themselves, but instead derive value by selling the information to others on so-called underground economy servers. There are several thousand known underground economy servers around the world that sell stolen information (about half of these are in the United States). **Table 5.2** lists some recently observed prices, which typically vary depending on the quantity being purchased. Experts believe the cost of stolen information has fallen as the tools of harvesting have increased the supply. On the demand side, the same efficiencies and opportunities provided by new technology have increased the number of people who want to use stolen information. It's a robust marketplace.

Finding these servers is difficult for the average user (and for law enforcement agencies), and you need to be vetted by other criminals before gaining access. This vetting process takes place through e-mail exchanges of information, money, and reputation. Criminals have fairly good, personalized security!

TABLE 5.2	THE CYBER BLACK MARKET FOR STOLEN DATA
Credit card	$2–$90
A full identity (U.S. bank account, credit card, date of birth, social security, etc.)	$3–$20
Bank account	$80–$700
Online accounts (PayPal, eBay, Facebook, Twitter, etc)	$10-$1500
E-mail accounts	$5-$12
Botnet rental	$15
A single compromised computer	$6–$20
Social security number	$5–$7
Attack toolkits	$120 per month

SOURCE: Based on data from PandaSecurity, 2012; Danchev, 2011; Symantec, Inc., 2011, 2010.

Not every cybercriminal is necessarily after money. In some cases, such criminals aim to just deface, vandalize, and/or disrupt a Web site, rather than actually steal goods or services. The cost of such an attack includes not only the time and effort to make repairs to the site but also damage done to the site's reputation and image, as well as revenues lost as a result of the attack. Ponemon Institute estimates that the average loss to corporations for a breach of data security in 2011 was $5.5 million (Ponemon Institute, 2012).

So, what can we can conclude about the overall size of cybercrime? Cybercrime against e-commerce sites is dynamic and changing all the time, with new risks appearing often. The amount of losses to businesses appears to be significant but stable, and may represent a declining percentage of overall sales because firms have invested in security measures to protect against the simplest crimes. Individuals face new risks of fraud, many of which (unlike credit cards where federal law limits the loss to $50 for individuals) involve substantial uninsured losses involving debit cards and bank accounts. The managers of e-commerce sites must prepare for an ever-changing variety of criminal assaults, and keep current in the latest security techniques.

WHAT IS GOOD E-COMMERCE SECURITY?

What is a secure commercial transaction? Anytime you go into a marketplace you take risks, including the loss of privacy (information about what you purchased). Your prime risk as a consumer is that you do not get what you paid for. In fact, you might pay and get nothing! Worse, someone steals your money while you are at the market! As a merchant in the market, your risk is that you don't get paid for what you sell. Thieves take merchandise and then either walk off without paying anything, or pay you with a fraudulent instrument, stolen credit card, or forged currency.

E-commerce merchants and consumers face many of the same risks as participants in traditional commerce, albeit in a new digital environment. Theft is theft, regardless of whether it is digital theft or traditional theft. Burglary, breaking and entering, embezzlement, trespass, malicious destruction, vandalism—all crimes in a traditional commercial environment—are also present in e-commerce. However, reducing risks in e-commerce is a complex process that involves new technologies, organizational policies and procedures, and new laws and industry standards that empower law enforcement officials to investigate and prosecute offenders. **Figure 5.1** on page 266 illustrates the multi-layered nature of e-commerce security.

To achieve the highest degree of security possible, new technologies are available and should be used. But these technologies by themselves do not solve the problem. Organizational policies and procedures are required to ensure the technologies are not subverted. Finally, industry standards and government laws are required to enforce payment mechanisms, as well as to investigate and prosecute violators of laws designed to protect the transfer of property in commercial transactions.

The history of security in commercial transactions teaches that any security system can be broken if enough resources are put against it. Security is not absolute. In addition, perfect security of every item is not needed forever, especially in the

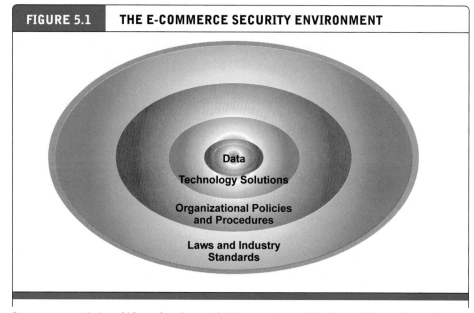

FIGURE 5.1   **THE E-COMMERCE SECURITY ENVIRONMENT**

E-commerce security is multi-layered, and must take into account new technology, policies and procedures, and laws and industry standards.

information age. There is a time value to information—just as there is to money. Sometimes it is sufficient to protect a message for a few hours, days, or years. Also, because security is costly, we always have to weigh the cost against the potential loss. Finally, we have also learned that security is a chain that breaks most often at the weakest link. Our locks are often much stronger than our management of the keys.

We can conclude then that good e-commerce security requires a set of laws, procedures, policies, and technologies that, to the extent feasible, protect individuals and organizations from unexpected behavior in the e-commerce marketplace.

DIMENSIONS OF E-COMMERCE SECURITY

integrity
the ability to ensure that information being displayed on a Web site or transmitted or received over the Internet has not been altered in any way by an unauthorized party

There are six key dimensions to e-commerce security: integrity, nonrepudiation, authenticity, confidentiality, privacy, and availability (see **Table 5.3**).

Integrity refers to the ability to ensure that information being displayed on a Web site, or transmitted or received over the Internet, has not been altered in any way by an unauthorized party. For example, if an unauthorized person intercepts and changes the contents of an online communication, such as by redirecting a bank wire transfer into a different account, the integrity of the message has been compromised because the communication no longer represents what the original sender intended.

nonrepudiation
the ability to ensure that e-commerce participants do not deny (i.e., repudiate) their online actions

Nonrepudiation refers to the ability to ensure that e-commerce participants do not deny (i.e., repudiate) their online actions. For instance, the availability of free e-mail accounts with alias names makes it easy for a person to post comments or send a message and perhaps later deny doing so. Even when a customer uses a real name and e-mail address, it is easy for that customer to order merchandise online and then

TABLE 5.3	CUSTOMER AND MERCHANT PERSPECTIVES ON THE DIFFERENT DIMENSIONS OF E-COMMERCE SECURITY	
DIMENSION	CUSTOMER'S PERSPECTIVE	MERCHANT'S PERSPECTIVE
Integrity	Has information I transmitted or received been altered?	Has data on the site been altered without authorization? Is data being received from customers valid?
Nonrepudiation	Can a party to an action with me later deny taking the action?	Can a customer deny ordering products?
Authenticity	Who am I dealing with? How can I be assured that the person or entity is who they claim to be?	What is the real identity of the customer?
Confidentiality	Can someone other than the intended recipient read my messages?	Are messages or confidential data accessible to anyone other than those authorized to view them?
Privacy	Can I control the use of information about myself transmitted to an e-commerce merchant?	What use, if any, can be made of personal data collected as part of an e-commerce transaction? Is the personal information of customers being used in an unauthorized manner?
Availability	Can I get access to the site?	Is the site operational?

later deny doing so. In most cases, because merchants typically do not obtain a physical copy of a signature, the credit card issuer will side with the customer because the merchant has no legally valid proof that the customer ordered the merchandise.

Authenticity refers to the ability to identify the identity of a person or entity with whom you are dealing on the Internet. How does the customer know that the Web site operator is who it claims to be? How can the merchant be assured that the customer is really who she says she is? Someone who claims to be someone he is not is "spoofing" or misrepresenting himself.

Confidentiality refers to the ability to ensure that messages and data are available only to those who are authorized to view them. Confidentiality is sometimes confused with **privacy**, which refers to the ability to control the use of information a customer provides about himself or herself to an e-commerce merchant.

E-commerce merchants have two concerns related to privacy. They must establish internal policies that govern their own use of customer information, and they must protect that information from illegitimate or unauthorized use. For example, if hackers break into an e-commerce site and gain access to credit card or other information, this not only violates the confidentiality of the data, but also the privacy of the individuals who supplied the information.

Availability refers to the ability to ensure that an e-commerce site continues to function as intended.

authenticity
the ability to identify the identity of a person or entity with whom you are dealing on the Internet

confidentiality
the ability to ensure that messages and data are available only to those who are authorized to view them

privacy
the ability to control the use of information about oneself

availability
the ability to ensure that an e-commerce site continues to function as intended

E-commerce security is designed to protect these six dimensions. When any one of them is compromised, it is a security issue.

THE TENSION BETWEEN SECURITY AND OTHER VALUES

Can there be too much security? The answer is yes. Contrary to what some may believe, security is not an unmitigated good. Computer security adds overhead and expense to business operations, and also gives criminals new opportunities to hide their intentions and their crimes.

Ease of Use

There are inevitable tensions between security and ease of use. When traditional merchants are so fearful of robbers that they do business in shops locked behind security gates, ordinary customers are discouraged from walking in. The same can be true on the Web. In general, the more security measures added to an e-commerce site, the more difficult it is to use and the slower the site becomes. As you will discover reading this chapter, digital security is purchased at the price of slowing down processors and adding significantly to data storage demands on storage devices. Security is a technological and business overhead that can detract from doing business. Too much security can harm profitability, while not enough security can potentially put you out of business.

Public Safety and the Criminal Uses of the Internet

There is also an inevitable tension between the desires of individuals to act anonymously (to hide their identity) and the needs of public officials to maintain public safety that can be threatened by criminals or terrorists. This is not a new problem, or even new to the electronic era. The U.S. government began informal tapping of telegraph wires during the Civil War in the mid-1860s in order to trap conspirators and terrorists, and the first police wiretaps of local telephone systems were in place by the 1890s—20 years after the invention of the phone (Schwartz, 2001). No nation-state has ever permitted a technological haven to exist where criminals can plan crimes or threaten the nation-state without fear of official surveillance or investigation. In this sense, the Internet is no different from any other communication system. Drug cartels make extensive use of voice, fax, the Internet, and encrypted e-mail; a number of large international organized crime groups steal information from commercial Web sites and resell it to other criminals who use it for financial fraud. Over the years, the U.S. government has successfully pursued various "carding forums" (Web sites that facilitate the sale of stolen credit card and debit card numbers), such as Shadowcrew, Carderplanet, and Cardersmarket resulting in the arrest and prosecution of a number of their members and the closing of the sites. However, other criminal organizations have emerged to take their place.

Terrorists are also fond users of the Internet and have been for many years. Encrypted files sent via e-mail were used by Ramzi Yousef—a member of the terrorist group responsible for bombing the World Trade Center in 1993—to hide plans for bombing 11 U.S. airliners. The Internet was also used to plan and coordinate the subsequent attacks on the World Trade Center on September 11, 2001. In 2010, Pentagon officials say the case of Umar Farouk Abdulmutallab illustrates how terrorists make effective use of the Internet to radicalize, recruit, train, and coordinate youthful terrorists. Abdulmutallab allegedly attempted to blow up an American airliner in Detroit on Christmas Day 2009. He was identified, contacted, recruited, and trained all within six weeks, according to a Pentagon counterterrorism official. That's much faster than the two and a half years it took for Osama bin Laden to hatch the plan to attack the United States in 2001.

5.2 SECURITY THREATS IN THE E-COMMERCE ENVIRONMENT

From a technology perspective, there are three key points of vulnerability when dealing with e-commerce: the client, the server, and the communications pipeline. **Figure 5.2** illustrates a typical e-commerce transaction with a consumer using a credit card to purchase a product. **Figure 5.3** on page 270 illustrates some of the things that can go wrong at each major vulnerability point in the transaction—over Internet communications channels, at the server level, and at the client level.

FIGURE 5.2 **A TYPICAL E-COMMERCE TRANSACTION**

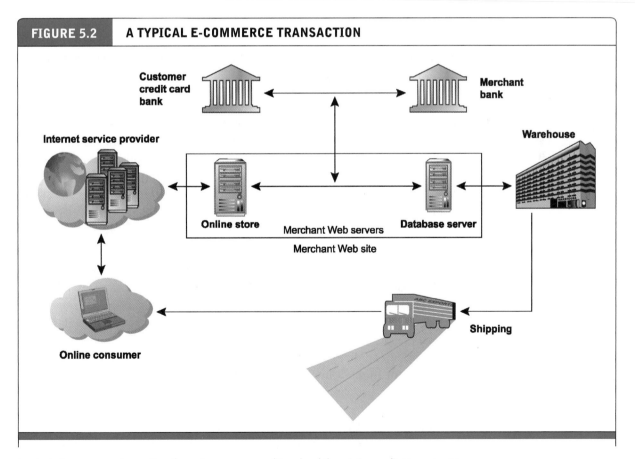

In a typical e-commerce transaction, the customer uses a credit card and the existing credit payment system.

FIGURE 5.3	VULNERABLE POINTS IN AN E-COMMERCE TRANSACTION

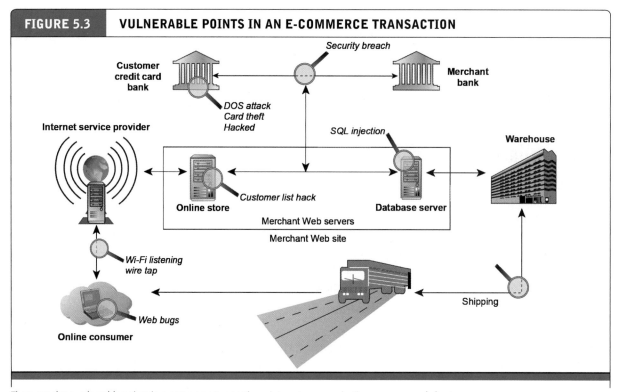

There are three vulnerable points in e-commerce transactions: Internet communications, servers, and clients.

In this section, we describe a number of the most common and most damaging forms of security threats to e-commerce consumers and site operators: malicious code, potentially unwanted programs, phishing and identity theft, hacking and cybervandalism, credit card fraud/theft, spoofing (pharming) and spam (junk) Web sites, Denial of Service (DoS) and DDoS attacks, sniffing, insider attacks, poorly designed server and client software, social network security issues, mobile platform security issues, and finally, cloud security issues.

MALICIOUS CODE

malicious code (malware)

includes a variety of threats such as viruses, worms, Trojan horses, and bots

Malicious code (sometimes referred to as "malware") includes a variety of threats such as viruses, worms, Trojan horses, and bots. Some malicious code, sometimes referred to as an *exploit,* is designed to take advantage of software vulnerabilities in a computer's operating system, Web browser, applications, or other software components. For example, Microsoft reported that the Blackhole exploit kit available for purchase or rent from various hacker forums lead to a significant increase in the number of exploits based on HTML or JavaScript reported in the second half of 2011. Java exploits, those that affected Adobe products, and those aimed at the Windows operating system were also quite common. Overall, according to Microsoft, exploits comprised 10% of the worldwide malware threats in the fourth quarter of 2011 (Microsoft, 2012). Security firm GData reported that there were more than 2.5 million malware programs on the Internet in 2011, an increase of almost 25% from the previous year (GData Security Labs, 2011). In the past, malicious code was often intended to simply impair computers, and was often authored by a lone hacker, but increasingly the intent is to steal e-mail addresses, logon credentials, personal data, and financial information. Malicious code is also used to develop integrated malware networks that organize the theft of information and money.

One of the latest innovations in malicious code distribution is to embed it in the online advertising chain, including in Google and other ad networks. As the ad network chain becomes more complicated, it becomes more and more difficult for Web sites to vet ads placed on their sites to ensure they are malware-free. Favorite targets are social media sites and large government agencies such as the National Institutes of Health (NIH), the U.S. Treasury, and the Environmental Protection Agency. More than 1.5 million malicious ads are served every day, including "drive-by downloads" and fake anti-virus campaigns. A **drive-by download** is malware that comes with a downloaded file that a user requests. Drive-by is now one of the most common methods of infecting computers. For instance, Web sites as disparate as eWeek.com (a technology site) to MLB.com (Major League Baseball) to AmericanIdol.com have experienced instances where ads placed on their sites either had malicious code embedded or directed clickers to malicious sites. Malicious code embedded in PDF files is also common. Malware authors are also increasingly using links embedded within e-mail instead of the more traditional file attachments to infect computers. The links lead directly to a malicious code download or Web sites that include malicious JavaScript code. Equally important, there has been a major shift in the writers of malware from amateur hackers and adventurers to organized criminal efforts to defraud companies and individuals. In other words, it's now more about the money than ever before.

drive-by download
malware that comes with a downloaded file that a user requests

A **virus** is a computer program that has the ability to replicate or make copies of itself, and spread to other files. In addition to the ability to replicate, most computer viruses deliver a "payload." The payload may be relatively benign, such as the display of a message or image, or it may be highly destructive—destroying files, reformatting the computer's hard drive, or causing programs to run improperly. According to Microsoft, viruses comprised 6.7% of the worldwide malware threats in the fourth quarter of 2011.

virus
a computer program that has the ability to replicate or make copies of itself, and spread to other files

Viruses are often combined with a worm. Instead of just spreading from file to file, a **worm** is designed to spread from computer to computer. A worm does not necessarily need to be activated by a user or program in order for it to replicate itself. In the fourth quarter of 2011, worms accounted for 17.2% of the worldwide malware threats, according to Microsoft. For example, the Slammer worm, which targeted a known vulnerability in Microsoft's SQL Server database software, infected more than 90% of vulnerable computers worldwide within 10 minutes of its release on the Internet; crashed Bank of America cash machines, especially in the southwestern part of the United States; affected cash registers at supermarkets such as the Publix chain in Atlanta, where staff could not dispense cash to frustrated buyers; and took down most Internet connections in South Korea, causing a dip in the stock market there. The Conficker worm, which first appeared in November 2008, is the most significant worm since Slammer, and reportedly infected 9 to 15 million computers worldwide (Symantec, 2010).

worm
malware that is designed to spread from computer to computer

Trojan horse

appears to be benign, but then does something other than expected. Often a way for viruses or other malicious code to be introduced into a computer system

A **Trojan horse** appears to be benign, but then does something other than expected. The Trojan horse is not itself a virus because it does not replicate, but is often a way for viruses or other malicious code such as bots or *rootkits* (a program whose aim is to subvert control of the computer's operating system) to be introduced into a computer system. The term *Trojan horse* refers to the huge wooden horse in Homer's *Iliad* that the Greeks gave their opponents, the Trojans—a gift that actually contained hundreds of Greek soldiers. Once the people of Troy let the massive horse within their gates, the soldiers revealed themselves and captured the city. In today's world, a Trojan horse may masquerade as a game, but actually hide a program to steal your passwords and e-mail them to another person. Miscellaneous Trojans and Trojan downloaders and droppers (Trojans that install malicious files to a computer it has infected by either downloading them from a remote computer or from a copy contained in its own code) were found on more than 40% of computers around the world reporting malware threats to Microsoft in the fourth quarter of 2011. In May 2011, Sony experienced the largest data breach in history when a Trojan horse took over the administrative computers of Sony's PlayStation game center and downloaded personal and credit card information involving 77 million registered users (Wakabayashi, 2011). In 2011, the most common Trojan horse was Zeus. Zeus steals information from users by keystroke logging. It is distributed through the Zeus botnet, which has millions of slave computers, and utilizes drive-by downloads and phishing tactics to persuade users to download files with the Trojan horse.

backdoor

feature of viruses, worms and Trojans that allows an attacker to remotely access a compromised computer.

A **backdoor** is a feature of viruses, worms and Trojans that allows an attacker to remotely access a compromised computer. Downadup, the fourth most prevalent malicious code family in 2011, is an example of a worm with a backdoor, while Virut, a virus that infects various file types that was the fifth most common malicious code family in 2011, also includes a backdoor that can be used to download and install additional threats.

bot

type of malicious code that can be covertly installed on a computer when attached to the Internet. Once installed, the bot responds to external commands sent by the attacker

botnet

collection of captured bot computers

Bots (short for robots) are a type of malicious code that can be covertly installed on your computer when attached to the Internet. Around 90% of the world's spam, and 80% of the world's malware, is delivered by botnets. Once installed, the bot responds to external commands sent by the attacker; your computer becomes a "zombie" and is able to be controlled by an external third party (the "bot-herder"). **Botnets** are collections of captured computers used for malicious activities such as sending spam, participating in a DDoS attack, stealing information from computers, and storing network traffic for later analysis. The number of botnets operating worldwide is not known but is estimated to be in the thousands. Bots and bot networks are an important threat to the Internet and e-commerce because they can be used to launch very large-scale attacks using many different techniques. In March 2011, federal marshals accompanied members of Microsoft's digital crimes unit in raids designed to disable the Rustock botnet, the leading source of spam in the world with nearly 500,000 slave PCs under the control of its command and control servers located at six Internet hosting services in the United States. Officials confiscated the Rustock control servers at the hosting sites, which claimed they had no idea what the Rustock servers were doing. The actual spam e-mails were sent by the slave PCs under the command of the Rustock servers. The control servers were owned by people giving their address as Azerbaijan (Wingfield, 2011). As a result, the amount of spam sent in 2011 declined significantly compared to the previous year.

Malicious code is a threat at both the client and the server level, although servers generally engage in much more thorough anti-virus activities than do consumers. At the server level, malicious code can bring down an entire Web site, preventing millions of people from using the site. Such incidents are infrequent. Much more frequent malicious code attacks occur at the client level, and the damage can quickly spread to millions of other computers connected to the Internet. **Table 5.4** lists some well-known examples of malicious code.

TABLE 5.4	NOTABLE EXAMPLES OF MALICIOUS CODE	
NAME	**TYPE**	**DESCRIPTION**
Ramnit	Virus/worm	Most common malicious code family in 2011. Infects various file types, including executable files, and copies itself to removable drives, excuting via AutoPlay when the drive is accessed on other computers
Sality.AE	Virus/worm	Second most common 2011 malware. First appeared in 2009. Disables security applications and services, connects to a botnet, then downloads and installs additional threats. Uses polymorphism to evade detection.
Downadup	Worm/backdoor	Fourth most common malware in 2011. Disables security software, copies itself to all drives at a location, and connects to a P2P botnet to download other malware.
Conficker	Worm	First appeared November 2008. Targets Microsoft operating systems. Uses advanced malware techniques. Largest worm infection since Slammer in 2003. Still considered a major threat.
Netsky.P	Worm/Trojan horse	First appeared in early 2003. It spreads by gathering target e-mail addresses from the computers, then infects and sends e-mail to all recipients from the infected computer. It is commonly used by bot networks to launch spam and DoS attacks.
Storm (Peacomm, NuWar)	Worm/Trojan horse	First appeared in January 2007. It spreads in a manner similar to the Netsky.P worm. May also download and run other Trojan programs and worms.
Nymex	Worm	First discovered in January 2006. Spreads by mass mailing; activates on the 3rd of every month, and attempts to destroy files of certain types.
Zotob	Worm	First appeared in August 2005. Well-known worm that infected a number of U.S. media companies.
Mydoom	Worm	First appeared in January 2004. One of the fastest spreading mass-mailer worms.
Slammer	Worm	Launched in January 2003. Caused widespread problems.
CodeRed	Worm	Appeared in 2001. It achieved an infection rate of over 20,000 systems within 10 minutes of release and ultimately spread to hundreds of thousands of systems.
Melissa	Macro virus/worm	First spotted in March 1999. At the time, the fastest spreading infectious program ever discovered. It attacked Microsoft Word's Normal.dot global template, ensuring infection of all newly created documents. It also mailed an infected Word file to the first 50 entries in each user's Microsoft Outlook Address Book.
Chernobyl	File-infecting virus	First appeared in 1998. It wipes out the first megabyte of data on a hard disk (making the rest useless) every April 26, the anniversary of the nuclear disaster at Chernobyl.

POTENTIALLY UNWANTED PROGRAMS (PUPS)

In addition to malicious code, the e-commerce security environment is further challenged by **potentially unwanted programs (PUPs)** such as adware, browser parasites, spyware, and other applications that install themselves on a computer, such as rogue security software, typically without the user's informed consent. Such programs are increasingly found on social network and user-generated content sites where users are fooled into downloading them. Once installed, these applications are usually exceedingly difficult to remove from the computer.

potentially unwanted program (PUP)
program that installs itself on a computer, typically without the user's informed consent

Adware is typically used to call for pop-up ads to display when the user visits certain sites. While annoying, adware is not typically used for criminal activities. ZangoSearch and PurityScan are examples of adware programs that open a partner site's Web pages or display the partner's pop-up ads when certain keywords are used in Internet searches. Adware was the most prevalent of the different categories of malware in the fourth quarter of 2011, according to Microsoft, and found on 37% of all computers reporting threats. A **browser parasite** is a program that can monitor and change the settings of a user's browser, for instance, changing the browser's home page, or sending information about the sites visited to a remote computer. Browser parasites are often a component of adware. For example, Websearch is an adware component that modifies Internet Explorer's default home page and search settings.

adware
a PUP that serves pop-up ads to your computer

browser parasite
a program that can monitor and change the settings of a user's browser

Spyware, on the other hand, can be used to obtain information such as a user's keystrokes, copies of e-mail and instant messages, and even take screenshots (and thereby capture passwords or other confidential data). One example of spyware is Vista Antispyware 2012 which infects PCs running the Vista operating system. Vista Antispyware poses as a legitimate anti-spyware program when in fact it is malware which, when installed, disables the user's security software, alters the user's Web browser, and diverts users to scam Web sites where more malware is downloaded. Spyware constituted the least reported PUP, with less than 1% of computers reporting it. Other miscellaneous PUPs were reported by 30% of computers worldwide.

spyware
a program used to obtain information such as a user's keystrokes, e-mail, instant messages, and so on

PHISHING AND IDENTITY THEFT

Social engineering relies on human curiosity, greed, and gullibility in order to trick people into taking an action that will result in the downloading of malware. Kevin Mitnick, until his capture and imprisonment in 1999, was one of America's most wanted computer criminals. Mitnick used simple deceptive techniques to obtain passwords, social security, and police records all without the use of any sophisticated technology (Mitnick, 2011).

Social engineering
exploitation of human fallibility and gullibility to distribute malware

Phishing is any deceptive, online attempt by a third party to obtain confidential information for financial gain. Phishing attacks do not involve malicious code but instead rely on straightforward misrepresentation and fraud, so-called "social engineering" techniques. The most popular phishing attack is the e-mail scam letter. The scam begins with an e-mail: a rich former oil minister of Nigeria is seeking a bank account to stash millions of dollars for a short period of time, and requests your bank account number where the money can be deposited. In return, you will receive a million

phishing
any deceptive, online attempt by a third party to obtain confidential information for financial gain

dollars. This type of e-mail scam is popularly known as a "Nigerian letter" scam (see **Figure 5.4**).

Thousands of other phishing attacks use other scams, some pretending to be eBay, PayPal, or Citibank writing to you for "account verification" (known as "spear phishing", or targeting a known customer of a specific bank or other type of business). Click on a link in the e-mail and you will be taken to a Web site controlled by the scammer, and prompted to enter confidential information about your accounts, such as your account number and PIN codes. On any given day, millions of these phishing attack e-mails are sent, and, unfortunately, some people are fooled and disclose their personal account information. For instance, in April 2011, the Oak Ridge National Laboratory (a highly classified atomic energy facility) was forced to disconnect Internet access for workers after the lab's computers were hacked as a result of a phishing attack. The intrusion resulted from a spear-phishing e-mail sent to lab employees purportedly from the Human Resources Department discussing their benefits, and included a link to a malicious Web page. Only two employees were ensnared, but that was enough to start a malicious data breach (Zetter, 2011).

Phishers rely on traditional "con man" tactics, but use e-mail to trick recipients into voluntarily giving up financial access codes, bank account numbers, credit card numbers, and other personal information. Often, phishers create (or "spoof") a Web site that purports to be a legitimate financial institution and con users into entering financial information, or the site downloads malware such as a keylogger to the vic-

| **FIGURE 5.4** | **AN EXAMPLE OF A NIGERIAN LETTER E-MAIL SCAM** |

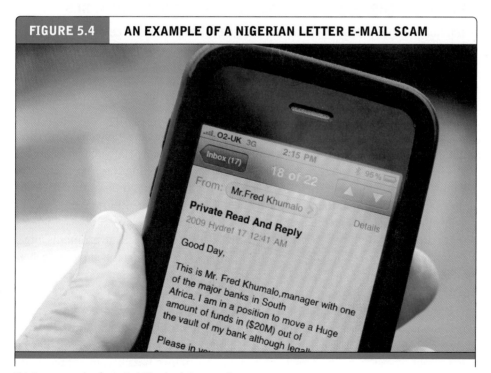

This is an example of a typical Nigerian letter e-mail scam.

© keith morris / Alamy

tim's computer. Phishers use the information they gather to commit fraudulent acts such as charging items to your credit cards or withdrawing funds from your bank account, or in other ways "steal your identity" (identity theft). Phishing attacks are one of the fastest growing forms of e-commerce crime. In the second half of 2011, there were 23% more phishing attacks than in the first half of 2011, according to the Anti-Phishing Working Group. The number of phishing Web sites detected ranged from a low of about 32,000 in July 2011 to a high of almost 50,000 in December 2011. The number of unique phishing e-mail compaigns reported by consumers to the Working Group similarly peaked in December, at a high of about 33,000, with each campaign typically involving potentially millions of e-mail sent to consumers (APWG, 2012). Symantec reported that in August 2012, about 1 in every 313 e-mails contained a phishing attack. The United States was the primary source of such attacks (Symantec, 2012b). Financial services are a primary brand used in phishing attacks. In July 2011, Tien Truong Nguyen was sentenced to over 12 years in prison for his role in a widespread phishing scam that used Web sites set up to look like they belonged to legitimate financial institutions to fleece more than 38,000 victims. Other top brands exploited by phishing attacks include e-commerce sites such as Amazon and eBay. In January 2012, leading e-mail service providers, including Google, Microsoft, Yahoo, and AOL, as well as financial services companies such as PayPal, Bank of America and others, joined together to form DMARC.org, an organization aimed at dramatically reducing phishing e-mail (DMARC.org, 2012).

HACKING, CYBERVANDALISM, HACKTIVISM, AND DATA BREACHES

hacker
an individual who intends to gain unauthorized access to a computer system

cracker
within the hacking community, a term typically used to denote a hacker with criminal intent

cybervandalism
intentionally disrupting, defacing, or even destroying a site

hacktivism
cybervandalism and data theft for political purposes

white hats
"good" hackers who help organizations locate and fix security flaws

A **hacker** is an individual who intends to gain unauthorized access to a computer system. Within the hacking community, the term **cracker** is typically used to denote a hacker with criminal intent, although in the public press, the terms hacker and cracker tend to be used interchangeably. Hackers and crackers gain unauthorized access by finding weaknesses in the security procedures of Web sites and computer systems, often taking advantage of various features of the Internet that make it an open system that is easy to use. In the past, hackers and crackers typically were computer aficionados excited by the challenge of breaking into corporate and government Web sites. Sometimes they were satisfied merely by breaking into the files of an e-commerce site. Today, hackers have malicious intentions to disrupt, deface, or destroy sites (**cybervandalism**) or to steal personal or corporate information they can use for financial gain (data breach).

Hacktivism adds a political twist. Hacktivists typically attack governments, organizations, and even individuals for political purposes, employing the tactics of cybervandalism, denial of service attacks, data thefts, and more. LulzSec and Anonymous are two prominent hacktivist groups.

Groups of hackers called *tiger teams* are sometimes used by corporate security departments to test their own security measures. By hiring hackers to break into the system from the outside, the company can identify weaknesses in the computer system's armor. These "good hackers" became known as **white hats** because of their role in helping organizations locate and fix security flaws. White hats do their work under contract, with agreement from clients that they will not be prosecuted for their efforts to break in.

In contrast, **black hats** are hackers who engage in the same kinds of activities but without pay or any buy-in from the targeted organization, and with the intention of causing harm. They break into Web sites and reveal the confidential or proprietary information they find. These hackers believe strongly that information should be free, so sharing previously secret information is part of their mission.

Somewhere in the middle are the **grey hats**, hackers who believe they are pursuing some greater good by breaking in and revealing system flaws. Grey hats discover weaknesses in a system's security, and then publish the weakness without disrupting the site or attempting to profit from their finds. Their only reward is the prestige of discovering the weakness. Grey hat actions are suspect, however, especially when the hackers reveal security flaws that make it easier for other criminals to gain access to a system.

A **data breach** occurs whenever organizations lose control over corporate information to outsiders. According to Symantec, data about more than 230 million people were exposed in 2011 as a result of data breaches. Breaches caused by hacker attacks were responsible for exposing more than 187 million identities. Many of the data breaches resulted from a hacking campaign called Operation AntiSec run by the hacker collectives Anonymous and LulzSec, which began in the spring of 2011, and which continued into 2012, despite some arrests (Symantec, 2012a; 2012b). The *Insight on Business* case, *Sony: Press the Reset Button*, describes the largest hacking data breach case of 2011.

black hats
hackers who act with the intention of causing harm

grey hats
hackers who believe they are pursuing some greater good by breaking in and revealing system flaws

data breach
occurs when an organization loses control over its information to outsiders

CREDIT CARD FRAUD/THEFT

Theft of credit card data is one of the most feared occurrences on the Internet. Fear that credit card information will be stolen prevents users from making online purchases in many cases. Interestingly, this fear appears to be largely unfounded. Incidences of stolen credit card information are much lower than users think, around .6% of all online card transactions (CyberSource, 2012). Several surveys have documented a slow drift downwards in the frequency and value of online credit card fraud due to better merchant screening systems and security improvements. Nevertheless, online credit card fraud is twice as common as offline card fraud.

There is substantial credit card fraud in traditional commerce, but the consumer is largely insured against losses by federal law. In the past, the most common cause of credit card fraud was a lost or stolen card that was used by someone else, followed by employee theft of customer numbers and stolen identities (criminals applying for credit cards using false identities). Federal law limits the liability of individuals to $50 for a stolen credit card. For amounts more than $50, the credit card company generally pays the amount, although in some cases, the merchant may be held liable if it failed to verify the account or consult published lists of invalid cards. Banks recoup the cost of credit card fraud by charging higher interest rates on unpaid balances, and by merchants who raise prices to cover the losses.

INSIGHT ON BUSINESS

SONY: PRESS THE RESET BUTTON

In the single largest data breach in Internet history, on April 19, 2011, system administrators at Sony's online gaming service PlayStation Network (PSN), with over 77 million users, began to notice suspicious activity on some of its 130 servers spread across the globe. On April 20, Sony engineers discovered that some data had likely been transferred from its servers to outside computers. The nature of the data transferred was not known at that time, but it could have included credit card and personal information of PlayStation customers. Because of the uncertainty of the data loss, Sony shut down the entire global PSN when it realized it no longer controlled the personal information contained on these servers. On April 22, Sony informed the FBI of the potential massive data leakage. On April 26, Sony notified the 49 U.S. states and territories that have legislation requiring corporations to announce their data breaches (there is no similar federal law at this time), and made a public announcement that hackers had stolen some personal information from all 77 million users, and possibly credit card information from 12 million users. Sony did not know exactly what personal information had been stolen.

The hackers corrupted Sony's servers, causing them to mysteriously reboot. The rogue program deleted all log files to hide its operation. Once inside Sony's servers, the rogue software transferred personal and credit card information on millions of PlayStation users. On May 2, Sony shut down a second service, Sony Online Entertainment, a San Diego–based subsidiary that makes multiplayer games for personal computers. Sony believed hackers had transferred personal customer information such as names, birth dates, and addresses from these servers as well. This was not the result of a second attack but rather part of the earlier attack that was not immediately discovered. On June 1, Sony Pictures Entertainment's Web site was also hacked, and drained of personal information on its several million customers, in addition to 75,000 "music codes" and 3.5 million coupons.

The Sony data breach was apparently the result of a "revenge hacking," the use of the Internet to destroy or disrupt political opponents, or to punish organizations for their public behavior. The hackers left a text file named Anonymous on Sony's server with the words "We are legion." Anonymous is the name of an Internet collective of hackers and vigilantes. Anonymous had previously attacked MasterCard and other company servers in retaliation for those companies cutting their financial relationships with WikiLeaks, a Web site devoted to releasing secret American government files. Sony and others believe the hacker attack, which followed weeks of a Denial of Service attack on the same Sony servers, was retaliation for Sony's civil suit against George Hotz, one of the world's best-known hackers. Hotz cracked the iPhone operating system in 2008; in 2010, he cracked the Sony PlayStation client operating system and later published the procedures on his Web site. Anonymous denied that, as an organization, it stole credit cards, but the statement is unclear about whether its members as individuals participated in the attack. Anonymous claimed Sony was simply trying to discredit Anonymous instead of admitting its own incompetence in computer security. Later, LulzSec, an offshoot group of Anonymous, claimed responsibility for both attacks.

Sony's chairman of the board apologized to its users and critics in the U.S. Congress for the security breakdown. Nevertheless, governments around the world reacted critically to the lapse in security at Sony. The U.S. House Committee on

(continued)

Commerce, Manufacturing, and Trading criticized Sony for not knowing what data had been transferred and for failing to inform customers immediately rather than waiting a week before going public. In a letter to Sony Chairman Kazuo Hirai, the committee demanded specifics on the kind of information the hackers stole and assurances that no credit card data was swiped. In a letter of apology to the committee and Sony customers, Chairman Hirai claimed that Sony had been the victim of a carefully planned, professional, and sophisticated cyberattack.

This is the "Darth Vader" defense that many organizations use when they experience a gross breach of security: whatever it was, it was extremely sophisticated, totally unprecedented, and could not possibly have been anticipated. But many experts in computer security did not buy Sony's explanation. In fact, most computer security breaches are the result of fairly simple tactics, management failures to anticipate well-known security risks, unwillingness to spend resources on expensive security measures, sloppy procedures, lack of training, carelessness, and outdated software. Many hacking attacks use simple, well-known approaches that seem obvious. The hack of Google's computers in late 2010 described in the opening case resulted from a single employee responding to a phishing e-mail from what he thought was Google's human resources department.

Appearing before the House Energy & Commerce Committee, Eugene Spafford, the executive director of the Purdue University Center for Education and Research in Information Assurance and Security (CERIAS), said the problem at Sony was that the PlayStation Network was using an older version of the Apache Web server software that had well-known security issues. In addition, Sony's Web site had very poor firewall protection. He said the problem was reported on an open forum months before the incident. A U.S. Secret Service agent told the committee that he believed that most attacks of this type were not that dif-ficult for hackers to carry out. Moreover, once hackers are on the inside, critical personal information and credit information is not encrypted. If it were encrypted, hackers would not be able to read the data. The reason most personal data is not encrypted in large-scale private databases is cost, and to a lesser extent, speed. Data encryption of the sort needed for an operation like Sony's could easily require a doubling of computing capacity at Sony. This would significantly eat into profits for an Internet-based enterprise like Sony simply because IT is such a huge part of their cost structure.

LulzSec itself claimed Sony's lax security allowed it to perform a standard SQL injection attack on a primitive security hole that allowed it to access whatever information it wanted. In September 2011, Cody Kretsinger, an Arizona college student was arrested and charged in connection with the attack. Kretsinger was the first alleged LulzSec member ever arrested in the United States. In April 2012, Kretsinger plead guilty and is currently awaiting sentencing. In August 2012, a second alleged LulzSec member, Raynaldo Rivera, was also arrested and charged.

Sony notified its customers of the data breach by posting a press release on its blog. It did not e-mail customers. Sony later offered customers privacy protection ("AllClear ID Plus") provided by a private security firm at Sony's expense for customers concerned about protecting their online identity. This offer was distributed to user e-mail accounts. The privacy protection plan does not include an insurance policy against potential losses but does help individuals monitor the use of their personal information by others. It took Sony four weeks to restore partial PlayStation Network service, and by May 31, 2011, the company had restored service to the United States, Europe, and Asia, except for Japan. So far, no law enforcement agency has reported illegal use of credit cards stolen in the Sony affair.

The Sony data breach followed a string of recent breaches that were larger and broader in

(continued)

scope than ever before. Prior to the Sony debacle, a data breach had occurred at Epsilon, the world's largest permission-based e-mail marketing services company, with more than 2,500 corporate customers, including many major banks and brokerage firms, TiVo, Walgreens, major universities, and others. Epsilon sends out 40 billion e-mail messages a year for its clients. In April 2011, Epsilon announced a security breach in which millions of e-mail addresses were transferred to outside servers. One result of this breach was millions of phishing e-mails to customers and the potential for the loss of financial assets.

As data breaches rise in significance and frequency, the Obama administration and Congress have proposed the Data Accountability and Trust Act, which would require firms to establish security requirements and policies, notify potential victims of a data loss without unreasonable delay, and notify a major media outlet and all major credit-reporting agencies within 60 days if the credit card data on more than 5,000 individuals is at risk. The Act has been passed by the House of Representatives, but remains stalled in the Senate as of September 2012. Currently, 49 states and U.S. territories have such legislation. In the past, many organizations failed to report data breaches for fear of harming their brand images. However, it is unclear if the proposed legislation, even if passed, would reduce the incidence of data breaches.

SOURCES: "Second Accused LulzSec Hacker Arrested in US," by Charlie Osborne, ZDNet.com, August 29, 2012; "Cody Kretsinger, Accused LulzSec Hacker, Pleads Guilty in Sony Hacking Case," by Reuters, April 5, 2012; "Cody Kretsinger, Arizona College Student, Charged in Sony Hacking Case," by Greg Risling, HuffingtonPost.com, September 22, 2011; "Senate Bills Would Require Data-Breach Notification," by Tim Peterson, Dmnews.com, July 29, 2011; "Hacker Group Claims Responsibility to New Sony Break-In," by Riva Richment, New York Times, June 2, 2011; "Sony Details Hacker Attack," by Ian Sherr and Amy Schatz, Wall Street Journal, May 5, 2011; "Expert: Sony Had Outdated Software, Lax Security," by Jesse Emspak, IBtimes.com, May 5, 2011; Testimony before the House Energy and Commerce Subcommittee on Commerce, Manufacturing, and Trade. Hearing on "The Threat of Data Theft to American Consumers" by Eugene Spafford, May 5, 2011; "Anonymous Press Release," Anonymous Enterprises LLC Bermuda, May 4, 2011; "Data Accountability and Trust Act" 112th Congress, H.R. 1707, May 4, 2011; "Letter to Honorable Mary Bono Black and Ranking Member Butterfield, Sub Committee on Commerce, Manufacturing, and Trade, United States Congress," by Kazuo Hirai, Chairman of the Board, Sony Corporation, May 3, 2011; "Hackers Breach Second Sony Service," by Ian Sherr, Wall Street Journal, May 2, 2011; "International Strategy for Cyberspace," Office of the President, May 2011; "Epsilon Notifies Clients of Unauthorized Entry into E-mail System," Epsilon Corporation, April 1, 2011.

But today, the most frequent cause of stolen cards and card information is the systematic hacking and looting of a corporate server where the information on millions of credit card purchases is stored. For instance, in March 2010, Albert Gonzalez was sentenced to 20 years in prison for organizing the largest theft of credit card numbers in American history. Along with two Russian co-conspirators, Gonzalez broke into the central computer systems of TJX, BJs, Barnes & Noble, and other companies, stealing over 160 million card numbers and costing these firms over $200 million in losses.

International orders have been particularly prone to repudiation. If an international customer places an order and then later disputes it, online merchants often have no way to verify that the package was actually delivered and that the credit card holder is the person who placed the order. Most online merchants will not process international orders.

A central security issue of e-commerce is the difficulty of establishing the customer's identity. Currently there is no technology that can identify a person with certainty. Until a customer's identity can be guaranteed, online companies are at a much higher risk of loss than traditional offline companies. The federal government has attempted to address this issue through the Electronic Signatures in Global and

National Commerce Act (the "E-Sign" law), which gives digital signatures the same authority as hand-written signatures in commerce. This law also intended to make digital signatures more commonplace and easier to use. Except for large businesses conducting transactions over the Internet, the law has had little impact on B2C e-commerce, but that may be changing.

SPOOFING (PHARMING) AND SPAM (JUNK) WEB SITES

Hackers attempting to hide their true identity often use **spoofing** tactics, misrepresenting themselves by using fake e-mail addresses or masquerading as someone else. Spoofing a Web site is also called "pharming," which involves redirecting a Web link to an address different from the intended one, with the site masquerading as the intended destination. Links that are designed to lead to one site can be reset to send users to a totally unrelated site—one that benefits the hacker.

spoofing
misrepresenting oneself by using fake e-mail addresses or masquerading as someone else

Although spoofing does not directly damage files or network servers, it threatens the integrity of a site. For example, if hackers redirect customers to a fake Web site that looks almost exactly like the true site, they can then collect and process orders, effectively stealing business from the true site. Or, if the intent is to disrupt rather than steal, hackers can alter orders—inflating them or changing products ordered—and then send them on to the true site for processing and delivery. Customers become dissatisfied with the improper order shipment, and the company may have huge inventory fluctuations that impact its operations.

In addition to threatening integrity, spoofing also threatens authenticity by making it difficult to discern the true sender of a message. Clever hackers can make it almost impossible to distinguish between a true and a fake identity or Web address. Spam (junk) Web sites are a little different. These are sites that promise to offer some product or service, but in fact are a collection of advertisements for other sites, some of which contain malicious code. For instance, you may search for "[name of town] weather," and then click on a link that promises your local weather, but then discover that all the site does is display ads for weather-related products or other Web sites.

Junk or spam Web sites typically appear on search results, and do not involve e-mail. These sites cloak their identities by using domain names similar to legitimate firm names, and redirect traffic to known spammer-redirection domains such as topsearch10.com.

DENIAL OF SERVICE (DOS) AND DISTRIBUTED DENIAL OF SERVICE (DDOS) ATTACKS

In a **Denial of Service (DoS)** attack, hackers flood a Web site with useless pings or page requests that inundate and overwhelm the site's Web servers. Increasingly, DoS attacks involve the use of bot networks and so-called "distributed attacks" built from thousands of compromised client computers. DoS attacks typically cause a Web site to shut down, making it impossible for users to access the site. For busy e-commerce sites, these attacks are costly; while the site is shut down, customers cannot make purchases. And the longer a site is shut down, the more damage is done to a site's reputation. Although such attacks do not destroy information or access restricted areas

Denial of Service (DoS) attack
flooding a Web site with useless traffic to inundate and overwhelm the network

of the server, they can destroy a firm's online business. Often, DoS attacks are accompanied by attempts at blackmailing site owners to pay tens or hundreds of thousands of dollars to the hackers in return for stopping the DoS attack.

Distributed Denial of Service (DDoS) attack
using numerous computers to attack the target network from numerous launch points

A **Distributed Denial of Service (DDoS)** attack uses hundreds or even thousands of computers to attack the target network from numerous launch points. DoS and DDoS attacks are threats to a system's operation because they can shut it down indefinitely. Major Web sites such as Yahoo and Microsoft have experienced such attacks, making the companies aware of their vulnerability and the need to continually introduce new measures to prevent future attacks. In August 2012, WikiLeaks, a site dedicated to the release of classified information, was hit by a massive DDoS attack that left its Web site effectively inoperable. According to WikiLeaks, the amount of bandwidth consumed by the attacks was in the 10 gigabits per second range, and the range of IP addresses used was so large that it believed whoever was running the attack either controlled thousands of computers or was able to simulate them. In an interesting twist, previously, one of the largest DDoS attacks had occurred in December 2010 when the hacker group Anonymous launched simultaneous attacks on MasterCard, Visa, PayPal, and other firms that had refused to handle online donations to WikiLeaks. The systems were slowed but none were forced to shut down.

SNIFFING

sniffer
a type of eavesdropping program that monitors information traveling over a network

A **sniffer** is a type of eavesdropping program that monitors information traveling over a network. When used legitimately, sniffers can help identify potential network trouble-spots, but when used for criminal purposes, they can be damaging and very difficult to detect. Sniffers enable hackers to steal proprietary information from anywhere on a network, including passwords, e-mail messages, company files, and confidential reports.

E-mail wiretaps are a variation on the sniffing threat. An e-mail wiretap is a method for recording or journaling e-mail traffic generally at the mail server level from any individual. E-mail wiretaps are used by employers to track employee messages, and by government agencies to surveil individuals or groups. E-mail wiretaps can be installed on servers and client computers. The USA PATRIOT Act permits the FBI to compel ISPs to install a black box on their mail servers that can impound the e-mail of a single person or group of persons for later analysis. In the case of American citizens communicating with other citizens, an FBI agent or government lawyer need only certify to a judge on the secret 11-member U.S. Foreign Intelligence Surveillance Court (FISC) that the information sought is "relevant to an ongoing criminal investigation" to get permission to install the program. Judges have no discretion. They must approve wiretaps based on government agents' unsubstantiated assertions. In the case of suspected terrorist activity, law enforcement does not have to inform a court prior to installing a wire or e-mail tap. A 2007 amendment to the 1978 Foreign Intelligence Surveillance Act, known as FISA, provided new powers to the National Security Agency to monitor international e-mail and telephone communications where one person is in the United States, and where the purpose of such interception is to collect foreign intelligence (Foreign Intelligence Surveillance Act of 1978; Protect America Act of 2007). In September 2012, the U.S. House of Representatives voted in favor of the FISA

Amendments Reauthorization Act, which, if also passed by the Senate, will extend the provisions of FISA for five more years, until 2017.

The Communications Assistance for Law Enforcement Act (CALEA) requires all communications carriers (including ISPs) to provide near-instant access to law enforcement agencies to their message traffic. Many Internet services (such as Facebook and LinkedIn) that have built-in ISP services are not technically covered by CALEA. One can only assume these non-ISP e-mail operators cooperate with law enforcement. Unlike the past where wiretaps required many hours to physically tap into phone lines, in today's digital phone systems, taps are arranged in a few minutes by the large carriers at their expense.

INSIDER ATTACKS

We tend to think of security threats to a business as originating outside the organization. In fact, the largest financial threats to business institutions come not from robberies but from embezzlement by insiders. Bank employees steal far more money than bank robbers. The same is true for e-commerce sites. Some of the largest disruptions to service, destruction to sites, and diversion of customer credit data and personal information have come from insiders—once trusted employees. Employees have access to privileged information, and, in the presence of sloppy internal security procedures, they are often able to roam throughout an organization's systems without leaving a trace. The 2010/2011 Computer Security Institute survey reports that insider abuse of systems was the fourth most frequent type of attack during the preceding 12 months, and that around 25% of survey respondents believed that insiders contributed to some portion of the firm's financial losses during the previous year (Computer Security Institute, 2011). In some instances, the insider might not have criminal intent, but inadvertently expose data that can then be exploited by others. For instance, a Ponemon Institute study found that negligent insiders are a top cause of data breaches.

POORLY DESIGNED SERVER AND CLIENT SOFTWARE

Many security threats prey on poorly designed server and client software, sometimes in the operating system and sometimes in the application software, including browsers. The increase in complexity and size of software programs, coupled with demands for timely delivery to markets, has contributed to an increase in software flaws or vulnerabilities that hackers can exploit. Each year, security firms identify thousands of software vulnerabilities in Internet and PC software. For instance, in its most recent semi-annual *Internet Security Threat Report,* Symantec identified almost 5,000 different software vulnerabilities. Browser vulnerabilities in particular are a popular target, as well as browser plug-ins such as for Adobe Reader. According to Kaspersky Labs, the number of browser-based attacks in 2011 increased to about 950 million, about 1.6 times the amount of the previous year (Kaspersky Labs, 2012). A **zero-day vulnerability** is one that has been previously unreported and for which no patch yet exists. For example, in December 2011, Adobe was hit with a zero-day vulnerability attack against its Reader and Acrobat products that persisted for over two weeks until it was able to release a patch (Symantec, 2012a). The very design of the personal computer includes

zero-day vulnerability
software vulnerability that has been previously unreported and for which no patch yet exists

many open communication ports that can be used, and indeed are designed to be used, by external computers to send and receive messages. The port typically attacked is TCP port 445. However, given their complexity and design objectives, all operating systems and application software, including Linux and Macintosh, have vulnerabilities.

SOCIAL NETWORK SECURITY ISSUES

Social networks like Facebook, Twitter, and LinkedIn provide a rich and rewarding environment for hackers. Viruses, site takeovers, identity theft, malware-loaded apps, click hijacking, phishing, and spam are all found on social networks (US-CERT, 2011). For instance, in 2011, hackers defaced Pfizer's Facebook page, took over the Twitter accounts of both USA Today and NBC News, and stole millions of LinkedIn passwords (Sophos, 2012). The Ramnit worm stole account information from more than 45,000 Facebook users. By sneaking in among our friends, hackers can masquerade as friends and dupe users into scams. Social network firms have thus far been relatively poor policemen because they have failed to aggressively weed out accounts that send visitors to malware sites (unlike Google, which maintains a list of known malware sites and patrols its search results looking for links to malware sites). Social networks are open: anyone can set up a personal page, even criminals. Most attacks are social engineering attacks that tempt visitors to click on links that sound reasonable. Social apps downloaded either from the social network or a foreign site are not certified by the social network to be clean of malware. It's "clicker beware."

MOBILE PLATFORM SECURITY ISSUES

The explosion in mobile devices has broadened opportunities for hackers. Mobile users are filling their devices with personal and financial information, making them excellent targets for hackers. In general, mobile devices face all the same risks as any Internet device as well as some new risks associated with wireless network security. While most PC users are aware their computers and Web sites may be hacked and contain malware, most cell phone users believe their cell phone is as secure as a traditional landline phone. As with social network members, mobile users are prone to think they are in a shared, trustworthy environment.

Mobile cell phone malware was developed as early as 2004 with Cabir, a Bluetooth worm affecting Symbian operating systems (Nokia phones) and causing the phone to continuously seek out other Bluetooth-enabled devices, quickly draining the battery. More recently, Ike4e.B appeared on jailbroken iPhones, turning the phones into botnet-controlled devices. An iPhone in Europe could be hacked by an iPhone in the United States, and all its private data sent to a server in Poland. Ike4e.B established the feasibility of cell phone botnets. Many—if not most—apps written for Android phones have poor protection for user information, and Google removed more than 100 malicious apps from the Android Market in 2011 (Sophos, 2012). The first malicious iPhone app was also discovered and removed from the iTunes Store. And it is not just rogue applications that are dangerous, but also popular legitimate applications that simply have little protection from hackers (Kolesnikov-Jessup, 2011; US-CERT 2010). ViaForensics, a mobile security firm in Chicago, found in a study of 50 popular iPhone apps that only three had adequate protection for usernames, passwords, and other sensitive data. Servers of mobile service providers like AT&T and Verizon are also vulnerable. In 2011, two computer hackers were arrested for allegedly breaking into AT&T's servers to gather e-mail addresses and other personal information of about 120,000 users of Apple's iPad, including corporate chiefs, U.S. government officials, and Hollywood moguls. The hackers did not use the information (Bray, 2011).

Vishing attacks target gullible cell phone users with verbal messages to call a certain number and, for example, donate money to starving children in Haiti. Smishing attacks exploit SMS messages. Compromised text messages can contain e-mail and Web site addresses that can lead the innocent user to a malware site. A small number of downloaded apps from app stores have also contained malware. Madware—innocent-looking apps that contain adware that launches pop-up ads and text messages on your mobile device—is also becoming an increasing problem.

Read the *Insight on Technology* case, *Think Your Smartphone Is Secure?* for a further discussion of some of the issues surrounding smartphone security.

CLOUD SECURITY ISSUES

The move of so many Internet services into the cloud also raises security risks. From an infrastructure standpoint, DDoS attacks threaten the availability of cloud services on which more and more companies are relying. Safeguarding data being maintained in a cloud environment is also a major concern. For example, researchers identified several ways data could be accessed without authorization on Dropbox, which offers a popular cloud file-sharing service. Dropbox has also experienced several security snafus, including leaving all of its users' files publicly accessible for four hours in June 2011 due to a software bug, the discovery of a security hole in its iOS app which allowed anyone with physical access to the phone to copy login credentials, and the theft of usernames and passwords in August 2012. To combat some of these issues, Dropbox has implemented a number of measures, including two-factor authentication, which relies on two separate elements—something you know, such as a password, coupled with a separately generated code. Around the same time, a hack into writer Mat Honan's Apple iCloud account using social engineering tactics allowed the hackers to wipe everything from his Mac computer, iPhone, and iPad, which were linked to the cloud service, as well as take over his Twitter and Gmail accounts (Honan, 2012). These incidents highlight the risks involved as devices, identities, and data become more and more interconnected in the cloud.

5.3 TECHNOLOGY SOLUTIONS

At first glance, it might seem like there is not much that can be done about the onslaught of security breaches on the Internet. Reviewing the security threats in the previous section, it is clear that the threats to e-commerce are very real, potentially devastating for individuals, businesses, and entire nations, and likely to be increasing in intensity along with the growth in e-commerce. But in fact a great deal of progress has been made by private security firms, corporate and home users, network administrators, technology firms, and government agencies. There are two lines of defense:

INSIGHT ON TECHNOLOGY

THINK YOUR SMARTPHONE IS SECURE?

So far, there have been few publicly identified, large-scale, smartphone security breaches. In 2012, the biggest security danger facing smartphone users is that they will lose their phone. In reality, all of the personal and corporate data stored on the device, as well as access to corporate data on remote servers, are at risk. In many Wall Street firms, losing your company phone means you lose your job. Still, criminals find stealing financial and personal data from PCs much easier and more lucrative than attacking cell phones. But with smartphones outselling PCs in 2012, and with smartphones increasingly being used as payment devices, they are likely to become a major avenue of malware.

Have you ever purchased anti-virus software for your smartphone? Probably not. Many users believe their iPhones and Androids are unlikely to be hacked because Apple and Google are protecting them from malware apps, and that the carriers like Verizon and AT&T can keep the cell phone network clean from malware just as they do the land-line phone system. Telephone systems are "closed" and therefore not subject to the kinds of attacks that occur on the open Internet.

To date, there has not been a major smartphone hack resulting in millions of dollars in losses, or the breach of millions of credit cards, or the breach of national security, but just because it has not happened yet doesn't mean that it won't. With 116 million smartphone users in the United States, 122 million people accessing the Internet from mobile devices, business firms increasingly switching their employees

to the mobile platform, consumers using their phones for financial transactions and even paying bills, the size and richness of the smartphone target for hackers is growing. The smartphone ecosystem is a very large target today, and rich with potential criminal opportunities. Users of smartphones download and open files with their browsers, and send and receive financial, personal, and commercial information. Hackers can do to a smartphone just about anything they can do to any Internet device: request malicious files without user intervention, delete files, transmit files, install programs running in the background that can monitor user actions, and potentially convert the smartphone into a robot that can be used in a botnet to send e-mail and text messages to anyone.

Apps are one avenue for potential security breaches. Apple, Google, and RIM (BlackBerry) now offer over 1.25 million apps collectively. Apple claims that it examines each and every app to ensure that it plays by Apple's iTunes rules, but risks remain. Most of the known cases that occurred thus far have involved jailbroken phones. The first iPhone app confirmed to have embedded malware made it past Apple into the iTunes store in July 2012. However, security company Kaspersky expects the iPhone to face an onslaught of malware within the next year. Apple iTunes app rules make some user information available to all apps by default, including the user's GPS position and name. However, a rogue app could easily do much more. Nicolas Seriot, a Swiss researcher, built a test app called "SpyPhone" that was capable of tracking users and all their activities, then transmitting this data to remote servers, all without

(continued)

user knowledge. The app harvested geolocation data, passwords, address book entries, and e-mail account information. Apple removed the app once it was identified. That this proof-of-concept app was accepted by the iTunes staff of reviewers suggests Apple cannot effectively review new apps prior to their use. Thousands of apps arrive each week.

Security on the Android platform is much less under the control of Google because it has an open app model. As a result, the Android has been the primary smartphone target, and instances of malware on the Android platform have reportedly increased by 400%. Google does not review any of the apps for the Android platform but instead relies on technical hurdles to limit the impact of malicious code, as well as user and security expert feedback. Google apps run in a "sandbox," where they cannot affect one another or manipulate device features without user permission. Android apps can use any personal information found on a Droid phone but they must also inform the user what each app is capable of doing, and what personal data it requires. Google removes from its official Android Market any apps that break its rules against malicious activity. One problem: users may not pay attention to permission requests and simply click "Yes" when asked to grant permissions. Apple's iPhone does not inform users what information apps are using, but does restrict the information that can be collected by any app.

Google can perform a remote wipe of offending apps from all Droid phones without user intervention. This is a wonderful capability, but is itself a security threat if hackers gain access to the remote wipe capability at Google. In one incident, Google pulled down dozens of mobile banking apps made by a developer called "09Droid." The apps claimed to give users access to their accounts at many banks throughout the world. In fact, the apps were unable to connect users to any bank, and were removed before they could do much harm. Google does take preventive steps to reduce malware apps such as vetting the backgrounds of developers, and requiring developers to register with its Google Wallet payment service (both to encourage users to pay for apps using their service but also to force developers to reveal their identities and financial information).

Beyond the threat of rogue apps, smartphones of all stripes are susceptible to browser-based malware that takes advantage of vulnerabilities in all browsers. In addition, most smartphones, including the iPhone, permit the manufacturers to remotely download configuration files to update operating systems and security protections. Unfortunately, flaws in the public key encryption procedures that permit remote server access to iPhones have been discovered, raising further questions about the security of such operations.

Some commentators dismiss these concerns as more hype than reality. But reality may be catching up with the hype.

SOURCES: "iPhone Malware: Spam App 'Find and Call' Invades App Store," by Zach Epstein, BGR.com, July 5, 2012; "iPhone Malware: Kaspersky Expects Apple's iOS to be Under Attack by Next Year," by Sara Gates, Huffington Post, May 15, 2012; "Android, Apple Face Growing Cyberattacks," by Byron Acohido, *USA Today*, June 3, 2011; "Security to Ward Off Crime on Phones," by Riva Richmond, *New York Times*, February 23, 2011; "AT&T Plans Smartphone Security Service for 2012," John Stankey, AT&T Enterprise CTO, interview May 16, 2012; "Smartphone Security Follies: A Brief History," by Brad Reed, *Network World*, April 18, 2011; "Experts: Android, iPhone Security Different But Matched," by Elinor Mills, CNET News, July 1, 2010; "Apple Security Breach Gives Complete Access to Your iPhone," by Jesus Diaz, Gizmodo.com, August 3, 2010; "iPhone Certificate Flaws, iPhone PKI Kandling flaws," by Cryptopath.com, January 2010.

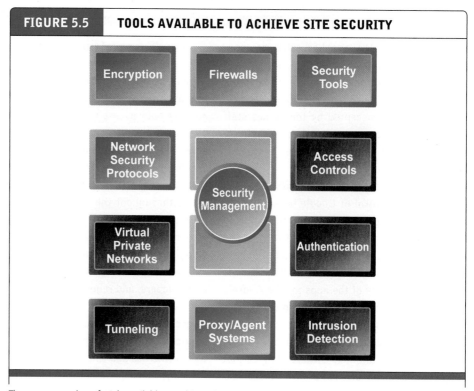

FIGURE 5.5   TOOLS AVAILABLE TO ACHIEVE SITE SECURITY

There are a number of tools available to achieve site security.

technology solutions and policy solutions. In this section, we consider some technology solutions, and in the following section, we look at some policy solutions that work.

The first line of defense against the wide variety of security threats to an e-commerce site is a set of tools that can make it difficult for outsiders to invade or destroy a site. **Figure 5.5** illustrates the major tools available to achieve site security.

PROTECTING INTERNET COMMUNICATIONS

Because e-commerce transactions must flow over the public Internet, and therefore involve thousands of routers and servers through which the transaction packets flow, security experts believe the greatest security threats occur at the level of Internet communications. This is very different from a private network where a dedicated communication line is established between two parties. A number of tools are available to protect the security of Internet communications, the most basic of which is message encryption.

ENCRYPTION

Encryption is the process of transforming plain text or data into **cipher text** that cannot be read by anyone other than the sender and the receiver. The purpose of encryption is (a) to secure stored information and (b) to secure information transmis-

encryption

the process of transforming plain text or data into cipher text that cannot be read by anyone other than the sender and the receiver. The purpose of encryption is (a) to secure stored information and (b) to secure information transmission

cipher text

text that has been encrypted and thus cannot be read by anyone other than the sender and the receiver sion. Encryption can provide four of the six key dimensions of e-commerce security referred to in Table 5.3 on page 267:

- *Message integrity*—provides assurance that the message has not been altered.
- *Nonrepudiation*—prevents the user from denying he or she sent the message.
- *Authentication*—provides verification of the identity of the person (or computer) sending the message.
- *Confidentiality*—gives assurance that the message was not read by others.

This transformation of plain text to cipher text is accomplished by using a key or cipher. A **key** (or **cipher**) is any method for transforming plain text to cipher text.

Encryption has been practiced since the earliest forms of writing and commercial transactions. Ancient Egyptian and Phoenician commercial records were encrypted using substitution and transposition ciphers. In a **substitution cipher**, every occurrence of a given letter is replaced systematically by another letter. For instance, if we used the cipher "letter plus two"—meaning replace every letter in a word with a new letter two places forward—then the word "Hello" in plain text would be transformed into the following cipher text: "JGNNQ." In a **transposition cipher**, the ordering of the letters in each word is changed in some systematic way. Leonardo Da Vinci recorded his shop notes in reverse order, making them readable only with a mirror. The word "Hello" can be written backwards as "OLLEH." A more complicated cipher would (a) break all words into two words and (b) spell the first word with every other letter beginning with the first letter, and then spell the second word with all the remaining letters. In this cipher, "HELLO" would be written as "HLO EL."

Symmetric Key Encryption

In order to decipher these messages, the receiver would have to know the secret cipher that was used to encrypt the plain text. This is called **symmetric key encryption** or **secret key encryption**. In symmetric key encryption, both the sender and the receiver use the same key to encrypt and decrypt the message. How do the sender and the receiver have the same key? They have to send it over some communication media or exchange the key in person. Symmetric key encryption was used extensively throughout World War II and is still a part of Internet encryption.

The possibilities for simple substitution and transposition ciphers are endless, but they all suffer from common flaws. First, in the digital age, computers are so powerful and fast that these ancient means of encryption can be broken quickly. Second, symmetric key encryption requires that both parties share the same key. In order to share the same key, they must send the key over a presumably *insecure* medium where it could be stolen and used to decipher messages. If the secret key is lost or stolen, the entire encryption system fails. Third, in commercial use, where we are not all part of the same team, you would need a secret key for each of the parties with whom you transacted, that is, one key for the bank, another for the department store, and another for the government. In a large population of users, this could result in as many as $n^{(n-1)}$ keys. In a population of millions of Internet users, thousands of millions of keys would be needed to accommodate all e-commerce customers (estimated at about 133[2]

key (cipher)
any method for transforming plain text to cipher text

substitution cipher
every occurrence of a given letter is replaced systematically by another letter

transposition cipher
the ordering of the letters in each word is changed in some systematic way

symmetric key encryption (secret key encryption)
both the sender and the receiver use the same key to encrypt and decrypt the message

million in the United States). Potentially, 133 million different keys would be needed. Clearly this situation would be too unwieldy to work in practice.

Modern encryption systems are digital. The ciphers or keys used to transform plain text into cipher text are digital strings. Computers store text or other data as binary strings composed of 0s and 1s. For instance, the binary representation of the capital letter "A" in ASCII computer code is accomplished with eight binary digits (bits): 01000001. One way in which digital strings can be transformed into cipher text is by multiplying each letter by another binary number, say, an eight-bit key number 0101 0101. If we multiplied every digital character in our text messages by this eight-bit key, sent the encrypted message to a friend along with the secret eight-bit key, the friend could decode the message easily.

The strength of modern security protection is measured in terms of the length of the binary key used to encrypt the data. In the preceding example, the eight-bit key is easily deciphered because there are only 2^8 or 256 possibilities. If the intruder knows you are using an eight-bit key, then he or she could decode the message in a few seconds using a modern desktop PC just by using the brute force method of checking each of the 256 possible keys. For this reason, modern digital encryption systems use keys with 56, 128, 256, or 512 binary digits. With encryption keys of 512 digits, there are 2^{512} possibilities to check out. It is estimated that all the computers in the world would need to work for 10 years before stumbling upon the answer.

The **Data Encryption Standard (DES)** was developed by the National Security Agency (NSA) and IBM in the 1950s. DES uses a 56-bit encryption key. To cope with much faster computers, it has been improved by *Triple DES*—essentially encrypting the message three times, each with a separate key. Today, the most widely used symmetric key encryption algorithm is **Advanced Encryption Standard (AES)**, which offers key sizes of 128, 192, and 256 bits. AES had been considered to be relatively secure, but in August 2011, researchers from Microsoft and a Belgian university announced that they had discovered a way to break the algorithm, and with this work, the "safety margin" of AES continues to erode. There are also many other symmetric key systems that are currently less widely used, with keys up to 2,048 bits.[1]

Public Key Encryption

In 1976, a new way of encrypting messages called **public key cryptography** was invented by Whitfield Diffie and Martin Hellman. Public key cryptography solves the problem of exchanging keys. In this method, two mathematically related digital keys are used: a public key and a private key. The private key is kept secret by the owner, and the public key is widely disseminated. Both keys can be used to encrypt and decrypt a message. However, once the keys are used to encrypt a message, that same key cannot be used to unencrypt the message. The mathematical algorithms used to produce the keys are one-way functions. A *one-way irreversible mathematical function* is one in which, once the algorithm is applied, the input cannot be subsequently derived from the output. Most food recipes are like this. For instance, it is easy to make

Data Encryption Standard (DES)
developed by the National Security Agency (NSA) and IBM. Uses a 56-bit encryption key

Advanced Encryption Standard (AES)
the most widely used symmetric key encryption algorithm, offering 128-, 192-, and 256-bit keys

public key cryptography
two mathematically related digital keys are used: a public key and a private key. The private key is kept secret by the owner, and the public key is widely disseminated. Both keys can be used to encrypt and decrypt a message. However, once the keys are used to encrypt a message, that same key cannot be used to unencrypt the message

[1] For instance: DESX and RDES with 168-bit keys; the RC Series: RC2, RC4, and RC5 with keys up to 2,048 bits; and the IDEA algorithm, the basis of PGP, e-mail public key encryption software described later in this chapter, which uses 128-bit keys.

scrambled eggs, but impossible to retrieve whole eggs from the scrambled eggs. Public key cryptography is based on the idea of irreversible mathematical functions. The keys are sufficiently long (128, 256, and 512 bits) that it would take enormous computing power to derive one key from the other using the largest and fastest computers available. **Figure 5.6** illustrates a simple use of public key cryptography and takes you through the important steps in using public and private keys.

FIGURE 5.6	PUBLIC KEY CRYPTOGRAPHY—A SIMPLE CASE
STEP	**DESCRIPTION**
1. The sender creates a digital message.	The message could be a document, spreadsheet, or any digital object.
2. The sender obtains the recipient's public key from a public directory and applies it to the message.	Public keys are distributed widely and can be obtained from recipients directly.
3. Application of the recipient's key produces an encrypted cipher text message.	Once encrypted using the public key, the message cannot be reverse-engineered or unencrypted using the same public key. The process is irreversible.
4. The encrypted message is sent over the Internet.	The encrypted message is broken into packets and sent through several different pathways, making interception of the entire message difficult (but not impossible).
5. The recipient uses his/her private key to decrypt the message.	The only person who can decrypt the message is the person who has possession of the recipient's private key. Hopefully, this is the legitimate recipient.

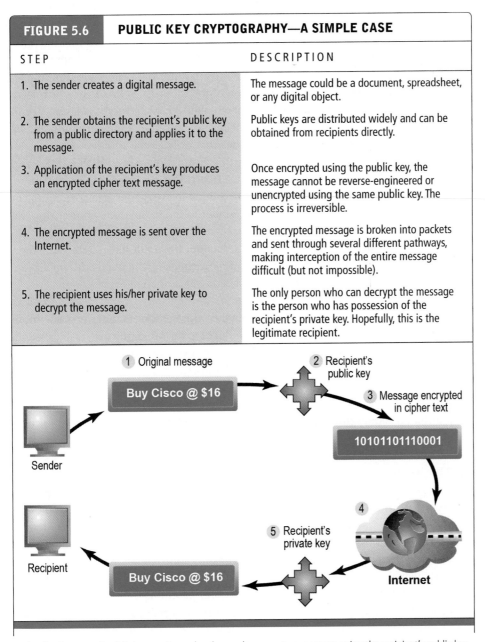

In the simplest use of public key cryptography, the sender encrypts a message using the recipient's public key, and then sends it over the Internet. The only person who can decrypt this message is the recipient, using his or her private key. However, this simple case does not ensure integrity or an authentic message.

Public Key Encryption Using Digital Signatures and Hash Digests

In public key encryption, some elements of security are missing. Although we can be quite sure the message was not understood or read by a third party (message confidentiality), there is no guarantee the sender really is the sender; that is, there is no authentication of the sender. This means the sender could deny ever sending the message (repudiation). And there is no assurance the message was not altered somehow in transit. For example, the message "Buy Cisco @ $16" could have been accidentally or intentionally altered to read "Sell Cisco @ $16." This suggests a potential lack of integrity in the system.

A more sophisticated use of public key cryptography can achieve authentication, nonrepudiation, and integrity. **Figure 5.7** illustrates this more powerful approach.

hash function

an algorithm that produces a fixed-length number called a hash or message digest

To check the integrity of a message and ensure it has not been altered in transit, a hash function is used first to create a digest of the message. A **hash function** is an algorithm that produces a fixed-length number called a *hash* or *message digest*. A hash function can be simple, and count the number of digital 1s in a message, or it can be more complex, and produce a 128-bit number that reflects the number of 0s and 1s, the number of 00s, 11s, and so on. Standard hash functions are available (MD4 and MD5 produce 128- and 160-bit hashes) (Stein, 1998). These more complex hash functions produce hashes or hash results that are unique to every message. The results of applying the hash function are sent by the sender to the recipient. Upon receipt, the recipient applies the hash function to the received message and checks to verify the same result is produced. If so, the message has not been altered. The sender then encrypts both the hash result and the original message using the recipient's public key (as in Figure 5.6 on page 291), producing a single block of cipher text.

One more step is required. To ensure the authenticity of the message and to ensure nonrepudiation, the sender encrypts the entire block of cipher text one more time using the sender's private key. This produces a **digital signature** (also called an *e-signature*) or "signed" cipher text that can be sent over the Internet.

digital signature (e-signature)

"signed" cipher text that can be sent over the Internet

A digital signature is a close parallel to a handwritten signature. Like a handwritten signature, a digital signature is unique—only one person presumably possesses the private key. When used with a hash function, the digital signature is even more unique than a handwritten signature. In addition to being exclusive to a particular individual, when used to sign a hashed document, the digital signature is also unique to the document, and changes for every document.

The recipient of this signed cipher text first uses the sender's public key to authenticate the message. Once authenticated, the recipient uses his or her private key to obtain the hash result and original message. As a final step, the recipient applies the same hash function to the original text, and compares the result with the result sent by the sender. If the results are the same, the recipient now knows the message has not been changed during transmission. The message has integrity.

Early digital signature programs required the user to have a digital certificate, and were far too difficult for an individual to use. Newer programs from several small companies are Internet-based and do not require users to install software, or understand digital certificate technology. DocuSign, EchoSign, and Sertifi are companies offering online digital signatures. Many insurance, finance, and surety companies now permit customers to electronically sign documents.

FIGURE 5.7 — PUBLIC KEY CRYPTOGRAPHY WITH DIGITAL SIGNATURES

STEP	DESCRIPTION
1. The sender creates an original message.	The message can be any digital file.
2. The sender applies a hash function, producing a 128-bit hash result.	Hash functions create a unique digest of the message based on the message contents.
3. The sender encrypts the message and hash result using recipient's public key.	This irreversible process creates a cipher text that can be read only by the recipient using his or her private key.
4. The sender encrypts the result, again using his or her private key.	The sender's private key is a digital signature. There is only one person who can create this digital mark.
5. The result of this double encryption is sent over the Internet.	The message traverses the Internet as a series of independent packets.
6. The receiver uses the sender's public key to authenticate the message.	Only one person can send this message, namely, the sender.
7. The receiver uses his or her private key to decrypt the hash function and the original message. The receiver checks to ensure the original message and the hash function results conform to one another.	The hash function is used here to check the original message. This ensures the message was not changed in transit.

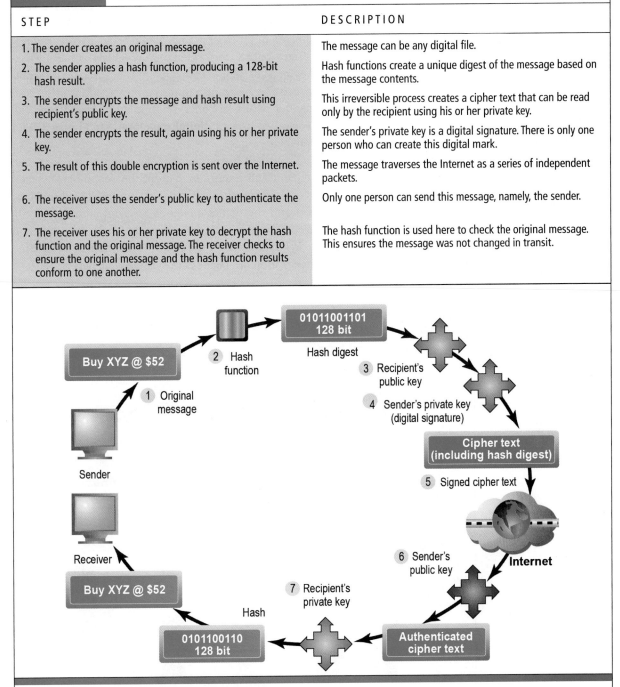

A more realistic use of public key cryptography uses hash functions and digital signatures to both ensure the confidentiality of the message and authenticate the sender. The only person who could have sent the above message is the owner or the sender using his/her private key. This authenticates the message. The hash function ensures the message was not altered in transit. As before, the only person who can decipher the message is the recipient, using his/her private key.

Digital Envelopes

Public key encryption is computationally slow. If one used 128- or 256-bit keys to encode large documents—such as this chapter or the entire book—significant declines in transmission speeds and increases in processing time would occur. Symmetric key encryption is computationally faster, but as we pointed out previously, it has a weakness—namely, the symmetric key must be sent to the recipient over insecure transmission lines. One solution is to use the more efficient symmetric encryption and decryption for large documents, but public key encryption to encrypt and send the symmetric key. This technique is called using a **digital envelope**. See **Figure 5.8** for an illustration of how a digital envelope works.

In Figure 5.8, a diplomatic document is encrypted using a symmetric key. The symmetric key—which the recipient will require to decrypt the document—is itself encrypted, using the recipient's public key. So we have a "key within a key" (a *digital envelope*). The encrypted report and the digital envelope are sent across the Web. The recipient first uses his/her private key to decrypt the symmetric key, and then the recipient uses the symmetric key to decrypt the report. This method saves time because both encryption and decryption are faster with symmetric keys.

digital envelope

a technique that uses symmetric encryption for large documents, but public key encryption to encrypt and send the symmetric key

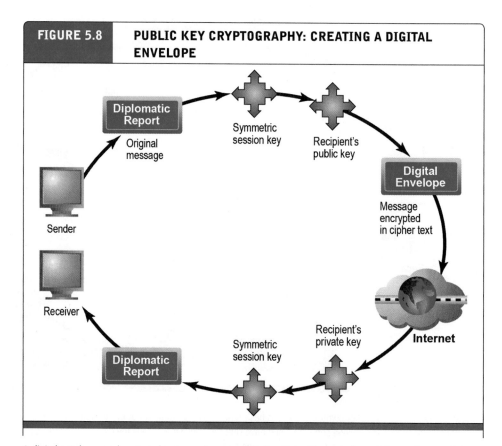

| FIGURE 5.8 | PUBLIC KEY CRYPTOGRAPHY: CREATING A DIGITAL ENVELOPE |

A digital envelope can be created to transmit a symmetric key that will permit the recipient to decrypt the message and be assured the message was not intercepted in transit.

Digital Certificates and Public Key Infrastructure (PKI)

There are still some deficiencies in the message security regime described previously. How do we know that people and institutions are who they claim to be? Anyone can make up a private and public key combination and claim to be someone they are not. Before you place an order with an online merchant such as Amazon, you want to be sure it really is Amazon.com you have on the screen and not a spoofer masquerading as Amazon. In the physical world, if someone asks who you are and you show a social security number, they may well ask to see a picture ID or a second form of certifiable or acceptable identification. If they really doubt who you are, they may ask for references to other authorities and actually interview these other authorities. Similarly, in the digital world, we need a way to know who people and institutions really are.

Digital certificates, and the supporting public key infrastructure, are an attempt to solve this problem of digital identity. A **digital certificate** is a digital document issued by a trusted third-party institution known as a **certification authority (CA)** that contains the name of the subject or company, the subject's public key, a digital certificate serial number, an expiration date, an issuance date, the digital signature of the certification authority (the name of the CA encrypted using the CA's private key), and other identifying information (see **Figure 5.9**).

In the United States, private corporations such as VeriSign, browser manufacturers, security firms, and government agencies such as the U.S. Postal Service and the

digital certificate
a digital document issued by a certification authority that contains the name of the subject or company, the subject's public key, a digital certificate serial number, an expiration date, an issuance date, the digital signature of the certification authority, and other identifying information

certification authority (CA)
a trusted third party that issues digital certificates

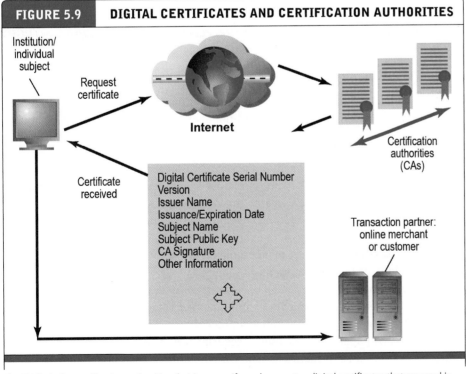

| FIGURE 5.9 | DIGITAL CERTIFICATES AND CERTIFICATION AUTHORITIES |

The PKI includes certification authorities that issue, verify, and guarantee digital certificates that are used in e-commerce to assure the identity of transaction partners.

public key infrastructure (PKI)
CAs and digital certificate procedures that are accepted by all parties

Federal Reserve issue CAs. Worldwide, thousands of organizations issue CAs. A hierarchy of CAs has emerged with less-well-known CAs being certified by larger and better-known CAs, creating a community of mutually verifying institutions. **Public key infrastructure (PKI)** refers to the CAs and digital certificate procedures that are accepted by all parties. When you sign into a "secure" site, the URL will begin with "https" and a closed lock icon will appear on your browser. This means the site has a digital certificate issued by a trusted CA. It is not, presumably, a spoof site.

To create a digital certificate, the user generates a public/private key pair and sends a request for certification to a CA along with the user's public key. The CA verifies the information (how this is accomplished differs from CA to CA). The CA issues a certificate containing the user's public key and other related information. Finally, the CA creates a message digest from the certificate itself (just like a hash digest) and signs it with the CA's private key. This signed digest is called the *signed certificate*. We end up with a totally unique cipher text document—there can be only one signed certificate like this in the world.

There are several ways the certificates are used in commerce. Before initiating a transaction, the customer can request the signed digital certificate of the merchant and decrypt it using the merchant's public key to obtain both the message digest and the certificate as issued. If the message digest matches the certificate, then the merchant and the public key are authenticated. The merchant may in return request certification of the user, in which case the user would send the merchant his or her individual certificate. There are many types of certificates: personal, institutional, Web server, software publisher, and CAs themselves.

Pretty Good Privacy (PGP)
a widely used e-mail public key encryption software program

You can easily obtain a public and private key for personal, noncommercial use at the International PGP Home Page Web site, Pgpi.org. **Pretty Good Privacy (PGP)** was invented in 1991 by Phil Zimmerman, and has become one of the most widely used e-mail public key encryption software tools in the world. Using PGP software installed on your computer, you can compress and encrypt your messages as well as authenticate both yourself and the recipient. The *Insight on Society* story, *Web Dogs and Anonymity: Identity 2.0*, describes additional efforts to ensure e-mail security.

Limitations to Encryption Solutions

PKI is a powerful technological solution to security issues, but it has many limitations, especially concerning CAs. PKI applies mainly to protecting messages in transit on the Internet and is not effective against insiders—employees—who have legitimate access to corporate systems including customer information. Most e-commerce sites do not store customer information in encrypted form. Other limitations are apparent. For one, how is your private key to be protected? Most private keys will be stored on insecure desktop or laptop computers.

There is no guarantee the person using your computer—and your private key—is really you. For instance, you may lose your laptop or smartphone, and therefore lose the private key. Likewise, there is no assurance that someone else in the world uses your personal ID papers such as a social security card, to obtain a PKI authenticated online ID in your name. If there's no real world identification system, there can be no Internet identification system. Under many digital signature laws, you are responsible for whatever your private key does even if you were not the person using the key. This

INSIGHT ON SOCIETY

WEB DOGS AND ANONYMITY: IDENTITY 2.0

One of the many problems with Internet security is people sometimes don't really know just who they are dealing with on the Web. It could be anyone, even a dog, as humorously suggested by the iconic *New Yorker* magazine cartoon by Peter Steiner that shows two dogs in front of a computer screen, one entering data. On the Web, you don't know who to trust, and you may not feel comfortable putting your personal information online, either by purchasing, socializing, or communicating. Spammers may even be sending out spam that appears to come from you, potentially destroying your credibility and reputation. Even Google employees get fooled into opening e-mails from their supposed friends, or their boss, only to find they clicked on an attachment, imported destructive malware, and lost valuable intellectual property to Chinese government-sponsored hackers.

It gets worse. Most Web users have multiple identities across the Web, with large numbers of user accounts, passwords, and personal identifier attributes (for instance, your mother's maiden name) across multiple providers of Web services, all of whom have different data-sharing and privacy policies. On social network sites, many people reveal their unique personal attributes or they can be found with artful searching. As a result, most Web users don't have a clue about who has what information about them, how it is used, or who has access to it. Most computers on the Internet do not really know who they are communicating with. Routers, the work horse computers that direct traffic on the Internet, send messages to one another about where to route packets of information. Routers trust that the instructions they receive from other routers are valid and legitimate. On numerous occasions in the past three years, significant portions of the global Internet traffic were routed to China by mistake, or intentionally, by rogue computer programs. When it comes to identity, or lack thereof (anonymity), the Internet is an information asylum based on the fiction that we know who we are really dealing with in our transactions.

There are several groups trying to establish secure identity on the Internet. An international group led by large business firms and 85 governments have started a global system of authentication in an effort to reduce spam, scams, and hacking. Dubbed "Secure DNS," short for Domain Name System Security Extensions (DNSSEC), the system is designed to replace the existing DNS authority structure operated by private industry (and which is widely regarded as insecure) with a new international system operated by a consortium of countries. When implemented, it would be impossible, according to supporters, for spammers and hackers to hide their location and identity. Comcast is the first large ISP to have completed DNSSEC deployment. However, much work remains to be done. For instance, security company Secure64 found that none of the nearly 300 financial institutions in the United States and around the world that they surveyed have fully implemented DNSSEC, despite the fact that it has been endorsed by the FCC, White House, Department of Homeland Security, ICANN, and many others.

The federal government, along with private industry, is also trying to fix parts of the identity problem in the United States with a program called "Identity 2.0." In April 2011, the White House released the National Strategy for Trusted Identities in Cyberspace (NSTIC), a policy document describing a "voluntary trusted identity" system that would provide all members of the online community (people, institutions, computers, network routers, and other appliances including

(continued)

cell phones) with an incontrovertible digital identity. The strategy calls for the creation of a new identity ecosystem, a kind of walled garden where people can safely play. The identity system would rely on a strong credential that would work like a combination of a digital key (a private digital key that uniquely identifies your computer), a fingerprint (or some bio marker that uniquely identifies you), and perhaps a digitized photo (or other attribute like your mother's maiden name).

The idea is that finally there will be agreed-upon standards for individuals and organizations to obtain and authenticate their digital identities. No more anonymous netizens who could be dogs, or worse. No more e-mails from servers in Russia that cannot be authenticated. Although NSTIC is part of the National Institute of Technology and Standards (NIST), it will work with private industry to develop the new ecosystem rather than have the government control personal identity credentials.

Where would the identity credential be stored? According to NSTIC, the credential could be stored on a smart card the user carries in his or her pocket like a credit card, or it could be stored on the user's computer, or a smartphone. You can think of it as an Internet driver's license, or a credit card on steroids. Internet users would not be required to have a strong credential, but they could not get access to most popular Web sites without it.

With this strong credential you would be able to sign in to any Web site requesting your ID, from a bank, or university, to a government agency, either by swiping the smart card or waving your smartphone, or sending a digital ID file. It's a single sign-on: you have one password and one login across all sites. Google and Microsoft have single sign-on systems (SSOs) to gain access to a wide variety of their proprietary services, but the SSOs don't work outside of the walled gardens created by Google and Microsoft. Anonymity, the bane of the Internet because it allows people to abuse the Internet and its users while hiding their identity, would presumably be eliminated or greatly reduced.

A computer captured by a botnet theoretically would not be allowed to send spam to any other computer, or a request for service, without first authenticating itself (or the owner of the computer). This would also greatly reduce phishing. A commanding computer controlling a botnet would not be able to launch a million spam e-mails at once across the Internet without identifying itself (IP address), sending its own authentication, and using digital keys to activate all its slave computers. You would not be allowed to post to a blog or Web site without first authenticating who you are. You would not be able to send e-mail to anyone without first authenticating who you are. In this plan, anonymity is not possible.

Who would control this identity system? NSTIC calls for a federation of private and public online identity systems. Banks, federal agencies, Google, the U.S. Postal Service, VeriSign, and other trusted institutions would provide the electronic smart ID cards, or digital files, once they have identified who you are. This would be similar to credit cards that are issued by multiple financial institutions and are widely accepted. The other alternative for organizing strong identity regimes is a single federal agency. This alternative is supported primarily by academic and government computer scientists who believe such a solution would be less chaotic and easier to implement. Most privacy advocates and private firms want a mix of public and private entities to control the identity ecosystem.

According to Steven Bellovin, a prominent security researcher, one of the biggest problems for Internet security is the issue of software vulnerabilities in whatever authentication system is implemented. A more mundane problem is ensuring that the digital identity granted by the security system matches the real physical identity of the person or institution applying for an online ID. Credit card companies are often fooled into

(continued)

issuing credit cards and credit card clearing services to criminals and imposters who have stolen identities; banks and government agencies often provide services to people with stolen social security numbers. If offline authentication is flawed, then online authentication is hopeless.

Commentators point out that while the strategy of having private industry create and hold the IDs of millions of Americans sounds good, and totally American, why should people trust big businesses with their personal information any more than big government? Who trusts Facebook or Google with their personal information? It's businesses that have been profiting by invading the privacy of citizens, and we currently have a private business Internet security system that is a failure by most accounts. On the other hand, the American public has never signed up for a government national identity card system like many European nations use. Privacy advocates are wary of any national identity system regardless of who runs it. It may be that continuing Internet anonymity is the least worst choice.

SOURCES: "Financial Services Industry Receives 'Incomplete' Grade on DNSSEC Deployment," Secure64 Software Corporation, August 7, 2012; "Recommendations for Establishing an Identity Ecosystem Governance Structure," Department of Commerce, National Institute of Standards and Technology, February 2012; "Comcast Finishes DNSSEC Rollout," by Karl Bode, DSLReports.com, January 11, 2012; "A Stronger Net Security System is Deployed," John Markoff, *New York Times*, June 24, 2011; "Wave of the Future: Trusted Identities in Cyberspace," by Dan Rowinski, *New York Times*, April 20, 2011; "Enhancing Online Choice, Efficiency, Security, and Privacy," The White House, April 2011; "White House's Trusted Identities Strategy Doesn't Inspire Trust," by Matthew Harwood, Securitymanagement.com, July 27, 2010; "A Major Milestone for Internet Security," by Andrew McLaughlin, Office of Science and Technology Policy, Whitehouse.gov, July 22, 2010; "Real ID Online? New Federal Online Identity Plan Raises Privacy and Free Speech," by Lee Tien and Seth Schoe, Electronic Frontier Foundation, July 20, 2010; "Taking the Mystery Out of Web Anonymity," John Markoff, *New York Times*, July 2, 2010; "White House Strategy For Secure Cyberspace Based on Identity-theft-flawed Meatspace," by Joe Campana, Examiner.com, June 29, 2010.

is very different from mail-order or telephone order credit card rules, where you have a right to dispute the credit card charge. Second, there is no guarantee the verifying computer of the merchant is secure. Third, CAs are self-selected organizations seeking to gain access to the business of authorization. They may not be authorities on the corporations or individuals they certify. For instance, how can a CA know about all the corporations within an industry to determine who is or is not legitimate? A related question concerns the method used by the CA to identify the certificate holder. Was this an e-mail transaction verified only by claims of the applicants who filled out an online form? For instance, VeriSign acknowledged in one case that it had mistakenly issued two digital certificates to someone fraudulently claiming to represent Microsoft. Digital certificates have been hijacked by hackers, tricking consumers into giving up personal information. For example, in 2011, the CA-granting firm Comodo was hacked by an Iranian hacker and lost control of its CA-granting process. The hacker issued hundreds of CAs to servers that appeared to the user to be legitimate sites operated by Google, Yahoo, and others. The Dutch company DigiNotar was hit by a similar attack, and hackers were thought to have obtained more than 200 digital certificates, including ones for Google, Mozilla, and Yahoo, among others. Last, what are the policies for revoking or renewing certificates? The expected life of a digital certificate or private key is a function of the frequency of use and the vulnerability of systems that use the certificate. Yet most CAs have no policy or just an annual policy for reissuing certificates. If Microsoft, Apple, or Cisco ever rescinded a number of CAs, millions of users would not be able to access sites. The CA system is difficult and costly to police.

SECURING CHANNELS OF COMMUNICATION

The concepts of public key encryption are used routinely for securing channels of communication.

Secure Sockets Layer (SSL) and Transport Layer Security (TLS)

secure negotiated session

a client-server session in which the URL of the requested document, along with the contents, contents of forms, and the cookies exchanged, are encrypted

session key

a unique symmetric encryption key chosen for a single secure session

The most common form of securing channels is through the *Secure Sockets Layer (SSL)* and *Transport Layer Security (TLS)* protocols. When you receive a message from a server on the Web with which you will be communicating through a secure channel, this means you will be using SSL/TLS to establish a secure negotiated session. (Notice that the URL changes from HTTP to HTTPS.) A **secure negotiated session** is a client-server session in which the URL of the requested document, along with the contents, contents of forms, and the cookies exchanged, are encrypted (see **Figure 5.10**). For instance, your credit card number that you entered into a form would be encrypted. Through a series of handshakes and communications, the browser and the server establish one another's identity by exchanging digital certificates, decide on the strongest shared form of encryption, and then proceed to communicate using an agreed-upon session key. A **session key** is a unique symmetric encryption key chosen just

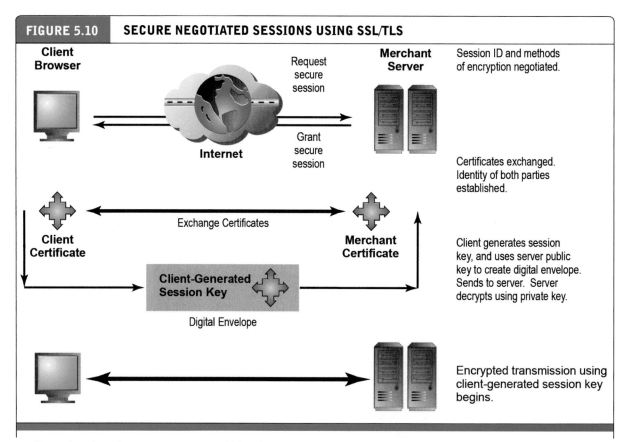

| FIGURE 5.10 | SECURE NEGOTIATED SESSIONS USING SSL/TLS |

Client Browser

Request secure session

Merchant Server

Session ID and methods of encryption negotiated.

Internet

Grant secure session

Client Certificate

Exchange Certificates

Merchant Certificate

Certificates exchanged. Identity of both parties established.

Client-Generated Session Key

Digital Envelope

Client generates session key, and uses server public key to create digital envelope. Sends to server. Server decrypts using private key.

Encrypted transmission using client-generated session key begins.

Certificates play a key role in using SSL/TLS to establish a secure communications channel.

for this single secure session. Once used, it is gone forever. Figure 5.10 shows how this works.

In practice, most private individuals do not have a digital certificate. In this case, the merchant server will not request a certificate, but the client browser will request the merchant certificate once a secure session is called for by the server.

SSL/TLS provides data encryption, server authentication, optional client authentication, and message integrity for TCP/IP connections. SSL/TLS addresses the issue of authenticity by allowing users to verify another user's identity or the identity of a server. It also protects the integrity of the messages exchanged. However, once the merchant receives the encrypted credit and order information, that information is typically stored in unencrypted format on the merchant's servers. While the SSL/TLS provides secure transactions between merchant and consumer, it only guarantees server-side authentication. Client authentication is optional.

In addition, SSL/TLS cannot provide irrefutability—consumers can order goods or download information products, and then claim the transaction never occurred. Recently, social network sites such as Facebook and Twitter have begun to use SSL/TLS to thwart account hijacking using Firesheep over wireless networks. Firesheep, an add-on for Firefox, can be used by hackers to grab unencrypted cookies used to "remember" a user and allow the hacker to immediately log on to a Web site as that user. SSL/TLS can thwart such an attack because it encrypts the cookie.

Virtual Private Networks (VPNs)

A **virtual private network (VPN)** allows remote users to securely access a corporation's local area network via the Internet, using a variety of VPN protocols. VPNs use both authentication and encryption to secure information from unauthorized persons. VPNs are able to block message intercepts and packet sniffing (providing confidentiality and integrity). Authentication prevents spoofing and misrepresentation of identities. A remote user can connect to a remote private local network using a local ISP. The VPN protocols will establish the link from the client to the corporate network as if the user had dialed into the corporate network directly. The process of connecting one protocol through another (IP) is called *tunneling,* because the VPN creates a private connection by adding an invisible wrapper around a message to hide its content. As the message travels through the Internet between the ISP and the corporate network, it is shielded from prying eyes by an encrypted wrapper.

A VPN is "virtual" in the sense that it appears to users as a dedicated secure line when in fact it is a temporary secure line. The primary use of VPNs is to establish secure communications among business partners—larger suppliers or customers, and employees working remotely. A dedicated connection to a business partner can be very expensive. Using the Internet and VPN as the connection method significantly reduces the cost of secure communications.

virtual private network (VPN)
allows remote users to securely access internal networks via the Internet, using the Point-to-Point Tunneling Protocol (PPTP)

PROTECTING NETWORKS

Once you have protected communications as well as possible, the next set of tools to consider are those that can protect your networks, as well as the servers and clients on those networks.

Firewalls

Firewalls and proxy servers are intended to build a wall around your network and the attached servers and clients, just like physical-world firewalls protect you from fires for a limited period of time. Firewalls and proxy servers share some similar functions, but they are quite different.

firewall

refers to either hardware or software that filters communication packets and prevents some packets from entering the network based on a security policy

A **firewall** refers to either hardware or software that filters communication packets and prevents some packets from entering the network based on a security policy. The firewall controls traffic to and from servers and clients, forbidding communications from untrustworthy sources, and allowing other communications from trusted sources to proceed. Every message that is to be sent or received from the network is processed by the firewall, which determines if the message meets security guidelines established by the business. If it does, it is permitted to be distributed, and if it doesn't, the message is blocked. Firewalls can filter traffic based on packet attributes such as source IP address, destination port or IP address, type of service (such as WWW or HTTP), the domain name of the source, and many other dimensions. Most hardware firewalls that protect local area networks connected to the Internet have default settings that require little if any administrator intervention and accomplish simple but effective rules that deny incoming packets from a connection that does not originate from an internal request—the firewall only allows connections from servers that you requested service from. A common default setting on hardware firewalls (DSL and cable modem routers) simply ignores efforts to communicate with TCP port 445, the most commonly attacked port. The increasing use of firewalls by home and business Internet users has greatly reduced the effectiveness of attacks, and forced hackers to focus more on e-mail attachments to distribute worms and viruses.

There are two major methods firewalls use to validate traffic: packet filters and application gateways. *Packet filters* examine data packets to determine whether they are destined for a prohibited port or originate from a prohibited IP address (as specified by the security administrator). The filter specifically looks at the source and destination information, as well as the port and packet type, when determining whether the information may be transmitted. One downside of the packet filtering method is that it is susceptible to spoofing, since authentication is not one of its roles.

Application gateways are a type of firewall that filters communications based on the application being requested, rather than the source or destination of the message. Such firewalls also process requests at the application level, farther away from the client computer than packet filters. By providing a central filtering point, application gateways provide greater security than packet filters but can compromise system performance.

proxy server (proxy)

software server that handles all communications originating from or being sent to the Internet, acting as a spokesperson or bodyguard for the organization

Proxy servers (proxies) are software servers (often a dedicated computer) that handle all communications originating from or being sent to the Internet by local clients, acting as a spokesperson or bodyguard for the organization. Proxies act primar-

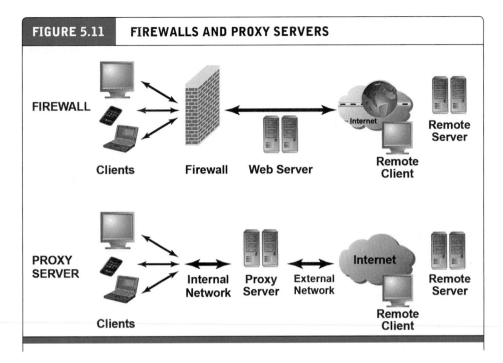

FIGURE 5.11   **FIREWALLS AND PROXY SERVERS**

The primary function of a firewall is to deny access by remote client computers to local computers. The primary purpose of a proxy server is to provide controlled access from local computers to remote computers.

ily to limit access of internal clients to external Internet servers, although some proxy servers act as firewalls as well. Proxy servers are sometimes called *dual-home systems* because they have two network interfaces. To internal computers, a proxy server is known as the *gateway*, while to external computers it is known as a *mail server* or *numeric address*.

When a user on an internal network requests a Web page, the request is routed first to the proxy server. The proxy server validates the user and the nature of the request, and then sends the request onto the Internet. A Web page sent by an external Internet server first passes to the proxy server. If acceptable, the Web page passes onto the internal network Web server and then to the client desktop. By prohibiting users from communicating directly with the Internet, companies can restrict access to certain types of sites, such as pornographic, auction, or stock-trading sites. Proxy servers also improve Web performance by storing frequently requested Web pages locally, reducing upload times, and hiding the internal network's address, thus making it more difficult for hackers to monitor. **Figure 5.11** illustrates how firewalls and proxy servers protect a local area network from Internet intruders and prevent internal clients from reaching prohibited Web servers.

PROTECTING SERVERS AND CLIENTS

Operating system features and anti-virus software can help further protect servers and clients from certain types of attacks.

Operating System Security Enhancements

The most obvious way to protect servers and clients is to take advantage of Microsoft's and Apple's automatic computer security upgrades. Microsoft and Apple continuously update their operating systems to patch vulnerabilities discovered by hackers. These patches are autonomic; that is, when using these operating systems on the Internet, you are prompted and informed that operating system enhancements are available. Users can easily download these security patches for free. The most common known worms and viruses can be prevented by simply keeping your server and client operating systems and applications up to date. Application vulnerabilities are also fixed in the same manner. For instance, most popular Internet browsers are updated automatically with little user intervention.

Anti-Virus Software

The easiest and least-expensive way to prevent threats to system integrity is to install anti-virus software. Programs by McAfee, Symantec (Norton AntiVirus), and many others provide inexpensive tools to identify and eradicate the most common types of malicious code as they enter a computer, as well as destroy those already lurking on a hard drive. Anti-virus programs can be set up so that e-mail attachments are inspected prior to you clicking on them, and the attachments are eliminated if they contain a known virus or worm. It is not enough, however, to simply install the software once. Since new viruses are developed and released every day, daily routine updates are needed in order to prevent new threats from being loaded. Some premium-level anti-virus software is updated hourly.

Anti-virus suite packages and stand-alone programs are available to eliminate intruders such as bot programs, adware, and other security risks. Such programs work much like anti-virus software in that they look for recognized hacker tools or signature actions of known intruders.

5.4 MANAGEMENT POLICIES, BUSINESS PROCEDURES, AND PUBLIC LAWS

Worldwide, in 2012, companies are expected to spend $60 billion on security hardware, software, and services (Gartner, 2012). However, most CEOs and CIOs believe that technology is not the sole answer to managing the risk of e-commerce. The technology provides a foundation, but in the absence of intelligent management policies, even the best technology can be easily defeated. Public laws and active enforcement of cybercrime statutes are also required to both raise the costs of illegal behavior on the Internet and guard against corporate abuse of information. Let's consider briefly the development of management policy.

A SECURITY PLAN: MANAGEMENT POLICIES

In order to minimize security threats, e-commerce firms must develop a coherent corporate policy that takes into account the nature of the risks, the information assets

FIGURE 5.12	DEVELOPING AN E-COMMERCE SECURITY PLAN

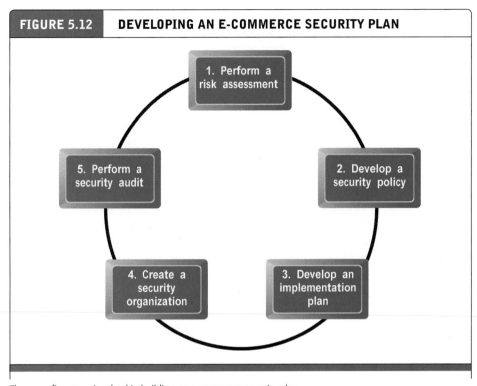

There are five steps involved in building an e-commerce security plan.

that need protecting, and the procedures and technologies required to address the risk, as well as implementation and auditing mechanisms. **Figure 5.12** illustrates the key steps in developing a solid security plan.

A security plan begins with **risk assessment**—an assessment of the risks and points of vulnerability. The first step is to inventory the information and knowledge assets of the e-commerce site and company. What information is at risk? Is it customer information, proprietary designs, business activities, secret processes, or other internal information, such as price schedules, executive compensation, or payroll? For each type of information asset, try to estimate the dollar value to the firm if this information were compromised, and then multiply that amount by the probability of the loss occurring. Once you have done so, rank order the results. You now have a list of information assets prioritized by their value to the firm.

Based on your quantified list of risks, you can start to develop a **security policy**— a set of statements prioritizing the information risks, identifying acceptable risk targets, and identifying the mechanisms for achieving these targets. You will obviously want to start with the information assets that you determined to be the highest priority in your risk assessment. Who generates and controls this information in the firm? What existing security policies are in place to protect the information? What enhancements can you recommend to improve security of these most valuable assets? What level of risk are you willing to accept for each of these assets? Are you willing, for instance, to lose customer credit card data once every 10 years? Or will you pursue a

risk assessment
an assessment of the risks and points of vulnerability

security policy
a set of statements prioritizing the information risks, identifying acceptable risk targets, and identifying the mechanisms for achieving these targets

100-year hurricane strategy by building a security edifice for credit card data that can withstand the once-in-100-year disaster? You will need to estimate how much it will cost to achieve this level of acceptable risk. Remember, total and complete security may require extraordinary financial resources. By answering these questions, you will have the beginnings of a security policy.

Next, consider an **implementation plan**—the steps you will take to achieve the security plan goals. Specifically, you must determine how you will translate the levels of acceptable risk into a set of tools, technologies, policies, and procedures. What new technologies will you deploy to achieve the goals, and what new employee procedures will be needed?

To implement your plan, you will need an organizational unit in charge of security, and a security officer—someone who is in charge of security on a daily basis. For a small e-commerce site, the security officer will likely be the person in charge of Internet services or the site manager, whereas for larger firms, there typically is a dedicated team with a supporting budget. The **security organization** educates and trains users, keeps management aware of security threats and breakdowns, and maintains the tools chosen to implement security.

The security organization typically administers access controls, authentication procedures, and authorization policies. **Access controls** determine which outsiders and insiders can gain legitimate access to your networks. Outsider access controls include firewalls and proxy servers, while insider access controls typically consist of login procedures (usernames, passwords, and access codes).

Authentication procedures include the use of digital signatures, certificates of authority, and PKI. Now that e-signatures have been given the same legal weight as an original pen-and-ink version, companies are in the process of devising ways to test and confirm a signer's identity. Companies frequently have signers type their full name and click on a button indicating their understanding that they have just signed a contract or document.

Biometric devices can also be used to verify physical attributes associated with an individual, such as a fingerprint or retina (eye) scan or speech recognition system. (**Biometrics** is the study of measurable biological, or physical, characteristics.) A company could require, for example, that an individual undergo a fingerprint scan before being allowed access to a Web site, or before being allowed to pay for merchandise with a credit card. Biometric devices make it even more difficult for hackers to break into sites or facilities, significantly reducing the opportunity for spoofing. **Security tokens** (such as RSA's SecurID Tokens) are used by millions of corporation and government workers to log on to corporate clients and servers. Tokens generate six-digit passwords continuously and prevent hackers from stealing passwords.

Authorization policies determine differing levels of access to information assets for differing levels of users. **Authorization management systems** establish where and when a user is permitted to access certain parts of a Web site. Their primary function is to restrict access to private information within a company's Internet infrastructure. Although there are several authorization management products currently available, most operate in the same way: the system encrypts a user session to function like a passkey that follows the user from page to page, allowing access only to those

implementation plan
the action steps you will take to achieve the security plan goals

security organization
educates and trains users, keeps management aware of security threats and breakdowns, and maintains the tools chosen to implement security

access controls
determine who can gain legitimate access to a network

authentication procedures
include the use of digital signatures, certificates of authority, and public key infrastructure

biometrics
the study of measurable biological or physical characteristics

security tokens
small devices that continuously generate six-digit passwords to prevent theft of passwords

authorization policies
determine differing levels of access to information assets for differing levels of users

authorization management system
establishes where and when a user is permitted to access certain parts of a Web site

areas that the user is permitted to enter, based on information set at the system data-base. By establishing entry rules up front for each user, the authorization management system knows who is permitted to go where at all times.

The last step in developing an e-commerce security plan is performing a security audit. A **security audit** involves the routine review of access logs (identifying how outsiders are using the site as well as how insiders are accessing the site's assets). A monthly report should be produced that establishes the routine and non-routine accesses to the systems and identifies unusual patterns of activities. As previously noted, tiger teams are often used by large corporate sites to evaluate the strength of existing security procedures. Many small firms have sprung up in the last five years to provide these services to large corporate sites.

security audit
involves the routine review of access logs (identifying how outsiders are using the site as well as how insiders are accessing the site's assets)

THE ROLE OF LAWS AND PUBLIC POLICY

The public policy environment today is very different from the early days of e-com-merce. The net result is that the Internet is no longer an ungoverned, unsupervised, self-controlled technology juggernaut. Just as with financial markets in the last 70 years, there is a growing awareness that e-commerce markets work only when a pow-erful institutional set of laws and enforcement mechanisms are in place. These laws help ensure orderly, rational, and fair markets. This growing public policy environ-ment is becoming just as global as e-commerce itself. Despite some spectacular inter-nationally based attacks on U.S. e-commerce sites, the sources and persons involved in major harmful attacks have almost always been uncovered and, where possible, prosecuted.

Voluntary and private efforts have played a very large role in identifying criminal hackers and assisting law enforcement. Since 1995, as e-commerce has grown in sig-nificance, national and local law enforcement activities have expanded greatly. New laws have been passed that grant local and national authorities new tools and mecha-nisms for identifying, tracing, and prosecuting cybercriminals. **Table 5.5** on page 308 lists the most significant federal e-commerce security legislation.

Following passage of the National Information Infrastructure Protection Act of 1996, which makes DoS attacks and virus distribution federal crimes, the FBI and the Department of Justice established the National Infrastructure Protection Center (NIPC). Now subsumed within the National Cyber Security Division of the Department of Homeland Security, this organization's sole mission is to identify and combat threats against the United States' technology and telecommunications infrastructure.

By increasing the punishment for cybercrimes, the U.S. government is attempting to create a deterrent to further hacker actions. And by making such actions federal crimes, the government is able to extradite international hackers and prosecute them within the United States.

After September 11, 2001, Congress passed the USA PATRIOT Act, which broadly expanded law enforcement's investigative and surveillance powers. The act has provisions for monitoring e-mail and Internet use. The Homeland Security Act of 2002 also attempts to fight cyberterrorism and increases the government's ability to compel information disclosure by computer and ISP sources. Recent proposed legisla-

TABLE 5.5	E-COMMERCE SECURITY LEGISLATION
LEGISLATION	SIGNIFICANCE
Computer Fraud and Abuse Act (1986)	Primary federal statute used to combat computer crime.
Electronic Communications Privacy Act (1986)	Imposes fines and imprisonment for individuals who access, intercept, or disclose the private e-mail communications of others.
National Information Infrastructure Protection Act (1996)	Makes DoS attacks illegal; creates NIPC in the FBI.
Health Insurance Portability and Accountability Act (1996)	Requires certain health care facilities to report data breaches.
Financial Modernization Act (Gramm-Leach-Bliley Act (1999)	Requires certain financial institutions to report data breaches.
Cyberspace Electronic Security Act (2000)	Reduces export restrictions.
Computer Security Enhancement Act (2000)	Protects federal government systems from hacking.
Electronic Signatures in Global and National Commerce Act (the "E-Sign Law") (2000)	Authorizes the use of electronic signatures in legal documents.
USA PATRIOT Act (2001)	Authorizes use of computer-based surveillance of suspected terrorists.
Homeland Security Act (2002)	Authorizes establishment of the Department of Homeland Security, which is responsible for developing a comprehensive national plan for security of the key resources and critical infrastructures of the United States; DHS becomes the central coordinator for all cyberspace security efforts.
CAN-SPAM Act (2003)	Although primarily a mechanism for civil and regulatory lawsuits against spammers, the CAN-SPAM Act also creates several new criminal offenses intended to address situations in which the perpetrator has taken steps to hide his or her identity or the source of the spam from recipients, ISPs, or law enforcement agencies. Also contains criminal sanctions for sending sexually explicit e-mail without designating it as such.
U.S. SAFE WEB Act (2006)	Enhances FTC's ability to obtain monetary redress for consumers in cases involving spyware, spam, Internet fraud, and deception; also improves FTC's ability to gather information and coordinate investigations with foreign counterparts.

tion focuses on requiring firms to report data breaches to the FTC, protection of the national electric grid, and cybersecurity have all failed to pass.

Private and Private-Public Cooperation Efforts

The good news is that e-commerce sites are not alone in their battle to achieve security on the Internet. Several organizations—some public and some private—are devoted to tracking down criminal organizations and individuals engaged in attacks against Internet and e-commerce sites. One of the better-known private organizations is the **CERT Coordination Center** (formerly known as the Computer Emergency Response Team) at Carnegie Mellon University. CERT monitors and tracks online criminal activity reported to it by private corporations and government agencies that seek out its help. CERT is composed of full-time and part-time computer experts who can trace the origins of attacks against sites despite the complexity of the Internet. Its staff members also assist organizations in identifying security problems, developing solutions, and communicating with the public about widespread hacker threats. The CERT Coordination Center also provides product assessments, reports, and training in order to improve the public's knowledge and understanding of security threats and solutions. The U.S. Department of Homeland Security (DHS) operates the **United States Computer Emergency Readiness Team (US-CERT)**, which coordinates cyber incident warnings and responses across both the government and private sectors.

CERT Coordination Center
monitors and tracks online criminal activity reported to it by private corporations and government agencies that seek out its help

US-CERT
division of the U.S. Department of Homeland Security that coordinates cyber incident warnings and responses across government and private sectors

Government Policies and Controls on Encryption Software

As noted in the beginning of this chapter, governments have sought to restrict availability and export of encryption systems as a means of detecting and preventing crime and terrorism. In the United States, both Congress and the executive branch have sought to regulate the uses of encryption. At the international level, four organizations have influenced the international traffic in encryption software: the Organization for Economic Cooperation and Development (OECD), G-7/G-8 (the heads of state of the top eight industrialized countries in the world), the Council of Europe, and the Wassenar Arrangement (law enforcement personnel from the top 33 industrialized counties in the world) (EPIC, 2000). Various governments have proposed schemes for controlling encryption software or at least preventing criminals from obtaining strong encryption tools (see **Table 5.6**).

TABLE 5.6	GOVERNMENT EFFORTS TO REGULATE AND CONTROL ENCRYPTION
REGULATORY EFFORT	**IMPACT**
Restricted export of strong security systems	Supported primarily by the United States. Widespread distribution of encryption schemes weakens this policy. The policy is changing to permit exports except to pariah countries.
Key escrow/key recovery schemes	France, the United Kingdom, and the United States supported this effort in the late 1990s but now have largely abandoned it. There are few trusted third parties.
Lawful access and forced disclosure	Growing support in recent U.S. legislation and in OECD countries.
Official hacking	All countries are rapidly expanding budgets and training for law enforcement "technical centers" aimed at monitoring and cracking computer-based, encryption activities of suspected criminals.

5.5   PAYMENT SYSTEMS

TYPES OF PAYMENT SYSTEMS

In order to understand e-commerce payment systems, you first need to be familiar with the various types of generic payment systems. Then you will be able to clarify the different requirements that e-commerce payment systems must meet and identify the opportunities provided by e-commerce technology for developing new types of payment systems. There are five main types of payment systems: cash, checking transfer, credit cards, stored value, and accumulating balance.

Cash

cash
legal tender defined by a national authority to represent value

Cash, which is legal tender defined by a national authority to represent value, is the most common form of payment in terms of number of transactions. The key feature of cash is that it is instantly convertible into other forms of value without the intermediation of any other institution. For instance, free airline miles are not cash because they are not instantly convertible into other forms of value—they require intermediation by a third party (the airline) in order to be exchanged for value (an airline ticket). Private organizations sometimes create a form of private cash called scrip that can be instantly redeemed by participating organizations for goods or cash. Examples include trading stamps, "point" programs, and other forms of consumer loyalty currency.

Why is cash still so popular today? Cash is portable, requires no authentication, and provides instant purchasing power for those who possess it. Cash allows for micropayments (payments of small amounts). The use of cash is "free" in that neither merchants nor consumers pay a transaction fee for using it. Using cash does not require any complementary assets, such as special hardware or the existence of an account, and it puts very low cognitive demands on the user. Cash is anonymous and difficult to trace, and in that sense it is "private." Other forms of payment require significant use of third parties and leave an extensive digital or paper trail.

float
the period of time between a purchase and actual payment for the purchase

On the other hand, cash is limited to smaller transactions (you can't easily buy a car or house with cash), it is easily stolen, and it does not provide any **float** (the period of time between a purchase and actual payment for the purchase); when it is spent, it is gone. With cash, purchases tend to be final and irreversible (i.e., they are irrefutable) unless otherwise agreed by the seller.

checking transfer
funds transferred directly via a signed draft or check from a consumer's checking account to a merchant or other individual

Checking Transfer

A **checking transfer**, which represents funds transferred directly via a signed draft or check from a consumer's checking account to a merchant or other individual, is the second most common form of payment in the United States in terms of number of transactions, and the most common in terms of total amount spent.

Checks can be used for both small and large transactions, although typically they are not used for micropayments (less than $1). Checks have some float (it can take up to 10 days for out-of-state checks to clear), and the unspent balances can earn interest. Checks are not anonymous and require third-party institutions to work. Checks also introduce security risks for merchants: They can be forged more easily than cash, so authentication is required. For merchants, checks also present some additional risk compared to cash because they can be canceled before they clear the account or they may bounce if there is not enough money in the account.

Credit Card

A **credit card** represents an account that extends credit to consumers, permits consumers to purchase items while deferring payment, and allows consumers to make payments to multiple vendors with one instrument. **Credit card associations** such as Visa and MasterCard are nonprofit associations that set standards for the **issuing banks**—such as Citibank—that actually issue the credit cards and process transactions. Other third parties (called **processing centers** or **clearinghouses**) usually handle verification of accounts and balances. Credit card issuing banks act as financial intermediaries, minimizing the risk to transacting parties.

Credit cards offer consumers a line of credit and the ability to make small and large purchases instantly. They are widely accepted as a form of payment, reduce the risk of theft associated with carrying cash, and increase consumer convenience. Credit cards also offer consumers considerable float. With a credit card, for instance, a consumer typically need not actually pay for goods purchased until receiving a credit card bill 30 days later. Merchants benefit from increased consumer spending resulting from credit card use, but they pay a hefty transaction fee of 3% to 5% of the purchase price to the issuing banks. In addition, federal Regulation Z places the risks of the transaction (such as credit card fraud, repudiation of the transaction, or nonpayment) largely on the merchant and credit card issuing bank. Regulation Z limits cardholder liability to $50 for unauthorized transactions that occur before the card issuer is notified. Once a card is reported stolen, consumers are not liable for any subsequent charges.

Credit cards have less finality than other payment systems because consumers can refute or repudiate purchases under certain circumstances, and they limit risk for consumers while raising risk for merchants and bankers.

Stored Value

Accounts created by depositing funds into an account and from which funds are paid out or withdrawn as needed are **stored value payment systems**. Stored value payment systems are similar in some respects to checking transfers—which also store funds—but do not involve writing a check. Examples include debit cards, gift certificates, prepaid cards, and smart cards (described in greater detail later in the chapter). **Debit cards** immediately debit a checking or other demand-deposit account. For many consumers, the use of a debit card eliminates the need to write a paper check. There were almost 550 million debit cards in use nationwide in 2011 (The Nilson Report,

credit card
represents an account that extends credit to consumers, permits consumers to purchase items while deferring payment, and allows consumers to make payments to multiple vendors at one time

credit card association
nonprofit association that sets standards for issuing banks

issuing bank
bank that actually issues credit cards and processes transactions

processing center (clearinghouse)
institution that handles verification of accounts and balances

stored value payment system
account created by depositing funds into an account and from which funds are paid out or withdrawn as needed

debit card
immediately debits a checking or other demand-deposit account

2012). However, because debit cards are dependent on funds being available in a consumer's bank account, larger purchases are still typically paid for by credit card, and their use in the United States still lags behind that of other developed nations, in part because they do not have the protections provided by Regulation Z and they do not provide any float.

Peer-to-peer (P2P) payment systems such as PayPal (discussed further in Section 5.6) are variations on the stored value concept. P2P payment systems do not insist on prepayment but do require an account with a stored value, either a checking account with funds available or a credit card with an available credit balance. PayPal is often referred to as a P2P payment system because it allows small merchants and individuals to accept payments without using a merchant bank or processor to clear the transaction.

Accumulating Balance

accumulating balance payment system

account that accumulates expenditures and to which consumers makes periodic payments

Accounts that accumulate expenditures and to which consumers make periodic payments are **accumulating balance payment systems**. Traditional examples include utility, phone, and American Express accounts, all of which accumulate balances, usually over a specified period (typically a month), and then are paid in full at the end of the period.

PAYMENT SYSTEMS STAKEHOLDERS

The main stakeholders in payment systems are consumers, merchants, financial intermediaries, and government regulators. Each of these stakeholders have different preferences. Consumers are interested primarily in low-risk, low-cost, refutable (able to be repudiated or denied), convenient, and reliable payment mechanisms. Consumers have demonstrated they will not use new payment mechanisms unless they are equally or more beneficial to them than existing systems. In general, most consumers use cash, checks, and/or credit cards. The specific payment system chosen will change depending on the transaction situation. For instance, cash may be preferred to keep certain transactions private and anonymous, but the same consumer may want a record of transaction for the purchase of a car.

Merchants are interested primarily in low-risk, low-cost, irrefutable (i.e., final), secure, and reliable payment mechanisms. Merchants currently carry much of the risk of checking and credit card fraud, refutability of charges, and much of the hardware cost of verifying payments. Merchants typically prefer payments made by cash, check, and to a lesser extent credit cards, which usually carry high fees and allow transactions to be repudiated after the fact by consumers.

Financial intermediaries, such as banks and credit card networks, are primarily interested in secure payment systems that transfer risks and costs to consumers and merchants, while maximizing transaction fees payable to themselves. The preferred payment mechanisms for financial intermediaries are checking transfers, debit cards, and credit cards.

Government regulators are interested in maintaining trust in the financial system. Regulators seek to protect against fraud and abuse in the use of payment systems;

ensure that the interests of consumers and merchants are balanced against the interests of the financial intermediaries whom they regulate; and enforce information reporting laws. The most important regulations of payment systems in the United States are Regulation Z, Regulation E, and the Electronic Funds Transfer Act (EFTA) of 1978, regulating ATM machines. Regulation Z limits the risk to consumers when using credit cards. In contrast, EFTA and Regulation E place more risk on consumers when using debit or ATM cards. For instance, if you lose an ATM card or debit card, you are potentially liable for any losses to the account. However, in reality, Visa and MasterCard have issued policies that limit consumer risk for loss of debit cards to the same $50 that applies to credit cards.

5.6 E-COMMERCE PAYMENT SYSTEMS

For the most part, existing payment mechanisms have been able to be adapted to the online environment, albeit with some significant limitations that have led to efforts to develop alternatives. In addition, new types of purchasing relationships, such as between individuals online, and new technologies, such as the development of the mobile platform, have also created both a need and an opportunity for the development of new payment systems. In this section, we provide an overview of the major e-commerce payment systems in use today. **Table 5.7** lists some of the major trends in e-commerce payments in 2012–2013.

Online payment represents a market of more than $360 billion in 2012. Institutions and business firms that can handle this volume of transactions (mostly the large banking and credit firms) generally extract 2%–3% of the transactions in the form of fees, or about $7 to $10 billion a year in revenue. Given the size of the market, competition for online payments is spirited.

In the United States, the primary form of online payment is still the existing credit card system. Although credit card usage slipped somewhat during the recession, the total payments volume for online use of credit cards by U.S. consumers is expected to climb by over 50% in the five-year period from 2011 to 2016, compared to just a 2% increase for debit card usage during the same period. Alternative payments, although currently representing less than 20% of e-commerce transactions, are also expected

TABLE 5.7	MAJOR TRENDS IN E-COMMERCE PAYMENTS 2012–2013

- Payment by credit and/or debit card remains the dominant form of online payment.
- PayPal remains the most popular alternative payment method online.
- Start-up Square begins to gain traction with a smartphone app, credit card reader, and credit card processing service that permits anyone to accept credit card payments.
- Google introduces Google Wallet, a mobile payment system based on near field communication (NFC) chips.

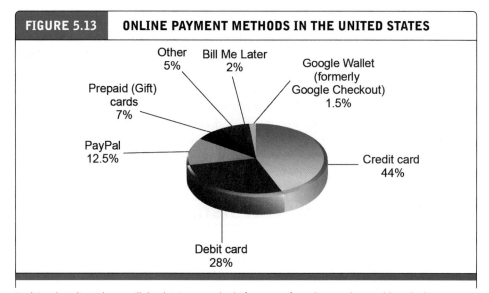

FIGURE 5.13 ONLINE PAYMENT METHODS IN THE UNITED STATES

Traditional credit cards are still the dominant method of payment for online purchases, although alternative methods such as PayPal and mobile payments are faster growing.

SOURCES: Based on data from Internet Retailer, 2012; Javelin Strategy & Research, 2011; industry sources.

to continue to make inroads into traditional payment methods (Javelin Strategy & Research, 2011). **Figure 5.13** illustrates the approximate usage of various payment types. PayPal is the most popular alternative to usage of credit and debit cards online.

In other parts of the world, e-commerce payments can be very different depending on traditions and infrastructure. Credit cards are not nearly as dominant a form of online payment as they are in the United States. If you plan on operating a Web site in Europe, Asia, or Latin America, you will need to develop different payment systems for each region. Consumers in Europe rely for the most part on bank debit cards (especially in Germany) and some credit cards. Online purchases in China are typically paid for by check or cash when the consumer picks up the goods at a local store. In Japan, consumers use postal and bank transfers and CODs, using local convenience stores (konbini) as the pickup and payment point. Japanese consumers also use accumulated balance accounts with the telephone company for Internet purchases made from their home computers. Japan and some European countries make extensive use of mobile phones for payment of small purchases (and even parking tickets).

ONLINE CREDIT CARD TRANSACTIONS

Because credit and debit cards are the dominant form of online payment, it is important to understand how they work and to recognize the strengths and weaknesses of this payment system. Online credit card transactions are processed in much the same way that in-store purchases are, with the major differences being that online merchants never see the actual card being used, no card impression is taken, and no signature is available. Online credit card transactions most closely resemble Mail Order-Telephone Order (MOTO) transactions. These types of purchases are also called Cardholder Not Present (CNP) transactions and are the major reason that charges can be disputed later by consumers. Since the merchant never sees the credit card, nor receives a hand-signed agreement to pay from the customer, when disputes arise, the merchant faces the risk that the transaction may be disallowed and reversed, even though he has already shipped the goods or the user has downloaded a digital product.

Figure 5.14 illustrates the online credit card purchasing cycle. There are five parties involved in an online credit card purchase: consumer, merchant, clearinghouse, merchant bank (sometimes called the "acquiring bank"), and the consumer's card-issuing bank. In order to accept payments by credit card, online merchants must have a merchant account established with a bank or financial institution. A **merchant account** is simply a bank account that allows companies to process credit card payments and receive funds from those transactions.

As shown in Figure 5.14, an online credit card transaction begins with a purchase (1). When a consumer wants to make a purchase, he or she adds the item to the merchant's shopping cart. When the consumer wants to pay for the items in the shopping cart, a secure tunnel through the Internet is created using SSL. Using encryption, SSL secures the session during which credit card information will be sent to the mer-

merchant account
a bank account that allows companies to process credit card payments and receive funds from those transactions

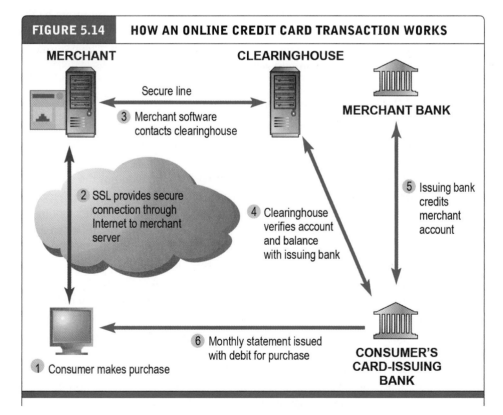

FIGURE 5.14   HOW AN ONLINE CREDIT CARD TRANSACTION WORKS

MERCHANT

CLEARINGHOUSE

Secure line

3 Merchant software contacts clearinghouse

MERCHANT BANK

5 Issuing bank credits merchant account

2 SSL provides secure connection through Internet to merchant server

4 Clearinghouse verifies account and balance with issuing bank

6 Monthly statement issued with debit for purchase

1 Consumer makes purchase

CONSUMER'S CARD-ISSUING BANK

chant and protects the information from interlopers on the Internet (2). SSL does not authenticate either the merchant or the consumer. The transacting parties have to trust one another.

Once the consumer credit card information is received by the merchant, the merchant software contacts a clearinghouse (3). As previously noted, a clearinghouse is a financial intermediary that authenticates credit cards and verifies account balances. The clearinghouse contacts the issuing bank to verify the account information (4). Once verified, the issuing bank credits the account of the merchant at the merchant's bank (usually this occurs at night in a batch process) (5). The debit to the consumer account is transmitted to the consumer in a monthly statement (6).

Credit Card E-commerce Enablers

Companies that have a merchant account still need to buy or build a means of handling the online transaction; securing the merchant account is only step one in a two-part process. Today, Internet payment service providers (sometimes referred to as payment gateways) can provide both a merchant account and the software tools needed to process credit card purchases online.

For instance, Authorize.net is an Internet payment service provider. The company helps a merchant secure an account with one of its merchant account provider partners and then provides payment processing software for installation on the merchant's server. The software collects the transaction information from the merchant's site and then routes it via the Authorize.net "payment gateway" to the appropriate bank, ensuring that customers are authorized to make their purchases. The funds for the transaction are then transferred to the merchant's merchant account. CyberSource is another well-known Internet payment service provider.

Limitations of Online Credit Card Payment Systems

There are a number of limitations to the existing credit card payment system. The most important limitations involve security, merchant risk, administrative and transaction costs, and social equity.

The existing system offers poor security. Neither the merchant nor the consumer can be fully authenticated. The merchant could be a criminal organization designed to collect credit card numbers, and the consumer could be a thief using stolen or fraudulent cards. The risk facing merchants is high: consumers can repudiate charges even though the goods have been shipped or the product downloaded. The banking industry attempted to develop a secure electronic transaction (SET) protocol, but this effort failed because it was too complex for consumers and merchants alike.

The administrative costs of setting up an online credit card system and becoming authorized to accept credit cards are high. Transaction costs for merchants are also significant—roughly 3.5% of the purchase plus a transaction fee of 20–30 cents per transaction, plus other setup fees.

Credit cards are not very democratic, even though they seem ubiquitous. Millions of young adults do not have credit cards, along with almost 100 million other adult Americans who cannot afford cards or who are considered poor risks because of low incomes.

ALTERNATIVE ONLINE PAYMENT SYSTEMS

The limitations of the online credit card system have opened the way for the development of a number of alternative online payment systems. Chief among them is PayPal. PayPal (purchased by eBay in 2002) enables individuals and businesses with e-mail accounts to make and receive payments up to a specified limit. Paypal is an example of an **online stored value payment system**, which permits consumers to make instant, online payments to merchants and other individuals based on value stored in an online account. In 2011, PayPal processed $118 billion in payments ($40 billion of which were generated on eBay, and $78 billion elsewhere on the Web), and had 104 million active registered users. PayPal builds on the existing financial infrastructure of the countries in which it operates. You establish a PayPal account by specifying a credit, debit, or checking account you wish to have charged or paid when conducting online transactions. When you make a payment using PayPal, you e-mail the payment to the merchant's PayPal account. PayPal transfers the amount from your credit or checking account to the merchant's bank account. The beauty of PayPal is that no personal credit information has to be shared among the users, and the service can be used by individuals to pay one another even in small amounts. Issues with PayPal include its high cost (in addition to paying the credit card fee of 3.5%, PayPal tacks on a variable fee of from 1.5%–3% depending on the size of the transaction) and its lack of consumer protections when a fraud occurs or a charge is repudiated. PayPal is discussed in further depth in the case study at the end of the chapter.

> **online stored value payment system**
> permits consumers to make instant, online payments to merchants and other individuals based on value stored in an online account

Although PayPal is by far the most well-known and commonly used online credit/debit card alternative, there are a number of other alternatives as well. Amazon Payments is aimed at consumers who have concerns about entrusting their credit card information to unfamiliar online retailers. Consumers can purchase goods and services at non-Amazon Web sites using the payment methods stored in their Amazon accounts, without having to reenter their payment information at the merchant's site. Amazon provides the payment processing. Google Checkout (now merged into Google Wallet, described further in the following section on Mobile Payments) offers similar functionality, enabling consumers to sign in once and then shop online at thousands of different stores without having to reenter account information.

Bill Me Later also appeals to consumers to do not wish to enter their credit card information online. Bill Me Later describes itself as an open-ended credit account. Users select the Bill Me Later option at checkout and are asked to provide their birth date and the last four digits of their social security number. They are then billed for the purchase by Bill Me Later within 10 to 14 days. Bill Me Later is currently offered by more than 1,000 online merchants.

WUPay (formerly eBillme, and now operated by Western Union) offers a similar service. WUPay customers who select the WUPay option at firms such as Sears, Kmart, Buy.com, and other retailers do not have to provide any credit card information. Instead they are e-mailed a bill, which they can pay via their bank's online bill payment service, or in person at any Western Union location. Dwolla is a similar cash-based payment network for both individuals and merchants. It bypasses the credit card network and instead connects directly into a bank account. Dwolla is free for transactions under $10 and only 25 cents per transaction for those over $10, and is currently available at more than 15,000 merchants.

Like Dwolla, Stripe is another company that is attempting to provide an alternative to the traditional online credit card system. Stripe focuses on the merchant side of the process. It provides simple software code that enables companies to bypass much of the administrative costs involved in setting up an online credit card system, and instead lets companies begin accepting credit card payments almost immediately without the need to obtain a merchant account or use a gateway provider. Unlike PayPal, the customer doesn't need a Stripe account to pay, and all payments are made directly to company rather than being routed through a third party.

MOBILE PAYMENT SYSTEMS: YOUR SMARTPHONE WALLET

near field communication (NFC)

a set of short-range wireless technologies used to share information among devices

The use of mobile devices as payment mechanisms is already well established in Europe, Japan, and South Korea and is expanding rapidly in the United States, where the infrastructure to support mobile payment is finally being put in place, especially with the advent of smartphones equipped with near field communication chips. **Near field communication (NFC)** is a set of short-range wireless technologies used to share information among devices within about 2 inches of each other (50 mm). NFC devices are either powered or passive. A connection requires one powered unit (the initiator), and one target unpowered unit that can respond to requests from the powered unit. NFC targets can be very simple forms such as tags, stickers, key fobs, or readers. NFC peer-to-peer communication is possible where both devices are powered. An NFC-equipped smartphone, for instance, can be swiped by a merchant's reader to record a payment wirelessly and without contact. In September 2011, Google introduced Google Wallet, a mobile app designed to work with NFC chips. Google Wallet currently works with the MasterCard PayPass contactless payment card system. It is also designed to work with Android smartphones that are equipped with NFC chips, although, as of September 2012, there are few such smartphones on the market in the United States. PayPal and start-up Square are attacking the mobile payment market from a different direction, with apps and credit card readers that attach to smartphones.

In 2012, mobile retail purchases are expected to total around $11.6 billion. The promise of riches beyond description to a firm that is able to dominate the mobile payments marketplace has set off what one commentator has called a goat rodeo surrounding the development of new technologies and methods of mobile payment. The end-of-chapter case study, *Online Payment Marketplace: Goat Rodeo,* provides a further look at the future of online and mobile payment in the United States, including the efforts of PayPal, Google, Square, and others.

DIGITAL CASH AND VIRTUAL CURRENCIES

digital cash

an alternative payment system in which unique, authenticated tokens represent cash value

Although the terms digital cash and virtual currencies are often used synonymously, they actually refer to two separate types of alternative payment systems. **Digital cash** is typically based on an algorithm that generates unique authenticated tokens representing cash value that can be used "in the real world." Examples of digital cash include Bitcoin and Ukash. Bitcoins are encrypted numbers (sometimes referred to as cryptocurrency) that are generated by a complex algorithm using a peer-to-peer network in a process referred to as "mining," that requires extensive computing power. Like real currency, Bitcoins have a fluctuating value tied to open-market trading. Like cash, Bitcoins are anonymous—they are exchanged via a 34-character alphanumeric address that the user has, and do not require any other identifying information. Bitcoins have recently attracted a lot of attention as a potential money laundering tool for cyber-criminals, and have also been plagued by security issues, with some high-profile heists. For example, in September 2012, hackers stole $250,000 worth of Bitcoins from BitFloor, a New York-based company that allows account holders to buy and sell Bitcoins and exchange them for U.S. dollars using the Automated Clearing House (ACH) system. Another group of hacktivists threatened to release Mitt Romney's tax returns unless they were paid $1 million in Bitcoins. Nonetheless, there are companies, such as BitPay, that are touting Bitcoins as a legitimate alternative payment system, and trying to make it easier for merchants to accept them. Ukash is another digital cash system that uses a unique 19-digit code, and can be stored online in an eWallet. Ukash can be purchased at more than 420,000 retail locations around the globe, and used wherever it is accepted.

Virtual currencies, on the other hand, typically circulate primarily within an internal virtual world community, such as Linden Dollars, created by Linden Lab for use in its virtual world, Second Life, or are associated with a specific corporation, such as Facebook Credits. Both types are typically used for purchasing virtual goods.

virtual currency
typically circulates within an internal virtual world community or is issued by a specific corporate entity, and used to purchase virtual goods

5.7 ELECTRONIC BILLING PRESENTMENT AND PAYMENT

In 2007, for the first time, the number of bill payments made online exceeded the number of physical checks written (Fiserv, 2007). In the $15.6 trillion U.S. economy with an $11.1 trillion consumer sector for goods and services, there are a lot of bills to pay. No one knows for sure, but some experts believe the life-cycle cost of a paper bill for a business, from point of issuance to point of payment, ranges from $3 to $7. This calculation does not include the value of time to consumers, who must open bills, read them, write checks, address envelopes, stamp, and then mail remittances. The billing market represents an extraordinary opportunity for using the Internet as an electronic billing and payment system that potentially could greatly reduce both the cost of paying bills and the time consumers spend paying them. Estimates vary, but online payments are believed to cost between only 20 to 30 cents to process.

Electronic billing presentment and payment (EBPP) systems are systems that enable the online delivery and payment of monthly bills. EBPP services allow consumers to view bills electronically and pay them through electronic funds transfers from bank or credit card accounts. More and more companies are choosing to issue statements and bills electronically, rather than mailing out paper versions. But even those businesses that do mail paper bills are increasingly offering online bill payment as an option to customers, allowing them to immediately transfer funds from a bank or credit card account to pay a bill somewhere else.

electronic billing presentment and payment (EBPP) system
form of online payment systems for monthly bills

MARKET SIZE AND GROWTH

There were just 12 million U.S households (11% of all households) using online bill payment in 2001. In 2011, according to the financial technology firm Fiserv, an estimated 40 million U.S. households used online bill payment at a financial institution, while 53 million used biller-direct bill payment, in each case an 11% increase over 2010. Online bill payments now account for half of all bill payments, while paper checks now account for less than 25% (Fiserv, 2012).

One major reason for the surge in EBPP usage is that companies are starting to realize how much money they can save through online billing. Not only is there the savings in postage and processing, but payments can be received more quickly (3 to 12 days faster, compared to paper bills sent via regular mail), thereby improving cash flow. In order to realize these savings, many companies are becoming more aggressive in encouraging their customers to move to EBPP by instituting a charge for the privilege of continuing to receive a paper bill.

Financials don't tell the whole story, however. Companies are discovering that a bill is both a sales opportunity and a customer retention opportunity, and that the electronic medium provides many more options when it comes to marketing and promotion. Rebates, savings offers, cross-selling, and upselling are all possible in the digital realm.

Consumers are also becoming more receptive to online bill payment. A survey by Fiserv found that over 30% of the online banking customers not already using online bill payment had expressed interest in using the service within the coming year. The primary benefits cited by users were speed, ease of use, and control (Fiserv, 2012).

EBPP BUSINESS MODELS

There are two main competing business models in the EBPP marketspace: biller-direct and consolidator. The biller-direct system was originally created by utility companies that send millions of bills each month. Their purpose is to make it easier for their customers to pay their utility bills routinely online. Today, telephone and credit card companies also frequently offer this service, as well as a number of individual stores. Companies implementing a biller-direct system can either develop their own system in-house (usually only an option for the very largest companies), install a system acquired from a third-party EBPP software vendor, use a third-party EBPP service bureau (the service bureau hosts a biller-branded Web site that enables consumers to view and pay bills and handles all customer enrollment, bill presentment, and payment processing), or use an application service provider (similar to a service bureau, but runs on the biller's Web site rather than being hosted on the service provider's Web site).

In the consolidator model, a third party, such as a financial institution or portal (either a general portal such as Yahoo! Bill Pay, or a focused portal such Intuit's Paytrust.com), aggregates all bills for consumers and ideally permits one-stop bill payment (pay anyone). Currently, financial institutions have been more successful than portals in attracting online bill payers. The consolidator model faces several challenges. For billers, using the consolidator model means an increased time lag between billing and payment, and also inserts an intermediary between the company and its customer. For consumers, security continues to be a major issue. Most consumers are unwilling to pay any kind of fee to pay bills online, and many are concerned about sharing personal financial information with non-financial institutions. Today, more and more banks are offering online bill payment free to some or all of their customers as an enticement.

Supporting these two primary business models are infrastructure providers such as Fiserv, Yodlee, FIS, Online Resources, MasterCard RPPS (Remote Payment and Presentment Service), and others that provide the software to create the EBPP system or handle billing and payment collection for the biller. **Figure 5.15** categorizes the major players in the EBPP marketspace.

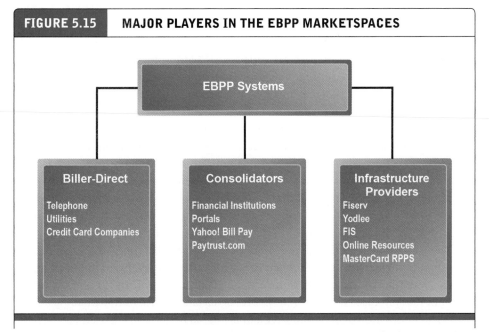

FIGURE 5.15   MAJOR PLAYERS IN THE EBPP MARKETSPACES

The main business models in the EBPP marketspace are biller-direct and consolidator. Infrastructure providers support both of these competing models and sometimes operate their own online payment portals.

| 5.8 | **CASE STUDY** |

Online Payment Marketplace:
Goat Rodeo

Nearly every day, it seems, a new online or mobile payment system is announced. The online payment marketplace is experiencing an explosion of innovative ideas, plans, and announcements, which one commentator has likened to a goat rodeo, a chaotic situation in which powerful players with different agendas compete with one another for public acceptance, and above all, huge potential revenues.

Others liken the payment marketplace to a battle among the titans of online payment and retailing: PayPal, credit card companies, telecommunications carriers like Verizon, AT&T, and T-Mobile, mobile hardware and software companies like Apple and Google, and even large retailers like Walmart and Target are all working to develop their very own online and mobile payment systems.

Each of these titans has its own version of a future payment system that challenges the other players. They all want to help us spend money and increase the convenience of shopping. They all want to not only gather the fees that such systems can produce, but also use it to gather oceans of personal consumer information and display ads throughout the payment transaction process, along with coupons, daily deals, and flash sales based on their knowledge of the consumer.

The continuing double-digit growth of e-commerce is certainly one factor driving market participants, but a more important factor is the emergence of the mobile platform of smartphones and tablets that opens the door for new firms to enter the online payment marketplace based on new technologies and control of the mobile platform itself. The future growth of online payment is mobile because that's where consumers are increasingly making their purchases and because the market is not yet dominated by any single player.

The overall online payment market in the United States is estimated to be worth about $362 billion in 2012 and is growing at more than 15% a year. While small compared to the total e-commerce picture, mobile commerce, driven by smartphones, tablets, and cellular networks, is growing at more than 20% a year, and a recent study by Juniper Research estimates that in 2015, mobile payment volume worldwide will reach $670 billion. And according to the Federal Reserve, U.S. consumers spent an estimated $3.3 trillion on 60 billion credit and debit card transactions in 2010. Even if a small percentage of these transactions move from plastic to mobile payments, the potential revenue is very large. This is enough to drive even old goats into a frenzy.

While credit and debit cards remain the dominant method of online payment, PayPal is currently the most successful alternative. Founded in 1998, PayPal was initially aimed at individuals buying and selling goods on eBay. PayPal allowed account holders to both receive and make payments in eBay auctions without revealing their

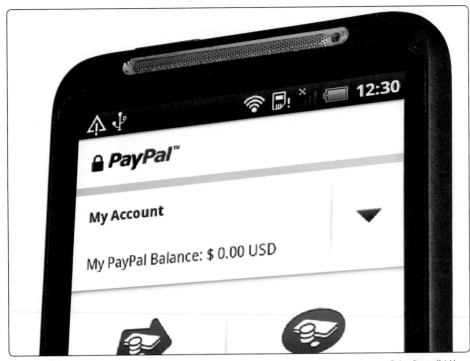

© Ian Dagnall / Alamy

credit card numbers, and without having to establish a credit card processing account with the credit card companies or merchant banks. Merchants did not have to purchase an expensive credit card swiping device or pay additional monthly fees. Sometimes called a "peer-to-peer" payment system, PayPal permitted users to e-mail payments to one another. Users established accounts by giving PayPal either a credit card number or a bank account number. PayPal offered security and convenience for both consumers and merchants. PayPal charged users a fee of 2%–3% for a retail transaction and 4% for a money transfer. eBay purchased PayPal in 2002, and PayPal has since expanded from its eBay foundation to the larger world of online payments at e-commerce sites.

PayPal is currently the largest alternative online payment service and accounts for about 78% of the alternative payment market. In 2011, PayPal cleared about $118 billion in payments worldwide. In the mobile payment marketplace, PayPal cleared about $4 billion in payments, about 30% of the overall mobile payment market. In mobile payments, PayPal is a much smaller player than in the larger alternative payment market. This situation gives competitors an opening to challenge PayPal.

Until March 2012, PayPal's mobile payment solution consisted of using an existing PayPal account with a mobile phone browser, just like paying from a desktop computer. While this system worked for purchasing goods while shopping online, it was of little use paying for coffee at the local Starbucks or purchasing goods and services from a local merchant. In March 2012, PayPal introduced PayPal Here, a card reader that plugs into a cell phone and can accept credit card payments, as well as check payments by taking a photo of the check. The card reader device and local accounting for payments is powered by a free smartphone app. PayPal charges 2.7% of each mobile transaction.

PayPal was late to the smartphone mobile payment market, beaten to the punch by a start-up firm called Square. Square started in 2009 with a smartphone app, credit card reader, and credit card processing service that allows anyone—businesses and individuals--to accept credit card payments. Square is one of the fastest growing e-commerce payment firms. Co-founder Jack Dorsey is a serial entrepreneur: he is a co-founder of Twitter. Initial funding for Square was provided by its founders and a $10 million investment led by Khosla Ventures in December 2009. The company was valued at $45 million and had 25 employees. In January 2011, Square received a $27.5 million venture investment led by Sequoia Capital, which valued the company at $240 million. In June 2011, Square received a $100 million investment from Kleiner Perkins Caufield and Byers, which valued the company at $1 billion. Finally, in September 2012, the company raised $200 million from Citibank, Visa, and Starbucks. The company is now valued at $3.9 billion, and the firm now has 400 employees.

Today more than 2 million Square users are swiping away. The technology is quite simple: a square-shaped credit card reader plugs into smartphones and tablet computers loaded with a Square app that processes the credit card information. Versions are available for iOS and Android devices. Users can sign up online by registering a credit card with Square. Square charges merchants 2.75% of each transaction for the service, and there are no additional fees, minimums, or financial statements to file. In contrast, credit card fees for merchants typically range from 3% to 5%. Analysts believe that Square loses money on transactions less than $10, given that it must pay credit companies over 2% for their payment clearance. The future of Square will depend on the revenues it can derive from selling consumer information and placing ads on its payment system.

Square's initial credit card reader product was aimed at a market that was poorly served by credit card companies: small businesses like coffee shops, news stands, small retailers, and farmers' market merchants, as well as piano teachers, baby sitters, and taxi drivers. A poll by the National Retail Federation in 2012 found that 50% of businesses planned to use a mobile device as a cash register in the next 18 months. How many "small businesses" are there? There are 7.6 million businesses in the United States, and 6.5 million have fewer than 20 employees. These small firms employ about 30 million people and generate about $1 trillion in revenues. Mobile payment systems are aimed directly at this large, underserved marketplace.

In March 2011, Square introduced its second product: Square Register, an app for the iPad that turns the iPad into a cash register. Voila: restaurants and small shops no longer needed to buy an expensive digital cash register or a credit card swiping machine from Verifone. What's more, the merchant can take the iPad home to watch movies when not used as a cash register! In May 2012, Square released the second version of Square Register, which has a more sophisticated business suite of accounting, inventory, and analytics software that allows merchants to identify best-selling items and time-of-day purchase patterns.

With a new app called Pay With Square introduced in July 2012, Square plans to make contact-less payments possible by simply entering the premises of a business, and using a photo as a personal ID in combination with a Square Register. In this system, there's no need to swipe a credit card. Here's how it will work. You enter your name, photo, and credit card number into your smartphone's Pay With Square app. Using the phone's GPS, the app identifies merchants nearby that use Pay With Square. On entering the shop, you press an icon and the app sends your payment information and photo to the Square Register. After ordering your sandwich, you pay by saying your name to the merchant who checks your photo on the Square Register to ensure it's really you.

Square claims that 75,000 merchants now use Square Registers and that the company clears more than $8 billion in transactions annually. PayPal, Groupon, and Intuit have developed copycat versions of the same idea: payments for very small businesses based on smartphone and tablet card readers. Groupon's card reader system is linked to its daily deals.

The key for all these payment systems is scale: getting enough consumers and merchants to adopt the Square dongle and purchase the iPads needed for the Square Register. Square received a tremendous boost in achieving scale in August 2012 when Starbucks agreed to use Square for all its credit card transactions in the United States. Starbucks has plenty of scale: 17,000 stores worldwide and 13,000 in the United States. Analysts believe that with Starbucks as a partner, Square will come to dominate the card swiping marketplace, and potentially play a large role in other contact-less payment schemes.

While PayPal and Square duke it out in the card swiping payment market for small merchants, other payment schemes and plans that take advantage of the full capabilities of mobile devices are being announced monthly, if not daily. The greatest potential in the next five years for mobile payment systems are systems based on NFC. So-called "swipe and pay" systems, NFC enables a direct secure communication link between the consumer's smartphone and the merchant's cash register. All that's needed is to bring the smartphone in close proximity (six inches) to the cash register. The two biggest players in the NFC payment market are the telecommunication carriers' Isis system and Google's Google Wallet. A third stealth player is Merchant Customer Exchange (MCX), which is being created by some of the largest retailers in the United States.

Isis is a mobile swipe and pay venture backed by Verizon, AT&T, and T-Mobile, originally announced in 2010. To date, Isis has lined up Chase, Visa, MasterCard, Capital One, and American Express to process credit card transactions. While a beta test was planned in September 2012, the tests have been delayed by difficulties in lining up merchants who will need to purchase NFC terminals or cash registers, and consumers who will need smartphones that have NFC chips built into them. When the Apple iPhone 5 did not include an NFC chip, the prospects for an NFC payment system in the United States dimmed a bit, but are certainly not extinguished given that Samsung's Android phones now have NFC chips installed. Isis planned a test of its payment system for September 2012 in Salt Lake City and Austin. Why Salt Lake City? Its metro transit system already uses NFC terminals to accept payment from riders' smartphones. The test was postponed for undisclosed reasons.

Google Wallet is an online payment system originally designed for desktop PCs, but Google has now extended it to include a mobile component in partnership with Sprint, Citibank, and MasterCard. Google has included support for the operation of

SOURCES: "Groupon Launches Credit Card Payment Business," by Alistair Barr and Nivedita Bhattachrjee, Reuters, September 19, 2012; "Delays Strike Mobile-Payments Test," by Robin Sidel, Wall Street Journal, September 13, 2012; "Square Closes Financing Round," by Evelyn M. Rusli, New York Times, September 17, 2012; "Can Square Remain Hip?" by Petere Eavis, New York Times, August 31, 2012; "Big Retailers Team Up On Mobile Payments Plan," Reuters, August 15, 2012; "Payments Network Takes on Google," by Robin Sidel, Wall Street Journal, August 15, 2012; "Square Gets a Jolt From Starbucks," by Rolfe Winkler and Andrew R. Johnson, Wall Street Journal, August 8, 2012; "Starbucks and Square to Team Up" by Claire Cain Miller, New York Times, August 8, 2012; "Pay By Voice? So Long Wallet," by David Pogue, New York Times, July 18, 2012; "Many Competing Paths on the Road to the Phone Wallet," by Joshua Brustein, New York Times, May 6, 2012; "PayPal Takes on Start-Up," by Stu Woo, Wall Street Journal,

March 16, 2012; "Retailers Join Payment Chase," by Robin Sidel, *Wall Street Journal*, March 2, 2012; "Mobile Payments: Moving Closer to a World without Wallets," by eMarketer, Inc., September 2011; "Look at All Those Zeros: Square Raises $100 Million at $1 Billion Valuation," by Tricia Duryee, Allthingsd.com, June 28, 2011; Verizon to Add Payment Option," by Roger Cheng, *Wall Street Journal*, June 10, 2011; "Google Unveils Smartphone Pay Service, PayPal Sues," by Peter Svenson and Michael Liedtke, *Wall Street Journal*, May 27, 2011; "Payment Method Bypasses the Wallet," by Claire Cain Miller, *New York Times*, May 23, 2011; "Visa Advances Toward a Digital Wallet," by Jenna Wortham, *New York Times*, May 11, 2011; "Bill Paying Made Easier, But For a Fee," by Ann Cairns, *New York Times*, May 10, 2011; "Isis Says Carrier-backed Mobile Payments 'Accelerated,' Not 'Dialing Back,'" Matt Hamblen, *Computerworld*, May 4, 2011; "Google Sets Role in Mobile Payment," by Amir Efrati and Robin Sidel, *Wall Street Journal*, March 28, 2011; "Swiping Is the Easy Part," by Tara Bernard and Claire Miller, *New York Times*, March 21, 2011; "The Technology Behind Mobile Payments," by Nick Bilton, *New York Times*, March 21, 2011; "Your Mobile Phone is Becoming Your Wallet," by Laurie Segall, CNN Money, January 19, 2011; "Bump Technologies Expands and Raises Money," by Claire Cain Miller, *New York Times*, January 11, 2011

NFC chips into the latest version of its Android smartphone operating system. Samsung's Galaxy phones are the only phones sold in the United States that have a built-in NFC chip. Google Wallet is the only NFC system that is operational, and Google claims that it is available at 150,000 merchants. In Google's system, customers tap the merchant's NFC terminal at check out. Called Tap & Go, Google offers its payment system with no charge to credit card companies and will not take a slice of transactions like Isis, and other mobile payment systems. Instead, Google will retain the right to display ads, coupons, loyalty programs, and daily deals by local merchants nearby on the user's mobile screen. As with the Isis program, widespread use of Google Wallet will require cooperation from handset makers and merchants who will be required to invest in new hardware.

Merchant Customer Exchange (MCX) is an NFC payment system being developed by Walmart, Target, Sears, 7-Eleven Inc., Sunoco, and 10 other national pharmacies, supermarkets, and restaurant chains. Announced in March 2012, the backers of this effort have annual sales of more than $1 trillion dollars. That's enough to make everyone involved in mobile payments stand up and listen, even Google.

So far, MCX has not released a system, but when it does, it will reportedly use NFC. Customers will be able to download an app to their smartphone and make purchases by tapping the phone against an NFC reader by the cash register. Why are these nationwide merchants willing to invest billions in a mobile payment system when financial service firms and technology players are also investing billions in competing systems? The answer is control over the customer during the transaction, and the information on customer purchase history that the apps will be recording. The merchants do not want this valuable marketing asset of personal information to flow to financial service firms or Google.

The future for smartphone mobile payments is assured given the size of the players involved, the potential rewards for successful players, and the demands of consumers for a payment system that does not involve swiping plastic cards and dealing with slips of paper. But it is unlikely that all the payment systems described above will survive, and also quite likely that consumers will remain confused by all their payment options for some time yet to come.

Case Study Questions

1. What is the value proposition that Square offers consumers? How about merchants? What are some of the weaknesses of Square's system?

2. Why would telecommunications carriers like AT&T and Verizon want to move into the payments business? What chance do they have to compete against Google? What's their advantage?

3. What advantages does PayPal have in the mobile payment market? What are its weaknesses?

4. What strategies would you recommend that PayPal pursue in order to translate its dominance in alternative online payments into a strong position in the emerging mobile payment market, especially in on-premise payments?

5.9 REVIEW

KEY CONCEPTS

■ **Understand the scope of e-commerce crime and security problems.**

While the overall size of cybercrime is unclear at this time, cybercrime against e-commerce sites is growing rapidly, the amount of losses is growing, and the management of e-commerce sites must prepare for a variety of criminal assaults.

■ **Describe the key dimensions of e-commerce security.**

There are six key dimensions to e-commerce security:
- *Integrity*—ensures that information displayed on a Web site or sent or received via the Internet has not been altered in any way by an unauthorized party.
- *Nonrepudiation*—ensures that e-commerce participants do not deny (repudiate) their online actions.
- *Authenticity*—verifies an individual's or business's identity.
- *Confidentiality*—determines whether information shared online, such as through e-mail communication or an order process, can be viewed by anyone other than the intended recipient.
- *Privacy*—deals with the use of information shared during an online transaction. Consumers want to limit the extent to which their personal information can be divulged to other organizations, while merchants want to protect such information from falling into the wrong hands.
- *Availability*—determines whether a Web site is accessible and operational at any given moment.

■ **Understand the tension between security and other values.**

Although computer security is considered necessary to protect e-commerce activities, it is not without a downside. Two major areas where there are tensions between security and Web site operations include:
- *Ease of use*—The more security measures that are added to an e-commerce site, the more difficult it is to use and the slower the site becomes, hampering ease of use. Security is purchased at the price of slowing down processors and adding significantly to data storage demands. Too much security can harm profitability, while not enough can potentially put a company out of business.
- *Public safety*—There is a tension between the claims of individuals to act anonymously and the needs of public officials to maintain public safety that can be threatened by criminals or terrorists.

■ **Identify the key security threats in the e-commerce environment.**

The most common and most damaging forms of security threats to e-commerce sites include:
- *Malicious code*—viruses, worms, Trojan horses, and bot networks are a threat to a system's integrity and continued operation, often changing how a system functions or altering documents created on the system.

- *Potentially unwanted programs (adware, spyware, etc.)*—a kind of security threat that arises when programs are surreptitiously installed on your computer or computer network without your consent.
- *Phishing*—any deceptive, online attempt by a third party to obtain confidential information for financial gain.
- *Hacking and cybervandalism*—intentionally disrupting, defacing, or even destroying a site.
- *Credit card fraud/theft*—one of the most-feared occurrences and one of the main reasons more consumers do not participate in e-commerce. The most common cause of credit card fraud is a lost or stolen card that is used by someone else, followed by employee theft of customer numbers and stolen identities (criminals applying for credit cards using false identities).
- *Spoofing*—occurs when hackers attempt to hide their true identities or misrepresent themselves by using fake e-mail addresses or masquerading as someone else. Spoofing also can involve redirecting a Web link to an address different from the intended one, with the site masquerading as the intended destination.
- *Denial of Service (DoS) and Distributed Denial of Service (DDoS) attacks*—hackers flood a Web site with useless traffic to inundate and overwhelm the network, frequently causing it to shut down and damaging a site's reputation and customer relationships.
- *Sniffing*—a type of eavesdropping program that monitors information traveling over a network, enabling hackers to steal proprietary information from anywhere on a network, including e-mail messages, company files, and confidential reports. The threat of sniffing is that confidential or personal information will be made public.
- *Insider jobs*—although the bulk of Internet security efforts are focused on keeping outsiders out, the biggest threat is from employees who have access to sensitive information and procedures.
- *Poorly designed server and client software*—the increase in complexity and size of software programs has contributed to an increase in software flaws or vulnerabilities that hackers can exploit.
- *Social network security issues*—malicious code, PUPs, phishing, data breaches, identity theft and other e-commerce security threats have all infiltrated social networks.
- *Mobile platform security issues*—the mobile platform presents an alluring target for hackers and cybercriminals, and faces all the same risks as other Internet devices, as well as new risks associated with wireless networks security.
- *Cloud security issues*—as devices, identities, and data become more and more intertwined in the cloud, safeguarding data in the cloud becomes a major concern.

■ **Describe how technology helps protect the security of messages sent over the Internet.**

Encryption is the process of transforming plain text or data into cipher text that cannot be read by anyone other than the sender and the receiver. Encryption can provide four of the six key dimensions of e-commerce security:
- *Message integrity*—provides assurance that the sent message has not been altered.
- *Nonrepudiation*—prevents the user from denying that he or she sent a message.
- *Authentication*—provides verification of the identity of the person (or computer) sending the message.

- *Confidentiality*—gives assurance that the message was not read by others.

There are a variety of different forms of encryption technology currently in use. They include:

- *Symmetric key encryption*—Both the sender and the receiver use the same key to encrypt and decrypt a message. Advanced Encryption Standard (AES) is the most widely used symmetric key encryption system on the Internet today.
- *Public key cryptography*—Two mathematically related digital keys are used: a public key and a private key. The private key is kept secret by the owner, and the public key is widely disseminated. Both keys can be used to encrypt and decrypt a message. Once the keys are used to encrypt a message, the same keys cannot be used to unencrypt the message.
- *Public key encryption using digital signatures and hash digests*—This method uses a mathematical algorithm called a hash function to produce a fixed-length number called a hash digest. The results of applying the hash function are sent by the sender to the recipient. Upon receipt, the recipient applies the hash function to the received message and checks to verify that the same result is produced. The sender then encrypts both the hash result and the original message using the recipient's public key, producing a single block of cipher text. To ensure both the authenticity of the message and nonrepudiation, the sender encrypts the entire block of cipher text one more time using the sender's private key. This produces a digital signature or "signed" cipher text that can be sent over the Internet to ensure the confidentiality of the message and authenticate the sender.
- *Digital envelope*—This method uses symmetric encryption to encrypt and decrypt the document, but public key encryption to encrypt and send the symmetric key.
- *Digital certificates and public key infrastructure*—This method relies on certification authorities who issue, verify, and guarantee digital certificates (a digital document that contains the name of the subject or company, the subject's public key, a digital certificate serial number, an expiration date, an issuance date, the digital signature of the certification authority, and other identifying information).

■ **Identify the tools used to establish secure Internet communications channels and protect networks, servers, and clients.**

In addition to encryption, there are several other tools that are used to secure Internet channels of communication, including:

- *Secure Sockets Layer (SSL)*—This is the most common form of securing channels. The SSL protocol provides data encryption, server authentication, client authentication, and message integrity for TCP/IP connections.
- *Virtual private networks (VPNs)*—These allow remote users to securely access internal networks via the Internet, using PPTP, an encoding mechanism that allows one local network to connect to another using the Internet as the conduit.

After communications channels are secured, tools to protect networks, the servers, and clients should be implemented. These include:

- *Firewalls*—software applications that act as filters between a company's private network and the Internet itself, denying unauthorized remote client computers from attaching to your internal network.
- *Proxies*—software servers that act primarily to limit access of internal clients to external Internet servers and are frequently referred to as the gateway.

- *Operating system controls*—built-in username and password requirements that provide a level of authentication. Some operating systems also have an access control function that controls user access to various areas of a network.
- *Anti-virus software*—a cheap and easy way to identify and eradicate the most common types of viruses as they enter a computer, as well as to destroy those already lurking on a hard drive.

■ **Appreciate the importance of policies, procedures, and laws in creating security.**

In order to minimize security threats:
- E-commerce firms must develop a coherent corporate policy that takes into account the nature of the risks, the information assets that need protecting, and the procedures and technologies required to address the risk, as well as implementation and auditing mechanisms.
- Public laws and active enforcement of cybercrime statutes are also required to both raise the costs of illegal behavior on the Internet and guard against corporate abuse of information.

The key steps in developing a security plan are:
- *Perform a risk assessment*—an assessment of the risks and points of vulnerability.
- *Develop a security policy*—a set of statements prioritizing the information risks, identifying acceptable risk targets, and identifying the mechanisms for achieving these targets.
- *Create an implementation plan*—a plan that determines how you will translate the levels of acceptable risk into a set of tools, technologies, policies, and procedures.
- *Create a security team*—the individuals who will be responsible for ongoing maintenance, audits, and improvements.
- *Perform periodic security audits*—routine reviews of access logs and any unusual patterns of activity.

■ **Describe the features of traditional payment systems.**

Traditional payment systems include:
- *Cash*, whose key feature is that it is instantly convertible into other forms of value without the intermediation of any other institution.
- *Checking transfers*, which are funds transferred directly through a signed draft or check from a consumer's checking account to a merchant or other individual; these are the second most common forms of payment.
- *Credit card accounts*, which are accounts that extend credit to a consumer and allow consumers to make payments to multiple vendors at one time.
- *Stored value systems*, which are created by depositing funds into an account and from which funds are paid out or are withdrawn as needed. Stored value payments systems include debit cards, phone cards, and smart cards.
- *Accumulating balance systems*, which accumulate expenditures and to which consumers make periodic payments.

■ **Identify the major e-commerce payment systems in use today.**

The major types of e-commerce payment systems in use today include:
- *Online credit card transactions,* which are the primary form of online payment system. There are five parties involved in an online credit card purchase: consumer, merchant, clearinghouse, merchant bank (sometimes called the "acquir-

ing bank"), and the consumer's card-issuing bank. However, the online credit card system has a number of limitations involving security, merchant risk, cost, and social equity.

- *PayPal*, which is an example of an online stored value payment system that permits consumers to make instant, online payments to merchants and other individuals based on value stored in an online account.
- *Alternative payment services* such as Amazon Payments, Google Checkout/ Google Wallet, and Bill Me Later, which enable consumers to shop online at a wide variety of merchants without having to provide credit card information each time they make a purchase.
- *Mobile payment systems*, using either credit card readers attached to a smartphone (Square, PayPal Here) or near field communication (NFC) chips, which enable contactless payment.
- *Digital cash* such as Bitcoin, which is based on an algorithm that generates unique authenticated tokens representing cash value, and virtual currencies, that typically circulate within an internal virtual world or are issued by a corporation, and usually used for the purchase of virtual goods.

■ **Describe the features and functionality of electronic billing presentment and payment systems.**

Electronic billing presentment and payment (EBPP) systems are a form of online payment systems for monthly bills. EBPP services allow consumers to view bills electronically and pay them through electronic funds transfers from bank or credit card accounts. Major players in the EBPP marketspace include:

- *Biller-direct systems*, which were originally created by large utilities to facilitate routine payment of utility bills, but which are increasingly being used by other billers.
- *Consolidators*, which attempt to aggregate all bills for consumers in one place and ideally permit one-stop bill payment.
- *Infrastructure providers*, which support the biller-direct and consolidator business models.

QUESTIONS

1. Why is it less risky to steal online? Explain some of the ways criminals deceive consumers and merchants.
2. Explain why an e-commerce site might not want to report being the target of cybercriminals.
3. Give an example of security breaches as they relate to each of the six dimensions of e-commerce security. For instance, what would be a privacy incident?
4. How would you protect your firm against a Denial of Service attack?
5. Explain why the U.S. government wants to restrict the export of strong encryption systems. And why would other countries be against it?
6. Name the major points of vulnerability in a typical online transaction.
7. How does spoofing threaten a Web site's operations?
8. Why is adware or spyware considered to be a security threat?
9. What are some of the steps a company can take to curtail cybercriminal activity from within a business?
10. Explain some of the modern-day flaws associated with encryption. Why is encryption not as secure today as it was earlier in the century?

11. Briefly explain how public key cryptography works.
12. Compare and contrast firewalls and proxy servers and their security functions.
13. Is a computer with anti-virus software protected from viruses? Why or why not?
14. Identify and discuss the five steps in developing an e-commerce security plan.
15. How do biometric devices help improve security? What particular type of security breach do they particularly reduce?
16. What are tiger teams, who uses them, and what are some of the tactics they use in their work?
17. How do the interests of the four major payment systems stakeholders impact each other?
18. Compare and contrast stored value payment systems and checking transfers.
19. Why is a credit card not considered an accumulating balance payment system?
20. Name six advantages and six disadvantages of using cash as a form of payment.
21. Describe the relationship between credit card associations and issuing banks.
22. What is Regulation Z, and how does it protect the consumer?
23. Briefly discuss the disadvantages of credit cards as the standard for online payments. How does requiring a credit card for payment discriminate against some consumers?
24. Describe the major steps involved in an online credit card transaction.
25. Compare and contrast smart cards and traditional credit cards.
26. How is money transferred in transactions using wireless devices?
27. Discuss why EBPP systems are becoming increasingly popular.
28. How are the two main types of EBPP systems both alike and different from each other?

PROJECTS

1. Imagine you are the owner of an e-commerce Web site. What are some of the signs that your site has been hacked? Discuss the major types of attacks you could expect to experience and the resulting damage to your site. Prepare a brief summary presentation.

2. Given the shift toward mobile commerce, do a search on "mobile commerce crime." Identify and discuss the new security threats this type of technology creates. Prepare a presentation outlining your vision of the new opportunities for cybercrime.

3. Find three certification authorities and compare the features of each company's digital certificates. Provide a brief description of each company as well, including number of clients. Prepare a brief presentation of your findings.

4. Research the challenges associated with payments across international borders and prepare a brief presentation of your findings. Do most e-commerce companies conduct business internationally? How do they protect themselves from repudiation? How do exchange rates impact online purchases? What about shipping charges? Summarize by describing the differences between a U.S. customer and an international customer who each make a purchase from a U.S. e-commerce merchant.

PART 3

Business Concepts
and Social Issues

CHAPTER **6**

E-commerce Marketing Concepts: Social, Mobile, Local

After reading this chapter, you will be able to:

- Identify the key features of the Internet audience.
- Discuss the basic concepts of consumer behavior and purchasing decisions.
- Understand how consumers behave online.
- Describe the basic marketing concepts needed to understand Internet marketing.
- Identify and describe the main technologies that support online marketing.
- Identify and describe basic e-commerce marketing and branding strategies.

Facebook:

Does Social Marketing Work?

When Facebook issued its stock for sale in an initial public offering on May 18, 2012, it followed a very long buildup of excitement based on the opportunity to turn the company, with its 190 million users in North America and its 1 billion global audience into a marketing behemoth to rival or exceed Google, Yahoo, and Amazon.

© digitallife / Alamy

The question both investors and marketers face is straightforward: does Facebook's social marketing and advertising platform work? Does it mean anything if millions of Facebook users Like your marketing campaign? Do Likes turn into sales? Is Facebook better for marketing (brand recognition and awareness) than it is for driving sales through advertisements? And, if Facebook's marketing platform does work, how well does it work when compared to other online marketing techniques such as search, e-mail, display ads, and affiliate programs? The answer to these questions will determine how much money Facebook can charge marketers for ad space and other marketing products.

In an effort to strengthen its marketing platform, Facebook has introduced a number of new products. Of course, the main marketing product it offers is the ability to create a Facebook page. From there, businesses can launch a variety of different engagement tools from contests, to coupons, to games. However, Facebook makes little or no revenue from these services. New money-making tools introduced in 2012 include a Timeline format for brand pages that can be used to highlight the history and development of the brand's products or of new products; Sponsored Stories in which Likes are reported to users' friends' news feeds, creating a viral effect for marketers; and Reach Generator, which can take a selected post from a consumer and push it out to the brand's fans over a month.

Early market research has raised questions about the effectiveness of social networks as marketing platforms. Research by Goldman Sachs found that social network sites are not very effective at driving purchases. Less than 5% of online purchasers in the study ranked social network sites as the most important factor in purchasing. Surveys by market research firm Compete found that social network sites were the least influential sources used by consumers prior to purchase, ranging from 2% to 7%. The most influential factors in purchasing are the retailers' Web site, search engines, display ads, and e-mails. To counter this research, Facebook commissioned a study by comScore to demonstrate the value of marketing on Facebook. Among the findings was the claim that being a fan of a brand on Facebook leads to more frequent purchases of the brand. A Facebook executive claimed that it's a myth that Facebook advertising does not work.

There are many marketing success stories, from both large Fortune 500 firms and small start-ups, that lend credibility to Facebook's claim that its social network marketing platform does, in fact, work. Currently, 88% of U.S. companies use Facebook for marketing purposes. One of the best known social media marketing campaigns is Ford Motor Company's Doug campaign, designed to attract a younger audience to its 2012 Ford Focus economy car. The brand image of earlier Ford Focus models was that they were an "econo-box" with little to offer more adventuresome younger consumers. The new Ford Focus was designed with a much younger audience in mind, and Ford needed a way to rebuild the brand's image, discover and engage with younger drivers, and create a market buzz that would drive people to showrooms. Ford wanted to get the attention and engagement of Facebook users, a younger demographic than traditional Internet advertising typically provides, and get them to pass on the experience to their friends. The answer was Doug.

Doug was an orange-color spokespuppet that appeared in 48 videos on the Ford Focus, covering topics from the dashboard interface, to interior features, and performance features of the car. Doug was possibly the first social marketing animal, appearing in a coordinated Facebook, Twitter, and YouTube campaign. Doug had his own Facebook page and his own channel on YouTube—FocusDoug. Ford hoped Doug would get 10,000 Facebook fans, but in the first few months quickly exceeded this, eventually totaling around 43,000 fans. More than 350,000 people watched the first YouTube video. More than 75% of those who saw any of the videos had a more favorable view towards the Focus and a greater likelihood of considering a Focus purchase. About 40% of online conversations about Ford's Focus have been about Doug, the spokespuppet.

By any measure, Ford's Doug campaign was a creative use of several social media channels and a marketing success story. It demonstrated the potential of Facebook to go far beyond search ads, display ads, and e-mail campaigns in bringing a new product to a new audience, creating buzz and viral excitement, and increasing favorability ratings with its intended demographic. Yet it was not a financial success for Facebook. Ford created its own Facebook page for Doug and the Focus and did not use any of Facebook's paid ad capabilities (like Sponsored Stories). Once Doug had succeeded on Facebook, Ford bought display ads on Yahoo's e-mail login page and paid Microsoft to sponsor videos and articles about Doug and the Focus. Ford did buy some Facebook display ads urging users to like Doug, but stopped when Doug reached 10,000 fans. Once Doug went viral there was no need to keep paying Facebook for its ads. Doug's campaign had a life of its own. Ford spent $95 million promoting the Focus but less than 5% of that went to Facebook.

Other large Fortune 500 advertisers report similar experiences with Facebook marketing. Only a tiny percentage of their online marketing budget goes to Facebook. After experimenting with Facebook, the really large advertisers found they could reach their target audience quickly at a steep discount using Facebook pages. While U.S. consumers spend 15% of their time online at Facebook, Facebook captures only 6.4% of total online ad spending, generating about $2 billion in U.S. ad revenues in 2012. Google remains the Internet marketing and ad giant with 2011 revenues of $38 billion. Still, there are hopeful signs that Facebook's larger advertiser base will expand. In 2012, Sony is moving 30% of its online advertising to social sites, and Diageo (maker of Smirnoff and Guinness) plans to spend $10 million on Facebook ads in 2012.

While large firms have not committed wholeheartedly to Facebook's marketing platform and are still experimenting, Facebook's real strength has been with smaller firms. One such firm is Pacific Rim, a winery in Portland, Oregon, that produces affordable Riesling wines. Riesling is a white wine that originated in the Rhine Valley in Germany, but today is grown in many regions, including Oregon.

Shawn Bavaresco founded Pacific Rim in 2006 with two other partners. Riesling is not a big seller like other white wines such as sauvignon blanc or pinot grigio. But the founders decided to focus on a single niche wine ignored by many retailers and wine drinkers rather than compete with wineries producing more popular varietals. And they decided to focus their marketing on millennials, people between the ages of 26 to 34, because they consume a large amount of wine and are willing to experiment with new wines.

Their first marketing step shortly after founding Pacific Rim was to create a Web site, reiselingrules.com. The focus was achieving brand awareness and credibility with wine retailers across the country by sharing their passion for riesling and educating wine drinkers about the wine. As it turns out, riesling is not a simple product, and there are different riesling wines that vary by sweetness and boldness. With a 30-page book available for free, and online forums, they hoped to become the leading voice on the riesling category. But what they lacked was a committed online community of wine drinkers that shared their passion and was engaged with the brand and the wine.

In 2010, they launched a Facebook page, Pacific Rim Riesling Rules, aimed at building an online community of riesling lovers as well as creating retail point of sale. The page used contests to drive Likes, videos to engage users, animations to illustrate the wine production process, and the ability to purchase the wine directly from Pacific Rim. When visitors clicked on a photo of a bottle they were taken to a shopping cart on the company's Web site. They also launched seasonal contests, asking visitors to write 150-word essays on why they loved riesling. The Facebook community voted on the submissions, and the winner received $1,000. Pacific Rim gave away $15,000 over 15 weeks, and generated 15,000 Likes in this period.

Currently, the winery has 25,000 fans talking about its wines and sells 200,000 cases of wine a year. The Facebook fan base increased brand awareness among retailers, according to Bavaresco, making it much easier to convince wine retailers to sell Pacific Rim wine. Today, Pacific Rim's Facebook page has more than 29,000 Likes. You can find Pacific Rim wines at all major retailers throughout the United States. Pacific Rim was able to establish a direct connection with its customers, which is unusual in the wine industry. And most importantly, it experienced a 15% increase in revenue and 73% increase in transactions since the Facebook page launch.

The Ford and Pacific Rim examples illustrate successful uses of the Facebook platform. But in both cases, Facebook itself made little revenue. There are several Fortune

SOURCES: "Summer 2012 Online Shopper," Compete Inc., August 2012; "Facebook Marketing: Reaching Consumers in a Changing Environment," eMarketer Inc., August 2012; "Likeonomics: The Unexpected Truth Behind Earning Trust, Influencing Behavior, and Inspiring Action," by Rohit Bhargava, Wiley, 2012; "Face-book's Growth Slows," by Shayndi Raice, *Wall Street Journal,* July 27, 2012; "Facebook Combats Criticism Over Ads," by Shayndi Raice, *Wall Street Journal,* June 12, 2012; "Facebook IPO Sputters," by Shayndi Raice, *New York Times,* May 18, 2012; "Big Brands Like Facebook, But They Don't Like to Pay," by Emily Steel and Geoffrey Fowler, *Wall Street Journal,* November 2, 2012; "RIP, Doug: Ford Sends Focus Spokespuppet Packing," by Dale Buss, Brand-channel.com, September 28, 2011.

500 firms that have withdrawn from using Facebook as an advertising platform while still using Facebook's free marketing platform (Facebook pages are free). General Motors, for instance, which spends $40 million a year with Facebook, withdrew $10 million in 2012 devoted to Facebook ads because it found no relationship between its Facebook ads and purchases by consumers. GM retains its $30 million effort to use Facebook as a marketing site to increase brand awareness and engage consumers. Ford also found no relationship between sales of the Ford Focus and Facebook fans.

The biggest challenge facing Facebook is proving that ads on its platform lead to increases in sales, somewhere, somehow, down the line. One key issue is discovering what a Like means. Do a million Likes lead to increases in sales, and if so, by how much? What does it mean when 40% of people discussing your brand mention your Facebook campaign? No one knows at this point if Sponsored Stories work or if the new Reach Generator service will add up to new sales.

Google's business model is much simpler than Facebook's and it's proven to work. Someone searches for something online, and he or she is shown ads as part of the search results. With Facebook, users are shown ads even when they are not searching for something, similar to other display ad sites like Yahoo. Facebook needs to be careful to avoid annoying its users who do not use the site generally as a place to shop. Likewise with Facebook's fledgling mobile offerings: the small mobile screen makes it very difficult to show ads of any kind without annoying users.

Despite having the largest online social audience in the world, it remains unclear if Facebook can monetize its user base and continue growing revenues at double-digit rates as it has done in the past. It will require several years of experimentation by marketers and Facebook to discover if social marketing on Facebook really works.

Facebook provides an example of how new Internet technologies and practices can disrupt and challenge existing industries. Perhaps no area of business has been more affected than marketing and marketing communications. As a communications tool, the Internet affords marketers new ways of contacting millions of potential customers at costs far lower than traditional media. The Internet also provides new ways—often instantaneous and spontaneous—to gather information from customers, adjust product offerings, and increase customer value. In the case of Facebook, and in the other cases in this and the following chapter, the Internet has spawned entirely new ways to identify and communicate with customers, including search engine marketing, social network marketing, behavioral targeting, recommender systems, and targeted e-mail.

The Internet was just the first transformation. Today, the mobile platform based on smartphones and tablet computers is transforming online marketing and communications yet again. The key changes in 2012 involve social networks, mobile marketing, and location-based services, including local marketing. In the next few years, the social, mobile, and local trends will accelerate as the technology improves and the always-on, social culture intensifies.

In this new environment in 2012–2013, advertisers are following huge shifts in audience away from traditional media and towards social networks, user-generated content, and online content destinations offering videos, music, and games. For instance, according to *Internet Retailer*, almost 95% of its Top 500 e-retailers have a presence on Facebook, more than 90% have a Twitter feed, and more than 75% have posted commercials, product demos, or other types of videos on YouTube (Internet Retailer, 2012). **Table 6.1** on page 340 summarizes some of the significant new developments in Internet marketing for 2012–2013.

The subject of online marketing, branding, and market communications is very broad and deep. We created two chapters to cover the material. Chapter 6 focuses on the basic online marketing and branding concepts and strategies you need to understand in order to evaluate e-commerce marketing programs. Here, we examine consumer behavior on the Web, the major types of online marketing and branding, and the technologies that support advances in online marketing. In Chapter 7 we focus on online marketing communications, including a detailed look at various online advertising methods and strategies. You will need this material in order to build effective online marketing and advertising campaigns. For readers who have no background in marketing, we have created an online Learning Track that discusses basic marketing and branding concepts.

6.1 CONSUMERS ONLINE: THE INTERNET AUDIENCE AND CONSUMER BEHAVIOR

Before firms can begin to sell their products online, they must first understand what kinds of people they will find online and how those people behave in the online marketplace. In this section, we focus primarily on individual consumers in the

TABLE 6.1	**WHAT'S NEW IN ONLINE MARKETING 2012–2013**

BUSINESS

- All forms of online marketing grow at double-digit rates, faster than traditional offline marketing (with the exception of television).
- Social media marketing channels expand, but search and display marketing remains dominant.
- Local marketing based on geolocation services like Groupon and LivingSocial take off.
- Mobile marketing grows at twice the rate of traditional online marketing.
- Flash marketing remakes online fashion sales.

TECHNOLOGY

- Powerful, low-power, handheld mobile devices challenge the PC as the major online marketing platform. Smartphones and tablet computers become prevalent Web access devices.
- Big data: online tracking produces oceans of data, challenging business analytics programs.
- Cloud computing makes rich marketing content and multi-channel, cross-platform marketing a reality.
- The Twitter and Facebook platforms grow into valuable social customer relationship management tools, enabling businesses to connect with customers on social network sites.

SOCIETY

- Behavioral tracking on social networks leads to growing privacy awareness and fears.
- Social network sites are accused of abusing customer profile information without providing sufficient user controls over profile distribution.
- Social network sites implement facial tracking technology, which allows users to tag their friends' faces, to identify pictures with a name, and potentially to track people across the entire Web based on their photos.
- Mobile GPS tracking of individual location information built into smartphones and other mobile devices raises privacy concerns.
- Apple and Google affirm they tracked personal location information.

business-to-consumer (B2C) arena. However, many of the factors discussed apply to the B2B arena as well, insofar as purchasing decisions by firms are made by individuals.

INTERNET TRAFFIC PATTERNS: THE ONLINE CONSUMER PROFILE

We will start with an analysis of some basic background demographics of Web consumers in the United States. The first principle of marketing and sales is "know thy customer." Who uses the Web, who shops on the Web and why, and what do they buy? In 2012, around 239 million people of all ages and more than 89 million U.S. households (about 75% of all U.S. households) will have access to the Internet (eMarketer, Inc., 2012a). By comparison, 98% of all U.S. households currently have televisions and 94% have telephones. Worldwide, around 2.26 billion people are online.

Although the number of new online users increased at a rate of 30% a year or higher in the early 2000s, over the last several years, this growth rate has slowed to about 2%–3% a year. E-commerce businesses can no longer count on a double-digit growth rate in the online population to fuel their revenues. The days of extremely rapid growth in the U.S. Internet population are over.

Intensity and Scope of Usage

The slowing rate of growth in the U.S. Internet population is compensated for, in part, by an increasing intensity and scope of use. Several studies show that a greater amount of time is being spent online by Internet users. Overall, users are going online more frequently, with 82% of adult users in the United States (158 million people) logging on in a typical day (Pew Internet & American Life Project, 2012a). In 2012, mobile smartphones and tablets are major new access points to the Internet and online commerce. About 122 million people, about half of all U.S. Internet users, access the Internet using a mobile device. In 2012, 102 million mobile users play games, 61 million view videos, 77 million visit a social site, and millions of others listen to music, shop, and text (eMarketer, Inc., 2012b, 2012c). The more time users spend online, becoming more comfortable and familiar with Internet features and services, the more services they are likely to explore, according to the Pew Internet & American Life Project.

People who go online are engaging in a wider range of activities than in the past. While e-mail and using search engines remain the most-used Internet services, other popular activities include visiting social network sites like Facebook, researching products and services, catching up on news, gathering hobby-related information, watching video on a video-sharing site such as YouTube, and banking online. **Table 6.2** on page 342 identifies the range of online activities for the typical adult U.S. Internet user. Each percent translates into about 1.9 million adults.

Demographics and Access

The demographic profile of the Internet—and e-commerce—has changed greatly since 1995. Up until 2000, single, white, young, college-educated males with high incomes dominated the Internet. This inequality in access and usage led to concerns about a possible "digital divide." However, in recent years, there has been a marked increase in Internet usage by females, minorities, seniors, and families with modest incomes, resulting in a notable decrease—but not elimination—in the earlier inequality of access and usage. The following discussion is based on data collected in surveys conducted by the Pew Internet & American Life Project. The people least likely to go online are senior citizens, adults with less than a high school education, and those living in households earning less than $30,000 a year (Pew Internet & American Life Project, 2012b).

Gender An equal percentage (85%) of both men and women use the Internet today, in contrast to 10 years ago, when the percentage of women online compared to men was slightly higher.

TABLE 6.2	A GROWING RANGE OF ONLINE ACTIVITIES: AN AVERAGE DAY IN THE LIFE OF AN INTERNET USER	
ACTIVITY	**PERCENT OF INTERNET USERS WHO REPORTED ENGAGING IN ACTIVITY "YESTERDAY" IN 2012**
Use the Internet	82%
Send or read e-mail	59%
Use a search engine to find information	59%
Use a social networking site like Facebook, LinkedIn, or Google+	48%
Get news	45%
Go online just for fun or to pass the time	44%
Look for info on a hobby or interest	35%
Check the weather	34%
Look online for news or information about politics	28%
Look for information online about a product or service	28%
Watch a video on a video-sharing site	28%
Do banking online	24%
Send instant messages	18%
Look for information on Wikipedia	17%
Search for a map or driving directions	17%
Play online games	13%
Visit a government Web site	13%
Get financial information online	12%
Categorize or tag online content	11%
Look online for job information	11%
Look for "how to" or "DIY" or repair information	11%
Use online classified ads or sites	11%
Pay to access or download digital content online	10%
Look for health/medical info	10%
Use Twitter	8%
Participate in an online discussion, listserv, or other online group forum	7%
Buy a product	6%
Take a virtual tour of a location online	6%
Look for religious/spiritual information	5%
Make a phone call online	4%
Buy or make a reservation for travel	4%
Create or work on own online journal or blog	4%
Participate in an online auction	4%
Post a comment or review online about a product or service	4%
Rate a product, service, or person using an online rating system	4%
Download a podcast	3%
Make a donation to a charity online	1%

SOURCE: Based on Pew Internet & American Life Project, "Online Activities, Daily," (last updated February 2012) http://pewinternet.org/Trend-Data-(Adults)/Online-Activities-Daily.aspx, accessed September 12, 2012a.

Age Young adults (18–29) form the age group with the highest percentage of Internet use, at 96%. Adults in the 30–49 group (93%) are also strongly represented. Another fast-growing group online is the 65 and over segment, 58% of whom now use the Internet, more than triple the level of 2002. Although not included in the Pew Internet & American report survey, teens (12–17) actually have the highest percentage of their age group online (97%). The percentage of very young children (1–11 years) online has also spurted, to 43% of that age group (eMarketer, Inc., 2012a).

Ethnicity Variation across ethnic groups is not as wide as across age groups. In 2002, there were significant differences among ethnic groups, but this has receded. In 2012, user participation by whites is 86%, African Americans, 86%, and Hispanics, 80%. The growth rates for both Hispanics and African Americans over the period from 2002 to 2010 is higher than for whites, which has helped close the gap.

Income Level About 99% of households with income levels above $75,000 have Internet access, compared to only 75% of households earning less than $30,000. However, those households with lower earnings are gaining Internet access at faster rates than households with incomes of $75,000 and above. Over time, income differences have declined but they remain significant. Income is not significantly related to exposure or hours using the Internet.

Education Amount of education also makes a significant difference when it comes to online access. Of those individuals with less than a high school education, 61% were online in 2012, compared to 97% of individuals with a college degree or more. Even a high school education boosted Internet usage, with that segment reaching 80%. In general, educational disparities far exceed other disparities in Internet access and usage.

Overall, there remains a strong relationship between age, income, ethnicity, and education on one hand and Internet usage on the other. The so-called "digital divide" has indeed moderated, but it still persists along the income, education, age, and ethnic dimensions. Gender, income, education, age, and ethnicity also impact online behavior. According to the Pew Internet & American Life Project, adults over the age of 65, those who have not completed high school, those who make less than $30,000 a year, and Hispanics are all less likely to purchase products online. Women are slightly more likely to purchase online than men, but not significantly so. With respect to online banking, the demographics are similar—those 65 and older are less likely than any age group to bank online, while those with at least some college are more likely than those with a high school diploma or less. Online banking is also more popular with men than women. No significant differences were found in terms of ethnicity (Pew Internet & American Life Project, 2012c). Other commentators have observed that children of poorer and less educated families are spending considerably more time using their access devices for entertainment (movies, games, Facebook, and texting) than children from wealthier households. For all children and teenagers, the majority of time spent on the Internet has been labeled "wasted time" because the majority of online use is for entertainment, and not education or learning (Richtel, 2012).

Table 6.3 summarizes some of the major intergroup differences discussed above and their pace of change.

Type of Internet Connection: Broadband and Mobile Impacts

While a great deal of progress has been made in reducing glaring gaps in access to the Internet, there are significant inequalities in access to broadband service. In 2012, around 83 million households had broadband service in their homes—69% of all households and 96% of Internet households (eMarketer, Inc., 2012d). Research suggests the broadband audience is different from the dial-up audience: the broadband audience is more educated and affluent. The Federal Communications Commission reports that

TABLE 6.3	CHANGING DEMOGRAPHIC DIFFERENCES IN INTERNET ACCESS	
GROUP	THE PERCENT OF EACH GROUP ONLINE	
	2012	2002
Total Adults	85%	50%
Men	85%	56%
Women	85%	60%
AGE		
18–29	96%	74%
30–49	93%	67%
50–64	85%	52%
65+	58%	18%
RACE/ETHNICITY		
White, Non-Hispanic	86%	60%
Black, Non-Hispanic	86%	45%
Hispanic	80%	54%
HOUSEHOLD INCOME		
Less than $30,000/yr	75%	38%
$30,000–$49,999	90%	65%
$50,000–$74,999	93%	74%
$75,000 and over	99%	86%
EDUCATIONAL ATTAINMENT		
Less than High School	61%	N/A
High School	80%	45%
Some College	94%	72%
College +	97%	82%

SOURCE: Based on data from Pew Internet & American Life Project, "Demographics of Internet Users," (last updated August 2012) http://pewinternet.org/Trend-Data-(Adults)/Whos-Online.aspx, accessed September 12, 2012b, 2005a, 2005b.

only 50% of Hispanic and African American homes have broadband, and only 40% of those homes with less than $20,000 in annual income (Federal Communications Commission, 2012). The broadband audience is much more intensely involved with the Internet and much more capable of using the Internet. For marketers, this audience offers unique opportunities for the use of multimedia marketing campaigns, and for the positioning of products especially suited for this audience. On the other hand, the dial-up households still buy products online, visit news sites, and use social network sites—just not as frequently or intensely as broadband households. The explosive growth of smartphones and tablet computers connected to broadband cellular and Wi-Fi networks is the foundation for a truly mobile e-commerce and marketing platform, which did not exist a few years ago. more than 122 million Americans access the Internet from mobile devices, and there are more than 300 million cell phone subscriptions. More than 115 million use smartphones, and 70 million use iPad tablet computers (eMarketer, Inc., 2012e). Marketers are just beginning to use this new platform for brand development.

Community Effects: Social Contagion in Social Networks

For a physical retail store, the most important factor in shaping sales is location, location, location. If you are located where thousands of people pass by every day, you will tend to do well. But for Internet retailers, physical location has almost no consequence as long as customers can be served by shipping services such as UPS or the post office or their services downloaded to anywhere. What does make a difference for consumer purchases on the Internet is whether or not the consumer is located in "neighborhoods" where others purchase on the Internet. These neighborhoods can be either face-to-face and truly personal, or digital. These so-called neighborhood effects, and the role of social emulation in consumption decisions, are well-known for goods such as personal computers. In general, there is a relationship between being a member of a social network and purchasing decisions. Research on an Internet grocery found that being located near other users of the online grocery increased the likelihood of purchasing at the site by 50% (Bell and Song, 2004). Yet the relationship between "connectedness" (either offline or online) and purchase decisions is not straightforward or simple. People who score in the top 10%–15% of connectedness "do their own thing" to differentiate themselves and often do not share purchase decisions with friends. In fact, highly connected users often stop purchasing what their friends purchase. One can think of them as iconoclasts. The middle 50% of connected people very often share purchase patterns of their friends. One can think of these people as "keeping up with the Joneses" (Iyengar, et al., 2009). A Forrester Research study found that less than 2% of online purchases could be traced back to social networks, although for short-term, flash sales, the percentage rises to 6% (Forrester Research, 2011a). Other research reported by Goldman Sachs shows that social networks account for about 5% of online purchase activity, compared to search engines (31%) and recommendation engines (27%) (Dyer, 2011).

Membership in social networks has a large influence on discovering new independent music, but less influence on already well-known products (Garg, 2009). Membership in an online brand community like Ford's Facebook page and community has a direct effect on sales (Adjei, et al., 2009). Amazon's recommender systems ("Consumers who bought this item also bought ...") create co-purchase networks where people do not know one another personally, but nevertheless triples the influence of complementary products (Oestereicher-Singer and Sundarajan, 2008). The value of social networks to marketers rests on the proposition that brand strength and purchase decisions are closely related to network membership, rank, prominence, and central-ity. At this point, the strength and scope of the relationship between social network membership, brand awareness, and purchase decisions is not completely understood, although all researchers agree that it exists in a variety of contexts and in varying degrees (Guo, et al., 2011).

Lifestyle and Sociological Impacts

There are some worrisome potential impacts to intensive Internet use. The Internet's impacts on social life, both positive and negative, have implications for marketing and branding. For instance, if you are hoping to attract young people who are continu-ally texting and who are often distracted by multitasking to your brand, then your marketing messages will have to be appropriately created and shaped. Ask many parents of young teenagers, and they will often complain their children are spending too much time instant messaging and playing games online. Early research suggested that the Internet might be causing a decline in traditional social activities, such as talking face-to-face with neighbors and family members, encouraging users to spend less time with family and friends, and working more often, whether at home or at the office. According to an early study performed at Stanford University by a group of political scientists, Internet users lose touch with those around them; individuals spending just two to five hours a week online spend far less time talking with friends and family face-to-face and on the phone. Users who spend up to five hours a week online frequently experience an increase in time spent working while at home, while those who spend more than five hours a week online find themselves working more at work as well; the Internet is taking up a larger portion of what used to be free time for some workers. On the other hand, e-mail, instant messaging, and chat groups, all decidedly social activities, albeit not face-to-face ones, are among the most popular uses of the Internet.

More recent research has found that the use of the Internet strengthens and complements traditional face-to-face relationships. While Internet use involves a single user sitting in front of a screen—much like television—it is very different from televi-sion because of the high levels of social interaction possible on the Internet. Insofar as Internet use deters children from face-to-face interaction or from undirected "play" out of doors, undesirable effects on child social development may result (Nie and Erbring, 2000). On the other hand, a recent study demonstrated that the Internet has strengthened ties among cousins (the "clicking cousins effect"), children, and parents through the use of e-mail to stay in touch on a daily basis. A meta-analysis of multiple studies on the impact of the Internet on social interaction from 1995–2003 found mixed results, with offline and online interaction stimulating one another, but online communication did not translate into more visiting face-to-face (Saunders and Chester, 2008; Shklovski, et al., 2004).

The contemporary "always on" Internet culture driven by smartphones and mobile Internet access has raised concerns among scientists that focused search engines are truncating scientific research efforts, narrowing their focus; and that addiction to smartphones causes a decline in intra-family communication, weakening family ties, and merging work and family. Critics point to a much darker side of social network sites and texting behavior. They point to teens sending 6,000 texts a month and avoiding face-to-face talk and phone conversations, and ultimately not being able to converse very well at all; couples dining out, but texting their dinners away; students engaging their smartphones instead of engaging the material. As much as we hope social networking sites bring us closer together, they also demonstrate how far apart we are. Instead of real friends, we "friend" complete strangers on Facebook. Instead of talking on the phone (never mind face-to-face), we text and tweet, or post a photo to all our friends as if it were a blast e-mail. (Turkle, 2011). Researchers are finding that multitaskers, and students distracted in class with digital devices, perform poorly when compared to people who turn off their computers and focus (Carr, 2010; Greenfield, 2009). Other research points to declines in productivity due to e-mail, instant messaging, and texting interruptions during the day, coupled with mindless wandering on the Internet while at work. Research on the use of computers in middle schools and at home suggests that computer usage lowers school achievement tests in English and math but raises computer skills (Malamud and Pop-Eleches, 2010).

Media Choices and Multitasking: The Internet versus Other Media Channels

What may be of even more interest to marketers, however, is that the more time individuals spend using the Internet, "the more they turn their back on traditional media," according to the Stanford study. For every additional hour users spend online, they reduce their corresponding time spent with traditional media, such as television, newspapers, and radio. Traditional media are competing with the Internet for consumer attention, and so far, the Internet appears to be gaining on print media (newspapers and magazines) but not television. Television viewing has increased as the Internet has grown in popularity. About 60% of TV viewers use the Internet simultaneously (mostly chatting, searching, e-mailing, and using Facebook or Twitter). Media multitasking is rising: over 100 million U.S. adult Internet users watch television while going online. Others listen to the radio, read magazines, or newspapers. A USC study found that more than 80% of Internet users multitasked at least some of the time they spent online (USC Annenberg School, 2011). Multitasking makes measurement of media exposure difficult because people can "expand" their media time by using multiple media at once. We discuss media consumption in greater depth in Chapter 10.

CONSUMER BEHAVIOR MODELS

Once firms have an understanding of who is online, they need to focus on how consumers behave online. The study of **consumer behavior** is a social science discipline that attempts to model and understand the behavior of humans in a marketplace. Several social science disciplines play roles in this study, including sociology, psychology, and economics. Models of consumer behavior attempt to predict or "explain" what consumers purchase and where, when, how much, and why they buy. The expectation

consumer behavior
a social science discipline that attempts to model and understand the behavior of humans in a marketplace

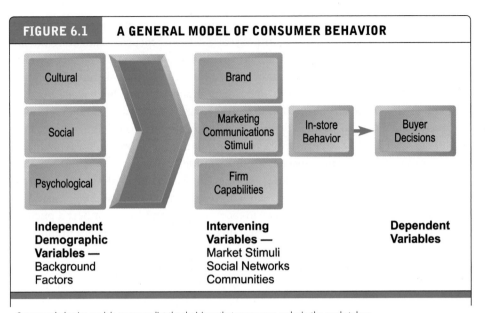

FIGURE 6.1 A GENERAL MODEL OF CONSUMER BEHAVIOR

Consumer behavior models try to predict the decisions that consumers make in the marketplace.
SOURCE: Adapted from Kotler and Armstrong, 2009.

is that if the consumer decision-making process can be understood, firms will have a much better idea how to market and sell their products. **Figure 6.1** illustrates a general consumer behavior model that takes into account a wide range of factors that influence a consumer's marketplace decisions.

Consumer behavior models seek to predict the wide range of decisions that consumers make on the basis of background demographic factors, and on a set of intervening, more immediate variables that shape the consumer's ultimate decisions.

Background factors are cultural, social, and psychological in nature. Firms must recognize and understand the behavioral significance of these background factors and adjust their marketing efforts accordingly. **Culture** is the broadest factor in consumer behavior because it shapes basic human values, wants, perceptions, and behaviors. Culture creates basic expectations that consumers bring to the marketplace, such as what should be bought in different markets, how things should be bought, and how things should be paid for. Generally, culture affects an entire nation, and takes on major significance in international marketing. For instance, an American-style e-commerce site that sells cooking spices might have difficulty in an Asian culture such as China or Japan, where food and spice shopping takes place at local neighborhood markets, large food stores do not exist, and shoppers tend to pick out and smell each spice before purchasing it.

Within nations, subcultures are extremely important in consumer behavior. **Subcultures** are subsets of cultures that form around major social differences such as ethnicity, age, lifestyle, and geography. In the United States, ethnicity plays a very large role in consumer behavior. There are an estimated 40 million African Americans with an annual purchasing power of around $950 billion, about 47

culture
shapes basic human values, wants, perceptions, and behaviors

subculture
subset of cultures that form around major social differences

million Hispanics with a total annual purchasing power of also about $1 trillion, and almost 15.5 million Asian Americans with a total purchasing power of about $610 billion (Catalyst, 2012). Each of these ethnic groups represents a significant market segment that firms can target. For instance, Toyota was one of the first automotive manufacturers to use the Internet to target Hispanic customers. Toyota places Web advertisements on Spanish-language portals such as MSN Latino, Yahoo en Español, AOL Latino, and Univision to direct Hispanic customers to its Toyota.com Spanish-language Web site. As a result, Toyota now ranks first in the new vehicle sales registered by Latinos. A number of major retailers, such as Best Buy, Lowe's, and Sears, now have Spanish-language Web sites as well. Among the important social factors that shape consumer behavior are the many reference groups to which all consumers "belong," either as direct participating members, or as indirect members by affiliation, association, or aspiration. Among the more powerful intervening variables are the social networks and communities to which a person belongs and which invariably send market stimuli. In the offline face-to-face world, these groups are referred to as **direct reference groups** and include one's family, profession or occupation, religion, neighborhood, and schools. In the online world, these groups are simply referred to as online social and professional networks and communities to which consumers belong. **Indirect reference groups** include one's life-cycle stage, social class, and lifestyle group (discussed later). In the online world, an analog would be celebrity blog and news sites, commentary sites of all sorts, fashion sites, and fan sites where consumers tend to be consumers of content and identify with the content and activities at the site. Online social networks are important for understanding how viral marketing works on the Internet.

direct reference groups
one's family, profession or occupation, religion, neighborhood, and schools

indirect reference groups
one's life-cycle stage, social class, and lifestyle group

Within each of these reference groups, there are **opinion leaders** (or **viral influencers**, as they are termed by online marketers), who because of their personality, skills, or other factors, influence the behavior of others. Marketers seek out opinion leaders (so-called influentials) in their communications and promotional efforts because of their presumed influence over other people. Some have argued that these "influentials" are about 10% of any population and directly influence the other 90% in the population (Barry and Keller, 2003). For instance, many Web sites include testimonials submitted by successful adopters of a product or service. Generally, those giving the testimonials are portrayed as opinion leaders—"smart people in the know." At Procter & Gamble's Web site, for example, testimonials come from "P&G Advisors," who are consumers who take an active interest in Procter & Gamble products.

opinion leaders (viral influencers)
influence the behavior of others through their personality, skills, or other factors

The concept of "influentials," while intuitively attractive, may not in fact describe how or why viral messages spread across the Web (Barry and Keller, 2003). A counterview is that the "Like" buttons on Web sites are not very powerful in influencing brand identification or sales because they spread messages from one person to another regardless of their social position in a network.

A unique kind of reference group is a **lifestyle group**, which can be defined as an integrated pattern of activities (hobbies, sports, shopping likes and dislikes, social events typically attended), interests (food, fashion, family, recreation), and opinions (social issues, business, government).

lifestyle group
an integrated pattern of activities, interests, and opinions

Lifestyle group classification systems—of which there are several—attempt to create a classification scheme that captures a person's whole pattern of living, consuming, and acting. The theory is that once you understand a consumer's lifestyle, or the lifestyles typical of a group of people—such as college students, for instance—then you can design products and marketing messages that appeal specifically to that lifestyle group. Lifestyle classification then becomes another method of segmenting the market.

In addition to lifestyle classification, marketers are interested in a consumer's psychological profile. A **psychological profile** is a set of needs, drives, motivations, perceptions, and learned behaviors—including attitudes and beliefs. Marketers attempt to appeal to psychological profiles through product design, product positioning, and marketing communications. For instance, many health e-commerce sites emphasize that they help consumers achieve a sense of control over their health destiny by providing them with information about diseases and treatments. This message is a powerful appeal to the needs of a wealthy, educated, professional, and technically advanced set of Web users for self-control and mastery over what might be a complex, health-threatening situation.

psychological profile
set of needs, drives, motivations, perceptions, and learned behaviors

Marketers cannot influence demographic background factors, but they can adjust their branding, communications, and firm capabilities to appeal to demographic realities. For instance, the National Basketball Association's Web site, NBA.com, appeals to a variety of basketball fan subgroups from avid fans interested in specific team statistics, to fashion-conscious fans who can purchase clothing for specific NBA teams, to fans who want to auction memorabilia.

PROFILES OF ONLINE CONSUMERS

Online consumer behavior parallels that of offline consumer behavior with some obvious differences. It is important to first understand why people choose the Internet channel to conduct transactions. **Table 6.4** lists the main reasons consumers choose the online channel.

While price appears on this list, overwhelmingly, consumers shop on the Web because of convenience, which in turn is produced largely by saving them time. Overall transaction cost reduction appears to be the major motivator for choosing the online channel, followed by other cost reductions in the product or service.

THE ONLINE PURCHASING DECISION

Once online, why do consumers actually purchase a product or service at a specific site? There are many models and several research studies that attempt to provide answers to this question. **Psychographic research** (research that combines both demographic and psychological data and divides a market into different groups based on social class, lifestyle, and/or personality characteristics) on the profile of active e-commerce shoppers attempts to understand the characteristics of users—in particular their various lifestyles—that lead to online buying behavior. For instance, in a study by the Wharton Forum on Electronic Commerce, a panel of 2,500 people was surveyed to understand the factors that predict e-commerce purchases (Lohse, Bellman, and Johnson, 2000). The survey found that the most important factors in predicting buying behavior were (1) looking for product information online,

psychographic research
divides a market into different groups based on social class, lifestyle, and/or personality characteristics

TABLE 6.4	WHY CONSUMERS CHOOSE THE ONLINE CHANNEL
REASON	PERCENTAGE OF RESPONDENTS
24-hour shopping convenience	35.1%
Easier to compare prices	33.1%
Free shipping offers	31.5%
No crowds like in mall/traditional stores	30.8%
More convenient to shop online	29.2%
Easier to find items online than in stores	17.5%
Better variety online	17.4%
No sales tax	14.9%
Direct shipping to gift recipients	13.8%
Easier to compare products	11.4%

SOURCE: Based on data from eMarketer, Inc., 2011a.

(2) leading a "wired lifestyle" (one where consumers spend a considerable amount of their working and home lives online), and (3) recently ordering from a catalog. Online recommendations can double the sales of soft and hard goods (Senecal and Nantel, 2004). **Table 6.5** also lists some of the most important factors that influence consumers' decisions to purchase online.

But aside from individual characteristics, you need to consider the process that buyers follow when making a purchase decision, and how the Internet environment affects consumers' decisions. There are five stages in the consumer decision process: awareness of need, search for more information, evaluation of alternatives, the actual

TABLE 6.5	FACTORS THAT INFLUENCE ONLINE PURCHASE DECISIONS
FACTOR	PERCENTAGE OF RESPONDENTS
Price	95%
Free shipping	90%
Trusted seller status	75%
No tax	60%
Online coupon availability	58%
Return policy	55%
Customer loyalty/rewards program	35%

SOURCE: Based on data from Channel Advisor, 2010.

purchase decision, and post-purchase contact with the firm (Kotler and Armstrong, 2011). **Figure 6.2** shows the consumer decision process and the types of offline and online marketing communications that support this process and seek to influence the consumer before, during, and after the purchase decision.

As shown in Figure 6.2, traditional mass media, along with catalogs and direct mail campaigns, are used to drive potential buyers to Web sites. What's new about online purchasing is the new media marketing communications capabilities afforded by the Web: search engines, social media such as blogs, social networks and social shopping sites, online product reviews, video ads, targeted banner ads and permission e-mail, bulletin boards, chat rooms, and the like. Simply put, the Web offers marketers an extraordinary increase in marketing communications tools and power, and the ability to envelop the consumer in a very rich information and purchasing environment (Awad, et al., 2007). In Chapter 7, we describe these new communications techniques and gauge their effectiveness in greater detail.

Both offline and online communications tools can be used to support the online consumer decision process at each of the five stages of the process.

A MODEL OF ONLINE CONSUMER BEHAVIOR

Is offline consumer behavior fundamentally different from online consumer behavior? Arguably not. The e-commerce world is not quite so revolutionary as some would have us believe. For instance, the stages of the consumer decision process are basically the same whether the consumer is offline or online. On the other hand, the general model of consumer behavior requires modification to take into account new factors and the unique features of the Internet that allow new opportunities to interact with the customer online also need to be accounted for. In **Figure 6.3**, we have modified the general model of consumer behavior to focus on user characteristics, product

FIGURE 6.2	THE CONSUMER DECISION PROCESS AND SUPPORTING COMMUNICATIONS				
MARKET COMMUNICATIONS	Awareness—Need Recognition	Search	Evaluation of Alternatives	Purchase	Post-purchase Behavior—Loyalty
Offline Communications	Mass media TV Radio Print media Social networks	Catalogs Print ads Mass media Sales people Product raters Store visits Social networks	Reference groups Opinion leaders Mass media Product raters Store visits Social networks	Promotions Direct mail Mass media Print media	Warranties Service calls Parts and repair Consumer groups Social networks
Online Communications	Targeted banner ads Interstitials Targeted event promotions Social networks	Search engines Online catalogs Site visits Targeted e-mail Social networks	Search engines Online catalogs Site visits Product reviews User evaluations Social networks	Online promotions Lotteries Discounts Targeted e-mail Flash sales	Communities of consumption Newsletters Customer e-mail Online updates Social networks

FIGURE 6.3	A MODEL OF ONLINE CONSUMER BEHAVIOR

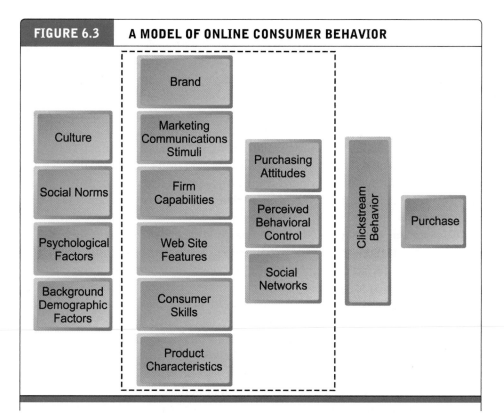

In this general model of online consumer behavior, the decision to purchase is shaped by background demographic factors, several intervening factors, and, finally, influenced greatly by clickstream behavior very near to the precise moment of purchase.

characteristics, and Web site features, along with traditional factors such as brand strength and specific market communications (advertising) and the influence of both online and offline social networks (Watts, 2004; Lohse, et al. 2000; Pavlou and Fygenson, 2005; Pavlou and Dimoka, 2006). Figure 6.3 attempts to summarize and simplify current research.

In the online model, Web site features, along with consumer skills, product characteristics, attitudes towards online purchasing, and perceptions about control over the Web environment come to the fore. Web site features include latency (delay in downloads), navigability, and confidence in a Web site's security. (We examine Web site design issues as they relate to marketing more fully in Chapter 7.) There are parallels in the analog world. For instance, it is well known that consumer behavior can be influenced by store design, and that understanding the precise movements of consumers through a physical store can enhance sales if goods and promotions are arranged along the most likely consumer tracks. For instance, because consumers almost invariably enter a store and move to the right, high-margin items—jewelry and cosmetics—tend to be located there. And because it is known that consumers purchase fresh dairy products frequently, they are put at the back of grocery stores, forcing customers to wend their way through many aisles. Walmart uses consumer-tracking databases within its stores to optimize the convenience to consumers—putting clothing nearest the entry, and electronics and cameras toward the back. Proper store design and precision tracking of consumers are not new, but the technical implementation, lowered cost, ubiquity, and comprehensiveness on the Web are new.

Consumer skills refers to the knowledge that consumers have about how to conduct online transactions (which increases with experience). *Product characteristics* refers to the fact that some products can be easily described, packaged, and shipped over the Internet (such as books, software, and DVDs), whereas others cannot. Combined with traditional factors, such as brand, advertising, and firm capabilities, these factors lead to specific attitudes about purchasing at a Web site (trust in the Web site and favorable customer experience) and a sense that the consumer can control his or her environment on the Web site.

clickstream behavior
the transaction log that consumers establish as they move about the Web

Clickstream behavior refers to the transaction log that consumers establish as they move about the Web, from search engine to a variety of sites, then to a single site, then to a single page, and then, finally, to a decision to purchase. These precious moments are similar to "point-of-purchase" moments in traditional retail.

A number of researchers have argued that understanding the background demographics of Internet users is no longer necessary, and not that predictive in any event. In most studies of consumer behavior, background demographics usually account for less than 5% of the observed behavior. Many believe instead that the most important predictors of online consumer behavior are the session characteristics and the clickstream behavior of people close to the moment of purchase, which can include also the history of their clickstream behavior prior to visiting a specific site. Advertising networks can keep histories of consumer clickstream behavior for many months. The theory is that this information will enable marketers to understand what the consumer was looking for at each moment, and how much they were willing to pay, thus allowing the marketers to precisely target their communications in an effort to sway the purchase decision in their favor.

A study of over 10,000 visits to an online wine store found that detailed and general clickstream behavior were as important as customer demographics and prior purchase behavior in predicting a current purchase (Van den Poel and Buckinx, 2005). The most important clickstream factors were:

- Number of days since last visit
- Speed of clickstream behavior
- Number of products viewed during last visit
- Number of pages viewed
- Number of products viewed
- Supplying personal information (trust)
- Number of days since last purchase
- Number of past purchases

Clickstream marketing takes maximum advantage of the Internet environment. It presupposes no prior "deep" knowledge of the customer (and in that sense is "privacy-regarding"), and can be developed dynamically as customers use the Internet. For instance, the success of search engine marketing (the display of paid advertisements

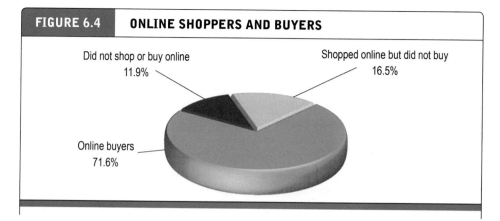

FIGURE 6.4   ONLINE SHOPPERS AND BUYERS

Did not shop or buy online
11.9%

Shopped online but did not buy
16.5%

Online buyers
71.6%

About 88% of U.S Internet users, age 14 and older, shop online, either by researching products or by purchasing products online. The percentage of those actually purchasing has increased to about 72%. Only about 12% do not buy or shop online.
SOURCE: Based on data from eMarketer, Inc., 2012f.

on Web search pages) is based in large part on what the consumer is looking for at the moment and how they go about looking (detailed clickstream data). After examining the detailed data, general clickstream data is used (days since last visit, past purchases). If available, demographic data is used (region, city, and gender).

SHOPPERS: BROWSERS AND BUYERS

The picture of Internet use sketched in the previous section emphasizes the complexity of behavior online. Although the Internet audience still tends to be concentrated among the well educated, affluent, and youthful, the audience is increasingly becoming more diverse. Clickstream analysis shows us that people go online for many different reasons. Online shopping is similarly complex. Beneath the surface of the $362 billion B2C e-commerce market in 2012 are substantial differences in how users shop online.

For instance, as shown in **Figure 6.4**, about 72% of U.S. Internet users, age 14 and older, are "buyers" who actually purchase something entirely online. Another 16.5% research products on the Web ("browsers"), but purchase them offline. With the teen and adult U.S. Internet audience (14 years or older) estimated at about 209 million in 2012, online shoppers (the combination of buyers and browsers, totalling 88%) add up to a market size of around 184 million consumers. Most marketers find this number exciting.

The significance of online browsing for offline purchasing should not be underestimated. Although it is difficult to precisely measure the amount of offline sales that occur because of online product research, several different studies have found that about one-third of all offline retail purchasing is influenced by online product research, blogs, banner ads, and other Internet exposure. The offline influence varies by product. This amounts to about $1.2 trillion in annual retail sales, a truly extraordinary number (Forrester Research, 2011b).

E-commerce is a major conduit and generator of offline commerce. The reverse is also true: online traffic is driven by offline brands and shopping. While online research influences offline purchases, it is also the case that offline marketing media heavily influence online behavior including sales. Traditional print media (magazines and newspapers) and television are by far the most powerful media for reaching and engaging consumers with information about new products and directing them to the Web (see **Table 6.6**). Online communities and blogging are also very influential but not yet as powerful as traditional media. This may be surprising to many given the attention to social networks as marketing vehicles, but it reflects the diversity of influences on consumer behavior and the real-world marketing budgets of firms that are still heavily dominated by traditional media. Even more surprising in the era of Facebook, face-to-face interactions are a more powerful influence than participation in online social communities.

TABLE 6.6	MEDIA THAT INFLUENCE CONSUMERS TO START SEARCH FOR MERCHANDISE ONLINE
MEDIA	PERCENTAGE OF RESPONDENTS
Magazines	47%
Reading an article	43%
Broadcast TV	43%
Newspapers	41%
Face-to-face communication	39%
Cable TV	36%
Coupons	36%
Direct mail	30%
Radio	29%
In-store promotions	27%
Online advertising	26%
E-mail advertising	25%
Online communities (Facebook, LinkedIn)	19%
Outdoor billboards	12%
Blogs	10%
Instant messaging	8%
Mobile phone	7%
Yellow pages	7%
Text messaging	6%
Other	6%
Mobile pictures/video	4%

SOURCES: Based on data from Retail Advertising & Marketing Association (RAMA), 2010; industry sources, authors' estimates.

These considerations strongly suggest that e-commerce and traditional commerce are coupled and should be viewed by merchants (and researchers) as part of a continuum of consuming behavior and not as radical alternatives to one another. Commerce is commerce; the customers are often the same people. Customers use a wide variety of media, sometimes multiple media at once. The significance of these findings for marketers is very clear. Online merchants should build the information content of their sites to attract browsers looking for information, build content to rank high in search engines, put less attention on selling per se, and promote services and products (especially new products) in offline media settings in order to support their online stores.

WHAT CONSUMERS SHOP FOR AND BUY ONLINE

You can look at online sales as divided roughly into two groups: small-ticket and big-ticket items. Big-ticket items include computer equipment and consumer electronics, where orders can easily be more than $1,000. Small-ticket items include apparel, books, health and beauty supplies, office supplies, music, software, videos, and toys, where the average purchase is typically less than $100. In the early days of e-commerce, sales of small-ticket items vastly outnumbered those of large-ticket items for a variety of reasons. First movers on the Web sold these products early on; the purchase price was low (reduced consumer risk); the items were physically small (shipping costs were low); margins were high (at least on CDs and software); and there was a broad selection of products (e-commerce vendors could compete on scope when compared to traditional offline stores). But the recent growth of big-ticket items such as computer hardware, consumer electronics, furniture, and jewelry has changed the overall sales mix. Consumers are now much more confident spending online for big-ticket items. Although furniture and large appliances were initially perceived as too bulky to sell online, these categories have rapidly expanded in the last few years. Free shipping offered by Amazon and other large retailers has also contributed to consumers buying many more expensive and large items online such as air conditioners. The types of purchases made also depend on levels of experience with the Web. New Web users tend primarily to buy small-ticket items, while experienced Web users are more willing to buy large-ticket items in addition to small-ticket items. Refer to Table 1.6 to see how much consumers spent online for various categories of goods at the top 500 Internet retailers in 2011.

INTENTIONAL ACTS: HOW SHOPPERS FIND VENDORS ONLINE

Given the prevalence of "click here" banner ads, one might think customers are "driven" to online vendors by spur-of-the-moment decisions. In fact, only a tiny percentage of shoppers click on banners to find vendors. Once they are online, 59% of consumers use a search engine as their preferred method of research for purchasing a product, 28% go to marketplaces such as Amazon or eBay, 10% go direct to retail Web sites, and 3% use other methods (Channel Advisor, 2010). E-commerce shoppers are highly intentional. Typically, they are focused browsers looking for specific products, companies, and services. Merchants can convert these "goal-oriented," intentional shoppers into buyers if the merchants can target their communications to the shoppers and design their sites in such a way as to provide easy-to-access and useful product information, full selection, and customer service, and do this at the very moment the customer is searching for the product (Wolfinbarger and Gilly, 2001). This is no small task. There are, of course, exceptions. Some people go on the Web and are not quite clear what they are looking for. StumbleUpon.com is a site for these unintentional searchers who, for the most part, are subject and community searchers rather than product searchers. StumbleUpon identifies the general topic of interest for the user and then relies on collaborative filtering tools to direct visitors to other sites on the Web that similarly interested people have visited and found interesting. eBay is building a recommender system that introduces interesting products to consumers regardless of their intentions.

WHY MORE PEOPLE DON'T SHOP ONLINE

A final consumer behavior question to address is: Why don't more online Web users shop online? About 28% of Internet users do not buy online. Why not? **Table 6.7** lists the major online buying concerns among Internet users in the United States.

Arguably, the largest factor preventing more people from shopping online is the "trust factor," the fear that online merchants will cheat you, lose your credit card information, or use personal information you give them to invade your personal privacy, bombarding you with unwanted e-mail and pop-up ads. Secondary factors can be summarized as "hassle factors," like shipping costs, returns, and inability to touch and feel the product (Doolin, et al., 2007).

TRUST, UTILITY, AND OPPORTUNISM IN ONLINE MARKETS

A long tradition of research shows that the two most important factors shaping the decision to purchase online are utility and trust (Brookings Institute, 2011; Kim, et al., 2009; Ba and Pavlou, 2002). Consumers want good deals, bargains, convenience, and

TABLE 6.7	WHY INTERNET USERS DO NOT BUY ONLINE
Want to see and touch before buying	34%
Concerns about pesonal financial information	31%
Delivery costs are too high	30%
Concerns that returns will be a hassle	26%
Prefer to research online, then buy in a store	24%
No need to buy products online	23%
Can't speak to a sales assistant in person	14%

SOURCE: Based on data from eMarketer, Inc., 2011a.

speed of delivery. In short, consumers are looking for utility. On the other hand, in any seller-buyer relationship, there is an asymmetry of information. The seller usually knows a lot more than the consumer about the quality of goods and terms of sale. This can lead to opportunistic behavior by sellers (Akerlof, 1970; Williamson, 1985; Mishra, 1998). Consumers need to trust a merchant before they make a purchase. Sellers can develop trust among online consumers by building strong reputations of honesty, fairness, and delivery of quality products—the basic elements of a brand. Feedback forums such as Epinions.com (now part of Shopping.com), Amazon's book reviews from reviewers, and eBay's feedback forum are examples of trust-building online mechanisms (NielsenWire, 2012; Opinion Research Corporation, 2009). Online sellers who develop trust among consumers are able to charge a premium price for their online products and services (Kim and Benbasat, 2006, 2007; Pavlou, 2002). A review of the literature suggests that the most important factors leading to a trusting online relationship are perception of Web site credibility, ease of use, and perceived risk (Corritore, et al., 2006). An important brake on the growth of e-commerce is lack of trust. Newspaper and television ads are far more trusted than online ads (Nielsen, 2011). Personal friends and family are far more powerful determinants of online purchases than membership in social networks (eMarketer, Inc., 2010a). These attitudes have grown more positive over time, but new concerns about the use of personal information by Web marketers is raising trust issues among consumers again.

6.2   THE DIGITAL COMMERCE MARKETING PLATFORM: AN OVERVIEW

Building and maintaining brands online has been transformed by the growth of online social networks and social sites, and the rapid deployment of smartphones and tablet computers. With well over 200 million U.S. Internet users visiting a variety of social network sites and spending nearly an hour there each day, firms need to have a presence on these sites. Likewise with mobile phones and tablets: about 60% of U.S. Internet users access the Web or use apps from their mobile devices, and soon, sales of tablet computers will exceed sales of PCs. Firms need to have a mobile solution to the problem of potential customers wanting to access their Web site through their devices.

In the past, from 2000 to 2010, the first step in building an online brand was to build a Web site, and then try to attract an audience. The most common "traditional" marketing techniques for establishing a brand and attracting customers were search engine marketing, display ads, e-mail campaigns, and affiliate programs. This is still the case: building a Web site is still a first step, and the "traditional" online marketing techniques are still the main powerhouses of brand creation and online sales revenue in 2012. But today, marketers need to take a much broader view of the online marketing challenge, and to consider other media channels for attracting an audience such as social network sites and mobile devices, in concert with traditional Web sites.

The five main elements of a comprehensive multi-channel marketing plan are: Web site, traditional online marketing, social marketing, mobile marketing, and offline marketing. **Table 6.8** illustrates these five main platforms, central elements within each type, some examples, and the primary function of marketing in each situation. Each of the main types of online marketing are discussed in Section 6.3 and throughout the chapter in greater detail.

STRATEGIC ISSUES AND QUESTIONS

Immediately, by examining Table 6.8, you can understand the management complexity of building brands online. There are five major types of marketing, and a variety of different platforms that perform different functions. If you're a manager of a start-up, or the Web site manager of an existing commercial Web site, you face a number of

TABLE 6.8	THE DIGITAL MARKETING ROADMAP		
TYPE OF MARKETING	**PLATFORMS**	**EXAMPLES**	**FUNCTION**
Web Site	Traditional Web site	Ford.com	Anchor site
Traditional Online Marketing	Search engine marketing	Google; Bing; Yahoo	Query-based intention marketing
	Display advertising	Yahoo; Google; MSN	Interest- and context-based marketing; targeted marketing
	E-mail	Major retailers	Permission marketing
	Affiliates	Amazon	Brand extension
Social Marketing	Social networks	Facebook/Google +1	Conversations; sharing
	Micro blogging sites	Twitter	News, quick updates
	Blogs/forums	Pinterest; TheFancy	Communities of interest; sharing
	Video marketing	YouTube	Engage; inform
	Game marketing	Farmville; SimCity	Identification
Mobile Marketing	Smartphone site	m.ford.com	Quick access; news; updates
	Tablet site	t.ford.com	Visual engagement
	Apps	Ford Mustang Customerizer; Discover the 2012 Mustang	Visual engagement
Offline Marketing	Television	Cadillac CTS Olympics 2012	Brand anchoring; inform
	Newspapers	Nike Olympics ambush campaign	Brand anchoring; inform
	Magazines	BMW Expression of Joy print and video campaign	Brand anchoring; inform

strategic questions. Where should you focus first? Build a Web site, develop a blog, or jump into developing a Facebook presence? If you have a successful Web site that already uses search engine marketing and display ads, where should you go next: develop a social network presence or use offline media? Does your firm have the resources to maintain a social media marketing campaign? We discuss how real firms and marketing executives are making these decisions in Section 6.3.

A second strategic management issue involves the integration of all these different marketing platforms into a single coherent branding message. Often, there are different groups with different skills sets involved in Web site design, search engine and display marketing, social media marketing, and offline marketing. Getting all these different specialties to work together and coordinate their campaigns can be very difficult. The danger is that a firm ends up with different teams managing each of the four platforms rather than a single team managing the digital online presence, or for that matter, marketing for the entire firm including retail outlets.

A third strategic management question involves resource allocation. There are actually two problems here. Each of the different major types of marketing, and each of the different platforms, have different metrics to measure their effectiveness. In some cases, for new social marketing platforms, there is no commonly accepted metric, and few which have withstood critical scrutiny or have a deep experience base providing empirical data. For instance, in Facebook marketing, an important metric is how many Likes your Facebook page produces. The connection between Likes and sales is still being explored. In search engine marketing, effectiveness is measured by how many clicks your ads are receiving; in display advertising, how many impressions of your ads are served. Second, each of these platforms has different costs for Likes, impressions, and clicks. In order to choose where your marketing resources should be deployed, you will have to link each of these activities to sales revenue. You will need to determine how much clicks, Likes, and impressions are worth. We address these questions in greater detail in Chapter 7.

CAN BRANDS SURVIVE THE INTERNET? BRANDS AND PRICE DISPERSION ON THE INTERNET

As we noted in Chapter 1, during the early years of e-commerce, many academics and business consultants predicted that the Web would lead to a new world of information symmetry and "frictionless" commerce. In this world, newly empowered customers, using intelligent shopping agents and the nearly infinite product and price information available on the Internet, would shop around the world (and around the clock) with minimal effort, driving prices down to their marginal cost and driving intermediaries out of the market as customers began to deal directly with producers (Wigand and Benjamin, 1995; Rayport and Sviokla, 1995; Evans and Wurster, 1999; Sinha, 2000). The result was supposed to be an instance of the "**Law of One Price**": with complete price transparency in a perfect information marketplace, one world price for every product would emerge. "Frictionless commerce" would, of course, mean the end of marketing based on brands.

Law of One Price
with complete price transparency in a perfect information marketplace, there will be one world price for every product

But it didn't work out this way. Price has not proven to be the only determinant of online consumer behavior. E-commerce firms continue to rely heavily on brands to attract customers and charge premium prices. For instance, online retailers use "flash pricing," where some popular products are marked down significantly for a day or even a few hours to create market buzz, and then are increased significantly the next day. Internet technologies can be used to infinitely differentiate products by using personalization, customization, and community marketing techniques (described in Section 6.3), thereby overcoming the price-lowering effects of lower search costs and a large number of worldwide suppliers for goods. By introducing information asymmetries into the marketplace, merchants can avoid direct price competition.

Whether or not prices are lower online than offline is still a point of debate. For instance, Bailey and Brynjolfsson (1997) found that prices for books, music CDs, and software were not substantially lower at e-commerce sites than in traditional stores or catalogs (see also Clay, et al., 1999 for similar results). Later studies found that prices at e-commerce sites were 9%–16% lower than at conventional retail outlets for music CDs (depending on whether taxes and shipping costs were included in the price), but also found substantial price dispersion—nearly as much as in traditional markets for the same goods (Brynjolfsson and Smith, 2000). Other research finds that online prices vary with season: during the holiday season of October–December, online prices rise, and then fall in the spring. This phenomenon is not dissimilar from traditional retail stores.

price dispersion

the difference between the highest and lowest prices in a market

Price dispersion refers to the difference between the highest and lowest prices in a market. In a perfect market, with perfect information, there is not supposed to be any price dispersion. Other evidence suggests that many suppliers and price comparisons can overwhelm consumers, and that consumers achieve efficiencies by quickly purchasing from a trusted, high-price provider. In general, the most frequently visited and used e-commerce sites are not the lowest-price sites (Smith, et al., 1999).

Research on brands and price dispersion illustrates the complexities of Internet marketing as well as the continuing power of brands, customer loyalty, and information symmetries. Some found that online prices were higher relative to offline prices (Baye, et al., 2002a; Scholten and Smith, 2002). Others found that, in general, online prices were less than offline prices depending on the product category and other variables. Price dispersion, a measure of competitiveness, typically is less for commodities (memory chips) than for books or other differentiated products. Moreover, Internet-savvy users systematically seek out the lowest prices by visiting shopping comparison sites, while other Internet users choose not to inform themselves and just purchase from a well-known online brand like Amazon. Sellers invest heavily in ways to differentiate their product or service—they create online brands that permit charging a premium for many products. The result is large differences in price sensitivity for the same products. For instance, researchers estimate that a 1% increase in prices at Amazon decreases sales by about 0.5%, while at Barnes & Noble, a 1% increase in prices results in a decrease in sales of about 4% (Baye, et al., 2002b). Price dispersion is also heavily influenced by "market thickness," the number of competitors selling the same undifferentiated goods. The more sellers in an online market (like photography), the less the price dispersion (Leiter and Warin, 2007). Price dispersion as measured by actual sale price is quite a bit lower than dispersion using posted prices, and there are many drivers of dispersion in online markets such as cost, order time, and quantity (Ghose and Yao, 2011). Online markets, as it turns out, are not "friction free" perfect markets although they probably have less friction than traditional markets.

Another tactic used by online sellers is the **library effect** (or catalog effect). How much is it worth to you to shop at a store that has everything? Just one stop, and chances are that you can get what you want. Would you rather visit a library with 10 million volumes or one with a few hundred thousand? The number of books on sale at Amazon is 23 times larger than the number of books found at a typical Barnes & Noble superstore and 57 times larger than the number of books typically found at a large independent bookstore. One analysis puts the gain in economic value (or "consumer welfare") produced by online bookstores at about $1 billion annually, five times larger than the gain in economic value produced by lower prices on the Internet (Brynjolfsson, Smith, and Hu, 2003). Stores such as Amazon make the size of their product offerings a part of their brand image and marketing communications in order to charge premium prices. Obviously, library effects apply only where there is a large number of SKUs or products available to sell—like music, DVDs, CDs, books, travel arrangements, airline tickets, and many of the products available on the Web—but not for unique collector items.

library effect
an attempt to appeal to consumers on the basis of the total number of products offered

We can conclude from the research evidence that brands are alive and well on the Web, that consumers are willing to pay premium prices for products and services they perceive as differentiated, that consumers are willing to shop online as opposed to offline at stores where product variety is high, and that in many instances, Web prices may be higher than those available in retail stores because of the premium consumers will pay for convenience. The evidence also suggests some solid reasons for the adage popular during the early days of e-commerce: "Get Big Fast." Selection, not price, may be your e-commerce site's biggest advantage and largest contributor to consumer welfare. Another strategic way to look at these data is to expect growing ownership concentration among Internet merchants as they pursue scale economies and library effects that derive from size.

Now that you have covered these basic concepts, the next section describes what makes Internet marketing different from ordinary marketing.

ONLINE SEGMENTING, TARGETING, AND POSITIONING

Markets are not unitary, but in fact are composed of many different kinds of customers with different needs. Firms seek to segment markets into distinct groups of customers who differ from one another in terms of product needs. Once the segments are established, each segment can be targeted with differentiated products. Within each segment, the product is positioned and branded as a unique, high-value product, especially suited to the needs of segment customers.

TABLE 6.9	MAJOR TYPES OF ONLINE MARKET SEGMENTATION AND TARGETING
Behavioral	Segmenting on the basis of behavior in the marketplace. In traditional stores, this involves observing how customers walk through stores. On the Internet, Web site owners and members of advertising networks can dynamically assign users to groups, and merge their behavioral information with other data. Using preferences and mentions on social networks to assign ads to individuals and network groups of friends.
Demographic	Using age, ethnicity, religion, and other demographic factors to segment. On the Internet, using registration data or other self-revelations. Sites visited also serves as proxy measures of age, e.g., music sites are visited by young persons.
Psychographic	Using common interests, values, and opinions along with personality, attitude, and lifestyle preferences to segment consumers into groups. On the Internet, Web sites visited can substitute for direct measurement, e.g., the fashion Web sites visited by consumers reflect a self-chosen lifestyle and values.
Technical	Using information gathered by a shopping technology as a basis for segmentation. Nearly everyone who shops at malls owns a car. On the Internet, each consumer visit generates a record of the user's domain, IP address, browser, computer platform, and connection type, as well as what URL the user linked to the site from and the date and time. People who connect using broadband media, for instance, are much more likely to download music from the Internet.
Contextual	Using the context of an event, or the content of an event, as a basis for segmentation. People who attend rock concerts tend to purchase music CDs as well. On the Internet, people who read the online *Wall Street Journal* are very good targets for financial service advertising.
Search	Using consumers' explicitly expressed interest at this moment to segment and target. Perhaps the simplest of all segmenting, search direct response follows the ageless maxim "sell them what they want."

There are six major ways in which marketers segment and target markets (**Table 6.9**). By segmenting markets, firms can differentiate their products to more closely fit the needs of customers in each segment. Rather than charge one price for the same product, firms can maximize revenues by creating several different variations on the same product and charging different prices in each market segment. While segmenting and targeting are not new, the Internet offers an unusual opportunity for very fine-grained segmenting down to the level of the individual. Potentially, with enough personal information, marketers on the Internet can personalize market messages to precisely fit an individual's needs and wants. In the physical world of marketing using other technologies like newspapers, radio, and television, it is difficult and sometimes impossible to personalize messages. Once markets are segmented, the branding process proceeds within each segment by appealing to the segment members. For instance, automobile manufacturers segment their markets on many dimensions: demographics (age, sex, income, and occupation), geographic (region), benefits (special performance features), and psychographics (self-image and emotional needs). For each market segment, they offer a uniquely branded product.

6.3 THE DIGITAL COMMERCE MARKETING PLATFORM: STRATEGIES AND TOOLS

Internet marketing has many similarities to, and differences from, ordinary marketing. The objective of Internet marketing—as in all marketing—is to build customer relationships so that the firm can achieve above-average returns (both by offering superior products or services and by communicating the brand's features to the consumer). These relationships are a foundation for the firm's brand. But Internet marketing, including all forms of digital marketing, is also very different from ordinary marketing because the nature of the medium and its capabilities are so different from anything that has come before.

There are four features of Internet marketing that distinguish it from traditional marketing channels. Compared to traditional print and television marketing, Internet marketing can be more personalized, participatory, peer-to-peer, and communal. Not all types of Internet marketing has these four features. For instance, there's not much difference between a marketing video splashed on your computer screen without your consent and watching a television commercial. However the same marketing video can be targeted to your personal interests, community memberships, and allow you to share it with others using a Like or + tag. Marketers are learning that the most effective Internet marketing has all four of these features.

CONVERSATIONS AND CUSTOMER ENGAGEMENT

In today's online marketing environment, the key phrases are "customer engagement" and "conversations." The point of contemporary online marketing today is to enter into conversations with customers about a firm's services and products, how customers use them, how they "feel" about them, and even what they don't like about them. These customer conversations take place using a variety of interactive online channels from the Web site, to blogs, Facebook pages, mobile devices, and Twitter feeds, to name a few. These conversations collectively are referred to as **customer engagement**. Soft is the new hard: it's not how many people were blasted by a television ad by your firm, but rather how many people entered into conversations with other viewers and company marketers, and hence were "engaged" as a result of your marketing campaign. How many Liked your product, or shared with friends in other ways? Both of these new metrics—Likes and sharing—point to the capabilities of the Internet

customer engagement
the totality of conversations a firm has with its customers through a variety of media and marketing channels

to enable a much closer relationship between brands and consumers than was ever possible with traditional technologies and media.

In this section, we describe a variety of Internet marketing strategies for market entry, brand development, customer acquisition, customer retention, pricing, and dealing with channel conflict. It is important to note that although B2C and B2B e-commerce do have differentiating features (for instance, in B2C e-commerce, marketing is aimed at individual consumers, whereas in B2B e-commerce, typically more than just one individual is involved with the purchase decision), the strategies discussed in this section in most instances can be, and are, applied in both the B2C and B2B arenas.

MARKET ENTRY STRATEGIES

Both new firms and traditional existing firms have choices about how to enter the market, and ways to establish the objectives of their online presence. **Figure 6.5** illustrates four basic market entry strategies. As you explore the Internet today you will find that successful online firms had many different origins. Some were unheard of start-ups with no brand to begin with, while other firms had brands that were decades old, and were able to establish a successful online presence.

Let's examine the situation facing new firms—quadrants 1 and 2 in Figure 6.5. One common strategy is pure clicks/first-mover advantage, utilized by such companies as Amazon, Netflix, Pinterest, LinkedIn, and Groupon (quadrant 1). Indeed, this start-up strategy is what most commonly comes to mind when people think about e-commerce even though start-up firms are just one part of the e-commerce story.

The ideas are beguiling and simplistic: enter the market first and experience first-mover advantages—heightened user awareness, followed rapidly by successful consumer transactions and experiences—and grow brand strength. According to leading consultants, first movers experience a short-lived mini-monopoly. They are the only providers for a few months, and then other copycats may enter the market

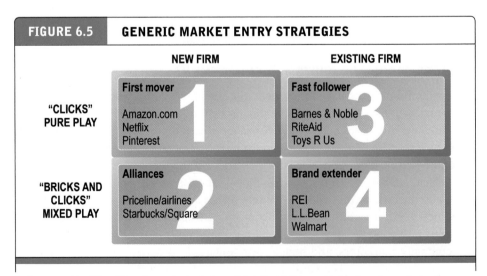

FIGURE 6.5	GENERIC MARKET ENTRY STRATEGIES

	NEW FIRM	EXISTING FIRM
"CLICKS" PURE PLAY	**First mover** 1 Amazon.com Netflix Pinterest	**Fast follower** 3 Barnes & Noble RiteAid Toys R Us
"BRICKS AND CLICKS" MIXED PLAY	**Alliances** 2 Priceline/airlines Starbucks/Square	**Brand extender** 4 REI L.L.Bean Walmart

Both new and traditional firms face a basic choice—"clicks" or "clicks and bricks"—when entering the e-commerce marketplace.

because entry costs are so low. To prevent new competitors from entering the market, growing audience size very rapidly is the most important corporate goal rather than profits and revenue.

Firms following this strategy typically spend the majority of their marketing budget (which, in and of itself, may constitute a large part of their available capital) on building brand and Web site awareness by purchasing display ads, search engine keywords, social network sites and promoted ads, along with high-visibility advertising in traditional mass media such as television (Super Bowl game ads), radio, newspapers, and magazines. If the first mover gathers most of the customers in a particular category (photo sharing, payments, pets, wine, gardening supplies, and so forth), the belief is that new entrants are not able to enter as easily because customers may not be willing to pay the switching costs. Customers would be "locked in" to the first-mover's interface. Moreover, the strength of the brand inhibits switching, even though competitors are just a click away.

For many firms, pursuing first-mover advantage as a marketing strategy has not always worked. Although first movers may have interesting advantages, they also have significant liabilities. For example, first movers often lack the complementary assets and resources required to compete over the long term. While innovative, first movers usually lack financial depth, marketing and sales resources, loyal customers, strong brands, and production or fulfillment facilities needed to meet customer demands once the product succeeds (Teece, 1986). Research on Internet marketing indicates that while expensive ad campaigns may increase brand awareness, the other components of a brand such as trust, loyalty, and reputation do not automatically follow, and more important, site visits do not necessarily translate into purchases (Fournier and Lee, 2009; Ha and Perks, 2005; Ellison, 2000).

Another possibility for new firms is to pursue a mixed bricks-and-clicks strategy, coupling an online presence with other sales channels (quadrant 2) by striking alliances. However, few new firms can afford the "bricks" part of this strategy. Therefore, firms following this entrance strategy often ally themselves with established firms that have already developed brand names, physical presence, production and distribution facilities, and the financial resources needed to launch a successful Internet business. For instance, Priceline struck alliances with the major airlines to provide unused inventory (passenger seats) to Priceline that would then sell the seats at a profit and share some of the proceeds with the airlines. For the airlines, Priceline offered a quick and useful way to develop an online presence. In 2012, Starbucks and Square, the mobile payment firm, struck an alliance that allows Starbucks coffee shops to accept smartphone payments from customers using the Square payment system. In this case we have a "bricks"-based business, Starbucks, working with a start-up online payments firm.

Now let's look at traditional firms. Traditional firms face some similar choices, with of course one difference: they have significant amounts of cash flow and capital to fund their e-commerce ventures over a long period of time. For example, Barnes & Noble, the world's largest physical store book retailer, formed Barnesandnoble.com (quadrant 3), a follower site, when faced with the success of upstart Amazon (quadrant 1). While

Barnes & Noble originally established its Web site as an independent firm, by 2012, it had rolled the Web business into its larger retail and publishing business, recognizing that today the digital business is integral to the entire business. Likewise, Rite Aid followed the success of online pharmacies such as Drugstore.com by establishing its own Web site (Riteaid.com).

The most common strategy for existing firms is to extend their businesses and brands by using a mixed bricks-and-clicks strategy in which online marketing is closely integrated with offline physical stores (quadrant 4). These "brand-extension" strategies characterize REI, L.L.Bean, Walmart, and many other established retail firms. Like fast followers, they have the advantage of existing brands and relationships. However, even more than fast followers, the brand extenders do not set up separate pure-play online stores, but instead typically integrate the online firm with the traditional firm from the very beginning. L.L.Bean and Walmart both saw the Web as an extension of their existing order processing and fulfillment, marketing, and branding efforts.

Each of the market entry strategies discussed above has seen its share of successes and failures. While the ultimate choice of strategy depends on a firm's existing brands, management strengths, operational strengths, and capital resources, most of today's firms with traditional stores are opting for a mixed bricks-and-clicks strategy in the hope that it will enable them to reach profitability more quickly.

THE WEB SITE AS A MARKETING PLATFORM: ESTABLISHING THE CUSTOMER RELATIONSHIP

Once a firm chooses a market entry strategy, the next task is establishing a relationship with the customer. A firm's Web site is a major tool for establishing the initial relationship with the customer. The Web site performs four important functions: establishing the brand identity and consumer expectations, informing and educating the consumer, shaping the customer experience, and anchoring the brand in an ocean of marketing messages coming from different sources. The Web site is the one place the consumer can turn to find the complete story. This is not true of apps, e-mails, or search engine ads.

The first function of a Web site is to establish the brand's identity and to act as an anchor for the firm's other Web marketing activities, thereby driving sales revenue. This involves identifying for the consumer the differentiating features of the product or service in terms of quality, price, product support, and reliability. Identifying the differentiating features of the product on the Web site's home page is intended to create expectations in the user of what it will be like to consume the product. For instance, Coke's Web site creates the expectation that the consumer will experience happiness by opening a Coke. Ford's Web site focuses on automobile technology and high miles per gallon. The expectation created by Ford's Web site is that if you buy a Ford, you'll be experiencing the latest automotive technology and the highest mileage. At the location-based social network Web site for Foursquare, the focus is on meeting friends, discovering local places, and saving money with coupons and rewards.

Web sites also function to anchor the brand online, acting as a central point where all the branding messages that emanate from the firm's multiple digital presences, such as Facebook, Twitter, mobile apps, or e-mail, come together at a single online location.

Aside from branding, Web sites also perform the typical functions of any commercial establishment by informing customers of the company's products and services. Web sites, with their online catalogs and associated shopping carts, are important elements of the online customer experience. **Customer experience** refers to the totality of experiences that a customer has with a firm, including the search, informing, purchase, consumption, and after-sales support for the product (Gartner, 2012; Verhoef, et al., 2008). The concept "customer experience" is broader than the traditional concept of "customer satisfaction" in that a much broader range of impacts is considered, including the customer's cognitive, affective, emotional, social, and physical relationship to the firm and its products. The totality of customer experiences will generally involve multiple retail channels. This means that, in the customer's mind, the Web site, Facebook page, Twitter feed, physical store, and television advertisements are all connected as part of his or her experience with the company.

For instance, Apple's extraordinary success in the market for smartphones and tablet computers is often attributed to Steve Jobs' nearly single-minded devotion to pursuing an optimal customer experience for consumers of Apple products, including the look and touch of the products, how they performed, and how durable they were. Beyond this, Jobs sought to create a sense of awe and magic in the mind of the consumer when using Apple products (Isaacson, 2012). Jobs extended these brand product features beyond the products to include Apple's retail stores, the Apple Web site, and the iTunes Store. The objective was, no matter where or how the consumer touched Apple products and services, the consumer would receive similar and coordinated branding messages.

TRADITIONAL ONLINE MARKETING TOOLS

Traditional online marketing tools include search engine marketing, display ad marketing, e-mail and permission marketing, affiliate marketing, lead generation marketing, and sponsorship marketing.

Search Engine Marketing

Search engines are the largest marketing and advertising platform on the Internet. In 2012, companies are expected to spend $17.6 billion on search engine marketing, almost half of all spending for digital marketing.

Search engine marketing (SEM) refers to the use of search engines to build and sustain brands. **Search engine advertising** refers to the use of search engines to support direct sales to online consumers.

Search engines are often thought of as mostly direct sales channels focused on making sales in response to advertisements. While this is a major use of search engines, they are also used more subtly to strengthen brand awareness, drive traffic to other Web sites or blogs to support customer engagement, gain deeper insight into customers' perceptions of the brand, support other related advertising (for instance, sending consumers to local dealer sites), and to support the brand indirectly. Search engines can also provide marketers insight into customer search patterns, opinions

customer experience
the totality of experiences that a customer has with a firm, including the search, informing, purchase, consumption, and after-sales support for its products, services, and various retail channels

search engine marketing (SEM)
involves the use of search engines to build and sustain brands

search engine advertising
involves the use of search engines to support direct sales to online

customers hold about their products, top trending search keywords, and what their competitors are using as keywords and the customer response.

A good example is Pepsico Inc., home to mega brands like Pepsi and Doritos chips, and many others. Pepsico makes no sales on the Web, but has several branding Web sites aimed at consumers, investors, and shareholders. The focus is on building, sustaining, and updating the Pepsi collection of branded consumer goods. A search on Pepsi will generate numerous search results that link to Pepsi marketing materials.

When users enter a search term at Google, Bing, Yahoo, or any of the other sites serviced by these search engines, they receive two types of listings: sponsored links, for which advertisers have paid to be listed (usually at the top of the search results page), and unsponsored "organic" search results. In addition, advertisers can purchase small text boxes on the side of search results pages. The paid, sponsored advertisements (Google's AdSense program) are powerful marketing tools that precisely match consumer intentions and interests with advertising messages at the right moment. Search engine marketing monetizes the value of the search process.

Marketers use search engines generally by purchasing key words that result in their firm's listings appearing on search results pages in response to user queries. Online publishers (which could include anyone from an individual blogger to a small business) can join an AdSense program (Google's term) and allow marketers to place ads on their Web sites based on the content of their sites, collecting some revenue for each click.

Because search engine marketing is so effective (it has the highest click-through rate and the highest return on ad investment), companies optimize their Web sites for search engine recognition. The better optimized the page is, the higher a ranking it will achieve in search engine result listings, and the more likely it will appear on the top of the page in search engine results. **Search engine optimization (SEO)** is the

search engine optimization (SEO)

techniques to improve the ranking of Web pages generated by search engine algorithms

process of improving the ranking of Web pages with search engines by altering the content and design of the Web pages and site. By carefully selecting key words used on the Web pages, updating content frequently, and designing the site so it can be easily read by search engine programs, marketers can improve the impact and return on investment in their Web marketing programs.

For instance, marketers need to make sure that the keywords used on their Web site match the keywords likely to be used as search terms by prospective customers. For example, if prospective customers search for "lighting" rather than "lamps," it makes sense to use the keyword "lighting" often on your Web site. It would also be advisable to have links on the Web site to other "lighting" sources. Search engines rank Web pages in part on the basis of how many links they have to other, well-known sites. Search engine programs make the assumption that the more links there are to and from a Web site, the more useful the Web site must be. We discuss search engine marketing and advertising techniques in more detail in Chapter 7.

Display Ad Marketing

Display ad marketing is the second largest form of online marketing. In 2012, companies spent around $13.4 billion on display ad marketing of all types, about 36% of all spending for digital marketing (eMarketer, Inc., 2012g). The display ad market is highly concentrated. The top five display ad companies are Google, Yahoo, Microsoft,

Facebook, and AOL, and they account for almost 50% of U.S. display ad revenue. Display ads includes four different kinds of ads: banner ads, rich media ads (animated ads), sponsorships, and video ads. Banner ads are the oldest and most familiar form of display marketing, and its difficult to avoid being exposed to hundreds of these ads every day on the Web, and increasingly on mobile devices. They are also the least effective and the lowest cost form of online marketing. The strong growth in display marketing is coming from two sources: the rapid growth of mobile devices, especially tablets, and the growing use and power of video ads and rich media ads on all platforms, from desktop PCs to tablets. Video ads are among the most powerful ads on the Internet in terms of user response and clicks.

Advertising Networks In the early years of e-commerce, firms placed ads on the few popular Web sites in existence, but by early 2000, there were hundreds of thousands of sites where ads could be displayed, and it became very inefficient for a single firm to purchase ads on each individual Web site. Most firms, even very large firms, did not have the capability by themselves to place banner ads and marketing messages on thousands of Web sites and monitor the results. Specialized marketing firms called advertising networks appeared to help firms take advantage of the powerful marketing potential of the Internet, and to make the entire process of buying and selling online ads more efficient and transparent. These ad networks have proliferated and have greatly increased the scale and liquidity of online marketing.

Advertising networks represent the most sophisticated application of Internet database capabilities to date, and illustrate just how different Internet marketing is from traditional marketing. **Advertising networks** sell advertising and marketing opportunities (slots) to companies who wish to buy exposure to an online audience (advertisers). Advertising networks obtain their inventory of ad opportunities from a network of participating sites that want to display ads on their sites in return for receiving a payment from advertisers everytime a visitor clicks on an ad. These sites are usually referred to as Web publishers. Marketers buy audiences and publishers sell audiences by attracting an audience and capturing audience information. Ad networks are the intermediaries who make this market work efficiently.

advertising networks
connect online marketers with publishers by displaying ads to consumers based on detailed customer information

The advertising network shares the revenue earned from marketers with the publisher. Audience information is collected by advertising networks, as well as other third-party data firms, who have developed software that tracks customer movements among the network members' sites, say, from Amazon to Travelocity, to Google, to Ford, and then on to AT&T, Yahoo, and eBay. At each visit, the ad network software decides which banner ads, videos, and other ads to show the customer, based in part on the customer's behavior at various sites on the network, recent clickstream behavior, demographics, prior searches, memberships, location, and interests, as well as a variety of other psychographic profiles. For instance, at Travelocity, the customer may research a vacation to England. On Google, the same customer may search for English cities. When the customer goes to Yahoo, he or she may be shown ads for raincoats. The advertiser works with the network to determine the rules for showing ads.

Perhaps the best-known advertising network is DoubleClick, which released its first-generation tracking system, DART, in 1996. Google purchased DoubleClick for $3.1 billion in April 2007, and the network is now called Google Display Network (GDN). Other

FIGURE 6.6	HOW AN ADVERTISING NETWORK SUCH AS DOUBLECLICK WORKS

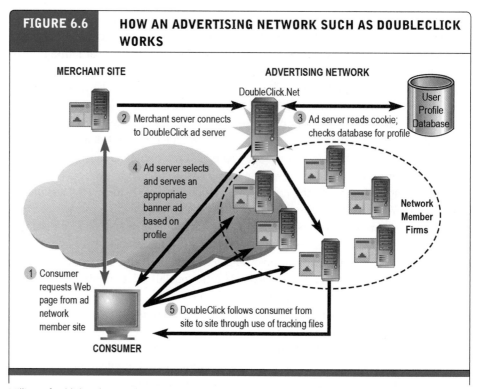

Millions of publishers have audiences to sell, and pages to fill with ads. Thousands of advertisers are looking for audiences. Ad networks are intermediaries that connect publishers with marketers.

advertising networks include 24/7 Real Media's Open AdStream (purchased by WPP, the world's largest advertising firm, for $649 million in June 2007), and Microsoft Advertising.

Figure 6.6 illustrates how these systems work. Advertising networks begin with a consumer requesting a page from a member of the advertising network (1). A connection is established with the third-party ad server (2). The ad server identifies the user by reading the cookie file on the user's hard drive and checks its user profile database for the user's profile (3). The ad server selects an appropriate banner ad based on the user's previous purchases, interests, demographics, or other data in the profile (4). Whenever the user later goes online and visits any of the network member sites, the ad server recognizes the user and serves up the same or different ads regardless of the site content. The advertising network follows users from site to site through the use of Web tracking files (5).

ad exchanges

create a market where many ad networks sell ad space to marketers

real-time bidding process (RTB)

online auctions where advertisers bid for audience slots

Advertising Exchanges and Real-Time Bidding. **Ad exchanges** take the online advertising market a step further by aggregating the supply side of advertising slots available at publishers across several ad networks, and establishing a **real-time bidding process (RTB)** where marketers can bid for slots based on their marketing criteria. Want to contact males age 18 to 34, recent visitors to a car site, unmarried, high risk-taking profile, located in New York or California, urban home, and financial service industry employment? An ad exchange will allow you to bid in real time on this audience against other advertisers, and then manage the placement of ads, accounting, and measurement for your firm. Ad exchanges offer tremendous global scale and efficiency. About 60%

of display ads are now placed through ad exchanges. One of the best known is Google's DoubleClick Ad Exchange, which is based on more than 100 ad networks (the supply side), and provides a computer-based market for buyers to purchase audiences (the demand side). This exchange sells audiences sliced into 1,000 interest categories. It displays more than 3 billion ads a day across 2 million Web sites worldwide, and maintains or distributes more than 100 million user profiles of Internet users (Google, 2011). These profiles are based on Web tracking files, offline purchase information, and social network data. Marketing firms, the buyers from publishers of Web sites, can target their audience and control the frequency and timing of ads during the day.

E-mail and Permission Marketing

In 2012, companies will spend an estimated $220 million on e-mail marketing, a relatively small market when compared to search and display ad marketing (eMarketer, Inc. 2012g). But these numbers can be deceiving. E-mail marketing still carries a punch with solid customer response in the form of clicks (upwards of 3% in targeted campaigns) and is very inexpensive. One result is that e-mail marketing is more prevalent than ever. It's a rare person who reports they don't receive any e-mail advertising messages every day. More than 183 million Americans use e-mail at least once a month. Daily deal firms like Groupon and LivingSocial, and flash marketers like Gilt, all built their firms on e-mail. While the amount spent on e-mail campaigns will be relatively flat in the coming years, marketers are becoming increasingly sophisticated in targeting e-mails to people most likely to be responsive. The growth of mobile devices will also drive additional e-mail campaigns. About one-third of e-mails will be opened on mobile devices in 2012, and mobile users have much higher e-mail utilization rates than desktop users. Upwards of 88% of smartphone users check their e-mail daily. While e-mail marketing often is sales oriented, it can also be used as an integral feature of a multi-channel marketing campaign designed to strengthen brand recognition. For instance, in 2012, Jeep created an e-mail campaign to a targeted audience of people who had searched on SUVs, and visited Chrysler and Jeep Facebook pages. The e-mail campaign announced a contest based on a game users could play online that involved tracking an arctic beast with a Jeep. Recipients could sign up on Facebook, Twitter, or the Jeep blog.

Permission Marketing The phrase "permission marketing" was coined by author and consultant Seth Godin to describe the strategy of obtaining permission from consumers before sending them information or promotional messages (Godin, 1999). Godin's premise was that by obtaining permission to send information to consumers up front, companies are much more likely to be able to develop a customer relationship. When consumers agree to receive promotional messages, they are opting in; when they decide they do not want to receive such messages, they opt out.

Permission marketing is a key component of e-mail. Typically, when placing an order online, consumers are given the option of receiving newsletters or announcements of products and sales via e-mail. In the United States, the default is usually "opt-in," and the consumer is required to check off an option to not receive e-mail. Federal law now requires merchants sending e-mail to consumers to provide an Unsubscribe link for all e-mail. We discuss e-mail as a marketing communication tool in greater detail in Chapter 7.

permission marketing marketing
strategy in which companies obtain permission from consumers before sending them information or promotional messages

Affiliate Marketing

affiliate marketing
commissions paid by advertisers to affiliate Web sites for referring potential customers to their Web site

Affiliate marketing is a form of marketing where a firm pays a commission to other Web sites (including blogs) for sending customers to their Web site. Affiliate marketing generally involves pay-for-performance: the affiliate or affiliate network gets paid only if users click on a link or purchase a product. In 2012, companies will spend about $2.5 billion on affiliate marketing (Forrester, 2012). Industry experts estimate that around 10% of all retail online sales are generated through affiliate programs (as compared to search engine ads, which account for more than 30% of online sales).

Visitors to an affiliate Web site typically click on ads and are taken to the advertiser's Web site. In return, the advertiser pays the affiliate a fee, either on a per-click basis or as a percentage of whatever the customer spends on the advertisers site. Paying commissions for referrals or recommendations long pre-dated the Web.

For instance, Amazon has a strong affiliate program consisting of more than 1 million participant sites, called Associates, which receive up to 15% on sales their referrals generate. Affiliates attract people to their blogs or Web sites where they can click on ads for products at Amazon.com Amazon pays affiliates a percentage on the sales generated within 24 hours of a visitor's click. Members of eBay's Affiliates Program can earn between $20 and $35 for each active registered user sent to eBay. Amazon, eBay, and other large e-commerce companies with affiliate programs typically administer such programs themselves. Smaller e-commerce firms who wish to use affiliate marketing often decide to join an affiliate network (sometimes called an affiliate broker), which acts as an intermediary. Bloggers often sign up for Google's AdSense program to attract advertisers to their sites. They are paid for each click on an ad and sometimes for subsequent purchases made by visitors.

Affiliate networks are firms that bring would-be affiliates (bloggers and Web publishers) and merchants seeking affiliates together, helps affiliates set up the necessary links on their Web sites, tracks all activity, and arranges all payments. Leading affiliate networks include Commission Junction and LinkShare. In return for their services, affiliate networks typically take about 20% of any fee that would be payable to the affiliate.

A key benefit of affiliate marketing is the fact that it typically operates on a "pay-for-performance" basis. Affiliates provide qualified sales leads in return for compensation. Another advantage is the existence of an established user base that a marketer can immediately tap into through an affiliate. For affiliates, the appeal is a steady income—potentially large—that can result from such relationships. In addition, the presence of another company's logo or brand name can provide a measure of prestige and credibility.

Lead Generation Marketing

Lead generation marketing uses multiple e-commerce presences to generate leads for businesses who later can be contacted and converted into customers through sales calls, e-mails, or other means. In one sense, all Internet marketing campaigns attempt to develop leads. But lead generation marketing is a specialized sub-set of the Internet marketing industry that provides consulting services and software tools to collect and manage leads for firms, and to convert these leads to customers. Companies will spend an estimated $1.7 billion on lead generation marketing in 2012. Sometimes called "inbound marketing," lead generation marketing firms help other firms build Web sites, launch e-mail campaigns, use social network sites and blogs to optimize the generation of leads, and then manage those leads by initiating further contacts, tracking interactions, and interfacing with customer relationship management systems to keep track of customer-firm interactions. One of the foremost lead generation marketing firms is Hubspot.com, which has developed a software suite for generating and managing leads.

Sponsorship Marketing

A **sponsorship** is a paid effort to tie an advertiser's name to particular information, an event, or a venue in a way that reinforces its brand in a positive yet not overtly commercial manner. In 2012, companies spent about $1.6 billion for sponsorship marketing (eMarketer, Inc., 2012g). Sponsorships typically are more about branding than immediate sales. A common form of sponsorship is targeted content (or advertorials), in which editorial content is combined with an ad message to make the message more valuable and attractive to its intended audience. For instance, WebMD.com, the leading medical information Web site in the United States, offers "sponsorship sites" on the WebMD Web site to companies such as Phillips to describe its home defibrillators, and Lilly to describe its pharmaceutical solutions for attention deficit disorders among children.

> **sponsorship**
> a paid effort to tie an advertiser's name to information, an event, or a venue in a way that reinforces its brand in a positive yet not overtly commercial manner

SOCIAL MARKETING: SHARING AND ENGAGING

Social marketing includes marketing on social networks sites such as Facebook, Google+, and Twitter, marketing on blogs, and "old-fashioned" viral marketing.

Social Marketing

Social marketing involves the use of online social networks and communities to build brands and drive sales revenues. There are several kinds of social networks, from Facebook and Twitter, to social apps, social games, blogs, and forums (Web sites that attract people who share a community of interests or skills). In 2012, companies will spend about $3.1 billion on social marketing, and this is expected to grow to about $5 billion by 2014. Next to mobile marketing, it is the fastest growing type of online marketing. Nevertheless, in 2012, it represents only 8% of all online marketing (eMarketer, Inc., 2012h). The long-term prospects of social marketing are not known at this time. Marketers cannot ignore the huge audiences that social networks such as Facebook, Twitter, and LinkedIn are gathering, which rival television and radio in size. Over 80% of U.S. businesses now have Facebook pages and a presence on many other social network sites. Companies will spend over 90% of their social marketing budgets on social networks, and the vast majority (70%) on Facebook. Nevertheless, all types of social networks are experiencing significant ad revenue growth despite the dominance of Facebook. Facebook will generate nearly $4 billion in online ad revenues in 2012. We examine social network advertising expenditures and effectiveness more closely in Chapter 7.

> **social marketing**
> the use of online social networks and communities to build brands and drive sales

Social marketing is grounded in the idea of the digital social graph. The digital social graph is a mapping of all significant online social relationships. The **social graph** is synonymous with the idea of a "social network" used to describe offline

> **social graph**
> a mapping of all significant online social relationships

relationships. You can map your own social graph (network) by drawing lines from yourself to the 10 closest people you know.

If they know one another, draw lines between these people. If you are ambitious, ask these 10 friends to list and draw in the names of the 10 people closest to them. What emerges from this exercise is a preliminary map of your social network. Now imagine if everyone on the Internet did the same, and then posted the results to a very large database with a Web site. Ultimately, you would end up with Facebook or a site like it. The collection of all these personal social networks is called "the social graph."

According to small-world theory, you are only six links away from any other person on earth. Let's say you sent a list of 100 names from your personal address book to your friends. They in turn entered 50 names of their friends to the list, and so on, six times. The social network created would encompass 31 billion people! The social graph is therefore a collection of millions of personal social graphs (and all the people in them). So it's a small world indeed, and we are all more closely linked than we ever thought.

If you understand the inter-connectedness of people, you will see just how important this concept is to e-commerce: the products and services you buy will influence the decisions of your friends, and their decisions will in turn influence you. If you are a marketer trying to build and strengthen a brand, the implication is clear: take advantage of the fact that people are enmeshed in social networks, share interests and values, and communicate and influence one another. As a marketer, your target audience is not a million isolated people watching a TV show, but the social network of people who watch the show, and the viewers' personal networks.

Social networks in the offline world are collections of people who voluntarily communicate with one another over an extended period of time. Online social networks, such as Facebook, LinkedIn, Twitter, Tumblr, and Google+, along with tens of other sites with social components, are Web sites that enable users to communicate with one another, form group and individual relationships, and share interests, values, and ideas. Individuals establish online profiles with text and photos, creating an online profile of how they want others to see them, and then invite their friends to link to their profile. The network grows by word of mouth and through e-mail links. One of the most ubiquitous graphical elements on Web sites in 2012 is Facebook's Like button, which allows users to tell their friends they like a product, service, or content.

There are four features of social marketing that are driving its growth:

- *Social sign-on:* Signing in to various Web sites through social network pages like Facebook. This allows Web sites to receive valuable social profile information from Facebook and use it in their own marketing efforts.

- *Collaborative shopping:* Creating an environment where consumers can share their shopping experiences with one another by viewing products, chatting, or texting. Instead of talking about the weather, friends can chat online about brands, products, and services.

- *Network notification:* Creating an environment where consumers can share their approval (or disapproval) of products, services, or content, or share their geolocation, perhaps a restaurant or club, with friends. Facebook's ubiquitous "Like" button is an example. Twitter tweets and followers are another example.

- *Social search (recommendation):* Enabling an environment where consumers can ask their friends for advice on purchases of products, services, and content. While Google can help you find things, social search can help you evaluate the quality of things by listening to the evaluations of your friends or their friends. For instance, Amazon's social recommender system can use your Facebook social profile to recommend products.

Twitter Marketing: All the News and Views Now

Twitter is a microblogging social networking site that allows users to send and receive 140-character messages. Twitter has an estimated 30 million users in the United States (about 12% of Internet users) (eMarketer, Inc., 2012h). Twitter claims over 140 million users worldwide. Twitter offers advertisers and marketers a chance to interact and engage with their customers in real time and in a fairly intimate, one-on-one manner. Advertisers can buy ads that look like organic tweets (the kind you receive from friends), and these ads can tie into and enhance marketing events like new product announcements or pricing changes. Twitter began offering advertising in 2010 and according to eMarketer, in 2012, over 50% of companies with more than 100 employees are now using it for marketing purposes. Examples include Volkswagen (product announcement), Google (announcing Google Instant Search), Old Spice (product promotion), Ford (product announcement), MTV (sponsorship and branding), and Papa John's Pizza (branding). See Chapters 2 and 7 for additional discussions of Twitter.

There are three kinds of Twitter marketing products:

- *Promoted Tweets:* Advertisers pay to have their tweets appear in users' search results. The tweets appear as "promoted" in the search results, and the pricing is based on an auction run on the Twitter ad platform.
- *Promoted Trends:* Advertisers pay to move their hashtags (# symbol used to mark keywords in a tweet) to the top of Twitter's Trends List. Otherwise, hashtags are found by the Twitter search engine, and only those that are organically popular make it to the Trends List. Promoted Trends cost about $120,000 a day in 2012.
- *Promoted Accounts:* Advertisers pay to have their branded account moved to the top of their Who to Follow list on the Twitter home page.

While marketers are just learning how to use Twitter, researchers find that about 21% of Twitter users follow at least one brand. Millions of users flood the Twitter Web site to follow fast developing stories, celebrities, and trending topics. It is clear that Twitter's marketing platform will expand with its user base.

Blog Marketing

Blogs have been around for a decade and are a part of the mainstream online culture (see Chapter 3 for a description of blogs). Thousands of high-ranking corporate officials, politicians, journalists, academics, and government officials have created blogs, along with the rest of us. Blogs play a vital role in online marketing. Around 43% of all U.S. companies use blogs for marketing in 2012. Although more firms use Twitter and Facebook, these sites have not replaced blogs, and in fact often point to blogs for long-form content. Blog creators tend to be young, broadband users, Internet veterans, wealthy, and educated. It did not take long for marketers to discover this large number of "eyeballs" and seek out ways to market and advertise to them. Because blogs are based on the personal opinions of the writers, they are ideal locations to start a viral marketing campaign. Blogs, like ordinary Web sites, can be used to display both branding ads not geared towards sales, as well as advertising aimed at making sales. But because blogs are usually created by private individuals wishing to make a public statement, bloggers do not have the Web marketing and advertising resources of large corporations, and the number of eyeballs viewing any one site is miniscule compared to portal Web sites such as Yahoo. The problem is how to efficiently aggregate these tiny audiences into a significant block of eyeballs worthy of an advertiser's attention. One solution is to build an advertising network of bloggers and allow bloggers to subscribe to this network, agreeing to display ads on their blogs, and then paying them a fee for each visitor who clicks on the ad.

Two major players in the blogging industry, Technorati and Six Apart, have launched blog advertising networks designed to connect blog sites with advertisers. Blogads.com provides a similar service. Google's AdSense is also a major blog marketer. The AdSense service "reads" a blog and identifies the subject of the blog's postings. Then AdSense places appropriate ads on the blog, adjusted to the blog's content. For instance, BoingBoing.net, a very popular technology blog known for its love of gadgets, displays ads from major advertisers like HP, Verizon, and Rackspace. Blog marketing is showing steady growth and will show substantial gains over the next several years. In 2011, blog marketing spending was about $640 million, estimated to rise to $775 million in 2015. The rapid growth of blogs and blog marketing has led to a small industry of "brand advocates." Brand advocates are Internet users who support and promote specific brands. Often, firms hire active bloggers to become brand advocates for a fee, or bloggers receive discounts on products or other deals. One problem: payments to brand advocates without letting readers know of the relationship threatens to reduce the credibility and effectiveness of blog marketing, and makes larger advertisers fearful of advertising on blogs when they cannot control the content of the blog.

Viral Marketing

viral marketing

the process of getting customers to pass along a company's marketing message to friends, family, and colleagues

Just as affiliate marketing involves using a trusted Web site to encourage users to visit other sites, **viral marketing** is a form of social marketing that involves getting customers to pass along a company's marketing message to friends, family, and colleagues. It's the online version of word-of-mouth advertising, which spreads even faster and further than in the real world. In the offline world, next to television, word of mouth is the second most important means by which consumers find out about new products. And the most important factor in the decision to purchase is the face-to-face recommendations of parents, friends, and colleagues. Millions of online adults in the United States are "influencers" who share their opinions about products in a variety of online settings. In addition to increasing the size of a company's customer base, customer referrals also have other advantages: they are less expensive to acquire since existing customers do all the acquisition work, and they tend to use online support services less, preferring to turn back to the person who referred them for advice. Also, because they cost so little to acquire and keep, referred customers begin to generate profits for a company much earlier than customers acquired through other marketing methods. There are a number of online venues where viral marketing appears. E-mail used to be the primary online venue for viral marketing ("please forward this e-mail to your friends"), but venues such as Facebook, Google+, YouTube, blogs, and social game sites now play a major role. For example, as of August 2012, Blendtec's "Will It Blend" and Evian's "Live Young" videos head up the top 10 viral video advertisements of all time, both with more than 100 million views on YouTube. Volkswagen's "The Force" video advertisement is in fourth place, with more than 58 million views.

The process of viral marketing can also involve users who do not know each other. When a consumer decides to make a major purchase, such as a new mountain bike, getting advice and opinions from people who own such bikes is usually the first step. And with the Internet, it is fairly easy to find and read reviews of various bike models written by knowledgeable consumers. Sites such as Epinions and ConsumerReports. org provide objective product reviews by people who have bought and used a long list of products and services. Armed with feedback and input from online aficionados, consumers can then click through to an e-commerce site and make a purchase. Epinions has links to a number of affiliate online retailers who pay a fee back to the site for each purchase that originates there.

MOBILE AND LOCAL MARKETING

Mobile marketing reaches consumers via their mobile devices such as smartphones and tablet computers. Local marketing typically employs mobile devices as well, but also uses the traditional desktop platform.

Mobile Marketing

Marketing on the mobile platform is growing rapidly although it remains a small part (7%) of the overall $37.3 billion online marketing spending. In 2012, spending on all forms of mobile marketing amounted to $2.6 billion, and it is growing at over 80% a year (eMarketer, Inc., 2012i).

Although still in its infancy, mobile marketing includes the use of display banner ads, rich media, video, games, e-mail, text messaging, in-store messaging, Quick Response (QR) codes, and couponing. Over 90% of retail marketing professionals have plans for mobile marketing campaigns in 2012, and mobile is now a required part of the standard marketing budget. **Table 6.10** shows the major formats and growth rates.

TABLE 6.10	U.S. MOBILE AD SPENDING BY FORMAT AND GROWTH (2012)	
FORMAT	SPENDING (MILLIONS)	GROWTH RATE
Messaging (SMS)	$227	−9.5%
Display	$953	99%
Search	$1,280	96%
Video	$152	122%
Total	$2,612	80%

SOURCE: Based on data from eMarketer, Inc., 2012i, 2012j.

TABLE 6.11	MOBILE MARKETING CAMPAIGNS OF SELECTED FIRMS 2012
Kraft Foods	Created a mobile campaign to promote the launch of its new instant coffee products, Jacobs 3in1 and Jacobs 2in1. The campaign was to be integrated with traditional media and was intended to provide consumers with an uncomplicated way of ordering product samples via mobile devices.
Gatorade G Series Campaign	Uses Pandora's ad platform to place banner ads leading users to an optimized mobile Web site promoting new drink products. Users can view NFL videos and share products and videos on Facebook and Twitter.
Chevrolet	Chevrolet ran a mobile video advertising campaign to support the Volt, Chevrolet's hybrid car. Mobile consumers can also learn more about the car's features through additional videos on Chevy's mobile site. The mobile ads are running in the Hulu Plus iPhone app.
Ikea	Uses the Apple iAd platform to display banner ads promoting the Ikea catalog. Users are redirected to the Apple App Store where they can download an app and view the catalog, find products by swiping pages, and discover pricing and store locations.
OfficeMax	Uses iPhone and Android platforms for loyalty marketing. OfficeMax uses SMS texting to deliver offers and daily deals, and directs users to apps where they can subscribe, participate in promotions, and find stores. Display ads redirect users to apps that can be downloaded.
BMW	BMW is promoting its new 3 Series and its DESIR3 campaign with short video clips in between commercial breaks while consumers are watching television shows and movies on their mobile devices. The ads connect to a mobile-optimized site where users can learn about the 3 Series and find a BMW dealership.
Ford Motor Company	Uses the Mobile Posse platform for an awareness and consideration campaign for the new Ford Taurus. Users opt in to see ads on their phones when their screens are idle and are redirected to Ford's mobile Web after clicking on a display ad.

Mobile marketing is uniquely suited for branding purposes, raising awareness through the use of video and rich interactive media such as games. Read the *Insight on Business* case, *Mobile Marketing: Land Rover Seeks Engagement on the Small Screen*, for a further look.

The entrance of Google and Apple into the mobile marketing arena has transformed mobile marketing into a major growth area. Google acquired AdMob, a mobile marketing pioneer. Apple acquired Quattro Wireless in response. After introducing the iPad tablet in early 2010, Apple introduced the iAd mobile ad platform, which offers marketers a platform for managing their mobile campaigns and metrics to gauge their effectiveness. **Table 6.11** provides examples of how several firms are using mobile marketing to promote their brands. The leading mobile platforms are iAd and AdMob (each with about 25% market share), followed by Jumptap, Millenial Media, and Yahoo. Publishers with a broad appeal like Pandora also have developed mobile ad platforms.

INSIGHT ON BUSINESS

MOBILE MARKETING: LAND ROVER SEEKS ENGAGEMENT ON THE SMALL SCREEN

Why is mobile marketing any different from ordinary online marketing? In one sense, it isn't. The same kinds of ad formats you find on Web sites are also used on smartphones—in order of importance, search, display, video, and text messages. In another sense, mobile marketing can be very different from other types of online marketing because of the unique features of the smartphone, which include a built-in GPS, a gyroscope, and an accelerometer. This means marketers can know the location of the user, and they can present rich media and video ads where the user can control the action in a way not possible with an ordinary PC. Smartphones use a touch interface, which increases user involvement. Mobile ads can therefore be more engaging and interactive than traditional PCs. Location information can be used to market local businesses at the very point of consumer purchase, namely, on the street or in the store while browsing. Other unique smartphone features are that people almost always carry them and keep them turned on while moving about. This means that smartphone users can be exposed to marketing messages throughout the day (and sometimes the night). Of course, smartphones have limitations as well. The screens are much smaller than tablets and laptops, making it difficult to squeeze ads onto the screen when the user is looking at other content. Expectations are important as well: unlike "free" advertising-supported Web sites, consumers pay for cell phone service and may not wish to be annoyed by bothersome ads interrupting their service and consuming valuable screen real estate.

Mobile devices are used by consumers throughout the purchase cycle: over 50% of smartphone users research products before entering a store, and 36% use their phones in retail stores.

The use of mobile devices to actually purchase products online (as opposed to just shopping and browsing online) is also growing commensurately. U.S. mobile commerce grew by more than 90% in 2011, and is expected to grow by 48% in 2012 to $11.6 billion. By 2015, mobile commerce is expected to nearly triple to $31 billion.

Only about half of smartphone online shoppers actually buy something using their phones, compared to more than 80% of desktop PC shoppers who actually purchase online. In part, this relatively low number of purchasers reflects the novelty and comfort level of consumers, as well as the fact that many online retailers do not have mobile Web sites or apps, and instead offer only their standard Web pages to mobile users. Many consumers feel the small screens on smartphones prevent them from examining retail products closely, and using a credit card with a smartphone is difficult. Yet for certain commodity goods that the consumer is familiar with, for sites that have an easy-to-use one-click shopping capability, and for purchases of content like books and movies, mobile purchasing can be convenient. Nearly half of smartphone customers have purchased digital goods, and more than a third have purchased clothing, tickets, and deals offered by firms like Gilt and LivingSocial. Also for local marketing, mobile is an ideal platform for merchants to attract consumers in the neighborhood. Restaurants, museums, and entertainment venues are ideal candidates to use mobile marketing aimed at local consumers.

A good example of the use of smartphones for marketing is Land Rover's use of Apple's iAd platform to introduce the Range Rover Evoque to a new audience in 2012. The Range Rover Evoque (pronounced e-voke) is a compact SUV aimed at young urban buyers. Land Rover is known for its

(continued)

line of very luxurious and expensive SUVs which appeal to an older consumer. The Evoque is a smaller, more fuel-efficient, less-polluting SUV than its much larger luxury SUV models. Land Rover wanted to introduce the car to an entirely new demographic: young affluents. The problem was how to introduce this new concept for Land Rover to an audience that most likely never intended to buy a Land Rover.

Land Rover worked with Mindshare (an Internet marketing firm), Y&R Group (a New York-based marketing firm), and Apple's iAd Network team to build an immersive and engaging interactive app that would allow consumers to explore and configure the interior and exterior of the car using the finger gestures of the iPhone. Users are shown a mobile ad on their cell phones, and tapping the ad, they are taken to the Land Rover app to explore the car. iAd used iTunes-based targeting to pinpoint the right audience based on the kinds of music they liked to listen to. The music people listen to on iTunes, or select as favorites, provide clues to their age, personal tastes, passions, and interests. Demographic data was also available. The ad could be shown at several points, but the most effective was showing the ad when consumers were using their favorite apps. When using apps, a person's attention and engagement is quite high.

Using Land Rover's configuration app, customers can change the Evoque's body style, color, and wheels. They can take a photo of their car and send it to others by e-mail or SMS. There's an immersive 360-degree view of the interior that puts viewers inside the car. Using the iPhone's built-in gyroscope and accelerometer, viewers can tilt and turn the device to see a 360-view of the interior.

According to Land Rover, the iAd mobile marketing effort has been a success. As one Land Rover marketer noted, there's a difference between looking at a 30-second TV commercial, and someone using their iPhone to explore a new product. With the mobile ad, people are more engaged, in control, and attentive to the message.

On average, people spent on average nearly 80 seconds whenever they engaged with the ad.

Other marketers have also been pleased with their iAd campaigns. Unilever, the global consumer products company, has run three iAd campaigns for brands like Dove Soap and Ben & Jerry's ice cream. Unilever marketers report that consumers were spending an amazing 68 seconds with some of their mobile ads, and that this allows marketers to tell much deeper stories and engage the viewer. Unilever has used iAd mobile advertising formats to create 13 ads across 11 brands in six countries. Dove Men, Knorr, Lynx, and Magnum have all been featured in mobile ad campaigns.

While ad networks like iAd and Google AdMob are the largest mobile marketing platforms, the micro-blogging service Twitter is fast becoming a mobile marketer as well, using its own platform and audience with 140 million monthly visitors. Currently, Twitter is generating more than 50% of its revenue from ads delivered to its users on mobile phones, rather than from ads on Twitter.com. One reason: people who see a mobile Twitter ad are more likely to click on it than people who access Twitter on their PC. About 60% of Twitter's users access the service with mobile devices, and this is growing rapidly. Twitter does not produce customized interactive experiences for its advertisers yet, although in the future it may well present engaging interactive ads. The format of Twitter mobile ads is the same as its Web site ads, and they cost the same.

Mobile marketing is still in its infancy, and most firms are having trouble monetizing their huge and growing mobile audiences through marketing campaigns. The format is often novel, the screens small, the targeting is less sophisticated than is available on Web sites, and the large advertisers are uncertain about how the mobile platform can be used. Twitter is enjoying considerable success with mobile ads, and in 2012, Google said it would generate $2.5 billion on its mobile ad network (compared to its $36 billion in total ad revenue) serving up search and display ads just like it does

(continued)

for traditional PCs. Google's CEO notes that mobile ads do not monetize well for Google because they are still learning how to target mobile ads as they do for traditional Web ads. Facebook has stumbled in its approach to the mobile market by being slow to develop a mobile screen despite the fact that 50% of its audience in the United States is accessing Facebook using smartphones. Facebook derives no significant revenue from mobile ads. Facebook has begun experimenting with mobile ads using its Sponsored Stories product which republishes favorable mentions of products. As more and more people rely on their smartphones for shopping and purchasing, marketers cannot afford to ignore the unique capabilities of smartphones for engaging consumers.

SOURCES: "Twitter's Mobile Ads Begin to Click," by Shira Ovide, *Wall Street Journal*, June 28, 2012; "Land Rover Reaches New Audience with iAd for Brands," Apple Inc., 2012; "Land Rover iAd Campaign Delivers Highest Engagement Levels," by Chantal Tode, Mobile Marketer, August 8, 2012; "Majority of US Smartphone Owners Use Devices to Aid Shopping," eMarketer, Inc., April 12, 2012; "US Mobile Commerce Forecast," by eMarketer, Inc., [Jeffrey Grau], January 2012; "Mobile Channel Strategy," by Carrie Johnson, Forrester Research, June 2, 2011; "The Effect of Mobile On the Path to Purchase," by eMarketer, Inc., February 29, 2012.

App Marketing

Apps on mobile devices constitute a new marketing platform that did not exist a few years ago. Apps are a non-browser pathway for users to experience the Web and perform a number of tasks from reading the newspaper to shopping, searching, and buying. Apps provide users much faster access to content than multi-purpose browsers. Apps are also starting to influence the design and function of traditional Web sites as consumers are attracted to the look and feel of apps, and their speed of operation. There are about a million apps on Apple iTunes and Google Apps Marketplace and another million apps provided by Internet carriers and third-party storefronts like GetJar and PocketGear, app portals like dev.appia.com, and the Amazon Appstore. An estimated one billion people use apps in 2012 worldwide, with about 200 million in the United States (eMarketer, Inc., 2012k). By 2012, more than 32 billion apps have been downloaded (Strategy Analytics, 2012).

Apps provide four potential sources of revenue for their creators and marketers: pay-per-app download of the app itself, in-app purchases, subscriptions, and advertising. According to the research firm ABI, apps produce about $9 billion in revenue in 2012, and this is expected to grow to $46 billion by 2016. The largest revenue component is in-app purchases. The most essential apps for American users are social network and community, banking, specific information (street addresses, phone numbers), search sites, and general news and information (newspapers, magazines, and news channels).

Firms are experimenting with apps as marketing and purchase platforms. Walmart has both tablet and smartphone apps, one for browsing products while sitting on the sofa (tablet app), and the other for on-the-go purchases and price checking. Nutrisystem, a weight loss program, has expanded into the mobile market with apps for meal planning, calorie counting, and exercise. Many of the major online newspapers have apps. Retailers like Lowe's and Zappos offer apps for mobile devices that allow customers to browse products, see video demonstrations, and create shopping lists for later purchase.

Local Marketing: The Local-Social-Mobile Nexus

Along with social marketing (discussed below) and mobile marketing, local marketing is the third major trend in e-commerce marketing in 2012–2013. The local search market is growing impressively (around 7% annually), and the growth of mobile devices has accelerated the growth of local search and purchasing since 2007. According to Google, local searches represent 20% of all searches, and 40% of all mobile searches in 2012. New marketing tools like local advertisements on social networks and daily deal sites are also contributing to local marketing growth.

Spending on online local ads in the United States is expected to total around $24 billion in 2012 and grow to more than $38 billion by 2016 (BIA/Kelsey, 2012). In contrast, spending on traditional local advertising is expected to be flat during the same time period. The most common local marketing tools are geotargeting using Google Maps (local stores appearing on a Google map), display ads in hyperlocal publications like those created by Patch Properties, aimed at narrowly defined communities, daily deals, and coupons.

The most commonly used venues include Facebook, Google, Amazon Local, Groupon, LivingSocial, LinkedIn, Yahoo, Bing, and Twitter, as well as more specific location-based offerings such as Google Places, Yahoo Local, Citysearch, YellowBook, SuperPages, and Yelp. The "daily deal" coupon sites, Groupon and LivingSocial, and location-based mobile firms such as Foursquare are also a significant part of this trend. Industry analysts believe about 92 million adult U.S. Internet users in 2012 will use online coupons, and research indicates that retail stores and those in the hospitality and entertainment industries have much to gain from adding online coupons to their local search listings. Findings from comScore indicate that around 40% of U.S. Internet users search for local businesses at least once a week (comScore, 2012).

MULTI-CHANNEL MARKETING: INTEGRATING ONLINE AND OFFLINE MARKETING

Without an audience, marketing is not possible. With the rapid growth of the Internet, media consumption patterns have changed greatly as consumers are more and more likely to engage with online media, from videos and news sites, to blogs, Twitter feeds, Facebook friends, and Pinterest posts. Increasingly, marketers are using multiple online channels to "touch" customers, from e-mail to Facebook, search ads, display ads on mobile devices, and affiliate programs. Forrester Research reports, for instance, that most customers purchased online following some Web marketing influence, and nearly half of online purchases followed multiple exposures to Web marketing efforts (Forrester Research, 2011b).

Yet the average American spends only about 24% of his or her time with the Internet, and a whopping 75% with other media (**Figure 6.7**). While television accounts for a large percentage of time spent with media, setting that aside, radio, newspapers, magazines, and "other" account for an additional 36% of time spent with media, larger than the Internet per se. An increasing percentage of American media consumers multitask by using several media at once in order to increase the total media exposure. In this environment, marketers increasingly are developing multi-channel marketing programs that can take advantage of the strengths of various media, and reinforce branding messages across media. Online marketing is not the only way, or by itself the best way, to engage consumers. Internet campaigns can be significantly strengthened by also using e-mail, TV, print, and radio.

For instance, Applebee's (a national family dining chain) introduced a new menu in 2011 designed to get noon-time customers in and out of the restaurants in fourteen minutes. The marketing campaign used a multi-channel approach involving traditional TV and radio, in addition to digital media like Facebook, YouTube, and Twitter.

In 2012, the Indiana Office of Tourism Development worked with the *Indianapolis Monthly* magazine to encourage visitors to the Super Bowl in Indianapolis to try local foods and locally owned restaurants. Using Web sites, blogs, e-mail, and print media, the campaign significantly increased the sales of local restaurants.

OTHER ONLINE MARKETING STRATEGIES

Leveraging Brands

Brand leveraging is one of the most successful online customer acquisition strategies. **Brand leveraging** refers to the process of using the power of an existing brand to acquire new customers for a new product or service. For instance, while Tab was the first to discover a huge market for diet cola drinks, Coca-Cola ultimately succeeded in dominating the market by leveraging the Coke brand to a new product called Diet Coke.

brand leveraging
using the power of an existing brand to acquire new customers for a new product or service

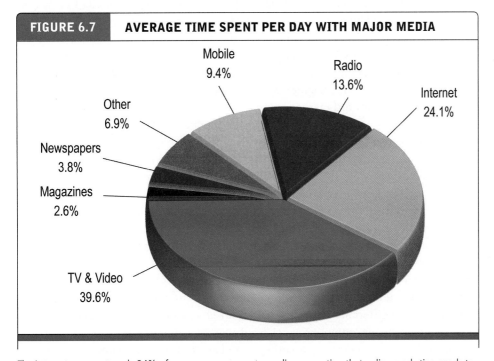

| FIGURE 6.7 | AVERAGE TIME SPENT PER DAY WITH MAJOR MEDIA |

The Internet represents only 24% of consumer exposure to media, suggesting that online marketing needs to be coupled with offline marketing to achieve optimal effectiveness.

SOURCE: Based on data from eMarketer, Inc., 2012l.

In the online world, some researchers predicted that offline brands would not be able to make the transition to the Web because customers would soon learn who was offering products at the cheapest prices and brand premiums would disappear (price transparency). But this has not occurred. In retail, firms such as Walmart and JCPenney have leaped into the top 10 online retail firms in a very short period in large part because of the strength of their offline brand, which gave them the ability to attract millions of their offline customers to their Web sites. In the financial service industry sector, firms such as Wells Fargo, Citibank, Fidelity, and TD Ameritrade have all succeeded in acquiring millions of online customers based on their large offline customer bases and brands. In the content provider industry, the *Wall Street Journal* and *Consumer Reports* have become among the most successful subscription-based content providers. A major advantage of brand leveraging—when compared to a start-up venture with no brand recognition—is that it significantly reduces the costs of acquiring new customers (Kotler and Armstrong, 2009).

Customer Retention Strategies

The Internet offers several extraordinary marketing techniques for building a strong relationship with customers and for differentiating products and services.

Personalization and One-to-One Marketing   No Internet-based marketing technique has received more popular and academic comment than "one-to-one" or "personalized marketing." **One-to-one marketing (personalization)** segments the market on the basis of individuals (not groups), based on a precise and timely understanding of their needs, targeting specific marketing messages to these individuals, and then positioning the product vis-à-vis competitors to be truly unique (Peppers and Rogers, 1997). One-to-one marketing is the ultimate form of market segmentation, targeting, and positioning—where the segments are individuals.

The movement toward market segmentation has been ongoing since the development of systematic market research and mass media in the 1930s. However, e-commerce and the Internet are different in that they enable personalized one-to-one marketing to occur on a mass scale. **Figure 6.8** depicts the continuum of marketing: from mass marketing of undifferentiated products, where one size and one price fits all, to personalized one-to-one marketing.

Mass marketing, based on national media messages aimed at a single national audience and with a single national price, is appropriate for products that are relatively simple and attractive to all consumers in a single form. Think of Coke, Tide, and McDonalds. *Direct marketing*, which is based on direct mail or phone messages and aimed at segments of the market likely to purchase and which has little variation in price (but special offers to loyal customers), is most often used for products that can be stratified into different categories. *Micromarketing*, which is aimed at geographical units (neighborhoods, cities) or specialized market segments (technology buffs), is the first form of true database marketing. Frito-Lay, for instance, maintains a national sales database for each of 10,000 route sales personnel and over 50,000 store outlets. Frito-Lay marketers know precisely at the end of every day how many small bags of Salsa Chips sell in Los Angeles, and how many bags of Ranch Chips sell in Cambridge, Massachusetts, store by store. Although seemingly simple, the corn chip can take

one-to-one marketing (personalization)

segmenting the market based on a precise and timely understanding of an individual's needs, targeting specific marketing messages to these individuals, and then positioning the product vis-à-vis competitors to be truly unique on fairly complex and nuanced taste experiences that attract different customers in different neighborhoods. Using its database, Frito-Lay dynamically adjusts prices to market conditions and competitor product and pricing, every day.

Personalized one-to-one marketing is suitable for products (1) that can be produced in very complex forms, depending on individual tastes, (2) whose price can be adjusted to the level of personalization, and (3) where the individual's tastes and preferences can be effectively gauged.

A good example of personalization at work is Amazon or Barnesandnoble.com. Both sites greet registered visitors (based on cookie files), recommend recent books based on user preferences (stored in a user profile in their database) as well as what other consumers purchased, and expedite checkout procedures based on prior purchases.

Is Web-based personalization as good as the personal attention you would receive from a local, independent bookstore owner? Probably not. Nevertheless, these Web-based techniques use more individual knowledge and personalization than traditional mass media, and more than a direct mail post card.

Personalization is not necessarily an unmitigated good, however. Research indicates that most consumers appreciate personalization when it increases their sense of control and freedom, such as through personalized order tracking, purchase histories, databases of personalized information to ensure quicker transactions during future sessions, and opt-in e-mail notification of new products and special deals. Furthermore, although

FIGURE 6.8	THE MASS MARKET-PERSONALIZATION CONTINUUM			
MARKETING STRATEGIES	**MARKETING ATTRIBUTES**			
	Product	**Target**	**Pricing**	**Techniques**
Mass Marketing	Simple	All consumers	One nation, one price	Mass media
Direct Marketing	Stratified	Segments	One price	Targeted communications, e.g., mail and phone
Micromarketing	Complex	Micro-segments	Variable pricing	Segment profiles
Personalized, One-to-one Marketing	Highly complex	Individual	Unique pricing	Individual and social network profiles

Personalized one-to-one marketing is part of a continuum of marketing strategies. The choice of strategy depends on the nature of the product as well as the technologies that are available to enable various strategies.

personalization technologies have made significant advances over the past several years, it is still difficult for a computer to accurately understand and anticipate the interests and needs of a customer. "Personalized" offers that miss the mark can lead to more customer disdain than satisfaction (Lambrecht and Tucker, 2011). How often do you open up a Web site such as Yahoo and find ads that are totally irrelevant to your interests?

customization

changing the product, not just the marketing message, according to user preferences

customer co-production

in the Web environment, takes customization one step further by allowing the customer to interactively create the product

Customization and Customer Co-Production Customization is an extension of personalization. **Customization** means changing the product—not just the marketing message—according to user preferences. **Customer co-production** means the users actually think up the innovation and help create the new product. For instance, studies of new and improved products find that many come directly from intensive users. The operating system Linux is built by users, and innovations in mountain bikes, sail boards, sailboats and gear, ski equipment, and thousands of other industrial products often came from "lead users" (von Hippel, 2005, 1994). Customer co-production in the Web environment takes customization one step further by allowing the customer to interactively create the product.

Many leading companies now offer "build-to-order" customized products on the Internet on a large scale, creating product differentiation and, hopefully, customer loyalty. Customers appear to be willing to pay a little more for a unique product. The key to making the process affordable is to build a standardized architecture that lets consumers combine a variety of options. For example, Nike offers customized sneakers through its Nike iD program on its Web site. Consumers can choose the type of shoe, colors, material, and even a logo of up to eight characters. Nike transmits the orders via computers to specially equipped plants in China and Korea. The sneakers cost only $10 extra and take about three weeks to reach the customer. At the Shop M&M's Web site, customers can get their own message printed on custom-made M&Ms; Timberland. com also offers online customization of its boots.

Information goods—goods whose value is based on information content—are also ideal for this level of differentiation. For instance, the New York Times—and many other content distributors—allows customers to select the news they want to see on a daily basis. Many Web sites, particularly portal sites such as Yahoo, MSN, and AOL, allow customers to create their own customized version of the Web site. Such pages frequently require security measures such as usernames and passwords to ensure privacy and confidentiality.

Customer Service A Web site's approach to customer service can significantly help or hurt its marketing efforts. Online customer service is more than simply following through on order fulfillment; it has to do with users' ability to communicate with a company and obtain desired information in a timely manner. Customer service can help reduce consumer frustration, cut the number of abandoned shopping carts, and increase sales.

Most consumers want to, and will, serve themselves as long as the information they need to do so is relatively easy to find. Online buyers largely do not expect or desire "high-touch" service unless they have questions or problems, in which case they want relatively speedy answers that are responsive to their individual issue. Researchers have found that online consumers strongly attach to brands when they have a problem with an order. Customer loyalty increases substantially when online buyers learn that customer service representatives are available online or at an 800-number and were willing and able to resolve the situation quickly. Conversely, online buyers who do not receive satisfaction at these critical moments often terminate their relationship with the business and switch to merchants that may charge more but deliver superior customer service (Ba, et al., 2010; Wolfinbarger and Gilly, 2001).

There are a number of tools that companies can use to encourage interaction with prospects and customers and provide customer service—FAQs, customer service chat systems, intelligent agents, and automated response systems—in addition to the customer relationship management systems described in the preceding section.

Frequently asked questions (**FAQs**), a text-based listing of common questions and answers, provide an inexpensive way to anticipate and address customer concerns. Adding an FAQ page on a Web site linked to a search engine helps users track down needed information more quickly, enabling them to help themselves resolve questions and concerns. By directing customers to the FAQs page first, Web sites can give customers answers to common questions. If a question and answer do not appear, it is important for sites to make contact with a live person simple and easy. Offering an e-mail link to customer service at the bottom of the FAQs page is one solution.

frequently asked questions (FAQs)
a text-based listing of common questions and answers

Real-time customer service chat systems (in which a company's customer service representatives interactively exchange text-based messages with one or more customers on a real-time basis) are an increasingly popular way for companies to assist online shoppers during a purchase. Chats with online customer service representatives can provide direction, answer questions, and troubleshoot technical glitches that can kill a sale. Leading vendors of customer service chat systems include LivePerson and InstantService. Vendors claim that chat is significantly less expensive than telephone-based customer service. However, critics point out this conclusion may be based on optimistic assumptions that chat representatives can assist three or four customers at once, and that chat sessions are shorter than phone sessions. Also, chat sessions are text sessions, and not as rich as talking with a human being over the phone. On the plus side, chat has been reported to raise per-order sales figures, providing sales assistance by allowing companies to "touch" customers during the decision-making process. Evidence suggests that chat can lower shopping cart abandonment rates, increase the number of items purchased per transaction, and increase the dollar value of transactions. "Click to call" or "live call" is another version of a real-time online customer service system, in which the customer clicks a link or accepts an invitation to have a customer service representative call them on the telephone.

real-time customer service chat systems
a company's customer service representatives interactively exchange text-based messages with one or more customers on a real-time basis

Intelligent agent technology is another way customers are providing assistance to online shoppers. Intelligent agents are part of an effort to reduce costly contact with customer service representatives. **Automated response systems** send e-mail order confirmations and acknowledgments of e-mailed inquiries, in some cases letting the customer know that it may take a day or two to actually research an answer to their question. Automating shipping confirmations and order status reports are also common.

automated response system
sends e-mail order confirmations and acknowledgments of e-mailed inquiries

Net Pricing Strategies

In a competitive market, firms compete for customers through price as well as product features, scope of operations, and focus. **Pricing** (putting a value on goods

pricing
putting a value on goods and services

and services) is an integral part of marketing strategy. Together, price and quality determine customer value. Pricing of e-commerce goods has proved very difficult for both entrepreneurs and investors to understand.

In traditional firms, the prices of traditional goods—such as books, drugs, and automobiles—are usually based on their fixed and variable costs as well as the market's **demand curve** (the quantity of goods that can be sold at various prices). *Fixed costs* are the costs of building the production facility. *Variable costs* are costs involved in running the production facility—mostly labor. In a competitive market, with undifferentiated goods, prices tend toward their *marginal costs* (the incremental cost of producing the next unit) once manufacturers have paid the fixed costs to enter the business.

Firms usually "discover" their demand curves by testing various price and volume bundles, while closely watching their cost structure. Normally, prices are set to maximize profits. A profit-maximizing company sets its prices so that the *marginal revenue* (the revenue a company receives from the next unit sold) from a product just equals its marginal costs. If a firm's marginal revenue is higher than its marginal costs, it would want to lower prices a bit and sell more product (why leave money on the table when you can sell a few more units?). If its marginal revenue for selling a product is lower than its marginal costs, then the company would want to reduce volume a bit and charge a higher price (why lose money on each additional sale?).

In the early years of e-commerce, something unusual happened. Sellers were pricing their products far below their marginal costs. Some sites were losing money on every sale. How could this be? New economics? New technology? The Internet age? No. Internet merchants could sell below their marginal costs (even giving away products for free) simply because a large number of entrepreneurs and their venture capitalist backers thought this was a worthwhile activity, at least in the short term. The idea was to attract "eyeballs" with free goods and services, and then later, once the consumer was part of a large, committed audience, charge advertisers enough money to make a profit, and (maybe) charge customers subscription fees for value-added services (the so-called "*piggyback*" *strategy* in which a small number of users can be convinced to pay for premium services that are piggybacked upon a larger audience that receives standard or reduced value services). To a large extent, social networking sites and user-generated content sites have resurrected this revenue model with a focus on the growth in audience size and not short-term profits. To understand the behavior of entrepreneurial firms, it is helpful to examine a traditional demand curve (see **Figure 6.9**).

A small number of customers are willing to pay a great deal for the product—far above P_1. A larger number of customers would happily pay P_1, and an even larger number of customers would pay less than P_1. If the price were zero, the demand might approach infinity! Ideally, in order to maximize sales and profits, a firm would like to pick up all the money in the market by selling the product at the price each customer is willing to pay. This is called **price discrimination**—selling products to different people and groups based on their willingness to pay. If some people really want the product, sell it to them at a high price. But sell it to indifferent people at a much lower price; otherwise, they will not buy. This only works if the firm can (a) identify the price each individual would be willing to pay, and (b) segregate the customers from one another so they cannot find out what the others are paying. Therefore, most

demand curve

the quantity of goods that can be sold at various prices

price discrimination

selling products to different people and groups based on their willingness to pay

FIGURE 6.9 · A DEMAND CURVE

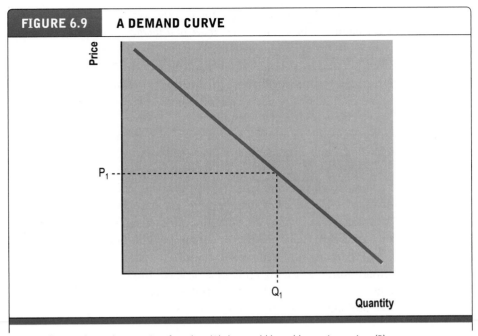

A demand curve shows the quantity of product (Q) that could be sold at various prices (P).

firms adopt a fixed price for their goods (P_1), or a small number of prices for different versions of their products.

What if the marginal cost of producing a good is zero? What should the price be for these goods? It would be impossible then to set prices based on equalizing marginal revenue and marginal cost—because marginal cost is zero. The Internet is primarily filled with information goods—from music to research reports, to stock quotes, stories, weather reports, articles, pictures, and opinions—whose marginal cost of production is zero when distributed over the Internet. Thus, another reason certain goods, such as some information goods, may be free on the Internet is that they are "selling" for what it costs to produce them—next to nothing. Content that is stolen from television, CDs, and Hollywood movies has zero production costs. Content that is contributed by users also has zero production costs for the Web sites themselves.

Free and Freemium Let's examine free pricing of Internet services. Everyone likes a bargain, and the best bargain is something for free. Businesses give away free PCs, free data storage, free music, free Web sites, free photo storage, and free Internet connections. Free is not new: banks used to give away "free" toasters to depositors in the 1950s. Google offers free office apps, free e-mail, and free collaboration sites. There can be a sensible economic logic to giving things away. Free content can help build market awareness (such as the free online *New York Times* that contains only the daily stories—not the archived stories) and can lead to sales of other follow-on products. Finally, free products and services knock out potential and actual competitors (the free browser Internet Explorer from Microsoft spoiled the market for Netscape's browser) (Shapiro and Varian, 1999).

Today, online "free" is increasingly being implemented as "freemium" to borrow a phrase from Chris Anderson's book *Free: The Future of a Radical Price.* The freemium pricing model is a cross-subsidy online marketing strategy where users are offered a basic service for free, but must pay for premium or add-on services. The people who pay for the premium services hopefully will pay for all the free riders on the service. Skype uses a freemium model: millions of users can call other Skype users on the Internet for free, but there's a charge for calling a land line or cell phone. Flickr, Google Sites, Yahoo, and a host of others offer premium services at a price in order to support "free" services. Even YouTube is launching a premium movie service where Hollywood movies are streamed for a price. Evernote.com offers online users a "universal memory drawer" that allows you to store any digital information (photos, videos, and documents) on the Evernote site, and then coordinate all of your digital devices from laptops, desktops, and smartphones. The basic service is free, but additional storage and special services cost $5 a month (Takahashi, 2010). Pandora offers free Internet radio, but it is restricted to a few hours a month. Premium unlimited service costs $36 a year.

"Free" and "freemium" as pricing strategies do have limits. In the past, many e-commerce businesses found it difficult to convert the eyeballs into paying customers. YouTube is still not profitable. Free sites attract hundreds of millions of price-sensitive "free loaders" who have no intention of ever paying for anything, and who switch from one free service to another at the very mention of charges. The piggyback strategy has not been a universal success. "Free" eliminates a rich price discrimination strategy. Clearly some of the free loaders would indeed pay a small amount each month, and this revenue is lost to the firms who offer significant services for free. Some argue that everything digital will one day be free in part because Internet users expect it to be so. But the history of "free" includes broadcast television, which used to be "free" (it was advertising-supported) but the public eventually had no problem moving to cable television and DVDs as paid services. The exceptions to "free" are really valuable streams of information that are exclusive, expensive to produce, not widely distributed, unique, and have immediate consumption or investment value. Even in the age of the Internet, these digital streams will sell for a price greater than zero. There probably is no free lunch after all, at least not one that's worth eating.

versioning

creating multiple versions of information goods and selling essentially the same product to different market segments at different prices

Versioning One solution to the problem of free information goods is **versioning**—creating multiple versions of the goods and selling essentially the same product to different market segments at different prices. In this situation, the price depends on the value to the consumer. Consumers will segment themselves into groups that are willing to pay different amounts for various versions (Shapiro and Varian, 1998). Versioning fits well with a modified "free" strategy. A reduced-value version can be offered for free, while premium versions can be offered at higher prices. What are characteristics of a "reduced-value version?" Low-priced—or in the case of information goods, even "free"—versions might be less convenient to use, less comprehensive, slower, less powerful, and offer less support than the high-priced versions. Just as there are different General Motors car brands appealing to different market segments (Cadillac, Buick, Chevrolet, and GMC), and within these divisions, hundreds of models from the most basic to the more powerful and functional, so can information goods be "versioned" in order to segment and target the market and position the products. In the realm of information goods, online magazines, music companies, and book publishers offer sample content for free, but charge for more powerful content. The *New York Times*, for instance, offers free daily content for several days after publication, but then charges per article for access to the more powerful archive of past issues. Writers, editors, and analysts are more than willing to pay for access to archived, organized content. Some Web sites offer "free services" with annoying advertising, but turn off the ads for a monthly fee.

Bundling "Ziggy" Ziegfeld, a vaudeville entrepreneur at the turn of the twentieth century in New York, noticed that nearly one-third of his theater seats were empty on some Friday nights, and during the week, matinee shows were often half empty. He came up with an idea for bundling tickets into "twofers": pay for one full-price ticket and get the next ticket free. Twofers are still a Broadway theater tradition in New York. They are based on the idea that (a) the marginal cost of seating another patron is zero, and (b) a great many people who would not otherwise buy a single ticket would buy a "bundle" of tickets for the same or even a slightly higher price.

Bundling of information goods online extends the concept of a twofer. **Bundling** offers consumers two or more goods for a price that is less than the goods would cost when purchased individually. The key idea behind the concept of bundling is that although consumers typically have very diverse ideas about the value of a single product, they tend to agree much more on the value of a bundle of products offered at a fixed price. In fact, the per-product price people are willing to pay for the bundle is often higher than when the products are sold separately. Bundling reduces the variance (dispersion) in market demand for goods. **Figure 6.10** illustrates how the demand curve changes when information goods are offered in a bundle.

bundling
offers consumers two or more goods for a reduced price

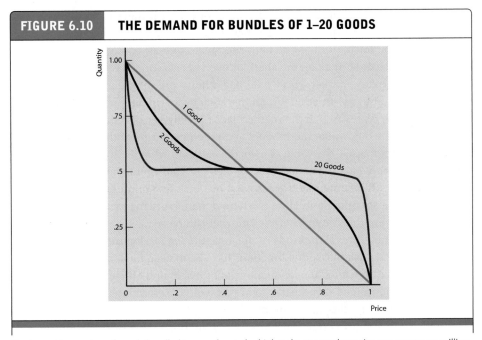

| FIGURE 6.10 | **THE DEMAND FOR BUNDLES OF 1–20 GOODS** |

The larger the number of goods bundled in a package, the higher the per-product price consumers are willing to pay.

Examples of bundling abound in the information goods marketplace. Microsoft bundles its separate Office tools (Word, Excel, PowerPoint, and Access) into a single Microsoft Office package. Even though many people want to use Word and Excel, far fewer want Access or PowerPoint. However, when all products are put into a single bundle, a very large number of people will agree that about $399 (or around $100 per tool) is a "fair" price for so many products. Likewise, the more software applications that Microsoft bundles with its basic operating system, the more the marketplace agrees that as a package of functionality, it is reasonably priced. On the Web, many content sites bundle as opposed to charge individual prices. Electronic libraries such as NetLibrary.com offer access to thousands of publications for a fixed annual fee. Theoretically, bundlers have distinct competitive advantages over those who do not or cannot bundle. Specifically, on the supply side, bundler firms can pay higher prices for content, and on the demand side, bundlers can charge higher prices for their bundles than can single-good firms (Bakos and Brynjolfsson, 2000).

However, bundling of digital goods does not always work. It depends on the bundle and the price. For instance, Reed Elsevier, the world's largest publisher of scientific journals, created a bundle of 1,500 digital scientific journals for American universities, and priced the bundle at a substantial markup to what universities were paying for a much smaller number of journals. It then raised the price to universities that did not want the bundle. The result was a marketplace rebellion shaped in part by the fact that much of the research in these journals was paid for by taxpayers through government grants.

Dynamic Pricing and Flash Marketing The pricing strategies we have discussed so far are all fixed-price strategies. Versions and bundles are sold for fixed prices based on the firm's best effort at maximizing its profits. But what if there is product still left on the shelf along with the knowledge that someone, somewhere, would be willing to pay something for it? It might be better to obtain at least some revenue from the product, rather than let it sit on the shelf, or even perish. Imagine also that there are some people in every market who would pay a hefty premium for a product if they could have it right away. In other situations, such as for an antique, the value of the product has to be discovered in the marketplace (usually because there is a belief that the marketplace would value the product at a much higher price than its owner paid as a cost). In other cases, the value of a good is equal to what the market is willing to pay (and has nothing to do with its cost). Or let's say you want to build frequent visits to your site and offer some really great bargains for a few minutes each day, or the whole day with a set time limit. Here is where dynamic pricing mechanisms come to the fore, and where the strengths of the Internet can be seen.

There are three prevalent kinds of *dynamic pricing mechanisms:* auctions, yield management, and flash marketing. Auctions have been used for centuries to establish the instant market price for goods. Auctions are flexible and efficient market mechanisms for pricing unique or unusual goods, as well as commonplace goods such as computers, flower bundles, and cameras.

Yield management is quite different from auctions. In *auctions*, thousands of consumers establish a price by bidding against one another. In *yield management*, managers set prices in different markets, appealing to different segments, in order to sell excess capacity. Airlines exemplify yield management techniques. Every few minutes during the day, they adjust prices of empty airline seats to ensure at least some of the 50,000 empty airline seats are sold at some reasonable price—even below marginal cost of production. Frito-Lay, as mentioned earlier, also uses yield management techniques to ensure products move off the shelf in a timely fashion. Amazon and other large online retailers frequently use yield management techniques that involve changing prices hourly to stimulate demand and maximize revenues.

Yield management works under a limited set of conditions. Generally, the product is perishable (an empty airline seat perishes when the plane takes off without a full load); there are seasonal variations in demand; market segments are clearly defined; markets are competitive; and market conditions change rapidly (Cross, 1997). In general, only very large firms with extensive monitoring and database systems in place have been able to afford yield management techniques.

A third dynamic pricing technique is *flash marketing*, which has proved extraordinarily effective for travel services, luxury clothing goods, and other goods. Using e-mail or dedicated Web site features to notify loyal customers (repeat purchasers), merchants offer goods and services for a limited time (usually hours) at very low prices. JetBlue has offered $14 flights between New York and Los Angeles. Deluxe hotel rooms are flash marketed at $1 a night. Companies like Rue La La, HauteLook, and Gilt Groupe are based on flash marketing techniques. Blink and you can easily miss these great prices. Gilt.com purchases overstocked items from major fashion brands and then offers them to their subscribers at discounted prices via daily e-mail and SMS flash messages. Typically, the sale of an item lasts for two hours or until the inventory is depleted. On many occasions, Gilt.com rises to the top of most frequently visited Web sites when it conducts a sale. Critics point out that these sites take advantage of compulsive shoppers and leads to over-shopping for unneeded goods. In another example of mass retail dynamic pricing, in May 2011, Amazon used its new cloud music service to offer a flash one-day sale of Lady Gaga's latest album for 99 cents. Response was so great that Amazon's cloud servers could not meet the demand, and the offer has not been repeated.

The Internet has truly revolutionized the possibilities to engage in dynamic, and even misleading, pricing strategies. With millions of consumers using a site every hour, and access to powerful databases, merchants can raise prices one minute and drop them another minute when a competitor threatens. Bait-and-switch tactics become more common: a really low price on one product is used to attract people to a site when in fact the product is not available.

We discuss dynamic pricing, auctions, and yield management techniques in greater detail in Chapter 11.

Long Tail Marketing

Consider that Amazon sells a larger number of obscure books than it does of "hit" books (defined as the top 20% of books sold). Nevertheless, the hit books generate 80% of Amazon's revenues. Consumers distribute themselves in many markets according to a power curve where 80% of the demand is for the hit products, and demand for non-hits quickly recedes to a small number of units sold. In a traditional market, niche products are so obscure no one ever hears about them. One impact of the Internet and e-commerce on sales of obscure products with little demand is that obscure products become more visible to consumers through search engines, recommendation engines, and social networks. Hence, online retailers can earn substantial revenue selling products for which demand and price is low. In fact, with near zero inventory costs, and a good search engine, the sales of obscure products can become a much larger percentage of total revenue. Amazon, for instance, has millions of book titles for sale at $2.99 or less, many written by obscure authors. Because of its search and recommendation engines, Amazon is able to generate profits from the sale of this large number of obscure titles. This is called the "**long tail**" effect. See *Insight on Technology: The Long Tail: Big Hits and Big Misses*.

CHANNEL STRATEGIES: MANAGING CHANNEL CONFLICT

In the context of commerce, the term **channel** refers to different methods by which goods can be distributed and sold. Traditional channels include sales by manufacturers, both directly and through intermediaries such as manufacturer representatives, distributors, and retailers. The emergence of e-commerce on the Web has created a new channel and has led to channel conflict. **Channel conflict** occurs when a new venue for selling products or services threatens to destroy existing venues for selling goods. Channel conflict is not new, but the Web creates incentives for producers of goods and services to establish direct relationships with consumers and thereby eliminate "middle persons" such as distributors and retailers.

For instance, Levi Strauss & Co. decided to begin selling Levi's jeans and Dockers on its Levi.com and Dockers.com sites. Initially, it forbade retailers (such as Macy's—one of Levi's largest retailers) from selling Levi's products on the Web. However, the storm of protest from retailers, falling sales, and drooping profits forced Levi's to allow retailers to sell through their Web channels.

Rather than engage in direct confrontation with alternative channels, some manufacturers have turned toward a partnership model. For instance, Ethan Allen developed its own Web site for direct sales of its entire line of furniture. At the same time, Ethan Allen recognizes the importance of its independent retail stores for delivery, service, and support, and pays dealers in a local area 25% of the Internet sale for delivery and service, and 10% of the Internet sale even if the dealer does not participate in any way.

At the other end of the spectrum, some manufacturers use the Web solely as a marketing and branding mechanism in order to prevent channel conflict. For instance, Ford, General Motors, and most automobile manufacturers continue to rely on sales made by their dealerships rather than attempt to sell their cars directly online.

6.4 INTERNET MARKETING TECHNOLOGIES

Internet marketing has many similarities to and differences from ordinary marketing. The objective of Internet marketing—as in all marketing—is to build customer

---

long tail
a colloquial name given to various statistical distributions characterized by a small number of events of high amplitude and a very large number of events with low amplitude

channel
refers to different methods by which goods can be distributed and sold

channel conflict
occurs when a new venue for selling products or services threatens to destroy existing venues for selling goods

INSIGHT ON TECHNOLOGY

THE LONG TAIL: BIG HITS AND BIG MISSES

The "Long Tail" is a colloquial name given to various statistical distributions characterized by a small group of events of high amplitude and a very large group of events with low amplitude. Coined by *Wired Magazine* writer Chris Anderson in 2004, the Web's Long Tail has since gone on to fascinate academics and challenge online marketers. The concept is straightforward. Think Hollywood movies: there are big hits that really hit big, and thousands of films that no one ever hears about and only a few people ever see. In economics, it's the Pareto principle: 20% of anything produces 80% of the effects. That means 20% of the hits produce 80% of the revenue, and by extension, 80% of the product line only returns 20% of the revenue. It's these non-hit misses that make up the Long Tail. Anderson claims to have discovered a new 98% rule: no matter how much content you put online, someone, somewhere will show up to buy it. Rather than 20:80, Anderson suggests the Internet changes the Pareto principle by making it easier for consumers to find more obscure products that are very satisfying. Likewise, demand for very popular products declines according to Anderson. Other researchers argue that, over time, Internet sales channels have a less concentrated sales distribution when compared to traditional channels. Internet search, recommendation engines, and online social networks enable niche products to be discovered and purchased. Marketers and Web designers are starting to focus on "long tail keywords," phrases that a small but significant number of people might use to find products. eBay would seem to be a perfect example. The online tag sale contains millions of items drawn from every Aunt Tilly's closet in the world and still seems to find a buyer somewhere for just about anything, revenue that would not be realized without an online marketplace.

On the Internet, where search costs are tiny, and storage and distribution costs are near zero, Amazon is able to offer millions of books for sale compared to a typical large bookstore with 40,000–100,000 titles. The same is true of CDs, DVDs, digital cameras, e-books, and streaming videos. Wherever you look on the Web, you find huge inventories, and a great many items that few people are interested in buying. But someone is almost always searching for something. With a billion people online, even a one-in-a-million product will find 1,000 buyers. Researchers note that it isn't just that some people search for strange things, but rather most shoppers have a taste for both popular as well as niche products. The strength of "infinite inventory" online retailers like Amazon is that they can satisfy the broadest range of individual tastes. According to Anderson, online music sites sell access to 98% of their titles once a quarter, and 15% of Netflix's revenue comes from titles ranked 3,000 or below. According to Netflix, over 50% of its 100,000 titles are rented at least once a day by someone. Unlike physical stores, such as Walmart and Sears, online merchants have much lower overhead costs because they do not have physical stores and have lower labor costs. Therefore, they can load up on inventory, including items that rarely sell. Researchers argue that one impact of the Internet is to alter the 20:80 rule to something more like 30:70, where the niche products make up a larger share of the revenues than in traditional catalogs or stores.

There are several implications of the Long Tail phenomenon for Web marketing. Some writers such as Anderson claim that the Internet revolutionizes digital content by making even niche products highly profitable, and that the revenues produced by small niche products will ultimately outweigh the revenues of hit movies, songs, and books. For Hollywood, and all content producers, this means

(continued)

less focus on the blockbusters that bust the budget, and more emphasis on the steady base—hit titles that have smaller audiences but make up for it in numbers of titles. The Long Tail is a democratizing phenomenon: even less well-known movies, songs, and books can now find a market on the Web. There's hope for your e-book, blog, and garage band! For economists, the Long Tail represents a net gain for social welfare because now customers can find exactly the niche content they really want rather than accept the "big hits" on the shelf. The Web's Long Tail makes more customers happy, and the possibility of making money on niche products should encourage more production of "indie" music and film.

The problem with all these misses in the Long Tail is that few people can find them because they are—by definition—largely unknown. Search engines help but return so much information that choice is difficult. Faced with hundreds of titles the user never heard of is perplexing, delays decision, raises consumer anxiety levels, and potentially wastes consumer time. Hence, in their native state, the revenue value of low-demand products is locked up in collective ignorance. Here's where recommender systems come into play: they can guide consumers to obscure but wonderful works based on the recommendations of others. Netflix just spent $1 million in recent years on improving its recommender system by 10%.

Social networks also make the Long Tail phenomenon even stronger. One online person discovers an unheard-of niche product and shares his or her feelings with others. A recent study found that popularity information of the sort produced in a social network spurs sales of niche products more than mainstream products because of the higher perceived quality of the niche product. If a lot of people say they like an obscure product, it means more to consumers than if the same popularity attaches to a mainstream product.

But recent research casts some doubt on the revenue potential in the Long Tail. In an odd twist, the number of DVD titles online that never get played is increasing rapidly, while the big blockbuster "winner-take-all" titles are increasing. Solid best sellers have expanded and produce the vast part of online media revenues. Over time, the number of titles in the Long Tail has exploded, and the no-play rate has expanded at music sites from 2% to 12%. A massive study of millions of digital downloads in England found that 75% of the digital titles were not downloaded even once. The Long Tail is a very lonely, quiet place. In reality, there seems to be more selling of less (the hits) than less selling of more (the misses). A U.S. study similarly found that 10% of the music titles at Rhapsody, a music site, produced 78% of the revenues. Researchers at Wharton examined over 17,000 movies at Netflix viewed by 480,000 users between 2000 and 2005. They found Long Tail effects missing: demand for the top 20% of movies actually expanded from 86% to 90%. While recommender systems are helpful for revealing niche content, they aren't very smart, and you still need several people to discover the niche product before alerting their friends. Recommender systems tend to recommend what the crowd likes. But niche products need serendipity to be discovered. When you go to a store to buy three things, you usually end up with ten things, some of which you never thought about before.

eBay is a company with a huge Long Tail problem that it is trying to convert into a lucrative virtue. eBay's 97 million users have stuffed its pages with over 200 million product listings, a great many of which are truly at the end of the Long Tail, desired by just a few people in the world, or worse, not even thought about by more than a few. eBay is working on a solution called Discover, which scours the listings to identify how intensely people interact with the listing, the history of the seller offering unusual items, and the emotional intensity of the product's description. Discover's algorithm attempts to serve up not recommended items but items that are really a surprise, therefore interesting, and therefore likely to be purchased. The objective of Discover is to increase the chances that users will

(continued)

experience the unexpected, the surprises which delight a consumer, and that are so much a part of the fun of shopping in the traditional stores.

Both the Long Tail and the winner-take-all approaches have implications for marketers and product designers. In the Long Tail approach, online merchants, especially those selling digital goods such as content, should build up huge libraries of content because they can make significant revenues from niche products that have small audiences. In the winner-take-all approach, the niche products produce little revenue, and firms should concentrate on hugely popular titles and services. Surprisingly, contrary to what Anderson originally theorized, the evidence for online digital content increasingly supports a winner-take-all perspective. George Clooney: do not worry.

■■■ SOURCES: "Article Marketing Tips: Using Long-Tail Keywords," by Steve Shaw, Internet Business, ezinearticles.com, August 26, 2012; "Goodbye Pareto Principle, Hello Long Tail: The Effect of Search Costs on the Concentration of Product Sales," by Eric Brynjolfsson, et al., *Management Science*, July 2012; "Recommendation Networks and the Long Tail of Electronic Commerce," by Gail Oestreicher-Singer, New York University, 2012; "Long Tail Pricing in Business-to-Business Markets," by Just Schurman, Boston Consulting Group, bcgperspectives.com, July 3, 2012; "Research Commentary - Long Tails vs. Superstars: The Effect of Information Technology on Product Variety and Sales Concentration Patterns" by Erik Brynjolfsson, Yu (Jeffrey) Hu, and Michael D. Smith, Information Systerms Research, December 2010; "Anatomy of the Long Tail:Ordinary People With Extraordinary Tastes," by Sharad Goel, et. al., Proceedings of the Third ACM Conference on Web Search and Data Mining, 2010; "EBay Tests Serendipitous Shopping," by Elizabeth Woyke, *Forbes*, August 22, 2011; "The Long Tail of E-commerce," by Jack Jia, *E-commerce Times*, August 18, 2011; "How Does Popularity Affect Choices? A Field Experiment," by Catherine Tucker and Juanjuan Zhang, *Management Science*, May 2011; "Keyword Strategies—The Long Tail," by Matt Daily, Searchengineguide.com, July 2010; "Anatomy of the Long Tail: Ordinary People with Extraordinary Tastes," by Sharad Goel, et al., (Yahoo Research). Proceedings of the Third ACM International Conference on Web Search and Data Mining, New York, New York, 2010; "Rethinking the Long Tail Theory: How to Define Hits and Misses," by Serguei Netessine and Tom Tan, Knowledge@Wharton, October 7, 2009; "The Long Tail of P2P," by Will Page and Eric Garland, *Economic Insight*, August 14, 2009; "Should You Invest in the Long Tail?," by Anita Elberse, *Harvard Business Review*, July–August 2008; "Superstars and Underdogs: An Examination of the Long Tail Phenomenon in Video Sales," by Anita Elberse and Felix Oberholzer-Gee, Harvard Business School Working Paper Series, No. 07-015, December, 2006; "From Niches to Riches: Anatomy of the Long Tail," by Eric Brynjolfsson, Yu Hu, and Michael Smith, *MIT Sloan Management Review*, Summer 2006; "The Long Tail," by Chris Anderson, *Wired Magazine*, October 2004.

relationships so that the firm can achieve above-average returns (both by offering superior products or services and by communicating the product's features to the consumer). But Internet marketing is also very different from ordinary marketing because the nature of the medium and its capabilities are so different from anything that has come before. In order to understand just how different Internet marketing can be and in what ways, you first need to become familiar with some basic Internet marketing technologies.

THE REVOLUTION IN INTERNET MARKETING TECHNOLOGIES

In Chapter 1, we listed eight unique features of e-commerce technology. **Table 6.12** on page 400 describes how marketing has changed as a result of these new technical capabilities.

On balance, the Internet has had four very powerful impacts on marketing. First, the Internet, as a communications medium, has broadened the scope of marketing communications—in the sense of the number of people who can be easily reached as well as the locations where they can be reached, from desktops to mobile smartphones (in short, everywhere). Second, the Internet has increased the richness of marketing

TABLE 6.12	IMPACT OF UNIQUE FEATURES OF E-COMMERCE TECHNOLOGY ON MARKETING
E-COMMERCE TECHNOLOGY DIMENSION	SIGNIFICANCE FOR MARKETING
Ubiquity	Marketing communications have been extended to the home, work, and mobile platforms; geographic limits on marketing have been reduced. The marketplace has been replaced by "marketspace" and is removed from a temporal and geographic location. Customer convenience has been enhanced, and shopping costs have been reduced.
Global reach	Worldwide customer service and marketing communications have been enabled. Potentially hundreds of millions of consumers can be reached with marketing messages.
Universal standards	The cost of delivering marketing messages and receiving feedback from users is reduced because of shared, global standards of the Internet.
Richness	Video, audio, and text marketing messages can be integrated into a single marketing message and consuming experience.
Interactivity	Consumers can be engaged in a dialog, dynamically adjusting the experience to the consumer, and making the consumer a co-producer of the goods and services being sold.
Information density	Fine-grained, highly detailed information on consumers' real-time behavior can be gathered and analyzed for the first time. "Data mining" Internet technology permits the analysis of terabytes of consumer data everyday for marketing purposes.
Personalization/ Customization	This feature potentially enables product and service differentiation down to the level of the individual, thus strengthening the ability of marketers to create brands.
Social technology	User-generated content and social networking sites, along with blogs, have created new, large, online audiences where the content is provided by users. These audiences have greatly expanded the opportunity for marketers to reach new potential customers in a nontraditional media format. Entirely new kinds of marketing techniques are evolving. These same technologies expose marketers to the risk of falling afoul of popular opinion by providing more market power to users who now can "talk back."

communications by combining text, video, and audio content into rich messages. Arguably, the Web is richer as a medium than even television or video because of the complexity of messages available, the enormous content accessible on a wide range of subjects, and the ability of users to interactively control the experience. Third, the Internet has greatly expanded the information intensity of the marketplace by providing marketers (and customers) with unparalleled fine-grained, detailed, real-time information about consumers as they transact in the marketplace.

Fourth, the always-on, always-attached, environment created by mobile devices results in consumers being much more available to receive marketing messages. One result is an extraordinary expansion in marketing opportunities for firms.

WEB TRANSACTION LOGS

How can e-commerce sites know more than a department store or the local grocery store does about consumer behavior? A primary source of consumer information on the Web is the transaction log maintained by all Web servers. A **transaction log** records user activity at a Web site. The transaction log is built into Web server software. Transaction log data becomes even more useful when combined with two other visitor-generated data trails: registration forms and the shopping cart database. Users are enticed through various means (such as free gifts or special services) to fill out registration forms. **Registration forms** gather personal data on name, address, phone, zip code, e-mail address (usually required), and other optional self-confessed information on interests and tastes. When users make a purchase, they also enter additional information into the shopping cart database. The **shopping cart database** captures all the item selection, purchase, and payment data. Other potential additional sources of data are information users submit on product forms, contribute to chat groups, or send via e-mail messages using the "Contact Us" option on most sites.

For a Web site that has a million visitors per month, and where, on average, a visitor makes 15 page requests per visit, there will be 15 million entries in the log each month. These transaction logs, coupled with data from the registration forms and shopping cart database, represent a treasure trove of marketing information for both individual sites and the online industry as a whole. Nearly all the new Internet marketing capabilities are based on these data-gathering tools. For instance, here are just a few of the interesting marketing questions that can be answered by examining a site's Web transaction logs, registration forms, and shopping cart database:

- What are the major patterns of interest and purchase for groups and individuals?
- After the home page, where do most users go first, and then second and third?
- What are the interests of specific individuals (those we can identify)?
- How can we make it easier for people to use our site so they can find what they want?
- How can we change the design of the site to encourage visitors to purchase our high-margin products?
- Where are visitors coming from (and how can we optimize our presence on these referral sites)?
- How can we personalize our messages, offerings, and products to individual users?

Answering these questions requires some additional technologies. As noted by Jupiter Research, businesses can choke on the massive quantity of information found in a typical site's log file. We describe some technologies that help firms more effectively utilize this information below.

SUPPLEMENTING THE LOGS: TRACKING FILES

While transaction logs create the foundation of online data collection at a single Web site, marketers use tracking files to follow users across the entire Web as they visit other sites. They are four kinds of tracking files: cookies, beacons, Flash cookies, and

transaction log
records user activity at a Web site

registration forms
gather personal data on name, address, phone, zip code, e-mail address, and other optional self-confessed information on interests and tastes

shopping cart database
captures all the item selection, purchase, and payment data

apps (software programs used on smartphones and Web sites). As described in Chapter 3, a cookie is small text file that Web sites place on the hard disk of visitors' client computers every time they visit, and during the visit, as specific pages are visited. Cookies allow a Web site to store data on a user's computer and then later retrieve it. The cookie typically includes a name, a unique ID number for each visitor that is stored on the user's computer, the domain (which specifies the Web server/domain that can access the cookie), a path (if a cookie comes from a particular part of a Web site instead of the main page, a path will be given), a security setting that provides whether the cookie can only be transmitted by a secure server, and an expiration date (not required). First-party cookies come from the same domain name as the page the user is visiting, while third-party cookies come from another domain, such as ad serving or adware companies, affiliate marketers, or spyware servers. On some Web sites, there are literally hundreds of tracking files on the main pages.

A cookie provides Web marketers with a very quick means of identifying the customer and understanding his or her prior behavior at the site. Web sites use cookies to determine how many people are visiting the site, whether they are new or repeat visitors, and how often they have visited, although this data may be somewhat inaccurate because people share computers, they often use more than one computer, and cookies may have been inadvertently or intentionally erased. Cookies make shopping carts and "quick checkout" options possible by allowing a site to keep track of a user as he or she adds to the shopping cart. Each item added to the shopping cart is stored in the site's database along with the visitor's unique ID value.

Ordinary cookies are easy to spot using your browser, but Flash cookies, beacons, and tracking codes are not easily visible. All common browsers allow users to see the cookies placed in their cookies file. Users can delete cookies, or adjust their settings so that third-party cookies are blocked, while first-party cookies are allowed.

With growing privacy concerns, over time the percentage of people deleting cookies has risen. The more cookies are deleted, the less accurate are Web page and ad server metrics, and the less likely marketers will be able to understand who is visiting their sites or where they came from. As a result, advertisers have sought other methods. One way is using Adobe Flash software, which creates its own cookie files, known as Flash cookies. Flash cookies can be set to never expire, and can store about 5 MB of information compared to the 1,024 bytes stored by regular cookies. A 2009 study by researchers at the University of California-Berkeley analyzed the use of Flash cookies at the top 100 Web sites, and found that 98% used regular cookies and 54% used Flash cookies, many to store the same information at the regular cookie. Some used the Flash cookies to re-create cookies that consumers had previously deleted.

Although cookies are site-specific (a Web site can only receive the data it has stored on a client computer and cannot look at any other cookie), when combined with Web beacons (also called "bugs"), they can be used to create cross-site profiles. Web bugs are tiny (1-pixel) graphic files embedded in e-mail messages and on Web sites. Web bugs are used to automatically transmit information about the user and the page being viewed to a monitoring server in order to collect personal browsing behavior and other personal information. For instance, when a recipient opens an e-mail in HTML format or opens a Web page, a message is sent to a server calling for graphic information. This tells the marketer that the e-mail was opened, indicating that the recipient was at least interested in the subject header. Web beacons are not visible to users. They are often clear or colored white so they are not visible to the recipient. You may be able to determine if a Web page is using Web bugs by using the View Source option of your browser and examining the IMG (image) tags on the page. As noted above, Web bugs are typically 1 pixel in size and contain the URL of a server that differs from the one that served the page itself (see w2.eff.org/Privacy/Marketing/web_bug.html). *Insight on Society: Every Move You Take, Every Click You Make, We'll Be Tracking You* examines the use of Web tracking files.

DATABASES, DATA WAREHOUSES, DATA MINING, AND BIG DATA

Databases, data warehouses, data mining, and the variety of marketing decision-making techniques loosely called *profiling* are at the heart of the revolution in Internet marketing. **Profiling** uses a variety of tools to create a digital image for each consumer. This image can be quite inexact, even primitive, but it can also be as detailed as a character in a novel. The quality of a consumer profile depends on the amount of data used to create it, and the analytical power of the firm's software and hardware. Together, these techniques attempt to identify precisely who the online customer is and what they want, and then, to fulfill the customer's criteria exactly. These techniques are more powerful, far more precise, and more fine-grained than the gross levels of demographic and market segmentation techniques used in mass marketing media or by telemarketing.

In order to understand the data in transaction logs, registration forms, shopping carts, cookies, Web bugs, and other unstructured data sources like e-mails, Tweets, and Likes, Internet marketers need massively powerful and capacious databases, database management systems, and analytic tools.

Databases

The first step in interpreting huge transaction streams is to store the information systematically. A **database** is a software application that stores records and attributes. A telephone book is a physical database that stores records of individuals and their attributes such as names, addresses, and phone numbers. A **database management system (DBMS)** is a software application used by organizations to create, maintain, and access databases. The most common DBMS are DB2 from IBM and a variety of SQL databases from Oracle, Sybase, and other providers. **Structured query language (SQL)** is an industry-standard database query and manipulation language used in relational databases. **Relational databases** such as DB2 and SQL represent data as two-dimensional tables with records organized in rows, and attributes in columns, much like a spreadsheet. The tables—and all the data in them—can be flexibly related to one another as long as the tables share a common data element.

Relational databases are extraordinarily flexible and allow marketers and other managers to view and analyze data from different perspectives very quickly.

profiling
profiling uses a variety of tools to create a digital image for each consumer.

database
a software application that stores records and attributes

database management system (DBMS)
a software application used by organizations to create, maintain, and access databases

structured query language (SQL)
industry-standard database query language used in relational databases

relational databases
represent data as two-dimensional tables with records organized in rows and attributes in columns; data within different tables can be flexibly related as long as the tables share a common data element

INSIGHT ON SOCIETY

EVERY MOVE YOU TAKE, EVERY CLICK YOU MAKE, WE'LL BE TRACKING YOU

When's the last time you visited your favorite Web portal page and saw ads that you had no interest in seeing? Don't think long! Most people online are treated to hundreds of irrelevant ads every day. The solution to the problem of annoying, irrelevant ads is "targeted ads," which reflect your current or even longer term interests. One major reason why Web display advertising is growing so fast is that advertisers can target ads at specific individuals with great specificity. The "free" Web depends on knowing as much personal information as possible about you. How personal? How about your pants and shirt size, favorite songs, health status, education, current location, or any of the thousands of pieces of information that make you who you are.

One of the main ways ad firms discover your personal information is by placing so-called "tracking files" on your computer's browser. There are four kinds of third-party tracking files on Web pages. Cookies are the best-known. These simple text files are placed in your browser and assign a unique number to your computer (regardless of which person is using it), and then are used by advertisers to track you across the Web as you move from one site to another (without telling you). Beacons are a little more pernicious. Beacons are small software files that track your clicks, choices, and purchases, and even location data from mobile devices, and then send that information, often in real time, to advertisers tracking you. Beacons can also assign your computer a unique number and track you across the Web. A Flash cookie is a third kind of tracking file. Installed by Adobe Flash as you watch movies, these files can be useful but are also used to install regular cookies on your computer and even restore cookies you have deleted. Tracking can also be performed by apps on cell phones as well as Facebook. Apps are built by third parties. The top 10 Facebook apps, for instance, all send personal information, including names, to dozens of advertising and Internet tracking companies.

So how common is Web tracking? In a path-breaking series of articles in the *Wall Street Journal* in 2010 and 2011, researchers examined the tracking files on 50 of the most popular U.S Web sites. What they found revealed a very widespread surveillance system. On the 50 sites, they discovered 3,180 tracking files installed on visitor computers. Only one site, Wikipedia, had no tracking files. Some popular sites such as Dictionary.com, MSN, and Comcast, installed more than 100 tracking files! Two-thirds of the tracking files came from 131 companies whose primary business is identifying and tracking Internet users to create consumer profiles that can be sold to advertising firms looking for specific types of customers. The biggest trackers were Google, Microsoft, and Quantcast, all of whom are in the business of selling ads to advertising firms and marketers. Another third of the tracking files came from database firms that gather and bundle the information and then sell it to marketers. Many of the tracking tools gather incredibly personal information such as age, gender, race, income, marital status, health concerns (heath topics you search on), TV shows and movies viewed, magazines and newspapers read, and books purchased. While tracking firms claim the information they gather is anonymous, this is true in name only. Scholars have shown that with just a few pieces of information, such as age, gender, zip code, and marital status, specific individuals can be easily identified. A 2012 study

(continued)

by data management company Krux found the situation worsened since 2010: tracking on the 50 most popular Web sites had risen nearly five fold! The cause: growth of online ad auctions where advertisers buy data about users' Web browsing behavior. When you visit a site, your visit is auctioned and the winner gets to show you some ads. All this takes place in a few milliseconds so you don't know its happening. Welcome to the brave new world of Internet marketing!

The leading Web tracker is Google Analytics, followed by Google Syndication, Google, Yahoo, Amazon, and your favorite Web 2.0 sites, YouTube, Photobucket, and Flickr. All of Google's sites together account for about 20% of Web beacons. Anytime you use these sites, your every move is tracked. Collectively, these sites capture a significant portion of the Web behavior of 232 million Internet users in the United States. The activities of these Web trackers are largely beyond current federal or state regulations or law.

The Privacy Foundation has issued guidelines for Web beacon usage. The guidelines suggest that Web beacons should be visible as an icon on the screen, the icon should be labeled to indicate its function, and it should identify the name of the company that placed the Web beacon on the page. In addition, if a user clicks on the Web beacon, it should display a disclosure statement indicating what data is being collected, how the data is used after it is collected, what companies receive the data, what other data the Web beacon is combined with, and whether or not a cookie is associated with the Web beacon. Users should be able to opt out of any data collection done by the Web beacon, and the Web beacon should not be used to collect information from Web pages of a sensitive nature, such as medical, financial, job-related, or sexual matters. None of these ideas are found in current law.

In an effort to address growing congressional concerns about privacy, and build consumer trust online, an industry advertising group, the Network Advertising Initiative (NAI), released self-regulatory guidelines for the industry. Major advertising industry groups have adopted the Self Regulatory Principles for Online Behavioral Advertising, which emphasize transparency (tell consumers how you use their information) and choice (opt-in and opt-out). The NAI renamed Web bugs as "Web beacons" and requires online firms to notify customers of Web beacon usage whether in e-mail or on Web sites, state the purpose of their use, and disclose any data that could be released to third parties. The NAI also called for users to be given a choice (whether opt-in or opt-out) of any release of personally identifiable information (PII) to third parties, and to provide an opt-in choice for any release of information related to PII. These restrictions do not apply to the Web site itself (agents). In addition, the NAI provides a capability open to all Web users to opt out of online advertising networks collecting non-personal information on them. However, for this to work, users need to have a cookie downloaded to their browser that will inform the networks not to collect information on this user.

Currently, there are no laws or regulations in the United States that prevent firms from installing tracking files on your computer or using that information in any way they please. This situation began to change in 2010, and by, 2012, there is considerable legislative and government interest in protecting the privacy of consumers, driven in part by public fear of the loss of privacy and the lack of transparency in the world of Web tracking.

In December 2010, the Federal Trade Commission issued a staff report that proposed a new balance between the privacy interests of consumers with continued innovation on the Web that relies on consumer information. The report argued that industry self-regulation had failed to protect consumer privacy. The Commission recommended consumers be given a simple way to opt out of tracking through a "Do Not Track" mechanism in the user's browser that would prevent Web sites from installing tracking software on the user's

(continued)

browser. In March, the White House issued a call for privacy legislation.

In April 2011, Senators John Kerry and John McCain proposed bipartisan legislation that would create a "privacy bill of rights" to protect people from an unregulated, invasive commercial data-collection industry. Labeled the "Commercial Privacy Bill of Rights Act of 2011," the legislation would allow consumers on a site-by-site basis to demand Web sites stop tracking them and selling their information online. In 2012, this legislation is unlikely to pass because of election year politics.

In addition, government itself also has an interest in maximizing the amount of information it keeps on its citizens, usually in the name of law enforcement and national security. In 2012, Senators Lieberman, Collins, Rockefeller, Feinstein, and Carper introduced the Cybersecurity Act of 2012 (S. 3414). While ostensibly designed to protect U.S. computer networks from cyberattacks, the legislation authorizes information sharing between private firms like Yahoo, Google, and Amazon, and the federal government. Sensitive personal and financial data would be shared. Both big business and big government would seem to be on the same side when it comes to tracking people online.

In February 2012 federal regulators, members of advertising trade groups, and technology companies like Microsoft, Google, and Yahoo met in Washington to announce new measures to protect consumer privacy online. The argument involves the meaning of "do not track." Industry wants an opt-in, default Track Me feature allowable on all Web sites, while the government and privacy groups are pushing for an opt-out Do Not Track feature at Web sites in which the default is Do Not Track. Many first-party sites, such as Google, Amazon, and the New York Times, would be unaffected. The idea is that firms can track and behaviorally target visitors on their own sites. Display ads are considered "third party" ads and would be effected. There are no technical standards for what "do not track" means.

Under pressure from Congress and public opinion, Mozilla was the first browser to add a Do Not Track feature to its Firefox browser. But users had to remember to turn it on. Over strong objections from the online advertising industry, Microsoft, in July 2012, added a default-on "do not track" feature to its Internet Explorer 10 browser saying that consumers favor products designed with their privacy in mind. Major Web sites have agreed to honor the request to do not track but refuse to stop gathering tracking data. Major Web sites and the online advertising industry insist their industry can self-regulate itself and preserve individual privacy. This solution has not worked in the past.

SOURCES: "Online Data Collection Explodes Year Over Year in US," eMarketer, July 19, 2012; "Online Tracking Ramps Up," by Julia Angwin, *Wall Street Journal*, June 17, 2012; "Microsoft's "Do Not Track" Mover Angers Advertising Industry," by Julia Angwin, *Wall Street Journal*, May 31, 2012; "Opt-Out Provision Would Halt Some, but Not All, Web Tracking," by Tanzina Vega, *New York Times*, February 28, 2012; "How Companies Learn Your Secrets," by Charles Duhigg, *New York Times Magazine*, February 16, 2012; "Recommendations for the Implementation of a Comprehensive and Constitutional Cybersecurity Policy," The Constitution Project, January 27, 2012; "Latest in Web Tracking: Stealthy 'Supercookies,'" by Julia Angwin, *Wall Street Journal*, August 18, 2011; "WPP Ad Unit Has Your Profile," by Emily Steel, *Wall Street Journal*, June 27, 2011; "Not Me Dot Com," by Luke O'Neil, *Wall Street Journal*, June 18, 2011; "Do-Not-Track Online Act of 2011," Senate 913, U.S. Senate, May 9, 2011; "Do Not Track Bill Appears in Congress," by Tanzina Vega, *New York Times*, May 6, 2011; "Show Us the Data. (It's Ours, After All)," by Richard Thaler, *New York Times*, April 23, 2011; "Commercial Privacy Bill of Rights Act," Senate 799; U.S. Senate, April 13, 2011; "Protecting Consumer Privacy," Preliminary FTC Staff Report. Federal Trade Commission, March 10, 2011; "What They Know About You," by Jennifer Valentino-Devries, *Wall Street Journal*, July 31, 2010; "Sites Feed Personal Details to New Tracking Industry," Julia Angwin and Tom McGinty, *Wall Street Journal*, July 30, 2010; "FTC Staff Issues Privacy Report, Offers Framework for Consumers, Businesses, and Policymakers," Federal Trade Commission, Press Release, December 10, 2010; "Facebook in Privacy Breach," by Emily Steel and Geoffrey Fowler, *Wall Street Journal*, October 18, 2010; "Technology Coalition Seeks Stronger Privacy Laws," by Miguel Helft, *New York Times*, March 30, 2010; "Study Finds Behaviorally-Targeted Ads More Than Twice As Valuable, Twice as Effective As Non-targeted Online Ads," Network Advertising Initiative, March 24, 2010.

Data Warehouses and Data Mining

A **data warehouse** is a database that collects a firm's transactional and customer data in a single location for offline analysis by marketers and site managers. The data originate in many core operational areas of the firm, such as Web site transaction logs, shopping carts, point-of-sale terminals (product scanners) in stores, warehouse inventory levels, field sales reports, external scanner data supplied by third parties, and financial payment data. The purpose of a data warehouse is to gather all the firm's transaction and customer data into one logical repository where it can be analyzed and modeled by managers without disrupting or taxing the firm's primary transactional systems and databases. Data warehouses grow quickly into storage repositories containing terabytes of data (trillions of bytes) on consumer behavior at a firm's stores and Web sites. With a data warehouse, firms can answer such questions as: What products are the most profitable by region and city? What regional marketing campaigns are working? How effective is store promotion of the firm's Web site? Data warehouses can provide business managers with a more complete awareness of customers through data that can be accessed quickly.

Data mining is a set of analytical techniques that look for patterns in the data of a database or data warehouse, or seek to model the behavior of customers. Web site data can be "mined" to develop profiles of visitors and customers. A **customer profile** is simply a set of rules that describe the typical behavior of a customer or a group of customers at a Web site. Customer profiles help to identify the patterns in group and individual behavior that occur online as millions of visitors use a firm's Web site. For example, almost every financial transaction you engage in is processed by a data mining application to detect fraud. Phone companies closely monitor your cell phone use as well to detect stolen phones and unusual calling patterns. Financial institutions and cell phone firms use data mining to develop fraud profiles. When a user's behavior conforms to a fraud profile, the transaction is not allowed or terminated (Mobasher, 2007).

There are many different types of data mining. The simplest type is **query-driven data mining**, which is based on specific queries. For instance, based on hunches of marketers who suspect a relationship in the database or who need to answer a specific question, such as "What is the relationship between time of day and purchases of various products at the Web site?", marketers can easily query the data warehouse and produce a database table that rank-orders the top 10 products sold at a Web site by each hour of the day. Marketers can then change the content of the Web site to stimulate more sales by highlighting different products over time or placing particular products on the home page at certain times of day or night.

Another form of data mining is model-driven. **Model-driven data mining** involves the use of a model that analyzes the key variables of interest to decision makers. For example, marketers may want to reduce the inventory carried on the Web site by removing unprofitable items that do not sell well. A financial model can be built showing the profitability of each product on the site so that an informed decision can be made.

data warehouse
a database that collects a firm's transactional and customer data in a single location for offline analysis

data mining
a set of analytical techniques that look for patterns in the data of a database or data warehouse, or seek to model the behavior of customers

customer profile
a description of the typical behavior of a customer or a group of customers at a Web site

query-driven data mining
data mining based on specific queries

model-driven data mining
involves the use of a model that analyzes the key variables of interest to decision makers

A more fine-grained behavioral approach that seeks to deal with individuals as opposed to market segments derives rules from individual consumer behavior (along with some demographic information) (Adomavicius and Tuzhilin, 2001a; Chan, 1999; Fawcett and Provost, 1996, 1997). Here, the pages actually visited by specific users are stored as a set of conjunctive rules. For example, if an individual visits a site and typically ("as a rule") moves from the home page to the financial news section to the Asian report section, and then often purchases articles from the "Recent Developments in Banking" section, this person—based on purely past behavioral patterns—might be shown an advertisement for a book on Asian money markets. These rules can be constructed to follow an individual across many different Web sites.

There are many drawbacks to all these techniques, not least of which is that there may be millions of rules, many of them nonsensical, and many others of short-term duration. Hence, the rules need extensive validation and culling (Adomavicius and Tuzhilin, 2001b). Also, there can be millions of affinity groups and other patterns in the data that are temporal or meaningless. The difficulty is isolating the valid, powerful (profitable) patterns in the data and then acting on the observed pattern fast enough to make a sale that otherwise would not have been made. As we see later, there are practical difficulties and trade-offs involved in achieving these levels of granularity, precision, and speed.

Hadoop and the Challenge of Big Data

Up until about five years ago, most data collected by organizations consisted of structured transaction data that could easily fit into rows and columns of relational database management systems. Since then, there has been an explosion of data from Web traffic, e-mail messages, and social media content (tweets, status messages), even music playlists, as well as machine-generated data from sensors. These data may be unstructured or semi-structured and thus not suitable for relational database products that organize data in the form of columns and rows. The popular term "big data" refers to this avalanche of digital data flowing into firms around the world largely from Web sites and Internet click stream data. The volumes of data are so large that traditional DBMS cannot capture, store, and analyze the data in a reasonable time. Some examples of "big data" challenges are analyzing 12 terabytes of tweets created each day to improve your understanding of consumer sentiment towards your products; 100 million e-mails in order to place appropriate ads alongside the e-mail messages; or 500 million call detail records to find patterns of fraud and churn. Big data and the tools needed to deal with it really started with Google and other search engines. Google's problem: it has to deal with 500 million searches a day, and within milliseconds, display search results and place ads. For fun, do a search on "big data" and you'll see Google respond with more than 1 billion results in 38 milliseconds (about a third of a second). That's much faster than you can read this sentence!

big data

big data refers to very large data sets in the petabyte and exabyte range

Big data usually refers to data in the petabyte and exabyte range—in other words, billions to trillions of records, all from different sources. Big data are produced in much larger quantities and much more rapidly than traditional data. Even though "tweets" are limited to 140 characters each, Twitter generates more than 8 terabytes of data daily. According to the IDC technology research firm, data is more than doubling every two years, so the amount of data available to organizations is skyrocketing. Making sense out of it quickly in order to gain a market advantage is critical.

Businesses are interested in big data because they contain more patterns and interesting anomalies than smaller data sets, with the potential to provide new insights into customer behavior, weather patterns, financial market activity, or other phenomena. However, to derive business value from these data, organizations need new technologies and tools capable of managing and analyzing nontraditional data along with their traditional enterprise data.

To handle unstructured and semi-structured data in vast quantities, as well as structured data, organizations are using Hadoop. **Hadoop** is an open source software framework managed by the Apache Software Foundation that enables distributed parallel processing of huge amounts of data across inexpensive computers. It breaks a big data problem down into sub-problems, distributes them among up to thousands of inexpensive computer processing nodes, and then combines the result into a smaller data set that is easier to analyze. You've probably used Hadoop to find the best airfare on the Internet, get directions to a restaurant, search on Google, or connect with a friend on Facebook.

Hadoop
a software framework for working with various big data sets

Hadoop can process large quantities of any kind of data, including structured transactional data, loosely structured data such as Facebook and Twitter feeds, complex data such as Web server log files, and unstructured audio and video data. Hadoop runs on a cluster of inexpensive servers, and processors can be added or removed as needed. Companies use Hadoop to analyze very large volumes of data as well as for a staging area for unstructured and semi-structured data before they are loaded into a data warehouse. Facebook stores much of its data on its massive Hadoop cluster, which holds an estimated 100 petabytes, about 10,000 times more information than the Library of Congress. Yahoo uses Hadoop to track user behavior so it can modify its home page to fit user interests. Life sciences research firm NextBio uses Hadoop and HBase to process data for pharmaceutical companies conducting genomic research. Top database vendors such as IBM, Hewlett-Packard, Oracle, and Microsoft have their own Hadoop software distributions. Other vendors offer tools for moving data into and out of Hadoop or for analyzing data within Hadoop.

CUSTOMER RELATIONSHIP MANAGEMENT (CRM) SYSTEMS

Customer relationship management systems are another important Internet marketing technology. A **customer relationship management (CRM) system** is a repository of customer information that records all of the contacts that a customer has with a firm (including Web sites) and generates a customer profile available to everyone in the firm with a need to "know the customer." CRM systems also supply the analytical software required to analyze and use customer information. Customers come to firms not just over the Web but also through telephone call centers, customer service representatives, sales representatives, automated voice response systems, ATMs and kiosks, in-store point-of-sale terminals, and mobile devices (m-commerce). Collectively, these are referred to as "**customer touchpoints**." In the past, firms generally did not maintain a single repository of customer information, but instead

customer relationship management (CRM) system
a repository of customer information that records all of the contacts that a customer has with a firm and generates a customer profile available to everyone in the firm with a need to "know the customer"

customer touchpoints
the ways in which customers interact with the firm

were organized along product lines, with each product line maintaining a customer list (and often not sharing it with others in the same firm).

In general, firms did not know who their customers were, how profitable they were, or how they responded to marketing campaigns. For instance, a bank customer might see a television advertisement for a low-cost auto loan that included an 800-number to call. However, if the customer came to the bank's Web site instead, rather than calling the 800-number, marketers would have no idea how effective the television campaign was because this Web customer contact data was not related to the 800-number call center data. **Figure 6.11** illustrates how a CRM system integrates customer contact data into a single system.

CRMs are part of the evolution of firms toward a customer-centric and marketing-segment–based business, and away from a product-line–centered business. CRMs are essentially a database technology with extraordinary capabilities for addressing the needs of each customer and differentiating the product or service on the basis of treating each customer as a unique person. Customer profiles can contain the following information:

- A map of the customer's relationship with the institution
- Product and usage summary data
- Demographic and psychographic data
- Profitability measures
- Contact history summarizing the customer's contacts with the institution across most delivery channels
- Marketing and sales information containing programs received by the customer and the customer's responses
- E-mail campaign responses
- Web site visits

With these profiles, CRMs can be used to sell additional products and services, develop new products, increase product utilization, reduce marketing costs, identify and retain profitable customers, optimize service delivery costs, retain high lifetime value customers, enable personal communications, improve customer loyalty, and increase product profitability.

For instance, Home Depot saw increased competition from online hardware stores and decided to emphasize e-commerce as part of its business strategy. The company sought a comprehensive CRM solution that could organize and analyze information from both clicks and mortar. They used a CRM software package called Epiphany Insight to gain a better understanding of which Home Depot products were selling on the Web and enabled their customer service focus from their stores to exist on the Web as well. Epiphany has since been acquired by Infor. Other leading CRM vendors include SAP, SalesForce.com, Oracle, Kana, and eGain.

| FIGURE 6.11 | **A CUSTOMER RELATIONSHIP MANAGEMENT SYSTEM** |

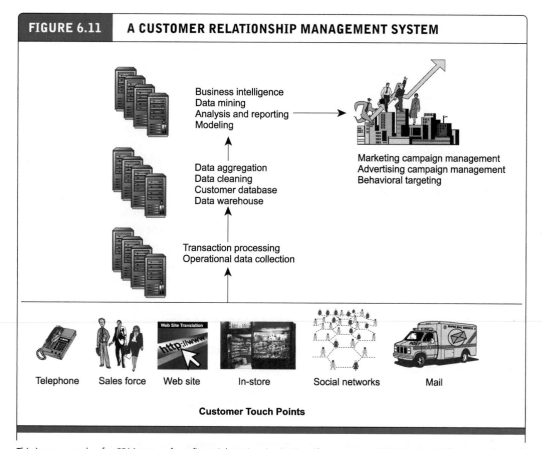

This is an example of a CRM system for a financial services institution. The system captures customer information from all customer touchpoints as well as other data sources, merges the data, and aggregates it into a single customer data repository or data warehouse where it can be used to provide better service, as well as to construct customer profiles for marketing purposes. Online analytical processing (OLAP) allows managers to dynamically analyze customer activities to spot trends or problems involving customers. Other analytical software programs analyze aggregate customer behavior to identify profitable and unprofitable customers as well as customer activities.

CASE STUDY

Building a Brand:

ExchangeHunterJumper.com

he Internet and Web have enabled thousands of business ideas to become online realities. The Internet has reduced the costs of starting a small business, and allowed small players to effectively use the same marketing and selling tools as major corporations. Small businesses usually occupy a market niche not occupied by big players or corporations. One such market niche in America is the high-end horse show circuit. These are people who are willing to drop $200,000 on a horse that can jump a five-foot fence with ease. This may be a very small market, but its members are highly motivated to both buy and sell horses, and they are willing to spend in the process. ExchangeHunterJumper.com is one example of how a small business focusing on a tiny niche market was able to successfully build an online brand.

According to Dagny Amber Aslin, founder and owner of ExchangeHunterJumper. com (The Exchange), a Web site created to help owners and professional trainers sell high-end competition horses, it's hard to "get rich" or even make money on the Internet. She adds, "There are a lot of preconceived notions ... I beat down a path

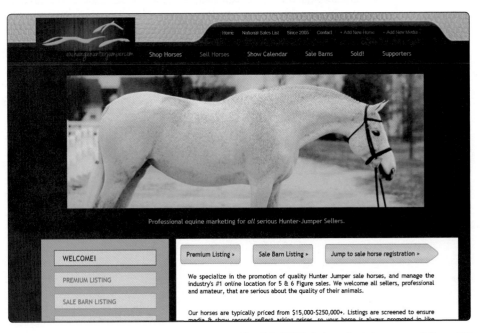

previously unplowed. It cost us a lot of money and we suffered many setbacks from our mistakes." Yet the site is still growing and has succeeded where others failed. How did Aslin break through and develop a site that works for professionals buying and selling alike? How did she build trust? How did she market her services?

Experience helped. Aslin started with applicable experience—in the horse world and in the world of Internet marketing. In addition to riding and competing as a child, Aslin spent several years working as a professional trainer. Working six-day weeks, including weekends, and spending most of her time outdoors riding, teaching, and competing, she saw first-hand the challenges facing professional horsemen, and she gained valuable credibility with those who would become her audience.

While working in the horse business, and learning how difficult it was to make a living, she took a part-time job as an assistant to a top California real estate agent, helping him market and sell high-end real estate in the Santa Barbara area. Among other activities, she helped him develop and expand his Web site. Through that experience, she realized that "selling six-figure horses and seven-figure houses are ridiculously similar—both tend to be overpriced, have emotional strings attached, require vettings and exhaustive negotiations, involve agents, and the list goes on." In 2005, when she moved from California back to the Midwest, where she had spent her childhood, The Exchange was born. Seven years later, the equine marketing model she has built is "a customized carbon copy" of the real estate program she assisted with in Santa Barbara.

Aslin knew busy horse professionals needed a high-quality, reliable source of suitable mounts for their clients, but their day-to-day business lives left them little time to thoroughly search the market, and they often lacked a good grasp of modern media technology. The same dilemma applied when it came to selling high-end horses. In response, she created an organized, professional process for preparing online horse sale advertisements. It included detailed forms for sellers to fill out, and she insisted that quality photos and video be provided for each horse advertised, enabling her to turn the descriptions into accurate portrayals of each animal and its capabilities. She created a fee structure that was reasonable and affordable, and she developed a multi-channel marketing program.

Aslin understood that her business plan needed to be a living document, evolving over time based on what the market was telling her. This helped her make inroads in a traditional industry that is very resistant to change. Most horse professionals spend their days outside, and tend to do business only with those they know personally—the level of trust is very low. Most existing horse sale Web sites are no more than online classifieds with information that is often unreliable and not given much credence. Although professional horsemen have been slow to use computers and the Internet, the rise of smartphones has helped increase their comfort level with e-mail and Web technology.

The Exchange took all of these things into account, and Aslin went further. In order to remain true to her business goal of providing a *reliable* service to professionals in the horse industry that would become a source of good horses described accurately, Aslin personally reviewed all potential advertisers. In some cases she went back to sellers and insisted on higher quality photographs and video, and in other cases where she determined the horse was not as represented, she turned down their business. The initial business plan process involved strict screening, and it meant turning away money and valuing quality over quantity in every area—horses, buyers, traffic, and ads. It was a hard and expensive premise to adhere to when building a reputation from scratch, but through persistence and dedication it has worked, and today, The Exchange's reputation and "brand" has become one of its most valuable assets.

In discussing some of the obstacles she faced in getting The Exchange up and running, Aslin starts with education—her own or lack thereof, specifically in the areas of graphic design and Web technology. While she knew what professional horsemen needed, she did not know how to translate that into graphic design or onto the Web. She says that looking back on the original logo and print designs is "a painful exercise," but she is happy with the current direction.

The budget was also an initial obstacle, as there wasn't a lot of money to spend up front. However, in hindsight, she believes that gave her an advantage because she had to learn what her market wanted and was able to do so without breaking the bank. Conversely, her main competitor took an opposite track, spent big up front, missed the mark with customers, and is now defunct.

In addition, she faced the negative perception among industry professionals and prospective buyers that equine Internet advertising was "worthless." Further, much of her target audience barely knew how to use a computer, didn't have e-mail addresses, and had been doing business in the same old-school manner for decades. For a few key players this worked very well, but it left a void for those outside of that inner circle to move horses. Through a combination of knowledge of the marketplace, on-the-job training, perseverance, and listening to what the market was telling her, The Exchange has successfully begun to fill that void.

Here's how it works. The Exchange handles advertising for sellers and trainers across the country. In 2012, show horses advertised on The Exchange are typically priced from $15,000 to $250,000. The recession caused prices to fall significantly, but in 2012, the prices in certain parts of the market have started to rebound. The Exchange specializes strictly in hunter-jumper show horses, and specifically those suited for high-level competition.

Trainers/sellers who sign up for a premium listing pay a flat $250 fee for the initial advertisement and a subscription fee of $35/month, which includes a listing on The Exchange's Web site featuring the horse's details, photos, show record, lineage, and videos. The Exchange provides copy-writing services and professionally edits all videos supplied by sellers, hosting them on its private server and making them available to download, embed, and share. Each listing typically takes 8–10 hours to prepare. In 2012, The Exchange added a second listing alternative—a Sale Barn listing for $300 a month or $3,000 a year, that allows for listing of up to 10 horses. A three-month commitment is required, but there are no initial or other fees. Aimed at high volume operations with frequent turnover, the Sale Barn page can link to the seller's Web site, YouTube, Facebook, and Twitter feeds, if available, with the goal of increasing overall brand awareness for the seller's business. Aslin designed the Sale Barn as an affordable option for professionals might otherwise be reluctant to spend on marketing. International sellers are given a slight additional discount.

Statistics show that a horse's first month online is most successful in terms of the number of Web page visits. With the addition of monthly campaign management, The Exchange helps keep each horse's marketing fresh and up to date. Updates can immediately escalate a horse's popularity as much as 30% and attract new potential buyers. Sellers are encouraged to provide updates as frequently as possible. Useful updates include upcoming competition appearances, recent competitions with impressive results, changes to listing details (such as a price adjustment), new photos, and video. Online videos add to the brand of the horse for sale and are especially important for young horses or those "growing into" their price tags. Updates are added to the Web site and promoted through various media outlets including Facebook and e-mail campaigns.

Sellers currently fill out two separate forms: a credit card registration form and an equine fact sheet. The fact sheet includes a long series of checkboxes from which sellers select pre-worded traits, coupled with space for additional written descriptions. This saves some production time, although writing the actual copy is still a major part of the value that The Exchange provides. To implement this option, Aslin spent time investigating form-building tools. Custom-built form solutions were likely to be too expensive, so she played with numerous online form generators and ultimately was able to find some that offered great functionality at a relatively low cost. So, for example, a seller can indicate that the horse is a "jumper" and questions specific to jumpers will be displayed.

The Exchange develops a specific marketing strategy for each horse listed. This includes reviewing information submitted, combing through a horse's official show record, considering impartial impressions, and identifying the most likely buyers. If The Exchange thinks that the photos or videos don't help to sell the horse, they advise the seller on how to improve them. This advice stems from experience in marketing all types of horses from coast to coast, and an understanding of varied buyer profiles and geographic trends that exist in the market.

The Exchange's Web site is at the core of its marketing efforts. The company recently shifted to Google Analytics to analyze its Web site traffic, finding that this free service provides much more thorough site statistics than any of the options it had previously been paying for.

In addition to the Web site, The Exchange uses a variety of multi-channel marketing strategies. For instance, in 2011 and 2012, The Exchange distributed more than 3,500 copies of a high-quality, four-color, printed National Sales List booklet at around 30 different horse shows around the country. The booklets included a QR code for each horse on the sales list, which when scanned with a smartphone using any one of many freely available apps, takes the reader directly to the horse's videos on The Exchange Web site. The booklet is also available on The Exchange's Web site, using technology provided by YUDU, an online publishing platform. The booklet replaced DVD video catalogs that, in the past, had been prepared at great expense by The Exchange and mailed directly to professionals and distributed at horse shows. The Exchange also uses e-mail campaigns, magazine advertising, and word of mouth.

Starting in 2009, The Exchange began experimenting with viral marketing and social media including RSS feeds, YouTube, Facebook, Twitter, and now, Pinterest. Aslin notes that when she began The Exchange, social media was not yet the phenomenon that it is today, but when its significance started to became apparent, she had no choice but to jump in and begin using it, learning as she went. The Exchange has experienced varying success with social media. For instance, The Exchange runs multiple RSS feeds through the free service, FeedBurner, although thus far, the equestrian set does not appear to be particularly interested in RSS feed subscriptions. The company's YouTube channel has been largely supplanted by a professional video management system from Vzaar that hosts all of its videos, serves to most smartphones, and provides more control, branding, and flexibility than YouTube without any annoying advertisements. Facebook has been the most resounding social media success. For the first six months of 2012, Facebook generated more than 35,000 visits to The Exchange's Web site (about 18% of new visits). The Exchange has more than 3,700 Likes on Facebook. Aslin's Twitter account has more than 1,300 followers, and links with both The Exchange's Facebook page and its YouTube channel. The latest social media platform now in The Exchange's sights is Pinterest, which Aslin believes may be very beneficial, since visuals such as photos and video play such an important role in the marketing of show horses. Because every business is different, The Exchange's experience suggests it's important for e-commerce sites to experiment with social media to determine which outlets are most effective in reaching their specific target audiences. The Exchange's successful use of social media in the equestrian industry was recognized when it was named one of 10 finalists for the 2012 PagePlay Equestrian Social Media Awards for best use of social media in North America.

Aslin has also been continually reviewing the design of the Web site with an eye to making it the most effective marketing tool possible. She built the original site herself in 2005 and updated it almost yearly in response to her target market's needs. In 2012, Aslin relaunched the site for a fifth time, and for the first time ever hired a professional Web development team to convert the static HTML site into a dynamically driven content management system on the Expression Engine platform. While she was able to keep costs low by designing and developing the site's CSS layout, the advanced functionality that was desired, such as the sale horse filter that enables shoppers to sort horses based on price, location, gender, type, and size, still required a hefty five-figure investment. Aslin believes the ability to get to know the market and update the site accordingly has kept The Exchange fresh and innovative. Every iteration of the Web site and overall multi-channel marketing strategy has been focused on meeting the target market's needs. For instance, she has also spent considerable time and expense to make sure The Exchange's Web site, including video, works just as well on mobile devices as it does on a traditional laptop or desktop computer.

Aslin has found it has been extremely helpful to have the Web development experience she has honed over the years. Here are some of her words of wisdom: She feels that entrepreneurs don't necessarily have to know how to build sites, but do need to be familiar with what is and what is not possible in site construction. It is important to understand which functions are complicated and which are not, so that overly complicated add-ons that don't really add to the user experience can be eliminated from tight budgets. It's also important to know what technology is popular now and what technology is just around the corner. Even if you think you are proficient in all the tasks you will need to launch your business, with the rapid pace of technology, you inevitably spend much of your time learning something totally new, whether you want to or not.

By paying attention to these words of wisdom, as well as to detail at every step of the marketing process, The Exchange has managed to build a successful brand, one the horse community has come to rely upon.

SOURCES: Exchangehunter-jumper.com, accessed October 1, 2012; Interview with Amber Aslin, founder of ExchangeHunterJumper, September 2012.

Case Study Questions

1. Find a site on the Web that offers classified ads for horses. Compare this site to exchangehunterjumper.com in terms of the services offered (the customer value proposition). What does The Exchange offer that other sites do not?

2. In what ways were social media effective in promoting The Exchange brand? Which media led to the highest increase in sales and inquiries? Why?

3. Make a list of all the ways The Exchange attempts to personalize its services to both buyers and sellers.

6.6 REVIEW

KEY CONCEPTS

■ Identify the key features of the Internet audience.

Key features of the Internet audience include:
- *The number of users online in the United States.* In 2011, the total was around 232 million. However, the rate of growth in the U.S. Internet population has begun to slow.
- *Intensity and scope of use.* Both are increasing, with around 77% of adult users in the United States logging on in a typical day and engaging in a wider set of activities, including sending and reading e-mail, gathering hobby-related information, catching up on news, browsing for fun, buying products, seeking health information, conducting work-related research, and reviewing financial information.
- *Demographics and access.* Although the Internet population is growing increasingly diverse, some demographic groups have much higher percentages of online usage than other groups, and different patterns of usage exist across various groups.
- *Lifestyle impacts.* Intensive Internet use may cause a decline in traditional social activities. The social development of children who use the Internet intensively instead of engaging in face-to-face interactions or undirected play out of doors may also be negatively impacted.
- *Media choices.* The more time individuals spend using the Internet, the less time they spend using traditional media.

■ **Discuss the basic concepts of consumer behavior and purchasing decisions.**

Models of consumer behavior attempt to predict or explain what consumers purchase, and where, when, how much, and why they buy. Factors that impact buying behavior include:
- Cultural factors
- Social factors
- Psychological factors

There are five stages in the consumer decision process:
- Awareness of need
- Search for more information
- Evaluation of alternatives
- The actual purchase decision
- Post-purchase contact with the firm

The online consumer decision process is basically the same, with the addition of two new factors:
- *Web site capabilities*—the content, design, and functionality of a site.
- *Consumer clickstream behavior*—the transaction log that consumers establish as they move about the Web and through specific sites. Analysts believe the most important predictors of online consumer behavior are the session characteristics and the clickstream behavior of people online, rather than demographic data.

■ **Understand how consumers behave online.**

Clickstream analysis shows us that people go online for many different reasons, at different times, and for numerous purposes.
- About 72% of online users are "buyers" who actually purchase something entirely online. Another 16.5% of online users research products on the Web, but purchase them offline. This combined group, referred to as "shoppers," constitutes approximately 88% of the online Internet audience.
- Online sales are divided roughly into two groups: small-ticket and big-ticket items. In the early days of e-commerce, sales of small-ticket items vastly outnumbered those of large-ticket items. However, the recent growth of big-ticket items such as computer hardware and consumer electronics has changed the overall sales mix.
- There are a number of actions that e-commerce vendors could take to increase the likelihood that shoppers and non-shoppers would purchase online more frequently. These include better security of credit card information and privacy of personal information, lower shipping costs, and easier returns.

■ **Describe the basic marketing concepts needed to understand Internet marketing.**

The key objective of Internet marketing is to use the Web—as well as traditional channels—to develop a positive, long-term relationship with customers (who may be online or offline) and thereby create a competitive advantage for the firm by allowing it to charge a higher price for products or services than its competitors can charge.
- Firms within an industry compete with one another on four dimensions: differentiation, cost, focus, and scope. "Competitive markets" are ones with lots of

substitute products, easy entry, low differentiation among suppliers, and strong bargaining power of customers and suppliers.

- Marketing is an activity designed to avoid pure price competition, and to create imperfect markets where returns on investment are above average, competition is limited, and consumers are convinced to pay premium prices for products that have no substitute because they are unique. Marketing encourages customers to buy on the basis of perceived and actual nonmarket, that is, non-price, qualities of products.

- A product's brand is what makes products truly unique and differentiable in the minds of consumers. A brand is a set of expectations, such as quality, reliability, consistency, trust, affection, and loyalty, that consumers have when consuming, or thinking about consuming, a product or service from a specific company.

- Marketers devise and implement brand strategies—a set of plans for differentiating a product from its competitors and communicating these differences effectively to the marketplace. Segmenting the market, targeting different market segments with differentiated products, and positioning products to appeal to the needs of segment customers are key parts of brand strategy.

- Brand equity is the estimated value of the premium customers are willing to pay for using a branded product when compared to unbranded competitors. Consumers are willing to pay more for branded products in part because they reduce consumers' search and decision-making costs. The ability of brands to attain brand equity also provides incentive for firms to build products that serve customer needs better than other products. Brands also lower customer acquisition cost and increase customer retention.

- Although some predicted that the Web would lead to "frictionless commerce" and the end of marketing based on brands, recent research has shown that brands are alive and well on the Web and that consumers are still willing to pay price premiums for products and services they can perceive and differentiate.

■ **Identify and describe the main technologies that support online marketing.**

- *Web transaction logs*—records that document user activity at a Web site. Coupled with data from the registration forms and shopping cart database, these represent a treasure trove of marketing information for both individual sites and the online industry as a whole.

- *Tracking files*—Various files, like cookies, Web beacons, Flash cookies, and apps, that follow users and track their behavior as they visit sites across the entire Web. Cookies are small text files that Web sites place on visitors' client computers every time they visit, and during the visit, as specific pages are visited. Web beacons are tiny (1 pixel) graphic files hidden in marketing e-mail messages and on Web sites. Flash cookies are created using Adobe Flash, can be set never to expire, and can store more information than regular cookies. Smartphone and Web apps also contain tracking files.

- *Databases, data warehouses, data mining, and profiling*—technologies that allow marketers to identify exactly who the online customer is and what they want, and then to present the customer with exactly what they want, when they want it, for the right price.

- *CRM systems*—a repository of customer information that records all of the contacts a customer has with a firm and generates a customer profile available to everyone in the firm who has a need to "know the customer."

■ **Identify and describe basic e-commerce marketing and branding strategies.**

The marketing technologies described above have spawned a new generation of marketing techniques and added power to some traditional techniques.

- Internet marketing strategies for market entry for new firms include pure clicks/first-mover and mixed bricks-and-clicks/alliances; and for existing firms include pure clicks/fast-follower and mixed bricks-and-clicks/brand extender.
- Online marketing techniques to online customers include the use of advertising networks and exchanges, permission marketing, affiliate marketing, viral marketing, blog marketing, social network marketing, mobile marketing, local marketing, and brand leveraging.
- Online techniques for strengthening customer relationships include one-to-one marketing, customization and customer co-production, and customer service (such as CRMs, FAQs, live chat, intelligent agents, and automated response systems).
- Online pricing strategies include offering products and services for free, versioning, bundling, and dynamic pricing.
- Companies operating in the e-commerce environment must also have marketing strategies in place to handle the possibility of channel conflict.

QUESTIONS

1. Is growth of the Internet, in terms of users, expected to continue indefinitely? What, if anything, will cause it to slow?
2. Other than search engines, what are some of the most popular uses of the Internet?
3. Would you say that the Internet fosters or impedes social activity? Explain your position.
4. Why would the amount of experience someone has using the Internet likely increase future Internet usage?
5. Research has shown that many consumers use the Internet to investigate purchases before actually buying, which is often done in a physical storefront. What implication does this have for online merchants? What can they do to entice more online buying, rather than pure research?
6. Name four improvements Web merchants could make to encourage more browsers to become buyers.
7. Name the five stages in the buyer decision process and briefly describe the online and offline marketing activities used to influence each.
8. Why are "little monopolies" desirable from a marketer's point of view?
9. Describe a perfect market from the supplier's and customer's perspectives.
10. Explain why an imperfect market is more advantageous for businesses.
11. What are the components of the core product, actual product, and augmented product in a feature set?
12. List some of the major advantages of having a strong brand. How does a strong brand positively influence consumer purchasing?
13. How are product positioning and branding related? How are they different?
14. List the differences among databases, data warehouses, and data mining.
15. Name some of the drawbacks to the four data mining techniques used in Internet marketing.

16. Why have advertising networks become controversial? What, if anything, can be done to overcome any resistance to this technique?
17. Which of the four market entry strategies is most lucrative?
18. Compare and contrast four marketing strategies used in mass marketing, direct marketing, micromarketing, and one-to-one marketing.
19. What pricing strategy turned out to be deadly for many e-commerce ventures during the early days of e-commerce? Why?
20. Is price discrimination different from versioning? If so, how?
21. What are some of the reasons that freebies, such as free Internet service and giveaways, don't work to generate sales at a Web site?
22. Explain how versioning works. How is this different from dynamic pricing?
23. Why do companies that bundle products and services have an advantage over those that don't or can't offer this option?

PROJECTS

1. Go to www.strategicbusinessinsights.com/vals/presurvey.shtml. Take the survey to determine which lifestyle category you fit into. Then write a two-page paper describing how your lifestyle and values impact your use of the Web for e-commerce. How is your online consumer behavior affected by your lifestyle?

2. Find an example of a Web site you feel does a good job appealing to both goal-directed and experiential consumers. Explain your choice.

3. Choose a digital content product available on the Web and describe its feature set.

4. Visit Net-a-porter.com and create an Internet marketing plan for it that includes each of the following:
   - One-to-one marketing
   - Affiliate marketing
   - Viral marketing
   - Blog marketing
   - Social network marketing

   Describe how each plays a role in growing the business, and create an electronic slide presentation of your marketing plan.

CHAPTER 7

E-commerce Marketing Communications

LEARNING OBJECTIVES

After reading this chapter, you will be able to:

- Identify the major forms of online marketing communications.
- Understand the costs and benefits of online marketing communications.
- Discuss the ways in which a Web site can be used as a marketing communications tool.

V i d e o   A d s :

Shoot, Click, Buy

The age of online video ads is upon us, just in case you haven't noticed. Improvements in video production tools, higher bandwidth, and better streaming quality have fueled an online video surge. Video production is no longer the exclusive province of just a few major players in New York and Hollywood, but instead has expanded to a much larger group of potential creators, including users themselves. In addition, the ways online video can be viewed have also expanded, from desktop PCs and laptops to smartphones, tablet computers, netbooks, and Web-enabled television sets.

The online audience for videos is huge. In July 2012, 184 million U.S. Internet users watched online video content during the month, with each

viewer spending an average of 22.25 hours! Because this is where the eyeballs are, video is an obvious advertising medium. And just in time: Internet users have learned how to avoid traditional banner ads by instinctively moving their eyes to a different part of the screen. Click-throughs on banner ads are miniscule but videos are another story: next to search engine advertising and focused e-mail campaigns, videos have the highest click-through rate. In addition, nearly 100% of online spenders are video viewers, and they provide a highly desirable demographic with strong buying power. Research by comScore has also found that retail site viewers who view videos are 64% more likely to purchase. As a result, advertisers are jumping on the bandwagon. More than 75% of the top 500 online retailers post commercials, product demos, or other types of video on YouTube. Americans viewed nearly 9.6 billion video ads in July 2012, almost double the amount in July 2011. Video ads reached 52% of the total U.S population. Google Sites (YouTube) delivered the highest number of video ads, with 1.5 billion, followed by Hulu with 1.2 billion, Adap.tv with 1.1 billion, and the SpotXchange Video Ad marketplace with 1 billion.

Firms are using online video for marketing in a variety of ways. Many companies produce their own videos to promote their brands and sell products. User-generated video reviews are another effective marketing mechanism. EXPO is a consumer network that aggregates hundreds of thousands of video reviews created by over 160,000 members on its Web site, ExpoTV.com. EXPO also distributes the product review videos to retailers such as Amazon, to social media sites such as Facebook and YouTube, to manufacturer Web sites and mobile apps, and as paid media, including pre-roll, rich media campaigns, and newsletters via such firms as WebCollege, a leading provider of rich product informa-tion to a network of more than 1,000 retailers in North America and Europe. EXPO has created a trusted database of videos that can be used as advertising by accepting reviews for any nationally available product and publishing all videos received, regardless of posi-tive or negative opinion, as long as they meet quality standards. EXPO screens each video for relevance and quality, and rewards members who submit quality reviews by offering recognition, contests, loyalty points, and special consumer programs. By 2012, over 350,000 videos related to over 120,000 different products have been produced by EXPO members, and these videos have generated over 40 million views. A study by comScore and EXPO using a sample of 25 video product reviews across various categories, such as electronics and consumer packaged goods, found that the highest performing reviews contained many of the same effective elements seen in professionally produced televi-sion commercials, and that the rates of presence of many of these elements were greater than those seen in regular online display ads. EXPO's clients include consumer packaged goods brands such as Nabisco, Clairol, Febreze, and many others, as well as consumer electronics firms such as LG. For example, for LG, EXPO collected 720 video product reviews of LG products that were viewed over 280,000 times, totaling over 6,000 hours of engagement. On ExpoTV, there is an 11% click-to-commerce rate for the electronics category, which EXPO believes is driven by genuine and credible video reviews posted by peers that provide deeper knowledge and greater purchasing confidence to consumers.

Many large firms are moving into the online video advertising marketplace with sophisticated campaigns and big budgets. For instance, Rite Aid was searching for ways to boost sales in a recessionary period. One idea was to use its Web site to drive sales at its 4,700 retail stores. In 2010, Rite Aid introduced its Video Values program. Online visitors who watch videos about Rite Aid products receive a coupon that can be redeemed at the store. If you watch 20 videos, you receive a $5 bonus coupon in addition to product coupons. Currently, Rite Aid is streaming 500,000 videos a month, which are generating a 20% coupon redemption rate. The coupons are personalized and participants have to register. Rite Aid generates extensive demographic data on its most engaged custom-ers who can later be contacted in e-mail campaigns. In turn, bargain hunting sites and blogs add a social component to the effort by driving bargain hunters to Rite Aid's site. Almost 80% of the companies in the Fortune Global 100 have YouTube channels where they control the video content and ad environment, up from 57% in 2011. Allstate has an entire YouTube channel devoted to explaining storm risks to its potential customers and building its brand name.

Smaller firms are also using video. Online fashion retailer KarmaLoop offers KarmaLoopTV, which places all its videos under a single tab on its Web site, with the objective of creating a community focused on Verge Culture, a demographic of young people heavily involved in music, fashion, sports, and the arts. The videos feature exclusive interviews with fashion designers, brands, artists, and musicians. As of October 2012, KarmaLoopTV has more than 16,000 subscribers and over 10 million video views.

Orabrush is another small firm that has successfully used video ads on YouTube, in its case, to build its business from the ground up. Dr. Robert Wagstaff, a dentist who invented a breath-freshening tongue cleaner, was unsuccessful marketing it through traditional channels. Jeffrey Harmon, an MBA student at nearby Brigham Young University, who Wagstaff had hired on a part-time basis, convinced him to give video ads a try. He initially posted a YouTube video called "How to tell if you have bad breath" on Orabrush's landing page, and found that it tripled Orabrush's conversion rate. From there, they decided to create Orabrush's own YouTube video channel. Today the channel has more than 100 videos, 185,000 subscribers, and almost 50 million video views, and more importantly, has resulted in sales of over 2.1 million units. YouTube continues to account for 80% of Orabrush's marketing effort, although it now also has a Facebook page.

People care and get excited about videos far more than banner ads and e-mail. This makes videos an ideal advertising medium. Several changes in the underlying technology of video advertising are helping to increase the effectiveness of these ads. For instance, it is now possible to make video ads interactive so viewers can click on a product and add it to their shopping cart as the video is playing. It's sort of like "streaming e-commerce." These "interactive video ads" are appearing throughout the Web, especially at newspaper sites as an alternative to display ads that are increasingly ignored. Video ads can also be optimized, allowing retailers to change elements of the videos and measure the impact in near real time. The introduction of the iPad in 2010 made viewing videos much more pleasant and mobile. Interaction rates with videos displayed on iPads are six times higher than desktop PCs. The challenge is figuring out how to package advertising messages more directly with the videos, and how to piggyback advertising onto millions of user-generated videos and measure the impact on sales. Google, Yahoo, AOL, and literally hundreds of smaller firms are hard at work trying to attach the right ads to the right videos, a tricky process since computers cannot "understand" the content of videos (although they can "understand" the audio script—sort of). One start-up firm, YuMe.com, specializes in matching ads to popular online videos. One risk: your ad is attached to a perfectly inappropriate video. No one wants their product ads attached to stolen, pornographic, or inappropriate videos.

Another challenge is to figure out how to show the ad while the video plays without destroying the viewing experience. The final challenge is to avoid turning the viewer off, and causing a kind of video blindness on a mass scale, which is the fate of display ads today. One solution: YouTube now offers the TrueView ad format, which provides "skippable" ads that allow users to skip the pre-roll ad embedded in videos and which doesn't charge the advertiser for skipped ads. Skippable ads offer the prospect that the video ad marketplace will be self-cleansing with really unpopular, annoying, frequently skipped ads disappearing. And for those ads where "the creative" works, as they say in the ad industry, the rewards are potentially huge. For instance, Toyota's Swagger Wagon campaign, featuring a couple of unhip GenX parents rapping, went a long way toward advancing the Toyota brand in a demographic that they otherwise had difficulty reaching.

SOURCES: Corp.ExpoTV.com, accessed October 1, 2012; "Global Social Media Check-Up 2012," Burson-Marsteller, July 2012; "As Seen on YouTube! Orabrush Reinvents the Infomercial," by Joseph Flaherty, Wired.com, May 21, 2012; "comScore Releases July 2012 U.S. Online Video Rankings," comScore, August 17, 2012; "YouTube Sees 'TrueView' Boosting Best Ads, *eMarketer,* December 28, 2011; "Yahoo Study Shows Changes in Online Video Audience," Zacks.com, June 29, 2011; "The Video Viewing Audience," eMarketer (Lisa Phillips), February 2011; "Persuasive Potential of Consumer Produced Content," comScore, December 2010; "YouTube to Introduce 'Skippable' Ads," *Wall Street Journal*, June 29, 2010; "Video E-Commerce: Innovative Models Drive Sales," by Jeffrey Grant, eMarketer, May, 2010; "How EXPO Helped LG Learn More about Their Customers," EXPO, February 17, 2010; "Video Ad Start-Up YuMe Raises $25 Million," by Brad Stone, *New York Times*, February 17, 2010.

The opening case provides an interesting glimpse into how the increasing broadband video capacity of homes and businesses, coupled with new Internet technologies and widespread distribution of digital video cameras, is being used to influence consumer choice and build brand awareness. It also illustrates some of the challenges that marketers should be aware of when using these new forms of advertising. The emergence of a powerful digital Internet platform of smartphones and tablet computers, which users rarely turn off, has multiplied opportunities for advertising.

In the last few years, online advertising has been on a tear. While the recession in 2008 and 2009 caused a decline in online advertising, growth resumed in 2010. In 2011, online ad spending increased by more than 20%, and is expected to continue to grow by more than 15% in 2012. In contrast, ad spending in traditional media is relatively flat. In the meantime, the advertising industry as a whole—both offline and online—is going through a period of tumultuous change. The Internet and online advertising have disrupted the traditional advertising business, which was dominated by television and print media. Advertising budgets are following customer eyeballs and moving onto the Web and mobile platform, while expenditures for print and television are static or declining. **Table 7.1** summarizes the significant changes in the advertising industry for 2012–2013.

In 2011, advertisers delivered 4.8 trillion display ad impressions of all kinds, increasingly targeted at individuals based on their personal online behavior (comScore, 2012a). Aggressive forms of "push" advertising, such as animated banners and pop-ups that greet you on entering and leaving Web sites, have exploded, along with unsolicited e-mail or "spam," which now consumes about 75%–80% of all e-mail traffic on the Internet. Paid search advertising (also called "pull" advertising)—where consumers search for and find information and advertisers pay for text ads, such as that offered by Google, Microsoft, Yahoo, and many others—still accounts for the largest share of digital ad spending, although it is no longer considered a high-growth ad marketplace. Instead, the high-growth action has shifted to social networks and the mobile platform. Video advertising is still a small part of the overall Internet ad pie, but with the advent of larger, high-resolution mobile screens, such as those available on the iPad and tablet computers, it is one of the fastest growing forms of advertising, growing by almost 50% in 2012. Online advertising has also become less costly as the supply of Web pages to show ads has mushroomed.

In Chapter 6, we described brands as a set of expectations that consumers have about products offered for sale. We discussed some of the marketing activities that companies engage in to create those expectations. In this chapter, we focus on understanding **online marketing communications**—all the major methods that online firms use to communicate to the consumer, create strong brand expectations, and drive sales. What are the best methods for attracting people to a Web site and converting them into customers? What are the new opportunities for social, mobile, and local advertising? How do you measure the effectiveness of social advertising? We also examine the Web site as a marketing communications tool. How does the design of a Web site affect sales? How can you optimize a Web site for search engines?

online marketing communications

methods used by online firms to communicate to the consumer and create strong brand expectations

TABLE 7.1	WHAT'S NEW IN ONLINE ADVERTISING 2012–2013
TREND	**IMPACT**
Online advertising grows as a share of the total advertising budget, at the expense of traditional media.	Online advertising spending increases by more than 15% to $37.3 billion, and now constitutes about 22% of all advertising spending, while advertising in traditional media is relatively flat.
Social advertising expands.	Social media ad spending grows by more than 25% to $3.1 billion. Facebook, Twitter, and LinkedIn dominate the social ad platform.
Mobile and local advertising expands.	Mobile ad spending grows by 80% to $2.6 billion. Local advertising accounts for about 50% of this amount. Apple and Google dominate the mobile platform.
Video advertising continues to be one of the fastest growing ad formats.	Spending on video advertising grows by almost 50% to $2.9 billion.
Search engine advertising continues to be the dominant form of online advertising, but rate of growth is slowing somewhat compared to other formats.	Search engine advertising spending increases to more than $17.5 billion, over twice the size of the display banner ad format ($8.7 billion).
Display ad marketing continues strong growth as new ad platforms appear on social sites and mobile platforms.	Display advertising spending grows by 20% to $13.4 billion, with more than 5 trillion display ads shown.
New ad formats emerge.	The simple banner display ad, in all its forms, gives way to an explosion in rich media, video, app ads, and game ads.
Targeted advertising based on behavioral tracking expands rapidly.	Behavioral tracking is used by more than 75% of North American advertisers in display ads. The ideal of showing ads at the right time, to the right person, comes closer to realization.
Privacy disputes grow.	The online advertising industry is challenged by growing public and congressional resistance to behavioral targeting.
Apple and Google compete for dominance in the mobile ad market.	Both Apple and Google purchase firms with strong mobile advertising platforms.
Metrics become more challenging.	Social network and mobile advertising require new metrics for measuring impact.

7.1 MARKETING COMMUNICATIONS

Marketing communications have a dual purpose: branding and sales. One purpose of marketing communications is to develop and strengthen a firm's brands by informing consumers about the differentiating features of the firm's products and services. In addition, marketing communications are used to promote sales directly by encouraging the consumer to buy products (the sooner, the better). The distinction between the branding and sales purposes of marketing communications is subtle but important

promotional sales communications

suggest the consumer "buy now" and make offers to encourage immediate purchase

branding communications

focus on extolling the differentiable benefits of consuming the product or service

online advertising

a paid message on a Web site, online service, or other interactive medium

because branding communications differ from promotional communications. **Promotional sales communications** almost always suggest that the consumer "buy now," and they make offers to encourage immediate purchase. **Branding communications** rarely encourage consumers to buy now, but instead emphasize the differentiable benefits of consuming the product or service.

There are many different forms of online marketing communications, including online advertising, e-mail marketing, and public relations. Even the Web site itself can be viewed as a marketing communications tool.

ONLINE ADVERTISING

Advertising is the most common and familiar marketing communications tool. Companies will spend an estimated $166 billion on advertising in 2012, and an estimated $37.3 billion of that amount on **online advertising**, which includes display (banners, video, and rich media), search, mobile messaging, sponsorships, classifieds, lead generation, and e-mail, on desktop, laptop, and tablet computers, as well as mobile phones (see **Figure 7.1**) (eMarketer, Inc., 2012a).

In the last five years, advertisers have aggressively increased online spending and cut outlays on traditional channels such as newspapers and magazines (both down over 30% in the last few years) while outdoor, television, and radio advertising

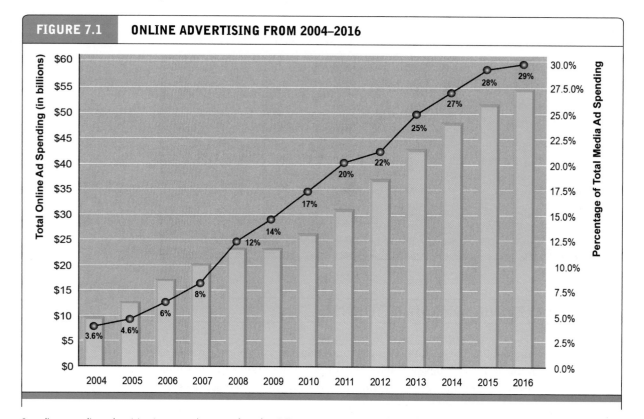

| FIGURE 7.1 | ONLINE ADVERTISING FROM 2004–2016 |

Spending on online advertising is expected to grow from $37 billion in 2012 to around $55 billion by 2016, and comprise an increasing percentage of total media ad spending.

SOURCES: Based on data from eMarketer, Inc., 2012a, 2012b.

have shown modest growth. Over the next five years, online advertising is expected to continue to be the fastest growing form of advertising, and by 2016, it is expected to be the second largest ad channel with a 29% share.

Spending on online advertising among different industries is somewhat skewed. Retail accounts for the highest percentage (22%), followed by financial services (13%), telecommunications (12%), automotive (11%), computers (8%), leisure travel (8%), consumer packaged goods (6%), media (5%), and entertainment (4%) (Interactive Advertising Bureau/PricewaterhouseCoopers, 2012). Online advertising has both advantages and disadvantages when compared to advertising in traditional media, such as television, radio, and print (magazines and newspapers). One big advantage for online advertising is that the Internet is where the audience is moving, especially the very desirable 18–34 age group, as well as the ballooning baby boomers who are over 65 years of age. A second big advantage for online advertising is the ability to target ads to individuals and small groups and to track performance of advertisements in almost real time. **Ad targeting**, the sending of market messages to specific subgroups in the population in an effort to increase the likelihood of a purchase, is as old as advertising itself, but prior to the Internet, it could only be done with much less precision, certainly not down to the level of individuals. Ad targeting is also the foundation of price discrimination: the ability to charge different types of consumers different prices for the same product or service. With online advertising, it's theoretically possible to charge every customer a different price. The six major online segmentation and targeting methods (behaviorial, demographic, pyschographic, technical, contextual, and search) were described in Table 6.9 in Chapter 6. We further discuss ad targeting later in this section.

ad targeting
the sending of market messages to specific subgroups in the population

Theoretically, online advertising can personalize every ad message to precisely fit the needs, interests, and values of each consumer. In practice, as we all know from spam and constant exposure to pop-up ads that are of little interest, the reality is very different. Online advertisements also provide greater opportunities for interactivity—two-way communication between advertisers and potential customers. The primary disadvantages of online advertising are concerns about its cost versus its benefits, how to adequately measure its results, and the supply of good venues to display ads. For instance, the owners of Web sites who sell advertising space ("publishers") do not have agreed-upon standards or routine audits to verify their claimed numbers as do traditional media outlets. We examine the costs and benefits of online advertising as well as research on its effectiveness in Section 7.2.

There are a number of different forms of digital advertisements:

- Display ads (banners and pop-ups)
- Rich media ads
- Video ads
- Search engine advertising
- Mobile and local advertising
- Social network advertising: social networks, blogs, and games
- Sponsorships
- Referrals (affiliate relationship marketing)
- E-mail marketing

TABLE 7.2	ONLINE ADVERTISING SPENDING FOR SELECTED FORMATS (IN BILLIONS)		
FORMAT	2012	2016	AVERAGE GROWTH RATE
Search	$17.6	$24.4	10%
Banner ads	$8.7	$11.3	8.4%
Video	$2.9	$8.0	32.6%
Classifieds	$2.6	$2.9	2.7%
Rich media	$1.8	$3.0	12.9%
Lead generation	$1.7	$2.2	7.8%
Sponsorships	$1.6	$2.9	21%
E-mail	$0.22	$0.24	2.7%
Total	$37.3	$55.3	11.6%

SOURCES: Based on data from eMarketer, Inc., 2012a.

Table 7.2 provides some comparative data on the amount of spending for certain advertising formats. The online advertising format that currently produces the highest revenue is paid search, followed by display ads, but the fastest growing online ad format is video ads. We discuss the various online ad formats in more depth next.

Display Ads: Banners and Pop-Ups

banner ad

displays a promotional message in a rectangular box at the top or bottom of a computer screen

Display ads were the first Internet advertisements. A **banner ad** displays a promotional message in a rectangular box at the top or bottom of a computer screen. A banner ad is similar to a traditional ad in a printed publication but has some added advantages. If clicked on, it can bring a potential customer directly to the advertiser's Web site. It also is much more dynamic than a printed ad: it can present multiple images or otherwise change its appearance. Even more important, the Web site where the ad appears can observe the click and the user's behavior on the site. The most distinguishing feature of online advertising when compared to other forms is this ability to identify and track the user.

Banner ads often feature Flash video and animations or animated GIFs, which display different images in relatively quick succession, creating an animated effect. The Interactive Advertising Bureau (IAB), an industry organization, has established voluntary industry guidelines for display ads. Publishers are not required to use these guidelines, but many do. One objective of IAB is to give the consumer a consistent experience across all Web sites. The various types of ads (including the rich media/ video ads discussed in the next section) are designed to help advertisers break through the "noise" and clutter created by the high number of display ad impressions that a typical user is exposed to within a given day. Advertising networks such as Double-

| FIGURE 7.2 | TYPES OF DISPLAY ADS |

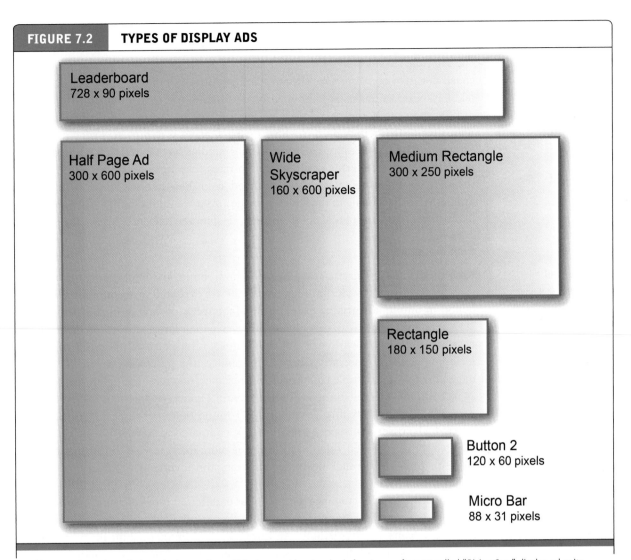

In addition to the various display ads shown above, IAB also provides standards for six new formats called "Rising Star" display ad units.
SOURCE: Based on data from Interactive Advertising Bureau, 2011.

Click serve more than 30 billion impressions a day (Google, 2010). **Figure 7.2** shows examples of the seven core standard ad units, as specified by the IAB. The top three ad formats—the medium rectangle, the leaderboard, and the wide skyscraper, account for nearly 80% of all display ad impressions served (Google, 2012). Eye-tracking research has found that for both desktop and tablet computers, leaderboard ads are the most effective in grabbing a user's attention and holding it (Tobii/Mediative, 2012).

Pop-up ads are display ads that are appear "on top of" the Web page that a user is visiting without the user calling for them. IAB guidelines state that each user should be exposed to no more than one pop-up ad for each visit to an online site. Pop-under

pop-up ad
display ad that appears on top of the user's browser window without the user calling for it

ads, which open underneath the user's active browser window and do not appear until after the user has closed it, are no longer supported by the IAB.

Multiple surveys have found that pop-up ads that appear over a user's Web page cause negative consumer sentiment. Online consumers rate pop-ups right next to telemarketing as the most annoying form of marketing communication. A number of ISPs and search engine/portal sites, such as Yahoo, Google, AOL, and Earthlink, now offer consumers pop-up blocking toolbars, as do Web browsers such as Mozilla Firefox and Internet Explorer. Unfortunately, studies have found that pop-up ads are twice as effective in terms of click-through rates than normal banner ads (although this may occur because people get confused about how to close the ads and end up unintentionally clicking to the advertised site). As a result, the number of pop-ups are likely to decline but not disappear entirely, despite the backlash.

Rich Media Ads

rich media ad

ad employing animation, sound, and interactivity, using Flash, HTML5 Java, and JavaScript

Rich media ads are ads that employ animation, sound, and interactivity, using Flash, HTML5, Java, and JavaScript. Rich media ads are expected to account for about $1.8 billion in online advertising expenditures (about 5% of total online advertising) in 2012. Rich media ads (with or without video) have their largest impact on brand awareness and online ad awareness. But they impact all aspects of the purchase funnel including message association, brand favorability, and purchase intent. They are far more effective than simple banner ads. For instance, one research report that analyzed 24,000 different rich media ads with more than 12 billion impressions served in North America between July and December 2011 found that exposure to rich media ads boosted advertiser site visits by nearly 300% compared to standard banner ads. Rich media ads that included video were six times more likely to visit the advertiser's Web site, either by directly clicking on the ad, typing the advertiser's URL, or by searching (MediaMind, 2012a).

interstitial ad

a way of placing a full-page message between the current and destination pages of a user

The IAB provides guidance for a number of different types of rich media ads, such as those that contain in-banner video, those that are expandable/retractable, pop-ups, floating versions, and interstitials. An **interstitial ad** (interstitial means "in between") is a way of placing a full-page message between the current and destination pages of a user. Interstitials are usually inserted within a single Web site, and displayed as the user moves from one page to the next. The interstitial is typically contained in its own browser window and moves automatically to the page the user requested after allowing enough time for the ad to be read. Interstitials can also be deployed over an advertising network and appear as users move among Web sites.

Since the Web is such a busy place, people have to find ways to cope with overstimulation. One means of coping is known as *sensory input filtering*. This means that people learn to filter out the vast majority of the messages coming at them. Internet users quickly learn at some level to recognize banner ads or anything that looks like a banner ad and to filter out most of the ads that are not exceptionally relevant. Interstitial messages, like TV commercials, attempt to make viewers a captive of the message. Typical interstitials last 10 seconds or less and force the user to look at the ad for that time period. IAB standards for pre-roll ads also limit their length. To avoid boring users, ads typically use animated graphics and music to entertain and inform them. A good interstitial will also have a "skip through" or "stop" option for users who have no interest in the message.

The IAB also provides mobile rich media ad interface definitions (MRAID) in an effort to provide a set of standards designed to work with HTML5 and JavaScript that developers can use to create rich media ads to work with apps running on different mobile devices. The hope is make it easier to display ads across a wide variety of devices without having to rewrite code (Interactive Advertising Bureau, 2012).

Video Ads

Video ads are TV-like advertisements that appear as in-page video commercials or before, during, or after a variety of content. **Table 7.3** describes some of the IAB standards for video ads.

Video ads are one of the fastest growing forms of online advertisement, accounting for about $2.9 billion in online advertising spending, which is expected to almost triple to $8.0 billion by 2016. However, from a total spending standpoint, online video ads are still very small when compared to the amount spent on search engine advertising, and of course, are dwarfed by the amount spent on television advertising.

The explosion of online video content across major news and entertainment sites, Web portals, and humor and user-generated sites has created huge opportunities for brand marketers to better reach their target audiences. As noted in the opening case, about 184 million U.S. Internet users watched online video content in July 2012, and 9.6 billion video ads. The rapid growth in video ads is due to the fact that video ads are far more effective than other display ad formats. For instance, according to research analyzing a variety of ad formats, in-stream video ads had click-through rates 12 times that of rich media and 27 times that of standard banner ads (MediaMind, 2012b).

Exactly how to best take advantage of this opportunity is still somewhat of a puzzle. Internet users are apparently willing to tolerate advertising in order to watch online as long as the ads are not too long and don't interfere too much with the viewing experience. There are many formats for displaying ads with videos. Currently, the

video ad
TV-like advertisement that appears as an in-page video commercial or before, during, or after content

TABLE 7.3	TYPES OF VIDEO ADS		
FORMAT	DESCRIPTION	WHEN USED	USED WITH
Linear video ad	Pre-roll; takeover; ad takes over video for a certain period of time	Before, between, after video	Text, banners, rich media video player skins
Non-linear video ad	Overlay; ad runs at same time as video content and does not take over full screen	During, over, or within video	
In-banner video ad	Rich media; ad is triggered within banner, may expand outside banner	Within Web page, generally surrounded by content	None
In-text video ad	Rich media; ad is delivered when user mouses over relevant text	Within Web page, identified as a highlighted word within relevant content	None

most widely used format is the "pre-roll" (followed by the mid-roll and the post-roll) where users are forced to watch a video ad either before, in the middle of, or at the end of the video they originally clicked on.

There are many specialized video advertising networks such as SAY Media, Advertising.com, and others who run video advertising campaigns for national advertisers and place these videos on their respective networks of Web sites. Firms can also establish their own video and television sites to promote their products. Retail sites are among the largest users of advertising videos. In 2011, Zappos, the largest online shoe retailer, created a video for every one of its products, adding 100,000 videos to its Web sites.

Regardless of the type of advertising, most large advertisers work through intermediaries such as advertising networks (e.g., Google's DoubleClick), or advertising agencies that have an ad placement and creative staff. Other options include swapping ad space with other sites and dealing directly with the publisher (the Web site that will post the advertisement).

Search Engine Advertising: Paid Search Engine Inclusion and Placement

Search engine advertising is the largest type of online advertising, and until recently, the fastest growing (see **Figure 7.3**). More than any other form of online advertising, search engine advertising has altered the entire marketing communications industry. Spending on search engine advertising has grown from 1% of total online advertising spending in 2000 to 46.5% in 2012, although the rate of growth is slowing somewhat (eMarketer, Inc., 2012a). On an average day in the United States, around 114 million American adults (around 59% of the adult online population) will use a search engine (Pew Internet & American Life Project, 2012). Collectively, they generate around 17 billion searches a month (comScore, 2012b). Briefly, this is where the eyeballs are (at least for a few moments) and this is where advertising can be very effective by responding with ads that match the interests and intentions of the user. The click-through rate for search engine advertising is generally 1%–5% and has been fairly steady over the years.

Today, there are hundreds of search engines on the Internet, with about 25 "major" search sites that generate most of the search traffic. Search engine advertising is highly concentrated. The top three search engine providers (Google, Microsoft/Bing, and Yahoo) supply more than 95% of all online searches (see Figure 3.20).

organic search

inclusion and ranking of sites depends on a more or less unbiased application of a set of rules imposed by the search engine

Types of Search Engine Advertising There are at least three different types of search engine advertising: keyword paid inclusion (so-called "sponsored links"), advertising keywords (such as Google's AdWords), and search engine context ads (such as Google's AdSense). Search engine sites originally performed unbiased searches of the Web's huge collection of Web pages and derived most of their revenue from banner advertisements. This form of search engine results is often called **organic search** because the inclusion and ranking of Web sites depends on a more or less "unbiased" application of a set of rules (an algorithm) imposed by the search engine. Since 1998, search engine sites slowly transformed themselves into digital yellow pages, where firms pay

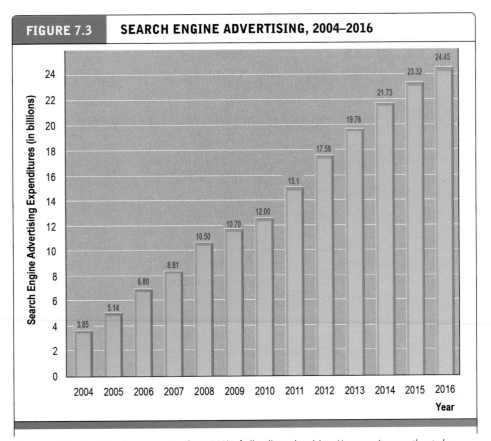

| FIGURE 7.3 | SEARCH ENGINE ADVERTISING, 2004–2016 |

Search engine advertising has grown to about 50% of all online advertising. However, its growth rate has slowed somewhat.

SOURCES: Based on data from eMarketer, Inc., 2012a.

for inclusion in the search engine index, pay for keywords to show up in search results, or pay for keywords to show up in other vendors ads.

Most search engines offer **paid inclusion** (also called sponsored link) programs which, for a fee, guarantee a Web site's inclusion in its list of search results, more frequent visits by its Web crawler, and suggestions for improving the results of organic searching. Search engines claim that these payments—costing some merchants hundreds of thousands a year—do not influence the organic ranking of a Web site in search results, just inclusion in the results. However, it is the case that page inclusion ads get more hits, and the rank of the page appreciates, causing the organic search algorithm to rank it higher in the organic results.

Google claims it does not permit firms to pay for their rank in the organic results, although it does allocate two to three sponsored links at the very top of their pages, albeit labeling them as "Sponsored Links." Merchants who refuse to pay for inclusion or for keywords typically fall far down on the list of results, and off the first page of results, which is akin to commercial death.

paid inclusion

for a fee, guarantees a Web site's inclusion in its list of sites, more frequent visits by its Web crawler, and suggestions for improving the results of organic searching

Research demonstrates the significance of rank in both organic and paid placements, and equally important, the greater power that users attach to organic search results (see **Figure 7.4**). Researchers used an eye-tracking tool to gauge Web users' behavior at search engines. They discovered an "F" shaped pattern (sometimes referred to as a "golden triangle") in which viewers scan search result pages from top to bottom, with greater attention to the left side of the page looking for clues. They spend less time on the right side of the page looking at paid text advertisements, and usually only at the top three advertisements. Users always viewed the first three organic listings, but were much less likely to view the sponsored listings. These results have been replicated several times using eye heat maps (Usercentric, 2011; Google, 2009; Shrestha and Lenz, 2007; Nielsen, 2006).

The two other types of search engine advertising rely on selling keywords in online auctions.

keyword advertising

merchants purchase keywords through a bidding process at search sites, and whenever a consumer searches for that word, their advertisement shows up somewhere on the page

In **keyword advertising**, merchants purchase keywords through a bidding process at search sites, and whenever a consumer searches for that word, their advertisement shows up somewhere on the page, usually as a small text-based advertisement on the right, but also as a listing on the very top of the page. The more merchants pay, the higher the rank and greater the visibility of their ads on the page. Generally, the search engines do not exercise editorial judgment about quality or content of the ads although they do monitor the use of language. In addition, some search engines rank the ads in terms of their popularity rather than merely the money paid by the advertiser so that the rank of the ad depends both on the amount paid and the number of clicks per

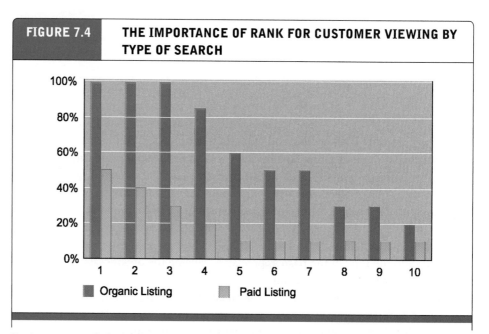

| FIGURE 7.4 | THE IMPORTANCE OF RANK FOR CUSTOMER VIEWING BY TYPE OF SEARCH |

Nearly everyone reads the top three-ranked results in organic search results, but readership drops off rather dramatically for the 4th through 10th-ranked results. Sponsored links are heavily discounted by readers—only 50% read the top-ranked sponsored results listed, and readership drops off sharply after that.
SOURCE: Based on data from Hotchkiss, et al., 2007.

unit time. Google's keyword advertising program is called AdWords, Yahoo's is called Sponsored Search, and Microsoft's is called adCenter.

Network keyword advertising (**context advertising**), introduced by Google as its AdSense product in 2002, differs from ordinary keyword advertising described previously. Publishers (Web sites that want to show ads) join these networks and allow the search engine to place "relevant" ads on their sites. The ads are paid for by advertisers who want their messages to appear across the Web. Google-like text messages are the most common. The revenue from the resulting clicks is split between the search engine and the site publisher, although the publisher gets much more than half in some cases. The publisher has no direct control over what ads are shown on its site. The advertiser has no control over where its ads appear either. But the search engines use a variety of tools (keyword analysis and propinquity of keywords) to ensure only "relevant" and "appropriate" ads appear. For this reason, network keyword advertising is often called "context marketing" because an effort is made to understand the context where the ad will be shown. Google calls this "AdSense," knowing where to place ads based on the surrounding context. Yahoo's program is called Content Match. Together, keyword and network keyword context advertising account for most of the growth in spending for search engine advertising. About half of Google's revenue comes from AdWords and the rest comes from AdSense.

In this manner, search engines have greatly extended their keyword advertising beyond their own sites (where users do not linger) to tens of thousands of other sites on the Web. Unfortunately, these programs have also led to the creation of "junk AdSense" sites composed of re-hashed links from the Web, and an entire industry of illegitimate poachers who nevertheless are paid when their Web site visitors click an AdSense link.

Keywords for both types of keyword advertising range in price from a few pennies per click to $100 or above for high-priced popular items. According to a recent survey, the highest cost category was insurance (for example "auto insurance price quotes") with a top cost of $55 per click, followed by loans, mortgages, and attorneys (all in the $44–$47 range) (Wordstream, 2011). How much would you pay (or should you pay) to place your company's listing in front of the consumer just as the consumer is looking for products provided by your company? This depends, of course, on how much customers are likely to spend at your site. And it depends on how much your competitors are willing to pay for the same keyword. In an auction environment, it is easy to overpay.

Search engine advertising is nearly an ideal targeted marketing technique: at precisely the moment that a consumer is looking for a product, an advertisement for that product is presented. While originally this was the idea behind advertising networks such as DoubleClick and Real Media 24/7, their database techniques could not deliver the advertisement with as much accuracy or speed at the moment of interest. Unlike traditional online and offline targeted marketing approaches, which are based on searching large databases for customer profiles and information, search engine advertising is based on the much more efficient idea of responding to keyword searches at that moment (although prior searches from the IP address, or keywords gleaned from other sources such as Google's Gmail, can also influence the results). No

network keyword advertising (context advertising)
publishers accept ads placed by Google on their Web sites, and receive a fee for any click-throughs from those ads

databases on clickstream behavior or background demographics are generally used. The most important fact for search engine marketers is that the customer is looking for a product like the one sold by the merchant.

In general, search engines have been very helpful to businesses that cannot afford extensive marketing campaigns. Because shoppers are looking for a specific product or service when they use search engines, they are what marketers call "hot prospects"— people who are looking for information and often intending to buy. Moreover, search engines charge only for a click-through to a site. Merchants do not have to pay for ads that don't work, only for ads that receive a click. In rare cases, a business can land on the first search page through organic search without paying for the privilege. In most cases this is unlikely to happen, and far more commonly, a firm has to pay to appear on the first page.

Consumers benefit from search engine advertising because ads for merchants appear only when consumers are looking for a specific product. There are no pop-ups, Flash animations, videos, interstitials, e-mails, or other irrelevant communications to deal with. Thus, search engine advertising saves consumers cognitive energy and reduces search costs (including the cost of cars or trains needed to do physical searches for products). In a recent study, the global value of search to both merchants and consumers was estimated to be more than $800 billion, with about 65% of the benefit going to consumers in the form of lower search costs and lower prices (McKinsey, 2011).

social search

effort to provide fewer, more relevant, and trustworthy results based on the social graph

Social Search **Social search** is an attempt to use your social contacts (and your entire social graph) to provide search results. In contrast to the top search engines that use a mathematical algorithm to find pages that satisfy your query, a social search Web site reviews your friends' recommendations (and their friends), past Web visits, and use of Like buttons. One problem with Google and mechanical search engines is that they are so thorough: enter a search for "smartphone" and in .28 seconds you will receive 504 million results, some of them providing helpful information and others that are suspect. Social search is an effort to provide fewer, more relevant, and trustworthy results based on the social graph. For instance, Google has developed Google +1 as a social layer on top of its existing search engine. Users can place a +1 next to Web sites they found helpful, and their friends will be automatically notified. Subsequent searches by their friends would list the +1 sites recommended by friends higher up on the page. Facebook's Like button is a similar social search tool. So far, neither Facebook nor Google has fully implemented a social search engine (Efrati, 2011). One problem with social search is that your close friends may not be interested in or have knowledge of topics that you want to explore.

Search Engine Issues While search engines have provided significant benefits to merchants and customers, they also present risks and costs. For instance, search engines have the power to crush a small business by placing its ads on the back pages of search results. Merchants are at the mercy of search engines for access to the online marketplace, and this access is dominated by a single firm, Google. How Google decides to rank one company over another in search results is not known. No one really knows how to improve in its rankings (although there are hundreds of firms who claim otherwise). Google editors intervene in unknown ways to punish certain Web sites and reward others. Using paid sponsored listings, as opposed to relying on organic search results, eliminates some of this uncertainty but not all.

Other practices that degrade the results and usefulness of search engines include:

- **Link farms** are groups of Web sites that link to one another, thereby boosting their ranking in search engines that use a PageRank algorithm to judge the "usefulness" of a site. For instance, in the 2010 holiday season, JCPenney was found to be the highest ranked merchant for a large number of clothing products. On examination, it was discovered that this resulted from Penney's hiring a search engine optimization company to create thousands of Web sites that linked to JCPenney's Web site. As a result, JCPenney's Web site became the most popular (most linked-to) Web site for products like dresses, shirts, and pants. No matter what popular clothing item people searched for, JCPenney came out on top. Experts believe this was the largest search engine fraud in history. There is no federal law against link farming, and JCPenney denied knowledge of the firm it hired to optimize its search results (Siegel, 2011). In April 2012, Google released Google Penguin, an update to its search results algorithm aimed at sites that participate in link schemes and other search engine optimization techniques that violate Google's guidelines.

  link farms
  groups of Web sites that link to one another, thereby boosting their ranking in search engines

- **Content farms** are companies that generate large volumes of textual content for multiple Web sites designed to attract viewers and search engines. Content farms profit by attracting large numbers of readers to their sites and exposing them to ads. The content typically is not original but is artfully copied or summarized from legitimate content sites. For instance, a single article in the *New York Times* will generate thousands of articles at content sites and blogs that report on the article's content. Typically, content farm freelance writers are told to write articles on "trending" or "hot topics" on the Web. Demand Media is one of the largest content farms. It produces more than 1 million articles a month that are posted on a variety of sites. These sites are then picked up by search engines and ranked high because of their "popular" articles, and receive revenue from ads being placed on the pages. In 2011, Google updated its search results ranking algorithm with Google Panda, which introduced many new ranking features aimed at downgrading Web sites that provide poor user experiences. The update targeted content farms and scraper sites that previously had been able to gain top listings based on shallow, low-quality, or copied content. Since then, Google has released a number of further Panda updates.

  content farms
  companies that generate large volumes of textual content for multiple Web sites designed to attract viewers and search engines

- **Click fraud** occurs when a competitor clicks on search engine results and ads, forcing the advertiser to pay for the click even though the click is not legitimate. Competitors can hire offshore firms to perform fraudulent clicks or hire botnets to automate the process. Click fraud can quickly run up a large bill for merchants, and not result in any growth in sales. There is some debate about the incidence of click fraud, with estimates ranging from 2% to 20% (Chambers, 2012). Search engines have developed some protections for merchants and offer rebates when they identify click fraud, but these are not foolproof.

  click fraud
  occurs when a competitor clicks on search engine results and ads, forcing the advertiser to pay for the click even though the click is not legitimates

Mobile and Local Advertising

A number of factors are driving advertisers to the mobile platform of smartphones and tablets, including much more powerful devices, faster networks, wireless local networks, rich media and video ads, and growing demand for local advertising by small business and consumers. Most important, mobile is where the eyeballs are now and increasingly will be in the future: 122 million people access the Internet at least some of the time from mobile devices.

Refer to Table 6.10 (in Chapter 6) for a review of the four major mobile ad formats in 2012 and ad spending levels. Overall, spending on all forms of mobile advertising reached about $2.6 billion in 2012 and is expected to grow to about $12 billion by 2016.

In 2012, search engine advertising is the most popular mobile advertising format, accounting for almost 50% of all mobile ad spending, and not surprising given that search is the second most common smartphone application (after voice and text communication). Search engine ads can be further optimized for the mobile platform by showing ads based on the physical location of the user. Display ads are also a popular format, accounting for about 36% of mobile ad spending. Display ads can be served as a part of a mobile Web site or inside apps and games. Mobile messaging generally involves SMS text messaging to consumers offering coupons or flash marketing messages. Messaging is especially effective for local advertising because consumers can be sent messages and coupons as they pass by or visit locations. Video advertising currently accounts for the smallest percentage of mobile ad spending, but it is the fastest growing format. Ad networks such as Google's AdMob, Apple's iAd, and Millennial Media are the largest providers of mobile advertising

Local marketers are also increasingly moving online. Spending on U.S local online advertising in 2012 (about $24 billion) comprises 17% of all local ad spending, and that percentage is expected to increase to more than 25% by 2016. Local advertising is intimately connected with mobile advertising, as the mobile platform inherently enables location-based advertising. Currently, local advertising accounts for about 50% of mobile advertising, and this share is expected to increase to around 65% by 2016 (BIA/Kelsey, 2012). Local advertising is also directly connected to search as well. Findings from comScore indicate that around 75% of U.S. Internet users turn first to search engines such as Google, Bing, and Yahoo to search for local businesses. Consumers are increasingly expecting local business search listings to have add-ons like phone numbers, images, and coupons as standard elements, and surveys show that adding such elements can greatly benefit the business (eMarketer, 2011a). Many small businesses are also beginning to use location-based offerings such as Google Places and Yahoo Local to promote their businesses as well.

Social Advertising: Social Networks, Blogs and Games

In Chapter 6, we described how social networks are being used to build and strengthen brands, and to create a social e-commerce where transactions take place in the context of, and are enabled by, the linkages among people in a social graph. There we described social marketing as being composed of four elements: social sign-on, collaborative shopping, network notification ("Like" feature), and social search.

Social advertising is another aspect of social commerce, namely, using the social graph to communicate brand images and to directly promote sales of products and services. Social advertising differs from traditional print and other media advertising that uses a one-to-many model of communication. For example, in a traditional broadcast one-to-many model, Procter & Gamble's marketing department seeks to communicate to millions of mid-day television viewers. In contrast, social network advertising adopts a many-to-many model where the object is not to directly contact millions of viewers, but instead to rely on the viewers themselves to pass the message along (hopefully with positive remarks). For instance, research has found that social network users are more likely to talk about and recommend a company or product they follow on Facebook or Twitter (eMarketer, Inc., 2012c).

Disney has proven to be a master at leveraging the power of social media. Its main Facebook page is the third most popular corporate brand on Facebook with more than 38 million Likes and with more than half a million talking about it, and its separate pages for its theme parks, movies, and TV series boost those numbers even higher. Disney's Facebook pages are all highly interactive and encourage its fans to share with friends, gaining even more exposure. Disney also uses types of social media to advertise. For instance, when Disney released its *Toy Story 3* video trailer on YouTube, it quickly generated 13 million views. More than 1 million viewers shared it with friends, and another 800,000 clicked Like to share it with their friends on Facebook. An existing social network composed of many people and their friends distributed the Disney message to a great many other people. In another example, Adobe succeeded in increasing the number of Likes of its Photoshop Facebook page from 240,000 in 2010 to more than 4.4 million in 2012. After examining the customer conversations on Facebook, Adobe sought to enter the customer conversations in an authentic way by asking and answering questions, providing sneak previews of product enhancements, and adding videos, tips, and tutorials. It essentially relied on its customers to lead the conversation and interact with the brand. This is a very different kind of marketing communication than, say, broadcast television. Measuring its impact on sales is also very difficult.

Social Network Advertising In 2012, there are an estimated 1 billion Facebook members, 140 million active Twitter users, and more than 175 million who have joined LinkedIn worldwide. In the United States, in August 2012, Facebook had around 152 million unique visitors. Around two-thirds of the U.S. Internet population visits social sites. It's little wonder that marketers and advertisers are joyous at the prospect of connecting with this large audience. Although in the past, major brands were reluctant to risk advertising on sites whose content they cannot control, they are beginning to experiment with a number of new ad formats. In 2012, 72% of the U.S. Fortune 500 companies had a Twitter account, 66% had a Facebook account, 62% had a YouTube account, and 28% had a corporate blog (Barnes et al., 2012). Social network sites are, above all, advertising platforms in the business of aggregating large audiences and selling the advertising opportunity to other firms.

In 2012, U.S. companies are expected to spend around $3.1 billion on social advertising, about 8% of all digital advertising. Around $2 billion of this spending is directed

social advertising
using the social graph to communicate brand images and promote sales

to Facebook alone. more than 80% of companies in the United States use Facebook for marketing purposes in 2012. Social advertising spending has grown by about 30% compared to 2011, and by 2014 is expected to exceed 10% of all digital advertising, about $5 billion. Still, social advertising spending is still dwarfed by the amount spent on search engine advertising and display advertising (eMarketer Inc., 2012d, 2012e). In this sense, social network advertising has to be part of a broader mix of tactics used by firms.

Social networks offer advertisers all the formats found on portal and search sites including banner ads (the most common), short pre-roll and post-roll ads associated with videos, and sponsorship of content. Having a corporate Facebook page is in itself an advertising portal for brands just like a Web page. Many firms, such as Coca-Cola, have shut down product-specific Web pages and instead use Facebook pages.

A typical social network advertising campaign for Facebook will include the following elements:

- Establish a Facebook page.
- Use comment and feedback tools to develop fan comments.
- Develop a community of users.
- Encourage brand involvement through videos and rich media showing product in use by real customers.
- Use contests and competitions to deepen fan involvement intensity.
- Develop display ads for use on other Facebook pages.
- Develop display ads for use in response to social search queries.
- Liberally display the Like button so fans share the experience with their friends.
- Enable e-commerce by using Facebook Connect (social sign on) to direct fans to product sale Web sites.

Twitter is another social site that offers advertisers and marketers a chance to interact and engage with their customers in real time and in a fairly intimate, one-on-one manner. As you learned in Chapter 6, there are three kinds of Twitter ads: Promoted Tweets, Promoted Trends, and Promoted Accounts. Twitter has also recently jumped on the visual bandwagon and is allowing company's to customize their brand's Twitter profile page with a head photo, profile background, and pinned tweet.

Cirque du Soleil, an international circus troupe, is one company that has used Twitter advertising with good results. Cirque du Soleil uses Promoted Accounts and Promoted Tweets to grow its follower base and engage with them in real time to answer questions, get feedback, and announce promotions for coming shows. Bonobos, an online retailer of men's apparel, held a 24-hour sale exclusively on Twitter and realized a return on investment of more than 1,200%, also finding it 13 times more cost-effective than acquiring a new customer from other marketing channels.

There are several issues to be aware of when using social advertising. User comments can sometimes be negative and brand destruction can result. Corporate users carefully watch submissions to their social network sites. Social networks can be influential, but not under all circumstances. For instance, research has shown that social network influence may extend to closest friends but not to distant friends (influence is inversely related to size of the friendship group). The 100th most distant friend of yours could care less about what you buy or think. Measuring the results of social advertising is in its infancy and not well understood. It is possible that some of your "friends" would react negatively to whatever you purchased, while others would not care or are not interested (Iyengar, 2010). If Facebook Likes do not turn into sales, then you will have to re-evaluate your objectives on social sites.

Given the uncertain, even experimental, nature of social advertising, marketers are continuing to invest in search engine and display advertising. Over the next five years, with current trends, it is possible that social network sites will equal the audience share of major portals and search engines, challenging these "older" venues for dominance in advertising platforms.

Blog Advertising Blogs are high on the list of advertising tactics that marketing executives consider, given that 72 million people read blogs and 26 million write blogs. In 2011, spending on blog advertising was about $640 million, and estimated to rise to $775 million by 2015. Advertising dollars tend to be concentrated in the top 100 blogs, which have coherent themes that consistently attracts larger audiences. Because blog readers and creators tend to be more educated, have higher incomes, and be opinion leaders, they are ideal recipients of ads for many products and services that cater to this kind of an audience. Advertising networks that specialize in blogs provide some efficiency in placing ads, as do blog networks, which are collections of a small number of popular blogs, coordinated by a central management team, and which can deliver a larger audience to advertisers.

Game Advertising The online gaming marketplace continues to expand rapidly as users are able to play games on smartphones and tablets, as well as PCs and consoles. The story of game advertising in 2012 is social, local, and mobile: social games are ascendant, mobile devices are the high-growth platform, and location-based local advertising is starting to show real traction. The objective of game advertising is both branding and driving customers to purchase moments at restaurants and retail stores.

In 2012, 102 million people will play games on their mobile devices, another 40 million on consoles, and another 94 million will play online games with a PC. Of the online gamers, about 76 million will play social games, such as Zynga's FarmVille, CityVille, and Words With Friends. Gaming is growing at nearly 50%, driven largely by mobile app games and social site games. The concept of a game is changing as social apps like Foursquare, Facebook Places, and Gowalla take ordinary real-world events (visiting a restaurant) and turn them into a game-like experience. For example, with Foursquare, if you visit a place often enough, you can become Mayor, and receive reward points and discounts. Advertisers can also sponsor a location and offer rewards for visiting. Social gaming apps are the fastest growing games in terms of players. Where the audience goes, ads are quick to follow. In the United States, spending on social game advertising in 2012 is around $210 million, and is estimated to grow by 75% to $371 million in 2014 (eMarketer, Inc., 2012f; 2012g).

There are many kinds of in-game advertising opportunities:

- *In-game billboard display ads:* Honda's billboard ad for its CR-Z Car Town.
- *Branded virtual goods:* 7-Eleven's FarmVille virtual drink is YoVille Big Gulp.
- *Sponsored banners:* National Geographic overlaid its logo on the soccer-themed game *Bola*.
- *Branded games (advergames):* Companies create their own games on their Web site or Facebook pages to promote their brands, such as Travelocity's *Roam with the Gnome* game.

More than 800 million sponsored games were downloaded in 2011 to millions of users (NPD Group, 2011). Coca-Cola, Burger King, and Taco Bell, along with many other national brands, have used advergames. *Insight on Society: Marketing to Children of the Web in the Age of Social Networks* considers some of the social issues that marketing to children on the Web presents.

Obviously, marketers need to be cautious about where they place ads and maintain control over game content. Action and combat games have few advertisers or advergames. Social games with benign friendly characters are favorable to ad placements, as are location-based games.

Sponsorships

sponsorship

a paid effort to tie an advertiser's name to information, an event, or a venue in a way that reinforces its brand in a positive yet not overtly commercial manner

A **sponsorship** is a paid effort to tie an advertiser's name to particular information, an event, or a venue in a way that reinforces its brand in a positive yet not overtly commercial manner. Sponsorships typically are more about branding than immediate sales. A common form of sponsorship is targeted content (or advertorials), in which editorial content is combined with an ad message to make the message more valuable and attractive to its intended audience. For instance, WebMD.com, the leading medical information Web site in the United States, offers "sponsorship sites" on the WebMD Web site to companies such as Phillips to describe its home defibrillators, and Lilly to describe its pharmaceutical solutions for attention deficit disorders among children. In 2012, companies spent about $1.6 billion on sponsorship marketing, and this is expected to grow to about $1.9 billion in 2013 (eMarketer, 2012a). Social media sponsorships, in which marketers pay for mentions in social media, such as in blogs, tweets, or in online video, have also become a popular tactic.

Referrals (Affiliate Relationship Marketing)

affiliate relationships

permit a firm to put its logo or banner ad on another firm's Web site from which users of that site can click through to the affiliate's site

An **affiliate relationship** permits a firm (the originating Web site) to place its logo, banner ad, or text link on another firm's Web site (called the affiliate) from which users of that site can click through to the originating site. For instance, millions of personal Web sites have Amazon logos that, when clicked, will take the visitor to Amazon and generate revenue for the Web site. A recent Forrester Research survey found that spending on affiliate marketing will grow by double-digit percentages over the next five years, rising from about $2.5 billion in 2012 to $4.5 billion in 2016. Forrester also found affiliate marketing produces new customers, and that buyers who use affiliate channels spend more online than the average online shopper, making them valuable to advertisers. In addition, the study found that a company's presence

INSIGHT ON SOCIETY

MARKETING TO CHILDREN OF THE WEB IN THE AGE OF SOCIAL NETWORKS

Children grow up today in an Internet world where more than 75% of all American households are online. There are around 46 million kids under the age of 18 online, with tens of millions of them visiting Web sites such as Wrigley's Candystand, Post Cereal's Pebbles Play (Flintstones games), and Disney's Playdom. Kids spend more time on these sites than they do watching TV commercials. Industry self-regulation requires firms not to advertise to children younger than 12, but sites such as Kraft's NabiscoWorld.com include games that appeal to younger audiences, such as Race for the Stuf, where a player-controlled character can twist, lick, and dunk oversize Oreo cookies. A Federal Trade Commission (FTC) report concluded that U.S. food firms were spending $1.6 billion on advertising to children, about half of that to children under 12. Critics argue, and the FTC expresses concern, that most of this advertising is for foods that make children obese and pose a health threat.

Children as young as three or four years old can often recognize brands and status items before they can even read, and almost 75% of four-year-olds generally ask their parents for specific brands. These findings are cause for celebration for some marketers. In the United States, estimates are that children influence over $1 trillion in overall family spending. In order to capture a portion of this spending and position themselves for future purchases as the child ages, marketers are becoming increasingly interested in advertising aimed at children. In addition to investing in television advertising, marketers are also focusing on children who have migrated to the Web and mobile devices. Around 20% of all Internet users in the United States are children, totaling more than 46 million users under the age of 18, split fairly evenly between the 2–11 age group (22 million) and the 12–17 age group (24 million).

The Web provides marketers an entirely new arsenal to influence really young children. What's in the arsenal? Here are some of the most common child-advertiser tools: mobile phone marketing, behavioral profiling, digital "360 buzz" campaigns, commercialized online communities, viral videos, game advertising, and avatar advertising. Using online custom banner ads, product characters, games, virtual worlds, and surveys, marketers are both influencing behaviors and gathering valuable data about purchasing preferences and family members. Coupled with in-bedroom televisions, video games, cell phones, and other digital paraphernalia, a children's digital culture has been created with built-in avenues to the psyche of very young minds—minds that are so young they are unlikely to know when they are being marketed to and when they are given misleading or even harmful information.

And as if this wasn't enough—then came social network sites. Marketers have moved aggressively to use online social networks and viral marketing to get kids hooked on brands early in life. For instance, Red Bull does little traditional TV advertising in the 100 countries where it sells energy drinks. Instead, it has been using Web-based contests, games, and apps such as Urban Futbol, an Angry Birds-like game app based on the Red Bull Balcony Shot events, where Red Bull takes over a street and lets people kick soccer balls at balconies.

As another example, consider the Unilever product called AXE. AXE is a deodorant for young

(continued)

men. Unilever's sales pitch is simple: "Hey, dude, spray AXE deodorant all over your body, and you will become irresistible to beautiful young women." Armed with this powerful message to the world's teenagers, Unilever launched the product in the United States by posting online videos that supposedly showed the AXE effect: women chasing men who used AXE. The response was sensational: millions of people forwarded the videos to friends in a massive viral outpouring. Marketers also created an online game that allowed guys to indicate the kind of young woman they were interested in and get recommendations on which AXE fragrance to buy. You can bet that many of these postings and shared experiences were written by children. Using social networks, blogs, and YouTube, in a way much more powerful than earlier Web marketing to children, marketers are able to circumvent what few restrictions exist on marketing to children.

While such moves may be savvy marketing, are they ethical? Some people say no. Research conducted in 1996 by the Center for Media Education (CME) showed that young children cannot understand the potential effects of revealing their personal information; neither can they distinguish between substantive material on Web sites and the advertisements surrounding it. Experts argue that since children don't understand persuasive intent until they are eight or nine years old, it is unethical to advertise to them before they can distinguish between advertising and the real world. Others believe that fair advertising is an important and necessary part of the maturation process for future adults in today's society. But does that argument hold when children are gaining increased access to information about unhealthy activities, such as beer drinking through Web sites geared to a young adult audience? Although brewers admit they are targeting a younger market segment—twenty-somethings—they have set up warning screens and registration pages that require users to enter a birth date

proving they are of legal drinking age. Of course, there is no process to verify such data, making it easy for underage consumers to gain access to, and be influenced by, entertaining content at drinking-oriented Web sites.

In 1998, Congress passed the Children's Online Privacy Protection Act (COPPA) after the FTC discovered that 80% of Web sites were collecting personal information from children, but only 1% required their parents' permission. Under COPPA, companies must post a privacy policy on their Web sites, detailing exactly how they collect information from consumers, how they'll use it, and the degrees to which they'll protect consumer privacy. Companies are not permitted to use personal information collected from children under 13 years of age without the prior, verifiable consent of parents. But the problem is that the FTC and others have been unable to specify exactly what "verifiable consent" means. The FTC recognized this fact by issuing a ruling requiring a sliding scale of verifiable parental consent. If firms want to use the personal information of children for internal uses only, the FTC requires an e-mail from the parent plus one other form of verification (such as a credit card or phone number). A stricter standard is required of firms who want to sell personal information about children: these Web sites are required to use one of the following means of verification in addition to an e-mail: a print-and-send consent form, credit card transaction, a toll free number staffed by trained personnel, or an e-mail with a password or PIN.

Industry trade groups claim that voluntary compliance with COPPA has been good in general, and that most Web sites are careful to avoid gathering personal information on children as a part of their marketing effort. However, a 2011 study by the Center for Digital Democracy found that 54 Web sites popular with children, including Nick. com and Disney.go.com, were making extensive

(continued)

use of tracking technologies. In addition, some Web sites are directly aimed at very young children. Sites such as ClubPenguin, Webkinz (one of the most popular children's sites), and NeoPets provide online tools and play environments that enable young users to interact, adopt pets, play sponsored games, and reveal personal information. In the process of playing the games, children produce marketing information for product designers. While each of these Web sites' privacy policies claim strict adherence to the restrictions of COPPA, it is unclear how they ascertain who is over 13 and who is under 13, or if those under 13 have parental consent.

Since the law took effect, the FTC has obtained a number of settlements and fined a number of companies for violations of COPPA. In October 2012, the operator of fan sites for Justin Bieber, Selena Gomez, Rihanna, and others agreed to pay a $1 million penalty for collecting personal information from children such as names, e-mail addresses, street addresses, and cell phone numbers without their parents' permission. Previously, in May 2011, Disney's Playdom was fined $3 million, the largest penalty to date, for collecting and disclosing children's information without parental approval. According to the FTC, many of Playdom's games, particularly Pony Stars, allowed children under the age of 13 to register at the site, and required that they share their ages and e-mail addresses during registration. The site then allowed those children to publicly post their full names, e-mail addresses, instant messenger IDs, and location on personal profile pages and in online community forums.

In August 2011, the FTC announced its first-ever COPPA enforcement action involving mobile apps. W3 Innovations, doing business as Broken Thumbs Apps, was fined $50,000 for collecting personal information such as e-mail addresses from children in connection with numerous apps, such as Emily's Girl World and Emily's Dress

Up. Shortly thereafter, in response to the explosion in children's use of mobile devices, the proliferation of online social networks, and interactive gaming, the FTC announced long-awaited proposed revisions to its COPPA regulations. The revisions would expand the definition of personal information to include a child's location, along with any personal data collected through the use of cookies for the purposes of targeted advertising, and require that Web sites that collect a child's information ensure that they can protect it, hold on to it for only as long as is reasonably necessary, and thereafter delete the information. Parental consent would be able to be obtained via a scanned version of a signed consent form, or through video conferencing. The FTC also proposed regulations with respect to facial recognition technology. In September 2012, in response to comments on its proposed revisions, the FTC issued a second round of proposed modifications to COPPA. The new proposed regulations make clear that a company that uses the services of an ad network or software plug-in to collect personal information from children is covered by COPPA, as are the ad network and plug-in developer. They also seek to make clear that personal information includes persistent identifiers that can be used for behavioral advertising and tracking across Web sites, although they permit their use for some internal operations such as contextual advertising and anti-fraud measures. The new proposed regulations also provide that mixed-use Web sites (those that contain child-oriented content but also appeal to those who are older) may age-screen visitors in order to provide COPPA's protections only to those under 13. Final comments on the proposed rules were due by September 10, 2012. Not surprisingly, major corporations such as Apple, Facebook, Google, Microsoft, and Viacom had submitted comments arguing that the proposed changes are so unworkable that they will deter companies from providing sites and online

(continued)

services for children. Facebook particularly objects to the possibility that the use its social plug-in to embed a Like button on a Web site may subject Facebook to COPPA. It claims doing so would infringe a child's freedom of speech.

Some version of the new rules are expected to be finalized by the end of the year. They do not require congressional approval. As the FTC chairman, Jon Leibowitz, noted, children may be "tech savvy, but judgment-poor." Privacy groups applaud the effort, but whether the new regulations will really affect the way Internet companies do business is not yet clear, and enforcement is likely to continue to be an issue.

SOURCES: "Fan Sites for Pop Stars Settle Children's Privacy Charges," by Natasha Singer, *New York Times*, October 3, 2012; "Facebook Says Child Privacy Laws Should Not Apply to 'Like' Buttons," by Somini Sengupta, *New York Times*, October 1, 2012; "U.S. Is Tightening Web Privacy Rule to Shield Young," by Natasha Singer, *New York Times*, September 27, 2012; "Update Urged on Children's Online Privacy," by Somini Sengupta, *New York Times*, September 15, 2011; "FTC Announces First-Ever COPPA Enforcement Action Against Mobile Apps," by David Silverman, Privsecblog.com, August 17, 2011; "FTC Fine on App Developer Prompts Calls for Updated Privacy Policies," by Josh Smith, *National Journal*, August 15, 2011; "Marketing to Kids Gets More Savvy with New Technologies," by Martin E. Klimek, *USA Today,* July 27, 2011; "Virtual Worlds are Scary for Parents, Liberating for Kids," by Audrey Watters, PBS.org, June 30, 2011; "FTC: Disney's Playdom Violated Child Protection Act," by Don Reisinger, News.cnet.com, May 13, 2011; "House Releases 'Do Not Track' Bill," by Steve Stecklow and Julia Angwin, *Wall Street Journal,* May 7, 2011; "Watchdog Group Calls For Stronger Online Child Privacy Law," by Mike Sachoff, Webpronews.com, April 29, 2010; "Virtual Worlds and Kids: Mapping the Risks. A Report to Congress," Federal Trade Commission, December 2009; "Iconix Brand Group Settles Charges Its Apparel Web Sites Violated Children's Online Privacy Protection Act," Federal Trade Commission, Press Release, October 20, 2009; "The Maine Act: Preventing Predatory Marketing Practices Against Minors," by Eric Sinrod, Blog.findlaw.com/technologist, August 11, 2009; "Ad It Up: Kids in a Commercial World," Federal Trade Commission, March 12, 2009.

on multiple affiliate channels improved the company's brand image and enhanced brand loyalty (Forrester Research, 2012).

E-MAIL MARKETING AND THE SPAM EXPLOSION

direct e-mail marketing
e-mail marketing messages sent directly to interested users

When e-mail marketing began, unsolicited e-mail was not common. **Direct e-mail marketing** (e-mail marketing messages sent directly to interested users) was one of the first and most effective forms of online marketing communications. Direct e-mail marketing messages are sent to an opt-in audience of Internet users who, at one time or another, have expressed an interest in receiving messages from the advertiser. By sending e-mail to an opt-in audience, advertisers were targeting interested consumers. Response rates to legitimate, opt-in e-mail campaigns average just over 6%, depending on the targeting and freshness of the list. By far, in-house e-mail lists are more effective than purchased e-mail lists. Because of the comparatively high response rates and low cost, direct e-mail marketing remains a common form of online marketing communications. Other benefits of e-mail marketing include its mass reach, the ability to track and measure response, the ability to personalize content and tailor offers, the ability to drive traffic to Web sites for more interaction, the ability to test and optimize content and offers and the ability to target by region, demographic, time of day, or other criteria. In 2012, the total amount U.S. companies spend on e-mail marketing is about $220 million, an increase of about 4.5% from the previous year (eMarketer, Inc., 2012a). Click-through rates for legitimate e-mails depend on the promotion (the offer), the product, and the amount of targeting, but average over 7% for an in-house list, higher than postal mail response rates (3.5%) (Direct Marketing Association, 2012). Despite the deluge of spam mail, e-mail remains a highly cost-effective way of communicating with existing customers, and to a lesser extent, finding new customers. Data from the CMO Council shows that almost two-thirds of marketers surveyed rated e-mail as the most successful digital marketing tactic (eMarketer, Inc., 2012h). E-mail is also increasingly being accessed via mobile devices, which has the potential to create both opportunities and issues for marketers.

E-mail marketing and advertising is inexpensive and somewhat invariant to the number of mails sent. The cost of sending 1,000 mails is about the same as the cost to send 1 million. The primary cost of e-mail marketing is for the purchase of the list of names to which the e-mail will be sent. This generally costs anywhere from 5 to 20 cents a name, depending on how targeted the list is. Sending the e-mail is virtually cost-free. In contrast, the cost to send a direct mail 5 x 7-inch post card is about 15 cents per name, but printing and mailing costs raise the overall cost to around 75 to 80 cents a name. While the cost of legitimate e-mail messages based on high-quality commercial opt-in e-mail lists is $5 to $10 per thousand, the direct mail cost is $500 to $700 per thousand.

In 2012, however, e-mail no longer commands quite as much respect as it once did because of three factors: spam, software tools used to control spam that eliminate much e-mail from user inboxes, and poorly targeted purchased e-mail lists. **Spam** is "junk e-mail," and *spammers* are people who send unsolicited e-mail to a mass audience that has not expressed any interest in the product. Spammers tend to market pornography, fraudulent deals and services, scams, and other products not widely approved in most civilized societies. Legitimate direct opt-in e-mail marketing is not growing as fast as behaviorally targeted banners, pop-ups, and search engine advertising because of the explosion in spam. Consumer response to even legitimate e-mail campaigns has become more sophisticated. Almost three-quarters of Internet users say they see value in e-mail from companies they do business with, while only 17% saw value when the e-mail came from companies they do not do business with. As Internet users become more experienced with spam filters, more and more (currently around 70%) delete spam before opening based on the "From" line or the "Subject" line. More than 60% of users find commercial spam unpleasant and 20% report reducing their use of e-mail due to spam. In general, e-mail works well for maintaining customer relationships but poorly for acquiring new customers.

spam
unsolicited commercial e-mail

While click fraud may be the Achilles' heel of search engine advertising, spam is the nemesis of effective e-mail marketing and advertising. The percentage of all e-mail that is spam is estimated at around 72% in 2012 (Symantec, 2012) (see **Figure 7.5** on page 450). Most spam originates from bot networks, which consist of thousands of captured PCs that can initiate and relay spam messages (see Chapter 5). Spam volume has declined somewhat since authorities took down the Rustock botnet in 2011. Spam is seasonally cyclical, and varies monthly due to the impact of new technologies (both supportive and discouraging of spammers), new prosecutions, and seasonal demand for products and services.

The cost of entry to the spam business or "mass bulk e-mailing business" is small. Hundreds of programs that can be purchased on the Web allow spammers to harvest e-mail addresses across the Web from message boards and chat rooms; downloads of millions of names are available. Spammers do not generally pay anything for the

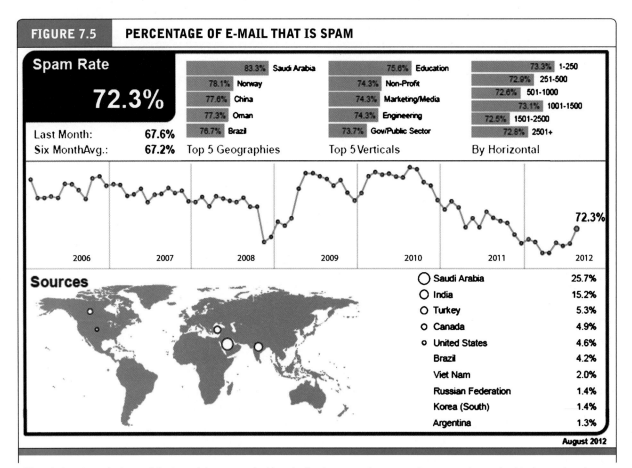

FIGURE 7.5 **PERCENTAGE OF E-MAIL THAT IS SPAM**

Spam Rate		
72.3%		
Last Month:	**67.6%**	
Six MonthAvg.:	**67.2%**	

Top 5 Geographies

83.3%	Saudi Arabia
78.1%	Norway
77.6%	China
77.3%	Oman
76.7%	Brazil

Top 5 Verticals

75.6%	Education
74.3%	Non-Profit
74.3%	Marketing/Media
74.3%	Engineering
73.7%	Gov/Public Sector

By Horizontal

73.3%	1-250
72.9%	251-500
72.6%	501-1000
73.1%	1001-1500
72.5%	1501-2500
72.8%	2501+

2006   2007   2008   2009   2010   2011   2012

72.3%

Sources

Saudi Arabia	25.7%
India	15.2%
Turkey	5.3%
Canada	4.9%
United States	4.6%
Brazil	4.2%
Viet Nam	2.0%
Russian Federation	1.4%
Korea (South)	1.4%
Argentina	1.3%

August 2012

Although the 2011 takedown of the Rustock botnet resulted in a decline in spam volume, spam has resumed growth with the continued development of tools that can circumvent anti-spam technologies and efforts. Spam is seasonally cyclical, and varies monthly due to the impact of new technologies (both supportive and discouraging of spammers), new prosecutions, and seasonal demand for products and services.
SOURCE: Based on data from Symantec, 2012.

cost of distributing their spam because they send the messages using captured client and server computers. The explosion in spam has led to many unsuccessful efforts to control the deluge. There are four solutions to spam: technology, such as filtering software, government legislation, voluntary self-regulation, and volunteer efforts to identify spammers and either shut them down or inform authorities. Obviously, none of these approaches has been successful to date, each approach has many advocates and entrepreneurs, and all approaches combined just might make a difference.

Legislative attempts to control spam have been mostly unsuccessful. Thirty-seven states in the United States have laws regulating or prohibiting spam (National Conference of State Legislatures, 2010). State legislation typically requires that unsolicited mail (spam) contain a label in the subject line ("ADV") indicating the message is an advertisement, require a clear opt-out choice for consumers, and prohibit e-mail that contains false routing and domain name information (nearly all spammers hide their own domain, ISP, and IP address). Some states, such as California and Delaware, are much stricter and prohibit all unsolicited e-mail to or from state citizens and require a specific opt-in choice before consumers can be sent e-mail. In Virginia, sending spam is a criminal felony offense.

Congress passed the first national anti-spam law ("Controlling the Assault of Non-Solicited Pornography and Marketing" or CAN-SPAM Act) in 2003, and it went into effect in January 2004. The act does not prohibit unsolicited e-mail (spam) but instead requires unsolicited commercial e-mail messages to be labeled (though not by a standard method) and to include opt-out instructions and the sender's physical address. It prohibits the use of deceptive subject lines and false headers in such messages. The FTC is authorized (but not required) to establish a "Do Not E-mail" registry. State laws that require labels on unsolicited commercial e-mail or prohibit such messages entirely are pre-empted, although provisions merely addressing falsity and deception may remain in place. The act imposes fines of $10 for each unsolicited pornographic e-mail and authorizes state attorneys general to bring lawsuits against spammers. The act obviously makes lawful legitimate bulk mailing of unsolicited e-mail messages (what most people call spam), yet seeks to prohibit certain deceptive practices and provide a small measure of consumer control by requiring opt-out notices. In this sense, critics point out, CAN-SPAM ironically legalizes spam as long as spammers follow the rules. For this reason, large spammers have been among the bill's biggest supporters, and consumer groups have been the act's most vociferous critics.

There have been a number of state and federal prosecutions of spammers, and private civil suits by large ISPs such as Microsoft. Volunteer efforts by industry are another potential control point. Notably, the Direct Marketing Association (DMA), an industry trade group that represents companies that use the postal mail system as well as e-mail for solicitations, is now strongly supporting legislative controls over spam, in addition to its voluntary guidelines. The DMA would like to preserve the legitimate use of e-mail as a marketing technique. The DMA has formed a 15-person anti-spam group and spends $500,000 a year trying to identify spammers. The DMA is also a supporter of the National Cyber-Forensics & Training Alliance (NCFTA), a non-profit organization with "close ties" to the FBI. NCFTA operates a variety of initiatives aimed at combating cybercrime, including digital phishing via spam.

BEHAVIORAL TARGETING: GETTING PERSONAL

In Chapter 6, you learned about the six major ways that marketers target markets (refer to Table 6.9)—through behavioral, demographic, psychographic, technical, contextual, and search data collected online. Behavioral targeting of ads involves using the online and offline behavior of consumers to adjust the advertising message delivered online, often in real time (milliseconds from the consumers first URL entry). The intent is to increase the efficiency of marketing and advertising, and to increase the revenue streams of firms who are in a position to behaviorally target visitors. Because "behavioral targeting" as a label has somewhat unfavorable connotations, the online advertising industry, led by Google, has introduced a new name for behavioral targeting. They call it **interest-based advertising**. As you learned in Chapter 6, personal

interest-based advertising
using search queries and clicks on results to behaviorally target consumers

profile information, and information on your relationships with others, on social networks to target consumers is called social marketing by the industry.

One of the original promises of the Web has been that it can deliver a marketing message tailored to each consumer based on this data, and then measure the results in terms of click-throughs and purchases. In the past, Yahoo, Google, and other Web sites would show you ads based on the content of the page you were visiting. This is called context advertising. If you are visiting a jewelry site, you would be shown jewelry ads. If you entered a search query like "diamonds," you would be shown text ads for diamonds and other jewelry. This was taken one step further by advertising networks composed of several thousand sites. An advertising network could follow you across thousands of Web sites and come up with an idea of what you are interested in as you browse, and then display ads related to those interests. For instance, if you visit a few men's clothing sites in the course of a few hours, you will be shown ads for men's clothing on most other sites you visit subsequently, regardless of their subject content. If you search for a certain pair of shoes at Zappos, and like them to your friends on Facebook, you will be shown ads for the exact same shoes at other sites (including Facebook). Behavioral targeting combines nearly all of your online behavioral data into a collection of interest areas, and then shows you ads based on those interests, as well as the interests of your friends. What's new about today's behavioral targeting is the breadth of data collected: your e-mail content, social network page content, friends, purchases online, books read or purchased, newspaper sites visited, and many other behaviors. And finally, ad exchanges take the marketing of all this information one step further. Most popular Web sites have more than 100 tracking programs on their home pages that are owned by third-party data collector firms who then sell this information in real time to the highest bidding advertiser in real-time online auctions. Ad exchanges make it possible for advertisers to retarget ads at individuals as they roam across the Internet. **Retargeting ads** involves showing the same or similar ad to individuals across multiple Web sites. Retargeted ads are nearly as effective as the original ad (eMarketer, 2011a).

There are four methods that online advertisers use to behaviorally target ads: search engine queries, the collection of data on individual browsing history online (monitoring the clickstream), the collection of data from social network sites, and increasingly, the integration of this online data with offline data like income, education, address, purchase patterns, credit records, driving records, and hundreds of other personal descriptors tied to specific, identifiable persons. This level of integration of both "anonymous" as well as identifiable information is routinely engaged in by Google, Microsoft, Yahoo, Facebook, and legions of small and medium-sized marketing firms that use their data, or collect data from thousands of Web sites using Web beacons and cookies. (See Chapter 6 for a more detailed discussion.) On average, online information bureaus maintain 2,000 data elements on each adult person in their database. The currency and accuracy of this data is never examined, and the retention periods are not known. Currently, there are no federal laws or regulations governing this data.

Earlier in the chapter we described search engine advertising in some detail. Search engine advertising has turned out to be the most effective online advertising

retargeting ads
showing the same ad to individuals across multiple Web sites

format by several orders of magnitude, and provides more than 95% of the revenue of Google, the world's largest online advertising agency. Why is search engine advertising so effective? Most agree that when users enter a query into a search engine, it reveals a very specific intention to shop, compare, and possibly purchase. When ads are shown at these very moments of customer behavior, they are 4 to 10 times as effective as other formats. The author John Battelle coined the phrase and the notion that the Web is a database of intentions composed of the results from every search ever made and every path that searchers have followed, since the beginning of the Web. In total, this database contains the intentions of all mankind. This treasure trove of intentions, desires, likes, wants, and needs is owned by only a few private business firms, namely, Google, Microsoft, and to a lesser extent, Yahoo, in massive, global databases (Battelle, 2003). Batelle later extended the concept of a database of intentions beyond search to include the social graph (Facebook and Google+), status updates (Twitter and Facebook), and the "check-in" (Foursquare and Yelp) (Battelle, 2010). The database of intentions can be exploited to track and target individuals and groups. Not only is this capability unprecedented, but it's growing exponentially into the foreseeable future. The potential for abuse is also growing exponentially.

The decline in the growth rate of search engine advertising, from the early days of double-digit growth to today's growth of high single digits, has caused the major search engine firms to seek out alternative forms of future growth, which include display, rich media, and video advertising on millions of Web publisher sites. Web publishers have responded by producing billions of pages of content. In this environment, the effectiveness of display ads has been falling in terms of response rates and prices for ads. Behavioral targeting is an effective way to solve this problem and increase response rates. Behavioral targeting of both search and display advertising is currently driving the expansion in online advertising.

Behavioral targeting seeks to optimize consumer response by using information that Web visitors reveal about themselves online, and if possible, combine this with offline identity and consumption information gathered by companies such as Acxiom. Behavioral targeting is based on real-time information about visitors' use of Web sites, including pages visited, content viewed, search queries, ads clicked, videos watched, content shared, and products they purchased. Once this information is collected and analyzed on the fly, behavioral targeting programs attempt to develop profiles of individual users, and then show advertisements most likely to be of interest to the user. In 2011, more than 75% of North American advertisers used some form of targeting in their online display ads (eMarketer, 2012i).

For a variety of technical and other reasons, this vision has, thus far, not been widely achieved. The percentage of ads that are actually targeted is unknown, but most display ads are not targeted. Instead, advertisers use less expensive context ads displayed to a general audience with no targeting, or very minimal demographic targeting. The quality of the data, largely owned by the online advertising networks, is quite good but hardly perfect. The ability to understand and respond—the business intelligence and real-time analytics—are weak, preventing companies from being able to respond quickly in meaningful ways when the consumer is online. The firms who sell targeted ads to their clients claim the targeted ads are two or three times more effective than general ads. There is not very good data to support these claims from independent sources. Generally these claims confound the impact of brands on targeted audiences, and the impact of the ads placed to this targeted audience. Advertisers target groups that are most likely to buy their product even in the absence of targeting ads at them. The additional impact of a targeted ad is much smaller than ad platforms claim. A recent research report based on real data from 18 ad campaigns on Yahoo, involving 18.4 million users, found that brand interest is the largest single factor in determining targeted ad effectiveness, and not the targeted ad itself (Farahat and Bailey, 2012). And marketing companies are not yet prepared to accept the idea that there needs to be several hundred or a thousand variations on the same display ad depending on the customer's profile. Such a move would raise costs. Last, consumer resistance to targeting continues. In a recent Truste/Harris Interactive Poll, more than 58% of those surveyed said that they do not like online behavioral ads (TRUSTe, 2012). A survey found that the percentage of people who plan to opt for Do Not Track options has doubled from 27% in 2011 to 50% in 2012 (Gigaom, 2012). Behavioral tracking does not work very well if half the audience declines to be targeted. On average, consumers can expect that at least 80% of the ads they see online are not very well targeted at them. This situation will no doubt improve.

Nevertheless, firms are experimenting with more precise targeting methods and ad budgets for targeting are expanding rapidly. Snapple used behavioral targeting methods (with the help of online ad firm Tacoda) to identify the types of people attracted to Snapple Green Tea. Answer: people who like the arts and literature, travel international-ally, and visit health sites. Microsoft offers MSN advertisers access to personal data derived from nearly 500 million worldwide Windows Live users. Some advertisers have reported more than 50% increases in click-through rates. General Motors uses Digitas (a Boston-based online ad firm) to create several hundred versions of a single ad for its Acadia crossover vehicle. Viewers are initially shown ads that emphasize brand, features, and communities. On subsequent viewings, they are shown different ads based on demographics, lifestyle, and behavioral considerations. Men are shown ver-sions of the ads emphasizing engines, specifications, and performance, while women are shown versions that emphasize comfort, accessibility, and families.

The growth of targeting continues to raise privacy issues. The public and congres-sional reaction to behavioral targeting is described more fully in Chapter 8.

MIXING OFFLINE AND ONLINE MARKETING COMMUNICATIONS

Many early proponents of e-commerce believed that the traditional world of market-ing based on mass media was no longer relevant to the exploding online commercial world, and that in the "new Internet economy," nearly all marketing communica-tions would be online. As it turned out, this did not happen. What did happen is that offline marketing powerhouses in consumer-oriented industries learned how to use the Web to extend their brand images and sales campaigns to an educated, wealthy, and computer-literate, online audience. The large advertising agencies that specialized in mass media opened up Internet practices, and learned quickly how to integrate online and offline campaigns. Pure online companies learned how to use traditional print and television advertising as a means for driving sales to their Web sites. As it turns out, physical catalogs are excellent drivers of Web sales.

The marketing communications campaigns most successful at driving traffic to a Web site have incorporated both online and offline tactics, rather than relying solely on one or the other. The objective is to draw the attention of people who are already online and persuade them to visit a new Web site, as well as attract the attention of people who will be going online in the near future in order to suggest that they, too, visit the Web site. Several research studies have shown that the most effective online advertisements are those that use consistent imagery with campaigns running in other media at the same time. For instance, research by iProspect found that search queries were prompted by the following traditional media outlets: television (44%), word of mouth (41%), magazines and newspapers (35%), radio (23%), and billboards (13%) (iProspect, 2011). Offline mass media such as television and radio have nearly a 100% market penetration into the 119 million households in the United States. U.S. daily newspapers have a total circulation of around 46 million. It would be foolish for pure online companies not to use these popular media to drive traffic to the online world of commerce. In the early days of e-commerce, the Internet audience was quite different from the general population, and perhaps was best reached by using online marketing alone. This is no longer true as the Internet population becomes much more like the general population.

Many online ventures have used offline marketing techniques to drive traffic to their Web sites, increase awareness, and build brand equity. For instance, LendingTree.com has used television advertising to direct people to its Web site to look for mortgages. Barnes & Noble, as well as JCPenney and REI Inc., use print media to inform customers of their in-store Web kiosks. Such "tie-ins" between a print product and a firm's Web site have proven to be very successful in driving Web traffic. Another example of the online/offline marketing connection is the use of print catalogs by heretofore entirely online ventures. Some online ventures have created paper catalogs and mailed them to their customers to improve their relationship with that group.

The development of multi-channel marketing and communications reflects the fact that the behavior of consumers is increasingly multi-channel (see Chapter 9). For instance, a recent survey reported that almost half of consumers surveyed said that they now shop in stores, online, and also using their mobile devices. In 2012, about $1.2 trillion of offline retail sales (43% of total U.S. retail sales) will be influenced by online research, almost 80% of Internet users research products online before buying them offline, and 35% of the online retail sales generated by Internet Retailer's Top 500 Web sites were made by mass merchant, multi-channel retailers—retailers who had physical stores and catalogs in addition to Web sites.

Insight on Business: Are the Very Rich Different from You and Me? examines how luxury goods providers use online marketing in conjunction with their offline marketing efforts.

INSIGHT ON BUSINESS

ARE THE VERY RICH DIFFERENT FROM YOU AND ME?

"Let me tell you about the very rich. They are different from you and me." So observed F. Scott Fitzgerald in the short story, "The Rich Boy." Palm Beach has its Worth Avenue, New York has its Fifth Avenue, Los Angeles has its Rodeo Drive, and Chicago has the Magnificent Mile. So where do the rich go on the Web to get that $5,000 cocktail dress, or that $3,000 Italian suit? How about a Jimmy Choo handbag? Something Armani? Well, today, it turns out they may not be so different from the rest of us: they look for online deals, say, the $5,000 cocktail dress for only $3,500. At Net-a-Porter, a leading fashion site that combines an online magazine with a strong sales component, you can find that Gucci silk crepe jumpsuit ($1,995) that looks smashing over a pair of Gucci stretch-suede over-the-knee boots ($2,495). Who could resist?

There are almost 14 million affluent households in the United States with a net worth of more than $500,000. Around 58 million U.S. adults live in households with $100,000 or more in yearly income. Retail consumption in general is highly skewed: the wealthiest top 10% of households account for 50% of all retail spending, and 37% of all e-commerce retail spending.

Yet even the rich are not immune to the economy around them. Let's say you have a "mere" $5 million in net worth (placing you in the "minor rich"), including the house, the second house, three cars (all still with money owed on them), and stocks and bonds, and then all this booty sinks in value by 30% to 40% in the Big Recession. What to do? You have a job, so you cut back on spending, sell one of the cars, engage in a little "cheap chic" by shopping at Walmart, and look for incredible sales at luxury spending stores

such as Tiffany, Neiman Marcus, and Marni. Online, you learn to pay attention to your e-mail because that's where luxe retailers like Gilt.com offer flash discounts on designer clothing to preferred customers.

The problem is the real luxe online stores typically don't have sales, at least not in public. Luxe retailers are loathe to offer sales because they believe sales detract from their reputations for timeless quality. However, change is in the air (or online as it were). LVMH, the world's largest luxe brand holding company, put up a Web site in 2011 called Nowness featuring all manner of daily specials. Times are changing when Lacoste (the polo shirts with the crocodile logo) pulls the plug on print advertising and puts all its U.S. marketing dollars on the Internet. You know something is different when Faberge introduces its first new line of luxe jewelery in 90 years with a Web-only marketing effort on a single Web site. The site offers 100 pieces of jewelry ranging in price from $48,000 to $10 million. A Faberge marketing report found the rich like to buy online if they have plenty of personal attention. Shopping carts? Please, are you kidding? "No, thank you." A personal sales rep to walk you through the Web site? "Yes, of course."

It used to be that luxe brands either avoided the Web entirely or just put up sites with Flash videos and high-end photography. But when ordinary department stores are discounting even luxe-branded goods, the high-end brands are getting down and dirty on the Web, rebuilding their sites for active competition with the department stores.

Luxe retailers are in fact offering more discounts—but they're secret. How can a sale be secret? Whispered discounts at the physical

(continued)

stores ("Shhhh! There's a special sale in the dress department!") have their online counterpart in flash e-mail campaigns and "private online sales" in which selected online customers are e-mailed alerts such as "A $3,000 handbag on sale for the next two hours for $800." Neiman Marcus calls them "Midday Dash" sales. Two-hour online-only sales promise 50% off on luxe goods that can be purchased only by clicking on a link in the e-mail. One week's "dash sale" featured a $697 Burberry handbag, marked down from $1,395. A Carmen Marc Valvo chiffon gown, just right for that special charity party, was offered at $575, down from $1,150. Cole Haan flats only $82, down from $165.

With in-store sales suffering as a result of the recession, the action has moved to the Internet where luxe retailers can offer discreet sales to a select group of customers without tarnishing the brand, preserving exclusivity, and creating a sense of urgency by limiting the time to purchase. At the same time, they can deny they discount their items. If prices were public, customers would know that the $800 Marni skirt they bought today was on sale the next day for $400. They might conclude that none of these goods are worth the price charged, certainly not the retail price, no matter what it is. Online dash sales are sort of like impulse buying at Walmart, but instead of 20 batteries for $5, it's more like one Burberry bag for $1,000. Rich people can indulge bigger impulses. But like the rest of us, the rich just can't seem to get enough of a good thing, especially if it's half price.

A study by Bain estimated online sales of luxury goods are expected to climb by 20% a year through 2015 as producers of luxe goods build networks of potential customers on social media Web sites such as Facebook. Worldwide revenue from fashion, jewelry, and other luxury products is likely to reach $15 billion by 2015 from a mere $7 billion in 2011. The explosion of social media and the increasing investments in the online channel by luxury companies has reinforced and enlarged the community of those who explore, comment upon, and eventually purchase luxury goods. Luxury companies are more than doubling their "friends" on Facebook annually in recognition of the link between online and offline purchases. Burberry Group Plc, the U.K.'s largest luxury goods maker, reports that it obtains the most reach and most response from digital initiatives compared with other media. To promote the Burberry Body fragrance, which hit shelves in 2011, the London-based company offered exclusive samples to its Facebook fans. It received more than 225,000 requests in little more than a week.

Tiffany, the quintessential luxe firm, experienced lower profits in the recession of 2008–2009, but never experienced a loss. Since then, however, revenues have expanded sharply worldwide, increasing by 18% in 2011. Tiffany's strategy, echoed by Hermes, is not to lower prices but to add more lower-priced items to the marketing mix. For instance, pendants are going for as little as $150 to "only" $15,000 (those are the ones with the big shiny things). Neiman Marcus, Saks Inc., and Hermes International reported similar results despite the recession.

Yet luxury retailers such as Neiman Marcus, Tiffany, Armani, and Christian Dior have had a difficult time developing an online presence for their wealthy customers. Critics argue many luxe manufacturers and retailers have had a difficult time understanding their wealthy online customers. A recent report from the Luxury Institute found that online luxe goods retailers fall short in community building. Most sites do not track online customer comments on rating and review sites, or blogs (let alone Twitter), although most use search engine optimization. When you're really good and charging accordingly, why ask customers what they think?

Luxury brands and retailers do face a difficult market where they must try to please not only their wealthy older customers, but also those customers' children and grandchildren who are

(continued)

used to shopping online. And they have had a hard time coming up with a credible online image that supports their brand, but is still an online site that appeals to the online customer.

For instance, when Neiman Marcus introduced its first Web site with two virtual boutiques, featuring tours of Kate Spade handbags and John Hardy silver cuff links, Web designers were awed by the display of graphics and motion. But most customers were turned off because they could not find enough goods for sale, and could not easily navigate the site. Pretty snazzy stuff, but today it's all gone. Neimanmarcus.com no longer features any animations or Flash graphics, but instead has much more merchandise neatly arranged by category and designer: in short, an online catalog much like JCPenney's catalog. The current Neiman Marcus Web site gets generally high marks for the simplicity of design and efficiency of navigation, although critics point out that it's still somewhat difficult to find the online version of Neiman Marcus's most popular offline marketing tool: its Christmas catalog that features "over the top" luxury items such as a "his and hers" double portrait in chocolate for $100,000 and an underwater personal submarine for $1.4 million.

Developing an online marketing approach that increases a company's access to consumers while retaining an image of exclusivity was the challenge faced by Tiffany & Co. when it redesigned its Web site in 1999. The company was in the enviable position of being perhaps the most famous jewelry company in the United States. Tiffany's offline marketing communications sought to engender feelings of beauty, quality, and timeless style—all hallmarks of the Tiffany brand. How could Tiffany maintain its approach on the Web, a medium that often emphasizes speed and flashy graphics over grace and elegance, and low-cost bargains over high-priced exclusive fashion? The Web, at least in its early days, was all about low prices and great deals—concepts that are anathema to the high-fashion merchant.

Tiffany's first effort on the Web was designed by Oven Digital Inc., who built a Web site that used soft, neutral colors throughout, sparse wording, and pictures that faded slowly onto the screen. The shopping portion of the Web site showed just one large item, with some smaller photos that could be enlarged by clicking at the bottom of the screen. But that same "reserved" quality made it difficult for consumers to find out what was for sale. Critics complained that the Tiffany Web site had too few products online, the Flash graphics were slow, there were too many animations, and the product line available was poorly organized. While Tiffany claimed there were 2,000 products online, finding them and buying them was an arduous process. The site was redesigned by an in-house team with a view toward making it more focused. Today, Tiffany has shifted more of its direct marketing effort from the offline catalog to the online catalog. The results improved dramatically. It has Web sites in 13 different countries, including Canada, the United Kingdom, Japan, and Australia. Tiffany sites carry over 2,800 products in six categories of goods: engagement, jewelry, watches, designers and collections, gifts, and accessories. In 2011, Tiffany's online sales were over $215 million, 6% of its $3.6 billion worldwide sales, placing it in second place in the online jewelry industry. (Blue Nile is first with almost $350 million in online sales.)

Other cutting-edge fashion houses such as Christian Dior, Armani, and Bottega Veneta insisted on managing their own Web sites initially. The results were not impressive. The Web sites were typically a collection of photos with directions to the nearest store. Embracing the Internet ran counter to their strategies to keep tight control over their images and customers. As a result of the difficulties they encountered, some luxury sites began reluctantly to outsource their Web sites. For instance, Louis Vuitton, DKNY, and Armani have all outsourced their online boutiques to Web operations companies such as Yoox, a

(continued)

fashion retailer with a long history on the Web. In the case of Armani, Emporio Armani personally directed the online effort. To avoid the cheaper catalog look, he had his store design team hand over architectural plans to the flagship store in Milan so that Yoox could use it as a metaphor and model for the Web site. Now visitors can turn left or right as they would at the Milan store, and take a virtual tour of the goods on display. Armani wanted a three-dimensional look, and the ability to shine bright lights on the products being examined, a trick used in his stores to impart the sense of elegance. The cost of opening the site has been a fraction of the cost of launching a new store, and less risky. A trip to the Armani Web site is a trip all unto itself: stunning video images of the latest seasonal collections, Armani Jeans, and the Armani Exchange, where you can actually buy something from the Emporio Armani retail collection.

Selling luxe to men has been difficult because they hate to shop. But help is on the way, men: don't despair. Net-a-Porter has launched a new site for men called Mrporter.com. They are offering Dolce & Gabbana washed indigo jeans for $450. And there's a contest on the home page: open an account and provide some personal details, and you stand a chance of winning a $2,500 certificate to spend at the store. Life is good at the top.

■ **SOURCES:** Tiffany & Co. Annual Report on 10-K, March 28, 2012; "Affluents: Demographic Profile and Marketing Approach," *eMarketer* (Mark Dolliver), January 2012; "Affluent Shoppers and Luxury Brand Retailers Online," *eMarketer* (Jeffrey Grau), September 2011; "High Fashion Relents to Web's Pull," by Stephanie Clifford, *New York Times*, July 11, 2010; "Luxury Brands Warming to the Web," by Mark Porter, Reuters, June 3, 2011; "Mr Porter to Test Men's Urge to Shop Online," by Ray Smith, *Wall Street Journal,* February 10, 2011; "Fashion Week Tips Hat to Blog Site," by Elizabeth Holmes, *Wall Street Journal,* February 9, 2011; "Luxe Lowdown: Tony Sites Begin to Invite Buyer Reviews," by Rachel Dodes, *Wall Street Journal,* October 16, 2010.

7.2 UNDERSTANDING THE COSTS AND BENEFITS OF ONLINE MARKETING COMMUNICATIONS

As we saw in Section 7.1, online marketing communications still comprise only a very small part of the total marketing communications universe. While there are several reasons why this is the case, two of the main ones are concerns about how well online advertising really works and about how to adequately measure the costs and benefits of online advertising. We will address both of these topics in this section. But first, we will define some important terms used when examining the effectiveness of online marketing.

ONLINE MARKETING METRICS: LEXICON

In order to understand the process of attracting prospects to your firm's Web site or Facebook page via marketing communications and converting them into customers, you will need to be familiar with Web marketing terminology. **Table 7.4** on page 460 lists some terms commonly used to describe the impacts and results of online marketing for display ads, social network ads, and e-mail campaigns.

The first nine metrics focus primarily on the success of a Web site in achieving audience or market share by "driving" shoppers to the site. These measures often substitute for solid information on sales revenue as e-commerce entrepreneurs seek

TABLE 7.4	MARKETING METRICS LEXICON
COMMON MARKETING DISPLAY AD METRICS	**DESCRIPTION**
Impressions	Number of times an ad is served
Click-through rate (CTR)	Percentage of times an ad is clicked
View-through rate (VTR)	Percentage of times an ad is not clicked immediately but the Web site is visited within 30 days
Hits	Number of HTTP requests
Page views	Number of pages viewed
Stickiness (duration)	Average length of stay at a Web site
Unique visitors	Number of unique visitors in a period
Loyalty	Measured variously as the number of page views, frequency of single-user visits to the Web site, or percentage of customers who return to the site in a year to make additional purchases
Reach	Percentage of Web site visitors who are potential buyers; or the percentage of total market buyers who buy at a site
Recency	Time elapsed since the last action taken by a buyer, such as a Web site visit or purchase
Acquisition rate	Percentage of visitors who indicate an interest in the Web site's products by registering or visiting product pages
Conversion rate	Percentage of visitors who become customers
Browse-to-buy ratio	Ratio of items purchased to product views
View-to-cart ratio	Ratio of "Add to cart" clicks to product views
Cart conversion rate	Ratio of actual orders to "Add to cart" clicks
Checkout conversion rate	Ratio of actual orders to checkouts started
Abandonment rate	Percentage of shoppers who begin a shopping cart purchase but then leave the Web site without completing a purchase (similar to above)
Retention rate	Percentage of existing customers who continue to buy on a regular basis (similar to loyalty)
Attrition rate	Percentage of customers who do not return during the next year after an initial purchase
SOCIAL MARKETING METRICS	
Gross rating points	Audience size times frequency of views (audience reach)
Applause ratio	Number of Likes per post
Conversation ratio	Ratio of number of comments per post
Amplification	Number of shares (or re-tweets) per post
Sentiment ratio	Ratio of positive comments to total comments
Duration of engagement	Average time on site
E-MAIL METRICS	
Open rate	Percentage of e-mail recipients who open the e-mail and are exposed to the message
Delivery rate	Percentage of e-mail recipients who received the e-mail
Click-through rate (e-mail)	Percentage of recipients who clicked through to offers
Bounce-back rate	Percentage of e-mails that could not be delivered
Unsubscribe rate	Percentage of recipients who click unsubscribe
Conversion rate (e-mail)	Percentage of recipients who actually buy

to have investors and the public focus on the success of the Web site in "attracting eyeballs" (viewers).

Impressions are the number of times an ad is served. **Click-through rate (CTR)** measures the percentage of people exposed to an online advertisement who actually click on the advertisement. Because not all ads lead to an immediate click, the industry has invented a new term for a long-term hit called **view-through rate (VTR)**, which measures the 30-day response rate to an ad. **Hits** are the number of HTTP requests received by a firm's server. Hits can be misleading as a measure of Web site activity because a "hit" does not equal a page. A single page may account for several hits if the page contains multiple images or graphics. A single Web site visitor can generate hundreds of hits. For this reason, hits are not an accurate representation of Web traffic or visits, even though they are generally easy to measure; the sheer volume of hits can be huge—and sound impressive—but not be a true measure of activity. **Page views** are the number of pages requested by visitors. However, with increased usage of Web frames that divide pages into separate sections, a single page that has three frames will generate three page views. Hence, page views per se are also not a very useful metric.

Stickiness (sometimes called *duration*) is the average length of time visitors remain at a Web site. Stickiness is important to marketers because the longer the amount of time a visitor spends at a Web site, the greater the probability of a purchase. In December 2011, for instance, Google's 173 million unique visitors stayed on-site an average of one and a half hours during a month's time; Yahoo's 144 million visitors stayed an average of 2 hours and 17 minutes; Facebook's 153 million visitors stayed on-site an average of almost 7 hours! While Facebook generates a great deal of stickiness, it's not the case that this translates directly into more advertisements, more sales, and more revenue. Equally important is what people do when they visit a Web site and not just how much time they spend there. People don't go to Facebook to buy or research goods, whereas Google visitors are more likely to visit because they are searching for something to buy (Nielsen, 2012).

The number of unique visitors is perhaps the most widely used measure of a Web site's popularity. The measurement of **unique visitors** counts the number of distinct, unique visitors to a Web site, regardless of how many pages they view. **Loyalty** measures the percentage of visitors who return in a year. This can be a good indicator of a site's Web following, and perhaps the trust shoppers place in a site. **Reach** is typically a percentage of the total number of consumers in a market who visit a Web site; for example, 10% of all book purchasers in a year will visit Amazon at least once to shop for a book. This provides an idea of the power of a Web site to attract market share. **Recency**—like loyalty—measures the power of a Web site to produce repeat visits and is generally measured as the average number of days elapsed between shopper or customer visits. For example, a recency value of 25 days means the average customer will return once every 25 days.

The metrics described so far do not say much about commercial activity nor help you understand the conversion from visitor to customer. Several other measures are more helpful in this regard. **Acquisition rate** measures the percentage of visitors who register or visit product pages (indicating interest in the product). **Conversion rate**

---

impressions
number of times an ad is served

click-through rate (CTR)
the percentage of people exposed to an online advertisement who actually click on the banner

view-through rate (VTR)
measures the 30-day response rate to an ad

hits
number of http requests received by a firm's server

page views
number of pages requested by visitors

stickiness (duration)
average length of time visitors remain at a site

unique visitors
the number of distinct, unique visitors to a site

loyalty
percentage of purchasers who return in a year

reach
percentage of the total number of consumers in a market who will visit a site

recency
average number of days elapsed between visits

acquisition rate
percentage of visitors who register or visit product pages

conversion rate
percentage of visitors who purchase something

browse-to-buy ratio
ratio of items purchased to product views

view-to-cart ratio
ratio of "Add to cart" clicks to product views

cart conversion rate
ratio of actual orders to "Add to cart" clicks

checkout conversion ratio
ratio of actual orders to checkouts started

abandonment rate
% of shoppers who begin a shopping cart, but then fail to complete it

retention rate
% of existing customers who continue to buy

attrition rate
% of customers who purchase once, but do not return within a year

conversation ratio
number of comments produced per post

applause ratio
number of Likes or Shares per post

amplification
number of re-tweets or re-shares per post

sentiment ratio
ratio of positive comments to total comments

open rate
% of customers who open e-mail

measures the percentage of visitors who actually purchase something. Conversion rates can vary widely, depending on the success of the site. Fireclick, a provider of Web analytics software, publishes conversion rate statistics, and cites a global conversion rate of around 2%–3% (Fireclick, 2012). The **browse-to-buy ratio** measures the ratio of items purchased to product views. The **view-to-cart ratio** calculates the ratio of "Add to cart" clicks to product views. **Cart conversion rate** measures the ratio of actual orders to "Add to cart" clicks. **Checkout conversion rate** calculates the ratio of actual orders to checkouts started. **Abandonment rate** measures the percentage of shoppers who begin a shopping cart form but then fail to complete the form and leave the Web site. Abandonment rates can signal a number of potential problems—poor form design, lack of consumer trust, or consumer purchase uncertainty caused by other factors. A recent study on shopping cart abandonment found that, on average, 65% of carts were abandoned in 2012 (Baymard, 2012). Among the reasons for abandonment were security concerns, customer just checking prices, couldn't find customer support, couldn't find preferred payment option, and the item being unavailable at checkout. Given that more than 80% of online shoppers generally have a purchase in mind when they visit a Web site, a high abandonment rate signals many lost sales. **Retention rate** indicates the percentage of existing customers who continue to buy on a regular basis. **Attrition rate** measures the percentage of customers who purchase once but never return within a year (the opposite of loyalty and retention rates).

Social network marketing differs from display ad marketing because the objective is to create word-of-mouth impact and alter the interaction among your visitors, and between your visitors and your brand. While unique visitors is important, it's even more important what they do when they arrive on-site. **Conversation ratio** measures the number of comments produced per post to your site. **Applause ratio** measures the number of Likes or Shares per post. **Amplification** measures the number of re-tweets or re-shares per post. All three of these measures are different dimensions of "word of mouth" advertising on social network sites. **Sentiment ratio** is the ratio of positive comments to total comments.

Facebook, Nielsen, and comScore are also measuring Facebook exposure using gross rating points, a traditional ad metric that multiplies the reach, or size, of an audience by the frequency with which that audience sees a brand. By using this metric, marketers can discuss online advertising in the same terms that they already use for TV, print, or outdoor ads (Raice, 2011; Nielsen, 2011). Facebook's application software development package provides extensive measures of user interactions and demographics. On the other hand, this measure does not measure dimensions of consumer engagement, which is the main strength of social network advertising.

E-mail campaigns have their own set of metrics. **Open rate** measures the percentage of customers who open the e-mail and are exposed to the message. Generally, open rates are quite high, in the area of 50% or greater. However, some browsers open mail as soon as the mouse cursor moves over the subject line, and therefore this measure can be difficult to interpret. **Delivery rate** measures the percentage of e-mail recipients who received the e-mail. **Click-through rate (e-mail)** measures the percentage of e-mail recipients who clicked through to the offer. Finally, **bounce-back rate** measures the percentage of e-mails that could not be delivered.

There is a lengthy path from simple online ad impressions, Web site visits, and page views to the purchase of a product and the company making a profit (see **Figure 7.6**). You first need to make customers aware of their needs for your product and somehow drive them to your Web site. Once there, you need to convince them you have the best value—quality and price—when compared to alternative providers. You then must persuade them to trust your firm to handle the transaction (by providing a secure environment and fast fulfillment). Based on your success, a percentage of customers will remain loyal and purchase again or recommend your Web site to others.

HOW WELL DOES ONLINE ADVERTISING WORK?

What is the most effective kind of online advertising? How does online advertising compare to offline advertising? The answers depend on the goals of the campaign, the

delivery rate
% of e-mail recipients who received e-mail

click-through rate (e-mail)
% of e-mail recipients who clicked through to the offer

bounce-back rate
percentage of e-mails that could not be delivered

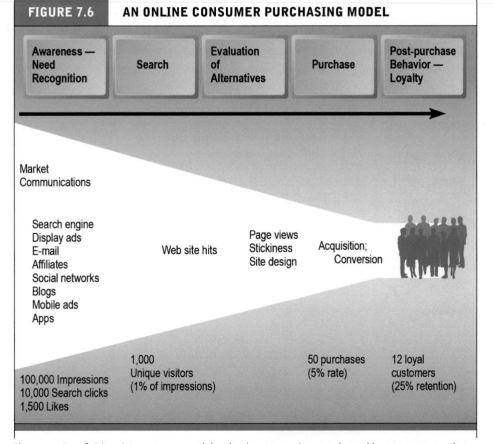

FIGURE 7.6   AN ONLINE CONSUMER PURCHASING MODEL

| Awareness — Need Recognition | Search | Evaluation of Alternatives | Purchase | Post-purchase Behavior — Loyalty |

Market Communications

Search engine
Display ads
E-mail
Affiliates
Social networks
Blogs
Mobile ads
Apps

Web site hits

Page views
Stickiness
Site design

Acquisition;
Conversion

100,000 Impressions
10,000 Search clicks
1,500 Likes

1,000
Unique visitors
(1% of impressions)

50 purchases
(5% rate)

12 loyal
customers
(25% retention)

The conversion of visitors into customers, and then loyal customers, is a complex and long-term process that may take several months.

nature of the product, and the quality of the Web site you direct customers toward. The answers also depend on what you measure. Click-through rates are interesting, but ultimately it's the return on the investment in the ad campaign that counts. A broader understanding of the matter requires that you consider the cost of purchasing the promotional materials and mailing lists, and the studio production costs for radio and TV ads. Also, each media has a different revenue-per-contact potential because the products advertised differ. For instance, online purchases tend to be for smaller items when compared to newspaper, magazine, and television ads (although this too seems to be changing).

Table 7.5 lists the click-through rates for various types of online marketing communications tools. There is a great deal of variability within any of these types, so the figures in Table 7.5 should be viewed as general estimates. Click-through rates on all these formats are a function of personalization and other targeting techniques. For instance, several studies have found that e-mail response rates can be increased 20% or more by adding social sharing links. And while the average Google click-through rate is .5%, some merchants can hit 10% or more by making their ads more specific and attracting only the most interested people. Permission e-mail click-through rates have been fairly consistent over the last five years, in the 5%–6% range. Putting the recipient's name in the subject line can double the click-through rate. (For unsolicited e-mail and outright spam, response rates are much lower, even though about 20% of U.S. e-mail users report clicking occasionally on an unsolicited e-mail.)

In general, Facebook ads have a far lower click-through rate, in part because Facebook users do not go to their pages to purchase goods or experience ads of any

TABLE 7.5	ONLINE MARKETING COMMUNICATIONS: TYPICAL CLICK-THROUGH RATES
MARKETING METHODS	TYPICAL CLICK-THROUGH RATES
Display ads	.03%–.30%
Interstitials	.02%–.16%
Search engine keyword purchase	.50%–4.00%
Video and rich media	.50%–2.65%
Sponsorships	1.50%–3.00%
Affiliate relationships	.20%–.40%
E-mail marketing in-house list	5.00%–6.00%
E-mail marketing purchased list	.01%–1.50%
Social site display ads	.02%–.25%
Mobile display ads	.50%–.80%

SOURCES: Based on data from eMarketer, Inc., 2011b; 2011c; industry sources; authors' estimates.

kind. While Facebook now accounts for about one-quarter of all display advertising (1 trillion display ads a year), its share of display ad revenue is far lower because the click-through on its site is so weak. Mobile ads outperform standard banner ads by up to six times, and rich media and video ads are much more effective than banner ads (eMarketer, 2011c).

The click-through rate for video ads may seem low, but it is twice as high as the rate for display ads. The "interaction rate" (sometimes referred to as "dwell rate") with rich media ads and video ads is about 7%–8%. "Interaction" means the user clicks on the video, plays it, stops it, or takes some other action (possibly skips the ad altogether) (eMarketer, 2009; Eyeblaster, 2009). Although click-through rate is an important metric for video ads, advertising agencies also focus on other metrics to assess the success of an online video campaign, such as number of unique viewers, target impressions, brand lift, sales impact, and conversions (Brightroll, 2012).

As consumers become more accustomed to new online advertising formats, click-through rates tend to fall. Response rates to banner ads have fallen about 50% over the last four years, and e-mail response has also fallen from its initial high rates. This is not true of video and rich media, where response rates have remained steady, perhaps due to the growing quality and novelty of online video.

How effective is online advertising compared to offline advertising? **Figure 7.7** provides some insight into this question. In general, the online channels (e-mail,

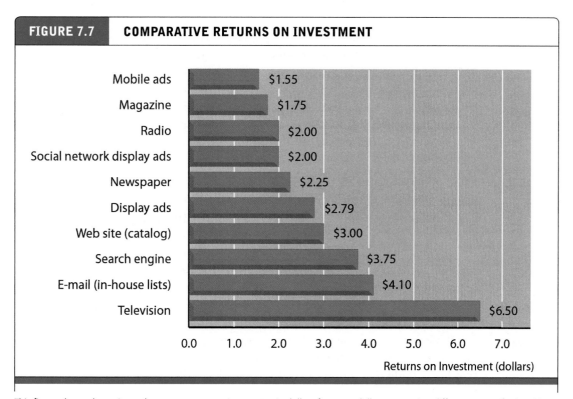

FIGURE 7.7 **COMPARATIVE RETURNS ON INVESTMENT**

Channel	Returns on Investment (dollars)
Mobile ads	$1.55
Magazine	$1.75
Radio	$2.00
Social network display ads	$2.00
Newspaper	$2.25
Display ads	$2.79
Web site (catalog)	$3.00
Search engine	$3.75
E-mail (in-house lists)	$4.10
Television	$6.50

This figure shows the estimated average return on investment in dollars for every dollar spent using different types of advertising techniques. These amounts are estimates and will vary by product, effectiveness, page placement, and degree of targeting.
SOURCES: Industry sources; authors' estimates.

search engine, banner ads, and video) compare very favorably with traditional channels. This explains in large part why online advertising has grown so rapidly in the last five years. Search engine advertising over the last five years has grown to be one of the most cost-effective forms of marketing communications and accounts for, in large part, the growth of Google, as well as other search engines. Surprisingly, direct opt-in e-mail is nearly twice as cost-effective as search engine advertising. This is, in part, because e-mail lists are so inexpensive compared to keywords, and because opt-in e-mail is a form of targeting people who are already interested in receiving more information.

There is growing evidence that the cost-effectiveness of search engine advertising has peaked, and may actually be declining because the cost of keywords has grown significantly, and the number of keywords being purchased has also expanded as retailers branch out from their core keywords into more peripheral words. The result is a rising cost per click and a declining efficacy of keywords that are peripheral to the brand. Growth in search engine advertising revenues are likely to slow in the near future, and search engine firms such as Google and Microsoft are seeking other opportunities for growth by purchasing advertising networks, display ad firms, and mobile ad firms. Future growth in online advertising does not lie in search, but in mobile, local, and social arenas.

A study of the comparative impacts of offline and online marketing concluded that the most powerful marketing campaigns used multiple forms of marketing, including online, catalog, television, radio, newspapers, and retail store. Traditional media like television and print media remain the primary means for consumers to find out about new products even though advertisers have reduced their budgets for print media ads. The consensus conclusion is that consumers who shop multiple channels are spending more than consumers who shop only with a single channel, in part because they have more discretionary income but also because of the combined number of "touchpoints" that marketers are making with the consumers. The fastest growing channel in consumer marketing is the multi-channel shopper.

THE COSTS OF ONLINE ADVERTISING

cost per thousand (CPM)
advertiser pays for impressions in 1,000 unit lots

cost per click (CPC)
advertiser pays prenegotiated fee for each click an ad receives

cost per action (CPA)
advertiser pays only for those users who perform a specific action

Effectiveness cannot be considered without an analysis of costs. Initially, most online ads were sold on a barter or **cost per thousand (CPM) impressions** basis, with advertisers purchasing impressions in 1,000-unit lots. Today, other pricing models have developed, including **cost per click (CPC)**, where the advertiser pays a prenegotiated fee for each click an ad receives, **cost per action (CPA)**, where the advertiser pays a prenegotiated amount only when a user performs a specific action, such as a registration or a purchase, and hybrid arrangements, combining two or more of these models (see **Table 7.6**).

While in the early days of e-commerce, a few online sites spent as much as $400 on marketing and advertising to acquire one customer, the average cost was never that high. **Table 7.7** shows the estimated average cost per acquisition for various types of media.

TABLE 7.6	DIFFERENT PRICING MODELS FOR ONLINE ADVERTISEMENTS
PRICING MODEL	DESCRIPTION
Barter	Exchange of ad space for something of equal value
Cost per thousand (CPM)	Advertiser pays for impressions in 1,000-unit lots
Cost per click (CPC)	Advertiser pays prenegotiated fee for each click ad received
Cost per action (CPA)	Advertiser pays only for those users who perform a specific action, such as registering, purchasing, etc.
Hybrid	Two or more of the above models used together
Sponsorship	Term-based; advertiser pays fixed fee for a slot on a Web site

While the costs for offline customer acquisition are higher than online, the offline items are typically far more expensive. If you advertise in the *Wall Street Journal,* you are tapping into a wealthy demographic that may be interested in buying islands, jets, other corporations, and expensive homes in France. A full-page black and white ad in the *Wall Street Journal* National Edition costs about $350,000, whereas other papers are in the $10,000 to $100,000 range. For these kinds of prices, you will need to either sell quite a few apples or a small number of corporate jet lease agreements.

One of the advantages of online marketing is that online sales can generally be directly correlated with online marketing efforts. If online merchants can obtain offline purchase data from a data broker, the merchants can measure precisely just how much revenue is generated by specific banners or e-mail messages sent to prospective customers. One way to measure the effectiveness of online marketing is by looking at the ratio of additional revenue received divided by the cost of the campaign (Revenue/Cost). Any positive whole number means the campaign was worthwhile.

TABLE 7.7	AVERAGE COST PER CUSTOMER ACQUISITION FOR SELECT MEDIA IN THE UNITED STATES, 2012
Internet search engine	$8.50
E-mail (opt-in)	$10.00
Television	$11.00
Magazine	$19.00
Yellow pages	$20.00
Newspaper	$25.00
Online display ads	$50.00
Direct mail	$50.00

SOURCES: Industry sources; authors' estimates.

A more complex situation arises when both online and offline sales revenues are affected by an online marketing effort. A large percentage of the online audience uses the Web to "shop" but not buy. These shoppers buy at physical stores. Merchants such as Sears and Walmart use e-mail to inform their registered customers of special offers available for purchase either online or at stores. Unfortunately, purchases at physical stores cannot be tied precisely with the online e-mail campaign. In these cases, merchants have to rely on less precise measures such as customer surveys at store locations to determine the effectiveness of online campaigns.

In either case, measuring the effectiveness of online marketing communications—and specifying precisely the objective (branding versus sales)—is critical to profitability. To measure marketing effectiveness, you need to understand the costs of various marketing media and the process of converting online prospects into online customers.

In general, online marketing communications are more costly on a CPM basis than traditional mass media marketing, but are more efficient in producing sales. **Table 7.8** shows costs for typical online and offline marketing communications. For instance, a local television spot (30 seconds) can cost $4,000–$40,000 to run the ad

TABLE 7.8	TRADITIONAL AND ONLINE ADVERTISING COSTS COMPARED
TRADITIONAL ADVERTISING	
Local television	$4,000 for a 30-second commercial during a movie; $45,000 for a highly rated show
Network television	$80,000–$600,000 for a 30-second spot during prime time; the average is $120,000 to $140,000
Cable television	$5,000–$8,000 for a 30-second ad during prime time
Radio	$200–$1,000 for a 60-second spot, depending on the time of day and program ratings
Newspaper	$120 per 1,000 circulation for a full-page ad
Magazine	$50 per 1,000 circulation for an ad in a regional edition of a national magazine, versus $120 per 1,000 for a local magazine
Direct mail	$15–$20 per 1,000 delivered for coupon mailings; $25–$40 per 1,000 for simple newspaper inserts
Billboard	$5,000–$25,000 for a 1–3 month rental of a freeway sign
ONLINE ADVERTISING	
Banner ads	$2–$15 per 1,000 impressions on a Web site, depending on how targeted the ad is (the more targeted, the higher the price)
Video and rich media	$20–$25 per 1,000 ads, depending on the Web site's demographics
E-mail	$5–$15 per 1,000 targeted e-mail addresses
Sponsorships	$30–$75 per 1,000 viewers, depending on the exclusivity of the sponsorship (the more exclusive, the higher the price)
Social network ads	$0.50–$3.00 per 1,000 impressions, with news feed ads at the high end of the range

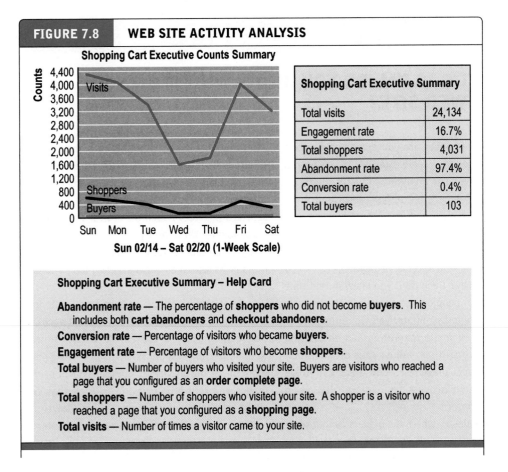

FIGURE 7.8 **WEB SITE ACTIVITY ANALYSIS**

Shopping Cart Executive Counts Summary

Sun 02/14 – Sat 02/20 (1-Week Scale)

Shopping Cart Executive Summary	
Total visits	24,134
Engagement rate	16.7%
Total shoppers	4,031
Abandonment rate	97.4%
Conversion rate	0.4%
Total buyers	103

Shopping Cart Executive Summary – Help Card

Abandonment rate — The percentage of **shoppers** who did not become **buyers**. This includes both **cart abandoners** and **checkout abandoners**.

Conversion rate — Percentage of visitors who became **buyers**.

Engagement rate — Percentage of visitors who become **shoppers**.

Total buyers — Number of buyers who visited your site. Buyers are visitors who reached a page that you configured as an **order complete page**.

Total shoppers — Number of shoppers who visited your site. A shopper is a visitor who reached a page that you configured as a **shopping page**.

Total visits — Number of times a visitor came to your site.

and an additional $40,000 to produce the ad, for a total cost of $44,000–$80,000. The ad may be seen by a population of, say, 2 million persons (impressions) in a local area for a CPM ranging from 2 to 4 cents, which makes television very inexpensive for reaching large audiences quickly. A Web site banner ad costs virtually nothing to produce and can be purchased at Web sites for a cost of from $2–$15 per thousand impressions. Direct postal mail can cost 80 cents to $1 per household drop for a post card, but e-mail can be sent for virtually nothing and costs only $5–$15 per thousand targeted names. Hence, e-mail is far less expensive than postal mail on a CPM basis.

SOFTWARE FOR MEASURING ONLINE MARKETING RESULTS

A number of software programs are available to automatically calculate activities at a Web site. **Figure 7.8** illustrates the information that a Web site activity analysis might provide.

Other software programs and services assist marketing managers in identifying exactly which marketing initiatives are paying off and which are not. See *Insight on Technology: It's 10 P.M. Do You Know Who Is On Your Web Site?* for a description of one such program.

INSIGHT ON TECHNOLOGY

IT'S 10 P.M. DO YOU KNOW WHO IS ON YOUR WEB SITE?

Chances are you don't know who is on your Web site, but if you used a Web site analytics software suite such as Adobe SiteCatalyst, you would. And if you did pay attention to these matters, you most surely would be making more money from your Web site, increasing your conversion rates by about 5% and your receive vs. payment (RVP) by up to 8%. Why? Because if you knew in real time what types of people were on your Web site hour by hour, minute by minute, you would be able to adjust your Web site marketing and advertising messages in real time, adjust your product mix, change product placement, and greatly improve the conversion process from mere visitors to actual purchasers.

In an industry where the players cannot seem to agree on standards for measuring Web site performance, and where webmasters are over-whelmed with literally millions of bits of information about the behavior of consumers on their Web sites, SiteCatalyst is working to help Web managers make sense of their clickstream traffic. SiteCatalyst is software as a service (SaaS) provided over the Internet to customers rather than installed on their firms' servers.

The company that created SiteCatalyst, Omniture, was purchased by Adobe Systems in 2009. Omniture has more than 5,100 customers across 91 countries, including six of the top 10 retailers, four of the top five travel companies, six of the top 10 media companies, and more. SiteCatalyst provides managers with the ability to measure, analyze, and integrate data from multiple marketing channels and technologies, including Web sites, social media, mobile, and video.

Other competitors in the same business include IBM Coremetrics and Yahoo WebAnalyt-ics; network management software and business intelligence vendors such as IBM SPSS, which offer Web analytics as part of their larger product offerings; and digital marketing and e-commerce services providers such as Digital River, which incorporate Web analytics in their services. Google markets its Google Analytics program to users of its search engine marketing tools AdSense and AdWords.

SiteCatalyst allows webmasters to monitor and analyze their Web traffic in real time, collect visitor intelligence, and enable faster adjustments to underperforming pages. It also provides most, if not all, of the answers to questions about performance and return on investment (ROI) that Web site marketing managers want. SiteCatalyst collects, processes, stores, and reports on Internet user behavior based on browser activity. Reports allow companies to measure which marketing initiatives visitors responded to, what search engines they used, what keywords they entered, how much time they spent on pages, what they bought online, when they abandoned shopping carts, and where they live. It also includes the ability to identify visitors across the different devices they use. The available reports and features include Web site navigation analysis, conversion rate analysis including calculating the long-term value of customers, marketing campaign measurement, and executive dashboards.

SiteCatalyst can evaluate a page-by-page navigation path a visitor has taken through a Web site. The service works by embedding a small piece of code into each HTML page a client wants to track and analyze. One benefit to clients is that SiteCatalyst eliminates the need to capture, store, and process log files, which are expensive to analyze and consume a good bit of a company's

(continued)

time and resources. SiteCatalyst does not need to be installed on a customer's own computers and infrastructure, but instead operates on a Web service (SaaS) model. There is no "installation" involved. Hence, maintenance and operational costs are borne by SiteCatalyst.

SiteCatalyst is able to segment customers in real time as they poke around a Web site. For instance, some visitors come for replacement parts and can be cross-sold other products from your firm in the process. Looking for a printer cartridge? Why not consider buying a whole new printer on sale today? Most visitors come to Web sites (especially brand-name Web sites like Microsoft, HP, or Macy's) looking for specific products. But as long as they are on your site, why not entice them to consider related products or services? If an L.L.Bean customer comes to LLBean.com looking for pajamas, SiteCatalyst is able to determine which ads and prompts lead to additional sales. In general, people looking for pajamas can be sold sleep- and warmth-related products like underwear, blankets, and pillows.

Not to be left behind by the rise of social media, the mobile platform, and video, Site-Catalyst also provides analytics aimed at each of those areas. If you have social media elements on your Web site like user comments, user-generated content, video with sharing possibilities, or bookmarking, SiteCatalyst's tools can help you understand the consumption and creation habits of visitors, identify how much the social elements add to sales, engage users with content that is motivational, and help create emotional links to your products and brand. Want to know who is clicking on the Like button and responding favorably to your site? SiteCatalyst can provide deep social profile information for your biggest fans. Site-Catalyst also enables you to track specific social media campaigns and make real-time adjustments as the effort unfolds, rather than after the fact.

On the mobile front, SiteCatalyst allows you to profile mobile audiences, devices, and applications on all major platforms; measure the performance of mobile content including mobile optimized Web sites, native mobile apps, and video; and optimize mobile app content for higher conversion. SiteCatalyst also offers its own interactive iPad application that provides on-the-fly exploration of key metrics.

SiteCatalyst also provides information on video performance that allows you to understand the impact of video across all marketing channels and by defined audience segments, as well as in-depth data on individual videos, comparisons between videos, and which part of a video is most engaging.

NBC Universal used all of these aspects of SiteCatalyst to understand how online visitors interact with its videos, including sharing and commenting on content and social networks such as Facebook, Tumblr, Google+, and others. Over five months, it collected and analyzed millions of viewer interactions and found, for example, that someone who went beyond merely viewing a video but instead opted to Like, share, or comment on it was much more likely to view additional video or digital content on NBC Universal's Web site. For instance, viewers who commented on a video watched seven times more video on the site.

Cars.com, a leading destination for online car shoppers, is another company that is using SiteCatalyst. Cars.com relies heavily on its Web site to drive its business. It has both a mobile Web site and an iPhone app to complement its traditional site, and managers wanted a better understanding of how its customers were using the technology. They also wanted a way for company marketers to gather data. Cars.com adopted SiteCatalyst to compile mobile and Web traffic data and gain a finer understanding of how their customers interact with content across all of its media platforms. For example, Cars.com is known for its splashy Super Bowl commercials. Using SiteCatalyst allowed the company to measure the return on its significant investment in the commercials, and to concretely determine the benefits of the ad to their mobile offerings. SiteCatalyst

(continued)

has made it easier and more efficient to generate reports because it centralizes data under a single dashboard. Cars.com is reaping the benefits of SiteCatalyst: its mobile traffic has grown significantly.

SteveMadden.com adopted SiteCatalyst to remove guessing from its marketing and Web site designs and replace it with hard data on consumer behavior. Steven Madden, Ltd. designs, sources, and sells footwear, handbags, and accessories. Its biggest customers include Macy's, DSW, Nordstrom, Famous Footwear, Dillard's, Lord & Taylor, and Victoria's Secret. Its own Web site, SteveMadden.com, plays an important part in the overall profit picture at the firm.

Prior to using SiteCatalyst, marketers at the firm's Web site did not know why visitors converted to shoppers, and had to guess which products and which promotional messages worked best. Marketers lacked real-time, actionable data on visitors to the site. What they wanted was the ability to

make changes to the Web site and see immediately how visitor behavior changed. Using SiteCatalyst, they are able to change offers, content, page functions, and other features, and measure results. In one test, for instance, marketers sought to reduce shopping cart abandonment by testing different versions of the shopping cart banner. A new version of the banner was shown to visitors from states where Steve Madden had retail stores: "Shop With Confidence." A second version was shown to visitors from states without Steve Madden stores: "Enjoy no sales tax." Both uses of what had been blank screen real estate boosted conversion ratios by 5%. In a second promotional test of e-mail messages to shoppers who signed up for Steve Madden marketing e-mails, customers were shown different banners involving countdown ("flash") sales, free shipping banners, and personalized messages based on prior purchases. These micro-level changes in marketing messages resulted in an average 7% increase in conversion.

SOURCES: "Adobe SiteCatalyst Product Overview," Adobe, 2012; "NBC Universal," Adobe Digital Marketing Suite Success Story, 2012; "SEC Form 10K for the fiscal year ending December 31, 2010," Steve Madden, Ltd., filed February 28, 2011; "SEC Form 10K for the fiscal year ending December 3, 2010," Adobe Systems Incorporated, filed January 27, 2011; "Steve Madden Mobile Revenue Exceeds $1M in 2010," by Rimma Kats, Mobilecommercenews.com, January 27, 2011; "SteveMadden.com Increases Sales and Continuously Optimizes E-commerce Site," Case Study, SteveMadden.com, August 2010; "Cars.com uses Adobe SiteCatalyst to Measure Mobile Application Adoption," August 2010.

7.3 THE WEB SITE AS A MARKETING COMMUNICATIONS TOOL

One of the strongest online marketing communications tools is a functional Web site that customers can find easily, and, once there, locate what they are looking for quickly. In some ways, a Web site can be viewed as an extended online advertisement. An appropriate domain name, search engine optimization, and proper Web site design are integral parts of a coordinated marketing communications strategy, and ultimately, necessary conditions for e-commerce success.

DOMAIN NAMES

One of the first communications an e-commerce Web site has with a prospective customer is via its URL. Domain names play an important role in reinforcing an existing brand and/or developing a new brand. There are a number of considerations to take into account in choosing a domain name. Ideally, a domain name should be short, memorable, not easily confused with others, and difficult to misspell. The name of a Web site may or may not reflect the nature of the company's business. The name of most major brands do not. Companies that choose a name unrelated to the nature of their business must be willing to spend extra time, effort, and money to establish the name as a brand. Dot-com domain names (as opposed to .net or .org) are still considered the most preferable, especially in the United States.

Today, however, it may be difficult to find a domain name that satisfies all of the above criteria. While it may appear that most of the "good" and simplest names have been taken, recent very high growth firms like Instagram, Pinterest, Glam, Gilt, and many others suggest the supply of workable names is quite large. A number of companies exist that list domain names for sale (such as GreatDomains.com and BuyDomains.com). Most of the online domain registration sites such as Networksolutions.com, Godaddy.com, and Register.com have tools that can help you find appropriate names.

SEARCH ENGINE OPTIMIZATION

Given that around 115 million adult Americans use search engines daily, it makes sense for a company to optimize its Web site for search engine recognition. Despite the fact that most major search engines allow Web sites to pay for inclusion in their search results listing (but not the organic ranking), and most major search engines have also adopted a paid search engine advertising model, it is still advisable to take the steps needed to objectively improve a Web site's visibility to search engines. Even if you use paid search engine marketing, by optimizing your Web site to improve its rank in the organic listings, you increase the chances of being noticed by consumers on the all-important first page of search results, and reduce your customer acquisition costs. For small firms, organic ranking is the primary tool for driving sales.

Search engines today operate with the use of Web crawlers, software programs that search the Web for pages, index their content, identify the number of sites linking to the page, and report the content to very large databases where it can be searched.

The method of indexing and ranking Web pages varies across search engines and is proprietary. Typically, Web pages are organically ranked using a kind of popularity index called "page rank" in which very popular pages (many sites link to these pages, and these pages link to many other sites) are ranked higher, and therefore appear higher on the search results page. Sponsored links, where the firm pays search engines for appearing on a search page, will generally rank higher than organic links. There are many consulting firms, books, and online sources that provide guidance on how to enhance the visibility of a Web site to crawler programs. Most of this advice is quite commonsensical and none of it is guaranteed to work despite the promises.

The first step in improving a firm's search engine ranking is to register with as many search engines as possible, so that a user looking for similar Web sites has a chance of coming across the firm's site. Nearly all search engines have registration pages.

The second step to improve a firm's ranking is to ensure that keywords used in the Web site description match keywords likely to be used as search terms by prospective customers. Using the keyword "lamps," for example, will not help your search engine ranking if most prospective customers are searching for "lights." Search engines differ, but most search engines read home page title tags, metatags, and other text on the home page in order to understand and index the content of the page.

Third, place keywords in a Web site's metatag and page title. A *metatag* is an HTML tag containing a list of words describing the Web site. Metatags are heavily used by search engines to determine the relevance of Web sites to search terms used frequently by users. The title tag provides a brief description of the Web site's content. The words in both the metatags and the title tags should match words on the home page. In addition, it is wise to include many references on the home page to the subject matter of likely consumer searches. Most crawlers will index the text content of the home page and may not go deeper into the Web site's secondary pages.

Fourth, link the Web site to as many other Web sites as possible, both in-coming links and out-going links. Search engines evaluate both kinds of links, and their quality, to identify how popular a page is and the number of links it has to other content on the Web. Search engines such as Google are guessing that when you enter a query for a product, chances are good that the product is located at one of the highly connected Web sites. The assumption is that the more links there are to a Web site, the more useful the Web site must be. How can a firm increase links to its Web site? Placing advertising is one way: banner ads, buttons, and interstitials are all links to a firm's Web site. You can also create Web sites, even hundreds of Web sites, whose only function is to link to your main Web site, although search engines can discover this and place you on the last page of search returns. Entering into affiliate relationships with other Web sites is another method. Search engines attempt to identify all efforts to mislead their search engines with varying and unknown success.

While the steps listed above are a beginning, increasing a firm's ranking is still a bit of an art form and usually requires a full-time professional effort to tweak metatags, keywords, and network links before solid results are obtained. The task often requires several months and is complicated by the fact that each search engine uses slightly different indexing methods, and changes their indexing methods in order to fool search engine optimizers.

WEB SITE FUNCTIONALITY

Attracting users to a company's Web site is the objective of marketing, but once a consumer is at a Web site, the sales process begins. This means that whatever brought the individuals to the Web site becomes much less relevant, and what they find at the Web site will ultimately determine whether they will make a purchase or return. Recall that a Web page and Web site are, first and foremost, a software interface. The question is: What makes for an effective software interface? In general, people use software interfaces that they perceive to be useful and easy to use (a literature that is referred to as the "technology acceptance model"). Utility and ease of use are, therefore, the main factors to focus on when designing a site. Other factors involved in the credibility and trust that users place in a Web site—both are very important for making decisions—are described in a growing literature on Web site design (Garzotta, 2010; Hausman, et al., 2009; Fogg, et al., 2003). In an exploratory study of Web site credibility based on 2,600 participants, the top three factors in Web site credibility were

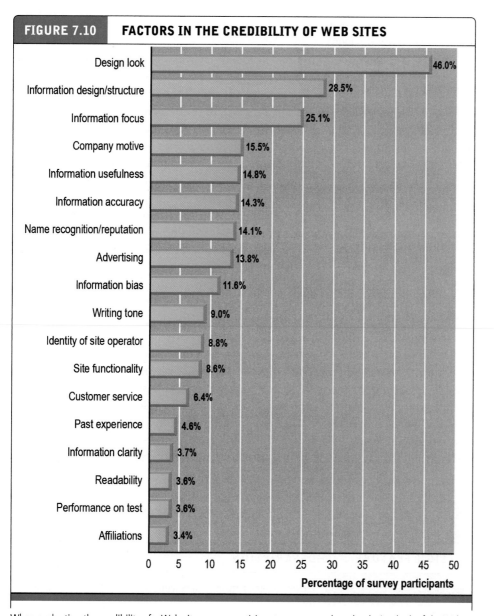

FIGURE 7.10 **FACTORS IN THE CREDIBILITY OF WEB SITES**

Factor	Percentage
Design look	46.0%
Information design/structure	28.5%
Information focus	25.1%
Company motive	15.5%
Information usefulness	14.8%
Information accuracy	14.3%
Name recognition/reputation	14.1%
Advertising	13.8%
Information bias	11.6%
Writing tone	9.0%
Identity of site operator	8.8%
Site functionality	8.6%
Customer service	6.4%
Past experience	4.6%
Information clarity	3.7%
Readability	3.6%
Performance on test	3.6%
Affiliations	3.4%

Percentage of survey participants

When evaluating the credibility of a Web site, survey participants commented on the design look of the Web site more than any other Web site feature.

SOURCE: Based on data from Fogg, et al., 2003.

design look, information design/structure, and information focus (Fogg, et al., 2003) (see **Figure 7.10**). Similar results were reported by Flanigan and Metzger in a 2007 study (Flanigan and Metzger, 2007). The message is: design counts. The authors of this study were disappointed that users were most impressed by the design look of a Web site rather than its utility or ease of use. While important, design is one of many factors effecting consumer purchases. In a study weighing the relative importance of Web site design quality versus service quality, service quality was a much stronger predictor of trust and satisfaction, which in turn was related to repurchase (customer loyalty) (Zhou, et al., 2008).

Research on Web site utilization has found that the way information is organized on a Web site, while important for first-time users, declines in importance over time. Gradually, information content becomes the major factor attracting further visits (Tarafdar and Zhang, 2008; Davern, et al., 2001). In this research, frequency of Web site use is a function of four independent variables: content quality, Web site organization, perceived usefulness of the Web site, and perceived ease of use. Over time, people get used to the organization of a Web site and learn how to use it effectively to gather information. This suggests that improving content and usefulness ought to be the first priority of a firm, and that Web site redesign should be implemented carefully and incrementally. Radically redesigning a site runs the risk of losing the "lock-in" effects that Web sites can induce (Davern, et al., 2001). Most firms risk user discomfort and eventually abandon old designs and seek out more useful and interesting designs that produce more sales: 65% of the top 500 Internet retailers redesigned their sites at least somewhat in 2010 (Internet Retailer, 2010). Web site design evolves over short periods of time, and requires continual reassessment of existing designs to ensure they are contemporary (Golander and Tractinsky, 2012).

In Chapter 4 (Section 4.4, especially Table 4.11), we identified eight basic design features that were necessary, from a business point of view, to attract and retain customers. The Web site must be functional, informative, employ simple navigation (ease of use), use redundant navigation, make it easy for customers to purchase, and feature multi-browser functionality, simple graphics, and legible text. Researchers have also found a number of other design factors that marketing managers should be aware of (see **Table 7.9**). In a study weighing the relative importance of Web site design quality versus service quality, service quality was a much stronger predictor

TABLE 7.9	WEB SITE DESIGN FEATURES THAT IMPACT ONLINE PURCHASING
DESIGN FEATURE	**DESCRIPTION**
Compelling experience	Provide interactivity, entertainment, human interest; site is fun to use
Editorial content	Provide helpful content, opinions, and features on subjects of interest to visitors in order to increase stickiness
Fast download times	Quicker is better; if longer, provide amusement
Easy product list navigation	Consumers easily find the products they want
Few clicks to purchase	The shorter the click list, the greater the chance of a sale
Customer choice agents	Recommendation agents/configurators help the consumer make quick, correct choices
Customer support	Personal e-mail response; 1-800 phone capability shown on Web site

of trust and satisfaction, which in turn was related to repurchase (customer loyalty) (Zhou, et al., 2008).

Sites that offer a "compelling experience" in the sense of providing entertainment with commerce or interactivity, or that are perceived as "fun" to use, are more successful in attracting and keeping visitors (Internet Retailer, 2010; Novak, et al., 2000). Web sites with editorial content that informs users also increases the time users spend on the Web site and increases the chance of them purchasing a product or service. While simplicity of design is hard to define, Lohse et al. (2000) found that the most important factor in predicting monthly sales was product list navigation and choice features that save consumers time. Thus, Amazon's "one-click" purchase capability is a powerful tool for increasing sales.

More and more Web sites are using interactive consumer-decision aids to help the shopper make choices. Recommendation agents are programs that can suggest a product based on either consumer surveys or a review of a consumer's profile. For example, Dell uses an online configurator to help consumers decide which computer to order.

Responsiveness of Web sites is also important to credibility. Firms are improving but have a long way to go. An eGain survey found that 70% of leading North American enterprise businesses were rated "below average" or "poor" in multi-channel customer service experience, although the online retail sector was a bright spot, with better scores than the previous year (eGain, 2010). In general, large companies with Web sites receive favorable respect ratings for "simplicity of design and use" but weak ratings on responding to customers. Other researchers have found that consumers purchase more at sites where there are strong privacy policies and these are known to visitors (Tsai, et al., 2007).

No matter how successful the offline and online marketing campaign, a Web site that fails to deliver information, customer convenience, and responsiveness spells disaster. Attention to these Web site design features will help ensure success.

Instant Ads:
Real-Time Marketing on Exchanges

The holy grail of advertising and marketing is to deliver the right message to the right person at the right time. If this were possible, no one would receive ads they did not want to see, and then no advertising dollars would be wasted, reducing the costs to end users and increasing the efficiency of each ad dollar. In the physical world, only a very rough approximation of this ideal is possible. Advertisers can buy television and radio spots, newspaper ads, and billboards based on broad demographics and interests of likely potential customers. The Internet promised to change this. On the Internet, ads supposedly could be targeted to individual consumers based on their personal characteristics, interests, and recent clickstream behavior. One early vision of e-commerce was a trade-off between privacy and efficiency: let us know a little more about you, and we will show you only the advertising and products you are interested in seeing, and even offer free content. E-commerce was supposed to end the mass advertising that exploded in the television era.

But contrary to popular impressions and the fears of privacy advocates, most of the display ads shown to site visitors are marvelously irrelevant to visitors' interests, both short term and long term. For this reason, the click-through rate for banner advertising is a stunningly low 0.03%, and the price of display ads has fallen to a few cents because of their poor performance. Check this out: point your browser at Yahoo (the largest display advertiser on earth), look at the prominent ads shown on the right, and ask yourself if you are really interested in the ad content at this moment in time. How about ever? Chances are slim you are interested at this moment even if the ad is somewhat appropriate to your demographics. Often, it's an ad for something you are totally not interested in and never have been. In 2011, only 20% of Internet users find display ads on Web sites are relevant to their interests, up only slightly from previous years.

A part of the problem is that online display ad publishers like Yahoo, and the advertising networks they ended up owning, did not know very much about you (until recently), and what they did know was quite general: gender, zip code, age, and perhaps some prior purchases. They could build a "profile" of you, but it was very imprecise. The resulting ads displayed were frequently far off the mark of what you were interested in at the moment. And even if they knew everything about you, the advertising networks did not have the mechanism to sell that information instantly to a potential advertiser. For this reason, banner ads displayed on the Web sites you visited in the past rarely had anything to do with your interests at the time. Rather than achieve the holy grail of advertising, much of Web-based display advertising was extraordinarily ignorant of who you were or what you were looking for. Search engine advertising was typically better, since it would be responding to search terms you yourself had entered.

Behavioral targeting and tracking of online behavior have begun to improve the situation for display advertisers by expanding the scope, breadth, and depth of personal information, making it possible for advertisers to fine-tune their display ads and to develop a much finer-grained, digital image of individual customers—real people, not just profiles. Using beacons, Web bugs, cookies, and Flash cookies, almost all the top Web sites now install tracking software onto visitor computers. A *Wall Street Journal* study of the 50 top Web sites in the United States, accounting for 40% of U.S. page views, found these sites installed 3,180 tracking files on a test computer that visited each site. Only one top-50 site installed no tracking files: Wikipedia. Over two-thirds of the tracking files were installed by 131 companies. Guess who the biggest trackers were? Google, Microsoft, and Yahoo. The vast majority of these tracking files are third-party cookies and beacons. (They are not installed by the Web site you are visiting, but through a commercial arrangement with the Web site you are visiting, tracking firms are allowed to place cookies and beacons.) What the *Journal* stumbled onto was an entire ecosystem of firms ranging from Internet giants like Yahoo, Google, and Microsoft, to smaller data aggregators, and finally to huge advertising firms that pay for the data their clients want to use in targeting ads.

Today, when a user visits a site, a tracking number or cookie is assigned to the user. Often a "beacon" or Web bug is installed, which captures what people are typing on a Web site. For instance, a beacon will record your comments on automobiles, illness, or favorite movies, as well as the fact you like *Dancing With the Stars*, do crossword puzzles, bought a Kindle, purchased romantic titles, have an iPad, and installed the *New York Times* reader. When the user visits other sites where the tracking firm has installed its software, the user is recognized, more behavior is observed, and this information is added to the original cookie file on the user's computer, or sent to the firm's tracking server using the installed beacon. The file keeps growing the more the user visits Web sites. Facebook has three tools in 2011 for targeting ads: it sells advertisers the topics you are interested in, the sites you follow as a fan, and profile information such as newlyweds, moving, college, as well as personal education and other data.

So what happens to all this information about you and others? The cookie and beacon owners collect all this information and sell it to advertisers. On the basis of all this personal and clickstream information, a profile of the individual user is developed by data exchange firms such as BlueKai Inc. and eXelate Media as well as the three big players. EXelate claims to have anonymous data on more than 400 million unique users who visit more than 500 of the most popular Web sites.

The information and the profile are sold to advertisers usually for 10 cents a piece. Advertisers specify the profiles they are looking for: male, 24 to 35 years old, urban, drives a sports sedan, sports fan, high income, and likes books (think possible BMW customer). Once individuals fitting this profile appear at a Web site, the advertiser pays to have a pre-fabricated ad displayed to that person. Voila! Targeting, personalization! A more efficient market communications process, happier Internet users who see what they are interested in looking at, and users who click more often.

Not quite yet. One thing is missing from this heady mix of behavioral tracking and targeting: immediacy. When you click on a search engine result, it's because you are interested in that product or service right now, this moment, this instant. Google, which is currently used by 75% of global Internet users, or approximately 1.5 billion people, is believed to be the largest and best repository of immediate user interests. For display ads, even targeted ones, this has not been possible until recently. Previously, online advertisers reserved slots (available pages, location on page, time of day/week) based on their best guesstimates of the types of people (i.e., profiles) who would show up to see those pages and be exposed to the ad. They really were clueless when it came to who you are and what you were interested in at the moment of opening a Web page. Advertisers could not make on-the-fly, instant decisions about ads to show Web site visitors based on what they were doing just before this instant, and just before they landed on a page.

In 2012, this situation is changing, and for the first time display advertisers, portals, and ad networks they own are building the capability to display banner ads that are based on the granular behavior of individuals just prior to displaying the ad. There are two players here: the often small-fry data collection firms (the third-party owners of cookies and beacons) and the large players. Both are developing data exchanges where advertisers can purchase all the individual-level data available. The second part of the change is the really large Web advertisers like Google, Microsoft, Facebook, and Yahoo who have each developed real-time ad exchanges that permit advertisers to bid for ad spaces in the few milliseconds between a user entering a Web address (or clicking on a search query) and the page appearing, based on the data purchased from data exchanges. Ad exchanges are middlemen who stand between Web site publishers who have ad space to sell and advertisers who want to display ads to highly targeted audiences. Generally, publishers prefer to sell most of their inventory directly to advertisers and avoid paying a middleman, like Google's Ad Exchange. But they often have excess inventory and use ad exchanges to sell this unused inventory. Ad exchanges use real-time bidding (RTB) to allocate publisher ad spaces to advertisers.

Ad exchanges allow advertisers to purchase inventory in an eBay-like auction environment. Advertisers can enter the kind of ad they want from display, pre-roll to a video, or other rich media ad, enter the desired demographics and audience characteristics, and the price range, and then click a button. When users enter a Web site, they are screened in a few milliseconds to see if they fit the profile, and if so, they are shown the ad.

For instance, Google has developed a real-time bidding (RTB) system or exchange for selling and buying display ads. Ad sellers (Web publishers) provide the inventory of slots available on the Internet. Ad buyers bid on these slots based on the likelihood their ads will be seen by the kinds of people they are targeting. Google calls this the DoubleClick Ad Exchange; Yahoo calls its exchange Right Media. Currently, more than 50 advertising networks buy display ads through Google's network. With ad exchanges, advertisers buy ads in milliseconds between the time you enter a URL on your keyboard and the time the Web page loads. In that interval, advertisers can decide, based on your cookies and beacon data they have acquired, what ad to show you.

According to Forrester, advertisers spent $353 million in the United States on RTB advertising in 2010, and this more than doubled in 2011 to $823 million—roughly 8% of total display spending. These ad exchanges have moved closer to the ideal Web advertising environment by allowing advertisers to decide where to place their ads on the fly, based on fairly solid data on the people most likely to see the ad. This is far different from the traditional ad placement process, which placed ads weeks and months in advance of the ad being displayed.

Facebook launched its own ad exchange in September 2012 as a way to monetize its huge audience. Facebook Exchange allows ad technology companies called "demand side platforms," which gather pools of targeted audiences, to sell these audiences to advertisers through automated systems that allow buyers to bid for targeted audiences. For instance, an airline with extra seats for flights from New York to Los Angeles could target an ad on Facebook to people who had searched for a Los Angeles flight but didn't buy a ticket, or an ad for a Los Angeles hotel for someone who booked a flight but not a hotel room. The Facebook Exchange will only sell standard Marketplace ads (small ads on the right side of a users page). How does Facebook know what its users have searched for? There are two ways. Facebook can place a cookie on its users' browsers that records the users' searches, including search terms on Google or another search engine. A second way is to work with ad networks who have placed cookies on users' browsers prior to visiting Facebook. Facebook will not allow advertisers to gain access to users' Facebook data (Likes, friends, and content posts) and will not be selling user profiles. So for now, the Facebook Exchange is simply a way for advertisers to gain access to people when they are on Facebook. Because Facebook does not allow Google, or other content miners, to gain access to Facebook pages, and that Facebook is therefore a kind of walled garden that advertisers can only reach by going through Facebook Exchange or other ad services owned by Facebook.

One problem that has arisen with instant real-time auctions of access to customers is that there are no agreed-on audience measures to assure advertisers that the ads were really delivered to the target audience. For instance, when advertisers buy a 6 p.m. local news slot for a 60-second ad, a variety of audience measuring firms from Nielsen to comScore will verify the ads were actually delivered. But with instant ad selection and delivery, there is no direct way to ensure the target audience actually received the ads. Several firms have stepped into this market in 2011 and 2012 with tools for proving the intended audience really did receive the ads.

SOURCES: "Ad Tech Company eXelate Raises $12M," by Ted O'Hear, Techcrunch.com, September 24, 2012; "Facebook Efforts on Advertising Face a Day of Judgment," by Somini Sengupta, *New York Times*, July 22, 2012; "Facebook Exchange and the Rise of Real-Time Ad Bidding," by Michael Baker, *Forbes*, June 14, 2012; "Facebook to Debut Ad Exchange in Bid to Boost Revenues" by Robert Hof, *Forbes*, June 13, 2012; "What's a Facebook Ad Exchange?" by Peter Kafka, *All Things Digital*, June 13, 2012; "ComScore, eXelate Cleaning Up 'Garbage In, Garbage Out,'" by Erin Griffith, *Ad Week,* August 16, 2011; "Tracking the Trackers: Early Results," by Jonathon River, Stanford Center for Internet and Society, July 121, 2011; "Real-Time Bidding Becomes a $832 Million Market in 2011," by Michael Barrett, AdAgeDigital, February 8, 2011; "Google Agonizes on Privacy as Ad World Vaults Ahead," by Jessica Vascellaro, *Wall Street Journal,* August 10, 2010; "Sites Feed Personal Details to New Tracking Industry," by Julia Angwin and Tom McGinty, *Wall Street Journal,* July 30, 2010; "Yahoo Finally Allows Real-Time Bidding on Network and Exchange," Kate Kaye, ClickZ.com, March 15, 2010; "Instant Ads Set the Pace on the Web," by Stephanie Clifford, *New York Times;* March 10, 2010; "Online Ad Auctions," by Hal Varian, Draft, University of California and Google, February 16, 2009.

Case Study Questions

1. Pay a visit to your favorite portal and count the total ads on the opening page. Count how many of these ads are (a) immediately of interest and relevant to you, (b) sort of interesting or relevant but not now, and (c) not interesting or relevant. Do this 10 times and calculate the percentage of the three kinds of situations. Describe what you find and explain the results using this case.

2. Advertisers use different kinds of "profiles" in the decision to display ads to customers. Identify the different kinds of profiles described in this case, and explain why they are relevant to online display advertising.

3. How can display ads achieve search-engine–like results?

4. Do you think instant display ads based on your immediately prior clickstream will be as effective as search engine marketing techniques? Why or why not?

7.5 REVIEW

KEY CONCEPTS

- **Identify the major forms of online marketing communications.**

Marketing communications include promotional sales communications that encourage immediate purchases and branding communications that focus on extolling the differentiable benefits of consuming a product or service. There are a number of different forms of marketing communications:

- *Banner and rich media/video ads* are promotional messages that users can respond to by clicking on the banner and following the link to a product description or offering. Variations include different size banners, buttons, skyscrapers, pop-ups, and pop-unders. Rich media ads use Flash, HTML5, Java, JavaScript, and streaming audio and/or video, and typically seek to involve users more deeply than static banner ads.
- *Paid search engine inclusion and placement* allows firms to pay search engines for inclusion in the search engine index (formerly free and based on "objective" criteria), receiving a guarantee that their firm will appear in the results of relevant searches.
- *Mobile advertising* involves using display ads, search engine advertising, video ads, and mobile messaging on mobile devices such as smartphones and tablet computers.
- *Social advertising*, on social networks, blogs, and in games, involves using the social graph to communicate brand images and directly promote sales of products and services.
- *Local advertising* involves advertising products and services based on the geographic location of the user, and is intimately connected with both mobile advertising and search advertising.
- *Sponsorships* are paid efforts to tie an advertiser's name to particular information, an event, or a venue in a way that reinforces its brand in a positive yet not overtly commercial manner. Advertorials are a common form of online sponsorship.
- *Affiliate relationships* permit a firm to put its logo or banner ad on another firm's Web site from which users of that site can click through to the affiliate's site.
- *Direct e-mail marketing* sends e-mail directly to interested users, and has proven to be one of the most effective forms of marketing communications. The key to effective direct e-mail marketing is "interested users"—Internet users who, at one time or another, have expressed an interest in receiving messages from the advertiser (people who have "opted in").
- *Offline marketing* combined with *online marketing* communications is typically the most effective. Although many e-commerce ventures want to rely heavily on online communications, marketing communications campaigns most successful at driving traffic have incorporated both online and offline tactics.

- **Understand the costs and benefits of online marketing communications.**

Key terms that one must know in order to understand evaluations of online marketing communications' effectiveness and its costs and benefits include:

- *Impressions*—the number of times an ad is served.
- *Click-through rate*—the number of times an ad is clicked.
- *View-through rate*—the 30-day response rate to an ad.
- *Hits*—the number of http requests received by a firm's server.
- *Page views*—the number of pages viewed by visitors.
- *Stickiness (duration)*—the average length of time visitors remain at a site.
- *Unique visitors*—the number of distinct, unique visitors to a site.
- *Loyalty*—the percentage of purchasers who return in a year.
- *Reach*—the percentage of total consumers in a market who will visit a site.
- *Recency*—the average number of days elapsed between visits.
- *Acquisition rate*—the percentage of visitors who indicate an interest in the site's product, by registering or visiting product pages.
- *Conversion rate*—the percentage of visitors who purchase something.
- *Browse-to-buy ratio*—the ratio of items purchased to product views.
- *View-to-cart ratio*—the ratio of "Add to cart" clicks to product views.
- *Cart conversion rate*—the ratio of actual orders to "Add to cart" clicks.
- *Checkout conversion rate*—the ratio of actual orders to checkouts started.
- *Abandonment rate*—the percentage of shoppers who begin a shopping cart form, but then fail to complete the form.
- *Retention rate*—the percentage of existing customers who continue to buy on a regular basis.
- *Attrition rate*—the percentage of customers who purchase once, but do not return within a year.
- *Conversation ratio*—the number of comments produced per post to a site.
- *Applause ratio*—the number of Likes or Shares per post.
- *Amplification*—the number of re-tweets or re-shares per post.
- *Sentiment ratio*—the ratio of positive comments to total comments.
- *Open rate*—the percentage of customers who open the mail and are exposed to the message.
- *Delivery rate*—the percentage of e-mail recipients who received the e-mail.
- *Click-through rate (e-mail)*—the percentage of e-mail recipients who clicked through to the offer.
- *Bounce-back rate*—the percentage of e-mails that could not be delivered.

Studies have shown that low click-through rates are not indicative of a lack of commercial impact of online advertising, and that advertising communication does occur even when users do not directly respond by clicking. Online advertising in its various forms has been shown to boost brand awareness and brand recall, create positive brand perceptions, and increase intent to purchase.

Effectiveness cannot be considered without analysis of cost. Typical pricing models for online marketing communications include:

- *Barter*—the exchange of ad space for something of equal value.
- *Cost per thousand (CPM)*—the advertiser pays for impressions in 1,000-unit lots.
- *Cost per click (CPC)*—the advertiser pays a prenegotiated fee for each click an ad receives.
- *Cost per action (CPA)*—the advertiser pays only for those users who perform a specific action.
- *Hybrid models*—combines two or more other models.
- *Sponsorships*—the advertiser pays a fixed fee for a particular term.

Online marketing communications are typically less costly than traditional mass media marketing. Also, online sales can generally be directly correlated with online marketing efforts, unlike traditional marketing communications tactics.

The online merchant can measure precisely just how much revenue is generated by specific banners or specific e-mail messages sent to prospective customers.

■ **Discuss the ways in which a Web site can be used as a marketing communications tool.**

A functional Web site that customers can find is one of the strongest online communications tools. The following are all integral parts of a coordinated marketing communications strategy:

- *Appropriate domain name*—Companies should choose a domain name that is short, memorable, hard to confuse or misspell, and indicative of a firm's business functions, and that preferably uses .com as its top-level domain.
- *Search engine optimization*—Companies should register with all the major search engines so that a user looking for similar sites has a better chance of finding that particular site, ensure that keywords used in the Web site description match keywords likely to be used as search terms by prospective customers, and link the site to as many other sites as possible.
- *Web site functionality*—Once at a Web site, visitors need to be enticed to stay and to buy. Web site design features that impact online purchasing include how compelling the experience of using the Web site is, download time, product list navigation, the number of clicks required to purchase, the existence of customer choice agents, and the Web site's responsiveness to customer needs.

QUESTIONS

1. Explain the difference between marketing and marketing communications.
2. Explain the difference between branding communications and sales/promotional communications.
3. What are some reasons why online advertising constitutes only about 15% of the total advertising market?
4. What kinds of products are most suited to being advertised online?
5. What is the difference between an interstitial ad and a superstitial ad?
6. What are some of the reasons for the decline in click-through rates on banner ads today? How can banner ads be made more effective?
7. Why are some affiliate relationships called "tenancy" deals? How do they differ from pure affiliate arrangements?
8. There is some controversy surrounding paid placements on search engines. What are the issues surrounding paid-placement search engines? Why might consumers object to this practice?
9. What are some of the advantages of direct e-mail marketing?
10. Why is offline advertising still important?
11. What is the difference between hits and page views? Why are these not the best measurements of Web traffic? Which is the preferred metric for traffic counts?
12. Define CTR, CPM, CPC, CPA, and VTR.

13. What are the key attributes of a good domain name?

14. What are some of the steps a firm can take to optimize its search engine rankings?

15. List and describe some Web site design features that impact online purchasing.

PROJECTS

1. Use the Online Consumer Purchasing Model (Figure 7.7) to assess the effectiveness of an e-mail campaign at a small Web site devoted to the sales of apparel to the ages 18–26 young adult market in the United States. Assume a marketing campaign of 100,000 e-mails (at 25 cents per e-mail address). The expected click-through rate is 5%, the customer conversion rate is 10%, and the loyal customer retention rate is 25%. The average sale is $60, and the profit margin is 50% (the cost of the goods is $30). Does the campaign produce a profit? What would you advise doing to increase the number of purchases and loyal customers? What Web design factors? What communications messages?

2. Surf the Web for at least 15 minutes. Visit at least two different e-commerce sites. Make a list describing in detail all the different marketing communication tools you see being used. Which do you believe is the most effective and why?

3. Do a search for a product of your choice on at least three search engines. Examine the results page carefully. Can you discern which results, if any, are a result of a paid placement? If so, how did you determine this? What other marketing communications related to your search appear on the page?

4. Examine the use of rich media and video in advertising. Find and describe at least two examples of advertising using streaming video, sound, or other rich media technologies. (Hint: Check the sites of Internet advertising agencies for case studies or examples of their work.) What are the advantages and/or disadvantages of this kind of advertising? Prepare a 3- to 5-page report on your findings.

5. Visit your Facebook page and examine the ads shown in the right margin. What is being advertised and how do you believe it is relevant to your interests or online behavior? You could also search on a retail product on Google several times, and related products, then visit Yahoo or another popular site to see if your past behavior is helping advertisers track you.

CHAPTER 8

Ethical, Social, and Political Issues in E-commerce

After reading this chapter, you will be able to:

■ Understand why e-commerce raises ethical, social, and political issues.

■ Recognize the main ethical, social, and political issues raised by e-commerce.

■ Identify a process for analyzing ethical dilemmas.

■ Understand basic concepts related to privacy.

■ Identify the practices of e-commerce companies that threaten privacy.

■ Describe the different methods used to protect online privacy.

■ Understand the various forms of intellectual property and the challenges involved in protecting it.

■ Understand how governance of the Internet has evolved over time.

■ Explain why taxation of e-commerce raises governance and jurisdiction issues.

■ Identify major public safety and welfare issues raised by e-commerce.

Internet Free Speech:
Who Decides?

Now that nearly all of our public and private life has moved online, who determines whether what we choose to say can be disseminated to the rest of the world via the Internet? There seem to be several possibilities here. One is that the private companies that now dominate and control the primary communication channels on the Internet, namely Google (including YouTube), Facebook, and Twitter, are actually the ones who can and do control what can be distributed with the click of a mouse. The second possibility is that governments are the ones that make the determination. As powerful as some private companies are, they are totally dependent on the good will of the governments of the countries in which they

© kentoh / Shutterstock

operate, which, if deemed necessary, could pull the plug on those firms or make their life difficult in other ways. There now also seems to be a third possibility: any group that is powerful enough to threaten the social order appears to be able to influence what is disseminated on the Internet.

As a case in point, in July 2012, a 14-minute movie trailer from a reputed feature-length film called *The Innocence of Muslims* was released on the Internet. The amateurish trailer was a scathing, satirical attack that ridiculed the prophet Muhammad. Muhammad is portrayed by an actor in the video as a mortal with several character defects. Any image or graphic depicting Muhammad is considered blasphemous in the Islamic faith, and public criticism of Islam is generally not tolerated in Muslim countries. The 1971 Broadway musical *Jesus Christ Superstar* similarly portrayed Jesus and his disciples as mortals, with less than holy motivations and attitudes. The trailer, apparently shot in the United States, was translated into Arabic by unknown persons. In September, after several months of languishing in the backwaters of the Internet, the video suddenly went viral throughout the Arab world, via Google and other search engines in response to user queries, and on Google's YouTube. An international firestorm ensued. Islamic groups, first in the Middle East and then throughout the Muslim world, protested the video, and in some cases, riots ensued, along with attacks on American embassies led by armed and organized militant groups. In Benghazi, Libya, the American consulate was attacked and burned, and U.S. Ambassador J. Christopher Stevens, along with three other Americans, was killed on September 11, 2012. Protests and riots around the world continued for an entire week.

A full-feature length film does not apparently exist. The filmmaker has been identified as a California man named Nakoula Basseley Nakoula, who used the alias "Sam Bacile." The actors in the video claim to have been duped, with anti-Islamic words dubbed over the lines they spoke when making the film. One actor is suing the producer and YouTube for distributing her likeness around the world. Nakoula is an Egyptian-born resident of the United States, a Coptic Christian, and has a criminal record. He was out of jail on parole when the video was released.

In response to growing unrest in the Islamic world, the Obama administration requested that Google remove links to the video on the Google search engine (refusing to answer search queries on the topic and removing references to any and all URLs where the video might be viewed), as well as remove the video from YouTube. The government argued that the video constituted "hate speech," which Google prohibits under its Terms of Service. Google disagreed, saying the video did not clearly violate its Terms of Service. However, a day after refusing to remove the video from YouTube, Google did block access to it in Egypt and Libya because, it said, the situation in those countries was exceptional and the ban was temporary. It did continue to allow the video to circulate in the rest of the Muslim world, including Indonesia, the largest Muslim country in the world.

Nearly all developed countries, and many developing countries, have laws that prohibit "hate speech." Hate speech is defined in most of these laws (as it is in Google's Terms of Service) as speech that may promote or incite hate or violence against a group or individual. These laws often identify protected groups by disability, ethnicity, religion, gender identity, nationality, race, or other characteristic. Hate speech is prohibited in England, Germany, France, the Netherlands, and other European countries. Europe has prohibited Neo-Nazi speech and banned materials that are offensive to various religious and ethnic groups, long before the Internet existed. Generally, Google, Facebook, and Yahoo follow the requirements of local laws. For instance, Google has removed videos that ridiculed Pakistani officials and blocked access to videos that exposed private information about Turkish officials, in both instances because the content violated local laws

In contrast, hate speech is not prohibited in the United States. The United States has a more absolutist view of the right to freedom of speech because of the First Amendment to the Constitution which declares "Congress shall make no law respecting an establishment of religion; or abridging the freedom of speech, or of the press; or the right of the people peaceably to assemble, and to petition the Government for a redress of grievances." Like all rights, there are limitations in the United States with respect to the right to free speech. Speech can be prohibited if there is an imminent and immediate likelihood that there will be violence in close proximity to the speech in time and space. This situation has occurred when speakers are addressing crowds face-to-face, for instance. Incitement to riot, and the use of "fighting words," which by their very utterance inflict injury or tend to incite an immediate and violent breach of the peace, can lead to criminal arrest. Although more than 350 colleges and universities in the United States, along with many local governments, have policies or laws that prohibit hate speech, these policies and laws have not withstood judicial challenge. Secondary school systems attempting to limit off-campus speech of students, especially that involving criticism of teachers or administrators, bullying of other students, and vulgar behavior, have received scant support from courts in the United States.

Strong advocates of free speech criticized Google for bowing to the demands of protestors in Egypt and Libya. Will freedom of speech on the Internet be determined by mobs in the street? Civil libertarians warned that to allow Google, a private corporation, to determine what is or is not published on the Web is a worrisome development. Freedom of speech is guaranteed in the Constitution, and they question whether or not Google has the right to regulate a "public speech platform." For instance, the *New York Times* has editorialized that nobody should be banned from the Internet because it is a fundamental tool for enabling free speech. Yet few of these critics would deny the editorial right of the *New York Times*, or any other newspaper to refuse to publish any material, for whatever reason. Indeed, this happens all the time. On the other hand, Google does not believe it is a publisher that potentially can be held liable for failing to monitor content. Google believes it is a utility carrier, like a telephone company, and that therefore it cannot be held liable for content, or conspiracies, that users distribute and create on its various services.

Others question Google's administration of its own content policies: surely Google managers knew, or should have known, that distributing *The Innocence of Muslims* on YouTube would be a violation of local laws in most, if not all, Muslim countries, and that they should have, and could have, anticipated the riots that ensued. In this view, the right to freedom of speech has limits, and one of them is imminent danger to violence. However, in this case, there was a long gap between distribution of the video and the resulting violence. The violence and protests appeared to have been planned for the anniversary date of the World Trade Center attacks on September 11, 2001. Violence was not imminent, immediate, or proximate in physical space. If there are to be limits to the freedom speech on the Internet because of the potential for violence, then new criteria may be needed to replace imminence, immediacy, and proximity because these conditions are rarely met on the Internet.

Today, what speech should be protected on the Internet, and who should protect it, is suddenly not clear at all. Ironically, the very technology that was supposed to bring people together into one big global community, can have just the opposite impact, dividing nations, religions, and peoples. The Internet can become a platform for wicked individuals to sow violence with their user-generated content. Like bringing the extended family together for holidays, bringing the world's diverse populations together on YouTube can have unexpected, and even dangerous, consequences.

SOURCES: "Held Dear in the U.S., Free Speech Perplexing Abroad," National Public Radio, September 19, 2012; "State of the Web: Online Speech Is Only as Free as Google Wants It to Be," by Andrew Couts, Digitaltrends.com, September 18, 2012; "On the Web, a Fine Line on Free Speech Across the Globe," by Somini Sengupta, *New York Times*, September 16, 2012; "As Violence Spreads in the Arab World, Google Blocks Access to Inflammatory Video," Claire Cain Miller, *Wall Street Journal*, September 13, 2012; "Google Groups Content Policy," Google Inc., http://support.google.com/groups, September 2012; "Free Speech and the Internet," *New York Times*, July 3, 2011; "Supreme Court Plays Hooky, Leaves Student Online Free Speech Rights Murky," by David Kravets, *Wired*, November 1, 2011; "The Role of Telecommunications in Hate Crimes," National Telecommunication and Information Administration, U.S. Department of Commerce, December 1993.

Determining how or whether to regulate behavior on the Internet is just one of many ethical, social, and political issues raised by the rapid evolution of the Internet and e-commerce. For instance, as described in the opening case, whether U.S. principles of free speech should govern on the Internet, or the principles of other nations, has not been determined. These questions are not just ethical questions that we as individuals have to answer; they also involve social institutions such as family, schools, business firms, and in some cases, entire nation-states. And these questions have obvious political dimensions because they involve collective choices about how we should live and what laws we would like to live under.

In this chapter, we discuss the ethical, social, and political issues raised in e-commerce, provide a framework for organizing the issues, and make recommendations for managers who are given the responsibility of operating e-commerce companies within commonly accepted standards of appropriateness.

8.1   UNDERSTANDING ETHICAL, SOCIAL, AND POLITICAL ISSUES IN E-COMMERCE

The Internet and its use in e-commerce have raised pervasive ethical, social, and political issues on a scale unprecedented for computer technology. Entire sections of daily newspapers and weekly magazines are devoted to the social impact of the Internet. But why is this so? Why is the Internet at the root of so many contemporary controversies? Part of the answer lies in the underlying features of Internet technology itself, and the ways in which it has been exploited by business firms. Internet technology and its use in e-commerce disrupt existing social and business relationships and understandings.

Consider for instance Table 1.2 (in Chapter 1), which lists the unique features of Internet technology. Instead of considering the business consequences of each unique feature, **Table 8.1** examines the actual or potential ethical, social, and/or political consequences of the technology.

We live in an "information society," where power and wealth increasingly depend on information and knowledge as central assets. Controversies over information are often disagreements over power, wealth, influence, and other things thought to be valuable. Like other technologies, such as steam, electricity, telephones, and television, the Internet and e-commerce can be used to achieve social progress, and for the most part, this has occurred. However, the same technologies can be used to commit crimes, despoil the environment, and threaten cherished social values. Before automobiles, there was very little interstate crime and very little federal jurisdiction over crime. Likewise with the Internet: before the Internet, there was very little "cybercrime."

Many business firms and individuals are benefiting from the commercial development of the Internet, but this development also exacts a price from individuals, organizations, and societies. These costs and benefits must be carefully considered by those seeking to make ethical and socially responsible decisions in this new environment. The question is: How can you as a manager make reasoned judgments

TABLE 8.1	UNIQUE FEATURES OF E-COMMERCE TECHNOLOGY AND THEIR POTENTIAL ETHICAL, SOCIAL, AND/OR POLITICAL IMPLICATIONS
E-COMMERCE TECHNOLOGY DIMENSION	POTENTIAL ETHICAL, SOCIAL, AND POLITICAL SIGNIFICANCE
Ubiquity—Internet/Web technology is available everywhere: at work, at home, and elsewhere via mobile devices, anytime.	Work and shopping can invade family life; shopping can distract workers at work, lowering productivity; use of mobile devices can lead to automobile and industrial accidents. Presents confusing issues of "nexus" to taxation authorities.
Global reach—The technology reaches across national boundaries, around the Earth.	Reduces cultural diversity in products; weakens local small firms while strengthening large global firms; moves manufacturing production to low-wage areas of the world; weakens the ability of all nations—large and small—to control their information destiny.
Universal standards—There is one set of technology standards, namely Internet standards.	Increases vulnerability to viruses and hacking attacks worldwide, affecting millions of people at once. Increases the likelihood of "information" crime, crimes against systems, and deception.
Richness—Video, audio, and text messages are possible.	A "screen technology" that reduces use of text and potentially the ability to read by focusing instead on video and audio messages. Potentially very persuasive messages that may reduce reliance on multiple independent sources of information.
Interactivity—The technology works through interaction with the user.	The nature of interactivity at commercial sites can be shallow and meaningless. Customer e-mails are frequently not read by human beings. Customers do not really "co-produce" the product as much as they "co-produce" the sale. The amount of "customization" of products that occurs is minimal, occurring within predefined platforms and plug-in options.
Information density—The technology reduces information costs, and raises quality.	While the total amount of information available to all parties increases, so does the possibility of false and misleading information, unwanted information, and invasion of solitude. Trust, authenticity, accuracy, completeness, and other quality features of information can be degraded. The ability of individuals and organizations to make sense out of this plethora of information is limited.
Personalization/Customization—The technology allows personalized messages to be delivered to individuals as well as groups.	Opens up the possibility of intensive invasion of privacy for commercial and governmental purposes that is unprecedented.
Social technology—The technology enables user content generation and social networking.	Creates opportunities for cyberbullying, abusive language, and predation; challenges concepts of privacy, fair use, and consent to use posted information; creates new opportunities for surveillance by authorities and corporations into private lives.

about what your firm should do in a number of e-commerce areas—from securing the privacy of your customer's clickstream to ensuring the integrity of your company's domain name?

A MODEL FOR ORGANIZING THE ISSUES

E-commerce—and the Internet—have raised so many ethical, social, and political issues that it is difficult to classify them all, and hence, complicated to see their relationship to one another. Clearly, ethical, social, and political issues are interrelated. One way to organize the ethical, social, and political dimensions surrounding e-commerce is shown in **Figure 8.1**. At the individual level, what appears as an ethical issue—"What should I do?"—is reflected at the social and political levels—"What should we as a society and government do?" The ethical dilemmas you face as a manager of a business using the Web reverberate and are reflected in social and political debates. The major ethical, social, and political issues that have developed around e-commerce over the past 10 years can be loosely categorized into four major dimensions: information rights, property rights, governance, and public safety and welfare.

Some of the ethical, social, and political issues raised in each of these areas include the following:

- **Information rights:** What rights to their own personal information do individuals have in a public marketplace, or in their private homes, when Internet technologies make information collection so pervasive and efficient? What rights do individuals have to access information about business firms and other organizations?
- **Property rights:** How can traditional intellectual property rights be enforced in an Internet world where perfect copies of protected works can be made and easily distributed worldwide in seconds?
- **Governance:** Should the Internet and e-commerce be subject to public laws? And if so, what law-making bodies have jurisdiction—state, federal, and/or international?

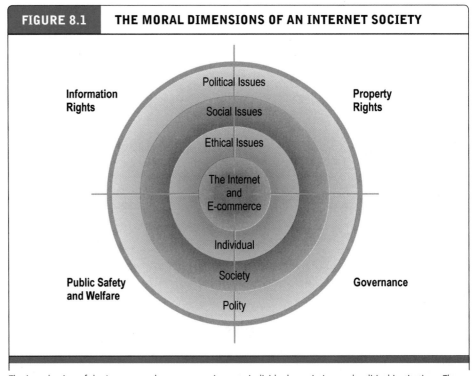

FIGURE 8.1	THE MORAL DIMENSIONS OF AN INTERNET SOCIETY

The introduction of the Internet and e-commerce impacts individuals, societies, and political institutions. These impacts can be classified into four moral dimensions: property rights, information rights, governance, and public safety and welfare.

- **Public safety and welfare:** What efforts should be undertaken to ensure equitable access to the Internet and e-commerce channels? Should governments be responsible for ensuring that schools and colleges have access to the Internet? Are certain online content and activities—such as pornography and gambling—a threat to public safety and welfare? Should mobile commerce be allowed from moving vehicles?

To illustrate, imagine that at any given moment, society and individuals are more or less in an ethical equilibrium brought about by a delicate balancing of individuals, social organizations, and political institutions. Individuals know what is expected of them, social organizations such as business firms know their limits, capabilities, and roles, and political institutions provide a supportive framework of market regulation, banking, and commercial law that provides sanctions against violators.

Now, imagine we drop into the middle of this calm setting a powerful new technology such as the Internet and e-commerce. Suddenly, individuals, business firms, and political institutions are confronted by new possibilities of behavior. For instance, individuals discover that they can download perfect digital copies of music tracks from Web sites without paying anyone, something that, under the old technology of CDs, would have been impossible. This can be done, despite the fact that these music tracks still legally belong to the owners of the copyright—musicians and record label companies. Then, business firms discover that they can make a business out of aggregating these digital musical tracks—or creating a mechanism for sharing musical tracks—even though they do not "own" them in the traditional sense. The record companies, courts, and Congress were not prepared at first to cope with the onslaught of online digital copying. Courts and legislative bodies will have to make new laws and reach new judgments about who owns digital copies of copyrighted works and under what conditions such works can be "shared." It may take years to develop new understandings, laws, and acceptable behavior in just this one area of social impact. In the meantime, as an individual and a manager, you will have to decide what you and your firm should do in legal "gray" areas, where there is conflict between ethical principles but no clear-cut legal or cultural guidelines. How can you make good decisions in this type of situation?

Before examining the four moral dimensions of e-commerce in greater depth, we will briefly review some basic concepts of ethical reasoning that you can use as a guide to ethical decision making, and provide general reasoning principles about the social and political issues of the Internet that you will face in the future.

BASIC ETHICAL CONCEPTS: RESPONSIBILITY, ACCOUNTABILITY, AND LIABILITY

Ethics is at the heart of social and political debates about the Internet. **Ethics** is the study of principles that individuals and organizations can use to determine right and wrong courses of action. It is assumed in ethics that individuals are free moral agents who are in a position to make choices. When faced with alternative courses of action, what is the correct moral choice? Extending ethics from individuals to business firms and even entire societies can be difficult, but it is not impossible. As long as there is a decision-making body or individual (such as a board of directors or CEO in a business firm, or a governmental body in a society), their decisions can be judged against a variety of ethical principles.

ethics
the study of principles that individuals and organizations can use to determine right and wrong courses of action

If you understand some basic ethical principles, your ability to reason about larger social and political debates will be improved. In western culture, there are three basic principles that all ethical schools of thought share: responsibility, accountability, and liability. **Responsibility** means that as free moral agents, individuals, organizations, and societies are responsible for the actions they take. **Accountability** means that individuals, organizations, and societies should be held accountable to others for the consequences of their actions. The third principle—liability—extends the concepts of responsibility and accountability to the area of law. **Liability** is a feature of political systems in which a body of law is in place that permits individuals to recover the damages done to them by other actors, systems, or organizations. **Due process** is a feature of law-governed societies and refers to a process in which laws are known and understood, and there is an ability to appeal to higher authorities to ensure that the laws have been correctly applied.

You can use these concepts immediately to understand some contemporary Internet debates. For instance, consider the 2005 U.S. Supreme Court decision in the case of *Metro-Goldwyn-Mayer Studios v. Grokster, et al.* MGM had sued Grokster and other P2P networks for copyright infringement. The court decided that because the primary and intended use of Internet P2P file-sharing services such as Grokster, StreamCast, and Kazaa was the swapping of copyright-protected music and video files, the file-sharing services should be held accountable and shut down. Although Grokster and the other networks acknowledged that the most common use of the software was for illegal digital music file-swapping, they argued that there were substantial, nontrivial uses of the same networks for legally sharing files. They also argued they should not be held accountable for what individuals do with their software, any more than Sony could be held accountable for how people use VCRs, or Xerox for how people use copying machines. Ultimately, the Supreme Court ruled that Grokster and other P2P networks could be held accountable for the illegal actions of their users if it could be shown that they intended their software to be used for illegal downloading and sharing, and had marketed the software for that purpose. The court relied on copyright laws to arrive at its decisions, but these laws reflect some basic underlying ethical principles of responsibility, accountability, and liability.

Underlying the *Grokster* Supreme Court decision is a fundamental rejection of the notion that the Internet is an ungoverned "Wild West" environment that cannot be controlled. Under certain defined circumstances, the courts will intervene into the uses of the Internet. No organized civilized society has ever accepted the proposition that technology can flaunt basic underlying social and cultural values. Through all of the industrial and technological developments that have taken place, societies have intervened by means of legal and political decisions to ensure that the technology serves socially acceptable ends without stifling the positive consequences of innovation and wealth creation. The Internet in this sense is no different, and we can expect societies around the world to exercise more regulatory control over the Internet and e-commerce in an effort to arrive at a new balance between innovation and wealth creation, on the one hand, and other socially desirable objectives on the other. This is a difficult balancing act, and reasonable people will arrive at different conclusions.

ANALYZING ETHICAL DILEMMAS

Ethical, social, and political controversies usually present themselves as dilemmas. A **dilemma** is a situation in which there are at least two diametrically opposed actions, each of which supports a desirable outcome. When confronted with a situation that seems to present an ethical dilemma, how can you analyze and reason about the situation? The following is a five-step process that should help:

1. **Identify and clearly describe the facts.** Find out who did what to whom, and where, when, and how. In many instances, you will be surprised at the errors in the initially reported facts, and often you will find that simply getting the facts straight helps define the solution. It also helps to get the opposing parties involved in an ethical dilemma to agree on the facts.

2. **Define the conflict or dilemma and identify the higher-order values involved.** Ethical, social, and political issues always reference higher values. Otherwise, there would be no debate. The parties to a dispute all claim to be pursuing higher values (e.g., freedom, privacy, protection of property, and the free enterprise system). For example, supporters of the use of advertising networks such as DoubleClick argue that the tracking of consumer movements on the Web increases market efficiency and the wealth of the entire society. Opponents argue this claimed efficiency comes at the expense of individual privacy, and advertising networks should cease their activities or offer Web users the option of not participating in such tracking.

3. **Identify the stakeholders.** Every ethical, social, and political issue has stakeholders: players in the game who have an interest in the outcome, who have invested in the situation, and usually who have vocal opinions. Find out the identity of these groups and what they want. This will be useful later when designing a solution.

4. **Identify the options that you can reasonably take.** You may find that none of the options satisfies all the interests involved, but that some options do a better job than others. Sometimes, arriving at a "good" or ethical solution may not always be a balancing of consequences to stakeholders.

5. **Identify the potential consequences of your options.** Some options may be ethically correct but disastrous from other points of view. Other options may work in this one instance but not in other similar instances. Always ask yourself, "What if I choose this option consistently over time?"

Once your analysis is complete, you can refer to the following well-established ethical principles to help decide the matter.

CANDIDATE ETHICAL PRINCIPLES

Although you are the only one who can decide which ethical principles you will follow and how you will prioritize them, it is helpful to consider some ethical principles with deep roots in many cultures that have survived throughout recorded history:

dilemma
a situation in which there are at least two diametrically opposed actions, each of which supports a desirable outcome

- **The Golden Rule:** Do unto others as you would have them do unto you. Putting yourself into the place of others and thinking of yourself as the object of the decision can help you think about fairness in decision making.

- **Universalism:** If an action is not right for all situations, then it is not right for any specific situation (Immanuel Kant's categorical imperative). Ask yourself, "If we adopted this rule in every case, could the organization, or society, survive?"

- **Slippery Slope:** If an action cannot be taken repeatedly, then it is not right to take at all (Descartes' rule of change). An action may appear to work in one instance to solve a problem, but if repeated, would result in a negative outcome. In plain English, this rule might be stated as "once started down a slippery path, you may not be able to stop."

- **Collective Utilitarian Principle:** Take the action that achieves the greater value for all of society. This rule assumes you can prioritize values in a rank order and understand the consequences of various courses of action.

- **Risk Aversion:** Take the action that produces the least harm, or the least potential cost. Some actions have extremely high failure costs of very low probability (e.g., building a nuclear generating facility in an urban area) or extremely high failure costs of moderate probability (speeding and automobile accidents). Avoid the high-failure cost actions and choose those actions whose consequences would not be catastrophic, even if there were a failure.

- **No Free Lunch:** Assume that virtually all tangible and intangible objects are owned by someone else unless there is a specific declaration otherwise. (This is the ethical "no free lunch" rule.) If something someone else has created is useful to you, it has value and you should assume the creator wants compensation for this work.

- **The New York Times Test (Perfect Information Rule):** Assume that the results of your decision on a matter will be the subject of the lead article in the *New York Times* the next day. Will the reaction of readers be positive or negative? Would your parents, friends, and children be proud of your decision? Most criminals and unethical actors assume imperfect information, and therefore they assume their decisions and actions will never be revealed. When making decisions involving ethical dilemmas, it is wise to assume perfect information markets.

- **The Social Contract Rule:** Would you like to live in a society where the principle you are supporting would become an organizing principle of the entire society?

For instance, you might think it is wonderful to download illegal copies of music tracks, but you might not want to live in a society that does not respect property rights, such as your property rights to the car in your driveway, or your rights to a term paper or original art.

None of these rules is an absolute guide, and there are exceptions and logical difficulties with all of them. Nevertheless, actions that do not easily pass these guidelines deserve some very close attention and a great deal of caution because the appearance of unethical behavior may do as much harm to you and your company as the actual behavior.

Now that you have an understanding of some basic ethical reasoning concepts, let's take a closer look at each of the major types of ethical, social, and political debates that have arisen in e-commerce.

<table>
<tr><td>**8.2**</td><td>**PRIVACY AND INFORMATION RIGHTS**</td></tr>
</table>

Privacy is the moral right of individuals to be left alone, free from surveillance or interference from other individuals or organizations, including the state. Privacy is a girder supporting freedom: Without the privacy required to think, write, plan, and associate independently and without fear, social and political freedom is weakened, and perhaps destroyed. **Information privacy** is a subset of privacy. The right to information privacy includes both the claim that certain information should not be collected at all by governments or business firms, and the claim of individuals to control the use of whatever information that is collected about them. Individual control over personal information is at the core of the privacy concept.

Due process also plays an important role in defining privacy. The best statement of due process in record keeping is given by the Fair Information Practices doctrine developed in the early 1970s and extended to the online privacy debate in the late 1990s (described later in this section).

There are two kinds of threats to individual privacy posed by the Internet. One threat originates in the private sector and concerns how much personal information is collected by commercial Web sites and how it will be used. A second threat originates in the public sector and concerns how much personal information federal, state, and local government authorities collect, and how they use it. While these threats are conceptually distinct, in practice they are related as the federal government increasingly relies on Internet companies to provide intelligence on specific individuals and groups, and as Internet records held by search engine companies and others (like Amazon) are sought by legal authorities and attornies.

Privacy claims—and thinking about privacy—mushroomed in the United States at the end of the nineteenth century as the technology of photography and tabloid journalism enabled the invasion of the heretofore private lives of wealthy industrialists. For most of the twentieth century, however, privacy thinking and legislation focused on restraining the government from collecting and using personal information. With the explosion in the collection of private personal information by Web-based marketing firms since 1995, privacy concerns are increasingly directed toward restraining the activities of private firms in the collection and use of information on the Web. Claims to privacy are also involved at the workplace. Millions of employees are subject to various forms of electronic surveillance that in many cases is enhanced by firm intranets and Web technologies. For instance, the majority of U.S. companies monitor which Web sites their workers visit, as well as employee e-mail and instant messages. Employee posts on message boards and blogs are also coming under scrutiny.

In 2012, the public discussion of privacy has broadened from a concern about tracking the behavior of individuals while they use the Internet, especially on social

privacy
the moral right of individuals to be left alone, free from surveillance or interference from other individuals or organizations, including the state

information privacy
includes both the claim that certain information should not be collected at all by governments or business firms, and the claim of individuals to control the use of whatever information that is collected about them

networks, to include the impact of mobile devices for tracking the location of people via their smartphones, and collecting information on their personal behavior including the shops, churches, political rallies, bars, and other locations they have visited. Smartphone apps that tap user information have also received critical attention. The falling costs of personal tracking technology like mobile cameras, the ubiquitous use of always-on smartphones fitted out with GPS, and the growth of powerful storage and analytic capabilities, has resulted in a torrent of data, referred to as "Big Data," pouring into marketing and law enforcement databases. Private and government investigations have found both Apple and Google are collecting personal location and behavior data, and potentially sharing this information with marketers and government agencies. The cell phone carriers receive more than a million requests each year from law enforcement agencies for call data (Maass and Rajagopalen, 2012). Apart from smartphone surveillance, new wireless cameras mounted on cars (a kind of remote sensing device) have led to a new industry of license plate tracking, resulting in hundreds of millions of license plate photos collected by private firms and police forces, regardless of whether or not the car's owners have done anything wrong (Angwin and Valentino-Devries, 2012).

In general, the Internet and the Web provide an ideal environment for both business and government to invade the personal privacy of millions of users on a scale unprecedented in history. Perhaps no other recent issue has raised as much widespread social and political concern as protecting the privacy of 239 million Internet users in the United States alone. The major ethical issues related to e-commerce and privacy include the following: Under what conditions should we collect information about others? What legitimates intruding into others' lives through unobtrusive surveillance, online tracking programs, market research, or other means? Do people have a right to be informed when Web sites are collecting data about them? The major social issues related to e-commerce and privacy concern the development of "expectations of privacy" or privacy norms, as well as public attitudes. In what areas of life should we as a society encourage people to think they are in "private territory" as opposed to public view? The major political issues related to e-commerce and privacy concern the development of statutes that govern the relations between record keepers and individuals. How should both public and private organizations—which may be reluctant to remit the advantages that come from the unfettered flow of information on individuals—be restrained, if at all? In the following section, we look first at the various practices of e-commerce companies that pose a threat to privacy.

INFORMATION COLLECTED AT E-COMMERCE SITES

personally identifiable information (PII)
any data that can be used to identify, locate, or contact an individual

anonymous information
demographic and behavioral information that does not include any personal identifiers

As you have learned in previous chapters, e-commerce sites routinely collect a variety of information from or about consumers who visit their site and/or make purchases. Some of this data constitutes **personally identifiable information (PII)**, which is defined as any data that can be used to identify, locate, or contact an individual (Federal Trade Commission, 2000a). Other data is **anonymous information**, composed of demographic and behavioral information, such as age, occupation, income, zip code, ethnicity, and other data that characterizes your life such as Web browsing behavior without identifying who you are. **Table 8.2** lists some of the personal identi-

TABLE 8.2	PERSONAL INFORMATION COLLECTED BY E-COMMERCE SITES		
Name	Gender	Education
Address	Age	Preference data
Phone number	Occupation	Transaction data
E-mail address	Location	Clickstream data
Social security number	Location history	Device used for access
Bank accounts	Likes	Browser type
Credit card accounts	Photograph	

fiers routinely collected by online e-commerce sites including mobile sites and apps. This is not an exhaustive list, and in fact many Web sites collect hundreds of different data points on visitors.

Advertising networks and search engines also track the behavior of consumers across thousands of popular sites, not just at one site, via cookies, Web beacons, tracking software, spyware, and other techniques

Table 8.3 on page 502 illustrates some of the major ways online firms gather information about consumers.

SOCIAL NETWORKS AND PRIVACY

Social networks pose a unique challenge for the maintenance of personal privacy because they encourage people to reveal details about their personal lives (passions, loves, favorites, photos, videos, and personal interests), and to share them with their friends. While Google's search engine is a massive database of personal intentions, Facebook has created a massive database of friends, preferences, Likes, posts, and activities. An Austrian researcher was able to obtain his Facebook file (possible under European laws) and received a 1,222 page document of messages, photos, posts, and friends (Sengupta, 2012a). Some social networkers share these personal details with everyone on the social network. On the face of it, this would seem to indicate that people who participate in social networks voluntarily give up their rights to personal privacy. How could they claim an expectation of privacy? When everything is shared, what's private?

But the reality is that many adult (18 or over) participants in social networks have a very keen sense of their personal privacy. Every time a leading social network has sought to use the personal information provided by participants as a method of monetizing social networks by displaying ads and targeting individuals, it has been vociferously rejected by members of the networks. Facebook is a prime example of senior management pushing the envelope of privacy, and experiencing a number of public relations reversals and growing government concern. In its most recent gaffe, Facebook had deployed facial recognition technology without any previous notice, which compromised its users' privacy by allowing them to be tagged in photos without their consent. Researchers at Carnegie Mellon found that it is possible to identify people,

TABLE 8.3	THE INTERNET'S MAJOR INFORMATION-GATHERING TOOLS AND THEIR IMPACT ON PRIVACY
INTERNET CAPABILITY	**IMPACT ON PRIVACY**
Smartphones and apps	Used to track location and share photos, addresses, phone numbers, search, and other behavior to marketers.
Advertising networks	Used to track individuals as they move among thousands of Web sites.
Social networks	Used to gather information on user-provided content such as books, music, friends, and other interests, preferences, and lifestyles.
Cookies and Super Cookies	Used to track individuals at a single site. Super Cookies are nearly impossible to identify or remove.
Third-party cookies	Cookies placed by third-party advertising networks. Used to monitor and track online behavior, searches, and sites visited across thousands of sites that belong to the advertising network for the purpose of displaying "relevant" advertising.
Spyware	Can be used to record all the keyboard activity of a user, including Web sites visited and security codes used; also used to display advertisements to users based on their searches or other behavior.
Search engine behavioral targeting (Google and other search engines)	Uses prior search history, demographics, expressed interests, geographic, or other user-entered data to target advertising.
Deep packet inspection	Uses software installed at the ISP level to track all user clickstream behavior.
Shopping carts	Can be used to collect detailed payment and purchase information.
Forms	Online forms that users voluntarily fill out in return for a promised benefit or reward that are linked with clickstream or other behavioral data to create a personal profile.
Site transaction logs	Can be used to collect and analyze detailed information on page content viewed by users.
Search engines	Can be used to trace user statements and views on newsgroups, chat groups, and other public forums on the Web, and profile users' social and political views. Google returns name, address, and links to a map with directions to the address when a phone number is entered.
Digital wallets (single sign-on services)	Client-side wallets and software that reveal personal information to Web sites verifying the identity of the consumer.
Digital Rights Management (DRM)	Software (Windows Media Player) that requires users of online media to identify themselves before viewing copyrighted content.
Trusted Computing Environments	Hardware and software that controls the viewing of copyrighted content and requires users identification, e.g., Amazon Kindle.

even their social security numbers, based on a single Facebook photograph and using facial recognition programs (Angwin, 2011; Acquisti, et al., 2011).

After consumer uproar and challenges from various state attorney generals, Facebook reversed course and made it easier for users to opt out of the technology. In 2012, Facebook began pushing ads on its users based on their use of apps, and offering advertisers the ability to serve ads to Facebook users even while not using Facebook. For a review of Facebook's various positions on online privacy over the years, and public and congressional reaction to these issues, refer back to the *Insight on Society* case, *Facebook and the Age of Privacy,* in Chapter 1.

The result of these conflicts suggests that social network participants do indeed have a strong expectation of privacy in the sense that they want to control how "their" information is used. People who contribute user-generated content have a strong sense of ownership over that content that is not diminished by posting the information on a social network for one's friends. What's involved are some basic tenets of privacy thinking: personal control over the uses of personal information, choice, informed consent, participation in formulation of information policies, and due process. Some of these ideas are foreign to managers and owners seeking to monetize huge social network audiences. As for members who post information to everyone, not just friends, these should be seen as "public performances" where the contributors voluntarily publish their performances, just as writers or other artists do. This does not mean they want the entirety of their personal lives thrown open to every Web tracking automaton on the Internet.

MOBILE AND LOCATION-BASED PRIVACY ISSUES

As the mobile platform becomes more and more important, issues about mobile and location-based privacy are also becoming a major concern. In 2012, investigators discovered that iOS and Android apps were funneling location information to mobile advertisers, along with users' address books and photos (Bilton, 2012). In April 2012, Congress opened an investigation into the privacy policies of smartphone manufacturers, along with Facebook, Pinterest, Yahoo, Google and 30 others in the app marketplace. Twitter announced that anyone using its "Find Friends" feature on smartphones was also sending every phone number and e-mail address in their address books to the company (Sarno, 2012).

In April 2011, a furor erupted over news that Apple iPhones and iPads and Google Android smartphones were able to track and store user location information. In July 2012, Facebook launched a new mobile advertising service that tracks what apps people use on their smartphones, and what they do while using the apps. The tracking starts when users sign on to Facebook Connect with their smartphones. Apple and Google track users' apps also. Apple disclosed that it can target ads based on the apps that a person has downloaded, while Google does not currently do this. Google and Apple do not track what users do on apps, while the Facebook program goes this additional step. For instance, Facebook can target a frequent player of Zynga games with ads using the player's Facebook News Feed, which is a major channel for Facebook ads (the other being display ads on the user's page) (Raice, 2012). Apps on both Android and Apple smartphones share user information with advertisers seeking to target their ads by location, time of day, and personal data shared with the app. Apple and Google have not settled on industry standards defining how mobile user data should be used, and what kinds of notice to users are required to protect users. In June 2011, a bill was proposed in the U.S. Senate that would require mobile companies to obtain a user's consent before collecting location-based data and before sharing that data with third parties. In 2012, investigators discovered that some cell phone companies had installed tracking devices inside phones to improve customer service. This ignited a flurry of criticism. In 2012, Congressman Ed Markey introduced the Mobile Device Privacy Act. The Act requires any firm performing consumer data collection on cell phones, other devices, or on Web sites, to inform consumers, and the Federal Trade Commission. However, the Act has not yet passed in Congress.

According to a 2012 TRUSTe/Harris Interactive survey, 42% of smartphone users said privacy and security are their top concerns. Only 31% said they would exchange personal information in return for free apps (TRUSTe, 2012). Refer back to the *Insight on Society* case, *Foursquare Checks Out a Revenue Model*, in Chapter 2, for more discussion of some of the issues associated with mobile and location-based privacy.

PROFILING AND BEHAVIORAL TARGETING

On an average day, around 158 million adult Americans go online (Pew Internet & American Life Project, 2012). Marketers would like to know who these people are, what they are interested in, and what they buy. The more precise the information, the more complete the information, and the more valuable it is as a predictive and marketing tool. Armed with this information, marketers can make their ad campaigns more efficient by targeting specific ads at specific groups or individuals, and they can even adjust the ads for specific groups.

Many Web sites allow third parties—including online advertising networks such as Microsoft Advertising, DoubleClick, and others—to place "third-party" cookies and Web tracking software on a visitor's computer in order to engage in profiling the user's behavior across thousands of Web sites. A third-party cookie is used to track users across hundreds or thousands of other Web sites who are members of the advertising network. **Profiling** is the creation of digital images that characterize online individual and group behavior. **Anonymous profiles** identify people as belonging to highly specific and targeted groups, for example, 20- to 30-year-old males, with college degrees and incomes greater than $30,000 a year, and interested in high-fashion clothing (based on recent search engine use). **Personal profiles** add a personal e-mail address, postal address, and/or phone number to behavioral data. Increasingly, online firms are linking their online profiles to personal offline consumer data collected by database firms tracking credit card purchases, as well as established retail and catalog firms. In the past, individual stores collected data on customer movement through a single store in order to understand consumer behavior and alter the design of stores accordingly. Also, purchase and expenditure data was gathered on consumers purchasing from multiple stores—usually long after the purchases were made—and the data was used to target direct mail and in-store campaigns, in addition to mass-media advertising.

profiling
the creation of digital images that characterize online individual and group behavior

anonymous profiles
identify people as belonging to highly specific and targeted groups

personal profiles
add a personal e-mail address, postal address, and/or phone number to behavioral data

The online advertising networks such as DoubleClick and 24/7 Real Media have added several new dimensions to established offline marketing techniques. First, they have the ability to precisely track not just consumer purchases, but all browsing behavior on the Web at thousands of the most popular member sites, including browsing book lists, filling out preference forms, and viewing content pages. Second, they can dynamically adjust what the shopper sees on screen—including prices. Third, they can build and continually refresh high-resolution data images or behavioral profiles of consumers. Other advertising firms have created spyware software that, when placed on a consumer's computer, can report back to the advertiser's server on all consumer Internet use, and is also used to display advertising on the consumer's computer.

A different kind of profiling and a more recent form of behavioral targeting is Google's results-based personalization of advertising. Google has a patent on a program that allows advertisers using Google's AdWords program to target ads to users based on their prior search histories and profiles, which Google constructs based on user searches, along with any other information the user submits to Google or that Google can obtain, such as age, demographics, region, and other Web activities (such as blogging). Google also applied for a second patent on a program that allows Google to help advertisers select keywords and design ads for various market segments based on search histories, such as helping a clothing Web site create and test ads targeted at teenage females. In 2007, Google began using behavioral targeting to help it display more relevant ads based on keywords. According to Google, the feature is aimed at capturing a more robust understanding of user intent, and thereby delivering a better ad. Google's Gmail, a free e-mail service, offers a powerful interface, and more than 7 gigabytes of free storage. In return, Google computers read all incoming and outgoing e-mail and place "relevant" advertising in the margins of the mail. Profiles are developed on individual users based on the content in their e-mail. Google's Chrome browser has a Suggest feature that automatically suggests related queries and Web sites when the user enters search terms. Critics pointed out this was a "key logger" device that would record every keystroke of users forever. Google has since announced it will anonymize the data within 24 hours. In 2010, Google began "personalizing" search results without asking users. Opt-in is the default option. Google uses your past personal search history to influence the ads you see on the page. It also can track the pages you subsequently visit if you have the Google toolbar turned on.

Deep packet inspection is another technology for recording every keystroke at the ISP level of every Internet user (no matter where they ultimately go on the Web), and then using that information to make suggestions, and target ads. While advertising networks are limited, and even Google does not constitute the universe of search, deep packet inspection at the ISP level really does capture the universe of all Internet users. The leading firm in this technology was NebuAd. After testing the hardware and software with several ISPs in 2008, the outcry from privacy advocates and Congress caused these ISPs to withdraw from the experiment, and NebuAd withdrew the product from the market and subsequently closed its doors in 2009. However, in 2012, using deep packet inspection for ad targeting is making a comeback. Two U.S. companies, Kindsight and Phorm, are pitching deep packet inspection as a way for ISPs to

deep packet inspection
a technology for recording every key stroke at the ISP level

participate in the online targeted ad market and for consumers to protect their online identities.

Network advertising firms argue that Web profiling benefits both consumers and businesses. Profiling permits targeting of ads, ensuring that consumers see advertisements mostly for products and services in which they are actually interested. Businesses benefit by not paying for wasted advertising sent to consumers who have no interest in their product or service. The industry argues that by increasing the effectiveness of advertising, more advertising revenues go to the Internet, which in turn subsidizes free content on the Internet. Last, product designers and entrepreneurs benefit by sensing demand for new products and services by examining user searches and profiles.

Critics argue that profiling undermines the expectation of anonymity and privacy that most people have when using the Internet, and changes what should be a private experience into one where an individual's every move is recorded. As people become aware that their every move is being watched, they will be far less likely to explore sensitive topics, browse pages, or read about controversial issues. In most cases, the profiling is invisible to users, and even hidden. Consumers are not notified that profiling is occurring. Profiling permits data aggregation on hundreds or even thousands of unrelated sites on the Web. The cookies placed by ad networks are persistent, and they can be set to last days, months, years, or even forever. Their tracking occurs over an extended period of time and resumes each time the individual logs on to the Internet. This clickstream data is used to create profiles that can include hundreds of distinct data fields for each consumer. Associating so-called anonymous profiles with personal information is fairly easy, and companies can change policies quickly without informing the consumer. Although the information gathered by network advertisers is often anonymous (non-PII data), in many cases, the profiles derived from tracking consumers' activities on the Web are linked or merged with personally identifiable information. Anonymous behavioral data is far more valuable if it can be linked with offline consumer behavior, e-mail addresses, and postal addresses.

From a privacy protection perspective, the advertising network raises issues about who will see and use the information held by private companies, whether the user profiles will be linked to actual personally identifying information (such as name, social security number, and bank and credit accounts), the absence of consumer control over the use of the information, the lack of consumer choice, the absence of consumer notice, and the lack of review and amendment procedures.

The pervasive and largely unregulated collection of personal information online has raised significant fears and opposition among consumers. Contrary to what the online advertising industry has often said, namely, that the public really does not care about its online privacy, there is a long history of opinion polls that document the public's fear of losing control over their personal information when visiting e-commerce sites. A 2012 survey by TRUSTe and Harris Interactive found that 94% of online consumers think privacy is an important issue, with 55% saying online privacy is really important to them. Targeted advertising makes 40% of those surveyed uncomfortable. More than 75% do not allow companies to share their personal information with a third party. More than two-thirds say they have stopped doing business with an online company because of privacy concerns (TRUSTe, 2012). In an earlier survey of 2,111 respondents, 81% said they were "somewhat" or "very" concerned about companies tracking their Web surfing habits and using that information for advertising, while 88% said it was "unfair" for companies to do such tracking without a user's permission. Another independent survey found that two-thirds of American Internet users objected to online tracking. About 80% said they would favor implementation of a "Do Not Track" list (Gruenwald, 2010). More than two-thirds of respondents had decided against registering or making a purchase online because those actions required them to provide information that they did not want to divulge. The actual amount of lost sales due to online privacy concerns is not known. This deep-seated and well-documented concern with respect to online privacy provides support for a steady stream of legislation seeking to redress this concern.

THE INTERNET AND GOVERNMENT INVASIONS OF PRIVACY: E-COMMERCE SURVEILLANCE

Today, the online and mobile behavior, profiles, and transactions of consumers are routinely available to a wide range of government agencies and law enforcement authorities, contributing to rising fears among online consumers, and in many cases, their withdrawal from the online marketplace. In 2012, there has been a surge in the use of cell phone tracking and surveillance of citizen movements by law enforcement authorities. While the Internet used to be thought of as impossible for governments to control or monitor, nothing could be actually further from the truth. Law enforcement authorities have long claimed the right under numerous statutes to monitor any form of electronic communication pursuant to a court order and judicial review and based on the reasonable belief that a crime is being committed. This includes the surveillance of consumers engaged in e-commerce. In the case of the Internet, this is accomplished by placing sniffer software and servers at the ISP being used by the target suspect, in a manner similar to pen registers and trap-and-trace devices used for telephone surveillance. The Communications Assistance for Law Enforcement Act (CALEA), the USA PATRIOT Act, the Cyber Security Enhancement Act, and the Homeland Security Act all strengthen the ability of law enforcement agencies to monitor Internet users without their knowledge and, under certain circumstances when life is purportedly at stake, without judicial oversight. The Patriot Act designed to combat terrorism inside the borders of the United States permits nearly unlimited government surveillance without court oversight, according to several Senators (Savage, 2012).

In 2011 and 2012. there were several Congressional initiatives to strengthen the privacy protections for electronic communications and personal location data. In 2011, Senator Patrick Leahy introduced the "Electronic Communications Privacy Act Amendments Act of 2011," which would require a probable cause warrant for access to e-mail and other electronic communications no matter how long they were saved or where they were saved, whether on a personal computer or an online storage system. Under current law, there is no warrant requirement after an e-mail has been stored for 180 days. The bill also applies warrant requirements to the use of some location data. In 2012, Senator Ron Wyden and Representative Jason Chaffetz introduced the

Geolocation Privacy and Surveillance Act to protect location privacy. The bill requires law enforcement to get a warrant based on probable cause before accessing location information and also regulates the use of this information by businesses. With location tracking cases rising all over the country, this would provide a strong and clear national standard for law enforcement.

Government agencies are among the largest users of private sector commercial data brokers, such as ChoicePoint, Acxiom, Experian, and TransUnion Corporation, that collect a vast amount of information about consumers from various offline and online public sources, such as public records and the telephone directory, and non-public sources, such as "credit header" information from credit bureaus (which typically contains name, aliases, birth date, social security number, current and prior addresses, and phone numbers). Acxiom is the largest private personal database in the world with records on more than 500,000 people and about 1,500 data points per person (Singer, 2012a). Information contained in individual reference services' databases ranges from purely identifying information (e.g., name and phone number) to much more extensive data (e.g., driving records, criminal and civil court records, property records, and licensing records). This information can be linked to online behavior information collected from other commercial sources to compile an extensive profile of an individual's online and offline behavior.

In July 2011, a U.S. House of Representatives committee approved a bill that forces ISPs to keep logs of their customers' activities for one year. Information required to be stored includes customers' names, addresses, phone numbers, credit card numbers, bank account numbers, and temporarily assigned IP addresses. The logs would be accessible to police investigating any crime and possibly to attorneys litigating civil disputes as well. Currently, ISPs typically discard log files that are no longer required for business reasons. Passage of the bill by the full House and Senate is required before it becomes law. The European Union's Data Retention Directive (DRD) is similar in nature but more limited in scope, requiring electronic communications providers to store usage and location data for a period of at least six months but for no longer than two years. Not to be outdone by the Americans, the British government proposed in April 2012 to permit intelligence and security services to monitor all of the communications of everyone in the country. It is unclear if this was intended to involve only digital media communications, including cell calls, or also casual conversation on the street or in bars and restaurants (Cowell, 2012).

Retention of search engine query data is also an issue. Although the amount of time such data is retained is not governed by U.S. law, the European Union has indicated that it should not be retained for more than six months. The three major search engines (Google, Bing, and Yahoo) have varying policies. In January 2010, Microsoft agreed to reduce the amount of time that it retains certain data, such as IP addresses, to six months to comply with the E.U. standard, although it retains other data, such as cookie IDs and cross-session IDs for 18 months. Google has refused, however, and retains search records for 18 months, claiming that this amount of time is necessary for it to improve services and prevent fraud. In April 2011, Yahoo, which had previously prided itself for retaining search records for only three months, announced that it too would extend that time to 18 months, for competitive reasons.

LEGAL PROTECTIONS

In the United States, Canada, and Germany, rights to privacy are explicitly granted in, or can be derived from, founding documents such as constitutions, as well as in specific statutes. In England and the United States, there is also protection of privacy in the common law, a body of court decisions involving torts or personal injuries. For instance, in the United States, four privacy-related torts have been defined in court decisions involving claims of injury to individuals caused by other private parties: intrusion on solitude, public disclosure of private facts, publicity placing a person in a false light, and appropriation of a person's name or likeness (mostly concerning celebrities) for a commercial purpose (Laudon, 1996). In the United States, the claim to privacy against government intrusion is protected primarily by the First Amendment guarantees of freedom of speech and association, the Fourth Amendment protections against unreasonable search and seizure of one's personal documents or home, and the Fourteenth Amendment's guarantee of due process.

In addition to common law and the Constitution, there are both federal laws and state laws that protect individuals against government intrusion and in some cases define privacy rights vis-à-vis private organizations such as financial, educational, and media institutions (cable television and video rentals) (see **Table 8.4** on page 510).

Informed Consent

The concept of **informed consent** (defined as consent given with knowledge of all material facts needed to make a rational decision) also plays an important role in protecting privacy. In the United States, business firms (and government agencies) can gather transaction information generated in the marketplace and then use that information for other marketing purposes, without obtaining the informed consent of the individual. For instance, in the United States, if a Web shopper purchases books about baseball at a site that belongs to an advertising network such as DoubleClick, a cookie can be placed on the consumer's hard drive and used by other member sites to sell the shopper sports clothing without the explicit permission or even knowledge of the user. This online preference information may also be linked with personally identifying information. In Europe, this would be illegal. A business in Europe cannot use marketplace transaction information for any purpose other than supporting the current transaction, unless of course it obtains the individual's consent in writing or by filling out an on-screen form.

There are traditionally two models for informed consent: opt-in and opt-out. The **opt-in** model requires an affirmative action by the consumer to allow collection and use of information. For instance, using opt-in, consumers would first be asked if they approved of the collection and use of information, and then directed to check a selection box if they agreed. Otherwise, the default is not to approve the collection of data. In the **opt-out** model, the default is to collect information unless the consumer takes an affirmative action to prevent the collection of data by checking a box or by filling out a form.

Until recently, many U.S. e-commerce companies rejected the concept of informed consent and instead simply published their information use policy on their site. U.S.

informed consent
consent given with knowledge of all material facts needed to make a rational decision

opt-in
requires an affirmative action by the consumer to allow collection and use of consumer information

opt-out
the default is to collect information unless the consumer takes an affirmative action to prevent the collection of data

TABLE 8.4	FEDERAL AND STATE PRIVACY LAWS
NAME	DESCRIPTION

GENERAL FEDERAL PRIVACY LAWS

NAME	DESCRIPTION
Freedom of Information Act of 1966	Gives people the right to inspect information about themselves held in government files; also allows other individuals and organizations the right to request disclosure of government records based on the public's right to know.
Privacy Act of 1974, as amended	Regulates the federal government's collection, use, and disclosure of data collected by federal agencies. Gives individuals a right to inspect and correct records.
Electronic Communications Privacy Act of 1986	Makes conduct that would infringe on the security of electronic communications illegal.
Computer Security Act of 1987	Makes conduct that would infringe on the security of computer-based files illegal.
Computer Matching and Privacy Protection Act of 1988	Regulates computerized matching of files held by different government agencies.
Driver's Privacy Protection Act of 1994	Limits access to personal information maintained by state motor vehicle departments to those with legitimate business purposes. Also gives drivers the option to prevent disclosure of driver's license information to marketers and the general public.
E-Government Act of 2002	Regulates the collection and use of personal information by federal agencies.

FEDERAL PRIVACY LAWS AFFECTING PRIVATE INSTITUTIONS

NAME	DESCRIPTION
Fair Credit Reporting Act of 1970	Regulates the credit investigating and reporting industry. Gives people the right to inspect credit records if they have been denied credit and provides procedures for correcting information.
Family Educational Rights and Privacy Act of 1974	Requires schools and colleges to give students and their parents access to student records and to allow them to challenge and correct information; limits disclosure of such records to third parties.
Right to Financial Privacy Act of 1978	Regulates the financial industry's use of personal financial records; establishes procedures that federal agencies must follow to gain access to such records.
Privacy Protection Act of 1980	Prohibits government agents from conducting unannounced searches of press offices and files if no one in the office is suspected of committing a crime.
Cable Communications Policy Act of 1984	Regulates the cable industry's collection and disclosure of information concerning subscribers.
Video Privacy Protection Act of 1988	Prevents disclosure of a person's video rental records without court order or consent.
Children's Online Privacy Protection Act (1998)	Prohibits deceptive practices in connection with the collection, use, and/or disclosure of personal information from and about children on the Internet.
Health Insurance Portability and Accountability Act of 1996 (HIPAA)	Requires healthcare providers and insurers and other third parties to promulgate privacy policies to consumers and establishes due process procedures.
Financial Modernization Act (Gramm-Leach-Bliley Act) (1999)	Requires financial institutions to inform consumers of their privacy policies and permits consumers some control over their records.

TABLE 8.4	FEDERAL AND STATE PRIVACY LAWS (CONT'D)
NAME	**DESCRIPTION**
SELECTED STATE PRIVACY LAWS	
Online privacy policies	The California Online Privacy Protection Act of 2003 was the first state law in the United States requiring owners of commercial Web sites or online services to post a privacy policy. The policy must, among other things, identify the categories of PII collected about site visitors and categories of third parties with whom the information may be shared. Failure to comply can result in a civil suit for unfair business practices. Nebraska and Pennsylvania prohibit false and misleading statements in online privacy policies. At least 16 states require government Web sites to establish privacy policies or procedures or incorporate machine-readable privacy policies into their Web sites.
Spyware legislation	A number of states, including California, Utah, Arizona, Arkansas, and Virginia, among others, have passed laws that outlaw the installation of spyware on a user's computer without consent.
Disclosure of security breaches	In 2002, California enacted legislation that requires state agencies or businesses that own or license computer data with personal information to notify state residents if they experience a security breach involving that information; today, nearly every state has enacted similar legislation.
Privacy of personal information	Two states, Nevada and Minnesota, require ISPs to keep their customers' PII private unless the customer consents to disclose the information. Minnesota also requires ISPs to get permission from subscribers before disclosing information about subscribers' online surfing habits.
Data encryption	In October 2007, Nevada passed the first law that requires encryption for the transmission of customer personal information. The law took effect October 1, 2008.

businesses argue that informing consumers about how the information will be used is sufficient to obtain the users' informed consent. Most U.S. sites that offer informed consent make opting in the default option, and require users to go to special pages to request to opt out of promotional campaigns. Some sites have an opt-out selection box at the very bottom of their information policy statements where the consumer is unlikely to see it. On Yahoo's home page there is an Ad Choice box that allows users to opt out of interest-based advertising although the user has to allow cookies from Yahoo and sign into a Yahoo account before the choices take effect. Privacy advocates argue that many information/privacy policy statements on U.S. Web sites are obscure and difficult to read, and legitimate just about any use of personal information. For instance, Yahoo's privacy policy begins by stating that Yahoo takes the user's privacy seriously and Yahoo does not rent, sell, or share personal information about users with others or non-affiliated companies. However, there are a number of exceptions that significantly weaken this statement. For instance, Yahoo may share the information with trusted partners, which could be anyone that Yahoo does business with, although perhaps not a company that the user might choose to do business with. In its privacy policy, Yahoo also says it places web beacons on its Web pages and e-mails in order to track user clickstream behavior across the Web.

The Federal Trade Commission's Fair Information Practices Principles

In the United States, the Federal Trade Commission (FTC) has taken the lead in conducting research on online privacy and recommending legislation to Congress. The FTC is a cabinet-level agency charged with promoting the efficient functioning of the marketplace by protecting consumers from unfair or deceptive practices and increasing consumer choice by promoting competition. In addition to reports and recommendations, the FTC enforces existing legislation by suing corporations it believes are in violation of federal fair trade laws.

In 1998, the FTC issued its Fair Information Practice (FIP) principles, on which it has based its assessments and recommendations for online privacy. **Table 8.5** describes these principles. Two of the five are designated as basic, "core" principles that must be present to protect privacy, whereas the other practices are less central.

TABLE 8.5	FEDERAL TRADE COMMISSION'S FAIR INFORMATION PRACTICE PRINCIPLES
Notice/Awareness (core principle)	Sites must disclose their information practices before collecting data. Includes identification of collector, uses of data, other recipients of data, nature of collection (active/inactive), voluntary or required, consequences of refusal, and steps taken to protect confidentiality, integrity, and quality of the data.
Choice/Consent (core principle)	There must be a choice regime in place allowing consumers to choose how their information will be used for secondary purposes other than supporting the transaction, including internal use and transfer to third parties. Opt-in/opt-out must be available.
Access/Participation	Consumers should be able to review and contest the accuracy and completeness of data collected about them in a timely, inexpensive process.
Security	Data collectors must take reasonable steps to assure that consumer information is accurate and secure from unauthorized use.
Enforcement	There must be a mechanism to enforce FIP principles in place. This can involve self-regulation, legislation giving consumers legal remedies for violations, or federal statutes and regulation.

SOURCE: Based on data from Federal Trade Commission, 1998, 2000a.

TABLE 8.6	FTC RECOMMENDATIONS REGARDING ONLINE PROFILING
PRINCIPLE	DESCRIPTION OF RECOMMENDATION
Notice	Complete transparency to user by providing disclosure and choice options on the host Web site. "Robust" notice for PII (time/place of collection; before collection begins). Clear and conspicuous notice for non-PII.
Choice	Opt-in for PII, opt-out for non-PII. No conversion of non-PII to PII without consent. Opt-out from any or all network advertisers from a single page provided by the host Web site.
Access	Reasonable provisions to allow inspection and correction.
Security	Reasonable efforts to secure information from loss, misuse, or improper access.
Enforcement	Done by independent third parties, such as seal programs and accounting firms.
Restricted collection	Advertising networks will not collect information about sensitive financial or medical topics, sexual behavior or sexual orientation, or use social security numbers for profiling.

SOURCE: Based on data from Federal Trade Commission, 2000b.

The FTC's FIP principles restate and strengthen in a form suitable to deal with online privacy the Fair Information Practices doctrine developed in 1973 by a government study group (U.S. Department of Health, Education and Welfare, 1973).

The FTC's FIP principles set the ground rules for what constitutes due process privacy protection procedures at e-commerce and all other Web sites—including government and nonprofit Web sites—in the United States.

The FTC's FIP principles are guidelines, not laws. They have stimulated private firms and industry associations to develop their own private guidelines (discussed next). However, the FTC's FIP guidelines are often used as the basis of legislation. The most important online privacy legislation to date that has been directly influenced by the FTC's FIP principles is the Children's Online Privacy Protection Act (COPPA) (1998), which requires Web sites to obtain parental permission before collecting information on children under 13 years of age.

In 2000, the FTC recommended legislation to Congress to protect online consumer privacy from the threat posed by advertising networks. **Table 8.6** summarizes the commission's recommendations. The FTC profiling recommendations significantly strengthened the FIP principles of notification and choice, while also including restrictions on information that may be collected.[1] Although the FTC supported industry

---

[1] Much general privacy legislation affecting government, e.g., the Privacy Act of 1974, precludes the government from collecting information on political and social behavior of citizens. The FTC restrictions are significant because they are the FTC's first effort at limiting the collection of certain information.

efforts at self-regulation, it nevertheless recommended legislation to ensure that all Web sites using network advertising and all network advertisers complied.

In the last decade, the FTC's privacy approach has shifted somewhat, away from notice and choice requirements and into a harm-based approach targeting practices that are likely to cause harm or unwarranted intrusion in consumers' daily lives. However, in recent years, the FTC has recognized the limitations of both the notice-and-choice and harm-based models. In 2009, the FTC held a series of three public roundtables to explore the effectiveness of these approaches in light of rapidly evolving technology and the market for consumer data. The major concepts that emerged from these roundtables were:

- The increasing collection and use of consumer data
- Consumers' lack of understanding about the collection and use of their personal data, and the resulting inability to make informed choices
- Consumers' interest in and concern about their privacy
- Benefits of data collection and use to both businesses and consumers
- Decreasing relevance of the distinction between PII and non-PII.

As a result of the roundtables, the FTC has now developed a new framework to address consumer privacy. **Table 8.7** summarizes the important aspects of this framework. Among the most noteworthy is the call for a "Do Not Track" mechanism for online behavioral advertising. The mechanism would involve placing a persistent cookie on a consumer's browser and conveying its setting to sites that the browser visits to signal whether or not the consumer wants to be tracked or receive targeted advertisements. In 2011, several bills were introduced in Congress to implement Do Not Track, but as yet none have been passed.

In response to growing public and congressional concern with online and mobile privacy violations, in 2011 and 2012, the FTC began taking a much more aggressive stance based on its new privacy policies developed over several years. In March 2011, the FTC reached an agreement with Google concerning charges it used deceptive tactics and violated its own privacy policies when it launched its Google Buzz social network, forcing people to join the network even if they selected not to join. Under the settlement, Google agreed to start a privacy program, permit independent privacy audits for 20 years, and face $16,000 fines for every future privacy misrepresentation. This was the first time the FTC had charged a company with such violations and ordered it to start a privacy program (Federal Trade Commission, 2011). In August 2012, the FTC fined Google $22.5 million to settle charges that it had bypassed privacy settings in Apple's Safari browser to be able to track users of the browser and show them advertisements, and violated the earlier privacy settlement with the agency. This fine is the largest civil penalty levied by the FTC to date, which has been cracking down on tech companies for privacy violations and is also investigating Google for antitrust violations (Federal Trade Commission, 2012a). In August 2012, the FTC also reached a settlement with Facebook resolving charges that Facebook deceived its users by telling them they could keep their information on Facebook private, but then repeatedly allowing it to be shared and made public. The settlement requires Facebook to live up

TABLE 8.7	THE FTC'S NEW PRIVACY FRAMEWORK
PRINCIPLE	**APPLICATION**
Scope	Applies to all commercial entities that collect or use consumer data; not limited to those that just collect PII.
Privacy by Design	Companies should promote consumer privacy throughout the organization and at every stage of development of products and services: • Data security • Reasonable collection limits • Reasonable and appropriate data retention policies • Data accuracy • Comprehensive data management procedures
Simplified Choice	Companies should simplify consumer choice. Need not provide choice before collecting and using data for commonly accepted practices: • Product and fulfillment • Internal operations, fraud prevention • Legal compliance • First-party marketing
	For all other commercial data collection and use, choice is required, and should be clearly and conspicuously offered at a time and in context in which consumer is providing data. Some types of information or practices (children, financial, and medical information, deep packet inspection) may require additional protection through enhanced consent. Special choice mechanism for online behavioral advertising: "Do Not Track."
Greater Transparency	Increase transparency of data practices by: • Making privacy notices clearer, shorter, and more standardized to enable better comprehension and comparison • Providing consumers with reasonable access to data about themselves • Providing prominent disclosures and obtaining express affirmative consent before using consumer data in a materially different manner than claimed when data was collected • Educating consumers about commercial data privacy practices

SOURCE: Based on data from Federal Trade Commission, 2010.

to its promises by giving consumers clear and prominent notice and obtaining their express consent before sharing their information beyond the user's privacy settings. It also requires Facebook to develop a comprehensive privacy program, and obtain independent biennial privacy audits for a period of 20 years (Federal Trade Commission, 2012b). In September 2012, the FTC also reached a settlement with Myspace for misrepresenting its privacy policies. The settlement bars Myspace from future misrepresentations, requires the company to implement a comprehensive privacy program, and calls for regular, independent privacy assessments for the next 20 years (Federal Trade Commission, 2012c).

In March 2012, the FTC released a final report based on its work in the previous two years. The report describes industry best practices for protecting the privacy of Americans and focuses on five areas: Do Not Track, mobile privacy, data brokers, large platform providers (advertising networks, operating systems, browsers, and social media companies), and the development of self-regulatory codes. The report called for implementation of an easy to use, persistent, and effective Do Not Track system; improved disclosures for use of mobile data; making it easier for people to see the files about themselves compiled by data brokers; development of a central Web site where data brokers identify themselves; development of a privacy policy by large platform providers to regulate comprehensive tracking across the Internet; and enforcement of self-regulatory rules to ensure firms adhere to industry codes of conduct. The report warned that unless the industry developed a Do Not Track button for Web browsers by the end of the year, and developed policies for reigning in rampant online tracking without user consent by data brokers, it would seek legislation to force these requirements on the industry (Federal Trade Commission, 2012d). The FTC report is supported by the White House, which in February 2012 issued its own framework for protecting online privacy. One provision of this framework is the development of a one-click, one-touch process by which users can tell Internet companies whether they want their online activities tracked. In July 2012, eight members of Congress launched an investigation of data brokers who collect both online and offline data on consumers.

Facing fines, congressional investigations, and public embarrassment over their privacy invading behaviors, with the potential loss of some business and credibility, the major players in the e-commerce industry in the United States are beginning to change some of their policies regarding the treatment of consumer data.

The European Data Protection Directive

In Europe, privacy protection is much stronger than it is in the United States. In the United States, private organizations and businesses are permitted to use PII gathered in commercial transactions for other business purposes without the prior consent of the consumer (so-called secondary uses of PII). In the United States, there is no federal agency charged with enforcing privacy laws. Instead, privacy laws are enforced largely through self-regulation by businesses, and by individuals who must sue agencies or companies in court to recover damages. This is expensive and rarely done. The European approach to privacy protection is more comprehensive and regulatory in nature. European countries do not allow business firms to use PII without the prior consent of consumers. They enforce their privacy laws by creating data protection agencies to pursue complaints brought by citizens and actively enforce privacy laws.

On October 25, 1998, the European Commission's Data Protection Directive went into effect, standardizing and broadening privacy protection in the E.U. nations. The Directive is based on the Fair Information Practices doctrine but extends the control individuals can exercise over their personal information. The Directive requires companies to inform people when they collect information about them and to disclose how it will be stored and used. Customers must provide their informed consent before any company can legally use data about them, and they have the right to access that information, correct it, and request that no further data be collected. Further, the Directive prohibits the transfer of PII to organizations or countries that do not have similarly strong privacy protection policies. This means that data collected in Europe by American business firms cannot be transferred or processed in the United States (which has weaker privacy protection laws). This would potentially interfere with a $3.5 trillion annual trade flow in goods, services, and investment between the United States and Europe.

The U.S. Department of Commerce, working with the European Commission, developed a safe harbor framework for U.S. firms. A **safe harbor** is a private self-regulating policy and enforcement mechanism that meets the objectives of government regulators and legislation, but does not involve government regulation or enforcement. The government plays a role in certifying safe harbors, however. Organizations that decide to participate in the safe harbor program must develop policies that meet European standards, and they must publicly sign on to a Web-based register maintained by the Department of Commerce. Enforcement occurs in the United States and relies to a large extent on self-policing and regulation, backed up by government enforcement of fair trade statutes. For more information on the safe harbor procedures and the E.U. Data Directive, see www.export.gov/safeharbor.

In January 2012, the E.U. issued significant proposed changes to its data protection rules, the first overhaul since 1995 (European Commission, 2012). The new rules would apply to all companies providing services in Europe, and require Internet companies like Amazon, Facebook, Apple, Google, and others to obtain explicit consent from consumers about the use of their personal data, delete information at the user's request (based on the "right to be forgotten"), and retain information only as long as absolutely necessary. The proposed rules provide for fines up to 2% of the annual gross revenue of offending firms. In the case of Google, for instance, with annual revenue of $38 billion, a maximum fine would amount to $760 million. The requirement for user consent includes the use of cookies and super cookies used for tracking purposes across the Web (third-party cookies), and not for cookies used on a Web site. Like the FTC's proposed framework, the EU's new proposed rules have a strong emphasis on regulating tracking, enforcing transparency, limiting data retention periods, and obtaining user consent.

safe harbor
a private self-regulating policy and enforcement mechanism that meets the objectives of government regulators and legislation but does not involve government regulation or enforcement

PRIVATE INDUSTRY SELF-REGULATION

The online industry in the United States has historically opposed online privacy legislation, arguing that industry can do a better job of protecting privacy than government. However, individual firms such as Facebook, Apple, Yahoo, and Google have adopted policies on their own in an effort to address the concerns of the public about personal privacy on the Internet. The online industry formed the Online Privacy Alliance (OPA) in 1998 to encourage self-regulation in part as a reaction to growing public concerns and the threat of legislation being proposed by FTC and privacy advocacy groups.

The FTC and private industry in the United States has created the idea of safe harbors from government regulation. For instance, COPPA includes a provision enabling industry groups or others to submit for the FTC's approval self-regulatory guidelines that implement the protections of the FIP principles and FTC rules. In May

2001, the FTC approved the TRUSTe Internet privacy protection program under the terms of COPPA as a safe harbor.

OPA has developed a set of privacy guidelines that members are required to implement. The primary focus of industry efforts has been the development of online "seals" that attest to the privacy policies on a site. The Better Business Bureau (BBB), TRUSTe, WebTrust, and major accounting firms—among them PricewaterhouseCoopers' BetterWeb—have established seals for Web sites. To display a seal, Web site operators must conform to certain privacy principles, a complaint resolution process, and monitoring by the seal originator. More than 4,000 companies subscribe to TRUSTe and 7,000 Web sites now display the TRUSTe seal, while more than 140,000 display the BBB's Accredited Business seal. Nevertheless, online privacy seal programs have had a limited impact on Web privacy practices. Critics argue that the seal programs are not particularly effective in safeguarding privacy. For these reasons, the FTC has not deemed the seal programs as "safe harbors" yet (with the exception of TRUSTe's children's privacy seal under COPPA), and the agency continues to push for legislation to enforce privacy protection principles.

The advertising network industry has also formed an industry association, the Network Advertising Initiative (NAI), to develop privacy policies. The NAI policies have two objectives: to offer consumers a chance to opt out of advertising network programs (including e-mail campaigns), and to provide consumers redress from abuses. In order to opt out, the NAI has created a Web site—Networkadvertising.org—where consumers can use a global opt-out feature to prevent network advertising agencies from placing their cookies on a user's computer. If a consumer has a complaint, the NAI has a link to the Truste.org Web site where the complaints can be filed. Consumers still receive Internet advertising just as before, but the ads will not be targeted to their browsing behavior (Network Advertising Initiative, 2010; 2011).

In general, industry efforts at self-regulation in online privacy have not succeeded in reducing American fears of privacy invasion during online transactions, or in reducing the level of privacy invasion. At best, self-regulation has offered consumers notice about whether a privacy policy exists, but usually says little about the actual use of the information, does not offer consumers a chance to see and correct the information or control its use in any significant way, offers no promises for the security of that information, and offers no enforcement mechanism (Hoofnagle, 2005).

PRIVACY ADVOCACY GROUPS

There are a number of privacy advocacy groups on the Web that monitor developments in privacy. Some of these sites are industry-supported, while others rely on private foundations and contributions. Some of the better-known sites are listed in **Table 8.8**.

THE EMERGING PRIVACY PROTECTION BUSINESS

As Web sites become more invasive and aggressive in their use of personal information, and as public concern grows, a number of firms have sprung up to sell products that they claim will help people protect their privacy. Venture capital firms have picked up the scent and are investing millions in small start-up companies based on the premise

TABLE 8.8	PRIVACY ADVOCACY GROUPS
ADVOCACY GROUP	**FOCUS**
Epic.org (Electronic Privacy Information Center)	Washington-based watch-dog group
Privacyinternational.org	Watch-dog organization focused on privacy intrusions by government and businesses
Cdt.org (Center for Democracy and Technology)	Foundation- and business-supported group with a legislative focus
Privacy.org	Clearinghouse sponsored by EPIC and Privacy International
Privacyrights.org	Educational clearinghouse
Privacyalliance.org	Industry-supported clearinghouse

that people will pay to protect their reputations. For instance, Reputation.com received $15 million in financing in June 2010 and an additional $41 million in June 2011. Other firms raising money in the business of reputation protection include SocialShield and Abine. For as little as $14.95 a month, you can monitor what people are saying about you, or about your children, on social Web sites. A small number of firms are trying to help users put a price on their personal information, and sell it to the highest bidders if they want (Laudon, 1996). Personal.com and LockerProject are firms that create a personal data locker for users which stores all their online behavioral information in a single location. Users can then decide who they want to give access to, and how much to charge. The idea is to make it possible for people to control the users of their information. Personal.com raised $7 million in venture backing in 2011. These and reputation management firms can succeed only if people are willing to pay out of pocket for privacy protection. Economists studying this issue have found that people are not willing to pay much to protect their privacy (at most about $30), and are willing to give up their privacy for small discounts (Brustein, 2012; Acquisti, et. al., 2009).

TECHNOLOGICAL SOLUTIONS

A number of privacy-enhancing technologies have been developed for protecting user privacy during interactions with Web sites such as spyware blockers, pop-up blockers, cookie managers, and secure e-mail (see **Table 8.9** on page 520). However, the most powerful tools for protecting privacy need to be built into browsers. Responding to pressure from privacy advocates in 2012, browsers have a number of tools that can help users protect their privacy, such as eliminating third party cookies. One of the most powerful browser-based protections is a built-in Do Not Track capability. Microsoft, Mozilla, Google, and Apple have all committed to introducing a default Do Not Track capability by 2013. Most of these tools emphasize security—the ability of individuals to protect their communications and files from illegitimate snoopers.

TABLE 8.9	TECHNOLOGICAL PROTECTIONS FOR ONLINE PRIVACY	
TECHNOLOGY	PRODUCTS	PROTECTION
Spyware blockers	Spyware Doctor, ZoneAlarm, Ad-Aware, and Spybot—Search & Destroy (Spybot-S&D) (freeware)	Detects and removes spyware, adware, keyloggers, and other malware
Pop-up blockers	Browsers: Firefox, IE 7/8/9, Safari, Opera Toolbars: Google, Yahoo, MSN Add-on programs: STOPzilla, Adblock, PopUpMaster	Prevents calls to ad servers that push pop-up, pop-under, and leave-behind ads; restricts downloading of images at user request
Secure e-mail	ZL Technologies; SafeMessage.com, Hushmail.com, Pretty Good Privacy (PGP)	E-mail and document encryption
Anonymous remailers	Jack B. Nymble, Java Anonymous Proxy, QuickSilver, Mixmaster	Send e-mail without trace
Anonymous surfing	Freedom Websecure, Anonymizer.com, Tor, GhostSurf	Surf without a trace
Cookie managers	Cookie Monster and most browsers	Prevents client computer from accepting cookies
Disk/file erasing programs	Mutilate File Wiper, Eraser, Wipe File	Completely erases hard drive and floppy files
Policy generators	OECD Privacy Policy Generator	Automates the development of an OECD privacy compliance policy
Privacy Policy Reader	P3P	Software for automating the communication of privacy policies to users
Public Key Encryption	PGP Desktop	Program that encrypts your mail and documents

8.3   INTELLECTUAL PROPERTY RIGHTS

Congress shall have the power to "promote the progress of science and useful arts, by securing for limited times to authors and inventors the exclusive right to their respective writings and discoveries."

—Article I, Section 8, Constitution of the United States, 1788.

Next to privacy, the most controversial ethical, social, and political issue related to e-commerce is the fate of intellectual property rights. Intellectual property encompasses all the tangible and intangible products of the human mind. As a general rule, in the United States, the creator of intellectual property owns it. For instance, if you personally create an e-commerce site, it belongs entirely to you, and you have exclusive rights to use this "property" in any lawful way you see fit. But the Internet potentially changes things. Once intellectual works become digital, it becomes difficult to control access, use, distribution, and copying. These are precisely the areas that intellectual property seeks to control.

Digital media differ from books, periodicals, and other media in terms of ease of replication, transmission, and alteration; difficulty in classifying a software work as a program, book, or even music; compactness—making theft easy; and difficulty in establishing uniqueness. Before widespread use of the Internet, copies of software, books, magazine articles, or films had to be stored on physical media, such as paper, computer disks, or videotape, creating some hurdles to distribution.

The Internet technically permits millions of people to make perfect digital copies of various works—from music to plays, poems, and journal articles—and then to distribute them nearly cost-free to hundreds of millions of Web users. The proliferation of innovation has occurred so rapidly that few entrepreneurs have stopped to consider who owns the patent on a business technique or method that they are using on their site. The spirit of the Web has been so free-wheeling that many entrepreneurs ignored trademark law and registered domain names that can easily be confused with another company's registered trademarks. In short, the Internet has demonstrated the potential for destroying traditional conceptions and implementations of intellectual property law developed over the last two centuries.

The major ethical issue related to e-commerce and intellectual property concerns how we (both as individuals and as business professionals) should treat property that belongs to others. From a social point of view, the main questions are: Is there continued value in protecting intellectual property in the Internet age? In what ways is society better off, or worse off, for having the concept of property apply to intangible ideas? Should society make certain technology illegal just because it has an adverse impact on some intellectual property owners? From a political perspective, we need to ask how the Internet and e-commerce can be regulated or governed to protect the institution of intellectual property while at the same time encouraging the growth of e-commerce and the Internet.

TYPES OF INTELLECTUAL PROPERTY PROTECTION

There are three main types of intellectual property protection: copyright, patent, and trademark law. In the United States, the development of intellectual property law begins in the U.S. Constitution in 1788, which mandated Congress to devise a system of laws to promote "the progress of science and the useful arts." Congress passed the first copyright law in 1790 to protect original written works for a period of 14 years, with a 14-year renewal if the author was still alive. Since then, the idea of copyright has been extended to include music, films, translations, photographs, and most recently the designs of vessels under 200 feet (Fisher, 1999). The copyright law has been amended (mostly extended) 11 times in the last 40 years.

The goal of intellectual property law is to balance two competing interests—the public and the private. The public interest is served by the creation and distribution of inventions, works of art, music, literature, and other forms of intellectual expression.

The private interest is served by rewarding people for creating these works through the creation of a time-limited monopoly granting exclusive use to the creator.

Maintaining this balance of interests is always challenged by the invention of new technologies. In general, the information technologies of the last century—from radio and television to CD-ROMs, DVDs, and the Internet—have at first tended to weaken the protections afforded by intellectual property law. Owners of intellectual property have often, but not always, been successful in pressuring Congress and the courts to strengthen the intellectual property laws to compensate for any technological threat, and even to extend protection for longer periods of time and to entirely new areas of expression. In the case of the Internet and e-commerce technologies, once again, intellectual property rights are severely challenged. In the next few sections, we discuss the significant developments in each area: copyright, patent, and trademark.

COPYRIGHT: THE PROBLEM OF PERFECT COPIES AND ENCRYPTION

copyright law

protects original forms of expression such as writings, art, drawings, photographs, music, motion pictures, performances, and computer programs from being copied by others for a minimum of 70 years

In the United States, **copyright law** protects original forms of expression such as writings (books, periodicals, lecture notes), art, drawings, photographs, music, motion pictures, performances, and computer programs from being copied by others for a period of time. Up until 1998, the copyright law protected works of individuals for their lifetime plus 50 years beyond their life, and works created for hire and owned by corporations, such as Mickey Mouse of the Disney Corporation, for 75 years after initial creation. Copyright does not protect ideas—just their expression in a tangible medium such as paper, cassette tape, or handwritten notes.

In 1998, Congress extended the period of copyright protection for an additional 20 years, for a total of 95 years for corporate-owned works, and life plus 70 years of protection for works created by individuals (the Copyright Term Extension Act, also known as CTEA). In *Eldred v. Ashcroft*, the Supreme Court ruled on January 16, 2003, that CTEA was constitutional, over the objections of groups arguing that Congress had given copyright holders a permanent monopoly over the expression of ideas, which ultimately would work to inhibit the flow of ideas and creation of new works by making existing works too expensive (Greenhouse, 2003a). Librarians, academics, and others who depend on inexpensive access to copyrighted material opposed the legislation.

In the mid-1960s, the Copyright Office began registering software programs, and in 1980, Congress passed the Computer Software Copyright Act, which clearly provides protection for source and object code and for copies of the original sold in commerce, and sets forth the rights of the purchaser to use the software while the creator retains legal title. For instance, the HTML code for a Web page—even though easily available to every browser—cannot be lawfully copied and used for a commercial purpose, say, to create a new Web site that looks identical.

Copyright protection is clear-cut: it protects against copying of entire programs or their parts. Damages and relief are readily obtained for infringement. The drawback to copyright protection is that the underlying ideas behind a work are not protected, only their expression in a work. A competitor can view the source code on your Web site to see how various effects were created and then reuse those techniques to create a different Web site without infringing on your copyright.

Look and Feel

"Look and feel" copyright infringement lawsuits are precisely about the distinction between an idea and its expression. For instance, in 1988, Apple Computer sued Microsoft Corporation and Hewlett-Packard Inc. for infringing Apple's copyright on the Macintosh interface. Among other claims, Apple claimed that the defendants copied the expression of overlapping windows. Apple failed to patent the idea of overlapping windows when it invented this method of presenting information on a computer screen in the late 1960s. The defendants counterclaimed that the idea of overlapping windows could only be expressed in a single way and, therefore, was not protectable under the "merger" doctrine of copyright law. When ideas and their expression merge (i.e., if there is only one way to express an idea), the expression cannot be copyrighted, although the method of producing the expression might be patentable (*Apple Computer, Inc. v. Microsoft*, 1989). In general, courts appear to be following the reasoning of a 1992 case—*Brown Bag Software vs. Symantec Corp.*—in which the court dissected the elements of software alleged to be infringing. There, the Federal Circuit Court of Appeals found that neither similar concept, function, general functional features (e.g., drop-down menus), nor colors were protectable by copyright law (*Brown Bag vs. Symantec Corp.*, 1992).

Fair Use Doctrine

Copyrights, like all rights, are not absolute. There are situations where strict copyright observance could be harmful to society, potentially inhibiting other rights such as the right to freedom of expression and thought. As a result, the doctrine of fair use has been created. The **doctrine of fair use** permits teachers and writers to use copyrighted materials without permission under certain circumstances. **Table 8.10** describes the five factors that courts consider when assessing what constitutes fair use.

doctrine of fair use
under certain circumstances, permits use of copyrighted material without permission

TABLE 8.10	FAIR USE CONSIDERATIONS TO COPYRIGHT PROTECTIONS
FAIR USE FACTOR	**INTERPRETATION**
Character of use	Nonprofit or educational use versus for-profit use.
Nature of the work	Creative works such as plays or novels receive greater protection than factual accounts, e.g., newspaper accounts.
Amount of work used	A stanza from a poem or a single page from a book would be allowed, but not the entire poem or a book chapter.
Market effect of use	Will the use harm the marketability of the original product? Has it already harmed the product in the marketplace?
Context of use	A last-minute, unplanned use in a classroom versus a planned infringement.

The fair use doctrine draws upon the First Amendment's protection of freedom of speech (and writing). Journalists, writers, and academics must be able to refer to, and cite from, copyrighted works in order to criticize or even discuss copyrighted works. Professors are allowed to clip a contemporary article just before class, copy it, and hand it out to students as an example of a topic under discussion. However, they are not permitted to add this article to the class syllabus for the next semester without compensating the copyright holder.

What constitutes fair use has been at issue in a number of recent cases, including the Google Books Library Project described in the case study at the end of the chapter, and in several recent lawsuits. In *Kelly v. Arriba Soft* (2003) and *Perfect 10, Inc. v. Amazon.com, Inc. et al.,* (2007), the Federal Circuit Court of Appeals for the 9th Circuit held that the display of thumbnail images in response to search requests constituted fair use. A similar result was reached by the district court for the District of Nevada with respect to Google's storage and display of Web sites from cache memory, in *Field v. Google, Inc.* (2006). In all of these cases, the courts accepted the argument that caching the material and displaying it in response to a search request was not only a public benefit, but also a form of marketing of the material on behalf of its copyright owner, thereby enhancing the material's commercial value. Fair use is also at issue in the lawsuit filed by Viacom against Google and YouTube described further in the next section.

The Digital Millennium Copyright Act of 1998

Digital Millennium Copyright Act (DMCA)

the first major effort to adjust the copyright laws to the Internet age

The Digital Millennium Copyright Act (DMCA) of 1998 is the first major effort to adjust the copyright laws to the Internet age. This legislation was the result of a confrontation between the major copyright holders in the United States (publishing, sheet music, record label, and commercial film industries), ISPs, and users of copyrighted materials such as libraries, universities, and consumers. While social and political institutions are sometimes thought of as "slow" and the Internet as "fast," in this instance, powerful groups of copyright owners anticipated Web music services such as Napster by several years. Napster was formed in 1999, but work by the World Intellectual Property Organization (WIPO)—a worldwide body formed by the major copyright-holding nations of North America, Europe, and Japan—began in 1995. **Table 8.11** summarizes the major provisions of the DMCA.

The penalties for willfully violating the DMCA include restitution to the injured parties of any losses due to infringement. Criminal remedies may include fines up to $500,000 or five years imprisonment for a first offense, and up to $1 million in fines and 10 years in prison for repeat offenders. These are serious remedies.

The DMCA attempts to answer two vexing questions in the Internet age. First, how can society protect copyrights online when any practical encryption scheme imaginable can be broken by hackers and the results distributed worldwide? Second, how can society control the behavior of thousands of ISPs, who often host infringing Web sites or who provide Internet service to individuals who are routine infringers? ISPs claim to be like telephone utilities—just carrying messages—and they do not want to put their users under surveillance or invade the privacy of users. The DMCA recognizes that ISPs have some control over how their customers use their facilities.

TABLE 8.11	THE DIGITAL MILLENNIUM COPYRIGHT ACT
SECTION	**IMPORTANCE**
Title I, WIPO Copyright and Performances and Phonograms Treaties Implementation	Makes it illegal to circumvent technological measures to protect works for either access or copying or to circumvent any electronic rights management information.
Title II, Online Copyright Infringement Liability Limitation	Requires ISPs to "take down" sites they host if they are infringing copyrights, and requires search engines to block access to infringing sites. Limits liability of ISPs and search engines.
Title III, Computer Maintenance Competition Assurance	Permits users to make a copy of a computer program for maintenance or repair of the computer.
Title IV, Miscellaneous Provisions	Requires the Copyright Office to report to Congress on the use of copyright materials for distance education; allows libraries to make digital copies of works for internal use only; extends musical copyrights to include "webcasting."

SOURCE: Based on data from United States Copyright Office, 1998.

The DMCA implements the WIPO Copyright Treaty of 1996, which declares it illegal to make, distribute, or use devices that circumvent technology-based protections of copyrighted materials, and attaches stiff fines and prison sentences for violations. WIPO is an organization within the United Nations. Recognizing that these provisions alone cannot stop hackers from devising circumventions, the DMCA makes it difficult for such inventors to reap the fruits of their labors by making the ISPs (including universities) responsible and accountable for hosting Web sites or providing services to infringers once the ISP has been notified. ISPs are not required to intrude on their users. However, after copyright holders inform the ISP that a hosted site or individual users are infringing, they must "take down" the site immediately to avoid liability and potential fines. ISPs must also inform their subscribers of the ISP's copyright management policies. Copyright owners can subpoena the personal identities of any infringers using an ISP. There are important limitations on these ISP prohibitions that are mostly concerned with the transitory caching of materials for short periods without the knowledge of the ISP. However, should the ISP be deriving revenues from the infringement, it is as liable as the infringer, and is subject to the same penalties.

Title I of the DMCA provides a partial answer to the dilemma of hacking. It is probably true that skilled hackers can easily break any usable encryption scheme, and the means to do so on a large scale through distribution of decryption programs already exists. The WIPO provisions accept this possibility and simply make it illegal to do so, or to disseminate or enable such dissemination, or even store and transmit decrypted products or tools. These provisions put large ISPs on legal notice.

There are a number of exceptions to the strong prohibitions against defeating a copyright protection scheme outlined above. There are exceptions for libraries to examine works for adoption, for reverse engineering to achieve interoperability with other software, for encryption research, for privacy protection purposes, and for security testing. Many companies, such as YouTube and Google, have latched on to the provision of the DMCA that relates to removing infringing material upon request of the copyright owner as a "safe harbor" that precludes them from being held responsible for copyright infringement. This position is currently being tested in a $1 billion lawsuit originally brought by Viacom in 2007 against Google and YouTube for willful copyright infringement.

In the Viacom case, Viacom alleges that YouTube and Google engaged in massive copyright infringement by deliberately and knowingly building up a library of infringing works to draw traffic to the YouTube site and enhance its commercial value. In response, Google and YouTube claim that they are protected by the DMCA's safe harbor and fair use, and that it is often impossible to know whether a video is infringing or not. YouTube also does not display ads on pages where consumers can view videos unless it has an agreement with the content owner. In October 2007, Google announced a filtering system (ContentID) aimed at addressing the problem. It requires content owners to give Google a copy of their content so Google can load it into an auto-identification system. The copyright owner can specify whether it will allow others to post the material. Then after a video is uploaded to YouTube, the system attempts to match it with its database of copyrighted material and removes any unauthorized material. Whether content owners will be satisfied with this system is unknown, particularly since guidelines issued by a coalition of major media and Internet companies with respect to the handling of copyrighted videos on user-generated Web sites calls for the use of filtering technology that can block infringing material before it is posted online. In June 2010, the federal district court ruled against Viacom, on the grounds that YouTube had taken down more than 100,000 videos requested by Viacom, as required by the DMCA, and that YouTube was protected by the safe harbor provisions of DMCA. In 2011, Viacom continues to appeal the case. In April 2012, a U.S. appeals court reversed the lower court decision, allowing the case to move forward. The court ruled that YouTube had specific knowledge or awareness of the infringing activity, and ample ability to prevent it.

The entertainment industry continues to be aggressive in pursuing online copyright infringement. In 2011, in a suit brought by the Motion Picture Association of America, a federal judge ordered DVD-streaming service Zediva to shut down. Zediva had argued that its service was just like one person lending a physical DVD to another, but just using the Web to accomplish the task. The court did not agree and said that the service threatened the growing Internet-based video-on-demand market.

File-sharing continues to be an ongoing copyright issue as well. File sharing sites keep popping up and are just as quickly being sued. Grooveshark, a U.S. digital music service that lets subscribers stream several million of songs for free, is being sued by the four major music firms for copyright infringement. Grooveshark obtains its music in part by encouraging users to upload their music to Grooveshark servers in order to share with others. Grooveshark claims that under DMCA's Safe Harbor provisions, it can store music tracks as long as it agrees to take them down when asked by copyright holders (Sisario, 2012). Grooveshark argues that its users have a right to share their own music with whomever they want. In 2012, both Google and Apple have removed Grooveshark apps from their stores.

Refer back to the case study at the end of Chapter 1, *The Pirate Bay: The World's Most Resilient Copyright Infringer?* for further discussion of copyright issues in e-commerce.

PATENTS: BUSINESS METHODS AND PROCESSES

> "Whoever invents or discovers any new and useful process, machine, manufacture, or composition of matter, or any new and useful improvement thereof, may obtain a patent therefore, subject to the conditions and requirements of this title."
>
> —Section 101, U.S. Patent Act

A **patent** grants the owner a 20-year exclusive monopoly on the ideas behind an invention. The congressional intent behind patent law was to ensure that inventors of new machines, devices, or industrial methods would receive the full financial and other rewards of their labor and still make widespread use of the invention possible by providing detailed diagrams for those wishing to use the idea under license from the patent's owner. Patents are obtained from the United States Patent and Trademark Office (USPTO), which was created in 1812. Obtaining a patent is much more difficult and time-consuming than obtaining copyright protection (which is automatic with the creation of the work). Patents must be formally applied for, and the granting of a patent is determined by Patent Office examiners who follow a set of rigorous rules. Ultimately, federal courts decide when patents are valid and when infringement occurs.

patent
grants the owner an exclusive monopoly on the ideas behind an invention for 20 years

Patents are very different from copyrights because patents protect the ideas themselves and not merely the expression of ideas. There are four types of inventions for which patents are granted under patent law: machines, man-made products, compositions of matter, and processing methods. The Supreme Court has determined that patents extend to "anything under the sun that is made by man" (*Diamond v. Chakrabarty*, 1980) as long as the other requirements of the Patent Act are met. There are three things that cannot be patented: laws of nature, natural phenomena, and abstract ideas. For instance, a mathematical algorithm cannot be patented unless it is realized in a tangible machine or process that has a "useful" result (the mathematical algorithm exception).

In order to be granted a patent, the applicant must show that the invention is new, original, novel, nonobvious, and not evident in prior arts and practice. As with copyrights, the granting of patents has moved far beyond the original intent of Congress's first patent statute, which sought to protect industrial designs and machines. Patent protection has been extended to articles of manufacture (1842), plants (1930), surgical and medical procedures (1950), and software (1981). The Patent Office did not accept applications for software patents until a 1981 Supreme Court decision that held that computer programs could be a part of a patentable process. Since that time, thousands of software patents have been granted. Virtually any software program can be patented as long as it is novel and not obvious.

Essentially, as technology and industrial arts progress, patents have been extended to both encourage entrepreneurs to invent useful devices and promote widespread dissemination of the new techniques through licensing and artful imitation of the published patents (the creation of devices that provide the same functionality as the invention but use different methods) (Winston, 1998). Patents encourage inventors to come up with unique ways of achieving the same functionality as existing patents. For instance, Amazon's patent on one-click purchasing caused Barnesandnoble.com to invent a simplified two-click method of purchasing.

The danger of patents is that they stifle competition by raising barriers to entry into an industry. Patents force new entrants to pay licensing fees to incumbents, and thus slow down the development of technical applications of new ideas by creating lengthy licensing applications and delays. The *Insight on Technology* case, *Theft and Innovation: The Patent Trial of the Century*, examines these issues in the context of the Apple-Samsung lawsuit with respect to infringement of Apple's patents for the iPhone.

E-commerce Patents

Much of the Internet's infrastructure and software was developed under the auspices of publicly funded scientific and military programs in the United States and Europe. Unlike Samuel F. B. Morse, who patented the idea of Morse code and made the telegraph useful, most of the inventions that make the Internet and e-commerce possible were not patented by their inventors. The early Internet was characterized by a spirit of worldwide community development and sharing of ideas without consideration of personal wealth (Winston, 1998). This early Internet spirit changed in the mid-1990s with the commercial development of the World Wide Web.

In 1998, a landmark legal decision, *State Street Bank & Trust v. Signature Financial Group, Inc.*, paved the way for business firms to begin applying for "business methods" patents. In this case, a Federal Circuit Court of Appeals upheld the claims of Signature Financial to a valid patent for a business method that allows managers to monitor and record financial information flows generated by a partner fund. Previously, it was thought business methods could not be patented. However, the court ruled there was no reason to disallow business methods from patent protection, or any "step by step process, be it electronic or chemical or mechanical, [that] involves an algorithm in the broad sense of the term" (*State Street Bank & Trust Co. v. Signature Financial Group*, 1998). The State Street decision led to an explosion in applications for e-commerce "business methods" patents. In June 2010, the U.S. Supreme Court issued a divided opinion on business methods patents in the *Bilski et al. v. Kappos* case (*Bilski et al. v. Kappos*, 2010). The majority argued that business methods patents were allowable even though they did not meet the traditional "machine or transformation test," in which patents are granted to devices that are tied to a particular machine, are a machine, or transform articles from one state to another. The minority wanted to flatly declare business methods are not patentable in part because any series of steps could be considered a business method (Schwartz, 2010).

INSIGHT ON TECHNOLOGY

THEFT AND INNOVATION: THE PATENT TRIAL OF THE CENTURY

Imagine you have just bought the car of your dreams, one with an unmistakable, unique, look on the outside and with some very unique features on the inside. You drive the car home to show friends and relatives. Across the street, a neighbor has parked his newly purchased car in his driveway. It looks strikingly similar but was manufactured by a different firm. On the inside, you find that it has all the features that your car dealer claimed were unique to your car. Your neighbor bought the car for substantially less than you paid. You might feel "cheated" as a consumer, paying so much more for an identical product. How would you feel if you were the manufacturer?

Apple found itself in a situation similar to the one above when Samsung introduced its line of Galaxy smartphones in 2010, phones that Apple claimed were nearly identical in design and functionality to Apple's iPhone, right down to the icons that bounced when clicked and the polished metal band around the phone. Apple sued Samsung for violating its patents for iPhones, iPads, and iPods in 2011 and on August 24, 2012, a California jury in federal district court delivered a decisive victory to Apple and a stunning defeat to Samsung. The jury awarded Apple $1 billion in damages in what some have called the patent trial of the century because it established criteria for determining just how close a competitor can come to an industry-leading and standard setting product like Apple's iPhone before it violates its patents. The same court ruled that Samsung could not sell its new tablet computer (Galaxy 10.1) in the United States. This was not just a loss for Samsung, but a warning shot across the bow for Google,

which developed the Android operating system, and all other makers of Android phones.

In January 2007, Apple introduced the first iPhone. The iPhone was a truly remarkable advance in design and technology. It was the first smartphone that combined, in a single device, the functionality of a phone with a music and video player and an Internet browser. The iPhone turned out to be wildly popular and quickly captured more than 70% of the smartphone market worldwide at its high point. Apple refused to license the iPhone iOS operating system to other manufacturers, and tied it closely to its iTunes store and its newly introduced App Store.

In the same year, Google introduced the Android operating system and licensed it without charge to smartphone manufacturers in return for retaining the rights to place mobile ads on Android devices and other considerations. Android is an open source operating system. Thousands of programmers around the world contribute to its development, which is led by the Android Open Source Project controlled by Google. The Open Handset Alliance was also formed in 2007 by 86 hardware, software, and telecommunications companies, led by Google, to advance open standards for mobile devices. Aside from Google, the Alliance included HTC, a Korean cell phone maker, and Samsung, the largest electronics component, consumer device, and cell phone manufacturer in the world. Samsung is also based in Korea. The Alliance was clearly a coordinated effort of the firms involved to develop a smartphone that was competitive with the iPhone. The iPhone had caught the world's other phone manufacturers completely flatfooted. The first HTC Android phones were sold in 2008, followed shortly by a

(continued)

Samsung Android phone. By 2012, nearly 1 billion people in the world used smartphones (115 million in the United States), and Android phones had grabbed the lead in global smartphone sales, with a 60% market share, Apple's share had dwindled to about 30%. For every iPhone sold, three Androids are sold in the global market. Nevertheless, Apple is the largest single manufacturer of smartphones, the most valuable company in the United States, and is expected to be the first company in history to attain a stock market valuation of $1 trillion dollars.

Samsung introduced the Galaxy S in September 2010. While the early Samsung smartphones of 2008-2010 did not look like Apple's iPhones or have the same functionality, the Galaxy S was clearly designed to compete against the iPhone, with similar functionality, and it looked strikingly like an iPhone—so much so that Apple sued Samsung in June 2011 for trademark and patent infringement, unfair competition, and other violations of law.

Apple alleged in its complaint that Samsung had quite literally copied the functionality and design of the Apple iPhone. Apple claimed that Samsung violated Apple's so-called "utility patents" like the multi-touch interface (which enables gestures such as selecting, scrolling, pinching, and zooming); arrangement of text on screen; arrangement and actions of images (such as bounce-back when user scrolls down too far), and the movement of buttons when pressed. Apple had been granted patents for these "fundamental features" that the world has come associate with Apple products.

Apple also claimed infringement of its "trade dress" patents. Trade dress patents cover non-functional design elements of physical devices such as the unique and ornamental appearance of the iPhone: the black face, bezel, a matrix of on-screen icons, a black thin rim surrounding a flat screen, a rectangular product with four rounded corners, a display screen under a clear glass surface, a thin metallic band around the outside edge, a row of small dots on the display screen, screen icons with evenly rounded corners, and a bottom dock of evenly rounded square icons.

Apple also claimed Samsung violated its registered trademarks, principally by copying the design of its interface icons. For instance, Apple trademarked its phone icon that users tap to dial a phone. The icon is green in color with a white silhouette of a phone handset arranged at a 45 degree angle and centered on the icon that represents the application for making telephone calls. All the icons on the iPhone screen are similarly trademarked. Samsung's Galaxy interface icons are identical according to Apple's complaint.

In a counter-complaint, Samsung denied infringing any Apple patents, and questioned the integrity of the patents issued by the U.S. Patent Office on the grounds that functionality of the utility patents had already been prior art that Apple itself copied. Samsung simply denied the trade dress and trademark infringement claims. Samsung claimed as well that Apple had violated its patents on various electronic components that perform critical functions in cell and smartphones. Samsung asked for $422 million in damages. Usually patent and trademark cases are settled out of court after a fair amount of posturing. But in this case, the parties could not come to an agreement, and the case went to a jury trial, a rare, risky, and expensive endeavor.

On August 24, 2012, the jury delivered a decisive victory to Apple and a stunning defeat to Samsung, and awarded Apple $1 billion in damages. The jury found in over 700 determinations that Samsung had violated Apple's utility patents covering things like the "bounce back" effect at the end of lists, and the ability to distinguish between one-finger scrolling and two-finger scrolling. The jury found Samsung had

(continued)

also violated Apple's trade dress patents protecting the physical design of the iPhone, and the trademarked icons as well. The jury flatly denied Samsung's claims that Apple violated its patents on various components, and rejected Samsung's claim for $422 million in damages. Samsung is appealing. Generally in these cases an out-of-court settlement is reached, but given the hostility between the firms, Apple may not settle if only as a warning to Google and other Android phone makers that they may not copy the design and functionality of the iPhone. An Apple spokeswoman said the decision sent a clear message that stealing is not right, and that Apple builds to delight its customers, not for competitors to flagrantly copy. Shortly before his death in 2012, Steve Jobs characterized the Android Samsung and other similar copycats as stolen products.

The Apple vs. Samsung case raises several issues for manufacturers of smartphones, consumers, and the development of the smartphone market. But it also raises ethical issues having to do with what's right and what's wrong. Few, if any, would argue that it's ethically acceptable to copy another person's work (their intellectual property), claim it is your own, and be well rewarded by the marketplace for the theft. In a society that respects property rights, this would seem to be a contradiction: people could take your house or car if they wanted and sell them. Nobody wants this outcome. Copycat designs challenge one of the foundations of intellectual (and other property) which argues that people (and companies) deserve the rewards of their investments and efforts—the "sweat of the brow" theory.

Business critics of the decision argue that innovation in the marketplace will be harmed and slowed down because the inventions of one firm cannot be built upon, but will have to be designed around, slowing the introduction of innovations. They also argue that some of the features Apple claims to own are part of the "standard design" of a smartphone without which a contemporary smartphone can't be built, or only built by the one firm that owns the patents. This would include features of Apple's multi-touch interface like pinching, zooming, and active icons. This is the "steering wheel" argument: you can't build a car without a steering wheel because it's become the standard design in the market. Owners of the steering wheel patent must therefore license the steering wheel patent for a reasonable fee. If smartphone makers could not use some of Apple's patented features, the smartphone market would become fractionated into a plethora of designs, and some phones would have missing features that consumers expect (like pinch to zoom).

Supporters of the decision argue that it provides incentives for firms to invest in design, and come up with new innovations, rather than just copy existing state of the art designs. They point to Windows Phone, Microsoft's operating system for smartphones, which looks nothing like the iOS interface and has received praise for its distinctive design. Moreover, innovative firms like Apple deserve to be rewarded for their research and successful designs and products. Without financial incentives, innovation will decline or disappear. Why should firms innovate if they cannot be rewarded in the marketplace?

SOURCES: United States Patent Office, "Intelligent Automated Assistant," Apple Inc., United States Patent Application, 20120245944, September 27, 2012; "Apple Seeks U.S. Samsung Sales Ban, $707 Million More in Damages," *Reuters*, September 22, 2012; "Samsung Fails to Defeat Galaxy Table Sale Ban in Apple Case," by Joel Rosenblatt, Bloomberg News, September 19, 2012; "Apple Did Not Violate Samsung Patents: U.S. Trade Judge," by Diane Bartz, *Reuters*, September 14, 2012; " Apple Case Muddies the Future of Innovations," by Nick Wingfield, *New York Times*, August 26, 2012; "Apple-Samsung Case Shows Smartphone as Legal Magnet," by Steve Lohr, *New York Times*, August 25, 2012; "Jury Awards $1 Billion to Apple in Samsung Patent Case," by Nick Wingfield, *New York Times*, August 24, 2012; "Apple v. Samsung: The Patent Trial of the Century," by Ashby Jones and Jessica Vascellaro, *Wall Street Journal*, July 24, 2012; Apple v. Samsung, Complaint, United States District Court, Northern District of California, Case No. 11-cv-01846-LHK, June 16, 2011.

Table 8.12 lists some of the better-known, controversial e-commerce patents. Reviewing these, you can understand the concerns of commentators and corporations. Some of the patent claims are very broad (for example, "name your price" sales methods), have historical precedents in the pre-Internet era (shopping carts), and seem "obvious" (one-click purchasing). Critics of online business methods patents argue that the Patent Office has been too lenient in granting such patents, and that in most instances, the supposed inventions merely copy pre-Internet business methods and thus do not constitute "inventions" (Harmon, 2003; Thurm, 2000; Chiappetta, 2001). The Patent Office argues, on the contrary, that its Internet inventions staff is composed of engineers, lawyers, and specialists with many years of experience with Internet and network technologies, and that it consults with outside technology experts before granting patents. To complicate matters, the European Patent Convention and the patent laws of most European countries do not recognize business methods per se unless the method is implemented through some technology (Takenaka, 2001).

Patent Reform

Issues related to business methods patents, patent "trolls" (companies such as Acacia Technologies that buy up broadly worded patents on a speculative basis and then use them to threaten companies that are purportedly violating the patent), and confusing legal decisions led to increasing calls for patent reform over the last few years, particularly by companies in the technology sector. One target of such legislation are firms that produce nothing but simply collect patents and then seek to enforce them. In 2000, Nathan Myhrvold formed a new kind of patent investment firm called Intellectual Ventures. A former Microsoft chief technology officer, Myhrvold has amassed a collection of more than 20,000 patents in the digital technology field, including e-commerce, by purchasing them from small companies and entrepreneurs. He discovers large firms that may be violating those patents and threatens to sue. Sony, Google, Verizon, and many other large firms have paid up, and in addition, have invested in the company so they can participate in future revenues (Sharma and Clark, 2008). In 2010, Microsoft co-founder Paul Allen, one of the world's richest men, sued most of Silicon Valley, including Google, Facebook, and eBay, claiming that he had invented many elements of their operations years before. Allen claims his former company, Interval Research, invented pop-up stock quotes, suggestions for related reading, and videos alongside a screen, among other common elements of today's Web sites. In another patent troll case, in 2011, Walker Digital, which calls itself a research and development laboratory for technology patents, filed 15 lawsuits against 100 different companies, including Apple, Microsoft, eBay, Amazon, and Google.

In September 2011, after many years of back-and-forth in Congress, a patent reform bill, the America Invents Act, was finally passed and signed into law. Among other changes, it will switch the U.S. patent system from a "first-to-invent" system to a "first-to-file" system, which many believe will be less prone to litigation. It also provides a new way to challenge patents out of court, and will allow start-up firms to get fast-track consideration of their patent applications, within 12 months, rather than the 30-plus months they typically must wait.

TABLE 8.12	SELECTED E-COMMERCE PATENTS	
COMPANY	SUBJECT	UPDATE
Amazon	One-click purchasing	Amazon attempted to use patent originally granted to it in 1999 to force changes to Barnes & Noble's Web site, but a federal court overturned a previously issued injunction. Eventually settled out of court. In September 2007, a USPTO panel rejected some of the patent because of evidence another patent predated it, sending it back to the patent examiner for reconsideration. Amazon amended the patent, and the revised version was confirmed in March 2010.
Eolas Technologies	Embedding interactive content in a Web site	Eolas Technologies, a spin-off of the University of California, obtained patent in 1998. Eolas filed suit against Microsoft in 1999 for infringing the patent in Internet Explorer and was awarded a $520 million judgment in 2003.
Priceline	Buyer-driven "name your price" sales	Originally invented by Walker Digital, an intellectual property laboratory, and then assigned to Priceline. Granted by the USPTO in 1999. Shortly thereafter, Priceline sued Microsoft and Expedia for copying its patented business method.
Sightsound	Music downloads	Sightsound won a settlement in 2004 against Bertelsmann subsidiaries CDNow and N2K music sites for infringing its patent.
Akamai	Internet content delivery global hosting system	A broad patent granted in 2000 covering techniques for expediting the flow of information over the Internet. Akamai sued Digital Island (subsequently acquired by Cable & Wireless) for violating the patent and, in 2001, a jury found in its favor.
DoubleClick	Dynamic delivery of online advertising	The patent underlying DoubleClick's business of online banner ad delivery, originally granted in 2000. DoubleClick sued competitors 24/7 Real Media and L90 for violating the patent and ultimately reached a settlement with them.
Overture	Pay for performance search	System and method for influencing position on search result list generated by computer search engine, granted in 2001. Competitor FindWhat.com sued Overture, charging that patent was obtained illegally; Overture countered by suing both FindWhat and Google for violating patent. Google agreed to pay a license fee to Overture in 2004 to settle.
Acacia Technologies	Streaming video media transmission	Patents for the receipt and transmission of streaming digital audio and or video content originally granted to founders of Greenwich Information Technologies in 1990s. Patents were purchased by Acacia, a firm founded solely to enforce the patents, in 2001.
Soverain Software	Purchase technology	The so-called "shopping cart" patent for network-based systems, which involves any transaction over a network involving a seller, buyer, and payment system. In other words, e-commerce! Originally owned by Open Markets, then Divine Inc., and now Soverain. Soverain filed suit against Amazon for patent infringement, which Amazon paid $40 million to settle.
MercExchange (Thomas Woolston)	Auction technology	Patents on person-to-person auctions and database search, originally granted in 1995. eBay ordered to pay $25 million in 2003 for infringing on patent. In July 2007, the U.S. district court denied a motion for permanent patent injunction against eBay using the "Buy It Now" feature. MercExchange and eBay settled the dispute in 2008 on confidential terms.
Google	Search technology	Google PageRank patent was filed in 1998 and granted in 2001. Becomes non-exclusive in 2011 and expires in 2017.
Google	Location technology	Google issued a patent in 2010 for a method of using location information in an advertising system.
Apple	Social technology	Apple applied for a patent in 2010 that allows groups of friends attending events to stay in communication with each other and share reactions to live events as they are occurring.

TRADEMARKS: ONLINE INFRINGEMENT AND DILUTION

A trademark is "any word, name, symbol, or device, or any combination thereof ... used in commerce ... to identify and distinguish ... goods ... from those manufactured or sold by others and to indicate the source of the goods."

—The Trademark Act, 1946

trademark
a mark used to identify and distinguish goods and indicate their source

Trademark law is a form of intellectual property protection for **trademarks**—a mark used to identify and distinguish goods and indicate their source. Trademark protections exist at both the federal and state levels in the United States. The purpose of trademark law is twofold. First, trademark law protects the public in the marketplace by ensuring that it gets what it pays for and wants to receive. Second, trademark law protects the owner—who has spent time, money, and energy bringing the product to the marketplace—against piracy and misappropriation. Trademarks have been extended from single words to pictures, shapes, packaging, and colors. Some things may not be trademarked such as common words that are merely descriptive ("clock"). Federal trademarks are obtained, first, by use in interstate commerce, and second, by registration with the U.S. Patent and Trademark Office (USPTO). Federal trademarks are granted for a period of 10 years and can be renewed indefinitely.

Disputes over federal trademarks involve establishing infringement. The test for infringement is twofold: market confusion and bad faith. Use of a trademark that creates confusion with existing trademarks, causes consumers to make market mistakes, or misrepresents the origins of goods is an infringement. In addition, the intentional misuse of words and symbols in the marketplace to extort revenue from legitimate trademark owners ("bad faith") is proscribed.

dilution
any behavior that would weaken the connection between the trademark and the product

In 1995, Congress passed the Federal Trademark Dilution Act (FTDA), which created a federal cause of action for dilution of famous marks. This legislation dispenses with the test of market confusion (although that is still required to claim infringement), and extends protection to owners of famous trademarks against **dilution**, which is defined as any behavior that would weaken the connection between the trademark and the product. In 2006, the FTDA was amended by the Trademark Dilution Revision Act (TDRA), which allows a trademark owner to file a claim based on a "likelihood of dilution" standard, rather than having to provide evidence of actual dilution. The TDRA also expressly provides that dilution may occur through blurring (weakening the connection between the trademark and the goods) and tarnishment (using the trademark in a way that makes the underlying products appear unsavory or unwholesome).

Trademarks and the Internet

The rapid growth and commercialization of the Internet have provided unusual opportunities for existing firms with distinctive and famous trademarks to extend their brands to the Internet. These same developments have provided malicious individuals and firms the opportunity to squat on Internet domain names built upon famous marks, as well as attempt to confuse consumers and dilute famous or distinctive marks (including your personal name or a movie star's name). The conflict between legitimate trademark owners and malicious firms was allowed to fester and grow because Network Solutions Inc. (NSI), originally the Internet's sole agency for domain name registration for many years, had a policy of "first come, first served." This meant anyone could register any domain name that had not already been registered, regardless of the trademark status of the domain name. NSI was not authorized to decide trademark issues (Nash, 1997).

In response to a growing number of complaints from owners of famous trademarks who found their trademark names being appropriated by Web entrepreneurs, Congress passed the **Anticybersquatting Consumer Protection Act (ACPA)** in November 1999. The ACPA creates civil liabilities for anyone who attempts in bad faith to profit from an existing famous or distinctive trademark by registering an Internet domain name that is identical or confusingly similar to, or "dilutive" of, that trademark. The act does not establish criminal sanctions. The act proscribes using "bad-faith" domain names to extort money from the owners of the existing trademark **(cybersquatting)**, or using the bad-faith domain to divert Web traffic to the bad-faith domain that could harm the good will represented by the trademark, create market confusion, tarnish, or disparage the mark **(cyberpiracy)**. The act also proscribes the use of a domain name that consists of the name of a living person, or a name confusingly similar to an existing personal name, without that person's consent, if the registrant is registering the name with the intent to profit by selling the domain name to that person.

Trademark abuse can take many forms on the Web. **Table 8.13** on page 536 lists the major behaviors on the Internet that have run afoul of trademark law, and some of the court cases that resulted.

Cybersquatting and Brandjacking

In one of the first cases involving the ACPA, E. & J. Gallo Winery, owner of the registered mark "Ernest and Julio Gallo" for alcoholic beverages, sued Spider Webs Ltd. for using the domain name Ernestandjuliogallo.com. Spider Webs Ltd. was a domain name speculator that owned numerous domain names consisting of famous company names. The Ernestandjuliogallo.com Web site contained information on the risks of alcohol use, anti-corporate articles about E. & J. Gallo Winery, and was poorly constructed. The court concluded that Spider Webs Ltd. was in violation of the ACPA and that its actions constituted dilution by blurring because the Ernestandjuliogallo.com domain name appeared on every page printed off the Web site accessed by that name, and that Spider Webs Ltd. was not free to use this particular mark as a domain name (*E. & J. Gallo Winery v. Spider Webs Ltd.*, 2001). In August 2009, a court upheld the largest cybersquatting judgment to date: a $33 million verdict in favor of Verizon against OnlineNIC, an Internet domain registration company that had used over 660 names that could easily be confused with legitimate Verizon domain names. Although there have not been many cases decided under the ACPA, that does not mean the problem has gone away. For instance, in 2011, MarkMonitor looked at incidents of brandjacking in the online sports apparel industry, and found almost 500 cybersquatting sites. A previous study of the luxury industry found more than 1,200 cybersquatting Web sites.

Anticybersquatting Consumer Protection Act (ACPA)

creates civil liabilities for anyone who attempts in bad faith to profit from an existing famous or distinctive trademark by registering an Internet domain name that is identical or confusingly similar to, or "dilutive" of, that trademark

cybersquatting

involves the registration of an infringing domain name, or other Internet use of an existing trademark, for the purpose of extorting payments from the legitimate owners

cyberpiracy

involves the same behavior as cybersquatting, but with the intent of diverting traffic from the legitimate site to an infringing site

TABLE 8.13	INTERNET AND TRADEMARK LAW EXAMPLES	
ACTIVITY	DESCRIPTION	EXAMPLE CASE
Cybersquatting	Registering domain names similar or identical to trademarks of others to extort profits from legitimate holders	*E. & J. Gallo Winery v. Spider Webs Ltd.*, 129 F. Supp. 2d 1033 (S.D. Tex., 2001) aff'd 286 F. 3d 270 (5th Cir., 2002)
Cyberpiracy	Registering domain names similar or identical to trademarks of others to divert Web traffic to their own sites	*Ford Motor Co. v. Lapertosa*, 2001 U.S. Dist. LEXIS 253 (E.D. Mich., 2001); *PaineWebber Inc. v. Fortuny*, Civ. A. No. 99-0456-A (E.D. Va., 1999); *Playboy Enterprises, Inc. v. Global Site Designs, Inc.*, 1999 WL 311707 (S.D. Fla., 1999), *Audi AG and Volkswagen of America Inc. v. Bob D'Amato* (No. 05-2359; 6th Cir., November 27, 2006)
Metatagging	Using trademarked words in a site's metatags	*Bernina of America, Inc. v. Fashion Fabrics Int'l, Inc.*, 2001 U.S. Dist. LEXIS 1211 (N.D. Ill., 2001); *Nissan Motor Co., Ltd. v. Nissan Computer Corp.*, 289 F. Supp. 2d 1154 (C.D. Cal., 2000), aff'd, 246 F. 3rd 675 (9th Cir., 2000)
Keywording	Placing trademarked keywords on Web pages, either visible or invisible	*Playboy Enterprises, Inc. v. Netscape Communications, Inc.*, 354 F. 3rd 1020 (9th Cir., 2004); *Nettis Environment Ltd. v. IWI, Inc.*, 46 F. Supp. 2d 722 (N.D. Ohio, 1999); *Government Employees Insurance Company v. Google, Inc.*, Civ. Action No. 1:04cv507 (E.D. VA, 2004); *Google, Inc. v. American Blind & Wallpaper Factory, Inc.*, Case No. 03-5340 JF (RS) (N.D. Cal., April 18, 2007)
Linking	Linking to content pages on other sites, bypassing the home page	*Ticketmaster Corp. v. Tickets.com*, 2000 U.S. Dist. Lexis 4553 (C.D. Cal., 2000)
Framing	Placing the content of other sites in a frame on the infringer's site	*The Washington Post, et al. v. TotalNews, Inc., et al.*, (S.D.N.Y., Civil Action Number 97-1190)

Cyberpiracy

Cyberpiracy involves the same behavior as cybersquatting, but with the intent of diverting traffic from the legitimate site to an infringing site. In *Ford Motor Co. v. Lapertosa*, Lapertosa had registered and used a Web site called Fordrecalls.com as an adult entertainment Web site. The court ruled that Fordrecalls.com was in violation of the ACPA in that it was a bad-faith attempt to divert traffic to the Lapertosa site and diluted Ford's wholesome trademark (*Ford Motor Co. v. Lapertosa*, 2001).

The Ford decision reflects two other famous cases of cyberpiracy. In the *Paine Webber Inc. v. Fortuny* case, the court enjoined Fortuny from using the domain name Wwwpainewebber.com—a site that specialized in pornographic materials—because it diluted and tarnished Paine Webber's trademark and diverted Web traffic from Paine Webber's legitimate site—Painewebber.com (*Paine Webber Inc. v. Fortuny*, 1999). In the *Playboy Enterprises, Inc. v. Global Site Designs, Inc.* case, the court enjoined the defendants from using the Playboy and Playmate marks in their domain names Playboyonline.net and Playmatesearch.net and from including the Playboy trademark in their metatags. In these cases, the defendants' intention was diversion for financial gain (*Playboy Enterprises, Inc. v. Global Site Designs, Inc.*, 1999).

In a more recent case, *Audi AG and Volkswagen of America Inc. v. Bob D'Amato*, the Federal Circuit Court of Appeals for the Sixth Circuit affirmed the district court's ruling that the defendant Bob D'Amato infringed and diluted the plaintiffs' Audi, Quattro, and Audi Four Rings logo marks, and violated the ACPA by operating the Audisport.com Web site (*Audi AG and Volkswagen of America Inc. v. Bob D'Amato*, 2006).

Typosquatting is a form of cyberpiracy in which a domain name contains a common misspelling of another site's name. Often the user ends up at a site very different from one they intended to visit. For instance, John Zuccarini is an infamous typosquatter who was jailed in 2002 for setting up pornographic Web sites with URLs based on misspellings of popular children's brands, such as Bob the Builder and Teletubbies. The FTC fined him again in October 2007 for engaging in similar practices (McMillan, 2007). Harvard Business School professor Ben Edelman conducted a study in 2010 that found that there were at least 938,000 domains typosquatting on the top 3,264 ".com" Web sites, and that 57% of these domains included Google pay-per click ads. In July 2011, Facebook filed a lawsuit against 25 typosquatters who established Web sites with such domain names as Faceboook, Facemook, Facebik, and Facebooki.

Metatagging

The legal status of using famous or distinctive marks as metatags is more complex and subtle. The use of trademarks in metatags is permitted if the use does not mislead or confuse consumers. Usually this depends on the content of the site. A car dealer would be permitted to use a famous automobile trademark in its metatags if the dealer sold this brand of automobiles, but a pornography site could not use the same trademark, nor a dealer for a rival manufacturer. A Ford dealer would most likely be infringing if it used "Honda" in its metatags, but would not be infringing if it used "Ford" in its metatags. (Ford Motor Company would be unlikely to seek an injunction against one of its dealers.)

In the *Bernina of America, Inc. v. Fashion Fabrics Int'l, Inc.* case, the court enjoined Fashion Fabrics, an independent dealer of sewing machines, from using the trademarks "Bernina" and "Bernette," which belonged to the manufacturer Bernina, as metatags. The court found the defendant's site contained misleading claims about Fashion Fabrics' knowledge of Bernina products that were likely to confuse customers. The use of the Bernina trademarks as metatags per se was not a violation of ACPA, according to the court, but in combination with the misleading claims on the site would cause confusion and hence infringement (*Bernina of America, Inc. v. Fashion Fabrics Int'l, Inc.*, 2001).

In the *Nissan Motor Co., Ltd. v. Nissan Computer Corp.* case, Uzi Nissan had used his surname "Nissan" as a trade name for various businesses since 1980, including Nissan Computer Corp. He registered Nissan.com in 1994 and Nissan.net in 1996. Nissan.com had no relationship with Nissan Motor, but over the years began selling auto parts that competed with Nissan Motor. Nissan Motor Company objected to the use of the domain name Nissan.com and the use of "Nissan" in the metatags for both sites on grounds it would confuse customers and infringe on Nissan Motor's trademarks. Uzi Nissan offered to sell his sites to Nissan Motor for several million dollars. Nissan Motor refused. The court ruled that Nissan Computer's behavior did indeed infringe on Nissan Motor's trademarks, but it refused to shut the site down. Instead, the court ruled Nissan Computer could continue to use the Nissan name, and metatags, but must post notices on its site that it was not affiliated with Nissan Motor (*Nissan Motor Co., Ltd. v. Nissan Computer Corp.*, 2000).

Keywording

The permissibility of using trademarks as keywords on search engines is also subtle and depends (1) on the extent to which such use is considered to be a "use in commerce" and causes "initial customer confusion" and (2) on the content of the search results.

In *Playboy Enterprises, Inc. v. Netscape Communications, Inc.*, Playboy objected to the practice of Netscape's and Excite's search engines displaying banner ads unrelated to *Playboy Magazine* when users entered search arguments such as "playboy," "playmate," and "playgirl." The Ninth Circuit Court of Appeals denied the defendant's motion for a summary judgment and held that when an advertiser's banner ad is not labeled so as to identify its source, the practice could result in trademark infringement due to consumer confusion (*Playboy Enterprises, Inc. v. Netscape Communications, Inc.*, 2004).

In the *Nettis Environmental Ltd. v. IWI, Inc.* case, Nettis and IWI, Inc. were competitors in the ventilation business. IWI had registered the trademarks "nettis" and "nettis environmental" on more than 400 search engines, and in addition, used these marks as metatags on its site. The court required IWI to remove the metatags and de-register the keywords with all search engines because consumers would be confused—searching for Nettis products would lead them to an IWI Web site (*Nettis Environmental Ltd. v. IWI, Inc.*, 1999).

Google has also faced lawsuits alleging that its advertising network illegally exploits others' trademarks. For instance, insurance company GEICO challenged Google's practice of allowing competitors' ads to appear when a searcher types "Geico" as the search query. In December 2004, a U.S. district court ruled that this practice did not violate federal trademark laws as long as the word "Geico" was not used in the ads' text (*Government Employees Insurance Company v. Google, Inc.*, 2004). Google quickly discontinued allowing the latter, and settled the case (Associated Press, 2005). In 2009, Google expanded its policy of allowing anyone to buy someone else's trademark as a keyword trigger for ads to more than 190 new countries. Google also announced that it would allow the limited use of other companies' trademarks in the text of some search ads, even if the trademark owner objected. In July 2009, Rosetta Stone, the language-learning software firm, filed a lawsuit against Google for trademark infringement, alleging its AdWords program allowed other companies to use Rosetta Stone's trademarks for online advertisements without permission. The suit was dismissed by a federal district court judge in August 2010, but was appealed by Rosetta Stone. In April 2012, the 4th Circuit Court of Appeals overturned the decision by the federal district court, finding that a trier of fact could find that Google could be held liable for trademark infringement. The court pointed to evidence that an internal Google study found that even sophisticated users were sometimes unaware that sponsored links were advertisements.

In 2009, the European Court of Justice handed Google a victory against luxury brand behemoth LVMH by allowing Google to continue selling advertisements based on keyword searches for luxury goods makers. Even competitor firms can bid on LVMH brand names (Ram, 2009). Currently Google allows anyone to buy anyone else's trademark as a keyword. In February 2011, Microsoft decided to follow this practice as well with Bing and Yahoo Search.

Linking

Linking refers to building hypertext links from one site to another site. This is obviously a major design feature and benefit of the Web. **Deep linking** involves bypassing the target site's home page and going directly to a content page. In *Ticketmaster Corp. v. Tickets.com*, Tickets.com—owned by Microsoft—competed directly against Ticketmaster in the events ticket market. When Tickets.com did not have tickets for an event, it would direct users to Ticketmaster's internal pages, bypassing the Ticketmaster home page. Even though its logo was displayed on the internal pages, Ticketmaster objected on the grounds that such "deep linking" violated the terms and conditions of use for its site (stated on a separate page altogether and construed by Ticketmaster as equivalent to a shrink-wrap license), and constituted false advertising, as well as the violation of copyright. The court found, however, that deep linking per se is not illegal, no violation of copyright occurred because no copies were made, the terms and conditions of use were not obvious to users, and users were not required to read the page on which the terms and conditions of use appeared in any event. The court refused to rule in favor of Ticketmaster, but left open further argument on the licensing issue. In an out-of-court settlement, Tickets.com nevertheless agreed to stop the practice of deep linking (*Ticketmaster v. Tickets.com*, 2000).

linking
building hypertext links from one site to another site

deep linking
involves bypassing the target site's home page, and going directly to a content page

Framing

Framing involves displaying the content of another Web site inside your own Web site within a frame or window. The user never leaves the framer's site and can be exposed to advertising while the target site's advertising is distorted or eliminated. Framers may or may not acknowledge the source of the content. In *The Washington Post, et al. v. TotalNews, Inc. case*, The Washington Post Company, CNN, Reuters, and several other news organizations filed suit against TotalNews, Inc., claiming that TotalNews's use of frames on its Web site, TotalNews.com, infringed upon the respective plaintiffs' copyrights and trademarks, and diluted the content of their individual Web sites. The plaintiffs claimed additionally that TotalNews's framing practice effectively deprived the plaintiffs' Web sites of advertising revenue.

framing
involves displaying the content of another Web site inside your own Web site within a frame or window

TotalNews's Web site employed four frames. The TotalNews logo appeared in the lower left frame, various links were located in a vertical frame on the left side of the screen, TotalNews's advertising was framed across the screen bottom, and the "news frame," the largest frame, appeared in the center and right. Clicking on a specific news organization's link allowed the reader to view the content of that particular organization's Web site, including any related advertising, within the context of the "news frame." In some instances, the framing distorted or modified the appearance of the linked Web site, including the advertisements, while the appearance of Total-News's advertisements, in a separate frame, remained unchanged. In addition, the URL remained fixed on the TotalNews address, even though the content in the largest frame on the Web site was from the linked Web site. The "news frame" did not, however, eliminate the linked Web site's identifying features.

The case was settled out of court. The news organizations allowed TotalNews to link to their Web sites, but prohibited framing and any attempt to imply affiliation with the news organizations (*The Washington Post, et al. v. TotalNews, Inc.*, 1997).

CHALLENGE: BALANCING THE PROTECTION OF PROPERTY WITH OTHER VALUES

The challenge in intellectual property ethics and law is to ensure that creators of intellectual property can receive the benefits of their inventions and works, while also making it possible for their works and designs to be disseminated and used by the widest possible audience. Protections from rampant theft of intellectual property inevitably lead to restrictions on distribution, and the payments to creators for the use of their works—which in itself can slow down the distribution process. Without these protections, however, and without the benefits that flow to creators of intellectual property, the pace of innovation will decline. In the early years of e-commerce, up to 2005, the balance has been struck more towards Internet distributors and their claim to be free from restrictions on intellectual content, particularly music. Since the development of the iTunes store, smartphones, and tablets, after 2005, the balance has swung back towards content owners in large part because Internet distributors depend on high-quality content to attract audiences, and in part because of the effectiveness of lawsuits in raising the costs to Internet firms that fail to protect intellectual property.

8.4 GOVERNANCE

governance
has to do with social control: who will control e-commerce, what elements will be controlled, and how the controls will be implemented

Governance has to do with social control: Who will control the Internet? Who will control the processes of e-commerce, the content, and the activities? What elements will be controlled, and how will the controls be implemented? A natural question arises and needs to be answered: Why do we as a society need to "control" e-commerce? Because e-commerce and the Internet are so closely intertwined (though not identical), controlling e-commerce also involves regulating the Internet.

WHO GOVERNS THE INTERNET AND E-COMMERCE?

Governance of both the Internet and e-commerce has gone through four stages. **Table 8.14** summarizes these stages in the evolution of e-commerce governance.

Prior to 1995, the Internet was a government program. Beginning in 1995, private corporations were given control of the technical infrastructure as well as the process of granting IP addresses and domain names. However, the NSI monopoly created in this period did not represent international users of the Internet, and was unable to

TABLE 8.14	THE EVOLUTION OF GOVERNANCE OF THE INTERNET
INTERNET GOVERNANCE PERIOD	DESCRIPTION
Government control, 1970–1994	DARPA and the National Science Foundation control the Internet as a fully government-funded program.
Privatization, 1995–1998	Network Solutions Inc. is given a monopoly to assign and track high-level Internet domains. Backbone is sold to private telecommunications companies. Policy issues are not decided.
Self-regulation, 1995–present	President Clinton and the U.S. Department of Commerce encourage the creation of a semiprivate body, ICANN, to deal with emerging conflicts and establish policies. ICANN currently holds a contract with the Department of Commerce to govern some aspects of the Internet.
Governmental regulation, 1998–present	Executive, legislative, and judicial bodies worldwide begin to implement direct controls over the Internet and e-commerce.

cope with emerging public policy issues such as trademark and intellectual property protection, fair policies for allocating domains, and growing concerns that a small group of firms were benefiting from growth in the Internet.

In 1995, President Clinton, using funds from the Department of Commerce, encouraged the establishment of an international body, the Internet Corporation for Assigned Names and Numbers (ICANN), that hopefully could better represent a wider range of countries and a broad range of interests, and begin to address emerging public policy issues. ICANN was intended to be an Internet/e-commerce industry self-governing body, not another government agency.

The explosive growth of the Web and e-commerce created a number of issues over which ICANN had no authority. Content issues such as pornography, gambling, and offensive written expressions and graphics, along with commercial issue of intellectual property protection, ushered in the current era of growing governmental regulation of the Internet and e-commerce throughout the world. Currently, we are in a mixed-mode policy environment where self-regulation through a variety of Internet policy and technical bodies co-exists with limited government regulation.

Today, ICANN remains in charge of the domain name system that translates domain names (such as www.company.com) into IP addresses. It has subcontracted the work of maintaining the databases of the domain registries to several private corporations. The U.S. government controls the "A-root" server. However, these arrangements are increasingly challenged by other countries, including China, Russia, Saudi Arabia, and most of the European Union, all of whom want the United States to give up control over the Internet to an international body such as the International Telecommunication Union (ITU) (a U.N. agency). In 2005, an Internet Summit sponsored by the ITU agreed to leave control over the Internet domain servers with the United States and instead called for an international forum to meet in future years to discuss Internet policy issues (Miller and Rhoads, 2005). The position of the United States with respect to international governance of the Internet changed significantly after the terrorist attacks of September 11, 2001. Currently, the United States has no intention of diminishing its role in control over the global or domestic Internet.

Can the Internet Be Controlled?

Early Internet advocates argued that the Internet was different from all previous technologies. They contended that the Internet could not be controlled, given its inherent decentralized design, its ability to cross borders, and its underlying packet-switching technology that made monitoring and controlling message content impossible. Many still believe this to be true today. The slogans are "Information wants to be free," and "The Net is everywhere" (but not in any central location). The implication of these slogans is that the content and behavior of e-commerce sites—indeed Internet sites of any kind—cannot be "controlled" in the same way as traditional media such as radio and television. However, attitudes have changed as many governments and corporations extend their control over the Internet and the World Wide Web (Stone, 2010).

In fact, as you learned in the Chapter 3 *Insight on Society* case, *Government Regulation and Surveillance of the Internet*, the Internet is technically very easily controlled, monitored, and regulated from central locations (such as network access points, as well as servers and routers throughout the network). For instance, in China, Saudi Arabia, Iran, North Korea, Thailand, Singapore, and many other countries, access to the Web is controlled from government-owned centralized routers that direct traffic across their borders and within the country (such as China's "Great Firewall of China," which permits the government to block access to certain U.S. or European Web sites), or via tightly regulated ISPs operating within the countries. In China, for instance, all ISPs need a license from the Ministry of Information Industry (MII), and are prohibited from disseminating any information that may harm the state or permit pornography, gambling, or the advocacy of cults. In addition, ISPs and search engines such as Google, Yahoo, and Bing typically self-censor their Asian content by using only government-approved news sources. China has also recently instituted new regulations that require cafes, restaurants, hotels, and bookstores to install Web monitoring software that identifies those using wireless services and monitors Web activity.

Following the outbreak of street demonstrations in June 2009 protesting a rigged election, the Iranian government unleashed one of the world's most sophisticated mechanisms for controlling and censoring the Web. Built with the assistance of Western companies like Siemens and Nokia, the system uses deep packet inspection to open every packet, look for keywords, reseal it, and send it on the network. In Great Britain, Prime Minister David Cameron suggested that he might temporarily block social network sites such as Facebook and Twitter during periods of social unrest such as the rioting that hit the country in August 2011.

In the United States, as we have seen in our discussion of intellectual property, e-commerce sites can be put out of business for violating existing laws, and ISPs can be forced to "take down" offending or stolen content. Government security agencies such as the FBI can obtain court orders to monitor ISP traffic and engage in widespread monitoring of millions of e-mail messages. Under the USA PATRIOT Act, passed after the World Trade Center attack on September 11, 2001, American intelligence authorities are permitted to tap into whatever Internet traffic they believe is relevant to the campaign against terrorism, in some circumstances without judicial review. Working with the large ISP firms such as AT&T, Verizon, and others, U.S. security agencies have access to nearly all Internet communications throughout the country. And many American corporations are developing restrictions on their employees' at-work use of the Web to prevent gambling, shopping, and other activities not related to a business purpose.

In the United States, as discussed in the opening case, efforts to control media content on the Web have run up against equally powerful social and political values that protect freedom of expression, including several rulings by the Supreme Court that have struck down laws attempting to limit Web content in the United States. The U.S. Constitution's First Amendment says, "Congress shall make no law ... abridging the freedom of speech, or of the press." As it turns out, the 200-year-old Bill of Rights has been a powerful brake on efforts to control twenty-first-century online content.

Public Government and Law

The reason we have governments is ostensibly to regulate and control activities within the borders of the nation. What happens in other nations, for the most part, we generally ignore, although clearly environmental and international trade issues require multinational cooperation. E-commerce and the Internet pose some unique problems to public government that center on the ability of the nation-state to govern activities within its borders. Nations have considerable powers to shape the Internet.

TAXATION

Few questions illustrate the complexity of governance and jurisdiction more potently than taxation of e-commerce sales. In both Europe and the United States, governments rely on sales taxes based on the type and value of goods sold. In Europe, these taxes are collected along the entire value chain, including the final sale to the consumer, and are called "value-added taxes" (VAT), whereas in the United States, taxes are collected by states and localities on final sales to consumers and are called consumption and use taxes. In the United States, there are 50 states, 3,000 counties, and 12,000 municipalities, each with unique tax rates and policies. Cheese may be taxable in one state as a "snack food" but not taxable in another state (such as Wisconsin), where it is considered a basic food. Consumption taxes are generally recognized to be regressive because they disproportionately tax poorer people, for whom consumption is a larger part of total income.

Sales taxes were first implemented in the United States in the late 1930s as a Depression-era method of raising money for localities. Ostensibly, the money was to be used to build infrastructure such as roads, schools, and utilities to support business development, but over the years the funds have been used for general government purposes of the states and localities. In most states, there is a state-based sales tax, and a smaller local sales tax. The total sales tax ranges from zero in some states (North Dakota) to as much as 13% in New York City.

The development of "remote sales" such as mail order/telephone order (MOTO) retail in the United States in the 1970s broke the relationship between physical presence and commerce, complicating the plans of state and local tax authorities to tax all retail commerce. States sought to force MOTO retailers to collect sales taxes for them based on the address of the recipient, but Supreme Court decisions in 1967 and 1992 established that states had no authority to force MOTO retailers to collect state taxes unless the businesses had a "nexus" of operations (physical presence) in the state. Congress could, however, create legislation giving states this authority. But every congressional effort to tax catalog merchants has been beaten back by a torrent of opposition from catalog merchants and consumers, leaving intact an effective tax subsidy for MOTO merchants.

The explosive growth of e-commerce, the latest type of "remote sales," has once again raised the issue of how—and if—to tax remote sales. Since its inception, e-commerce has benefited from a tax subsidy of up to 13% for goods shipped to high sales-tax areas. Local retail merchants have complained bitterly about the e-commerce tax subsidy. E-commerce merchants have argued that this form of commerce needs to be nurtured and encouraged, and that in any event, the crazy quilt of sales and use tax regimes would be difficult to administer for Internet merchants. Online giants like Amazon claim they should not have to pay taxes in states where they have no operations because they do not benefit from local schools, police, fire, and other governmental services. State and local governments meanwhile see billions of tax dollars slipping from their reach. In 2012, thousands of online retailers, including Amazon, Blue Nile, eBay, and Overstock, pay no taxes in states where they do not have a presence.

In 1998, Congress passed the Internet Tax Freedom Act, which placed a moratorium on "multiple or discriminatory taxes on electronic commerce," as well as on taxes on Internet access, for three years until October 2001. Since that time, the moratorium has been extended several times, most currently until 2014.

The merger of online e-commerce with offline commerce further complicates the taxation question. Currently, almost all of the top 100 online retailers collect taxes when orders ship to states where these firms have a physical presence. But others, like eBay, still refuse to collect and pay local taxes, arguing that the so-called tax simplification project ended up with taxes for each of 49,000 zip codes, hardly a simplification. The taxation situation is also very complex in services. For instance, none of the major online travel sites collect the full amount of state and local hotel occupancy taxes, or state and local airline taxes. Instead of remitting sales tax on the full amount of the consumer's purchase, these sites instead collect taxes on the basis of the wholesale price they pay for the hotel rooms or tickets. The states have not given up on collecting hundreds of millions of dollars from Internet merchants. The *Insight on Business* case, *Internet Sales Tax Battle*, provides further information on the fight over e-commerce sales taxes.

The taxation situation in Europe, and trade between Europe and the United States, is similarly complex. The Organization for Economic Cooperation and Development (OECD), the economic policy coordinating body of European, American, and Japanese

INSIGHT ON BUSINESS

INTERNET SALES TAX BATTLE

Most people are happy when they discover they don't have to pay any sales tax on a purchase they make online. However, few stop to consider the implications that this may have. According to the Brookings Institute, since the end of the recession and subsequent phasing out of the American Recovery and Reinvestment (Stimulus) Act, more than 350,000 public sector employees, such as teachers, police officers, firefighters, and emergency responders, have lost their jobs. These public sector jobs are typically paid for by state or local governments, which typically derive almost a third of their revenue from sales and use taxes. States in the last few years have been suffering a persistent budget crunch. Constitutionally bound to balance their budgets, starved for revenue, and simultaneously facing increased demand for public services, many of the 45 states that levy sales taxes have been eying the lost revenue from e-commerce sales, estimated at $11.4 billion nationwide in 2012.

Internet sales tax policy has been dictated by the Supreme Court decision in *Quill v. North Dakota*, which held that retailers without a store or other physical presence (nexus) in a state could not be forced to collect state sales taxes. Citizens were supposed to be responsible for remitting unpaid sales tax along with their state income tax returns. This unsurprisingly proved to be unworkable, with nearly universal noncompliance. The rationale for not closing this loophole, which resulted from a MOTO (Mail Order/Telephone Order) case, was to provide protection for a nascent market. With total 2012 B2C e-commerce sales topping $362 billion, this argument had lost its punch.

Internet retail kingpin Amazon has been at the center of the political battle. Multiple states,

frustrated by the lost revenue that could have been used to balance their budgets and prevent further layoffs, have taken Amazon on. In 2010, Texas levied a $269 million sales tax bill against Amazon covering a period of four years. In response, Amazon, which asserted that a warehouse did not constitute a nexus, shuttered its Dallas-vicinity warehouse, laying off 119 employees. In 2011, Illinois, which estimated that the state had lost up to $170 million in sales tax revenue every year, enacted legislation requiring all retailers with a marketing affiliate in the state to collect sales taxes. Amazon retaliated by severing all ties to its Illinois affiliates while big bricks and clicks retailers quickly offered themselves as replacements. The Illinois law was fashioned after a 2008 New York law with which Amazon has complied while simultaneously challenging its constitutionality. It did not drop its New York affiliates, but when Rhode Island and North Carolina followed New York's lead in 2009, Amazon terminated its affiliate relationships in those states, a pattern it continued in Arkansas in 2011. California, which estimated that it lost $1.1 billion per year in uncollected sales tax, passed its legislation expanding the definition of nexus in September 2011, but delayed tax collection until September 2012.

Facing a continuing state-by-state assault, with Arizona, Connecticut, Hawaii, Minnesota, Mississippi, and Vermont all considering similar legislation, and pushed as well at the federal level by Senate legislation crafted by Senators Durbin, Alexander, and Enzi, Amazon recognized that its former competitive advantage was ultimately going to come to an end. It devised a dual-pronged strategy. In the short term, it negotiated deals with states in which it planned to open distribution centers. These distribution centers were strategi-

(continued)

cally located to support its long-term goal and what it hopes will become its new competitive advantage—same day delivery.

For example, in April 2012, Amazon settled its dispute with Texas when it agreed to create 2,500 local jobs over four years' time, pay an undisclosed amount to resolve its tax bill, and begin collecting sales tax from Texas residents. Similarly, in May 2012, Amazon reached an agreement with New Jersey that allowed it to build two distribution centers in the state. New Jersey will gain approximately 1,500 full-time jobs and between $30 and $40 million in sales tax revenue when Amazon starts collecting sales tax from New Jersey residents in July 2013. Amazon will also receive yet to be determined tax incentives from the state Economic Development Authority. In California, in exchange for the one-year tax reprieve, Amazon is opening facilities in Patterson—85 miles from San Francisco—and outside of Los Angeles. This agreement to spend $500 million building new facilities in the state and garnering it approximately 10,000 new full-time jobs positioned Amazon for same-day delivery to two major metropolitan areas.

In November 2011, apparently fatigued by the state-by-state offensive, Amazon threw its support behind the Durbin-Enzi-Alexander bill, the Main Street Fairness Act. Durbin had tried for several years and in various iterations to get a bill to the Senate floor. He was able to gain the sponsorship of two Republican senators by incorporating a small business exemption. Businesses with less than $500,000 in annual sales will not have to comply. States will also have to agree to the Streamlined Sales and Use Tax Agreement, which simplifies their tax policies so that it will be easier for Internet retailers to conform. While the majority of Republican governors support the bill, gaining enough Republican support to surmount the 60 vote threshold necessary for Senate passage is expected to be difficult. Proponents

of the bill argue that this is not a new tax, it is an already owed tax that has gone uncollected, and the National Conference of State Legislatures agrees.

Also supporting the bill are the major retail chains, including Walmart, Best Buy, Lowe's, Target, and Sears, which have predictably been grumbling for years about the unfair advantage given to Internet-only retailers. While their group, the Alliance for Main Street Fairness, includes the giants, small bricks-and-clicks retailers such as Sides Family Music Center in Williamsport, PA and BookPeople in Austin, Texas are featured in their press releases. Additional retail groups supporting the bill include the National Retail Federation, Consumer Electronics Association, and the International Council of Shopping Centers.

On the opposing side is a new coalition, WE R HERE (Web Enabled Retailers Helping Expand Retail Employment), headed by a former Under Secretary for Technology in the Bush administration Department of Commerce, Phil Bond. The heavy hitter in this group is auction giant eBay, which was not mollified by the $500,000 small business exemption. Many of eBay's small sellers and more than 1,000 other small online retailers have joined the fray, fearful of the burden of being forced to remit sales taxes to "thousands of jurisdictions." (Many counties, cities, and towns also levy a sales tax.) Bond's argument is that these small sellers do not live, have a business presence, or use government services in the jurisdictions for which they will be required to collect taxes and that burdening them in tough economic times will have the opposite of the intended effect, dampening job creation and ultimately further reducing state coffers.

The real sticking point appears to be the yearly sales figure that will define a "small business." While Amazon would like to see it set as low as $150,000, NetChoice, an older lobbying group to which eBay also belongs along with

(continued)

Overstock.com, Facebook, Expedia, VeriSign, Yahoo, Oracle, and IAC Interactive Corp, the parent company of Shoebuy.com, would like to see this figure raised to $5 million per year in remote sales. Senator Enzi has indicated that a $1 million figure is certainly feasible and that he is open to discussion and adaptation to whatever consensus is arrived at in the Senate.

While Enzi, Durbin, and Alexander had hoped to bring their bill to a vote at the end of 2012, it is unlikely to happen until 2013. The influential anti-tax lobbying group, Americans for Tax Reform, is another formidable foe that has the ear of Republican legislators in both houses of Congress. Senate Majority Leader Harry Reid has indicated that without the support of at least a dozen Republican senators (15 to 20 are needed to pass the bill), he will not schedule it for a vote. Passing the companion bill in the House of Representatives could be even tougher.

On balance, bill proponents have the stronger hand and are likely to prevail eventually. eBay and other online marketplaces have created unique environments in which lowered barriers to entry enable entrepreneurs to either work for themselves or start their own businesses and further, they present new opportunities to developing markets to offer their goods directly to buyers. It is these small undertakings that are still in need of protection, not, it must be noted, the large retailers that now proliferate on eBay's storefronts. A $1 million annual remote sales cap would give them a leg up, support innovation where govern-

ment intervention is necessary to do so, and avoid unduly burdening small sellers whose contribution to state revenue is minor in comparison.

The big players such as Amazon are now operating in a mature market in which they must adapt and formulate new strategies for remaining competitive. Whether or not Amazon will succeed in its ambitious same-day delivery plan remains to be seen, but it is operating as all businesses must—evolving with changing circumstances in an ever-changing business environment. Clearly Walmart and the other big-box retailers are not suffering from lack of a level playing field. They are simply using their political clout to benefit themselves and erect barriers for smaller competitors. However, they do have a point vis-à-vis tax fairness and civic duty.

Sales taxes have been an established method for raising revenue at the state and local level for more than half a century. First adopted by Mississippi in 1932, the idea quickly caught on spreading to 22 additional states by 1940 and extending to 45 states and the District of Columbia by 1969 when Vermont was the final adopter. Alaska, Montana, Oregon, Delaware, and New Hampshire are the holdouts. We have all enjoyed purchasing online goods from out-of-state sellers and evading the sales tax, but this is not a new tax. It is a tax that we have enjoyed evading, and one which the states desperately need to pay for the services and professions we rely on every day.

SOURCES: "Small E-retailers Mobilize to Lobby Against Online Sales Tax Collection," by Paul Demery, Internet Retailer, September, 14, 2012; "Coalition Launched to Oppose Internet Sales Tax Legislation," by Juliana Gruenwald, NextGov Newsletter, September 13, 2012; "Amazon, Forced to Collect a Tax, Is Adding Roots," by David Streitfeld, New York Times, September 11, 2012; "10 Surprising Facts About Online Sales Taxes," by Robert W. Wood, Forbes, September 11, 2012; "Durbin Still Hopeful for Action on Net Sales Tax Bill," by Juliana Gruenwald, " National Journal, June 12, 2012; "Amazon.com to Begin Collecting Sales Tax on N.J. Orders Next Year," by Matt Friedman and Jarrett Renshaw, NJ.com, May 30, 2012; "Tax Revenues Continue to Grow in Early 2012," by Lucy Dadayan, The Nelson A. Rockefeller Institute of Government State Revenue Report No. 88, August, 2012; "Durbin Gains Key Support for Revitalized Internet Sales Tax Bill," by Paul Merrion, Crain's Chicago Business, November 9, 2011; "Revenue Declines Less Severe, But States' Fiscal Crisis Is Far From Over," by Donald J. Boyd and Lucy Dadayan, The Nelson A. Rockefeller Institute of Government State Revenue Report No. 79, April, 2010.

governments, is currently investigating different schemes for applying consumption and business profit taxes for digitally downloaded goods. The E.U. began collecting a VAT on digital goods such as music and software delivered to consumers by foreign companies in 2003. Previously, European Union companies were required to collect the VAT on sales to E.U. customers, but U.S. companies were not. This gave American companies a huge tax edge.

Thus, there is no integrated rational approach to taxation of domestic or international e-commerce (Varian, 2001). In the United States, the national and international character of Internet sales is wreaking havoc on taxation schemes that were built in the 1930s and based on local commerce and local jurisdictions. Although there appears to be acquiescence among large Internet retailers such as Amazon to the idea of some kind of sales tax on e-commerce sales, their insistence on uniformity will probably delay taxation for many years, and any proposal to tax e-commerce will likely incur the wrath of around 148 million U.S. e-commerce consumers. Congress is not likely to ignore their voices.

NET NEUTRALITY

"Net neutrality" is more a political slogan than a concept. It means different things to different people. Currently, all Internet traffic is treated equally (or "neutrally") by Internet backbone owners in the sense that all activities—word processing, e-mailing, video downloading, music and video files, etc.—are charged the same flat rate regardless of how much bandwidth is used. However, the telephone and cable companies that provide the Internet backbone (Internet Service Providers or ISPs) would like to be able to charge differentiated prices based on the amount of bandwidth consumed by content being delivered over the Internet, much like a utility company charges according to how much electricity consumers use. The carriers claim they need to introduce differential pricing in order to properly manage and finance their networks.

cap pricing
Putting caps on bandwidth usage, charging more for additional usage in tiers of prices

speed tiers
charging more for higher speed Internet service

usage-based billing
charging on the basis of metered units of Internet service

congestion pricing
charging more for peak hour Internet service

There are three basic ways to achieve a rationing of bandwidth using the pricing mechanism: cap plans (also known as "tiered plans"), usage metering, and "highway" or "toll" pricing. Each of these plans have historical precedents in highway, electrical, and telephone pricing. **Cap pricing** plans place a cap on usage, say 300 gigabytes a month in a basic plan, with more bandwidth available in 50 gigabyte chunks for, say, an additional $50 a month. The additional increments can also be formalized as tiers where users agree to purchase, say, 400 gigabytes each month as a Tier II plan. Additional tiers could be offered.

A variation on tier pricing is to offer **speed tiers**. Comcast offers its Xfinity Platinum Internet plan with download speeds of 300 megabits per second for $300, and Verizon offers its FiOS high-speed tier for $204 a month. An alternative to cap plans are metered or **usage-based billing**. Time Warner is testing usage plans which start at five gigabytes a month (the equivalent of two high definition movie downloads) and charge $1 for every additional gigabyte (much like an electric usage meter in a home).One variation on metering is **congestion pricing**, where, as with electric "demand pricing," the price of bandwidth goes up at peak times, say, Saturday and Sunday evening from 6:00 P.M. to 12 midnight—just when everyone wants to watch a movie! Still a third pricing model is **highway (toll) pricing** where the firms that use high levels of bandwidth for their business pay a toll based on their usage of the Internet. Highway pricing is a common way for governments to charge trucking companies based on the weight of their vehicles to compensate for the damage that heavy vehicles inflict on roadways. In the case of the Internet, YouTube, Netflix, Hulu, and other heavy bandwidth providers would pay fees to the Internet carriers based on their utilization of the networks in order to compensate the carriers for the additional capacity they are required to supply to these heavy user firms. Presumably, these fees would be passed on to customers by the industry players by charging users a distribution expense. The only way to do this fairly is to charge fees to users based on how much they download, e.g., a short YouTube video might cost 10 cents, a feature-length movie might cost $1.

Plans to ration bandwidth are controversial, and in some cases bring legal, regulatory, and political scrutiny. For instance, in September 2007, Comcast, the largest ISP in the United States, began to slow down traffic and specific Web sites using the BitTorrent protocol not because the content was pirated, but because these video users were consuming huge chunks of the Comcast network capacity during peak load times. Comcast claims its policy was a legitimate effort to manage capacity. In August 2008 the Federal Communications Commission (FCC) disagreed and ordered Comcast to stop discriminating against certain Web sites. Comcast filed suit and in April 2010, a federal appeals court ruled against the FCC and for Comcast, arguing that Comcast had the right to manage its own network, including charging some users more for bandwidth or slowing down certain traffic such as BitTorrent files (Watt, 2010).

In 2009, the FCC began developing a national broadband strategy. In December 2010, the FCC approved "compromise" net neutrality rules (Schatz, 2010). The rules force ISPs to be transparent about how they handle network congestion, prohibit them from blocking traffic such as BitTorrent or Skype protocols on wired networks, and outlawed "unreasonable" discrimination on such networks. The regulations do not cover wireless cellular networks, nor do they prohibit "paid prioritization," in which broadband companies could enable premium customers to have access to higher-speed, higher-priced "fast lanes." For instance, telecommunications providers such as Verizon and AT&T, and Internet distributors such as Google, have reached a market-based compromise: maintain existing rules for landlines, but implement differential pricing for mobile wireless networks. Currently, for instance, for new wireless customers, AT&T no longer offers a flat-rate plan. Instead, consumers must choose between plans with different data limits, ranging from $15/ month for 200 MB/month of data to up to $45/month for 4 GB/month. In September 2011, Verizon sued the FCC to stop its net neutrality rules from going into effect (Wyatt, 2011a). In November 2011, the FCC implemented its new rules despite Verizon's law suit. In 2012, the U.S. Court of Appeals began consideration of the Verizon case, which will not be decided until 2013 (Sasso, 2012).

Meanwhile, public interest groups have filed suits against the FCC for not going far enough to regulate ISPs, claiming that to allow ISPs to manage their networks will reduce innovation on the Internet. Politicians of all stripes have lined up on

highway (toll) pricing
charging service providers like Netflix for their use of the Internet based on their bandwidth use

one side or the other. The U.S. Senate in November 2011, defeated a Republican proposal to prevent the FCC from regulating the ISPs. For instance, opponents of the legislation argued that if ISPs are allowed to manage their networks, they would impose costs on heavy bandwidth users like YouTube, Netflix, Skype, and other innovative services. New start-up companies offering high-bandwidth innovative services might not be able to get traction if they had to charge their customers for network distribution. Supporters of the FCC net neutrality regulations argue that, without net neutrality, Netflix or Hulu customers might find their cable company (which also happens to be their Internet service provider) blocking Internet access to online streaming video from Netflix in order to force customers to use the cable company's on-demand movie rental platform from which the cable company makes a much larger profit.

How the net neutrality debate impacts the use of the mobile platform in the future is anyone's guess. Will consumers be less likely to want to use the mobile platform once they start to bump up against the data limits of their plans and pay additional fees? For instance, in 2012, AT&T restricted FaceTime calls on Apple's iPhones to customers signed up to a premium data plan. 4G networks in 2012 are already generating public criticism for their high monthly charges. This would put a big kibosh on the plans of content distributors, and they are not likely to be happy if that occurs. At the end of the day, both the content distributors and network providers need one another, and they are likely to work out a plan that is mutually beneficial (Stelter, 2012).

In the end, net neutrality is about generating revenue for content distributors and Internet service providers. Keep your eyes on the money.

8.5   PUBLIC SAFETY AND WELFARE

Governments everywhere claim to pursue public safety, health, and welfare. This effort produces laws governing everything from weights and measures to national highways, to the content of radio and television programs. Electronic media of all kinds (telegraph, telephone, radio, and television) have historically been regulated by governments seeking to develop a rational commercial telecommunications environment and to control the content of the media—which may be critical of government or offensive to powerful groups in a society. Historically, in the United States, newspapers and print media have been beyond government controls because of constitutional guarantees of freedom of speech. Electronic media such as radio and television have, on the other hand, always been subject to content regulation because they use the publicly owned frequency spectrum. Telephones have also been regulated as public utilities and "common carriers," with special social burdens to provide service and access, but with no limitations on content.

In the United States, critical issues in e-commerce center around the protection of children, strong sentiments against pornography in any public media, efforts to control gambling, and the protection of public health through restricting sales of drugs and cigarettes.

PROTECTING CHILDREN

Pornography is an immensely successful Internet business. The most recent statistics with respect to revenues generated by online pornography are now several years old and range widely. However, it is probably safe to estimate that the online pornography industry in 2012 generates more than $3 billion in revenue. Adult Web sites reportedly attract more than 75 million unique visitors a month and make up 12% of the Internet (New York Times, 2009; Worthen, 2009; Wondracek et al., 2010).

To control the Web as a distribution medium for pornography, in 1996, Congress passed the Communications Decency Act (CDA). This act made it a felony criminal offense to use any telecommunications device to transmit "any comment, request, suggestion, proposal, image, or other communications which is obscene, lewd, lascivious, filthy, or indecent" to anyone, and in particular, to persons under 18 years of age (Section 502, Communications Decency Act of 1996). In 1997, the Supreme Court struck down the CDA as an unconstitutional abridgement of freedom of speech protected by the First Amendment. While the government argued the CDA was like a zoning ordinance designed to allow "adult" Web sites for people 18 years of age or over, the Court found the CDA was a blanket proscription on content and rejected the "cyberzoning" argument as impossible to administer. In 2002, the Supreme Court struck down another law, the Child Pornography Prevention Act of 1996, which made it a crime to create, distribute, or possess "virtual" child pornography that uses computer-generated images or young adults rather than real children, as overly broad (*Ashcroft v. Free Speech Coalition*).

In 1998, Congress passed the Children's Online Protection Act (COPA). This act made it a felony criminal offense to communicate for "commercial purposes" "any material harmful to minors." Harmful material was defined as prurient, depicting sexual acts, and lacking value for minors. The act differed from the CDA by focusing on "commercial speech" and minors exclusively. In February 1999, a federal district court in Pennsylvania struck down COPA as an unconstitutional restriction on Web content that was protected under the First Amendment. The court nevertheless recognized the interest of Congress and society to protect children on the Internet and in e-commerce. In May 2002, the U.S. Supreme Court returned the case to the court of appeals for a decision, leaving in place an injunction barring enforcement of the law. In March 2003, the Third Circuit Court of Appeals ruled for the second time that COPA was unconstitutional, finding that the law violated the First Amendment because it improperly restricted access to a substantial amount of online speech that is lawful for adults. In 2004, the Supreme Court blocked enforcement of the law again, saying that it likely violated the First Amendment, but remanded it to the district court for a further trial examining Internet filtering technologies that might be used to achieve the law's goals. In January 2006, it was revealed that in preparation for this trial, the Department of Justice had issued subpoenas to Google, AOL, Yahoo, and Microsoft seeking a week's worth of search queries and a random sampling of 1 million Web addresses in the effort to understand the prevalence of material that could be deemed harmful to minors and the effectiveness of filtering technology, raising a storm of additional controversy. AOL, Microsoft, and Yahoo all agreed to supply the requested data, but Google refused on a variety of grounds, including protection of its trade secrets, privacy, and public relations (Hafner and Richtel, 2006). In response, the court limited the subpoena to just a sample of URLs in Google's database. In March 2007, the district court struck down COPA, ruling once again that the law violated the First and Fifth Amendments, and issued an order permanently prohibiting the government from enforcing COPA. The government once again appealed, and in July 2008, the Third Circuit Court of Appeals upheld the district court opinion that COPA violated the First Amendment. On January 21, 2009, the Supreme Court refused an appeal of the circuit court decision, putting an end to the saga of litigation over the act.

The 2003 Protect Act is an omnibus bill intended to prevent child abuse that includes prohibitions against computer-generated child pornography. Part of that statute was previously held to be unconstitutional by the Eleventh Circuit Court of Appeals, but in May 2008, the Supreme Court reversed the circuit court and upheld the provision (Greenhouse, 2008).

In 1998, Congress made one more effort to protect children online when it passed the Children's Online Privacy Protection Act (COPPA) (1998). COPPA prohibits Web sites from collecting information on children under the age of 13. It does permit such data collection if parental consent is obtained. Because COPPA does not interfere with speech or expression, it has not been challenged in the courts. Unfortunately, it has been impossible to verify a person's age when they sign up for an account at Web sites, and in many cases, parents are helping children under 13 years of age to sign up for sites like Facebook (which has an official policy prohibiting users under age 13).

In 2001, Congress passed the Children's Internet Protection Act (CIPA), which requires schools and libraries in the United States to install "technology protection measures" (filtering software) in an effort to shield children from pornography. In June 2003, the Supreme Court upheld CIPA, overturning a federal district court that found the law interfered with the First Amendment guarantee of freedom of expression. The Supreme Court, in a 6–3 opinion, held that the law's limitations on access to the Internet posed no more a threat to freedom of expression than limitations on access to books that librarians choose for whatever reason not to acquire. The dissenting justices found this analogy inappropriate and instead argued the proper analogy was if librarians were to purchase encyclopedias and then rip out pages they thought were or might be offensive to patrons. All the justices agreed that existing blocking software was overly blunt, unable to distinguish child pornography from sexually explicit material (which is protected by the First Amendment), and generally unreliable (Greenhouse, 2003b). Other legislation such as the 2002 Domain Names Act seeks to prevent unscrupulous Web site operators from luring children to pornography using misleading domain names or characters known to children, while the 2002 Dot Kids Act authorizes the creation of a second-level domain on the Internet where all Web sites would have to declare they contain no material harmful to children. An alternative plan, to create an .xxx domain for adult Web site content, was finally approved by ICANN in June 2010, and in September 2011, limited registration for .xxx domains began. Trademark holders who do not wish their brand to be associated with an .xxx domain can block requests by other companies for domain names that include their brand name.

COPPA, then, is the only federal legislation that has survived legal challenge and has been partially protective of children. Yet it has never had the support of industries trying to sell products to children (see the Chapter 7 *Insight on Society* case, *Marketing to Children of the Web in the Age of Social Networks*). In addition, it is extremely difficult to verify the age of someone who signs up for an account. Since 1998, entirely new technologies like social networks, online tracking, advertising networks, online gaming, and mobile apps have appeared that are now being used to gather data on children and which were not specifically addressed in COPPA or FTC regulations. In August 2012, a group of 20 children's advocacy, health, and public interest groups filed complaints with the FTC alleging that McDonald's, General Mills, Viacom (Nickelodeon), and Turner's Cartoon Network were collecting data on children (Singer, 2012b). Instead of collecting information directly from children, these sites use "tell a friend" or "Play this game and share with a friend" features to gather the e-mail addresses of children. These addresses can later be used for marketing messages directly to children.

Responding to these changes in technology and public pressure, the FTC announced a new set of rules in early September 2012 (Singer, 2012c). The new rules seek to prohibit online tracking of children across the Web with cookies or any other technology such as persistent identifiers; prohibit ad networks from following children across the Web and advertising to them without parental consent; makes clear that mobile devices are subject to COPPA, including games and software apps; and makes clear that third-party data collection firms that collect data on Web sites are responsible for any unlawful data collection. The new rules potentially will prevent Facebook from tracking the Likes of children generated when they click on the Like software plugin on other Web sites because the Like button is a tracking device that sends information back to Facebook (Sengupta, 2012b). A *Consumer Reports* study in June 2012 discovered that Facebook has more than 5 million children registered even though its policies forbid under age members (Reuters, 2012). The new rules are opposed by the Interactive Advertising Bureau trade group, and many well-known firms who market products like breakfast cereal and fast foods to children. These firms point out that they do not knowingly collect information on children, but a study of 54 Web sites in 2011 found that sites aimed at children (Disney.com and Nick.com) use tracking technologies extensively to follow children when they are online. The new regulations are not expected to be implemented until the end of the 2012.

CIGARETTES, GAMBLING, AND DRUGS: IS THE WEB REALLY BORDERLESS?

In the United States, both the states and the federal government have adopted legislation to control certain activities and products in order to protect public health and welfare. Cigarettes, gambling, medical drugs, and of course addictive recreational drugs, are either banned or tightly regulated by federal and state laws (see *Insight on Society: The Internet Drug Bazaar*). Yet these products and services are ideal for distribution over the Internet through e-commerce sites. Because the sites can be located offshore, they can operate beyond the jurisdiction of state and federal prosecutors. Or so it seemed until recently. In the case of cigarettes, state and federal authorities have been quite successful in shutting down tax-free cigarette Web sites within the United States by pressuring PayPal and credit card firms to drop cigarette merchants

INSIGHT ON SOCIETY

THE INTERNET DRUG BAZAAR

In October 2012, in the largest operation of its kind to date, 100 countries participated in a concerted action targeting the online sale of counterfeit and illegal drugs. Worldwide, the effort resulted in 79 arrests and the seizure of 3.7 million doses of counterfeit drugs. As part of the effort, in the United States, federal authorities shut down and seized 686 Web sites that believed to be selling counterfeit drugs, bringing the two-year total of such seized domains to 1,525. Despite successes such as this, however, the Internet drug bazaar operated by rogue Internet drug outlets remains a continuing public health and safety issue. For instance, a Massachusetts General study found that the increase in Internet access parallels the growth in prescription drug abuse, and posits that increasing access to rogue online pharmacies and easy online availability of controlled drugs without a prescription might be an important factor behind the rapid increase.

According to a study done by the Treatment Research Institute at the University of Pennsylvania, addictive and potentially lethal medications are available without prescription from more than 2 million Web sites around the world, with many sites based in countries that impose little if any regulation on pharmaceuticals. A Google search on "drugs no prescription" returns more than 14 million results. According to the National Association of Boards of Pharmacy (NABP), 97% of more than 10,600 Web sites it has analyzed operate without compliance with U.S. pharmacy laws and provide an outlet for counterfeit drugs to enter the United States, fueling prescription drug use and misuse.

The International Narcotics Control Board, a U.N. narcotics watchdog agency has provided guidelines and a framework for governments struggling to contain growing abuse of prescription drugs on the Internet. According to the report, a U.S. study found that only two of 365 so-called Internet pharmacies it surveyed were legitimate. In many countries, the report said, trafficking in illegal prescription drugs now equals or exceeds the sale of heroin, cocaine, and amphetamines. According to the World Health Organization, 8% of the bulk drugs imported into the United States in 2010 were counterfeit or substandard, and illegal pharmacies accountfor 10% of the worldwide pharmaceutical trade. While properly regulated Internet pharmacies offer a valuable service by increasing competition and access to treatments in underserved regions, Web pharmacies are a long way from proper regulation. In 2011, the INCB issued a follow-up report urging countries that had not implemented its guidelines to do so, and warned of the increasing number of illegal online pharmacies targeting the young, particularly through social media.

The sale of drugs without a prescription is not the only danger posed by the Internet drug bazaar. Rogue online pharmacy sites may be selling counterfeit drugs or unapproved drugs. For instance, in the past, the FDA has issued warnings that a number of consumers who had purchased Ambien, Xanax, and Lexapro online from several different Web sites had instead received a product containing haloperial, a powerful anti-psychotic drug. Drug pushers on the Internet also include legitimate U.S. pharmaceutical firms who have discovered search engine advertising. Enter a search for "high choles-

(continued)

terol" on Bing or Google and you will be faced with multiple ads extolling the benefits of Lipitor (Pfizer's leading statin drug).

But despite these dangers, online pharmacies remain alluring and are one of the fastest growing business models, with, oddly, senior citizens— usually some of the most law-abiding citizens— leading the charge for cheaper drugs. The main attraction of online drug sites is price. Typically, online pharmacies are located in countries where prescription drugs are price-controlled, or where the price structure is much lower, such as Canada, the United Kingdom, and European countries, as well as India and Mexico. U.S. citizens can often save 50%–75% by purchasing from online pharmacies located in other countries. In 2011, the Justice Department began a criminal investigation of Google for allowing Canadian pharmacies to advertise prescription drugs for distribution in the United States. The Justice Department viewed Google as an accomplice to the crime by enhancing the ability of the Canadian pharmacies to reach American consumers. In August 2011, Google agreed to a nonprosecution agreement, and forfeited $500 million, which represented both its advertising revenue from the Canadian pharmacies and the revenues the pharmacies received from American customers buying the drugs. Google also agreed to enhance its compliance program for drug advertisers.

Currently, a patchwork regulatory structure governs the sale of drugs online. At the federal level, the 1938 Food, Drug, and Cosmetic Act (FDCA) requires that certain drugs may only be purchased with a valid doctor's prescription and must be dispensed by a state-licensed pharmacy. To get around this requirement, some online pharmacies use questionnaires to diagnose disease and have these questionnaires reviewed by doctors who write the prescription. The Ryan Haight Online Pharmacy Consumer Act, which took effect

in 2009, was designed to give the Drug Enforcement Agency authority to address rogue Internet pharmacies selling controlled substances without a valid prescription. The act bans the sale of prescription drugs over the Internet without a legitimate prescription issued by a medical practitioner who has examined the patient in person at least once. The act is named after teenager Ryan Haight, who died from a drug overdose using drugs purchased on the Internet. The act requires online pharmacies to comply with pharmacy licensing laws in every state where they do business, and to register with the FDA before beginning to sell drugs online. This requirement is virtually unenforceable because foreign online pharmacies can easily run their Web sites from an offshore location, making it difficult for federal and state authorities to exercise jurisdiction over them. In 2011, LegitScript, a company aimed at identifying and shutting down rogue pharmacies, issued a report assessing the DEA's implementation of the Ryan Haight Act. The report documented 1,000 sample rogue Internet pharmacies (which it said was just a small fraction of those that exist) that it found marketing controlled substances in violation of the act. Most importantly, it noted that 55%–75% of these sites were using U.S.–based servers or domain name registrars, bringing them within the ambit of U.S. law. According to LegitScript, as of October 2012, there are 43,820 active Internet pharmacies, of which 42,179 (96.3%) are not legitimate.

In the meantime, the Food and Drug Administration recommends that consumers look for the NABP Verified Internet Pharmacy Practices Sites (VIPPS) seal, which verifies that the site is legitimate with respect to conformance with state laws, and requires a prescription for controlled drugs. So far, 32 major Internet pharmacies have signed on, including Drugstore.com, Caremark.com, Walgreens.com, and many other U.S. online

(continued)

pharmacies. LegitScript also offers a seal program endorsed by the NABP and has thus far verified 250 online pharmacies. However, it is important to note that, as an American trade association, the NABP does not deal with Canadian or European pharmacies, thereby potentially locking the American consumer into high-priced drugs.

■ **SOURCES:** Legitscript.com, accessed October 4, 2012; "HSI Seizes 686 Websites Selling Counterfeit Medicine to Unsuspecting Consumers," U.S. Immigration and Customs Enforcement, October 4, 2012; VIPPS, National Association of Boards of Pharmacy, October 1, 2012; "The Wrong Way to Stop Fake Drugs," by Roger Bate, *New York Times*, April 22, 2012; "In Whom We Trust: The Role of Certification Agencies in Online Drug Markets," by Roger Bate et. al, NBER Working Paper, March 2012; "UN Cracks Down on International Drug Fraudsters," by Natalie Morrison, In-pharmatechnologist.com, March 1, 2012; "Behind Google's $500 Million Settlement with the U.S.," by Peter J. Henning, *New York Times*, August 30, 2011; "Internet Drug Outlet Identification Program: Progress Report for State and Federal Regulators: July 2011," Nabp.net, July 11, 2011; "Drug Dealers on the Internet: Is the DEA Enforcing the Ryan Haight Act?", Legitscript.com, June 2011; "Increase in Internet Access Parallels Growth in Prescription Drug Abuse," Massgeneral.org, May 12, 2011; "Rogue Pharmacies Still a Problem For Search Engines," by Lance Whitney, CNET News, August 19, 2009; "FDA Warns Drug Firms Over Internet Ads," by Jerod Favole, *Wall Street Journal*, April 4, 2009; "U.N. Issues Guidelines on Illegal Web Pharmacies," by Reuters, *PC Magazine*, March 17, 2009; "Don't Put Your Health in the Hands of Crooks," Federal Bureau of Investigation, Headline Archives, March 3, 2009; "Ryan Haight Online Pharmacy Consumer Protection Act," H.R. 6353, 110th Congress, 2008.

from their systems. The major shipping companies—UPS, FedEx, and DHL—have been pressured into refusing shipment of untaxed cigarettes. Philip Morris has also agreed not to ship cigarettes to any resellers that have been found to be engaging in illegal Internet and mail order sales. However, a few off-shore Web sites continue to operate using checks and money orders as payments and the postal system as a logistics partner, but their level of business has plummeted as consumers fear state tax authorities will present them with huge tax bills if they are discovered using these sites. In 2010, President Obama signed the Prevent All Cigarette Trafficking Act. The law restricts the sale of untaxed cigarettes and other tobacco products over the Internet and bans the delivery of tobacco products through the U.S. mail.

Gambling also provides an interesting example of the clash between traditional jurisdictional boundaries and claims to a borderless, uncontrollable Web. The online gambling market, based almost entirely offshore—primarily in the United Kingdom and various Caribbean Islands—grew by leaps and bounds between 2000 and 2006, generating as much as $50 billion to $60 billion a year, and with much of the action (some estimate up to 50%) coming from customers based in the United States. Although the federal government contended online gambling was illegal under U.S. federal law (the "Wire Act" of 1961 prohibits use of wire communications for sports betting), they were initially unable to stop it, with various federal courts offering mixed opinions. However, in the summer of 2006, federal officials turned up the heat and arrested two executive officers of offshore gambling operations as they passed through the United States, leading their companies to cease U.S. operations. Then in October 2006, Congress passed the Unlawful Internet Gambling Enforcement Act, which makes it a crime to use credit cards or online payment systems for Internet betting. This effectively bars online gambling companies from operating legally in the United States, and shortly thereafter a number of the leading, publicly traded companies suspended their business in the United States. However, the bill has not eliminated all online gambling in the United States, with some smaller companies still offering offshore gambling. An association of online gambling groups challenged the law as unconstitutional, claiming that Internet gambling is protected by First Amendment privacy rights and that filtering technology exists to make sure that children and compulsive gamblers cannot access offshore betting sites. These arguments were rejected by the Third Circuit Court of Appeals in September 2009. Several countries are also seeking compensation from the United States on the basis of a World Trade Organization ruling that American Internet gambling restrictions are illegal.

More recently, however, perhaps because of the recession which depleted state budgets, or the widespread use and popularity of state lotteries, the political climate in the United States seems to have shifted towards tolerance and even support for online gambling operations. In 2010, legislation was introduced in the House of Representatives calling for legalization of online gambling and taxation of gambling revenues by both states and the federal government, and in 2011, a bipartisan group of legislators introduced a more narrowly drawn bill that would legalize only online poker. Proponents argue that Internet gambling goes on anyway, so why not regulate and tax the activity? In the meantime, online gambling continues, as do prosecutions. For instance, in April 2011, federal prosecutors filed fraud and money laundering charges against the operators of three of the most popular online poker sites, Full Tilt Poker, PokerStars, and Absolute Poker, basing the suit not only on federal law but also New York state law. The three sites together have about 6 million monthly unique visitors.

By the end of 2011, however, the Justice Department reversed its stance against Internet gambling, removing a major obstacle for states like New York and Illinois that want to legalize online gambling so they can tax the proceeds (Wyatt, 2011b). In June 2012, the State of Delaware became the first state to legalize online gambling in all its forms (Berzo, 2012). With the promise of enormous profits, Amazon, Facebook, Apple, and Zynga are rumored to be developing online betting apps (Winkler, 2012). The ethical issues surrounding online gambling may have less influence on the public debate than the need for new tax revenues, and for firms, the hope for additional revenues.

The Google Books Settlement:
Is It Fair?

In the Internet age, books are supposed to die off and go away. Who wants to read books when YouTube streams more than 4 billion videos every day in 2012, covering most topics known to man, and Google can provide online access to the world's information? Steve Jobs noted in an interview about the Kindle e-book reader, "It doesn't matter how good or bad the product [Kindle e-book reader] is, the fact is that people don't read anymore. Around 40% of the people in the U.S. read one book or less last year. The whole conception is flawed at the top because people don't read anymore."

Actually, in 2011, approximately 2.5 billion books were sold, generating around $27.2 billion in revenue. Although that represented a drop of 2.5% from 2010, e-book sales continued to grow rapidly, increasing to $2.07 billion in 2011 from $869 million in 2010, accounting for 15% of all trade sales in 2011. Books continue to be a very hot topic in 2012 as e-readers and tablets have exploded in popularity and Google battles the major heavy-hitter tech companies, authors, publishing firms, the United States

© Cyberstock / Alamy

Congress, the Department of Justice, and the European Commission over the future of online digital books.

Google is on a tear to put everything digital on its servers and then, as the founders promise in ceaseless self-congratulatory announcements, provide access to "all the world's information" through its efforts. And make a buck, as it turns out, by selling ads aimed at you that are "relevant" to your searches. A problem arises, however, when what Google wants to put on its servers does not belong to them. We're all familiar with the copyrighted music and video situation, where firms often operate offshore, beyond the law (or so they think), and enable, induce, and encourage Internet users to illegally download copyrighted material without paying a dime for it, while in the meantime raking in millions of advertising dollars from companies willing to advertise on their networks.

But Google is no criminal organization. For a firm whose motto is "Don't be evil," it seems out of character for it to initiate a program of scanning millions of copyrighted books it does not own and then, without permission, providing its search engine users with access to those books without charge, while selling ad space and pocketing millions for its own account without sharing that revenue with publishers or authors. One major difference between Google and most file-sharing firms is that Google has very deep pockets filled with cash, and they are based in the United States, making it an excellent legal target.

It all started with Google's secret 2002 project to scan all the books in libraries and make parts ("snippets") available online, and of course, display ads next to the results of book searches, even on the pages of snippets. In 2004, Google announced a program it first called Google Print and now just calls Google Books. There are two parts to the project. Under the Partner Program, publishers give permission to Google to scan their books, or make scans available, and then make parts of the work, or simply bibliographic information (title, author, and publisher), available on Google's search engine. No problem there: publishers and authors get a chance to find a wider market, and Google sells more ads. Publishers may even choose to sell online editions of their books on their own Web sites. And publishers were promised a hefty 70% of the display ad revenues and book sales (far better than Amazon's cut of book sales which is about 50%).

It's the second part of the project that became controversial. Under the Library Project, Google proposed to scan millions of books in university and public libraries, allow users to search for key phrases, and then display "relevant" portions of the text ("snippets"), all without contacting the publisher or seeking permission or paying a royalty fee. Google said it would "never show a full page without the right from the copyright holder," just the "relevant" portion. Google gave the publishing industry until November 2005 to opt out by providing Google with a list of books they did not want included. In addition, Google proposed to scan millions of books for which the copyright has lapsed and make those available on its servers for free. In these early days, Google's public stance towards authors and publishers was, "Stop us if you can."

Google has the backing of a number of prestigious libraries, such as the University of Michigan, Harvard University, Stanford University, the New York Public Library, and Oxford University. But not all librarians agree. Some believe this is a marvelous extension of public access to library collections, while other librarians fear it is harmful to book authors and publishers. A number of well-known libraries, such as the Smithsonian Institution and the Boston Public Library, as well as a consortium of 19 research and academic libraries in the Northeast, have refused to participate, in part because of restrictions that Google wants to place on the collection. Libraries that work with Google must agree to make the material unavailable to other commercial search services. Google claims it is performing a public service by making an index of books, and relevant portions, available to millions on the Internet, and perhaps even helping publishers sell new copies of books that currently sit on dusty library shelves. Google wants a monopoly on the books it has scanned (which is pretty much the universe of all books).

In 2005, the publishing industry struck back at Google's book-scanning program and two lawsuits were filed in federal court in New York, one a class-action suit by the Authors Guild and the second by five major publishing companies (McGraw Hill, Pearson Education, Penguin Group, Simon & Schuster, and John Wiley & Sons), claiming copyright infringement. The publishers' consortium, the American Association of Publishers (AAP), alleged that Google was claiming the right to "unilaterally change copyright law and copy anything unless somebody tells [them] "No" [making it] impossible for people in the intellectual property community to operate. They [Google] keep talking about doing this because it is good for the world. That has never been a principle in law. They 'do no evil' except they are stealing people's property." Or, as one commentator put it, it's like having a thief break into your house and clean the kitchen—it's still breaking and entering.

Google, on the other hand, claimed its use was "fair" under the "fair use" doctrine that has emerged from a number of court decisions issued over the years, and which is codified in the Copyright Act in 1976. The copying and lending of books by libraries has been considered a fair use since the late 1930s under a "gentleman's agreement" between libraries and publishers, and a library exemption was codified as Section 108 of the Copyright Act of 1976. Libraries loan books to patrons for a limited period, and must purchase at least one copy. Many people read books borrowed from libraries and recommend them to friends, who often buy the books rather than take the time and effort to go to a library. Libraries are also considered by many in the publishing industry as helping to market a book to a larger public, and libraries are believed to be performing a public service by increasing literacy and education.

In 2008, Google agreed to a settlement of the lawsuit with the authors and publishers. In return for the nonexclusive right to sell books scanned into its database, place advertisements on those pages, display snippets, and make other commercial uses of its database of scanned books, Google agreed to pay about $125 million to the parties. All books that Google digitizes will be listed in the central registry available to the public on the Internet. In 2009, a group of companies and organizations, including Microsoft, Yahoo, and Amazon, the American Association of Publishers, members of the Author's Guild, and publishers in the European Union all filed briefs with the court disputing the settlement. The technology companies formed the Open Book Alliance to oppose the settlement. They were joined by privacy protection groups who claimed that Google would be able to track whatever e-books people accessed and read. In September 2009, representatives of those groups spoke out at a hearing sponsored by the European Commission against the proposed deal. They said it would give Google too much power, including exclusive rights to sell out-of-print works that remain under copyright, a category that includes millions of books.

The Justice Department is continuing its investigation into the antitrust implications of the settlement. Critics argue the settlement will create a de facto monopoly position for Google, make it difficult for competitors to enter the field, and give Google broad copyright immunity. The settlement provides that Google's access to publishers' books is "non-exclusive," but competitors would have to scan all the same books over again in order to establish a competitive position, something that experts believe is financially prohibitive. Google, they argue, would end up owning the digital book, which is like owning the libraries of the future. Google counters that the settlement will expand digital access to millions of books that are gathering dust on library shelves.

Currently, Google has reportedly scanned about 20 million of the estimated 130 million books in the world. About 2 million of those are in the public domain, and can be viewed for free through Google's Book Search. Google Book users can also view previews of another 2 million books that are in copyright and in print, under agreements with various publishers. The remainder of the scanned books are out of print but still in copyright. These are currently available only in short "snippet view." The settlement would have allowed users to preview longer parts of those works and potentially purchase them in their entirety, but in March 2011, Federal Judge Denny Chin rejected the settlement, throwing the project into legal limbo once again. Citing copyright, antitrust, and other concerns, Chin said that the settlement went too far, and agreed with critics that it would give Google a "de facto monopoly" and the right to exploit and profit from books without the permission of copyright owners, particularly the authors of "orphaned" works whose content owners Google could not identify. The judge said that he would consider a revised settlement that addressed these concerns, suggesting that copyright owners be given the right to "opt in" to the settlement rather than "opt out" as originally proposed. An "opt in" structure had previously been rejected by Google as unworkable.

In September 2011, in a related action, the Authors Guild filed a new lawsuit related to the Library Project, suing Google, the university consortium HathiTrust, and five universities that are participating in the book-scanning project. The suit charges that the scanning of 9.5 million works in the HathiTrust repository constitutes massive copyright infringement, and also takes issue with HathiTrust's planned October 2011 launch of its Orphan Works Project, which would make available scans of books it had concluded were available after failing to locate valid copyright holders. Interestingly, as soon as the list was made public, a crowdsourcing effort quickly located some of the authors that purportedly could not be found. That suit must also wind its way through the legal process, presenting a further bar to Google's efforts to provide access to, and potentially profit from, all of the books in the world.

SOURCES: "Book Sales Fell 2.5% in 2011," by Jim Milliot, *Publishers Weekly*, July 18, 2012; "Suit Over Google Book Scanning Delayed on Appeal," by Chad Bray, *Wall Street Journal*, September 17, 2012; "Google Suit Gets Class-Action Status," by Jeffrey A. Trachtenberg, *Wall Street Journal,* May 31, 2012; "Google Deal Gives Publishers a Choice: Digitize or Not," by Claire Cain Miller, *New York Times*, October 4, 2012; "Suit Over Google Book Scanning Delayed on Appeal," by Chad Bray, *Wall Street Journal*, September 17, 2012; "Book Sales Fell 2.5% in 2011," by Jim Milliot, *Publishers Weekly*, July 18, 2012; "Google Suit Gets Class-Action Status," by Jeffrey A. Trachtenberg, *Wall Street Journal*, May 31, 2012 "Authors Organizations File Fresh Lawsuit Challenging Google Library Scans and Pending 'Orphan Works' Access," by Michael Cader, PublishersLunch, September 13, 2011; "New Publishing Industry Survey Details Strong Three-Year Growth in Net Revenue Unit," by Andi Sporkin, Publishers.org, August 9, 2011; "Judge Rejects Google Books Settlement," by Amir Efrati and Jeffrey A. Trachtenberg, *Wall Street Journal*, March 23, 2011; "Judge Rejects Google's Deal to Digitize Books," by Miguel Helft, *New York Times*, March 22, 2011; "What Is Google Editions?" by Peter Osnos, Theatlantic.com, July 10, 2010; "11th Hour Filings Oppose Google's Book Settlement," by Miguel Helft, *New York Times*, September 9, 2009; "Congress to Weigh Google Books Settlement," *New York Times*, September 9, 2009; "Tech Heavyweights Put Google's Books Deal in Crosshairs," by Jessica Vascellaro and Geoffrey Fowler, *Wall Street Journal*, August 21,2009; "Probe of Google Book Deal Heats Up," by Elizabeth Williamson, J. Trachtenberg and J. Vascellaro, *Wall Street Journal*, June 10, 2009; "Justice Department Opens Antitrust Inquiry Into Google Books Deal," by Miguel Helft, *New York Times*, April 29, 2009; *The Authors Guild, Inc., Association of American Publishers,*

Inc., et al., v. Google Inc., Preliminary Settlement, Case 1:05-cv-08136-JES Document 56, Filed 10/28/2008; *The McGraw Hill Companies, et al., v. Google Inc.,* United States Southern District Court, Southern District of New York, October 19, 2005.

In 2012, the legality of the Google Books project was still up in the air. In May 2012, Judge Chin granted class-action certification to the lawsuit, allowing authors to sue Google as a group. Google had argued that copyright claims needed to be brought individually by authors, which would have made things much more difficult for them in their fight against Google. After Google appealed Judge Chin's latest decision, the case was once again delayed. In October 2012, Google and the publishers reached an out-of-court settlement (after seven years of litigation) that allows the publishers to choose whether to permit Google to scan their out-of-print books that are still under copyright. If Google scans these permitted books, then it must provide the publishers with a digital copy for their own use. The economic value of this victory for publishers is difficult to perceive. Google will be giving away the scanned books for free and receive revenue from ads displayed on some book pages or a pre-rolls. It's unlikely the publishers will be able to sell these e-books when free books will be available.

Case Study Questions

1. Who is harmed by the Library Project? Make a list of harmed groups, and for each group, try to devise a solution that would eliminate or lessen the harm.

2. Why is Google pursuing the Library Project? What is in it for Google? Make a list of benefits to Google.

3. If you were a librarian, would you support the Library Project? Why or why not?

4. Why have firms like Amazon, Yahoo, and Microsoft opposed the Library Project? Why would a firm like Sony support Google?

5. Do you think the Library Project will result in a de facto monopoly in e-books, or will there be other competitors?

8.7 REVIEW

KEY CONCEPTS

■ Understand why e-commerce raises ethical, social, and political issues.

Internet technology and its use in e-commerce disrupts existing social and business relationships and understandings. Suddenly, individuals, business firms, and political institutions are confronted by new possibilities of behavior for which understandings, laws, and rules of acceptable behavior have not yet been developed. Many business firms and individuals are benefiting from the commercial development of the Internet, but this development also has costs for individuals, organizations, and societies. These costs and benefits must be carefully considered by those seeking to make ethical and socially responsible decisions in this new environment, particularly where there are as yet no clear-cut legal or cultural guidelines.

- ■ **Recognize the main ethical, social, and political issues raised by e-commerce.**

The major issues raised by e-commerce can be loosely categorized into four major dimensions:

- *Information rights*—What rights do individuals have to control their own personal information when Internet technologies make information collection so pervasive and efficient?
- *Property rights*—How can traditional intellectual property rights be enforced when perfect copies of protected works can be made and easily distributed worldwide via the Internet?
- *Governance*—Should the Internet and e-commerce be subject to public laws? If so, what law-making bodies have jurisdiction—state, federal, and/or international?
- *Public safety and welfare*—What efforts should be undertaken to ensure equitable access to the Internet and e-commerce channels? Do certain online content and activities pose a threat to public safety and welfare?

- ■ **Identify a process for analyzing ethical dilemmas.**

Ethical, social, and political controversies usually present themselves as dilemmas. Ethical dilemmas can be analyzed via the following process:
- Identify and clearly describe the facts.
- Define the conflict or dilemma and identify the higher-order values involved.
- Identify the stakeholders.
- Identify the options that you can reasonably take.
- Identify the potential consequences of your options.
- Refer to well-established ethical principles, such as the Golden Rule, Universalism, Descartes' Rule of Change, the Collective Utilitarian Principle, Risk Aversion, the No Free Lunch Rule, the *New York Times* Test, and the Social Contract Rule to help you decide the matter.

- ■ **Understand basic concepts related to privacy.**

To understand the issues concerning online privacy, you must first understand some basic concepts:
- *Privacy* is the moral right of individuals to be left alone, free from surveillance or interference from others.
- *Information privacy* includes both the claim that certain information should not be collected at all by governments or business firms, and the claim of individuals to control the use of information about themselves.
- *Due process* as embodied by the Fair Information Practices doctrine, informed consent, and opt-in/opt-out policies also play an important role in privacy.

- ■ **Identify the practices of e-commerce companies that threaten privacy.**

Almost all e-commerce companies collect some personally identifiable information in addition to anonymous information and use cookies to track clickstream behavior of visitors. Advertising networks and search engines also track the behavior of consumers across thousands of popular sites, not just at one site, via cookies, spyware, search engine behavioral targeting, and other techniques

■ **Describe the different methods used to protect online privacy.**

There are a number of different methods used to protect online privacy. They include:

- Legal protections deriving from constitutions, common law, federal law, state laws, and government regulations. In the United States, rights to online privacy may be derived from the U.S. Constitution, tort law, federal laws such as the Children's Online Privacy Protection Act (COPPA), the Federal Trade Commission's Fair Information Practice principles, and a variety of state laws. In Europe, the European Commission's Data Protection Directive has standardized and broadened privacy protection in the European Union nations.
- Industry self-regulation via industry alliances, such as the Online Privacy Alliance and the Network Advertising Initiative, that seek to gain voluntary adherence to industry privacy guidelines and safe harbors. Some firms also hire chief privacy officers.
- Privacy-enhancing technological solutions include secure e-mail, anonymous remailers, anonymous surfing, cookie managers, disk file-erasing programs, policy generators, and privacy policy readers.

■ **Understand the various forms of intellectual property and the challenge of protecting it.**

There are three main types of intellectual property protection: copyright, patent, and trademark law.

- *Copyright law* protects original forms of expression such as writings, drawings, and computer programs from being copied by others for a minimum of 70 years. It does not protect ideas—just their expression in a tangible medium. "Look and feel" copyright infringement lawsuits are precisely about the distinction between an idea and its expression. If there is only one way to express an idea, then the expression cannot be copyrighted. Copyrights, like all rights, are not absolute. The doctrine of fair use permits certain parties under certain circumstances to use copyrighted material without permission. The Digital Millennium Copyright Act (DMCA) is the first major effort to adjust the copyright laws to the Internet age. The DMCA implements a World Intellectual Property Organization treaty, which declares it illegal to make, distribute, or use devices that circumvent technology-based protections of copyrighted materials, and attaches stiff fines and prison sentences for violations.
- *Patent law* grants the owner of a patent an exclusive monopoly to the ideas behind an invention for 20 years. Patents are very different from copyrights in that they protect the ideas themselves and not merely the expression of ideas. There are four types of inventions for which patents are granted under patent law: machines, man-made products, compositions of matter, and processing methods. In order to be granted a patent, the applicant must show that the invention is new, original, novel, nonobvious, and not evident in prior arts and practice. Most of the inventions that make the Internet and e-commerce possible were not patented by their inventors. This changed in the mid-1990s with

the commercial development of the World Wide Web. Business firms began applying for "business methods" and software patents.

- *Trademark protections* exist at both the federal and state levels in the United States. The purpose of trademark law is twofold. First, trademark law protects the public in the marketplace by ensuring that it gets what it pays for and wants to receive. Second, trademark law protects the owner who has spent time, money, and energy bringing the product to market against piracy and misappropriation. Federal trademarks are obtained, first, by use in interstate commerce, and second, by registration with the U.S. Patent and Trademark Office (USPTO). Trademarks are granted for a period of 10 years and can be renewed indefinitely. Use of a trademark that creates confusion with existing trademarks, causes consumers to make market mistakes, or misrepresents the origins of goods is an infringement. In addition, the intentional misuse of words and symbols in the marketplace to extort revenue from legitimate trademark owners ("bad faith") is proscribed. The Anticybersquatting Consumer Protection Act (ACPA) creates civil liabilities for anyone who attempts in bad faith to profit from an existing famous or distinctive trademark by registering an Internet domain name that is identical or confusingly similar to, or "dilutive" of, that trademark. Trademark abuse can take many forms on the Web. The major behaviors on the Internet that have run afoul of trademark law include cybersquatting, cyberpiracy, metatagging, keywording, linking, and framing.

■ **Understand how governance of the Internet has evolved over time.**

Governance has to do with social control: who will control e-commerce, what elements will be controlled, and how the controls will be implemented. Governance of both the Internet and e-commerce has gone through four stages:

- *Government control (1970–1994).* During this period, DARPA and the National Science Foundation controlled the Internet as a fully government-funded program.
- *Privatization (1995–1998).* Network Solutions was given a monopoly to assign and track high-level Internet domain names. The backbone was sold to private telecommunications companies and policy issues remained undecided.
- *Self-regulation (1995–present).* President Clinton and the Department of Commerce encouraged creation of ICANN, a semi-private body, to deal with emerging conflicts and to establish policies.
- *Governmental regulation (1998–present).* Executive, legislative, and judicial bodies worldwide began to implement direct controls over the Internet and e-commerce.

We are currently in a mixed-mode policy environment where self-regulation, through a variety of Internet policy and technical bodies, co-exists with limited government regulation.

■ **Explain why taxation of e-commerce raises governance and jurisdiction issues.**

E-commerce raises the issue of how—and if—to tax remote sales. The national and international character of Internet sales is wreaking havoc on taxation schemes in the United States that were built in the 1930s and based on local commerce and local jurisdictions. E-commerce has benefited from a tax subsidy since its inception.

E-commerce merchants have argued that this new form of commerce needs to be nurtured and encouraged, and that in any event, the crazy quilt of sales and use tax regimes would be difficult to administer for Internet merchants. In 1998, Congress passed the Internet Tax Freedom Act, which placed a moratorium on multiple or discriminatory taxes on electronic commerce, and any taxation of Internet access, and since that time has extended the moratorium three times, most recently until November 2014. In November 2002, delegates from 32 states approved model legislation designed to create a system to tax Web sales, and by 2007, 15 states had agreed to support the program. Although there appears to be acquiescence among large Internet retailers to the idea of some kind of sales tax on e-commerce sales, insistence on uniformity will delay taxation for many years, and any proposal to tax e-commerce will likely incur the wrath of U.S. e-commerce consumers.

■ **Identify major public safety and welfare issues raised by e-commerce.**

Critical public safety and welfare issues in e-commerce include:
- The protection of children and strong sentiments against pornography. The Children's Online Protection Act (COPA) of 1998 made it a felony criminal offense to communicate for commercial purposes any material harmful to minors. This law has thus far been struck down as an unconstitutional restriction on Web content that is protected under the First Amendment. The Children's Internet Protection Act (CIPA), which requires schools and libraries in the United States to install "technology protection measures" (filtering software) in an effort to shield children from pornography, has, however, been upheld by the Supreme Court. In addition to government regulation, private pressure from organized groups has also been successful in forcing some Web sites to eliminate the display of pornographic materials.
- Efforts to control gambling and restrict sales of cigarettes and drugs. In the United States, cigarettes, gambling, medical drugs, and addictive recreational drugs are either banned or tightly regulated by federal and state laws. Yet these products and services are often distributed via offshore e-commerce sites operating beyond the jurisdiction of federal and state prosecutors. At this point, it is not clear that the Web will remain borderless or that e-commerce can continue to flaunt national, state, and local laws with impunity.

QUESTIONS

1. What basic assumption does the study of ethics make about individuals?
2. What are the three basic principles of ethics? How does due process factor in?
3. Explain Google's position that YouTube does not violate the intellectual property rights of copyright owners.
4. Define universalism, slippery slope, the *New York Times* test, and the social contract rule as they apply to ethics.
5. Explain why someone with a serious medical condition might be concerned about researching his or her condition online, through medical search engines or pharmaceutical sites, for example. What is one technology that could prevent one's identity from being revealed?

6. Name some of the personal information collected by Web sites about their visitors.
7. How does information collected through online forms differ from site transaction logs? Which potentially provides a more complete consumer profile?
8. How is the opt-in model of informed consent different from opt-out? In which type of model does the consumer retain more control?
9. What are the two core principles of the FTC's Fair Information Practice principles?
10. How do safe harbors work? What is the government's role in them?
11. Name three ways online advertising networks have improved on, or added to, traditional offline marketing techniques.
12. Explain how Web profiling is supposed to benefit both consumers and businesses.
13. What are some of the challenges that chief privacy officers (CPOs) face in their jobs?
14. How could the Internet potentially change protection given to intellectual property? What capabilities make it more difficult to enforce intellectual property law?
15. What does the Digital Millennium Copyright Act (DMCA) attempt to do? Why was it enacted? What types of violations does it try to prevent?
16. Define cybersquatting. How is it different from cyberpiracy? What type of intellectual property violation does cybersquatting entail?
17. What is deep linking and why is it a trademark issue? Compare it to framing—how is it similar and different?
18. What are some of the tactics illegal businesses, such as betting parlors and casinos, successfully use to operate outside the law on the Internet?

PROJECTS

1. Go to Google, click the Options icon in the upper-right corner of the home page, and then click on Search Settings. Examine its SafeSearch filtering options available on the Preferences page. Surf the Web in search of content that could be considered objectionable for children using each of the options. What are the pros and cons of such restrictions? Are there terms that could be considered inappropriate to the filtering software but be approved by parents? Name five questionable terms. Prepare a brief presentation to report on your experiences and to explain the positive and negative aspects of such filtering software.

2. Develop a list of privacy protection features that should be present if a Web site is serious about protecting privacy. Then, visit at least four well-known Web sites and examine their privacy policies. Write a report that rates each of the Web sites on the criteria you have developed.

3. Review the provisions of the Digital Millennium Copyright Act of 1998. Examine each of the major sections of the legislation and make a list of the protections afforded property owners and users of copyrighted materials. Do you believe this legislation balances the interests of owners and users appropri-

ately? Do you have suggestions for strengthening "fair use" provisions in this legislation?

4. Visit at least four Web sites that take a position on e-commerce taxation, beginning with the National Conference of State Legislatures (Ncsl.org) and the National Governors Association (Nga.org). You might also include national associations of local businesses or citizen groups opposed to e-commerce taxation. Develop a reasoned argument for, or against, taxation of e-commerce.

5. Consider the issue of the Department of Justice's subpoena of search query records discussed on 549–550. Prepare a list of reasons why the firms subpoenaed should or should not have complied with this request. What moral dilemmas are presented? What higher-order values, and what kind of value conflicts, are revealed in this list? How do you propose that we as a society resolve these dilemmas? You might conclude by applying each of the Candidate Ethical Principles described in Section 8.1.

PART **4**

E-commerce
in Action

CHAPTER 9

Online Retail and Services

Blue Nile Sparkles

for Your Cleopatra

Men: looking for that special gift for your Cleopatra but don't want to spend a lot of time shopping? Want to give the "Big Rock" certified by the independent Gemological Institute of America (GIA) or the American Gem Society Laboratories (AGSL) without spending a mountain of cash for the engagement experience? How about 35% less than retail prices? Not sure about the future value of diamonds? Then how about pearls, gold, or platinum?

Your answer has arrived: BlueNile offers you an online selection of about 80,000 diamonds for that special someone. You can buy

© Ken Gillespie Photography / Alamy

them cut and polished, or put them into settings like rings, bracelets, earrings, necklaces, pendants, watches, and brooches that you choose online. All the diamonds are graded by the 4Cs: carats (size), cut, color, and clarity, and a report for each diamond prepared by the GIA is available online. To make it easier, the carats are translated into milligrams, and one carat is exactly 200 milligrams of mass (if that helps). Just ask her what size she wants, and then look in your wallet.

In 2007, Blue Nile sold the biggest item in Internet history, a $1.5 million single diamond of around 10 carats, a size that would cover your finger with a penny-size rock. In 2010, another diamond sold for $500,000.

BlueNile.com started out as RockShop.com in March 1999 in Seattle, Washington. In November 1999, the company launched the Blue Nile brand and changed its name to Blue Nile Inc., opening up its Web site, BlueNile.com, in December 1999. In 2004, it went public.

Back in the early days of e-commerce, no one ever thought that the Internet would be a place where fine jewelry was sold. Typically, gifts of jewelry such as diamonds are associated with a significant emotional event, such as an engagement, marriage, or an anniversary. Generally, the event is shared with a significant other and often involves shopping together for the gem. Shopping on the Web (alone or together) hardly matches the emotional impact of walking into Tiffany's or another established retail store, with marvelous clear glass cases filled with brilliantly shining baubles, attended by a small army of unctuous perfumed sales clerks that make you feel so special. Diamonds represent a significant cost, and there is significant uncertainty about their value and pricing. Surveys show that most shoppers believe jewelry is highly overpriced, but they lack the knowledge and information to negotiate a better price or even judge the quality of what they are buying. Consumers generally have no rational way to compare diamonds, and face a limited selection at a single store, often in a high-pressure environment where sales employees are helping several customers at the same time. Most experts thought that, given the emotional significance and uncertainty of purchasing diamonds, few consumers would heighten the built-in anxiety by going to a strange Web site and plunking down $5,000 or more for a diamond they could not see or touch for several days.

But jewelry and high-fashion retailers are leading the second act of online retailing, bursting on the scene with high-growth rates and spectacular average sales transaction levels. As it turns out, the retail jewelry industry is an ideal candidate for Web sales. Here's why.

The $65 billion traditional jewelry industry is a byzantine, fragmented collection of about 25,000 specialty jewelry stores and another 100,000-plus that sell jewelry along with other products. To supply this fragmented market, several layers of wholesalers and middlemen intervene, from rough diamond brokers to diamond cutters, diamond wholesalers, jewelry manufacturers, jewelry wholesalers, and finally, regional distributors. Oddly, the source of raw mined diamonds is monopolized by a single company, De Beers, which controls around half of the world market. The fragmented supply and distribution chains add to huge markups based on monopoly-set prices for the raw diamonds. Currently, the typical retail store markup for diamonds is between 50% and 100%. Blue Nile's markup is around 30%.

Blue Nile's 2011 revenues were $348 million, up from $332 million in 2010, but the company experienced slower sales in the critical fourth quarter, which accounts for the lion's share of Blue Nile's revenues. International sales (in more than 40 countries worldwide) continued to be a bright spot, growing from $43.3 million in 2010 to $55.9 million in 2011. At least somebody has money! In the first half of 2012, Blue Nile's sales bounced back from the tough final quarter of 2011, increasing 13 percent over 2011 totals and landing the company at the top of lists of the strongest online retailers. International sales continued to grow as well.

Blue Nile's online competitors include Tiffany, Ice.com, Bidz, an online auction jewelry discount site, Tiffany, and even Amazon. Together, these companies are transforming the byzantine jewelry business. Blue Nile, for instance, has simplified the supply-side of diamonds by ordering and paying for a diamond, after the customer has ordered it. Blue Nile has cut out several supply-side layers of middlemen and instead deals directly with wholesale diamond owners and jewelry manufacturers.

Blue Nile minimizes its inventory costs and limits its risk of inventory markdowns. On the sell side of distribution, Blue Nile has eliminated the expensive stores, sales clerks, and beautiful but expensive glass cases. Instead, Blue Nile offers a Web site at which it can aggregate the demand of thousands of unique visitors for diamonds and present them with a more attractive shopping experience than a typical retail store. The result of rationalizing the supply and distribution chain is much lower markups. For example, Blue Nile will purchase a pair of oval emerald and diamond earrings from a supplier for $850 and charge the consumer $1,020. A traditional retailer would charge the consumer $1,258.

Blue Nile has improved the shopping experience primarily by creating a trust- and knowledge-based environment that reduces consumer anxiety about the value of diamonds.

In essence, Blue Nile and the other online retailers give the consumer as much information as a professional gemologist would give them. The Web site contains educational guides to diamonds and diamond grading systems, and provides independent quality ratings for each diamond provided by nonprofit industry associations, such as the GIA. There's a 30-day, money-back, no-questions-asked guarantee. The company's focus is "empowering the customer with information." And empower they do. The average customer visits the Web site repeatedly over several weeks, views at least 200 pages, and typically calls Blue Nile's live customer service line at least once. Repeat business accounts for around 25% of revenue.

In 2009, Blue Nile rebuilt its Web site, strengthening its appeal to its mostly male customer base while attempting to draw more women to the site. The new site removed the left menu so common to older Web designs, enlarged the pictures, added visualization software so visitors can see the jewelry with shadows and sparkles, expanded the product detail, and improved the search engine. The site's "Build Your Own Ring" feature has a new layout that's easier to use and to see more precisely what you're building. Another addition was the Recently Purchased Engagement Rings feature that showcases custom-ordered engagement rings. Blue Nile also added functionality to the Web site that allows customers to transact in their local currency, and now supports 24 different currencies in addition to the U.S. dollar, helping fuel the increase in international sales. In 2010, it introduced a mobile Web site and iPhone/iPad app, and reported that traffic and sales from both are growing rapidly. The iPhone app provides users with a quick way to set specifications for a diamond and see the price. A Dream Box button allows users to view the latest rings being sold by Blue Nile and share selections with friends via e-mail or Facebook. The app also features a Call button that provides a direct link to the Blue Nile call center for phone orders. In 2012, 25% of Blue Nile's traffic comes to it via smartphones, and the average smartphone shopper spends more than the traditional Web shopper. The biggest smartphone sale to date: a $300,000 engagement ring!

In 2012, Blue Nile began a shift in its strategy driven by the possibility that online retailers will have to begin collecting Internet sales taxes in most jurisdictions (see the *Insight on Society* case, *Internet Sales Tax Battle*, in Chapter 8). The company is moving towards fashion jewelry and higher price points and away from simply offering the lowest prices. Blue Nile has begun offering a proprietary line of high-end jewelry, and has added a design director and a new chief merchant to retool its product offerings. Still, even with additional sales taxes, Blue Nile's Internet-based distribution methods and lack of overhead from physical stores will allow them to continue to offer competitive prices.

So far, the "Blue Nile" effect of lower margins and Internet efficiency has mainly impacted the small mom-and-pop jewelry stores. About 3,000 small retailers have disappeared in the last few years for a variety of reasons. The big retailers, such as Tiffany, Zales, and others, sell more than Blue Nile, and continue to benefit from consumer interest in diamond engagement and wedding rings. Both Tiffany and Zales have active Web sites. Tiffany's site is primarily a branding site, but it has greatly improved its online graphics and online sales capabilities. The Zales site is a much more effective sales site than Tiffany's, with a marvelous build-a-ring capability, but still not quite up to the level of Blue Nile with respect to certification. Still, Blue Nile will have to keep a keen watch on its competitors, who are not far behind, to keep its edge online.

SOURCES: "Blue Nile's New Direction, and What it Says about Our Industry," by Rob Bates, JCKOnline.com, September 7, 2012; "Blue Nile Carries the Week in the Internet Retailer Online Retail Index," by Thad Rueter, Internetretailer.com, August 6, 2012; "Blue Nile Announces Second Quarter 2012 Financial Results," Bluenile.com, August 2, 2012; "Blue Nile Announces Fourth Quarter and Fiscal Year 2011 Financial Results," Bluenile.com, February 15, 2012; "Customer Says 'I Do' To a $300,000 Mobile Transaction," by Bill Siwicki, InternetRetailer.com, September 15, 2011; "Blue Nile CEO: More Shoppers Saying 'I Do,'" by Christina Berk, Cnbc.com, November 29, 2010; "Shopping on a Phone Finds Its Customer," by Geoffrey Fowler, *Wall Street Journal,* November 26, 2010; "Blue Nile Works to Build Repeat Business," Internet Retailer, September 22, 2010; "Blue Nile's App Is a Girl's Best Friend (And Maybe a Boy's Too)," by Christina Berk, Cnbc.com, September 16, 2010; "Selling Information, Not Diamonds," by Kaihan Krippendorf, Fastcompany.com, September 1, 2010; "Blue Nile Sparkles," by Kaihan Krippendorf, Fastcompany.com, August 30, 2010; "Digital Bling: Diamonds For Sale Online," by Wendy Kaufman, NPR.org, February 14, 2010; "Blue Nile Gets Makeover to Please Ladies," by Geoffrey Fowler, *Wall Street Journal,* September 1, 2009; "New Blue Site Hits Web," *New York Times,* September 1, 2009; "Blue Nile Aims to Sparkle With Re-designed Web Site," Internet Retailer, September 1, 2009; "Blue Nile: A Guy's Best Friend," by Jay Greene, *Business Week,* May 29, 2008.

The Blue Nile case illustrates some of the advantages that a pure-play, start-up retail company has over traditional offline retailers, and some of the disadvantages. A pure-play consumer service company can radically simplify the existing industry supply chain and develop an entirely new Web-based distribution system that is far more efficient than traditional retail outlets. At the same time, an online pure-play retailer can create a better value proposition for the customer, improving customer service and satisfaction in the process. On the other hand, pure-play start-up companies often have razor-thin profit margins, lack a physical store network to bolster sales to the non-Internet audience, and are often based on unproven business assumptions that, in the long term, may not prove out. In contrast, large offline retailers such as Walmart, JCPenney, Sears, and Target have established brand names, a huge real estate investment, a loyal customer base, and extraordinarily efficient inventory control and fulfillment systems. As we shall see in this chapter, traditional offline catalog merchants are even more advantaged. We will also see that, in order to leverage their assets and core competencies, established offline retailers need to cultivate new competencies and a carefully developed business plan to succeed on the Web.

As with retail goods, the promise of pure-online service providers is that they can deliver superior-quality service and greater convenience to millions of consumers at a lower cost than established bricks-and-mortar service providers, and still make a respectable return on invested capital. The service sector is one of the most natural avenues for e-commerce because so much of the value in services is based on collecting, storing, and exchanging information—something for which the Web is ideally suited. And, in fact, online services have been extraordinarily successful in attracting banking, brokerage, travel, and job-hunting customers. The quality and amount of information online to support consumer decisions in finance, travel, and career placement is extraordinary, especially when compared to what was available to consumers before e-commerce.

The online service sector—like online retail—has shown both explosive growth and some recent impressive failures. Despite the failures, online services have established a significant beachhead and are coming to play a large role in consumer time on the Internet. In areas such as brokerage, banking, and travel, online services are an extraordinary success story, and are transforming their industries. As with the retail sector, many of the early innovators—delivery services such as Kozmo and Webvan and consulting firms such as BizConsult.com—are gone. However, some early innovators, such as E*Trade, Schwab, Expedia, and Monster, have been successful, while many established service providers, such as Citigroup, JPMorgan Chase, Wells Fargo, Bank of America, and the large airlines, have developed successful online e-commerce service delivery sites. In Sections 9.5–9.7 of this chapter, we take a close look at three of the most successful online services: financial services (including insurance and real estate), travel services, and career services.

9.1 THE ONLINE RETAIL SECTOR

Table 9.1 summarizes some of these leading trends in online retailing for 2012–2013. Perhaps the most important theme in online retailing is the effort by retailers—both offline and online—to integrate their operations so they can serve customers in the various ways they want to be served.

By any measure, the size of the U.S. retail market is huge. In a $15.6 trillion economy, personal consumption of retail goods and services accounts for about $11.1

TABLE 9.1	WHAT'S NEW IN ONLINE RETAIL 2012–2013

- Mobile commerce exploded, almost doubling from $6.7 billion in 2011 to an estimated $11.6 billion in 2012. It is expected to continue to grow significantly in 2013, to around $17.2 billion.
- Continued rapid growth in social networks and user-generated content sites encourages "social commerce," where users pass on their opinions and recommendations to others in several online viral networks. Social commerce in the United States tripled, from $1 billion in 2011 to $3 billion in 2012, and is expected to almost double again, to $5 billion in 2013.
- Local commerce, headlined by daily deal sites such as Groupon and LivingSocial, continues to be popular with consumers, increasing to $2.9 billion in 2012, and an estimated $4.3 billion in 2013.
- The number of online buyers increased to almost 150 million in 2012, and the average annual purchase is up 10% to $1,497.
- Online retailers remain generally profitable by focusing on revenue growth, increasing the size of average purchase amounts, and improving efficiency of operations.
- Online retail remains the fastest growing retail channel.
- Buying online has become a normal, mainstream, everyday experience. Around 88% of Internet users in the United States are now online shoppers.
- The selection of goods for purchase online continues to increase to include luxury goods, such as jewelry, gourmet groceries, furniture, and wine, as customer trust and experience increase.
- Informational shopping for big-ticket items such as cars and appliances continues to expand rapidly to include nearly all retail goods (both durables and non-durables).
- Specialty retail sites show rapid growth in online retail as they develop customized retail goods and customer online configuration of goods.
- Online retailers place an increased emphasis on providing an improved "shopping experience," including ease of navigation and use, online inventory updates, interactive tools, customer feedback and ratings, and social shopping opportunities.
- Online retailers increase the use of interactive marketing technologies and techniques such as blogs, user-generated content, and video that exploit the dominance of broadband connections and offer features such as zoom, color switch, product configuration, and virtual simulations of households and businesses.
- Retailers become increasingly efficient in integrating multiple retailing channels, beyond "bricks-and-clicks" to "click-and-drive" and in-store Web kiosk ordering.
- More than half of online shopping and nearly a third of online purchases occur at work. However, growth of at-home broadband connections increases, making evening purchases from home the fastest growing time segment for retail purchases online and relieving some pressure on workplace purchasing.

trillion (about 71%) of the total gross domestic product (GDP) (Bureau of Economic Analysis, U.S. Department of Commerce, 2012).

If we examine the personal consumption sector more closely, we find that about 66% of personal consumption is for services, 11% is for durable goods, and 23% is for nondurable goods. Services include medical, educational, financial, and food services. **Durable goods** are those that are consumed over a longer period of time (generally more than a year), such as automobiles, appliances, building supplies, and furniture. **Nondurable goods** are consumed quickly and have shorter life spans, and include general merchandise, clothing, music, drugs, and groceries.

durable goods

goods that are consumed over a longer period of time (generally more than a year)

nondurable goods

goods that are consumed quickly and have shorter life spans

The distinction between a "good" and a "service" is not always clear, and is becoming more ambiguous over time. Increasingly, manufacturers and retailers of physical goods sell support services that add value to the physical product. It is difficult to think of a sophisticated physical good that does not include significant services in the purchase price. The movement toward "product-based services" can be seen in the packaged software market. Microsoft offers purchasers of its Windows and Office suite products additional value-added services from a variety of Microsoft Web sites. Charging for services, particularly on a monthly subscription basis, can be highly profitable. For instance, warranties, insurance policies, after-sale repairs, and purchase loans are increasingly a large source of revenue for manufacturers and retailers. Nevertheless, in this chapter, retail goods refer to physical products, and retailers refer to firms that sell physical goods to consumers, recognizing that retail goods include many services.

THE RETAIL INDUSTRY

The retail industry is composed of many different types of firms. **Figure 9.1** divides the retail industry into seven segments: durable goods, general merchandise, food and beverage, specialty stores, gasoline and fuel, mail order/telephone order (MOTO), and online retail firms.

Each of these segments offers opportunities for online retail, and yet in each segment, the uses of the Internet may differ. Some eating and drinking establishments use the Web to inform people of their physical locations and menus, while others offer delivery via Web orders (although this has not been a successful model). Retailers of durable goods typically use the Web as an informational tool rather than as a direct purchasing tool, although this is beginning to change as consumers have begun to purchase furniture and building supplies over the Internet. For instance, automobile manufacturers still do not directly sell cars over the Web, but they do provide information to assist customers in choosing among competing models.

The largest segment of the U.S. retail market is consumer durables, followed by general merchandise. These segments, particularly general merchandise, are highly concentrated, with large firms dominating sales. These very large firms have developed highly automated real-time inventory control systems (systems that collect point-of-sale data from cash registers, update inventory records, and inform vendors of stock levels), large national customer bases, and customer databases containing detailed purchasing information.

FIGURE 9.1 — COMPOSITION OF THE U.S. RETAIL INDUSTRY

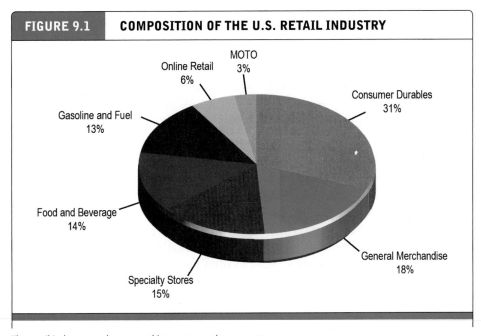

The retail industry can be grouped into seven major segments.
SOURCE: Based on data from U.S. Census Bureau, 2012.

General merchandisers have always competed against a more traditional form of retail commerce called specialty retailers. In fact, modern retail trade began as a collection of small retail shops in a concentrated location that customers visited in serial order. Shopping used to mean a visit to a shoemaker, dressmaker, pharmacy, butcher, and dry goods store. While mass-market general department stores were the fastest growing form of retail commerce for most of the twentieth century, in the 1960s, boutique and specialty stores catering to much smaller market segments with higher priced goods became the fastest growing form of physical retail stores. Stores such as The Gap, Banana Republic, Athlete's Foot, Sports Authority, Victoria's Secret, Staples, and many others developed national and international chain store strategies based on upscale youth market segments. The success of specialty retailing depends on building unique products for a market segment, offering strong customer service, and providing a persuasive shopping experience to support the brand image.

The MOTO sector is the most similar to the online retail sales sector. In the absence of physical stores, MOTO retailers distribute millions of physical catalogs (their largest expense) and operate large telephone call centers to accept orders. They have developed extraordinarily efficient order fulfillment centers that generally ship customer orders within 24 hours of receipt. MOTO was the fastest growing retail segment throughout the 1970s and 1980s. It grew as a direct result of improvements in the national toll-free call system, the implementation of digital switching in telephone systems, falling long distance telecommunications prices, and of course, the expansion of the credit card industry and associated technologies, without which neither MOTO nor e-commerce would be possible on a large national scale. MOTO was the last "technological" retailing revolution that preceded e-commerce. Because of their experience in fulfilling small orders rapidly, MOTO firms are advantaged when competing in e-commerce, and the transition to e-commerce has not been difficult for these firms.

ONLINE RETAILING

Online retail is perhaps the most high-profile sector of e-commerce on the Web. Over the past decade, this sector has experienced both explosive growth and spectacular failures.

Many of the early pure-play online-only firms that pioneered the retail marketspace failed. Entrepreneurs and their investors seriously misjudged the factors needed to succeed in this market. But the survivors of this early period emerged much stronger, and along with traditional offline general and specialty merchants, as well as new start-ups, the e-tail space is growing very rapidly and is increasing its reach and size.

E-commerce Retail: The Vision

In the early years of e-commerce, literally thousands of entrepreneurial Web-based retailers were drawn to the marketplace for retail goods, simply because it was one of the largest market opportunities in the U.S. economy. Many entrepreneurs initially believed it was easy to enter the retail market. Early writers predicted that the retail industry would be revolutionized, literally "blown to bits"—as prophesized by two consultants in a famous Harvard Business School book (Evans and Wurster, 2000). The basis of this revolution would be fourfold. First, because the Internet greatly reduced both search costs and transaction costs, consumers would use the Web to find the lowest-cost products. Several results would follow. Consumers would increasingly drift to the Web for shopping and purchasing, and only low-cost, high-service, quality online retail merchants would survive. Economists assumed that the Web consumer was rational and cost-driven—not driven by perceived value or brand, both of which are nonrational factors.

Second, it was assumed that the entry costs to the online retail market were much less than those needed to establish physical storefronts, and that online merchants were inherently more efficient at marketing and order fulfillment than offline stores. The costs of establishing a powerful Web site were thought to be minuscule compared to the costs of warehouses, fulfillment centers, and physical stores. There would be no difficulty building sophisticated order entry, shopping cart, and fulfillment systems because this technology was well known, and the cost of technology was falling by 50% each year. Even the cost of acquiring consumers was thought to be much lower on the Web because of search engines that could almost instantly connect customers to online vendors.

Third, as prices fell, traditional offline physical store merchants would be forced out of business. New entrepreneurial companies—such as Amazon—would replace the traditional stores. It was thought that if online merchants grew very quickly, they would have first-mover advantages and lock out the older traditional firms that were too slow to enter the online market.

Fourth, in some industries—such as electronics, apparel, and digital content—the market would be disintermediated as manufacturers or their distributors entered to build a direct relationship with the consumer, destroying the retail intermediaries or middlemen. In this scenario, traditional retail channels—such as physical stores, sales clerks, and sales forces—would be replaced by a single dominant channel: the Web.

Many predicted, on the other hand, a kind of hypermediation based on the concept of a virtual firm in which online retailers would gain advantage over established offline merchants by building an online brand name that attracted millions of customers, and outsourcing the expensive warehousing and order fulfillment functions—the original concept of Amazon and Drugstore.com.

As it turned out, few of these assumptions and visions were correct, and the structure of the retail marketplace in the United States, with some notable exceptions, has not been blown to bits, disintermediated, or revolutionized in the traditional meaning of the word "revolution." With several notable exceptions, online retail has often not been successful as an independent platform on which to build a successful "pure-play" Web-only business. As it turns out, the consumer is not primarily price-driven when shopping on the Internet but instead considers brand name, trust, reliability, delivery time, convenience, ease of use, and above all "the experience," as at least as important as price (Brynjolfsson, Dick, and Smith, 2004).

However, the Internet has created an entirely new venue for multi-channel firms that have a strong offline brand, and in some cases, the Internet has supported the development of pure-play online-only merchants, both general merchandisers as well as specialty retailers. As predicted, online retail has indeed become the fastest growing and most dynamic retail channel in the sense of channel innovation. The Web has created a new marketplace for millions of consumers to conveniently shop. The Internet and Web have continued to provide new opportunities for entirely new firms using new business models and new online products—such as Blue Nile, as previously described. The new online channel can conflict with a merchant's other channels, such as direct sales forces, physical stores, and mail order, but this multi-channel conflict can be managed and turned into a strength.

The Online Retail Sector Today

Although online retailing is one of the smallest segments of the retail industry, constituting about 5%–6% of the total retail market today, it is growing at a faster rate than its offline counterparts, with new functionality and product lines being added every day (see **Figure 9.2**). Due to the recession, online retail revenues were basically flat from 2008 to 2009, but they since have resumed their upward trajectory. When we refer to online retail, we will not be including online services revenues such as travel, job-

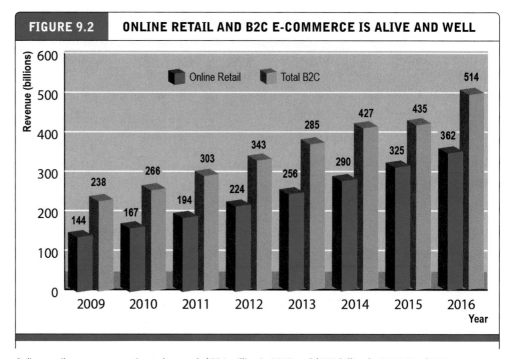

FIGURE 9.2 **ONLINE RETAIL AND B2C E-COMMERCE IS ALIVE AND WELL**

Online retail revenues are estimated to reach $224 million in 2012 and $362 billion by 2016. Total B2C e-commerce revenues (including travel, other services, and digital downloads) are projected to reach around $514 billion by 2016.

SOURCES: Based on data from eMarketer, 2012a; author estimates.

hunting, or the purchase of digital downloads such as software applications and music. Instead, for the purposes of this chapter, online retail refers solely to sales of physical goods over the Internet. The Internet provides a number of unique advantages and challenges to online retailers. **Table 9.2** summarizes these advantages and challenges.

Despite the high failure rate of online retailers in the early years, more consumers than ever are shopping online. For most consumers, the advantages of shopping on the Web overcome the disadvantages. In 2012, it is estimated that around 72% of Internet users over the age of 14 (around 150 million people) will buy at an online retail store, generating about $224 billion in online retail sales. While the number of new Internet users in the United States is not growing as rapidly at it was, with over 75% of the U.S. population already on the Internet, this slowdown will not necessarily slow the growth in online retail e-commerce because the average shopper is spending more on the Internet each year, and finding many new categories of items to buy. For instance, in 2003, the average annual amount spent online by users was $675, but by 2012, it had jumped to around $1,500 (eMarketer, Inc., 2012a, 2005). Also, as noted in Chapter 6, millions of additional consumers research products on the Web and are influenced in their purchase decisions at offline stores.

The primary beneficiaries of this growing consumer support are not only the pure online companies, but also the established offline retailers who have the brand-name

TABLE 9.2	ADVANTAGES AND CHALLENGES TO ONLINE RETAIL	
ADVANTAGES	**CHALLENGES**
Lower supply chain costs by aggregating demand at a single site and increasing purchasing power	Consumer concerns about the security of transactions
Lower cost of distribution using Web sites rather than physical stores	Consumer concerns about the privacy of personal information given to Web sites
Ability to reach and serve a much larger geographically distributed group of customers	Delays in delivery of goods when compared to store shopping
Ability to react quickly to customer tastes and demand	Inconvenience associated with return of damaged or exchange goods
Ability to change prices nearly instantly	Overcoming lack of consumer trust in online brand names
Ability to rapidly change visual presentation of goods	Added expenses for online photography, video and animated presentations
Avoidance of direct marketing costs of catalogs and physical mail	Online marketing costs for search, e-mail, and displays
Increased opportunities for personalization, customization	Added complexity to product offerings and customer service
Ability to greatly improve information and knowledge delivered to consumer	Greater customer information can translate into price competition and lower profits
Ability to lower consumers' overall market transaction costs	

recognition, supportive infrastructure, and financial resources to enter the online marketplace successfully. Table 1.7 on page 42 lists the top online retail firms ranked by online sales. The list contains pure-play online retailers for whom the Internet is the only sales channel, such as Amazon (in first place) and Newegg (in 13th); multi-channel firms that have established brand names and for whom e-commerce plays a relatively small role when compared to their offline physical store channels, such as Staples (2nd), Walmart (4th), Office Depot (6th), Sears (8th), Best Buy (11th), OfficeMax (12th), and Macy's (14th), and manufacturers of computer and electronic equipment, such as Apple (3rd), Dell (5th), and Sony (16th). The top 25 retailers account for over 60% of all online retail. For pure-play firms heavily dependent on Web sales, the challenge is to turn visitors into customers, and to develop efficient operations that permit them to achieve long-term profitability. For traditional firms that are much less dependent on e-commerce sales, their challenge is to integrate the offline and online channels so customers can move seamlessly from one environment to another.

TABLE 9.3	RETAIL E-COMMERCE: MULTI-CHANNEL INTEGRATION METHODS
INTEGRATION TYPE	**DESCRIPTION**
Online order, in-store pickup	Probably one of the first types of integration.
Online order, store directory, and inventory	When items are out of stock online, customer is directed to physical store network inventory and store location.
In-store kiosk Web order, home delivery	When retail store is out of stock, customer orders in store and receives at home. Presumes customer is Web familiar.
In-store retail clerk Web order, home delivery	Similar to above, but the retail clerk searches Web inventory if local store is out of stock as a normal part of the in-store checkout process.
Web order, in-store returns, and adjustments	Defective or rejected products ordered on the Web can be returned to any store location.
Online Web catalog	Online Web catalog supplements offline physical catalog and often the online catalog has substantially more product on display.
Manufacturers use online Web site promotions to drive customers to their distributors' retail stores	Consumer product manufacturers such as Colgate-Palmolive and Procter & Gamble use their Web channels to design new products and promote existing product retail sales.
Gift card, loyalty program points can be used in any channel	Recipient of gift card, loyalty program points can use it to purchase in-store, online, or via catalog, if offered by merchant.
Mobile order, Web site and physical store sales	Apps take users directly to specially formatted Web site for ordering, or to in-store bargains.
Geo-fencing mobile notification, in-store sales	Use of smartphone geo-location technology to target ads for nearby stores and restaurants.

Multi-Channel Integration

Clearly one of the most important e-commerce retail themes of 2012–2013, and into the future, is the ability of offline traditional firms such as Walmart, Target, JCPenney, Staples, and others to continue to integrate their Web and mobile operations with their physical store operations in order to provide an "integrated shopping customer experience," and leverage the value of their physical stores. **Table 9.3** illustrates some of the various ways in which traditional retailers have integrated the Web, the mobile platform, and store operations to develop nearly seamless multi-channel shopping. This list is not exclusive, and retailers continue to develop new links between channels.

Rather than demonstrate disintermediation, online retailing provides an example of the powerful role that intermediaries continue to play in retail trade. Established offline retailers have rapidly gained online market share. Increasingly, consumers are attracted to stable, well-known, trusted retail brands and retailers. The online audience is very sensitive to brand names (as described in Chapter 6) and is not primarily cost-driven. Other factors such as reliability, trust, fulfillment, and customer service are equally important.

The most significant changes in retail e-commerce in 2012 are the explosive growth in social e-commerce, the growing ability of firms to market local services and products through the use of location-based marketing, and not least, the rapidly growing mobile platform composed of smartphones and tablet computers. In retail circles, tablets are being called "the ultimate shopping machine," enabling consumers to browse media-rich online catalogs just like they used to do with physical catalogs, and then buy when they feel the urge.

Social e-commerce refers to marketing and purchasing on social network sites like Facebook, Twitter, Tumblr, and others. To date, these sites have not become major locations from which consumers actually purchase products. Instead they have developed into major marketing and advertising platforms, directing consumers to external Web sites to purchase products. For instance, over 25% of the 4.8 trillion display ads shown in the United States in 2012 appeared on Facebook, more than double that of Yahoo (comScore, 2012a). In 2012, social commerce is estimated to reach $3 billion and is expected to almost double that, to $5 billion, in 2013. More than 2.5 million Web sites have integrated with Facebook and more than 250 million people engage with Facebook from other Web sites (Paglia, 2012). Facebook has has around 190 million North American members, and getting the marketing message out on the social graph can happen very quickly. In the near future, it is likely that Facebook will develop on-site shopping, competing with Amazon for the role of largest online store.

Whereas in the past only large firms could afford to run marketing and ad campaigns on the Web, this changed radically with the development of local marketing firms like Groupon and LivingSocial, and tens of others, who make it possible for consumers to receive discount deals and coupons from local merchants based on their geographic location. Using billions of daily e-mails, these so-called daily deal sites have sold millions of coupons to purchase local goods and services at steep discounts. For the first time, local merchants can inexpensively use the Web to advertise their products and services. In 2012, local commerce is estimated to generate about $2.9 billion in revenues, and this is expected to grow to around $7 billion by 2015 (eMarketer, Inc, 2011a).

Social and local e-commerce are enabled by the tremendous growth in mobile Internet devices, both smartphones and tablet computers. In 2012, mobile commerce is expected to generate over $4 billion in sales at Amazon, and around $11.6 billion overall. In 2012, about 35% of smartphone users are expected to make a purchase with their phone, and it is estimated that this percentage will grow to over 42% by 2015. More than 40% of tablet owners are also expected to make a purchase using their tablet in 2012 (eMarketer, Inc., 2011b; 2012b).

9.2 ANALYZING THE VIABILITY OF ONLINE FIRMS

In this and the following chapters, we analyze the viability of a number of online companies that exemplify specific e-commerce models. We are primarily interested in understanding the near-to-medium term (1–3 years) economic viability of these firms and their business models. **Economic viability** refers to the ability of firms to survive as profitable business firms during the specified period. To answer the question of economic viability, we take two business analysis approaches: strategic analysis and financial analysis.

economic viability
refers to the ability of firms to survive as profitable business firms during a specified period

STRATEGIC ANALYSIS

Strategic approaches to economic viability focus on both the industry in which a firm operates and the firm itself (see Chapter 2, Sections 2.2 and 2.5). The key industry strategic factors are:

- *Barriers to entry*: Can new entrants be barred from entering the industry through high capital costs or intellectual property barriers (such as patents and copyrights)?

- *Power of suppliers*: Can suppliers dictate high prices to the industry or can vendors choose from among many suppliers? Have firms achieved sufficient scale to bargain effectively for lower prices from suppliers?

- *Power of customers*: Can customers choose from many competing suppliers and hence challenge high prices and high margins?

- *Existence of substitute products*: Can the functionality of the product or service be obtained from alternative channels or competing products in different industries? Are substitute products and services likely to emerge in the near future?

- *Industry value chain*: Is the chain of production and distribution in the industry changing in ways that benefit or harm the firm?

- *Nature of intra-industry competition*: Is the basis of competition within the industry based on differentiated products and services, price, scope of offerings, or focus of offerings? How is the nature of competition changing? Will these changes benefit the firm?

The strategic factors that pertain specifically to the firm and its related businesses include:

- *Firm value chain*: Has the firm adopted business processes and methods of operation that allow it to achieve the most efficient operations in its industry? Will changes in technology force the firm to realign its business processes?

- *Core competencies*: Does the firm have unique competencies and skills that cannot be easily duplicated by other firms? Will changes in technology invalidate the firm's competencies or strengthen them?

- *Synergies*: Does the firm have access to the competencies and assets of related firms either owned outright or through strategic partnerships and alliances?

- *Technology*: Has the firm developed proprietary technologies that allow it to scale with demand? Has the firm developed the operational technologies (e.g., customer relationship management, fulfillment, supply chain management, inventory control, and human resource systems) to survive?

- *Social and legal challenges*: Has the firm put in place policies to address consumer trust issues (privacy and security of personal information)? Is the firm the subject of lawsuits challenging its business model, such as intellectual property ownership issues? Will the firm be affected by changes in Internet taxation laws or other foreseeable statutory developments?

FINANCIAL ANALYSIS

Strategic analysis helps us comprehend the competitive situation of the firm. Financial analysis helps us understand how in fact the firm is performing. There are two parts to a financial analysis: the statement of operations and the balance sheet. The statement of operations tells us how much money (or loss) the firm is achieving based on current sales and costs. The balance sheet tells us how many assets the firm has to support its current and future operations.

Here are some of the key factors to look for in a firm's statement of operations:

- *Revenues*: Are revenues growing and at what rate? Many e-commerce companies have experienced impressive, even explosive, revenue growth as an entirely new channel is created.

- *Cost of sales*: What is the cost of sales compared to revenues? Cost of sales typically includes the cost of the products sold and related costs. The lower the cost of sales compared to revenue, the higher the gross profit.

- *Gross margin*: What is the firm's gross margin, and is it increasing or decreasing? **Gross margin** is calculated by dividing gross profit by net sales revenues. Gross margin can tell you if the firm is gaining or losing market power vis-à-vis its key suppliers.

  gross margin
  gross profit divided by net sales

- *Operating expenses*: What are the firm's operating expenses, and are they increasing or decreasing? Operating expenses typically include the cost of marketing, technology, and administrative overhead. They also include, in accordance with professional accounting standards (see below), stock-based compensation to employees and executives, amortization of goodwill and other intangibles, and impairment of investments. In e-commerce companies, these turn out to be very important expenses. Many e-commerce firms compensated their employees with stock shares (or options), and many e-commerce firms purchased other e-commerce firms as a part of their growth strategy. Many of the companies were purchased at extremely high values using company stock rather than cash; in numerous instances, the purchased companies fell dramatically in market value. All these items are counted as normal operating expenses.

- *Operating margin*: What did the firm earn from its current operations? **Operating margin** is calculated by dividing operating income or loss by net sales revenue. Operating margin is an indication of a company's ability to turn sales into pre-tax profit after operating expenses have been deducted. Operating margin tells us if the firm's current operations are covering its operating expenses, not including interest expenses and other non-operating expenses.

  operating margin
  calculated by dividing operating income or loss by net sales revenue

net margin
the percentage of its gross sales revenue the firm is able to retain after all expenses are deducted; calculated by dividing net income or loss by net sales revenue

- *Net margin*: **Net margin** tells us the percentage of its gross sales revenue the firm was able to retain after all expenses are deducted. Net margin is calculated by dividing net income or loss by net sales revenue. Net margin sums up in one number how successful a company has been at the business of making a profit on each dollar of sales revenues. Net margin also tells us something about the efficiency of the firm by measuring the percentage of sales revenue it is able to retain after all expenses are deducted from gross revenues, and within a single industry can be used to measure the relative efficiency of competing firms. Net margin takes into account many non-operating expenses such as interest and stock compensation plans.

When examining the financial announcements of e-commerce companies, it is important to realize that online firms often choose not to announce their net income according to generally accepted accounting principles (GAAP). These principles have been promulgated by the Financial Accounting Standards Board (FASB), a board of professional accountants that establishes accounting rules for the profession, and which has played a vital role since the 1934 Securities Act, which sought to improve financial accounting during the Great Depression. Many e-commerce firms in the early years instead reported an entirely new calculation called *pro forma earnings* (also called EBITDA—earnings before income taxes, depreciation, and amortization). Pro forma earnings generally do not deduct stock-based compensation, depreciation, or amortization. The result is that pro forma earnings are always better than GAAP earnings. The firms that report in this manner typically claim these expenses are non-recurring and special and "unusual." In 2002 and 2003, the SEC issued new guidelines (Regulation G) that prohibit firms from reporting pro forma earnings in official reports to the SEC, but still allow firms to announce pro forma earnings in public statements (Weil, 2003). Throughout this book, we consider a firm's income or loss based on GAAP accounting standards only.

balance sheet
provides a financial snapshot of a company on a given date and shows its financial assets and liabilities

assets
refers to stored value

current assets
assets such as cash, securities, accounts receivable, inventory, or other investments that are likely to be able to be converted to cash within one year

A **balance sheet** provides a financial snapshot of a company's assets and liabilities (debts) on a given date. **Assets** refer to stored value. **Current assets** are those assets such as cash, securities, accounts receivable, inventory, or other investments that are likely to be able to be converted to cash within one year. **Liabilities** are outstanding obligations of the firm. **Current liabilities** are debts of the firm that will be due within one year. Liabilities that are not due until the passage of a year or more are characterized as **long-term debt**. For a quick check of a firm's short-term financial health, examine its **working capital** (the firm's current assets minus current liabilities). If working capital is only marginally positive, or negative, the firm will likely have trouble meeting its short-term obligations. Alternatively, if a firm has a large amount of current assets, it can sustain operational losses for a period of time.

liabilities
outstanding obligations of the firm

current liabilities
debts of the firm that will be due within one year

long-term debt
liabilities that are not due until the passage of a year or more

working capital
firm's current assets minus current liabilities

9.3   E-COMMERCE IN ACTION: E-TAILING BUSINESS MODELS

So far, we have been discussing online retail as if it were a single entity. In fact, as we briefly discussed in Chapter 2, there are four main types of online retail business models: virtual merchants, multi-channel merchandisers (sometimes referred to as bricks-and-clicks or clicks-and-bricks), catalog merchants, and manufacturer-direct firms. In addition, there are small mom-and-pop retailers that use eBay, Amazon, and Yahoo Stores sales platforms, as well as affiliate merchants whose primary revenue derives from sending traffic to their "mother" sites. Each of these different types of online retailers faces a different strategic environment, as well as different industry and firm economics.

VIRTUAL MERCHANTS

Virtual merchants are single-channel Web firms that generate almost all their revenue from online sales. Virtual merchants face extraordinary strategic challenges. They must build a business and brand name from scratch, quickly, in an entirely new channel and confront many virtual merchant competitors (especially in smaller niche areas). Because these firms are totally online stores, they do not have to bear the costs associated with building and maintaining physical stores, but they face large costs in building and maintaining a Web site, building an order fulfillment infrastructure, and developing a brand name. Customer acquisition costs are high, and the learning curve is steep. Like all retail firms, their gross margins (the difference between the retail price of goods sold and the cost of goods to the retailer) are low. Therefore, virtual merchants must achieve highly efficient operations in order to preserve a profit, while building a brand name as quickly as possible in order to attract sufficient customers to cover their costs of operations. Most merchants in this category adopt low-cost and convenience strategies, coupled with extremely effective and efficient fulfillment processes to ensure customers receive what they ordered as fast as possible. In the following *E-commerce in Action* section, we take an in-depth look at the strategic and financial situation of Amazon, the leading online virtual merchant. In addition to Amazon, other successful virtual merchants include Newegg, Netflix, Zappos (now part of Amazon), Overstock.com, Drugstore.com, Buy.com, Gilt Group, Wayfair, Rue La La, Blue Nile (profiled in the opening case), Bluefly, Hayneedle, Net-a-Porter, and Shoebuy.

virtual merchant
single-channel Web firms that generate almost all of their revenue from online sales

E-COMMERCE IN ACTION

AMAZON.COM

Amazon, the Seattle-based pure-online merchant, is one of the most best-known names on the Web. Never suffering from modesty, Amazon's founder, Jeff Bezos, has proclaimed in the company's annual report that the objective of Amazon is to "offer the Earth's Biggest Selection and to be Earth's most customer-centric company where customers can find and discover anything they may want to buy." Exactly what these claims mean, and how it might be possible to achieve them, is a matter of speculation for both customers and investors. Yet this has not stopped Bezos and his team from becoming the Web's most successful and innovative pure-play, online retailer.

Few business enterprises have experienced a similar roller-coaster ride from explosive early growth, to huge losses, and then on to profitability. No Internet business has been both so widely reviled and so hotly praised. Its stock reflects these changing fortunes, fluctuating over the past 10 years, from an early high of $106 in 1999, to a low of $6 a share in 2001, and then bouncing back and forth between 2003–2009 between $50–$90, then climbing toward its current price of $242 in October 2012. While controversial, Amazon has also been one of the most innovative online retailing stories in the history of e-commerce. From the earliest days of e-commerce, Amazon has continuously adapted its business model based both on its market experience and its insight into the online consumer.

The Vision

The original vision of founder Jeff Bezos and his friends was that the Internet was a revolutionary new form of commerce and that only companies that became really big early on (ignoring profitability) would survive. The path to success, according to founder Bezos, was to offer consumers three things: the lowest prices, the best selection, and convenience (which translates into feature-rich content, user-generated reviews of books and products, fast and reliable fulfillment, and ease of use). Currently, Amazon offers consumers millions of unique new, used, and collectible items in a variety of different categories, both physical and digital. Its physical goods include books; movies, music, and games; electronics and computers; home, garden, and tools; grocery, health, and beauty; toys, kids, and baby; clothing, shoes, and jewelry; sports and outdoors; and auto and industrial. Its digital products include unlimited instant videos, digital games and software, MP3s and Cloud Player, Audible audiobooks, and Kindle e-book reader products. And if Amazon does not carry it, they have created systems for helping you find it at online merchants who rent space from Amazon, or even at other places on the Web. In short, Amazon has come close to becoming the largest, single one-stop merchant on the Web, a kind of combined "shopping portal" and "product search portal" that puts it in direct competition with other large online general merchants, eBay, and general portals such as Yahoo, MSN, and even Google. As Amazon has succeeded in becoming the world's largest online store, it expanded its original vision to become one of the Web's largest suppliers of merchant and search services.

Business Model

Amazon's business is currently organized into two basic segments, North American and International. Within those segments, it serves not only retail customers but also merchants and developers. The retail component of the business sells physical and digital products that Amazon has purchased and then resells to consumers just like a traditional retailer. It also manufactures and sells a variety of versions of its Kindle e-reader and Kindle Fire tablet computer.

Another major component of Amazon's business is its third-party merchant segment. Amazon Services enables third parties to integrate their products into Amazon's Web site, and use Amazon's customer technologies. In the early years of its business, Amazon entered into partnerships with large merchants such as Toys"R"Us, Borders, and Target, and created storefronts for these companies within the larger Amazon site. Today, Amazon has increasingly left the enterprise-level business to competitors and instead it has focused its efforts on small and medium-sized retail merchants.

Thousands of these types of merchants have signed on with Amazon, offering products that in some instances even compete with those that Amazon itself sells. For instance, a single product on the Amazon Web site may be listed for sale simultaneously by Amazon, by a large branded merchant participant such as Target, and by a business or individual selling a new, used, or collectible version of the product through Amazon Marketplace or an Amazon Webstore created by the merchant. For these types of merchants, Amazon is not the seller of record, does not own these products, and the shipping of products is usually handled by the third party (although in some instances, Amazon provides fulfillment services as well). Amazon collects a monthly fixed fee, sales commission (generally estimated to be between 10% and 20% of the sale), per-unit activity fee, or some combination thereof from the third party. In this segment, Amazon acts as an online shopping mall, collecting "rents" from other merchants and providing "site" services such as order entry and payment.

In many respects, Amazon's third-party seller segment is an effort to compete directly with eBay, the Web's most successful third-party merchant sales platform. At any given time, eBay has a registered trading community of over 113 million active buyers and sellers. Amazon has even developed its own version of PayPal: Checkout by Amazon. At the same time, eBay itself has moved closer to Amazon's business model by encouraging merchants to sell rather than auction goods on its sites.

Another major part of Amazon's business is Amazon Web Services (AWS). Through this segment, Amazon offers a variety of Web services that provide developers with direct access to Amazon's technology platform, and allow them to build their own applications based on that platform. The company launched the program in 2002. Bezos, however, was not satisfied with only a slew of cool new applications for his company's Web site. In 2006, Amazon introduced the first of several services that Bezos hoped would transform the future of Amazon as a business. With Simple Storage Service (S3) and, later, Elastic Compute Cloud (EC2), Amazon entered the utility computing market. The company realized that the benefits of the billions it had invested in technology could also be valuable to other companies. Amazon has tremendous computing capacity, but like most companies, only uses a small portion of it at any one time. Moreover, the Amazon infrastructure is considered by many to be among the most robust in the world. Amazon began to sell its computing power on a per-usage basis, just like a power company sells electricity.

S3, for example, is a data storage service that is designed to make Web-scale computing easier and more affordable for developers. New customers get a certain amount of storage and services for free (5 gigabytes of storage and 15 gigabytes of data transfer out each month.) Therafter, U.S. customers pay 12.5 cents per gigabyte of data for the first terabyte stored per month on Amazon's network of disk drives, and a declining amount for additional storage. There is no charge for data transferred in or for the first gigabyte of data transferred out. Data transferred out over 1 gigabyte and up to 10 terabytes costs 12 cents per gigabyte with a declining price for additional transfers over that amount. Customers pay for exactly what they use and no more. Working in conjunction with S3, EC2 enables businesses to utilize Amazon's servers for computing tasks, such as testing software. An initial tier of EC2 usage is free, and thereafter incurs charges of 8 cents per standard (small-instance) hour consumed for Linux/Unix usage and 11.5 cents per hour for Windows usage. A standard "small instance" supplies the user with the equivalent of 1.7 GB of RAM, 1 virtual core with 1 EC2 compute unit, a 160 GB storage, a 32-bit or 64-bit platform, and 250 MB of bandwidth on the network. Other "infrastructure" Web services offered by Amazon include messaging services such as Simple Queue Service (SQS), Simple Notification Service (SNS), and Simple Email Service (SES); database services such as SimpleDB, Relational Database Service, and ElastiCache; content delivery services called CloudFront; deployment and management services such as Elastic Beanstalk and CloudFormation; monitoring services such as CloudWatch; and Elastic MapReduce, a Web service that enables users to perform data-intensive tasks.

In addition to these Web services, Amazon offers networking services such as Route 53 (a DNS service in the cloud enabling businesses to direct Internet traffic to Web applications), Elastic Load Balancing, Direct Connect, and Virtual Private Cloud (VPC), which can be used to create a VPN between the Amazon cloud and a company's existing IT infrastructure. Flexible Payments Service (FPS) provides a payments service for developers. DevPay is an online billing and account management service for developers who create Amazon cloud applications. Amazon Mechanical Turk provides a marketplace for work that requires human intelligence. Alexa Web Information Service provides Web traffic data and information for developers. Fulfillment Web Services (FWS) allows merchants to access Amazon's fulfillment capabilities through a simple Web services interface.

Amazon does not break out its revenues from AWS, but analysts believe it will generate $1.5 billion in 2012 revenue. Because AWS provides cloud computing to thousands of Web sites, one research firm concluded that one-third of all Internet users access an AWS cloud site once a day on average, and that 1% of all Internet traffic runs through AWS infrastructure. These numbers place Amazon at the forefront of the "infrastructure as a service market." Even with the success of AWS, Amazon still continues to generate revenue primarily by selling products. While Amazon started out as an online merchant of books, CDs, and DVDs, since 2002, it has diversified into becoming a general merchandiser of millions of other products. Amazon has turned itself into a major online media and content firm. In 2011, 36% of its revenue comes from the sales of media (including MP3 tracks, CDs, DVDs, and books) and 60% comes from sales of electronics and general merchandise

In addition to Amazon.com in the United States, Amazon also operates localized sites in Japan, Germany, the United Kingdom, France, Italy, and Canada. The success of its international business often does not attract much attention. For instance, in 2011, Amazon derived almost $21.3 billion, or about 45%, of its $48 billion of gross revenue offshore, and international sales grew by 37% for the year. In 2012, Amazon, following its success with Kindle e-books, is also making a strong move into the music

| TABLE 9.4 | AMAZON'S CONSOLIDATED STATEMENTS OF OPERATIONS AND SUMMARY BALANCE SHEET DATA 2009–2011 | | |

CONSOLIDATED STATEMENTS OF OPERATIONS (in millions)			
For the fiscal year ended December 31,	**2011**	**2010**	**2009**
Revenue			
Net sales..........	48,077	$ 34,204	$ 24,509
Cost of sales.....	37,288	26,561	18,978
Gross profit	**10,789**	**7,643**	**5,531**
Gross margin.......	**22.4%**	**22.3%**	**22.5%**
Operating expenses			
Marketing......	1,630	1,029	680
Fulfillment......	4,576	2,898	2,052
Technology and content.....	2,909	1,029	1,240
General and administrative.....	658	470	328
Other operating expense (income), net........	154	106	102
Total operating expenses.....	9,927	6,237	4,402
Income from operations.....	**862**	**1,406**	**1,129**
Operating margin.....	**1.8%**	**4.1%**	**4.6%**
Total non-operating income.....	72	91	32
Income before income taxes.....	934	1,497	1,161
Provision for income taxes.....	(291)	(352)	(253)
Equity-method investment activity, net of tax.....	(12)	7	(6)
Net income (loss).....	**631**	**1,152**	**902**
Net margin.....	**1.3%**	**3.3%**	**3.7%**
SUMMARY BALANCE SHEET DATA (in millions)			
At December 31,	**2011**	**2010**	**2009**
Assets			
Cash, cash equivalents and marketable securities.....	9,576	8,762	6,366
Total current assets.....	17,490	13,747	9,797
Total assets.....	25,278	18,797	13,813
Liabilities			
Total current liabilities.....	14,896	10,372	7,364
Long-term liabilities.....	2,625	1,561	1,192
Working capital.....	2,594	3,102	2,433
Stockholders' Equity (Deficit).....	7,757	6,864	5,257

SOURCE: Amazon.com, Inc, 2012.

and streaming video business, with its Cloud Drive, Cloud Player, and Instant Video services.

Financial Analysis

Amazon's revenues have increased from about $600 million in 1998 to $48.1 billion in 2011. From 2009 to 2011, Amazon's revenues have almost doubled (see **Table 9.4**). This is very impressive, explosive revenue growth. In an effort to attract sales, Amazon has offered free shipping on orders over $25 and all orders to Amazon Prime members who pay $79 a year. Wall Street analysts detest free shipping because it increases Amazon's operating costs and lowers net margins. However, Amazon has been able to compensate for the cost of its low price strategy and free shipping policies by focusing on operating expenses and by eliminating marketing in offline magazines and television. This means that Amazon's increase in sales did not come about by increases in marketing, head count, or administrative overhead. Amazon instead relies heavily on affiliates and third-party merchants to drive sales. In addition, it has demonstrated an ability to scale its operations without rapidly increasing its administrative expenditures. However, Amazon's growth strategies have made it difficult for the company to increase its net income. In 2011, Amazon only earned a profit of about 1 cent per share—positive but not wonderful and not any better than a lot of bricks-and-mortar retailers. Nevertheless, the prospect for Amazon based on this financial analysis looks much improved from earlier years when it was showing negative margins and losing money on every sale. Even though investors are unhappy with Amazon's poor earnings record, they have driven the price of the stock to around $242 a share in October 2012, giving Amazon's stock a price earnings ratio (P/E) of 242, which is astounding. In contrast, Apple's P/E ratio is around 16 times earnings in 2012. What this means is that investors are betting that Amazon will keep growing at about the same rate for a long time.

Amazon's balance sheet has improved significantly since 2009. At the end of December 2011, it had about $9.5 billion in cash and marketable securities. The cash and securities were obtained from sales, sales of stock and notes to the public, venture capital investors, and institutional investors in return for equity (shares) in the company or debt securities. Total assets are listed at about $25.3 billion. The company emphasizes the strength of its "free cash flow" as a sign of financial strength, suggesting it has more than enough cash available to cover short-term liabilities (such as financing holiday season purchasing). Amazon's cash assets should certainly be enough to cover future short-term deficits should they occur.

Strategic Analysis—Business Strategy

Amazon engages in a number of business strategies that seek to maximize growth in sales volume, while cutting prices to the bare bones. Its revenue growth strategies include driving the growth of e-book sales by offering continuing enhancements of its Kindle e-reader and Kindle Fire tablet computer, both in the United States and internationally, as well as new e-book publishing initiatives; expanding into the music and streaming video business, with its Cloud Drive, Cloud Player, and Instant Video services, and a planned tablet computer to rival the iPad; expanding its Amazon Web Services offerings and extending their geographic reach; moving towards a broader trading platform by expanding the third-party seller segment; and moving towards greater product focus by grouping its offerings into major categories called stores. Amazon is still following Walmart's and eBay's examples by attempting to be a mass-market, low-price, high-volume online supermarket where you can get just about anything. To achieve profitability in this environment, Amazon has invested heavily in supply chain management and fulfillment strategies to reduce its costs to the bare minimum while providing excellent customer service and even free shipping.

Specific programs to increase retail revenues are the continuation of free shipping from Amazon Retail (a strategy that has increased order sizes by 25%), Amazon Prime (which for $79 a year provides free two-day shipping and one-day delivery upgrades for $3.99), greater product selection, and shorter order fulfillment times. Amazon offers customers same-day shipping in seven major cities without charging additional fees. Internet customers have long been frustrated both by high shipping and handling charges as well as long delays in receiving goods. A ticking clock can be seen next to some Amazon sale items indicating the hours remaining for an order to make it to the customer by the next day.

Amazon made several strategic acquisitions in 2011 and 2012, including its block-buster acquisition of warehouse robot manufacturer Kiva Systems in March 2012. Amazon acquired Kiva Systems for $775 million with an eye towards automating its expensive fulfillment process. In July 2012, Amazon also announced that it expanded a content licensing agreement from 2011 with NBC Universal to add content to Amazon's Instant Video library, bringing the total of movies and TV shows available for instant streaming to more than 22,000. This came on the heels of similar agreements with Viacom and nearly every major Hollywood studio. In 2011, Amazon struck a similar deal with CBS.

Amazon has moved strongly into the mobile shopping space as well, with shopping apps for the iPhone, BlackBerry, Android, Windows Phone 7, and iPad. It also has Deals, Price Check, and Student apps for the iPhone and has opened an Appstore for Android applications. In 2012, Amazon is expected to earn around $4 billion from mobile commerce. Reports have also surfaced that Amazon is developing its own smartphone to better compete in the mobile content marketplace.

In 2012, Amazon continues to build on the rousing success of its Kindle e-book reader platform, which Amazon has touted as the best-selling product in its history. In 2011, it introduced a lower-cost version, the Kindle with Special Offers (i.e., a Kindle with advertising), in both Wi-Fi and 3G versions, joining the regular Kindle 3G/Kindle Wi-Fi, a smaller, lighter version with better contrast and increased book storage (and without advertising), and the Kindle DX, a large-screen version more appropriate for newspapers, magazines, and textbooks. In September 2011, it introduced new touch-screen versions, as well as the Kindle Fire, a tablet version with a color display. It also introduced a variety of new Kindle apps, such as the Kindle Cloud Reader, that allows Kindle readers to access their Kindle books online using a Safari or Chrome Web browser. In 2012, Amazon released the Kindle Fire HD, with prices as low as $200 for the 7-inch screen version. According to Amazon, it now sells more Kindle books than all print books combined.

On the cost side, Amazon has taken significant steps to lower costs in the past three years. Important initiatives included the hiring of mathematicians and operations specialists to optimize the location of storing goods in Amazon's six warehouses, optimizing the size of shipments, and consolidating orders into larger batches prior to shipping. The company increasingly uses "postal injection" for shipping, in which Amazon trucks deliver pre-posted packages to U.S. Postal System centers. In 2012, Amazon also began an aggressive strategy to build warehouses all across the country to improve its delivery speeds. Many of Amazon's customers who had previously not paid sales taxes will soon be forced to pay them, so Amazon has prepared by seeking an insurmountable advantage in the entirely different area of delivery speeds. The ultimate goal for Bezos and Amazon: same-day delivery in many areas of the country.

Strategic Analysis—Competition

Amazon's competitors are general merchandisers who are both offline and online, and increasingly both. This includes the largest online competitor, eBay, and multi-channel retailers such as Walmart, Sears, and JCPenney. Amazon also competes with catalog merchants such as L.L.Bean and Lands' End in a number of product areas. As the Web's largest bookseller, Amazon is in competition with bookstores such as Barnesandnoble.com. Insofar as other portal sites such as MSN and Yahoo are involved in operating online stores or auctions, or selling their own products, Amazon also competes with these portals. In addition, Amazon competes with other firms who sell Web services such as hosting, shopping cart, and fulfillment services. Amazon has also engaged iTunes and Netflix in competition by offering video and audio downloads and Amazon Cloud Player, which allows users to store and play music on the Web. In September 2012, Amazon now offers over 20 million DRM-free MP3 songs from all four major music labels and thousands of independent labels that can be played on virtually any hardware device and managed with any music software. Amazon also offers Amazon Instant Video, which offers over 100,000 movies and TV shows to rent or buy.

Strategic Analysis—Technology

The person who said that "IT doesn't make a difference" clearly does not know much about Amazon. Amazon arguably has the largest and most sophisticated collection of online retailing technologies available at any single site on the Web. Amazon has implemented numerous Web site management, search, customer interaction, recommendation, transaction processing, and fulfillment services and systems using a combination of its own proprietary technologies and commercially available, licensed technologies. Amazon's transaction-processing systems handle millions of items, a number of different status inquiries, gift-wrapping requests, and multiple shipment methods. These systems allow customers to choose whether to receive single or several shipments based on availability and to track the progress of each order. Amazon's technology extends to its employees as well. Every warehouse worker carries a shoehorn-size device that combines a bar code scanner, a display screen, and a two-way data transmitter. It continues to invest heavily in AWS and the new versions of the Kindle e-reader, and in consumer electronics, with the Kindle Fire tablet and reportedly, a new smartphone. In 2011, Amazon spent over $2.9 billion on technology and new content, and is on track to spend even more in 2012.

Strategic Analysis—Social and Legal Challenges

Amazon faces a number of lawsuits concerning various aspects of its business. One series of lawsuits alleges that Amazon wrongfully failed to collect and remit sales and use taxes for sales of personal property, and knowingly created records and statements falsely stating it was not required to collect or remit such taxes. Amazon historically has also faced a number of patent infringement suits, which it typically settles out of court. Currently, there are several pending patent suits, including some involving Amazon's Kindle.

In 2012, Amazon faced increased challenges from states who were eager to begin collecting sales taxes from Amazon's sales. In the past, only customers in five states were required to pay sales taxes, but at least 23 states have now enacted legislation that will force companies like Amazon to begin charging sales tax. Amazon has already lost several legal battles involving the imposition of sales taxes. Many states had offered Amazon sweetened deals with tax breaks several years ago to lure Amazon's business, perhaps not expecting that Amazon would grow so large that the untaxed sales amount to billions of dollars in lost potential tax revenue. As many of those deals expire, Amazon has already begun, and, as mentioned previously, has begun an aggressive (and costly) expansion of its warehousing infrastructure across the United States.

Future Prospects

Amazon clearly has improved its financial performance through consistent gains in operational efficiency and extraordinary growth in sales. In 2011, net sales grew 40% to $48 billion. Through the second quarter of 2012, Amazon showed a significant gain over the previous year in net sales. For the first six months of the year, the company registered over $26 billion in sales, as opposed to $19.7 billion for the same period in 2011, paced by increases in Kindle Fire, Amazon Web Services, third-party sales, retail, and mobile sales. Still, net income dropped in 2011 from the previous year and has continued to drop in 2012, due primarily to increased spending on new technology initiatives and new warehouses. Although many worry about its ability to maintain high levels of customer service, Amazon routinely ranks among the top five online e-commerce sites for customer service, accuracy of delivery, and speed of fulfillment.

When compared to Walmart, a very profitable retailing giant, Amazon's recent track record is impressive. It has turned the corner and achieved several years of consecutive profitability. And while Walmart's same store sales have slumped to a crawl, Amazon's double-digit revenue growth in the last two years has been remarkable.

MULTI-CHANNEL MERCHANTS: BRICKS-AND-CLICKS

bricks-and-clicks

companies that have a network of physical stores as their primary retail channel, but have also introduced online offerings

Also called multi-channel merchants, **bricks-and-clicks** companies have a network of physical stores as their primary retail channel, but have also introduced online offerings. These are multi-channel firms such as Walmart, Sears, JCPenney, Staples, OfficeMax, Costco, Macy's, Target, and other brand-name merchants. While bricks-and-clicks merchants face high costs of physical buildings and large sales staffs, they also have many advantages such as a brand name, a national customer base, warehouses, large scale (giving them leverage with suppliers), and a trained staff. Acquiring customers is less expensive because of their brand names, but these firms face challenges in coordinating prices across channels and handling returns of Web purchases at their retail outlets. However, these retail players are used to operating on very thin margins and have invested heavily in purchasing and inventory control systems to control costs, and in coordinating returns from multiple locations. Bricks-and-clicks companies face the challenge of leveraging their strengths and assets to the Web, building a credible Web site, hiring new skilled staff, and building rapid-response order entry and fulfillment systems. According to Internet Retailer, in 2011, the chain retailers accounted for around $65 billion (around 30%) of all online retail sales. However, there remains much room for growth (Internet Retailer, 2012).

JCPenney is a prime example of a traditional merchant based on physical stores and a catalog operation moving successfully to a multi-channel online store. In 2011, JCPenney.com ranked 20th on Internet Retailer's list of the top 500 retail Web sites ranked by annual sales.

James Cash Penney opened the first Golden Rule store in 1902, and incorporated his growing business as the J. C. Penney Company in 1913. Penney's original vision was to create a nationwide chain of stores based on the newly emerging business model called a "department store," which aggregated a wide variety of general merchandise at a central location, usually near local transportation hubs formed by streets, highways, and street car lines. In addition, Penney envisioned a national catalog mail-order business to rival the successful Sears model. Today, JCPenney is one of the largest national department store chains, with more than 1,100 department stores in the United States and Puerto Rico. In addition to its department stores, JCPenney had one of the largest catalog operations in the United States, but in December 2009, it announced that its twice-yearly "big-book" catalog was being phased out, because "big-book catalogs have become less relevant as customers have embraced shopping online." In September 2010, JCPenney decided to stop publishing its remaining dozen specialty catalogs as well, although it continues to send monthly catalogs to about 14 million homes.

Like many traditional retailers, however, JCPenney has had to change its business model to accommodate the Internet and consumer demands for low cost and unparalleled product depth and selection, which could only be achieved by enhancing its Web operations. JCPenney opened its Web site for business in 1998 and placed its full catalog inventory online. Its department stores and Internet channels primarily serve the same target market: "modern spenders" and "starting-outers," or two-income families with median annual incomes of $50,000.

At JCPenney.com, customers can buy family clothing, jewelry, shoes, accessories, and home furnishings. And whether they buy merchandise in a bricks-and-mortar store, through the catalog, or on the Internet, customers can return items either at a store or through the mail. Indeed, the current essence of multi-channel retailing is the nearly complete integration of offline and online sales and operations while presenting a single branded experience to the customer. A second feature of successful multi-channel retailing is understanding customer preferences so that each channel sells products appropriate to that channel. For instance, not only can customers pick up and return at a local store what they order from JCPenney.com, but they can also order items from the store's counters that are only available online. The in-store point-of-sale system is integrated with Penney's Web catalog, and they both share a common inventory system. Many items are too expensive to hold in physical store inventory, but they can be offered economically on the Web site. The company has also invested in state-of-the-art interactivity and imaging tools for the Web site, such as a tool that lets shoppers mix and match 142,000 combinations of window treatments, and fitting guides that enable shoppers to zoom in on products such as jeans and create more custom-fitted orders. It has also embraced social media, with a presence on Facebook, YouTube, and Twitter, and mobile commerce. Its mobile site has won praise for its performance. It has also begun to advertise using the mobile platform, running ads inside the Hulu Plus iPhone app that let users shop via JCPenney's mobile site.

The company has achieved online success through some savvy decisions: putting approximately 250,000 products online, from lingerie to home furnishings, surpassing the competition in terms of selection, targeting women as the primary consumer, and making it easy to move from one category to the next on the site. JCPenney is able to directly compete against Amazon given its large selection, especially in apparel lines. In doing so, online sales are attracting new, younger JCPenney shoppers, 25% of whom have never bought anything in a JCPenney store. According to Internet Retailer, 90% of JCPenney Web customers also shop in their stores. Online sales are complementing, rather than cannibalizing, store and catalog sales. Shoppers who buy through all three channels spend four times more—$1,000—than the shopper who makes purchases only at the retail store. In 2011, JCPenney implemented a new e-commerce platform from ATG that provides the technology it needs to launch even more sophisticated online marketing programs. In 2012, it plans to roll out WiFi in all its stores, and has plans to install mobile checkout.

As a result, JCPenney appears to have successfully made the transition from department store/catalog merchant to store/Web merchant. Web sales in 2011 were $1.59 billion, about 4% higher than 2010. Continued improvement in this segment, coupled with a strong focus on high-margin apparel products for families, an area where Amazon and eBay are weak, offers a chance for continuing improved long-term performance (JCPenney, 2012; Internet Retailer, 2012).

CATALOG MERCHANTS

Catalog merchants such as Lands' End, L.L.Bean, CDW Corp., PC Connection, Cabela's, and Victoria's Secret are established companies that have a national offline catalog operation, but who have also developed online capabilities. Catalog merchants face very high costs for printing and mailing millions of catalogs each year—many of which have a half-life of 30 seconds after the customer receives them. Catalog merchants

catalog merchants
established companies that have a national offline catalog operation that is their largest retail channel, but who have recently developed online capabilities

typically have developed centralized fulfillment and call centers, extraordinary service, and excellent fulfillment in partnership with package delivery firms such as FedEx and UPS. Catalog firms have suffered in recent years as catalog sales growth rates have fallen. As a result, catalog merchants have had to diversify their channels either by building stores (L.L.Bean), being bought by store-based firms (Sears purchased Lands' End), or by building a strong Web presence.

Catalog merchants face many of the same challenges as bricks-and-mortar stores—they must leverage their existing assets and competencies to a new technology environment, build a credible Web presence, and hire new staff. Catalog firms are uniquely advantaged, however, because they already possess very efficient order entry and fulfillment systems. Nevertheless, in 2011, according to Internet Retailer, catalog merchants generated combined Web sales of about $22.3 billion (Internet Retailer, 2012).

Arguably one of the most successful online catalog merchants is LandsEnd.com. Lands' End started out in 1963 in a basement of Chicago's tannery district selling sailboat equipment and clothing, handling 15 orders on a good day. Since then it expanded into a direct catalog merchant, distributing over 200 million catalogs annually and selling a much expanded line of "traditionally" styled sport clothing, soft luggage, and products for the home. Lands' End launched its Web site in 1995 with 100 products and travelogue essays. Located in Racine, Wisconsin, it has since grown into one of the Web's most successful apparel sites.

Lands' End has always been on the leading edge of online retailing technologies, most of which emphasize personal marketing and customized products. Lands' End was the first e-commerce Web site to allow customers to create a 3-D model of themselves to "try on" clothing. Lands' End "Get Live Help" enables customers to chat online with customer service representatives; Lands' End Custom allows customers to create custom-crafted clothing built for their personal measurements. While customized clothing built online was thought to be a gimmick in the early years of online retailing, today, 40% of Lands' End clothing sold online is customized. In 2003, Lands' End was purchased by Sears (which itself was purchased by Kmart in 2004) but retains an independent online presence and catalog operation. In 2012, Lands' End took 7th place in the National Retail Foundation's ranking of best customer service. Features that garnered praise include live video chat, product recommendations that reflect a shopper's preferences, content display based on the shopper's location and referral source, and iPhone and iPad apps that deliver Lands' End catalogs to mobile users. Sears has incorporated many of Lands' End's online techniques into its own Web site, Sears.com (Landsend.com, 2012; Demery, 2012; Wagner, 2011).

MANUFACTURER-DIRECT

manufacturer-direct
single- or multi-channel manufacturers who sell directly online to consumers without the intervention of retailers

Manufacturer-direct firms are either single- or multi-channel manufacturers that sell directly online to consumers without the intervention of retailers. Manufacturer-direct firms were predicted to play a very large role in e-commerce, but this has generally not happened. The primary exceptions are computer hardware, where firms such as Apple, Dell, Sony, and Hewlett-Packard account for over 70% of computer retail sales online, and apparel manufacturers, such as Ralph Lauren, Nike,

Under Armour, Fossil, Crocs, Jones Retail, and Vera Bradley. Most consumer products manufacturers do not sell directly online, although this has started to change. For instance, in 2010, Procter & Gamble launched PGeStore.com, which carries over 50 different Procter & Gamble brands. Overall, according to Internet Retailer, consumer brand manufacturers account for about $20.3 billion in online retail sales (Internet Retailer, 2012).

As discussed in Chapter 6, manufacturer-direct firms face channel conflict challenges. Channel conflict occurs when physical retailers of products must compete on price and currency of inventory directly against the manufacturer, who does not face the cost of maintaining inventory, physical stores, or sales staffs. Firms with no prior direct marketing experience face the additional challenges of developing a fast-response online order and fulfillment system, acquiring customers, and coordinating their supply chains with market demand. Switching from a **supply-push model** (where products are made prior to orders received based on estimated demand and then stored in warehouses awaiting sale) to a **demand-pull model** (where products are not built until an order is received) has proved extremely difficult for traditional manufacturers. Yet for many products, manufacturer-direct firms have the advantage of an established national brand name, an existing large customer base, and a lower cost structure than even catalog merchants because they are the manufacturer of the goods and thus do not pay profits to anyone else. Therefore, manufacturer-direct firms should have higher margins.

One of the most frequently cited manufacturer-direct retailers is Dell Inc., the world's largest direct computer systems supplier, providing corporations, government agencies, small-to-medium businesses, and individuals with computer products and services ordered straight from the manufacturer's headquarters in Austin, Texas. Although sales representatives support corporate customers, individuals and smaller businesses buy direct from Dell by phone, fax, and via the Internet, with about $4.6 billion in sales generated online in 2011 (ranking 2nd only to Apple among consumer brand manufacturers and 5th on Internet Retailer's list of top 500 online retailers) (Internet Retailer, 2012).

When Michael Dell started the company in 1984 in his college dorm room, his idea was to custom-build computers for customers, to eliminate the middleman, and more effectively meet the technology needs of his customers. Today, the company sells much more than individual computer systems; it also offers enterprise systems, desktop, and laptop computers, as well as installation, financing, repair, and management services. By relying on a build-to-order manufacturing process, the company achieves faster inventory turnover (five days), and reduced component and finished goods inventory levels; this strategy virtually eliminates the chance of product obsolescence.

The direct model simplifies the company's operations, eliminating the need to support a wholesale and retail sales network, as well as cutting out the costly associated markup, and gives Dell complete control over its customer database. In addition, Dell can build and ship custom computers nearly as fast as a mail-order supplier can pull a computer out of inventory and ship it to the customer.

supply-push model
products are made prior to orders received based on estimated demand

demand-pull model
products are not built until an order is received

To extend the benefits of its direct sales model, Dell has aggressively moved sales, service, and support online. Each month, the company typically has about 7 million unique visitors at Dell.com, where it maintains an estimated 80 country-specific Web sites. Dell's Premier service enables companies to investigate product offerings, complete order forms and purchase orders, track orders in real time, and review order histories all online. For its small business customers, it has created an online virtual account executive, as well as a spare-parts ordering system and virtual help desk with direct access to technical support data. Dell has also continued to broaden its offerings beyond pure hardware product sales, adding warranty services, product integration and installation services, Internet access, software, and technology consulting, referring to them as "beyond the box" offerings. These include nearly 30,000 software and peripheral products from leading manufacturers that can be bundled with Dell products. Dell has also embraced social media. It has a presence on Facebook, YouTube, and Twitter, and posts Twitter-exclusive sales for those who follow Dell Outlet. In 2012, Dell redesigned its two-year-old mobile site, with a new layout, updated HTML5 navigation, and a host of new functionalities, including shopping assistance, Dell's full product image gallery, social sharing, mobile live chat, a product comparison tool, and simpler, more intuitive purchase process (Dell, Inc., 2012; Internet Retailer, 2012; Dusto, 2012).

COMMON THEMES IN ONLINE RETAILING

We have looked at some very different companies in the preceding section, from entrepreneurial Web-only merchants to established offline giants. Online retail is the fastest growing channel in retail commerce, has the fastest growing consumer base, and has growing penetration across many categories of goods. On the other hand, profits for many start-up ventures have been difficult to achieve, and it took even Amazon eight years to show its first profit.

The reasons for the difficulties experienced by many online retailers in achieving profits are also now clear. The path to success in any form of retail involves having a central location in order to attract a larger number of shoppers, charging high enough prices to cover the costs of goods as well as marketing, and developing highly efficient inventory and fulfillment systems so that the company can offer goods at lower costs than competitors and still make a profit. Many online merchants failed to follow these fundamental ideas, and lowered prices below the total costs of goods and operations, failed to develop efficient business processes, failed to attract a large enough audience to their Web sites, and spent far too much on customer acquisition and marketing. By 2012, the lessons of the past have been learned, and far fewer online merchants are selling below cost, especially if they are start-up companies. There's also been a change in consumer culture and attitudes. Whereas in the past consumers looked to the Web for really cheap prices, in 2012, they look to online purchasing for convenience, time savings, and time shifting (buying retail goods at night from the sofa). Consumers have been willing to accept higher prices in return for the convenience of shopping online and avoiding the inconvenience of shopping at stores and malls. This allows online merchants more pricing freedom.

A second common theme in retail e-commerce is that, for the most part, disintermediation did not occur and the retail middleman did not disappear. Indeed, virtual merchants, along with powerful offline merchants who moved online, maintained their powerful grip on the retail customer, with some notable exceptions in electronics and software. Manufacturers—with the exception of electronic goods—have used the Web primarily as an informational resource, driving consumers to the traditional retail channels for transactions. Leaving Amazon aside, the most significant online growth has been that of offline general merchandiser giant intermediaries such as Walmart, Sears, Costco, JCPenney, Macy's, Target, and Nordstrom. Many of the first-mover, Web pure-play merchants (online intermediaries) failed to achieve profitability and closed their doors en masse as their venture capital funds were depleted. Traditional retailers have been the fast followers (although many of them cannot be characterized as particularly "fast") and are most likely to succeed on the Web by extending their traditional brands, competencies, and assets. In this sense, e-commerce technological innovation is following the historical pattern of other technology-driven commercial changes, from automobiles to radio and television, where an explosion of start-up firms attracts significant investment, but quickly fail, and are consolidated into larger existing firms.

A third theme is that in order to succeed online, established merchants need to create an integrated shopping environment that combines their catalog, store, and online experiences into one. Customers want to shop wherever they want, using any device, and at any time. Established retailers have significant fulfillment, inventory management, supply chain management, and other competencies that apply directly to the online channel. To succeed online, established retailers need to extend their brands, provide incentives to consumers to use the online channel (which given the same prices for goods is more efficient to operate than a physical store), avoid channel conflict, and build advertising campaigns using online search engines such as Google, Yahoo, and Bing, and shopping comparison sites, as described further in *Insight on Technology: Using the Web to Shop 'Till You Drop*.

A fourth theme is the growth of online specialty merchants selling high-end, fashionable and luxury goods such as diamonds (Blue Nile), jewelry (Tiffany), and high fashion (Emporio Armani and Gilt.com) or selling discounted electronics (BestBuy.com), apparel (Gap.com), or office products (OfficeDepot.com). These firms are demonstrating the vitality and openness of the Internet for innovation and extending the range of products available on the Web. Many virtual merchants have developed large, online customer bases, as well as the online tools required to market to their customer base. These online brands can be strengthened further through alliances and partnerships that add the required competencies in inventory management and fulfillment services. Virtual merchants need to build operational strength and efficiency before they can become profitable.

A final theme in 2012 is the continuing extraordinary growth in social commerce, local marketing and commerce, and mobile commerce. In the space of five years since the first iPhone appeared, the mobile platform has emerged as a retail marketing and shopping tool, which will greatly expand e-commerce, potentially driving e-commerce

INSIGHT ON TECHNOLOGY

USING THE WEB TO SHOP 'TILL YOU DROP

The original idea was simple and leveraged many of the unique features of e-commerce technology: Create a Web site listing thousands of products where consumers can compare prices, features, consumer reviews of the actual product performance, and reputations of merchants. Then, when visitors click on a product and price they like, they are taken to the merchant's Web site where they can make the purchase. The merchant pays the Web site a fee or commission for sending the customer, as well as a listing fee usually determined by bidding on key words. The idea: Shoppers would not have to shop till they dropped, but instead could conveniently compare prices at one site, and then buy from the lowest-price merchant on the Web. Merchants would support this service because they would obtain additional customers and sales. Merchants join the shopping services and deliver a digital feed to the comparison sites providing information on both products and prices.

The idea first appeared in the mid-1990s in academic papers on potential uses of the Web and Internet, and was referred to as "shopping robots." Shopping robots are essentially search engines that scour the Web for prices on specific products. Now referred to much more descriptively as comparison shopping sites, they have become big business, with products tracked numbering in the millions. No one knows for sure, but observers believe there are over 100 price comparison sites on the Web in 2012. The top sites include Nextag, PriceGrabber, Shopping.com (which also includes Epinions.com, and is owned by eBay), Shopzilla/BizRate (owned by Scripps), Pronto, TheFind, Become, and Smarter. Nextag says more than 21 million people a month use

its site to research and compare products and services online. According to Channel Advisor, a leading e-commerce software and services provider, comparison shopping sites drive about 15% of e-commerce, making them an important channel for retailers. Shopzilla, PriceGrabber, Shopping.com, and Pronto, among others, are used by over 50% of Internet Retailer's top 500 online merchants.

General merchandisers such as Amazon and search engines such as Google and Bing have also developed their own comparison shopping capabilities. Shopping sites make money by charging participating merchants on a per-click basis regardless of whether a sale is made. A twist on shopping search engines is comparison shopping coupon systems. Sites like Wow-Coupons, CurrentCodes, FatWallet, and Bing Deals search the Web for deals and coupons.

Comparison shopping sites focused originally on tracking online prices for electronic consumer goods and computers. Consumer electronics are fairly commoditized products by a few branded manufacturers, with standard features, making it relatively easy to compare one product to another. Type in "digital camera," select the number of megapixels you want, enter the zoom range and price, press the Enter key on your keyboard, and you will receive a long list of cameras and dealers. You can refine your search as you move along the purchase process, and explore the reputations of dealers before you decide to purchase.

However, although Shopping.com tracks over 60 million products and about 2,700 different brands, very few of these items are so-called "soft goods" purchased by women, who have risen to equal the purchasing power of men on the Web. In 1998, 65% of Web purchases were made by men,

(continued)

while today, over 60% are made by women who are much more likely to be looking for soft goods, such as apparel, jewelry, accessories, luggage, and gifts. In fact, these are among the fastest growing consumer product categories on the Web. For this reason, the shopping comparison sites are currently adding soft goods to their services.

But the process of comparison shopping for soft goods is not as simple as for hard goods such as digital TVs or digital cameras. The strength of a comparison shopping site is to present highly similar or identical items from different merchants at varying prices and reputation levels. Generally, these kinds of electronic goods have a limited number of suppliers (mostly solid brand names) and limited features. But in more complex product areas, such as apparel or jewelry, such standards do not exist. In fact, manufacturers of these products emphasize their uniqueness, not their similarity. One solution is to focus on the brands of soft goods and not the price: bags from Gucci, sweaters from Benetton, and mountain climbing gear from REI. Yahoo and search engines such as Bing and Google are moving closer to the brand model of comparison shopping as price becomes a less powerful factor in consumer purchases of soft goods.

As more attention focuses on comparison shopping sites, the sites themselves continue to innovate and add features, and they attempt to go beyond simply finding customers the lowest-price products. Shopping.com tracks its visitors to help consumers decide what to buy, and where to buy. It does this by showing visitors the most popular sites for each category of product selected. It has moved strongly into the mobile arena and has both iPhone and Android apps that allow consumers to research products and compare prices while they are in a store. Shopzilla has developed a data categorization technology that it calls Robozilla, designed to help expedite the shopping process. Shopzilla also redesigned its Web site seeking to enhance the customer experience by adding speed, a better search engine, and more product detail. Shopzilla was able to reduce the search time for products from 6 to 9 seconds, down to 1.2 seconds on average. PriceGrabber has added product tours and a local availability feature to its Web site, and more content, such as user and third-party reviews, and discussion boards. In 2011, it added price alerts and local availability to its iPhone and iPad apps as well. Nextag also offers consumers e-mail price alerts and product price history charting, and for merchants, a data feed auto-import option. Most of the larger sites are adding user-generated reviews and opinions of products.

As the number of shoppers using mobile to make purchases continues to rise rapidly, comparison shopping on mobile has grown as well. Half of the U.S. respondents in a 2012 survey report using their mobile devices to compare prices while out shopping. Comparison shopping sites have adjusted accordingly. Shopping.com has moved strongly into the mobile arena and has both iPhone and Android apps that allow consumers to research products and compare prices while they are in a store. In 2011, Nextag introduced a mobile app for its Radar feature, which searches for products and alerts consumers to price changes. The mobile app allows users to add items to their Radar list by taking a photo of the item. Radar uses image recognition and is integrated with the core Nextag Mobile app.

In 2012, perhaps the biggest news in comparison shopping came from Google when it announced that its free Google Product Search service would become a paid service called Google Shopping. This was bad news to merchants who were used to receiving this service for free from Google, but Google's unbeatable amounts of eyeballs and potential traffic will likely be too much for most merchants to ignore, and Google Shopping should maintain its position as the

(continued)

most popular comparison shopping engine. Merchants will be able to have their products appear more frequently than competitors and be listed as a "Trusted Store" if they share data with Google that proves reliable shipping and quality customer service. Merchants will pay Google at a cost per click rate. Search engines like Google and Bing are in direct competition with the stand-alone comparison shopping sites for business.

SOURCES: "Survey: Younger Shoppers Increasingly Using Mobiles To Buy and Compare", by Natasha Lomas, TechCrunch.com, September 28, 2012; "The 10 Best Shopping Engines," by Andrew Davis, Searchenginewatch.com, June 19, 2012; "The New Google Shopping: 15 FAQs," by Mary Weinstein, Cpcstrategy.com, June 14, 2012; "Nextag's Radar Picks Up a Smartphone App," by Kevin Woodward, *Internet Retailer*, August 24, 2011; "PriceGrabber Adds Price Alerts and Local Availability to its Mobile Apps," by Katie Deatsch, *Internet Retailer*, January 5, 2011; "Comparison Shopping Engines: Strategies for Smaller Merchants," *Practical eCommerce*, August 25, 2010; "Amazon Moves Up in a Ranking of Comparison Shopping Sites," by Don Davis, *Internet Retailer*, July 20, 2010; "Beyond Compare," by Don Davis, *Internet Retailer*, May 27, 2010; "8 Top Sites for Online Shopping Deals," by Jennifer Mulrean, moneycentral. msn.com, September 14, 2009; "Shopzilla Site Redo—You Get What You Measure," by Philip Dixon, en.oreilly.com, June 24, 2009.

to 20% of all commerce in the next five years. Local merchants will be a major benefactor of the growing mobile commerce platform. In an equally short time, Americans have begun to spend a quarter of their Internet time on social network sites where they share attitudes and experiences about business firms, products, and services. In a few years, social sites will turn into large purchasing venues.

9.4 THE SERVICE SECTOR: OFFLINE AND ONLINE

The service sector is typically the largest and most rapidly expanding part of the economies in advanced industrial nations such as the United States and in European and some Asian countries. In the United States, the service sector (broadly defined) employs about four out of every five workers and accounts for about 75% of all economic activity (Bartash, 2011). E-commerce in the service sector offers extraordinary opportunities to deliver information, knowledge, and transaction efficiencies.

WHAT ARE SERVICES?

service occupations
occupations concerned with performing tasks in and around households, business firms, and institutions

service industries
establishments providing services to consumers, businesses, governments, and other organizations

Just what are services? The U.S. Department of Labor defines **service occupations** as "concerned with performing tasks" in and around households, business firms, and institutions (U.S. Department of Labor, 1991). The U.S. Census Bureau defines **service industries** as those "domestic establishments providing services to consumers, businesses, governments, and other organizations" (U.S. Census Bureau, 2001). The major service industry groups are finance, insurance, real estate, travel, professional services such as legal and accounting, business services, health services, and educational services. Business services include activities such as consulting, advertising and marketing, and information processing.

CATEGORIZING SERVICE INDUSTRIES

Within these service industry groups, companies can be further categorized into those that involve **transaction brokering** (acting as an intermediary to facilitate a transaction) and those that involve providing a "hands-on" service. For instance, one type of financial service involves stockbrokers who act as the middle person in a transaction between buyers and sellers. Online mortgage companies such as LendingTree.com refer customers to mortgage companies that actually issue the mortgage. Employment agencies put a seller of labor in contact with a buyer of labor. The service involved in all these examples is brokering a transaction.

transaction brokering
acting as an intermediary to facilitate a transaction

In contrast, some industries perform specific hands-on activities for consumers. In order to provide their service, these professionals need to interact directly and personally with the "client." For these service industries, the opportunities for e-commerce are somewhat different. Currently, doctors and dentists cannot treat patients over the Internet. However, the Internet can assist their services by providing consumers with information, knowledge, and communication.

KNOWLEDGE AND INFORMATION INTENSITY

With some exceptions (for example, providers of physical services, such as cleaning, gardening, and so on), perhaps the most important feature of service industries (and occupations) is that they are knowledge- and information-intense. In order to provide value, service industries process a great deal of information and employ a highly skilled, educated workforce. For instance, to provide legal services, you need lawyers with law degrees. Law firms are required to process enormous amounts of textual information. Likewise with medical services. Financial services are not so knowledge-intensive, but require much larger investments in information processing just to keep track of transactions and investments. In fact, the financial services sector is the largest investor in information technology, with over 80% of invested capital going to information technology equipment and services (Laudon and Laudon, 2012).

For these reasons, many services are uniquely suited to e-commerce applications and the strengths of the Internet, which are to collect, store, and disseminate high-value information and to provide reliable, fast communication.

PERSONALIZATION AND CUSTOMIZATION

Services differ in the amount of personalization and customization required, although just about all services entail some personalization or customization. Some services, such as legal, medical, and accounting services, require extensive personalization—the adjustment of a service to the precise needs of a single individual or object. Others, such as financial services, benefit from customization by allowing individuals to choose from a restricted menu. The ability of Internet and e-commerce technology to personalize and customize service, or components of service, is a major factor undergirding the extremely rapid growth of e-commerce services. Future expansion of e-services will depend in part on the ability of e-commerce firms to transform their customized services—choosing from a list—into truly personalized services, such as providing unique advice and consultation based on a digital yet intimate understanding of the client (at least as intimate as professional service providers).

9.5 ONLINE FINANCIAL SERVICES

The online financial services sector is a shining example of an e-commerce success story, but one with many twists and turns. While the innovative, pure-online firms such as E*Trade have been instrumental in transforming the brokerage industry, the impacts of e-commerce on the large, powerful banking, insurance, and real estate firms have been delayed by consumer resistance and the lack of industry innovation. For instance, online-only banks have not displaced or transformed the large national banks or even regional and local banks. But e-commerce has nevertheless transformed the banking and financial industries, as the major institutions have deployed their own online applications to service an increasingly connected online customer base. A 2011 survey by the American Bankers Association found that 62% of customers preferred online banking compared with any other method (American Bankers Association, 2012). Insurance has become more standardized and easier to purchase on the Web. Although security is still a concern, consumers are much more willing to trust online sites with their financial information than in the past. Firms such as Mint.com (now owned by Quicken), SmartyPig, and Credit Karma continue to show growth. Multi-channel, established financial services firms—the slow followers—also continue to show modest gains in online transactions of about 2%–4% annually.

FINANCIAL SERVICES INDUSTRY TRENDS

The financial services industry provides four generic kinds of services: storage of and access to funds, protection of assets, means to grow assets, and movement of funds. Historically, in the United States and elsewhere, separate institutions provided these financial services (see **Table 9.5**).

TABLE 9.5	TRADITIONAL PROVIDERS OF FINANCIAL SERVICES
FINANCIAL SERVICE	INSTITUTIONAL PROVIDER
Storage of and access to funds	Banking, lending
Protection of assets	Insurance
Growth	Investment and brokerage firms
Movement of funds (payment)	Banks, credit card firms

| FIGURE 9.3 | INDUSTRY CONSOLIDATION AND INTEGRATED FINANCIAL SERVICES |

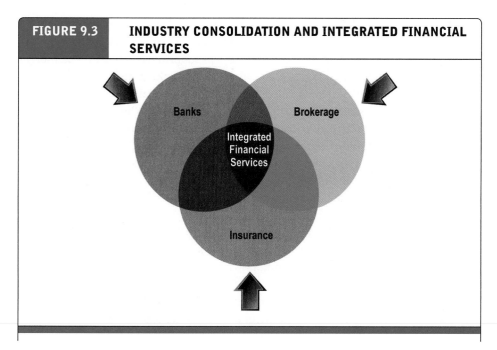

The major trends in financial services are industry consolidation and the provision of integrated financial services to consumers.

However, two important global trends in the financial services industry that have direct consequences for online financial services firms are changing the institutional structure of financial services. The first trend is industry consolidation (see **Figure 9.3**).

In the United States, the banking, finance, brokerage, and insurance industries were legally separated by the Glass-Steagall Act of 1934, which prohibited banks, insurance firms, and brokerages from having significant financial interests in one another in order to prevent a repetition of the calamitous financial institution failures that followed the stock market crash of 1929 and the ensuing Depression. The Glass-Steagall Act also prevented large banks from owning banks in other states. This legal separation meant that financial institutions in the United States could not provide customers with integrated financial services, and could not operate nationwide. One result was the proliferation of small, inefficient, local banks in the United States, arguably the most "over-banked" country in the world. West European and Japanese financial institutions did not face similar restrictions, putting the American industry at a disadvantage. The Financial Reform Act of 1998 amended Glass-Steagall and permitted banks, brokerages, and insurance firms to merge and to develop nationwide banks. This new law touched off an avalanche of financial service sector consolidations.

The financial meltdown of 2008–2009 demonstrated the risks of permitting financial institution consolidation. The rapid growth of risk-transfer instruments (credit default swaps), and collateralized debt obligations, which began in the late 1990s, greatly expanded the pools of capital available for investment, allowing banks to greatly expand their leverage, and to make loans to subprime customers. The merger of commercial banks with insurance and investment banking meant that they now shared risks: if investment banks failed, so would commercial banks, and the insurance companies that guaranteed all these new instruments. When the U.S. housing and credit markets collapsed in 2007 and 2008, so did the foundation of banking and investment institutions worldwide. Suddenly, what looked like solid assets were worth very little, sometimes nothing. One result is that large money center banks are buying up failed regional and local commercial banks, as well as investment banks and brokerage firms. Consolidation in the banking and investment sphere continues on an accelerated schedule.

A second related trend is the movement toward integrated financial services. Once banks, brokerages, and insurance companies are permitted to own one another, it becomes possible to provide consumers with what countless surveys have documented they really want: trust, service, and convenience. The movement toward financial service integration began in the 1980s when Merrill Lynch developed the first "cash management account" that integrated the brokerage and cash management services provided to Merrill Lynch's customers into a single account. Spare cash in each customer account was invested at the close of business each day into a money market fund. In the 1990s, Citibank and other large money center banks developed the concept of a financial supermarket, where consumers can find any financial product or service at a single physical center or branch bank. Nearly all large national banks now provide some form of financial planning and investment service. As a result of the financial meltdown in 2008, Bank of America took over a failed Merrill Lynch (brokerage and investment banking). Citibank continues its former integrated business model of banking, investment banking, insurance, and brokerage.

The Internet has created the technical foundations for an online financial supermarket to operate, but, for the most part, it has still not arrived. It is not yet possible to arrange for a car loan, obtain a mortgage, receive investment planning advice, and establish a pension fund at any single financial institution with one account. Nevertheless, this is the direction in which large banking institutions are attempting to move.

The promise of the Internet in the long term is to take the financial supermarket model one step further by providing a truly personalized, customized, and integrated offering to consumers based on a complete understanding of the consumer and his or her financial behavior, life cycle status, and unique needs. It will take many years to develop the technical infrastructure, as well as change consumer behavior toward a much deeper relationship with online financial services institutions.

ONLINE FINANCIAL CONSUMER BEHAVIOR

Surveys show that consumers are attracted to financial sites because of their desire to save time and access information rather than save money, although saving money is an important goal among the most sophisticated online financial households. According to financial services technology provider Fiserv, around 79 million households

TABLE 9.6	TOP ONLINE BANKS: OCTOBER 2012
BANK (RANKED BY VISITORS)	PERCENTAGE OF TOTAL WEB BANK VISITS
Wells Fargo Online Banking	8.98%
Chase Online	7.85%
Bank of America Online Banking	2.58%
Capital One Online Banking	2.54%
PNC Online Banking	2.05%

SOURCES: Based on data from eMarketer, Inc., 2012c.

used online banking in 2011 compared to just 46.7 million in 2005. Over 53 million households paid bills directly at company Web sites, and over 40 million used online bill payment at a financial institution (Fiserv, 2012). Most online consumers use financial services sites for mundane financial management, such as checking balances of existing accounts, and paying bills, most of which were established offline. Once accustomed to performing mundane financial management activities, consumers move on to more sophisticated capabilities such as using personal financial management tools, making loan payments, and considering offers from online institutions. The number of people using mobile devices for financial service needs is also surging. According to FiServ, about 25% of online households had used a mobile banking service, primarily to check their account balance, pay bills, and transfer money (FiServ, 2012). comScore found that mobile banking app usage increased dramatically in 2011, rising by almost 75% from the previous year. Over 36 million accessed either banking, credit card, insurance, or brokerage information from a mobile deivce (comScore, 2012b).

ONLINE BANKING AND BROKERAGE

NetBank and Wingspan Bank pioneered online banking in the United States in 1996 and 1997, respectively. Traditional banks had developed earlier versions of telephone banking but did not use online services until 1998. Although late by a year or two, the established brand-name national banks have taken a substantial lead in market share as the percentage of their customers who bank online has grown rapidly. **Table 9.6** lists the top five online banks in 2012, ranked by the percentage of all Web visits to online banks. The top banks are all large, national banks. In 2011, Capital One acquired ING Direct, leaving VirtualBank as one of the last pure online banks.

Around 107 million U.S. consumers are expected to conduct some online banking activity in 2012, and this number is expected to grow 4%–5% a year, to around 116 million by 2014 (eMarketer, Inc., 2010; comScore, 2010a) (see **Figure 9.4**). Over 32 million in the U.S. access banking information from a mobile device (comScore, 2012b).

The history of online brokerage has been similar to that of online banking. Early innovators such as E*Trade have been displaced from their leadership positions in

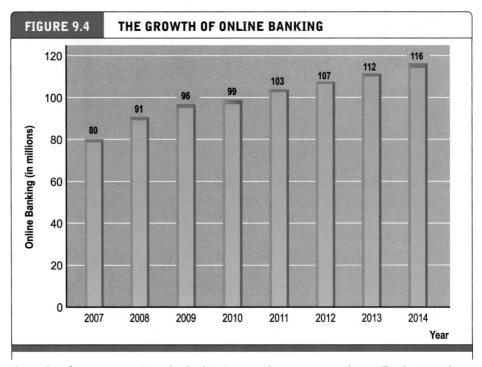

FIGURE 9.4	THE GROWTH OF ONLINE BANKING

The number of Internet users using online banking is expected to grow to around 116 million by 2014. About 60% of the U.S. Internet population visits at least one of the top 20 online banks. Increases in mobile banking may impact these numbers over the next three years.

SOURCES: Based on data from comScore, 2010a; eMarketer, 2010; authors' estimates.

terms of numbers of online accounts by discount broker pioneer Charles Schwab and financial industry giant Fidelity (which has more mutual fund customers and more funds under management than any other U.S. firm).

Today, according to Nielsen Net Ratings, 20 million U.S. investors trade online, a number expected to increase to approximately 29 million by 2013. According to comScore, almost 10 million use a mobile device to access brokerage or stock information (comScore, 2012b). The top trading Web site among U.S. Internet users in 2012 is Fidelity Investments, with around 6.5 million monthly unique visitors (see **Table 9.7)**. The major online brokerage firms are investing significantly in search engine marketing, and are among the biggest spenders in the paid search market. They are also increasingly using social media to engage with customers, although they must be careful to comply with all regulations and rules as they do so. For instance, some brokerage firms use Twitter to deliver commentary, company information, marketing, and customer service (eMarketer, Inc., 2011c).

Multi-Channel vs. Pure Online Financial Services Firms

Online consumers prefer to visit financial services sites that have physical outlets or branches. In general, multi-channel financial services firms that have both physical

TABLE 9.7	TOP ONLINE BROKERAGES, 2012
FIRM	NUMBER OF UNIQUE VISITORS (IN MILLIONS)
Fidelity.com	6.50
Charles Schwab	2.31
Vanguard	2.27
Scottrade	2.02
TD Ameritrade	1.50
Merrill Lynch	1.30
E*Trade	1.20
ShareBuilder	0.88
Troweprice.com	0.83

SOURCES: Based on data from Compete.com, 2012

branches or offices and solid online offerings are growing faster than pure-online firms that have no physical presence, and they are assuming market leadership as well. Traditional banking firms have literally thousands of branches where customers can open accounts, deposit money, take out loans, find home mortgages, and rent a safety deposit box. Top online brokerage firms do not have the same physical footprint as the banks do, but each has a strong physical presence or telephone presence to strengthen its online presence. Fidelity has urban walk-in service center branches, but it relies primarily on the telephone for interacting with investors. Charles Schwab has investment centers around the country as an integral part of its online strategy. Pure-online banks and brokerages cannot provide customers with some services that still require a face-to-face interaction.

Financial Portals and Account Aggregators

Financial portals are sites that provide consumers with comparison shopping services, independent financial advice, and financial planning. Independent portals do not themselves offer financial services, but act as steering mechanisms to online providers. They generate revenue from advertising, referral fees, and subscription fees. For example, Yahoo's financial portal, Yahoo Finance, offers consumers credit card purchase tracking, market overviews, real-time stock quotes, news, financial advice, streaming video interviews with financial leaders, and Yahoo Bill Pay, an EBPP system. Other independent financial portals include Intuit's Quicken.com, MSN's MSN Money, CNNMoney, and America Online's Money & Finance channel. A host of

financial portals
sites that provide consumers with comparison shopping services, independent financial advice, and financial planning

financial portal sites have sprung up to help consumers with financial management and planning such as Mint.com (owned by Quicken), SmartPiggy, and Credit Karma.

In general, the financial portals do not offer financial services (they make their money from advertising); instead, they add to the online price competition in the industry and run counter to the strategy of large banking institutions to ensnare consumers into a single branded, financial institutional system, with a single account and high switching costs.

account aggregation

the process of pulling together all of a customer's financial (and even nonfinancial) data at a single personalized Web site

Account aggregation is the process of pulling together all of a customer's financial (and even nonfinancial) data at a single personalized Web site, including brokerage, banking, insurance, loans, frequent flyer miles, personalized news, and much more. For example, a consumer can see his or her TD Ameritrade brokerage account, Fidelity 401(k) account, Travelers Insurance annuity account, and American Airlines frequent flyer miles all displayed on a single site. The idea is to provide consumers with a holistic view of their entire portfolio of assets, no matter what financial institution actually holds those assets.

The leading provider of account aggregation technology is Yodlee. It uses screen-scraping and other techniques to pull information from over 12,000 different data sources. A smart-mapping technology is also used so that if the underlying Web sites change, the scraping software can adapt and still find the relevant information. Today, Yodlee has more than 40 million personal financial management (PFM) users worldwide and is used by 600 leading financial institutions and companies (Yodlee, 2012).

ONLINE MORTGAGE AND LENDING SERVICES

During the early days of e-commerce, hundreds of firms launched pure-play online mortgage sites to capture the U.S. home mortgage market. Early entrants hoped to radically simplify and transform the traditional mortgage value chain process, dramatically speed up the loan closing process, and share the economies with consumers by offering lower rates.

By 2003, over half of these early-entry, pure-online firms had failed. Early pure-play online mortgage institutions had difficulties developing a brand name at an affordable price and failed to simplify the mortgage generation process. They ended up suffering from high start-up and administrative costs, high customer acquisition costs, rising interest rates, and poor execution of their strategies.

Despite this rocky start, the online mortgage market is slowly growing; it is dominated by established online banks and other online financial services firms, traditional mortgage vendors, and a few successful online mortgage firms.

More than half of all mortgage shoppers research mortgages online, but few actually apply online because of the complexity of mortgages. Most mortgages today are written by intermediary mortgage brokers, with banks still playing an important origination role but generally not servicing mortgages they originate.

Although online mortgage originations currently represent a small percentage of all mortgages, their number is expected to continue to grow slowly but surely over the next several years, although in 2012 the number of mortgages being originated in all forms continues to be negatively impacted by the subprime mortgage crisis.

There are three kinds of online mortgage vendors:

- Established banks, brokerages, and lending organizations such as Chase, Bank of America, Wells Fargo, Ameriquest Mortgage, and Citigroup.
- Pure online mortgage bankers/brokers such as E-Loan, Quicken Loans, and E*Trade. These companies aim to expedite the mortgage shopping and initiation process, but still require extensive paperwork to complete a mortgage.
- Mortgage brokers such as LendingTree.com. These companies offer visitors access to hundreds of mortgage vendors who bid for their business.

Consumer benefits from online mortgages include reduced application times, market interest rate intelligence, and process simplification that occurs when participants in the mortgage process (title, insurance, and lending companies) share a common information base. Mortgage lenders benefit from the cost reduction involved in online processing of applications, while charging rates marginally lower than traditional bricks-and-mortar institutions.

Nevertheless, the online mortgage industry has not transformed the process of obtaining a mortgage. A significant brake on market expansion is the complexity of the mortgage process, which requires physical signatures and documents, multiple institutions, and complex financing details—such as closing costs and points—that are difficult for shoppers to compare across vendors. Nevertheless, as in other areas, the ability of shoppers to find low mortgage rates on the Web has helped reduce the fees and interest rates charged by traditional mortgage lenders.

ONLINE INSURANCE SERVICES

In 1995, the price of a $500,000 20-year term life policy for a healthy 40-year-old male was $995 a year. In 2012, the same policy could be had for around $400—a decline of about 60%—while other prices have risen 15% in the same period. In a study of the term life insurance business, Brown and Goolsbee discovered that Internet usage led to an 8%–15% decline in term life insurance prices industry-wide (both offline and online), and increased consumer surplus by about $115 million per year (and hence reduced industry profits by the same amount) (Brown and Goolsbee, 2000). Price dispersion for term life policies initially increased, but then fell as more and more people began using the Internet to obtain insurance quotes.

Unlike books and CDs, where online price dispersion is higher than offline, and in many cases online prices are higher than offline, term life insurance stands out as one product group supporting the conventional wisdom that the Internet will lower search costs, increase price comparison, and lower prices to consumers. Term life insurance is a commodity product, however, and in other insurance product lines, the Web offers insurance companies new opportunities for product and service differentiation and price discrimination.

The insurance industry forms a major part of the financial services sector. It has four major segments: automobile, life, health, and property and casualty. Insurance products can be very complex. For example, there are many different types of non-automotive property and casualty insurance: liability, fire, homeowners, commercial, workers' compensation, marine, accident, and other lines such as vacation insurance. Writing an insurance policy in any of these areas is very information-intense, often necessitating personal inspection of the properties, and it requires considerable actuarial experience and data. The life insurance industry has also developed life insurance policies that defy easy comparison and can only be explained and sold by an experienced sales agent. Historically, the insurance industry has relied on thousands of local insurance offices and agents to sell complex products uniquely suited to the circumstances of the insured person and the property. Complicating the insurance marketplace is the fact that the insurance industry is not federally regulated, but rather is regulated by 50 different state insurance commissions that are strongly influenced by local insurance agents. Before a Web site can offer quotations on insurance, it must obtain a license to enter the insurance business in all the states where it provides quotation services or sells insurance.

Like the online mortgage industry, the online insurance industry has been very successful in attracting visitors who are looking to obtain prices and terms of insurance policies. While many national insurance underwriting companies initially did not offer competitive products directly on the Web because it might injure the business operations of their traditional local agents, the Web sites of almost all of the major firms now provide the ability to obtain an online quote. Even if consumers do not actually purchase insurance policies online, the Internet has proven to have a powerful influence on consumer insurance decisions by dramatically reducing search costs and changing the price discovery process. Some of the leading online insurance services companies are InsWeb, Insure.com, Insurance.com, QuickQuote, and NetQuote. For instance, a recent survey found that almost 60% of consumers surveyed would use the Internet to conduct research if they were to make a life insurance purchase, although they ultimately would buy from an insurance agent, and 20% said they would both research and buy life insurance online (LIMRA and Life Insurance Foundation for Education, 2011). Other forms of insurance are more likely to be purchased online. For instance, according to a 2012 comScore study, online auto insurance policy sales grew by 6% to 3.1 million online policy sales in 2011. The survey also found that the online channel continues to be consumers' preferred method for shopping for auto insurance policies, with nearly 70% of shoppers getting an online quote (comScore, 2012c).

ONLINE REAL ESTATE SERVICES

During the early days of e-commerce, real estate seemed ripe for an Internet revolution that would rationalize this historically local, complex, and local agent-driven industry that monopolized the flow of consumer information. Potentially, the Internet and e-commerce might have disintermediated this huge marketspace, allowing buyers and sellers, renters, and owners to transact directly, lower search costs to near zero, and dramatically reduce prices. However, this did not happen. What did happen is extremely beneficial to buyers and sellers, as well as to real estate agents. At one point, there were an estimated 100,000 real estate sites on the Internet worldwide. Many of these sites have disappeared. However, the remaining online sites have started to make headway toward transforming the industry. In addition, most local real estate brokers in the United States have their own agency Web sites to deal with clients, in addition to participating with thousands of other agencies in multiple listing services that list homes online. Some of the major online real estate sites are Realtor.com, HomeGain, RealEstate.com, ZipRealty, Move.com, Craigslist, Zillow, and Trulia.

Real estate differs from other types of online financial services because it is impossible to complete a property transaction online. Clearly, the major impact of Internet real estate sites is in influencing offline decisions. The Internet has become a compelling method for real estate professionals, homebuilders, property managers and owners, and ancillary service providers to communicate with and provide information to consumers. According to a survey conducted by the National Association of Realtors, 90% of buyers surf the Internet to search for a home. Although buyers also use other resources, most start the search process online and then contact an agent, with about 85% purchasing through an agent. Almost 40% of buyers said that they first learned of the home that they ultimately purchased via the Internet (National Association of Realtors, 2010).

The primary service offered by real estate sites is a listing of houses available. In 2012, Realtor.com, the official site of the National Association of Realtors, is one of the top Web sites in terms of market share of visits. Realtor.com listed over 4 million homes, and had over 9 million unique visitors in October 2012. The offerings have become sophisticated and integrated. Listings typically feature detailed property descriptions, multiple photographs, and virtual 360-degree tours. Consumers can link to mortgage lenders, credit reporting agencies, house inspectors, and surveyors. There are also online loan calculators, appraisal reports, sales price histories by neighborhood, school district data, crime reports, and social and historical information on neighborhoods. Some online real estate brokers now charge substantially less than traditional offline brokers who typically charge 6% of the sale price. They can do this because the buyers (and in some cases, the seller) do much of the work of traditional real estate agents, such as prospecting, choosing neighborhoods, and identifying houses of interest prior to contacting an online agent. For instance, Move.com (the parent company of Realtor.com) also offers a "Find a Neighborhood" feature that allows users to choose the type of neighborhood they want to live in by weighing factors such as the quality (and tax costs) of schools, age of the population, number of families with children nearby, and available social and recreational services. Move.com also offers mobile apps for the iPad and iPhone, Android, and Windows phones. For instance, the Area Scout function allows users to see the list prices of all homes in a neighborhood on the street level.

Despite the revolution in available information, there has not been a revolution in the industry value chain. The listings available on Web sites are provided by local multiple listing services supported by local real estate agents. Sometimes, addresses of the houses are not available, and online users are directed to the local listing agent who is hired by the seller of house. Traditional hands-on real estate brokers will show the house and handle all transactions with the owner to preserve their fees, typically ranging from 5% to 6% of the transaction.

9.6 ONLINE TRAVEL SERVICES

Online travel is one of the most successful B2C e-commerce segments. The Internet is becoming the most common channel used by consumers to research travel options, seek the best possible prices, and book reservations for airline tickets, hotel rooms, rental cars, cruises, and tours. Today, more travel is booked online than offline. Online travel services revenues are expected to reach almost $120 billion in 2012, and continue growing to over $150 billion in 2016 (see **Figure 9.5**) (eMarketer, Inc., 2012d).

WHY ARE ONLINE TRAVEL SERVICES SO POPULAR?

Online travel sites offer consumers a one-stop, convenient, leisure and business travel experience where travelers can find content (descriptions of vacations and facilities), community (chat groups and bulletin boards), commerce (purchase of all travel elements), and customer service (usually through call centers). Online sites offer much more information and many more travel options than traditional travel agents. For suppliers—the owners of hotels, rental cars, and airlines—the online sites aggregate millions of consumers into singular, focused customer pools that can be efficiently reached through on-site advertising and promotions. Online sites create a much more efficient marketplace, bringing consumers and suppliers together in a low-transaction cost environment.

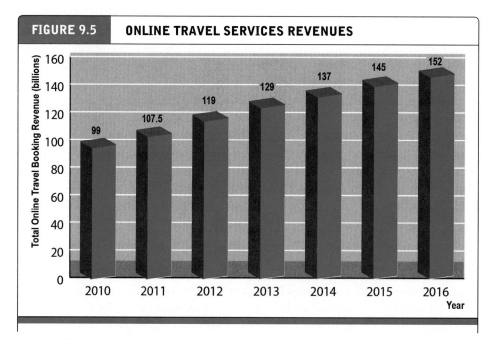

FIGURE 9.5 ONLINE TRAVEL SERVICES REVENUES

U.S. online leisure/unmanaged business travel service revenues has resumed growing and is expected to reach over $150 billion by 2016.

SOURCE: Based on data from eMarketer, Inc., 2012d.

Travel services appear to be an ideal service for the Internet, and therefore e-commerce business models should work well for this product. Travel is an information-intensive product requiring significant consumer research. It is an electronic product in the sense that travel requirements—planning, researching, comparison shopping, reserving, and payment—can be accomplished for the most part online in a digital environment. On the travel reservation side, travel does not require any "inventory": there are no physical assets. And the suppliers of the product—owners of hotels, airlines, rental cars, vacation rooms, and tour guides—are highly fragmented and often have excess capacity. Always looking for customers to fill vacant rooms and rent idle cars, suppliers will be anxious to lower prices and willing to advertise on Web sites that can attract millions of consumers. The online agencies—such as Travelocity, Expedia, and others—do not have to deploy thousands of travel agents in physical offices across the country but can instead concentrate on a single interface with a national consumer audience. Travel services may not require the kind of expensive multi-channel "physical presence" strategy required of financial services (although they generally operate centralized call centers to provide personal customer service). Therefore, travel services might "scale" better, permitting earnings to grow faster than costs. But these efficiencies also make it hard for reservation sites to make a profit.

THE ONLINE TRAVEL MARKET

There are four major sectors in the travel market: airline tickets, hotel reservations, car rentals, and cruises/tours. Airline tickets are the source of the greatest amount of revenue in online travel. Airline reservations are largely a commodity. They can be easily described over the Web. According to a 2011 survey, 57% of respondents purchased airline tickets on the airline's Web site, while 22% used a travel booking Web site such as Expedia or Orbitz. Only 5% reported using a traditional travel agent (MarketTools, 2011). The same is true with car rentals; most people can reliably rent a car over the phone or the Web and expect to obtain what they ordered (see *Insight on Business: Zipcar Shifts into High Gear* for a different kind of car rental business model). Although hotels are somewhat more difficult to describe, hotel branding, supplemented by Web sites that include descriptions, photographs, and virtual tours, typically provide enough information to most consumers to allow them to feel as if they know what they are purchasing, making them more comfortable making hotel reservations online.

Increasingly, corporations are outsourcing their travel offices entirely to vendors who can provide Web-based solutions, high-quality service, and lower costs. Online vendors to corporations provide **corporate online booking solutions (COBS)** that provide integrated airline, hotel, conference center, and auto rental services at a single site.

corporate online-booking solutions (COBS)
provide integrated airline, hotel, conference center, and auto rental services at a single site

ONLINE TRAVEL INDUSTRY DYNAMICS

Because much of what travel agency sites offer is a commodity, and thus they face the same costs, competition among online providers is intense. Price competition is difficult because shoppers, as well as online site managers, can comparison shop easily. Therefore, competition among sites tends to focus on scope of offerings, ease

INSIGHT ON BUSINESS

ZIPCAR SHIFTS INTO HIGH GEAR

How would you like to have all the functionality of a car but not have to deal with any of the headaches typically associated with ownership of a car or even the hassles involved with renting a car from a traditional car rental agency? This might sound like an impossible dream, but it's not. In the late 1990s, a new business model for renting cars was imported from Europe by a group of environmentally conscious entrepreneurs that leverages the power of the Web. Today, Zipcar, along with a number of other smaller companies, are using this model on their way towards sustained growth.

Zipcar began in 1999 with a single limegreen Volkswagen Bug in Cambridge, Massachusetts, and slowly grew within the city. Members could pick up cars at any one of several parking spots around Cambridge, use them for as long as they wanted, and then return them to the same parking spot. Today, the combined company has over 11,000 cars and 700,000 members. The company operates in 15 major metropolitan areas in the United States, more than 250 college campuses, and in London, Toronto and Vancouver.

Zipcar brings the Web 2.0 culture of sharing online videos and tweets to the car transportation market. An online application costs $25 and takes minutes to complete, and 94% of applicants are accepted. Zipcars are parked mostly in small clusters—between 2 and 20—in neighborhood garages, shoulder to shoulder with the owned and leased cars of the unenlightened. In Manhattan, a mix of Honda Civics, Toyotas, Volkswagens, Volvos, and Mini Coopers are available. Zipcar's predicate is that sharing is big business—bigger, potentially, than anyone can fathom. Its claim is

that the winners in the new economy will be those who crack the puzzle posed by scarce resources. In other words, in certain circles, using a Zipcar is cooler than owning a BMW!

In order to make the business work, Zipcar uses a lot of technology and tries to reduce the human-customer contact as much as possible to keep expenses low. Here's how it works. Customers pay an annual subscription fee and are issued a Zipcard, a card subscribers use to lock and unlock Zipcars that they've reserved. Customers go online or call an automated central number to reserve a car. Rates start at $7 per hour and vary depending on the vehicle, or a flat rate for a full day. Once a customer rents a car, a central computer activates the car's key card entry system to permit that customer to enter the car and start the engine. Customers return cars to the same locations and their credit cards are billed. Using wireless technology, the Internet, and automated voice recognition software at each city's central office, Zipcar is able to keep costs very low.

Zipcar is supported by universities as well as city governments looking for ways to discourage car ownership, and encourage car sharing, to reduce pollution and congestion. Zipcar has exclusive arrangements with a number of major universities. In these deals, the universities promise the car will make a certain revenue level per year (usually about $100,000) and make up the difference if they do not hit that revenue target. In San Francisco, when the Bay Bridge closed for repairs in 2009, over 350 Zipcars were located near BART rapid transit terminals in the Bay Area so residents could take trains to stations, and hop into Zipcars to drive to their final destinations. In an emergency, Zipcars can act as a reserve mini-mass transportation system.

(continued)

In 2012, Zipcar launched its Zipvan service, which allows Zipcar members in major cities to use vans to transport items that are too large for cars or pickup trucks. After a successful launch of the program in San Francisco, Zipvan service has been added in a host of major U.S. cities. Zipcar plans to introduce Zipvan service to the rest of the metropolitan markets in which it operates over the course of 2013.

Zipcar's customers are not Middle America, the people who own 200 million cars. Instead, most of Zipcar's customers are young urban professionals or college students, a market shunned by traditional car rental companies who typically will not rent to drivers under 21. The attraction for college students is that they save money compared to owning cars that sit idle while they are in classes. In urban areas, Zipcar users report they are saving over $500 a month on car operational and parking costs alone. Consider that in Manhattan, where studio apartments rent for $2,500 a month, garage parking for your personal four-wheeler will run another $300.

Car sharing is also green: national studies show that each shared car replaces up to 20 privately owned vehicles. Some corporations in major cities are thinking about eliminating their urban fleets and using car-sharing services.

However, it's unclear that Zipcar can expand beyond large cities and universities. The idea might not work as well in the suburbs, because customers would have to drive a car to pick up a Zipcar rental. On the other hand, Zipcar executives see a fleet of about 1 million cars in the future just in urban areas. This fleet would replace 20 million privately owned vehicles, one-tenth of the U.S. private fleet. Who needs the burbs? Traditional car rental companies have begun to respond to Zipcar by opening small neighborhood rental shops that make it much more convenient to rent cars. In 2009, Hertz started its own car-sharing service, Connect by Hertz, in New York, London, and Paris, with a fleet of Mini Coopers in each city. Hertz charges a flat hourly fee and its rates are lower than Zipcar's. In the New York area, Hertz has over 40,000 vehicles, many of which could ultimately be put into the program. Although Hertz has been sidetracked by its 2012 acquisition of top competitor Dollar Thrifty for $2.6 billion, the company still represents Zipcar's biggest competitor moving forward. But these firms are not as Web-enabled as Zipcar, and currently still lack the technology infrastructure to compete effectively. Zipcar, for instance, spent over $500,000 on a fleet reservation system that connects users, its Web site, and the cars themselves.

So far, Zipcar is not worrying about the competition. In April 2011, Zipcar went public and raised almost $175 million to fuel its expansion. Although analysts have predicted that the car-sharing industry could grow into a multi-billion dollar industry by 2016, in 2012, Zipcar stock has lost some ground. Valued at $1.2 billion at its opening price, Zipcar's market capitalization is now estimated at around $300 million. Although Zipcar's revenue and membership have continued to grow, they haven't kept pace with the company's aggressive spending in a down economic climate. Still, Zipcar is the undisputed leader in a growing market, and as with many companies that grow very quickly, the bottom-line numbers are likely to improve when the company reaches sufficient size.

■ **SOURCES:** "Zipcar Now Offers Campus Car Sharing With More Than 300 North American Colleges and Universities," Zipcar Inc., October 9, 2012; "Why Zipcar Is Worth $18," by Trefis Team, *Forbes*, June 15, 2012; "Is Zipcar as Bad as the Chart Suggests?" Seekingalpha.com, August 28, 2012; "Zipcar Expands 'Zipvan' Cargo Van Service to Boston and Washington D.C.," Zipcar.com, May 27, 2012; "Ford and Zipcar Join Forces," by Bill Vlasic, *New York Times*, August 31, 2011; Zipcar Quarterly Report on Form 10-Q for the period ended June 30, 2011, Sec.gov, August 5, 2011; "Zipcar Soars in Market Debut," by Evelyn M. Rusli, *New York Times*, April 14, 2011; "Car Sharing: Ownership by the Hour," by Ken Belson, *New York Times*, September 10, 2010.

of use, payment options, and personalization. Some well-known travel sites are listed in **Table 9.8**.

The online travel services industry has gone through a period of consolidation with stronger offline, established firms such as Sabre Holdings (which now owns Travelocity, Lastminute, and Site59, among others) purchasing weaker and relatively inexpensive online travel agencies in order to build stronger multi-channel travel sites. Orbitz and Expedia have also been involved in the industry consolidation. Orbitz was initially an industry consortium, then went public, then was purchased by Cendant (along with other travel firms such as CheapTickets and Trip.com), then sold by Cendant to Blackstone Group, and finally went public again in 2007. Expedia, originally begun by Microsoft, was purchased by Barry Diller's conglomerate IAC/InterActiveCorp, but has now been spun off as an independent company once again, picking up IAC's Hotels.com, Hotwire, TripAdvisor, and TravelNow in the process.

In addition to industry consolidation, the online travel industry has been roiled by meta-search engines that scour the Web for the best prices on travel and lodging, and then collect finder or affiliate fees for sending consumers to the lowest-price sites. For instance, TripAdvisor has created a one-stop Web site where consumers can find

TABLE 9.8	MAJOR ONLINE TRAVEL SITES
NAME	DESCRIPTION
LEISURE/UNMANAGED BUSINESS TRAVEL	
Expedia	Largest online travel service; leisure focus.
Travelocity	Second-largest online travel service; leisure focus. Owned by Sabre Holdings.
TripAdvisor	Travel shopping bot that searches for the lowest fares across all other sites.
Orbitz	Began as supplier-owned reservation system; now part of Orbitz Worldwide, a public company.
Priceline	Name Your Price model; leisure focus.
CheapTickets	Discount airline tickets, hotel reservations, and auto rentals. Part of Orbitz Worldwide.
Hotels.com	Largest hotel reservation network; leisure and corporate focus. Owned by Expedia.
Hotwire	Seeks out discount fares based on airline excess inventory. Owned by Expedia.
MANAGED BUSINESS TRAVEL	
GetThere.com	Corporate online booking solution (COBS). Owned by Sabre Holdings.
Travelocity Business	Full-service corporate travel agency.

the lowest price airfares and hotels by searching over 100 other Web travel sites and presenting the fares in rank order. Similar "travel aggregator" sites are Kayak, Fly.com, and Mobissimo. These sites, in the eyes of many industry leaders, commoditize the online travel industry even further, cause excessive price competition, and divert revenues from the leading, branded firms who have made extensive investments in inventory and systems.

Mobile devices and apps used for pre-trip planning, booking, check-in, and context and location-based destination information are also transforming the online travel industry (see also the case study on Orbitz' mobile strategy in Chapter 4). For instance, in 2012, over 36 million are expected to use a mobile device to research travel, and that number is estimated to double, to over 72 million by 2016 (eMarketer, 2012e). During the past year, most of the major airlines have launched apps for a variety of mobile platforms to enable flight research, booking, and management. Apps from hotels and car rental companies are still somewhat less prevalent, but available from most of the major players such as Hertz and Avis for car rentals, and Best Western, Choice Hotels, Hilton, and Starwood for hotels. Apps may sometimes target specific consumer behavior. For instance, the Wyndham Hotel group discovered that about 70% of its mobile bookings come on the same day, in many cases within a few miles of the hotel (eMarketer, Inc., 2012e).

Social media is also having a big impact on the online travel industry. User-generated content and online reviews are having an increasing influence on travel-buying decisions. The *Insight on Society* story, *Phony Reviews,* examines some of the issues this presents for the industry.

9.7 ONLINE CAREER SERVICES

Next to travel services, one of the Internet's most successful online services has been job services (recruitment sites) that provide a free posting of individual resumes, plus many other related career services; for a fee, they also list job openings posted by companies. Career services sites collect revenue from other sources as well, by providing value-added services to users and collecting fees from related service providers.

The online job market is dominated by two large players: CareerBuilder (which provides job listings for AOL and MSN), with about 15 million unique monthly visitors in October 2012, and Monster, with about 18 million. (Yahoo HotJobs, which had been the third large player, was acquired by Monster for $225 million in 2010.) Other popular sites include Indeed (24 million unique visitors), SimplyHired (5.5 million), and SnagAJob (5.8 million). These top sites generate more than $1 billion annually in revenue from employers' fees and consumer fees. Rising unemployment during late 2008 to 2010 has led to an increasing number of Americans seeking jobs and career opportunities online, with career services and development Web sites among the top 10 fastest growing site categories (comScore, 2010b, 2011). The professional social network site LinkedIn is also becoming an increasingly important player in this market (see the opening case in Chapter 11). In 2011, it added a plug-in, Apply with LinkedIn, that allows job seekers to easily submit their LinkedIn profile to an employer's Web site.

INSIGHT ON SOCIETY

PHONY REVIEWS

People used to rely on travel agents for professional recommendations about travel destinations and hotels. Today, however, that function has been largely usurped by sites like TripAdvisor, which aggregates consumer reviews. TripAdvisor has been a smashing success, with more than 75 million user-generated reviews, and is often one of the first places consumers go as they try to decide where to travel and what hotels to book. A good rating can be worth thousands of dollars in bookings. But are all those reviews for real? Can they be trusted?

In the United Kingdom, TripAdvisor is under investigation by the U.K Advertising Standards Authority as a result of complaints that TripAdvisor's review problem has reached "epidemic levels." According to online reputation management KwikChex, as many as 10 million of the most current reviews on TripAdvisor could be fake. KwikChex alleges that hotels are paying people to create false identities and post favorable reviews on their properties, and also to slam competing venues. A *Times of London* investigation had previously found that hotel owners were paying thousands of dollars to companies that employ teams of writers to post hundreds of fake reviews. On various forums and classified sites, such as Craigslist, Fiverr, and Digital Point, ads can easily be found promising payment for positive feedback on various review sites. Some establishments offer guests future discounts for "honest but positive" reviews. In 2012, TripAdvisor was told by the ASA to remove wording on its site claiming that its reviews were "trusted and honest."

Another problem is the disgruntled consumer with an axe to grind. For instance, Dancing Deer Mountain, a small wedding venue in Junction City, Oregon, had steady business until one wedding went horribly wrong. The proprietors said that rules about bringing in outside alcohol were broken; the situation with the wedding-goers purportedly became combative as a result. Afterwards, five scathing online reviews were posted, including one that claimed "The owner is absolutely crazy and needs professional help," with another exclaiming "DO NOT USE THIS VENUE." As a result, business dropped off precipitously. The owners tried suing the reviewers but lost under Oregon's anti-SLAPP (Strategic Lawsuit Against Public Participation) legislation, which protects individual free speech, particularly speech that qualifies as an opinion. About half the states in the United States have an anti-SLAPP law, which many believe is vital to consumer free speech.

For sites like Yelp, which are primarily focused on business ratings and reviews, the growth in phony reviews presents a considerable challenge. The authenticity and accuracy of reviews are critically important to Yelp's success, but garnering a high review score is equally important to the restaurants and other businesses listed on the site. If site visitors have no reason to trust Yelp's reviews, there isn't much incentive for those visitors to return in the future. With this in mind, Yelp has begun to remove suspect reviews from its site, including those from a Californian marketing and business networking group. Members of the group were giving five-star reviews to all of the other members of the group to inflate their ratings. Yelp caught on and removed those reviews from its site. Yelp is also developing its own algorithms which are intended to detect phony reviews. Phony

(continued)

reviews are getting to be an expensive proposition for Yelp because they have to hire staff to read and evaluate the reviews.

TripAdvisor also claims it uses an algorithm to help filter out false reviews, although it rejects requiring would-be reviewers to supply a reservation number in order to prove that they have actually stayed at the property that they are reviewing. According to TripAdvisor, it takes the authenticity of its reviews very seriously, and has numerous methods to ensure their legitimacy, including automated site tools and a team of review integrity experts. It also relies on the review community itself to identify suspicious content and trolls the sites where businesses advertise for fake reviewers.

There may soon be another tool in TripAdvisor's toolbox. Researchers at Cornell University have developed an algorithm that they say can identify language features specific to fake and truthful reviews. To train the algorithm, they created a database of 20 truthful and 20 fake reviews for 20 hotels, for a total of 800 reviews. According to the researchers, the algorithm accurately identified fake reviews 90% of the time. The truthful reviews tended to talk about the specific details, using specific nouns and adjectives as descriptors. Since those who wrote the fake reviews were not necessarily familiar with the physical location they were reviewing, the fake reviewers, not surprisingly, tended to talk more about themselves, reasons for the trip, and traveling companions. The algorithm has attracted the attention of a number of companies, including TripAdvisor, Hilton, and several specialist travel sites.

Are the days of phony reviews over as a result? Probably not. So best to take what you read with a grain of salt, discarding both the overwhelmingly positive and the unrelentingly negative reviews.

SOURCES: "Yelp Reviews: Can You Trust Them? Some Firms Game the System," by Jessica Guynn and Andrea Chang, *Los Angeles Times,* July 4, 2012; "TripAdvisor Told to Stop Claiming Reviews are 'Trusted and Honest,'" *Daily Mail,* February 1, 2012; "A Lie Detector Test for Online Reviewers," by Karen Weise, *BusinessWeek,* September 29, 2011; "Cornell Researchers Work to Spot Fake Reviews," by Emma Court, *The Cornell Daily Sun,* September 23, 2011; "TripAdvisor Called into Question Over 'Fake' Reviews," by Melanie Naylor, Boston.com, September 7, 2011; "Investigation Launched into TripAdvisor Following Claims up to 10 Million Reviews are Fake," News.com.au, September 5, 2011; "TripAdvisor's Fake Reviews Sickness Goes Critical," by Phillip Butler, Argophilia.com, September 2, 2011; "TripAdvisor's Fake Battle," by Gulliver, *The Economist,* August 22, 2011; "The Yelp Wars: False Reviews, Anti-SLAPP, and Slander – What's Ethical in Online Reviewing?", by Kathleen Miles, Scpr.org, August 25, 2011; "In a Race to Out-Rave, 5-Star Web Reviews Go for $5," by David Streitfeld, *New York Times,* August 19, 2011.

Traditionally, companies have relied on five employee recruitment tools: classified and print advertising, career expos (or trade shows), on-campus recruiting, private employment agencies (now called "staffing firms"), and internal referral programs. In comparison to online recruiting, these tools have severe limitations. Print advertising usually includes a per-word charge that limits the amount of detail employers provide about a job opening, as well as a limited time period within which the job is posted. Career expos do not allow for pre-screening of attendees and are limited by the amount of time a recruiter can spend with each candidate. Staffing firms charge high fees and have a limited, usually local, selection of job hunters. On-campus recruiting also restricts the number of candidates a recruiter can speak with during a normal visit and requires that employers visit numerous campuses. And internal referral programs may encourage employees to propose unqualified candidates for openings in order to qualify for rewards or incentives offered.

Online recruiting overcomes these limitations, providing a more efficient and cost-effective means of linking employers and potential employees, while reducing the total time to hire. Online recruiting enables job hunters to more easily build, update, and distribute their resumes while gathering information about prospective employers and conducting job searches.

IT'S JUST INFORMATION: THE IDEAL WEB BUSINESS?

Online recruitment is ideally suited for the Web. The hiring process is an information-intense business process that involves discovering the skills and salary requirements of individuals and matching them with available jobs. In order to accomplish this match up, there does not initially need to be face-to-face interaction, or a great deal of personalization. Prior to the Internet, this information sharing was accomplished locally by human networks of friends, acquaintances, former employers, and relatives, in addition to employment agencies that developed paper files on job hunters. The Internet can clearly automate this flow of information, reducing search time and costs for all parties.

Table 9.9 lists some of the most popular recruitment sites.

Why are so many job hunters and employers using Internet job sites? Recruitment sites are popular largely because they save time and money for both job hunters and employers seeking recruits. For employers, the job boards expand the geographical reach of their searches, lower costs, and result in faster hiring decisions.

For job seekers, online sites are popular not only because their resumes can be made widely available to recruiters but also because of a variety of other related job-hunting services. The services delivered by online recruitment sites have greatly expanded since their emergence in 1996. Originally, online recruitment sites just provided a digital version of newspaper classified ads. Today's sites offer many other services, including skills assessment, personality assessment questionnaires, personalized account management for job hunters, organizational culture assessments, job search tools, employer blocking (prevents your employer from seeing your posting), employee blocking (prevents your employees from seeing your listings if you are their employer), and e-mail notification. Online sites also provide a number of educational services such as resume writing advice, software skills preparation, and interview tips.

For the most part, online recruitment sites work, in the sense of linking job hunters with jobs, but they are just one of many ways people actually find jobs. A survey by The Conference Board found that the majority (70%) of job seekers rely equally on both the Internet and newspapers to look for jobs, with about half relying on word-of-mouth leads, and about a quarter on employment agencies. Given that the cost of posting a resume online is zero, the marginal returns are very high.

The ease with which resumes can be posted online has also raised new issues for both job recruiters and job seekers. If you are an employer, how do you sort through the thousands of resumes you may receive when posting an open job? If you are a job seeker, how do you stand out among the thousands or even millions of others? Perhaps

TABLE 9.9	POPULAR ONLINE RECRUITMENT SITES
RECRUITMENT SITE	**BRIEF DESCRIPTION**
GENERAL RECRUITMENT SITES	
CareerBuilder	Owned by Gannett, Tribune, McClatchy (all newspaper companies), and Microsoft. Provides job search centers for more than 9,000 Web sites, including AOL and MSN, and 140 newspapers; 1.6 million jobs listed.
Monster	One of the first commercial sites on the Web in 1994. Today, a public company offering general job searches in 50 countries.
Yahoo HotJobs	General job searches. Partners with consortium of newspapers, including Hearst, Cox, MediaNews General, Scripps, and others for cross-listing of job postings. Purchased by Monster in 2010 for $225 million.
Indeed.com	Job site aggregator
SimplyHired	Job site aggregator
Craigslist	Popular classified listing service focused on local recruiting
EXECUTIVE SEARCH SITES	
Futurestep	Korn/Ferry site, low-end executive recruiting
Spencerstuart.com	Middle-level executive recruiting
ExecuNet	Executive search firm
NICHE JOB SITES	
SnagAJob	Part-time and hourly jobs
USAJobs	Federal government jobs
HigherEdJobs	Education industry
EngineerJobs	Engineering jobs
Medzilla	Medical industry
Showbizjobs	Entertainment industry
Salesjobs	Sales and marketing
Dice	Information technology jobs
MBAGlobalNet	MBA-oriented community site

one way is to post a video resume. In a survey by Vault, nearly nine in 10 employers said they would watch a video resume if it were submitted to them, in part because it would help them better assess a candidate's professional presentation and demeanor, and over half said they believed video would become a common addition to future job applications. CareerBuilder became the first major online job site to implement a video resume tool for job candidates, following a previous launch for an online video brand-building tool for employers.

Perhaps the most important function of online recruitment sites is not so much their capacity to actually match employees with job hunters but their ability to establish market prices and terms, as well as trends in the labor market. Online recruitment sites identify salary levels for both employers and job hunters, and categorize the skill sets required to achieve those salary levels. In this sense, online recruitment sites are online national marketplaces that establish the terms of trade in the labor markets. For instance, Monster.com offers its U.S. Monster Employment Index. This index is based on a large, representative selection of corporate career sites and job boards, and calculates employment demand for the nation, regions, and specific occupations. The existence of these online national job sites should lead to a rationalization of wages, greater labor mobility, and higher efficiency in recruitment and operations because employers will be able to quickly find the people they need.

ONLINE RECRUITMENT INDUSTRY TRENDS

Trends for 2012–2013 in the online recruitment services industry include the following:

- **Consolidation:** The two major job services are CareerBuilder (owned by newspapers and Microsoft) and Monster (which now owns Yahoo HotJobs). In 2012, these two sites continue to dominate the market, and are expected to do so for some time to come.
- **Diversification:** While the national online market is becoming larger and consolidating into a few general sites, there is an explosion in specialty niche employment sites that focus on specific occupations. This is creating greater online job market diversity and choice.
- **Localization:** While local classified ads in newspapers remain a significant source of jobs, the large national online sites are also developing local boards in large metropolitan areas that compete more directly against local newspapers. The local newspapers themselves have responded by building Web sites that focus on local job markets, especially hourly and contract jobs that often do not appear on the large national job boards. Craigslist is another source of local job listings. Hence there is a growing focus on local job markets by all participants in the marketplace because this is where so many new jobs first appear.
- **Job search engines/aggregators:** As with travel services, search engines that focus specifically on jobs are posing a new threat to established online career sites. For instance, Indeed, SimplyHired, and Us.jobs "scrape" listings from thousands of online job sites such as Monster, CareerBuilder, specialty recruiting services, and

the sites of individual employers to provide a free, searchable index of thousands of job listings in one spot. Because these firms do not charge employers a listing fee, they are currently using a pay-per-click or other advertising revenue model.

- **Social networking:** LinkedIn, probably the most well-known business-oriented social network, has grown significantly to over 175 million members representing over 170 different industries in over 200 countries as of October 2012. LinkedIn's corporate hiring solutions are used by 85 of the Fortune 100 companies, and more than 2 million companies have a LinkedIn page. Consumers are using sites such as LinkedIn to establish business contacts and networks. For instance, according to LinkedIn, its members will do an estimated 5.3 billion professionally-oriented searches on LinkedIn in 2012. Employers are also using LinkedIn to conduct searches to find potential job candidates that may not be actively job hunting. For instance, LinkedIn offers companies a feature called LinkedIn Talent Advantage that includes tools that help corporate recruiters find "passive talent" (people who are not actively looking for a new job), as well as custom company profiles that are specifically designed for recruitment. CareerBuilder offers a job and internship matching application on Facebook that allows users to receive continuously updated listings based on the information found in their profiles. Social network sites are also being used by employers to "check up" on the background of job candidates. A study by Harris Interactive of 2,667 managers and human resource employees found that 45% are using social networks to screen job candidates, and 35% have rejected candidates because of content on a social site. Employers typically search Facebook, Twitter, and LinkedIn. Provocative photos were the biggest negative factor followed by drinking and drug references. Another 2011 survey found that 91% of employers surveyed used social network sites to screen applicants. Almost 70% reported rejecting a candidate because of what they saw.

- **Mobile:** As with other forms of services, career services firms have also moved onto the mobile platform. A 2011 study found that around 20% of job seekers who are 18 to 34 years old reported that they searched for jobs and researched companies using mobile devices. To reach this audience, CareerBuilder has a mobile Web site, as well as iPhone and Android apps that allow job seekers to create and upload resumes, search jobs by keyword, location, and company, e-mail jobs, browse and apply, and more. Monster offers similar functionality. CareerBuilder also has a mobile app for employers that allows them to sync directly to their existing CareerBuilder accounts and gain access to job applicants.

CASE STUDY

OpenTable:
Your Reservation Is Waiting

OpenTable is the leading supplier of reservation, table management, and guest management software for restaurants. In addition, the company operates OpenTable.com, the world's most popular Web site for making restaurant reservations online. In 13 years, OpenTable has gone from a start-up to a successful and growing public company that counts around two-thirds of the nation's reservation-taking restaurants as clients.

Today, more than 25,000 restaurants in the United States, Canada, Mexico, the United Kingdom, Germany, and Japan use the OpenTable hardware and software system. OpenTable also owns and operates Toptable.com, a leading restaurant site in the United Kingdom, which it acquired in 2010. This system automates the reservation-taking and table management process, while allowing restaurants to build diner databases for improved guest recognition and targeted e-mail marketing. The OpenTable Web site, OpenTable for Mobile Web (its mobile Web site), and OpenTable Mobile (its mobile app), provide a fast, efficient way for diners to find available tables in real time. The Web sites and app connect directly to the thousands of computerized reservation

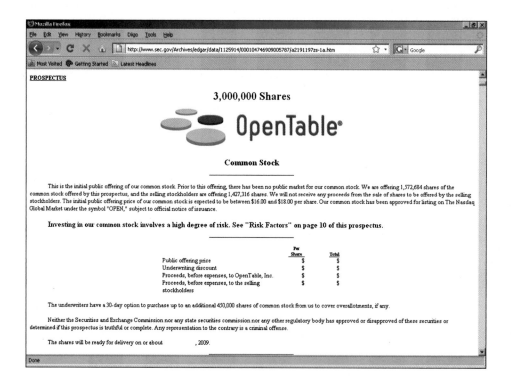

systems at OpenTable restaurants, and reservations are immediately recorded in a restaurant's electronic reservation book.

Restaurants subscribe to the OpenTable Electronic Reservation Book (ERB), the company's proprietary software, which is installed on a touch-screen computer system and supported by asset-protection and security tools. The ERB software provides a real-time map of the restaurant floor and enables the restaurant to retain meal patterns of all parties, serving as a customer relationship management (CRM) system for restaurants. The software is upgraded periodically, and the latest version, introduced in August 2010, was designed to provide increased ease of use and a more thorough view of table availability to help turn more tables, enhance guest service, personalize responses to diners, coordinate the seating process, and maximize guest seating. The ERBs at OpenTable's customer restaurants connect via the Internet to form an online network of restaurant reservation books. For restaurants that rely less heavily on reservations, OpenTable offers Connect, a web-based service that lets restaurants accept online reservations.

OpenTable's revenue comes from two sources. Restaurants pay a one-time fee for on-site installation and training, a monthly subscription fee of $199 for software and hardware, and a $1 transaction fee for each restaurant guest seated through online reservations. The online reservation service is free to diners. The business model encourages diners to assist in viral marketing. When an individual makes a reservation, the site "suggests" that they send e-vites to their dinner companions directly from OpenTable.com. The e-vites include a link back to the OpenTable site.

OpenTable is a service-based (software as service, or SaaS) e-commerce company. In other words, customers don't buy software and install it on their computers, but instead go online and get the software functionality through subscriptions. OpenTable is also an online service that does not sell goods, but instead enables diners to make reservations, like social networking sites provide services.

The restaurant industry was slow to leverage the power of the Internet. This was in part because the industry was, and continues to be, highly fragmented and local—made up of more than 30,000 small, independent businesses or local restaurant-owning groups.

The founders of OpenTable knew that dealing with these restaurants as a single market would be difficult. They also realized that the Internet was changing things for diners by providing them with instant access to reviews, menus, and other information about dining options. And there was no method for making reservations online—we all know reserving by phone is time-consuming, inefficient, and prone to errors. In order to make the system work, reach and scale were very important. For diners to use an online reservation system, they would need real-time access to a number of local restaurants, and the ability to instantly book confirmed reservations around the clock. If customers were planning a trip to another city, OpenTable would need participating restaurants in those cities.

The company was originally incorporated in San Francisco in 1998 as Easyeats.com. In 1999, its name was changed to OpenTable.com, Inc. When the company was founded, most restaurants did not have computers, let alone systems that would allow online reservations made through a central Web site. OpenTable's initial strategy of paying online restaurant reviewers for links to its Web site and targeting national chains for fast expansions got the company into 50 cities, but it was spending $1 million a month and bringing in only $100,000 in revenue. Not exactly a formula for success. The original investors still felt there was a viable business to be built, and they made a number of management changes, including installing investor and board member Thomas Layton, founder of CitySearch.com, as OpenTable's CEO. Layton cut staff, shut down marketing efforts, and got the company out of all but four cities: Chicago, New York, San Francisco, and Washington, D.C.

The company retooled its hardware and software to create the user-friendly ERB system, and deployed a door-to-door sales force to solicit subscriptions from high-end restaurants. The combination of e-commerce, user-friendly technology, and the personal touch worked. The four markets OpenTable targeted initially developed into active, local networks of restaurants and diners that continue to grow. OpenTable has implemented the same strategy across the country, and now includes approximately 25,000 OpenTable restaurant customers. In 13 years, the company has seated approximately 350 million diners, and it is currently averaging 10 million diners seated per month.

As the company grew, investors began making plans for it to go public. Layton stepped down from his position as CEO in 2007, though he remains a board member. He was replaced by Jeffrey Jordan, former president of PayPal. Jordan had some experience with public companies from working with eBay on its acquisition of PayPal. In 2009, he chose an aggressive strategy—going ahead with an initial public offering (IPO) despite a terrible economy and worse financial markets. So far, the gamble has paid off. On its first day of trading, OpenTable's shares climbed 59%. The share price at the end of September 2012 was in the mid-$40 range, more than double the $20 IPO price.

Despite the challenging economy, OpenTable's numbers at the time of the IPO were strong, and since then, it has continued to grow. In 2011, the company's total revenues were $139.5 million, up 41% over 2010's figure of $99 million. OpenTable has shown no signs of slowing down in 2012. Revenues for the second quarter of 2012 increased by 15% to $39.6 million, and the company's earnings per share have continued to grow.

The company has benefited from having e-commerce revenue streams from subscription fees and per-transaction charges, instead of from advertising. Further, more than 50% of OpenTable's revenue comes from B2B subscriptions, which are typically part of long-term contracts. Restaurants that have invested in OpenTable's software package are less likely to want to incur the switching costs associated with changing to a different reservation management package.

Another reason for its success is that OpenTable has a large number of satisfied customers. Restaurant owners report that they and their staff members find the software easy to use, and it helps them manage their business better. Specifically, it streamlines operations, helps fill additional seats, and improves quality of service, providing a concrete return on investment. This has led to both high customer satisfaction and high retention rates.

OpenTable has also taken advantage of the interconnected needs of restaurants and diners. Restaurants want cost-effective ways to attract guests and manage their reservations, while diners want convenient ways to find available restaurants, choose among them, and make reservations. By creating an online network of restaurants and diners that transact with each other through real-time reservations, OpenTable has figured out how to successfully address the needs of both.

OpenTable's market is susceptible to network effects: the more people use it, the more utility the system delivers. OpenTable's growth continually provides diners with expanded choices. More diners discover the benefits of using the online reservation system, which in turn delivers value to restaurant customers, and helps attract more restaurants to the network. Diners serve as a source of viral marketing, as the OpenTable Web site encourages them to e-vite their dinner companions to the meal. When they do so, the e-mail provides links back to the OpenTable Web site. And the OpenTable link appears on the restaurant's Web site, linking directly to the reservation page. OpenTable has been able to improve its efficiency even as diners are staying home more often.

While OpenTable is the biggest, most successful online player in the restaurant reservations market, it does have competitors. MenuPages.com offers access to restaurant menus and reviews, but visitors to the site can't make reservations, and the site covers only eight U.S. cities. Urbanspoon.com offers a reservation service, but its technology is not compatible with OpenTable, so those reservations must be entered manually into the OpenTable system. Like OpenTable, Urbanspoon charges $1 for each diner. Looming on the horizon is Google, which purchased online restaurant guide Zagat in September 2011, raising the specter that it might try to compete with OpenTable, although Zagat does not yet possess that functionality.

While some may argue that there are better ways to make reservations that don't take visitors away from restaurant's Web sites (once someone clicks on the OpenTable link, they navigate away), restaurant owners like the OpenTable software, and diners have an enormous range of dining choices. Those two factors make this argument a relatively weak one.

The company is committed to innovation when it makes sense. For example, it has both a mobile Web site and mobile applications that work on just about every smartphone platform. These applications help users find restaurants with the use of GPS and make reservations. OpenTable also launched Facebook Connect, allowing users to share their reservations on Facebook, as well as a Facebook application called Reservations, which allows partner restaurants to offer reservations directly on Facebook.

Along with innovation, OpenTable continues to use its tried-and-true business model that combines technology with old-fashioned door-to-door sales. Using this model, OpenTable's North American markets have grown over time, and this growth is projected to continue. OpenTable plans a selective international expansion into countries where there are large numbers of online consumer transactions and reservation-taking restaurants. The company currently has operations in Germany, Japan, and the United Kingdom, each supported with a direct sales force, and has signed on approximately 1,000 restaurant customers in these markets.

The company's international strategy is to replicate the successful U.S. model by focusing initially on building a restaurant customer base. OpenTable believes the

SOURCES: "OpenTable Shares Drop After Analyst Cuts Rating," Businessweek.com, September 17, 2012; "OpenTable Hits 15 million Restaurant Reviews," by Anita Li, Mashable.com, September 6, 2012; "OpenTable, Inc. Form 10-Q, filed with the SEC, August 6, 2012; "OpenTable Inc. Announces Fourth Quarter and Full Year 2011 Financial Results," Opentable.com, February 7, 2012; "Google Buys Zagat to View the OpenTable, Yelp," by Alexei Oreskovic, Reuters, September 8, 2011; Form 10-Q for the quarterly period ended June 30, 2011, Sec.gov, August 4, 2011; Form 10-K for the year ended December 31, 2010, Sec.gov, March 9, 2011; "Behind Open-Table's Success," Kevin Kelleher, CNNMoney.com, September 23, 2010; "OpenTable Introduces the Next Generation of Its Electronic Reservation Book Software," RestaurantNews.com, August 17, 2010; "OpenTable: the Hottest Spot in Town," by Maha Atal, CNNMoney.con, August 14, 2009;

"OpenTable Unveils Version 2.0 of its iPhone App," AppScout.com, August 14, 2009; "Gadgetell: Fight for Your Dinner: Urbanspoon vs. Open Table," NewsFactor.com, August 8, 2009; "Urbanspoon is Now Taking Online Reservations: Takes on OpenTable," by Frederic Lardinois, ReadWriteWeb.com, August 7, 2009; "Yelp vs. OpenTable—Where Should Restaurants Spend Their Marketing Dollars," Dinner Rush Blog, reservationdc. wordpress.com, July 19, 2009; May 22, 2009; "What Media Companies Could Learn from OpenTable," The Media Wonk, May 20, 2009; Open Table S-1/A Amendment #6, filed with the Securities and Exchange Commission, May 19, 2009.

localized versions of its software will compare favorably against competitive software offerings, enabling them to expand across a broad selection of local restaurants.

The company is well-positioned for future growth. Its size, track record of growth, and high customer satisfaction rates should continue to work in its favor.

Case Study Questions

1. Why will OpenTable competitors have a difficult time competing against Open-Table?

2. What characteristics of the restaurant market make it difficult for a reservation system to work?

3. How did OpenTable change its marketing strategy to succeed?

4. Why would restaurants find the SaaS model very attractive?

9.9 REVIEW

KEY CONCEPTS

■ **Understand the environment in which the online retail sector operates today.**

Personal consumption of retail goods and services comprise about 71% and account for about $11.1 trillion of total GDP. The retail sector can be broken down into three main categories:
- Services, which account for 66% of total retail sales
- Durable goods, which account for 11% of total retail sales
- Nondurable goods, which account for 23% of total retail sales

Although the distinction between a good and a service is not always clear, and "product-based services" are becoming the norm, we use the term retail goods to refer to physical products and retailers to refer to firms that sell physical goods to consumers. The retail industry can be further divided into seven major firm types:
- General merchandise
- Durable goods
- Specialty stores
- Food and beverage
- Gasoline and fuel
- MOTO
- Online retail firms

Each type offers opportunities for online retail. The biggest opportunities for direct online sales are within those segments that sell small-ticket items (less than $100). This includes specialty stores, general merchandisers, mail-order catalogers, and grocery stores. The MOTO sector is the most similar to the online retail sales sector, and MOTO retailers are among the fastest growing online retail firms.

During the early days of e-commerce, some predicted that the retail industry would be revolutionized, based on the following beliefs:

- Greatly reduced search costs on the Internet would encourage consumers to abandon traditional marketplaces in order to find the lowest prices for goods. First movers who provided low-cost goods and high-quality service would succeed.
- Market entry costs would be much lower than those for physical storefront merchants, and online merchants would be more efficient at marketing and order fulfillment than their offline competitors because they had command of the technology (technology prices were falling sharply).
- Online companies would replace traditional stores as physical store merchants were forced out of business. Older traditional firms that were too slow to enter the online market would be locked out of the marketplace.
- In certain industries, the "middleman" would be eliminated (disintermediation) as manufacturers or their distributors entered the market and built a direct relationship with the consumer. This cost savings would ensure the emergence of the Web as the dominant marketing channel.
- In other industries, online retailers would gain the advantage over traditional merchants by outsourcing functions such as warehousing and order fulfillment, resulting in a kind of hypermediation, in which the online retailer gained the upper hand by eliminating inventory purchasing and storage costs.

Today, it has become clear that few of the initial assumptions about the future of online retail were correct. Also, the structure of the retail marketplace in the United States has not been revolutionized. The reality is that:

- Online consumers are not primarily cost-driven—instead, they are as brand-driven and influenced by perceived value as their offline counterparts.
- Online market entry costs were underestimated, as was the cost of acquiring new customers.
- Older traditional firms, such as the general merchandising giants and the established catalog-based retailers, are taking over as the top online retail sites.
- Disintermediation did not occur. On the contrary, online retailing has become an example of the powerful role that intermediaries play in retail trade.

■ **Explain how to analyze the economic viability of an online firm.**

The economic viability, or ability of a firm to survive during a specified time period, can be analyzed by examining the key industry strategic factors, the strategic factors that pertain specifically to the firm, and the financial statements for the firm. The key industry strategic factors include:

- *Barriers to entry*, which are expenses that will make it difficult for new entrants to join the industry.
- *Power of suppliers*, which refers to the ability of firms in the industry to bargain effectively for lower prices from suppliers.
- *Power of customers*, which refers to the ability of the customers for a particular product to shop among the firm's competitors, thus keeping prices down.
- *Existence of substitute products*, which refers to the present or future availability of products with a similar function.
- The *industry value chain*, which must be evaluated to determine if the chain of production and distribution for the industry is changing in ways that will benefit or harm the firm.

- *The nature of intra-industry competition*, which must be evaluated to determine if the competition within the industry is based on differentiated products and services, price, the scope of the offerings, or the focus of the offerings and whether any imminent changes in the nature of the competition will benefit or harm the firm.

The key firm strategic factors include:

- The *firm value chain*, which must be evaluated to determine if the firm has adopted business systems that will enable it to operate at peak efficiency and whether there are any looming technological changes that might force the firm to change its processes or methods.
- *Core competencies*, which refer to unique skills that a firm has that cannot be easily duplicated. When analyzing the economic viability of a firm, it is important to consider whether technological changes might invalidate these competencies.
- *Synergies*, which refer to the availability to the firm of the competencies and assets of related firms that it owns or with which it has formed strategic partnerships.
- The firm's current *technology*, which must be evaluated to determine if it has proprietary technologies that will allow it to scale with demand and if it has developed the customer relationship, fulfillment, supply chain management, and human resources systems that it will need in order to be viable.
- The *social and legal challenges facing the firm*, which should be examined to determine if the firm has taken into account consumer trust issues such as the privacy and security of personal information and if the firm may be vulnerable to legal challenges.

The key financial factors include:

- *Revenues*, which must be examined to determine if they are growing and at what rate.
- *Cost of sales*, which is the cost of the products sold, including all related costs. The lower the cost of sales compared to revenue, the higher the gross profit.
- *Gross margin*, which is calculated by dividing gross profit by net sales revenue. If the gross margin is improving consistently, the economic outlook for the firm is enhanced.
- *Operating expenses*, which should be evaluated to determine if the firm's needs in the near interim will necessitate increased outlays. Large increases in operating expenses may result in net losses for the firm.
- *Operating margin*, which is calculated by dividing operating income or loss by net sales revenue, and is an indication of a company's ability to turn sales into pre-tax profit after operating expenses are deducted.
- *Net margin,* which is calculated by dividing net income or net loss by net sales revenue. It evaluates the net profit or loss for each dollar of net sales. For example, a net margin of -24% indicates that a firm is losing 24 cents on each dollar of net sales revenue.
- The firm's *balance sheet,* which is a financial snapshot of a company on a given date that displays its financial assets and liabilities. If current assets are less than or not much more than current liabilities, the firm will likely have trouble meeting its short-term obligations.

■ Identify the challenges faced by the different types of online retailers.

There are four major types of online retail business models, and each faces its own particular challenges:

- *Virtual merchants* are single-channel Web firms that generate all of their revenues from online sales. Their challenges include building a business and a brand name quickly, many competitors in the virtual marketplace, substantial costs to build and maintain a Web site, considerable marketing expenses, large customer acquisition costs, a steep learning curve, and the need to quickly achieve operating efficiencies in order to preserve a profit. Amazon is the most well-known example of a virtual merchant.

- *Multi-channel merchants* (bricks-and-clicks) have a network of physical stores as their primary retail channel, but have also begun online operations. Their challenges include high cost of physical buildings, high cost of large sales staffs, the need to coordinate prices across channels, the need to develop methods of handling cross-channel returns from multiple locations, building a credible Web site, hiring new skilled staff, and building rapid-response order entry and fulfillment systems. JCPenney.com is an example of a bricks-and-clicks company.

- *Catalog merchants* are established companies that have a national offline catalog operation as their largest retail channel, but who have recently developed online capabilities. Their challenges include high costs for printing and mailing, the need to leverage their existing assets and competencies to the new technology environment, the need to develop methods of handling cross-channel returns, building a credible Web site, and hiring new skilled staff. Lands' End is an example of a catalog merchant.

- *Manufacturer-direct merchants* are either single- or multi-channel manufacturers who sell to consumers directly online without the intervention of retailers. They were predicted to play a very large role in e-commerce, but this has not generally happened. Their challenges include channel conflict, which occurs when physical retailers of a manufacturer's products must compete on price and currency of inventory with the manufacturer who does not face the cost of maintaining inventory, physical stores, and a sales staff; quickly developing a rapid-response online order and fulfillment system; switching from a supply-push (products are made prior to orders being received based on estimated demand) to a demand-pull model (products are not built until an order is received); and creating sales, service, and support operations online. Dell.com is an example of a manufacturer-direct merchant.

■ Describe the major features of the online service sector.

The service sector is the largest and most rapidly expanding part of the economy of advanced industrial nations. Service industries are companies that provide services (i.e., perform tasks) for consumers, businesses, governments, and other organizations. The major service industry groups are financial services, insurance, real estate, business services, and health services. Within these service industry groups, companies can be further categorized into those that involve transaction brokering and those that involve providing a "hands-on" service. With some exceptions, the service sector is by and large a knowledge- and information-intense industry. For this reason, many services are uniquely suited to e-commerce and the strengths of the Internet.

The rapid expansion of e-commerce services in the areas of finance, including insurance and real estate, travel, and job placement can be explained by the ability of these firms to:

- Collect, store, and disseminate high value information
- Provide reliable, fast communication
- Personalize and customize service or components of service

E-commerce offers extraordinary opportunities to improve transaction efficiencies and thus productivity in a sector where productivity has so far not been markedly affected by the explosion in information technology.

■ **Discuss the trends taking place in the online financial services industry.**

The online financial services sector is a good example of an e-commerce success story, but the success is somewhat different than what had been predicted in the early days of e-commerce. Today, the multi-channel established financial firms are growing the most rapidly and have the best prospects for long-term viability. Other significant trends include the following:

- Management of financial assets online is growing rapidly.
- In the insurance and real estate industries, consumers still generally utilize the Internet just for research and use a conventional transaction broker to complete the purchase.
- Historically, separate institutions have provided the four generic types of services provided by financial institutions. Today, as a result of the Financial Reform Act of 1998, which permitted banks, brokerage firms, and insurance companies to merge, this is no longer true. This has resulted in two important and related global trends in the financial services industry that have direct consequences for online financial services firms: the move toward industry consolidation and the provision of integrated financial services.

Key features of the online banking and brokerage industries include the following:

- Multi-channel firms that have both physical branches and solid online offerings have assumed market leadership over the pure-online firms that cannot provide customers with many services that still require hands-on interaction.
- Customer acquisition costs are significantly higher for Internet-only banks and brokerages that must invest heavily in marketing versus their established brand-name bricks-and-mortar competitors, which can simply convert existing branch customers to online customers at a much lower cost.
- Financial portals provide comparison shopping services and steer consumers to online providers for independent financial advice and financial planning.
- Account aggregation is another rapidly growing online financial service, which pulls together all of a customer's financial data on a single personalized Web site.
- During the early days of e-commerce, a radically altered online mortgage and lending services market was envisioned in which the mortgage value chain would be simplified and the loan closing process speeded up, with the resulting cost savings passed on to consumers. Affordably building a brand name, the resulting high customer acquisition costs, and instituting these value chain changes proved to be too difficult. Today, the established banks and lenders are reaping the benefits of a relatively small but growing market.

- There are three basic types of online mortgage lenders, including established banks, brokerages, and lending organizations; pure-online bankers/brokers; and mortgage brokers.

Key features of the online insurance industry include the following:

- Term life insurance stands out as one product group supporting the early visions of lower search costs, increased price transparency, and the resulting consumer savings. However, in other insurance product lines, the Web offers insurance companies new opportunities for product and service differentiation and price discrimination.
- The insurance industry has several other distinguishing characteristics that make it difficult for it to be completely transferred to the new online channel, such as policies that defy easy comparison and that can only be explained by an experienced sales agent, a traditional reliance on local insurance offices and agents to sell complex products uniquely suited to the circumstances of the insured person and/or property, and a marketplace that is coordinated by state insurance commissions in each state with differing regulations. Although search costs have been dramatically reduced and price comparison shopping is done in an entirely new way, the industry value chain has so far not been significantly impacted.

Key features of the online real estate services industry include the following:

- The early vision that the historically local, complex, and agent-driven real estate industry would be transformed into a disintermediated marketplace where buyers and sellers could transact directly has not been realized. What has happened has been beneficial to buyers, sellers, and real estate agents alike.
- Since it is not possible to complete a property transaction online, the major impact of the online real estate industry is in influencing offline purchases.
- The primary service is a listing of available houses, with secondary links to mortgage lenders, credit reporting agencies, neighborhood information, loan calculators, appraisal reports, sales price histories by neighborhood, school district data, and crime reports.
- The industry value chain, however, has remained unchanged. Home addresses are not available online and users are directed back to the local listing agent for further information about the house.
- Buyers benefit because they can quickly and easily access a wealth of valuable information; sellers benefit because they receive free online advertising for their property; and real estate agents have reported that Internet-informed customers ask to see fewer properties.

- ◼ Discuss the major trends in the online travel services industry today.

Online travel services attract the largest single e-commerce audience and the largest slice of B2C revenues. The Internet has become the most common channel used by consumers to research travel options. It is also the most common way for people to search for the best possible prices and book reservations for airline tickets, rental cars, hotel rooms, cruises, and tours. Some of the reasons why online travel services have been so successful include the following:

- Online travel sites offer consumers a one-stop, convenient, leisure and business travel experience where travelers can find content, community, commerce, and customer service. Online sites offer more information and travel options than traditional travel agents, with such services as descriptions of vacations and facilities, chat groups and bulletin boards, and the convenience of purchasing all travel elements at one stop. They also bring consumers and suppliers together in a low transaction cost environment.

- Travel is an information-intensive product as well as an electronic product in the sense that travel requirements can be accomplished for the most part online. Since travel does not require any inventory, suppliers (which are highly fragmented) are always looking for customers to fill excess capacity. Also, travel services do not require an expensive multi-channel physical presence. For these reasons, travel services appear to be particularly well suited for the online marketplace.

- It is important to note that various segments of the travel industry fit this description better than others—for instance, airline reservations, auto rentals, and to a lesser extent, hotels. Cruises and tours are more differentiated with varying quality and a more complex level of information required for the decision-making process.

- Corporations are increasingly outsourcing their travel offices entirely to vendors who can provide Web-based solutions, high-quality service, and lower costs.

The major trends in online travel services include the following:

- The online travel services industry is going through a period of consolidation as stronger offline, established firms purchase weaker and relatively inexpensive online travel agencies in order to build stronger multi-channel travel sites that combine physical presence, television sales outlets, and online sites.

- Suppliers—such as airlines, hotels, and auto rental firms—are attempting to eliminate intermediaries and develop a direct relationship with consumers. At the same time, successful online travel agencies are attempting to turn themselves into merchants by purchasing large blocks of travel inventory and then reselling it to the public, eliminating the global distributors and earning much higher returns.

■ **Identify current trends in the online career services industry.**

Next to travel services, job-hunting services have been one of the Internet's most successful online services because they save money for both job hunters and employers. In comparison to online recruiting, traditional recruitment tools have severe limitations:

- Online recruiting provides a more efficient and cost-effective means of linking employers and job hunters and reduces the total time to hire.

- Job hunters can easily build, update, and distribute their resumes, conduct job searches, and gather information on employers at their convenience and leisure.

- It is an information-intense business process that the Internet can automate, and thus reduce search time and costs for all parties.

Online recruiting can also serve to establish market prices and terms, thereby identifying both the salary levels for specific jobs and the skill sets required to achieve those salary levels. This should lead to a rationalization of wages, greater labor mobility, and higher efficiency in recruitment and operations as employers are able to more quickly fill positions.

The major trends in the online career services industry are:

- *Consolidation*—The online recruitment industry is going through a period of rapid consolidation led by Monster.
- *Diversification*—There is an explosion of specialty niche employment sites that focus on specific occupations.
- *Localization*—There is a growing focus on local job markets.
- *Job search engines*—New online job search engines that scrape listings from thousands of online job sites pose a threat to established career sites.
- *Social networking*—Many Internet users are beginning to use social networking sites to establish business contacts and find jobs; employers are also using them to identify and find out further information about job candidates.
- *Mobile*—As with other forms of services, career services firms have also moved onto the mobile platform.

QUESTIONS

1. Why were so many entrepreneurs drawn to start businesses in the online retail sector initially?
2. What frequently makes the difference between profitable and unprofitable online businesses today?
3. Which segment of the offline retail business is most like online retailing? Why?
4. Name the largest segment of U.S. retail sales. Explain why businesses in this segment have achieved and continue to dominate online retailing.
5. Describe the technological retail revolution that preceded the growth of e-commerce. What were some of the innovations that made later online retailing possible?
6. Name two assumptions e-commerce analysts made early on about consumers and their buying behavior that turned out to be false.
7. Why were customer acquisition costs assumed early on to be lower on the Web? What was supposed to reduce those costs?
8. Explain the distinction between disintermediation and hypermediation as it relates to online retailing.
9. How would you describe the top 10 online retailers as a group? Do they account for a small or a large percentage of online business, for example?
10. Compare and contrast virtual merchants and bricks-and-clicks firms. What other type of online retailer is most like the virtual merchant?
11. What is the difference between a supply-push and a demand-pull sales model? Why do most manufacturer-direct firms have difficulty switching to one of these?
12. What are five strategic issues specifically related to a firm's capabilities? How are they different from industry-related strategic issues?
13. Which is a better measure of a firm's financial health: revenues, gross margin, or net margin? Why?
14. What are some of the difficulties in providing services in an online environment? What factors differentiate the services sector from the retail sector, for example?
15. Compare and contrast the two major types of online services industries. What two major features differentiate services from other industries?

16. Name and describe the types of online mortgage vendors. What are the major advantages of using an online mortgage site? What factors are slowing the growth of such service businesses?

17. What is the biggest deterrent to growth of the online insurance industry nationally?

18. Define channel conflict and explain how it currently applies to the mortgage and insurance industries. Name two online insurance companies or brokers.

19. What is the most common use of real estate Web sites? What do most consumers do when they go there?

20. Name and describe the four types of services provided by financial services firms on the Web.

21. Who are the major players in the financial industry consolidation currently occurring worldwide?

22. Explain the two global trends impacting the structure of the financial services industry and their impact on online operations.

23. How have travel services suppliers benefited from consumer use of travel Web sites?

24. Name and describe five traditional recruitment tools companies have used to identify and attract employees. What are the disadvantages of such tools compared to online career sites?

25. In addition to matching job applicants with available positions, what larger function do online job sites fill? Explain how such sites can affect salaries and going rates.

PROJECTS

1. Find the Securities and Exchange Commission Web site at Sec.gov, and access the EDGAR archives, where you can review 10-K filings for all public companies. Search for the 10-K report for the most recent completed fiscal year for two online retail companies of your choice (preferably ones operating in the same industry, such as Staples Inc. and Office Depot Inc.). Prepare a presentation that compares the financial stability and prospects of the two businesses, focusing specifically on the performance of their respective Internet operations.

2. Examine the financial statements for Amazon and Best Buy Co., Inc. What observations can you make about the two businesses? Which one is stronger financially and why? Which one's business model appears to be weaker and why? If you could identify two major problem areas for each, what would they be? Prepare a presentation that makes your case.

3. Conduct a thorough analysis—strategic and financial—of one of the following companies or another of your own choosing: Bluefly Inc., Drugstore.com, Inc., or 1-800-Flowers.com, Inc. Prepare a presentation that summarizes your observations about the company's Internet operations and future prospects.

4. Find an example not mentioned in the text of each of the four types of online retailing business models. Prepare a short report describing each firm and why it is an example of the particular business model.

5. Drawing on material in the chapter and your own research, prepare a short paper describing your views on the major social and legal issues facing online retailers.

6. Conduct a thorough analysis—strategic and financial—of one of the following Web sites: Progressive.com, Insure.com, or Insweb.com. Prepare a presentation that summarizes your observations about the company's operations and future prospects.

7. Choose a services industry not discussed in the chapter (such as legal services, medical services, accounting services, or another of your choosing). Prepare a 3- to 5-page report discussing recent trends affecting online provision of these services.

8. Together with a teammate, investigate the use of mobile apps in the financial services industries. Prepare a short joint presentation on your findings.

9. Find at least two examples of companies not mentioned in the text that act as transaction brokers and at least two examples of companies that provide a hands-on service. Prepare a short memo describing the services each company offers and explaining why the company should be categorized as a transaction broker or a hands-on service provider.

CHAPTER 10

Online Content and Media

After reading this chapter, you will be able to:

- Identify the major trends in the consumption of media and online content, and the major revenue models for digital content delivery.
- Understand digital rights management.
- Discuss the concept of media convergence and the challenges it faces.
- Understand the key factors affecting the online publishing industry.
- Understand the key factors affecting the online entertainment industry.

YouTube
and the Emerging Internet Broadcasting System (IBS)

In 2012, YouTube began implementing its $100 million initiative to create 100 YouTube channels devoted to a wide variety of topics, from sports to music, food, and news. The new channel experiment was so successful in its first eight months that Google doubled down and put another $150 million into the experiment in July 2012. When completed, and assuming the audience appears, YouTube will be on its way to developing a new kind of television network, one based on the Internet. This new network will go head to head with cable and broadcast television giants competing for viewers, and of course, advertising dollars, which make it all happen.

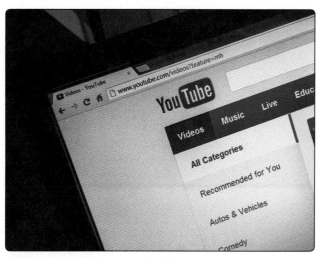

© Ingvar Björk / Alamy

When YouTube was launched in 2005, no one envisaged that within seven years it would grow into a possible alternative to the cable and broadcast television system. Starting out with 8 million videos streamed daily in 2005, YouTube today supports 4 billion video streams a day, in some cases rivaling the audience sizes of cable and broadcast television, still the most popular source of video in the United States. Despite this success in building a very large global audience of 800 million monthly unique visitors, YouTube has only recently shown a profit.

The most popular television shows in 2012 (*The Big Bang Theory* and *American Idol*) routinely draw six million viewers each, and they stay for the full show. Reruns and syndication over the lifetime of the show can easily triple these numbers. Thus far, the highest number of concurrent livestream viewers that YouTube has ever drawn is the 8 million that watched Felix Baumgartner's record-breaking skydive from 24 miles above the earth in October 2012. However, many YouTube videos have more than 500 million total views. For instance, as of October 2012, the three most popular YouTube videos in history are music videos of Justin Bieber's *Baby* (785 million views), Jennifer Lopez's *On the Floor* (604 million views), and Eminem's *Love the Way You Lie* (501 million views). In the first 24 hours, these singers can easily attract around 500,000 views. Unfortunately, no one knows how many views are generated by the same people, so the measures are not equivalent.

The average YouTube visitor stays for 14 minutes, hardly enough time to get a word in from advertisers whose ads appear next to the video, or are themselves videos pre-run before the real video you want to see. Television advertising in the United States generates $70 billion in revenues, dwarfing YouTube's expected $3.2 billion in revenue in 2012. In the last few years, rivals such as Hulu, Apple, and Amazon have developed new Internet audiences for high-quality video, both from television series to movie rentals.

And there's the problem: While YouTube's overall unique audience in the United States is about 146 million a month in 2012, it cannot easily be "monetized" if that audience only stays for a few minutes.

YouTube has figured out the solution to this problem: improve the quality and length of videos so visitors stay longer than a five-minute music video, or worse, a few seconds to watch a dancing cat. While YouTube built its huge audience using amateur videos of less than professional quality, it cannot grow advertising revenues without substantially increasing the quality, length, and popularity of its videos. If Web 2.0 meant user-generated content, Web 3.0 means professional content that can generate ad revenues.

There are three sources of high-quality entertainment videos in the United States: Hollywood studios, broadcast and cable television producers, and independent producers. While YouTube executives claim YouTube will never enter the media production business because it's too hard to get it right, YouTube is coming perilously close to being both a producer of video content and the world's largest Internet video distributor. In reality, it is becoming a third platform, right alongside cable television and broadcast television. YouTube is being joined by other Internet juggernauts Apple, Netflix, and Amazon, all of whom are reshaping the television and movie video industry. Together, these new Internet broadcasters threaten to disrupt the highly successful 50-year-old cable television industry, reshaping television and movies with their Internet Broadcasting System.

In 2011, Google initiated a number of new projects to improve the quality and advertising potential of its videos. Like its rivals who hold dominant positions in Internet distribution (Apple, Facebook, Netflix, and Microsoft), YouTube has reached out to Hollywood movie and New York television producers to offer streaming movies and television series. It has struck deals with Sony, Lionsgate, television networks, and MGM to rent full-length movies and television series. In April 2012, YouTube and MGM struck a deal to bring 600 new rental titles to YouTube. Google is late to the streaming movie business, compared to Netflix, with 20,000 titles, and Amazon, with 5,000 streaming titles tied to its Prime Advantage program of free shipping. All these Web broadcasters have to share ad revenues with the copyright owners of the content, reducing profitability. One possible solution to this profit-reducing situation is for Web broadcasters to create their own content designed specifically for the Web audience of 12- to 34-year-olds who are watching less TV on traditional television sets than 34+ viewers, and instead, watching their tablets and smartphones more.

In October 2011, YouTube announced the $100 million initiative to create 100 YouTube channels mentioned at the beginning of this case. By 2012, a very diverse group of about 50 channels has been created. The idea is for Google to provide seed funding of up to several million dollars for independent and even well-known sources to produce video content and develop their brands online. Control over content is entirely with the producers, and Google receives all the ad revenue until the seed money is repaid, and then splits the ad revenues thereafter. About 50 channels are now online, running the gamut from the IGN Entertainment game channel, MyIsh (a channel for discovering new music), celebrity channels (Madonna), a slew of sports channels (ESPN for kids), to the *Wall Street Journal*'s channel featuring *Off Duty*, a daily lifestyle show, and regular contributions from the *Journal*'s name-brand reporters. Yes, that's right: the *Wall Street Journal* newspaper is a major new online source of video, along with the *New York Times* and other papers. Foodies don't despair: Bruce Seidel, who produced shows for the Food Network, including the *Iron Chef*, is working with a YouTube media company, Electus, to produce a food channel that will drive the Internet food conversation. YouTube is providing $5 million in seed money to Electus. Electus, a production studio, is not an amateur outfit, formed by Ben Silverman, former co-chairman of NBC Entertainment, and owned by Barry Diller's IAC Inc., a firm with 30 years of television and Internet content development.

While YouTube's channels are aimed at niche audiences (just like the hundreds of cable channels), collectively they will play to an audience of 800 million people worldwide, who are viewing 4 billion hours of video each month. The YouTube content will not require a monthly subscription fee (outside of an Internet connection), and content will be paid for by advertising (as in existing television systems). Moreover, the user determines the schedule for on-demand viewing and the device on which to view the show. What's not to like?

To celebrate its early success with launching video channels, YouTube hosted 1,000 top advertisers, agencies, and content producers in May 2012 in New York in a coordinated effort called Digital Content Newfronts. YouTube joined Web broadcasters Yahoo, AOL, Microsoft, and Hulu in an effort to tap off a portion of the $70 billion TV ad budget. YouTube was pushing ad packages for up to $62 million to advertisers for multi-channel slots, with single channel ad packages selling for $2–$4 million. By August 2012, YouTube had secured commitments for $150 million in advertising.

Across town, the traditional cable and television advertising industry was holding its annual meeting called the Upfronts, where advertisers, agencies, and TV executives haggle over the next year's advertising packages. The cable and broadcast television audience for 12–34-year-olds has begun to shrink for the first time since basic cable television began in 1976 with Ted Turner's network. The implication for the traditional television industry is that advertising dollars will slip away to the new Internet Broadcasting System.

SOURCES: "Felix Baumgartner Jump: Record 8m Watch Live on YouTube," by John Plunkett, *The Guardian*, October 14, 2012; "YouTube to Double Down on Its 'Channel' Experiment," by Amir Efrati, *New York Times*, July 30, 2012; "CW Network's Rush to Web Rankles Some TV Stations," by Sam Schechner and Christopher Stewart, *Wall Street Journal*, April 19, 2012; "Youths Are Watching, but Less Often on TV," by Brian Stelter, *New York Times*, February 8, 2012; "Wall Street Journal Launches Video Channel For YouTube," *Wall Street Journal*, February 1, 2012; "New YouTube Channel is All About Games, Brands," by Tom Loftus, *Wall Street Journal*, January 30, 2012; "Hulu to Create More Original Shows," by Sam Schechner and Christopher Stewart, *Wall Street Journal*, January 17, 2012; "Food Network Executive to Run YouTube Channel," by Brian Stelter, *New York Times*, January 29, 2012; "New Rules for the Way We Watch," by David Carr, *New York Times*, December 24, 2011; "YouTube Announces Channels: Video Site Will Feel a Little More Like Cable TV," by D.M. Levine, *Adweek*, October 28, 2011; "New Layer of Content Amid Chaos on YouTube," by Ben Sisario, *New York Times*, March 12, 2011.

The opening case illustrates how online content distributors like YouTube are both moving into premium content production and sales, and also becoming Internet stores for traditional television and movie content, possibly rivaling existing cable and satellite distributors. If consumers can find their favorite television shows and movies online, then why should they pay for cable or satellite TV? If consumers can watch their favorite shows on a smartphone or tablet, why should they buy a TV? As Internet users increasingly change their reading and viewing habits, spurred on by the growth of mobile media devices, they are challenging existing business models that worked for decades to support newspapers, books, magazines, television, and Hollywood movies. Clearly, the future of content—news, music, and video—is online. Today, the print industry, including newspapers, books and magazines, is having a difficult time coping with the movement of their readership to the Web. Broadcast and cable television, along with Hollywood and the music labels, are also wrestling with outdated business models based on physical media. Established media giants are continuing to make extraordinary investments in unique online content, new technology, new digital distribution channels, and entirely new business models. Internet giants like Apple, Google, Amazon, and Facebook are competing to dominate online content distribution. In this chapter, we focus primarily on the publishing and entertainment industries as they attempt to transform their traditional media into Web-deliverable forms and experiences for consumers, while at the same time, earning profits.

10.1 ONLINE CONTENT

No other sector of the American economy has been so challenged by the Internet and the Web than the content industries. The online content industries are organized into two major categories: the print industries (newspapers, books, and magazines), and the online entertainment industries of television, feature-length movies, radio, video games, and music. Together, the online content industries generate revenues of about $15 billion in 2012 (including the online versions of print products).

As a communications medium, the Web is, by definition, a source of online content as well as a powerful new distribution platform. In this chapter, we will look closely at publishing (newspapers, books, and magazines) and entertainment (music, film, games, and television). These industries make up the largest share of the commercial content marketplace, both offline and online. In each of these industries, there are powerful offline brands, significant new pure-play online providers and distributors, consumer constraints and opportunities, a variety of legal issues, and new mobile technology platforms that offer an entirely new content distribution system in the form of smartphones and tablet computers.

Table 10.1 describes the most recent trends in online content for 2012–2013.

TABLE 10.1	WHAT'S NEW IN CONTENT 2012–2013

BUSINESS

- Vertical integration: Amazon, Google (YouTube), Hulu, and Netflix (owners of the distribution channel) enter the content production business for video, books, and online TV-like channels.

- Netflix transitions to a TV show distributor, along with Hulu, AOL, and Amazon, in order to capture television advertising dollars and find reliable high-quality content partners.

- YouTube launches over 100 entertainment channels offering TV-like amateur productions aimed at the twenty-something marketplace.

- Internet content begins to challenge cable TV for the home viewing audience.

- Physical media (DVDs and Blu-Ray) retain 88% of the home video market, but online delivered video grows to 12%.

- Music: digital music sales top physical sales.

- Radio: online radio attracts 100 million listeners each month. AM/FM radio revenues and audience remain stable.

- TV: almost 100 million Americans watch TV online (41% of the Internet audience). iTunes hosts 550 TV series and has sold more than 450,000 million TV shows.

- E-book sales rise to 50% of all book sales, while the overall book market expands.

- Movies: Americans spend more on online movies than for DVDs. In 2012, there are 3.4 billion online movie transactions compared to 2.4 billion DVD transactions.

- Magazines experience a small comeback via high-resolution tablet displays. Personalized magazine apps like Flipboard and Zinio gain acceptance. *Atlantic Magazine* (154 years old) reports digital ad revenues exceed physical ad revenues.

- Newspapers: online readership exceeds print readership. Print ad revenues fall from $47 billion in 2005 to $21 billion. Digital ad revenue increases 50% in this period, from $2 billion to $3.2 billion. Online ad revenues cannot make up for lost print ad revenues. Online newspaper audience grows at double digits as newspapers implement paywalls.

- Gaming market: console game sales stagnate as online social and casual gaming soars.

- The four Internet Titans compete: Apple, Google, Amazon, and Facebook vie for ownership of the online entertainment and content ecosystem, selling experiences as well as content.

- Business models: content owners adopt a mixture of business models: advertising-supported (free), subscriptions, and a la carte payment.

- Paid content and free content coexist: the common notion of the Internet means free information is being replaced by consumer acceptance of paying for premium content.

- Revenues from online media are the fastest growing media revenues, reducing revenues from physical products such as DVDs, CDs, newspapers, magazines, and printed books.

- Content gets social: social network sites become a major source of content recommendations and content distribution partners for content.

(continued)

TABLE 10.1	WHAT'S NEW IN CONTENT 2012–2013 (CONT.)

TECHNOLOGY

- "Smart" mobile platform users grow to 116 million smartphone users in the United States, 55 million tablet users, and 46 million e-reader users. Globally, the smartphone population reaches 1 billion units.

- The personal computer morphs into a mobile multimedia entertainment device. Tablet sales grow to 50% of PC sales.

- Netflix becomes the largest consumer of bandwidth, consuming upwards of 29% of downstream Internet traffic.

- With more than 1 billion now available, apps become the foundation for an "app economy" as they morph into content-distribution platforms that are proprietary, where users can be charged for content.

- Cloud storage services grow to serve the huge market for mobile device content. Apple launches iCloud video service that allows users to watch purchased videos on multiple Apple devices (iPhones, iPads, and Macs). Amazon and Google develop similar cloud services.

- Amazon's dedicated e-book reader (Kindle Fire) expands to tablet-like functionality, suitable for video and Web browsing.

SOCIETY

- Media consumption: Americans spend around 4,200 hours a year consuming various types of media, more than twice as many hours as they work.

- Internet time exposure continues to grow rapidly, surpassing newspapers and music, but is still behind traditional television.

- Content consumption goes mobile: in 2012, 25% of mobile phone users listen to music on mobile phones, 30% watch videos, and 42% play games.

- Revenue from streamed movies exceeds revenue from DVDs.

- Young adults watch more TV on the Internet, less on cable.

- Television, radio, print, games, and video converge on the tablet screen, and the divisions between these forms of content becomes blurred.

- Multi-device experiences: around 70% of smartphone and tablet owners use their devices while watching TV.

- The Justice Department sues the five major book publishers over e-book price fixing, allowing Amazon to continue selling e-books below cost.

CONTENT AUDIENCE AND MARKET: WHERE ARE THE EYEBALLS AND THE MONEY?

The average American adult spends around 4,200 hours each year consuming various media, twice the amount of time spent at work (2,000 hours/year) (see **Figure 10.1**). U.S. entertainment and media (E & M) revenues (both online and offline) in 2012 are estimated to be $488 billion, and they are expected to grow at a compound rate of 6% to a total of $598 billion in 2016 (U.S. Census Bureau, 2012; PWC, 2012). Sales of tablets and smartphones have created new revenue streams for entertainment and media firms as consumer behavior changes in response to the new technologies. Content is no longer tied to physical products, and can be delivered over the Internet to multiple mobile devices, reducing costs for consumers. Currently, online digital E&M revenue is 24% of total E&M revenue, or $117 billion in 2012. Analysts estimate that by 2016, digital E&M revenue will be 32% of E&M revenue or about $188 billion (PWC, 2012).

Media Utilization

The proliferation of new mobile media devices—tablets and smartphones—has led to an increase in the total amount of time spent listening to radio, watching TV and movies, and reading books, newspapers, and even magazines. An increasing percentage of this media engagement is digital, although traditional TV and radio audiences

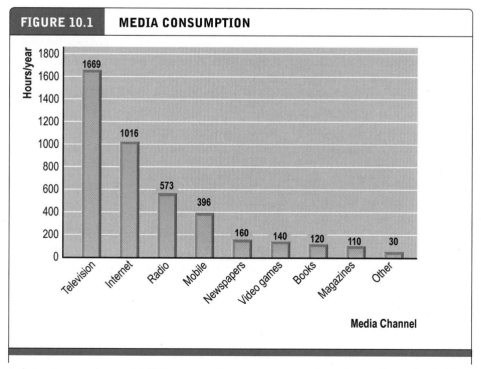

| FIGURE 10.1 | MEDIA CONSUMPTION |

Each American spends around 4,200 hours annually, on average, consuming various media, mostly television, the Internet, radio, and mobile media, including games.

SOURCES: Based on data from eMarketer, Inc., 2012a; authors' estimates.

remain stable (Arbitron, 2012). The most popular medium is television, followed by the Internet, and then radio. Together, these three media account for more than 77% of the hours spent consuming various media. While the Internet is currently second, far behind television, Internet utilization has been growing rapidly (U.S. Census Bureau, 2012). Nielsen, a media rating service, reports that television viewing is down slightly in 2012 (.5%). More interesting is the finding that the number of Americans owning a TV set has declined by 1 million, a small but unprecedented event. Both economics and technology are involved. Because traditional viewers are spending more time playing games, watching Web video, and socializing with friends, there is a slight decline in their television viewing hours. Still, cable and broadcast TV retains the largest share of viewers' media time, while Internet usage in 2012 is about 2.8 hours a day (more than 1,000 hours a year) and growing at 6% annually. Surveys report that 20% of online users read newspapers, books, and magazines less, but Internet usage does not reduce their television viewing (Nielsen, 2012a). Well over 50% of television viewers multitask while watching television, usually using a smartphone or tablet computer, texting with friends, reading e-mail, searching the Web, or visiting social network sites (eMarketer, Inc., 2012a).

Internet and Traditional Media: Cannibalization versus Complementarity

Several studies reveal that time spent on the Internet reduces consumer time available for other media (Pew Internet & American Life Project, 2011). True, there has been a massive shift of the general audience to the Web, and once there, a large percentage of time is spent on viewing content. Yet more recent data finds a more complex picture. Despite the availability of the Internet on high-resolution tablet computers, television viewing remains strong, video viewing on all devices has increased, and the reading of all kinds of books, including physical books, has increased. Total music consumption measured in hours a day listening to music has increased dramatically even as CDs decline, and movie consumption has increased dramatically even as DVD sales decline markedly. The impact of the Internet on media appears to be increasing the total demand for media, and even in some cases, stimulating demand for traditional products like books. It is also the case that content firms' physical products—printed newspapers, magazines, music CDs, and movie DVDs—are being replaced by digital versions.

Consumers are spending about 38% of their time online at social network sites, 34% shopping and buying, 10% playing games, 8% using e-mail, and 7% at entertainment sites (Nielsen, 2011b). In general, Internet users spend 15%–20% less time reading traditional books, newspapers, and magazines, watching broadcast television and box office movies, talking on the phone, or listening to broadcast radio. On the other hand, Internet users consume more media of all types than non-Internet users. This reflects the demographics of the Internet user as more literate, wealthier, more technically savvy, and more media-aware. In addition, Internet users multitask when using the Internet, frequently listening to music, watching television, and using instant messaging while working on other tasks.

Multimedia use reduces the cannibalization impact of the Internet for some visual and aural media, but obviously not for reading physical books or newspapers. And even for these print media, the Internet is simply an alternative source; Internet users are increasing the time they spend online reading newspapers, magazines, and even books. Ironically, the new mobile media platform of smartphones and tablet computers has led to an explosion in reading of both newspapers and books, but digital versions, not the printed versions.

Media Revenues

An examination of media revenues reveals a somewhat different pattern when compared to media consumption (see **Figure 10.2**). Television accounts for 28% of media revenues, print media (books, newspapers, and magazines) accounts for 37%, video games 9%, Internet media (video) 7%, music media (radio and recorded music) 11%, and box office 4%. Internet media, while small now, is growing at 12% annually, far faster than traditional media revenues.

Three Revenue Models for Digital Content Delivery: Subscription, A La Carte, and Advertising-Supported (Free and Freemium)

There are three revenue models for delivering content on the Internet. The two "pay" models are subscriptions (usually all you can eat) and a la carte (pay for what you use). The third model uses advertising revenue to provide content for free, usually with a "freemium" (higher price) option. There is also completely free, user-generated content, which we will discuss later. Contrary to early analysts' projections that

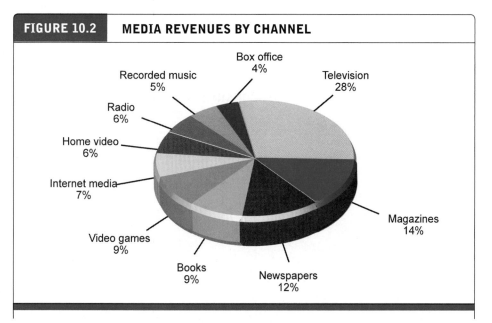

| FIGURE 10.2 | **MEDIA REVENUES BY CHANNEL** |

Traditional media still dominate the entertainment and media market, but Internet media (streaming videos, music, and content) is the fastest growing segment.

SOURCES: Based on data from industry sources; authors' estimates.

"free" would drive "paid" out of business ("information wants to be free"), it turns out that both models are viable now and in the near future. Consumers increasingly choose to pay for high-quality, convenient, and unique content, and they have gladly accepted "free" advertiser-supported content when that content is deemed not worth paying for but entertaining nevertheless. There's nothing contradictory about all three models working in tandem and cooperatively: free content can drive customers to paid content, as the recorded music firms have discovered with services like Pandora.

Online Content Consumption

Now let's look at what kinds of online content Internet users purchase or view online (**Figure 10.3**). Nearly 50% of Internet users read newspapers and 43% listen to radio, the two most popular activities. Newspapers and radio? Not what we would expect. Casual games (41%) and TV shows (41%) are nearly as popular, followed by movies and music downloads and streams. E-book consumption (23%) has grown at triple-digit rates since the Kindle was introduced in 2007 and the iPad in 2010. What this reveals is that Internet users retain their affinity to traditional formats—newspapers, radio, TV shows, and music tracks and albums—and bring these tastes to the Internet.

Figure 10.4 shows the estimated revenues from the online entertainment and media industries, projected to 2015. In 2012, total paid online content is estimated to be $11.2 billion, and to reach $17 billion by 2015. Online video (including premium movies) and music are the largest and projected fastest growing online segments, followed by TV.

Now let's look at the fastest growing paid content area: videos (which includes movies, short videos, and TV shows). This audience is huge and growing very rapidly. **Figure 10.5** on page 652 shows the top online video sites in April 2012. The top 10 sites had over 180 million video viewers. The largest site remains Google (YouTube) with 157 million viewers of 17.6 million videos, followed by Yahoo, and the fast growing

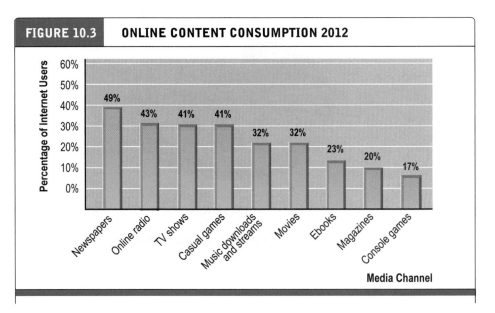

FIGURE 10.3 **ONLINE CONTENT CONSUMPTION 2012**

SOURCES: Based on data from industry sources; authors' estimates.

music video site, VEVO. The monetary value of all these videos is that they attract large audiences that can be shown ads. In March 2012, 9.4 billion video ads were shown on the Internet, about 3.9 billion ad minutes watched, reaching 52% of the Internet population (about 120 million people) (comScore, 2012).

The overall size of the online video audience (with more than 180 million monthly unique viewers in the United States) is about the same size as the traditional television audience. There are 115 million households with televisions, representing about 200 million individuals who tune in every month. However, major TV events tend to draw a much higher viewership. For instance, 111.3 million people watched Super Bowl XLVI in 2012. No Internet video has drawn such a large audience during a single time period.

Free or Fee: Attitudes About Paying for Content and the Tolerance for Advertising

In the early years of online content, multiple surveys found that large majorities of the Internet audience expected to pay nothing for online content although equally large majorities were willing to accept advertising as a way to pay for free content. In reality, on the early Web, there wasn't much high-quality content. By 2012, attitudes towards paying for content have greatly changed. Until Internet services such as iTunes arrived, few thought the "fee" model could compete with the "free" model, and most Internet aficionados and experts concluded that information on the Internet wants to be free. Cable TV systems (networks themselves) offer a totally different

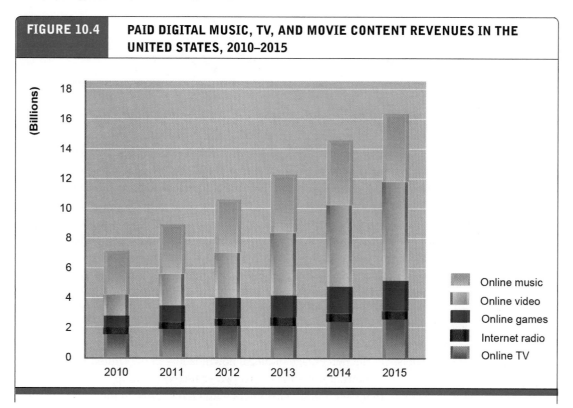

FIGURE 10.4 **PAID DIGITAL MUSIC, TV, AND MOVIE CONTENT REVENUES IN THE UNITED STATES, 2010–2015**

Legend:
- Online music
- Online video
- Online games
- Internet radio
- Online TV

SOURCES: Based on data from industry sources; authors' estimates.

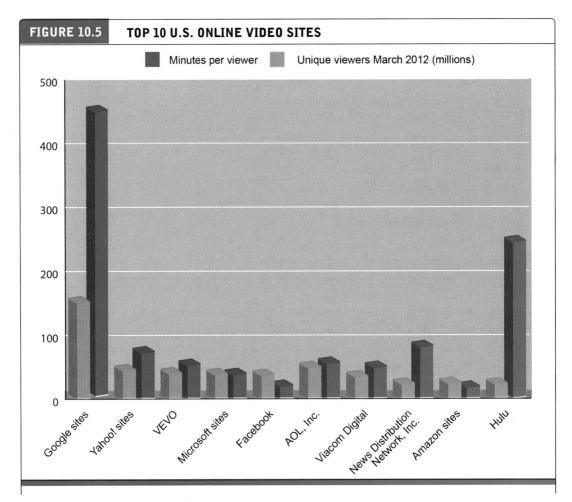

FIGURE 10.5   **TOP 10 U.S. ONLINE VIDEO SITES**

Minutes per viewer   Unique viewers March 2012 (millions)

SOURCES: Based on data from comScore, 2012

history: they always charged for service and content, and cable TV experts never thought information wanted to be free. Neither did the Hollywood and New York media companies that paid for and provided the content to television and movie theaters. In 2012, millions of Internet users pay for high-quality content delivered on a convenient device such as a smartphone or tablet computer. Like cable TV, Apple iTunes charges for service and content as well. In a demonstration of just how much quality online content is worth paying for, by 2012, Apple had sold 20 billion songs, 450 million TV shows, and more than 100 million movies. Pandora, the second largest source of Internet music, and the largest streaming service, has 20 million monthly unique visitors. While an estimated 16 million Internet users in the United States still download songs from illegal P2P sites, 80 million buy music from legal sites in 2012, generating $3.6 billion in sales (eMarketer, Inc., 2012a). Most experts thought free would drive out fee models. Yet the percentage of illegal downloaders in the United States shrunk from 16% to 9% of Internet users in the last two years (NPD Group, 2011). Worldwide, iTunes has more than 400 million customers with credit cards on file.

The culture of the Internet is beginning to change when firms such as YouTube (and its parent Google), which started out with a business model based on amateur videos and illegally uploaded music videos, begin cooperating closely with Hollywood and New York production studios for premium content. As it turns out, free content isn't worth very much and should be free, especially if producers give it away. Premium content is worth a great deal, and should be priced accordingly.

DIGITAL RIGHTS MANAGEMENT (DRM) AND WALLED GARDENS

Content producers—newspapers, book publishers, television, movie, and music producers—generate revenue and profits from their creations, and they protect these revenue streams through copyright. Created by Congress in Article I, Section 8 of the United States Constitution, Congress granted authors and inventors copyrights and patent rights to "the progress of science and useful arts." The first Copyright Act was passed in 1790. In the digital age, when exact copies and widescale distribution of works is possible, protecting the copyrights to content is a major challenge.

Digital rights management (DRM) refers to a combination of technical (both hardware and software) and legal means for protecting digital content from unlimited reproduction and distribution without permission. Essentially, DRM can prevent users from purchasing and making copies for widespread distribution over the Internet without compensating the content owners. While music tracks in the iTunes Store were originally protected by DRM, in 2009, Apple abandoned the practice because of user objections, and because Amazon had opened an online music store in 2007 without any DRM protections, with the support of music label firms, who came to realize that DRM prevented them from exploiting the opportunities of the Internet and perhaps encouraged an illegal market. Most music firms with subscription services use technologies that limit the time period that a song can be played without re-subscribing. For instance, songs downloaded from Rhapsody, the largest music subscription service, will not play after 30 days unless the user pays the monthly subscription fee. And if you don't pay, you will lose access to all your songs. Movies streamed from Netflix are technically difficult for the average user to capture and share. Likewise, music streamed from Pandora is cumbersome to record and share. These newer digital services, including both Apple and Amazon, use a kind of DRM called "walled garden" to restrict the widespread sharing of content. E-books purchased from Amazon can only be played on Kindles or Kindle apps running on smartphones, tablets, computers, or browsers. Kindle books cannot be converted to other formats, like epubs or Adobe PDF files. By locking the content to a physical device, or a digital stream with no local storage, the appliance makers derive additional revenues and profits by locking customers into their service or device.

While the issue of DRM is often cast as a moral contest between content owners and hackers bent on distributing and using free music, films, and books, the industry titans themselves are divided on DRM. The telecommunications and digital device industries directly benefit from the illegal and unfettered downloading of music and other content. For instance, Apple, Intel, Sony, and Microsoft all benefited in the early 2000s from the explosion in illegal sharing of intellectual property simply because users will buy more devices. A mantra voiced first by Steve Jobs as "Rip. Mix. Burn"

digital rights management (DRM)
refers to the combination of technical and legal means for protecting digital content from unlimited reproduction without permission

became an Apple advertising slogan and popular rationale for copying CDs and sharing or posting the music online for commercial purposes. [In subsequent interviews, Jobs said he did not intend this remark to encourage people to steal music, and in fact, he was strong supporter of protecting the intellectual property rights of all artists and their production firms (Isaacson, 2011)]. Likewise, Verizon, SBC Communications, and Time Warner Cable (and the major Internet trunk line owners) also depend on their networks being kept as busy as possible. In 2012, an estimated 23% of global Internet bandwidth consists of unauthorized stolen material. Around 20% of U.S. Internet traffic consists of BitTorrent torrents of illegal content (mostly videos, but music and books as well) (Envisional, 2012). Internet service providers, telecom providers, and even search engines like Google derive revenue from an environment where users can share any content whether or not it is legally obtained content. In contrast, content creators and owners often insist on DRM, and are supportive of walled gardens that make their content unusable on more general purpose platforms such as PCs, using Adobe Flash or PDF files. Content producers make nothing on the delivery devices or the telecommunications infrastructure. To understand all this, you need to keep your eye on the money.

In 2003, iTunes provided a partial but game-changing solution to illegal downloading and sharing by creating iTunes, and managed to make it a popular alternative to file-sharing services like Kazaa, eDonkey, and Limewire. Of all the device makers, Apple has turned out to be the most friendly to artists and music labels. Google Play and Amazon's Store are closely following in the iTunes footsteps by providing an environment where users can conveniently download or stream legal content for a very low cost. By 2012, it is clear to the major online content distributors that more revenue can be generated from legal distribution of content than illegal distribution.

MEDIA INDUSTRY STRUCTURE

The media content industry prior to 1990 was composed of many smaller independent corporations specializing in content creation and distribution in the separate industries of film, television, book and magazine publishing, and newspaper publishing. During the 1990s and into this century, after an extensive period of consolidation, huge entertainment and publishing media conglomerates emerged.

The media industry is still organized largely into three separate vertical stovepipes: print, movies, and music. Each segment is dominated by a few key players. We do not include the delivery platform firms here, such as AT&T, Verizon, Sprint, Dish Network, or Comcast, because in general they do not create content but instead move content across cable, satellite, and telephone lines. Generally, there is very little crossover from one segment to another. Newspapers do not also produce Hollywood films, and publishing firms do not own newspapers or film production studios. Even within media conglomerates that span several different media segments, separate divisions control each media segment. The competition between corporate divisions in mega-sized corporations is often more severe than with marketplace competitors.

While the commercial media industry is highly concentrated within each segment, the much larger media ecosystem includes literally millions of individuals and independent entrepreneurs creating content in the form of blogs, videos on YouTube and VEVO, and music on indie sites like madeloud.com. At times, the viewership (or readership) of these much smaller but numerous players exceeds that of the media titans.

MEDIA CONVERGENCE: TECHNOLOGY, CONTENT, AND INDUSTRY STRUCTURE

Media convergence is a much used but poorly defined term. There are at least three dimensions of media where the term convergence has been applied: technology, content (artistic design, production, and distribution), and to the industry's structure as a whole. Ultimately for the consumer, convergence means being able to get any content you want, when you want it, on whatever platform you want it—from an iPod to an iPad, Android phone, or home PC, or set-top device like Google TV.

Technological Convergence

Convergence from a technology perspective **(technological convergence)** has to do with the development of hybrid devices that can combine the functionality of two or more existing media platforms, such as books, newspapers, television, movies, radio, and games, into a single device. Examples of technological convergence include the iPad, iPhone, and Android ("smartphones") that combine print, music, pictures, and video in a single device.

technological convergence
development of hybrid devices that can combine the functionality of two or more existing media platforms into a single device

Content Convergence

A second dimension of convergence is **content convergence**. There are three aspects to content convergence: design, production, and distribution.

There is a historical pattern in which content created in an older media technology migrates to the new technology largely intact, with little artistic change. Slowly, the different media are integrated so that consumers can move seamlessly back and forth among them, and artists (and producers) learn more about how to deliver content in the new media. Later, the content itself is transformed by the new media as artists learn how to fully exploit the capabilities in the creation process. At this point, content convergence and transformation has occurred—the art is different because of the new capabilities inherent to new tools. For instance, European master painters of the fifteenth century in Italy, France, and the Netherlands (such as van Eyck, Caravaggio, Lotto, and Vermeer) quickly adopted new optical devices such as lenses, mirrors, and early projectors called *camera obscura* that could cast near-photographic quality images on canvases, and in the process they developed new theories of perspective and new techniques of painting landscapes and portraits. Suddenly, paintings took on the qualities of precision, detail, and realism found later in photographs (Boxer, 2001). A similar process is occurring today as artists and writers assimilate new digital and Internet tools into their toolkits. For instance, GarageBand from Apple enables low-budget independent bands (literally working in garages) to mix and control eight

content convergence
convergence in the design, production, and distribution of content

different digital music tracks to produce professional sounding recordings on a shoe-string budget. Writers of books are beginning to think about video and interactive versions of their books. Online newspapers are turning to live video as an enhancement to their stories.

On the production side, tools for digital editing and processing (for film and television) are driving content convergence. Given that the most significant cost of content is its creation, if there is a wide diversity of target delivery platforms, then it is wise to develop and produce only once using technology that can deliver to multiple platforms. Generally, this means creating content on digital devices (hardware and software) so that it can be delivered on multiple digital platforms. Once captured on digital devices, the same content can be archived, sliced into atomistic units, and repurposed for a wide variety of other platforms and distribution channels.

On the distribution side, it is important that distributors and the ultimate consumers have the devices needed to receive, store, and experience the product. While for the most part technology companies have succeeded in giving consumers portable devices to receive online content, it has been more difficult for the content owners to come up with new, profitable distribution platforms.

Figure 10.6 depicts the process of media convergence and transformation using the example of books. For example, consider this book. In 2012, this book was written with a view to appearing on iPads and Kindle e-book readers, and is moving closer

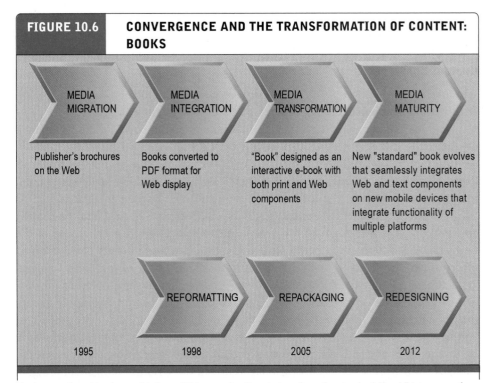

| FIGURE 10.6 | CONVERGENCE AND THE TRANSFORMATION OF CONTENT: BOOKS |

MEDIA MIGRATION — Publisher's brochures on the Web

MEDIA INTEGRATION — Books converted to PDF format for Web display

MEDIA TRANSFORMATION — "Book" designed as an interactive e-book with both print and Web components

MEDIA MATURITY — New "standard" book evolves that seamlessly integrates Web and text components on new mobile devices that integrate functionality of multiple platforms

REFORMATTING   REPACKAGING   REDESIGNING

1995   1998   2005   2012

The Internet is making it possible for publishers and writers to transform the standard "book" into a new form that integrates features of both text and the Internet, and also transforms the content of the book itself.

to the media maturity stage, in which the book will be available mostly as a purely digital product with substantial visual and aural content that can be displayed on many different digital devices. By that time, the "learning experience" will be transformed. Traditional bound books will probably still be available (books have many advantages), but most likely, print editions will be printed on demand by customers using their own print facilities.

Industry Structure Convergence

A third dimension of convergence is the structure of the various media industries. **Industry convergence** refers to the merger of media enterprises into powerful, synergistic combinations that can cross-market content on many different platforms and create new works that use multiple platforms. This can take place either through purchases or through strategic alliances. Traditionally, each type of media—film, text, music, television—had its own separate industry, typically composed of very large players. For instance, the entertainment film industry has been dominated by a few large Hollywood-based production studios, book publication is dominated by a few large book publishers, and music production is dominated by four global record label firms.

industry convergence merger of media enterprises into synergistic combinations that create and cross-market content on different platforms

However, the Internet has created forces that make mergers and partnerships among media and Internet firms a necessary business proposition. Media industry convergence may be necessary to finance the substantial changes in both the technology platform and the content. Traditional media firms who create the content generally do not possess the core competencies or financial heft to distribute it on the Internet. Technology companies that dominate the Internet (Google, Apple, Amazon, and Facebook) have the competency and wealth to pursue Internet channel strategies, but do not have the competencies needed to create content. Business combinations and partnerships are made to solve these issues.

While traditional media companies have not done well in purchases of Internet platform companies, the technology owners such as Apple, Amazon, Facebook, Microsoft, and Google have generally avoided merging with media companies, and instead rely on contractual arrangements with media companies to protect intellectual property rights and to create a business pricing model that both parties can accept. However, this pattern may be changing. For instance, in 2012, CBS Inc. is planning to produce a television show for Netflix; Netflix and Hulu have begun production and distribution of their own original TV shows; Google's Channels are producing original content designed for Internet distribution on YouTube. Amazon created its own book imprint, Amazon Books Publishing, and entered the book publishing business.

In the end, consumers' demands for content anywhere, anytime, and on any device is pushing the technology and content companies towards cooperation or outright purchases.

MAKING A PROFIT WITH ONLINE CONTENT: FROM FREE TO FEE

Despite the resistance of users in the early years of e-commerce, there is broad consensus that many online consumers, perhaps 25%, are increasingly willing to pay for high-quality content, at their discretion, and that sites offering a mix of free and fee content can be successful. In 2012, this is still an untested idea in many content areas, especially newspapers.

There appear to be four factors required to charge for online content: focused market, specialized content, sole-source monopoly, and high perceived net value (see **Figure 10.7**). **Net value** refers to that portion of perceived customer value that can be attributed to the fact that content is available on the Internet. Net value derives from the ability of consumers to instantaneously access the information on the Web or mobile device, search large and deep historical archives, and move the online information to other documents or devices easily. Customer convenience is a large part of net value. For instance, Hoover's provides four different subscriptions ranging from $75 a month to $2,995 for a professional subscription. Hoover's content addresses a focused market (business analysts and executive search firms); it has specialized content (data gathered by its own reporters and other sources); it is the sole source for some of this information; and it has high perceived value because it can be quickly accessed, searched, and downloaded into other documents and made a part of business decision making. And the consumers are in a hurry to get the information. In general, the opportunity for paid content varies by the nature of the content and the audience.

net value

that portion of perceived customer value that can be attributed to the fact that content is available on the Internet

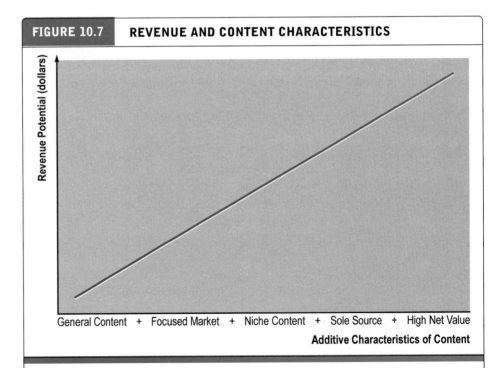

FIGURE 10.7 **REVENUE AND CONTENT CHARACTERISTICS**

Revenue Potential (dollars)

General Content + Focused Market + Niche Content + Sole Source + High Net Value

Additive Characteristics of Content

As content becomes more focused and more specialized, is controlled by a single source and provides real value to consumers for an Internet delivery (i.e., speed, searchability, and portability), the prospects for charging fees for access increase.

10.2 THE ONLINE PUBLISHING INDUSTRY

Nothing is quite so fundamental to a civilized society as reading text. Text is the way we record our history, current events, thoughts, and aspirations, and transmit them to all others in the civilization who can read. Even videos require scripts. Today, the publishing industry (composed of books, newspapers, magazines, and periodicals) is a $82 billion media sector based originally on print, and now moving rapidly to the Internet (U.S. Census Bureau, 2012). The Internet offers the text publishing industry an opportunity to move toward a new generation of newspapers, magazines, and books that are produced, processed, stored, distributed, and sold over the Web, available anytime, anywhere, and on any device. The same Internet offers the possibility of destroying many existing print-based businesses that may not be able to make this transition and remain profitable.

ONLINE NEWSPAPERS

Newspapers in 2012 are the most troubled segment of the publishing industry, troubles that result almost exclusively from the availability of alternatives to the printed newspaper, as well as a sluggish response by management to the opportunities on the Internet for news, if not newspapers. Also important is the failure of newspaper management to protect its valuable content from being distributed for free by headline aggregators such as Yahoo, MSN, and Google, as well as tens of millions of bloggers and tweeters. These search firms can index online newspaper content, and provide search results to users' queries (as they display ads to those same users and derive revenue). While these search firms do link to the actual newspaper articles, they have in the meantime generated revenue for themselves based on the newspaper article contents. As it turns out, there wouldn't be a Google or Yahoo news functionality without traditional reporters and editors who work for newspapers and create the content. As you may have noticed, a single, original, high-quality newspaper article generates hundreds if not thousands of Internet knockoff articles on blogs, news aggregation sites, and content generator sites.

Over 60% of newspapers have reduced news staff in the last three years, and 61% report shrinking the size of the newspaper. Readership has been declining for 10 years, print edition advertising is down 15% a year, subscriptions are down, and old print readers are not being replaced by young readers, who instead get their news online. To make matters worse, in the slow growth period of 2009–2012, online ads declined another 28%, and the amount spent on Internet advertising in general now equals that spent on newspaper advertising. Alternative online sources such as Yahoo, Google, and even blogs, have became major sources of news for many Americans. Much of this "news" is redistributed content generated by newspapers! Alternatives to newspaper classified ads like Craigslist have decimated newspaper classified revenues.

But there is some good news too. Online readership of newspapers is growing at more than 10% a year. New reading devices from smartphones to e-readers, iPads, and tablet PCs connected to wireless networks offer opportunities for online newspapers to be read everywhere. A new Internet culture is supportive of paying for quality content. Newspaper owners, faced with extinction, are exploring ways to protect their content, and are introducing paid "premium" news and views, a la carte purchase of articles, subscriptions to digital versions, and online apps for mobile devices. Pure Internet aggregators of news such as Google and Yahoo are beginning to recognize that if the newspaper industry disappears, there will be little news to aggregate, distribute, and place ads against. Amateur blogs and tweets may be wonderful for expressing opinions, or making instant reports on events as they occur, but they are no substitute for professional reporters and editors, and not a place for brand-conscious advertisers. Therefore, the Internet distributors are recognizing they have a vested interest in keeping the newspaper content industry in working order.

According to the Newspaper Association of America, in 2012, print newspapers have around 46 million paid subscribers, down from 62 million in 1990. On an average day in 2011, 49 million people read a print newspaper and 150 million read a newspaper online. Even when compared to YouTube (5 million unique visitors a day), these are impressive audience sizes. Offline newspaper readership of physical papers has declined at about 2% a year for several years, while online readership is at an all-time high of about 113 million daily readers with online traffic growing at 10% annually in 2012. The important 21–34 age group is growing at 17%. Nearly 50% of all Web users on a typical day visit an online newspaper. The online audience increases the overall footprint of the newspaper media. Total print edition advertising in newspapers in 2012 is expected to be around $18 billion, and declining at 10% a year. Since 2002, advertising revenues have fallen by 50%. Partially offsetting these negative trends is that subscription revenues produced by loyal daily readers have been stable over the decade at around $10 billion. However, online newspaper ad revenues in 2012 are expected to be about $3.5 billion, growing at 7% a year. Still, the online ad revenues represent only 13% of all revenues, not nearly enough to support current operations. In a nutshell, the problem confronting newspapers is how to grow online revenues fast enough so as to offset the losses from print advertising (Myers, 2012; Pew Research, 2012; Newspaper Association of America, 2012). To date, this has been an elusive target.

Audience Size and Growth

There are more than 10,000 online newspapers in the world. Globally, online newspaper readership is growing at 17% a year. According to comScore, online newspapers experienced very strong growth in recent quarters. (See **Figure 10.8** for a list of the top eight.) The online newspapers attract a wealthy and consumer-intense demographic, reaching 64% of 25- to 34-year-olds and 75% of individuals in households earning more than $100,000 a year on average throughout the quarter. The online newspaper audience is also highly engaged, generating 4.1 billion page views each month, spending nearly 3.4 billion minutes browsing the sites (comScore, 2011). The average online visitor stayed on the site for 35 to 45 minutes. Online newspapers are the dominant local Web site: 62% of Internet users look for local news on a local newspaper Web site. Given this huge online newspaper audience, it is clear that the future of newspapers lies in the online mobile market even as readership and subscriptions to the traditional print newspapers continue to decline at a steady pace.

Next to social networks, newspapers produce the largest online audiences of any media, and in that sense, contrary to popular opinion, are one of the most successful

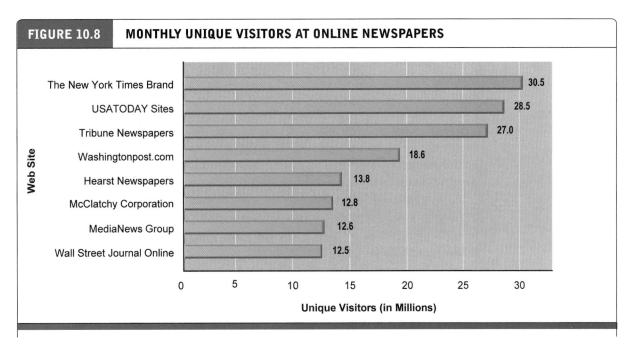

FIGURE 10.8   MONTHLY UNIQUE VISITORS AT ONLINE NEWSPAPERS

Online newspaper readership is expanding rapidly as more people get their news online, and as smartphone and tablet apps become more widespread.

SOURCES: Based on data from Myers, 2012.

forms of online content to date. The Internet provides existing branded newspapers the opportunity to extend their brands to a new online audience, and also gives entrepreneurial firms the opportunity to offer services—such as classified job listings—on the Web that were previously delivered by newspapers. Online newspapers are the top choice for local news and information for Internet users in the United States.

While newspapers have done an excellent job at increasing their Web presence and audience, few have reached break-even operations. Instead, online classified and advertising revenues have not kept pace with the fall in revenues from their traditional print editions. There are several reasons for this, including increased competition from general portal sites moving into the content aggregation business, loss of classified ads to online portals and job sites, and free listing services such as Craigslist. Craigslist is reported to have wiped out $50 million in classified ads for the *San Francisco Chronicle* alone.

The Web has provided an opportunity for newspapers to extend their offline brands, but at the same time it has given entrepreneurs the opportunity to disaggregate newspaper content—such as weather, classified ads, or current national and international news—and create stand-alone Web sites that compete with online and offline newspapers.

Newspaper Business Models

The online newspaper industry has gone through several business models, from fee to free, and most recently, struggling to return to a fee-based metered and subscription business model. In the past, a few online newspapers such as the *New York Times*, *Wall Street Journal*, and *Financial Times* (U.K.) charged for some or all online content, especially premium content. In the case of the *New York Times*, access to the *New York Times* archives was a paid service. Most newspapers did not charge for online content, and even the *New York Times* abandoned its Times Select subscription service for archived content. The result was that content generated by newspapers became freely available across the Web, where it could be indexed by search engines that redistributed the headlines and content. Newspaper headlines became the primary content on Google News and Yahoo News. Newspapers benefited from this because a Google listing brought readers to the newspaper, where readers could be exposed to advertising. In 2012, the threatened destruction of the newspaper industry is causing newspaper management to rethink free content supported by online ads placed at the newspapers' sites. The Associated Press has negotiated licensing agreements with Google, Yahoo, and other online news portals. The *Wall Street Journal* was prepared to abandon the fee model in 2008, but in 2009, the parent News Corp., the largest owner of newspapers in the world, announced plans to begin charging for all its online content across the world.

Starting in March 2011, the *New York Times*, the world's largest online newspaper, started charging for online access. Print subscribers pay $300 a year for seven days of home or business-delivered editions, and complete free access to any online editions from the Web to smartphone apps. Unlimited digital access is about $420 a year. Those who are not a print or digital subscriber are limited to 10 free articles a month, after which readers will have to become digital subscribers at $15 to $35 a month depending on the devices used to access the *Times*. In the first month of operation, the online edition had 100,000 paid subscribers, and in March 2012, the paper hit 480,000 paid subscribers. The *Times* online subscriptions produce more than $200 million in revenue, nearly 10% of its overall revenues.

Many, but not all, efforts by newspapers to adapt to the Internet involve making alliances with Internet titans such as Google and Yahoo, which have huge online audiences. These efforts involve sharing revenue with Internet partners. A different strategy is emerging based on the proliferation of e-reader devices such as smartphones, tablets like the iPad, and dedicated devices like the Kindle and Barnes & Noble's Nook. Each of these devices has reader apps that present newspaper content in a way that closely matches the offline editions and is familiar to readers.

These new reader devices offer newspapers an opportunity to connect directly with their readers anytime and anywhere. What has been missing is a kind of online newsstand, a newspaper version of the iTunes Store, where you can find newspaper content from any newspaper in the United States or the world. But this is changing with the appearance of Google and Apple newsstand apps, where newspapers can display their apps. Apple takes a 30% cut of sales, Google somewhat less. Newspaper-Direct is an online store that has same-day online editions of nearly 2,210 newspapers from 94 countries in 54 languages. Unlimited subscriptions are $29.00 a month, economy editions are $9.95 for 31 articles, and most individual articles cost 99 cents. See the *Insight on Society* case, *Can Apps and Video Save Newspapers?*

INSIGHT ON SOCIETY

CAN APPS AND VIDEO SAVE NEWSPAPERS?

In the past decade, Internet pundits have buried the newspaper industry several times, just as they did books and other print media. Rejected as a relic of the age of the Gutenberg press of 1467, published by old firms incapable of adopting new technology, newspapers would one day be replaced by free content from amateurs in the field and on the scene. Indeed, the newspaper industry has been disrupted by the Internet: ad revenues have been cut in half over the last 10 years, and classified ad revenue has been decimated by sites such as Craigslist and Angie's List.

The initial reaction of the newspaper industry to the Internet and Web was to build Web sites as a way to attract an Internet audience and advertisers. It didn't work. Newspaper executives now concede it was a terrible mistake to give away news content for free.

But the game is not over. Just the beginning is over. Because of the Internet, newspaper readership is actually up, not down. In 2012, more than half of newspaper readers get their news from an online edition. Online readership is growing: over 113 million people read newspapers online in 2012, nearly half of all adult users of the Internet, and readership is growing at 10% a year. Just as books rose from the ashes of technorati critical commentary, newspapers might be able to adapt to newer technologies and opportunities. The social, local, mobile platform driven by smartphones and tablet computers offers newspapers many new opportunities to attract subscribers and advertisers. There are four factors that might just keep newspapers around for a long time.

The first is the paid subscription business model. Newspapers are increasingly using a free-mium business model and charging for online content. Typically, the freemium model gives readers the choice of some free articles (10 to 20) every day, or paying for a premium subscription to all the news, and then paying in addition for various platform choices (smartphones and tablet app versions). The *Wall Street Journal, New York Times, Minneapolis Tribune, Boston Globe, Dallas Morning News*, and the Gannett papers are just some of the major national and regional newspapers adopting online subscriptions.

Information wants to be expensive if it's current, relevant, accurate, and timely. The *Wall Street Journal* led the way in the United States with an online premium service: $260 a year for both the print and online editions, and $207 a year for the digital edition. Today, the *Journal* has nearly 600,000 online subscribers, 80,000 of whom use tablets and smartphones. With over 2.1 million worldwide subscribers, roughly a quarter are now reading online. One key to the *Wall Street Journal*'s success is that a subscription gives users access to premium content in the form of 25,000 in-depth background reports on companies, an archive of news articles going back to 1996, and access to the Dow Jones Publication Library, which features current and past articles from 7,000 newspapers, magazines, and business-news sources. If you are a stock analyst or an individual investor looking for information on a specific company, this archive of material is worth the small annual subscription fee.

The *New York Times* led the pay revolution for general-purpose newspapers by announcing a paid subscription freemium service in 2011: everyone gets 20 free articles a day. While most experts predicted the pay model for general interest newspapers could not work in the Internet age,

(continued)

they were wrong. Today, the *Times* has more than 450,000 online subscribers, although the ad revenue does not match the revenues lost from declining physical paper sales. In May 2012, the *Times* reduced the number of free articles to 10 per day in an effort to encourage more paid subscriptions.

The second factor is the arrival of the mobile platform in the form of smartphones and tablets, which is proving to be a boon for online newspapers. In a survey by comScore, over 67% of online newspaper readers said they use multiple devices—PCs, tablets, and/or smartphones. It's a multiplatform world that plays to the strengths of newspapers. Apps enable the newspapers to charge a la carte for articles, develop different versions at different price points, personalize the content, and above all, protect the content from being copied without payment. The *Washington Post's* Trove app allows readers to create their own personal newspaper. Apps are a proprietary, walled garden where content cannot easily be copied, in contrast to the public Web where just about anything can be copied and distributed. From a customer experience point of view, high-resolution tablets are uniquely suited for the large format, pictures, and videos found in today's online newspapers. Tablets allow readers the chance to read newspapers anywhere, anytime, even while traveling. Rather than a "morning" or "evening" event, reading the newspaper online becomes a convenient, continuous event on demand. A number of "newsstands" have sprung up, including Flipboard, Zite, and AOL Editions, which aggregate content from partners (some of them newspapers) for display on tablets. Both Apple and Google feature newsstands that put all of a users' subscriptions in one place. So far, only magazines have signed up, but newspapers may strike a deal with both distributors.

The third factor is video content. If you visit online or app-based newspapers, you'll see that online newspapers are increasingly differentiated from traditional print newspapers because of extensive use of video. Online newspapers are redesigning themselves to be more like CNN or MSNBC television shows. For instance, in 2012, the *Wall Street Journal* produces over five hours of live video each day to accompany its text articles; the *New York Times* is running a live morning newscast, and a taped daily show called *TimesCast*. Newspapers are being helped in this transition to video on demand by Google, which is encouraging newspapers to establish YouTube channels. The news agency Reuters publishes live video segments on its channel every day, and the *Wall Street Journal* has established its own channel with live and taped programming featuring sections on live news, lifestyle, digital news, Wall Street views, and opinion. The attraction of extensive use of video by online newspapers is that ads displayed alongside videos pay over $50 per CPM (cost per thousand clicks), whereas ordinary display ads pay only $5 per CPM or less. For newspapers starved for revenue, the future is video, driven by a professional reporting and editorial staff.

The final factor is that news is predominantly local. While many wrote off the local town newspaper as advertising disappeared from their pages bound for Craigslist, Angie's List, and other locally oriented classified sites, and search engines like Google, instead they have proliferated. In 2012, there are over 500 local online newspapers supported by local advertisers from local car dealerships, to local pizza stores, restaurants, nail salons, and drug stores appealing to a local client base with local news and views. While not as sophisticated in their use of video or apps, these local papers are building a strong local readership, and hopefully a successful business model.

There are many challenges ahead for the newspaper industry. Online revenues are not high enough right now to overcome the loss of ad rev-

(continued)

enues from the print editions but they are a fast growing revenue stream. These revenues soften the blow of declining print revenues, and give newspapers some breathing room to innovate and experiment. So far, the experiments online have been successful.

SOURCES: "Newspaper Websites See Increases in Unique and Average Daily Visitors in First Quarter," by Marianna Hendricks, Newspaper Association of America, April 25, 2012; "Smart Devices Attract News Readers," eMarketer, April 11, 2012; "New York Times Nears Half-million Online Subscriber Mark, Halves Free Article Allowance to Celebrate," New York Times Communications Group, March 12, 2012; "Papers Put Faith in Paywalls," by Russell Adams, *Wall Street Journal*, March 4, 2012.

Challenges: Disruptive Technologies

The online newspaper industry would appear at first glance to be a classic case of disruptive technology destroying a traditional business model based on physical products and physical distribution. This may turn out to be the case, but it cannot be the final assessment just yet. The industry is changing rapidly. There are significant assets that newspapers have—excellent content and writing, strong local readership, strong local advertising, and a fragmented but huge audience of over 100 million readers that rivals Yahoo, Google, and Microsoft's audience. Content is still king: the thousands of blogs in the blogosphere depend on traditional reporting media like television and newspapers to create the content that blog writers can react to. Without the original content creators in the form of professional reporters and news organizations, the blogosphere would be a dull place. The people who read newspapers are very different from the people who visit YouTube: they are wealthier, more educated, and older. This is an ideal demographic for advertisers and a potential gold mine for newspapers. The online audience for newspapers will continue to grow in both sheer numbers and sophistication, demanding higher quality online delivery and more services. The industry has made significant investments in technology for Web content creation and delivery. The challenge is for newspaper owners and managers to invest heavily in the online editions even if they do not meet investment criteria at first. If the newspaper industry has a future, it will be online. The challenge for newspapers is to create value by focusing on differentiated, timely, and exclusive content available nowhere else. And to make this content available anywhere, anytime, anyplace, on any device.

E-BOOKS AND ONLINE BOOK PUBLISHING

In April 2000, Stephen King, one of America's most popular writers, published a novella called *Riding the Bullet*. This novella was only available as an e-book. King was the first major fiction writer to create an e-book-only volume of a new work. King's publisher, Simon & Schuster, arranged for sales online through online retailers such as Amazon. In the first day, there were 400,000 downloads, so many that Amazon's servers crashed several times. More than 600,000 downloads occurred in the first week. While Amazon gave the book away for free in the first two weeks, when it began charging $2.50 for a 66-page novella—about the same price per page as a standard King hardcover novel—sales continued to be brisk.

Ten years later, on April 15, 2010, Amanda Hocking, an unknown and unpublished self-publisher from Austin, Minnesota, uploaded one of her vampire novels, *My Blood Approves*, to Amazon's self-publishing site, and later to Barnes & Noble e-book store. Her novels had been rejected by many of the publishing houses in New York. By March 2011, she had sold more than 1 million copies of her e-books, which generally sell for 99 cents to $2.99, and earned more than $2 million. Starting out with sales of 5 to 10 books a day, Hocking's sales have reached as many as 100,000 a day when she first publishes a novel. In the same month, she signed a traditional publishing contract worth $2 million with St. Martin's Press. In 2012, Hocking is listed as one of the Amazon 99 cent millionaires.

In the space of a decade, e-books have gone from an unusual experiment by a major author, to an everyday experience for millions of Americans, and an exciting new market for authors. Sales of e-books have exploded in a few short years, and the process of writing, selling, and distributing books has radically changed. E-books sales in 2012 are expected to be $4.2 billion dollars (see **Figure 10.9**). An entire new channel for self-published authors now exists, a channel not controlled by the major

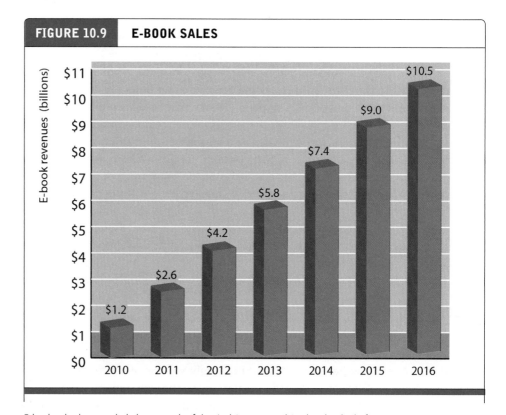

FIGURE 10.9	E-BOOK SALES

E-book sales have exploded as a result of the rival Amazon and Apple e-book platforms.
SOURCE: Based on data from eMarketer, Inc., 2012b.

New York publishing houses and their professional editors. In essence, by passing professional editors and publishers, authors can now "crowdsource" the distribution of their books. Recognizing the booming self-publishing market, Penguin (the second largest trade book publisher in the world after Random House) purchased the self-publishing company Author Solutions in July 2012. Author Solutions has published 150,000 authors and more than 190,000 books. Other publishers have made similar purchases in the hope that successful books and authors will emerge from the burgeoning online author crowd (Bosman, 2012).

Little of this was supposed to happen. E-books have had a glorious history of birth, death, and rebirth, starting in the early 1970s when Project Gutenberg at the Materials Research Lab at the University of Illinois put more than 2,000 classic books online at the University's Computer Center. The books were all in ASCII plain text without traditional book fonts or formatting. While not a joy to read, they were free. In 1990, Voyager Company, a New York-based media company, began putting books such as *Jurassic Park* and *Alice in Wonderland* on CDs for reading on PCs. However, with the exception of encyclopedias and large reference texts, books on CDs never were a commercial success. They were expensive to produce and distribute, and appeared in the marketplace before most PC users had CD-ROM drives. PC screens of this era had poor resolution, making text characters appear fuzzy. Stand-alone reader devices like the Franklin Reader (1999–2002) met with a similar fate of poor design, low-resolution screen, lack of integration with the Internet, the absence of an online book store, and a very limited inventory of e-books. Many experts and commentators in the last decade believed e-books would never become a popular reading platform. They just could not see the near-term future.

Amazon and Apple: The New Digital Media Ecosystems

Prospects for e-books picked up in 2001 with the introduction of Apple's iPod, which later became a platform for e-books (iPod Touch). In 2004, Sony introduced the first e-ink reader (Sony Librie). In 2007, the iPhone smartphone was released with a high definition color screen that could be used to read books.

The future of e-books was finally and firmly established when Amazon introduced its Kindle in 2007 to a skeptical public and critical industry observers. The early Kindle readers used electronic ink technology, providing a higher resolution than PCs and a longer battery life than portable book readers. The early Kindle had 16 megabytes of memory and could store 200 books. More important, the reader was linked to the Internet through AT&T's cell network, permitting users to access Amazon's bookstore where they could browse, search, and purchase e-books. Amazon's bookstore is the largest online bookstore on the Internet. The first Kindle readers in 2007 sold out in a few days, and were on backorder for five months until Amazon caught up with demand. Now in its 5th generation, the latest Kindle Fire has morphed into a small tablet computer with a 1-Ghz processor, Android operating system, high-resolution IPS color touch screen similar to an iPad, and 8 gigabytes of memory to store 6,000 books, plus 10 movies or 800 songs. Storage of all content in the Amazon cloud is free (which means you can watch your movies either on the Kindle or your home TV, or tablet). The Kindle Fire is no longer simply an e-book reader, but rather a media and entertainment portable device.

In 2012, Amazon's e-book and media store contains an estimated 1 million book titles. More than 800 million Kindles of all types have been sold in the United States, and there are 46 million adults who use e-readers like the Kindle (and other e-book readers like the Barnes & Noble Nook, and tablet computers like the iPad). Industry analysts believe that Amazon is racking up Kindle unit sales of over 20 million units a year, and $7.96 billion in Kindle + related revenue (content and hardware sales). The Kindle ecosystem sales represent about 17% of Amazon's $48 billion in annual revenues. For every sale of 100 print books, Amazon sells over 110 e-books. Kindle users are avid readers and typically purchase a book a week. At one point in 2010, prior to the introduction of the iPad tablet computers, Amazon accounted for 90% of the e-book market. This did not last long.

E-books received another large boost in 2010 when Apple introduced its first iPad tablet computer. With its large 11.7" screen and access to the iTunes Store of online music, video, TV, and book content, the iPad was an ideal media entertainment device. And with its high-resolution screen, the iPad was an even better e-book reader than the Kindle, albeit not easily slipped into a purse. While Amazon got the jump on Apple in dedicated e-book readers, Apple's approach from the beginning was a multipurpose device that could handle movies, music, magazines, and books, as well having a Wi-Fi connection to the Internet. Apple's iBookstore at launch in 2010 had 60,000 titles, and is estimated to have about 150,000 titles in 2012 (much smaller than Amazon's store). Apple has sold about 84 million iPads since 2007. It has a 60% market share of tablet computers in 2012, but only an estimated 15% of the e-book market. The Barnes & Noble Nook has a 25% share. The Google Play online store in 2012 is not a large book media and entertainment player yet, but will emerge in the next few years to challenge Amazon and Apple for the online content customer.

The result of the Amazon and Apple ecosystems, combining hardware, software, and online mega stores, is an explosion in online book content, readership, authorship, marketing, and at least a partial upending of the traditional book publishing and marketing channels. Increasingly, social networks play an important role in all book marketing as millions of social network members tell their friends about their favorite books. Traditional book publishing has similarly been altered. In the traditional process, authors worked with agents, who sold book manuscripts to editors and publishers, who sold books through bookstores, and at prices determined largely by the publishers. Because bookstores had a vested interest in selling books at a profit, there was only limited discounting during clearance sales. In the new publishing model, authors still write books, but then bypass traditional agent and publisher channels and instead publish their books electronically on the Amazon or Apple online stores. Prices are determined by the author, usually much lower than traditional books depending on the popularity of the author, and the platform takes a percentage of the sale (usually 30%). New self-published authors typically give away their early works to develop an audience, and then, when an audience appears, charge a small amount for their books, typically 99 cents to $2.99. Marketing occurs by word of mouth on social networks, author blogs, and public readings. While a small percentage of all books are produced this way, it is a growing and popular form of publishing and striking it rich, sometimes. They're called "99 cent millionaires," and there's enough around to arouse the passions of thousands of potential writers of the great American novel, as well as lesser genres from police procedurals to paranormal romance writers.

The book publishing industry is generally comfortable with the security and intellectual property protections offered by the online distributors. Both Amazon and Apple offer publishers walled gardens and tight controls over proprietary formats, devices, and files, thus preventing the large-scale theft of copyrighted materials. This is very different from the music industry, where the MP3 files can be easily copied and distributed. Apple and Amazon e-books are difficult to copy and upload to cyberlockers or to distribute on the Internet. Amazon Kindle titles can be put on six devices, and the files are stored both in the Amazon cloud and on the Kindle reader. Kindles can be passed around, but that is thought to be a minor issue, much like lending a physical book to a friend. Consumers cannot access books purchased from other Amazon accounts, although family members can share accounts. Apple books can't be read on Kindle or B&N devices. Kindle apps allow iPad users to read and purchase Amazon e-books using their iPads. In all these ways, the e-book online stores offer a very secure environment for book publisher intellectual content.

What Are the Challenges of the Digital E-Book Platform?

Despite, or because, of the rapid growth in e-books, the book publishing industry is in stable, even robust condition. There are two major challenges facing book publishers. Responses to these challenges will shape the future existence of the book publishing industry as we know it. These two challenges are cannibalization and finding the right business model.

Cannibalization in digital markets refers to the potential for new digital products to rapidly reduce the sales of existing physical products. This can be a threat to digital content firms insofar as the prices and profits available from selling digital products are much lower than prices and profits from physical products. Sometimes the situation is complicated by large online digital distributors such as Amazon, who want to maximize their sales of physical devices by offering free or low-priced content, and have little short-term interest protecting the profits of content owners and producers. Both the music and newspaper industries have suffered cannibalization, with revenues declining by 50% or more over the last decade.

cannibalization
when sales of new digital products replace sales of traditional products

The evidence from book publishing is mixed so far. Overall, book publishing revenues in 2011 were $27.2 billion, down 2.5% from 2010. As digital revenues have expanded, print book sales have gone down about $1 billion from the previous year. Trade book sales are flat, around $12.7 billion. In adult fiction ($4 billion in sales), e-books have doubled in sales over 2010 (from $900 million to $ 1.9 billion) and constitute about 50% of all adult fiction sales. The largest sales channel remains physical brick-and-mortar bookstores ($8.9 billion), and this has fallen 15% with the closing of Borders bookstore in 2011. Sales to online retailers grew 35% to $5 billion, reflecting in part the growth of e-book sales. Sales directly to individuals increased 58% to $1.1 billion (Caderon, 2012; Book Industry Study Group, 2012).

The overall picture that emerges is that the rapid growth of e-books and online sales has lowered sales of physical books in brick-and-mortar stores. However, much of this lost revenue is being made up by the growth in e-book sales online. Total readership has arguably increased with the popularity of e-books and the widespread adoption of Kindles and iPads. More than 40% of e-book readers use some kind of e-reader like Kindles and Nooks, 42% use a PC, 29% use cell phones, and 23% use tablet computers. In 2012, 21% of Americans have read an e-book (most using a PC or their smartphones) and 88% of e-book readers also read traditional books (Pew Internet, 2012).

E-Book Business Models

The e-book industry is composed of intermediary retailers (both brick-and-mortar stores and online merchants), traditional publishers, technology developers, device makers (e-readers), and vanity presses (self-publishing service companies). Together, these players have pursued a wide variety of business models and developed many alliances in an effort to move text onto the computer screen.

There are six very large publishers that dominate trade book, education, and religious book publishing. These traditional publishers have the largest content libraries for conversion to e-books. These large publishers started out using a **wholesale model** of distribution and pricing, in part because this is the same model they used with hard cover books. In this model, the retail store pays a wholesale price for the book and then decides at what price to sell it to the consumer. The retailer sets the price with, of course, some kind of understanding with the publisher that the book will not be given away for free. In the past, the wholesale price was 50% of the retail price. A retailer would pay the publisher a $10 wholesale price, and mark it up to $20 retail price. However, retailers could also determine to sell the book at a much lower sale price, say $5, as a way to attract readers to the store or as a close-out sale. Brick-and-mortar stores had a vested interest in selling most books above their wholesale cost. With e-books, publishers discovered that some online retailers like Amazon would gladly sell e-books below their own cost for a variety of reasons.

In the case of e-books, publishers sought to keep their prices high enough so as not to discourage hard cover sales. Generally, this meant publishers wanted e-books to sell at a retail price of $12.99 to $14.99, depending on the popularity of the book and the stage in the product life cycle (months since first publication). E-book distributors like Amazon were charged a wholesale price of about $9, and they were expected to mark up the product to around $12.99 to $14.99 or more. Instead, Amazon chose to sell e-books for $9.99, at or below its cost, in order to attract buyers to its content store to buy Kindles, and to attract new customers to its online retail store. Amazon lost $1 to $3 on every e-book sold, but recouped the money by selling Kindles for hundreds of dollars, and from additional sales at its stores. With the lowest e-book prices on the Internet, publishers were forced to sell their e-books on all other Web sites at the $9.99

wholesale model
prices are determined by the retailer

Amazon price, as were local independent book stores just getting into e-book sales. Using this strategy, Amazon not only sold millions of Kindles but also sold 90% of all e-book titles on the Web in 2010. Amazon had a near monopoly on e-books.

Publishers opposed Amazon's policy as debasing the perceived value of both physical and electronic books, and as a mortal threat to the publishers who could not survive if their e-books were priced at $9.99 across the Web. They claimed Amazon was engaging in "predatory pricing," designed to destroy traditional book publishers. In 2010, five of the largest publishers secretly met with Steve Jobs and Apple. They agreed to a new pricing model called "agency." In the agency model, the distributor is an agent of the publisher, and can be directed to sell e-books at a price determined by the publisher, around $14.99 and higher for certain titles. In return for a 30% commission, Apple agreed to support this model, as did Google, neither of whom were comfortable watching as Amazon dominated one of the hottest areas of Web content sales. In these meetings, publishing executives discussed a common pricing strategy.

The **agency model** temporarily turned the tables on Amazon: it now had to charge whatever price the publishers wanted or the publishers would not sell Amazon any books (they would not choose Amazon as an agent for their products). A result of the agency model was that Amazon prices on e-books rose to the publisher desired levels, and its market share fell to 60% in 2012. Apple, Google, Barnes & Noble, and the five major publishers were delighted. The Justice Department was not delighted: it sued the five publishers and Apple for price fixing in violation of antitrust laws. Three of the publishers settled, but Apple and two publishers have not settled. As a result, Amazon's e-book prices have fallen again to $9.99, and its market share is expected to return towards 90% of the e-book market, raising new concerns about Amazon's dominance of the e-book marketplace. The outcome of this conflict between the largest single e-book retailer (Amazon) and the large publishing houses will shape the future of e-books.

agency model
the retailer is an agent and prices are set by the manufacturer

Interactive Books: Converging Technologies

The future of e-books will also depend in part on changes in the concept of a book. The modern book is not really very different from the first two-facing page, bound books that began to appear in seventeenth-century Europe. The traditional book has a very simple, non-digital operating system: text appears left to right, pages are numbered, there is a front and back cover, and text pages are bound together by stitching or glue. In educational and reference books, there is an alphabetical index in the back of the book that permits direct access to the book's content. While these traditional books will be with us for many years given their portability, ease of use, and flexibility, a parallel new world of interactive e-books is expected to emerge in the next five years. Interactive books combine audio, video, and photography with text, providing the reader with a multimedia experience thought to be more powerful than simply reading a book. In 2012, Apple released iBook Author, an app to help authors create interactive books. Hundreds of children's books are already built as interactive books. In 2012, Apple also introduced iBook Textbooks, a line of interactive textbooks created by several of the largest textbook publishing firms. Some experts believe that traditional print books will be curiosities by 2020.

MAGAZINES REBOUND ON THE TABLET PLATFORM

Magazines in the United States reached their peak circulation in the early 1980s, with more than 40 million people reading some kind of weekly or monthly magazine. Most Americans got their national and international news from the three weekly news magazines, *Time*, *Newsweek*, and *U.S. News and World Report*. The "glossies," as general-interest magazines were known, attracted readers with superb writing, short form articles, and stunning photography brought to life by very high-resolution color printing (Vega, 2012).

Circulation fell after 2000 in part because of the Internet. At first, the Internet and the Web did not have much impact on magazine sales, in part because the PC was no match for the high-resolution, large-format pictures found in, say, *Life* or *Time*. Eventually, as screens improved, as video on the Web became common, and the economics of color publishing changed, magazine circulation began to plummet and advertisers turned their attention to the digital platform on the Web, where readers were increasingly getting their news, general-interest journalism, and photographic accounts of events.

Magazine newsstand sales dropped from 22 million units in 2001 to 11 million in 2011 (Sass, 2011). Yet special-interest, celebrity, homemaking, and automobile magazines remained stable. The largest monthly subscription magazine for several decades was the *AARP* magazine (American Association of Retired Persons), with a paid circulation of over 20 million readers. In the last half of 2011, sales continued a fall of nearly 10% from the previous year. Increasingly, magazine readers were turning to the Internet for celebrity gossip and news, unusual stories, pictures, and video.

Despite the shrinkage of print subscription and newsstand sales, the growth of digital magazine sales has been extraordinary. Almost one-third of the Internet population in the United States (about 74 million people) read magazines online, and digital magazine circulation has doubled in 2012 to 3.29 million copies. More than 35% of tablet computer owners read magazine content once a week (eMarketer, Inc., 2012a). Popular Web sites like Pinterest, an image-collecting site that attracts millions of women, and Facebook, Yahoo, and Twitter, are the largest drivers of traffic to digital magazines (Vega, 2012). The widespread adoption of tablet computers has helped create the "visual Internet," where glossy magazine publishers, who are inherently oriented to richly detailed color photography, can display their works and advertisements to great advantage.

magazine aggregator
a Web site or app that provides subscriptions and sales of many digital magazines

With hundreds of popular online magazines to choose from, magazine aggregators like Zinio and Apple's Newsstand make it possible for customers to find their favorite magazines using a single app. A **magazine aggregator** is a Web site or app that offers users online subscriptions and sales of many digital magazines. See the *Insight On Business* case, *Read All About It: Rival Digital Newsstands Fight.*

INSIGHT ON BUSINESS

READ ALL ABOUT IT: RIVAL DIGITAL NEWSSTANDS FIGHT

Newsstands, the street shop on the corner hawking magazines, newspapers, soda, candy, cigarettes, and chewing gum in the downtowns of major cities, airports, train stations, and malls, are a pillar of magazine sales. In 2011, more than 11 million copies of magazines were sold at newsstands. That's an impressive number, but it's half of what it was in 2001. The other pillar of magazine sales is paid subscriptions. Over 110 million readers have paid subscriptions to magazines, down about 10% from 2001. The most popular subscriber magazine is *AARP The Magazine* (American Assocation of Retired Persons) with 20 million subscribers; the most popular newsstand magazine is *Cosmopolitan*, with 1.6 million monthly sales. Despite declines in magazine advertising dollars and circulation, despite the threatened and actual digital disruption of new digital platforms for news and photos, magazines still attract a huge monthly audience of over 120 million readers. This is an audience worth fighting for—it's a more educated, wealthier, and aspirational audience than television or newspapers attract.

What really made magazines such a popular form of mass communication in the past was high-resolution photography, resulting in stunning, often full-page photos. In addition, magazines had longer, in-depth articles, written by some of the best writers in the business. Personal computer displays didn't stand a chance against color photography available in magazines. But with the introduction of high-resolution tablet computers, connected to an online content store, it was a short hop to the idea of a "digital news-

stand," where high-quality photography and long-form magazine articles could easily be presented and consumed. This short hop has turned into a fight among several start-ups, the owners of the content stores and devices (Apple, Google, and Nook), and the magazine publishers themselves.

In 2012, the largest digital newsstand, Zinio, rose to 13th on the AppData list of the top-grossing apps for iOS devices (iPad and iPhone), and 5th on the list of top-grossing news apps, behind giants like the *New York Times*, *Macworld*, and the *Economist*. Zinio is an online magazine newsstand where users can find 5,000 mostly magazine titles, 2,500 of them exclusive to the platform. Among the available titles are *Rolling Stone, Road & Track, Seventeen*, and the *Economist*. In addition to iOS devices, Zinio is now available on Android devices and Kindle. Zinio has partnerships with nearly all the largest magazine publishers including McGraw-Hill Companies, Wiley, Ziff Davis, Hearst Corporation, and Playboy Enterprises, Inc. The advantage of using Zinio, the company claims, is that a single app provides interface consistency across all the different magazines, and makes it easier for consumers to manage their subscriptions at one site.

Notably absent from Zinio's list is Time Inc., the largest U.S. magazine publisher with titles like *Time, Fortune*, and *People*; Condé Nast; the New York Times Company; and Wall Street Journal/Dow Jones. These publishers have their own proprietary apps available to consumers on the two largest mobile platforms, Apple's iOS and Android tablets and smartphones. Their message is clear: why sell to digital newsstand distributors at a discount when they can sell directly to the

(continued)

consumer using apps available for tablet computers? This works for readers who want to buy single issues (as a traditional newsstand), and pay the same price as they would for the physical magazine. Digital doesn't mean cheap. According to Hearst Publications, readers are willing to pay more for a tablet version than a physical version of its magazine simply because of its greater ease of use, portability, high resolution, and the inclusion of videos in some issues. Hearst aims to sell 1 million copies of its magazines per month in 2012, and currently sells about 600,000 copies a month at the same price as a physical magazine.

Adding to the competition for tablet magazine readers, the five largest publishers have launched their own newsstand called Next Issue Media with some of the most popular magazine titles in the United States, including *Better Homes and Gardens, Condé Nast Traveler, Esquire, Elle, Fortune, Glamour, Parents, People, Popular Mechanics, Real Simple, Sports Illustrated, Time, The New Yorker, Vanity Fair,* and many more. The top five publishers are Condé Nast, Meredith, Hearst, News Corp., and Time. Next Issue has developed a single app where, initially, 32 magazines will be available. For $9.99 per month, readers have unlimited access to 27 monthly and bi-weekly magazines. For $14.99 a month, weeklies such as *Time* and *Sports Illustrated* are available. With Next Issue, and like Hulu in the film industry, the major publishers are building their own digital distribution platform rather than cede the customer relationship

and revenues to start-up intermediaries like Zinio. Apple and Google are another matter.

The third player in the fight for the digital newsstand is the owners of the distribution platform (the tablet), and that means Apple and Google. Each has its own newsstand. Apple's Newsstand organizes magazine and newspaper subscriptions into a single app, provides a point of purchase for new subscriptions on iTunes, and sends the user notices as new issues become available. Google plans a similar service, as does Yahoo. Publishers are wary of Apple because it wants a 30% cut of subscription revenue, and worse, will not allow publishers to send users outside the Apple iOS sandbox to purchase subscriptions. Everything has to be purchased through the iTunes Store, and Apple retains ownership and personal data on the customer. The publishers and Apple are working on a compromise solution. Both need each other: Apple's Newsstand without magazines is a loser, and magazines want to sell digital subscriptions to iTunes' millions of users.

Whether or not digital newsstands can produce enough revenue to overcome the decline in physical magazine sales and advertising is not clear at this time. Yet as tablet computers evolve, and as the publishers and writers take advantage of the unique features of the tablet, the demand for digital magazines will likely increase significantly. The magazine industry suffered significant digital disruption of its traditional print products, but it has found a friend in the mobile platform.

SOURCES: "Hearst Hails the Age of the Tablet, Says Readers Are Willing to Pay More for Tablet Editions," by Doug Drinkwater, *Editor & Publisher*, May 15, 2012; "A Buffet of Magazines on a Tablet," by David Pogue, *New York Times*, April 11, 2012; "Zinio Makes the iPad a Viable Magazine Platform," by Jason O'Grady, ZDNet, April 4, 2012; "Magazine Newsstand Sales Suffered Sharp Falloff in Second Half of 2011," by Tanzina Vega, *New York Times*, February 7, 2012; "For the First Time, the Atlantic's Online Ad Revenue Exceeds Print," by Anna Heim, Thenextweb.com, November 21, 2011.

10.3 THE ONLINE ENTERTAINMENT INDUSTRY

The entertainment industry is generally considered to be composed of four traditional, commercial players and one new arrival: television, radio broadcasting, Hollywood films, music, and video games (the new arrival). **Figure 10.10** illustrates the estimated relative sizes of these commercial entertainment markets as of 2012. By far, the largest entertainment producer is television (broadcast, satellite, and cable), and then motion pictures, followed by music, radio, and video games (both stand-alone and online games). While online, computer, and console games have grown to be larger than film box office revenues, total Hollywood film revenues dwarf the game industry when DVD sales and rentals, licensing, and ancillary products are added.

Along with the other content industries, the entertainment segment is undergoing a transformation brought about by the Internet. Several forces are at work. Accelerated platform development such as the iPhone/iPad video and music platform, other smartphones and tablets, the Amazon music and video platform, not to mention the Netflix streaming platform, have changed consumer preferences and increased demand for music, video, television, and game entertainment delivered over Internet devices whether in subscription or a la carte pay-per-view forms. Other social network platforms are also spurring the delivery of entertainment content to desktop and laptop PCs and smartphones. In 2012, Facebook is attempting to become an important entertainment distribution site. iTunes and other legitimate music subscription services like Pandora, Spotify, and Rhapsody have demonstrated a viable business model where millions of consumers are willing to pay reasonable prices for high-quality content,

FIGURE 10.10 | **THE FIVE MAJOR PLAYERS IN THE ENTERTAINMENT INDUSTRY: 2012 ESTIMATED REVENUES**

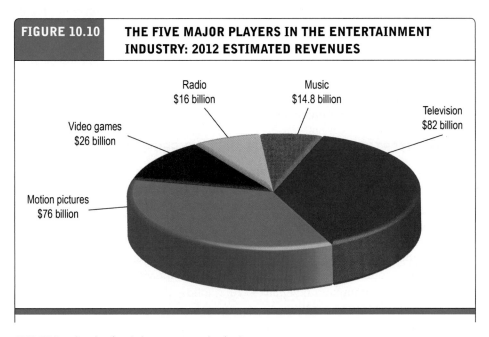

Radio $16 billion
Music $14.8 billion
Video games $26 billion
Television $82 billion
Motion pictures $76 billion

SOURCES: Based on data from industry sources; authors' estimates.

portability, and convenience. The growth in broadband has obviously made possible both wired and wireless delivery of all forms of entertainment over the Internet, potentially displacing cable and broadcast television networks. The development of high-quality customer experiences at online entertainment sites has in many cases eliminated the need for digital rights management restrictions. Closed platforms, like the Kindle, also work to obviate the need for DRM. Subscription services for streaming music and video are inherently copyright-protected because the content is never downloaded to a computer (similar to cable TV). All of these forces have combined in 2012 to bring about a transformation in the entertainment industries.

The ideal Internet content e-commerce world would allow consumers to watch any movie, listen to any music, watch any TV show, and play any game, when they want, where they want, and using whatever Internet device is convenient. Consumers would be billed monthly for these services by a single provider of Internet service. This idealized version of a convergent media world is many years away, but clearly this is the direction of the Internet-enabled entertainment industry.

When we think of the producers of entertainment in the offline world, we tend to think about television networks such as ABC, Fox, NBC, HBO, or CBS; Hollywood film studios such as MGM, Disney, Paramount, and Twentieth Century Fox; and music labels such as Sony BMG, Atlantic Records, Columbia Records, and Warner Records. Interestingly, none of these international brand names have a significant entertainment presence on the Internet. Although traditional forms of entertainment such as television shows and Hollywood movies are just now appearing on the Web, neither the television nor film industries have built an industry-wide delivery system. Instead, they are building alliances with portals like Yahoo, Google, Amazon, Facebook, MSN, and Apple, which has become a very significant player in media distribution.

While industry titans waiver, online consumers are redefining and considerably broadening the concept of entertainment. We refer to this development as "non-traditional" entertainment or what most refer to as user-generated content, which also has entertainment value including user videos uploaded to YouTube, photos uploaded to Photobucket, as well as blogs. User-generated content reflects some of the same shifts in consumer preferences experienced by traditional media: people want to participate in the creation and distribution of content.

ONLINE ENTERTAINMENT AUDIENCE SIZE AND GROWTH

Measuring the size and growth of the Internet content audience is far less precise than measuring a television audience. Recognizing the difficulties of measuring an Internet audience, let's first examine the use of "traditional" entertainment content, such as feature-length movies, music, online TV, online radio, and games; then we will look at non-traditional online entertainment. **Figure 10.11** shows the current and projected growth for commercial online entertainment revenues for the major players: music, Internet radio, online TV, online games, and online video. Music leads the list of commercial entertainment revenues in 2012, followed by online video, online TV, online games, and Internet radio.

There will be some interesting changes by 2015. Video surpasses music as the largest form of online entertainment. Online TV, online games, and radio remain

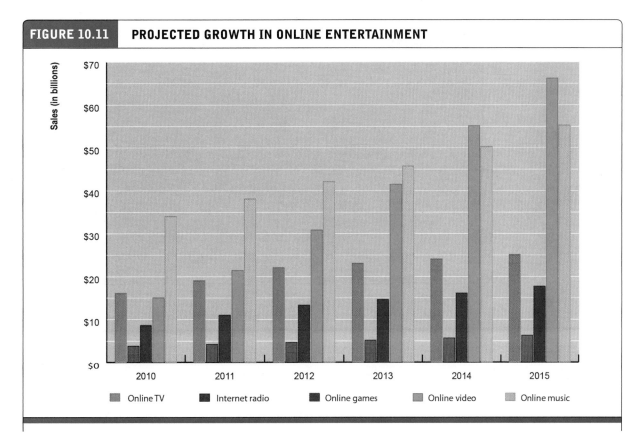

FIGURE 10.11 | **PROJECTED GROWTH IN ONLINE ENTERTAINMENT**

Among commercial forms of mass entertainment, online music downloads engage the largest number of people and generate the largest revenues on the Web in 2012. However, online video and games will grow dramatically in the next four years, with video becoming larger than music in 2015 revenues.

SOURCES: Based on data from industry sources; authors' estimates.

relatively smaller generators of revenue, declining in significance when compared to music and video.

User-Generated Content: Where Does It Fit?

Whereas traditional commercial entertainment is produced by professional entertainers and producers, user-generated entertainment involves all those other activities that people voluntarily engage in to have fun, such as shooting videos, taking pictures, recording music and sharing it, and writing blogs. We have extensively documented the user-generated phenomenon in previous chapters. One question for this chapter is, "How does this content fit into the overall entertainment picture?"

The answer appears to be that user-generated content is both a substitute for as well as a complement to traditional commercial entertainment. As people spend more time consuming user-generated content, one might think they would spend less time consuming commercial content. But this does not seem to be the case. Consumer-generated content seems to increase the acceptance of the Internet as

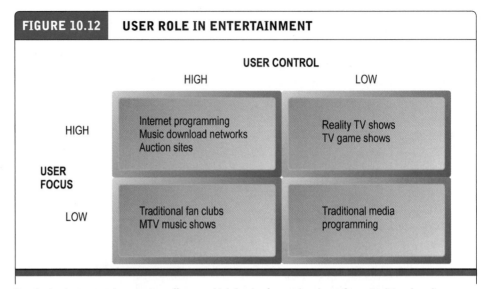

FIGURE 10.12 | **USER ROLE IN ENTERTAINMENT**

USER CONTROL

	HIGH	LOW
HIGH	Internet programming Music download networks Auction sites	Reality TV shows TV game shows
LOW	Traditional fan clubs MTV music shows	Traditional media programming

USER FOCUS

Popular Internet entertainment sites offer users high levels of control and user focus. Traditional media programming content is determined by programmers and has a celebrity focus. Traditional media has moved to become more participatory and more user-focused, but cannot match Internet levels of interactivity and user contribution to content.

a content channel, and consumption of all content seems to expand. **Figure 10.12** characterizes different types of Web entertainment experiences along two dimensions: user focus and user control. Sites that offer nontraditional user-generated forms of entertainment are unique not only because they afford access to large digital archives, promote fine-grained searching, and enable users to create their own archives, but also because they permit users high levels of control over both the program content and the program focus. For example, social network sites like Facebook or Google+ offer user-generated content that is viewed by others as "entertaining." The hypothesis is that sites that offer both high user focus and high user control will have the fastest rates of growth. Facebook is a good example of a site where user control is near absolute, and the focus is highly user centric.

TELEVISION AND PREMIUM VIDEO

In 2012, about 170 million Americans watch video online, about 70% of the Internet population (Nielsen, 2012a). Increasingly, the TV household is a cross-platform phenomenon. Every week, Americans watch about 35 hours of TV on traditional TV sets, but nearly 6 hours using a computer, 2.5 hours watching time-shifted TV using a digital video recorder or cable system with cloud storage, and 7 minutes watching video on a smartphone. While teens continue to spend more time texting than ever, 70% of college students ages 18 to 30 report watching streamed television shows (eMarketer, Inc., 2011a). Netflix is the second largest distributor of premium online video with $3.2 billion in 2012 revenues (half of which come from streaming video), 24 million subscribers, and annual growth at 50%. The largest online video distributor is Apple's iTunes (which provides downloads or cloud storage but not streaming). Netflix is close to exceeding iTunes video revenues.

The television industry, the major source of premium video on the Internet, is beginning a transition to a new delivery platform, the Internet and mobile smart-phones and tablet computers. This transition closely follows an earlier but related transition to digital video recorders and "time-shifting" by consumers who no longer were constrained by television executives' programming and scheduling decisions. The current transition to Internet delivery of television is not leading to a decline in traditional television viewing, which has in fact increased. The new platform is just changing how, when, and where consumers can watch TV. Cloud computing, the storage and streaming of content from large Internet datacenters rather than on individual personal devices, has created a large shift away from ownership of content, and a focus instead on access to content anywhere, anytime, from any device. Social networks have enabled a new kind of "social TV" where consumers share comments while viewing television shows. The most important activity in today's television household may not be what's on screen, but instead what's being said about what's on screen. Television rating agencies today do not have a methodology for measuring this kind of engagement.

Expansion of broadband networks, especially those serving mobile devices such as Wi-Fi and high-speed cellular networks, and the growth of cloud servers, has enabled the growth of a whole new class of television distributors. Cloud distributors, like Apple's iCloud service, allow users to purchase video and movies, store them in iCloud, and view the entertainment from any device, anywhere. Whereas the dominant way consumers obtained a TV signal in the past was from over-the-air broadcasters, cable TV, or satellite distributors, a new "over-the-top" channel has developed led by power-ful technology companies such as Apple, Google, Hulu, VUDU, Netflix, and many others, all of whom offer consumers access to television shows and some full-length feature movies. **Over-the-top (OTT)** entertainment services refers to the use of the Internet to deliver online entertainment services to the home. "Over-the-top" refers to the fact that the entertainment service rides "on top" of other network services like cable TV and telephone service. It's as if we have a new Internet Broadcasting System with many new players. This new network is obviously a threat to cable television and the other distributors, who, in turn, have their on-demand services for television series and movies. In addition, the leaders in the new Internet-based networks are at odds with the content producers over how the content-generated revenues are divided. In some cases, the new distributors like Apple are so powerful, they can dictate the terms. When content producers want to charge very high prices, Apple, Google, and others, including Hulu, have begun to get into the content production business by creating their own TV shows. The marketplace is very fluid, and filled with conflicts.

The largest content provider in the United States, and most of the world, is televi-sion. In terms of audience size, ad revenue generated, and hours watched per day, the biggest screen in the house dominates the entertainment landscape in all countries. While the print industries struggle to attract customers to their traditional products, and the music industry struggles to generate revenues from streaming and down-loaded music tracks, the television industry faces a nearly insatiable demand for its

over-the-top (OTT)
use of the Internet to deliver entertainment services to the home on cable TV or FiOS networks

traditional products—sports, drama, and news—on both traditional platforms and the new Internet platforms.

While the Internet has not diminished TV viewing, it has transformed how, when, and where TV shows are watched. Alongside traditional television viewing, and the traditional "TV household," is a whole new "digital household" with broadband connections to the Internet, and new mobile viewing devices: the smartphone, tablet, and game console. (Carr, 2011). While TV might be the biggest screen in the house, it has to compete or share with other digital devices. Increasingly, the television industry is providing high-quality content in the form of older versions of television series and some sporting events. These three factors—broadband penetration, new mobile platforms, and a willing industry that wants to monetize its library of high-quality content—are the leading factors in changing the television industry.

The Internet and the new mobile platform have also changed the viewing experience. The best screen when commuting or traveling is the smartphone and tablet. More importantly, Internet-enabled social networks like Facebook and Twitter have made TV viewing a social experience shared among neighbors, friends, and colleagues. In the past, television was often a social event involving family and friends in the same room watching a single TV show. In 2012, the social circle has expanded to include Facebook and Twitter friends in different locations, changing television from a "lean back and enjoy" experience into a "lean forward and engage" experience. Reality television shows encourage viewers to tweet while watching, and run a scrolling bar of viewer tweets. About 20% of viewers start watching a TV show after hearing about it on a social network. TV viewers are multitasking: co-viewing shows while texting, commenting, and chatting on line while the show unfolds. Around 32% of Internet users will use social media while watching TV, and this jumps to 64% for users who own smartphones and tablets (eMarketer, Inc., 2012c). Nearly 60% are watching TV show clips on social networks.

While the Internet so far has had an expansive and positive impact on the television industry, challenges lie ahead. The largest providers of television in virtually all countries are cable television systems that charge consumers a monthly service fee for providing service, often accompanied by Internet and/or telephone service. This service in the United States costs, on average, about $125 per month per household. Cable systems also generate advertising revenues from local and national advertisers. The revenues generated are used to maintain the physical cable network, and pay program producers (often called "cable networks") for their content. For instance, HBO (Home Box Office network) creates a variety of television shows for the nearly 11,000 local cable systems in the United States, and collects fees from the local cable systems and their subscribers. ESPN, the largest sports network on TV and the Internet, charges local and national cable systems per viewer fees. But with so much video available online for "free," many users are thinking about "cutting the cable cord" and just relying on the Internet for their video entertainment. Other viewers are "cord shavers," who have reduced their subscriptions to digital channels. Likewise, the improvement in over-the-air digital broadcasting of television signals has resulted in a slight increase in over-the-air viewers (about 15% of all television viewers). So far, cord cutting and shaving has been very limited, but the high service fees for cable television service, and expanding Internet capabilities, suggest the future of traditional cable systems, and their ungainly set-top boxes, may be challenged.

One response of the television production industry has been to set up their own online streaming services, the most popular of which is Hulu. Hulu is a joint venture of the Walt Disney Company, the News Corporation's Fox Broadcasting unit, Comcast's NBC Universal unit, and Providence Equity Partners. The original idea was that the movie and television studios would develop their own streaming and downloading service to counter the growth of online leaders like Apple, Netflix, and Amazon. The original plan called for advertising-supported "free content." While it has had its ups and downs, today Hulu has 38 million monthly visitors, and 2 million subscribers to its $8 a month subscription. The industry owners of Hulu have prevented it from developing a strong movie collection, and focused instead on selling access to dated television series. Despite funding Hulu, the television industry founders have prevented Hulu from showing current television series, limiting selection to older out-of-date series and shows, out of fear that consumers would never sign up for cable TV to see the newest shows (Schechner, 2012). Lacking current content, in 2012, Hulu began selling several self-produced television series, making it appear more like a traditional cable TV network (Cheney, 2012). Wall Street analysts believe Hulu has a confusing business model with conflicting interests. Other Internet distributors such as Apple, Google, and Netflix have all indicated they will begin producing their own "television" content for exclusive distribution on the Internet, as a way to obtain low-cost, current content.

MOVIES

The Hollywood movie industry is going through a difficult transition from a reliance on DVDs, its primary revenue generator over the last decade, to a new marketplace where consumers want to watch videos on their PCs, tablet computers, and their smartphones. Americans spent more money on online videos (both streaming and purchased films) than they did on DVDs. Consumers are expected to download or stream 3.4 billion movies in 2012, versus renting or purchasing 2.4 billion DVDs (IHS iSuppli, 2012a). A little over 60 million Americans watch movies online in 2012 (see **Figure 10.13** on page 682). Consumers increasingly want access to cloud-stored movies rather than downloading entire movies to their devices. There are many parallels with the television industry: a very rapid growth in the mobile platform, expansion of cloud computing to support instant streaming of movies, and a change in consumer behavior in which movie viewing becomes both more individualized (watch whatever you want on your phone) and more social (let's text as we watch the movie). Both the television and movie industries are concentrated oligopolies with little competition. Pundits may write about the "indie" television movement, along with indie films built for the Internet, and the hundreds of millions of non-premium movies on YouTube. But these sub-premium efforts produce sub-premium revenues or no revenues at all.

While the movie box office attendance in 2011 hit a 16-year low, and DVD sales continued to drop, Hollywood is nevertheless weathering the digital onslaught far better than the music industry. Hollywood has a potent weapon in its corner: no one goes online to see zeroes and ones. Instead, they go to online entertainment sites to be happy, sad, awed, romantically stimulated, or agitated. The future of online movies is

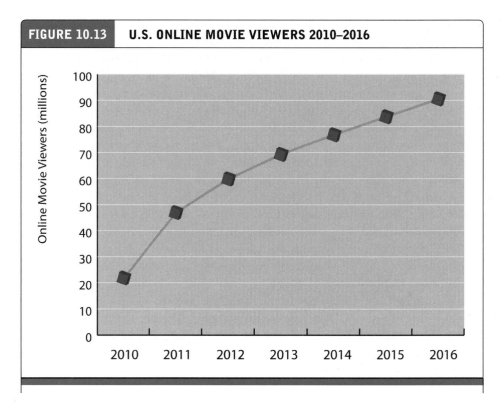

FIGURE 10.13 U.S. ONLINE MOVIE VIEWERS 2010–2016

SOURCE: Based on data from eMarketer, Inc., 2012d.

very bright: it is expected to rise continuously worldwide through 2016 (IHS, 2012b). Hollywood has few competitors. Also, movies are far larger than music tracks and much more difficult to illegally download and move around the Web without detection. And unlike the music labels, who allowed a single distributor (Apple iTunes) to dominate online sales, the movie producers have Apple, Google (YouTube), Amazon, Netflix, Hulu, VUDU, and others competing for distribution rights.

Major studios and production groups in Hollywood and New York still dominate profit-making movie and television content production. But the movie industry faces a more challenging environment than television because, unlike TV, it heavily depended for several decades on physical DVDs, which are rapidly losing favor with consumers who want to watch movies they can download or stream on any of several digital devices. DVD sales were cut in half from 2006 to 2011.

In 2012, for the first time, consumers will view more and pay more for Web-based movie downloads, rentals, and streams than for DVDs or related physical products (eMarketer, Inc., 2012e). As with television, the demand for feature-length Hollywood movies appears to be expanding in part because of the growth of smartphones and tablets. In addition, the surprising resurgence of music videos, led by VEVO, is attracting millions of younger viewers on smartphones and tablets. Online movies began a growth spurt in 2010 as broadband services spread throughout the country. In 2011, online movie viewing doubled in a single year. In 2012, about 60 million Internet users are expected to view movies, about one-third of the adult Internet audience. Online movie viewing is growing faster than all video viewing (which includes TV shows) (IHS iSuppli, 2012a; eMarketer, Inc., 2011b).

The size of the online movie business is difficult to ascertain because TV show rentals and premium video are often lumped together. Nevertheless, industry observers estimate the total online movie market at about $1 billion in 2012. To put this in perspective, the total annual revenues of Hollywood studios when all revenue streams are combined is about $70 billion. So at this point, the Internet and online distribution is a tiny part of the overall picture, but one that is growing very rapidly. Netflix is the largest Internet video distributor (44% of online video and movie revenues) by far, followed by Apple, and a then host of smaller services (IHS iSuppli, 2012b) (see **Figure 10.14**).

There are three kinds of online movie sales: subscription video on demand (SVOD) as offered by firms like Netflix ($454 million); transactional video on-demand (TVOD), which is the a la carte download of movies as provided by iTunes ($273 million); and electronic sell-through (streaming video on demand) ($236 million). Total online movie revenues doubled from 2010 to 2011. The fastest growing segment is SVOD (up triple digits), followed by TVOD (up 75%), and streaming video on demand (up 2.5%). Netflix has the largest market share, relying largely on older libraries of movies, and Apple has the second largest market share, relying largely on recent releases (IHS iSuppli, 2012c). Netflix has an estimated 24 million subscribers in the United States,

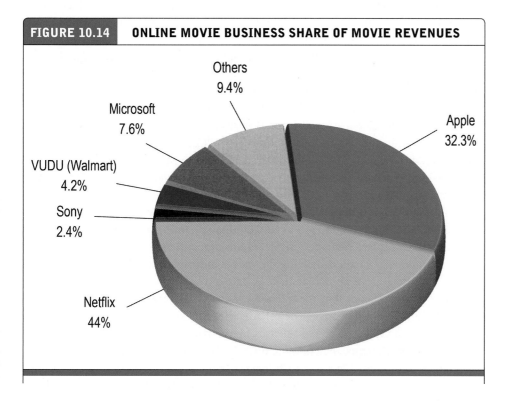

FIGURE 10.14 — **ONLINE MOVIE BUSINESS SHARE OF MOVIE REVENUES**

Others
9.4%

Microsoft
7.6%

VUDU (Walmart)
4.2%

Sony
2.4%

Apple
32.3%

Netflix
44%

SOURCE: Based on data from IHS iSuppli, 2012.

and a library of an estimated 50,000 films. However, in 2012, several thousand popular movies disappeared from the Netflix catalog because its contract with a major movie producer, Starz Premium Cable, expired. With growing difficulty obtaining recent premium movie titles from Hollywood studios, Netflix is increasingly dependent on re-runs of older television serials and shows.

The online movie industry is a complex web of competing forces with conflicting interests. The existing Hollywood movie industry, which creates the products that produce the revenues, is threatened by the piracy of its products, loss of control over its traditional and very profitable distribution channels (largely movie theaters, television networks, and retailers of its DVD products), and the growth of powerful technology players such as Apple, Google, and Amazon, who own online movie stores and also sell the physical devices used to watch movies.

The movie industry estimates that it loses over $5 billion a year in pirated movies copied from DVDs, early production copies, and in-theater videoing. But video piracy appears not to be growing. A Google research paper found that searches for pirated movies peaked in 2008, and have been dropping steadily, while searches for online rentals and streaming are up (Google, 2011). Insofar as searches are an indicator of consumer interest and intent, the public interest in pirated movies is declining rapidly. A recent academic study found no evidence that U.S. box office receipts since 2003 have been negatively impacted by BitTorrent (a popular protocol for peer-to-peer sharing of copyrighted materials), and that international piracy increases when Hollywood studios delay release of films in foreign countries (Danaher and Waldfogel, 2012).

However, the estimated losses due to piracy pale in comparison to the fall in DVD sales: in 2008, DVD sales of physical units were $10 billion, and by 2012 are estimated to be less than $4 billion. The DVD format is rapidly declining just as the digital rental, digital download-and-own, streaming, and video-on-demand markets show striking growth. Netflix is estimated to have 28.5 million customers in 2012, the majority of which stream movies and television. Digital streaming grew to $1 billion in sales in 2011 (about a 20% increase), and sales of movies through digital download services like Apple's iTunes rose 9% to $554 million (DEG, 2012). The download movie market is dominated by Apple (65%), Microsoft's Zune Video Marketplace, and Walmart's VUDU, where you can rent a movie for as little as $3.99 or purchase a digital downloaded copy for $14 to $16.

Hollywood studios depended heavily on DVD sales: they made an estimated $5 on each DVD sold at retail for $15 to $20. Online streaming and download sales and rentals produce far less revenue for the studios, depending on the timing and distribution channel. The challenge facing the movie industry is to rapidly find a replacement for the decline in DVD revenues. A part of the answer lies in maximizing its revenues by strictly controlling the "release windows" of movies despite pressures from online distributors for a change. The release windows system devised by Hollywood in the 1980s is a system of timed releases of a movie to distributors with the aim of maximizing film revenues by charging different audiences different prices based on the recency of the film. This is classic market segmentation. Typically, a new film is released to movie theaters first, where the most film-conscious customers are willing to pay a premium price for the newest films. This first window is usually four months. Next, the film is released to the DVD distribution chain, which could include Amazon, Walmart, and rental firms for a period of four months. Eight months after a film first appears, it is released to the pay television and cable systems, which provide video on-demand services to consumers for in-home viewing. This period varies, but generally lasts for another 4 months. A year after a new film appears, it begins to filter into less lucrative distribution chains like broadcast television (less popular films appear within a year) and, finally, Internet streaming services. At each point in the release windows system, the revenue generated per viewer declines. The Internet streaming and download window is the least profitable movie sale—around $4.00—of which the distributor (Apple, Amazon, VUDU, and others) takes about 30%.

If you've ever wondered why your favorite movie sites do not have recent hit movies, it's because the films are intentionally not available to the Internet market. Hollywood studios are not enthused about releasing films on the Internet and displacing sales of DVDs, box office revenues, or cable video-on-demand channels. The absence of current movies on services like Netflix is forcing the Internet distributors to focus on out-of-date television series. Ironically, this places a premium on pirated versions of recent movies. In 2012, several studios are experimenting with streamlining their traditional release windows and providing movies to Internet distributors within two months of release. Online engagement with movies is extremely high, and search engines record a growing interest in online movies, and a declining interest in DVDs.

In 2012, the movie and Internet industries are both cooperative and competitive, with an explosion in alliances and agreements, many at cross purposes with one another. In 2012, Apple, the leading digital-movie downloading site, reached an agreement with five movie studios that allows consumers to buy their films on Apple's iTunes Store on one Apple device, store them on Apple's iCloud movie service, and then watch the same film on any Apple device (Vascellaro, et al., 2012). The revenue split was not announced but movie studios much prefer users to own movies rather than rent because ownership generates more revenue. Meanwhile, 70 movie studios spent three years coming up with a cyberlocker service called UltraViolet that performs many of the same functions as iCloud. **UltraViolet** is a proof-of-purchase system where users enter a code into their UltraViolet online account attached to purchased DVDs, or online-purchased movies, which gives them access to that movie from any device, including Android and Apple smartphones. Walmart is offering its customers in-store assistance in setting up UltraViolet accounts, and storing their DVDs in the cloud (Kung, 2012). Most video services use an a la carte business model where consumers pay for each movie, although some of the largest streaming services such as Netflix use subscription models where users pay a flat fee for access to movies.

UltraViolet
movie industry proof of DVD purchase program that allows playback of DVDs to any digital device

MUSIC

In 2012, the online radio audience reached over 100 million listeners in the United States, four times larger than in 2002. Online radio consists of AM/FM station streams, and Internet pure-play programming from firms like Pandora, Spotify, and Songza. The growth of online radio provides a large opportunity for music labels and artists, while at the same time threatening their very existence because online streaming digital revenues are so much smaller than the CD-driven revenues, or broadcast station ad revenues in the past.

In 2011, the top-selling CD album was Adele's *21* with more than 5.8 million units sold. It was also the top-selling digital download album, with 1.8 million units sold. Both were a record in terms of sales for any album since 2004. After 12 years of bad digital news, with some predicting the record industry would collapse and albums were dead, the music industry is staging a steady comeback from the abyss created by new technology, and, in part, its own obstinacy.

More than any of the other content industries, the recorded music industry has suffered the most from the onslaught of digital devices and Internet distribution. For most of its history, the music industry depended on a variety of physical media to distribute music--acetate records, vinyl recordings, cassette tapes, and finally CD-ROMs. At the core of its revenue was a physical product. Since the 1950s, that physical product was an album—a collection of bundled songs that sold for a much higher price than singles. The Internet changed all that when, in 2000, a music service called Napster begin distributing pirated music tracks over the Internet to consumers using their PCs as record players. Despite the collapse of Napster due to legal challenges, hundreds of other illegal sites showed up, resulting in music industry revenues falling from $14 billion in 1999 to an estimated $5.4 billion in 2012. The appearance of powerful mobile media players beginning in 2001 that could be connected to the Internet, like Apple's iPod, iPhone, and iPad, further eroded sales of CD albums. With the growth of cloud computing and cloud-based music services, by 2012, the very concept of "owning" music has begun to shift instead to "access" to music from any device, anywhere.

The music industry initially resisted the development of legal digital channels of distribution, but ultimately and reluctantly struck deals with Apple's new iTunes Store in 2003, as well as with several small subscription music services, for online distribution. Nevertheless, revenues from the sales of digital downloads of individual songs from iTunes selling for 99 cents paled in comparison to revenues produced by CD albums selling for $15. Internet downloads of individual songs, which unbundled the album, decimated revenues as users created their own collections of songs. Despite the growth of Amazon, Walmart, and other online retailers of CDs, consumers increasingly shifted to digital downloads and, more recently, streams.

In 2011, for the first time in history, revenue from digital downloads and streams accounted for a majority (52%) of industry revenues. While the industry makes about 32 cents from a downloaded song, it makes less than a penny (about .63 of a penny) on a streamed version of the same song. This revenue is split with the artists who receive .32 of a penny. *Rolling Stone* calculated that a very popular song selling one million streams would produce revenue of $3,166 for the artist and a similar amount for the music label.

Yet in 2012, the outlook for the music industry is cautiously optimistic. It's a different industry from what it was, no longer totally dependent on highly profitable physical products, less able to sell bundled music as albums, but with a rapidly growing demand for its high-quality, popular products from a variety of Internet distributors who are competing with one another to buy musical content. The explosive growth in smartphones and tablets has further driven demand for cloud-based streaming music

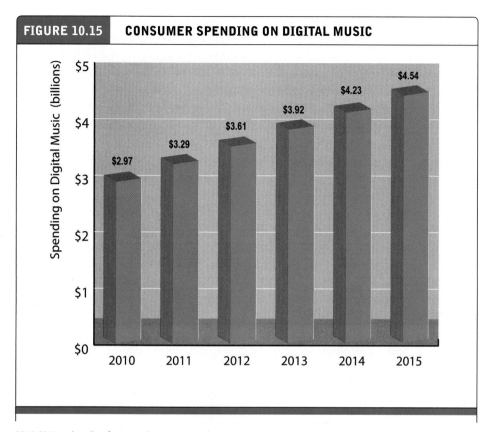

FIGURE 10.15 CONSUMER SPENDING ON DIGITAL MUSIC

SOURCE: Based on data from eMarketer, Inc., 2012f.

access. Online music monthly listening hours in the United States have doubled from 606 million in 2009 to 1,301 million in 2011, according to AccuStream Research. **Figure 10.15** shows consumer spending on digital music (both downloads and streams), which is expected to reach $4.54 billion in 2015, up from $3.61 billion in 2012 (IFPI, 2012; eMarketer, Inc., 2012f).

While the music industry's initial digital model involved downloading of songs from iTunes today, the fastest growth in digital music is streaming from cloud-based services. The streaming services (sometimes referred to as "Internet radio") provide cloud-based access from any device, personalized broadcasting through user-curation and selection, file storage, and social sharing by connecting to social networks. In 2012, online music streams reached nearly 500 million per week, up from 242 million in 2011, doubling in a single year. In contrast, in 2012, weekly sales of digital tracks as downloads only rose to 27 million from 22 million a year earlier (Nielsen Broadcast Data Systems, 2012).

The most popular streaming services are Amazon (Cloud Player), Apple (iTunes Match), Google (Google Play), iHeartRadio, Last.fm, MOGH, Pandora, Rdio, Slacker, and Spotify. Streaming music services are currently growing at nearly 100% annually although this is expected to slow. For instance, Pandora's revenues in 2012 are expected to be $274 million, up from $137 million in 2011 (eMarketer, Inc., 2012f). Next to iTunes, Pandora's is the second largest music service with over 150 million subscribers in 2012.

The streaming services use a variety of different business models: ad-supported, subscription fees, and device sales. Internet radio streaming services like Pandora and Spotify make over 85% of their revenue from advertisements, mostly to music sites where consumers can purchase CDs or downloads. In return for free but limited music, users agree to be exposed to ads. Less than 15% of revenues come from subscription fees for premium services. Amazon, Apple, and Google are not interested in music as a source of revenue, but rather in the sale of physical devices (from Kindles, to smartphones and tablets) which have much higher profit margins. Their operations with respect to music are break-even.

It is unclear if streaming of music is a viable business model for the recorded music industry. Clearly the revenues produced from streaming are tiny when compared to digital downloads or sales of CD albums. The only way streaming services generate revenue for record labels is by exposing consumers to music on free streaming services, and hoping some consumers purchase the music either as a CD or digital download, perhaps even a downloaded album. There is some evidence this is happening. Digital revenues grew by 8% globally in 2011 to $5.2 billion. In the United States, digital music sales are larger than CD sales (50% of all music purchased), digital tracks are up 8.4%, and digital album sales are up 20% to 103 million albums (Nielsen, 2012b). The album is not dead, yet.

GAMES

No Internet media content form has grown as explosively as online games. Well over 100 million Internet users play some kind of game online in the United States, and that number swells to over 300 million worldwide (Wakabayachi, 2012). There are four types of Internet gamers. Casual gamers play games on a PC or laptop computer. Social gamers play games using a Web browser on a social network like Facebook. Mobile gamers play games using their smartphones or tablet computers. Console gamers play games online (or offline) using a console like Xbox, PlayStation, or Wii. Often, console gamers are connected over the Internet to enable group play. **Figure 10-16** illustrates the relative size of these four online gaming audiences and their future growth prospects. Because people play games in a variety of different venues, the total number of online gamers is on the order of 105 million, about 40% of all Internet users. Estimates vary, but in 2012, industry analysts peg annual sales of console games (hardware and software) at around $17.5 billion, and sales of subscriptions, virtual goods, and services on social, mobile, and casual gaming platforms at around $8 billion. The most widely played mobile casual game is *Angry Birds*. In *Angry Birds,* players launch birds at green pigs hiding inside buildings using a sling shot to blast away the pig and the building. As mindless as this sounds, *Angry Birds* has been downloaded more than 700 million times by 2012 (Anderson, 2012).

Clearly, the fastest growing gaming venue is the mobile smartphone market, which is growing 26% in 2012. The smallest audience, and slowest growing, is the console games venue. Social and casual gaming—often lumped together in a single number—is growing at 10% in 2012, but is expected to slow over time to about 5% in 2016.

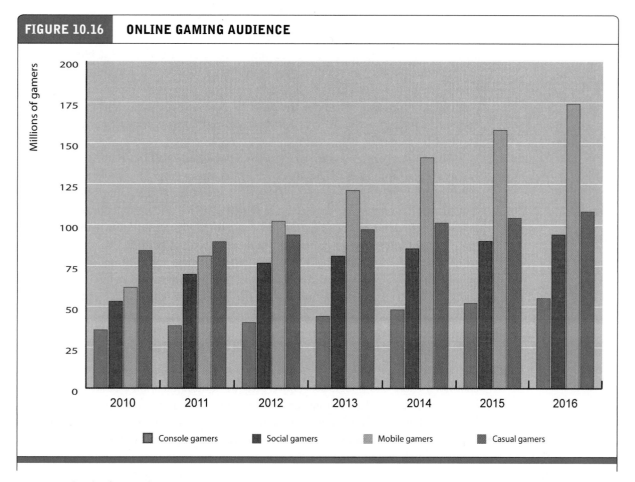

FIGURE 10.16 | **ONLINE GAMING AUDIENCE**

SOURCE: Based on data from eMarketer, Inc., 2012g.

Social gaming on sites like Facebook grew very rapidly in 2010–2012 in large part due to the success of Zynga games like *Farmville, CityVille,* and *Words With Friends.* Online social gaming enlarged the demographic of gamers to include women and older people, compared to console gamers who tend to be young and male. But like other game platforms, consumers tire of current games and are attracted to the latest market entrants. Users of various Zynga "ville" games have fallen in 2012 by up to 35%. Mobile gamers are the largest segment of the online gaming audience. There will be more than 100 million mobile gamers in 2012. These games are sometimes social, but more often focus on individual performance of short duration. The possibilities of selling virtual goods or displaying ads on these mobile games is very limited. Levels of engagement are low (eMarketer, Inc., 2012g).

The number of console gamers, about 40 million in 2012, has leveled off in recent years. In part this is due to the age of the platforms. The Xbox, PlayStation, and Wii are old, have not been able to expand much beyond the young male demographic, and the games typically have large initial sales that wane quickly. The exception is the Wii platform with its wireless remote that senses the user's direction and acceleration. Wii was the largest selling console in the first few years of its introduction after 2007, and appeals to a much broader family demographic. But Wii sales have slowed considerably in recent years, and the excitement surrounding the motion sensing remote has waned. In 2012, about 12 million game consoles will be sold according to industry estimates. In 2012, sales of console game software and hardware are down 8% over 2011, in part because of the rapid growth of casual, social, and mobile games.

While casual and social gaming rapidly grows, nearly all these online and mobile games are free and users do not stay in the games very long. These two features make it difficult for gaming firms to monetize their user base by showing advertisements and charging for services. The business model of social and casual gaming is still not settled. Marketers have just recently begun to build video marketing campaigns that increase a brand's engagement and interaction with customers who are playing at social mobile gaming sites (Olsen, 2012). Zynga has chosen a different route to profits by relying the sales of virtual goods to its customers with mixed results. For a discussion of Zynga's struggle to define a workable business model, see the chapter ending case, *Zynga Bets on Online Games*.

THE ONLINE ENTERTAINMENT INDUSTRY STRUCTURE

The most likely development in industry structure will be the movement of Internet channel owners like Google and Apple into the content creation business. By creating their own content, distributors can reduce their costs of content and develop entertainment that is uniquely suited to the Internet, not just copies of the Hollywood and television styles of content. The existing online entertainment industry value chain is highly inefficient and fractured. For the entertainment industry to survive and prosper on the Web, there needs to be a reorganization of the value chain either through corporate mergers, strategic alliances, or both. In the process of reorganization, traditional distributors (like cable TV and broadcast television) most likely will experience severe disruptions to their business models as Internet power houses like Google, Apple, and Amazon replace them as a distribution media for video and movies.

Figure 10.17 illustrates the existing players and industry value chain and three alternative arrangements. The entertainment industry has never been a neat and tidy industry to describe. There are many players and forces—including government regulators and courts—that shape the industry. In the existing model, creators of entertainment such as music labels or television producers sell to distributors, who in turn sell to local retail stores or local television stations, who then sell or rent to consumers.

In the film industry, court decisions in the 1930s and 1940s forced production studios to give up ownership of local theaters on antitrust grounds, fearing the large Hollywood production studios would monopolize the film industry. One possible alternative to this fractionated industry is the content owner direct model. The Internet offers entertainment content producers (the music labels, Hollywood studios, and television content producers) the opportunity to dominate the industry value chain by eliminating the distributors and retailers and selling directly to the consumer. This

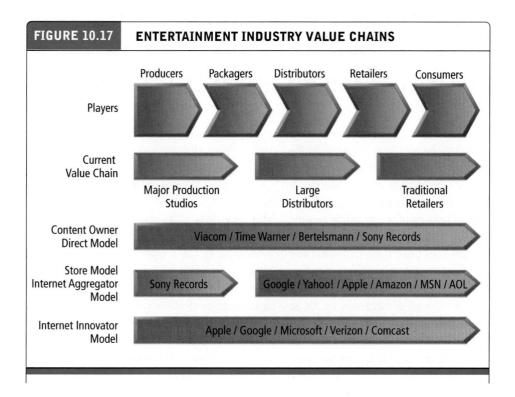

FIGURE 10.17 | **ENTERTAINMENT INDUSTRY VALUE CHAINS**

has not yet been a successful model to date because the content producers have not independently developed large Internet audiences and have not been successful on the Internet. A second possibility is the Internet aggregator model. In this model, Web-based intermediaries such as Yahoo, Google, Amazon, and MSN that aggregate large audiences enter into strategic alliances with content owners to provide content to the aggregators.

A third possible model is the Internet innovator model, in which successful Internet technology companies that develop the technology platforms (such as Apple, Google, Facebook, and Amazon, as well as Internet communications platform providers like Verizon and Comcast) move back into the value chain and begin creating their own content for exclusive distribution on their proprietary platform or channels. So far, Internet distributors have not chosen this path, but they might if the content owners refused to license their works on favorable terms for online distribution.

Insight on Technology: Hollywood and the Internet: Let's Cut a Deal describes how Hollywood studios and Internet distributors are cutting deals to provide more video and movie content online.

INSIGHT ON TECHNOLOGY

HOLLYWOOD AND THE INTERNET: LET'S CUT A DEAL

In tough times, real people go to the movies. All things considered, 2011 was an acceptable year for the movie industry. Despite the continuing effects of the recession, or because of it, box office receipts were $10.2 billion in North America, down only 4% from the previous year. However, global box office sales were up to $32 billion in 2011, a record, and 3% higher than the previous year. The number of films released in 2011 was up 7% to 607 new films. And Internet sales, rentals, and movie subscriptions exploded, and are estimated to be about $1 billion in 2012. By any measure, the Hollywood money machine has been transformed by the Internet. But, unlike the music business, it has not been substantially disrupted. Hollywood is still in control of its fate.

The year also boasted the continuing success of the highest-grossing movies of all time. *Avatar* (2009) grossed over $3 billion in global box office receipts by the end of the year. *Avatar*'s budget was estimated at $300 million. Continuing sales of DVDs, and revenues from online streaming services and sales at the iTunes Store, drove revenues for even older movies. The second highest grossing movie, *Titanic*, hit $2 billion in revenue in 2011 since its release in 1997. More recent blockbusters include the *Avengers* (2012), generating $1.5 billion, and *Harry Potter and the Deathly Hallows—Part 2* (2011), generating $1.3 billion. If only all movies could produce results like these, Hollywood would be golden again. One impact of the Internet on Hollywood revenues is that consumers can easily and inexpensively watch older movies that they did not see or that they want to revisit years after their release. The Internet is making Hollywood's backlist much more valuable.

But all is not well in Tinseltown. Once movies are shown in theaters, where Hollywood generates only 20% of its revenue, they move on to less-profitable venues, from DVDs (which are very profitable) to cable television video-on-demand services, and then to Internet distributors like Netflix and Apple for either purchase, rental downloads, or streaming. Eventually, movies end up with broadcast television stations years after they were released. This "release window" differs for various films based on the studio's estimate of the revenue potential for each film. A very popular film will be delayed all along the release window.

Hollywood is facing several problems moving forward to a world where most people will be watching movies on the Internet, either at home, or on the go, using tablet computers and smartphones. One problem is that the fastest growing segment of its business, the Internet, is also the least profitable. A second problem is that Hollywood does not control its own Internet distribution network, but instead is forced to rely on the likes of Netflix, Apple, Amazon, and Google, each of whom attract large online audiences. Likewise, the big Internet distributors face a content problem: they cannot attract large audiences without recently made movies. Old movies and movie libraries on Netflix have a limited appeal, and consumers are looking for the latest releases.

Initially, Hollywood was highly dependent on Amazon's sales of DVDs as physical rental stores declined. At one point, iTunes was the largest downloading service of movies a la carte (so-called electronic sell through, or EST). In 2012,

(continued)

things changed. Multiple buyers of movies have appeared, not just Amazon or iTunes. Google is developing its own home TV device (like Apple's iTV) that may be a platform for movie streaming.

Netflix continues to dominate online movie revenues, with a 44% market share compared to Apple at 32%. At one time, Apple had a 70% share of Internet movie revenue, and Hollywood studios feared Apple would be able to dominate Internet distribution and dictate prices. Now with Netflix dominating the streaming market, Hollywood fears it will be forced to sell its product for a pittance compared to DVD prices. For this reason, Hollywood has been restricting the release of movies to Netflix, doling out access to recent movies very carefully.

More and more large firms are entering the streaming market, and competing with one another for Hollywood movies, and driving up prices. Google is expanding its movie service beyond rentals to include sales of digital movies; Walmart's VUDU, and Best Buy's CinemaNow are promoting their movie rentals and sales. VUDU cut a deal with several major studios to supply rentals of movies on the same day they are released on DVDs, months before they become available on Netflix. Amazon is seeking to strike deals with the studios for digital a la carte purchases and streaming of recent movies. In 2012, Amazon struck a deal with Viacom to purchase TV episodes and movies to stock its forthcoming streaming service.

In late 2011, Google's YouTube announced the expansion of its movie rental service by adding 3,000 new films. YouTube finally signed deals with the major Hollywood studios including Warner Brothers, Sony, Universal, and Lionsgate. Most movies will be priced at $2.99. No subscriptions are required, it's a la carte. Hello Netflix and Hulu! In addition, Google is spending $100 million in 2011 to produce its own content,

making deals with Hollywood and New York production companies as a way to avoid hefty commissions paid to these same studios for their content. Imagine, "The Google Comedy Hour!"

One result of all this competition for Hollywood content is rising prices paid by the distributors, and a feeling in Hollywood that they can maintain some semblance of control over their fate, unlike the music industry. In fact, the prices being paid by Netflix and others exceed those paid by cable television video-on-demand services. For instance, Netflix cut a multi-year deal with the Weinstein Company for exclusive display of *The Artist* (an Academy Award–winning movie), and other films, before the films are released to leading pay-TV channels. The estimated size of this deal is over $200 million. Dreamworks, a Hollywood studio, has signed a deal with Netflix for exclusive access to films for $30 million a movie. Netflix will be spending nearly $2 billion in 2012 for content to stream to its 24 million subscribers. As a result, its profits have fallen significantly in 2012, and its share price has tanked from $250 in 2011 to $60 in 2012. Netflix may be the leading online movie site now, but it may be the equivalent of Blockbuster video stores in a few years.

The movie industry itself has launched a new movie service that would possibly give new life to DVDs. The new service is called UltraViolet. Designed to cut down on piracy, and make it possible for consumers to watch their movies on multiple devices, customers will purchase DVDs in retail stores and register the DVD serial number at the same time on the UltraViolet service. Once registered, consumers can watch a digital version of their movies stored on Walmart cloud servers streamed to their smartphones, tablets, or PCs. Apple's iCloud movie service avoids DVDs altogether. Can you imagine Steve Jobs wanting to

(continued)

preserve DVDs? iCloud offers a cyberlocker that allows consumers to purchase digital movies at iTunes and play them on other Apple devices, including Macs. Apple has struck deals with five major studios (Lionsgate, Sony Pictures, Walt Disney, Paramount, and Warner Brothers).

In the end, Hollywood and the Internet need each other, and the only question is how to find the price, define the terms of trade, and cut a deal where both parties come out winners. The flurry of deals in 2012 bodes well for consumers, and probably for both Internet distributors and Hollywood studios. Consumers are finding multiple services that will allow them to watch movies on whatever device is convenient, and move from one device to another with a lot less effort than in the past. Given the shift of eyeballs to online entertainment, Hollywood is expanding its audience while taking a haircut on pricing. With lots of Internet distributors competing, Hollywood gains in power from the competition among alternative distributors. And Internet companies are coming up with even more reasons why consumers should forget about cable TV and watch the Internet, which means more ad revenues for Internet distributors. How all these calculations will work out remains to be determined. Tune in next year on the same channel.

SOURCES: "Netflix Passes Apple to Take Lead in Online Movie Business," by Dan Graziano, BGR.com, June 6, 2012; "Hollywood Studios Warm to Apple's iCloud Effort," by Jessica Vascellaro and Erica Ordern, *Wall Street Journal,* March 12, 2012; "Theatrical Market Statistics," Motion Picture Industry Association, March 2012; "Walmart to Give Hollywood a Hand," by Michelle Kung, *Wall Street Journal,* February 28, 2012; "Web Deals Cheer Hollywood, Despite Drop in Moviegoers," by Brooks Barnes, *New York Times,* February 24, 2012; Netflix Secures Streaming Deal With DreamWorks," by Brooks Barnes and Brian Stelter, *New York Times,* September 25, 2011; "For Wal-Mart, a Rare Online Success," by Miguel Bustillo and Karen Talley, *Wall Street Journal,* August 20, 2011; "Painful Profits From Web Video," by Sam Schechner, *Wall Street Journal,* August 15, 2011; "YouTube Is Said to Be Near a Major Film Rental Deal," by Brooks Barnes and Claire Cain Miller, *New York Times,* April 26, 2011; "YouTube Recasts for New Profits," by Jessica Vascellaro, *Wall Street Journal,* April 7, 2011.

CASE STUDY

Zynga
Bets on Online Games

Until 2012, Zynga, an online social gaming company that used Facebook as its launchpad to the top of the gaming company industry, was riding high. Zynga was the leader in a movement that has brought online games to the social network platform. Zynga's games on Facebook have over 182 million active users. Its most popular games include *FarmVille*, *CityVille*, *Mafia Wars*, and *Words with Friends*. In 2011, Zynga generated $1.1 billion in revenue selling virtual goods, both "durables" like tractors and skyscrapers, and "non-durables" like clothing, and of course farm animals like chickens and cows. Zynga's 2011 revenues were twice 2010 revenues, and in two previous years it grew by several hundred percent a year to become the fastest growing mobile gaming service in history. But in a sign that not all is well in Zyngaville, the firm showed a $400 million loss in 2011 amid signs that the growth of new users was slowing, veteran players were leaving, and the firm was having a hard time coming up with new enticing games. Although Zynga is expanding to other social networks such as Google+, it remains heavily dependent on Facebook, where it is one of hundreds of businesses located almost exclusively on Facebook, and where it can directly appeal to Facebook's 1 billion members worldwide.

Founded in 2007 by Mark Pincus and a group of other entrepreneurs, Zynga is the leading developer of social network games. In October 2012, its *ChefVille*, *TexasHoldEm Poker*, *FarmVille2*, and *Zynga Slingo* were the top four Facebook apps in terms of

monthly average users, each of them with between 35 million to 39 million users. Zynga's games generate 3 terabytes of data every day. Since its inception, Zynga has made data analytics a priority for guiding the management of its games and the business decisions of the company. Zynga is not interested in individual user information, but instead in the trends displayed in the aggregated data it collects. The company relies heavily on its data to improve user retention and to increase collaboration among its gamers. Zynga uses a reporting team and an analytics team to work with the data and create concrete recommendations for increasing sales. Zynga's analytics system is, in reality, a very sophisticated customer relationship management system. If a gold halo around a virtual angel's head causes more purchases of virtual angels, then the change is made. Zynga's audience demographics are perhaps not what you would think. Like most social games, the audience is slightly more female, older (average age is 46 years), and wealthier than console or other online gamers.

Zynga went public in December 16, 2011, after delaying earlier efforts throughout the year due to questions about its accounting. Earlier in the year, other IPOs for Groupon, LinkedIn, and Zillow had gone well, with their share prices zooming upwards on the first day of trading in true Internet-frenzy style. Not so for Zynga: its shares, which were priced at $10, giving the company a value of $20 billion, fell to $9.50 in a matter of minutes. Since then, Zynga has faced a difficult time maintaining investor confidence.

Zynga's business model is to offer free games aimed at a larger, more casual gaming audience, and to make money by selling "virtual goods" in games initially, and later by exploiting the advertising possibilities of the games. The idea of "free games" is a blow to the existing video game business that depends on selling video games. The idea of virtual goods has been around for years, most notably in Second Life and other virtual worlds, where users can buy apparel and accessories for their in-game avatars. But Zynga's attention to detail and ability to glean important information from countless terabytes of data generated by its users on a daily basis has set it apart. For example, product managers of Zynga's *FishVille* Facebook game discovered that players bought a certain type of fish, the "translucent anglerfish," more frequently than the rest. Zynga began offering fish similar to the anglerfish for about $3 apiece, and Fish-Ville players responded by buying many more fish than usual. Analytics have also shown that Zynga's gamers tend to buy more in-game goods when they are offered as limited edition items. As a result of fine-tuning the games, Zynga sells about 38,000 virtual goods every second of operation.

Zynga also benefits from using Facebook as its game platform. When users install a Zynga application, they allow Zynga access to all of their profile information, including their names, genders, and lists of friends. Zynga then uses that information to determine what types of users are most likely to behave in certain ways. If Zynga updates its games, it sends messages to all your friends whether they play the game or not. By carefully analyzing the online behavior of its customers, Zynga hopes to determine which types of users are most likely to become "whales," or big spenders that buy hundreds of dollars of virtual goods each month. Though only a small percentage of its active users contribute to its revenue, that subset of users is so dedicated that they account for nearly all of the company's earnings.

Zynga's games also make heavy use of Facebook's social features. For example, in *CityVille*, users must find friends to fill fictional posts at their "City Hall" to successfully complete the structure. All of Zynga's games have features like this, but Facebook hasn't always fully supported all of Zynga's efforts. Facebook apps were formerly able to send messages directly to Facebook members, but Facebook disabled the feature after complaints that it was a form of spam. Still, if your friends use Zynga's Facebook apps, chances are you've seen advertisements encouraging you to play as well in your News Feed.

Zynga's initial success caused some consternation and criticism in the video game industry. Traditional video game companies begin with an idea for a game that they hope players will buy and enjoy, and then make the game. Zynga begins with a game, but then studies data to determine how its players play, what types of players are most active, and what virtual goods players buy. Then, Zynga uses the data to change the game, and to encourage players to play longer, tell more friends, and buy even more goods. Many game industry veterans believe Zynga's games are overly simplistic and have many of the same game elements. The company has also been the target of several lawsuits alleging that Zynga copied their games. And even developers within Zynga have sometimes bristled at the company's prioritization of data analysis over creativity in game design. Imagine writing a novel or a history based on what users liked. But of course this happens all the time, despite criticism from many purists.

After releasing exceptionally poor second quarter results in July 2012, Zynga's stock plunged 40%. Revenue growth had "slowed" down to 19% from 32% in the prior quarter. Investors had been expecting a doubling in sales for most of 2012. Selling at under $3 a share in July 2012, the company lost 70% of its IPO value in about six months. The company pointed to a number of factors to explain its slowing growth. Facebook changed its platform to highlight new games from competitors, and reduced Zynga's announcements of its frequent game updates. Zynga had not introduced enough new games according to investors, and other competitors were always coming along with "new" new games, causing the user base to churn. The average life span of a Zynga user declined from 14 months in 2011 to 9 months in 2012. An important new game, *The Ville*, was delayed, and another game, *Mafia Wars II*, was a flop. In late summer 2012, Zynga was reported to be looking at online gambling as the answer to its problems. CEO Mark Pincus announced that Zynga would launch its first online gambling poker game involving real money in the first half of 2013, most likely outside the United States, since online gambling using real money is still illegal in most states and under U.S. federal law.

No one knows the long-term prospects of Zynga, even if it succeeds in launching its new online gambling initiative, given that it is late to the online gambling game. It faces significant competition from established players, such as PokerStars and other upstarts like Big Fish Casino that have already beat Zynga to the table. In addition, its primary business in virtual goods looks increasingly suspect. What has sold on Zynga in the past are fashionable virtual goods, and what comes into fashion often goes quickly out of fashion.

Perhaps the biggest risk for Zynga is that it is still almost totally reliant on Facebook, to whom it pays 30% of all revenues from its games, including ad revenue, and has agreed to use Facebook Credits as the sole means of payment by its users for the next five years. (Facebook Credits is Facebook's internal virtual payment system—users buy Facebook Credits to pay vendors on Facebook. Facebook Credits are not good any-

SOURCES: "Facebook Apps Leaderboard," Appdata.com, accessed October 2012; "It's Too Late for Gambling to Save Zynga," by Jeff John Roberts, Gigaom.com, October 8, 2012; "Zynga to Launch Real-Money Gambling Online Games in 2013," by Dean Takahashi, Venturebeat.com, July 26, 2012; "Zynga Stock Dives on Loss," by John Letzing and Shayndi Raice, *New York Times*, July 26, 2012; "Zynga's Facebook Games Continue to Shed Players by the Millions," by Paul Tassi, *Forbes*, May 23, 2012; Zynga Inc., "Form 10K for the Fiscal Year Ending December 31, 2011," Securities and Exchange Commission, February 28, 2012; "Testing the Durability of Zynga's Virtual Business," by Rolfe Winkler, *Wall Street Journal*, September 28, 2011; "Zynga Filing Shows Slowing Growth," by Shayndi Raice and Randall Smith, *Wall Street Journal*,

September 21, 2011; "Virtual Products, Real Profits," *Wall Street Journal*, September 9, 2011, Jacquelyn Gavron; "Vertica: The Analytics Behind all the Zynga Games," ReadWrite Enterprise, July 18, 2011; "Crikey! Zynga's IPO By the Numbers," by Mathew Lynley, VentureBeat, July 1, 2011; "Social Gaming," by Paul Verna, eMarketer, January 2011.

where else on the Web.) The customer base is also very narrow, with the virtual goods revenues coming from only 5% of the users. Advertising currently produces less than 10% of Zynga's revenues. In the last year, Zynga has been working to get its games on other platforms like Google+, Yahoo, and the iPhone and iPad in order to reduce its dependence on Facebook. It has also been working to expand its international presence. However, it is not clear if Zynga is going to continue to be able to dominate the games market in the future. Instead, Zynga has many competitors with a chance to succeed.

Case Study Questions

1. Do you think Zynga would be a good advertising platform? What kinds of companies would be interested in reaching this audience, and how should the ads be presented to users?

2. How could firms use the Zynga platform to develop and sell branded virtual goods? Assume you were a manufacturer of sporting goods and wanted to use Zynga as a marketing platform. What concerns would you have about the Zynga platform? How would you use its social character to extend the reach of your campaign?

3. How would you judge the competitive situation facing Zynga?

4. What role does Zynga's customer relationship management system have on its success to date? Why is it effective and what are its limitations?

10.5 REVIEW

KEY CONCEPTS

■ **Identify the major trends in the consumption of media and online content, and the major revenue models for digital content delivery.**

Major trends in the consumption of media and online content include the following:
- The average American adult spends around 4,200 hours per year consuming various media. The most hours are spent viewing television, followed by using the Internet and listening to the radio.
- Although several studies indicate that time spent on the Internet reduces consumer time available for other media, recent data reveals a more complex picture, as Internet users multitask and consumer more media of all types than non-Internet users.
- In terms of revenue, print media (books, newspapers, and magazines) accounts for the most revenue (37%), followed by television (28%) and radio and recorded music (11%).
- The three major revenue models for digital content delivery are the subscription, a la carte, and advertising-supported (free and freemium) models.

- Online newspapers, online radio, online TV shows, and casual games are the top four categories of online content.
- The fastest growing paid content area is videos.

■ Understand Digital Rights Management (DRM)

- Digital rights management (DRM) refers to the combination of technical and legal means for protecting digital content from reproduction without permission.
- Walled gardens are a kind of DRM that restrict the widespread sharing of conent.

■ Discuss the concept of media convergence and the challenges it faces.

The concept of media convergence has three dimensions:
- Technological convergence, which refers to the development of hybrid devices that can combine the functionality of two or more media platforms, such as books, newspapers, television, radio, and stereo equipment, into a single device.
- Content convergence, with respect to content design, production, and distribution.
- Industry convergence, which refers to the merger of media enterprises into powerful, synergistic combinations that can cross-market content on many different platforms and create works that use multiple platforms.
- In the early years of e-commerce, many believed that media convergence would occur quickly. However, many early efforts failed, and new efforts are just now appearing.

■ Understand the key factors affecting the online publishing industry.

Key factors affecting online newspapers include:
- *Audience size and growth.* Although the newspaper industry as a whole is the most troubled part of the publishing industry, online readership of newspapers is growing at more than 10% a year, fueled by new reading devices such as smartphones, e-readers, and tablet computers, and online newspapers produce the largest online audience of any media, next to social networks.
- *Revenue models and results.* Online newspapers predominantly rely upon an advertising model. Some also supplement revenues by using a subscription revenue model.

Key factors affecting e-books and online book publishing include:
- *Audience size and growth.* E-book sales have exploded, fueled by the Amazon Kindle, Barnes & Noble Nook, and Apple iPad. The mobile platform of smartphones and tablets has made millions of books available online at a lower price than print books. The future of the book will be digital although printed books will not disappear for many years.
- *Challenges.* The two primary challenges of the digital e-book platform are cannibalization and finding the right business model.
- *Competing business models.* E-book business models include the wholesale model and the agency model.
- *Convergence.* The publishing industry is making steady progress toward media convergence. Newly authored e-books are appearing with interactive rich media, which allow the user to click on icons for videos or other material.

Key factors affecting online magazines include:

- *Online audience and growth:* Digital magazine sales have soared, with almost a third of the Internet population now reading magazines online.
- *Magazine aggregation:* Magazine aggregators (Web sites or apps) offer users online subscriptions and sales of many digital magazines.

■ **Understand the key factors affecting the online entertainment industry.**

There are five main players in the entertainment sector: television, motion pictures, music, video games, and radio broadcasting. The entertainment segment is currently undergoing great change, brought about by the Internet and the mobile platform. Consumers have begun to accept paying for content and also beginning to expect to be able to access online entertainment from any device at any time.

Key factors include the following:

- *Audience size and growth.* While music downloads are the most popular form of entertainment, the fast-paced growth of online video sees videos overtaking music in 2014–2015 as the most popular online entertainment. In addition, Internet users are defining new forms of non-traditional entertainment that do not involve the traditional media titans, such as blogs and user-generated content on social network sites.
- *The emergence of streaming services and the mobile platform.* In the movie and television industries, two major trends are the move to consumers purchasing streaming services, from Amazon, Apple, Hulu, and other channels and the continued increase in online purchases and downloads. Although physical sales of products (DVDs) are dropping significantly, more and more consumers are purchasing movies and television episodes on new mobile devices, such as smartphones and tablets. The music industry is experiencing similar trends as the movie industry: the growth of streaming services, or Internet radio, the continued expansion of online purchases, and increased downloads on mobile devices. However, the unbundling of a traditional music product, the album, into individual songs, has decimated music industry revenues. Of the four types of gamers—casual, social, mobile, and console—the greatest growth is anticipated for mobile gamers, as the mobile market is rapidly expanding along all e-commerce fronts.
- *Industry structure upheaval.* The online entertainment industry structure faces upheaval. The current structure is inefficient and fractured, with Internet channel owners, such as Google and Apple, owning advanced distribution technologies, and content producers and owners, such as television and movie studios, forced to find profitable distribution channels. Concurrently, Internet channel owners are moving into the content creation business.

QUESTIONS

1. What are the three dimensions in which the term "convergence" has been applied? What does each of these areas of convergence entail?
2. What are the basic revenue models for online content, and what is their major challenge?
3. What are the two primary e-book business models?

4. What effect is the growth of tablet computing having on online entertainment and content?
5. What techniques do music subscription services use to enforce DRM?
6. What type of convergence does the Kindle Fire represent?
7. How has the Internet impacted the content that newspapers can offer?
8. What changes have occurred for newspapers in the classified ads department?
9. What are the key challenges facing the online newspaper industry?
10. What are the advantages and disadvantages of e-book content?
11. How has the Internet changed the packaging, distribution, marketing, and sale of traditional music tracks?
12. What are the factors that make nontraditional, distinctly Web entertainment sites so popular with users?
13. What would complete content convergence in the entertainment industry look like? Has it occurred?
14. How has streaming technology impacted the television industry?
15. Why is the growth of cloud storage services important to the growth of mobile content delivery?
16. Has the average consumer become more receptive to advertising-supported Internet content? What developments support this?
17. What factors are needed to support succesfully charging the consumer for online content?
18. Why are apps helping the newspaper and magazine industries where Web sites failed?
19. What alternatives do magazine publishers have to using Apple and Google newsstands as distribution channels?

PROJECTS

1. Research the issue of media convergence in the newspaper industry. Do you believe that convergence will be good for the practice of journalism? Develop a reasoned argument on either side of the issue and write a 3- to 5-page report on the topic. Include in your discussion the barriers to convergence and whether these restrictions should be eased.

2. Go to Amazon and explore the different digital products that are available. Prepare a presentation to convey your findings to the class.

3. Go to TBO.com (Tampa Bay Online). Surf the site and sample the offerings. Prepare a presentation to describe and display the efforts you see at technology, content, and industry structure convergence as well as the revenue model being used. Who owns this site?

4. Examine and report on the progress made with respect to the delivery of movies on demand over the Internet.

5. Has technology platform, content design, or industry structure convergence occurred in the online magazine industry? Prepare a short report discussing this issue.

CHAPTER 11

Social Networks, Auctions, and Portals

Social Network Fever

Spreads to the Professions

When social networks first appeared a decade ago, it was widely believed the phenomenon would be limited to crazed teenagers already captive to online games and video game consoles. Most of the technorati in Silicon Valley and Wall Street felt this was a blip on the horizon, and their full attention was occupied by search engines, search engine marketing, and ad placement. But when the population of social network participants pushed past 50 million and on to 75 million, even the technical elite woke up to the fact that these huge audiences were not just a bunch of teenagers. Instead, a wide slice of American society was participating. Steve Ballmer, CEO of Microsoft, expressed the conviction as early as September 2007 that social networks would have some staying power, although he tempered that outlook with reservations about just how long that would be, given their youthful appeal and faddish nature. This was just before Microsoft paid $250 million for a small stake in Facebook, which valued the company at $15 billion. Trying to sound convincing, the month before his company spent $1.65 billion for YouTube, Google CEO Eric Schmidt asserted his belief that despite prevailing opinion, social networks were a bona fide business opportunity.

Courtesy of Carol Traver

By October 2012, Facebook had grown to about 1 billion subscribers worldwide, challenging Google and Yahoo for face time with the Internet audience. The social network craze obviously has awakened the technology giants, but they focus mostly on the really huge audiences attracted to general social network sites such as Facebook, Twitter, and YouTube. However, in the background there is a fast-growing collection of social networks that are aimed at communities of practitioners or specific interest groups.

Take LinkedIn, for example, probably the best-known and most popular business network site. LinkedIn is an online network with more than 175 million worldwide members in over 200 countries, representing 170 different industries. Two new members join LinkedIn approximately every second. LinkedIn allows a member to create a profile, including a photo, to summarize his or her professional accomplishments. Members' networks include their connections, their connections' connections, as well as people they know, potentially linking them to thousands of others. How members use LinkedIn depends somewhat on their position. Top executives use the site mainly for industry networking and promoting their businesses. Middle managers use LinkedIn primarily to keep in touch with others and also for industry networking. Lower-level employees typically use the site for job searching and networking with co-workers. On May 18, 2011, LinkedIn went public in what was, at the time, the biggest Internet IPO since Google, raising more than $350

SOURCES: "About Us," LinkedIn.com Press Center, accessed October 10, 2012; LinkedIn Corporation Market Cap," YCharts.com, accessed October 10, 2012; "Number of Active Users at Facebook Over the Years," Associated Press, October, 4, 2012; "Thirty-Seven Percent of Companies Use Social Networks to Research Potential Job Candidates, According to New CareerBuilder Survey," by Ryan Hunt, Career-Builder.com, April 18, 2012; "Managing Your Online Image Across Social Networks" The Reppler Effect, September 27, 2011; "LinkedIn Hits $10 Billion Market Cap; Valuation Ethereal," by Eric Savitz, *Forbes*, May 19, 2011; "How Professionals Use LinkedIn," eMarketer, August 5, 2011; "LinkedFA Offers Social Network for Financial Advisors," by David F. Carr, *Information Week*, June 1, 2011; "All About LinkedIn, Knowledge@Wharton, May 20, 2011; "The Social Network That Gets Down to Business," by Miguel Helft, *New York Times*, September 29, 2010; "Online Reputation in a Connected World," Cross-Tab Marketing, January 2010; "Influence Marketing With Social Networks," by Lee Oden, Toprankblog.com, September 16, 2009; "Online Social Networks Go to Work," by Xeni Jardin, Msnbc.com, September 16, 2009.

million and giving it a company valuation of $8.9 billion. The company priced its IPO at $45 per share. As of October 2012 its stock had risen to approximately $112 per share, making its market capitalization now well over $11.65 billion.

Those with a particular interest in the stock market can choose from a crop of Web sites aimed at stock investors who want to share their ideas with other investors. These social networks are not just bulletin boards with anonymous comments, but active communities where users are identified and ranked according to the performance of their stock picks. One network is SocialPicks. SocialPicks is a community where stock investors exchange ideas and track the performance of financial bloggers. Like the larger social network sites, the financial sites allow users to connect with other investors, discuss issues focused on the stock market, and sometimes just show off investing prowess. The Motley Fool, one of the best-known online stock investment services, started its CAPS stock-rating social network in 2006 and has around 170,000 members.

You can find similar social network sites for a variety of specific professional groups such as health care (DailyStrength.org), law (LawLink), physicians (Sermo), wireless industry executives (INmobile.org), advertising professionals (AdGabber), and financial advisors (LinkedFA). These social networks encourage members to discuss the realities of their professions and practices, sharing successes and failures. There are also general business social networks designed more to develop a network for career advancement, such as Ecademy and Ryze. The rapid growth of professional social networks, linked to industry and careers, demonstrates how widespread and nearly universal the appeal of social networks is. While e-mail remains the Web's most popular activity, it is about to be eclipsed by social networks. What explains the very broad attraction to social networks? E-mail is excellent for communicating with other individuals, or even a small group. But e-mail is not very good at getting a sense of what others in the group are thinking, especially if the group numbers more than a dozen people. The strength of social networks lies in their ability to reveal group attitudes and opinions, values, and practices.

Professionals who join social networks need to be careful about the content they provide, and the distribution of this content. As business social networks have grown, and as the number of participants expands, employers are finding them a great place to discover the "inner" person who applies for a job. An April 2012 survey by CareerBuilder, the most widely used employment site in the United States, found that 37% of employers use social networks to screen job candidates and another 11% plan to begin doing so. However six months earlier, Reppler, an online identity management service, surveyed 300 hiring professionals. An astonishing 91% reported that they used social network screening, 47% of those upon receiving an application, 27% after detailed conversation with the prospective employee, and another 4% right before making an offer. Almost 70% of those using this tool reported rejecting a candidate based upon information they discovered. Provocative photos and references to drinking and drugs are the most common factors in deciding not to offer a job. For this reason, it wise to use Facebook's and other sites' maximum privacy settings, and release to the public only the most innocuous content. Likewise, be cautious of social network sites that do not provide "take down" policies, which allow users to remove embarrassing materials from their pages.

I n this chapter, we discuss social networks, auctions, and portals. One might ask, "What do social networks, auctions, and portals have in common?" They are all based on feelings of shared interest and self-identification—in short, a sense of community. Social networks and online communities explicitly attract people with shared affinities, such as ethnicity, gender, religion, and political views, or shared interests, such as hobbies, sports, and vacations. The auction site eBay started as a community of people interested in trading unwanted but functional items for which there was no ready commercial market. That community turned out to be huge—much larger than anyone expected. Portals also contain strong elements of community by providing access to community-fostering technologies such as e-mail, chat groups, bulletin boards, and discussion forums.

11.1   SOCIAL NETWORKS AND ONLINE COMMUNITIES

The Internet was designed originally as a communications medium to connect scientists in computer science departments around the continental United States. From the beginning, the Internet was intended, in part, as a community-building technology that would allow scientists to share data, knowledge, and opinions in a real-time online environment (see Chapter 3) (Hiltzik, 1999). The result of this early Internet was the first "virtual communities" (Rheingold, 1993). As the Internet grew in the late 1980s to include scientists from many disciplines and university campuses, thousands of virtual communities sprang up among small groups of scientists in very different disciplines that communicated regularly using Internet e-mail, listservs, and bulletin boards. The first articles and books on the new electronic communities began appearing in the mid- to late 1980s (Kiesler et al., 1984; Kiesler, 1986). One of the earliest online communities, The Well, was formed in San Francisco in 1985 by a small group of people who once shared an 1,800-acre commune in Tennessee. It is now a part of Salon.com, an online community and magazine. The Well (Whole Earth 'Lectronic Link) is an online community that now has thousands of members devoted to discussion, debate, advice, and help (Hafner, 1997; Rheingold, 1998). With the development of the Web in the early 1990s, millions of people began obtaining Internet accounts and Web e-mail, and the community-building impact of the Internet strengthened. By the late 1990s, the commercial value of online communities was recognized as a potential new business model (Hagel and Armstrong, 1997).

The early online communities involved a relatively small number of Web aficionados, and users with intense interests in technology, politics, literature, and ideas. The technology was largely limited to posting text messages on bulletin boards sponsored by the community, and one-to-one or one-to-many e-mails. In addition to The Well, early networks included GeoCities, a Web site hosting service based on neighborhoods. By 2002, however, the nature of online communities had begun to change. User-created Web sites called blogs became inexpensive and easy to set up without any technical expertise. Photo sites enabled convenient sharing of photos. The growth of mobile devices like smartphones, tablet computers, digital cameras, and portable media devices enabled sharing of rich media such as photos, music, and videos. Suddenly there was a much wider audience for sharing interests and activities, and much more to share.

A new culture emerged as well. The broad democratization of the technology and its spread to the larger population meant that online social networks were no longer limited to a small group but instead broadened to include a much wider set of people and tastes, especially pre-teens, teens, and college students who were the fastest to adopt many of these new technologies. Entire families and friendship networks soon joined. The new social network culture is very personal and "me" centered, displaying photos and broadcasting personal activities, interests, hobbies, and relationships on social network profiles. In an online social network, the "news" is not something that happened somewhere else to other people; instead, the news is what's going on with your friends and colleagues. Today's social networks are as much a sociological phenomenon as they are a technology phenomenon.

Currently, social network participation is one of the most common usages of the Internet. About two-thirds of all Internet users in the United States—about 158 million Americans—use social networks on a regular basis, about 67% of all Internet users and 50% of all adults (eMarketer, 2012a). Facebook has about 1 billion active users worldwide (about 190 million in the North America) (Facebook, 2012). There are only seven markets in the world where Facebook is not the leading social network. Twitter is growing exponentially, with an estimated 140 million users worldwide and 40 million in the United States as of August 2012 (Twitter, 2012; eMarketer, Inc., 2012b; comScore, 2012a). Facebook may not always be the leading social network: the Google + social network exploded to 25 million users in its first month (Facebook took three years to reach that level), and now has 100 million worldwide users and 27 million in the United States (Gaudin, 2012). Facebook's mindshare trumps Google + by a huge margin, however, the average user spends three minutes a month on Google + versus seven hours on Facebook.

Worldwide, the social network phenomena is even stronger. According to Nielsen, in a look at a sample of 10 global markets, social networks are the top online destination in each country, accounting for the majority of time spent online, and reaching at least 60% of active Internet users. According to comScore, Israelis spend the most time, about 12 hours per month, followed closely by Russians, at 11 hours a month. About 20% of all online mintues worldwide is spent on social networks. Although Facebook dominates the global social network marketspace, in some countries, more localized social networks are signficant, such as Orkut (owned by Google) in Brazil, FC2 Blog in Japan, QQ and RenRen in China, Tuenti in Spain, and Vkontakte in Russia (Nielsen, 2011; comScore, 2012a). There is an online social network for you to join almost anywhere you go! Unfortunately, there's very little communication across social networks.

WHAT IS AN ONLINE SOCIAL NETWORK?

social network

involves a group of people, shared social interaction, common ties among members, and people who share an area for some period of time

So exactly how do we define an online social network, and how is it any different from, say, an offline social network? Sociologists, who frequently criticize modern society for having destroyed traditional communities, unfortunately have not given us very good definitions of social networks and community. One study examined 94 different sociological definitions of community and found four areas of agreement. **Social net-**

works involve (a) a group of people, (b) shared social interaction, (c) common ties among members, and (d) people who share an area for some period of time (Hillery, 1955). This will be our working definition of a social network. Social networks do not necessarily have shared goals, purposes, or intentions. Indeed, social networks can be places where people just "hang out," share space, and communicate.

It's a short step to defining an **online social network** as an area online where people who share common ties can interact with one another. This definition is very close to that of Howard Rheingold's—one of The Well's early participants—who coined the term *virtual communities* as "cultural aggregations that emerge when enough people bump into each other often enough in cyberspace." It is a group of people who may or may not meet one another face to face, and who exchange words and ideas through the mediation of an online social meeting space. The Internet removes the geographic and time limitations of offline social networks. To be in an online network, you don't need to meet face to face, in a common room, at a common time.

online social network
an area online, where people who share common ties can interact with one another

THE DIFFERENCE BETWEEN SOCIAL NETWORKS AND PORTALS

We describe portals in the last section of this chapter. Portals began as search engines and then added content, Internet, and e-commerce services. In order to survive, portals have added many community-building and social network features, such as chat groups, bulletin boards, and free Web site design and hosting, that encourage visitors to stay on the site and interact with others who share their interests. Yahoo, for instance, uses deep vertical content features to retain its audience on-site and maximize revenue opportunities. Portals have begun to measure their success in terms of their social network features. For instance, Yahoo has purchased several Web properties, such as Flickr (a photo-sharing site), which has social network features. Portals have moved toward becoming general community meeting places in an effort to enlarge and retain audience share and increase revenues. User-generated content on portals is one way to entice visitors to stay online at the site (and, of course, view more commercials).

Similarly, sites that began as narrowly focused content or affinity group community sites such as iVillage, a site devoted to women's issues, have added more general portal-like services, including general Web searching, general news, weather, travel information, and a wide variety of e-commerce services. Browsers such as Mozilla Firefox and Microsoft Internet Explorer include social network features as well. There is no reason why social networks have to be limited to self-proclaimed social network sites such as Facebook. Social networking is a functionality, not a Web site. For instance, many Web sites have online forums and blogs that are intended to create a sense of community and social network relationships. As a result, social networks and portals have moved closer together, and at times are indistinguishable from one another.

THE GROWTH OF SOCIAL NETWORKS AND ONLINE COMMUNITIES

Facebook, Twitter, LinkedIn, Google +, Pinterest, and Tumblr are all examples of popular online communities. **Figure 11.1** shows the top 10 social network sites, which together account for well over 90% of the Internet's social network activity.

In 2009, Facebook passed Myspace as the largest social network in terms of total members. Myspace has since fallen even farther from favor, with around only 28

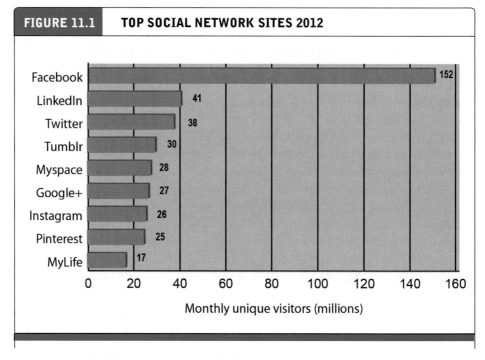

FIGURE 11.1 | **TOP SOCIAL NETWORK SITES 2012**

Monthly unique visitors (millions)

SOURCES: Based on data from comScore, 2012a; Gaudin, 2012; McGee, 2012.

million monthly unique visitors in the United States in 2012. While social networks originally attracted mostly young Internet users, social networks today are not just about teens and college students, but a much larger social phenomenon. More than 50% of Facebook's users are over 35.

While Facebook and Twitter dominate the news, a new kind of social network is appearing, and growing much faster than Facebook with respect to unique visitors and subscribers. These new sites are attracting marketers and advertisers as well. For instance, Pinterest, described in the opening case in Chapter 1, is a visually oriented site that allows users to curate their tastes and preferences, expressed in visual arts. You can think of Pinterest as a visual blog. Users post images to an online "pinboard." The images can come from any source. Users can also "re-pin" images they see on Pinterest. Pinterest's membership has skyrocketed since its launch and now has more than 25 million monthly unique visitors in the United States in August 2012. Tumblr is an easy-to-use blogging site with tools for visual and text curating, sharing with others, and re-blogging contents. Tumblr started in 2007 and has 30 million users in 2012.

Other new and fast growing sites are not necessarily competing with Facebook, but adding to the social network mix, and enlarging the total social network audience. Facebook's share of the total social market is declining. Facebook is not likely to be the sole place to meet your friends. **Table 11.1** describes some other social sites that are more focused.

TABLE 11.1	OTHER FAST-GROWING SOCIAL SITES
SOCIAL NETWORK	**DESCRIPTION**
Path	Personal journal for sharing photos, text
Stumbleupon	A search platform for sharing interests
Flickr	The original social photo-sharing site
Instagram	Social photo-sharing site (now owned by Facebook)
Ning	Platform for creating personal social networks
Polyvore	Topic-focused social network (fashion)
deviantART	Web site focused on art, sharing of images
Vevo	Video and music sharing site

It is easy to both overestimate and underestimate the significance of social networks. The top four social network sites in the United States (Facebook, LinkedIn, Twitter, and Tumblr) together have a total monthly unique audience of over 260 million. In contrast, the top four portal/search engine sites (Google, Yahoo, MSN, and AOL) together have a total monthly unique audience of over 630 million. (Obviously, with 239 million people on the Internet in the United States, users are unique to more than one site.) Although Facebook's 152 million monthly unique U.S. visitors seems high, consider that Yahoo's various sites have around 163 million in the United States. Still, since 2008, Facebook has grown from a very small Internet audience of less than 20 million, to an Internet behemoth among the top three to four Web sites on the Internet.

The number of unique visitors is just one way to measure the influence of a site. Time on site is another important metric. The more time people spend on a site, called engagement, the more time to display ads and generate revenue. In this sense, Facebook is three times more addictive and immersive than the other top sites on the Web. In the United States, Facebook visitors spend about seven hours a month on Facebook, compared to about three hours on Yahoo, and only 1.5 hours on Google (eMarketer, Inc., 2012a).

The amount of advertising revenue generated by sites is perhaps the ultimate metric for measuring the business potential of Web sites and brands. The top four search engine companies (Google, Yahoo, Microsoft, and AOL) will generate about $17.5 billion in U.S. advertising revenue in 2012 (eMarketer, Inc., 2012c). In contrast, social network sites in the United States in 2012 are expected to generate about $3.1 billion in advertising revenue (eMarketer, Inc., 2012d). Social network sites are the fastest growing form of Internet usage, but they are not yet as powerful as traditional search engines/portals in terms of ad dollars generated. A part of the problem is that subscribers do not go to social network sites to seek ads for relevant products, nor pay attention to the ads that are flashed before their eyes (see Chapters 6 and 7).

TURNING SOCIAL NETWORKS INTO BUSINESSES

While the early social networks had a difficult time raising capital and revenues, today's top social network sites are now learning how to monetize their huge audiences. Early social network sites relied on subscriptions, but today, most social networks rely on advertising or the investments of venture capitalists. Users of portals and search engines have come to accept advertising as the preferred means of supporting Web experiences rather than paying for it. One important exception is LinkedIn, which offers free memberships to individual job seekers but charges professional recruiters and business firms for premium services. **Figure 11.2** shows the amount of ad spending on social networks.

Social networks have had a profound impact on how businesses operate, communicate, and serve their customers. The most visible business firm use of social networks is as a marketing and branding tool. More than 90% of the Fortune 500 have established Facebook pages, where "fans" can follow the business and its products and share opinions with the company and other fans. More than 80% of corporations have Twitter feeds for this purpose as well (Newman, 2011). A less visible marketing use of networks is as a powerful listening tool that has strengthened the role of customers and customer feedback systems inside a business. The software drink industry is a good example. Dr Pepper, for instance, has built up a fan base of 10.9 million people who Like it on Facebook. Mountain Dew has about 6.3 million, Coca-Cola more than 36 million, and Red Bull about 22.5 million. Twitter has attracted more than 1,000 firms, and over 140 million active users worldwide, 20% of whom follow tweets from brand name firms (Efrati, 2011).

Social networks are where corporate brands and reputations are formed, and firms today take very seriously the topic of "online reputation," as evidenced by social

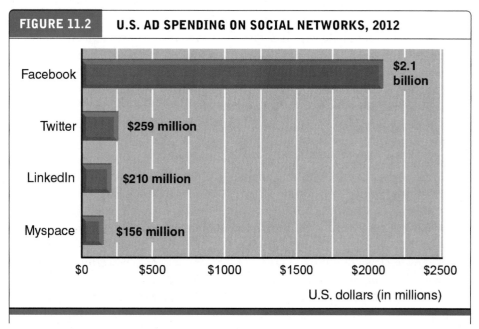

FIGURE 11.2   **U.S. AD SPENDING ON SOCIAL NETWORKS, 2012**

SOURCE: Based on data from eMarketer, 2012d.

network posts, commentary, chat sessions, and Likes. In this sense, social network sites become an extension of corporate customer relationship management systems and extend existing market research programs. Beyond branding, social network sites are being used increasingly as advertising platforms to contact a somewhat younger audience than Web sites and e-mail, and as customers increasingly shift their eyeballs to social networks. Rosetta Stone, for instance, uses its Facebook page to display videos of its learning technology, encourage discussions and reviews, and post changes in its learning tools. Yet the business use of social networks does not always go well. The *Insight on Society* case, *The Dark Side of Social Networks*, discusses some of the risks associated with social networks.

TYPES OF SOCIAL NETWORKS AND THEIR BUSINESS MODELS

There are many types and many ways of classifying social networks and online communities. While the most popular general social networks have adopted an advertising model, other kinds of networks have different revenue sources. Social networks have different types of sponsors and different kinds of members. For instance, some are created by firms such as IBM for the exclusive use of their sales force or other employees (intra-firm communities or B2E [business-to-employee] communities); others are built for suppliers and resellers (inter-organizational or B2B communities); and others are built by dedicated individuals for other similar persons with shared interests (P2P [people-to-people] communities). In this chapter, we will discuss B2C communities for the most part, although we also discuss briefly P2P communities of practice.

Table 11.2 describes in greater detail the five generic types of social networks and online communities: general, practice, interest, affinity, and sponsored. Each type of

TABLE 11.2	TYPES OF SOCIAL NETWORKS AND ONLINE COMMUNITIES
TYPE OF SOCIAL NETWORK / COMMUNITY	**DESCRIPTION**
General	Online social gathering place to meet and socialize with friends, share content, schedules, and interests. Examples: Facebook, Pinterest, Tumblr, and Myspace.
Practice	Social network of professionals and practitioners, creators of artifacts such as computer code or music. Examples: Just Plain Folks (musicians' community) and LinkedIn (business).
Interest	Community built around a common interest, such as games, sports, music, stock markets, politics, health, finance, foreign affairs, or lifestyle. Examples: E-democracy.org (political discussion group) and PredictWallStreet (stock market site).
Affinity	Community of members who self-identify with a demographic or geographic category, such as women, African Americans, or Arab Americans. Examples: BlackPlanet (African American community and social network site) and iVillage (focusing on women).
Sponsored	Network created by commercial, government, and nonprofit organizations for a variety of purposes. Examples: Nike, IBM, Cisco, and political candidates.

INSIGHT ON SOCIETY

THE DARK SIDE OF SOCIAL NETWORKS

ChapStick thought it had a great marketing idea when it decided to launch a new Facebook ad—a mildly provocative picture of a young woman on her disheveled sofa—derriere in the air—rummaging behind the couch. The ad proclaimed: WHERE DO LOST CHAPSTICKS GO? The subtitle—BE HEARD AT FACEBOOK.com/CHAPSTICK—invited user comment. Unfortunately, ChapStick had no social network advertising policy. The site administrator was rudderless when controversy erupted.

First, a blogger cited the ad in a post about the pervasiveness of sexist advertising. When she posted to ChapStick's Facebook page, her comment was deleted. Other Facebook posters followed suit. Their comments were also deleted. It wasn't long before a stream of comments mocking the "Be Heard" subtitle ensued, replete with references to ChapStick as a bunch of long-eared horse relatives. Incredibly, ChapStick still did not respond and continued deleting posts.

ChapStick treated Facebook as simply another broadcast channel. But social networks are interactive. When your customers have an immediate and visible "voice," you cannot simply stay silent, delete dissent, and, as ChapStick did, hope the whole thing will just go away on its own. While negative posts that can be clearly identified as trolling can either be ignored or quickly deleted, criticisms that have merit must be responded to with candor, admission of guilt when appropriate, and by outlining the steps that will be taken to remedy the problem.

ChapStick had an opportunity to begin a conversation with its customers that would have demonstrated its cognizance of and sensitivity to sexist advertising. Even if it had chosen to defend its ad as comparatively mild in our sexual imagery saturated advertising environment, it would have demonstrated its willingness to hear and engage with its customers. If the controversy had not abated, it could have chosen to pull the ad in deference to its most loyal customers. Rather than a public relations nightmare, it could have created a public relations coup, stamping itself as a company that cares about its most loyal fans. After all, if you have befriended ChapStick on Facebook, you are clearly a fan.

And, in fact, many of ChapStick's fans rose to its defense and were dismayed that its brand image was being negatively impacted. And still ChapStick remained inexplicably silent. Finally, when it could no longer delete the negative posts quickly enough, ChapStick pulled the ad and responded. However, not only was its response anemic, it did not even fully own up to the mass deletions it had perpetrated. It offered regret if fans "felt" this had happened and essentially blamed posters for being uncivil or posting "menacing" comments.

Even though the offending ad had been removed, the matter had not ended. The social media backlash from ChapStick's half-hearted apology continued. When ChapStick finally tried to assure its fans that it valued them and was listening, it was hardly credible. In short, ChapStick presented us with a textbook case in how not to conduct social network advertising!

Shell Oil also learned the hard way that once an idea is unleashed online it is difficult to control, even if the idea is a hoax. In June 2012, Greenpeace, the environmental activist group, published a video on YouTube of a supposed Shell Oil drillship launch party at the Seattle Space Needle. Two drillships could be seen in the harbor heading off to the inaugural Artic expedition. A model oil

(continued)

rig cake topped with a liquor dispenser graced the presenting dais. The "oil rig" malfunctioned, spewing alcohol all over the elderly widow of the oil rig designer. This incited a chaotic scene in which Shell principals attempted to contain the mess, disable the dispenser, and prevent the videographer from filming. Press releases appeared denying that Shell had held such a gathering and threatening legal action. A new Shell Web site went up—arcticready.com—proclaiming, "Let's Go! Shell in the Arctic." Users were invited to caption Arctic pictures. One user entered the slogan, "Our Money is Worth More than Any Animals Who Used to Live Here" atop a scene of melting, cracking Arctic ice. Next, the Twittersphere erupted in posts criticizing the inappropriate slogans and Shell's silence. A new Twitter account, @ShellisPrepared, began tweeting overwrought messages threatening legal action and attempting to suppress the false ads. Twitter users, amused at the ineptitude of Shell's social media team, not only retweeted the messages, but also passed on the Arctic Ready and video URLs as well. Voilà!

Greenpeace had created a successful viral social media hoax garnering it new converts, 900,000 petition signatures, and a host of publicity for their anti-Arctic drilling campaign. Meanwhile, Shell was caught completely flat-footed. An authentic press release disavowing any association with the video, fake press release, Web site, and Twitter account was finally issued six weeks later.

Fast food giant McDonald's confronted the dark side of social networks when it began a public relations campaign on Twitter. Using the hashtag #meetthefarmers, it inserted promotional tweets into the streams of Twitter users and paid for premium search engine results. The Supplier Stories campaign encouraged users to share stories about the farmers who sold their meat and produce to McDonald's. All was proceeding nicely until McDonald's replaced the hashtag with #McDStories. Now encouraging users to share their gen-

eral consumer stories, McDonald's almost immediately lost control of its advertising campaign. The Twittersphere exploded with tweets comparing McDonald's fare to dog food and diarrhea, sprinkled with barbs about Type II diabetes, obesity, and food poisoning. The best that can be said for McDonald's is that it was prepared to pull the plug on the campaign should anything go amiss. Within two hours, the promotion was halted.

The ChapStick, Shell, and McDonald's fiascos are instructive. Inadequate consideration and attentiveness can result in damage that is hard to ameliorate. ChapStick had no policies in place for how to respond to an ad campaign gone wrong. Shell had no social media network monitoring in place so that it could form a rapid response. McDonald's failed to fully recognize the polarizing nature of its product, making soliciting general comments a risky proposition. Even though its response was rapid, the sticky negative word associations will be hard to shake. Companies with controversial products or goods that can be detrimental to society must tread carefully. All three cases highlight that listening is fundamental. Ignoring and allowing a problem to fester is perilous. Negative comments must be met head on with rapid and repeated counter-speech or with problem-solving that demonstrates a willingness to engage customers and fix mistakes. Developing a positive reputation in the social media universe can insulate a company when problems arise, and understanding potential pitfalls is essential to developing a safe and effective social network advertising strategy.

But marketing is not the only social media hazard. For employees, privacy protection for Facebook posts is still being determined in the courts. For example, Danielle Mailhoit was the manager of a Home Depot store in Burbank, California. After she was fired, she filed suit claiming gender and disability discrimination due to her

(continued)

vertigo. The defense attorney filed a broad request for all of Malhoit's Facebook photos, profiles, postings, status updates, tagged photos, group memberships, and any blog entries or activity streams from any other social networking sites beginning from the date she identified as the first incident of discrimination. Specifically, the attorney wanted any communications that revealed her emotional or mental state. In September 2012, a federal judge ruled this request overly broad and limited discovery to only communications between the plaintiff and current or former Home Depot employees. Stating that they were unlikely to be relevant unless they were directly related to the lawsuit or her former employment, she also denied Home Depot's request for photos.

Employers must be careful with personal information gleaned from social networking sites. If it can be proven that membership in a protected group was discovered during the hiring process and used to reject a candidate or later used to terminate an employee, a claim can be filed under one of the Federal Equal Employment Opportunity (EEO) laws. These include Title VII of the Civil Rights Act of 1964, the Age Discrimination in Employment Act of 1967 (ADEA), Title I and Title V of the Americans with Disabilities Act of 1990 (ADA), and Title II of the Genetic Information Nondiscrimination Act of 2008 (GINA), which prohibits employment discrimination based on genetic information about an applicant, employee, or former employee. GINA's regulations provide a distinction between whether genetic information is acquired purposefully or inadvertently. Inadvertent acquisition includes acquisition through social media sites, equating it to accidentally overhearing a conversation at work.

However, data on a social media site with privacy controls equipped should not be able to be "inadvertently" acquired. The Stored Communications Act (SCA) covers privacy protection for e-mail and digital communications. The latest court rulings on its application to social network communications have held that Facebook wall postings and other social media comments are protected as long as they have not been made public.

Facebook, to protect its business model, is speaking out against recent hiring practices that have come to its attention—and threatening legal action. According to both Facebook and the American Civil Liberties Union (ACLU), some companies have been asking new hires either to befriend the hiring manager or to submit their password. Facebook's Privacy Page condemns this practice, stating that it violates both individual users' and their friends' expectations of privacy, jeopardizes security, and could reveal a user's membership in a protected group. Erin Egan, Facebook's chief privacy officer, assures users that Facebook will pursue all avenues to protect their privacy while gently reminding them that sharing passwords is already against Facebook's terms of service. She then advises companies that they could be exposing themselves to legal risks and warns them that litigation will be pursued if necessary.

Legislators in at least two states have decided to be proactive. In May 2012, a bill prohibiting employers from asking prospective employees for their social media user names and passwords unanimously passed the California State Assembly and was on its way to the Senate. In New Jersey, a committee for the State Assembly sent similar legislation, also applicable to educational institutions, on to the full Assembly.

Carefully crafted policies can help companies to avoid the dark side of social networking. Advertising and hiring are but two of the areas that must be monitored. The Human Resources department must also develop policies regarding employee use of social networks. Employee education programs must be implemented to apprise

(continued)

employees of infractions that can be grounds for disciplinary action. IT departments must develop stringent policies to protect proprietary data and defend company networks from cyberscams. Social networking is an exciting new tool, but one which requires safeguards.

SOURCES: "Judge: Home Depot Went Too Far in Seeking Worker's Social Posts, by Declan McCullagh, News.cnet.com, September 17, 2012; "Was Greenpeace's Shell Hoax Brilliant Or 'Villainous'? One of the Guys Behind It All Speaks," by Kashmir Hill, Forbes, July 19, 2012; "Shell's Fake Social Media Fiasco—What Would You Have Done?" by Vicki Flaugher, CommPro.biz, July 18, 2012; "California May Ban Employers from Asking for Facebook Passwords," by Jessica Guynn, Los Angeles Times, May 11, 2012; "N.J. Committee OKs Ban on Employers Seeking Passwords," by Doug Isenberg, GigaLaw.com, May 10, 2012; "Facebook Speaks Out Against Employers Asking for Passwords," by Doug Gross, CNN.com, March 23, 2012; "Why McDonald's Should Have Known Better," by Shelley DuBois, CNNMoney.com, January 31, 2012; "McDonald's Social Media Director Explains Twitter Fiasco," by Jeff John Roberts, paidContent.org, January 24, 2012; "Lessons from the ChapStick Social Media Fiasco," by Ted Rubin, Tedrubin.com, December 3, 2011; "ChapStick Gets Itself in a Social Media Death Spiral: A Brand's Silent War Against Its Facebook Fans," by Tim Nudd, Adweek, October 26, 2011; "The Social Media Pitfalls for Your Business: 10 Legal Issues Every Employer Should Consider," by Kevin Shook, FrostBrownTodd.com September 2, 2011; "The Dangers of Using Social Media Data in Hiring," by Gregg Skall, Radio Business Report, June 6, 2011; "Stored Communications Act Protects Facebook and MySpace Users' Private Communication," by Kathryn Freund, Jolt.law.harvard.edu, June 11, 2010.

community can have a commercial intent or commercial consequence. We use this schema to explore the business models of commercial communities.

General communities offer members opportunities to interact with a general audience organized into general topics. Within the topics, members can find hundreds of specific discussion groups attended by thousands of like-minded members who share an interest in that topic. The purpose of the general community is to attract enough members to populate a wide range of topics and discussion groups. The business model of general communities is typically advertising supported by selling ad space on pages and videos.

general communities
offer members opportunities to interact with a general audience organized into general topics

Practice networks offer members focused discussion groups, help, information, and knowledge relating to an area of shared practice. For instance, Linux.org is a non-profit community for the open source movement, a worldwide global effort involving thousands of programmers who develop computer code for the Linux operating system and share the results freely with all. Other online communities involve artists, educators, art dealers, photographers, and nurses. Practice networks can be either profit-based or nonprofit, and support themselves by advertising or user donations.

practice networks
offer members focused discussion groups, help, information, and knowledge relating to an area of shared practice

Interest-based social networks offer members focused discussion groups based on a shared interest in some specific subject, such as business careers, boats, horses, health, skiing, and thousands of other topics. Because the audience for interest communities is necessarily much smaller and more targeted, these communities have usually relied on advertising and tenancy/sponsorship deals. Sites such as Fool.com, Military.com, Sailing Anarchy, and Chronicle Forums all are examples of Web sites that attract people who share a common pursuit. Job markets and forums such as LinkedIn can be considered interest-based social networks as well.

interest-based social networks
offer members focused discussion groups based on a shared interest in some specific topic

Affinity communities offer members focused discussions and interaction with other people who share the same affinity. "Affinity" refers to self- and group identification. For instance, people can self-identify themselves on the basis of religion, ethnicity, gender, sexual orientation, political beliefs, geographical location, and hundreds of other categories. For instance, iVillage, Oxygen, and NaturallyCurly are affinity sites

affinity communities
offer members focused discussions and interaction with other people who share the same affinity

designed to attract women. These sites offer women discussion and services that focus on topics such as babies, beauty, books, diet and fitness, entertainment, health, and home and garden. These sites are supported by advertising along with revenues from sales of products.

sponsored communities

online communities created for the purpose of pursuing organizational (and often commercial) goals

Sponsored communities are online communities created by government, non-profit, or for-profit organizations for the purpose of pursuing organizational goals. These goals can be diverse, from increasing the information available to citizens; for instance, a local county government site such as Westchestergov.com, the Web site for Westchester County (New York) government; to an online auction site such as eBay; to a product site such as Tide.com, which is sponsored by an offline branded product company (Procter & Gamble). Cisco, IBM, HP, and hundreds of other companies have developed their internal corporate social networks as a way of sharing knowledge.

SOCIAL NETWORK FEATURES AND TECHNOLOGIES

Social networks have developed software applications that allow users to engage in a number of activities. Not all sites have the same features, but there is an emerging feature set among the larger communities. Some of these software tools are built into the site, while others can be added by users to their profile pages as widgets (described in earlier chapters). **Table 11.3** describes several social network functionalities.

TABLE 11.3	SOCIAL NETWORK FEATURES AND TECHNOLOGIES
FEATURE	DESCRIPTION
Profiles	User-created Web pages that describe themselves on a variety of dimensions
Friends network	Ability to create a linked group of friends
Network discovery	Ability to find other networks and find new groups and friends
Favorites	Ability to communicate favorite sites, bookmarks, content, and destinations
Games, widgets, and apps	Apps and games on the site, such as those offered by Facebook
E-mail	Ability to send e-mail within the social network site to friends
Storage	Storage space for network members' content
Instant messaging	Immediate one-to-one contact with friends through the community facility
Message boards	Posting of messages to groups of friends and other groups' members
Online polling	Polling of member opinion
Chat	Online immediate group discussion; Internet relay chat (IRC)
Discussion groups	Discussion groups and forums organized by topic
Experts online	Certified experts in selected areas respond to queries
Membership management tools	Ability of site managers to edit content, and dialog; remove objectionable material; protect security and privacy

THE FUTURE OF SOCIAL NETWORKS

Social networking in 2012 is one of the most popular online activities. Will it stay that way or grow even more popular? Today's social network scene is highly concentrated with the top site, Facebook, garnering about 50% of the social network audience, which has declined from a few years ago when Facebook represented over 65% of the market. Relative to other sites then, Facebook's growth has slowed, while newer social network sites have grown explosively. There has also been an explosion of social networks that are more focused on specific interests that tie members together, not some diffuse sense of "friendship." It may be more fun to network on a site dedicated to your central interests. As a result, Facebook's growth rate has inevitably declined, and future revenue growth will depend on how well it can monetize its very large subscriber base either by selling ads, virtual goods, or other revenue sources. Moreover, the success of Facebook is likely to attract some powerful competitors with their own ideas of how to build online versions of the social graph, namely, Google, Apple, and Amazon. See the *Insight on Technology* case *Facebook Has Friends.*

Many Facebook users report "network fatigue" caused by spending too much time keeping up with their close and distant friends on many social networks. Fatigue grows as users increase the number of social networks to which they belong (Rosenblum, 2011). One result is avoiding Facebook (and other sites) or spending less and less time on the sites. A 2012 Reuters' poll found that Facebook users were spending less time on the site than earlier, and 35% said they were less engaged. An Associated Press poll found that 80% of users said they had never been influenced by an ad on the site, and 43% said Facebook would fade away as new platforms appear (Oreskovic, 2012; Murphy, 2012). The fears that many users have about the privacy of their posts and content is also another factor in people either not joining Facebook, or pulling back from engagement.

The financial future of social networks is to become advertising and sales platforms. But social networks are not yet proven advertising platforms that drive sales. The relationship between Likes and sales is not clear yet. Response rates to display ads on Facebook are far lower than portal sites like Yahoo, or search ads like Google. In part this reflects the sentiment of users who go onto social sites without the intention of purchasing anything.

11.2 ONLINE AUCTIONS

Online auction sites are among the most popular consumer-to-consumer (C2C) e-commerce sites on the Internet, although the popularity of auctions and their growth rates have slowed in recent years due to customers' preferences for a "buy now" fixed-price model. The market leader in C2C auctions is eBay, which has 100 million active users in the United States and over 300 million items listed on any given day within 18,000 categories. In August 2012, eBay had around 75 million unique visitors, placing it 11th on the list of top 50 Web properties (comScore, 2012b). In 2011, eBay had $5.4 billion in net revenues from its Marketplaces segment, a 12% increase from 2010, and the total worth of goods sold was $68 billion (Gross Market Value) (eBay, 2012). eBay

INSIGHT ON TECHNOLOGY

FACEBOOK HAS FRIENDS

In the ongoing battles between hype and substance, fantasy and reality, and hubris and humility on the Internet, Silicon Valley takes no prisoners and has no equals. Google wants to organize the world's information, Amazon wants to be the world's store, Apple wants to be the most beloved company, and now Facebook wants to be the social operating system for the Internet, connecting the world in one big social network (that it owns). Mark Zuckerberg, Facebook's founder, says he wants Facebook to connect everyone in what he calls the social graph. Facebook is built on the assumption that there is just one social graph, including you, your friends, colleagues, relatives, and their friends, and so forth. It's one big family.

So far, Facebook has been right in its strategy. In October 2012, Facebook has an estimated 1 billion users worldwide, with about 152 million unique visitors a month in the United States (about 40% of the entire social network audience in the United States). About half of its users access the site every day to interact with 250 billion objects (posts to walls, photos, apps, and games) and 1.1 trillion Likes. According to Facebook, over 600 million people worldwide access Facebook using their mobile devices. Facebook is global: it's available in 70 languages. Facebook seems to have attained social network dominance, but its growth rate has slowed down (you can't get much bigger than 1 billion users), and minutes of engagement with the site have also begun to plateau.

On May 18, 2012, Facebook went public in the largest IPO in Internet history, with its stock offered at $38 a share, and a total market value of $104 billion. As a public company, Facebook had to reveal its revenues and income. In 2011, Facebook had revenues of $3.7 billion, and estimated revenues for 2012 are $5 billion, a hefty 35% growth rate, but much slower than the market anticipated. By September 2012, the stock had sunk to $20 a share amid questions about the efficacy of its ad business. Shareholders lost about $50 billion in market value. Skeptics were also critical of Facebook's failure to develop a mobile application when nearly 40% of its visitors access the site with smartphones.

But there are other players and forces at work. While Facebook has 152 million U.S. visitors, the other nine members of the top nine social networks together have around 230 million, and some of them are growing much faster than Facebook. For instance, in late 2012, one of the fastest growing sites is Tumblr, with nearly 30 million visitors. Tumblr is a short form, or microblogging, site where users post text, images, videos, and links that other users can follow and share. Tumblr is growing at more than 200% a year, and is a start-up based in Manhattan backed by venture capital investors. Tumblr's popularity is based on the idea of enhanced user control. Users control the look and feel of blog pages and can post anything, including documents as long as a book. Tumblr offers privacy controls that allow users to keep posts private. Users can create multiple groups of friends that include different people. Groups can create community-powered blogs to which anyone can contribute. Users own their own work (unlike Facebook), and Tumblr provides for automatic updates to Twitter and Facebook if users select that option. It's free, with no ads, forced banner ads, or logos (so far).

How Tumblr makes money is a bit of a mystery, just like other social network sites in their early days. Yet Tumbler attracts the investor crowd: in September 2011, it raised a cool $85 million from a group of venture capital firms. At this point, the firm was valued at $800 million. At some point

(continued)

Tumblr will have to monetize its audience, and earn revenue with premium features.

While its rapid growth might be interesting to Facebook, Tumblr is a speck on the wall. Google is not. With annual revenues of nearly $30 billion (96% comes from search and display advertising) and growth at about 30% a year, Google is one of the giants of the Internet. Facebook is a speck on Google's wall (no pun intended), albeit an irritant for all the press it receives and its huge, intense user base. After several failed efforts to enter the social network space, Google finally launched its Google+ site in June 2011, which is a serious competitor to Facebook. Google+ is based on the idea (similar to Tumblr) of sharing with multiple separate groups of friends who form the collection of real-world social networks that people participate in. Google+ assumes there are multiple social graphs and not just one. Google+ makes it really easy to have separate social networks for family, work colleagues, professional colleagues, fellow sports fanatics, and fashionistas who share your tastes, and to keep the messages separate. There's really no need for your parents to learn about your weekend parties. Rather than share with the entire online world, users share with their naturally formed groups called "circles," a much smaller audience. This is intended to eliminate "social network awkwardness" created when users post material on their walls that is embarrassing to some of their friends, or a real turn-off to their relatives (like Mom, Dad, or Aunt Bertha). It's called "oversharing" or "TMI" (too much information), and it's a major irritant to Facebook users (along with Facebook's privacy invading behavior).

Other features of Google+ include group video chatting (called "Hang Outs") and group mobile audio and video chatting (called "Huddles"). It is fully integrated with other Google products like Gmail, so you can drag and drop friends from your Gmail lists to request they join one of your circles. Gmail is used by an estimated 200 million users worldwide. The Google+ search feature now includes searching your friends' pages for relevant information, giving search a solid social quality and not just an algorithmic quality. "Sparks" is a feature that lets users declare what's interesting to them, and Google+ searches the Web for interesting news and stories on that topic, sort of like a personal research assistant. Google+ claims its solution to social networks is based on 100 new features not found on other sites. One feature found on Google+ (but not on Tumblr, for example) is Google's tracking of your interests and behaviors in all your circles so that it can, presumably, show you even better ads than it does now. Google+ is advertising-supported, you betcha!

Google launched Google+ to the public on September 20, 2011. By the end of September 2012, Google+ has rocketed to 27 million registered users. While Google+ is a contender for social network power, it lacks the engagement of other sites like Facebook, Tumblr, and Pinterest. For instance, the average Facebook user in the United States spends nearly seven hours a month on Facebook, whereas Google+ users spend three minutes in 2012. Google+ is a lonely place. At Tumblr and Pinterest, users spend 89 minutes, and at Twitter, about 21 minutes.

Of course, Microsoft wants to play in this new arena too. It invested $250 million in Facebook in October 2007 for a 1.6% stake. This valued Facebook at $15 billion, and was a sign of how desperate Microsoft was to play in this new field. However, Facebook and Microsoft have shared only a few technologies so far. Microsoft's search engine Bing is used by Facebook users. In May 2011, Microsoft purchased Skype, the Internet-based telephone service. Facebook needs Skype because it does not have a peer-to-peer network of its own that can handle video and voice services for users. In lending Skype's infrastructure to Facebook, Microsoft gains access to a huge audience. Google already has Google Voice, which performs these functions.

(continued)

It's unlikely that Microsoft will be satisfied with its tiny slice of Facebook. In May 2012, Microsoft launched a social network called So.cl (pronounced "social"). While not clearly aimed at Facebook, Microsoft claims So.cl is designed to help students find and share interesting Web pages, combining social with Bing search. So.cl has developed partnerships with several universities, including New York University. So.cl is closely integrated with Facebook and appears to be aimed at competing with Google+ by combining search and social with other features like e-mail and visual pin-up boards. Apple is also rumored to be building a social network system based on iOS mobile devices. A recent patent application from Apple describes a proximity or location-based sharing and communication system where mobile devices share their users' interests with other cell phones in the area, seeking a match. For instance, users could search for people in their nearby location who had downloaded a particular movie, or song. Apple abandoned its Ping music social network in iOS 6, and instead is rumored to be discussing an investment in Twitter.

While Facebook is the dominant social network site now, given the strength of its competitors, it is likely there will be many powerful social networks for users to join. One point competitors have already made is that there isn't "one social graph," but many social graphs that people want to keep separate. Journalists are already reporting a kind of "social network fatigue," where users are simply getting tired of following and updating their Facebook, Twitter, Tumblr, and LinkedIn networks. The next generation of entrepreneurs may solve this problem by creating an inter-network, inter-operable system where users can participate in all their networks from one interface. But for now, the big players in this field are determined to build their own walls (pun intended).

SOURCES: "Apple Officials Said to Consider Stake in Twitter," by Evelyn Rusli and Nick Bilton, *New York Times*, July 27, 2012; "Microsoft Launches New Social Network to Compete With Google," by Kelly Clay, *Forbes*, May 21, 2012; "The Mounting Minuses at Google+," by Amir Efrati, *Wall Street Journal*, February 28, 2012; "Google is Now in the Top Ten Social Networking Sites," by Matt Rosoff, *Business Insider*, September 26, 2011; "Google+ Traffic Floodgates Open," Rolfe Winkler, *Wall Street Journal*, September 22, 2011; "Microsoft Social Networking Accident Makes Perfect Sense," Nick Kolakowski, *eWeek*, July 18, 2011; "Going in Google+ Circles," by Katherine Boehret, *Wall Street Journal*, July 13, 2011; "Google Makes Facebook Look Socially Awkward," Rolfe Winkler, *Wall Street Journal*, July 7, 2011; "Google Takes on Friend Sprawl," by Amir Efrati, *Wall Street Journal*, June 29, 2010; "Another Try by Google to Take On Facebook," by Claire Cain Miller, *New York Times*, June 28, 2011.

is further discussed in the case study at the end of this chapter. In the United States alone, there are several hundred auction sites, some specializing in unique collectible products such as stamps and coins, others adopting a more generalist approach in which almost any good can be found for sale. Increasingly, established portals and online retail sites—from Yahoo and MSN to JCPenney and Sam's Club—are adding auctions to their sites. Auctions constitute a significant part of B2B e-commerce in 2012, and more than a third of procurement officers use auctions to procure goods. What explains the extraordinary popularity of auctions? Do consumers always get lower prices at auctions? Why do merchants auction their products if the prices they receive are so low?

DEFINING AND MEASURING THE GROWTH OF AUCTIONS AND DYNAMIC PRICING

auctions

markets in which prices are variable and based on the competition among participants who are buying or selling products and services

Auctions are markets in which prices are variable and based on the competition among participants who are buying or selling products and services. Auctions are one type of **dynamic pricing**, in which the price of the product varies, depending directly on the demand characteristics of the customer and the supply situation of the seller. There is a wide variety of dynamically priced markets, from simple haggling, bartering, and negotiating between one buyer and one seller, to much more sophisticated public auctions in which there may be thousands of sellers and thousands of buyers, as in a single stock market for a bundle of shares.

In dynamic pricing, merchants change their prices based on both their understanding of how much value the customer attaches to the product and their own desire to make a sale. Likewise, customers change their offers to buy based on both their perceptions of the seller's desire to sell and their own need for the product. If you as a customer really want the product right now, you will be charged a higher price in a dynamic pricing regime, and you will willingly pay a higher price than if you placed less value on the product and were willing to wait several days to buy it. For instance, if you want to travel from New York to San Francisco to attend a last-minute business conference, and then return as soon as possible, you will be charged twice as much as a tourist who agrees to stay over the weekend.

In contrast, traditional mass-market merchants generally use **fixed pricing**—one national price, everywhere, for everyone. Fixed pricing first appeared in the nineteenth century with the development of mass national markets and retail stores that could sell to a national audience. Prior to this period, all pricing was dynamic and local, with prices derived through a process of negotiation between the customer and the merchant. Computers and the development of the Internet have contributed to a return of dynamic pricing. The difference is that with the Internet, dynamic pricing can be conducted globally, continuously, and at a very low cost.

There are many other types of dynamic pricing that preceded the Internet. Airlines have used dynamic pricing since the early 1980s to change the price of airline tickets depending on available unused capacity and the willingness of business travelers to pay a premium for immediate bookings. Airline yield management software programs seek to ensure that a perishable item (an empty airline seat is useless after the plane takes off) is sold before flight time at some price above zero.

The use of coupons sent to selected customers, and even college scholarships given to selected students to encourage their enrollment, are a form of both price discrimination and dynamic pricing. In these examples, the price of the item is adjusted to demand and available supply, and certain consumers are discriminated against by charging them higher prices while others are advantaged by receiving lower prices for the same products, namely, a reduced price for an item or a college education.

Newer forms of dynamic pricing on the Internet include bundling, trigger pricing, utilization pricing, and personalization pricing. As discussed in Chapter 6, bundling of digital goods is the practice of including low-demand products in a bundle "for free" in order to increase total revenues. **Trigger pricing**, used in m-commerce applications, adjusts prices based on the location of the consumer—for example, walking within 400 yards of a restaurant may trigger an immediate 10% dinner coupon on a portable Web device. **Utilization pricing** adjusts prices based on utilization of the product; for example, Progressive Insurance Company adjusts the annual cost of automobile insurance based on mileage driven. **Personalization pricing** adjusts prices based on the

dynamic pricing
the price of the product varies, depending directly on the demand characteristics of the customer and the supply situation of the seller

fixed pricing
one national price, everywhere, for everyone

trigger pricing
adjusts prices based on the location of the consumer

utilization pricing
adjusts prices based on utilization of the product

personalization pricing
adjusts prices based on the merchant's estimate of how much the customer truly values the product

merchant's estimate of how much the customer truly values the product; for instance, Web merchants may charge committed fans of a musician higher prices for the privilege of receiving a new DVD before its official release to retail stores. Higher-cost hardbound books sell primarily to committed fans of writers, while less-committed fans wait for cheaper paperback versions to appear.

Auctions—one form of dynamic pricing mechanism—are used throughout the e-commerce landscape. The most widely known auctions are **consumer-to-consumer (C2C) auctions**, in which the auction house is simply an intermediary market maker, providing a forum where consumers—buyers and sellers—can discover prices and trade. Less well known are **business-to-consumer (B2C)** auctions, where a business owns or controls assets and uses dynamic pricing to establish the price. Established merchants on occasion use B2C auctions to sell excess goods. This form of auction or dynamic pricing will grow along with C2C auctions.

Some leading online auction sites are listed in **Table 11.4**. Auctions are not limited to goods and services. They can also be used to allocate resources, and bundles of resources, among any group of bidders. For instance, if you wanted to establish an optimal schedule for assigned tasks in an office among a group of clerical workers, an auction in which workers bid for assignments would come close to producing a nearly

consumer-to-consumer (C2C) auctions

auction house acts as an intermediary market maker, providing a forum where consumers can discover prices and trade

business-to-consumer (B2C) auctions

auction house sells goods it owns, or controls, using various dynamic pricing models

TABLE 11.4	LEADING ONLINE AUCTION SITES
GENERAL	
eBay	The world market leader in auctions: 75 million visitors a month and millions of products.
uBid	Marketplace for excess inventory from pre-approved merchants.
eBid	In business since 1998. Operates in 18 countries, including U.S. Currently, the top competitor to eBay. Offers much lower fees.
Bid4Assets	Liquidation of distressed assets from government and the public sector, corporations, restructurings, and bankruptcies.
Auctions.samsclub	Sam's Club brand merchandise in a variety of categories.
SPECIALIZED	
BidZ	Live auction format for online jewelry.
Racersauction	Specialized site for automobile racing parts.
Philatelic Phantasies	Stamp site for professionals, monthly online stamp auction.
Teletrade	America's largest fully automated auction company of certified coins including ancient gold, silver, and copper coins. Also offers sports cards.
Baseball-cards.com	The Internet's first baseball card store. Offers weekly auctions of baseball, football, basketball, hockey, wire photos, and more.
Oldandsold	Online auction service specializing in quality antiques. Dealers pay a 3% commission on merchandise sold.

optimal solution in a short amount of time (Parkes and Ungar, 2000). In short, auctions—like all markets—are ways of allocating resources among independent agents (bidders).

WHY ARE AUCTIONS SO POPULAR? BENEFITS AND COSTS OF AUCTIONS

The Internet is primarily responsible for the resurgence in auctions. Although electronic network-based auctions such as AUCNET in Japan (an electronic automobile auction for used cars) were developed in the late 1980s, these pre-Internet auctions required an expensive telecommunications network to implement. The Internet provides a global environment and very low fixed and operational costs for the aggregation of huge buyer audiences, composed of millions of consumers worldwide, who can use a universally available technology (Internet browsers) to shop for goods.

Benefits of Auctions

Aside from the sheer game-like fun of participating in auctions, consumers, merchants, and society as a whole derive a number of economic benefits from participating in Internet auctions. These benefits include:

- **Liquidity:** Sellers can find willing buyers, and buyers can find sellers. The Internet enormously increased the liquidity of traditional auctions that usually required all participants to be present in a single room. Now, sellers and buyers can be located anywhere around the globe. Just as important, buyers and sellers can find a global market for rare items that would not have existed before the Internet.

- **Price discovery:** Buyers and sellers can quickly and efficiently develop prices for items that are difficult to assess, where the price depends on demand and supply, and where the product is rare. For instance, how could a merchant (or buyer) price a Greek oil lamp made in 550 B.C. (to use just one example of the rare items that can be found on eBay)? How could a consumer even find a Greek oil lamp without the Internet? It would be difficult and costly for all parties.

- **Price transparency:** Public Internet auctions allow everyone in the world to see the asking and bidding prices for items. It is difficult for merchants to engage in price discrimination (charging some customers more) when the items are available on auctions. However, because even huge auction sites such as eBay do not include all the world's online auction items (there are other auction sites in the world), there still may be more than one world price for a given item (there are inter-market price differences).

- **Market efficiency:** Auctions can, and often do, lead to reduced prices, and hence reduced profits for merchants, leading to an increase in consumer welfare—one measure of market efficiency. Online auctions provide consumers the chance to find real bargains at potentially give-away prices; they also provide access to a very wide selection of goods that would be impossible for consumers to access physically by visiting stores.

- **Lower transaction costs:** Online auctions can lower the cost of selling and purchasing products, benefiting both merchants and consumers. Like other Internet markets, such as retail markets, Internet auctions have very low (but not zero) transaction costs. A sale at an auction can be consummated quickly and with very low transaction costs when compared to the physical world of markets.

- **Consumer aggregation:** Sellers benefit from large auction sites' ability to aggregate a large number of consumers who are motivated to purchase something in one marketspace. Auction-site search engines that lead consumers directly to the products they are seeking make it very likely that consumers who visit a specific auction really are interested and ready to buy at some price.
- **Network effects:** The larger an auction site becomes in terms of visitors and products for sale, the more valuable it becomes as a marketplace for everyone by providing liquidity and several other benefits listed previously, such as lower transaction costs, higher efficiency, and better price transparency. For instance, because eBay is so large—garnering close to 90% of all C2C auction commerce in the United States—it is quite likely you will find what you want to buy at a good price, and highly probable you will find a buyer for just about anything.

Risks and Costs of Auctions for Consumers and Businesses

There are a number of risks and costs involved in participating in auctions. In some cases, auction markets can fail—like all markets at times. (We describe auction market failure in more detail later.) Some of the more important risks and costs to keep in mind are:

- **Delayed consumption costs:** Internet auctions can go on for days, and shipping will take additional time. If you ordered from a mail-order catalog, you would likely receive the product much faster, or if you went to a physical store, you would immediately be able to obtain the product.
- **Monitoring costs:** Participation in auctions requires your time to monitor bidding.
- **Equipment costs:** Internet auctions require you to purchase a computer system, pay for Internet access, and learn a complex operating system.
- **Trust risks:** Online auctions are the single largest source of Internet fraud. Using auctions increases the risk of experiencing a loss.
- **Fulfillment costs:** Typically, the buyer pays fulfillment costs of packing, shipping, and insurance, whereas at a physical store these costs are included in the retail price.

watch lists
permit the consumer to monitor specific auctions of interest

proxy bidding
allows the consumer to enter a maximum price, and the auction software automatically bids for the goods up to that maximum price in small increments

Auction sites such as eBay have taken a number of steps to reduce consumer participation costs and trust risk. For instance, auction sites attempt to solve the trust problem by providing a rating system in which previous customers rate sellers based on their overall experience with the merchant. Although helpful, this solution does not always work. Auction fraud is the leading source of e-commerce complaints to federal law enforcement officials. One partial solution to high monitoring costs is, ironically, fixed pricing. At eBay, consumers can reduce the cost of monitoring and waiting for auctions to end by simply clicking on the "Buy It Now!" button and paying a premium price. The difference between the "Buy It Now" price and the auction price is the cost of monitoring. Also, most online auctions reduce monitoring costs by providing both a watch list and proxy bidding. **Watch lists** permit the consumer to monitor specific auctions of interest, requiring the consumer to pay close attention only in the last few minutes of bidding. **Proxy bidding** allows the consumer to enter a maximum price, and the auction software automatically bids for the goods up to that maximum price in small increments.

Nevertheless, given the costs of participating in online auctions, the generally lower cost of goods on Internet auctions is in part a compensation for the other additional costs consumers experience. On the other hand, consumers experience lower search costs and transaction costs because there usually are no intermediaries (unless, of course, the seller is an online business operating on an auction site, in which case there is a middleman cost), and usually there are no local or state taxes.

Merchants face considerable risks and costs as well. At auctions, merchants may end up selling goods for prices far below what they might have achieved in conventional markets. Merchants also face risks of nonpayment, false bidding, bid rigging, monitoring, transaction fees charged by the auction site, credit card transaction processing fees, and the administration costs of entering price and product information. We explore the benefits and risks for merchants later in this chapter.

Market-Maker Benefits: Auctions as an E-commerce Business Model

Online auctions have been among the most successful business models in retail and B2B commerce. eBay, the Internet's most lucrative auction site, has been profitable nearly since its inception. The strategy for eBay has been to make money off every stage in the auction cycle. eBay earns revenue from auctions in several ways: transaction fees based on the amount of the sale, listing fees for display of goods, financial service fees from payment systems such as PayPal, and advertising or placement fees where sellers pay extra for special services such as particular display or listing services.

However, it is on the cost side that online auctions have extraordinary advantages over ordinary retail or catalog sites. Auction sites carry no inventory and do not perform any fulfillment activities—they need no warehouses, shipping, or logistical facilities. Sellers and consumers provide these services and bear these costs. In this sense, online auctions are an ideal digital business because they involve simply the transfer of information.

Even though eBay has been extraordinarily successful, the success of online auctions is qualified by the fact that the marketplace for online auctions is highly concentrated. eBay dominates the online auction market, followed by eBid and uBid. Many of the smaller auction sites are not profitable because they lack sufficient sellers and buyers to achieve liquidity. In auctions, network effects are highly influential, and the tendency is for one or two very large auction sites to dominate, with hundreds of smaller specialty auction sites (sites that sell specialized goods such as stamps) being barely profitable.

TYPES AND EXAMPLES OF AUCTIONS

Auction theory is a well-established area of research, largely in economics (McAfee and McMillan, 1987; Milgrom, 1989; Vickrey, 1961). Much of this research is theoretical, and prior to the emergence of public Internet auctions, there was not a great deal of empirical data on auctions or consumer behavior in auctions. Previous literature has identified a wide range of auction types, some of which are seller-biased, and others

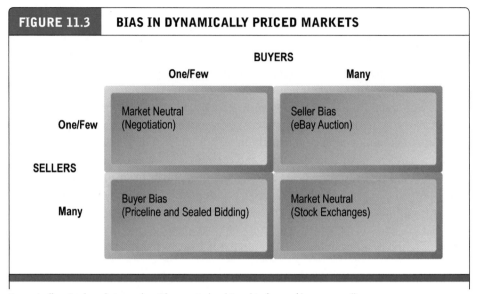

Dynamically priced markets can be either neutral or biased in favor of buyers or sellers.

of which are more buyer-biased. Internet auctions are very different from traditional auctions. Traditional auctions are relatively short-lived (such as a Sotheby's art auction), and have a fixed number of bidders, usually present in the same room. Online Internet auctions, in contrast, can go on much longer (a week), and have a variable number of bidders who come and go from the auction arena.

Internet Auction Basics

Before a business turns to auctions as a marketing channel, its managers need to understand some basic facts about online auctions.

Market Power and Bias in Dynamically Priced Markets Dynamically priced markets are not always "fair" in the sense of distributing market power to influence prices. **Figure 11.3** illustrates four different market bias situations that occur in dynamic markets.

In situations in which the number of buyers and sellers is few or equal in size, markets tend to be neutral, favoring neither the buyer nor the seller. One-on-one negotiations, barter markets, and stock exchanges all have this quality of neutrality, although specialists and market makers exact a commission for matching buy and sell orders. In stock markets, which are sometimes called a "double auction" because bids and offers are made continuously, many sellers and buyers call out prices for bundles of stock (of which there is a very large supply) until a deal is struck. In contrast, auctions such as those run by eBay and reverse auctions offered by companies such as Priceline have built-in biases. Usually on eBay, there is just one seller or a small number of sellers marketing goods that are in limited supply (or even rare goods) to millions of buyers who are competing on price. Priceline offers just the opposite bias and shares many features with a sealed-bid RFQ (request for quote) market. In Priceline's reverse auctions (described in greater detail later in this chapter), buyers post their unique needs for goods and services and a price they are willing to pay, while many sellers compete against one another for the available business. Of course, inherent bias in a marketplace does not mean consumers and merchants cannot find "good deals" and thousands of motivated customers willing to purchase goods at profitable prices.

However, the inherent biases should provide cautions to both merchants and consumers; namely, goods in auctions sometimes sell for far above their fair market value as they get bid too high, and sometimes for far less than their fair market value as merchants become too desperate for business. **Fair market value** could be defined here as the average of prices for that product or service in a variety of dynamic and fixed-price markets around the world. We explore other auction market failures in a later section.

Price Allocation Rules: Uniform vs. Discriminatory Pricing There are different rules for establishing the winning bids and prices in auctions where there are multiple units for sale, say, 10 Lenovo laptop PCs. With a **uniform pricing rule**, there are multiple winners and they all pay the same price (usually the lowest winning bid—sometimes called a market clearing price). Other auctions use **discriminatory pricing** in which winners pay different amounts depending on what they bid. See, for instance, Ubid.com, which typically auctions multiple units from manufacturers. Like so many other auction rules, price allocation can change bidding strategy in auctions. For instance, in a uniform pricing auction for 10 Lenovo laptops, you may bid a very high price for a few units, knowing that others will not follow, but you will only pay a price equal to the lowest winning bid needed to clear out the units from the market. The person who bid for the 10th unit may have only bid 75% as high as your offer. Nevertheless, that is the price you will actually pay—the price needed to "clear the market" of all units. However, under a discriminatory pricing rule, you would be forced to pay your high bid. Obviously, from a buyer's point of view, uniform pricing is better, but from a merchant's point of view, discriminatory pricing is much better.

Public vs. Private Information in Dynamically Priced Markets In some dynamic markets, the prices being bid are secret, and are known only to one party. For instance, a firm may issue a request for bid to electrical contractors for provision of electrical service on a new building. Bidders are requested to submit sealed bids, and the lowest bidder (subject to qualifications) will be the winner. In this instance, the bidders do not know what others are bidding, and must bid their "best" price. The danger here is **bid rigging**, in which bidders communicate prior to submitting their bids, and rig their bids to ensure that the lowest price is higher than it might otherwise be (which benefits the bidder, who in this instance is receiving the bid price as payment for services to be rendered). This is a common problem in sealed-bid markets. However, in auction markets, bid prices are usually public information, available to all. Here the risks are that bidders agree offline to limit their bids, that sellers use shills to submit false bids, or that sellers use the market itself as a signaling device, driving prices up. Open markets permit large players to signal prices or engage in **price matching**, where sellers agree informally or formally to set floor prices on auction items below which they will not sell. Generally such collusion exists on the sell side, where there are just a few sellers or auction houses in a position to fix prices.

fair market value
the average of prices for a product or service in a variety of dynamic and fixed-price markets around the world

uniform pricing rule
there are multiple winners and they all pay the same price

discriminatory pricing
winners pay different amounts depending on what they bid

bid rigging
bidders communicate prior to submitting their bids, and rig their bids to ensure that the lowest price is higher than it might otherwise be

price matching
sellers agree informally or formally to set floor prices on auction items below which they will not sell

Types of Auctions

Now that you have learned some basic auction market rules and practices, it's time to consider some of the major forms of dynamically priced markets and auctions, both online and offline. **Table 11.5** describes the major types of auctions, how they work, and their biases. As you can see in Table 11.5, aside from the different formats and rules, there are many other differences among auctions. As noted above, there are both discriminatory and uniform pricing rules, although the latter seem to be most common. Also, in some auctions, there are multiple units for sale, whereas in others, there is only a single unit for sale. The major types of Internet auctions are English, Dutch Internet, Name Your Own Price, and Group Buying.

English auction

most common form of auction; the highest bidder wins

English Auctions The **English auction** is the easiest to understand and the most common form of auction on eBay. Typically, there is a single item up for sale from a single seller. There is a time limit when the auction ends, a reserve price below which the seller will not sell (usually secret), and a minimum incremental bid set. Multiple buyers bid against one another until the auction time limit is reached. The highest bidder wins the item (if the reserve price of the seller has been met or exceeded). English auctions are considered to be seller-biased because multiple buyers compete against one another—usually anonymously.

Traditional Dutch Auctions In the traditional Dutch auction in Aalsmeer, Holland, 5,000 flower growers—who own the auction facility—sell bundles of graded flowers to 2,000 buyers. The Dutch auction uses a clock visible to all that displays the starting price growers want for their flowers. Every few seconds, the clock ticks to a lower price. When buyers want to buy at the displayed price, they push a button to accept the lot of flowers at that price. If buyers fail to bid in a timely fashion, their competitors will win the flowers. The auction is very efficient: on average, Aalsmeer conducts 50,000 transactions daily for 20 million flowers. Dutch flower auctions are now conducted over the Internet. Buyers no longer have to be present at the market to bid, and sellers no longer have to have their flowers present in adjacent warehouses, but can ship directly from their farms (Kambil and vanHeck, 1996).

Dutch Internet auction

public ascending price, multiple unit auction. Final price is lowest successful bid, which sets price for all higher bidders

Dutch Internet Auctions In **Dutch Internet auctions**, such as those on eBay, OnSale, and others, the rules and action are different from the classical Dutch auction. The Dutch Internet auction format is perfect for sellers that have many identical items to sell. Sellers start by listing a minimum price, or a starting bid for one item, and the number of items for sale. Bidders specify both a bid price and the quantity they want to buy. The uniform price reigns. Winning bidders pay the same price per item, which is the lowest successful bid. This market clearing price can be less than some bids. If there are more buyers than items, the earliest successful bids get the goods. In general, high bidders get the quantity they want at the lowest successful price, whereas low successful bidders might not get the quantity they want (but they will get something). The action is usually quite rapid, and proxy bidding is not used. **Table 11.6** shows closing data from a sample Dutch Internet auction for a bundle of laptop computers. In Table 11.6, the bids are arranged by price and then quantity. Under a uniform pricing rule, the lowest winning bid that clears the market of all 10 laptops is $736 and all winners pay this amount. However, the lowest winning bidder, JB505, will only receive three laptops, not four, because higher bidders are given their full allotments.

TABLE 11.5	TYPES OF AUCTIONS AND DYNAMIC PRICING MECHANISMS	
AUCTION TYPE	**MECHANISM**	**BIAS**
Sealed-bid auction (B2B e-procurement—Ariba Sourcing; Elance)	Sealed-bid auction, RFQs. Winner is chosen from lowest bidders at acceptable quality levels.	Buyer bias: Multiple vendors competing against one another
Vickrey auction (private auction)	Sealed-bid auction, single unit; highest bidder wins at the second-highest bid price.	Seller bias: Single seller and multiple buyers competing against one another
English auction (eBay)	Public ascending price, single unit; highest bidder wins at a price just above the second-highest bid. Buyers can skip bidding at each price, but return at higher prices.	Seller bias: Single seller and multiple buyers competing against one another
Traditional Dutch (Dutch flower market)	Public descending-price auction, single unit; seller lowers price until a buyer takes the product.	Seller bias: Single seller and multiple buyers competing against one another
Dutch Internet (eBay Dutch auction)	Public ascending price, multiple units. Buyers bid on quantity and price. Final per-unit price is lowest successful bid, which sets a uniform price for all higher bidders as well (uniform price rule).	Seller bias: Small number of sellers and many buyers
Japanese auction (private auction)	Public ascending price, single unit; highest bidder wins at a price just above second-highest bid (reservation price) and buyers must bid at each price to stay in auction.	Seller bias: Single seller and many buyers
Yankee Internet auction (variation on Dutch Internet auction)	Public ascending price, multiple units. Buyers bid on quantity and price per unit. Bidders ranked on price per unit, units, and time. Winners pay their actual bid prices (discriminatory rule).	Seller bias: Single seller and multiple buyers competing against one another
Reverse auction	Public reverse English auction, descending prices, single unit. Sellers bid on price to provide products or services; winning bid is the lowest-price provider. Similar to sealed-bid markets.	Buyer bias: Multiple sellers competing against one another
Group buying (demand aggregators)	Public reverse auction, descending prices, multiple units. Buyers bid on price per unit and units. Groups of sellers bid on price; winning bid is lowest-price provider.	Buyer bias: Multiple sellers competing against one another
Name Your Own Price (Priceline)	Similar to a reverse auction except the price the consumer is willing to pay is fixed and the price offered is nonpublic. Requires a commitment to purchase at the first offered price.	Buyer bias: Multiple sellers competing against one another for an individual's business
Double auction (Nasdaq and stock markets)	Public bid-ask negotiation; sellers ask, buyers bid. Sale consummated when participants agree on price and quantity.	Neutral: Multiple buyers and sellers competing against one another. Market bias: trading specialists (matchmakers)

NOTE: "Public" means all participants can observe prices offered.

TABLE 11.6	**A MULTI-UNIT DUTCH INTERNET AUCTION**

CLOSING AUCTION DATA

Lot number	8740240
Total Number of Units	10
Description	HP Pavilion DV6 Laptop; Win 7; Intel Core i5, 3 GHz, 17″ widescreen; 4 GB memory; 500 GB hard drive
Reserve Price	None

BIDDER	DATE	TIME	BID	QUANTITY
JDMTKIS	9/30/12	18:35	$750	4
KTTX	9/30/12	18:55	$745	3
JB505	9/30/12	19:05	$736	4
VAMP	9/30/12	19:10	$730	2
DPVS	9/30/12	19:20	$730	1
RSF34	9/30/12	19:24	$725	1
CMCAL	9/30/12	19:25	$725	2

Name Your Own Price auction

auction where users specify what they are willing to pay for goods or services

Name Your Own Price Auctions The **Name Your Own Price** auction was pioneered by Priceline, and is the second most-popular auction format on the Web. Although Priceline also acts as an intermediary, buying blocks of airline tickets and vacation packages at a discount and selling them at a reduced retail price or matching its inventory to bidders, it is best known for its Name Your Own Price auctions, where users specify what they are willing to pay for goods or services, and multiple providers bid for their business. Prices do not descend and are fixed: the initial consumer offer is a commitment to purchase at that price. In 2011, Priceline had more than $4.35 billion in revenues, and in 2012, attracts around 15 million unique visitors a month. It is one of the top-ranked travel sites in the United States. Today, it also arranges for the sale of new cars, hotel accommodations, car rentals, long distance telephone service, and home finance.

Table 11.7 describes the products and services available in Priceline's Name Your Own Price auctions. Clearly, a major attraction of Priceline is that it offers consumers a market biased in their favor and very low prices, up to 40% off. Brand-name suppliers compete with one another to supply services to consumers. However, it is unclear at this time if the Priceline business model can extend to other categories of products. Experiments to sell gasoline and groceries through Priceline failed.

But how can Priceline offer discounts up to 40% off prices for services provided by major brand-name providers? There are several answers. First, Priceline "shields the brand" by not publicizing the prices at which major brands sell. This reduces conflict with traditional channels, including direct sales. Second, the services being sold are perishable: if a Priceline customer did not pay something for the empty airline

TABLE 11.7	PRICELINE NAME YOUR OWN PRICE OFFERINGS
SERVICE/PRODUCT	DESCRIPTION
Airline seats	Brand-name carriers bid for individual consumer business—perishable items that airlines are motivated to sell at the last minute.
Hotel rooms	Brand-name hotels bid for consumer business—perishable services that hotels are motivated to sell on a last-minute basis.
Rental cars	Brand-name rental companies bid for consumer business—perishable services that rental companies are motivated to sell on a last-minute basis.
Vacation packages	Brand-name hotels and air carriers bid for consumer business—perishable services that providers are motivated to sell on a last-minute basis.
Cruises	Cruise ship companies bid for consumer business; especially active in off-season periods.

seat, rental car, or hotel room, sellers would not receive any revenue. Hence, sellers are highly motivated to at least cover the costs of their services by selling in a spot market at very low prices.

The strategy for sellers is to sell as much as possible through more profitable channels and then unload excess capacity on spot markets such as Priceline. This works to the advantage of consumers, sellers, and Priceline, which charges a transaction fee to sellers.

Group Buying Auctions: Demand Aggregators A **demand aggregator** facilitates group buying of products at dynamically adjusted discount prices based on high-volume purchases. The originator of demand aggregation was Mercata, formed in 1998, and the Web's largest retail demand aggregator until it ceased operations in January 2001, when needed venture capital financing did not materialize. Mercata holds several patents covering online demand aggregation. The largest supplier today of demand aggregation software (what it now calls "social buying") is Ewinwin. Demand aggregation has also found a home in B2B commerce as a way of organizing group buying. Trade associations and industry buying groups have traditionally pursued group buying plans in order to reduce costs from large suppliers.

Online demand aggregation is built on two principles. First, sellers are more likely to offer discounts to buyers purchasing in volume, and, second, buyers increase their purchases as prices fall. Prices are expected to adjust dynamically to the volume of the order and the motivations of the vendors. In general, demand aggregation is suitable for MRO products (commodity-like products) that are frequently purchased by a large number of organizations in high volume.

Professional Service Auctions Perhaps one of the more interesting uses for auctions on the Web is eBay's marketplace for professional services, Elance. This auction is a sealed-bid, dynamic-priced market for freelance professional services from legal

demand aggregators
suppliers or market makers who group unrelated buyers into a single purchase in return for offering a lower purchase price. Prices on multiple units fall as the number of buyers increases

and marketing services to graphics design and programming. Firms looking for professional services post a project description and request for bid on Elance. Providers of services bid for the work. The buyer can choose from among bidders on the basis of both cost and perceived quality of the providers that can be gauged from the feedback of clients posted on the site. This type of auction is a reverse Vickrey-like auction where sealed bids are submitted and the winner is usually the low-cost provider of services. Another similar site is SoloGig.

WHEN TO USE AUCTIONS (AND FOR WHAT) IN BUSINESS

There are many different situations in which auctions are an appropriate channel for businesses to consider. For much of this chapter, we have looked at auctions from a consumer point of view. The objective of consumers is to receive the greatest value for the lowest cost. Now, switch your perspective to that of a business. Remember that the objective of businesses using auctions is to maximize their revenue (their share of consumer surplus) by finding the true market value of products and services, a market value that hopefully is higher in the auction channel than in fixed-price channels. **Table 11.8** provides an overview of factors to consider.

The factors are described as follows:

- **Type of product:** Online auctions are most commonly used for rare and unique products for which prices are difficult to discover, and there may have been no market for the goods. However, Priceline has succeeded in developing auctions for perishable commodities (such as airline seats) for which retail prices have already been established, and some B2B auctions involve commodities such as steel (often sold at distress prices). New clothing items, new digital cameras, and new computers are generally not sold at auction because their prices are easy to discover, catalog

TABLE 11.8	FACTORS TO CONSIDER WHEN CHOOSING AUCTIONS
CONSIDERATIONS	DESCRIPTION
Type of product	Rare, unique, commodity, perishable
Stage of product life cycle	Early, mature, late
Channel-management issues	Conflict with retail distributors; differentiation
Type of auction	Seller vs. buyer bias
Initial pricing	Low vs. high
Bid increment amounts	Low vs. high
Auction length	Short vs. long
Number of items	Single vs. multiple
Price-allocation rule	Uniform vs. discriminatory
Information sharing	Closed vs. open bidding

prices are high, sustainable, and profitable, they are not perishable, and there exists an efficient market channel in the form of retail stores (online and offline).

- **Product life cycle:** For the most part, businesses have traditionally used auctions for goods at the end of their product life cycle and for products where auctions yield a higher price than fixed-price liquidation sales. However, products at the beginning of their life cycle are increasingly being sold at auction. Early releases of music, books, videos, games, and digital appliances can be sold to highly motivated early adopters who want to be the first in their neighborhood with new products. Online sales of event tickets from music concerts to sports events now account for upwards of 25% of all event ticket sales in the United States.

- **Channel management:** Established retailers such as JCPenney and Walmart, and manufacturers in general, must be careful not to allow their auction activity to interfere with their existing profitable channels. For this reason, items found on established retail-site auctions tend to be late in their product life cycle or have quantity purchase requirements.

- **Type of auction:** Sellers obviously should choose auctions where there are many buyers and only a few, or even one, seller. English ascending-price auctions such as those at eBay are best for sellers because as the number of bidders increases, the price tends to move higher.

- **Initial pricing:** Research suggests that auction items should start out with low initial bid prices in order to encourage more bidders to bid (see "Bid increments" below). The lower the price, the larger the number of bidders will appear. The larger the number of bidders, the higher the prices move.

- **Bid increments:** It is generally safest to keep bid increments low so as to increase the number of bidders and the frequency of their bids. If bidders can be convinced that, for just a few more dollars, they can win the auction, then they will tend to make the higher bid and forget about the total amount they are bidding.

- **Auction length:** In general, the longer auctions are scheduled, the larger the number of bidders and the higher the prices can go. However, once the new bid arrival rate drops off and approaches zero, bid prices stabilize. Most eBay auctions are scheduled for seven days.

- **Number of items:** When a business has a number of items to sell, buyers usually expect a "volume discount," and this expectation can cause lower bids in return. Therefore, sellers should consider breaking up very large bundles into smaller bundles auctioned at different times.

- **Price allocation rule:** Most buyers believe it is "fair" that everyone pay the same price in a multi-unit auction, and a uniform pricing rule is recommended. eBay Dutch Internet auctions encourage this expectation. The idea that some buyers should pay more based on their differential need for the product is not widely supported. Therefore, sellers who want to price discriminate should do so by holding auctions for the same goods on different auction markets, or at different times, to prevent direct price comparison.

- **Closed vs. open bidding:** Closed bidding has many advantages for the seller, and sellers should use this approach whenever possible because it permits price discrimination without offending buyers. However, open bidding carries the advantage of "herd effects" and "winning effects" (described later in the chapter) in which consumers' competitive instincts to "win" drive prices higher than even secret bidding would achieve.

SELLER AND CONSUMER BEHAVIOR AT AUCTIONS

In addition to these structural considerations, you should also consider the behavior of consumers at auction sites. Research on consumer behavior at online auction sites is growing, but is still in its infancy. However, early research has produced some interesting findings.

Seller Profits: Arrival Rate, Auction Length, and Number of Units

The profit to the seller is a function of the arrival rate, auction length, and the number of units for auction. However, each of these relationships suffers a declining return to scale and rapidly falls off after an optimal point is reached (Vakrat and Seidmann, 1998, 1999) (see **Figure 11.4**). For this reason, in real-world auctions on eBay, sellers with a large number of units to sell, say, hundreds of PC laptops, usually have multiple concurrent auctions with about 10 units for sale in each auction, with a duration of three days. The auction is just long enough to attract most of the likely bidders, but

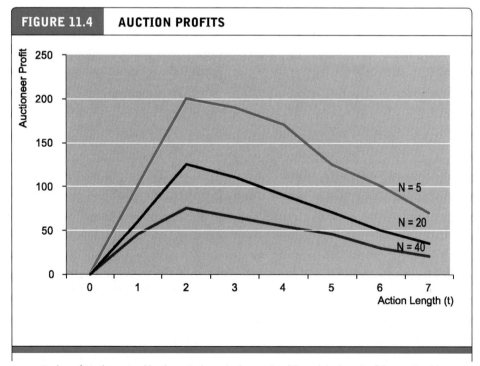

FIGURE 11.4 **AUCTION PROFITS**

An auction's profit is determined by the arrival rate at the auction (N), and the length of the auction (t). Profitability rises rapidly at first, but then falls off rapidly as costs rise. Profits also rise with the number of units auctioned up to a maximum point, and then rapidly fall off.

SOURCE: Based on data from Vakrat and Seidmann, 1998.

not so long as to run up the cost of posting the auction beyond a profitable level. The more popular an auction (the more bidders who arrive), the longer an auction should be, up to the point where the costs of maintaining the auction listing outweigh the additional profit brought by the last bidder. These dynamics suggest a kind of bidding frenzy for popular items, in which the prices bid depend on the number of bidders, length of time, and units offered.

Auction Prices: Are They the Lowest?

It is widely assumed that auction prices are lower than prices in other fixed-price markets. Empirical evidence is mixed on this assumption. Vakrat and Seidmann (1999) found auction prices were 25% lower on average than prices for the identical goods found in catalogs produced by the same retailers. Brynjolfsson and Smith (2000) also found that auction prices for CDs were lower than online store prices. Lee found, however, that auction prices for used cars in Japan on the AUCNET auction site were actually higher than fixed-price markets, in part because the quality of cars on the auction site was higher than cars found in car lots (Lee et al., 1999–2000).

There are many reasons why auction prices might be higher than those in fixed-price markets for items of identical quality, and why auction prices in one auction market may be higher than those in other auction markets. A considerable body of research has shown that consumers are not driven solely by value maximization, but instead are influenced by many situational factors, irrelevant and wrong information, and misperceptions when they make market decisions (Simonson and Tversky, 1992). Auctions are social events—shared social environments, where bidders adjust to one another (Hanson and Putler, 1996). Briefly, bidders base their bids on what others previously bid, and this can lead to an upward cascading effect (Arkes and Hutzel, 2000). In a study of hundreds of eBay auctions for Sony PlayStations, CD players, Mexican pottery, and Italian silk ties, Dholakia and Soltysinski (2001) found that bidders exhibited **herd behavior** (the tendency to gravitate toward, and bid for, auction listings with one or more existing bids) by making multiple bids on some auctions (coveted comparables), and making no bids at auctions for comparable items (overlooked comparables). Herd behavior was lower for products where there was more agreement and more objective clues on the value of the products—Sony PlayStations, for instance, compared to Italian silk ties. Herd behavior resulted in consumers paying higher prices than necessary for reasons having no foundation in economic reality.

The behavioral reality of participating in auctions can produce many unintended results. Winners can suffer **winner's regret**, the feeling after winning an auction that they paid too much for an item, which indicates that their winning bid does not reflect what they thought the item was worth but rather what the second bidder thought the item was worth. Sellers can experience **seller's lament**, reflecting the fact that they sold an item at a price just above the second place bidder, never knowing how much the ultimate winner might have paid or the true value to the final winner. Auction losers can experience **loser's lament**, the feeling of having been too cheap in bidding and failing to win. In summary, auctions can lead to both winners paying too much and sellers receiving too little. Both of these outcomes can be minimized when sellers

herd behavior
the tendency to gravitate toward, and bid for, auction listings with one or more existing bids

winner's regret
the winner's feeling after an auction that he or she paid too much for an item

seller's lament
concern that one will never know how much the ultimate winner might have paid, or the true value to the final winner

loser's lament
the feeling of having been too cheap in bidding and failing to win

and buyers have a very clear understanding of the prices for items in a variety of different online and offline markets.

Consumer Trust in Auctions

Auction sites have the same difficulties creating a sense of consumer trust as all other e-commerce Web sites, although in the case of auction sites, the operators of the marketplace do not directly control the quality of goods being offered and cannot directly vouch for the integrity of customers. This opens the possibility for criminal actors to appear as either sellers or buyers. eBay is the single largest source of consumer fraud on the Internet. Several studies have found that trust and credibility increase as users gain more experience, if trusted third-party seals are present, and if the site has a wide variety of consumer services for tracking purchases (or fraud), thus giving the user a sense of control (Krishnamurthy, 2001; Stanford-Makovsky, 2002; Nikander and Karnonen, 2002; Bailey, et al., 2002; Kollock, 1999). Because of the powerful role that trust plays in online consumer behavior, eBay and most auction sites make considerable efforts to develop automated trust-enhancing mechanisms such as seller and buyer ratings, escrow services, and authenticity guarantees (see the next section).

WHEN AUCTION MARKETS FAIL: FRAUD AND ABUSE IN AUCTIONS

Markets fail to produce socially desirable outcomes (maximizing consumer welfare) in four situations: information asymmetry, monopoly power, public goods, and externalities.

Online and offline auction markets can be prone to fraud, which produces information asymmetries between sellers and buyers and among buyers, which in turn causes auction markets to fail (see **Table 11.9**). According to the Internet Crime Complaint Center (IC3), Internet auto-auction fraud was one of the top 10 types of fraud reported in 2011. Victims of auto-auction fraud scams reported more than $8.2 million in losses, and an average reported loss of more than $2,000 (National White Collar Crime Center/FBI, 2012).

eBay and many other auction sites have investigation units that receive complaints from consumers and investigate reported abuses. Nevertheless, with millions of visitors per week and hundreds of thousands of auctions to monitor, eBay is highly dependent on the good faith of sellers and consumers to follow the rules.

11.3 E-COMMERCE PORTALS

Port: From the Latin porta, an entrance or gateway to a locality.

Portals are the most frequently visited sites on the Web if only because they often are the first page to which many users point their browser on startup. The top portals such as Yahoo, MSN, and AOL have hundreds of millions of unique visitors worldwide each month. Web portal sites are gateways to the more than 100 billion Web pages available on the Internet. Millions of users have set Facebook as their home

TABLE 11.9	TYPES OF AUCTION FRAUDS

TYPE OF FRAUD	DESCRIPTION
FEEDBACK OFFENSES	
Shill feedback	Using secondary IDs or other auction site members to inflate seller ratings
Feedback abuse	Engaging in abuse in the feedback forum
Feedback extortion	Threatening negative feedback in return for a benefit
Feedback solicitation	Offering to sell, trade, or buy feedback
BUYING OFFENSES	
Transaction interference	E-mailing buyers to warn them away from a seller
Invalid bid retraction	Using the retraction option to make high bids, discovering the maximum bid of current high bidder, then retracting bid
Persistent bidding	Persisting in making bids despite a warning that bids are not welcome
Unwelcome buyer	Buying in violation of seller's terms
Bid shielding	Using secondary user IDs or other members to artificially raise the bidding price of an item
Nonpayment after buying	Blocking legitimate buyers by bidding high, then not paying
SELLING OFFENSES	
Shill bidding	Using secondary user IDs or bidders who have no actual intention to buy to artificially raise the price of an item
Seller nonperformance	Accepting payment and failing to deliver the promised goods, either at all, or delivering goods not as described in auction (counterfeit or poor quality)
Nonselling seller	Refusing payment, failure to deliver after a successful auction
Fee avoidance	Any of a variety of mechanisms for avoiding paying listing fees
Transaction interception	Pretending you are a seller and accepting payment
Contact Information/Identity Offenses	
Misrepresentation of identity	Claiming to be an employee of the auction site; representing oneself as another auction site member
False or missing contact information	Providing false information or leaving information out
Dead/invalid e-mail addresses	Providing false contact information
Underage user	A minor claiming to be 18 years old or older
MISCELLANEOUS OFFENSES	
Interference with site	Using any software program that would interfere with auction site operations
Bid siphoning	E-mailing another seller's bidders and offering the same product for less
Sending spam	Sending unsolicited offers to bidders

page, choosing to start their sessions with news from their friends. We have already discussed Facebook in Section 11.1. Perhaps the most important service provided by portals is that of helping people find the information they are looking for on the Web. The original portals in the early days of e-commerce were search engines. Consumers would pass through search engine portals on their way to rich, detailed, in-depth content on the Web. But portals evolved into much more complex Web sites that provide news, entertainment, maps, images, social networks, in-depth information, and education on a growing variety of topics all contained at the portal site. Portals today seek to be a sticky destination site, not merely a gateway through which visitors pass. In this respect, Web portals are very much like television networks: destination sites for content supported by advertising revenues. Portals today want visitors to stay a long time—the longer the better. For the most part they succeed: portals are places where people linger for a long time.

enterprise portals

help employees navigate to the enterprise's human resource and corporate content

Portals also serve important functions within a business or organization. Most corporations, universities, churches, and other formal organizations have **enterprise portals** that help employees or members navigate to important content, such as human resources information, corporate news, or organizational announcements. For instance, your university has a portal through which you can register for courses, find classroom assignments, and perform a host of other important student activities. Increasingly, these enterprise portals also provide general-purpose news and real-time financial feeds provided by content providers outside the organization, such as MSNBC News and generalized Web search capabilities. Corporate portals and intranets are the subject of other textbooks focused on the corporate uses of Web technology and are beyond the scope of this book (see Laudon and Laudon, 2012). Our focus here is on e-commerce portals.

THE GROWTH AND EVOLUTION OF PORTALS

Web portals have changed a great deal from their initial function and role. As noted above, most of today's well-known portals, such as Yahoo, MSN, and AOL, began as search engines. The initial function provided by portals was to index Web page content and make this content available to users in a convenient form. Early portals expected visitors to stay only a few minutes at the site. As millions of people signed on to the Internet in the early 2000s, the number of visitors to basic search engine sites exploded commensurately. At first, few people understood how a Web search site could make money by passing customers on to other destinations. But search sites attracted huge audiences, and therein lay the foundation for their success as vehicles for marketing and advertising. Search sites, recognizing the potential for commerce, expanded their offerings from simple navigation to include commerce (the sale of items directly from the Web site as well as advertising for other retail sites), content (in the form of news at first, and later in the form of weather, investments, games, health, and other subject matter), and distribution of others' content. These three characteristics have become the basic definition of portal sites, namely, sites that provide three functions: navigation of the Web, commerce, and content.

Because the value of portals to advertisers and content owners is largely a function of the size of the audience each portal reaches, and the length of time visitors stay on

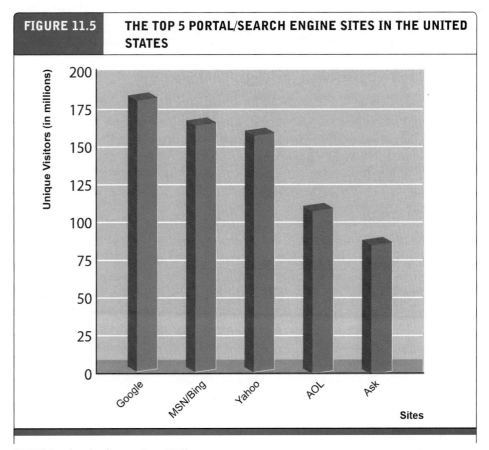

| FIGURE 11.5 | THE TOP 5 PORTAL/SEARCH ENGINE SITES IN THE UNITED STATES |

SOURCE: Based on data from comScore, 2012b.

site, portals compete with one another on reach and unique visitors. *Reach* is defined as the percentage of the Web audience that visits the site in a month (or some other time period), and *unique visitors* is defined as the number of uniquely identified individuals who visit in a month. Portals are inevitably subject to network effects: The value of the portal to advertisers and consumers increases geometrically as reach increases, which, in turn, attracts still more customers. These effects have resulted in the differentiation of the portal marketspace into three tiers: a few general-purpose mega portal sites that garner 60%–80% of the Web audience, second-tier general-purpose sites that hover around 20%–30% reach, and third-tier specialized vertical market portals that attract 2%–10% of the audience. As described in Chapter 3, the top five portals/search engines (Google, Yahoo, MSN/Bing, AOL, and Ask.com) account for more than 95% of online searches. A similar pattern of concentration is observed when considering the audience share of portals/search engines as illustrated in **Figure 11.5**. However, this picture is changing as large audiences move to social network sites, and millions of users make these sites their opening or home pages.

For more insight into the nature of the competition and change among the top portals, read *Insight on Business: The Transformation of AOL*.

INSIGHT ON BUSINESS

THE TRANSFORMATION OF AOL

You have to give it to AOL; its corporate DNA must include a gene for tenacity. From its inauspicious beginnings as an online game server for the Atari 2600 video game console to its dizzying heights as the leading ISP in the United States—a time that even spawned a Meg Ryan/Tom Hanks movie entitled *You've Got Mail* after the ubiquitous greeting AOL users heard each time they signed on—to its equally staggering decline after its failed merger with Time Warner—somehow AOL has found a way to survive.

Started in the early 1980s as Control Video Corporation, it provided an online service called Gameline for the Atari 2600. The company didn't make enough money, and in May 1983, it was reorganized as Quantum Computer Services, providing a dedicated online service for Commodore 64 and 128 computers called Quantum Link. In 1988, the company added online services called Apple Link and PC Link, and in 1989, its name was changed to America Online.

In February 1991, AOL launched an online program for the DOS operating system (the early Microsoft operating system that used text commands) and one for Windows the following year. In contrast to CompuServe, which served the technical community, AOL positioned itself as the online service for people who weren't comfortable with technology, a shrewd move at the time. Initially, it provided proprietary software and charged users hefty hourly fees. In 1996, it switched to a subscription-based model, charging $19.99 per month. Mass distribution of AOL CD-ROMs through the mail spurred adoption—AOL was everywhere, giving over 10 million people their

first exposure to the Web, e-mail, instant messaging, and chat rooms. However, the company was slow to provide access to the open Internet, and complaints erupted, in particular, about dropped connections and busy signals. Still, it continued to grow. In 1996, in another boon to its brand, AOL signed a five-year agreement that it would be bundled with Windows on new PCs. The first major Web portal for the general public was on its way.

In 1999, CEO Steve Case said that Windows was in the past, and predicted that AOL would be the next Microsoft. This is not exactly how the story unfolded. When AOL tried to exploit its tremendous name recognition and brand prominence, it failed repeatedly. Its biggest failure, though not its only one, was not anticipating the broadband transformation. But that's getting ahead of the story.

In 2000, before the company's spectacular fall began, Time Warner bought AOL for $165 billion. Despite the media fanfare, there were problems from the start with what is now acknowledged by current CEO Tim Armstrong to be the worst merger in corporate history. In the first year, the merged company already had difficulty reaching growth targets, possibly because AOL had improperly inflated its pre-merger revenue. In 2002, advertising revenue declined sharply. The number of AOL ISP subscribers peaked in the fall of that year, at 26.7 million, and has been declining ever since. There are only 3.03 million ISP subscribers today. However, these subscribers still generate a third of the company's revenue. Though 400,000 more users were lost between June 2011 and June 2012, the decline is slowing. Incredibly, these core dial-up holdouts have substantially helped to keep the company afloat.

(continued)

Some people believe the merger did not have to turn out that way. Marrying one of the foremost providers of "old fashioned" content to one of the largest distributors of "online" content might have made sense if it had been managed differently. But it wasn't. Key players at Time Warner resented the merger and thought it was a waste of time and money. To make matters worse, corporate leadership did little to persuade brand/division heads that it was their responsibility to make the merged company work.

And then came broadband. AOL underestimated just how attractive broadband would become. By 2004, broadband adoption was gathering speed. At the same time, Google's search engine advertising took off and banner advertising with it. Yahoo was successful with banner display ads, and it added content that drew the broadband audience. AOL was quickly perceived as stodgy, slow, and uncool. Even when AOL made its subscriber-only content freely available, it was too little, too late.

Between 2002 and 2007 the company occupied various positions on the continuum between misstep and turmoil. Its stock price plummeted, it was investigated by the SEC for several unorthodox advertising deals, the Justice Department conducted a criminal probe, financial reports had to be revised downward, and the positions of CEO and VP of Marketing became revolving doors.

In 2007, AOL began pursuing a new strategy, creating more than a dozen niche content sites.

The following year, Time Warner negotiated with both Microsoft and Google in an attempt to sell AOL. When this was unsuccessful, it decided to spin off the company instead. First, it repurchased Google's 5% stake for $283 million. Google's purchase price in 2005 had been $1 billion.

When Tim Armstrong came on board in 2009, he added senior staff members from Google and Yahoo with an eye towards turning the company into the biggest creator of premium content on the Web and the largest seller of online display ads. Positioning AOL to be ready when the line between online and broadcast programming permanently blurred, he began assembling the infrastructure. Acquisitions included StudioNow, a provider of a proprietary digital platform that allows clients to create and distribute professional-quality videos; 5Min Media, which provided a syndication platform for instructional, knowledge, and lifestyle videos; Thing Labs, a Web-based software company specializing in social media applications; and Pictela, which enables AOL to scale its delivery of video, photos, and apps within advertising and generally across AOL. The real blockbuster acquisition was the Huffington Post in March 2011 for $315 million. Armstrong appeared to be betting big on its charismatic leader, Arianna Huffington, and its 25 million unique monthly visitors. Around 20% of AOL's workforce was eliminated following the purchase.

It soon became clear that the big bet was actually on online video, with HuffPost Live as one significant part of the wager. Launched in the summer of 2012, HuffPost Live features live discussions on current events 12 hours a day, five days a week. These 12 hours are recorded and rebroadcast the second half of the day with compilations of weekly highlights shown on weekends. Essentially it is an online cable news network with hosts interacting with reporters, authors, and other topic experts through webcams. The unique twist and perceived draw is user interaction. Viewers submit chat comments as programs are airing and can also tweet and submit their own videos. Viewers will also increasingly be included in programming, also via webcam, so that they can engage with the host and his or her guest, creating a "social video" experience. Rather than scheduling specific programs at specific times of the day, or even for a set period of time, topics are conversational, not bound by timeframe, and

(continued)

not bound by the hot topic of the day—a sort of freeform television. To which, Armstrong is of course hoping to add live advertising. Cadillac and Verizon are two of the main investors in the venture.

AOL also has teams of video producers in both New York and Los Angeles which are creating branded entertainment video. Sometimes working with celebrities, these teams as well as video partners from around the world are producing hundreds of videos a day of an informational, how-to, or entertainment nature. Sources include wholly owned properties such as Engadget and TechCrunch, one of the most popular tech blogs on the Internet, with around 4.8 million unique monthly U.S. visitors. Partners include Martha Stewart Living Omnimedia, Travel Channel, and E!. These videos will attempt to tread the line between branded infomercial and useful and sought after information. Karen Cahn, AOL's general manager for branded entertainment, says that there are 40 to 50 original shows in production in which a brand is either an exclusive sponsor, the programs have brand ads wrapped around them, or the product is shown in the program. They will be distributed to different online outlets depending on where AOL thinks they will be most widely viewed. These outlets include various channels within HuffPost Live and the AOL On Network, AOL Advertising.com, and YouTube, on which AOL placed the 20,000 videos from its original library in October 2012. According to TechCrunch, only YouTube now exceeds AOL in the number of online video offerings.

Aiming to become a one-stop shop for consumers delivering the content they want when they want it, the AOL On Network debuted in April 2012. The launch of this central hub was organized by Ran Harnevo, senior vice president of video at AOL and CEO of 5Min Media. More than 420,000 videos are available on 14 channels divided into subject areas. iOS and Android apps were released in October 2012. The opposite approach from HuffPost Live is embraced. Organized, selected, programmed content, much more like traditional TV, is offered here and syndicated out to different outlets. Cahn sees it as the necessary home repository for AOL's video library where users will come to spend some time, but not as the optimum outlet for maximizing viewership. That, she believes, is the job of the vertical markets.

AOL's second quarter 2012 financial report in July 2012 registered a turnaround from a loss of $11.8 million in 2011 to earnings of $970.8 million in 2012. This was mainly attributed to a one-time patent deal that was completed with Microsoft in June. Revenue decline slowed to 2%, the smallest in seven years, and total advertising revenue was up 6%. So far, revenue from display advertising on Huffington Post and Patch, a community-specific news and information platform, as well as from a deal forged with Microsoft and Yahoo, showed little improvement. Patch, which serves at least 860 communities in 22 states and the District of Columbia, has been an investor concern. Armstrong appears not to have lost faith that Patch, in which more than $200 million has been invested, can become a revenue source. Citing traffic increases greater than 10% per year, projected 2012 revenues of $40 to 50 million, and a site rework that will enable community networking, he touted its ability to transition into local listings and commerce and an upcoming deal with a major national advertiser. However, one drag on AOL operating income included a now concluded proxy fight costing $8.8 million with investor group Starboard Value, which sought to eliminate Patch.

AOL's strategy to focus on video, content, and display advertising is risky. One-third of the company's revenue is still derived from its dwindling dial-up subscriptions. However, in August 2012, AOL instituted a $600 million stock buyback and one-time cash dividend of $5.15 per share to recompense investors for the completed Microsoft

(continued)

patent deal. It also enjoyed a tripling of its stock price from the previous year, and appears well positioned to capitalize on the popularity of online video. The combination is likely to mollify inves- tors in the short term while Armstrong continues to work towards consistent user growth, which he says will signify that the turnaround is complete.

SOURCES: "AOL: You've Got Apps," *New York Business Journal*, October 4, 2012; "AOL," Wikipedia.com, accessed September 26, 2012; "AOL CEO Tim Armstrong: 'We Haven't Won Yet'," by Daniel Terdiman, News.cnet.com, September 11, 2012; "AOL's Triple-Pronged Approach to Online Video," by Troy Dreier, Streamingmedia.com, August/September 2012; "$1.1B Microsoft Patent Deal Done, AOL Buys Back $600M In Stock, Offers Dividend Of $5.15 Per Share," by Ingrid Lunden,TechCrunch.com, August 27th, 2012; "AOL Dialup Just Had Its 'Best' Quarter In A Decade, And Still Has 3 Million Subscribers," by Dan Frommer, SplatF.com, July 26, 2012; "AOL Says Patch Continues to Double Its Revenue from Last Year," by Steve Myers, Poynter.org, July 25, 2012; "AOL's Ad Revenue Up; Armstrong Bullish on Video," by Tanzina Vega, *New York Times*, July 25, 2012; "AOL Buys TechCrunch, 5Min and Thing Labs," by Jessica E. Vascellaro and Emily Steel, *New York Times*, September 29, 2010; "Eleven Years of Ambition and Failure at AOL," by Saul Hansell, *New York Times*, July 24, 2009; "Daring to Dream of a Resurgent AOL," by Saul Hansell, *New York Times*, July 23, 2009; "Before Spin-off, AOL Tries for that Start-up Feeling," *New York Times*, July 20, 2009.

TYPES OF PORTALS: GENERAL-PURPOSE AND VERTICAL MARKET

There are two primary types of portals: general-purpose portals and vertical market portals. **General-purpose portals** attempt to attract a very large general audience and then retain the audience on-site by providing in-depth vertical content channels, such as information on news, finance, autos, movies, and weather. General-purpose portals typically offer Web search engines, free e-mail, personal home pages, chat rooms, community-building software, and bulletin boards. Vertical content channels on general-purpose portal sites offer content such as sports scores, stock tickers, health tips, instant messaging, automobile information, and auctions.

Vertical market portals (sometimes also referred to as destination sites or vortals) attempt to attract highly focused, loyal audiences with a deep interest either in com-munity or specialized content—from sports to the weather. In addition to their focused content, vertical market portals have recently begun adding many of the features found in general-purpose portals. For instance, in addition to being a social network, you can also think of Facebook as a portal—the home page for millions of users, and a gateway to the Internet. Facebook is an affinity group portal because it is based on friendships among people. Facebook offers e-mail, search (Bing), games, and apps. News is limited.

The concentration of audience share in the portal market reflects (in addition to network effects) the limited time budget of consumers. This limited time budget works to the advantage of general-purpose portals. Consumers have a finite amount of time to spend on the Web, and as a result, most consumers visit fewer than 30 unique domains each month. Facing limited time, consumers concentrate their visits at sites that can satisfy a broad range of interests, from weather and travel information, to stocks, sports, and entertainment content.

General-purpose sites such as Yahoo try to be all things to all people, and attract a broad audience with both generalized navigation services and in-depth content and community efforts. For instance, Yahoo has become the Web's largest source of news: more people visit Yahoo News than any other news site including online newspapers. Yet recent changes in consumer behavior on the Web show that consumers are spending less time "surfing the Web" and on general browsing, and more time doing focused searches, research, and participating in social networks. These trends will advantage special-purpose, vertical market sites that can provide focused, in-depth community and content.

general-purpose portals
attempt to attract a very large general audience and then retain the audience on-site by providing in-depth vertical content

vertical market portals
attempt to attract highly focused, loyal audiences with a deep interest in either community or specialized content

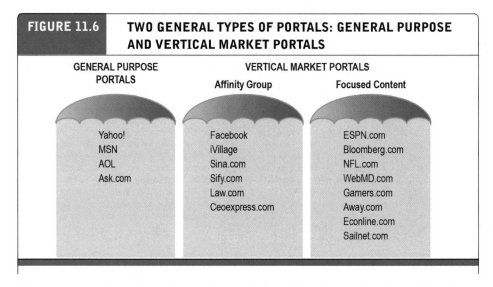

FIGURE 11.6 — TWO GENERAL TYPES OF PORTALS: GENERAL PURPOSE AND VERTICAL MARKET PORTALS

There are two general types of portals: general-purpose and vertical market. Vertical market portals may be based on affinity groups or on focused content.

As a general matter, the general-purpose portals are very well-known brands, while the vertical content and affinity group portals tend to have less well-known brands. **Figure 11.6** lists examples of general-purpose portals and the two main types of vertical market portals.

PORTAL BUSINESS MODELS

Portals receive income from a number of different sources. The revenue base of portals is changing and dynamic, with some of the largest sources of revenue declining. **Table 11.10** summarizes the major portal revenue sources.

The business strategies of both general-purpose and vertical portals have changed greatly because of the rapid growth in search engine advertising and intelligent ad placement networks such as Google's AdSense, which can place ads on thousands of Web sites based on the content of the Web site. General portal sites such as AOL and Yahoo did not have well-developed search engines, and hence have not grown as fast as Google, which has a powerful search engine. Microsoft, for instance, has invested billions of dollars in its Bing search engine to catch up with Google. On the other hand, general portals have content, which Google did not originally have, although it added to its content by purchasing YouTube, and adding Google sites devoted to news, financial information, images, and maps. Yahoo and MSN visitors stay on-site a long time reading news, content, and sending e-mail. Facebook users stay on-site and linger three times as long as visitors to traditional portals like Yahoo. For this reason social network sites, Facebook in particular, are direct competitors of Yahoo, Google, and the other portals. General portals are attempting to provide more premium content focused on sub-communities of their portal audience. Advertisers on portals are especially interested in focused, revenue-producing premium content available on Web portals because it attracts a more committed audience.

TABLE 11.10	TYPICAL PORTAL REVENUE SOURCES
PORTAL REVENUE SOURCE	DESCRIPTION
General advertising	Charging for impressions delivered
Tenancy deals	Fixed charge for guaranteed number of impressions, exclusive partnerships, "sole providers"
Commissions on sales	Revenue based on sales at the site by independent providers
Subscription fees	Charging for premium content
Applications and games	Games and apps are sold to users; advertising is placed within apps

For instance, financial service firms pay premium advertising rates to advertise on portal finance service areas such as Yahoo's Finance pages. As noted in Chapters 6 and 7, there is a direct relationship between the revenue derived from a customer and the focus of the customer segment (see **Figure 11.7**).

The survival strategy for general-purpose portals in the future is therefore to develop deep, rich, vertical content in order to reach and engage customers at the site. The strategy for much smaller vertical market portals is to put together a collection of vertical portals to form a vertical portal network, a collection of deep, rich content sites. The strategy for search engine sites such as Google is to obtain more content to attract users for a long time and expose them to more ad pages (or screens).

FIGURE 11.7	REVENUE PER CUSTOMER AND MARKET FOCUS

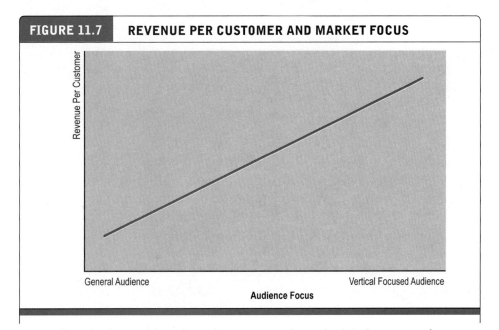

The more focused and targeted the audience, the more revenue that can be derived per customer for an appropriately targeted product or service.

11.4 | **CASE STUDY**

eBay Evolves

With the unveiling of its new, more reserved logo in September 2012, eBay announced its arrival to the mainstream. Gone are the jaunty, incongruent block letters that characterized the offbeat startup auction site founded by Pierre Omidyar in 1995. In their place, the bold primary colors intact, is a symmetrical set of block letters staidly observing the same parallel bottom line. With eBay now deriving 70% of its revenue from traditional e-commerce, and peer-to-peer auctions taking a backseat, the time had come. Underscoring this change, which was by no means sudden, the 2012 Fall Seller Update announced that sales of tarot card readings, potions, spells, and psychic readings would no longer be permitted. And, in a progression from the previous Christmas when it provided a tool to allow customers to locate in-stock items at local bricks-and-mortar chains, eBay instituted a rewards program with Toys "R" Us, Dick's Sporting Goods, and Aeropostale in which customers who spend $100 either at one of these merchants' eBay storefronts or at their Web sites receive a $10 in-store coupon. Eccentric was out; conventional in.

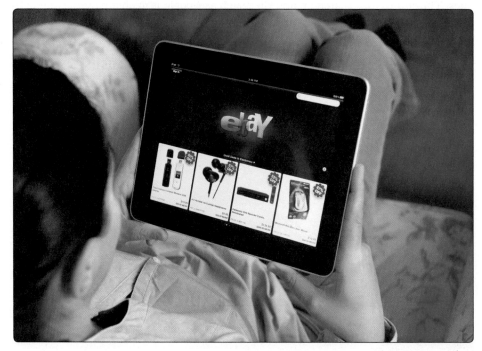

© Iain Masterton / Alamy

The transformation began in November 2007, when former CEO Meg Whitman exited and was replaced by former Bain & Company managing director, John Donahoe. The company had already begun to stall, and the trend continued through 2009. For many buyers, the novelty of online auctions had worn off, and they were returning to easier and simpler methods of buying fixed-price goods from fixed-price retailers such as Amazon, which, by comparison, had steady growth during the same time period. Search engines and comparison shopping sites were also taking away some of eBay's auction business by making items easier to find on the Web.

Inheriting as he did one of the world's most recognizable and well-known Web sites perhaps made Donahoe's heretofore never accomplished task of turning around an Internet company more achievable, but his path was not easy or without controversy. His three-year revival plan moved eBay away from its origins as an online flea market, and at first it began to resemble an outlet mall where retailers sold out-of-season, overstocked, refurbished, or discontinued merchandise. From there it was a straightforward progression to partnering with firms such as Toys"R"Us to simply serve as another channel for current merchandise.

Small sellers were encouraged to shift away from the auction format and move toward the fixed-price sales model. The fee structure was adjusted, listing fees for fixed-price sales were lowered, improvements were made to the search engine, and rather than displaying ending auctions first, a formula was devised that took into account price and seller reputation so that highly rated merchants appeared first and received more exposure.

Unsurprisingly, the growing pains during this period included increasing complaints from sellers about excessive fees and eBay's favoritism toward big retailers. The hundreds of thousands of people who support themselves by selling on eBay and many millions more who use eBay to supplement their income often felt slighted. With its stock continuing to drop from its $58 high in 2004 to a low of just over $10 in early 2009, analysts' faith that Donahoe could turn things around had dwindled. Fearing that eBay had strayed too far from its original corporate culture and that competition from Amazon and Google Search presented serious threats, most forecasters were negative or neutral on eBay's chance of recovery, This pessimism discounted eBay's history of sensible growth marked by a number of canny purchases.

Its signature purchase is, of course, PayPal, whose payment services enable the exchange of money between individuals over the Internet. At a decade old, this acquisition was the key to eBay's endurance through the lean years and the propeller that pushed it towards the future. At times accounting for as much as 40% of eBay's revenues, it was responsible for 32% of eBay's growth from the first quarter of 2011 through the first quarter of 2012. With active registered accounts up 12% over that same time period, and half its growth accruing from abroad, PayPal was clearly an asset ripe for further development.

In 2012, a system was installed in 2,000 Home Depot stores so that PayPal card holders could either swipe their cards or use a PIN and their cell phone number to pay for purchases. Other bricks-and-mortar venues will be similarly equipped in the near future. Further expansion is a credit card processing device called PayPal Here that allows small businesses to use smartphones and tablets to accept credit cards. In direct competition with Square, eBay plans to enable consumers to "check in" so that they can be personally greeted, complete purchases without a mobile device or a credit card, and receive a text message as their receipt.

The 2008 addition of BillMeLater to the PayPal wallet, an instant credit product offered at checkout, has also proved, so far, to be farsighted. BML, which lets online customers pay several months after they have made purchases, logged 64% loan growth between 2010 and 2011, making it one of eBay's fastest growing business segments. BML can reduce funding costs for PayPal and help it to develop into a true financial product. Currently, more than 50% of PayPal purchases are funded using Visa and MasterCard credit and debit cards, which come with substantial fees. Reducing this cost would naturally increase profit margins. Now ranked the third most popular online payment service behind PayPal and Amazon's payment service, BML was used by consumers to complete 14% of purchases in 2011, a stunning jump from just 1% in 2010.

One possible downside, however, is that as BML grows, it increases overall risk for the company putting downward pressure on stock price. Collecting fees for processing payments presents little in the way of risk. Expanding into the loan granting arena is coupled with the risk of default and with regulatory issues. BML's continued expansion would likely mean that PayPal, which is already a bank in Europe, would have to become a chartered financial institution in the United States. This lengthy and expensive process has so far been forestalled by using WebBank as the lender and purchasing the receivables from them. This set-up has already been tested in a California district court case charging that the true lender is BMI, and further, that it engages in usury lending practices because the loans carry close to a 20% annual interest rate. While the usury charges were dismissed, the remainder of the case was moved to a Utah district court. eBay will have to balance the risks and benefits of further BMI expansion.

Still, with possible PayPal challenges in the future, its success gave the Marketplaces segment time to rebound. And recover it did. In 2012, it delivered double-digit growth, 11% annualized, and eBay stock rose to its highest level in six years, close to $50 in September. As impressive and encouraging as the Marketplaces turnaround was, it was another of eBay's astute investments that truly fueled its resurgence—mobile technology. eBay's mobile investments began in 2010 with RedLaser, a barcode-scanning mobile application. This was followed by Critical Path, an industry leading mobile app developer, doubling the size of eBay's mobile team. WHERE, a location-based media and advertising company with a local discovery mobile application, and Zong, a provider of mobile payments through mobile carrier billing, were purchased in 2011. PayPal was used to purchase Fig Card, a small mobile payment startup in April 2011. A year later, these outlays were bearing fruit, reportedly supporting $15 billion in mobile transactions over the preceding year. Approximately 50% of these transactions were mobile Marketplaces sales, while the other half was mobile PayPal transactions.

eBay recognized the coming mobile revolution even before the first iPhone or the establishment of the App Store, according to Olivier Ropars, senior director of Mobile Commerce. This prescience resulted in two significant September 2012 milestones—

the 100 millionth download of eBay mobile apps and the 100 millionth mobile listing. eBay not only has a core app, but also an eBay Motors app, an eBay Fashion app, and a RedLaser price checking app, which they expect to drive mobile sales to $10 billion by the end of 2012, nearly double 2011.

While many other acquisitions through the years have also helped to transform eBay from an online garage sale to a mainstream competitor with Amazon, its adoption of the "social, mobile, local" driving theme was central to its survival. Positioning itself at the center of the online—offline—mobile triangle by offering a wide variety of services that enable merchants to more easily integrate their cross-channel retailing is the key to its 2012 resurgence and to its continued success. Still, in a nod to its innovative origins, eBay built a new online tool aimed at its original and still most active users—comic book and coin collectors. Described as a "Pinterest-like" service, it is called Setify in reference to enabling collectors to complete their "sets." The tool, still in beta as of October 2012, will enable avid collectors to compile and organize pictures of their treasures for display to other users and to create wish lists so that sellers can target market to them. iPhone and Android apps are in the works, and expansion to other collection categories will follow. eBay appears to be wisely adhering to two maxims for long-lived companies: Always be cognizant of your changing environment, and stay true to your core identity.

Case Study Questions

1. Contrast eBay's original business model with its latest proposed business model.

2. What are the problems that eBay is currently facing? How is eBay trying to solve these problems?

3. Are the solutions eBay is seeking to implement good solutions? Why or why not? Are there any other solutions that eBay should consider?

4. Who are eBay's top three competitors online, and how will eBay's new strategy help it compete? Will eBay be providing a differentiated service to customers?

SOURCES: "eBay Hits 100m Mobile App Download Mark," by Dervedia Thomas, Dailydeal-media.com, September 29, 2012; "With Setify, eBay Goes Back To Its Roots And Creates The Nerdiest Pinterest Ever," by Christina Chaey, *Fast Company*, September 25, 2012; "eBay: We Need to Behave More Like a Retailer," by Sarah Shearman, Tamebay.com, September 25, 2012; "eBay Logo Gets a Refresh; The Time Felt Right After 17 Years," by Mark Tyson, Hexus.com, September 14, 2012; "eBay Bans Magic Spells and Potions," by Katy Waldman, Slate.com, August 17, 2012; "Behind eBay's Comeback," by James B. Stewart, *New York Times*, July 27, 2012; "Bill Me Later, eBay's Credit Version of PayPal, Helps Company's Profits but Exposes It to Risk, by Alistair Barr, MercuryNews.com, July 12, 2012; "PayPal Strength Helps eBay Exceed Forecasts," by Somini Sengupta, *New York Times*, April 18, 2012; "eBay Favors Big-Box Retailers in Holiday Promotions," by Ina Steiner, eCommerce-Bytes.com, December, 16, 2011; "How Jack Abraham is Reinventing eBay," by Danielle Sacks, *Fast Company*, June 22, 2011; "Connecting the Dots on eBay's Local Shopping Strategy," by Leena Rao, Techcrunch.com, May 15, 2011; "eBay CEO Sees Opportunities in Online and Offline Commerce," by Scott Morrison, *Wall Street Journal,* February 10, 2011; "eBay Says Big Growth Is Not Over," by Verne G. Kopytoff, *New York Times*, February 6, 2011; "eBay Mobile Sales Rise to $2 Billion, Reach Top End of Forecast," by Joseph Galante, Bloomberg.com, January 5, 2011.

11.5 REVIEW

KEY CONCEPTS

■ **Explain the difference between a traditional social network and an online social network.**

Social networks involve:
- A group of people
- Shared social interaction
- Common ties among members
- A shared area for some period of time

By extension, an online social network is an area online where people who share common ties can interact with one another.

■ **Understand how a social network differs from a portal.**

The difference between social networks and portals has become blurred. Originally, portals began as search engines. Then they added content and eventually many community-building features such as chat rooms, bulletin boards, and free Web site design and hosting. Social network sites began as content-specific locations and added more general portal services such as Web searching, general news, weather, and travel information, as well as a wide variety of e-commerce services.

■ **Describe the different types of social networks and online communities and their business models.**
- *General communities:* Members can interact with a general audience segmented into numerous different groups. The purpose is to attract enough members to populate a wide range of topical discussion groups. Most general communities began as non-commercial subscription-based endeavors, but many have been purchased by larger community portal sites.
- *Practice networks:* Members can participate in discussion groups and get help or simply information relating to an area of shared practice, such as art, education, or medicine. These generally have a nonprofit business model in which they simply attempt to collect enough in subscription fees, sales commissions, and limited advertising to cover the cost of operations.
- *Interest-based communities:* Members can participate in focused discussion groups on a shared interest such as boats, horses, skiing, travel, or health. The advertising business model has worked because the targeted audience is attractive to marketers. Tenancy and sponsorship deals provide another similar revenue stream.
- *Affinity communities:* Members can participate in focused discussions with others who share the same affinity or group identification, such as religion, ethnicity, gender, sexual orientation, or political beliefs. The business model is a mixture of subscription revenue from premium content and services, advertising, tenancy/sponsorships, and distribution agreements.
- *Sponsored communities:* Members can participate in online communities created by government, nonprofit, or for-profit organizations for the purpose of pursuing organizational goals. These types of sites vary widely from local government sites to branded product sites. They use community technologies and tech-

niques to distribute information or extend brand influence. The goal of a branded product site is to increase offline product sales. These sites do not seek to make a profit and are often cost centers.

■ Describe the major types of auctions, their benefits and costs, and how they operate.

Auctions are markets where prices vary (dynamic pricing) depending on the competition among the participants who are buying or selling products or services. They can be classified broadly as C2C or B2C, although generally the term C2C auction refers to the venue in which the sale takes place, for example, a consumer-oriented Web site such as eBay, which also auctions items from established merchants. A B2C auction refers to an established online merchant that offers its own auctions. There are also numerous B2B online auctions for buyers of industrial parts, raw materials, commodities, and services. Within these three broad categories of auctions are several major auction types classified based upon how the bidding mechanisms work in each system:

- *English auctions:* A single item is up for sale from a single seller. Multiple buyers bid against one another within a specific time frame, with the highest bidder winning the object, as long as the high bid has exceeded the reserve bid set by the seller, below which he or she refuses to sell.
- *Traditional Dutch auctions:* Sellers with many identical items sold in lots list a starting price and time for the opening of bids. As the clock advances, the price for each lot falls until a buyer offers to buy at that price.
- *Dutch Internet auctions:* Sellers with many identical items for sale list a minimum price or starting bid, and buyers indicate both a bid price and a quantity desired. The lowest winning bid that clears the available quantity is paid by all winning bidders. Those with the highest bid are assured of receiving the quantity they desire, but only pay the amount of the lowest successful bid (uniform pricing rule).
- *Name Your Own Price or reverse auctions:* Buyers specify the price they are willing to pay for an item, and multiple sellers bid for their business. This is one example of discriminatory pricing in which winners may pay different amounts for the same product or service depending on how much they have bid.
- *Group buying or demand aggregation auctions:* In the group-buying format, the more users who sign on to buy an item, the lower the item's price falls. These are generally B2B or B2G sites where small businesses can collectively receive discount prices for items that are purchased in high volumes.

Benefits of auctions include:

- *Liquidity:* Sellers and buyers are connected in a global marketplace.
- *Price discovery:* Even difficult-to-price items can be competitively priced based on supply and demand.
- *Price transparency:* Everyone in the world can see the asking and bidding prices for items, although prices can vary from auction site to auction site.
- *Market efficiency:* Consumers are offered access to a selection of goods that would be impossible to access physically, and consumer welfare is often increased due to reduced prices.
- *Lower transaction costs:* Merchants and consumers alike are benefited by the reduced costs of selling and purchasing goods compared to the physical marketplace.

- *Consumer aggregation:* A large number of consumers who are motivated to buy are amassed in one marketplace—a great convenience to the seller.
- *Network effects:* The larger an auction site becomes in the numbers of both users and products, the greater the benefits become, and therefore the more valuable a marketplace it becomes.
- *Market-maker benefits:* Auction sites have no inventory carrying costs or shipping costs, making them perhaps the ideal online business in that their main function is the transfer of information.

Costs of auctions include:

- *Delayed consumption:* Auctions can go on for days, and the product must then be shipped to the buyer. Buyers will typically want to pay less for an item they cannot immediately obtain.
- *Monitoring costs:* Buyers must spend time monitoring the bidding.
- *Equipment costs:* Buyers must purchase, or have already purchased, computer systems and Internet service, and learned how to operate these systems.
- *Trust risks:* Consumers face an increased risk of experiencing a loss as online auctions are the largest source of Internet fraud.
- *Fulfillment costs:* Buyers must pay for packing, shipping, and insurance, and will factor this cost into their bid price.

Auction sites have sought to reduce these risks through various methods including:

- *Rating systems:* Previous customers rate sellers based on their experience with them and post them on the site for other buyers to see.
- *Watch lists:* These allow buyers to monitor specific auctions as they proceed over a number of days and only pay close attention in the last few minutes of bidding.
- *Proxy bidding:* Buyers can enter a maximum price they are willing to pay, and the auction software will automatically place incremental bids as their original bid is surpassed.

■ Understand when to use auctions in a business.

Auctions can be an appropriate channel for businesses to sell items in a variety of situations. The factors for businesses to consider include:

- *The type of product:* Rare and unique products are well suited to the auction marketplace as are perishable items such as airline tickets, hotel rooms, car rentals, and tickets to plays, concerts, and sporting events.
- *The product life cycle:* Traditionally, auctions have been used by businesses to generate a higher profit on items at the end of their life cycle than they would receive from product liquidation sales. However, they are now more frequently being used at the beginning of a product's life cycle to generate premium prices from highly motivated early adopters.
- *Channel management:* Businesses must be careful when deciding whether to pursue an auction strategy to ensure that products at auction do not compete with products in their existing profitable channels. This is why most established retail firms tend to use auctions for products at the end of their life cycles or to have quantity purchasing requirements.

- *The type of auction:* Businesses should choose seller-biased auctions where there are many buyers and only one or a few sellers, preferably using the English ascending price system to drive the price up as high as possible.
- *Initial pricing:* Auction items should start with a low initial bid in order to attract more bidders, because the more bidders an item has, the higher the final price will be.
- *Bid increments:* When increments are kept low, more bidders are attracted and the frequency of their bidding is increased. This can translate into a higher final price as bidders are prodded onward in small steps.
- *Auction length:* In general, the longer an auction runs, the more bidders will enter the auction, and the higher the final price will be. However, if an auction continues for too long, the bid prices will stabilize and the cost of posting the auction may outweigh the profit from any further price increases.
- *Number of items:* If a business has a large quantity of items to sell, it should break the lot up into smaller bundles and auction them at different times so that buyers do not expect a volume discount.
- *Price allocation rule:* Because most buyers are biased toward the uniform pricing rule, sellers should use different auction markets, or auction the same goods at different times in order to price discriminate.
- *Closed vs. open bidding:* Closed bidding should be used whenever possible because it benefits a seller by allowing price discrimination. However, open bidding can sometimes be beneficial when herd behavior kicks in, causing multiple bids on highly visited auctions, while overlooked and lightly trafficked auctions for the same or comparable items languish. This generally occurs when there are few objective measures of a product's true value in the marketplace.

■ Recognize the potential for auction abuse and fraud.

Auctions are particularly prone to fraud, which produces information asymmetries between buyers and sellers. Some of the possible abuses and frauds include:

- *Bid rigging:* Agreeing offline to limit bids or using shills to submit false bids that drive prices up.
- *Price matching:* Agreeing informally or formally to set floor prices on auction items below which sellers will not sell in open markets.
- *Shill feedback, defensive:* Using secondary IDs or other auction members to inflate seller ratings.
- *Shill feedback, offensive:* Using secondary IDs or other auction members to deflate ratings for another user (feedback bombs).
- *Feedback extortion:* Threatening negative feedback in return for a benefit.
- *Transaction interference:* E-mailing buyers to warn them away from a seller.
- *Bid manipulation:* Using the retraction option to make high bids, discovering the maximum bid of the current high bidder, and then retracting the bid.
- *Non-payment after winning:* Blocking legitimate buyers by bidding high, then not paying.
- *Shill bidding:* Using secondary user IDs or other auction members to artificially raise the price of an item.
- *Transaction non-performance:* Accepting payment and failing to deliver.
- *Non-selling seller:* Refusing payment or failing to deliver after a successful auction.
- *Bid siphoning:* E-mailing another seller's bidders and offering the same product for less.

■ **Describe the major types of Internet portals.**

Web portals are gateways to the more than 100 billion Web pages available on the Internet. Originally, their primary purpose was to help users find information on the Web, but they evolved into destination sites that provided a myriad of content from news to entertainment. Today, portals serve three main purposes: navigation of the Web, content, and commerce. Among the major portal types are:

- *Enterprise portals:* Corporations, universities, churches, and other organizations create these sites to help employees or members navigate to important content such as corporate news or organizational announcements.
- *General-purpose portals:* Examples are AOL, Yahoo, and MSN, which try to attract a very large general audience by providing many in-depth vertical content channels. Some also offer ISP services on a subscription basis, search engines, e-mail, chat, bulletin boards, and personal home pages.
- *Vertical market portals:* Also called destination sites, they attempt to attract a highly focused, loyal audience with an intense interest in either a community they belong to or an interest they hold. Recent studies have found that users with limited time resources are interested in concentrating their Web site visiting on focused searches in areas that appeal to them. Vertical market portals can be divided into two main classifications, although hybrids that overlap the two classifications also exist.
- *Affinity groups:* Statistical aggregates of people who identify themselves by their attitudes, values, beliefs, and behavior. Affinity portals exist to serve such broad constituencies as women, African Americans, and gays as well as much more focused constituencies such as union members, religious groups, and even home-schooling families.
- *Focused content portals:* These sites contain in-depth information on a particular topic that all members are interested in. They can provide content on such broad topics as sports, news, weather, entertainment, finance, or business, or they can appeal to a much more focused interest group such as boat, horse, or video game enthusiasts.

■ **Understand the business models of portals.**

Portals receive revenue from a number of different sources. The business model is presently changing and adapting to declines in certain revenue streams, particularly advertising revenues. Revenue sources can include:

- *General advertising:* Charging for impressions delivered
- *Tenancy deals:* Locking in long-term, multiple-year deals so a company is guaranteed a number of impressions with premium placement on home pages and through exclusive marketing deals
- *Subscription fees:* Charging for premium content
- *Commissions on sales:* Earning revenue based on sales at the site by independent merchants.

The survival strategy for general-purpose portals is to develop deep, rich, vertical content in order to attract advertisers to various niche groups that they can target with focused ads. The strategy for the small vertical market portals is to build a collection of vertical portals, thereby creating a network of deep, rich content sites for the same reason.

QUESTIONS

1. Why did most communities in the early days of e-commerce fail? What factors enable online social networks to prosper today?
2. How does a social network differ from a portal? How are the two similar?
3. What is an affinity community, and what is its business model?
4. What is personalization or personal value pricing, and how can it be used at the beginning of a product's life cycle to increase revenues?
5. List and briefly explain three of the benefits of auction markets.
6. What are the four major costs to consumers of participating in an auction?
7. Under what conditions does a seller bias exist in an auction market? When does a buyer bias exist?
8. What are the two price allocation rules in auction markets? Explain the difference between them.
9. What is an auction aggregator and how does it work?
10. What types of products are well suited for an auction market? At what points in the product life cycle can auction markets prove beneficial for marketers?
11. What three characteristics define a portal site today?
12. What is a vertical market portal, and how might recent trends in consumer behavior prove advantageous to this business model?
13. What are the two main types of vertical market portals, and how are they distinguished from one another?
14. List and briefly explain the main revenue sources for the portal business model.

PROJECTS

1. Find two examples of an affinity portal and two examples of a focused-content portal. Prepare a presentation explaining why each of your examples should be categorized as an affinity portal or a focused-content portal. For each example, surf the site and describe the services each site provides. Try to determine what revenue model each of your examples is using and, if possible, how many members or registered visitors the site has attracted.

2. Examine the use of auctions by businesses. Go to any auction site of your choosing and look for outlet auctions or auctions directly from merchants. Research at least three products for sale. What stage in the product life cycle do these products fall into? Are there quantity purchasing requirements? What was the opening bid price? What are the bid increments? What is the auction duration? Analyze why these firms have used the auction channel to sell these goods and prepare a short report on your findings.

3. Visit one for-profit-sponsored and one nonprofit-sponsored social network. Create a presentation to describe and demonstrate the offering at each site. What organizational objectives is each pursuing? How is the for-profit company using community-building technologies as a customer relations management tool?

CHAPTER 12

B2B E-commerce: Supply Chain Management and Collaborative Commerce

LEARNING OBJECTIVES

After reading this chapter, you will be able to:

- Define B2B commerce and understand its scope and history.
- Understand the procurement process, the supply chain, and collaborative commerce.
- Identify the main types of B2B e-commerce: Net marketplaces and private industrial networks.
- Understand the four types of Net marketplaces.
- Identify the major trends in the development of Net marketplaces.
- Identify the role of private industrial networks in transforming the supply chain.
- Understand the role of private industrial networks in supporting collaborative commerce.

Volkswagen

Builds Its B2B Platform

Volkswagen AG is the world's third largest car manufacturer, producing 8.3 million cars, trucks, and vans in 2011, and generating over $206 billion in revenue, up 25% from the year before. In addition to the Volkswagen brand, the Volkswagen Group also owns luxury carmakers such as Porsche, Audi, Bentley, Scania Bugatti, and Lamborghini, and family carmakers SEAT in Spain and Skoda in the Czech Republic. The company has almost 500,000 employees and operates plants in Europe, Africa, the Asian/Pacific rim, and the Americas. In the first half of 2012, Volkswagen Group continued its expansion despite a slowdown in Europe. New investments in China, India, and Mexico, along with a strong American market, pushed sales revenues up 22%, and its share of the global passenger car market to 12.4%, making Volkswagen the second largest producer in the world, behind General Motors.

© Julian Clune / Alamy

The various companies and 61 production plants in the Volkswagen Group annually purchase components, automotive parts, and indirect materials worth about 95 billion euros, or about $123 billion (which constitutes about 60% of Volkswagen's annual revenue). Obviously, the procurement process and relationships with suppliers are absolutely critical for Volkswagen's success.

Today, the Volkswagen Group manages almost all of its procurement needs via the Internet. It began building its Internet platform, VWGroupSupply.com, in 2000. The Volkswagen Group was looking for ways to create more efficient relationships with its suppliers and reduce the cost of paper-based procurement processes. However, the company did not want to automate procurement using a public independent exchange or an industry consortium because it would have had to adapt its own business processes to a common framework that could be used by many different organizations. Volkswagen hoped that by building its own B2B network, it could compete more effectively against other automakers. Volkswagen decided, for instance, not to participate in Covisint, the giant automotive industry consortium backed by major car manufacturers such as Ford, General Motors, and DaimlerChrysler, which provided procurement and other supply chain services for these companies, other automotive manufacturers, and their suppliers.

Instead, Volkswagen opted for a private platform that would allow it to integrate its suppliers more tightly with its own business processes, and where it could control more

SOURCES: "Facts and Figures," Volkswagen Group Supply, September 2012; Annual Report 2011, Volkswagen Group, March 9, 2012; "e-Procurement within the Volkswagen Group," by Alex Smith, Littleknowhow.com, September 25, 2011; "Customer Specific Quality Requirements of the Volkswagen Group," IATF Global Certification Body Conference, February 10, 2011; "Automotive B2B Developments at Odette25," GXS.com, June 22, 2010; "Best Practices: VW Revs Up its B2B Engine," by Martin Hoffman, *Optimize*, March 2004.

precisely who was invited to participate. VWGroupSupply now handles over 90% of all global purchasing for the Volkswagen Group, including all automotive and parts components. It is one of the most comprehensive e-procurement systems in the global automotive industry. Volkswagen refers to it as the Group Business Platform. From an initial seven applications in 2003, the platform now offers over 60 different online applications, such as requests for quotations (RFQs), contract negotiations, catalog purchases, purchase order management, engineering change management, vehicle program management, and payments, among others. The Volkswagen Group developed the platform using technology from a number of vendors, including Ariba, IBM, and i2 Technologies.

Suppliers of all sizes can access VWGroupSupply with standard Web browser software. The Web site is limited to suppliers who have done business with one or more companies in the Volkswagen Group and potential new suppliers who go through an authorization process. Currently, over 45,000 suppliers are registered, and there are over 206,000 users. The system maintains a common data repository with details on each supplier concerning procurement, logistics, production, quality, technical design, and finance.

VWGroupSupply's online catalog currently contains about 2.5 million items from 590 global suppliers. There are 14,200 internal users of the online catalog who have conducted over 1.5 million transactions with a value totaling 380 million euros ($447 million). The catalog uses the eCl@ss standard for classifying its contents. All suppliers who participate in the catalog ordering process classify their products using this standard.

Online negotiations involve multiple bids by suppliers for various purchasing contracts. VWGroupSupply ensures that all participants meet its technical and commercial qualifications. Before an online solicitation begins, the system informs vendors about the data and precise rules governing negotiations. About 13,000 different vendors have taken part in online negotiations. In 2011, VWGroupSupply conducted around 2,500 online contract negotiations online, with a value of 2.6 billion euros ($3.3 billion).

Shifts in market demand have a drastic impact on Volkswagen's production activities and affect the ability of suppliers to deliver. Production bottlenecks can result if suppliers are unprepared for a sudden upsurge in demand. If suppliers stock too much inventory, they may incur excess costs from running at overcapacity. VWGroupSupply has an application called electronic Capacity Management (eCAP) to alert both Volkswagen and its suppliers to changes in trends in advance. eCAP enables suppliers to track Volkswagen's continually updated production plans and materials requirements in real time online. This capability captures information about participating suppliers' planned maximum and minimum capacities. If Volkswagen production requirements go beyond these limits, the system sets off an alarm so both parties can react quickly. eCAP maintains information on over 400 suppliers and 4,000 critical parts.

The VWGroupSupply case illustrates the exciting potential for B2B e-commerce to lower production costs, increase collaboration among firms, speed up new product delivery, and ultimately revolutionize both the manufacturing process inherited from the early twentieth century and the way industrial products are designed and manufactured. VWGroupSupply is an example of just one type of B2B e-commerce, but there are many other equally promising efforts to using the Internet to change the relationships among manufacturers and their suppliers. In the fashion industry, the combination of high-speed value chains coupled with equally high-speed trendy design, not only clears shelves (and reduces the likelihood of clearance sales), but increases profits by increasing value to consumers (Cachon and Swinney, 2011). The success of VWGroupSupply and similar networks operated by the major automobile firms in the world stands in contrast to an earlier industry-sponsored Net marketplace called Covisint. Founded in 1999 by five of the world's largest automakers (General Motors, Ford, Chrysler, Nissan, and Peugeot), Covisint hoped to provide an electronic market connecting thousands of suppliers to a few huge buyers using auctions and procurement services. While initially successful, Covisint was sold in June 2004, although it continues as a B2B services firm in a number of industries. Its auction business was sold to FreeMarkets, an early B2B auction company, which itself was sold to another B2B e-commerce firm called Ariba later in 2004. In 2012, Ariba survives as a successful software firm focusing on the procurement process and the operation of a successful net marketplace.

The failure of Covisint (as well as Ford's AutoExchange) and the simultaneous growth in B2B e-commerce efforts such as VWGroupSupply illustrates the difficulties of achieving the broad visions established during the early days of e-commerce. From a high of 1,500 online B2B exchanges in 2000, the number has dwindled to less than 200 survivors today (Rosenzweig, et. al., 2011). Like B2C commerce, the B2B marketplace has consolidated, evolved, and moved on to more attainable visions. In the process, many B2B efforts have experienced extraordinary success. There are many failed efforts to consider as well; these provide important lessons to all managers.

In this chapter, we examine three different B2B e-commerce themes: procurement, supply chain management, and collaborative commerce. Each of these business processes has changed greatly with the evolution of B2B e-commerce systems. In Section 12.1, we define B2B commerce and place it in the context of trends in procurement, supply chain management, and collaborative commerce. The next two sections describe the two fundamental types of B2B e-commerce: Net marketplaces and private industrial networks. We describe four major types of Net marketplaces, their biases (seller, buyer, and neutral), ownership structure and accessibility (private versus public), and value creation dynamics.

Table 12.1 summarizes the leading trends in B2B e-commerce in the 2012–2013 period. Perhaps the most important themes are growing industry concern with supply chain risk and volatility, along with a growing public concern with the accountability of supply chains—in particular, violations of developed-world expectations of working conditions in third-world factories that play a key role in the production of goods sold in more developed countries. What many firms have learned in the last decade is that

TABLE 12.1	MAJOR TRENDS IN B2B E-COMMERCE, 2012–2013

BUSINESS

- B2B e-commerce growth accelerates in 2012 to pre-recession levels as the global economy expands especially in commodities, mining, and manufacturing.
- Risk management: sophisticated global supply chains blindsided by the Takeuchi nuclear accident, and floods in Thailand; chaos in financial markets, rapid increases in fuel costs, rising labor and commodity costs in Asia, and a global recession.
- Regional manufacturing: risks of far flung global networks lead to an increase in regional manufacturing and supply chains, moving production closer to market demand.
- Flexibility: growing emphasis on rapid-response and optimal supply chains rather than lowest cost supply chains which typically carry great risks.
- Supply chain visibility: growing calls for more real-time data that would allow managers to "see" across not only their production, but also "see into" the production and financial condition of their key suppliers.
- Social commerce and customer intimacy: buyers, like consumers, are tapping into their tablets, smartphones, and social network sites for purchasing, scheduling, exception handling, and deciding with their B2B customers and suppliers in order to manage supply chain risk.
- Large firms begin splintering single, global B2B platforms into product and region-centered systems to achieve lower risk, greater adaptability, and lower complexity.
- Market ownership: private B2B markets proliferate, especially as Web services, while public B2B markets stabilize in selected industries.

TECHNOLOGY

- Big data: global trade and logistics systems are generating huge repositories of B2B data, swamping management understanding and controls.
- Business analytics: growing emphasis on use of business analytics software (business intelligence) to understand very large data sets.
- Cloud: migration of B2B hardware and software to cloud computing and cloud apps, away from individual corporate data centers, as a means of slowing rising IT costs. B2B systems move to Cloud computing providers like IBM, Oracle, Amazon, Google, and HP as their core technology.
- Mobile platform: growing use of mobile platform for B2B systems (CRM, SCM, and enterprise), putting B2B commerce into managers' palms.
- Social networking platforms increasingly being used by B2B managers for feedback from customers, strengthening customer and supplier relationships, adjusting prices and orders, and enhancing decision making.

SOCIETY

- Accountability: growing demands for supply chain accountability and monitoring in developed countries driven by reports of poor working conditions in Asian factories. Apple and others under fire for harsh working conditions in their supply chains.
- Sustainable supply chains: growing public demand for businesses to mitigate their environmental impact leads from local environmental optimization to consideration of the entire supply chain from design, production, customer service, and post-use disposal.
- Acceptance and growth of B2B platforms: Ariba, the largest Net marketplace, has 300,000 firms participating, 80% of the Fortune 500 firms.
- B2B firms discover social networks: 66% of B2B firms user Twitter along with other social network sites to build communities and enable collaboration among engineers, sales, and procurement personnel.
- Decline in antitrust concerns raised by early B2B trading schemes.

supply chains can strengthen or weaken a company depending on a number of factors related to supply chain efficiency such as community engagement, labor relations, environmental protection, and sustainability. Yet many believe that all of these related factors are important to the long profitability of firms (Beard and Hornik, 2011). At the same time, in part because of the globalization of supply chains, B2B e-commerce systems are now used by nearly all of the American S&P 500 firms, where over half of all revenues are produced offshore. Thousands of smaller firms are now able to participate in B2B systems as low-cost cloud-based computing and software-as-a-service (SaaS) becomes widely available. The cost of participating in B2B e-commerce systems has fallen significantly, allowing smaller firms to participate along with giant firms. Taking advantage of the exploding mobile platform, more companies are using smartphones and tablet computers to run their businesses from any location. There are hundreds of iPhone and Android apps available from enterprise B2B vendors like SAP, IBM, Oracle and others that link to supply chain management systems (Bolukbasi, 2011; Melnyk, 2010). Social network tools are pushing into the B2B world as well as the consumer world. B2B managers are increasingly using public and private social network sites and technologies to enable long-term conversations with their customers and vendors.

12.1 B2B E-COMMERCE AND SUPPLY CHAIN MANAGEMENT

The trade between business firms represents a huge marketplace. The total amount of B2B trade in the United States in 2012 is about $11.5 trillion, with B2B e-commerce (online B2B) contributing about $4.1 trillion of that amount (U.S. Census Bureau, 2012a; authors' estimates). By 2016, B2B e-commerce should grow to about $5.6 trillion in the United States.

The process of conducting trade among business firms is complex and requires significant human intervention, and therefore, consumes significant resources. Some firms estimate that each corporate purchase order for support products costs them, on average, at least $100 in administrative overhead. Administrative overhead includes processing paper, approving purchase decisions, spending time using the telephone and fax machines to search for products and arrange for purchases, arranging for shipping, and receiving the goods. Across the economy, this adds up to trillions of dollars annually being spent for procurement processes that could potentially be automated. If even just a portion of inter-firm trade were automated, and parts of the entire procurement process assisted by the Internet, then literally trillions of dollars might be released for more productive uses, consumer prices potentially would fall, productivity would increase, and the economic wealth of the nation would expand. This is the promise of B2B e-commerce. The challenge of B2B e-commerce is changing existing patterns and systems of procurement, and designing and implementing new Internet-based B2B solutions.

DEFINING AND MEASURING THE GROWTH OF B2B COMMERCE

Before the Internet, business-to-business transactions were referred to simply as *trade* or the *procurement process*. The term **total inter-firm trade** refers to the total flow of value among firms. Today, we use the term **B2B commerce** to describe all types of

total inter-firm trade
the total flow of value among firms

B2B commerce
all types of inter-firm trade

inter-firm trade to exchange value across organizational boundaries. B2B commerce includes the following business processes insofar as they involve inter-firm trade: customer relationship management, demand management, order fulfillment, manufacturing management, procurement, product development, returns, logistics/transportation, and inventory management (Barlow, 2011). This definition of B2B commerce does not include transactions that occur within the boundaries of a single firm—for instance, the transfer of goods and value from one subsidiary to another, or the use of corporate intranets to manage the firm. We use the term **B2B e-commerce** (or **B2B digital commerce**) to describe specifically that portion of B2B commerce that is enabled by the Internet. The links that connect business firms in the production of goods and services are referred to as "the supply chain." **Supply chains** are a complex system of organizations, people, business processes, technology, and information, all of which need to work together to produce products efficiently (Global Supply Chain Forum, 2012). Today's supply chains are often global, connecting the smartphones in New York to the shipyards in Los Angeles and Quindow, and to the Foxconn factories that produce the phones. They are also local and national in scope.

THE EVOLUTION OF B2B COMMERCE

B2B commerce has evolved over a 35-year period through several technology-driven stages (see **Figure 12.1**). The first step in the development of B2B commerce in the mid-1970s was **automated order entry systems** that involved the use of telephone modems to send digital orders to health care products companies such as Baxter

B2B e-commerce (B2B digital commerce)
that portion of B2B commerce that is enabled by the Internet

Supply chain
the links that connect business firms with one another to coordinate production

automated order entry systems
involve the use of telephone modems to send digital orders

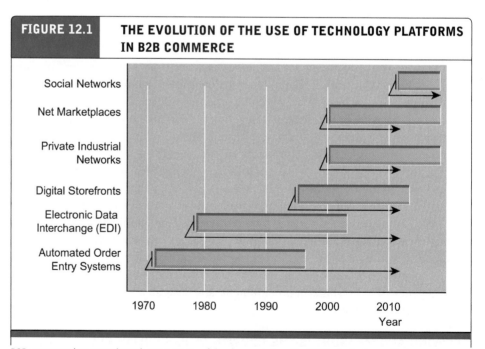

FIGURE 12.1   THE EVOLUTION OF THE USE OF TECHNOLOGY PLATFORMS IN B2B COMMERCE

B2B commerce has gone through many stages of development since the 1970s. Each stage reflects a major change in technology platforms from mainframes to private dedicated networks, and finally to the Internet. In 2012, social networks—both private and public—are being used to coordinate decision-making in B2B commerce.

Healthcare. Baxter, a diversified supplier of hospital supplies, placed telephone modems in its customers' procurement offices to automate re-ordering from Baxter's computerized inventory database (and to discourage re-ordering from competitors). This early technology was replaced by personal computers using private networks in the late 1980s, and by Internet workstations accessing electronic online catalogs in the late 1990s. Automated order entry systems are **seller-side solutions**. They are owned by the suppliers and are seller-biased markets—they show only goods from a single seller. Customers benefited from these systems because they reduced the costs of inventory replenishment and were paid for largely by the suppliers. Automated order entry systems continue to play an important role in B2B commerce.

By the late 1970s, a new form of computer-to-computer communication called **electronic data interchange (EDI)** emerged. We describe EDI in greater detail later in this chapter, but at this point, it is necessary only to know that EDI is a communications standard for sharing business documents such as invoices, purchase orders, shipping bills, product stocking numbers (SKUs), and settlement information among a small number of firms. Virtually all large firms have EDI systems, and most industry groups have industry standards for defining documents in that industry. EDI systems are owned by the buyers, hence they are **buyer-side solutions** and buyer-biased because they aim to reduce the procurement costs of supplies for the buyer. Of course, by automating the transaction, EDI systems also benefit the sellers through customer cost reduction. The topology of EDI systems is often referred to as a **hub-and-spoke system**, with the buyers in the center and the suppliers connected to the central hub via private dedicated networks.

EDI systems generally serve vertical markets. A **vertical market** is one that provides expertise and products for a specific industry, such as automobiles. In contrast, **horizontal markets** serve many different industries.

Electronic storefronts emerged in the mid-1990s along with the commercialization of the Internet. **B2B electronic storefronts** are perhaps the simplest and easiest form of B2B e-commerce to understand, because they are just online catalogs of products made available to the public marketplace by a single supplier—similar to Amazon for the B2C retail market. Owned by the suppliers, they are seller-side solutions and seller-biased because they show only the products offered by a single supplier.

Electronic storefronts are a natural descendant of automated order entry systems, but there are two important differences: (1) the far less expensive and more universal Internet becomes the communication media and displaces private networks, and (2) electronic storefronts tend to serve horizontal markets—they carry products that serve a wide variety of industries. Although electronic storefronts emerged prior to Net marketplaces (described next), they are usually considered a type of Net marketplace.

Net marketplaces emerged in the late 1990s as a natural extension and scaling-up of the electronic storefronts. There are many different kinds of Net marketplaces, which we describe in detail in Section 12.2, but the essential characteristic of a Net marketplace is that they bring hundreds to thousands of suppliers—each with electronic catalogs and potentially thousands of purchasing firms—into a single Internet-based environment to conduct trade.

---

seller-side solutions
seller-biased markets that are owned by, and show only goods from, a single seller

electronic data interchange (EDI)
a communications standard for sharing business documents and settlement information among a small number of firms

buyer-side solutions
buyer-biased markets that are owned by buyers and that aim to reduce the procurement costs of supplies for buyers

hub-and-spoke system
suppliers connected to a central hub of buyers via private dedicated networks

vertical market
one that provides expertise and products for a specific industry

horizontal markets
markets that serve many different industries

B2B electronic storefronts
online catalogs of products made available to the public marketplace by a single supplier

Net marketplace
brings hundreds to thousands of suppliers and buyers into a single Internet-based environment to conduct trade

Net marketplaces can be organized under a variety of ownership models. Some are owned by independent third parties backed by venture capital, some are owned by established firms who are the main or only market players, and some are a mix of both. Net marketplaces establish the prices of the goods they offer in four primary ways—fixed catalog prices, or more dynamic pricing, such as negotiation, auction, or bid/ask ("exchange" model). Net marketplaces earn revenue in a number of ways, including transaction fees, subscription fees, service fees, software licensing fees, advertising and marketing, and sales of data and information.

Although the primary benefits and biases of Net marketplaces have to be determined on a case-by-case basis depending on ownership and pricing mechanisms, it is often the case that Net marketplaces are biased against suppliers because they can force suppliers to reveal their prices and terms to other suppliers in the marketplace. Net marketplaces can also significantly extend the benefits of simple electronic storefronts by seeking to automate the procurement value chain of both selling and buying firms.

private industrial networks (private trading exchange, PTX)

Internet-based communication environments that extend far beyond procurement to encompass truly collaborative commerce

Private industrial networks also emerged in the late 1990s as natural extensions of EDI systems and the existing close relationships that developed between large industrial firms and their trusted suppliers. Described in more detail in Section 12.3, **private industrial networks** (sometimes also referred to as a *private trading exchange*, or *PTX*) are Internet-based communication environments that extend far beyond procurement to encompass supply chain efficiency enhancements and truly collaborative commerce. Private industrial networks permit buyer firms and their principal suppliers to share product design and development, marketing, inventory, production scheduling, and unstructured communications. Like EDI, private industrial networks are owned by the buyers and are buyer-side solutions with buyer biases. These systems are directly intended to improve the cost position and flexibility of large industrial firms (Yoo, et. al., 2011; Kumaran, 2002). These private industrial networks have a much higher survival rate than other Net marketplaces (Rosenzweig, 2011).

Naturally, private industrial networks have significant benefits for suppliers as well. Inclusion in the direct supply chain for a major industrial purchasing company can allow a supplier to increase both revenue and margins because the environment is not competitive—only a few suppliers are included in the private industrial network. These networks are the most prevalent form of Internet-based B2B commerce, and this will continue into the foreseeable future.

THE GROWTH OF B2B E-COMMERCE 2011–2016

During the period 2012–2016, B2B e-commerce is projected to grow from about 40% to 42% of total inter-firm trade in the United States, or from $4.1 trillion in 2012 to $5.6 trillion in 2016 (see **Figure 12.2**).

Several observations are important to note with respect to Figure 12.2. First, it shows that the initial belief that electronic marketplaces would become the dominant form of B2B e-commerce is not supported. Second, private industrial networks play a dominant role in B2B e-commerce, both now and in the future. Third, non-EDI B2B e-commerce is the most rapidly growing type of B2B e-commerce, and EDI is still quite large but is declining over time.

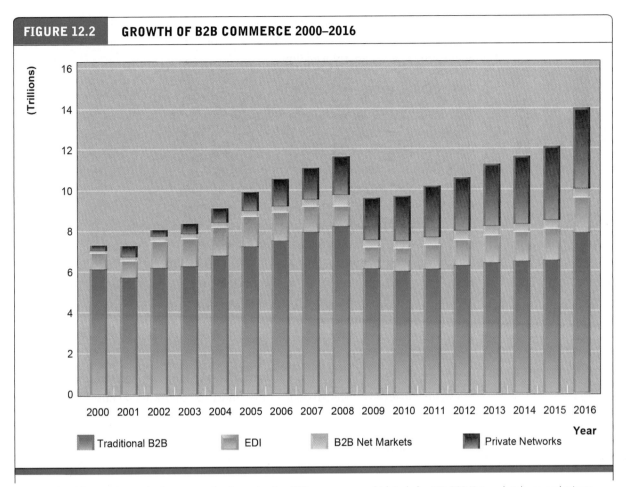

| FIGURE 12.2 | GROWTH OF B2B COMMERCE 2000–2016 |

Private industrial networks are the fastest growing form of online B2B e-commerce, which includes EDI, B2B Net marketplaces, and private industrial markets.

SOURCES: Based on data from U.S. Census Bureau, 2012a; authors' estimates.

Industry Forecasts

Not all industries will be similarly affected by B2B e-commerce, nor will all industries similarly benefit from B2B. Several factors influence the speed with which industries migrate to B2B e-commerce and the volume of transactions. Those industries in which there is already significant utilization of EDI (indicating concentration of buyers and suppliers) and large investments in information technology and Internet infrastructure can be expected to move first and fastest to B2B e-commerce utilization. The aerospace and defense, computer, and industrial equipment industries meet these criteria. Where the marketplace is highly concentrated on either the purchasing or selling side, or both, conditions are also ripe for rapid B2B e-commerce growth, as in the energy and chemical industries. In the case of health care, the federal government, health care providers (doctors and hospitals), and major insurance companies are moving rapidly towards a national medical record system and the use of Internet for managing medical payments. Coordinating the various players in the health care system is an extraordinary B2B challenge. Computer service firms like IBM, and B2B service firms like Covisint, are expanding the use of information ecosystems where health providers and insurers can share information.

POTENTIAL BENEFITS AND CHALLENGES OF B2B E-COMMERCE

Regardless of the specific type of B2B e-commerce, as a whole, Internet-based B2B commerce promises many strategic benefits to participating firms—both buyers and sellers—and impressive gains for the economy as a whole. B2B e-commerce can:

- Lower administrative costs
- Lower search costs for buyers
- Reduce inventory costs by increasing competition among suppliers (increasing price transparency) and reducing inventory to the bare minimum
- Lower transaction costs by eliminating paperwork and automating parts of the procurement process
- Increase production flexibility by ensuring delivery of parts "just in time"
- Improve quality of products by increasing cooperation among buyers and sellers and reducing quality issues
- Decrease product cycle time by sharing designs and production schedules with suppliers
- Increase opportunities for collaborating with suppliers and distributors
- Create greater price transparency—the ability to see the actual buy and sell prices in a market
- Increase the visibility and real-time information sharing among all participants in the supply chain network.

B2B e-commerce offers potential first-mover strategic benefits for individual firms as well. Firms that move their procurement processes online first will experience impressive gains in productivity, cost reduction, and potentially much faster introduction of new, higher-quality products. While these gains may be imitated by other competing firms, it is also clear from the brief history of B2B e-commerce that firms making sustained investments in information technology and Internet-based B2B commerce can adapt much faster to new technologies as they emerge, creating a string of first-mover advantages.

While there are many potential benefits to B2B e-commerce supply chains, there are also considerable risks and challenges. Often real-world supply chains fail to provide visibility into the supply chain because they lack real-time demand, production, and logistics data, along with inadequate financial data on suppliers. The result is unexpected supplier failure and disruption to the supply chain. Builders of B2B digital supply chains often had little concern for the environmental impacts of supply chains, the sensitivity of supply chains to natural events, fluctuating fuel and labor costs, or the impact of public values involving labor and environmental policies. The result in 2012-2013 is that many Fortune 1000 supply chains are risky and vulnerable. Read *Insight on Society: Where's MyiPad? Apple's Supply Chain Risks and Vulnerabilities* for a look at the impact the recent earthquake in Japan has had on global supply chains, as well as the reputational risk posed by supply chains.

INSIGHT ON SOCIETY

WHERE'S MY IPAD? SUPPLY CHAIN RISK AND VULNERABILITY

On Friday, March 11, 2011, a magnitude 9.0 earthquake occurred offshore of northern Japan and the Oshika Peninsula of Tohoku. The Tohoku earthquake was the largest in recorded history and it immediately created a number of tsunami waves, some of which exceeded 100 feet in height and penetrated up to six miles inland. In their path were six coastal nuclear reactors in the Fukushima Prefecture near the town of Okuma, the largest nuclear power site in the world. The earthquake and tsunami combined to cut off the nuclear plant's electrical power, which caused the water pumps that keep the nuclear material from overheating and melting to stop. Backup diesel generators were swamped by the tsunami waves. Several of the nuclear reactors exploded and began leaking dangerous levels of radiation as fuel rods melted at temperatures exceeding 5,000 degrees. The government evacuated the entire population within a radius of 20 miles, and radiation levels rose throughout Japan, contaminating the surrounding countryside and ocean. Over 13,000 people lost their lives directly from the earthquake and tsunami, and the death and disease tolls from the nuclear disaster may never be fully known.

The impact of the Tohoku earthquake on global supply chains was just as unexpected as the earthquake itself, although one wonders if either should have been unexpected. In fact, the earthquake exposed significant weaknesses and vulnerabilities in today's modern B2B supply chains. Technology, globalization of trade, and high levels of wage disparity between the developed and undeveloped worlds have led to a massive outsourcing of manufacturing around the world, mostly to low-wage countries but also to countries with unusual expertise as well as low wages like Japan. Today, every component of every manufactured product is carefully examined by company engineers and financial managers with an eye to finding the lowest cost and highest quality manufacturer in the world. Production inevitably tends to concentrate at single firms that are given very high order volumes if they can meet the price. Large orders make lower prices easier to grant because of scale economies. Rather than spread production among multiple suppliers using small production runs, why not concentrate orders among one or two preferred global suppliers with huge production runs? The answer: when you concentrate production globally on a few suppliers, you also concentrate risk.

As a result, the world's manufacturing base is less redundant, flexible, and adaptive than older traditional supply chains. Interdependencies have grown into a tightly coupled machine that is quite fragile. Risk assessment in supply chains has been weak or nonexistent.

Computers, cell phones, Caterpillar earth movers, Boeing airplanes, and automobiles from Toyota, Ford, GM, and Honda are just a few of the complex manufactured goods that rely on parts and subassemblies made thousands of miles away from their assembly plants. Most of these manufacturers know who their first-tier suppliers are but don't have a clue as to who supplies their suppliers, and so on down the line of the industrial spider's web that constitutes the real world of supply chains. None of the firms above had considered the impact of an earthquake on their supply chains, or a nuclear meltdown, or even a financial collapse in the global banking system—all typical risks found in the real world.

Take the Apple iPad. IHS iSuppli is a market research firm that tears apart consumer electronic devices to discover how they are made, who makes the components, and where they are made, in order

(continued)

to obtain market intelligence on producer prices and profits. In its tear down of the iPad 2, it identfied at least five major components sourced from Japanese suppliers, some of whom are located in northern Japan: NAND flash from Toshiba Corp., dynamic random access memory (DRAM) made by Elpida Memory Inc., an electronic compass from AKM Semiconductor, the touch screen overlay glass likely from Asahi Glass Co., and the system battery from Apple Japan Inc. Not all of these suppliers were directly impacted by the earthquake, but some were, and many have sub-suppliers of various hard-to-replace small components that were directly impacted. The iPad and iPhone's unusually shaped lithium batteries use a crucial polymer made by Kureha, a Japanese firm in the nuclear contamination zone. Kureha controls 70% of the global production of this polymer. Apple was not the only consumer product manufacturer hit hard: computer chips are built on silicon wafers, and 25% of the world's supply is made by two Japanese manufacturers, both of which have shut down wafer production.

Apple is especially susceptible to supply chain disruptions because its new products often experience huge surges in demand, stressing its supply chains in normal times, and causing 2-4 week delays in meeting orders. After the Japanese earthquake, the consumer order delivery reached eight weeks.

The new iPad released in March 2012 suggests that Apple has changed its supply chain sourcing in order to lessen the risk of disruption. In a tear down of the new iPad, UBM TechInsights took apart several iPads and found that many of the components were made by two or more manufacturers when comparing different iPads. The new retina display, for instance, was produced by three different manufacturers (Samsung, LG, and a third company not identified). Still, many of the major components were made by the same Asian companies that ran into difficulties with nuclear accidents and Asian floods. It's unclear if using multiple suppliers all from the same region mitigates Apple's supply chain risk, or if it is an effort to extract lower prices from competing suppliers.

Supply chain risk involves more than disruptions in production, as Apple and many other companies have discovered. Supply chains can produce reputational risks when key suppliers engage in labor and environmental policies and practices that are unacceptable to developed world audiences. For instance, for much of 2012, Apple was under attack in the United States and Europe after an audit by the Fair Labor Association found that workers at several assembly plants operated by Apple contractor Foxconn were exposed to toxic chemicals and forced to work over 60 hours a week under dangerous work conditions.

Apple was not the only manufacturer that learned a lesson in supply chain risk from the Japanese earthquake: Boeing was without carbon fiber airframe assemblies made in Japan; Ford and GM closed factories for lack of Japanese transmissions; and Caterpillar reduced production at its factories worldwide as it attempted to secure alternative suppliers.

One might think that in the so-called global and Internet economy, computer-based supply chains could quickly and effortlessly adjust to find new suppliers for just about any component or industrial material in a matter of minutes. Think again. New supply chains will need to be built that optimize not just cost but also survivability in the event of common disasters. They must also take into account efforts to reform labor and environmental practices of those involved in the supply chain.

SOURCES: "Disruptions: Too Much Silence on Working Conditions," by Nick Bilton, *New York Times*, April 8, 2012; "Audit Faults Apple Supplier," by Jessica Vascellaro, *Wall Street Journal*, March 30, 2012; "Under the Hood of Apple's Tablet," by Don Clark, *Wall Street Journal*, March 16, 2012; "In China, Human Costs Are Built Into an iPad," by Charles Duhigg and David Barboza, New York Times, January 25, 2012; "Japan: The Business After Shocks," by Andrew Dowell, *Wall Street Journal*, March 25, 2011; "Some Worry the Success of Apple Is Tied to Japan," by Miguel Helft, *New York Times*, March 22, 2011; "Crisis Tests Supply Chain's Weak Links," by James Hookway and Aries Poon, *Wall Street Journal*, March 18, 2011; "Caterpillar Warns of Supply Problems From Quake," by Bob Tita, *Wall Street Journal*, March 18, 2011; "Lacking Parts, G.M. Will Close Plant," by Nick Bunkley, *New York Times*, March 17, 2011.

THE PROCUREMENT PROCESS AND THE SUPPLY CHAIN

The subject of B2B e-commerce can be complex because there are so many ways the Internet can be used to support the exchange of goods and payments among organizations, efficient supply chains, and collaboration. At the most basic level, B2B digital e-commerce is about changing the **procurement process** (how business firms purchase goods they need to produce goods they will ultimately sell to consumers) of thousands of firms across the United States and the world.

procurement process
how firms purchase goods they need to produce goods for consumers

One way to enter this area of Internet-based B2B commerce is to examine the existing procurement business process (see **Figure 12.3**). Firms purchase goods from a set of suppliers, and they in turn purchase their inputs from a set of suppliers. The supply chain includes not just the firms themselves, but also the relationships among them and the processes that connect them.

There are seven separate steps in the procurement process. The first three steps involve the decision of who to buy from and what to pay: searching for suppliers of specific products; qualifying both the seller and the products they sell; and negotiating prices, credit terms, escrow requirements, quality, and scheduling of delivery. Once a supplier is identified, purchase orders are issued, the buyer is sent an invoice, the goods are shipped, and the buyer sends a payment. Each of these steps in the procurement process is composed of many separate business processes and sub-activities. Each of these activities must be recorded in the information systems of the seller, buyer, and shipper. Often, this data entry is not automatic and involves a great deal of manual labor, telephone calls, faxes, and e-mails.

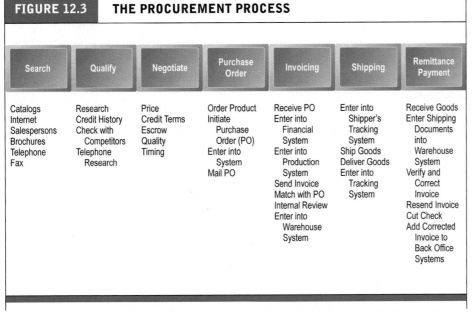

FIGURE 12.3	THE PROCUREMENT PROCESS

Search	Qualify	Negotiate	Purchase Order	Invoicing	Shipping	Remittance Payment
Catalogs	Research	Price	Order Product	Receive PO	Enter into	Receive Goods
Internet	Credit History	Credit Terms	Initiate	Enter into	Shipper's	Enter Shipping
Salespersons	Check with	Escrow	Purchase	Financial	Tracking	Documents
Brochures	Competitors	Quality	Order (PO)	System	System	into
Telephone	Telephone	Timing	Enter into	Enter into	Ship Goods	Warehouse
Fax	Research		System	Production	Deliver Goods	System
			Mail PO	System	Enter into	Verify and
				Send Invoice	Tracking	Correct
				Match with PO	System	Invoice
				Internal Review		Resend Invoice
				Enter into		Cut Check
				Warehouse		Add Corrected
				System		Invoice to
						Back Office
						Systems

The procurement process is a lengthy and complicated series of steps that involves the seller, buyer, and shipping companies in a series of connected transactions.

Types of Procurement

direct goods
goods directly involved in the production process

indirect goods
all other goods not directly involved in the production process

MRO goods
products for maintenance, repair, and operations

contract purchasing
involves long-term written agreements to purchase specified products, under agreed-upon terms and quality, for an extended period of time

spot purchasing
involves the purchase of goods based on immediate needs in larger marketplaces that involve many suppliers

Two distinctions are important for understanding how B2B e-commerce can improve the procurement process. First, firms make purchases of two kinds of goods from suppliers: direct goods and indirect goods. **Direct goods** are goods integrally involved in the production process; for instance, when an automobile manufacturer purchases sheet steel for auto body production. **Indirect goods** are all other goods not directly involved in the production process, such as office supplies and maintenance products. Often these goods are called **MRO goods**—products for maintenance, repair, and operations.

Second, firms use two different methods for purchasing goods: contract purchasing and spot purchasing. **Contract purchasing** involves long-term written agreements to purchase specified products, with agreed-upon terms and quality, for an extended period of time. Generally, firms purchase direct goods using long-term contracts. **Spot purchasing** involves the purchase of goods based on immediate needs in larger marketplaces that involve many suppliers. Generally, firms use spot purchasing for indirect goods, although in some cases, firms also use spot purchasing for direct goods.

According to several estimates, about 80% of inter-firm trade involves contract purchasing of direct goods, and 20% involves spot purchasing of indirect goods (Kaplan and Sawhney, 2000). This finding is significant for understanding B2B e-commerce.

Although the procurement process involves the purchasing of goods, it is extraordinarily information-intense, involving the movement of information among many existing corporate systems. The procurement process today is also very labor-intensive, directly involving over 1.2 million employees in the United States, not including those engaged in transportation, finance, insurance, or general office administration related to the process (U.S. Census Bureau, 2012).

In the long term, the success or failure of B2B e-commerce depends on changing the day-to-day behavior of these 1.2 million people. The key players in the procurement process are the purchasing managers. They ultimately decide who to buy from, what to buy, and on what terms. Purchasing managers ("procurement managers" in the business press) are also the key decision makers for the adoption of B2B e-commerce solutions.

Although Figure 12.3 captures some of the complexity of the procurement process, it is important to realize that firms purchase thousands of goods from thousands of suppliers. The suppliers, in turn, must purchase their inputs from their suppliers. Large manufacturers such as Ford Motor Company have over 20,000 suppliers of parts, packaging, and technology. The number of secondary and tertiary suppliers is at least as large. Together, this extended **multi-tier supply chain** (the chain of primary, secondary, and tertiary suppliers) constitutes a crucial aspect of the industrial infrastructure of the economy. **Figure 12.4** depicts a firm's multi-tier supply chain.

multi-tier supply chain
the chain of primary, secondary, and tertiary suppliers

The supply chain depicted in Figure 12.4 is a three-tier chain simplified for the sake of illustration. In fact, large Fortune 1000 firms have thousands of suppliers, who in turn have thousands of smaller suppliers. The complexity of the supply chain suggests a combinatorial explosion. Assuming a manufacturer has four primary suppliers and each one has three primary suppliers, and each of these has three primary

| FIGURE 12.4 | THE MULTI-TIER SUPPLY CHAIN |

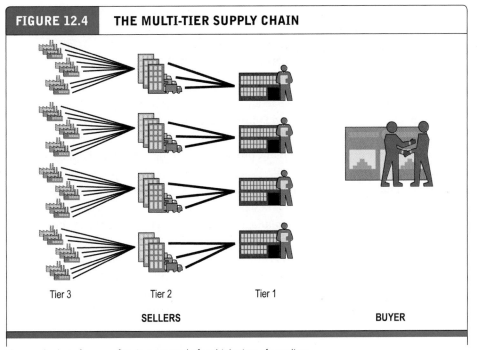

Tier 3   Tier 2   Tier 1

SELLERS   **BUYER**

The supply chain for every firm is composed of multiple tiers of suppliers.

suppliers, then the total number of suppliers in the chain (including the buying firm) rises to 53. This figure does not include the shippers, insurers, and financiers involved in the transactions.

Immediately, you can see from Figure 12.4 that the procurement process involves a very large number of suppliers, each of whom must be coordinated with the production needs of the ultimate purchaser—the buying firm. You can also understand how difficult it is to "manage" the supply chain, or obtain "visibility" into the supply chain simply because of its size and scope.

The Role of Existing Legacy Computer Systems and Enterprise Systems

Complicating any efforts to coordinate the many firms in a supply chain is the fact that each firm generally has its own set of legacy computer systems, sometimes homegrown or customized, that cannot easily pass information to other systems. **Legacy computer systems** generally are older systems used to manage key business processes within a firm in a variety of functional areas from manufacturing, logistics, finance, and human resources. **Enterprise systems** are corporate-wide systems that relate to all aspects of production, including finance, human resources, and procurement. Many large Fortune 500 global firms have implemented global enterprise-wide systems from major vendors such as IBM, SAP, Oracle, and others. These enterprise systems have supply chain management modules designed to automate key B2B processes.

With an enterprise-wide B2B system in place, incoming orders from customers can be translated into Bills of Material (BOM), production schedules, and human resource and financial requirements, including notifying the finance department to issue

legacy computer systems
older mainframe systems used to manage key business processes within a firm in a variety of functional areas

enterprise systems
corporate-wide systems that relate to all aspects of production, including finance, human resources, and procurement

invoices to customers and pay suppliers. Similarly, enterprise systems automate the procurement process, including logistics, and track the delivery of parts from suppliers.

TRENDS IN SUPPLY CHAIN MANAGEMENT AND COLLABORATIVE COMMERCE

It is impossible to comprehend the actual and potential contribution of Internet-based B2B commerce, or the successes and failures of B2B e-commerce vendors and markets, without understanding ongoing efforts to improve the procurement process through a variety of supply chain management programs that long preceded the development of e-commerce.

supply chain management (SCM)

refers to a wide variety of activities that firms and industries use to coordinate the key players in their procurement process

Supply chain management (SCM) refers to a wide variety of activities that firms and industries use to coordinate the key players in their procurement process. For the most part, today's procurement managers still work with telephones, e-mail, fax machines, face-to-face conversations, and instinct, relying on trusted long-term suppliers for their strategic purchases of goods directly involved in the production process.

There have been a number of major developments in supply chain management over the last two decades that set the ground rules for understanding how B2B e-commerce works (or fails to work). These developments include just-in-time and lean production, supply chain simplification, adaptive supply chains, sustainable supply chains, electronic data interchange (EDI), supply chain management systems, and collaborative commerce (Supply Chain Digest, 2012a).

Just-in-Time and Lean Production

just-in-time production

a method of inventory cost management which seeks to eliminate excess inventory to a bare minimum.

lean production

a set of production methods and tools that focuses on the elimination of waste throughout the customer value chain

One of the significant costs in any production process is the cost of in-process inventory: the parts and supplies needed to produce a product or service. **Just-in-time production** is a method of inventory cost management that seeks to eliminate excess inventory to a bare minimum. In just-in-time production, the parts needed for, say, an automobile, arrive at the assembly factory a few hours or even minutes before they are attached to a car. Payment for the parts does not occur until the parts are attached to a vehicle on the production line. In the past, producers used to order enough parts for a week or even a month's worth of production, creating huge, costly buffers in the production process. These buffers assured that parts would almost always be available, but at a large cost. **Lean production** is a set of production methods and tools that focuses on the elimination of waste throughout the customer value chain. It is an extension of just-in-time beyond inventory management to the full range of activities that create customer value. Originally, just-in-time and lean methods were implemented with phones, faxes, and paper documents to coordinate the flow of parts in inventory. Supply chain management systems now have largely automated the process of acquiring inventory from suppliers, and made possible significant savings on a global basis. Arguably, contemporary supply chain systems are the foundation of today's global B2B production system.

Supply Chain Simplification

Many manufacturing firms have spent the past two decades reducing the size of their supply chains and working more closely with a smaller group of "strategic" supplier firms to reduce both product costs and administrative costs, while improving quality. Following the lead of Japanese industry, for instance, the automobile industry has systematically reduced the number of its suppliers by over 50%. Instead of open bidding for orders, large manufacturers have chosen to work with strategic partner supply firms under long-term contracts that guarantee the supplier business and also establish quality, cost, and timing goals. These strategic partnership programs are essential for just-in-time production models, and often involve joint product development and design, integration of computer systems, and tight coupling of the production processes of two or more companies. **Tight coupling** is a method for ensuring that suppliers precisely deliver the ordered parts at a specific time and to a particular location, ensuring the production process is not interrupted for lack of parts.

tight coupling
a method for ensuring that suppliers precisely deliver the ordered parts, at a specific time and particular location, to ensure the production process is not interrupted for lack of parts

Supply Chain Black Swans: Adaptive Supply Chains

While firms have greatly simplified their supply chains in the last decade, they have also sought to centralize them by adopting a single, global supply chain system that integrates all the firm's vendor and logistics information into a single enterprise-wide system. Large software firms like Oracle, IBM, and SAP encourage firms to adopt a "one world, one firm, one database" enterprise-wide view of the world in order to achieve scale economies, simplicity, and to optimize global cost and value.

Beginning in earnest in 2000, managers in developed countries used these new technological capabilities to push manufacturing and production to the lowest cost labor regions of the world, specifically China and South East Asia. This movement of production to Asia was also enabled by the entrance of China into the World Trade Organization in September 2001. Suddenly, it was both technologically and politically possible to concentrate production wherever possible in the lowest cost region of the world. These developments were also supported by low-cost fuel, which made both transoceanic shipping and production inexpensive, and relative political stability in the region. By 2005, many economists believed a new world economic order had emerged based on cheap labor in Asia capable of producing inexpensive products for Western consumers, profits for global firms, and the opening of Asian markets to sophisticated Western goods and financial products.

As it turns out, there were many risks and costs to this strategy of concentrating production in China and Asia in a world of economic, financial, political, and even geological instability. For instance, in the global financial crisis of 2007–2009, relying on suppliers in parts of Europe where currencies and interest rates fluctuated greatly exposed many firms to higher costs than anticipated. Suddenly, key suppliers could not obtain financing for their production or shipments. In March 2011, following the earthquake and tsunami in Japan, key suppliers in Japan were forced to shut down or slow production because of nuclear contamination of the entire Fukushima region where, as its turns out, major Japanese and American firms had automobile parts factories. As a result, General Motors, could no longer obtain transmissions for its Volt electric car, and had to shut down a truck factory in Louisiana due to a lack of parts from Japan. Japanese and other global firms could not obtain batteries, switches, and axle assemblies. Production lead times in the automobile industry were very short, and inventories of parts were intentionally very lean, with only a few weeks supply on hand. Texas Instruments shut down several of its Japanese plants, as did Toshiba, putting a crimp on the world supply of NAND flash memory chips used in smartphones (Jolly, 2011; Bunkley, 2011). Caterpillar, Sony, Boeing, Volvo, and hundreds of other firms that are all part of a tightly coupled world supply chain also experienced supply chain disruptions. And then, in October of 2011, torrential rains in Thailand led to flooding of many of its key industrial regions, and the wiping out of a significant share of the world's electronics components from hard disk drives to automobile subsystems, cameras, and notebook PCs (Supply Chain Digest, 2012b; Hookway, 2012).

By 2012, the risks and costs of extended and concentrated supply chains had begun to change corporate strategies. To cope with unpredictable world events, firms are taking steps to break up single global supply chain systems into regional or product-based supply chains, with some level of centralization, but substantial autonomy for the smaller systems. Using regional supply chains, firms can decide to locate some production of parts in Latin America, rather than all their production or suppliers in a single country such as Japan. They will be able to move production around the world to temporary "safe harbors." This may result in higher short term costs, but provide substantial, longer term risk protection in the event any single region is disrupted. Increasingly, supply chains are being built based on the assumption that global disruptions in supply are inevitable, but not predictable (Simchi-Levi, et. al., 2011;Malik, et. al., 2011). The focus in 2012 is on "optimal-cost," not low-cost, supply chains, and more distributed manufacturing along with more flexible supply chains that can shift reliably from high risk to low risk areas. Regional manufacturing means shorter supply chains that can respond rapidly to changing consumer tastes and demand levels (Cachon and Swinney, 2011).

Accountable Supply Chains: Labor Standards

Accountable supply chains are those where the labor conditions in low-wage, underdeveloped producer countries are visible and morally acceptable to ultimate consumers in more developed industrial societies. For much of the last century, American and European manufacturers with global supply chains with large offshore production facilities sought to hide the realities of their offshore factories from Western reporters and ordinary citizens. For global firms with long supply chains, "visibility" did not mean their consumers could understand how their products were made.

Beginning in 2000, and in part because of the growing power of the Internet to empower citizen reporters around the world, the realities of global supply chains have slowly become more transparent to the public. For instance, for much of the past decade, beginning in 1997, Nike, the world's largest manufacturer of sporting goods, has been under intense criticism for exploiting foreign workers, operating sweat shops, employing children, and allowing dangerous conditions in its sub-contractor factories. As a result, Nike has introduced significant changes to its global supply chain.

With the emergence of truly global supply chains, and political changes at the World Trade Organization, which opened up European and American markets to Asian goods and services, many—if not most—of the electronics, toys, cosmetics, industrial supplies, footwear, apparel, and other goods consumed in the developed world are made by workers in factories in the less developed world, primarily in Asia and Latin America. Unfortunately, but quite understandably, the labor conditions in these factories in most cases do not meet the minimal labor standards of Europe or America even though these factories pay higher wages and offer better working conditions than other local jobs in the host country. In many cases, the cost for a worker of not having a job in what—to Western standards—are horrible working conditions is to sink deeper into poverty and even worse conditions. Many point out that labor conditions were brutal in the United States and Europe in the 19th and early 20th century when these countries were building industrial economies, and therefore, whatever conditions exist in offshore factories in 2012 are no worse than developed countries in their early years of rapid industrialization.

The argument results in a painful ethical dilemma, a terrible trade-off: cheap manufactured goods that increase consumer welfare in developed countries seem to require human misery in less developed countries. Indeed, these jobs would never have been moved to less developed parts of world without exceptionally low, even survival level, wages.

Notwithstanding the argument that having a job is better than being unemployed in low wage countries, or any country, there are some working conditions that are completely unacceptable to consumers and therefore to firms in developed countries. Among these unacceptable working conditions are slave or forced labor, child employment, routine exposure to toxic substances, more than 48 hours of work per week, harassment and abuse, sexual exploitation, and compensation beneath the minimal standard of living leaving no disposable income. These practices were, and are, in some cases typical, and certainly not atypical, in many low-wage countries.

A number of groups in the last decade have contributed to efforts to make global supply chains transparent to reporters and citizens, and to develop minimal standards of accountability. Among these groups are the National Consumers League, Human Rights First, the Maquilla Solidarity Network, the Global Fairness Initiative, the Clean Clothes Campaign, the International Labor Organization (UN), and the Fair Labor Association (FLA). The FLA is a coalition of business firms with offshore production and global supply chains, universities, and private organizations. For member firms, the FLA conducts interviews with workers, makes unannounced visits to factories to track progress, and investigates complaints. They are also one of the major international labor standard-setting organizations (Fair Labor Organization, 2012).

In March 2012, the FLA released its investigation of Hon Hai Precision Industry Company (a Taiwan-based company known as Foxconn), which is the assembler of nearly all iPhones and iPads in the world. Foxconn operates what is alleged to be the largest factory in the world in Longhua, Shenzhen, where over 250,000 workers assemble electronics goods. The audit of working conditions at Foxconn was authorized by Apple, a member of the FLA, and was based on 35,000 surveys of workers at the Longhua factory. The report found over 50 legal and code violations (sometimes in violation of Chinese laws) including requiring too many hours of work a week (over 60), failing to pay workers for overtime, and hazardous conditions which injured workers (Fair Labor Association, 2012).

Sustainable Supply Chains: Lean, Mean and Green

"Sustainable business" is a call for business to take social and ecological interests, and not just corporate profits, into account in all their decision-making throughout the firm. No small request. Since the United Nations World Commission on Environment and Development (WCED) published the first comprehensive report on sustainable business in 1987, firms around the globe have struggled with these concepts and in some cases ignored or resisted them as simply a threat to sustained profitability. The commission's report (*Our Common Future*) argued for a balance of profits, social community development, and minimal impact on the world environment, including of course, the carbon footprint of business. By 2012, the consensus among major firms in Europe, Asia, and the United States has become that in the long term, and through careful planning, sustainable business is just good business because it means using the most efficient environment-regarding means of production, distribution, and logistics. These efficient methods create value for consumers, investors, and communities.

Notions of sustainable business have had a powerful impact on supply chain thinking. In part, these efforts are good risk management: all advanced countries have substantially strengthened their environmental regulations. It makes good business sense for firms to prepare methods and operations suitable to this new environment.

For instance, all the major textiles brand and retailers have announced plans for a more sustainable supply chain in textiles. One of the world's truly ancient industries, textiles supports millions of workers while consuming extraordinary resources: it takes 1,000 gallons of water to make one pound of finished cotton (your jeans, for instance). While growing cotton has its issues (fertilizer), the subsequent dying, finishing, and cleaning of cotton makes it the number one industrial polluter on Earth (cKinetics, 2010). It's not a small matter then that Walmart, Gap, Levi's, Nike, and other large players in the industry are taking steps to reduce the environmental impact of their operations by improving the efficiency of the entire supply and distribution chains.

With the help of IBM, SAP, and Oracle, other firms and entire industries are working to develop sustainable supply chains. McKesson, North America's largest distributor of drugs, uses IBM's Supply Chain Sustainability Management Solution (SCSM), to minimize carbon dioxide emissions throughout its supply chain, while lowering its distribution costs. SCSM (a business analytics package that works with IBM's B2B software) can determine low-cost refrigeration alternatives for certain medicines (such as insulin and vaccines); identify the environmentally least harmful way to bring new products into its distribution network; and determine the best way to transport pharmaceuticals to customers (IBM, 2011a).

Electronic Data Interchange (EDI)

As noted in the previous section, B2B e-commerce did not originate with the Internet, but in fact has its roots in technologies such as EDI that were first developed in the mid-1970s and 1980s. EDI is a broadly defined communications protocol for exchanging documents among computers using technical standards developed by the American National Standards Institute (ANSI X12 standards) and international bodies such as the United Nations (EDIFACT standards).

EDI was developed to reduce the cost, delays, and errors inherent in the manual exchanges of documents such as purchase orders, shipping documents, price lists, payments, and customer data. EDI differs from an unstructured message because its messages are organized with distinct fields for each of the important pieces of information in a commercial transaction such as transaction date, product purchased, amount, sender's name, address, and recipient's name.

Each major industry in the United States and throughout much of the industrial world has EDI industry committees that define the structure and information fields of electronic documents for that industry. EDI communications at first relied on private point-to-point circuit-switched communication networks and private value-added networks that connected key participants in the supply chain (Laudon and Laudon, 2012). Estimates indicate that B2B e-commerce EDI transactions will total about $1.1 billion in 2012, about 30% of all B2B e-commerce. (U.S. Census Bureau, 2011a, authors' estimates). In this sense, EDI remains very important in the development of B2B e-commerce.

EDI has evolved significantly since the 1980s (see **Figure 12.5**). Initially, EDI focused on document automation (Stage 1). Procurement agents created purchase orders electronically and sent them to trading partners, who in turn shipped order fulfillment and shipping notices electronically back to the purchaser. Invoices, payments, and other documents followed. These early implementations replaced the postal system for document transmission, and resulted in same-day shipping of orders (rather than a week's delay caused by the postal system), reduced errors, and lower costs.

FIGURE 12.5	THE EVOLUTION OF EDI AS A B2B MEDIUM

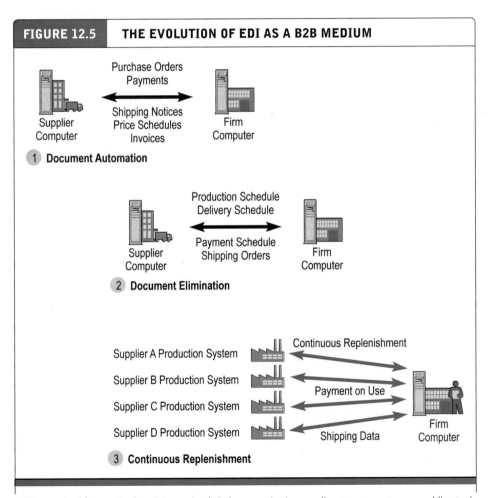

EDI has evolved from a simple point-to-point digital communications medium to a many-to-one enabling tool for continuous inventory replenishment.

The second stage of EDI development began in the early 1990s, driven largely by the automation of internal industrial processes and movement toward just-in-time production and continuous production. New methods of production called for greater flexibility in scheduling, shipping, and financing of supplies. EDI evolved to become a system for document elimination. To support the new automated production processes used by manufacturers, EDI was used to eliminate purchase orders and other documents entirely, replacing them with production schedules and inventory balances. Supplier firms were sent monthly statements of production requirements and precise scheduled delivery times, and the orders would be fulfilled continuously, with inventory and payments being adjusted at the end of each month.

In the third stage of EDI, beginning in the mid-1990s, suppliers were given online access to selected parts of the purchasing firm's production and delivery schedules, and, under long-term contracts, were required to meet those schedules on their own without intervention by firm purchasing agents. Movement toward this continuous access model of EDI was spurred in the 1990s by large manufacturing and process firms (such as oil and chemical companies) that were implementing enterprise systems. These systems required standardization of business processes and resulted in the automation of production, logistics, and many financial processes. These new processes required much closer relationships with suppliers, who were required to be more precise in delivery scheduling and more flexible in inventory management. This level of supplier precision could never be achieved economically by human purchasing agents. This third stage of EDI enabled the era of continuous replenishment. For instance, Walmart and Toys"R"Us provide their suppliers with access to their store inventories, and the suppliers are expected to keep the stock of items on the shelf within pre-specified targets. Similar developments occurred in the grocery industry.

Today, EDI must be viewed as a general enabling technology that provides for the exchange of critical business information between computer applications supporting a wide variety of business processes. EDI is an important industrial network technology, suited to support communications among a small set of strategic partners in direct, long-term trading relationships. The technical platform of EDI has changed from mainframes to personal computers, and the telecommunications environment is changing from private, dedicated networks to the Internet (referred to as Internet-based EDI, or just Internet EDI). Most industry groups are moving toward XML as the language for expressing EDI commercial documents and communications.

The strength of EDI is its ability to support direct commercial transactions among strategically related firms in an industrial network, but this is its weakness as well. EDI is not well suited for the development of electronic marketplaces, where thousands of suppliers and purchasers meet in a digital arena to negotiate prices. EDI supports direct bilateral communications among a small set of firms and does not permit the multilateral, dynamic relationships of a true marketplace. EDI does not provide for price transparency among a large number of suppliers, does not scale easily to include new participants, and is not a real-time communications environment. EDI does not have a rich communications environment that can simultaneously support e-mail messaging, sharing of graphic documents, network meetings, or user-friendly flexible database creation and management. For these features, Internet-based software has emerged (described below). EDI is also an expensive proposition, and a staff of dedicated programmers is required to implement it in large firms; in some cases, a considerable amount of time is also needed to reprogram existing enterprise systems to work with EDI protocols. Small firms are typically required to adopt EDI in order to supply large firms, and there are less-expensive, small-firm solutions for implementing EDI.

Supply Chain Management Systems: Mobile B2B in Your Palm

Supply chain simplification, lean production, focusing on strategic partners in the production process, enterprise systems, and continuous inventory replenishment, are the foundation for contemporary **supply chain management (SCM) systems**. Supply chain management systems continuously link the activities of buying, making, and moving products from suppliers to purchasing firms, as well as integrating the demand side of the business equation by including the order entry system in the process. With an SCM system and continuous replenishment, inventory is greatly reduced and production begins only when an order is received (see **Figure 12.6**). These systems enable just-in-time and lean-production methods. The growing use of smartphones has led software firms like SAP and Oracle to develop mobile apps for personal computers, smartphones, and other consumer devices to connect firms with their supply chain partners.

supply chain management (SCM) systems

continuously link the activities of buying, making, and moving products from suppliers to purchasing firms, as well as integrating the demand side of the business equation by including the order entry system in the process

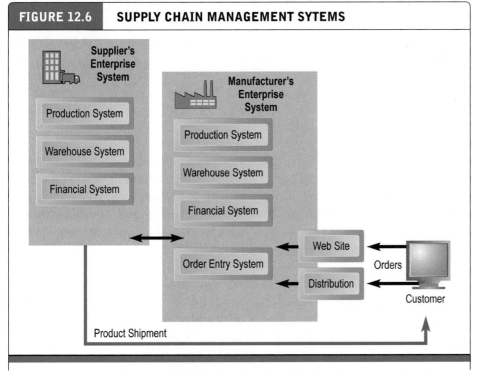

FIGURE 12.6   SUPPLY CHAIN MANAGEMENT SYTEMS

SCM systems coordinate the activities of suppliers, shippers, and order entry systems to automate order entry through production, payment, and shipping business processes. Increasingly customers, as well as employees working throughout the supply chain, are using smartphones and mobile apps to place and coordinate orders.

Hewlett-Packard (HP) is one of the largest technology companies in the world, with sales of $127 billion in 2011. With operations in 178 countries, sales in 43 currencies, and 15 languages, HP is truly a global firm with global supply chain issues that became even more complicated as HP expanded by making over 200 acquisitions in the last decade, including Palm Inc., manufacturer of Palm smartphones, in 2010. To cope with one of the most complex supply chains in the world, HP turned to supply chain management software.

HP has a Web-based, order-driven supply chain management system that begins with either a customer placing an order online or the receipt of an order from a dealer. The order is forwarded from the order entry system to HP's production and delivery system. From there, the order is routed to one of several HP contractor supplier firms. One such firm is Synnex in Fremont, California. At Synnex, computers verify the order with HP and validate the ordered configuration to ensure the PC can be manufactured (e.g., will not have missing parts or fail a design specification set by HP). The order is then forwarded to a computer-based production control system that issues a bar-coded production ticket to factory assemblers. Simultaneously, a parts order is forwarded to Synnex's warehouse and inventory management system. A worker assembles the computer, and then the computer is boxed, tagged, and shipped to the customer. The delivery is monitored and tracked by HP's supply chain management system, which links directly to one of several overnight delivery systems operated by Airborne Express, Federal Express, and UPS. The elapsed time from order entry to shipping is 48 hours. With this system, Synnex and HP have eliminated the need to hold PCs in inventory, reduced cycle time from one week to 48 hours, and reduced errors. HP has extended this system to become a global B2B order tracking, reporting, and support system for large HP customers (Synnex Corporation, 2012; Hewlett-Packard, 2012). In 2010, HP began a simplification of B2B applications from over 300 applications down to 30. Many of these applications were inherited from acquired companies (Gardner, 2010).

It isn't just huge technology companies that use supply chain software. There's nothing quite so perishable as fashionable underwear given the rate of fashion change. Under Armour, which calls itself "the world's No. 1 performance athletic brand," uses software from SAP to predict sales, plan inventory, and coordinate suppliers (Booen, 2011). Prior to using these tools, Under Armour often missed sales because it did not produce enough of popular items, or over-produced items that were not selling.

Implementing an order-driven, Web-based supply chain management system is not always easy, however, as *Insight on Technology: RFID AutoIdentification: Giving a Voice to Your Inventory* illustrates.

collaborative commerce

the use of digital technologies to permit organizations to collaboratively design, develop, build, and manage products through their life cycles

Collaborative Commerce

Collaborative commerce is a direct extension of supply chain management systems, as well as supply chain simplification. **Collaborative commerce** is defined as the use of digital technologies to permit organizations to collaboratively design, develop, build, and manage products through their life cycles. This is a much broader mission than EDI or simply managing the flow of information among organizations. Collaborative commerce involves a definitive move from a transaction focus to a relationship focus among the supply chain participants. Rather than having an arm's-length

INSIGHT ON TECHNOLOGY

RFID AUTOIDENTIFICATION: GIVING A VOICE TO YOUR INVENTORY

It's 10 p.m. Do you know where your containers are? Wouldn't it be nice if your containers could talk to you, call home every now and then to report their progress towards your loading docks? Radio frequency identification (RFID) makes that possible today, and as of 2012, even your jeans will be given a voice inside, and maybe outside, the store where you purchased them.

If you're in business anywhere in the world today, and that business involves physical goods, then chances are quite good that your business depends on the movement of goods in containers. In fact, there are more than 200 million sea cargo containers moving every year among the world's seaports, and nearly 50% of the value of all U.S. imports arrive via sea cargo containers each year. The containers are loaded onto ships, and stacked high on the deck. The containers also fit on the back of trucks and on railway carriages. So when the containers are unloaded from the ship, they continue their journey from the port on the back of trucks or trains. It is a fast and efficient way of moving cargo. A standard container is about 20 feet long, 8 feet wide, and 8 feet high, and can hold about 47,900 lbs of cargo.

Prior to the development of containers, all ocean-going cargo was loaded and unloaded onto ships in huge nets by dock workers, one package at a time. While the container revolutionized ocean shipping, vastly increasing productivity and reducing breakage, keeping track of 200 million cargo containers is difficult. While each container has its own permanent ID number painted on the side, as well as a bar code identification tag, this number must be entered manually by dock workers or scanned up close. Identification of containers is slow and prone

to errors. If you had to find one container on a dock containing over 1,000 containers, you would have to read each ID number until you found the one you wanted. All by themselves, containers can't talk.

Tracking containers is just one part of the larger B2B product identification problem. Retailers such as Walmart, Target, and Amazon find it difficult and expensive to track millions of annual shipments into and out of their warehouses and sales floors; the automotive industry finds it costly and difficult to synchronize the flow of parts into its factories; the U.S. Department of Defense logistics system finds it difficult to track the movement of troop supplies; and the airline industry often loses bags in transit.

Thirty years ago, the development of the Uniform Product Code (UPC) and the ubiquitous bar code label was an initial first step towards automating the identification of goods. But the bar code technology of the 1970s still required humans or sometimes machines to scan products. The problem with bar codes is that they don't talk—they are passive labels that must be read or scanned.

Today, a new technology to replace bar codes is being deployed among the largest manufacturing and retailing firms. RFID involves the use of tags attached to products or product containers that transmit a radio signal in the 850 megahertz to 2.5 gigahertz range that continuously identifies them to radio receivers in warehouses, factories, retail floors, or on board ships. RFID labels are really tiny computer chips and a battery that are used to transmit each product's electronic product code to receivers nearby.

RFID has several key advantages over the old bar code scanner technology. RFID eliminates the line-of-sight reading requirement of bar codes and greatly increases the distance from which scan-

(continued)

ning can be done from a few inches up to 90 feet. RFID systems can be used just about anywhere—from clothing tags to missiles to pet tags to food—anywhere that a unique identification system is needed. The tag can carry information as simple as a pet owner's name and address or the cleaning instructions on a sweater or as complex as instructions on how to assemble a car. Best of all, instead of looking at a warehouse filled with thousands of packages that can't talk, you could be listening to these same thousands of packages each chirping a unique code, identifying themselves to you. Finding the single package you are looking for is greatly simplified. RFID tags produce a steady stream of data that can be entered into Internet- and intranet-based corporate applications such as SCM and ERP systems.

In 2012, the global RFID market is estimated to be $5.3 billion, with a U.S. market of $3 billion. The RFID market is expanding rapidly because of the growing use of RFIDs by governments and private industry, as well as the explosive growth in item-level RFID.

Walmart, the world's largest retailer, made RFID an important part of its supply chain strategy in the 2000s. The company mandated that its suppliers place RFID tags on all cases and pallets headed for its Dallas distribution centers, and RFID funding increased dramatically in the wake of its decision. Many pundits thought that RFID had finally reached a tipping point and would become a mainstream technology used by the entire business world. When Walmart speaks, people listen. The problem was that the expense

and extra hours required to switch to RFID was too heavy a burden on many of Walmart's suppliers, and the movement toward RFID stalled. However, RFID has made a comeback at the item level. An increasing number of department stores, Walmart included, have begun tracking individual clothing items in stores, allowing them to more easily track which items need replenishing, right down to the specific sizes that are being purchased most frequently. Item-level RFID allows for instant inventory analysis, continuous restocking, and a significant bump in sales.

Retailers like JC Penney, Macy's, and Lord & Taylor have already rolled out item-level RFID in many outlets, and all of them report increases in sales and improved inventory visibility. Walmart, still leading the charge, has rolled out RFID in two non-apparel categories in 2012: tires and consumer electronics. In the future, item-level tracking might encompass every item in a store, and could include walk-by checkout, effectively eliminating checkout lines. That is still a long way off, but as implementation costs for RFID continue to decrease, more companies will be able to tag their goods and use RFID to manage inventory. Some analysts predict that sales of RFID readers will hit 250 million in 2012 and come close to doubling that by 2016.

As adoption of the technology increases, RFID will have a profound impact on B2B e-commerce by reducing the cost of tracking goods through industry supply chains, reducing errors, and increasing the chances that the right product will be sent to the right customer.

■■■ **SOURCES:** "Did Walmart Love RFID to Death?," by Matthew Malone, smartplanet.com, February 14, 2012; "Is the Tipping Point Really, Truly Here for Item Level RFID Tracking in Apparel Retail?," SCDigest.com, February 2, 2012; "RFID In Consumer Goods to Retail – A Comeback?," by Dan Gilmore, SCDigest.com, November 11, 2011; "Do JCPenney, Macy's Announcements Mean RFID to Finally Really Takeoff in Retail?," SCDigest.com, November 2, 2011; "Car2go Test Drive: RFID, GPS, and Mobile Apps Make for a Smarter Smart," by Tim Stevens, Engadget.com, March 14, 2011; "Suddenly RFID is Hot Again," by Dan Gilmore, Scdigest.com, August 17, 2010; "Walmart Will Track You and Your Undies With RFIDs," by Matthew Zuras, Switched.com, July 26, 2010; "Walmart Radio Tags to Track Clothing," by Miguel Bustillo, *Wall Street Journal*, July 23, 2010; "RFID Market Projected to Grow in 2010," by Ilya Leybovich, Thomasnet.com News, March 11, 2010; "RFID Printers Adapt to Changing Market Needs," by Brian Albright, Integrated Solutions, September 2009; "Bar Code Labelling, RFID, ASNs All Smooth the Flow of Goods," SCDigest.com, September 9, 2009; "Global RFID Market to be Worth USD 5.56 Billion in 2009," Report, ThePaypers.com, August 27, 2009; "IDTechEx Report: Apparel RFID 2008-2018," by Cathryn Hindle, Just-style.com, August 12, 2008; "The Up and Down of Walmart RFID Implementation," by EcoSensa, March 24, 2009; "Apparel RFID 2008-2018" by Cathryn Hindle, *IDTechEx Report*, August 12, 2008; "Walmart RFID Plan Has Mixed Results," *RFID News*, April 28, 2008; "Walmart Gets Tough on RFID," by Mary Hayes Weier, InformationWeek, January 19, 2008.

adversarial relationship with suppliers, collaborative commerce fosters sharing of sensitive internal information with suppliers and purchasers. Managing collaborative commerce requires knowing exactly what information to share with whom. Collaborative commerce extends beyond supply chain management activities to include the collaborative development of new products and services by multiple cooperating firms.

A good example of collaborative commerce is the long-term effort of P&G, the world's largest manufacturer of personal and health care products, from Crest toothpaste to Tide soap, to work with suppliers and even customers to develop 50% of its product line over time. In the past, for instance, P&G would design a bottle or product package in-house, and then turn to over 100 suppliers of packaging to find out what it would cost and try to bargain that down. In 2011, using Ariba's procurement network, P&G asks its suppliers to come up with innovative ideas for packaging and pricing. Taking it a step further, P&G's Web site, Pgconnectdevelop.com, solicits new product ideas from suppliers and customers. About 50% of P&G's new products originate with substantial input from its suppliers and customers (P&G, 2011; Vance, 2010). Other well-known companies using collaboration to develop and deliver products include Lego (DesignByMe), Harley Davidson, Starbucks, and GE's Ecomagination program (James, 2012; Esposito, 2012).

Although collaborative commerce can involve customers as well as suppliers in the development of products, for the most part, it is concerned with the development of a rich communications environment to enable inter-firm sharing of designs, production plans, inventory levels, delivery schedules, and the development of shared products (see **Figure 12.7**).

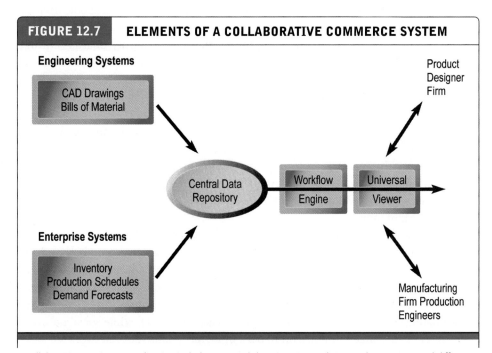

| **FIGURE 12.7** | **ELEMENTS OF A COLLABORATIVE COMMERCE SYSTEM** |

A collaborative commerce application includes a central data repository where employees at several different firms can store engineering drawings and other documents. A workflow engine determines who can see this data and what rules will apply for displaying the data on individual workstations. A viewer can be a browser operating on a workstation.

Collaborative commerce is very different from EDI, which is a technology for structured communications among firms. Collaborative commerce is more like an interactive teleconference among members of the supply chain. EDI and collaborative commerce share one characteristic: they are not open, competitive marketplaces, but instead are, technically, private industrial networks that connect strategic partners in a supply chain. New broadband video networks like Cisco's TelePresence Studios are beginning to play a role in enabling frequent, long distance, collaboration among supply chain partners. TelePresence is one of several very high bandwidth video systems from different vendors that give users the impression they are sharing physical space with other participants who are in fact located remotely, sometimes on the other side of the globe. In 2010, for instance, P&G installed forty TelePresence studios in its facilities around the world to encourage collaboration among its employees and suppliers (Cisco, 2011).

In Section 12.3, we discuss collaborative commerce in greater depth as a technology that enables private industrial networks.

SOCIAL NETWORKS AND B2B: THE EXTENDED SOCIAL ENTERPRISE

It's a short step from collaboration with vendors, suppliers, and customers, to a more personal relationship based on conversations with participants in the supply chain using social networks—both private and public. Here, the conversations and sharing of ideas are more unstructured, situational, and personal. Procurement officers, managers of supply chains, and logistics managers are people too, and they participate in the same social network culture provided by Facebook, Twitter, Tumblr, Instagram, and a host of other public social networks as we all do. Being able to respond to fast moving developments that effect supply chains requires something more than a Web site, e-mail, or telephone calls. Social networks can provide the intimate connections among customers, suppliers, and logistics partners that are needed to keep the supply chain functioning, and to make decisions based on current conditions (Red Prairie, 2012).

Participants in the supply chain network are tapping into their tablet computers, smartphones, and social network sites for purchasing, scheduling, exception handling, and deciding with their B2B customers and suppliers. In many cases, supply chain social networks are private—owned by the largest firm in the supply chain network. In other cases, firms develop Facebook pages to organize conversations among supply chain network members.

Some examples of social B2B include TradeSpace, a UK-based business social network where business people can share experiences and ideas, and buy and sell products. Cisco is using its Web site and Facebook pages to run new product campaigns for its business customers using social networks exclusively. Dell, like many businesses, uses its YouTube channel to engage suppliers and customers in conversations about existing products, and ideas for new products (Hird, 2011). While social networks have not yet had a large influence on B2B e-commerce, public social network sites like Facebook and Twitter are good listening posts for businesses involved in B2B trade.

FIGURE 12.8	TWO MAIN TYPES OF INTERNET-BASED B2B COMMERCE

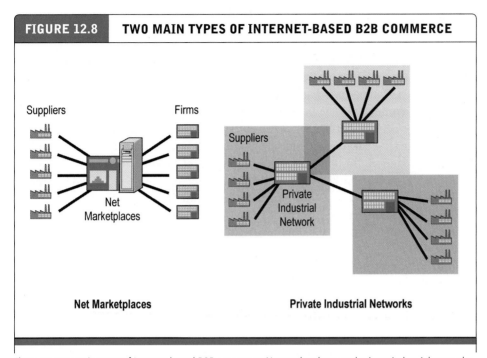

Net Marketplaces   **Private Industrial Networks**

There are two main types of Internet-based B2B commerce: Net marketplaces and private industrial networks.

MAIN TYPES OF INTERNET-BASED B2B COMMERCE

There are two generic types of Internet-based B2B commerce systems: Net market-places (which tend to be public) and private industrial networks (see **Figure 12.8**). Within each of these general categories are many different subtypes that we discuss in the following sections. (Yoo, et. al., 2011.)

Net marketplaces (also referred to as exchanges) bring together potentially thousands of sellers and buyers into a single digital marketplace operated over the Internet. Net marketplaces are transaction-based, support many-to-many as well as one-to-many relationships, and bear some resemblance to financial markets such as the New York Stock Exchange. There are many different types of Net marketplaces, with different pricing mechanisms, biases, and value propositions that will be explored in Section 12.2 (Kerrigan, et al., 2001). Private industrial networks bring together a small number of strategic business partner firms that collaborate to develop highly efficient supply chains and satisfy customer demand for products. Private industrial networks are relationship-based, support many-to-one or many-to-few relationships, and bear some resemblance to internal collaborative work environments. There are many different types of private industrial networks, as discussed in Section 12.3. Private industrial networks are by far the largest form of B2B e-commerce and account for over 10 times as much revenue as Net marketplaces.

12.2 NET MARKETPLACES

One of the most compelling visions of B2B e-commerce is that of an electronic marketplace on the Internet that would bring thousands of fragmented suppliers into contact with hundreds of major purchasers of industrial goods for the purpose of conducting "frictionless" commerce. The hope was that these suppliers would compete with one another on price, transactions would be automated and low cost, and as a result, the price of industrial supplies would fall. By extracting fees from buyers and sellers on each transaction, third-party intermediary market makers could earn significant revenues. These Net marketplaces could scale easily as volume increased by simply adding more computers and communications equipment.

In pursuit of this vision, well over 1,500 Net marketplaces sprang up in the early days of e-commerce. Unfortunately, many of them have since disappeared and the population is expected to stabilize at about 200. Still, many survive, and they are joined by other types of Net marketplaces—some private and some public—based on different assumptions that are quite successful.

THE VARIETY AND CHARACTERISTICS OF NET MARKETPLACES

There is a confusing variety of Net marketplaces today, and several different ways to classify them. For instance, some writers classify Net marketplaces on the basis of their pricing mechanisms—auction, bid/ask, negotiated price, and fixed prices—while others classify markets based on characteristics of the markets they serve (vertical versus horizontal, or sell-side versus buy-side), or ownership (industry-owned consortia versus independent third-party intermediaries). **Table 12.2** describes some of the important characteristics of Net marketplaces.

TYPES OF NET MARKETPLACES

Although each of these distinctions helps describe the phenomenon of Net marketplaces, they do not focus on the central business functionality provided, nor are they capable by themselves of describing the variety of Net marketplaces.

TABLE 12.2	OTHER CHARACTERISTICS OF NET MARKETPLACES: A B2B VOCABULARY
CHARACTERISTIC	**MEANING**
Bias	Sell-side vs. buy-side vs. neutral. Whose interests are advantaged: buyers, sellers, or no bias?
Ownership	Industry vs. third party. Who owns the marketplace?
Pricing mechanism	Fixed-price catalogs, auctions, bid/ask, and RFPs/RFQs.
Scope/Focus	Horizontal vs. vertical markets.
Value creation	What benefits do they offer customers or suppliers?
Access to market	In public markets, any firm can enter, but in private markets, entry is by invitation only.

In **Figure 12.9**, we present a classification of Net marketplaces that focuses on their business functionality; that is, what these Net marketplaces provide for businesses seeking solutions. We use two dimensions of Net marketplaces to create a four-cell classification table. We differentiate Net marketplaces as providing either indirect goods (goods used to support production) or direct goods (goods used in production), and we distinguish markets as providing either contractual purchasing (where purchases take place over many years according to a contract between the firm and its vendor) or spot purchasing (where purchases are episodic and anonymous—vendors and buyers do not have an ongoing relationship and may not know one another). The intersection of these dimensions produces four main types of Net marketplaces that are relatively straightforward: e-distributors, e-procurement networks, exchanges, and industry consortia. Note however, that in the real world, some Net marketplaces can be found in multiple parts of this figure as business models change and opportunities appear and disappear. Nevertheless, the discussion of "pure types" of Net marketplaces is a useful starting point.

Each of these Net marketplaces seeks to provide value to customers in different ways. We discuss each type of Net marketplace in more detail in the following sections.

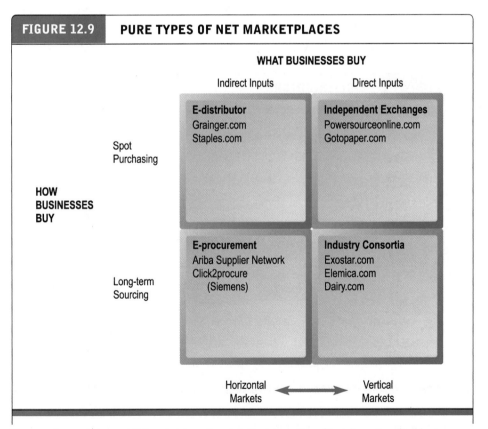

FIGURE 12.9   **PURE TYPES OF NET MARKETPLACES**

There are four main types of Net marketplaces based on the intersection of two dimensions: how businesses buy and what they buy. A third dimension—horizontal versus vertical markets—also distinguishes the different types of Net marketplaces.

E-distributors

e-distributor

provides electronic catalog that represents the products of thousands of direct manufacturers

E-distributors are the most common and most easily understood type of Net market-place. An **e-distributor** provides an electronic catalog that represents the products of thousands of direct manufacturers (see **Figure 12.10**). An e-distributor is the equivalent of Amazon for industry. E-distributors are independently owned intermediaries that offer industrial customers a single source from which to order indirect goods (often referred to as MRO) on a spot, as-needed basis. A significant percentage of corporate purchases cannot be satisfied under a company's existing contracts, and must be purchased on a spot basis. E-distributors make money by charging a markup on products they distribute.

Organizations and firms in all industries require MRO supplies. The MRO function maintains, repairs, and operates commercial buildings and maintains all the machinery of these buildings from heating, ventilating, and air conditioning systems to lighting fixtures.

E-distributors operate in horizontal markets because they serve many different industries with products from many different suppliers. E-distributors usually operate "public" markets in the sense that any firm can order from the catalog, as opposed to "private" markets, where membership is restricted to selected firms.

E-distributor prices are usually fixed, but large customers receive discounts and other incentives to purchase, such as credit, reporting on account activity, and limited forms of business purchasing rules (for instance, no purchases greater than $500 for

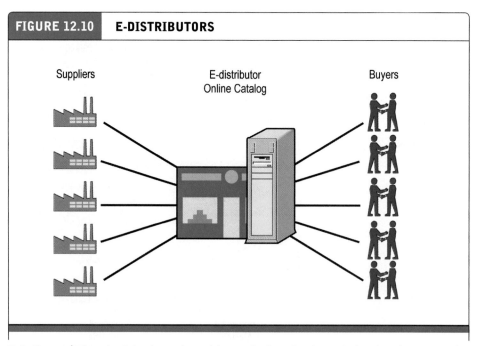

| FIGURE 12.10 | E-DISTRIBUTORS |

Suppliers   E-distributor   Buyers
                   Online Catalog

E-distributors are firms that bring the products of thousands of suppliers into a single online electronic catalog for sale to thousands of buyer firms. E-distributors are sometimes referred to as one-to-many markets, one seller serving many firms.

a single item without a purchase order). The primary benefits offered to industrial customers are lower search costs, lower transaction costs, wide selection, rapid delivery, and low prices.

The most frequently cited example of a public e-distribution market is W.W. Grainger. Grainger is involved in both long-term systematic sourcing as well as spot sourcing, but its emphasis is on spot sourcing. Grainger's business model is to become the world's leading source of MRO suppliers, and its revenue model is that of a typical retailer: it owns the products, and takes a markup on the products it sells to customers. At Grainger.com, users get an electronic online version of Grainger's famous seven-pound catalog, plus other parts not available in the catalog (adding up to around 900,000 parts), and complete electronic ordering and payment (W.W. Grainger Inc., 2012). Another example is McMaster-Carr.com, a New Jersey-based industrial parts mecca for manufacturers around the world.

E-procurement

An **e-procurement Net marketplace** is an independently owned intermediary that connects hundreds of online suppliers offering millions of maintenance and repair parts to business firms who pay fees to join the market (see **Figure 12.11**). E-procurement Net marketplaces are typically used for long-term contractual purchasing of indirect goods (MRO); they create online horizontal markets, but they

e-procurement Net marketplace

independently owned intermediary that connects hundreds of online suppliers offering millions of maintenance and repair parts to business firms who pay fees to join the market

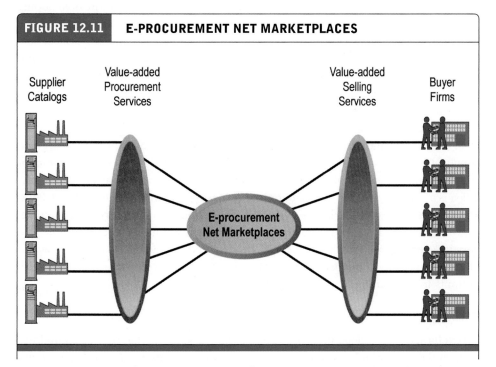

FIGURE 12.11   E-PROCUREMENT NET MARKETPLACES

E-procurement Net marketplaces aggregate hundreds of catalogs in a single marketplace and make them available to firms, often on a custom basis that reflects only the suppliers desired by the participating firms.

also provide for members' spot sourcing of MRO supplies. E-procurement companies make money by charging a percentage of each transaction, licensing consulting services and software, and assessing network use fees (Trkman and McCormack, 2010).

E-procurement companies expand on the business model of simpler e-distributors by including the online catalogs of hundreds of suppliers and offering value chain management services to both buyers and sellers. **Value chain management (VCM) services** provided by e-procurement companies include automation of a firm's entire procurement process on the buyer side and automation of the selling business processes on the seller side. For purchasers, e-procurement companies automate purchase orders, requisitions, sourcing, business rules enforcement, invoicing, and payment. For suppliers, e-procurement companies provide catalog creation and content management, order management, fulfillment, invoicing, shipment, and settlement.

E-procurement Net marketplaces are sometimes referred to as many-to-many markets. They are mediated by an independent third party that purports to represent both buyers and sellers, and hence claim to be neutral. On the other hand, because they may include the catalogs of both competing suppliers and competing e-distributors, they likely have a bias in favor of the buyers. Nevertheless, by aggregating huge buyer firms into their networks, they provide distinct marketing benefits for suppliers and reduce customer acquisition costs.

Ariba stands out as one of the poster children of the B2B age, a firm born before its time. Promising to revolutionize inter-firm trade, Ariba started out in 1996 hoping to build a global business network linking buyers and sellers—sort of an eBay for business. With little revenue, the stock shot past $1,000 a share by March 2000. But sellers and buyers did not join the network in large part because they did not understand the opportunity, were too wedded to their traditional procurement processes, and did not trust outsiders to control their purchasing and vendor relationship. In September 2001, Ariba's share price tanked to $2.20. Ariba survived largely by selling software that helped large firms understand their procurement processes and costs. Finally, by 2008, large and small firms had become more sophisticated in their purchasing and supply change management practices, and Ariba's original idea of a global network of suppliers and purchasers of a wide variety of industrial goods came back to life. Today, Ariba is a leading provider of collaborative business commerce solutions (Ariba, 2012; Levy, 2010; Vance, 2010). Players in this market segment include Perfect Commerce, BravoSolution, A.T. Kearney Procurement & Analytic Solutions, and Emptoris. The very large enterprise software firms—Oracle, SAP, and JDA Software Group—now also offer procurement solutions to their customers and compete directly against the early entrants in this market.

Exchanges

An **exchange** is an independently owned online marketplace that connects hundreds to potentially thousands of suppliers and buyers in a dynamic, real-time environment (see **Figure 12.12**). Although there are exceptions, exchanges generally create vertical markets that focus on the spot-purchasing requirements of large firms in a single industry, such as computers and telecommunications, electronics, food, and industrial

---

value chain management (VCM) services

include automation of a firm's entire procurement process on the buyer side and automation of the selling business processes on the seller side

---

exchange

independently owned online marketplace that connects hundreds to potentially thousands of suppliers and buyers in a dynamic, real-time environment equipment. Exchanges were the prototype Internet-based marketplace in the early days of e-commerce; as noted above, over 1,500 were created in this period, but most have failed.

Exchanges make money by charging a commission on the transaction. The pricing model can be through an online negotiation, auction, RFQ, or fixed buy-and-sell prices. The benefits offered to customers of exchanges include reduced search cost for parts and spare capacity. Other benefits include lower prices created by a global marketplace driven by competition among suppliers who would, presumably, sell goods at very low profit margins at one world-market price. The benefits offered suppliers are access to a global purchasing environment and the opportunity to unload production overruns (although at very competitive prices and low profit margins). Even though they are private intermediaries, exchanges are public in the sense of permitting any bona fide buyer or seller to participate.

Exchanges tend to be biased toward the buyer even though they are independently owned and presumably neutral. Suppliers are disadvantaged by the fact that exchanges put them in direct price competition with other similar suppliers around the globe, driving profit margins down. Exchanges have failed primarily because suppliers have refused to join them, and hence, the existing markets have very low liquidity, defeating the very purpose and benefits of an exchange. **Liquidity** is typically measured by the number of buyers and sellers in a market, the volume of transactions, and the size of transactions. You know a market is liquid when you can buy or sell just about any size

liquidity

typically measured by the number of buyers and sellers in a market, the volume of transactions, and the size of transactions

FIGURE 12.12 EXCHANGES

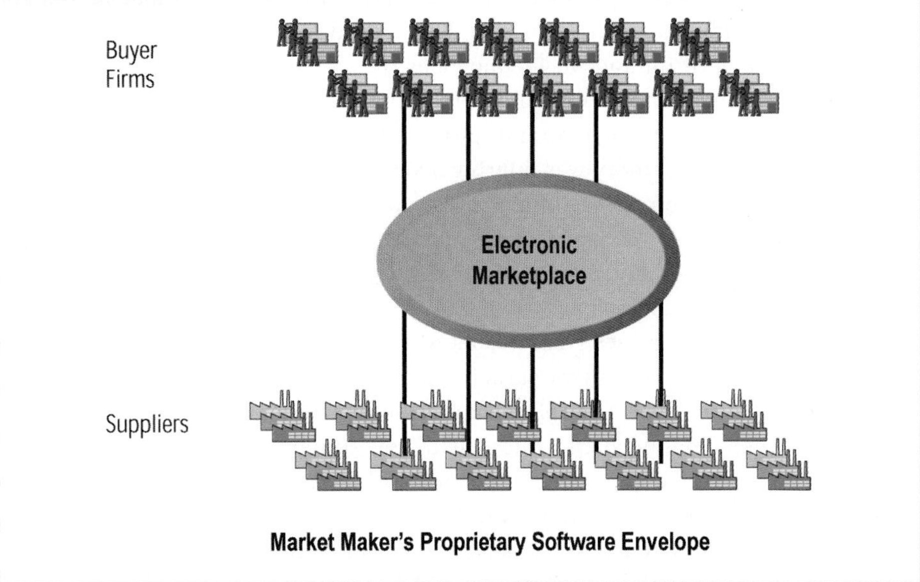

Buyer Firms

Electronic Marketplace

Suppliers

Market Maker's Proprietary Software Envelope

Independent exchanges bring potentially thousands of suppliers to a vertical (industry-specific) marketplace to sell their goods to potentially thousands of buyer firms. Exchanges are sometimes referred to as many-to-many markets because they have many suppliers serving many buyer firms.

TABLE 12.3	EXAMPLES OF INDEPENDENT EXCHANGES
EXCHANGE	FOCUS
PowerSource Online	Computer parts exchange
Converge	Semiconductors and computer peripherals
Smarterwork	Professional services from Web design to legal advice
Active International	Trading in underutilized manufacturing capacity
IntercontinentalExchange	International online marketplace for over 600 commodities

order at just about any time you want. On all of these measures, many exchanges failed, resulting in a very small number of participants, few trades, and small trade value per transaction. The most common reason for not using exchanges is the absence of traditional, trusted suppliers.

While most exchanges tend to be vertical marketplaces offering direct supplies, some exchanges offer indirect inputs as well, such as electricity and power, transportation services (usually to the transportation industry), and professional services. **Table 12.3** lists a few examples of some current independent exchanges.

The following capsule descriptions of two exchanges provide insight into their origins and current functions.

Global Wine & Spirits (GWS) (Globalwinespirits.com) is somewhat unique among independent exchanges, not only as a start-up that has managed to survive, but also as a latecomer to the B2B e-commerce community. GWS opened in 1999, but did not begin to trade products online until May 2001. Based in Montreal, Quebec, GWS is operated by Mediagrif Interactive Technologies Inc., a Canadian company that operates a number of independent exchanges in a variety of industries. GWS offers a spot marketplace for wines, where wine and spirit producers offer wines for sale (recently, for instance, an Italian winery was offering 500 cases of Tuscan Chianti wine for $30 a case , with 20 days left on the offer); a "call for tenders" market, where members make offers to purchase wines and spirits; a trade database with listings of thousands of industry professionals; and a wine and spirits catalog with over 35,000 products and 6,700 companies (Globalwinespirits.com, 2012).

Inventory Locator Service (ILS) has its roots as an offline intermediary, serving as a listing service for aftermarket parts in the aerospace industry. Upon opening in 1979, ILS initially provided a telephone and fax-based directory of aftermarket parts to airplane owners and mechanics, along with government procurement professionals. As early as 1984, ILS incorporated e-mail capabilities as part of its RFQ services, and by 1998, it had begun to conduct online auctions for hard-to-find parts. In 2012, ILS maintains an Internet-accessible database of over 5 billion aerospace and marine industry parts, and has also developed an eRFQ feature that helps users streamline their sourcing processes. The network's 22,000 subscribers in 93 different countries access the site over 60,000 times a day. (Inventory Locator Service, 2012).

Industry Consortia

An **industry consortium** is an industry-owned vertical market that enables buyers to purchase direct inputs (both goods and services) from a limited set of invited participants (see **Figure 12.13**). Industry consortia emphasize long-term contractual purchasing, the development of stable relationships (as opposed to merely an anonymous transaction emphasis), and the creation of industry-wide data standards and synchronization efforts. Industry consortia are more focused on optimizing long-term supply relationships than independent exchanges, which tend to focus more on short-term transactions. The ultimate objective of industry consortia is the unification of supply chains within entire industries, across many tiers, through common data definitions, network standards, and computing platforms. In addition, industry consortia, unlike independent exchanges described previously, take their marching orders from the industry and not from venture capitalists or investment bankers. This means any profits from operating industry consortia are returned to industry business firms.

industry consortium
industry-owned vertical market that enables buyers to purchase direct inputs (both goods and services) from a limited set of invited participants

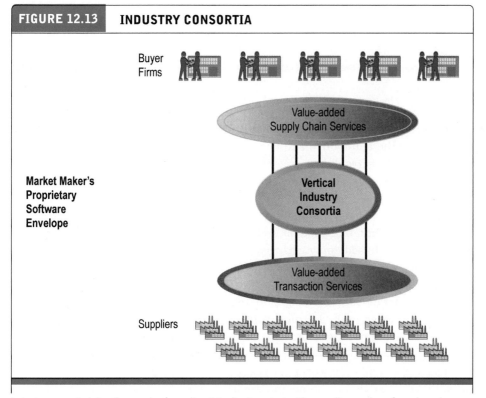

FIGURE 12.13	INDUSTRY CONSORTIA

Industry consortia bring thousands of suppliers into direct contact with a smaller number of very large buyers. The market makers provide value-added software services for procurement, transaction management, shipping, and payment for both buyers and suppliers. Industry consortia are sometimes referred to as many-to-few markets, where many suppliers (albeit selected by the buyers) serve a few very large buyers, mediated by a variety of value-added services.

TABLE 12.4	INDUSTRY CONSORTIA BY INDUSTRY (SEPTEMBER 2012)
INDUSTRY	NAME OF INDUSTRY CONSORTIA
Aerospace	Exostar
Automotive	SupplyOn
Chemical	Elemica
Food	Dairy.com
Hospitality	Avendra
Medical Services, Supplies	GHX (Global Healthcare Exchange)
Paper and Forest Products	PaperFiber
Shipping	OceanConnect
Textiles	The Seam (Cotton Consortium)
Transportation	Transplace

Industry consortia sprang up in 1999 and 2000 in part as a reaction to the earlier development of independently owned exchanges, which were viewed by large industries (such as the automotive and chemical industries) as market interlopers that would not directly serve the interests of large buyers, but would instead line their own pockets and those of their venture capital investors. Rather than "pay-to-play," large firms decided to "pay-to-own" their markets. Another concern of large firms was that Net marketplaces would work only if large suppliers and buyers participated, and only if there was liquidity. Independent exchanges were not attracting enough players to achieve liquidity. In addition, exchanges often failed to provide additional value-added services that would transform the value chain for the entire industry, including linking the new marketplaces to firms' ERP systems. A number of industry consortia now exist, with many industries having more than one (see **Table 12.4)**.

The industries with the most consortia are food, metals, and chemicals, although these are not necessarily the largest consortia in terms of revenue. Many very large Fortune 500 and private firms are investors in several industry consortia. For instance, Cargill—the world's largest private corporation—invested in six consortia that exist at various points in Cargill's and the food industry's tangled value chain.

Industry consortia make money in a number of ways. Industry members usually pay for the creation of the consortia's capabilities and contribute initial operating capital. Then industry consortia charge buyer and seller firms transaction and subscription fees. Industry members—both buyers and sellers—are expected to reap benefits far greater than their contributions through the rationalization of the procurement process, competition among vendors, and closer relationships with vendors.

Industry consortia offer many different pricing mechanisms, ranging from auctions to fixed prices to RFQs, depending on the products and the situation. Prices can also be negotiated, and the environment, while competitive, is nevertheless restricted to a smaller number of buyers—selected, reliable, and long-term suppliers who are often viewed as "strategic industry" partners. The bias of industry consortia is clearly toward the large buyers who control access to this lucrative market channel and can benefit from competitive pricing offered by alternative suppliers. Benefits to suppliers come from access to large buyer firm procurement systems, long-term stable relationships, and large order sizes.

Industry consortia can and often do force suppliers to use the consortia's networks and proprietary software as a condition of selling to the industry's members. Although exchanges failed for a lack of suppliers and liquidity, the market power of consortia members ensures suppliers will participate, so consortia may be able to avoid the fate of voluntary exchanges. Clearly, industry consortia are at an advantage when compared to independent exchanges because, unlike the venture-capital-backed exchanges, they have deep-pocket financial backing from the very start and guaranteed liquidity based on a steady flow of large firm orders. Yet industry consortia are a relatively new phenomenon, and the long-term profitability of these consortia, especially when several consortia exist for a single industry, has yet to be demonstrated.

Exostar is one example of an industry consortium. Its founding partners include BAE Systems, Boeing, Lockheed Martin, Raytheon, and Rolls-Royce, all companies in the aerospace industry. Exostar has taken a slow but steady approach to building its technology platform. It has kept its focus on the direct procurement and supply chain needs of its largest members, and taken its time developing a portfolio of technology solutions that meet its needs. Its current products include Supply Pass, an integrated suite of tools that enables suppliers to handle buyer transactions via the Internet; SourcePass, which provides a dynamic bidding environment for buyers and sellers; and ProcurePass, which enables buyers to handle supplier transactions online, among others. As of September 2012, Exostar served a community of more than 70,000 trading partners (Exostar, 2012).

THE LONG-TERM DYNAMICS OF NET MARKETPLACES

Net marketplaces are changing rapidly because of the widespread failures of early exchanges and a growing realization by key participants that real value will derive from B2B e-commerce only when it can change the entire procurement system, the supply chain, and the process of collaboration among firms. Several industry consortia have transformed themselves into industry data standards and synchronization forums. The consolidation of Net marketplaces has resulted in remaining firms that are much stronger and that are beginning to grow rapidly once again. In fact, B2B online transaction volumes are growing worldwide and within the United States at 20%–30% per year.

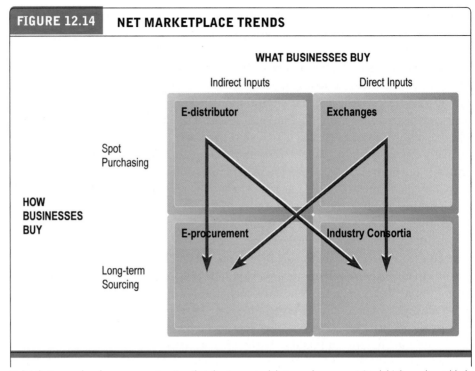

| FIGURE 12.14 | NET MARKETPLACE TRENDS |

E-distributors and exchanges are migrating their business models toward more sustained, higher value-added relationships with buyer firms by providing e-procurement services and participating in industry consortia.

Figure 12.14 depicts some of these changes. Pure Net marketplace exchanges are moving away from the simple "electronic marketplace" vision, and toward playing a more central role in changing the procurement process. Independent exchanges are ideal buy-out candidates for industry consortia because they have often developed the technology infrastructure. In any event, consortia and exchanges are beginning to work together in selected markets. Likewise, e-distributors are securing admission to large e-procurement systems and also seeking admission to industry consortia as suppliers of indirect goods.

Other notable trends include the movement from simple transactions involving spot purchasing to longer-term contractual relationships involving both indirect and direct goods (Wise and Morrison, 2000). The complexity and duration of transactions is increasing, and both buyers and suppliers are becoming accustomed to working in a digital environment, and making less use of the fax machine and telephone. To date, Net marketplaces, as well as private industrial networks, have emerged in a political climate friendly to large-scale cooperation among very large firms. However, the possibility exists that Net marketplaces may provide some firms with an ideal platform to collude on pricing, market sharing, and market access, all of which would be anti-competitive and reduce the efficiency of the marketplace.

12.3 PRIVATE INDUSTRIAL NETWORKS

Private industrial networks today form the largest part of B2B e-commerce, both on and off the Internet. Industry analysts estimate that in 2012, over 50% of B2B expenditures by large firms will be for the development of private industrial networks. Private industrial networks can be considered the foundation of the "extended enterprise," allowing firms to extend their boundaries and their business processes to include supply chain and logistics partners.

WHAT ARE PRIVATE INDUSTRIAL NETWORKS?

As noted at the beginning of this chapter, private industrial networks are direct descendants of existing EDI networks, and they are closely tied to existing ERP systems used by large firms. A private industrial network (sometimes referred to as a private trading exchange, or PTX) is a Web-enabled network for the coordination of trans-organizational business processes (sometimes also called collaborative commerce). **A trans-organizational business process** requires at least two independent firms to perform (Laudon and Laudon, 2012). For the most part, these networks originate in and closely involve the manufacturing and related support industries, and therefore we refer to them as "industrial" networks, although in the future they could just as easily apply to some services. These networks can be industry-wide, but often begin and sometimes focus on the voluntary coordination of a group of supplying firms centered about a single, very large manufacturing firm. Private industrial networks can be viewed as "extended enterprises" in the sense that they often begin as ERP systems in a single firm, and are then expanded to include (often using an extranet) the firm's major suppliers. **Figure 12.15** illustrates a private industrial network originally built by Procter & Gamble (P&G) in the United States to coordinate supply chains among its suppliers, distributors, truckers, and retailers.

trans-organizational business process
process that requires at least two independent firms to perform

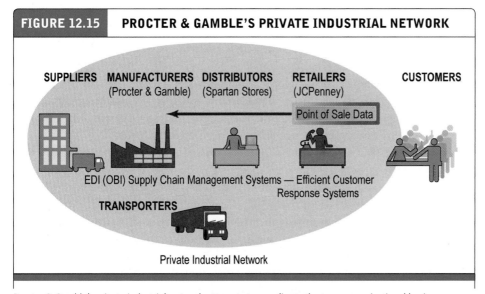

FIGURE 12.15   PROCTER & GAMBLE'S PRIVATE INDUSTRIAL NETWORK

SUPPLIERS   MANUFACTURERS   DISTRIBUTORS   RETAILERS   CUSTOMERS
(Procter & Gamble)   (Spartan Stores)   (JCPenney)

Point of Sale Data

EDI (OBI) Supply Chain Management Systems — Efficient Customer Response Systems

TRANSPORTERS

Private Industrial Network

Procter & Gamble's private industrial network attempts to coordinate the trans-organizational business processes of the many firms it deals with in the consumer products industry.

In P&G's private industrial network shown in Figure 12.15, customer sales are captured at the cash register, which then initiates a flow of information back to distributors, P&G, and its suppliers. This tells P&G and its suppliers the exact level of demand for thousands of products. This information is then used to initiate production, supply, and transportation to replenish products at the distributors and retailers. This process is called an efficient customer response system (a demand-pull production model), and it relies on an equally efficient supply chain management system to coordinate the supply side.

Not surprisingly, there is not a great deal of detailed information about private industrial networks. Most companies that originate and participate in these networks view them as a competitive advantage, and therefore they are reluctant to release information about how much they cost and how they operate.

GE, Dell Computer, Cisco Systems, Microsoft, IBM, Nike, Coca-Cola, Walmart, Nokia, and Hewlett-Packard are among the firms operating successful private industrial networks.

CHARACTERISTICS OF PRIVATE INDUSTRIAL NETWORKS

The central focus of private industrial networks is to provide an industry-wide global solution to achieve the highest levels of efficiency. The specific objectives of a private industrial network include:

- Developing efficient purchasing and selling business processes industry-wide
- Developing industry-wide resource planning to supplement enterprise-wide resource planning
- Increasing supply chain visibility—knowing the inventory levels of buyers and suppliers
- Achieving closer buyer-supplier relationships, including demand forecasting, communications, and conflict resolution
- Operating on a global scale—globalization
- Reducing industry risk by preventing imbalances of supply and demand, including developing financial derivatives, insurance, and futures markets

Private industrial networks serve different goals from Net marketplaces. Net marketplaces are primarily transaction-oriented, whereas private industrial networks focus on continuous business process coordination between companies. This can include much more than just supply chain management, such as product design, sourcing, demand forecasting, asset management, sales, and marketing. Private industrial networks do support transactions, but that is not their primary focus.

Private industrial networks usually focus on a single sponsoring company that "owns" the network, sets the rules, establishes governance (a structure of authority, rule enforcement, and control), and invites firms to participate at its sole discretion. Therefore, these networks are "private." This sets them apart from industry consortia, which are usually owned by major firms collectively through equity participation. Whereas Net marketplaces have a strong focus on indirect goods and services, private industrial networks focus on strategic, direct goods and services.

For instance, True Value is one of the largest retailer-owned hardware cooperatives with operations in 54 countries, 5,000 plus stores, and 12 regional distribution centers. The logistics are staggering to consider: in 2011 they processed 64,000 domestic inbound loads, and over 600 million pounds of freight. True Value imports roughly 3,500 containers through 20 international ports and 10 domestic ports. The existing inbound supply chain system was fragmented, did not permit real-time tracking of packages, and when shipments were short or damaged, could not alert stores. The supply chain was "invisible": suppliers could not see store inventory levels, and stores could not see supplier shipments. Using a Web-based solution from Sterling Commerce (an IBM company), True Value created its own private industrial network to which all suppliers, shippers, and stores have access. The network focuses on three processes: domestic prepaid shipping, domestic collect, and international direct shipping. For each process the network tracks in real-time the movement of goods from suppliers to shippers, warehouses, and stores. So far, the system has led to a 57% reduction in lead-time needed for orders, a 10% increase in the fill rate of orders, and an 85% reduction in back orders. If goods are delayed, damaged, or unavailable, the system alerts all parties automatically (True Value, 2012; IBM, 2011b).

Perhaps no single firm better illustrates the benefits of developing private industrial networks than Walmart, described in *Insight on Business: Walmart Develops a Private Industrial Network*.

PRIVATE INDUSTRIAL NETWORKS AND COLLABORATIVE COMMERCE

Private industrial networks can do much more than just serve a supply chain and efficient customer response system. They can also include other activities of a single large manufacturing firm, such as design of products and engineering diagrams, as well as marketing plans and demand forecasting. Collaboration among businesses can take many forms and involve a wide range of activities—from simple supply chain management to coordinating market feedback to designers at supply firms (see **Figure 12.16** on page 802).

One form of collaboration—and perhaps the most profound—is industry-wide **collaborative resource planning, forecasting, and replenishment (CPFR)**, which involves working with network members to forecast demand, develop production plans, and coordinate shipping, warehousing, and stocking activities to ensure retail and wholesale shelf space is replenished with just the right amount of goods. If this goal is achieved, hundreds of millions of dollars of excess inventory and capacity could be wrung out of an industry. This activity alone is likely to produce the largest benefits and justify the cost of developing private industrial networks.

A second area of collaboration is *demand chain visibility*. In the past, it was impossible to know where excess capacity or supplies existed in the supply and distribution chains. For instance, retailers might have significantly overstocked shelves, but suppliers and manufacturers—not knowing this—might be building excess capacity or supplies for even more production. These excess inventories would raise costs for the entire industry and create extraordinary pressures to discount merchandise, reducing profits for everyone.

A third area of collaboration is *marketing coordination and product design*. Manufacturers that use or produce highly engineered parts use private industrial networks

collaborative resource planning, forecasting, and replenishment (CPFR)
involves working with network members to forecast demand, develop production plans, and coordinate shipping, warehousing, and stocking activities to ensure that retail and wholesale shelf space is replenished with just the right amount of goods

INSIGHT ON BUSINESS

WALMART DEVELOPS A PRIVATE INDUSTRIAL NETWORK

Walmart is a well-known leader in the application of network technology to coordinate its supply chain. Walmart's supply chain is the secret sauce behind its claim of offering the lowest prices everyday. It's able to make this promise because it has possibly the most efficient B2B supply chain in the world. It doesn't hurt to also be the largest purchaser of consumer goods in the world. With sales of more than $443 billion for the fiscal year ending January 31, 2012, Walmart has been able to use information technology to achieve a decisive cost advantage over competitors. As you might imagine, the world's largest retailer also has the world's largest supply chain, with more than 60,000 suppliers worldwide. In the next five years, the company plans to expand from around 5,000 retail stores in the United States (including Sam's Clubs) to over 5,500 and increase its selection of goods. Internationally, Walmart has over 5,200 additional stores in 26 countries outside the United States, giving it a total of over 10,000 retail units. The rapid expansion in Walmart's international operations will require an even more capable private industrial network than what is now in place.

In the late 1980s, Walmart developed the beginnings of collaborative commerce using an EDI-based SCM system that required its large suppliers to use Walmart's proprietary EDI network to respond to orders from Walmart purchasing managers. In 1991, Walmart expanded the capabilities of its EDI-based network by introducing Retail Link. This system connected Walmart's largest suppliers to Walmart's own inventory management system, and it required large suppliers to track actual sales by stores and to replenish supplies as dictated by demand and following rules imposed by Walmart. Walmart also introduced financial payment systems that ensure that Walmart does not own the goods until they arrive and are shelved.

In 1997, Walmart moved Retail Link to an extranet that allowed suppliers to directly link over the Internet into Walmart's inventory management system. In 2000, Walmart hired an outside firm to upgrade Retail Link from being a supply chain management tool toward a more collaborative forecasting, planning, and replenishment system. Using demand aggregation software provided by Atlas Metaprise Software, Walmart purchasing agents can now aggregate demand from Walmart's 5,000 separate stores in the United States into a single RFQ from suppliers. This gives Walmart tremendous clout with even the largest suppliers. Previously, Walmart's foreign location buyers relied on a mix of telephones, fax, and e-mail to communicate their spending forecasts. The Atlas system allows them to submit forecasts via the Internet. Walmart headquarters issues worldwide RFQs for all stores. The Atlas software helps Walmart purchasing agents select a winning bid and negotiate final contracts.

In addition, suppliers can now immediately access information on inventories, purchase orders, invoice status, and sales forecasts, based on 104 weeks of online, real-time, item-level data. The system does not require smaller supplier firms to adopt expensive EDI software solutions. Instead, they can use standard browsers and PCs loaded with free software from Walmart. There are now over 20,000 suppliers—small and large—participating in Walmart's network.

In 2002, Walmart switched to an entirely Internet-based private network. Walmart adopted AS2, a software package from iSoft Corporation, a Dallas-based software company. AS2 implemented EDI-INT (an Internet-based standard version of EDI), and the result was a radical reduction in communications costs. In 2007, Walmart's rapid growth, especially global operations, forced it go outside for its financial services operation systems. Walmart hired SAP, an enterprise software mangement firm, to build a global financial management system for Walmart. Walmart had finally started to outgrow its home-grown systems.

By 2012, Walmart's B2B supply chain management system had mastered on a global scale the following capabilities: cross docking, demand planning, forecasting, inventory management, strategic sourcing, and distribution management. The future of Walmart's SCM lies in business analytics—working smarter—rather than simply making the movement and tracking of goods more efficient. For instance, in 2012 Walmart purhased Quintiq Inc., a supply chain management tool for improving load assignment and dispatch of trucks for large retailers. Quintiq's software will enable Walmart's managers to optimize the loading of its trucks and to reduce the time required to supply its retail stores.

Despite the economic slowdown in 2011–2012, Walmart's sales grew. In 2011, Walmart's revenues of $443 billion were up 6.4% from 2010, and its net income was $15.77 billion, up from $15.36 billion. In the first half of 2012, sales continued to grow by over 4%.

Like other large global firms, Walmart's global supply chain has been criticized for exploiting labor in underdeveloped countries where it buys products and in home markets where it sells them; bribing officials to look the other way; destroying environments; and wasting energy. In response to critics, Walmart has taken a number of steps. Walmart has set a goal of reducing carbon emissions in its supply chain by 20 million metric tons by 2015, and a goal of 100% renewable energy use in the United States. Walmart has made less progress in its labor policies: In January 2012, the ABP pension fund blacklisted Walmart for failing to comply with the United Nations' Global Compact principles. The Global Compact presents a set of core values relating to human rights, labor standards, the environment, and anti-corruption efforts. In April 2012 the Department of Justice opened an investigation into widespread allegations that Walmart had bribed Mexican officials to expand their stores and supply chain in Mexico.

Walmart's success spurred its competitors in the retail industry to develop industry-wide private industrial networks such as Global NetXchange (now Agentrics) in an effort to duplicate the success of Walmart. Walmart executives have said Walmart would not join these networks, or any industry-sponsored consortium or independent exchange, because doing so would only help its competitors achieve what Walmart has already accomplished with Retail Link. To compete with the efficiencies attained by Walmart, other retailers, such as JCPenney, have implemented their own extensive private industrial networks to link suppliers to their stores' inventories directly over the Internet. Target Stores has even given over some of its inventory control and product selection to its largest apparel provider, TAL Apparel Ltd. of Hong Kong.

SOURCES: "How Walmart is Changing Supplier Sustainability-Again," by Aran Rice, Renewablechoice.com, May 30, 2012; "Wal-Mart's Dirty Partners," by Josh Eidelson, Salon.com, July 6, 2012; "The Walmart Model and the Human Cost of Our Low Priced Goods," by Juan De Lara, The Guardian, July 25, 2012; "Supply Chain News: Walmart, Sustainability, and Troubles in Mexico," by Dan Gilmore, Supply Chain Digest, April 26, 2012; "Retail Giant Optimizes Supply Chain Processes With Quintiq Software," Supply&Demand Chain Executive, February 15, 2012; "Walmart Adds $7 Billion Through Acquisition in 2011," by Nate Holmes, InstoreTrends.com, May 11, 2012.

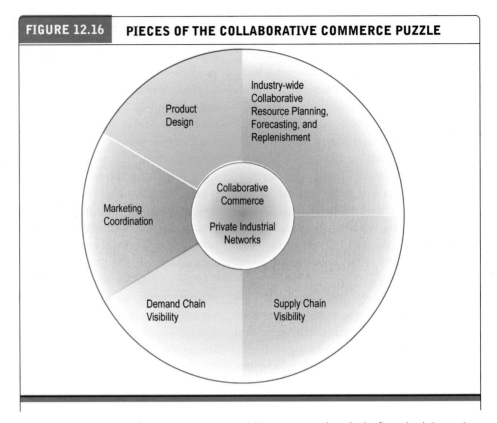

| FIGURE 12.16 | PIECES OF THE COLLABORATIVE COMMERCE PUZZLE |

Collaborative commerce involves many cooperative activities among supply and sales firms closely interacting with a single large firm through a private industrial network.

to coordinate both their internal design and marketing activities, as well as related activities of their supply and distribution chain partners. By involving their suppliers in product design and marketing initiatives, manufacturing firms can ensure that the parts produced actually fulfill the claims of marketers. On the reverse flow, feedback from customers can be used by marketers to speak directly to product designers at the firm and its suppliers. For the first time, "closed loop marketing"—customer feedback directly impacting design and production—described in Chapter 6—can become a reality.

IMPLEMENTATION BARRIERS

Although private industrial networks represent a large part of the future of B2B, there are many barriers to its complete implementation. Participating firms are required to share sensitive data with their business partners, up and down the supply chain. What in the past was considered proprietary and secret must now be shared. In a digital environment, it can be difficult to control the limits of information sharing. Information a firm freely gives to its largest customer may end up being shared with its closest competitor.

Integrating private industrial networks into existing enterprise systems and EDI networks poses a significant investment of time and money. The leading providers of enterprise systems to Fortune 500 companies (Oracle, IBM, and SAP) do offer B2B modules, and supply chain management capabilities, that can be added to their existing software suites. Nevertheless, implementing these modules is a very expensive proposition in part because the procurement side of many Fortune 500 firms is so fragmented and out-of-date. For smaller firms, cloud computing and software as a service (SaaS) alternatives are appearing on the market, which offer far less-expensive supply chain management capabilities.

Adopting private industrial networks also requires a change in mindset and behavior for employees. Essentially, employees must shift their loyalties from the firm to the wider trans-organizational enterprise and recognize that their fate is intertwined with the fate of their suppliers and distributors. Suppliers in turn are required to change the way they manage and allocate their resources because their own production is tightly coupled with the demands of their private industrial network partners. All participants in the supply and distribution chains, with the exception of the large network owner, lose some of their independence, and must initiate large behavioral change programs in order to participate (Laudon and Laudon, 2012).

Elemica:

Cooperation, Collaboration, and Community

I t may seem unusual to refer to an entire industry as a "community," a word reserved typically for collections of people who more or less know one another. Trade associations are one example of an industrial community. Trade associations form in an effort to pursue the interests of all members in the community although usually they do not include customers in the community. Elemica is a B2B industry trading hub aiming to revolutionize the entire supply chain of the chemical, tire and rubber, energy, and selected manufacturing industries worldwide. Elemica's purpose is not just to foster cooperation on a one-to-one inter-firm basis, or just to foster collaboration on multi-firm projects, but instead to lift all boats on an industry tide by making all firms more efficient. Elemica is one of the few survivors of the early B2B e-commerce years. In 2012, Elemica connects over 5,000 companies to its network and clears over $100 billion in transactions a year.

Elemica is a global e-commerce company originally founded by 22 leading corporations in the chemical industry (including oil and industrial gases) to provide cloud-based order management and supply chain applications and services. A single

platform provides one-stop shopping so that companies can buy and sell products to one another through their own enterprise systems or using a Web alternative. It also helps companies automate all of their business processes, creating efficiencies and economies of scale that lead to an improved bottom line.

How does Elemica achieve community among a diverse, global collection of firms where firms are often both customers and vendors to one another? It unites community members by linking together their enterprise systems. This is the "social glue" that sets Elemica apart. This "super platform" permits companies to communicate with one another electronically and to conduct transactions, handle logistics, and keep the books. The Elemica commerce platform has effectively standardized industry business transactions for all network members regardless of the type of enterprise system they have, and it's leveled the playing field for trade partners who are less technically sophisticated. This neutral platform facilitates millions of transactions for industry suppliers, customers, and third-party providers. In this sense, Elemica is one of the most sophisticated technology platforms in the B2B space.

One of the largest investments for a company is its enterprise system. Despite these investments, intercompany relationships—the backbone of their supply chain— are often left to outdated and unreliable processes. These shortcomings cost billions in lost productivity, revenue, and profit. Elemica's eCommerce platform changes that. It helps its clients leverage their enterprise system investment by incorporating transactions to external trade partners. Elemica's QuickLink ERP connectivity enables companies to link their internal IT systems through a neutral platform so that information is moved into each company's database while maintaining confidentiality and security. The chemical and oil industries were among the first users of enterprise systems (referred to in the early years as "manufacturing resource planning systems"). These large-scale systems were developed by single firms in order to rationalize and control the manufacturing process. They achieved this objective by identifying the outputs, inputs, and processes involved in manufacturing and automating key elements including inventory control and planning, process control, warehousing and storage, and shipping/logistics. If a company needed to produce 10 tons of polyethylene plastic, its enterprise system could tell it precisely how many tons of petrochemical inputs were required, when they should be delivered to manufacturing, the machinery and labor force required to manufacture the product, how long it would take, where it would be stored, and how it would be shipped. The systems can estimate the cost at any stage.

Elemica facilitates transactions of all types including order processing and billing, and logistics management. However, unlike some other companies in the field, Elemica does not buy, sell, or own raw material products. Instead it acts as an intermediary, or hub, linking companies together to automate confidential transactions. Like eBay or a credit card company, Elemica's revenue comes from charging transaction fees on a per-transaction basis. Its network of clients opens the door for companies to do business with all other connected buyers and sellers.

Elemica offers a variety of services for suppliers and customers, enabling them to automate both their business processes and internal purchasing. A modular, cloud-based solution simplifies sales, procurement, and financial processes; integrates supply chain partners to diminish communication barriers; and reduces overhead and errors.

Elemica integrates information flow among global trading partners using a cloud-based business process network. Each client needs only a single connection to Elemica, and Elemica manages the connections to that company's external trade partners. That means a company needs only maintain one connection to Elemica (important when it's time for enterprise system maintenance or upgrade) rather than maintain a variable number of connections and infrastructure to all its trade partners. Once a company connects to Elemica, it can have access to thousands of other customers. Clients are charged for the service based on volume of usage. This is much more efficient than older EDI solutions to inter-company transactions. Elemica provides the platform for collaborative commerce through a fully automated integrated network of suppliers, customers, and third-party providers.

Elemica offers cloud-based solutions for four areas: Logistics Management, Customer Management, Supplier Management, and Sourcing Management. Using these solutions, companies can automate ordering, invoicing, shipment tracking, and day-to-day business operations. Companies can sign up for one or more solutions depending on their needs.

Here's an example of how Elemica works. Let's say you need to order vinyl acetate from one of your suppliers. You put the order into your internal enterprise system, the order is automatically routed to Elemica, Elemica routes the order to your supplier's internal enterprise system, and you get a confirmed receipt of the order. Elemica's QuickLink Network ensures the accuracy of the item number and purchase order number and sends an alert if there's an issue. Once an order is confirmed, Elemica's platform can be leveraged to plan and coordinate delivery and automatically send an invoice and submit payment. For small or medium firms that may not have an enterprise system, Elemica has a Web portal with online software that allows firms to participate in the community with suppliers and customers. The platform offers a closed-loop process, end to end, from the purchase order, to acknowledgments, load tenders and responses, carrier status updates, and dock scheduling. All of this takes place in a few seconds with little or no human intervention. Elemica has even developed a solution that allows a customer to send a purchase order via e-mail or a print driver (alleviating fax processes) that's then routed to Elemica. The company then routes it to the supplier in its preferred format, integrated with its enterprise system as though it were a true electronic order. This holistic approach to order management allows suppliers to automate the process with both strategic and core customers, without asking its customers to change their processes. It's a win-win situation for suppliers and customers.

Unlike the automobile industry or the airline industry, where a few companies dominate, the $1.3 trillion chemical industry is made up of many companies of all sizes. The top 10 companies generate only 10% of the industry's annual revenue total, and the largest player, Dow Chemical, is responsible for 2%. In addition, unlike many other industries, chemical companies often buy the output from other chemical companies to use as raw materials for their products. Thus, chemical companies are often customers of one another as well as competitors.

By the late 1990s, senior leaders at some of the larger chemical companies were aware of changes in technology that made the adoption of information technology and the tools of e-commerce more appealing. The questions were how to best use these advances to benefit their businesses and how to establish industry standards for electronic transactions to make them accessible and attainable for all. Leaders from companies such as Dow Chemical and DuPont began discussing this subject and determined that a cooperative alliance would be the most efficient way to move forward. They were met with initial skepticism by marketing and sales staff, worried that online procurement would negatively affect relationships. Further, senior corporate leadership wasn't sure that e-commerce would have any use in the chemical industry at all. And companies were cautious about the expense of investing in the infrastructure necessary for e-commerce.

However, there were compelling opportunities that were impossible to dismiss, including lowering costs, creating closer connections with customers and suppliers, and differentiating companies on something other than price. At the same time, new start-ups like e-Chemicals and PlasticsNet were making traditional chemical companies nervous. What would happen if their efforts to use information technology to streamline an inefficient supply chain helped them capture market share? In other words, if the more traditional companies didn't move forward, they might end up losing the revenue race.

When Dow began looking at start-ups that were using e-commerce and talking to their customers, they found that customers were concerned about making an investment to establish online connections with multiple firms. Dow and DuPont decided that the best and most economically efficient option was to offer customers the choice of a neutral one-to-one link. This would remove the obstacle of multiple connections. A strong, third-party network addressed the community concern about loss of control. The two companies decided to create and invest in a neutral e-commerce company, partnering with other companies to create the critical mass needed to make it viable.

In 1999, the corporate boards of Dow and DuPont agreed that there were major advantages to online transaction processing and additional online connections among buyers and sellers. Since time and cost considerations made multiple connections unattractive to customers, a "hub" concept was adopted. It was also decided that a neutral community was the best approach.

All participants shared the common goal of creating a neutral platform to facilitate inter-company transactions and enhance business processes. Dow and DuPont also reviewed the concept with the relevant regulatory agencies and received up-front approval. Ultimately, 22 global chemical companies were involved in the launch of Elemica.

When Elemica opened its doors in 1999, there were 50 start-up B2B e-commerce companies in the chemical industry. Nearly all of these B2B companies were third-party owned Net marketplaces suitable at best for short-term sourcing of some direct inputs. In 2012, only a handful of these Net marketplaces for the chemical industry remain. Elemica focuses on building longer-term business relationships by creating

SOURCES: "About Elemica," Elemica.com, August 31, 2012; "Elemica Introduces Transportation Management Solution," Elemica Corporation, February 16, 2012; "Elemica Wins 2011 SDCExec Green Supply Chain Award for Helping Clients Incorporate Sustainability Within Their Supply Chains," Elemica Corporation, November 29, 2011; "Elemica Procurement Case Study: Dow," Elemica Corporation, September 2010; "Elemica Order Management Case Study: BP," Elemica Corporation, September 2010; "Elemica Case Study: LanXess," Elemica Corporation, September 2010; "Elemica and Rubber-Network Merge," SDCExec.com, August 25, 2009; "Case Study: Elemica," http://www.ebusiness-watch. org/studies, August 25, 2009; "Once Elemica Tackled the Hard Part, the Rest Was Easy," SupplyChainBrain.com August 05, 2009; "Elemica Merger with Rubber Network," Philly.com, August 3, 2009; "Elemica Automates B2B Transactions Between Trading Partners—Speeding Up Orders by 78%," Softwareag.com, January 2009; "Top Chemical Company Selects Elemica's Business Process Network to Automate Global Procurement," Redorbit.com, December 18, 2008; "Elemica: Standards and Business," by Mike McGuigan, CEO, November 6, 2007, www.pidx.org/events/upload/Elemica. ppt; "Elemica: Simplification + Efficiency = Increased Profitability," by Fran Keeth, Elemica Business Leadership Forum, Philadelphia, Pennsylvania, wwwstatic.shell.com, September 13, 2005; "The Journey of Elemica: An e-Commerce Consortium," by Andrew Liveris, Business Group President, Performance Chemicals. Strategic Alliances Conference, www.dow.com/ebusiness/news/ecs peech. htm, April 9, 2002

committed and contractual supply chains. The company acts only as a facilitator of business transactions and does not directly buy and sell chemical products.

Companies who sign on with Elemica have the support of Elemica's Professional Services & Implementation Team, which works with their staff to ensure a successful on-boarding process and acceptance of the business value of the endeavor. Many of Elemica's staff came from the chemical industry and are integral to the success of this training. Once companies witnessed that more orders were being delivered and received on time, and that their bills were going out faster and being paid faster, the enculturation and training processes became easier.

Today, Elemica, a privately held company, has 150 employees, more than 5,000 partners in its supply chain network, and conducts more than $100 billion in annual transactions. Its headquarters is in Pennsylvania, and it has overseas offices in Amsterdam, Frankfurt, London, Seoul, Shanghai, Singapore, and Tokyo.

Elemica's business model has been successful primarily because it addresses the needs of chemical, tire and rubber, energy and selected manufacturing companies of all sizes. It does this by offering multiple options for connecting to its hub system, multiple products that can be used alone or in combination, and by ensuring that only one connection integrated with a client's enterprise system is needed for all transactions. Customers can use Elemica, and take advantage of the technology it offers, without purchasing an additional internal system.

With Elemica, companies benefit from improved operational efficiency, reduced costs due to elimination of redundant systems and excess inventory, and a much higher percentage of safe and reliable deliveries. The flexibility of Elemica's solutions and network combines simplification, standardization, and efficiency. And clients have increased their profitability and improved cash flow through faster payment.

A number of very large companies use Elemica's platform. In Europe, Shell Oil started using Elemica after recognizing that it had ongoing problems with the coordination of paperwork processing and deliveries. Truck drivers would arrive at delivery sites and wait up to two hours while paperwork was filled out. These delays were costing Shell money. Once Shell began using Elemica, things improved. Today, paperwork is processed 24 hours a day, and truck waiting time has been cut from an average of two hours to an average of 15 minutes. Given this success, Shell continues to expand its relationship with Elemica.

Dow Chemical began to transition to full procurement automation with Elemica in 2007. More than 300 of their MRO suppliers are now linked to Elemica's platform. Errors are down 75%, and Dow has achieved economies of scale that have led to meaningful financial savings. Elemica helped Dow unify multiple, disparate business processes, reduced the cost of getting contracted items from suppliers, and increased efficiency in procurement, operations, IT, and accounts payable.

Air Products & Chemicals, Inc. is a global provider of gases and chemicals with 22,000 employees worldwide, and $10 billion in revenue. A major customer asked them for online ordering, but the initial method proposed would have required considerable additional work for both parties. Since both companies were connected to Elemica, there was a better option—the Elemica Supply Chain Hosted Solution.

Elemica has also developed a sustainability program. In November 2011, Elemica received the Green Supply Chain Award from an industry group for incorporating sustainability goals into its supply chain services. Elemica says it has delivered more than 160 million messages since 2004, which equates to 1,666 cubic meters of landfill space, 18,160,002 liters of water saved in paper production, 17,434 trees, and 196,128 kilograms of CO_2 emissions. In February 2012, Elemica introduced a transportation management solution (ETM) powered by Oracle. Available as a cloud-based software-as-a-service (SaaS) on a subscription basis, ETM will enable Elemica member firms to optimize logistics and transportation business processes, resulting in supply chain savings and a reduction of carbon emissions.

Case Study Questions

1. If you were a small chemical company, what concerns would you have about joining Elemica?

2. Elemica provides a community for participants where they can transact, coordinate, and cooperate to produce products for less. Yet these firms also compete with one another when they sell chemicals to end-user firms in the automobile, airline, and manufacturing industries. How is this possible?

3. Review the concept of private industrial networks and describe how Elemica illustrates many of the features of such a network.

12.5 REVIEW

KEY CONCEPTS

■ Define B2B commerce and understand its scope and history.

Before the Internet, business-to-business transactions were referred to simply as *trade* or the *procurement process*. Today, we use the term *B2B commerce* to describe all types of computer-assisted inter-firm trade, and the term *Internet-based B2B commerce* or *B2B e-commerce* to describe specifically that portion of B2B commerce that uses the Internet to assist firms in buying and selling a variety of goods to each other. The process of conducting trade among businesses consumes many business resources, including the time spent by employees processing orders, making and approving purchasing decisions, searching for products, and arranging for their purchase, shipment, receipt, and payment. Across the economy, this amounts to trillions of dollars spent annually on procurement processes. If a significant portion of this inter-firm trade could be automated and parts of the procurement process assisted by the Internet, millions or even trillions of dollars could be freed up for other uses, resulting in increased productivity and increased national economic wealth.

In order to understand the history of B2B commerce, you must understand several key stages including:

- *Automated order entry systems*, developed in the 1970s, used the telephone to send digital orders to companies. Telephone modems were placed in the offices of the customers for a particular business. This enabled procurement managers to directly access the firm's inventory database to automatically reorder products.
- *EDI* or *electronic data interchange*, developed in the late 1970s, is a communications standard for sharing various procurement documents including invoices, purchase orders, shipping bills, product stocking numbers (SKUs), and settlement information for an industry. It was developed to reduce the costs, delays, and errors inherent in the manual exchange of documents.
- *Electronic storefronts* emerged in the 1990s along with the commercialization of the Internet. They are online catalogs containing the products that are made available to the general public by a single vendor.
- *Net marketplaces* emerged in the late 1990s as a natural extension and scaling-up of the electronic storefront. The essential characteristic of all Net marketplaces is that they bring hundreds of suppliers, each with its own electronic catalog, together with potentially thousands of purchasing firms to form a single Internet-based marketplace.
- *Private industrial networks* also emerged in the late 1990s with the commercialization of the Internet as a natural extension of EDI systems and the existing close relationships that developed between large industrial firms and their suppliers.

Before you can understand each of the different types of Net marketplaces, you must be familiar with several other key concepts:

- *Seller-side solutions* are owned by the suppliers of goods and are seller-biased markets that only display goods from a single seller. Customers benefit because these systems reduce the costs of inventory replenishment and are paid for mainly by the suppliers. Automated order entry systems are seller-side solutions.
- *Buyer-side solutions* are owned by the buyers of goods and are buyer-biased markets because they reduce procurement costs for the buyer. Sellers also benefit because the cost of serving a company's customers is reduced. EDI systems are buyer-side solutions.
- *Vertical markets* provide expertise and products targeted to a specific industry. EDI systems usually serve vertical markets.
- *Horizontal markets* serve a myriad of different industries. Electronic storefronts are an example of a horizontal market in that they tend to carry a wide variety of products that are useful to any number of different industries.

■ Understand the procurement process, the supply chain, and collaborative commerce.

- The *procurement process* refers to the way business firms purchase the goods they need in order to produce the goods they will ultimately sell to consumers. Firms purchase goods from a set of suppliers who in turn purchase their inputs from a set of suppliers. These firms are linked in a series of connected transactions.
- The *supply chain* is the series of transactions that links sets of firms that do business with each other. It includes not only the firms themselves but also the relationships between them and the processes that connect them.

There are seven steps in the procurement process:
- Searching for suppliers for specific products
- Qualifying the sellers and the products they sell
- Negotiating prices, credit terms, escrow requirements, and quality requirements
- Scheduling delivery
- Issuing purchase orders
- Sending invoices
- Shipping the product

Each step is composed of separate sub-steps that must be recorded in the information systems of the buyer, seller, and shipper. There are two different types of procurements and two different methods of purchasing goods:
- *Purchases of direct goods*—goods that are directly involved in the production process.
- *Purchases of indirect goods*—goods needed to carry out the production process but that are not directly involved in creating the end product.
- *Contract purchases*—long-term agreements to buy a specified amount of a product. There are pre-specified quality requirements and pre-specified terms.
- *Spot purchases*—for acquisition of goods that meet the immediate needs of a firm. Indirect purchases are most often made on a spot-purchase basis in a large marketplace that includes many suppliers.

The term *multi-tier supply chain* is used to describe the complex series of transactions that exists between a single firm with multiple primary suppliers, the secondary suppliers who do business with those primary suppliers, and the tertiary suppliers who do business with the secondary suppliers.

Trends in supply chain management (the activities that firms and industries use to coordinate the key players in their procurement process) include:
- *Supply chain simplification,* which refers to the reduction of the size of a firm's supply chain. Firms today generally prefer to work closely with a strategic group of suppliers in order to reduce both product costs and administrative costs. Long-term contract purchases containing pre-specified product quality requirements and pre-specified timing goals have been shown to improve end-product quality and ensure uninterrupted production.
- *Supply chain management systems,* which coordinate and link the activities of suppliers, shippers, and order entry systems to automate the order entry process from start to finish, including the purchase, production, and moving of a product from a supplier to a purchasing firm.
- *Collaborative commerce,* which is a direct extension of supply chain management systems as well as supply chain simplification. It is the use of digital technologies to permit the supplier and the purchaser to share sensitive company information in order to collaboratively design, develop, build, and manage products throughout their life cycles.

- **Identify the main types of B2B commerce: Net marketplaces and private industrial networks.**

There are two generic types of B2B commerce and many different subtypes within those two main categories of Internet commerce:
- *Net marketplaces,* which are also referred to as exchanges or hubs, assemble hundreds to thousands of sellers and buyers in a single digital marketplace on

the Internet. They can be owned by either the buyer or the seller, or they can operate as independent intermediaries between the buyer and seller.

- *Private industrial networks* bring together a small number of strategic business partners who collaborate with one another to develop highly efficient supply chains and to satisfy customer demand for product. They are by far the largest form of B2B commerce.

■ **Understand the four types of Net marketplaces.**

There are four main types of "pure" Net marketplaces:

- *E-distributors* are independently owned intermediaries that offer industrial customers a single source from which to make spot purchases of indirect or MRO goods. E-distributors operate in a horizontal market that serves many ifferent industries with products from many different suppliers.
- *E-procurement Net marketplaces* are independently owned intermediaries connecting hundreds of online suppliers offering millions of MRO goods to business firms who pay a fee to join the market. E-procurement Net marketplaces operate in a horizontal market in which long-term contractual purchasing agreements are used to buy indirect goods.
- *Exchanges* are independently owned online marketplaces that connect hundreds to thousands of suppliers and buyers in a dynamic real-time environment. They are typically vertical markets in which spot purchases can be made for direct inputs (both goods and services). Exchanges make money by charging a commission on each transaction.
- *Industry consortia* are industry-owned vertical markets where long-term contractual purchases of direct inputs can be made from a limited set of invited participants. Consortia serve to reduce supply chain inefficiencies by unifying the supply chain for an industry through a common network and computing platform.

■ **Identify the major trends in the development of Net marketplaces.**

- In the early days of e-commerce, independent exchanges were the prototype Internet-based marketplace and over 1,500 of them were created; however, most of them did not succeed. The main reason independent exchanges failed is that they did not attract enough players to achieve liquidity (measured by the number of buyers and sellers in the market, the transaction volume, and the size of the transactions).
- Industry consortia sprang up partly in reaction to the earlier development of independently owned exchanges that were viewed by large industries as interlopers who would not directly serve their needs. Industry consortia are profitable because they charge the large buyer firms transaction and subscription fees, but the rationalization of the procurement process, the competition among the vendors, and the closer relationship with the vendors are benefits that more than offset the costs of membership to the firms. However, the long-term profitability of consortia has yet to be proven.
- The failure of the early exchanges is one reason Net marketplaces are changing so rapidly. Participants have come to realize that the real value of B2B e-commerce will only be realized when it succeeds in changing the entire procurement system, the supply chain, and the process of collaboration among firms.

■ Identify the role of private industrial networks in transforming the supply chain.

- Private industrial networks, which presently dominate B2B commerce, are Web-enabled networks for coordinating trans-organizational business processes (collaborative commerce). These networks range in scope from a single firm to an entire industry.

- Although the central purpose of a private industrial network is to provide industry-wide global solutions to achieve the highest levels of efficiency, they generally start with a single sponsoring company that "owns" the network. This differentiates private industrial networks from industry consortia that are usually owned collectively by major firms through equity participation.

- Private industrial networks are transforming the supply chain by focusing on continuous business process coordination between companies. This coordination includes much more than just transaction support and supply chain management. Product design, demand forecasting, asset management, and sales and marketing plans can all be coordinated among network members.

■ Understand the role of private industrial networks in supporting collaborative commerce.

Collaboration among businesses can take many forms and involve a wide range of activities. Some of the forms of collaboration used by private industrial networks include the following:

- *CPFR or industry-wide collaborative resource planning, forecasting, and replenishment* involves working with network members to forecast demand, develop production plans, and coordinate shipping, warehousing, and stocking activities. The goal is to ensure that retail and wholesale shelf space is precisely maintained.

- *Supply chain and distribution chain visibility* refers to the fact that, in the past, it was impossible to know where excess capacity existed in a supply or distribution chain. Eliminating excess inventories by halting the production of overstocked goods can raise the profit margins for all network members because products will no longer need to be discounted in order to move them off the shelves.

- *Marketing and product design collaboration* can be used to involve a firm's suppliers in product design and marketing activities as well as in the related activities of their supply and distribution chain partners. This can ensure that the parts used to build a product live up to the claims of the marketers. Collaborative commerce applications used in a private industrial network can also make possible closed loop marketing in which customer feedback will directly impact product design.

QUESTIONS

1. Explain the differences among total inter-firm trade, B2B commerce, and B2B e-commerce.
2. What are the key attributes of an electronic storefront? What early technology are they descended from?
3. List at least five potential benefits of B2B e-commerce.
4. Name and define the two distinct types of procurements firms make. Explain the difference between the two.
5. Name and define the two methods of purchasing goods.

6. Define the term supply chain and explain what SCM systems attempt to do. What does supply chain simplification entail?
7. Explain the difference between a horizontal market and a vertical market.
8. How do the value chain management services provided by e-procurement companies benefit buyers? What services do they provide to suppliers?
9. What are the three dimensions that characterize an e-procurement market based on its business functionality? Name two other market characteristics of an e-procurement Net marketplace.
10. Identify and briefly explain the anti-competitive possibilities inherent in Net marketplaces.
11. List three of the objectives of a private industrial network.
12. What is the main reason why many of the independent exchanges developed in the early days of e-commerce failed?
13. Explain the difference between an industry consortium and a private industrial network.
14. What is CPFR, and what benefits could it achieve for the members of a private industrial network?
15. What are the barriers to the complete implementation of private industrial networks?

PROJECTS

1. Choose an industry and a B2B vertical market maker that interests you. Investigate the site and prepare a report that describes the size of the industry served, the type of Net marketplace provided, the benefits promised by the site for both suppliers and purchasers, and the history of the company. You might also investigate the bias (buyer versus seller), ownership (suppliers, buyers, independents), pricing mechanism(s), scope and focus, and access (public versus private) of the Net marketplace.

2. Examine the Web site of one of the e-distributors listed in Figure 12.9, and compare and contrast it to one of the Web sites listed for e-procurement Net marketplaces. If you were a business manager of a medium-sized firm, how would you decide where to purchase your indirect inputs—from an e-distributor or an e-procurement Net marketplace? Write a short report detailing your analysis.

3. Assume you are a procurement officer for an office furniture manufacturer of steel office equipment. You have a single factory located in the Midwest with 2,000 employees. You sell about 40% of your office furniture to retail-oriented catalog outlets such as Quill in response to specific customer orders, and the remainder of your output is sold to resellers under long-term contracts. You have a choice of purchasing raw steel inputs—mostly cold-rolled sheet steel—from an exchange and/or from an industry consortium. Which alternative would you choose and why? Prepare a presentation for management supporting your position.

References

CHAPTER 1

Aguiar, Mark and Erik Hurst. "Life-Cycle Prices and Production." *American Economic Review* 97:5, 1533-1559. (January 1, 2008).

Alessandria, George. "Consumer Search, Price Dispersion, and International Relative Price Fluctuations." *International Economic Review* 50:3, 803-829 (September 1, 2009).

Bailey, Joseph P. *Intermediation and Electronic Markets: Aggregation and Pricing in Internet Commerce.* Ph. D., Technology, Management and Policy, Massachusetts Institute of Technology (1998a).

Bakos, Yannis. "Reducing Buyer Search Costs: Implications for Electronic Marketplaces." *Management Science* (December 1997).

Banerjee, Suman and Chakravarty, Amiya. "Price Setting and Price Discovery Strategies with a Mix of Frequent and Infrequent Internet Users." (April 15, 2005). SSRN: http://ssrn.com/abstract=650706.

Baye, Michael R. "Price Dispersion in the Lab and on the Internet: Theory and Evidence." *Rand Journal of Economics* (2004).

Baye, Michael R., John Morgan, and Patrick Scholten. "Temporal Price Dispersion: Evidence from an Online Consumer Electronics Market." *Journal of Interactive Marketing* (January 2004).

Brynjolfsson, Erik, and Michael Smith. "Frictionless Commerce? A Comparison of Internet and Conventional Retailers." *Management Science* (April 2000).

Buck, Stephanie. "The Beginner's Guide to Instagram." Mashable.com (May 29, 2012).

comScore. "comScore Releases April 2012 U.S. Online Video Rankings." (May 18, 2012a).

comScore. "comScore Media Metrix Ranks Top 50 U.S. Web Properties for April 2012." (May 24, 2012b).

Deatsch, 2010. "As Web Sales Grow, So Should Spending on Technology, Report Says." Internet Retailer (June 17, 2010).

eBay, Inc. "eBay Reports Strong Second Quarter 2012 Results." (July 18, 2012).

eMarketer, Inc. (Jeffrey Grau) "US Retail E-commerce Forecast: Entering the Age of Omnichannel Retailing." (March 1, 2012).

eMarketer, Inc. "Comparative Estimates: BC2 Ecommerce Sales Growth" for China, India, Brazil" (Accessed June 8, 2012a).

eMarketer, Inc. (Jeffrey Grau) "Mobile Commerce Forecast: Capitalizing on Consumers' Urgent Needs." (January 2012b).

eMarketer, Inc. (Krista Garcia) "Facebook Commerce: Reaching Shoppers Where They Socialize." (January 2012c).

eMarketer, Inc. "US Internet Users and Penetration, 2011-2016." (February 13, 2012d).

eMarketer, Inc. "US Internet Users, by Age, 2010-2016." (March 1, 2012e).

eMarketer, Inc. "US Fixed Broadband Households and Subscriptions, 2010-2016" (March 1, 2012f).

eMarketer, Inc. "Mobile Internet Users Worldwide, by Region and Country, 2010-2016." (April 17, 2012g).

eMarketer, Inc. "Comparative Estimates Broadband Households Worldwide, 2010-2015, and Mobile Internet Users Worldwide 2010-2016." (accessed June 7, 2012x).

eMarketer, Inc. (Lauren Fisher) "Local Online Advertising: Digital Trends, Challenges and Opportunities." (December 2011a).

eMarketer, Inc. "US Internet Households by Type, 2009-2015." (March 2011b).

Evans, Philip, and Thomas S. Wurster. "Getting Real About Virtual Commerce." *Harvard Business Review* (November-December 1999).

Evans, Philip, and Thomas S. Wurster. "Strategy and the New Economics of Information." *Harvard Business Review* (September-October 1997).

Fink, Eugene, Josh Johnson, and Jerry Hu. "Exchange Market for Complex Goods: Theory and Experiments." *Communications of the ACM.* (April, 2004).

Forrester Research. "Forrester Research Web Influenced Retail Sales Forecast, 2010 to 2015 (US)." (January 31, 2011).

Ghose, Anindya, and Yuliang Yao. "Using Transaction Prices to Re-Examine Price Dispersion in Electronic Markets." Information Systems Research, Vol. 22 No. 2. (June 2011).

Internet Retailer. "Top 400 Europe 2012 Edition." (2012a).

Internet Retailer. "Top 500 Guide 2012 Edition." (2012b).

Internet Systems Consortium, Inc. "ISC Internet Domain Survey." (June 2012).

Internet World Stats. "Internet Usage Statistics : The Internet Big Picture: World Internet Users and Population Stats." Internetworldstats.com (June 2012).

Kalakota, Ravi, and Marcia Robinson. *e-Business 2.0: Roadmap for Success, 2nd edition.* Reading, MA: Addison Wesley (2003).

Kambil, Ajit. "Doing Business in the Wired World." *IEEE Computer* (May 1997).

Lawler, Ryan. "YouTube Revenues More Than Double in 2010." Gigaom.com (January 20, 2011).

Levin, Jonathon. "The Economics of Internet Markets." Stanford University, Draft, February 18, 2011.

Mesenbourg, Thomas L. "Measuring Electronic Business: Definitions, Underlying Concepts, and Measurement Plans." U. S. Department of Commerce Bureau of the Census (August 2001).

National Retail Foundation. "NRF Forecasts Retail Industry Sales Growth of 3.4 Percent." (January 16, 2012).

Pew Internet & American Life Project. "What Internet Users Do on an Average Day." (September 2012).

PricewaterhouseCoopers/National Venture Capital Association. MoneyTree Report, Data: Thomson Reuters (2012).

Rayport, Jeffrey F., and Bernard J. Jaworski. *Introduction to E-commerce, 2nd edition*. New York: McGraw-Hill (2003).

Rosso, Mark and Bernard Janse. "Smart Marketing or Bait & Switch: Competitors' Brands as Keywords in Online Advertising." Proceedings of the 4th Workshop on Information Credibility. ACM (2010).

Shapiro, Carl, and Hal R. Varian. *Information Rules. A Strategic Guide to the Network Economy*. Cambridge, MA: Harvard Business School Press (1999).

Sinha, Indajit. "Cost Transparency: The Net's Threat to Prices and Brands." *Harvard Business Review* (March-April 2000).

Smith, Michael; Joseph Bailey; and Erik Brynjolfsson. "Understanding Digital Markets: Review and Assessment." In Erik Brynjolfsson and Brian Kahin (eds.) *Understanding the Digital Economy*. Cambridge MA: MIT Press (2000).

Tumblr.com "About." Accessed June 6, 2012

Tversky, A., and D. Kahneman. "The Framing of Decisions and the Psychology of Choice." *Science* (January 1981).

U.S. Census Bureau. "U.S. POPClock Projection." Census.gov (October 1, 2012a).

U.S. Census Bureau. "E-Stats." (May 10, 2012b).

Varian, Hal R. "When Commerce Moves On, Competition Can Work in Strange Ways." *New York Times* (August 24, 2000a).

Varian, Hal R. "5 Habits of Highly Effective Revolution." *Forbes ASAP* (February 21, 2000b).

Wikipedia.org. "Wikipedia: About." (accessed May 28, 2012).

Wikimedia Foundation. "Wikipedia Celebrates 10 Years of Free Knowledge." (January 12, 2011).

WordPress.com. "Stats." (accessed June 6, 2012).

Yahoo Finance. "YouTube Will Generate Ad Revenue of $1.6B in 2011." (November 3, 2011).

Yankee Group. "Mobile Apps and Cloud Forecast." (June 4, 2012).

YouTube.com. "Statistics." (accessed May 28, 2012).

CHAPTER 2

Arthur, W. Brian. "Increasing Returns and the New World of Business." *Harvard Business Review* (July-August 1996).

Bakos, Yannis. "The Emerging Role of Electronic Marketplaces on the Internet." *Communications of the ACM* (August 1998).

Barney, J. B. "Firm Resources and Sustained Competitive Advantage." *Journal of Management* Vol. 17, No. 1 (1991).

Bellman, Steven; Gerald L. Lohse; and Eric J. Johnson. "Predictors of Online Buying Behavior." *Communications of the ACM* (December 1999).

Bureau of Economic Analysis, U.S. Department of Commerce, Table 1.1.5 "Gross Domestic Product," (accessed August 20, 2012).

comScore, "comScore Releases July 2012 Search Engine Rankings." (August 10, 2012).

eBay, Inc. "eBay Inc. Reports Strong Second Quarter Revenue and Earnings Growth." (July 18, 2012).

Fisher, William W. III. "The Growth of Intellectual Property: A History of the Ownership of Ideas in the United States." Cyber.law.harvard.edu/people/tfisher/iphistory.pdf (1999).

Gerace, Thomas. "Encyclopedia Britannica." Harvard Business School Case Study 396-051 (1999).

Ghosh, Shikhar. "Making Business Sense of the Internet." Harvard Business Review (March- April 1998).

Kambil, Ajit. "Doing Business in the Wired World." *IEEE Computer* (May 1997).

Kambil, Ajit; Ari Ginsberg; and Michael Bloch. "Reinventing Value Propositions." Working Paper, NYU Center for Research on Information Systems (1998).

Kanter, Elizabeth Ross. "The Ten Deadly Mistakes of Wanna-Dots." *Harvard Business Review* (January 2001).

Kaplan, Steven, and Mohanbir Sawhney. "E-Hubs: The New B2B Marketplaces." *Harvard Business Review* (May-June 2000).

Kim, W. Chan, and Renee Mauborgne. "Knowing a Winning Business Idea When You See One." *Harvard Business Review* (September-October 2000).

Magretta, Joan. "Why Business Models Matter." *Harvard Business Review* (May 2002).

Porter, Michael E. "Strategy and the Internet." *Harvard Business Review* (March 2001).

Porter, Michael E. *Competitive Advantage: Creating and Sustaining Superior Performance*. New York: Free Press (1985).

Rigdon, Joan I. "The Second-Mover Advantage." *Red Herring* (September 1, 2000).

Teece, David J. "Profiting from Technological Innovation: Implications for Integration, Collaboration,

Licensing and Public Policy." *Research Policy* 15 (1986).

Timmers, Paul. "Business Models for Electronic Markets" *Electronic Markets* Vol. 8, No. 2 (1998).

U.S. Census Bureau. "E-Stats." (May 17, 2012).

CHAPTER 3

Arar, Yardena. "Google Play vs. Amazon vs. iTunes Store: How the Content Stores Stack Up." PCWorld.com (July 10, 2012).

Arstechnica.com. "Capitol Hill, The Internet, and Broadband: An Ars Technica Quarterly Report." (September 2010).

Berners-Lee, Tim; Robert Cailliau; Ari Luotonen; Henrik Frystyk Nielsen; and Arthur Secret. "The World Wide Web." *Communications of the ACM* (August 1994).

Bluetooth.com. "Press & Analysts." (2012).

Brandt, Richard. "Net Assets: How Stanford's Computer Science Department Changed the Way We Get Information." *Stanford Magazine* (November/December 2004).

Burger, Andrew. "Report: Business Adoption Fuels Growth in VoIP Services." Telecompetitor.com (April 10, 2012).

Bush, Vannevar. "As We May Think." *Atlantic Monthly* (July 1945).

Cerf, V., and R. Kahn, "A Protocol for Packet Network Intercommunication." *IEEE Transactions on Communications*, Vol. COM-22, No. 5, pp 637-648 (May 1974).

comScore. "comScore Releases July 2012 U.S. Search Engine Rankings." (August 10, 2012a).

comScore. "comScore Releases July 2012 U.S. Online Video Rankings." (August 17, 2012b).

eMarketer, Inc. "Mobile Phone Users Worldwide, by Region and Country, 2010-2016." (April 17, 2012a).

eMarketer, Inc. "US Fixed Broadband Households and Subscriptions, 2010-2016." (March 1, 2012b).

eMarketer, Inc. "Mobile Internet Users Worldwide, by Region and Country, 2010-2016." (April 17, 2012c).

eMarketer, Inc. "US Blog Readers, 2010-2016." (March 1, 2012d).

eMarketer, Inc. "US Bloggers, 2010-2016." (March 1, 2012e).

eMarketer, Inc. (Jeffrey Grau). "US Mobile Commerce Forecast: Capitalizing on Consumers' Urgent Needs." (January 2012f).

eMarketer, Inc. (Catherine Boyle). "Tablet Computing Fuels 'Couch and Pillow' Commerce." (June 13, 2012g).

Federal Networking Council. "FNC Resolution: Definition of 'Internet.'" (October 24, 1995).

Geni.net. "Global Environment for Network Innovations." (accessed September 2012).

Gross, Grant. "NSF Seeks Ambitious Next-Generation Internet Project." *Computerworld* (August 29, 2005).

International Data Corporation. "Worldwide Quarterly Mobile Phone Tracker." (March 15, 2012).

Internet2. "Internet2 Planned 100 Gigabit Infrastructure Topology; Internet2 Network." Internet2.edu (September 2011).

Internet Corporation for Assigned Names and Numbers (ICANN). "ICANN Approves Historic Change to Internet 's Domain System." (June 20, 2011a).

Internet Corporation for Assigned Names and Numbers (ICANN). "Top-Level Domains (gTLDs)." (2011b).

ISOC.org. "ISOC's Standards Actitivies." Internet Society. (September 2010).

Internet Society. " World IPv6 Launch on June 6, 2012, To Bring Permanent IPv6 Deployment." (January 2012).

Internet Society. "RFC 2616: Hypertext Transfer Protocol-HTTP/1.1." (June 1999).

Internet Society. "RFC 0959: File Transfer Protocol." (October, 1985).

Internetworldstats.com "Internet Usage Statistics : The Internet Big Picture-World Internet Users and Population Stats." (As of June 30, 2012.)

Juniper Research. "Mobile Payments for Digital & Physical Goods: Opportunity Analysis 2012-2017." (August 8, 2012).

Kleinrock, Leonard. *1964 Communication Nets: Stochastic Message Flow and Delay*. New York: McGraw-Hill (1964).

Leiner, Barry M.; Vinton G. Cerf; David D. Clark; Robert E. Kahn; Leonard Kleinrock; Daniel C. Lynch; Jon Postel; Larry G. Roberts; and Stephen Wolff. "All About the Internet: A Brief History of the Internet." *Internet Society* (ISOC) (August 2000).

Marketshare.hitslink.com. "Top Browser Share Trend." (September 2012).

National Research Foundation. "NSP Leadership in Discovery and Initiative Sparks White House US Ignite Initiative." (June 13, 2012).

Netcraft. "July 2012 Web Server Survey." (July 2012).

Nielsen. "Buzz in the Blogosphere: Millions More Bloggers and Blog Readers." (March 8, 2012a).

Nielsen. "Apps Dominate Mobile Time Spent Accessing Travel in the U.S." (August 29, 2012b).

Nielsen. "Mobile Apps Beat the Mobile Web Among US Android Smartphone Users." (August 18, 2011).

NLR.net. "National LambdaRail: About Us." (September 2010).

Oracle. "Mobile Trends: Consumer Views of Mobile Shopping and Mobile Service Providers." (April 2011).

PCWorld.com. "Google Play vs. Amazon vs. iTunes Store: How the Content Stores Stack Up." (July 10, 2012).

Pew Internet & American Life Project. "Daily Internet Activities." (September 2012).

Pfanner, Eric. "Ethics Fight Over Domain Names Intensifies." *New York Times* (March 18, 2012).

Radicati Group. "Email Statistics Report, 2012-2016." (May 2012).

Siegler, MG. "The Best Overlooked Numbers And Subtle Features From WWDC 2011." Techcrunch.com (June 7, 2011).

Troianovski, Anton. "Optical Delusion? Fiber Booms Again, Despite Bust." *Wall Street Journal* (April 2, 2012).

U.S. Department of Commerce. "Letter to ICANN Chairman." http://www.ntia.doc.gov/comments/2008/ICANN_080730.html (July 30, 2008).

Visualware, Inc., "VisualRoute Traceroute Server." (September 2011).

Zakon, Robert H. "Hobbes' Internet Timeline v8.1." Zakon.org (2005).

Ziff-Davis Publishing. "Ted Nelson: Hypertext Pioneer." Techtv.com (1998).

CHAPTER 4

Banker, Rajiv D., and Chris F. Kemerer. "Scale Economies in New Software Development." *IEEE Transactions on Software Engineering*, Vol. 15, No. 10 (1989).

Doyle, Barry and Cristina Videria Lopes. "Survey of Technologies for Web Application Development." ACM, Vol.2., No. 3. (June 2005).

Hostway. "Hostway Pet Peeves Survey." (2007).

IBM (High Volume Web Sites Team). "Best Practices for High-Volume Web Sites." *IBM Redbooks* (December 2002).

Laudon, Kenneth C. and Jane P. Laudon. Management Information Systems: *Managing the Digital Firm*. 13th edition. Upper Saddle River, NJ: Prentice Hall (2012).

Lientz, Bennet P., and E. Burton Swanson. Software *Maintenance Management*. Reading MA: Addison-Wesley (1980).

WebTrends, Inc. "WebTrends Analytics 10." (2011).

CHAPTER 5

Bray, Charles. "Two Arrested in iPad Security Breach." *Wall Street Journal* (January 11, 2011).

Channelinsider.com. "Network Solutions Suffers Large Data Breach." (July 24, 2009).

Computer Security Institute. "CSI Computer Crime and Security Survey 2012." (2012).

Cybersource, Inc. "Online Fraud Report-2012 Edition." (2012).

Danchev, Dancho. "Exposing the Market for Stolen Credit Cards Data." DDanchev.blogspot.com (October 31, 2011).

DMARC.org. "Leading Email Senders and Providers to Combat Email Phishing Through DMARC.org." (January 30, 2012).

Electronic Privacy Information Center (EPIC). "Cryptography and Liberty 2000. An International Survey of Encryption Policy." Washington D. C. (2000).

Fiserv. "2011 Fiserv Consumer Trends Survey: Financial Services Continue the Digital Shift." (February 2012).

Fiserv. "2007 Consumer Bill Payments Trends Survey: Volume of Electronic Payments." (2007).

Gartner. "Forecast Overview: Security Infrastructure Worldwide, 2010-2016, 2Q12 Update." (August 8, 2012).

GData SecurityLabs. Malware Report. Bi-annual Report July-December 2011 (December 2011).

Honan, Mat. "How Apple and Amazon Security Flaws Led to My Epic Hacking." Wired.com (August 6, 2012).

Internet Retailer. "The Internet Retailer Survey: Lower Debit Card Rates Elude Most Online Retailers, But It's Still Early." (April 1, 2012).

Javelin Strategy & Reseach. "2012 Identity Fraud Survey Report." (February 2012).

Javelin Strategy & Research. "Online Retail Payments Forecast 2011-2016: New Regulations Leave Credit Poised for a Comeback." (November 27, 2011).

Kaspersky Lab. "Kapersky Security Bulletin. Statistics 2011." (March 1, 2012).

Kolesnikov-Jessup, Sonia. "Hackers Go After the Smartphone." *New York Times* (February 13, 2011).

Microsoft. "Microsoft Security Intelligence Report Volume 12: July-December 2011 (2012).

Mitnick, Kevin. Ghost in the Wires. Little, Brown & Co. (2011).

National White Collar Crime Center and the Federal Bureau of Investigation. "Internet Crime Complaint Center 2011 Internet Crime Report." (2012).

Nilson Report. "General Purpose Cards -- U.S. 2011." (February 2012).

PandaSecurity, "Cyber-Crime Files." http://cybercrime.pandasecurity.com/blackmarket/how_works.php (accessed September 15, 2012).

Ponemon Institute. "2011 Cost of Data Breach Study: Global." (March 2012).

Schwartz, John. "Fighting Crime Online: Who is in Harm's Way?" *New York Times* (February 8, 2001).

Sophos. "Security Threat Report 2012." (2012).

Stein, Lincoln D. *Web Security: A Step-by-Step Reference Guide*. Reading, MA: Addison-Wesley (1998).

Symantec, Inc. "Internet Security Threat Report Volume XVII: May 2012." (May 2012a).

Symantec. "Symantec Intelligence Report: August 2012." (September 2012b).

Symantec, Inc. "Internet Security Threat Report: Trends for 2010, Volume 16: April 2011." (April 2011).

Symantec, Inc. "Internet Security Threat Report Volume XV: April 2010." (April 2010).

US-Cert "Socializing Securely: Using Social Networking Services." (January 2011).

US-Cert. "Cyber Threats to Mobile Devices." TIP 10-105-01 (April 2010).

Wakabayashi, Daisuke. "A Contrite Sony Vows Tighter Security." *Wall Street Journal* (May 1, 2011).

Wingfield, Nick. "Spam Network Shut Down." *Wall Street Journal* (March 18, 2011).

Zetter, Kim. "Top Federal Lab Hacked in Spear-Phishing Attack." Wired (April 20, 2011).

CHAPTER 6

Adjei, Mavis, and Stephanie Noble. "The Influence of C2C Communications in Online Brand Communities On Purchase Behavior." *Journal of the Academy of Marketing Science*, Vol. 38, No. 5 (2009).

Adomavicius, Gediminas, and Alexander Tuzhilin. "Using Data Mining Methods to Build Customer Profiles." *IEEE Computer* (February 2001a).

Adomavicius, Gediminas, and Alexander Tuzhilin. "Expert-Driven Validation of Rule-Based User Models in Personalization Applications." *Data Mining and Knowledge Discovery* (January 2001b).

Akerlof, G. "The Market for 'Lemons' Quality Under Uncertainty and the Market Mechanism." *Quarterly Journal of Economics* (August 1970).

Awad, Neveen; Michael Smith, and Mayuram Krishnan. "The Consumer Online Purchase Decision: A Model of Consideration Set Formation and Buyer Conversion Rate Across Market Leaders and Market Followers." Working Paper Series, SSRN (September 2007).

Ba, Sulin, and Jan Stallaert, and Zhang. "Balancing IT with the Human Touch: Optimal Investment in IT-Based Customer Service." Information Systems Research (September 2010).

Ba, Sulin, and Paul Pavlou. "Evidence on the Effect of Trust Building Technology in Electronic Markets: Price Premiums and Buyer Behavior." *MIS Quarterly* (September 2002).

Bailey, J., and Erik Brynjolfsson. "An Exploratory Study of the Emerging Role of Electronic Intermediaries." *International Journal of Electronic Commerce* (Spring, 1997).

Bakos, J. Y., and Erik Brynjolfsson. "Bundling and Competition on the Internet: Aggregation Strategies for Information Goods." *Marketing Science* (January 2000).

Barry, John and Ed Keller. *The Influentials: One American in Ten Tells the Other Nine How to Vote, Where to Eat, and What to Buy.* Free Press (2003).

Baye, Michael R.; John Morgan; and Patrick Scholten. "Price Dispersion in the Small and in the Large: Evidence from an Internet Price Comparison Site." Nash-equilibrium.com, (August 2002a).

Baye, Michael R.; John Morgan; and Patrick Scholten. "The Value of Information in an Online Consumer Market." *Journal of Public Policy and Marketing* (August 2002b).

Bell, David R. and Sangyoung Song. "Social Contagion and Trial on the Internet: Evidence from Online Grocery Retailing." Unpublished paper. The Wharton School, University of Pennsylvania (May 12, 2004).

BIA/Kelsey. "Annual U.S. Local Media Forecast 2011-2016." (March 20, 2012).

Brookings Institute. "Online Identity and Consumer Trust: Assessing Online Risk." (January 2011).

Brynjolfsson, Erik, and M. D. Smith. "Frictionless Commerce? A Comparison of Internet and Conventional Retailer." *Management Science* (April 2000).

Brynjolfsson, Erik; Michael D. Smith; and Yu Hu. "Consumer Surplus in the Digital Economy: Estimating the Value of Increased Product Variety at Online Booksellers." *Working Paper, Information, Operations, and Management Sciences Research Seminar Series*, Stern School of Business (April 17, 2003).

Carr, Nicholas. "Does the Internet Make You Dumber?" *New York Times* (June 5, 2010).

Catalyst. "Buying Power." (March 8, 2011).

Chan, P. K. "A Non-Invasive Learning Approach to Building Web User Profiles." In *Proceedings of ACM SIGKDD International Conference* (1999).

Channel Advisor, "Through the Eyes of the Consumer: 2010 Consumer Shopping Habits Survey." (2010).

Clay, K.; K. Ramayya; and E. Wolff. "Retail Strategies on the Web: Price and Non-Price Competition in the On Line Book Industry." Working Paper, *MIT E-commerce Forum* (1999).

comScore. "The Top 6 Trends Shaping Local Search in 2012 and Beyond." ComScore Webinar (April 2012).

Corritore, C.L., B. Kracher, S. Wiedenbeck, "On-line trust: concepts, evolving themes, a model," *International Journal of Human-Computer Studies* (2006).

Cross, Robert. "Launching the Revenue Rocket: How Revenue Management Can Work For Your Business." *Cornell Hotel and Restaurant Administration Quarterly* (April 1997).

Doolin, Bill; Stuart Dillion, and Fiona Thompson. "Perceived Risk, the Internet Shopping Experience, and Online Purchasing Behvaior." In Annie Becker (editor), Electronic Commerce: Concepts, Methodologies, Tools and Applications. Information Science Reference (2007).

Dyer, Pam. "Social Networks Have Little Influence on What You Buy Online." Pamarama.net (April 2011).

Ellison, Sarah. "Web-Brand Study Says Awareness Isn't Trust." *Wall Street Journal* (June 7, 2000).

eMarketer, Inc. "US Internet Users and Penetration, 2011-2016." (February 13, 2012a).

eMarketer, Inc. "Mobile Internet User Penetration Worldwide, by Region and Country, 2010-2016." (April 17, 2012b).

eMarketer, Inc. (Alison McCarthy) "US Mobile Usage Forecast." (September 2012c).

eMarketer, Inc. ""US Fixed Broadband Households and Subscriptions, 2010-2016." (March 1, 2012d).

eMarketer, Inc. "Mobile Data Dashboard." (accessed August 27, 2012e).

eMarketer, Inc. (Jeffrey Grau) "US Retail Ecommerce Forecast: Entering the Age of Omnichannel Retailing Growth Opportunities in a Maturing Channel." (March 1, 2012f).

eMarketer, Inc. "US Online Ad Spending, by Format, 2011-2016 (billions)." (September 1, 2012g).

eMarketer, Inc. (Alison McCarthy) "US Ad Spending Forecast: Fall 2012 Update." (October 1, 2012h).

eMarketer, Inc. "U.S. Mobile Ad Spending, by Format, 2010-2016 (millions)." (September 2012i).

eMarketer, Inc. "U.S. Mobile Ad Spending Growth, by Format, 2010-2016 (% change)." (September 2012j).

eMarketer, Inc. (Noah Elkin) "App-etite for Engagement: Marketing Beyond the Browser) (June 27, 2012k).

eMarketer, Inc. "Time Spent with Media." (March 2012l).

eMarketer, Inc. (Jeffrey Grau) "US Retail Ecommerce Forecast: Growth Opportunities in a Maturing Channel." (April 1, 2011a).

eMarketer, Inc. (Paul Verna). "Word of Mouth Marketing" (October 2010a).

Evans, P., and T. S. Wurster. "Getting Real About Virtual Commerce." *Harvard Business Review* (November-December 1999).

Fawcett, Tom, and Foster Provost. "Adaptive Fraud Detection." *Data Mining and Knowledge Discovery* (1997).

Fawcett, Tom, and Foster Provost. "Combining Data Mining and Machine Learning for Effective User Profiling." In *Proceedings of the Second International Conference on Knowledge Discovery and Data Mining* (1996).

Federal Communications Commission. "FCC Broadband Report Finds Significant Progress In Broadband Deployment, But Important Gaps Remain." (August 17, 2012).

Forrester Research. "Affiliate Marketing—The Direct and Indirect Values That Affiliates Deliver to Advertisers." (June 26, 2012).

Forrester Research. (Sucharita Mulpuru) "Will Facebook Ever Drive eCommerce?" (April 7, 2011a).

Forrester Research. "Web-Influenced Offline Retail Sales Forecast, 2009-2014." (July 13, 2011b).

Fournier, Susan and Lara Lee. "Getting Brand Communities Right." Harvard Business Review (April 2009).

Garg, Rajiv. "Peer Influence and Information Difusion in Online Networks: An Empricial Analysis." Carnegie Mellon University, School of Information Systems and Management, Working Paper, 2009.

Ghose, Anindya and Yuliang Yao. "Using Transaction Prices to Re-Examine Price Dispersion in Electronic Markets." Information Systems Research (June 2011).

Godin, Seth. *Permission Marketing.* New York: Simon & Schuster (1999).

Google, Inc. "The Arrival of Real-Time Bidding." (2011).

Greenfield, Patricia. "Technology and Informal Education: What Is Taught, What Is Learned. *Science Magazine* (January, 2009).

Guo, Stephen, M. Wang, and J. Leskovec. "The Role of Social Networks in Online Shopping Choice: Information Passing, Price of Trust, and Consumer Choice." Stanford University, June 2011.

Ha, Hong-Youl and Helen Perks. "Effects of Consumer Perceptions of Brand Experience on the Web: Brand Familiarity, Satisfaction and Brand Trust." Journal of Consumer Behavior (December 2005).

Internet Retailer. "Top 500 Guide 2012 Edition." (2012).

Kim, D. and I. Benbasat. "The Effects of Trust-Assuring Arguments on Consumer Trust in Internet Stores," *Information Systems Research* (2006).

Kim, D. and I. Benbasat. "Designs for Effective Implementation of Trust Assurances in Internet Stores," *Communications of the ACM* (July 2007).

Kim, Dan, Donald Ferrin, and Raghav Rao. "Trust and Satisfaction, Two Stepping Stones for Successful E-Commerce Relationships: A Longitudinal Exploration." Journal of Information Systems Research (June 2009).

Kotler, Philip, and Gary Armstrong. *Principles of Marketing, 13th Edition*. Upper Saddle River, NJ: Prentice Hall (2009).

Lambrecht, Anja and Catherine Tucker. "When does Retargeting Work? Timing Information Specificity." (July 29, 2011). SSRN: http://ssrn.com/abstract=1795105.

Leiter, Daniel B. and Thierry Warin. "An Empirical Study of Price Disperson in Homogeneous Goods Markets." Middlebury College Economics Discussion Paper No. 07-10. 2007.

Lohse, L. G., G. Bellman, and E. J. Johnson. "Consumer Buying Behavior on the Internet: Findings from

Panel Data." *Journal of Interactive Marketing* (Winter 2000).

Malamud, Ofer and Cristian Pop-Eleches. "Home Computer Use and the Development of Human Capital." University of Chicago and NBER Columbia University (January 2010).

Mishra, D. P., J. B. Heide, and S. G. Cort. "Information Asymmetry and Levels of Agency Relationships." *Journal of Marketing Research*. (1998).

Mobasher, Bamshad. "Data Mining for Web Personalization." Center for Web Intelligence, School of Computer Science, Telecommunication, and Information Systems, DePaul University, Chicago, Illinois. (2007).

Nie, Norman, and Lutz Erbring. "Internet and Society: A Preliminary Report." *Stanford Institute for the Quantitative Study of Society* (February 17, 2000).

Nielsen Company. "Global Online Consumer Survey." (May 2011).

Opinion Research Corporation. "Online Consumer Product Reviews Have Big Influence." Opinion Research Corporation (April 16, 2009).

Pavlou, Paul. "Institution-Based Trust in Interorganizational Exchange Relationships: The Role of Online B2B Marketplaces on Trust Formation." *Journal of Strategic Information Systems* (2002).

Pavlou, Paul A. and Angelika Dimoka. "The Nature and Role of Feedback Text Comments in Online Marketplaces: Implications for Trust Building, Price Premiums, and Seller Differentiation." *Information Systems Research* (August 2006).

Pavlou, P. A. and M. Fygenson (2005). "Understanding and Predicting Electronic Commerce Adoption: An Extension of the Theory of Planned Behavior." *MIS Quarterly* (2005).

Pew Internet & American Life Project. "May-June 2005 Tracking Survey." (August 9, 2005a).

Pew Internet & American Life Project (Amanda Lenhart, Mary Madden and Paul Hitlin). "Teens and Technology." (July 27, 2005b).

Pew Internet & American Life Project, "Online Activities, Daily." (February 2012a) http://pewinternet.org/Trend-Data-(Adults)/Online-Activities-Daily.aspx, accessed September 12, 2012.

Pew Internet & American Life Project. "Demographics of Internet Users," (August 2012b) http://pewinternet.org/Trend-Data-(Adults)/Whos-Online.aspx, accessed September 12, 2012.

Pew Internet & American Life Project. (Kathryn Zickuhr and Aaron Smith) "Digital Differences." (April 13, 2012c).

Rayport, J. F., and J. J. Sviokla. "Exploiting the Virtual Value Chain." *Harvard Business Review* (November-December 1995).

Retail Advertising & Marketing Association (RAMA). "Social Media: An Inside Look at the People Who Use It." (March 3, 2010).

Richtel, Matt. "Wasting Time is Divide in Digital Era." New York Times (May 29, 2012).

Saunders, Peter Lee, and Andrea Chester. "Shyness and the Internet: Social Problem or Panacea?" Division of Psychology, School of Health Sciences, RMIT University, City Campus, Melbourne, Victoria, Australia (2008).

Scholten, Patrick, and S. Adam Smith. "Price Dispersion Then and Now: Evidence from Retail and E-tail Markets." Nash-equilibrium.com. (July 2002).

Senecal, Sylvain and J. Nantel, "The Influence of Online Product Recommendations on Consumers' Online Choices." Journal of Retailing, Vol. 80 (2004).

Shapiro, Carl, and Hal Varian. *Information Rules: A Strategic Guide to the Network Economy.* Cambridge, MA: Harvard Business School Press (1999).

Shapiro, Carl, and Hal Varian. "Versioning: The Smart Way to Sell Information." *Harvard Business Review* (November-December 1998).

Shklovski, Irina; Sara Kiesler, and Robert Kraut. "The Internet and Social Interaction: A Meta-analysis and Critique of Studies, 1995-2003." Carnegie Mellon University (2004).

Sinha, Indrajit. "Cost Transparency: The Net's Real Threat to Prices and Brands." *Harvard Business Review* (March-April 2000).

Strategy Analytics. "Global Mobile Media Forecast" press release (April 20, 2012).

Takahashi, Dean. "Freemium Summit: Evernote shares the insider secrets of free apps," Mobileventurebeat.com (March 26, 2010).

Teece, David J. "Profiting from Technological Innovation: Implications for Integration, Collaboration, Licensing and Public Policy." *Research Policy*, 15 (1986).

Turkle, Sherry. "Alone Together: Why We Expect More From Technology and Less From Each Other." Basic Books, Inc. (2011).

USC Annenberg School, Center for the Digital Future. The Digital Future Report 2011. (June 3, 2011).

Van den Poel, Dirk and Wouter Buckinx. "Predicting Online Purchasing Behavior." *European Journal of Operations Research*, Vol. 166, Issue 2 (2005).

von Hippel, Eric. *The Sources of Innovation.* New York: Oxford University Press (1994).

von Hippel, Eric. *Democratizing Innovation.* Cambridge : MIT Press, (2005).

Watts, Duncan. *Six Degrees of Freedom.* W.W. Norton (2004).

Wigand, R. T., and R. I. Benjamin. "Electronic Commerce: Effects on Electronic Markets." *Journal of*

Computer Mediated Communication (December 1995).

Williamson, O. E. *The Economic Institutions of Capitalism.* New York: Free Press (1985).

Wolfinbarger, Mary, and Mary Gilly. "Shopping Online for Freedom, Control and Fun." *California Management Review* (Winter 2001).

CHAPTER 7

Barnes, Nora Ganim; Ava M. Lescault and Justina Andonian. "Social Media Surge by the 2012 Fortune 500: Increase Use of Blogs, Facebook , Twitter and More." (2012).

Battelle, John. "The Database of Intentions is Far Larger Than I Thought." Battellemedia.com (March 5, 2010).

Battelle, John. "Search Blog." Battellemedia.com (November 13, 2003).

Baymard Reserach, "15 Cart Abandonment Rate Statistics." Baymard.com (July 17, 2012))'

BIA/Kelsey. "Annual U.S. Local Media Forecast 2011-2016." (March 20, 2012).

Brightroll. "US Video Advertising Report." (June 7, 2012).

Chambers, Clem. "Click Fraud a Ticking Time Bomb Under Google." *Forbes* (June 18, 2012).

comScore. "2012 U.S. Digital Future in Focus." (February 2012a).

comScore. "comScore Releases July 2012 U.S. Search Engine Rankings." (August 10, 2012b).

Davern, Michael J.; Dov Te'eni; and Jae Yun Moon. "Information Environments and Human Behavior Over Time: From Initial Preferences to Mature Usage." Department of Information Systems, Stern School of Business, New York University (2001).

Direct Marketing Association (DMA). "Response Rate 2012 Report." (June 14, 2012).

Efrati, Amir. "Google Wants Search to Be More Social." *New York Times* (March 31, 2011).

eGain. "Multichannel Experience Most Dysfunctional Aspect of Customer Service, According to New North America Research Survey." (February 23, 2010).

eMarketer, Inc. "US Digital Ad Spending, by Format, 2012-2016." (September 1, 2012a).

eMarketer, Inc. "US Total Media Ad Spending, 2012-2016." (September 2012b).

eMarketer, Inc. (Kimberly Maul) "Brand Advocates: Scaling Social Media Word-of-Mouth." (May 23, 2012c).

eMarketer, Inc. (Alison McCarthy) "US Ad Spending Forecast: Fall 2012 Update." (October 1, 2012d).

eMarketer, Inc. (Kimberly Maul). "Facebook Marketing: Reaching Consumers in a Changing Environment." (August 22, 2012e).

eMarketer, Inc. (Alison McCarthy) "US Online Gaming Audience Forecast: Mobile and Social Lead the Way." (June 5, 2012f).

eMarketer, Inc. "Social Game Ad Revenues, US vs. Non-US, 2010-2014." (September 2012g).

eMarketer, Inc. "Latest Benchmarks Prove Email Still an Effective Marketing Channel." (July 6, 2012h).

eMarketer, Inc. "Online Ad Targeting Types." (April 30, 2012i).

eMarketer, Inc. "Integrating Search and Display: Tactics For More Effective Marketing. (April 2011a).

eMarketer, Inc. "Facebook Marketing: Turning Likes Into Loyalty." (May 2011b).

eMarketer, Inc. "Click Through and Like Rate of Facebook Ads." (August 2011c).

eMarketer, Inc. "How Much Time People Really Spend with Ads." (August 24, 2009).

Eyeblaster. "Trends of Time and Attention in Online Advertising." (July 22, 2009).

Farahat, Ayman and Michael Bailey. "How Effective is Targeted Advertising." International World Wide Web Conference Committee (April 26-20, 2012).

Flanigan, Andrew, and Miriam J. Metzger. "The Role of Site Features, User Attributes, and Information Verification Behaviors on the Perceived Credibility of Web-based Information." *New Media & Society*, Vol. 9, No. 2 (2007).

Fogg, B.J., Cathey Soohoo, David Danielson, Leslie Marable, Julliane Stanford, and Ellen Tauber. "How Do Users Evaluate the Credibility of Web Sites? A Study with Over 2,500 Participants." *Proceedings of DUX2003, Designing for User Experiences.* (2003).

Forrester Research. "Affiliate Marketing—The Direct and Indirect Value That Affiliates Deliver to Advertisers." (June 2012).

Garzotta, Franca. "Empirical Investigation of Web Design Attributes Affecting Brand Perception." *Proceedings of the Nordic Conference on Human Computer Interaction, New York* (2010).

Gigaom.com, "Survey: Percentage of Users Saying They Opt Out of Targeted Ads Has Nearly Doubled." Gigaom.com, (July 16, 2012).

Golander, Gill Korman and Noam Tractinsky. "Trends in Website Design." *AIS Transactions on Human Computer Interactions*, Vol 4, Issue 3 (2012).

Google, Inc. "What's Trending in Display for Publishers?" (May 29, 2012).

Google, Inc.. "Eye-tracking Studies: More than Meets the Eye." googleblog.blogspot.com (February 6, 2009).

Google, Inc. "Overview/DoubleClick for Advertisers." (2010).

Hausman, Angela V. and Jeffrey Sam Siekpe . "The Effect of Web Interface Features on Consumer

Online Purchase Intentions." *Journal of Business Research* (January 2009).

Hotchkiss, Gord, Tracy Sherman, Rick Tobin, Cory Bates and Krista Brown. "Search Engine Results 2010." Enquiroresearch.com (September, 2007).

Interactive Advertising Bureau. "Mobile Rich Media Ad Definitions (MRAID)" (September 2012).

Interactive Advertising Bureau. "IAB Standards and Guidelines." Iab.net (September 2011).

Interactive Advertising Bureau (IAB)/PriceWaterhouse-Coopers. "IAB Internet Advertising Revenue Report: 2011 Full Year Results." (April 2012).

Internet Retailer. 2010 Guide to Retail Web Site Design & Usability. (2010).

iProspect Inc. "How Offline Marketing Boosts Online Effect by 40%." iProspect.com (August 2011).

Iyengar, Raghuram, S. Han and S. Gupta. "Do Friends Influence Purchases in a Social Network." Harvard Business School. Working Paper, 2010.

Lohse, L. G.; G. Bellman; and E. J. Johnson. "Consumer Buying Behavior on the Internet: Findings from Panel Data." *Journal of Interactive Marketing* (Winter 2000).

McKinsey & Company. "The Impact of Internet Technologies: Search." (July 2011).

MediaMind Inc. "The Rich and the Powerful." (March 2012a).

MediaMind Inc. "Consumers 27 Times More Likely to Click-Through Online Video Ads than Standard Banners."(September 12, 2012b).

National Conference of State Legislatures. "State Laws Relating to Unsolicited Commercial of Bulk E-mail (SPAM)." (February 10, 2010).

Nielsen, Jakob. "F-Shaped Pattern For Reading Web Content, Nielsen's Alertbox." (April 17, 2006).

Nielsen Company. "December 2011—Top U.S. Web Brands." (January 25, 2012).

Nielsen Company. "Nielsen Receives MRC Accreditation for Nielsen Online Campaign Ratings." (September 7, 2011).

Novak, T. P.; D. L. Hoffman; and Y. F. Yung. "Measuring the Customer Experience in Online Environments: A Structural Modeling Approach." *Marketing Science* (Winter, 2000).

Pew Internet & American Life Project. "Daily Internet Activities." (September 2012).

Shrestha, Sav and Kelsi Lenz. "EyeGaze Patterns while Searching vs. Browsing a Website." Software Usability Research Laboratory, Department of Psychology, Wichita State University, Wichita, KS 67260-0034 (September, 2007).

Symantec. "Symantec Intelligence Report: August 2012 Report" (August 2012).

Tarafdar, Monideepa, and Jie Zhang. "Determinants of Reach and Loyalty- A study of Website Performance and Implications for Website Design." *Journal of Computer Information Systems*, (Winter 2008).

Tobii/Mediative. "The Effectiveness of Display Advertising on a Desktop PC vs. a Tablet Device." (August 2012).

TRUSTe. "U.S. Consumer Privacy Attitudes and Business Implications." (July 16, 2012).

Tsai, Janice; S. Egelman, L. Cranor, and A. Acquisti. "The Effect of Online Privacy Information on Purchasing Behavior: An Experimental Study." Paper presented at the Workshop on the Economics of Information Security, June 7-8, 2007, Pittsburgh, PA. (June 2007).

Usercentric. "Eye Tracking Bing vs. Google: A Second Look." (January 27, 2011).

Wordstream, Inc. "How Does Google Make Its Money: The 20 Most Expensive Keywords in Google AdWords." (2011).

Zhou, Tao, Y. Lin, and B. Wang, "The Relative Importance of Website Design Quality and Service Quality in Determining Consumers' Online Repurchase Behavior." *Information Systems Management*, Vol. 26, Issue 4 (2008).

CHAPTER 8

Acquisti, Alessandro, Ralph Gross, and Fred Stutzman. "Faces of Facebook: Privacy in the Age of Augmented Reality," Heinz College & CyLab Carnegie Mellon University (August 4, 2011).

Acquisti , Alessandro, Leslie John, and George Loewenstein. "What is Privacy Worth?" Twenty First Workshop on Information Systems and Economics (WISE) (December 14-15, 2009).

Angwin, Julia and Jennifer Valentino-Devries. "New Tracking Frontier: Your License Plates." *Wall Street Journal* (September 28, 2012).

Angwin, Julia. "Face-ID Tools Pose New Risk." *Wall Street Journal* (August 1, 2011).

Apple Computer, Inc. v. Microsoft Corp. 709 F. Supp. 925, 926 (N. D. Cal. 1989); 799 F. Supp. 1006, 1017 (N. D. Cal., 1992); 35 F. 3d 1435 (9th Cir.); cert. denied, 63 U. S. L. W. 3518 (U.S., Feb. 21, 1995) (No. 94-1121).

Associated Press. "Google Settles Final Piece of Geico Case." BizReport.com (September 8, 2005).

Audi AG and Volkswagen of America, Inc. v. Bob D'Amato No. 05-2359, 6th Circuit (November 27, 2006).

Bernina of America, Inc. v. Fashion Fabrics Int'l., Inc. 2001 U. S. Dist. LEXIS 1211 (N. D. Ill., Feb. 8, 2001).

Berzo, Alexandra. "Delaware Lawmakers Clear Online Gambling." *Wall Street Journal* (June 27, 2012).

Bilski et al. v. Kappos, 561 U.S. _____(2010).

Bilton, Nick. "Apple Loophole Gives Developers Access to Photos." *New York Times* (February 28, 2012).

Brown Bag vs. Symantec Corp., 960 F. 2d 1465 (9th Cir. 1992).

Brustein, Joshua. "Start-Ups Seek to Help Users Put a Price on Their Personal Data." *New York Times* (February 12, 2012).

Chiappetta, Vincent. "Defining the Proper Scope of Internet Patents: If We Don't Know Where We Want to Go, We're Unlikely to Get There." *Michigan Telecommunications Technology Law Review* (May 2001).

Cowell, Alan. "Britons Protest Proposal to Widen Surveillance." *New York Times* (April 2, 2012).

Diamond v. Chakrabarty, 447 US 303 (1980).

E. & J. Gallo Winery v. Spider Webs Ltd. 129 F. Supp. 2d 1033 (S.D. Tex., 2001) aff'd 286 F. 3d 270 (5th Cir., 2002).

European Commission, "Commission Proposes a Comprehensive Reform of the Data Protection Rules." (January 26, 2012).

Federal Trade Commission. "Google Will Pay $22.5 Million to Settle FTC Charges It Misrepresented Privacy Assurance to Users of Apple's Safari Internet Browser." (August 9, 2012a).

Federal Trade Commission. "Facebook Must Obtain Consumers' Consent Before Sharing Their Information Beyond Established Privacy Settings." (August 10, 2012b).

Federal Trade Commission. "FTC Finalizes Privacy Settlement with Myspace." (September 11, 2012c).

Federal Trade Commission. "Protecting Consumer Privacy in an Era of Rapid Change." (March 26, 2012d).

Federal Trade Commission. "FTC Charges Deceptive Privacy Practices in Google's Rollout of Its Buzz Network." (March 3, 2011).

Federal Trade Commission. "Privacy Online: Fair Information Practices in the Electronic Marketplace." (May 2000a).

Federal Trade Commission. "Online Profiling: A Report to Congress." (June 2000b).

Federal Trade Commission. "Privacy Online: A Report to Congress." (June 1998).

Field v. Google, Inc. 412 F.Supp. 2nd 1106 (D. Nev., 2006).

Fisher, William W. III. "The Growth of Intellectual Property: A History of the Ownership of Ideas in the United States." Law.harvard.edu/Academic_Affairs/coursepages/tfisher/iphistory.html (1999).

Ford Motor Co. v. Lapertosa 2001 U. S. Dist. LEXIS 253 (E. D. Mich. Jan. 3, 2001).

Google, Inc. v. American Blind & Wallpaper Factory, Inc. Case No. 03-5340 JF (RS) (N.D. Cal., April 18, 2007).

Government Employees Insurance Company v. Google, Inc. Civ. Action No. 1:04cv507 (E.D. VA, December 15, 2004).

Greenhouse, Linda. "Supreme Court Upholds Child Pornography Law." *New York Times* (May 20, 2008).

Greenhouse, Linda. "20 Year Extension of Existing Copyrights Is Upheld." *New York Times* (January 16, 2003a).

Greenhouse, Linda. "Justices Back Law to Make Libraries Use Internet Filters." *New York Times* (June 24, 2003b).

Gruenwald, Juliana. "Poll Finds Public Concern Over Online Privacy." National Journal.com (June 8, 2010).

Hafner, Katie and Matt Richtel. "Google Resists U.S. Subpoena of Search Data." *New York Times* (January 20, 2006).

Harmon, Amy. "Pondering Value of Copyright vs. Innovation." *New York Times* (March 3, 2003).

Hoofnagle, Chris Jay. "Privacy Self-Regulation: A Decade of Disappointment." Electronic Privacy Information Center (Epic.org) (March 4, 2005).

Kelly v. ArribaSoft. 336 F3rd 811 (CA 9th, 2003).

Laudon, Kenneth. "Markets and Privacy." *Communications of the ACM* (September 1996).

Maass, Peter and Megha Rajagopalen. "That's No Phone. That's My Tracker." *New York Times* (July 13, 2012).

McMillan, Robert. "Porn Typosquatter Fined Again by FTC." *InfoWorld* (October 16, 2007).

Miller, John W. and Christopher Rhoads, "U.S. Fights to Keep Control Of Global Internet Oversight." *Wall Street Journal* (November 16, 2005).

Nash, David B. "Orderly Expansion of the International Top-Level Domains: Concurrent Trademark Users Need a Way Out of the Internet Trademark Quagmire." *The John Marshall Journal of Computer and Information Law* Vol. 15, No. 3 (1997).

Nettis Environmental Ltd. v. IWI, Inc. 46 F. Supp. 2d 722 (N. D. Ohio 1999).

Network Advertising Initiative. "Network Advertising Initiative Releases 2010 Compliance Report." Networkadvertising.org (February 18, 2011).

Network Advertising Initiative. "Major Marketing/Media Trade Groups Launch Program to Give Consumers Enhanced Control over Collection and Use of Web Viewing Data for Online Behavioral Advertising." (October 4, 2010).

New York Times. "Bailouts Gone Wild. Porn Chiefs Seek $5 Billion." (January 7, 2009).

Nissan Motor Co., Ltd. v. Nissan Computer Corp. 289 F. Supp. 2d 1154 (C. D. Cal.), aff'd, 2000 U. S. App. LEXIS 33937 (9th Cir. Dec. 26, 2000).

PaineWebber Inc. v. Fortuny, Civ. A. No. 99-0456-A (E. D. Va. Apr. 9, 1999).

Perfect 10, Inc. v. Amazon.com, Inc. 487 F3rd 701 (CA 9th, 2007).

Pew Internet & American Life Project. "Daily Internet Activities." (September 2012).

Playboy Enterprises, Inc. v. Global Site Designs, Inc. 1999 WL 311707 (S. D. Fla. May 15, 1999).

Playboy Enterprises, Inc. v. Netscape Communications, Inc. 354 F. 3rd 1020 (9th Cir., 2004).

Raice, Shayndi. "Facebook to Target Ads Based on App Usage." *New York Times* (July 6, 2012).

Ram, Vidya. "Google's Luxury Victory." *Forbes* (September 22, 2009).

Reuters. "Why Are 5 Million Kids on Facebook If It Doesn't Want Them?" Reuters (September 19, 2012).

Sasso, Brendan. "FCC Urges Court to Uphold Net Neutrality Rules." TheHill.com (September 10, 2012).

Sarno, David. "SmartPhone Apps dial Up Privacy Worries." *Los Angeles Times* (February 16, 2012).

Savage, Charlie. "Democratic Senators Issue Strong Warning About Use of the Patriot Act." *New York Times* (March 16, 2012).

Schatz, Amy. "Net Neutrality' Rules Set to Pass." *Wall Street Journal* (December 21, 2010).

Schwartz, John. "Justices Take Broad View of Business Methods Patents." *New York Times* (June 28, 2010).

Sengupta, Somini. "Europe Weighs Tough Law on Online Privacy." *New York Times* (January 23, 2012a).

Sengupta, Somini. "Facebook Says Child Privacy Laws Should Not Apply to Like." *New York Times* (October 1, 2012b).

Sharma, Amol, and Don Clark. "Tech Guru Riles the Industry By Seeking Huge Patent Fees." *Wall Street Journal* (September 17, 2008).

Singer, Natasha. "Consumer Data, But Not For Consumers." *New York Times* (July 21, 2012a).

Singer, Natasha. "U.S. Is Tightening Web Privacy Rule to Shield Young." *New York Times* (September 27, 2012b).

Singer, Natasha. "Web Sites Accused of Collecting Data on Children." *New York Times* (August 22, 2012c).

State Street Bank & Trust Co. v. Signature Financial Group, 149 F. 3d 1368 (1998).

Stelter, Brian. "Sweeping Effects as Broadband Moves to Meters." *New York Times* (June 26, 2012).

Stone, Brad. "Scaling the Digital Wall in China." *New York Times,* January 15, 2010

Takenaka, Toshiko. "International and Comparative Law Perspective on Internet Patents." *Michigan Telecommunications Technology Law Review* (May 15, 2001).

Thurm, Scott. "The Ultimate Weapon: It's the Patent." *Wall Street Journal* (April 17, 2000a).

Ticketmaster v. Tickets.com. 2000 U.S. Dist. Lexis 4553 (C.D. Cal., August 2000).

TRUSTe, Inc.. "TRUSTe Releases U.S. Consumer Findings From 2012." (July 16, 2012).

United States Copyright Office. "Digital Millennium Copyright Act of 1998: U.S. Copyright Office Summary." (December 1998).

Varian, Hal, "Forget Taxing Internet Sales. In Fact, Just Forget Sales Taxes Altogether." *New York Times* (March 8, 2001).

Washington Post, The et al. v. TotalNews, Inc., et al., S.D.N.Y., Civil Action Number 97-1190 (February 1997).

Watt, Edward. "U.S. Court Curbs F.C.C. Authority on Web Traffic." *New York Times* (April 6, 2010).

Winkler, Rolfe. "Online Profits From Gambling in the Cards." *Wall Street Journal* (January 3, 2012).

Winston, Brian. *Media Technology and Society: A History From the Telegraph to the Internet.* Routledge (1998).

Wondracek, G. , Thorsen Holz, Christian Platzer, Engin Kirda, and Christopher Kruegel. "Is the Internet for Porn? An Insight into the Online Adult Industry." In *Proceedings (online) of the 9th Workshop on Economics of Information Security,* Cambridge, MA (June 2010).

Worthen, Ben. "Red Light Sites Give Green Light to IT Innovation." ITBusiness.ca (August 13, 2009).

Wyatt, Edward. "Verizon Sues F.C.C. to Overturn Order on Blocking Web Sites." *New York Times* (January 20, 2011a).

Wyatt, Edward. "Rule by Justice Department Opens a Door on Online Gambling." *New York Times* (December 24, 2011b).

CHAPTER 9

Amazon.com, Inc. Amazon.com Inc. Form 10-K for the fiscal year ended December 31, 2011, filed with the Securities and Exchange Commission (February 1, 2012).

Bartash, Jeremy. "U.S. Service Sector Expands Faster in August." Marketwatch.com (September 6, 2011).

Brown, Jeffrey, and Austan Goolsbee. "Does the Internet Make Markets More Competitive? Evidence from the Life Insurance Industry." John F. Kennedy School of Government, Harvard University. Research Working Paper RWP00-007 (2000).

Brynjolfsson, Erik; Astrid Andrea Dick and Michael D. Smith. "Search and Product Differentiation at an Internet Shopbot," Center for eBusiness@MIT (December, 2004).

Compete.com. "Site Profiles: Fidelity.com, Sharebuilder, Scottrade, TDAmeritrade, E-Trade, Vanguard, Charles Schwab, Merrill Lynch, and Troweprice." (September 2012).

comScore. "Government Sites Reach 40 Percent of Americans but Lag Behind Overall Internet Growth." (September 12, 2011).

comScore. "The 2010 State of Online Banking Report." (May 11, 2010a).

comScore. "comScore Media Metrix Ranks Top-Growing Properties and Site Categories for January 2010." (February 23, 2010b).

Dell Inc. Form 10-K for the fiscal year ended February 3, 2012, filed with the Securities and Exchange Commission (March 13, 2012).

Evans, Philip, and Thomas S. Wurster. *Blown to Bits: How the New Economics of Information Transforms Strategy*. Cambridge, MA: Harvard Business School Press (2000).

Internet Retailer. "Top 500 Guide 2012 Edition." (2012).

JC Penney Company, Inc. Report on Form 10-K for the fiscal year ended January 28, 2012, filed with the Securities and Exchange Commission (March 28, 2012).

Lands' End, Inc. "About Lands' End." Landsend.com (accessed October 1, 2012).

Laudon, Kenneth C., and Jane P. Laudon. *Management Information Systems: Managing the Digital Firm, 13th edition*. Upper Saddle River, NJ: Prentice Hall (2012).

LIMRA and Life Insurance Foundation for Education (LIFE). "The 2011 Insurance Barometer Study." (July 27, 2011).

MarketTools. "Satisfaction with US Airline Carriers." (May 25, 2011).

National Association of Realtors. "NAR Home Buyer and Seller Survey Show Value of Long-Term Home Ownership." Realtor.org (November 5, 2010).

U. S. Census Bureau. "Census of Service Industries." (2001).

U.S. Census Bureau. *Statistical Abstract of the United States 2012* (2012).

U.S. Department of Labor. Dictionary of Occupational Titles, 4th edition. (1991).

Weil, Jonathon. "Securities Rules Help to Close the Earning Reports GAAP." *Wall Street Journal* (April 24, 2003).

CHAPTER 10

Boxer, Sarah. "Paintings Too Perfect? The Great Optics Debate." *New York Times* (December 4, 2001).

Brand, Stuart. "The First Hackers conference in 1984." Transcript in The Media Lab: Inventing the Future at MIT, Viking Penguin, (1987).

Carr, David. "New Rules for the Ways We Watch." *New York Times* (December 24, 2011).

Cheney, Alexandra. "Hulu to Launch Three New Series, Seven Licensed Shows for Summer," *New York Times* (May 20, 2012).

comScore. "comScore Releases March 2012 U.S. Online Video Rankings." (April 19, 2012).

comScore. "Newspaper Websites Reach Nearly Two-thirds of all Internet Users in Fourth Quarter." (August 11, 2011).

DEG (Digital Entertainment Group). DEG Report 2011 U.S. Home Entertainment Consumer Spending by Format." (January 6, 2012).

eMarketer, Inc. (Mark Dolliver) "Time Spent With Media." (March 22, 2012a).

eMarketer, Inc. (Paul Verna) "Book Publishing: The Price of Disruption." (August 2012b).

eMarketer, Inc. "TV Related Activities of US Internet Users, 2012." (January 2012c).

eMarketer, Inc. "US Adult Online Movie Viewers, 2010-2016," (March 2012d).

eMarketer, Inc. "Online Movies Set to Overtake DVDs and Blu-rays." (April 2, 2012e).

eMarketer, Inc. (Paul Verna) "Cloud Based Music Streaming: Emerging Opportunities for Brands." (April 2012f).

eMarketer, Inc. (Alison McCarthy), "US Online Gaming Audience Forecast." (June 2012g).

eMarketer, Inc. "TV Video Viewing: Beyond Cord Cutters." (July 2011a).

eMarketer, Inc. "Premium Video: Audience, Devices and Content." (December 2011b).

Google. (Deborah Schwartz) "A Window Into Film." (April 2011).

IFPI. "Digital Music Report 2012." International Federation of Phonographic Industry (2012).

IHS iSuppli. "Movie Consumption Revenue Expected to Rise Continuously from 2012 to 2015." (March 13, 2012a).

IHS iSuppli. "Netflix Surpasses Apple to Take Lead in U.S. Online Movie Business in 2011." (June 1, 2012b).

Kung, Michelle and Miguel Bustillo. "Wal-Mart to Give Hollywood a Hand." *Wall Street Journal* (February 26, 2012).

Myers, Steve."Latest Numbers Indicate New York Times Traffic is Flat Since Paywall." Poynter.org (January 25, 2012).

Newspaper Association of America. "Annual Daily and Sunday Newspaper Circulation Expenditures." (September 04, 2012).

Nielsen. "The Cross Platform Report." (February 2012a).

Nielsen. "The Nielsen Company and Billboard's 2011 Music Industry Report." Nielsen SoundScan (January 5, 2012b).

Nielsen Broadcast Data Systems. "Music Streaming Activity." *Los Angeles Times* (March 14, 2012).

Nielsen. "Web 2012." (August 2011).

NPD Group. "Video Games Revenues." (January 2011).

Pew Research Center. "The State of the News Media 2012." (April 11, 2012).

Pew Internet & American Life Project. "The State of the News Media." (September 2011).

Schechner, Sam, and John Jannarone, "Media to Get More of Hulu." *Wall Street Journal* (April 26, 2012).

U.S. Census Bureau. Statistical Abstract of the United States 2012 (2012).

Vascellaro, Jessica, Erica Order, and Sam Schechner. "Hollywood Studios Warm to Apple's iCloud Effort." *Wall Street Journal* (March 12, 2012).

CHAPTER 11

Arkes, H. R., and L. Hutzel. "The Role of Probability of Success Estimates in the Sunk Cost Effect." Journal of Behavioral Decisionmaking (2000).

Bailey, Brian P.; Laura J. Gurak; and Joseph Konstan, "Do You Trust Me? An Examination of Trust in Computer-Mediated Exchange," In Human Factors and Web Development, 2nd Edition. Mahwah, NJ: Lawrence Erlbaum (2002).

Brynjolfsson, Erik, and Michael Smith. "Frictionless Commerce? A Comparison of Internet and Conventional Retailers." Management Science (April 2000).

comScore. "The State of Social Media." (February 2012a).

comScore. "comScore Media Metrix Ranks Top 50 U.S. Properties for July 2012." (August 2012b).

Dholakia, Utpal, and Kerry Soltysinski. "Coveted or Overlooked? The Psychology of Bidding for Comparable Listings in Digital Auctions." Marketing Letters (2001).

eBay, Inc. "Form 10-K For the Fiscal Year Ended December 31, 2011." Filed with the Securities and Exchange Commission. (January 31, 2012).

Efrati, Amir. "Twitter Tests New Ad Types." *Wall Street Journal* (July 29, 2011).

eMarketer, Inc. (Alison McCarthy and Debra Aho Williamson) "US Social Network User Forecast: Mass Audience, Slowing Growth." (May 2012a).

eMarketer, Inc. "US Twitter Users and Penetration, 2010-2014." (March 1, 2012b).

eMarketer, Inc. "US Digital Ad Spending by Format, 2009-2014." (October 1, 2012c).

eMarketer, Inc. "US Social Network Ad Revenues by Venue, 2010-2014." (September 1, 2012d).

Gaudin, Sharon. "Google+ Use Skyrockets, Says Report." Computerworld (July 30, 2012).

Hafner, Katie. "The Epic Saga of The Well: The World's Most Influential Online Community (and It's Not AOL)." Wired (May 1997).

Hagel, John III, and Arthur G. Armstrong. Net Gain: Expanding Markets Through Virtual Communities. Cambridge, MA: Harvard Business School Press (1997).

Hanson, Ward, and D. S. Putler. "Hits and Misses: Herd Behavior and Online Product Popularity." Marketing Letters (1996).

Hillery, George A. "Definitions of Community: Areas of Agreement." Rural Sociology (1955).

Hiltzik, Michael. *Dealers of Lightning: Xerox PARC and the Dawn of the Computer Age.* New York: Harper Collins (1999).

Kambil, Ajit, and Eric van Heck. "Competition in the Dutch Flower Market." New York University, Stern School of Business, Center for Information Systems Research (1996).

Kiesler, Sara. "The Hidden Messages in Computer Networks." Harvard Business Review (January-February 1986).

Kiesler, Sara; Jane Siegel; and Timothy W. McGuire. "Social Psychological Aspects of Computer-Mediated Communication." American Psychologist (October 1984).

Kollock, Peter. "The Production of Trust in Online Markets" In Advances in Group Processes (Vol 16) edited by E. J. Lawler, M. Macy, S. Thyne and H. A. Walker. Greenwich, CT: JAI Press (1999).

Krishnamurthy, Sandeep. "An Empirical Study of the Causal Antecedents of Customer Confidence in ETailers." First Monday (January 2001).

Laudon, Kenneth C. and Jane P. Laudon. *Management Information Systems: Managing the Digital Firm. 13th edition.* Upper Saddle River, NJ, Prentice Hall (2012).

Lee, H. G.; J. C. Westland; and S. Hong. "The Impact of Electronic Marketplaces on Product Prices: An Empirical Study of Aucnet." International Journal of Electronic Commerce (Winter 1999-2000).

McAfee R., and John McMillan. "Auctions and Bidding." Journal of Economic Literature (June 1987).

McGee, Matt. "Pinterest May Have More Visitors Than Tumblr: If Not, It Will Soon." Marketingland.com (October 10, 2012).

Milgrom, Paul R. "Auctions and Bidding: A Primer." Journal of Economic Perspectives (Summer 1989).

Murphy, Samantha. "Is Facebook a Passing Fad? Nearly Half of Americans Think So." Mashable.com (May 15, 2012).

National White Collar Crime Center and the Federal Bureau of Investigation. "Internet Crime Complaint Center 2011 Internet Crime Report." (2012).

Newman, Andrew Adam. "Brands Now Direct Their Followers to Social Media," *New York Times* (August 3, 2011).

Nielsen. "State of the Media: The Social Media Report Q3 2011." (September 11, 2011).

Nikander, Pekka, and Kristina Karvonen. "Users and Trust in Cyberspace." In the Proceedings of Cambridge Security Protocols Workshop 2000, April 3-5, 2000, Cambridge University (2002).

Oreskovic, Alexei. "Facebook Comments, Ads, Don't Sway Most Users." Reuters (June 4, 2012.)

Parkes, David C., and Lyle Ungar. "Iterative Combinatorial Auctions: Theory and Practice." *Proceedings of the 17th National Conference on Artificial Intelligence* (AAAI-00) (2000).

Rheingold, Howard. Hosting Web Communities. New York: John Wiley and Sons (1998). Also see Rheingold.com for more recent articles by Rheingold.

Rheingold, Howard. *The Virtual Community.* Cambridge MA: MIT Press (1993).

Rosenblum, Stephanie. "For the Plugged-In, Too Many Choices." *New York Times* (August 10, 2011).

Stanford Persuasive Technology Lab and Makovsky & Company. "Stanford-Makovsky Web Credibility Study 2002." Stanford Persuasive Technology Lab. (Spring 2002).

Twitter, Inc. "Twitter Stats," August 22, 2012. http://business.twitter.com/basics/

Vakrat, Yaniv, and Abraham Seidmann. "Can Online Auctions Beat Online Catalogs?" Proceedings of the 20th Conference on Information Systems (December 1999).

Vakrat, Yaniv, and Abraham Seidmann. "Analysis and Design Models for Online Auctions." *Proceedings of the 4th INFORMS Conference on Information Systems and Technology.* (May 1998).

Vickrey, William. "Counterspeculation, Auctions and Competitive Sealed Tenders." Journal of Finance (March 1961).

CHAPTER 12

Ariba Inc. "About Us." (September 2012).

Barlow, Alexis. "Web Technologies and Supply Chains." Glasgow Calendonian University, Scotland. In *Supply Chain Management: New Perspectives*, edited by S. Renko. (2011).

Beard, Alison and Richard Hornik, "It's Hard to Be Good," *Harvard Business Review Magazine,* November 2011

Bunkley, Nick. "Lacking Parts, GM Will Close Plant." *New York Times* (March 17, 2011).

Bolukbasi, Hande. "Putting the Business in the Palm of Your Hand." SAPInsider.com (January 2011).

Booen, Brett. "The Under Armour Success Story: How SAP Improves the UA Supply Chain." SupplyChainDigital.com (March 10, 2011).

Cachon, Gerard, and Robert Swinney, "The Value of Fast Fashion: Quick Response, Enhanced Design, and Strategic Consumer Behavior." *Management Science* Vol. 57 778-795 (April 2011).

Cisco Systems, Inc. "Proctor & Gamble Revolutionize Collaboration With Cisco TelePresence." (March, 2011).

Esposito, Carl. "What Are the Best Examples of Crowdsourcing." Crowdsourcing.org (2012).

Exostar LLC. "About Exostar." (September 2012).

Fair Labor Association. "Independent Investigation of Apple Supplier, Foxconn Report Highlights." Fairlabor.org (March 30, 2012).

Gardner, Dana. "HP Shows Benefits From Successful Application Consolidation With Own Massive Global Supply Chain Project." Zdnet.com (May 20, 2010).

Globalwinespirits.com. "About GWS." Globalwinespirts.com (September 2012).

Hewlett-Packard. "HP.com Business to Business." Hp.com (September 2012).

Hird, Jake. "25 Business-tastic B2B Social Media Case Studies." eConsultancy.com (October 11, 2011).

IBM Corporation. "No Resting Place." (July 2011a).

IBM Corporation, "True Value Company: True Value Optimizes Their Inbound Supply Process with IBM Sterling Supply Chain Visibility." (July 2011b).

Inventory Locator Service LLC. ILSmart.com "About Us." (September 2012).

James, Henry. "Crowdsourcing Trends in 2012." Crowdsourcing.org (April 9, 2012).

Jolly, David. "Long Pause for Japanese Industry Raises Concerns About Supply Chain." *New York Times* (March 16, 2011).

Kaplan, Steven, and Mohanbir Sawhney. "E-Hubs: The New B2B Marketplaces." Harvard Business Review (May-June 2000).

Kerrigan, Ryan; Eric Roegner; Dennis Swinford; and Craig Zawada. "B2B Basics." McKinsey Quarterly (2001).

Kumaran, S. "A Framework-Based Approach to Building Private Trading Exchanges." IBM Systems Journal (July 2002).

Laudon, Kenneth C. and Jane P. Laudon. *Management Information Systems: Managing the Digital Firm. 13th edition.* Upper Saddle River, NJ: Prentice Hall (2012).

Levy, James. "Ariba: Sustained Profitable Growth in B2B Collaborative Commerce Solutions." Seekingalpha.com (June 7, 2010).

Meinyk, Steven, et. al. "Supply Chain Management 2010 and Beyond." APICS Educational & Research Foundation (2010).

Red Prairie, Inc. "The B2B SoLoMo Imperative." (September 2012).

Rosenzweig, et. al., "Through the service operations strategy looking glass: Influence of industrial sector, ownership, and service offerings on B2B e-marketplace failures." *Journal of Operations Management*, (29) (2011).

Supply Chain Digest. "Building the Supply Chain from the Shelf Back Research." (April 4, 2012a).

Supply Chain Digest. "Global Supply Chain: Toyota Taking Massive Effort to Reduce Its Supply Chain Risk in Japan." (March 7, 2012b).

Synnex Corporation. Form 10-K for the fiscal year ended November 30, 2011, filed with the Securities and Exchange Commission (January 27, 2012).

Trkman, P.; McCormack, K.; "Estimating the Benefits of Implementing E-Procurement," Engineering Management, IEEE Transaction, Volume 57, Issue 2 (May 2010).

True Value. Annual Report 2011. (March 2012).

U.S. Census Bureau. "eStats Report 2010 E-commerce Multi-sector Report." (May 20, 2012).

U.S. Census Bureau. Statistical Abstract of the United States (2012b).

Vance, Ashlee. "For an Online Marketplace, It's Better Late Than Never." *New York Times* (November 20, 2010).

Wise, Richard, and Dave Morrison. "Beyond the Exchange: The Future of B2B." Harvard Business Review (November-December 2000).

W.W. Grainger. Inc. Form 10-K for the fiscal year ended December 31, 2011, filed with the Securities and Exchange Commission (February 28, 2012).

Yoo, Byungjoon; V. Choudray; and T. Mukhopadhyay. "Marketplaces or Web Service: Alternate Business Models for Electronic B2B Commerce." Proceedings of the 44th Hawaii International Conference on System Sciences (HICSS) (2011).

Index

Credits

continued from front inside cover